P9-ARZ-794

Hypercube Multiprocessors 1987

Proceedings of the Second Conference on Hypercube Multiprocessors, Knoxville, Tennessee, September 29-October 1, 1986.

This conference was sponsored by the Mathematical Sciences Section of Oak Ridge National Laboratory and the Society for Industrial and Applied Mathematics Activity Groups on Supercomputing and Linear Algebra. Funding provided by the Applied Mathematical Sciences Research Program of the U.S. Department of Energy.

Hypercube Multiprocessors 1987

EDITED BY
Michael T. Heath
Oak Ridge National Laboratory

Philadelphia 1987

All rights reserved. Printed in the United States of America. No part of this book may be reproduced, stored or transmitted in any manner without the written permission of the Publisher. For information, write the Society for Industrial and Applied Mathematics, 1400 Architects Building, 117 South 17th Street, Philadelphia, Pennsylvania 19103-5052.

Library of Congress Catalog Card Number 87-60443
ISBN 0-89871-215-7

Copyright © 1987 by the Society for Industrial and Applied Mathematics

Preface

P3.85

The Second Conference on Hypercube Multiprocessors was held in Knoxville, Tennessee on September 29–October 1, 1986. Nothing better illustrates the remarkably rapid growth of interest in hypercube architectures than the history of these conferences.

The first conference in August 1985, which was the first to be devoted specifically to hypercubes, was attended by 170 people despite the fact that hypercubes had been available commercially for only one month. Because few participants had had significant experience with the new architecture, the conference in the main considered its potential in abstract terms.

In the intervening year between the first and second conferences, the early model hypercubes achieved a surprising market success considering the novelty of the architecture. Initial models were upgraded, and new models were produced by additional commercial vendors. By the time of the second conference, hands-on access to hypercubes was widely available to researchers in parallel computing. As a consequence, attendance grew to around 300 people, and the number of speakers increased dramatically from 20 to 100.

Eighty of the papers given at the conference are represented in this proceedings. Most are based on experience with real hypercube hardware. Working within this new architectural paradigm has caused a re-thinking of traditional concepts of programming languages, data structures, operating systems and the like, and some novel proposals in these areas are presented. Several authors present detailed empirical studies of the performance of existing hypercubes, and numerous architectural and communication enhancements are proposed. An impressive range of applications is represented, from traditional "number-crunching" problems such as particle transport, fluid dynamics, and computational chemistry to purely combinatorial problems such as sorting and discrete optimization. Special emphasis is given to matrix computations and partial differential equations, both of which have always been at the forefront of supercomputer applications. The sheer number and variety of papers in this volume attest to the wide applicability and future promise of hypercubes for scientific computing.

Although it is always difficult to forecast the course of technological trends, it seems safe to assume that the current hypercube vendors, as well as possible additional manufacturers, will produce a second generation of more powerful hypercubes. These machines not only will feature faster processors and larger memories, but will also focus specifically on relieving some of the bottlenecks in current hypercubes such as internode communication speed and external I/O capacity. If these improvements in hardware can be matched by comparable progress in algorithm development, programming methodology, and software support, hypercubes may become the most cost-effective means of providing the supercomputing power necessary for the next decade of general-purpose scientific computing.

The Second Conference on Hypercube Multiprocessors was cosponsored by the Mathematical Sciences Section of Oak Ridge National Laboratory and the Activity Groups on Supercomputing and Linear Algebra of the Society for Industrial and Applied Mathematics (SIAM) and was supported by funds from the Applied Mathematical Sciences Research Program of the U.S. Department of Energy. The organizing committee of the conference consisted of Jack Fanselow of the Jet Propulsion Laboratory, John Hayes of the University of Michigan, David Krumme of Tufts University, and Martin Schultz of Yale University, with Michael Heath of Oak Ridge National Laboratory as conference chairman.

Michael T. Heath
Oak Ridge National Laboratory

List of Contributors

Tarek S. Abdel-Rahman, *Advanced Computer Architecture Laboratory, Department of Electrical Engineering and Computer Science, University of Michigan, Ann Arbor, Michigan 48109*

J. K. Aggarwal, *Computer and Vision Research Center, College of Engineering, University of Texas at Austin, Austin, Texas 78712*

D. P. Agrawal, *Department of Electrical and Computer Engineering, North Carolina State University, Raleigh, North Carolina 27695*

Steven Anderson, *Department of Computer Science, Yale University, New Haven, Connecticut 06520*

C. Aykanat, *Department of Electrical Engineering, Ohio State University, Columbus, Ohio 43210*

R. G. Babb, II, *Department of Computer Science and Engineering, Oregon Graduate Center, Beaverton, Oregon 97006*

B. Bagheri, *Department of Mathematics, University of Michigan, Ann Arbor, Michigan 48109*

J. Barhen, *Center for Engineering Systems Advanced Research, Oak Ridge National Laboratory, Oak Ridge, Tennessee 37831*

K. Barish, *Department of Physics, Mathematics and Astronomy, California Institute of Technology, Pasadena, California 91125*

N. Bauman, *Department of Computer and Information Science, Ohio State University, Columbus, Ohio 43210*

Adam Beguelin, *Computer Science Department, University of Colorado at Boulder, Boulder, Colorado 80302*

Maurice W. Benson, *Department of Mathematical Sciences, Lakehead University, Thunder Bay, Ontario, Canada P7B 5E1*

Donna Bergmark, *Department of Computer Services, Cornell University, Ithaca, New York 14853*

Christian Bischof, *Department of Computer Science, Cornell University, Ithaca, New York 14853*

Win Bo, *Department of Computer and Information Science, Ohio State University, Columbus, Ohio 43210*

Kimiko O. Bowman, *Engineering Physics and Mathematics Division, Oak Ridge National Laboratory, Oak Ridge, Tennessee 37831*

J. M. Boyle, *Mathematics and Computer Science Division, Argonne National Laboratory, Argonne, Illinois 60439*

Carl Braganza, *Distributed Artificial Intelligence Group, Computer Science Department, University of Southern California, Los Angeles, California 90089*

Alison A. Brown, *Cornell Theory Center, Cornell University, Ithaca, New York 14853*

Scott Shorey Brown, *General Electric Corporation, Valley Forge, Pennsylvania 19481*

Gregory D. Burns, *Cornell Theory Center, Cornell University, Ithaca, New York 14853*

W. H. Butler, *Metals and Ceramics Division, Oak Ridge National Laboratory, Oak Ridge, Tennessee 37831*

G. D. Buzzard, *Advanced Computer Architecture Laboratory, Department of Electrical Engineering and Computer Science, University of Michigan, Ann Arbor, Michigan 48109*

Christopher J. Catherasoo, *AMETEK Computer Research Division, Arcadia, California 91006*

R. M. Chamberlain, *Chr. Michelsen Institute, Fantoftveien 38, N-5036 Fantoft, Norway*

Tony F. Chan, *Department of Mathematics, University of California at Los Angeles, Los Angeles, California 90024*

Marina C. Chen, *Department of Computer Science, Yale University, New Haven, Connecticut 06520*

Ming-Syan Chen, *Advanced Computer Architecture Laboratory, Department of Electrical Engineering and Computer Science, University of Michigan, Ann Arbor, Michigan 48109*

A. Cisneros, *California Institute of Technology, Pasadena, California 91125*

Thomas F. Coleman, *Computer Science Department and Center for Applied Mathematics, Cornell University, Ithaca, New York 14853*

Tait Cyrus, *Department of Electrical and Computer Engineering, University of New Mexico, Albuquerque, New Mexico 87131*

G. J. Davis, *Department of Mathematics and Computer Science, Georgia State University, Atlanta, Georgia 30303*

Erik P. DeBenedictis, *AT&T Bell Laboratories, Holmdel, New Jersey 07733*

Sudarshan K. Dhall, *Parallel Processing Institute, School of Electrical Engineering and Computer Science, University of Oklahoma, Norman, Oklahoma 73019*

S. M. Doraivelu, *Universal Energy Systems, Dayton, Ohio 45432*

T. H. Dunigan, *Mathematical Sciences Section, Oak Ridge National Laboratory, Oak Ridge, Tennessee 37831*

P. J. Eberlein, *Department of Computer Science, State University of New York at Buffalo, Buffalo, New York 14260*

J. R. Einstein, *Center for Engineering Systems Advanced Research, Oak Ridge National Laboratory, Oak Ridge, Tennessee 37831*

F. Ercal, *Department of Computer and Information Science, Ohio State University, Columbus, Ohio 43210*

R. Fatland, *Department of Physics, Mathematics and Astronomy, California Institute of Technology, Pasadena, California 91125*

E. Felten, *Department of Physics, Mathematics and Astronomy, California Institute of Technology, Pasadena, California 91125*

Geoffrey C. Fox, *Concurrent Computation Program, California Institute of Technology, Pasadena, California 91125*

Joan M. Francioni, *Department of Mathematical and Computer Sciences, Michigan Technological University, Houghton, Michigan 49931*

Paul O. Frederickson, *Los Alamos National Laboratory, Los Alamos, New Mexico 87544*

R. E. Funderlic, *Department of Computer Science, North Carolina State University, Raleigh, North Carolina 27695*

Wojtek Furmanski, *Concurrent Computation Program, California Institute of Technology, Pasadena, California 91125*

Judith D. Gardiner, *Department of Electrical and Computer Engineering, University of California at Santa Barbara, Santa Barbara, California 93106*

Les Gasser, *Distributed Artificial Intelligence Group, Computer Science Department, University of Southern California, Los Angeles, California 90089*

Kevin Gates, *Department of Applied Mathematics, University of Washington, Seattle, Washington 98195*

G. A. Geist, *Engineering Physics and Mathematics Division, Mathematical Sciences Section, Oak Ridge National Laboratory, Oak Ridge, Tennessee 37831*

Alan George, *Mathematical Sciences Section, Oak Ridge National Laboratory, Oak Ridge, Tennessee 37831*

W. B. Gragg, *Department of Mathematics, University of Kentucky, Lexington, Kentucky 40506*

John J. Grefenstette, *Navy Center for Applied Research in Artificial Intelligence, Naval Research Laboratory, Washington, District of Columbia 20375*

Dirk C. Grunwald, *Department of Computer Science, University of Illinois at Urbana, Urbana, Illinois 61801*

John L. Gustafson, *Floating Point Systems, Incorporated, Beaverton, Oregon 97006*

J. P. Hayes, *Department of Electrical Engineering and Computer Science, University of Michigan, Ann Arbor, Michigan 48109*

Michael T. Heath, *Mathematical Sciences Section, Oak Ridge National Laboratory, Oak Ridge, Tennessee 37831*

Brenda K. Helminen, *Department of Mathematical and Computer Sciences, Michigan Technological University, Houghton, Michigan 49931*

Nava Herman, *Distributed Artificial Intelligence Group, Computer Science Department, University of Southern California, Los Angeles, California 90089*

Alex Ho, *Concurrent Computation Project, California Institute of Technology, Pasadena, California 91125*

Ching-Tien Ho, *Department of Computer Science, Yale University, New Haven, Connecticut 06520*

F. Ho, *Department of Physics, Mathematics and Astronomy, California Institute of Technology, Pasadena, California 91125*

Jung Hong, *Mechanical and Electronics Division, Data Systems, Los Alamos National Laboratory, Los Alamos, New Mexico 87544*

Ilse C. F. Ipsen, *Department of Computer Science, Yale University, New Haven, Connecticut 06520*

Jay Alan Jackson, *Department of Mathematical and Computer Sciences, Michigan Technological University, Houghton, Michigan 49931*

R. Jain, *Department of Electrical Engineering and Computer Science, University of Michigan, Ann Arbor, Michigan 48109*

D. Jefferson, *Computer Science Department, University of California at Los Angeles, Los Angeles, California 90024*

Elizabeth R. Jessup, *Department of Computer Science, Yale University, New Haven, Connecticut 06520*

Somesh Jha, *Department of Electrical Engineering, Pennsylvania State University, University Park, Pennsylvania 16802*

S. Lennart Johnsson, *Department of Computer Science, Yale University, New Haven, Connecticut 06520*

Howard P. Katseff, *AT&T Bell Laboratories, Holmdel, New Jersey 07733*

A. E. Kayaalp, *Department of Electrical Engineering and Computer Science, University of Michigan, Ann Arbor, Michigan 48109*

Rich Kellner, *Mechanical and Electronics Division, Data Systems, Los Alamos National Laboratory, Los Alamos, New Mexico 87544*

A. Kolawa, *Concurrent Computation Program, California Institute of Technology, Pasadena, California 91125*

S. Lakshmivarahan, *Parallel Processing Institute, School of Electrical Engineering and Computer Science, University of Oklahoma, Norman, Oklahoma 73019*

A. R. Larrabee, *Department of Computer Science and Engineering, Oregon Graduate Center, Beaverton, Oregon 97006*

Alan J. Laub, *Department of Electrical and Computer Engineering, University of California at Santa Barbara, Santa Barbara, California 93106*

S.-Y. Lee, *Computer and Vision Research Center, College of Engineering, University of Texas at Austin, Austin, Texas 78712*

Michael R. Leuze, *Department of Computer Science, Vanderbilt University, Nashville, Tennessee 37235*

Guangye Li, *Computer Science Department and Center for Applied Mathematics, Cornell University, Ithaca, New York 14853*

Davis S. Lim, *AMETEK Computer Research Division, Arcadia, California 91006*

J. Lindheim, *Chr. Michelsen Institute, Fantoftveien 38, N-5036 Fantoft, Norway*

Joseph Liu, *Department of Computer Science, York University, Downsview, Ontario, Canada M3J 1P3*

Steven E. Lucco, *AT&T Bell Laboratories, Holmdel, New Jersey 07733*

Gordon Lyon, *Systems Components Division, National Bureau of Standards, Gaithersburg, Maryland 20899*

S. Martin, *Universal Energy Systems, Dayton, Ohio 45432*

William R. Martin, *Department of Nuclear Engineering, University of Michigan, Ann Arbor, Michigan 48109*

Mike L. Mathews, *Space Systems Division, General Electric Company, Philadelphia, Pennsylvania 19101*

Oliver A. McBryan, *Los Alamos National Laboratory, Los Alamos, New Mexico 87545*

Russ Miller, *Department of Computer Science, State University of New York at Buffalo, Buffalo, New York 14260*

T. K. Miller, *Department of Electrical and Computer Engineering, North Carolina State University, Raleigh, North Carolina 27695*

Gary R. Montry, *Advanced Computer Science Project, Fluid and Thermal Sciences Department, Sandia National Laboratories, Albuquerque, New Mexico 87185*

Alexander P. Morgan, *Mathematics Department, General Motors Research Laboratories, Warren, Michigan 48090*

R. Morison, *Department of Physics, Mathematics and Astronomy, California Institute of Technology, Pasadena, California 91125*

Zhijing Mu, *Department of Computer Science, Yale University, New Haven, Connecticut 06520*

Trevor N. Mudge, *Advanced Computer Architecture Laboratory, Department of Electrical Engineering and Computer Science, University of Michigan, Ann Arbor, Michigan 48109*

Vijay K. Naik, *Institute for Computer Application in Science and Engineering, NASA Langley Research Center, Hampton, Virginia 23665*

Esmond Ng, *Mathematical Sciences Section, Oak Ridge National Laboratory, Oak Ridge, Tennessee 37831*

James M. Ortega, *Department of Applied Mathematics, University of Virginia, Charlottesville, Virginia 22901*

S. Otto, *Department of Physics, Mathematics and Astronomy, California Institute of Technology, Pasadena, California 91125*

F. Özgüner, *Department of Electrical Engineering, Ohio State University, Columbus, Ohio 43210*

Edward Page, III, *Department of Computer Science, Clemson University, Clemson, South Carolina 29634*

J. Petersen, *Chr. Michelsen Institute, Fantoftveien 38, N-5036 Fantoft, Norway*

Chrisila C. Pettey, *Department of Computer Science, Vanderbilt University, Nashville, Tennessee 37235*

Doug Poland, *Department of Nuclear Engineering, University of Michigan, Ann Arbor, Michigan 48109*

Howard Pollard, *Department of Electrical and Computer Engineering, University of New Mexico, Albuquerque, New Mexico 87131*

David A. Poplawski, *Department of Mathematical and Computer Sciences, Michigan Technological University, Houghton, Michigan 49931*

Alex Pothen, *Department of Computer Science, Pennsylvania State University, University Park, Pennsylvania 16802*

Jim Quinlan, *Department of Electrical and Computing Engineering, Carnegie Mellon University, Pittsburgh, Pennsylvania 15213*

Michael J. Quinn, *Parallel Computing Laboratory, Department of Computer Science, University of New Hampshire, Durham, New Hamphire 03824*

Daniel A. Reed, *Department of Computer Science, University of Illinois at Urbana, Urbana, Illinois 61801*

Lothar Reichel, *Department of Mathematics, University of Kentucky, Lexington, Kentucky 40506*

Diana C. Resasco, *Department of Computer Science, Yale University, New Haven, Connecticut 06520*

Mark T. Robinson, *Solid State Division, Oak Ridge National Laboratory, Oak Ridge, Tennessee 37831*

C. H. Romine, *Engineering Physics and Mathematics Division, Mathematical Sciences Section, Oak Ridge National Laboratory, Oak Ridge, Tennessee 37831*

P. Sadayappan, *Department of Computer and Information Science, Ohio State University, Columbus, Ohio 43210*

Shmuel Safra, *Department of Computer Science, Weizmann Institute of Science, Rehovot 76100, Israel*

Faisal Saied, *Department of Computer Science, Yale University, New Haven, Connecticut 06520*

John Salmon, *Physics Department, California Institute of Technology, Pasadena, California 91125*

Joel H. Saltz, *Department of Computer Science, Yale University, New Haven, Connecticut 06520*

Martin H. Schultz, *Department of Computer Science, Yale University, New Haven, Connecticut 06520*

Karsten Schwan, *Department of Computer and Information Science, Ohio State University, Columbus, Ohio 43210*

L. R. Scott, *Departments of Computer Science and Mathematics, Pennsylvania State University, University Park, Pennsylvania 16802*

Steven R. Seidel, *Department of Mathematical and Computer Sciences, Michigan Technological University, Houghton, Michigan 49931*

Ehud Shapiro, *Department of Computer Science, Weizmann Institute of Science, Rehovot 76100, Israel*

Kang G. Shin, *Advanced Computer Architecture Laboratory, Department of Electrical Engineering and Computer Science, University of Michigan, Ann Arbor, Michigan 48109*

Dan Siewiorek, *Department of Electrical and Computer Engineering, Carnegie Mellon University, Pittsburgh, Pennsylvania 15213*

David Socha, *Department of Computer Science, University of Washington, Seattle, Washington 98195*

John Stamey, Jr., *Department of Computer Science, Clemson University, Clemson, South Carolina 29634*

Quentin F. Stout, *Department of Electrical Engineering and Computer Science, University of Michigan, Ann Arbor, Michigan 48109*

Shlomo Ta'asan, *Institute for Computer Application in Science and Engineering, NASA Langley Research Center, Hampton, Virginia 23665*

Stephen Taylor, *Department of Computer Science, Weizmann Institute of Science, Rehovot 76100, Israel*

Rex V. Thanakij, *AMETEK Computer Research Division, Arcadia, California 91006*

Russell Therman, *Department of Electrical and Computer Engineering, University of New Mexico, Albuquerque, New Mexico 87131*

Bob Tomlinson, *Mechanical and Electronics Division, Data Systems, Los Alamos National Laboratory, Los Alamos, New Mexico 87544*

Ray S. Tuminaro, *Department of Computer Science, Stanford University, Stanford, California 94305*

D. J. Vasicek, *Amoco Production Company, Tulsa, Oklahoma 74102*

Courtenay T. Vaughan, *Department of Applied Mathematics, University of Virginia, Charlottesville, Virginia 22901*

Udaya Vemulapati, *Pennsylvania State University, University Park, Pennsylvania 16802*

Bruce Wagar, *Department of Electrical Engineering and Computer Science, University of Michigan, Ann Arbor, Michigan 48109*

David W. Walker, *Concurrent Computation Project, California Institute of Technology, Pasadena, California 91125*

Stephen R. Walton, *AMETEK Computer Research Division, Arcadia, California 91006*

Tzu-Chiang Wan, *Department of Nuclear Engineering, University of Michigan, Ann Arbor, Michigan 48109*

Richard C. Ward, *Computing and Telecommunications Division, Oak Ridge National Laboratory, Oak Ridge, Tennessee 37831*

Layne T. Watson, *Departments of Electrical Engineering and Computer Science, Industrial and Operations Engineering, and Mathematics, University of Michigan, Ann Arbor, Michigan 48109*

W. B. Wike, *Department of Electrical and Computer Engineering, North Carolina State University, Raleigh, North Carolina 27695*

R. Williams, *Concurrent Computation Program, California Institute of Technology, Pasadena, California 91125*

Winifred I. Williams, *Concurrent Processor Systems Group, Jet Propulsion Laboratory, Pasadena, California 91109*

Chen-Ping Yuan, *Technology Development CAD, Intel Company, Santa Clara, California 95052*

Lynn R. Ziegler, *Department of Mathematical and Computer Sciences, Michigan Technological University, Houghton, Michigan 49931*

Contents

PART I:
PROGRAMMING ENVIRONMENTS, LANGUAGES AND DATA STRUCTURES

CUBIX: Programming Hypercubes without Programming Hosts

JOHN SALMON*

Abstract. Typically, application programs for hypercubes consist of two parts, a master process running on the host and a server running in the nodes of the hypercube.

CUBIX adopts a different viewpoint. Once a program is loaded into the hypercube, that program assumes control of the machine. The host process only serves requests for operating system services. Since it is no more than a file server, the host program is universal; it is unchanged from one application to the next.

This programming model has some important advantages.

- Program development is easier because it is not necessary to write a separate program for the host.

- Hypercube programs are easier to develop and debug because they can use standard I/O routines rather than machine-dependent system calls.

- Hypercube programs can often be run on sequential machines with minimal modification.

Versions of CUBIX exist for both crystalline and amorphous applications. In crystalline applications operating system requests occur synchronously. Requests are either "singular" or "multiple" according to whether all nodes request the same or distinct actions. In amorphous applications requests occur completely asynchronously. The host process serves each request independently. Care is taken so that many processors may simultaneously access the same file.

1. Introduction

CUBIX was created to make programming hypercubes easier. It's goal is to eliminate significant duplication of effort on the part of hypercube programmers, and to make the hypercube environment appear much more familiar to application programmers. It is also intended to make hypercube programs more easily portable to sequential machines as

---

* Physics Department, California Institute of Technology, Pasadena, CA 91125

well as between different brands of hypercubes.

The motivation for CUBIX can probably best be understood by sitting down with one's favorite hypercube and trying to get each of the nodes to perform a trivial task involving input and output to the console. For example, have each processor identify itself, and multiply its processor number by a number entered on the console, printing an informative message like:

"I am processor 17 and 3 times 17 is 51."

in response to the number 3 being entered. This is an extraordinarily difficult exercise because the nodes of the hypercube do not have direct access to the operating system facilities available on the host. One can not, for instance, execute a "scanf" in the nodes to obtain data from the console. Instead, the host (intermediate host, cube manager, control processor, etc.) must allocate a buffer, read data from the console into it, pass the contents of the buffer to the nodes, read a message for each node containing the results of that node's calculation, format those messages and print the results. Programming this exercise requires two programs, one for the host and one for the nodes of the cube, often compiled with different compilers and different compiler options.

This example is obviously frivolous, but it illustrates an important shortcoming in hypercube programming environments. Maintaining and debugging "real" programs is unnecessarily difficult for exactly the same reason as in the exercise: it is too hard to use the host's operating system. Debugging is extremely difficult because programs cannot be easily modified to produce output tracing the flow of control. Additionally, when a program is modified, it often requires separate but coordinated changes to both the node program and the host program. The necessary coordination is a rich source of minor bugs.

A further deficiency in the hypercube environments is the duplication of effort involved in this programming style. Each programmer is forced to reinvent a host-cube protocol which resembles, functionally at least, the protocols that have been written hundreds, if not thousands, of times already. After writing a few protocols, each programmer tends to develop a characteristic signature. Programmers quickly learn to reuse their 'main' routines, but by then, their time has already been wasted.

Finally, after expending the effort to develop an application on the hypercube, the programmer finds that the program will not run on a sequential machine. The I/O protocol designed for the cube is completely foreign to the sequential machine. Even though the bulk of the application would operate correctly by linking with a very simple library of dummy communication routines, the host program and node program must be "glued" back together. Maintaining an evolving code intended to run on both sequential machines and hypercubes is quite difficult for this reason. (Note that the program, once glued, no longer runs on the hypercube.)

All these deficiencies can be traced to a single source. Hypercubes are viewed as high–speed peripherals attached to a host computer which controls their operation. As peripherals go, they are extremely flexible and programmable, but control, nevertheless, resides in the host. The host loads programs and data into the cube, which then computes and eventually returns results which are expected, in number and length, by the host. In more sophisticated applications, the cube analyzes various tokens passed by the host and may perform different computations based on their values. This general organizational style is familiar to most hypercube programmers.

2. A different perspective

The basic idea behind CUBIX is that the program running in the cube should control the operation of the associated program running on the host. This is exactly opposite to the common style of programming discussed above. In CUBIX, tokens are passed from the cube to the host requesting activities like opening and closing files, reading the time-of-day clock, reading and writing the file system, etc. The host program does nothing more than read requests from the cube, act on them and return appropriate responses. All such requests are generated by subroutine calls in the cube. The host program which serves the requests is universal; it is unchanged from one application to the next, and the programmer need not be concerned with its internal operation.

It is convenient to give the cube subroutines the same names and calling conventions as the system calls they generate on the host. This relieves the programmer of the task of learning a new lexicon of system calls. Any operation he would have performed in a host program can be encoded in a syntactically identical way in the cube. It is of no consequence that the subroutine called in the cube will actually collect its arguments into a message, add a token identifying the request, and send the message to the host for action. All the programmer sees is a call to, e.g., *write(fd, ptr, cnt)*.

High-level utilities are often written in terms of a set of standard system calls. Since the CUBIX system calls have the usual names and calling sequences, system utilities designed for the sequential host computer can be readily ported to the hypercube. For example, the C Standard I/O Library can be compiled and linked with CUBIX allowing various forms of formatted and unformatted buffered I/O. Under CUBIX, the exercise of Section 1 would be programmed as:

```
#include <stdio.h>

main()
{
    int entry, pnum;

    pnum = /* machine dependent specification of local processor number */;
    scanf("%d", &entry);
    fmulti(stdout);                 /* see section 4. */
    printf("I am processor %d, and %d times %d is %d\n",
        pnum, entry, pnum, pnum*entry);
    exit(0);
}
```

3. The catch

It is highly optimistic to think that a set of system calls designed for a sequential computer can be sufficient for use in a parallel environment without modifications or additions. In fact, the requirements of the parallel environment do force one to restrict the use of some routines and also to add a few additional ones. The details differ markedly between crystalline and amorphous environments. The two cases will be taken up in the next two sub-sections. In both cases, the issue addressed is the same:

How does one resolve the problem that different processors may need to do different things?

3.1 The crystalline case

Crystalline programs are characterized by uniformity from processor to processor and a computation that proceeds in loose lock-step. Synchronization is maintained by enforcing a rendez-vous whenever data is communicated between processors. Since loose synchronization is the norm in crystalline programs, it is not unreasonable to demand that system calls be made loosely synchronously. That is, it is permissible to call system sub-routines whenever all communication channels are free. Furthermore, when a system call is made in one processor, it must be made in all processors at the same time, and with identical arguments. (Exceptions will be discussed shortly.) This neatly resolves the prob-lem of how to deal with disparate requests from different nodes; such an event is declared to be in error.

Of course, there are times when different nodes need to request different actions from the host. The short program in Section 2 contains an example in which each proces-sor attempts to print a different string. CUBIX adds two system calls, *mread* and *mwrite*, to the usual set to allow for distinct I/O operations to be performed by different proces-sors. Both must be called loosely synchronously, but they may have different arguments in each node. Their effect is as follows:

mread(fd, ptr, cnt) causes cnt_0 bytes to be read from the file referred to by file descriptor fd, into the memory of processor 0 starting at ptr_0. The next cnt_1 bytes are read from the file into the memory of processor 1 starting at ptr_1, etc. Subscripts refer to the value of the argument in the corresponding proces-sor.

mwrite(fd, ptr, cnt) behaves like *mread*, except that data is copied from the memory of the various processors to the file.

In C programs, it is much more common to use the the Standard I/O Library rather than to use system calls like *read, write, open* and *close* directly. Thus, it is crucial to enhance the Standard I/O Library so users can take advantage of *mread* and *mwrite* along with the usual system calls. In the Standard I/O Library, I/O is directed to *streams,* declared as pointers to type FILE. In CUBIX, streams have a new attribute called *multi-plicity*. That is, streams can be in either the *singular* or *multiple* state. The functions, *fmulti(stream)* and *fsingl(stream)* are provided, which change the multiplicity of their argument to multiple and singular, respectively. Singular streams behave in the usual way, and are bound by the usual rules of loose synchronization and identical arguments. Multi-ple streams form the standard I/O interface to *mread* and *mwrite*. They allow the pro-grammer to read and write data which is distinct in each node of the hypercube. Since output is buffered, queueing data for output to multiple streams need not be synchronous.

On the other hand, flushing the buffer must be done explicitly, and it must be synchro-nous. Flushing a multiple stream causes the data stored in each processor's buffer to appear in order of increasing processor number. The buffer associated with a stream may be flushed by calling one of *fflush, fclose* or *exit*, simultaneously in all the nodes of the hypercube. Since the programmer has control over when buffers are flushed, he can con-trol,in detail, the appearance of his program's output. For example, the code fragment:

```
fmulti(stdout);
printf("hello\n");
fflush(stdout);
printf("goodbye\n");
fflush(stdout);
```

```
printf("CUBIX ");
printf("is flexible\n");
fflush(stdout);
```

produces the following output when executed in all processors loosely synchronously:

```
hello
hello
...
hello
goodbye
goodbye
...
goodbye
CUBIX is flexible
CUBIX is flexible
...
CUBIX is flexible
```

Multiple input streams are not quite as flexible as output streams because the data must be available to the program when the input routine returns. This is in contrast to output routines which do not guarantee that the data has appeared on the output device upon return from the function. Thus, when input functions like *scanf* and *getc* are applied to multiple streams, each node reads as much of the input stream as necessary and then passes control on to the next node in sequence. The function, *ungetc*, when applied to multiple input streams replaces the last character read by the last processor.

3.2 The amorphous case

Amorphous (i.e. non-crystalline) programs are naturally asynchronous. It would be extremely inconvenient for the programmer to synchronize his calculation every time he wished to produce output or interact with the operating system. The processors in an amorphous CUBIX program are treated as though they are executing separate and independent processes. There is no notion of singular I/O, and there are no requirements of loose synchronization or identical arguments. Most system calls behave in a completely straightforward way when used in an amorphous CUBIX program, but the programmer must beware of asking for system resources too frequently. With currently available hosts, it would be easy to swamp the host's operating system if every node were to simultaneously request the same resource.

There is some difficulty, however, in maintaining numerous open files. If the host's operating system allowed CUBIX to allocate several hundred file descriptors, CUBIX could simply return a distinct file descriptor to every process that requested one. Unfortunately, there is a limit of about twenty simultaneously open files, so the CUBIX host program must remember what files are already open and avoid reopening them. There is still a limit of about twenty simultaneously open file *names,* which means that the programmer usually cannot open a different file for each processor in the cube.

When a file is opened by a processor, that processor's pointer into the file is unchanged by the activity of other processors. Each processor maintains some information about the files it has opened, including the current offset at which to begin the next read or write operation. When a read or write request is sent to the host, this information is sent as well, so the host can "seek" to the correct place before reading or writing the data. Thus, each processor has complete control over the location of each byte it writes into the file. Using this system requires considerable care on the part of the programmer to keep processors using the same file from destroying one another's data. Nevertheless, such care often results in programs whose output is repeatable, so that the order of the data in output files does not depend on tiny variations in processor speed, etc. Aside from difficulty of use, there is another important disadvantage. In order for several processors to share a file, it must make sense for that file to have multiple pointers into it. This is simply not true of devices like terminals, to which data may only be appended.

The UNIX operating system provides for file output in *append* mode, in which each datum is placed at the end of the file, regardless of the offset of the process' current file pointer. CUBIX supports the same idea. Placing output files in append mode is a simple way of guaranteeing that data will not be lost because of several processors writing to the same offset. Output to files in append mode may also be directed to a terminal or other serial device. Append mode has the disadvantage that each record in the file must usually be tagged to indicate its originator. A system to automatically tag each record and record a "table–of–contents" at the end of the file upon closure is under development.

4. Experience with CUBIX

A crystalline version of CUBIX has been running at Caltech since early 1986. A version for amorphous applications was implemented about six months later. Since its introduction, CUBIX has become quite popular, and systems are now operating on the Caltech Mark II and Mark III machines as well as the Intel IpSC and the NCUBE. The prevailing attitude among users is that use of CUBIX is vastly simpler than the old host-cube protocols (even among persons not in the author's immediate family). Several programs have been written for which the same code can be compiled and run on a sequential machine, as well as a hypercube running CUBIX.

CUBIX's most significant drawback seems to be the increased code size in node programs. All computation that would have been done on the host is now done in the nodes of the hypercube. Although it is not any slower to perform inherently sequential tasks simultaneously in many processors, a copy of the code must reside in each processor. It is important to realize that both Standard I/O routines like *printf*, which usually does not appear in non-CUBIX programs, and application–dependent sequential code, which would have appeared in the host program, must now be included in the code that runs in every node. The size of this code can be significant, and reduces the amount of space available for data. The code and data linked by a call to *printf*, for example, requires about 6 kbytes on each node in our implementation. Measures can be taken to reduce the size of application–dependent sequential code. For example, filters can be used with UNIX pipes to massage the data prior to sending it into the cube, or after getting it back. So far, we have not needed more generality than that provided by simple input and output filters. Nevertheless, the possibility remains that in subsequent versions of CUBIX, application programs in the cube could call application–dependent subroutines linked into the host program.

5. Conclusion

Adopting the viewpoint that the program running in the nodes of the hypercube should control the behavior of the host program has some extremely desirable consequences.

- It is possible to write a universal host program which accepts commands generated by subroutine calls in the nodes of the hypercube.

- Given a universal host program, programmers only write one program (the one for the nodes) for any application, eliminating considerable labor and an annoying source of bugs.

- All details of the host-cube interface are hidden from the application programmer. Operating system services are obtained by system calls identical to those used on the host.

- Since applications require only one program to operate on the hypercube, it is usually a simple matter to run them on a sequential machine as a special case.

- Since operating system interaction is, for the most part, the same as in sequential programs, there is considerably less to learn before one can begin writing significant hypercube programs.

Protocol-Based Multiprocessors

ERIK P. DEBENEDICTIS*

This short paper describes a programming environment on a hypercube-style multiprocessor that utilizes protocol-based programming primitives and which has been used to make an effective circuit simulator. The paper first describes the programming technique for this environment in terms of *programming plans*. Programming plans are easily understood in terms of *protocols* or *distributed programming primitives*, the emulation of which is the primary function of the runtime environment of the multiprocessor. A description is then given of the programming of the circuit simulator, which is unusually concise given the irregularity of the problem and the high degree of parallelism achieved.

1. Introduction. Let us start by considering the way that people think about computer programming from a psychological rather than the usual mathematical viewpoint.

```
count := 0;
read(x);
while x < > SENTINEL do begin
   count := count+1;
   read(x);
end
```

The code shown above represents programming knowledge, or a plan, called the SENTINEL-CONTROLLED COUNTER-LOOP PLAN [1]. The plan reads a series of values until it encounters a particular sentinel value indicating the end. The plan tallies the number of values encountered before the sentinel.

The SENTINEL-CONTROLLED COUNTER-LOOP PLAN is an example of something that an experienced programmer has used many times, but usually through variants and in combination with other activities. Here, the counted values are obtained by reading input, whereas in a variant they might come from an array or a linked-list. A similar plan that adds a series of values can be imagined by adding the input to a running total, instead of incrementing the count variable, each time through the loop.

Figure 1 is a picture of a multiprocessor plan called the MASTER-AND-SLAVES, or SIMD PLAN (so called because the hardware of a SIMD multiprocessor operates this way).

---

* AT&T Bell Laboratories, Holmdel, New Jersey 07733.

The action in this plan starts with the master, who picks a task and makes the slaves work on the task. When the slaves are all done, the master is notified and it can then perform its next activity.

An example of this plan is when a person runs a multiprocessor program interactively. The person is the master and uses the program by repeatedly typing a command to the program and observing the output. The slaves are the processing elements (PE's) of the multiprocessor, and they repeatedly input commands from the master, compute something

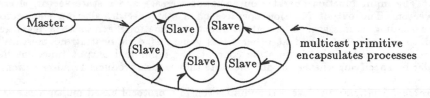

FIG. 1. MASTER-AND-SLAVES Plan

in conjunction with the other PE's, and collectively report completion to the master. Unlike a SIMD computer, however, the MASTER-AND-SLAVES plan is not restricted to having one master; [2] includes an example where many parts of a program are master for many other parts.

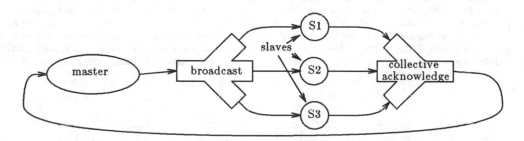

FIG. 2. Implementation of MASTER-AND-SLAVES

Figure 2 illustrates the information flow inherent in MASTER-AND-SLAVES. The master broadcasts commands to the slaves, and the slaves participate in some sort of collective acknowledgement protocol with other slaves, and the master, to indicate completion.

2. *Programming Primitives and Protocols.* I propose to represent distributed programming plans, or techniques, as manipulations of programming primitives. To some extent, this is already done. Multiprocessor algorithms are typically represented as sequences of message passing operations or accesses to shared memory. Currently, however, two implementations of one plan on machines with different distributed programming primitives are considered to be independent pieces of knowledge. I suggest that if an plan is most concisely represented as, say, broadcasting and collective acknowledgement, then this representation should prevail even if the target multiprocessor does not have that exact hardware.

When viewed as information flow on wires, programming primitives are nothing more than protocols. Again, this is done now to some extent. Protocols diagrams can be seen explicitly in the descriptions of shared memory [3] and RPC [4]. The combining elements in the fetch-and-add-based ($f\&a$-based) Ultracomputer [5] use a protocol to remember which $f\&a$ locations have outstanding requests.

The reader may, for tutorial purposes, consider shared-memory locations and pipes (or queues) as typical instances of protocols. A protocol is associated with each memory location in a shared-memory computer, and the programmer interacts with these protocols by issuing read or write requests from any PE. It should be easy to imagine a variant of the pipe structures found in many conventional operating systems applied to a multiprocessor. A protocol would be associated with each pipe (or queue) and it could be read from one PE and written from another.

2.1. Protocol Emulation. The protocol-based multiprocessor executes protocols from a representation similar to the finite state representation [6]. The system, therefore, includes a scheduler that executes the *input function* when a message arrives, and executes the *output function* when the network can accommodate a message and action is specified by a *state vector*.[1] The input function operates on an input message and a state vector, altering the state vector. The output function operates on a state vector, altering the vector, and perhaps sending a message. The output function sometimes generates a message when applied to a state vector and at other times generates ϕ, indicating no message. As a pragmatic extension to the finite state concept, the input and output functions help the scheduler by specifying whether or not the state they return produces requires action.

2.2. Protocol Multiplexing. Every communication in a protocol-based multiprocessor is part of a protocol that is interpreted by the system. Furthermore, the multiprocessor supports an essentially unlimited number of independently operating protocols. This facility requires two things: every message must be tagged with a *protocol number* to identify with which protocol the message is associated, and there must be a state vector to record data and state information about a protocol, for each protocol interacting with a particular PE.

A matter of practical concern arises here. Ease of programming suggests a large virtual space of protocols of which only a small fraction is used. Also, most protocols interact with only a few PEs, leaving their state vectors on other PEs in the *0 state* (initialization state). For example, protocol numbers of 32 bits are appropriate and so are programs where only a half dozen protocols ever leave the 0 state - implying that 6 out of 2^{32} state vectors are in a non-zero state. This suggests that the system should allocate state vectors on demand and deallocate them when no longer necessary. A system managed heap, or some similar structure, is necessary.

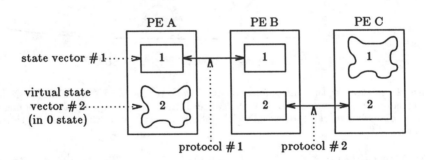

FIG. 3. Illustration of Protocol Multiplexing

Figure 3 illustrates protocol multiplexing. The PEs labeled A and B are interacting via protocol number 1, and B and C via number 2. These two instances of the protocol are functionally independent. While PE B must have a state vector allocated for each of the two instances of the protocol operating on that PE, A and C require only one each. In this case, the virtual protocol state facility avoids allocating memory for these state vectors until they are accessed, either by message receipt or user program access, and when accessed it appears in the 0 state. A protocol may interact with more than two PEs, although this is not illustrated.

3. An Example Protocol. This section illustrates protocol design with a detailed example.

---

1   The term *state vector* is used in the sense of a state machine, and can be thought of as a vector of bits (a binary number) or a data structure.

The example chosen is a simple message-passing implementation of shared memory. The example has been chosen because the semantics of shared memory are well known, and this implementation is simple if not efficient.

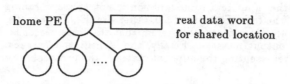

FIG. 4. Simple Implementation of Shared Memory

Figure 4 illustrates the chosen approach to shared memory. A protocol and a *home PE* (shown as the upper circle) are associated with each memory word. Within the home PE is a memory word (shown as a rectangle) which represents the actual value of the shared memory location. Accesses to this word from within the home PE are made by conventional accesses to this location. Accesses from other PEs are done by sending a R (read) or W (write) message to the home node and waiting for an A (acknowledge) message. The protocol is consistent with memory semantics where the actual read or write occurs at an unspecified time during the period between the R or W message and the A message.

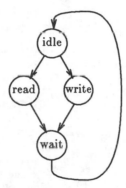

FIG. 5. Slave Node Protocol

A state transition diagram for the protocol executed by non-home PEs is illustrated in figure 5. The protocol is normally in the *idle* state. To start a read or write operation the application program changes the state from *idle* to *read* or *write*, writing a data word into the data part of the state vector if appropriate. If necessary, these operations are done in a critical region to assure they are atomic. The system is informed that the state vector is in an *active* state, indicating that the output function will generate a message, as opposed to a ϕ.

When network is ready to accept an output message, which may be immediately or after an unbounded delay, the protocol scheduler will invoke the output function. The output function will send a R or W message and change the state to *wait*. The data word is sent in the data portion of a W message.

When an A message is eventually received, the input function changes the state to *idle* and stores the data portion of the A message in the data portion of the state.

The input and output functions and the application program code to do a write for this protocol (on the non-home PE) are illustrated below in C. Both the input and output functions accept a pointer to the state vector as an argument; the state vector is a structure with attributes *state* and *data*. The input function takes a pointer to a message as an argument, and the message is a structure containing a *data* field. When the state vector returned by either the input or output function is not *active*, meaning it will not generate an output message, the function returns a 0, otherwise it does not. The write function uses the statement *activate(s)* to inform the system that the state vector is in a condition where it will generate an output message. Finally, the identifiers *idle*, *read*, *write*, and *wait* are manifest constants representing the different states of the protocol.

```
struct state_vector {
    int state;                              /* idle, read, write, or wait */
    int data; } ;                           /* data-to-write or read data */

struct message {
    char type;                              /* R, W, or A */
    int origin;                             /* originating PE */
    int data; } ;

input_function(s, m) state_vector *s; message *m; {
    s->state = idle;                        /* state part of state vector */
    s->data = m->data;                      /* data part of state vector */
    return(0);                              /* indicates no output message */
}

output_function(s) state_vector *s; {
    if (s->state == read)                   /* CPU requested read */
        /* send R message */
    else if (s->state == write)             /* CPU requested write */
        /* send W message with s->data */
    else return(0);                         /* indicates no output message */
    s->state = wait;                        /* change state */
    return(1);                              /* indicates output message */
}

write(x, s) state_vector *s; {
    /* enter critical region */
    s->data = x;                            /* data part of state vector */
    s->state = write;                       /* request write */
    activate(s);                            /* put on activity queue */
    /* leave critical region */
    while (s->state != idle) ;              /* busy wait until done */
}
```

4. *A Circuit Simulator*. Integrated circuit simulation is an important task in industry, and may be the most computing intensive computer-aided design task. Circuit simulations which use exact transistor models and accurately model the analog functional and timing behavior of integrated circuits are currently applied to portions of integrated circits with around 100 transistors. It is important to industry, however, that whole integrated circuits, containing perhaps 100,000 transistors be simulated. Whole integrated circuits can only be simulated by abstracting the analog and timing behavior of many small portions of the circuit and then functionally simulating the entire circuit on the basis of these abstractions. Functional simulation is relatively inaccurate at modeling timing and analog properties. This section discusses a distributed algorithm for a simulator midway between circuit and functional simulators. The simulator discussed here [7] allows larger circuits to be simulated as part of the integrated circuit design cycle that has been previously possible.

4.1. *Uniprocessor Circuit Simulation*. The type of simulator discussed here divides the simulation into into intervals (Δt) and repeatedly computes the voltage on each wire at time $t + \Delta t$ based on voltages at time t.

```
for each timestep
  for each element
    update voltages on output wires
```

The straightforward plan shown above must be merged with (what I call here) the SIMULTANEOUS UPDATE PLAN. This plan assures that the value computed for a wire at time $t + \Delta t$ is actually based on voltages at the input of the circuit element at time t. Simply associating a variable with each wire to hold its voltage does not work. When a wire goes from the output of one element to the input of another, and the first element happens to be updated first, then the second element is updated using the new voltage value. A common uniprocessor version of the SIMULTANEOUS UPDATE PLAN associates two variables with each wire, one for an *old* value and one for a *new* value. When each circuit element is updated values from the *old* variables are used to compute values for the *new* variables. A second phase iterates over each circuit element a second time moving the *new* variable to the *old* variable.

```
for each element
  new voltage = update(old voltage)
for each element
  old voltage = new voltage
```

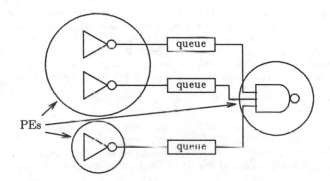

FIG. 6. Multiprocessor Simulator with Queues

4.2. Multiprocessor Circuit Simulation. Figure 6 illustrates a multiprocessor plan for circuit simulation. The SIMULTANEOUS UPDATE PLAN is managed by the use of queues which are written by circuit elements with outputs, and read by circuit elements with inputs. Different circuit elements may be on different PEs with only the requirement that the PEs refer to the wire by a single protocol number. If there is synchronization to assure that all PEs are computing for the same value of t, then there are a maximum of two voltage values in a queue.

Figure 7 illustrates the MASTER-AND-SLAVES plan in the context of the circuit simulator. The definition of the circuit simulation problem requires that there be a person running the program issuing commands such as *simulate for 100 ns*. Such a command must be delivered to every SLAVE with circuit elements, which simulate until done, and then participate in a collective acknowledgement directed toward the MASTER. The MASTER might then decides if more simulation is in order or if the answer is to be printed.

5. *Conclusions.* The approach presented in this paper addresses the spectrum of issues

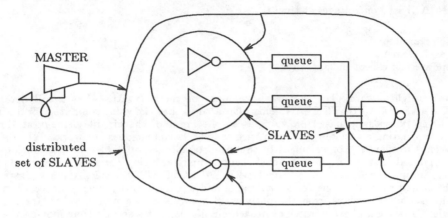

FIG. 7. Multiprocessor Simulator with Queues

between technology and programming technique consistently and with thought to future developments. It should be possible to write programs and build machines with up to 100,000 PEs and retain adequate efficiency. Research not reported here has explored computer architectures where protocol emulation is an intrinsic function of the hardware. The *communication to computation* cost ratio of a machine with such an architecture would be substantially lower, and would therefore support a broader class of applications (such as, for example logic simulation instead of just circuit simulation). An evolution in programming primitives is occurring in my laboratory as more programs are written; certain programming primitives (protocols) see increasing usage (and are enhanced) whereas others see decreasing usage (and are abandoned). There is a possibility that a standard set of distributed programming primitives will eventually emerge, in the same way as conventional computer hardware has standardized on 2's complement integers, pointers, and floating point as data types.

6. References.

[1] E. SOLOWAY, *Learning to Program = Learning to Construct Mechanisms and Explanations.* In *Communications of the ACM*, September 1986. Pages 850-858.

[2] E. DeBENEDICTIS, *Multiprocessor Programming with Distributed Variables.* In M. HEATH (ed.), *Hypercube Multiprocessors 1986* , August, 1985, pages 70-86.

[3] L. RUDOLPH, Z. SEGALL, *Dynamic Decentralized Cache Schemes for MIMD Parallel Processors.* In *Proceedings of the 11th Annual International Symposium on Computer Architecture*, June 1984. Pages 340-347.

[4] A. BIRRELL and B. NELSON, *Implementing Remote Procedure Calls.* In *ACM Transactions on Computer Systems*, February 1984. Pages 39-59.

[5] A. GOTTLIEB, R. GRISHMAN, C. KRUSKAL, K. McAULIFFE, L. RUDOLPH, M. SNIR, *The NYU Ultracomputer - Designing an MIMD Shared Memory Parallel Computer.* In *IEEE Transactions on Computers*, February 1983. Pages 175-189.

[6] A. DANTHINE, *Protocol Representation with Finite-State Models.* In *IEEE Transactions on Communications*, April 1980. Pages 632-643.

[7] B. ACKLAND, S. AHUJA, E. DeBENEDICTIS, T. LONDON, S. LUCCO, D. ROMERO, *MOS Timing Simulation on a Message Based Multiprocessor.* In *Proceedings of the IEEE International Conference on Computer Design* , October, 1986, pages 446-450.

Programming NCUBEs[*] with a Graphical Parallel Programming Environment versus an Extended Sequential Language

KEVIN GATES[†] AND DAVID SOCHA[‡]

Abstract. We compare the writing and execution of programs written in Cosmic Cube C with programs written in the graphical parallel programming environment and language Poker. Our example programs, an implementation of a Cholesky algorithm for a banded matrix, were written in both languages and compiled into object codes that ran on the Cosmic Cube. However, the program written in Poker is shorter, faster and easier to write, easier to debug, and portable without changes to other parallel architectures. The Poker program was slower than the program written directly in Cosmic Cube C; however, the experiments provided insights into changes that make Poker programs nearly as fast.

1 Introduction

Now that there are a number of parallel architectures, including n-cubes, there is an increased need for better parallel programming techniques. In particular, programmers need assistance handling the parallel aspects of their programs. One direction for improvement is in the design of better parallel programming languages and environments. At one extreme are very high-level languages such as Crystal [1] in which the programmer relies on the compiler to extract parallelism and optimize inter-process communication. At the other extreme are low-level languages/language-support-systems such as crystalline [2] which provide bare-bones message facilities and no algorithmic programming assistance but are tuned to maximizing execution speed. Poker [3] takes a more conservative intermediate position providing a high-level parallel programming abstraction supported by a graphical programming environment and language while still relying upon the programmer to extract the parallelism from algorithms. The key question is whether such a high-level language can provide this programming support while not compromising the speed of the programs.

This paper addresses this question by discussing the programming and execution of the modified Cholesky decomposition written in both Poker and the extended C [4] for the Cosmic Cube [5]. We provide timing results for the execution of both programs on the

---
* NCUBE Corporation, Tempe, Arizona
† Department of Applied Mathematics, FS-20, University of Washington, Seattle, WA, 98195
‡ Department of Computer Science, FR-35, University of Washington, Seattle, WA, 98195

Cosmic Cube.

2 The Algorithmic Test Case

Our basis of comparison between the two programming languages is an algorithm to solve the matrix equation:

$$Ax = b \tag{1}$$

where A is a symmetric, positive definite, $n \times n$ matrix, with semi-bandwidth β. The solution method that we use is an implementation of the modified Cholesky algorithm:

$$A = LDL^T$$

where L is a unit lower triangular matrix with semi-bandwidth β, and D is a diagonal matrix. The complete solution of (1) is then found by solving the following equations:

$$Lz = b \tag{2}$$
$$Dy = z \tag{3}$$
$$L^T x = y \tag{4}$$

We solve (2) for z with forward substitution, (3) for y by a vector division, and (4) for x with back substitution. Our implementation of the modified Cholesky algorithm has seven steps:

1. Load matrix A.

2. Load vector b.

3. Do Cholesky decomposition $A = LDL^T$.

4. Do forward substitution $Lz = b$.

5. Calculate $Dy = z$.

6. Do back substitution $L^T x = y$.

7. Dump resultant vector x.

The algorithm uses $(\beta + 1)^2$ processes conceptually arranged in a square grid. Steps 3, 4, and 6 require that each process be able to broadcast to every other process in its column, and that each process on the diagonal be able to broadcast across its row. Instead of fully connecting the columns and rows we acknowledged the high cost of message passing in current implementations of n-cubes and did our own message routing, using n-cube connections for the columns and trees, embedded in a n-cube, for the rows. These communication requirements can be realized with an n-cube interconnection scheme.

3 The Languages

Both Cosmic Cube C and Poker use a non-shared memory model of cooperating sequential processes communicating by message passing and a modified C to express the sequential details of the process's code. They differ chiefly in how they handle the parallel aspects of a program. The Cosmic Cube C provides no parallel structure while Poker uses a graphical environment for describing the parallel aspects of the program.

```
for i ← 0 to n − 1 do    (i = update row)
      for j ← i to min(n, i + β) do     (j = update column)
            for k ← max(0, i − β) to i do     (k = pivot row)
                  if k = i then
```
$$d_{kk} = a_{kk}$$
$$a_{kj} \leftarrow a_{kj} \; / \; d_{kk}$$
```
                  else
```
$$a_{ij} \leftarrow a_{ij} - (a_{ik} * a_{kj})$$
```
                  endif
            endfor
      endfor
endfor.
```

Figure 1: The Cholesky Decomposition Algorithm.

3.1   The Poker Language and Environment

Poker is both a parallel programming language for non-shared memory algorithms, and a parallel programming environment used to program and execute Poker programs. The Poker environment runs on a conventional computer. It allows the user to write Poker programs and serves as the front end when running Poker programs on the simulator, emulator, or target parallel architecture. Both the Poker language and the Poker environment are non-standard and intimately connected, so this section will interleave discussion of their features from the point of view of a programmer.

The description of a Poker program is based on the graph model so often used to describe a parallel program. This description has five logical components:

1. a graph whose vertices are processes and whose edges are communication channels between the processes,

2. a labeling of the vertices with the codes to run in the processes,

3. a labeling of the edges at each vertex,

4. the codes for the processes, and

5. a description of the inputs and outputs (the Cholesky decomposition has none).

Poker encodes parallel algorithms at this same level of abstraction, using separate "views" of a graphical programming environment to define four of the five parts; the process codes are programmed using a standard text editor.[3] For example, a Poker programmer for the Cholesky Decomposition step (step 3), Figure 1, codes the five components as shown in Figure 2:

1. *Communication Graph*: The programmer uses a mouse or number pad to explicitly *draw* the connections between the processes (boxes). This drawing is the *only* definition of the interconnection; there is no textual specification of the interconnection.

---

[3]The term "View" refers to the manner in which Poker programs are stored and recalled. The five parts form a database defining the program. Each "View" is a perspective on this database, perhaps incorporating information from more than one of the parts of the program, as in the graph programmed in the Communication Graph View is visible in the Process Assignment View.

Communication Graph

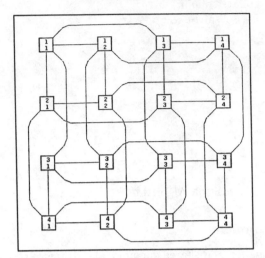

Process Assignment

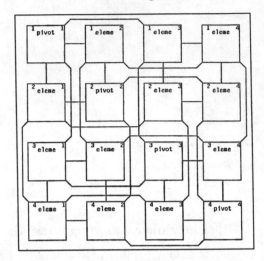

Port Name Assignment

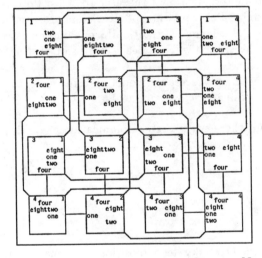

Process Definition

```
code pivot;
ports one,two,four,eight;
pivot() {
    short MatrixRow, MatrixCol;
    float A[2][4], b[4];
    port Row[2], Column[2], SendPort, RecvPort;
        ⋮
    import MatrixRow from MatrixRow;
    import MatrixCol from MatrixCol;
    import A from A;
    Row[1] = one;

    for (PivotRow = 1; PivotRow < 16; PivotRow ++) {
    if (PivotRow == MatrixRow + 4*UpdateRow) {
        Aii[0] = A[0][UpdateRow];
        bcst(Aii, MatrixRow, Row);
            ⋮
    SendPort = Column[PivotRow % 2];
    SendPort < - piv;
        ⋮
```

Stream Name Assignment

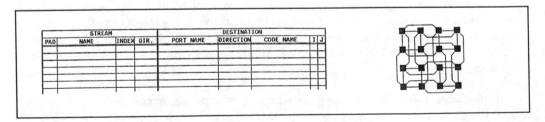

Figure 2: The five parts of a Poker program for the Cholesky decomposition step.

2. *Process Assignment*: The programmer assigns the code to run in each process by entering the code name at the top of the process box. Note that the Communication Graph is still visible here, aiding the programming of the Process Assignment.

3. *Port Name Assignment*: The programmer labels the edges from the perspective of each vertex; each edge has two names, one for each end or "port." Again, the communication graph is visible to aid the programmer.

4. *Process Definition*: The (usually small number of) process codes are written in a slightly modified version of C [6]. Section 3.2 on Poker C describes the modifications. Figure 2 shows only the code for `pivot`.

5. *Stream Name Assignment*: The dangling edges of the graph connect the algorithm to its inputs and outputs. The programmer labels dangling edges with the name of the input and output streams.[4]

These pictures are exact replicas of the lower part of the corresponding Poker views, showing the parallel parts of the Poker program as entered by the user. The upper part of a Poker View contains additional status information including the number of processes in the program (between 4 and 4096 processes) and the state of the programming environment during programming. Note that several views display the communication graph as context while programming the remaining parts of the parallel algorithm.

Three additional Views aid the user in initializing the size of the program and compiling and executing it:

- *CHiP Parameters View*: Used to select the logical CHiP architecture[5], including the number of processes.

- *Command Request View*: Used to compile, load, link, and so on, Poker programs so that they are ready to execute.

- *Trace View*: Used to watch the execution of the algorithm. The Trace View uses the same picture as in the Process Assignment, except that the last four lines of each box show the current values of up to four variables being traced in that process.

The Trace View is especially important when debugging Poker programs. The Poker generic simulator runs on a conventional von-Neuman computer and provides a much more interactive environment in which to debug Poker programs before tying up the Cosmic Cube or other parallel computer. If additional problems arise during Cosmic Cube execution, we can turn the tracing mechanism on to try to pinpoint the error, though such tracing changes the timing of the program making it exceedingly difficult to pinpoint timing problems.

What we have seen so far is one "phase" of a Poker program; that is, one unit of parallel execution. Most parallel programs are more complex, requiring a number of different parallel units, which we call phases. Each of these phases is defined using the five parts described above and a grid of processes of the same size. Processes occupying the same location on the grid in different phases may pass information between phases, using the `import`/`export` convention described in Section 3.2. Each phase may connect the processes in any graph independent of the connections used in other phases.

---

[4] A stream is a series of data values of arbitrary, and possibly mixed, types. Poker requires that the stream data in files are basic data types, *e.g.* `bool`, `char`, `short`, and so on.

[5] Poker was designed to program the CHiP architecture. Both CHiP Parameters View and the switches in the Communication Graph are vestiges of this decision.

Each phase executes as a unit and the processes synchronize after completing each phase. Phases can be invoked manually, from the Poker environment, or via a program written in a sequential phase-control language.

3.2   Poker C

Poker C code is standard C [6] with a few changes.[6] Using the Process Definition in Figure 2 as an example, we see that each code has a header specifying the name of the code (`pivot`), and the ports (`one`, `two`, `four`, `eight`) followed by a set of C routines. Variables exist only within routines; there are no external variables.

Processes occupying the same location on the grid communicate through an inter-phase data space that they, and only they, share. Variables in this inter-phase data space do not exist before being assigned values. However, once assigned, the variable exists forever. Hence, the most recently assigned value is available until the program terminates. The expression

$$\texttt{export}(local, inter\text{-}phase)$$

stores the value of the locally defined variable *local* into the inter-phase variable *inter-phase*. At any point in the future, from any phase, the expression

$$\texttt{import}(local, inter\text{-}phase)$$

loads the local variable *local* with the last value stored into *inter-phase*.

The statements

$$port \texttt{ <- } expression$$
$$variable \texttt{ <- } port$$

send and receive messages. *Port* is either a port name from the header's `ports` list, or a variable of type `port`. The run-time system checks receive messages to make sure that the message received is of the same type as the *variable*; incompatible types cause a fatal run-time error. Messages between processes may be any of the basic data types, arrays with statically defined size, or structures, as long as there are no pointers in the data.

4   Implementations

Since both languages use the same non-shared memory paradigm of communicating sequential processes and the same base language, C, the process codes are very similar in the two languages. However, we had to do some subtle programming in the Cosmic Cube C program to determine which messages to keep and which to pass. In our message passing scheme communications are difficult in the Cosmic Cube C version, but painless in Poker since Poker automatically encodes the "direction" of a message by the port from which it enters.

Both programs have three types of processes: (1) a host "controller" process that allocates a cube, spawns processes onto the Cosmic Cube, and controls their execution, (2) a host "file server" process that passes values between files and processes, and (3) 16 cube processes, one per node of a 4-cube, implementing the Cholesky algorithm. The Cosmic Cube C version combined the controller and file server into one process.

---

[6]A more complete description of Poker C is found in [7].

5   Mapping the Guest Graph to the Host Graph

Both programs used the communication links of an n-cube. We mapped the n-cube graph of the algorithm (guest graph) directly onto the n-cube of the host architecture (host graph) maintaining the node adjacencies. In general the mapping of the algorithm's interconnection, the guest graph, to the host graph of the architecture can be more complex.

Cosmic Cube C provides no explicit concept of either graph; instead the cube is logically completely connected and the definition and use of the guest graph is embedded into the program. This increases the difficulty of changing the mapping of the guest graph to the host graph. This difficulty could be eliminating by writing a more general spawning/message-passing scheme.

Poker simplifies the mapping problem by separating it from the program specification. The guest graph, defined by the Communication Graph, is automatically mapped onto the host graph and the resulting mapping stored in a file. The spawner reads this file at run-time to determine the process placement on the processors. Changing the mapping file changes the resultant mapping with no need to recompile.

This is an obvious place for an automatic mapping system. Currently, Poker does one mapping, a row-major assignment of process/node numbers to processes. It is easy to imagine a more sophisticated system that would try to improve the mapping, perhaps first using simulation to weight the use of the communication paths, and also automatically mapping from a family of guest graphs to a family of host graphs. Berman [8] describes one such system. This is a rich area for further research.

6   Results

The cube processes ran on an otherwise unloaded 4-cube, to avoid message contention with other cube programs, and the host processes ran on a Sun 2/120 directly connected to the cube, to avoid ethernet delays. We tried to keep the Sun otherwise unloaded during the runs. Each cube process cached its timing values until the end of the program to minimize measurement perturbations.

To estimate the variance we ran each program 8 or more times.[7] Each cube process recorded the start and end time of steps 3, 4–5, and 6 (step 5 was folded into step 4). This provided two measurements for each process: the "total" time from start of step 3 to end of step 6, and the "combined" time, a sum of the times between the beginning and end of steps 3–6.

The process/node number is on the x-axis (recall that there is one process/node) while the y-axis shows the execution time in milliseconds. The vertical bars are the 95% confidence regions for the averages.

Figure 3 emphasizes two trends. First, the cost of synchronization, estimated by the difference between the "combined" times (lower points) and "total" times, is quite large, ranging from 40% to 80% of the total execution time.

Second, processes with higher numbers have faster execution times, especially for the combined times. This reduction has at least two causes: (1) the controller starts the cube processes in ascending order of process number so that lower numbered processes block on input from higher numbered processes, (2) the lower numbered processes need to

---

[7]We attempted to execute 15 runs of each of the four program discussed below, randomly shuffling the executions into a sequence of 60 runs. However the Cosmic Cube has been having problems recently, so we were unable to get one set of 60 runs. The number of runs per figure are: 12 for Fig. 6, 13 for Fig. 6, and 8 for Fig. 5. The 15 runs for Fig. 4 came from an earlier batch. Note how the variance decreases with increasing number of runs.

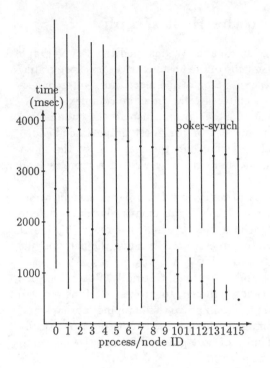

Figure 3: Timings for Poker program with synchronization between phases.

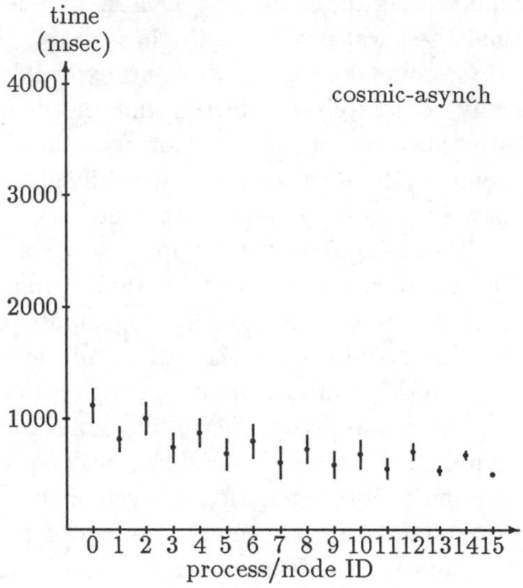

Figure 4: Timings for Cosmic Cube C program with no synchronization between steps.

forward messages between the host, connected to node 0, and the other processes. The Cholesky algorithm, with its low computation/communication ratio, accentuates this high communication cost. Also note that higher numbered processes have much less variance for the "combined" times indicating that message forwarding or idling for messages from processes that have yet to execute takes a heavy toll on lower numbered processes.

For comparison, Figure 4 shows the execution times for the Cosmic Cube C program. There is no synchronization between steps of this program so the total time equals the combined time. This program runs about 3 times faster than the Poker program. However the difference between "combined" Poker times and the Cosmic Cube C times decreased as the node number increases, suggesting that inter-step synchronization is killing Poker programs. Figures 5 and 6 demonstrate that the Poker program is not inherently slower than the Cosmic Cube C program. Figure 5 shows that the times for the same Cosmic Cube C program, but with synchronization between steps, approach those of synchronized Poker. One reason the synchronized Cosmic Cube C program does not slow down as much as the synchronized Poker program is that the controller and file server for the Cosmic Cube C program are one process, so the Cosmic Cube C program has about one third fewer synchronization messages than the Poker program. Going in the other direction, Figure 6 shows that the same Poker program without the inter-phase synchronization is as fast as the Cosmic Cube C program.

In conclusion, The Poker Cholesky program exhibits the same run-times as the Cosmic Cube C program, indicating that Poker's higher level programming abstraction does not sacrifice an efficient implementation for at least one communication intensive algorithm.

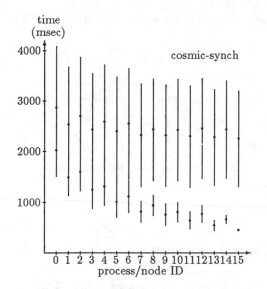

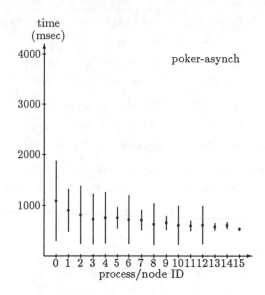

Figure 5: Timings for Cosmic Cube C program with synchronization between steps.

Figure 6: Timings for Poker program without synchronization between phases.

Programming in raw Cosmic Cube C could still be advantageous since it allows the following: message passing to simulate a completely connected graph of processes, dynamic process creation and deletion, dynamic reallocation of the cube, and the use of the programmer's knowledge of a program to optimize its run time with non-blocking sends and receives and no synchronization.

On the other hand, Poker provides the following: a higher level program abstraction that eases the definition of a parallel program, a visually oriented environment, automatic provision of routines to handle file input/output, process spawning, cube allocation, and process control so that the programmer can concentrate on the algorithm, and a parallel simulator/debugger for developing programs off-line. In addition, programs written in Poker are portable to different parallel architectures [9].

7   Improving the efficiency of Cosmic Poker

These experiments pointed to places where more effort on the part of compilers, host operating systems, or host hardware might improve the efficiency of parallel programs. The amount of improvement depends on the algorithm, its implementation, and the n-cube hardware available. In particular, Poker programs potentially could benefit from:

- Running phases without intervening synchronization. As a result of this work, we have decided that Cosmic Poker will provide a way to run phases asynchronously.

- Broadcasting, fanning-out, or fanning-in messages between the controller and cube processes. Support in the host operating system or hardware could substantially reduce synchronization costs. Fan-in synchronization could be made extremely cheap with the use of a hardware "AND" line raised when all processes have completed some task, such as a phase.

- Placing the controller on the cube, say on the opposite side from the host, to balance the message load and avoid the host/cube bottleneck.

- Using non-blocking sends and receives where possible. This requires extensive flow analysis.

- Statically initializing the message descriptors.

In most cases there are tradeoffs so that the modifications would speed some types of algorithms on some machines, and slow others.

8   Conclusion

This and other experiments indicate that high-level parallel programming languages and environments can substantially elevate the programmability of n-cubes while still producing efficient code. This is not to say that parallel programs will always be easier to write and execute more efficiently if written in Poker. An algorithm that *requires* complete connectivity or dynamic creation or destruction of processes does not fit into the current Poker framework. However, Poker does provide a cleaner approach to writing efficient programs for a large class of parallel algorithms.

9   Acknowledgments

A number of people assisted us in this project: Our advisors Larry Snyder and Loyce Adams provided motivation, advise, and helpful criticism; Bob Mitchell wrote portions of the Poker C compiler; James Schaad helped retarget Poker to the Cosmic Cube, producing good code under time pressure; Beth Ong helped with the design and programming of the numerical algorithm; Chuck Seitz and his group at Caltech were most helpful in providing access to the Cosmic Cube and its hosts and dealing promptly with our problems; Phil Nelson, Mary Bailey, and many fellow graduate students made helpful comments throughout the project. We thank all of these people.

This supported in part by National Science Foundation Grant DCR-8416878 and by Office of Naval Research Contract No. N000014-86-K-00264.

References

[1] Marina C. Chen. Very high-level parallel programming in crystal. *Proceedings of the Second Conference on Hypercube Multiprocessors*, 1986.

[2] Brian Beckman. Hypercube operating systems: development for performance and programmability. *Proceedings of the Second Conference on Hypercube Multiprocessors*, 1986.

[3] Lawrence Snyder. Parallel programming and the poker programming environment. *Computer*, 17(7):27–36, July 1984.

[4] Wen-King Su, Reese Faucette, and Chuck Seitz. *C Programmer's Guide to the Cosmic Cube*. Technical Report 5203:TR:85, Computer Science Department, California Institute of Technology, September 1985.

[5] Charles L. Seitz. The cosmic cube. *Communications of the ACM*, 28(1):22–33, January 1985.

[6] Brian W. Kernighan and Dennis M. Richie. *The C Programming Language*. Academic Press, New York, 1978.

[7] Lawrence Snyder. *Poker (4.0) Programmer's Reference Guide*. Technical Report 86–05–04, Computer Science Department, University of Washington, November 1986.

[8] Francine Berman, Michael Goodrich, Charles Koelbel, III W. J. Robison, and Karen Showell. Prep-P: a mapping preprocessor for CHiP architectures. *Proceedings of the 1985 International Conference on Parallel Processing*, 731–733, 1985.

[9] Lawrence Snyder and David Socha. Poker on the cosmic cube: the first retargettable parallel programming language and environment. *Proceedings of the International Conference on Parallel Processing, IEEE*, 628–635, 1986.

A Cellular Automata Interface to Hypercube Multiprocessors

JOHN W. STAMEY, JR.* AND EDWARD W. PAGE, III*

Abstract. Program development in parallel processing environments is a new issue in software engineering. The CA/Shell is an interface designed to ease the coding, testing and debugging of programs designed to execute on hypercube multiprocessors in a manner reflecting the underlying architecture of the machine.

Introduction. The notion of parallel processing has lead to many developments in parallel algorithms and architectures. Another logical step is the development of software tools for program development in these new parallel programming environments (PPE's).

This paper is a summary of a high level design for a PPE. The name of the environment is the "CA/Shell." CA refers to the model of computation known as cellular automata, while shell reflects the fact that the PPE is really a user interface. The concepts borrowed from the field of cellular automata include global-vs-local views of system evolution (computation) as well as a regular interconnection of processing elements similar to the cellular automata neighborhood. The anticipated ease of coding, testing and debugging of programs for hypercube machines will serve to make the advances of parallel computing more accessible to all programmers. The motivation for this user interface is based on the concept that the programming environment should reflect the underlying architecture of the machine in the most natural manner.

A good programming environment provides, among other

---

*Department of Computer Science, Clemson University, Clemson, S.C. 29634 things, a reasonable debugging facility (1).   Standard von Neumann architectures lead to programming environments which are sequential in their editing and testing capabilities. An example of this is the setting of break points in code or display selected data values as they are calculated.

As the constituant modules of a parallel program ensemble execute on multiple processors, facilities which would facilitate testing and debugging include tracking of local and global data objects (within each processor as well as within the ensemble of processors), tracing of interprocessor communication, and some type of I/O analysis.

Two modes of operation may be used to provide the facilities just described: a STEP mode of operation would let the programmer examine execution of the individual program statements so that data objects and channel activity can be effectively monitored; a FAST mode would allow the program ensenble to execute in the normal manner.   As the STEP mode does not actually require the power of multiple processors, the actual execution of this simulation tool may take place on one of the single processing units.

Design Of CA/Shell.   CA/Shell is a menu driven system which provides information on such topics as processor allocation, global and local views of computation, communication tracking and code editing.   The main menu (Screen 1) allows selection of the following eight options: environment setup, global hypercube view, local neighborhood view, processor view, communication monitor, editor (programming environment), program execution and exit.   Screen 2, the Environment Setup, is used to determine the number of actual processors (physical CPU's) to be allocated for the current computation as well as the number of virtual processors (CPU's to be used by the computation).   At this point, a heuristic assignment of processes to processors is the only allocation policy available in the CA/Shell.

Screens 3 through 4a provide different views of each individual processor.   Screen 3 contains a picture of the selected hypercube configuration mapped into a two-dimensional plane.   This global view of the hypercube allows the programmer to review all allocated processors as well as preview channel communication for the possibility of pre-execution deadlock detection.   Screen 4, the Local Neighborhood view allows the programmer to see each processor in its geometric relationship with other processors.   Features available include: multiple views of concurrent processes; the ability to navigate from one processor to another through the arrow keys; execution simulation (in STEP mode only) which designates active channels as well as the data transmitted; and a display of preselected global and local data objects.   Interaction between processes which execute in the neighborhood of a given process can be easily examined.   The programmer may: select a window giving the actual source code being executed; examine data as it is transmitted from processor to processor; and follow the active communication channels during program execution.

Screen 1

CA/Shell
Main Menu

1. Environment Setup
2. Global Hypercube View
3. Processor Neighborhood View
4. Processor Local View
5. Mode Selection
6. Programming Environment
7. Execution
8. Exit

Screen 2

CA/Shell
Environmental Setup

Number of Actual Processors 8

Number of Virtual Processors 7

Screen 4

CA/Shell
Local Neighborhood View

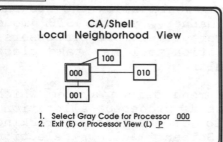

1. Select Gray Code for Processor 000
2. Exit (E) or Processor View (L) P

Screen 3

CA/Shell
Global Hypercube View

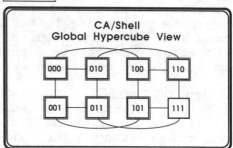

Screen 4a

CA/Shell
Local Processor View

Processor:	XXX	Program:	TEST

Local Data: Data Object 1
               Data Object 2
                    .
                    .
                    .

Code: Statement 1
               Statement 2
                    .
                    .
                    .

Screen 5

CA/Shell
Mode Selection

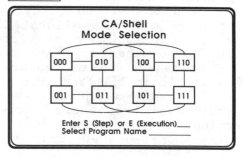

Enter S (Step) or E (Execution)____
Select Program Name _____

Screen 6

CA/Shell
Local Processor View

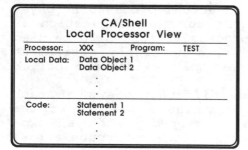

1. Select Processor to View/Edit: 000 (A=All)
2. Select Processor to Compile: 000 (A=All)
3. Select Program name: _____

Screen 6a

CA/Shell - Edit Processor 000,   Program 1DCA

Local Data: X(8) = (1,0,0,0,0,0,1)
               STATIC C_VAL = 0

1:   Y = INLEFT*4+C_VAL*2+INRIGHT
2:   C_VAL = X(Y)

Replication: Processor: _____ (A=All)
Line Range: _____ _____

Screen 5 allows selection of STEP mode for debugging or FAST mode for true execution. The programming environment, Screen 6, allows the option of selecting a particular programming ensemble or a particular processor whose code is to be displayed or compiled.

Screen 6a depicts a program displayed in the actual editing environment. This particular program generates the time-step evolution of a one-dimensional cellular automata with two states (0 and 1) per site (cell) and one connection link between the cells. For example, given a set of cells $(\ldots, a_{i-1}, a_i, a_{i+1}, \ldots)$, the state of the cells at time t+1 is completely determined by the function $(a_i, t+1) = r((a_{i-1}, t), (a_i, t), (a_{i+1}, t))$, for $a_i \varepsilon (0,1)$. The state transition function r can take on 256 possible values based upon the value of (a_i, t) over the eight neighborhoods (000, 001, 010, 011, 100, 101, 110, 111) determined by $((a_{i-1}, t), (a_i, t), (a_i))$. The example program uses the rule of 129, derived from the fact that r(111)=1, r(000)=1, otherwise r(xyz)=0. A more complete discussion of cellular automata may be found in (2).

A command called REPLICATE allows the programmer to copy sections of code from one processor to others as necessary. Such a facility can clearly speed program development when processors require similar code.

Summary. The CA/Shell project is currently being developed at Clemson University. Three goals of the project include: (i) creation of an enhanced programming environment for hypercube multiprocessors; (ii) availability of a facility with which to study human computer interaction and software engineering in a PPE; and (iii) ability to study various implementations of parallel algorithms.

REFERENCES

(1) T. PRATT, Programming Languages, 2nd Edition, Prentice-Hall, 1984.
(2) S. WOLFRAM, Statistical Mechanics of Cellular Automata, Rev. Mod. Phys., 55 (1983), pp. 601-644.

A Heuristic Linda Kernel for Hypercube Multiprocessors

STEVEN E. LUCCO*

Abstract

Linda is a parallel programming language distinguished by its support for distributed data structures and its simplicity. We have developed a new implementation strategy for Linda on hypercube multiprocessors; the new scheme uses a distributed hashing algorithm to emulate Linda's shared memory semantics. Using this scheme to program a 64 processor hypercube, we have completed a runtime system which executes all Linda communication primitives at speeds within a factor of two of those on an existing, bus-based, kernel. We have implemented a VLSI circuit simulator, called EMU, under the hypercube Linda kernel. Communication costs dominate runtime due to a simple transistor model, making EMU the first significant communication-bound application written entirely in Linda. EMU under Linda shows an almost linear speedup for 2 or more 12MHz MC68000 processors; using 64 processors, it executes 14 times faster than an optimal serial implementation. Moreover, use of Linda made the EMU communication kernel extremely elegant and easy to program.

Having achieved these results with a random hash function, we modified our runtime Linda system so that it could dynamically redistribute information (i.e. Linda "tuples") to better match an application's communication pattern. Under this heuristic kernel, EMU ran over 31 times faster than on a uniprocessor, and within ten percent of an EMU implementation meticulously written with direct message passing.

Introduction

Linda belongs to a class of parallel languages characterized by shared memory emulation. Such languages create the illusion of a global data space and provide communication primitives which manipulate objects in that space. Shared memory emulation has two major advantages. First, it allows the construction of

---

*AT&T Bell Laboratories, Holmdel, New Jersey 07733

distributed data structures. Several processes can access a global database, or communicate through the abstraction of a stream, pipeline or other structure. Second, it is simple. Instead of many message passing channels, the user works with a single shared data space.

Languages like Linda have been considered prohibitively expensive to implement on current hypercube multiprocessors because of the large communication costs typical of these architectures. The research presented below demonstrates that Linda can run on a hypercube with only a small (10-15%) overhead for many applications. We first give a brief overview of Linda and its previous implementation on a bus-based multiprocessor. Next, we present a new implementation strategy for Linda on a hypercube multiprocessor[1]. Third, we look at a sample Linda application, distributed MOS timing simulation, under the new kernel. Finally, we present heuristics which greatly reduce Linda kernel communication overhead.

Linda

Linda emulates a shared memory called Tuple Space. Tuple Space contains lists of typed data, called tuples. In Linda, processes access tuples through matching input templates. Linda creates this abstraction by adding three communication primitives--IN, OUT, and READ--to a host language such as C or FORTRAN.

Tuple Space acts like a bulletin board for information exchange among processes. OUT "posts" a tuple on the bulletin board. IN reads and removes a tuple from the board. READ non-destructively accesses a tuple, leaving it on the board for other processes to read or remove. This set of primitives helps the user avoid synchronization problems, as tuples can only be created or destroyed, not modified in place.

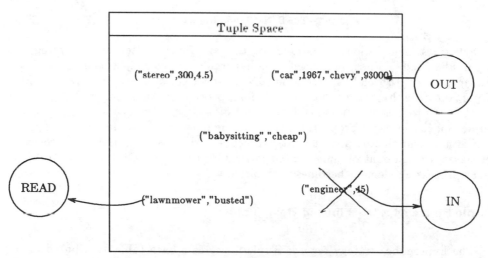

Figure 1--Tuple Space as a Bulletin Board

Linda uses a simple matching algorithm to determine whether a process can access a tuple. To request a tuple, a process specifies a *template* using IN or READ. The runtime Linda kernel tries to match this template against tuples in Tuple Space. To match a template, a tuple must have the same length and sequence of types as the template. In addition, for fields in the template filled in by an actual

value, the tuple's corresponding field must have the same value. In this example,
{
  int mileage;

  in("car",1967,"chevy",var mileage);
}
the specified template matches ("car",1967,"chevy",*any integer*), but not
("car",1967,"chevy"), ("car",1967,"chevy","brown"), or ("car",1978,"chevy",45000),
the mismatches due to length, type, and value respectively. Linda's associative,
asynchronous matching style simplifies the construction of distributed data structures such as streams and pipelines[2].

Linda has been implemented on a bus-based multiprocessor--the S/Net[3]. This
implementation uses the fast broadcast of the bus to maintain a complete copy of
Tuple Space on each processing element[4]. An OUT broadcasts the new tuple to
all processors. READ is very fast because it requires no communication. IN provides some difficulty, since the S/Net kernel must use a broadcast and response
protocol to determine whether it is OK to allow a process to delete a particular
tuple from Tuple Space.

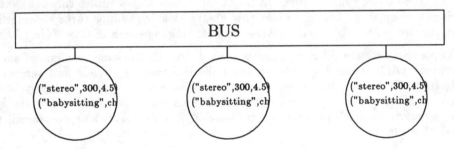

Figure 2--The S/Net Linda Implementation

Several considerations prompted us to look for an alternative strategy for
hypercube Linda. First, broadcast on a hypercube is not as fast as on a bus-based
multiprocessor. Second, the complex IN protocol slows the S/Net kernel. Most
important, the hypercube has many more processors than the S/Net. As the
number of processors increases, the amount of wasted memory for fully replicating
Tuple Space increases proportionally. The memory necessary for a large application is not available on any current hypercube. Also, as the number of processors
increases, the amount of time wasted in fielding broadcast OUT and IN traffic on
every processing element becomes prohibitive.

Tuple Space as a Distributed Hash Table

The hypercube strategy regards Tuple Space as a hash table distributed among
the processing elements. A hashing function takes as input any tuple, and places
that tuple in one of 64K slots in the distributed hash table. We assign 1024 of
these slots to each processing element so that, effectively, the hashing function
maps tuples to processors. The sets of table slots assigned to each processor do
not overlap; a tuple exists at only one location in the network. This makes the new
strategy more memory efficient and simplifies the implementation of Linda's three
communication primitives.

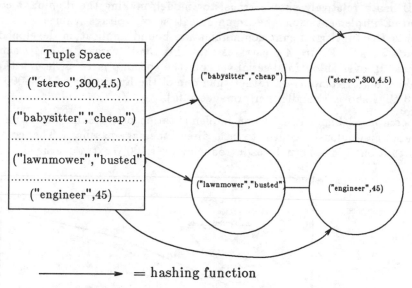

Tuple Space
("stereo",300,4.5)
("babysitter","cheap")
("lawnmower","busted")
("engineer",45)

⟶ = hashing function

Figure 3--Tuple Space as A Distributed Hash Table

All protocols in the hypercube Linda kernel use only point-to-point messages. The hashing function determines where a particular tuple or template belongs in the network without sending messages. It does this by only looking at the length and sequence of types in a tuple or template (as well as the first field, which must be literal). Only the processing element at the hashed location and the originating processing element are logically involved in the transaction (other processors may become involved in low level message routing for the transaction). To execute an OUT, a process simply sends a tuple to its hashed location. For an IN, a process first sends a template to its hashed location and blocks, waiting for a response. The process at the hashed location receives the template and either matches it immediately or stores it. Whenever a match is found, the process at the hashed location sends the matching tuple to the blocked requesting process which receives the tuple and returns from its IN call. READ is identical to IN, except that the the tuple is not deleted from its hashed location.

Distributed Timing Simulation under Hypercube Linda

We implemented a distributed MOS timing simulator, called EMU, under hypercube Linda[5]. EMU is part of the MULGA [6] VLSI design package developed at AT&T Bell Laboratories. The simulator partitions a MOS circuit into regions containing from one to several hundred transistors. It then uses a simple bin packing algorithm to assign these regions to processors, taking the number of transistors in a region as an approximation of its computational cost. Each processor simulates all its regions for a given timestep, and then exchanges voltage information with other processors. This algorithm has two communication requirements. First, the implementation must correctly transfer voltage values between regions on different processing elements. Second, EMU requires a global synchronization protocol to ensure that all processing elements are at the same timestep. We coded both these communication functions easily in Linda.

EMU has a relatively simple transistor model, making the dominant cost in a distributed implementation the communication of voltage values. As such it represents the first significant communication bound application developed under any Linda kernel. Figure 4 illustrates that this Linda version of EMU achieves a good speedup over an optimal serial version (the speedup is 14, although the figure uses a Vax780 for comparison rather than one of the hypercube's MC68000 processors and thus shows a smaller performance gain).

We compared Linda EMU to an implementation of the same algorithm on the hypercube meticulously coded to use direct message-passing. The comparison showed that out Linda kernel was introducing over 100% extra overhead.

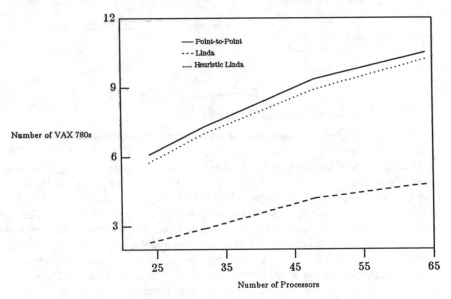

Figure 4--EMU Speedup on 64 processor Hypercube

Accelerating Linda Performance

There are several approaches to lessening this overhead. N. Carriero[7] has written a compiler which assosiates tags with tuples to minimize matching costs. The compiler also classifies tuples into types and provides information for a run-time system to use different storage methods for different tuple types based on difficulty of matching. Unfortunately, 87% of the hypercube Linda kernel overhead is due to interprocessor communication so such techniques could not significantly improve the kernel's performance.

Specialized hardware can also accelerate Linda execution. V. Krishnaswami and S. Ahuja recently proposed a Linda chip set [8] that handles almost all matching and communication functions currently done in S/Net Linda kernel.

Our approach is to make the runtime kernel capable of reducing communication overhead by relocating tuples. This strategy is similar to virtual memory algorithms. In virtual memory, the kernel notices an access to a page not in core, and retrieves it from disk. Various heuristics are used to keep in core the pages most likely to be accessed (thus decreasing the average page access cost). In a tuple relocation scheme, the Linda kernel notices a pathological access pattern to a particular tuple or template (e.g. page) and moves it to a spot where the most interested processes can more efficiently access it.

Specifically, our Linda kernel counts how many times each processing element uses a particular IN template. If the use of a given template is biased toward some processing element, the kernel annotates its hashing function so that the template and its corresponding tuples hash to that processing element. A relocation takes place in the following manner. First, the kernel running on the default location for a template notices (statistically) that some other processor requests a match for that template very frequently. Second, the kernel broadcasts an annotation to the hashing function that causes the template (and its corresponding tuples) to hash to the processor making these frequent requests. Finally, the kernel "mops up," by sending any of the now rehashed tuples or templates previously stored on to the new location.

This heuristic costs little in time or memory, especially compared to Tuple Space replication schemes. On average, a relocation costs the same as 2-3 INs. To avoid thrashing, the kernel collects statistics for 60-90 INs before relocating a particular template/tuple signature.

Tuple relocation dramatically increased Linda EMU performance. Figure 4 illustrates that EMU running under the heuristic kernel performed within 10% as fast as the hand-code message-passing version of EMU. Communications in EMU are predominantly point-to-point; it is rare that more than two processes are interested in a particular message. These results suggest that for EMU and for the many other point-to-point parallel applications, a relocation-based kernel can provide a powerful and efficient alternative to explicit message-passing.

Current Work

We are currently studying heuristics which would increase Linda performance for algorithms based on non-point-to-point communication patterns. Many parallel algorithms use a master/slave model of computation. One process acts as the master, allocating computing tasks to the remaining slave processes. Linda provides a natural mechanism for organizing such a programming plan. All slaves execute an IN on a particular template, get a tuple representing some computation, and output finished data tuples. The master process outputs computation tuples and gathers the finished product.

A runtime kernel can easily detect such a pattern; it is characterized by a particular process repeatedly outputing the same tuple type. To respond to this pattern, the kernel could rehash the tuple and its corresponding templates to the output (master) process. This still requires that slave processes send and receive a message to obtain a computational task; however, master/slave algorithms implemented with direct message passing also require two messages--one for the master to send a task to a slave, and another for the slave to notify the master when it has completed the task and needs a new one.

Many parallel algorithms also use database searches. Like the master/slave plan, database search is easily represented in Linda. A set of tuples constitutes a database inside of Tuple Space. Processes search the database by executing the READ primitive. Assuming that non-destructive operations occur much more frequently than destructive operations, the kernel can detect this pattern by noticing that a particular template has the READ primitive executed on it frequently and by many different processes. To respond, the kernel could mark such templates (and their corresponding tuples) as *broadcast* templates. The kernel would handle templates (and their corresponding tuples) designated *broadcast* not through the hash table, but through a replication and broadcast scheme similar to that used on the S/Net. As long as the database remained small, this would allow for very fast search operations. For larger databases, the kernel will have to become still cleverer, identifying some *subset* of the hypercube processing elements on which to replicate a particular tuple type.

An implementation for both these new heuristics is in progress. In addition, we are studying the behavior our original heuristic, varying the criteria for tuple relocation to observe overhead and thrashing effects. Finally, we are studying whether the relocation heuristic is useful in cases where the hashing function has produced an unusually skewed initial distribution of tuples.

Conclusions

Our Linda implementation of the MOS timing simulator, EMU, is significantly more elegant and compact than the version based on explicit message passing. This difference supports the contention in previous articles on Linda that the language's shared memory emulation provides a powerful tool for parallel programming. The heuristic hypercube Linda kernel demonstrates that languages like Linda--based on decoupled output and input primitives operating on a virtual shared memory--are not only conceptually useful but viable for real applications. A new kernel, based on a combination of heuristics, will extend this result to an even wider class of applications.

The usefulness of object relocation in distributed language systems goes beyond the minimization of communication cost. In cases (i.e. Smalltalk) where objects represent computational units as well as data, the same relocation techniques can be applied toward balancing computational load. Thus, even future multiprocessors, which may have offloaded much of present system's communication costs onto co-processors, can still benefit from language kernels capable of making intelligent decisions about object placement.

References

1.   Erik DeBenedictis, "Multiprocessor Programming with Distributed Variables," *Proceedings of Conference on Hypercube Multiprocessors*, (August, 1985).

2.   D. Gelernter, N. Carriero, S. Chandran, and S. Chang, "Parallel Programming in Linda," *Proceedings International Conference on Parallel Processing*, (August, 1985).

3.   S. R. Ahuja, "S/NET: A High Speed Interconnect for Multicomputers," *IEEE Journal on Selected Areas in Communications*, (November, 1983).

4.   N. Carriero and D. Gelernter, "The S/Net's Linda Kernel," *Proceedings of the SOSP*, (1985).

5.   Bryan Ackland et al, "MOS Timing Simulation on a Message Based Multiprocessor," *Proceedings of the ICCD*, pp. 446-450 IEEE Computer Society and IEEE Circuits and Systems Society, (October, 1986).

6.   B. Ackland and N. Weste, "Functional Verification in an Interactive Symbolic IC Design Environment," *Proc. of the 2nd Caltech Conference on VLSI*, pp. 2285-298 (January, 1981).

7.   N. Carriero, *private communication*.

8.   V. Krishnaswami, S. Ahuja, D. Gelernter, and N. Carriero, "Progress Towards a Linda Machine," *Proceedings of the ICCD*, pp. 97-101 IEEE Computer Society and IEEE Circuits and Systems Society, (October, 1986).

Very-High-Level Parallel Programming in Crystal

MARINA C. CHEN*

Abstract. Crystal is a functional language in which programs resemble concise, formal mathematical definitions, without explicit communication commands. The Crystal compiler transforms this very-high-level description into an assemblage of concurrent programs, each coded in some target machine language (e.g., any of the concurrent versions of C, FORTRAN, or LISP) with communication commands that establish its interaction with programs on other processors of the machine. At the center of these transformations are the concepts of *granulization* and *clustering* which automatically break down a Crystal program into many pieces of independent tasks. Granulization is based on two innovations in the language Crystal: (1) to treat all data as functions over some base domain (or index set), giving the generality and flexibility needed in expressing any parallel operation over any network of distributed data, and (2) to assign a process to each element in the base domain and exploit parallelism on the data level, as well as the expression level. Crystal provides powerful operators, or parallel programming idioms (a la APL), that have guaranteed efficiency in their parallel implementations. The Crystal compiler is capable of generating efficient code for machines with different granularities of parallelism. The Crystal run-time system [4] further ensures the performance of target programs over a spectrum of machine granularity. Together they resolve the portability issue in parallel programming.

1 Introduction

One of the most critical problems in parallel processing today is that of programming parallel machines. The difficulty lies in task decomposition: how to partition a given task into pieces, one for each processor, so that it can be accomplished by the cooperation of many processors in parallel. There have been two main approaches: (1) programming in a conventional sequential language, and relying on a parallelizing compiler to generate code for parallel machines (as in numerical computing) or relying on a parallelizing interpreter and run-time support for dynamically spawning parallel processes (as in functional programming); and (2) devising a parallel programming language and expressing parallelism explicitly in a program.

The first approach has the advantage that programs can be written in familiar languages and existing programs can be transformed by parallelizing compilers for execution on the new

---

*Department of Computer Science, Yale University, New Haven, CT 06520. chen-marina@yale. Work supported in part by the Office of Naval Research under Contract No. N00014-86-K-0296.

machines. However, the parallelism discovered this way is limited by the algorithm embodied by the program. It is unlikely that the transformations provided by the parallelizing compiler are sophisticated enough for the task of redesigning programs better suited for parallel processing. Such redesigning is necessary for using parallel resources to their full potential. Take the problem of sorting as an example. Consider parallelizing a quicksort program, which is a very good sequential solution. This can be done by spawning a process for each of the two recursive calls to quicksort. The time complexity is indeed improved from $O(n \log n)$ in the sequential version to $O(n)$ (since $O(n)$ comparisons are needed at the top level and the number of comparisons is halved at every level thereafter) by using $O(n)$ independent parallel processes. However, what can be achieved by various parallel sorting networks (e.g., [17]) with $O(n)$ processors is $O(\log^2 n)$, which is significantly faster for large n. Numerous other good sequential algorithms have the same property that they do not lend themselves to efficient parallel implementations, as exemplified by many of the newly devised parallel algorithms [5] which are considerably different from their sequential counterparts.

This point leads to the second approach — parallel programming, where parallelism is explicitly expressed in a program. This is flexible enough to be applied to either class of parallel machines (shared-memory machines or message-passing machines) as well as any kind of parallel algorithm. However, parallel programming and debugging can be extremely difficult with thousands of interacting processes. Most parallel languages, either proposed or in use, have explicit constructs for parallelism. Programmers specify how tasks should be partitioned and which ones can be run in parallel (e.g., futures in Multilisp [7,8], "in" and "out" in Linda [6]), or how processes are mapped to processors (e.g., annotation in ParAlfl [10]); or they specify explicitly the communication between processes (e.g., "?" and "!" in CSP [9]). But specifying communication is very tricky because it requires the programmer to keep track of both the processor's own state and its interactions with other processes, and explicit task decomposition by the user will yield inefficient code for a large class of problems for which an efficient decomposition cannot be known until run-time. In fact, early experience with programming machines such as the Intel iPSC reveals that the burden of specifying task decomposition and communication can be so great that it discourages extensive experiments on load balancing via different task decompositions.

A critical research question raised here is: can a parallel program be written in a highly abstract form such that the detailed interactions among processes in space and time are suppressed, and yet it is still possible to generate efficient code for an assemblage of communicating processors? The seemingly conflicting goals of *ease of programming* and *efficient target code* can be achieved. In this paper we will give an illustration of programming in Crystal, its parallel interpretation that yields automatic task decomposition, and the organization of the Crystal compiler. The Crystal run-time system is described in another presentation [4] of this proceedings.

The rest of the paper is organized as follows. Section 2 contains some example program segments. Section 3 gives a more formal description of the syntax and semantics of the language. Section 4 addresses the issue of parallelism and how to interpret a Crystal program as a collection of parallel processes. Section 5 describes operators for programming abstraction and the properties these operators must possess in order for them to be efficiently implemented on parallel machines. Section 6 contains a brief description of the Crystal compiler.

2   Example Program Segments

2.1   Operations over a set of elements

In problem solving, one often likes to say "the value x associated with some element p is defined as the minimum (or maximum, summation, union, etc.) of the set of all values y(q) for those elements q in set S such that the predicate z(p,q) is true." In Crystal, the above sentence translates to an equation of the form

```
x(p) = \min { y(q) | q in S, z(p,q)}
```

Below is an example excerpted from a Crystal program for computing the minimum spanning tree of a graph with vertex set **vset** and edge set **E**, where i is an index for iterations.

```
minWeight(v, i) =
  \ min { weight({v, u}) | u in vset, ({v, u} in E) and marked({v, u}, i)}
```

2.2 Sorting

Given an input tuple x, this program segment computes a tuple y of elements in sorted order. This program is based on a mesh-of-trees parallel sorting algorithm given in [17], but the Crystal version is portable to other architectures, such as the hypercube.

```
v(i, j) = << x[i] > x[j] -> 1,
             else -> 0
          >>
rank(i) = \+ {v(i, j) | j in 0:n-1}
w(i, j) = << rank(i) = j -> x[i],
             else -> 0
          >>
y = [( \+ {w(i, j) | i in 0:n-1} ) | j in 0:n-1]
```

For instance, if $x = [2, 5, 0, 11, 6, -1]$, then the values of function v can be displayed as an array (below left) with, say, row index i and column index j. The function rank has the values $2, 3, 1, 5, 4, 0$, for $i = 0, 1, \ldots, n-1$. The function w is displayed at right.

$$
\begin{pmatrix}
0 & 0 & 1 & 0 & 0 & 1 \\
1 & 0 & 1 & 0 & 0 & 1 \\
0 & 0 & 0 & 0 & 0 & 1 \\
1 & 1 & 1 & 0 & 1 & 1 \\
1 & 1 & 1 & 0 & 0 & 1 \\
0 & 0 & 0 & 0 & 0 & 0
\end{pmatrix}
\begin{pmatrix}
0 & 0 & 2 & 0 & 0 & 0 \\
0 & 0 & 0 & 5 & 0 & 0 \\
0 & 0 & 0 & 0 & 0 & 0 \\
0 & 0 & 0 & 0 & 0 & 11 \\
0 & 0 & 0 & 0 & 6 & 0 \\
-1 & 0 & 0 & 0 & 0 & 0
\end{pmatrix}
$$

Finally, the tuple $y = [-1, 0, 2, 5, 6, 11]$.

2.3 Parallel prefix

The scan operator is a familiar one in APL. Let tuple u be defined as $u = [1, 2, 3, 4, 5]$. Then the tuple v defined as $v = \text{scan}(u, +)$ has the value $[1,3,6,10,15]$. Since scan is used extensively and has an efficient implementation, it is supported as a primitive operator in Crystal. However, it can be defined in Crystal as follows:

```
scan(v, f) = u
    where u[i]= w(i, floor(log(i)))
        where w(i,j) = << j=0 -> v[i],
                          j>0 -> f(w(i,j-1), w(i-2 ^ (j-1), j-1))
                       >>
```

The above program is just a description of the parallel prefix operator [11]. Note that n-ary operations over a set of n elements (Section 2.1) can be done using the parallel prefix operation. The value x(p) of Section 2.1 is just the last element of the tuple scan([y(q) | q in S, z(p,q)], min). However, it is more efficient (by a logarithmic factor) to implement these directly.

2.4 Solving linear systems

The following segment of code defines a scalar value scalar_a and a vector q which are computed iteratively, where i is the index for iterations. Matrices A and B, vectors q0, r, and s are given as inputs. Subroutines for computing inner product inner, vector addition vectoradd, matrix vector multiplication mmult and forward solve fsolve are defined in the subprogram after the keyword where, in which i and j are used for indexing matrix and vector elements. The Crystal compiler will interprets i in the main program as a time index, and i and j in the subprogram as space indices.

```
scalar_a(i)= num/den where (num = inner(r, q(i))
                           den = inner(q(i), q(i)))
q(i)= << i = 0 -> fsolve(B, mmult(A, q0)),
         i > 0 -> vectoradd(s, q(i-1), scalar_a(i-1))
     >>
where (
     vectoradd(vec1, vec2, scalar) = [ vec(i) | i in 1:n ]
     where vec(i) = vec1[i] + scalar * vec2[i]
     inner(vec1, vec2) = \+ { vec1[i] * vec2[i] | i in 1:n }
     fsolve(B, y) = [x(i) | i in 1:n]
           where x(i) = y[i] -
           (\+ { B[i,j] * x(j) | j in 1:i-1 } )
     mmult(A, p) = [ap(i) | i = 1:n]
           where ap(i) = ({ A[i,j]*p[j] | j = 1:n }
     )
```

2.5   Particle membership

Given a list of particles **particleList**, this program segment partitions the list into 4 sublists of particles according to their locations. A particle k belongs to the list for box j if it is closest to the center of box j. The partition is done by first computing the square of the distance from the xy-coordinates of the particle **particleList(k).x** and **particleList(k).y**, to those of the center of the box **box(j).x** and **box(j).y**. The function **membership** computes for each particle k which box it belongs to. Conversely, a list of particles for each box is obtained by the function **particleInBox**.

```
distSqParticleToBox(k,j) =
    distSq(particleList(k).x, particleList(k).y, box(j).x, box(j).y)
    where distSq(x1, y1, x2, y2) = power((x1-x2),2.0) + power((y1-y2), 2.0)
membership(k) = \minarg{ [ distSqParticleToBox(k,j), j ] | j = 1:4 }
particlesInBox(j) = inverse(membership, particleList, union)(j)
    where ( inverse(f, D, mergeOp) = g
           where g(y) = \mergeOp  x | x in D, f(x) = y }
```

The binary associative operator **minarg** takes a set of pairs [value, arg] and returns the **arg** which has the minimum **value** over the set. The operator **inverse(f, D, mergeOp)** computes the inverse of a function **f** with domain **D**. The binary associative operator **mergeOp** specifies how the value of an inverse image should be computed when the function is not one-to-one. For instance, given a function $f(i,j) = i+j$ with domain $D = \{1:n\} \times \{1:n\}$, its inverse function **inverse(f, D, union)** will give a set of pairs $\{(i,j) | i+j = a\}$ as the image of each element a in its domain.

For more examples of Crystal programs, such as dynamic programming, LU-decomposition, matrix multiplication, and numerous toy examples, see [1,2,3].

3   Syntax and Semantics of Crystal

Crystal is a functional language that uses set notation, similar to SASL [16]. Syntactically, it uses infix operators to make programs as readable as familiar mathematical notation. Semantically, it has the standard fixed-point semantics.

$$F_1(\mathbf{v}) = \begin{cases} p_{11}(F_1(\tau_{111}(\mathbf{v})), F_2(\tau_{112}(\mathbf{v})), F_2(\tau_{113}(\mathbf{v})), \mathbf{x}_{114}(\mathbf{v})) \rightarrow \\ \quad \phi_{11}(F_1(\tau_{111}(\mathbf{v})), F_2(\tau_{112}(\mathbf{v})), F_2(\tau_{113}(\mathbf{v})), \mathbf{x}_{114}(\mathbf{v})) \\ p_{12}(F_1(\tau_{121}(\mathbf{v})), F_2(\tau_{122}(\mathbf{v})), \mathbf{x}_{123}(\mathbf{v})) \rightarrow \\ \quad \phi_{12}(F_1(\tau_{121}(\mathbf{v})), F_2(\tau_{122}(\mathbf{v})), \mathbf{x}_{123}(\mathbf{v})) \end{cases} \tag{1}$$

$$F_2(\mathbf{v}) = \begin{cases} p_{21}(F_1(\tau_{211}(\mathbf{v})), F_2(\tau_{212}(\mathbf{v})), \mathbf{x}_{213}(\mathbf{v}), \mathbf{x}_{214}(\mathbf{v})) \rightarrow \\ \quad \phi_{21}(F_1(\tau_{211}(\mathbf{v})), F_2(\tau_{212}(\mathbf{v})), \mathbf{x}_{213}(\mathbf{v}), \mathbf{x}_{214}(\mathbf{v})) \\ p_{22}(F_1(\tau_{221}(\mathbf{v})), F_1(\tau_{222}(\mathbf{v})), F_2(\tau_{223}(\mathbf{v})), \mathbf{x}_{224}(\mathbf{v})) \rightarrow \\ \quad \phi_{22}(F_1(\tau_{221}(\mathbf{v})), F_1(\tau_{222}(\mathbf{v})), F_2(\tau_{223}(\mathbf{v})), \mathbf{x}_{224}(\mathbf{v})) \end{cases} \tag{2}$$

Figure 1: The general form for a system of two recursion equations.

3.1   Functions

There are two ways a given function F can be used in a Crystal program. The first is the conventional one of using functions as a way of abstracting detailed operations, such as **vectoradd**, **scan**, **distSq**, and **inverse** in the examples above. The second way is new, using functions as a way for describing data structures. For example, the functions **w** and **v** in sorting, the functions **q(i)**, and **scalar_a(i)** for representing a vector and a scalar, and function **particleList** for a list of particles. Treating all data as functions over some base domain (or index set) instead of defining data structures separately gives the language the generality and flexibility needed in expressing any parallel operation over any network of distributed data.

3.2   Constructors

Three constructors are used in Crystal: sets, ordered tuples, and records, as shown in the above examples. These constructors are familiar either in conventional mathematical descriptions or in data processing tasks. They are essential for concise, clear, and intuitive expressions.

3.3   Syntactic constructs: a more formal description

Crystal syntax is quite intuitive since it very much resembles conventional mathematical notation. Formally, a Crystal program consists of a system of recursion equations. Figure 1 shows such a system. In describing the syntactical parts of recursion equations, three indices i, j, and k are used: the first index i is used for numbering the equations, the second index j for numbering the conditional branches within a given equation, and the third index for the number of occurrences of functions and/or constants within a given branch.

The system shown in Equations (1) and (2) defines two left-hand side functions F_i where $i = 1, 2$. Function F_i can be a tuple of functions or a field of a record of functions. Similarly, set notation may be used to express all arguments on the right hand side of each equation, as in the example of Section 2.1. Each equation can be defined by several conditional branches, such as the two cases satisfying boolean predicate p_{1j} for $j = 1, 2$ in the first equation. Certainly, each case can be defined by nested levels of conditionals. Any left hand side function value $F_i(\mathbf{v})$ of the i'th equation may depend on some *mutually recursive* function values $F_{i'}(\tau_{ijk}(\mathbf{v}))$ on the right-hand side as defined by functions ϕ_{ij} and τ_{ijk}. It may also depend on some *non-recursive* function values $\mathbf{x}_{ijk}(\mathbf{v})$, where any $\mathbf{x}_{ijk}$ is a function that does not appear on the left-hand side of any equation in the system. For example, there are 3 mutually recursive functional values (for $k = 1, 2, 3$) and a single non-recursive function value $\mathbf{x}_{114}$ in case 1 of Equation 1.

3.4   Semantics

The language Crystal is functional, and has fixed-point semantics [13]. Let V_i and all other value or functional domains over which functions and predicates ϕ_{ij}, τ_{ijk}, p_{ij}, and $\mathbf{x}_{ijk}$ are defined be continuous and complete lattices. Furthermore, let these functions and predicates be continuous. Then the solution of the system of recursion equations is its least fixed-point.

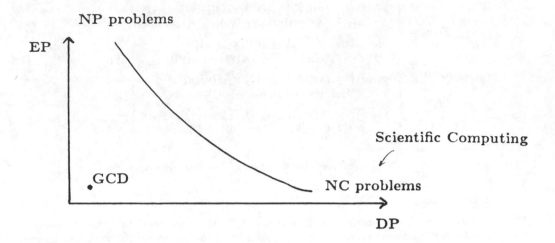

Figure 2: The distribution of problems with varying degree of DP and EP.

4   Parallelism

Parallelism in a Crystal program does not need to be specified explicitly by any particular syntactic constructs. Rather, it is a result of assigning an operational interpretation to familiar mathematical notation.

4.1   Dichotomy of operands/operations and interpretations

As described above, a Crystal function is used to describe a data structure (operands) or an operation (an operator). These two different interpretations of functions correspond to different sources of parallelism and both are supported in Crystal. An example illustrating the two types of parallelism and discussion of their relative merits can be found in [2].

4.1.1   Expression level parallelism (EP)

The first source, called expression level parallelism (EP), or applicative parallelism in [2], is well known in functional languages. This is the parallelism attainable by interpreting each function as a process. As long as two functions are not constrained by a dependency relation, the two processes can proceed in parallel. An analogous interpretation appears in logic programming languages, such as interpreting Prolog's conjuctive goals as a network of processes in Concurrent Prolog [14]. In the example of solving linear systems above, if we spawn two parallel processes that compute the values of `inner(r, q(i)` and `inner(q(i), q(i))` in the definition of `scalar_a(i)`, then we are exploiting EP. However, there is another kind of parallelism "inside of" the inner product operation on two vectors. This is called *data level parallelism*.

4.1.2   Data level parallelism (DP)

What's new in Crystal is the idea of interpreting each element of the domain of a function as a process, rather than the function itself as a process. The amount of parallelism that can be extracted this way is only limited by the size of the domain and eventually the available parallel resources. When the domain is very large, which is often the case with compute-intensive tasks, the available parallelism is correspondingly large. Parallelizing Fortran compilers tap this to a very limited extent, and one can do much better (in theory, anyway) by hand-coding everything. But until now there has no systematic way of fully exploiting such massive parallelism.

Problems in various application domains (strictly speaking, efficient algorithms for these problems), can be broadly categorized by their inherent EP and DP as shown in Figure 2. For a given amount of parallel resource, one needs to exploit as much parallelism as the problem allows. Some algorithms, such as the Euclidean algorithm for computing GCD (greatest common devisor) seem to be inherently sequential in the sense that they contain little EP or DP.

The significance of Crystal's new interpretation of functions lies in its ability to exploit DP, which is essential for virtually all fast parallel algorithms for problems in the class NC [5] (polynomial number of processors and polylogarithmic time complexity).

Crystal supports both DP and EP for a spectrum of problems lying on the continuum: predominantly EP for the class of problems clustered in the upper left corner of the figure, EP on top of DP for those along the middle part of the curve, and predominantly DP for those on the lower right corner. For the current generation of parallel machines, except for the Connection Machine, the potential of DP cannot be fully exploited due to the communication/computation ratio of the processors. As parallel computer technology progresses and the communication latency between processors becomes less, this will change.

4.2   Operational interpretation of DP

Since the idea of EP is well known only DP will be treated here. Consider a system of recursion equations as shown in Figure 1. Each element $\mathbf{v}$ in the domain V_i is interpreted as a process. Each of the mutually recursive functions F_i corresponds to the output of a process. A function ϕ_{ij}, called a *local processing* function, describes a part of the functionality of element $\mathbf{v}$ that produces output value $F_i(\mathbf{v})$. Function τ_{ijk}, called a *communication function*, describes which other element $\mathbf{u} = \tau_{ijk}(\mathbf{v})$, element $\mathbf{v}$ should receive its input. Function $\mathbf{x}_{ijk}$, called an *input function*, describes the input data. Predicates p_{ij}, called *control predicates*, describe the conditions under which a given process executes some particular processing functions ϕ_{ij}, obtains data from other processes defined by particular communication functions τ_{ijk}, and receives some particular inputs described by the input functions $\mathbf{x}_{ijk}$.

5   Programming Abstraction

One of the goals of Crystal is to provide a set of useful idioms for developing fast parallel algorithms. To this end, Crystal borrows several operators from APL, many similar to those used in Connection Machine Lisp [15]. In the context of parallel programming, in particular when different granularities are considered, these operators have two properties of particular interest:

1. *Granulizability*. Each operator can be implemented on machines of logarithmic diameter with near-linear speedup, independent of the machine granularity.

2. *Completeness*. There is a subset of Crystal operators which is complete in the sense that algorithms for all problems in NC can be programmed using these operators. A minimum such set consists of the **scan** operator, loop of polylogarithmic number of iterations, and constant-time local computations .

The granulizability property ensures portability over a spectrum of machines. The completeness property guarantees the power and generality of the language.

6   Organization of the Crystal Compiler

Figure 3 shows the organization of the Crystal compiler. The lexer and the parser are conventional. The (static) mapping generator performs a transformation that maps each index appearing in the source program to either time (a loop index) or space (logical process-id's). For more sophisticated mapping [1], a linear combination of indices in the source program is mapped to the time index in the implementation.

The granulizer performs task decomposition according to DP and EP, regardless of the machine granularity. It generates as many logical processes (represented as a parse tree) and *inter-process*

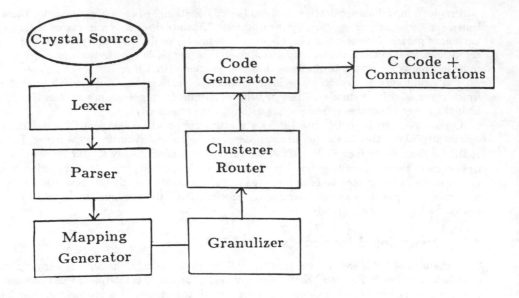

Figure 3: The organization of the Crystal compiler.

communications as possible, which contains the maximum amount of parallelism possible in a given program.

The clusterer then combines many logical processes into a single *nodal parse tree* to fit the particular granularity of the target machine. In the meantime, it eliminates those inter-process communications that are inside the same node and package those that go outside of the node. Furthermore, it determines efficient routing for these outgoing communications [12].

At this point, the original source code has been transformed to a collection nodal parse trees, one for each processor, plus the communications. Compiling a nodal parse tree to target sequential code on each processor requires no more than conventional code generation. Thus completes the compilation process.

One extremely important and interesting issue is how the clusterer chooses the appropriate collection of logical processes to combine into a single node. This is discussed in a companion paper [4] in this proceedings.

7   Concluding Remarks

This paper demonstrates the viability of programming for parallelism without user-specified task decomposition or explicit inter-process communications. The compiler is responsible for automatically breaking down a Crystal program into many pieces of independent tasks and generating efficient target code. At the center of these transformations are the concepts of *granulization* and *clustering*. Crystal also provides a set of high-level operators which can be supported efficiently on parallel machines and are powerful enough for expressing all fast parallel algorithms. Together with conventional mathematical notation, these high-level operators help to bring programming, debugging and testing to a new conceptual level. Before the advent of parallel machines, such operators wouldn't be supported in a sequential language (APL is an exception) because they are too expensive to implement. But now they can be supported very efficiently — polylogarithmic time complexity and always near-linear speedup — on parallel machines. As larger and larger machines become available, languages that exploit only EP will soon reach their limit and languages with explicit communication will become still more difficult to use, while Crystal will be able to exploit parallelism to the limit of the available DP.

Acknowledgement. I would like to thank Alan Perlis for many inspiring discussions, and Neil Immerman on the subject of the completeness of Crystal operators. My thanks also go to Joe Rodrigue for his comments and suggestions on the manuscript.

References

[1] M. C. Chen. A design methodology for synthesizing parallel algorithms and architectures. *Journal of Parallel and Distributed Computing*, December 1986.

[2] M. C. Chen. A parallel language and its compilation to multiprocessor machines. In *The Proceedings of the 13th Annual Symposium on POPL*, January 1986.

[3] M. C. Chen. Placement and interconnection of systolic processing elements: a new LU decomposition algorithm. In *Proceedings of the IEEE International Conference on Computer Design: VLSI in Computers*, pages 275–281, October 1986.

[4] M. C. Chen and Joel Saltz. A multi-level parallel programming environment. In *The Proceedings of the Hypercube Microprocessors Conf., Knoxville, TN*, September 1986.

[5] Stephen A. Cook. A taxonomy of problems with fast parallel algorithms. *Information and Control*, (64):2–22, 1985.

[6] David Gelerter. Linda and friends. *IEEE Computer*, August 1986.

[7] Jr. Halstead, Robert H. Multilisp: a language for concurrent symbolic computation. *ACM Transaction on Programming Language and Systems*, October 1985.

[8] Jr. Halstead, Robert H. Parallel symbolic computing. *IEEE Computer*, August 1986.

[9] C.A.R. Hoare. Communicating sequential processes. *Communication of ACM*, 21(8):666–677, 1978.

[10] Paul Hudak. Para-functional programming. *IEEE Computer*, August 1986.

[11] R. E. Ladner and M. J. Fischer. Parallel prefix computation. *JACM*, (4), October 1980.

[12] Zhijung Mu and M. C. Chen. Communication efficient distributed data structures on hypercube machines. In *The Proceedings of the Hypercube Microprocessors Conf., Knoxville, TN*, September 1986.

[13] D.S. Scott and C. Strachey. Toward a mathematical semantics for computer languages. In J. Fox, editor, *Proceedings of the Symposium on Computers and Automata*, pages 19–46, Polytechnic Institute of Brooklyn Press, New York, 1971.

[14] Ehud Shapiro. Concurrent prolog: a progress report. *IEEE Computer*, August 1986.

[15] Guy L. Steele Jr. and W. Daniel Hillis. Connection machine lisp: fine-grained parallel symbolic processing. In *Proceedings of the 1986 Symposium on Lisp and Functional Programming*, pages 279–297, 1986.

[16] D. A. Turner. *Recursion Equations as a Programming Language*, pages 1–28. Cambridge University Press, 1982.

[17] Jeffrey D. Ullman. *Computational Aspects of VLSI*. Computer Science Press, 1984.

A Hypercube Implementation of Flat Concurrent Prolog

STEPHEN TAYLOR*, SHMUEL SAFRA* AND EHUD SHAPIRO*

Abstract. Flat Concurrent Prolog is a simple, practical, concurrent programming language which has an efficient uni-processor implementation. This paper summarises the problems involved in implementing the language on a parallel architecture. The main concepts employed in an initial parallel interpreter are described; the interpreter has been implemented on an Intel iPSC Hypercube.

Introduction. Flat Concurrent Prolog (FCP) is a simple, process oriented, single assignment language [1]. It provides an interesting framework to investigate parallel processing problems for a variety of reasons:

- FCP supports meta-programming allowing many non-trivial system functions to be supported without complicating the language semantics [9]. These include methods for process and code mapping [11].

- Due to its simplicity and uniformity the language can be used to investigate a number of program transformation techniques aimed at improving efficiency. These include partial evaluation [10] and abstract interpretation.

- An efficient uni-processor implementation exists which is comparable in speed to commercially available Prolog compilers [6].

- FCP is a practical language which has been used for a number of non-trivial programming problems. These include a bootstrapping compiler, a programming environment, sections of an operating system and various parallel algorithms.

---

*Department of Computer Science, Weizmann Institute of Science, Rehovot 76100, Israel.

This paper briefly summarises the problems and concepts involved in implementing FCP on a parallel architecture. A full exposition of the material and a comprehensive explanation of an initial parallel interpreter are presented in [12]. The interpreter has been implemented on an Intel iPSC Hypercube and extends the uni-processor algorithm for FCP described in [8].

Language Overview. An FCP program comprises a set of rules of the following form:

$$H \leftarrow G \mid B.$$

where H is the head, G is the guard consisting of simple test predicates and B is the body. A process whose data state unifies (matches) with the head may be re-written to the processes described by the body if the guard predicates are true.

The semantics of FCP is based on non-deterministic process and clause selection [12]. Each state of a computation consists of a multi-set of processes (which form the resolvent), a program and the data state. A *reduction* transition involves non-deterministically selecting a process and a clause from the program. The transition involves the following operations:

- Making a new copy of the selected clause.

- Unifying the process with the head of the clause copy and solving the clause guard.

- Replacing the process by the body of the clause copy in the resolvent.

The notions of process, communication and synchronisation are supported directly in the language. Software processes communicate via shared streams and read-only variable annotations provide a means to specify data-flow synchronisation. The following program illustrates the formalism by simulating a memory cell:

$$cell(Is) \leftarrow cell(Is?, undefined). \quad \text{\% initial state undefined}$$

$$
\begin{aligned}
&cell([read(X) \mid Is], X) \leftarrow &&\text{\% receive read, return value}\\
&\quad cell(Is?, X). &&\text{\% wait for input with old state}\\
&cell([write(Y) \mid Is], X) \leftarrow &&\text{\% receive write}\\
&\quad cell(Is?, Y). &&\text{\% wait for input with new state}\\
&cell([], X). &&\text{\% terminate}
\end{aligned}
$$

The cell is accessed via a message stream Is and hides its internal state which is initially *undefined*. It accepts two forms of message: *read* or *write*. Reading the cell returns its internal state via an unbound variable in the message (i.e. X); writing to the cell changes its internal state. The cell terminates when its input stream is closed.

The example uses list structures (e.g. $[Car \mid Cdr]$) to represent streams. Variables (which begin with uppercase letters) may be read-only annotated e.g. $Is?$ (Is is read-only) to indicate data-flow synchronisation. A process may not bind a variable via a read-only occurrence but can only test the value of the variable when it gets bound by some other process. In the above program, a recursive call to *cell* suspends until another process has bound the *Is* variable because it has only read access to *Is*. Thus the cell process is forced to wait for a message and may then decide which rule to use in reducing the process.

Problems. A parallel implementation of FCP requires that a number of non-trivial problems be solved. Most of the problems are familiar and have been treated extensively in the literature on database systems, operating systems and data-flow languages. The most difficult task is to integrate solutions for solving these problems in a coherent, simple and efficient algorithm. In summary, the major problems are:

Mutual Exclusion. Processes must be mutually excluded when updating shared variables [4].

Deadlock Prevention. Deadlock [5] may occur when multiple processes attempt to access shared variables; these may be viewed as shared resources e.g.

$$f(X, Y), g(Y, X)$$

In this example f may gain access to variable X and prevent other processes from accessing it while attempting to access variable Y. If process g does likewise then deadlock occurs.

Infinite Structures. Infinite structures (e.g. streams) require special consideration when involved in communication [14,7].

Circular References. It is possible to generate circular references within terms. Consider the following unifications:

$$X = f(Y), X = Y$$

Unification may never terminate if this term is unified with a similar term. On a uni-processor the problem may be solved using a technique involving pointer comparison. On a parallel machine variables and structures may exist on different processors making pointer comparison difficult [7].

Data-flow Synchronization. To implement data-flow synchronisation on a uni-processor is relatively simple. Consider the process:

$$X? = a$$

If X is unbound the unification process is simply suspended using a data structure associated with the variable X; when the variable is bound by some other process, the unification process may be woken up to attempt reduction again. The situation is more complex on a parallel machine; the variable X may reside on another machine and may be bound by a process executing on it.

Housekeeping Overheads. Maintaining the status of inter-processor requests can require complex algorithms and data structures. Minimising the overheads involved presents a significant problem. In order to maintain uni-processor performance, if many processes access variables locally there should be no overhead incurred by the parallel algorithm.

Starvation. A process may recurse infinitely while holding access to variables and never writing on them; other processes will as a result never obtain access.

Concepts. Some simple concepts can be applied in order to attack the above problems:

Atomicity of Unification. Processes are mutually excluded when updating shared variables by ensuring that reduction is implemented as an atomic action. To achieve atomicity no communication is carried out during a reduction attempt; any *necessary* structures which must be read and variables to be written upon are brought locally (variable migration). These techniques ensure that all required data structures needed are local and that nothing can effect them during unification other than the actions of unification. This reduces the problem of multiprocessor atomicity to that of uni-processor atomicity solving it trivially.

Variable Occurrences. The implementation ensures that only a single occurrence of each variable exists; all other occurrences are represented by either local or remote references to it. A remote reference includes both the notion of processor and location within a processor. This effectively implements a global address space; it circumvents the problem of maintaining consistency between multiple copies of variable bindings.

Reading. It is possible to distinguish two operations performed during unification: reading the value of a term and attempting to write the value of a term onto a variable. Reading of remote values occurs more frequently than binding remote terms. The following table shows the percentage of the total number of messages transmitted (for both reading and writing) which were concerned with reading and transferring values. The tests were conducted on some simple initial parallel algorithms using the interpreter described in [12].

Program	% Reading
Virtual Machines	87.2
Matrix Multiplication	95.8
Insertion Sort	95.9
Symbolic Differentiation	96.6
Naive Reverse	98.8

Of the programs examined, matrix multiply, insertion sort and naive reverse are simple, regular, systolic applications. The symbolic differentiation application uses a dynamic load balancing algorithm. The virtual machines program is highly dynamic and comprises a number of different applications running concurrently on three virtual machines.

It is possible to determine locally at a processor whether reading or writing on a remote term is required. Reading requires less synchronisation and can be implemented more efficiently. When data is needed in several processors the data can be replicated (with remote references to unbound parts of the terms) and sent to each reading processor; this operation is legal because of the single assignment rule employed by the language.

Variable Migration. When a process needs to write on a variable which resides in another processor the variable is brought locally; this operation is termed *variable migration* since variables migrate between processors. Replicating structures and bringing variables locally provides the opportunity to detect circular references using pointer comparison.

Localisation. Chains of remote references can occur through processors. Messages are always forwarded through these chains until the destination is found to be either a variable or a value. If a message is received at its source processor after being forwarded through a remote chain, a technique termed *localisation* is applied. This operation effectively dereferences a chain of remote references and replaces it by a local reference.

Demand Copying. In order to deal with infinite structures a demand copying scheme [13,2] can be employed. If unification requires access to a term which resides on another processor the term is accessed incrementally by sending some constant number of levels in the structure at a time. Remote pointers can be used to access unbound variables. Demand copying copies only the *necessary* information to allow a process to commit; this is performed in response to demands generated by unification.

Relative References. All structures which may be transferred between processors are implemented using relative references. As a result, messages must be packed for sending to other processors but at the receiving processor can be simply loaded onto the heap and used immediately. Runable compiled code may be transferred between secondary storage and processors directly.

Broadcast Notes. A simple technique can be used to achieve data-flow synchronisation. When a remote processor attempts to read the value of an unbound variable a note is attached to it. This note can be used when the variable becomes bound to copy the value to the requesting processor.

Deadlock Prevention. Naive implementations of variable migration result in livelock; it is necessary to employ some form of locking when processes access shared variables. Unfortunately, deadlock may occur when processes lock some variables while requesting locks on others. Since deadlock may occur only in rare occasions involving multiple writers on multiple variables we seek a solution which requires little overhead for, the more common single writer programs.

A simple scheme is employed which assigns a priority to processors; the priority is only used to determine which processor obtains access to a variable in the event of competition. Locks are pooled (i.e. jointly owned by all local processes) at a processor for simplicity; this prevents competition for local locks since the atomicity of reduction ensures that only one process accesses a variable at a time. Each variable must have an associated number which specifies the processor locking it and each processor must hold a count of how many of its processes jointly require a lock. The following policy is followed when a process p in processing element P of priority i requests a lock on variable X:

1.   If no processor owns the lock, then p is granted ownership of the lock.

2. If a process (or processes) in another processing element P' with priority number h, where $h < i$, already owns the lock, then p is refused the lock and gives up ownership of all the locks that it currently owns, jointly or independently.

3. If another process in P has already been granted the lock, p is given joint ownership of the lock.

4. If a process (or processes) in another processing element P' with priority number j, where $j > i$, already owns the lock, then the request is temporarily deferred and p must wait for the lock until no processes in P' own the lock.

Locks are granted immediately if the variable is unlocked. If the variable is locked and the priority of a lock request is lower than the locking processor then the lock is refused and must be re-requested. Locks are granted within one queue cycle if the variable is locked and the incoming request is from a higher priority processor. If remote locks are required, all local variables required by the process are also locked; this prevents low priority processors from stealing locks until the process has gained sufficient locks to either commit or suspend. The algorithm ensures that there is always one processor in the system which will eventually gain all its locks, reduce and release locks to other processors; this prevents deadlock.

Integration of Reading and Writing. Consider an interrupt handling process which may modify some global structure and waits on an interrupt stream. The handler may never be executed thus it is imperative that the process does not hold locks on the global structure while waiting. Reading and writing are thus integrated such that processes hold their locks only while requesting locks that they have not yet obtained. Eventually all the necessary locks are granted and the process is re-scheduled. At this time the process either commits or still requires data to be read. In the latter case the process suspends releasing its locks. If the necessary data arrives the process must regain the locks it requires in order to commit.

Busy-Waiting. The interpreter forces processes to busy-wait for locks. This substantially reduces the overheads associated with maintaining the status of inter-processor lock availability.

Conclusion. The interpreter has been useful for providing insights into the major problems and includes a number of novel ideas. The implementation has been demonstrated on a range of applications including the code and process mapping techniques described in [11]. It represents the first parallel implementation of FCP and provides a workable basis for current and future research. Garbage collection and detection of global termination are discussed in [3]; system bootstrapping is discussed in [11].

Unfortunately, the data structures required by the interpreter are cumbersome; moreover the deadlock prevention scheme seems complex although it is by far the most simple of many proposed schemes. Perhaps most concerning is that the algorithm is sufficiently complex that it is difficult to reason about its correctness.

REFERENCES

(1) W. B. ACKERMAN, *Data Flow Languages*, Computer, Vol. 15, No. 2, February 1982, pp 15-25.

(2) ARVIND and R. E. THOMAS, *I-Structures: An Efficient Data Type for Functional Languages*, MIT Laboratory for Computer Science, Tech. Man. TM-178, MIT, Cambridge Mass., Sept. 1978.

(3) E. AV-RON and S. TAYLOR, *A Parallel Garbage Collector for Flat Concurrent Prolog*, Weizmann Institute of Science, Dept. of Computer Science, Rehovot, Israel.

(4) E. G. COFFMAN, and P. J. DENNING, Operating Systems Theory, Prentice-Hall, Englewood Cliffs, New Jersey, 1973.

(5) J. W. HAVENDER, *Avoiding Deadlock in Multitasking Systems*, IBM Systems Journal, Vol. 7, No.2, pp. 74-84, 1968.

(6) A. HOURI and E. SHAPIRO, *An abstract machine for Flat Concurrent Prolog*, Tech. Rep. CS86-20, Weizmann Institute of Science, July 1986.

(7) R. M. KELLER and G. LINDSTROM, *Applications of feedback in functional programming*, Conference on functional languages and computer architecture, pages 123-130, October 1981.

(8) C. MIEROWSKY, S. TAYLOR, E. SHAPIRO, J. LEVY, and S. SAFRA, *The Design and Implementation of Flat Concurrent Prolog*, Dept of Computer Science, Weizmann Institute of Science, Rehovot, Israel, Technical Report CS85-09, July, 1985.

(9) S. SAFRA and E. SHAPIRO, *Meta-Interpreters for Real*, To appear in: Proceedings of IFIP-86.

(10) S. SAFRA, *Partial Evaluation of Concurrent Prolog and its Implications*, CS86-24, Weizmann Institute of Science, July 1986.

(11) S. TAYLOR, E. AV-RON and E. SHAPIRO, *A Layered Method for Process and Code Mapping*, Journal of New Generation Computing, In Press.

(12) S. TAYLOR, S. SAFRA and E. SHAPIRO, *A Parallel Implementation of Flat Concurrent Prolog*, Submitted to: International Journal of Parallel Programming.

(13) P. C. TRELEAVEN, D. R. BROWNBRIDGE and R. P. HOPKINS, *Data-driven and demand-driven computer architecture*, Computing Surveys 14(1):93-143, March 1982.

(14) K. S. WENG, *Stream-oriented computation in recursive data flow schemes*, MIT Cambridge, MA., Tech. Rep. MTMM-68, October 1975.

Distributed Data Structures for Scientific Computation

L. R. SCOTT*, J. M. BOYLE† AND B. BAGHERI‡

ABSTRACT. We study language issues related to *sharing variables* in the context of programming *non-shared memory* multi-processors, such as the hypercube processors that are the subject of this conference. The language constructs developed are intended to support the technique of creating parallelism by distributing data structures, and operations on them, over several processors. We present two approaches to this problem and describe our implementation and experience with both. Computational results for both the NCUBE and Intel hypercubes are presented. Also described is an abstract framework that underlies the two approaches; this framework holds the promise of allowing automated subdivision of scientific computing problems.

1. INTRODUCTION. The most obvious way to utilize a parallel computer is to identify tasks that can be done independently of each other and assign them separately to individual processors. This approach works well for some applications, such as ray tracing in computer graphics, but in many others the structure of the problem does not immediately offer many such opportunities. When the possibilities of task independence have been exhausted, one way to "create" parallelism is to divide a problem's data structures, and the operations performed on them, and distribute them among the processors. Such an approach works well, e.g., for solving many problems in scientific computation, and its implementation on shared memory machines has been discussed before (see [3,4,8]). The main requirement is synchronization of individual processors (or processes), cf. Dongarra and Sorensen [5] and references therein, and techniques for doing this exist in some languages, e.g., in Ada.

In this paper, we focus on language issues related to automating this approach to programming parallel computers when the target is a parallel computer that does NOT have a shared memory, such as the hypercube-architecture machines that are the subject of this conference. The main new language constructs introduced here give the appearance

---

* Departments of Computer Science and of Mathematics, Pennsylvania State University, University Park, PA 16802

† Mathematics and Computer Science Division, Argonne National Laboratory, Argonne, IL 60439

‡ Department of Mathematics, University of Michigan, Ann Arbor, MI 48109

that *variables* are shared among processors (at the language level, without explicit recourse to message-passing or ports, cf. [6].). This is done in the context of the "single code" approach to programming multi-processors. Because the same code runs on all processors, each processor can *infer* from the code what data should be sent to another processor so that requests for data are not needed (and synchronization problems are avoided). The introduction of "variables," i.e., abstract names for values in storage locations, was a major step in automating programming, removing the need to keep track of storage locations when coding at the machine level. Here we propose two approaches to solving an analogous problem occurring with parallel, communicating programs.

We assume here that the programmer will explicitly subdivide the problem at the algorithm level, and we study language constructs that simplify the programming of the resulting algorithms. Near the end of the paper, we give a brief suggestion of how this might be further extended to allow automatic subdivision, a subject we intend to pursue in future work. The main body of the paper is devoted to describing our approach to language constructs for distributed data structures, its implementation and preliminary experience with it on model problems. We begin, however, with a digression concerning the style of management of the parallel processor to be used, as this affects the programming style in a fundamental way.

2. MANAGEMENT STYLE. Programming a parallel computer requires a choice, implicitly or explicitly, of a style of management of the processors. In this paper, we focus on a "single code" style of programming in which the multiple processors that make up what we view here as the "computer" under study each have a copy of the same code and do different work only because they interpret the code differently from their own individual perspective. We consider the case in which the individual perspective is determined only by the processor identification number (like a Social Security Number), which we represent by a reserved variable name, node_id. On different processors, this variable evaluates to a different value, and actions may occur differently as a result. Thus the variable node_id, when it occurs in a code, is interpreted by an individual processor to mean "me," and it is assumed that other processor values (e.g., node_id + 6) within a given range would refer to one of "them." We assume that the multiprocessor under study knows how to communicate with any other processor in the system given its identification number.

The "single code" style of programming reflects what might be called a "religious" style of management: there is (possibly) one leader (the host program), and all others have access to the same document for guidance, although they may interpret it differently depending on individual circumstances. Other styles of management are certainly possible. The HEP computer was organized according to what might be called a "job shop" approach in which there is a pool of tasks to be done, and each process(or) would simply pick the next available task to be done. (We note that much of the programming for the HEP was nevertheless done via a single-code approach, cf. [8].) This is the way a typing pool or a machine shop frequently works. Another management style that is often used for human groups is a pyramidal style with multiple levels of responsibility/authority and task granularity. Such a style might be of interest for a hypercube-connected multiprocessor because its connection network can be given a pyramidal structure. There is a natural way to divide a three-dimensional cube into two groups of four processors such that three processors in each group are nearest-neighbors of the fourth, which could be designated the "middle manager." Similarly, a seven-dimensional cube can be divided into sixteen groups of eight processors with each group consisting of the seven nearest neighbors of the eighth, as proved by Stout [9]. Still other management styles might prove useful for parallel computing, such as the current "networking" style of young urban professionals.

We have described alternate management styles to emphasize that the one under study here is not unique; it is simply the one we have chosen currently to examine. One reason for comparing computer management styles to similar ones for human groups is to predict possible strengths and weaknesses. For example, one question to ask is whether it seems reasonable to manage X number of individuals (persons or processors) with a given style. In some organizations (such as an automobile manufacturer), vast numbers of individuals are managed with a pyramidal style. On the other hand, it is hard to imagine a typing pool with a thousand typists managed by the traditional "job shop" approach. The "religious" management style is quite effective even with many millions of individuals, although its success depends heavily on the coarse-grained nature of the tasks involved and the limited need for (and local nature of) communication. Thus we can be cautiously optimistic about its prospects for managing large multiprocessors provided that the tasks to be done are sufficiently large and requirements for communication are kept small.

3. DISTRIBUTED DATA STRUCTURES. By "distributed" data structures we mean a (typically large) data structure, such as a vector or matrix, that is logically a single entity but that has been distributed over independent processor stores. Suppose X and Y are two such structures, and we wish to perform an operation on them of the form $Y = f(X)$. Suppose that a given processor holds in storage part of X, say S, and that it is required to compute part (call it T) of its contribution to $Y = f(X)$. If $T = f(S)$, i.e., if each element y in the subset T of Y can be computed knowing only the values of x in the subset S, then the computation can be done without disturbing other processors – it is naturally parallel. However, in general we may need values other than those just in the subset S to compute T, so data must be exchanged among processors to obtain the needed information in the remaining part of X. We discuss here ways to automate such communication in the context of extensions to Fortran, although the concepts apply to a wide range of languages. At the end of the paper, we discuss possible ways to automate the process even further by eliminating the need for subdivision at the algorithm level and replacing it with an automatic, optimized subdivision.

We shall use an intentionally trivial example throughout this paper to illustrate the basic ideas. It comes from considering iterative methods for solving the linear equations that arise in discrete approximations to partial differential equations (cf. Axelsson and Barker [1]) A fundamental operation in each iteration step of such methods is the multiplication of a highly structured, sparse matrix times a vector, with the latter being changed as a consequence of the iteration. In one spatial dimension, such a matrix would in the simplest case be tridiagonal, and a very elementary form of the iteration would be

(3.1) $$x(i) \leftarrow (x(i-1) + x(i+1) - f(i))/2$$

where f represents a given, fixed vector. Specifically, we assume that the subscript for x runs from 0 to $N + 1$, with the given "boundary" values $x(0)$ and $x(N + 1)$ being held fixed (thus the range of the index i in 3.1 is from 1 to N). In this example, the data structures X and Y are essentially the same, namely, the old and new values of the vector $\{x(i) : 1 \le i \le N\}$. Since the computation of each $x(i)$ depends on its neighbors, there is no way to subdivide to achieve parallelism without communication. A natural way to subdivide the problem among P processors is to assign N/P contiguous components of x to each processor (assuming, as we shall for simplicity, that N is an integer multiple, say k, of P). If the $j - th$ processor (where we number processors starting with zero and have $j < P$) is assigned indices $i = j*k+1, \ldots, j*k+k$, then only two components of x, $x(j*k)$ and $x((j+1)*k+1)$, are needed from other processors (namely processors $j-1$ and $j+1$) at each iteration (see Figure 1, where we have taken $k = 4$). We now discuss how such communications can be automated at the language level. We consider two approaches to distributed data structures in the context of the single code approach to parallel processing, one which we dub "local" and the other which we call "global."

4. THE LOCAL APPROACH. In the "local" approach, a processor p has the right to refer explicitly to a *variable* in the store of another processor, q . Since we are talking about a single-code style of programming, both p and q know about each other's variable names (which are presumably the same for a given distributed data structure). For example, a line of code might read "x(p) = y(q)" meaning that the value of y in the program of processor q should be transferred at this point in the execution of the code to the storage location for the variable x in processor p. Typically, q would be a function of the individual (requesting) processor identification number, node_id, and p would be equal to node_id. The reference to a processor p on the left hand side can be omitted, in which case the default is p = node_id. More complex expressions than single variables are of course needed in practice, and we have used them in our implementations. We do not take a stand on what sort of syntax should be used here. For simplicity of implementation, we have used one of the type

(4.1)   x[range_x ; p] = y[range_y ; q]

where range_x and range_y indicate array limits (possibly empty, for a single variable), p and q can be ranges of processors and q can be a function of the individual processor identifier, node_id. Different syntaxes have been suggested for a "range," such as in Alliant FX/Fortran and Cyber Fortran 200, and we shall not elaborate on the choices we have made as such questions are orthogonal to our direction of interest here. We hope our usage will be clear from the examples. The reference to the processor p is optional; when it occurs (on the left side of an "=") it is equivalent to a conditional in the sense that a given processor receives no data if its identifier is not equal to p (or a member of p if it is a range of processors). When the reference to p is omitted on the left side of an "=," all processors are to receive the designated data. Note that if q is a constant in (4.1), that is, if q is not a fucntion of node_id, then this amounts to a broadcast from q to all processors p . We refer to this approach as "local" because each processor views the data structure from the local perspective of the other processor.

$$x(4j). \ .x(4j+1) \qquad x(4j+4). \ .x(4j+5)$$

$$\text{processor } j-1 \ . \ . \qquad \text{processor } j \qquad . \ . \ \text{processor } j+1$$

Figure 1. A simple example of a distributed data structure (global indexing)

In the example (3.1) above, suppose that each processor has its portion of the array x stored in the variables $z(i)$ for $i = 1, ..., k$ (as shown in Figure 2). Then the algorithm (3.1) is easily implemented by the code

```
          dimension z(0:100000001)
               ⋮

          if( node_id .eq. 0 ) z(0) = left_value
          if( node_id .eq. P-1 ) z(k+1) = right_value

               ⋮

          z(0)  = z[ k ; node_id - 1 ]
          z(k+1) = z[ 1 ; node_id + 1 ]
          do 1 i = 1, k
           znew(i) = ( z(i-1) + z(i+1) - f(i) )/2
      1   continue
          do 2 i = 1, k
           z(i) = znew(i)
      2   continue
```

The crucial point here is that, since every processor has a copy of this same code, it can infer what data must be sent to other processors in order that they be able to receive the data they are requesting in a line of code such as "z(0) = z[k ; node_id - 1]." This example shows that it is useful to allow processor values outside the range zero to $P - 1$; in this case, the corresponding lines of code involve no receipt of data. In the above example, this implies that processor 0 will not change its "boundary" value $z(0) = x(0)$, and similarly processor $P - 1$ will leave $z(k+1) = x(N + 1)$ fixed; this is exactly what we want it to do in such algorithms. Note that it may be advisable to initialize the (rest of the) array z (say, to zero).

```
. . . . . . . . . .
            . .                              . .
  z[k;j-1]. .z[1;j]          z[k;j]. .z[1;j+1]
o      o . . o        o        o      o . . o        o
            . .                              . .
  processor j-1 . .       processor j     . . processor j+1
. . . . . . . . . . . .
```

Figure 2. "Local" indexing of a distributed data structure

5. THE GLOBAL APPROACH. An alternative to this approach involves an explicit global view of the distributed data structures. It involves a declaration of the form

```
local X( local_X_range1 ) ,..., Y( local_Y_range1 ) , ...
global X( global_X_range1 ) ,..., Y( global_Y_range1 ) , ...
```

where the ranges are possibly functions of the processor identifier, node_id. The global data is information that may be needed during program execution but is not necessarily stored in the local processor memory. The local statement describes the extent of what is kept in the processor storage, or more precisely, the range of variables that can appear on the left-hand side of an assignment statement in the code for that processor. From this information, it is possible to determine where needed information (the global variables) may be found. Information exchange can be signalled by some sort of command that requests values to be "updated." This command can of course limit the extent of variables to be exchanged, e.g., by saying "update(Y)" if only the Y variables need to be refreshed, and not X. The algorithm (3.1) in this case would be implemented via the code

```
dimension x(0:1000000000000000001)
local x( range( node_id * k + 1 , node_id * k + k ) )
global x( node_id * k ) , x( ( node_id + 1)* k + 1 )
        ⋮
update( x )
 do 1 i = node_id * k + 1 , node_id * k + k
  xnew(i) = ( x(i-1) + x(i+1) - f(i) )/2
1 continue
 do 2 i = node_id * k + 1 , node_id * k + k
  x(i) = xnew(i)
2 continue
```

One question that may be asked is whether the global declaration statement is really needed, i.e., whether one could not infer what data transfers must occur from the code. Consider the following code fragment:

```
local x( range(j,k) )
x( j ) = something
update( x )
do 1 i=j+1,k
1  x( i ) = f( x( g( x( i-1 ) ) ) )
```

It is impossible to infer, at compile time, what is meant because indices depend on previous computations involving the distributed variables themselves (even if, as we assume, the functions f and g are well-enough behaved for this algorithm to be well defined). Doing so at execution time would mean that the update statement execution would not occur at a specified time; it would have to get data on the fly. But then some sort of temporal element and appropriate synchronization mechanisms would have to be added to indicate which value of a variable was desired. Thus we conclude that it is useful to specify explicitly the "global" variables to simplify the problem and make its implementation possibly more efficient.

Note that we allow the global ranges to be sloppy in the sense that they can refer to indices that do not exist in any local range. In this case, no data transfer will be attempted. As in the local approach, this allows simplification in the coding of (3.1) as follows. Between the global and update statements, the "boundary values" would be set by code of the form

```
if( node_id .eq. 0 ) x(0) = left_value
if( node_id .eq. P-1 ) x(N+1) = right_value
```

The variable x(0) is not a local distributed variable for processor 0 because it does not appear in the local declaration; it is simply an ordinary variable for that processor. On the other hand, the global statement for processor 0 reads, in part, "global x(0),..." But since x(0) is not claimed by any processor through a local declaration, no attempt is made to alter its state. Note that in this case the conditionals "if(node_id.eq. ...)" are superfluous; if all processors set x(0) and x(N+1) to some value it will not effect the computation as these variables simply go unused by the other processors.

6. COMPARISONS AND LIMITATIONS OF THE APPROACHES. We should begin by stressing that the main goal of both approaches outlined above is to enable the programmer to think about the data transfers in terms of the data s/he needs rather than the particular communications protocol required to transfer it. By doing so, and by generating the communication statements automatically, both approaches improve the chance that the data communication will be carried out correctly. Such correctness is of paramount importance since program complexity in parallel computation is far greater than for conventional serial computation. Moreover, in scientific computation the character of the result of the program is often unknown, unlike other programming areas (e.g., an operating system) in which one knows what is supposed to happen and is simply trying to automate it. For many of the most important problems in scientific computation (for example, in solving partial differential equations), the outcome is unknown (the question might be, does the solution of a differential equation exist until a given time, or does the solution "blow up"?). In such a case, the correctness of the code is of critical importance. Both the "local" and "global" approach insure correct data transfer, so we now compare them in other ways.

One strength of the "global" approach discussed in section 5 is that it comes quite close to allowing the modification of a "dusty deck" to work in a parallel environment; it involves primarily the addition of non-executable declaration statements (the local and global statements), as well as the modification of certain limits on "do" loops. However, our present implementation is naive in that it makes no attempt to reduce the storage requirement on each processor. That is, the program for each processor declares the entire array from the original sequential code, even though it only uses about $1/P - th$ of it. For small problems, or on machines with virtual memory, this approach may be adequate. But to make the transfer of sequential programs to non-global-memory multiprocessors practical, the waste of storage would have to be eliminated. A systematic approach to doing so is sketched below.

(1) Infer a processor's storage requirements for a given variable from the union of the

ranges for that variable in the local and global statements. For the example program in section 5, the storage requirement for x is range(node_id* k,(node_id+1)* k +1).

(2) Propagate this limitation throughout the body of the program, reducing the bounds of loops to address no elements outside this range.

(3) Translate the bounds of the array and corresponding indices in the program body to eliminate the parameterization in node_id. In the example, the translated range of x becomes range(0 , k + 1). In the program body, subtract node_id * k from all subscripts of x.

(4) Simplify the subscripts, translating loop bounds where appropriate.

This process results in a version of the code that declares only the needed storage on each processor. Note that each step preserves the correctness of the program. As a consequence the derived program will be correct if the original, together with the local and global declarations, was correct. (This idea of correctness-preserving derivation is discussed further in [2].) Although it would be possible to implement TAMPR [2] transformations to carry out such a derivation, we have not yet done so, primarily because of the large amount of tedious algebra on subscripts that would be involved.

On the other hand, the "local" approach gives the programmer complete control over the data storage, at the expense (possibly) of a more radical modification of the code structure to exploit parallelism.

In either the "local" or "global" approach, there is a potential for deadlock if data exchange statements are hidden behind conditional barriers. A statement such as (in the "local" approach) "if(node_id .ne. 17) z(1) = z[k+1 ; node_id - 1]" could preclude processor number 17 from participating in the data exchange. Even if processor 17 did not need z[k+1 , 10], it may have data that processor 18 will want via this statement. If processor 17 skips this statement, processor 18 will deadlock waiting for it. Similarly, in the global approach, "if(node_id .ne. 17) update(x)" would produce a similar deadlock if processor 17 skipped the execution of "update." Our point of view has been to avoid such problems explicitly in the examples we have tried, but a more systematic approach to this difficulty may be warranted.

7. IMPLEMENTATIONS. The implementation strategy that we have used might be described as "The Golden Rule," namely that each processor takes the responsibility to communicate the information that it has and others want, without being asked. More precisely, the algorithm for the local data approach to implement the code

$$x[\text{ range\_x }] = y[\text{ range\_y } ; \text{ f(node\_id) }]$$

consists of the following:

(#) send y(range_y) to all processors whose node number i satisfies node_id = f(i)
    (that is, to all processors in the inverse image of node_id via the mapping f)

(##) receive y(range_y) from processor f(node_id) .

To insure correct receipt of the data, the "send" message is tagged with a) the sending processor number, b) the receiving processor number and c) an identifier (some counter) unique to this data exchange (i.e., to this execution of this line of code); this "tag" is used on receipt to identify the message. Note that the algorithm can be implemented via a simple subroutine in Fortran whose inputs are the variable names "x" and "y," the ranges and the function name "f."

The particular order and details of "sending" and "receiving" data are system dependent. For the NCUBE hypercube, our implementation first sends to other processors data that they will want, and then it receives from others data it wants. For the Intel hypercube, our implementation first initiates receipt of data that will be sent from other processors, then sends data to others that they want, and finally checks the "status" of the "receive" processes. (The detailed implementation could be different on other machines as appropriate.)

At this point it is useful to compare our approach to the concept of "port" for data exchange in parallel processing (cf. Filman and Friedman [6]), e.g., as implemented in Occam (and called "channel," cf. Hoare [7]). The reliance on "ports" as the sole programming construct for communication differs from our approach in that only *values* are passed via ports and not *variables*. That is, once a value has been sent to a port, it is no longer possible to determine what variable it corresponds to without further identifying information (which is not explicitly part of the Occam language). On the other hand, the language constructs discussed here explicitly describe the exchange of abstract variables between processes; the language recognizes "distributed" variables by their name and process(or) location. In the implementation described above, the "tag" that is sent along with the values plays the role of the variable "name" to insure that data exchange is done correctly. This type of language construct could be easily implemented in Occam by letting the "tag" information in a-c) define a unique port, or channel, identifier. Thus we are discussing a higher level construct than that of "port," yet one that is compatible with it.

There is potential for a type of ambiguity in this implementation if one processor only sends data and never expects to receive data. In this case, synchronization never occurs and an arbitrarily large number of messages could be sent, either overflowing the message buffers or causing the message counter in c) above to recycle inappropriately. Of course, if the communication buffers were infinite and the identifier in c) had no bound on its size, no problems could occur; but in a practical system difficulties would arise. However, as soon as a "receive" is initiated (but not necessarily from the same data exchange), synchronization will occur. A possible way to avoid this sort of problem completely would be

(###) acknowledge receipt of the message in (##) and wait for acknowledgement of data sent in (#)

but we have not experimented with this idea. Also, in our implementations on test problems, we have used explicit inverse functions in step (#) to achieve more efficiency.

In the "global" approach, the data exchange is only slightly more complicated. For example, if the declarations read

```
local X( local_range( node_id ) )
global X( global_range( node_id ) )
```

then "update(X)" (on processor node_id) means

(+) for processor indices i such that local_range(node_id) and global_range(i) intersect, send the intersection range of x values to processor i.

(++) for processor indices i such that local_range(i) and global_range(node_id) intersect, receive the intersection range of x values from processor i.

(Note the natural duality in steps (+) and (++) between the variables i and node_id.) As above, the "send's" and "receive's" are tagged with message identifiers as described in a-c). If there are multiple ranges occurring on the local or global declarations, all possible pairs of local and global ranges (for a given variable) are formed, and each individual pair is treated separately as above. (There is of course no need to pair a local range of one variable with a global range of another variable.) As in the "local" approach discussed previously, an unbounded number of "send's" by any processor can cause problems, but any "receive" it does will always force synchronization.

Experimental, preliminary implementations of the above algorithms have been carried out for the NCUBE and the Intel iPSC. For logistical reasons, the "global" approach has been implemented on the iPSC only, and it was done via program-transformation techniques using the TAMPR program [2]. Again for logistical reasons, the "local" approach has been implemented only for the NCUBE, and it was done via a Fortran pre-processor written in C. However, there is nothing special about the implementation tools used, and both could be used for both techniques on both machines.

8. APPLICATIONS. For the sake of simplicity (and because we suspect it is a better numerical algorithm), the Gauss-Seidel iteration (cf. Axelsson and Baker [1]) was used within each processor instead of the pure Jacobi iteration described previously to implement (3.1). More precisely, the "do" loop number 2 in both cases was eliminated; the active line of loop 1 was replaced by "x(i) = (x(i-1) + x(i+1) - f(i))/2" in the "global" case and, in the "local" case, by "z(i) = (z(i-1) + z(i+1) - f(i))/2". Tests were done on a problem where the solution for the corresponding o. d. e. was known, for the sake of comparison. Although the numerical algorithm being used is known theoretically to have poor convergence properties even on a single processor, we found that with $N = 32000$, one hundred iterations would nevertheless yield three digits of accuracy. We chose this N and this number of iterations not for algorithmic reasons, but simply for the purposes of timing.

The main purpose of this study was programmability, not performance, so the first result we would like to focus on concerns our experience with the code for this simple problem on the Intel iPSC using the "global" approach. A prototype code had been developed and debugged on a Vax, and then the code was ported to run on the cube by applying correctness-preserving program transformations to introduce the required communication. Not surprisingly, it worked correctly *the first time it was run* on the hypercube, yielding the same answers as obtained on the Vax (to within round-off error). The timings (for the complete code including set-up and evaluation of the difference between the final vector x and the corresponding values of the solution to the o. d. e.), and the corresponding efficiency obtained, were as shown in Table 1. The surprising supralinear speed-up shown in Table 1 is a result of the "polling" mode used by the operating system to transmit messages from the cube to the host. This has the effect of degrading individual processor performance as fewer processors are used, and the effect disappears when a different mode is used, as shown in Table 2. On the other hand, supralinear speed-up should not be unexpected on realistic machines, since performance on most processors degrades as problem size increases (as the problem overflows the cache and ultimately migrates out to disk storage). Thus running smaller problems on a larger number of processors could definitely yield supralinear speed-up. In fact, on machines where the charging algorithm is based on a simple multiple of the number of processors and time used, speed-up will need to be supralinear in order that using more than one processor be cost effective.

D := cube dimension	number P of processors	time T(P) (seconds)	speed-up S(P) :=T(P)/T(1)	% efficiency E(P) := 100 S(P)/P
0	1	603	(1.0)	(100)
1	2	238	2.53	127
2	4	108	5.58	140
3	8	54	11.2	140
4	16	28	21.5	138
5	32	17	35.5	111

TABLE 1. Computational experience with the "global" approach on the Intel iPSC (results computed in "polling mode")

Since the communication and computation frequently decouple in scientific computation problems of the kind studied here, we experimented with some simple code optimization techniques (implemented by hand) to achieve as much overlap as possible of communication and computation. For problems of the type considered here, this only involves isolating the computation of the new values at the boundary of each processor's segment of the data from the interior ones, as the latter never enter into the communication. Then by simple code movement, the communication can be initiated as soon as possible while the checking of its "status" is delayed as long as possible. This led to improved performance as shown in the results of Table 2 and indicates the importance of allowing simultaneous communication and computation. These results also show an improvement in using the "contention" mode on the iPSC (with less than 32 processors), in which case the anomalous supralinear speedup disappears.

		POLLING MODE			*CONTENTION MODE*		
D	P	T(P)	S(P)	E(P)	T(P)	S(P)	E(P)
0	1	571	(1.0)	(100)	358	(1.0)	(100)
2	4	99	5.77	144	90	3.98	99
3	8	47	12.1	152	46	7.78	97
5	32	13	43.9	137	15	23.9	75

TABLE 2. Computational experience with the "global" approach on the Intel iPSC with optimization of communication-code placement. (See Table 1 headings for notation.)

Similar tests were done on the NCUBE/6 using the "local" approach, and again it was successful in automating the production of correct code. Since the machine used was a "beta" version, agreements with the manufacturer prevent us from giving detailed timings at present. Concerning speed-up/efficiency, results were similar, except that faster communications times apparently contributed to greater efficiency: e.g., for $N = 16384$ and with 64 processors, we obtained an 88% efficiency. Instead of giving a more complete report of the tests, let us describe a further type of application that was done on the NCUBE using the "local" approach, namely direct methods in linear algebra. The column oriented algorithm for Gaussian elimination suggested by Moler (cf. his paper at this conference and references therein) can be written succinctly in the "local" notation as follows:

```
      do 20  j = 1 , n-1
       if( node_id .eq. node_loc(j) ) then
           a(j+1:n,col_loc(j)) = a(j+1:n,col_loc(j))/a(j,col_loc(j))
       endif
       m[j+1:n;node_loc[j+1:n]]=a[j+1:n,col_loc(j);node_loc(j)]
       do  10  k = j+1 , n
        if( node_id .eq. node_loc(k) ) then
      a(j+1:n,col_loc(k))=a(j+1:n,col_loc(k))-m(j+1:n)* a(j,col_loc(k))
        endif
   10  continue
   20  continue
```

In this code, "node_loc" is a function that says in which processor node a given column of the original matrix a is located, and "col_loc" describes the local storage location of columns in the appropriate processor. Note that only the line before the start of loop "10" involves communication and, except for this line of code and two "if" statements, the code is identical to the standard Fortran code for Gaussian elimination. Preliminary results for small problems run on the NCUBE/6 using the above code are shown in Table 3.

n	P = 2	P = 4	P = 8	P = 16	P = 32	P = 64
32	76	50	30	14	8	–
64	73	58	44	25	12	8
128	73	63	53	41	22	10

TABLE 3. Percentage efficiency (see definition of E(P) in Table 1) on the NCUBE for "local" data notation code for Gaussian elimination (P = number of processors used)

The only communication in this code is a broadcast from one processor to all other processors. We thus note that the performance of the algorithm depends strongly on the speed of "broadcast" on a given machine. For this reason it would seem valuable to have optimized "broadcast's" available for different parallel systems. Correspondingly, in iterative methods such as the conjugate gradient method (cf. [1]), a global "sum" over all processors must be done, and it would be advisable to have this optimized for a given machine.

9. AN ABSTRACT APPROACH.

Recall some notation from section 3. Suppose X and Y are two distributed data structures, and suppose we perform an operation of the form $Y = f(X)$. When two data structures interact in this way, we can describe the interaction by a graph, or equivalently by a matrix A whose rows and columns are indexed by the structures X and Y respectively and whose entries are 0 if corresponding entries in the data structures do not interact and 1 if they do. Suppose that a given processor holds in storage part of X, say S, and part of Y, say T, and that it is required to compute its contribution to $Y = f(X)$. If $A(x, y) = 0$ for all y in T and x NOT in S, i.e., if $T = f(S)$, then this is a completely separate operation, a naturally parallel one. However, we may need values other than those just in the subset S to compute T (if A is not reducible), so some sort of communication must go on between processors to obtain the needed information in the remaining part of X. We can predict which processors will need to communicate as follows. Suppose we introduce two more graphs, or matrices as above, that describe the storage structure for X and Y. That is, let $B(i, x) = 1$ if processor number i is assigned to store x (and zero otherwise), and let $C(i, y) = 1$ if processor number i is assigned to store y (and zero otherwise). If

$$(9.1) \qquad B(j, x) \cdot A(x, y) \cdot C^t(y, i) \neq 0 \quad \text{(and thus } = 1)$$

(i.e., if processor j stores x, x is needed to compute y and y is stored in processor i) then this means that processor i will have to get x from processor j in order to compute y. In fact, the number of x values that i will have to get from j in order to compute y is therefore $(BA)(j, y) \cdot C^t(y, i)$ where BA is the matrix product of B times A. The *total* number of elements that must be sent from j to i for the computation of all the y values by processor i is thus

$$(9.2) \qquad (BAC^t)(j, i).$$

If $(BAC^t)(j, i) = 0$, then processor i does not need to hear from j for this part of the computation. Thus the non-zero entries in the matrix BAC^t describe the communication network necessary to compute $f(X)$, and the individual values measure the amount of traffic that will be sent over a given link.

The interaction matrix A is completely determined by the need to compute $Y = f(X)$, but the matrices B and C can be chosen arbitrarily. In the previous part of the paper, we have assumed that the programmer specifies B and C. (In the "global" approach, the information contained in B and C is essentially represented in the "local" and "global" declarations and is used to effect data transfers.) However, we can imagine B and C left unspecified by the programmer, with their choice optimized to achieve efficiency on a given machine according to whatever criterion is appropriate. (We imagine initially that this optimization would be done statically, at "compile" time, but it is conceivable that it could ultimately also be done dynamically to some extent, which would be useful for problems in scientific computation with adaptive meshes.) Various optimality measures would be appropriate. For example, it may be important to make the number of communications paths as small as possible, which would mean to make BAC^t as sparse as possible (while still utilizing available processors effectively). On the other hand, we may wish to limit total message lengths, which means that we constrain the size of the maximum entry of BAC^t. Limits on the choices of B and C would have to be made so that the computational load on the processors is balanced. Other criteria could be used as well. Our point is simply that, since BAC^t contains a complete description of the communications that will go on, we can (in principle) choose B and C automatically to optimize efficiency for a given machine. Not only could this lead to more efficient use of parallel processors, it could remove the need for the programmer to perform a decomposition of the problem explicitly. We intend to pursue these ideas in future research.

10. CONCLUSIONS AND RECOMMENDATIONS. We have discussed two approaches to facilitate data transfers occurring in parallel, communicating programs. Each approach has advantages and drawbacks, but both appear effective in automating the programming of non-shared-memory multi-processors and in assuring the correct transfer of data in such programs. Based on our experience with these approaches, we make the following recommendations for future software systems for such multi-processors:

1) Implement distributed data structures with

2) Parallel execution of data exchange and computational tasks, and

3) Provide "built-in" utility functions such as "global sum" and "broadcast."

We have discussed only communications among the "node" processors in the hypercube architecture and essentially ignored the interaction between nodes and the host. One obvious extension of this work is to integrate the host and node codes and to automate the communication between them. This would reflect more directly the two-level management style being used, and it could lead to ways of implementing more complex, multi-level management schemes, such as a pyramidal one. Depending on the particular relationship between host and nodes, we might then add another recommendation to

4) Integrate host and node codes, including a distributed-data notation for data transfers.

We note that an alternate approach to integrating host functions into the node code (the Cubix operating system) has been described at this conference by Salmon.

REFERENCES

[1] O. Axelsson and V. A. Barker, **Finite Element Solutions of Boundary Value Problems: Theory and Computation**, Orlando: Academic Press, 1984.

[2] Boyle, J. M., and Muralidharan, M. N., *Program reusability through program transformation*, **IEEE Transactions on Software Engineering**, SE-10, 5 (Sept, 1984), 574-588.

[3] J. J. Dongarra, and D. C. Sorensen, *Linear algebra on high-performance computers*, **Proceedings Parallel Computing 85**, U. Schendel, ed., Amsterdam: North Holland, 1986, pp. 3-32.

[4] J. J. Dongarra, and D. C. Sorensen, *A fully parallel algorithm for the symmetric eigenvalue problem*, to appear in **SIAM J. SISSC**, March 1987.

[5] J. J. Dongarra and D. C. Sorensen, SCHEDULE: *An aid to programming explicitly parallel algorithms in Fortran*, Proceedings of the ARO Workshop: Parallel Processing and Medium Scale Multiprocessors, Stanford, California, Jan. 1986, A. Wouk, ed. (to be published in Philadelphia: SIAM).

[6] R. E. Filman and D. P. Friedman, **Coordinated Computing**, New York: McGraw-Hill, 1984.

[7] C. A. R. Hoare, **Communicating Sequential Processes**, Englewood Cliffs: Prentice Hall, 1985.

[8] J. S. Kowalik, ed., **Parallel MIMD Computation: HEP Supercomputer and Its Applications**, Cambridge: MIT Press, 1985.

[9] Q. Stout, private communication.

Communication-Efficient Distributed Data Structures on Hypercube Machines

ZHIJING MU* AND MARINA C. CHEN*

Abstract

Sets, as programming data structures, have become more important than before due to the emergence of parallel machines. Efficient communication over sets of distributed data therefore is the crucial issue in parallel computing. We identify three distributed set data structures and two general operations over sets. Algorithms are developed to support the operations over distributed set structures in poly-logarithmic time. The algorithms have been implemented on the iPSC and the performance is presented. A full example is given to demonstrate the usage of the data structures. Discussion is made on the spectrum of different granularities.

1 Introduction

The concept of the set is fundamental in mathematics. Its importance has been recognized and reflected in programming languages like SETL [5] and SASL [6]. However, the set as a data structure is not widely used in most conventional programming languages due to the inherent sequentiality imposed by the von Neumann machine model. The emergence of parallel computers might change the situation. When a set of data is distributed over multi-processors, an operation defined over the set may be carried out with the participation of all the processors involved. Therefore, sets have become sources of parallelism and perhaps the most important data structures in parallel languages [1].

Suppose that we want to compute a function that depends on the values distributed over a group of processors on machines like the iPSC, the time used depends on largely the communication speed. To avoid message congestion, which would slow down communication, programmers have to specify the tedious message routing explicitly. We intend to treat sets as data structures with some general built-in operators. The algorithms presented in this paper will take care of the message routing so that the level at which the parallel programs are designed can be elevated without sacrificing performance.

In general, operations over a set of distributed objects may require communications. For example, to increase each object by a constant, local computation is sufficient, but if

---

*Department of Computer Science, Yale University, P.O.Box 2158, Yale Station, New Haven, CT 06520-2158. Work supported in part by the Office of Naval Research under Contract No. N0014-86-0296

we want to get the sum of all objects, communication among the processors containing the objects is necessary. Operations that demand communication over a set often can be classified as one of the following two types: broadcast and merge (see Section 3). These two types of operations have been shown to be general and powerful enough to express a broad class of parallel algorithms [3] [4]. This paper will concentrate on algorithms to support broadcast and merge operations over sets.

In real problems, we can often find the situation where the same operations are to be carried out for many sets. For example, with a matrix, we may want to find the minimum for each row. As the sets are independent of each other, the operations ideally are to be done in parallel. Our algorithms are designed to carry out the operations on more than one set in parallel with complexities independent of the number of sets involved.

Ho and Johnsson have developed algorithms to support broadcast for static sets [1] distributed over a cube or subcubes [2], which can be used to support operations over uniform sized sets; Leiserson and Maggs [4] have considered communication issues over dynamic sets, and developed randomized algorithms for the fat-tree machine model. In this paper, we will consider static sets with non-uniform sizes, and deterministic algorithms for dynamic sets.

The paper is organized as follows: In the next section, we will specify and discuss the communication issues of distributed data structures. In Section 3, three set implementations with communication algorithms are introduced. The performance of the data structures implemented on the Intel iPSC is presented in Section 4. In Section 5 the connected components problem is used to demonstrate the usage of three data structures. The final section is concerned with the adaptation of the data structures over the spectrum of different granularities of parallelism.

2   Communication Issues in Distributed Data Structures

In some graph problems, we may want to find for *each* vertex an edge of the smallest weight adjacent to it; in scientific computing, we may sum over *each* row of a matrix. These kinds of computations can all be described by the following general operation:

Given *k disjoint sets of data* $S_1, \ldots, S_k$, *and an associative operator* $\oplus$, *compute* $\oplus_{a \in S_i} a$ *for* $i = 1, \ldots, k$.

There are two levels of parallelism in the operation. First of all, the computation for the k sets can be done in parallel since the sets are independent from each other. Secondly, for each set, the operation $\oplus$ can be performed via a spanning tree structure with cost logarithmic to the size of the set.

The simplest case is that of static sets with a uniform size, for instance, rows of a matrix. In this case, we can simply map each set into some subcube in a hypercube, and construct a spanning tree structure for each subcube to explore the parallelism at both levels [2].

However, we may encounter the case of k static sets of non-uniform sizes, e.g. the adjacency lists of a graph. As forcing each of the non-uniform sized sets into a subcube will waste processors, objects in one set should be distributed across the boundaries of subcubes. The first implementation of sets, what we call consecutive lists, will facilitate the operations over non-uniform size static sets with logarithmic time complexity.

When the operation is to be carried out over dynamically formed sets, the efficiency becomes a more complex issue. The locations of the elements of a dynamic set are unpredictable before run-time; therefore, efficient communication can only be supported by dynamic routing schemes.

---

[1] A set defined before run-time and not subject to change is static, otherwise is dynamic.

The problem with dynamic sets is further complicated by the following constraint: as dynamic sets may be changed by *union*, *intersection*, etc., operations, it is essential that the memory required to represent a set does not grow with the size of the set. This implies that information about elements' locations should be distributed rather than centralized at any one processor. One way of defining the scope of a set under the constraint is to have a pointer for each element designating another element in the same set.

We will present two implementations for dynamic sets. Non-consecutive lists are used to deal with the situation where the pointers link elements in a set into a list; rooted trees are for the situation where the pointers link the elements into a rooted tree. It will be shown that operations over both the two kinds of dynamic sets can be carried out in poly-logarithmic time.

3   Three Distributed Data Structures Implementing Sets

3.1   Preliminary

The development of the data structures is based on the following three principles:

- *Distributed Data*: the elements in sets are distributed over processors of a message-passing parallel machine.
- *Distributed Computations*: a function over a set is computed by all the processors where the elements reside, each processor computes part and only part of the function.
- *Distributed Information*: Each processor representing an element in a set has part and only part of the information about the entire set structure. The required local memory for storing the information should not grow with the size of the set.

We will consider the following two types of operations over distributed sets:

- *Broadcast*: given a set S and a value $v(x)$ associated with an element $x \in S$, send $v(x)$ from x to all elements in the set.
- *Merge*: given a set S, a value $v(x)$ associated with each $x \in S$, an associative and commutative binary operator $\oplus$, compute $\bigoplus_{x \in S} v(x)$.

The operations can be carried out in poly-logarithmic time if we can find some tree structure that has the following properties.

- All elements in the set are in the tree.
- The height and fan-in of the tree are bounded by $O(\log n)$ or $O(\log^k n)$ for some small constant k.
- It can be constructed in poly-logarithmic time.

The problem of supporting the set data structures therefore can be reduced to the problem of construction of such trees, which, following Leiserson and Maggs [4] will be referred to as communication trees (CTs) throughout the paper.

To simplify the discussion, in this section we assume:

- Time complexity of the algorithms is measured by the number of communication steps required. This assumption is well justified since local computations in our algorithms take constant time.
- Synchronized machine model. As the synchronization can be achieved by paying logarithmic factor in time [8] , the given complexities are valid within a logarithmic factor for asynchronous machines like the Intel iPSC.
- One and only one datum is mapped to one processor. (However, we will devote Section 4 to the discussion on the spectrum of machine granularity.)

3.2   Consecutive lists (C-lists)

Consecutive lists are the representation of static sets with non-uniform sizes, e.g., the adjacency lists of a graph. Notice that rows and columns of matrix are just special cases of C-lists.

Consider p static sets $S_1, \ldots, S_i, \ldots, S_p$ with arbitrary sizes $m_1, \ldots, m_i, \ldots, m_p$. For the jth elements in the ith set, we can assign a new index l by the following equation:

$$l = j + \sum_{k=1}^{i-1} m_k \tag{1}$$

The new indices actually impose a total order over elements in all sets. With the gray code we can map each element according to its index l onto the hypercube. Obviously, two elements will be physically adjacent in the cube if and only if they were adjacent elements in the sets, and therefore the processors containing all elements in one set form a consecutive list.

The following algorithm constructs CTs for the C-lists. It is a simple recursive process starting from the head of each C-list and terminating at the elements found to be leaves in the CT. The variables in all algorithms of this paper are local, global variables shared by all processors are not used.

Algorithm 1
All processors in parallel:
(1) if the processor contains the head element of a list $\{e_{l_1}, \ldots, e_{l_m}\}$, then
      FATHER := self;
      INTERVAL := $[l_1, l_m]$;
    else INTERVAL := NIL.
(2) if INTERVAL is not NIL , then
      if INTERVAL $= [s, f]$ and $s \neq f$ then
        for D := cube dimension to 0 do
          NB := the Dth dimension neighbor of the processor;
          if NB $> s$ and $\leq f$ then
            claim that NB is a son in CT;
            INTERVAL := $[s, \text{NB-1}]$;
            send INTERVAL $[\text{NB}, f]$ to the son processor.
      else the processor is a leaf of the CT.
    else
      receive (INTERVAL, sender);
      FATHER := sender;
      do step (2);
end.

An example of a C-list is given in Figure 1. The C-list consists of elements mapped to processors with IDs from 6 to 13 (gray code). The constructed CT is given on the right side of Figure 1.

The bound of the height of constructed CTs, though not very apparent, can be shown to be $2 \log n$ with the help of the following lemma:

Lemma 1 *From the root of the CT along any path to a leaf, the dimension of the link decreases by one in at most every two links.*

Following the lemma, we have,

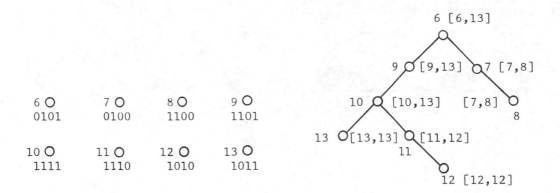

Figure 1: Building the CT for a C-list.

Theorem 1 *The height of a CT for a consecutive list is bounded by $2 \log n$; fan-in of any node in CT is bounded by $\log n$, where n is the length of the list.*

Notice that the CT for a C-list consists of only links connecting the elements in the list; therefore, when there is one or more consecutive lists, both the process of CT construction, and the broadcast or merge operation can proceed for all C-lists in parallel without communication interference from each other. Since the links of the CTs correspond to physical links between processors in the hypercube, a message sent across a link can arrive in unit time. Therefore, we conclude the time required for CT construction, broadcast, and merge operation are all $O(\log n)$ for a static set of arbitrary size n.

In fact, assume that each element in a C-list has information about the head and tail element indices, each elements can obtain the INTERVAL by local computation. So, the CTs for C-lists can be constructed with no communication cost.

3.3   Non-consecutive lists (N-lists)

Dynamically formed sets can be randomly located in a group of processors and two adjacent elements can be physically far away in the hypercube. According to the information distributing principle, the elements' locations are not known by any one processor. Instead, an element A knows of only element B in the same set by a pointer designating B. In the case where one element is pointed to by at most one other element in the set, the dynamic set forms what we call a non-consecutive list.

Algorithm 2 constructs CTs for the N-lists. The basic idea is simple: initially only the head of a list is inactive, all other elements will query first the left neighbor, and then the left neighbor of the left neighbor, and so on, until it reaches an inactive element. Then the inactive element reached becomes the father of the element in the CT and the element itself becomes inactive.

Algorithm 2
All processors in parallel:
(1) if the processor is correspondent to the head of a list then
      ACTIVE := false;
      FATHER := self;
   else

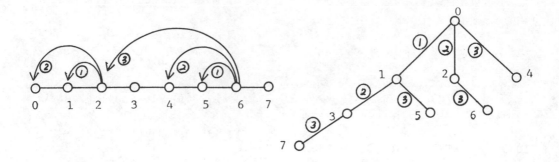

Figure 2: Building the CT for a N-list.

```
        ACTIVE := true;
        PRED := left-neigbor;
(2)  while ACTIVE = true do
        send query to PRED;
        if PRED is active then PRED := the PRED of PRED;
        else
           ACTIVE := false;
           FATHER := PRED;
end.
```

In Figure 2 we give a N-list with 8 elements.[2] Notice how element 6 queries node 5, 4 and 2 in sequence, and becomes the son of element 2, since element 2 was inactive when the query was made at step 3.

Theorem 2 *The height and fan-in of the CT for any N-list of length n are bounded by* $\log n$.

Proof: Let the time step of a query sent initially be 0, the time step of the second query be 1, and so on. Give the links of the CT labels which correspond to the final query's time step. Assume an element in CT has a path from the root labeled $l_0, l_1, \ldots, l_m$, then observe that the index of the element in the list is $\sum_{i=0}^{m} 2^{l_i}$.

Observe that at any step in constructing or using the CT, one processor is accessed by at most one other processor. The communication pattern at each step is therefore a partial permutation, and can be done in logarithmic time in the hypercube [8]. The number of steps is bounded by the height of CT, which is $\log n$. Broadcast and merge over N-lists can therefore be done in $O(\log^2 n)$ time.

Algorithm 2 is similar but essentially different from the "pointer doubling" technique [3]. Communication with "doubling" is achieved by handshaking between the head and each element in a list. In $\log n$ time step, the head must deal with n elements. To avoid message congestion $O(n)$ processors must be used for each element. By contrast, Algorithm 2 assumes only one processor for one element.

The CT constructed is either a partial or complete binomial tree [2] depending on whether or not the length of the list is a power of two. It can be shown for the purpose of

---

[2]The given indices of the elements do not correspond to the host processor IDs.

communication that binomial trees is superior to balanced trees for machines like iPSC, where the message start-up time is expensive.

We have treated the CT construction and operations as two separate phases. In fact the operations can be done while the CT is being constructed. In the process of CT construction, an element must reach an inactive element before it stops, but the inactive element is either the head of the list or an element that that has directly or indirectly reached the head. A message from the head thus can pass to each element in the list. Similarly, merge operation can also be done while the CT being constructed.[3]

3.4   Rooted trees (R-trees)

The rooted tree is another type of dynamic set. Similar to the N-list, a node is linked to the set only by a pointer to another node. While an element can be pointed by at most one element in a N-list, a node in a R-tree may be pointed by more than one other nodes in a R-tree.

As there is no restriction on the shape of the R-trees, a R-tree can be at one extreme very flat and fat and at another extreme very thin like a chain. In either case, using the R-tree itself to achieve the communication would require at least linear time.

Because a processor containing a node of R-tree knows of only another node, i.e., the father in R-tree, it must communicate with the father as the first step to communicate with other elements in the set. However in some cases, for example a flat tree, in the very first step serious message congestion will occur(see Fig.5.(right)). This problem suggests that something must be done between the source and destination of a message.

A technique, *message merge*, has been devised to overcome this problem: When a message x is being sent from processor S to processor D, passing processors $m_1, ..., m_i, ..., m_p$, each intermediate processor m_i will check if a message y of the destination and same type has passed before. If so, the message x will be held in processor m_i and will be responded to by the reply for y; otherwise it will be passed to processor m_{i+1}. It is clear that two message for the same destination and of the same type will never be sent through the same link in the cube with message merge technique.

The CT construction algorithm for R-trees with *message merge* technique is sketched below.

Algorithm 3
All processors in parallel:
(1)if the processor is correspondent to the root of R-tree then
     FATHER := self;
     ACTIVE := false;
   else
     ACTIVE := true;
     PRED := father in R-tree;
(2) while ACTIVE = true do
     send query to PRED;
     if PRED is active then PRED := the PRED of PRED;
     else

---

[3]Let the value associated with an element x be $v_0(x)$. While an element queries $x_1, ..., x_m$ do: $v_1(x) := v_0(x) \oplus v_0(x_1), ..., v_m(x) := v_{m-1}(x) \oplus v_m(x_m)$. Then $v_i(x)$ is the merge result with the 2^i elements to the left of x. When the tail element becomes inactive, it contains the result of merging all elements in the list.

Notice that an element x does not merge with an element y until it has merged with all elements to the right of y, hence, the binary operator $\oplus$ is allowed to be non-commutative. Moreover, the procedure actually computes the listfix function [4] with the result distributed over all the elements in the list.

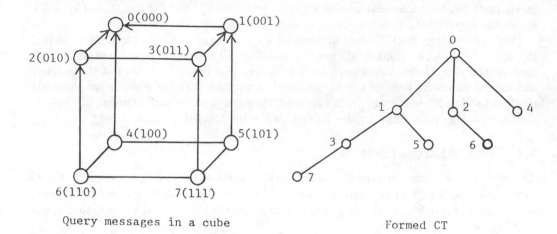

Query messages in a cube   Formed CT

Figure 3: Building the CT for a rooted tree.

      ACTIVE := false;
      if the query was merged at node M then FATHER := M;
      else FATHER := PRED;
end.

A R-tree is given in Figure 3 to illustrate the algorithm. The R-tree is flat, node 0 is the root and all other nodes are sons of node 0.

Theorem 3 *Let n be the size of a R-tree, N the size of cube; assume $N = O(\log n)$, then the height and fan-in of the CT for the R-tree are bounded by $O(\log n)$.*

Proof: The bound of the height can be shown with the same argument for N-lists. Because of message merge, a processor can at most have $\log N$ sons in the same CT, hence, the fan-in $<= O(\log n)$.

When a message is broadcasted through the CT, the left-most leaf of the left-most branch will receive the message in $O(\log^2 n)$ time, since each link of the CT may take up to $O(\log n)$ time and the height of the tree is $O(\log n)$. On the other hand, for the right-most leaf of the right-most branch in CT, the time used may add to another $O(\log n)$ factor, as at each level of the CT the processor may have to send $O(\log n)$ messages. The conclusion is that operations over a set of n data with R-tree structures can be carried out in $O(\log^3 n)$ time in the hypercube [4].

Notice that when $k > 1$ R-trees exists , a processor may become a node in more than one CT due to the message merge. The communication time certainly increases when taking the problem into account. However, poly-logarithmic time can be proven sufficient for any number of R-trees. [5]

---

[4]In comparison with N-lists, we are paying an extra $O(\log n)$ factor of time for the operations. The reason being that the shape of the CTs for N-lists is always a partial or perfect binomial tree, where the depth of a given branch is always smaller than the branch to its left.

[5]Limited by space, the proof cannot be given here. We are also working on another version of the algorithm, where a node can be in at most one CT.

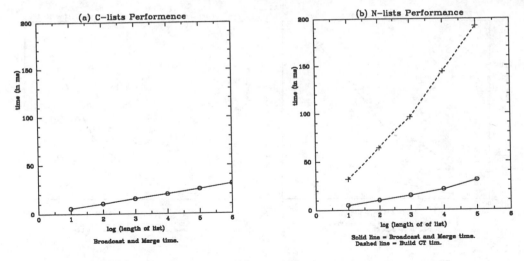

Figure 4: Performance of the CTs for C-lists and N-lists.

4   The Performance of the Algorithms

The data structures have been implemented on the Intel iPSC. The performance is given in Figures 4 and 5. [6] It can be observed that the time used for the CT construction and operations is indeed within the bound given by the theorem for each data structure.

The performance of R-trees algorithm can vary a great deal depending on the shapes the number of existing trees. The performance given in Figure 5(a) is only for the case of single flat trees. For comparison, we measured the time required to do the same operations over the same flat trees without the CTs. The results (Figure 5(b)) show that linear time is required.

5   On the Spectrum of the Granularity

Even with high dimension cubes, we may have to map more than one datum into one physical node for large scale problems. For algorithms supporting data structures to be really useful, they must be able to adapt to different granularities; moreover, the performance should scale well, i.e., the time cost should vary approximately linearly along with the number of given processors. This section is to show that the algorithms for the set structures indeed have the above properties.

Throughout the following discussion we will assume that n is the size of the data, m is the number of data mapped to one processor, and the size of the hypercube is $O(n/m)$.

(1) C-lists: Assume that the m elements are always in the same set. A CT can be constructed by Algorithm 1 if we treat each m elements in a processor as one element in the algorithm. One node of the CT still corresponds to one processor but contains m elements. The m elements can share the message broadcasted to the host processor and can merge with each other and send a single result up to the father processor of the CT. The amount of communication work of a processor in broadcasting and merge is therefore independent of the number m. The time required is decided by the height of the CT, i.e., $\log n/m$.

---

[6]The operation time given is the average of two hundred broadcast and merge over the CTs.

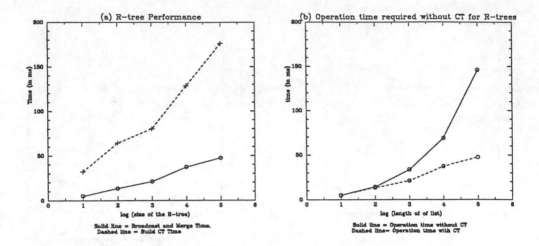

Figure 5: Performance for R-trees with CTs and without CTs.

(2) N-lists: As N-lists are dynamically formed sets, the m elements in one processor may belong to m different sets. We therefore have to apply Algorithm 2 to each element [7] in the processor and a factor of m is added to the complexity given by Theorem 2. The height of CT is still in the worst case $\log n$; however, each link of the CT may take less time for a message to go across as the cube size decreases when m increases. The time complexity is therefore $O(m \log n \log n/m)$.

(3) R-trees: Just as with Algorithm 2 in the N-lists, Algorithm 3 should be applied to each of the m nodes residing in one processor. With the same arguments as in (2), we can show that for one R-tree, the time cost of communications is bounded by $O(m \log n \log^2 n/m)$.

If n is fixed, the time complexities for N-lists and R-trees decrease linearly within a $\log n$ and $\log^2 n$ factor respectively when m decreases. Put in another way, the speed-up of the algorithms increases about linearly with the number of processors used.

6   An Application Example

A parallel algorithm for the connected component problem is as follows [7]:

Algorithm 4
Initial: each node is a partially connected component (PCC);
Iterate $2 \log n$ times:
    (1) for each node i in G in parallel do
            compute $m_i = $ minimum PCC of a neighbor of i;
    (2) for each PCC p in parallel do
            find $n_p = $ minimum of p and the $m_i's$ for i in p;
    (3) for each PCC p in parallel do
            find h_p, the limit of the sequence $p, n_p, n_{n_p}, ...$;
    (4) for each node i in parallel do
            $p_i := h_p$;
end.

---

[7]A more sophisticated algorithm is to find out which of the m elements indeed belong to one set by local computation, and package the messages of those elements together. The message traffic will be certainly reduced when elements in that same set tend to reside in the same processors.

The above algorithm is independent of the implementation. Now assume we map the adjacency lists with gray code onto a hypercube (Section 3.2). Then obviously step (1) is a merge over consecutive lists with a binary operator MIN. The partially connected components are dynamically formed sets of vertices of the graph, and step (2) is just a merge over non-consecutive lists with again the MIN operator. In step (3), if we regard the h_p as a pointer from one PCC to another, all the pointers can be shown to define a rooted forest [7], and the limit of the sequence $p, n_p, n_{n_p}, ...$, for a PCC p actually is the value of the root of a R-tree; hence, step (3) can be achieved by broadcasting over R-trees. Finally step (4) can be done by broadcasting over PCCs, which are N-lists.

The algorithm iterate $2\log n$ times, and each step of the algorithm can be done in poly-logarithmic time. Therefore, the implementation of the connected component algorithm with the data structures has poly-logarithmic complexity.

Let V be the number of vertices, E the number of edges of a graph. As adjacency lists are used in the above implementation, we use $O(\log E)$ processors. By contrast, implementations that require an adjacency matrix as input use $O(\log V^2)$ processors [7] [3]. For sparse graphs, (where $E = O(V)$), the implementation with the data structures can save $O(V)$ number of processors and still gives poly-logarithmic performance.

7 Concluding Remarks

It is obvious that the C-lists are just special cases of the N-lists whereas the N-lists are special cases of the R-trees. The trade-off between the generality and efficiency among the three data structures should be observed.

The set structures with the supported operations are general enough to be applied to a wide class of graph, combinatorial, set operation and system programming problems such as minimum spanning tree, max-flow, garbage collection and load balancing problems.

References

[1] M. C. Chen, *Very-high-level Parallel Programing by Aggregate Set Operations*, Research Report YALEEU/DCS/RR-499, Yale University, 1986.

[2] C. -T. Ho and S.L. Johnsson *Distributed Routing Algorithms and for Broadcasting and Personalized Communication in Hypercube*, 1986 ICPP p640 - p648.

[3] M-D A. Huang, *Solving Graph Problems with Optimal Speed up on Mesh-of-Tree Networks*, 26th Annual Symposium on Foundations of Computer Science. 1985.

[4] C. E. Leiserson and C. M. Maggs, *Communication-Efficient Graph Algorithms*, Proceeding of the 1986 International Conference on Parallel Processing.

[5] J. T. Schwartz *On Programming - An Interim Report on the SETL Project*, New York University, 1973.

[6] D. A. Turner *SASL Language Manual*, St Andrews University Technical Report, 1976.

[7] J. D. Ullman, *Computational Aspects of VLSI*. Computer Science Press, Inc., 1984.

[8] L. G. Valiant, *A Scheme for Fast Parallel Communication*,. SIAM J. Computing 11:2. 1981.

A Fast, Message-Based Tagless Marking

GORDON LYON*

Abstract. The parallel implementation of a marking algorithm provides an object lesson on the importance of memory domains for some classes of parallel application, especially searchings. A new tagless marking algorithm for list-structures has an underlying linear mode that initiates an independent O(n) cycle test (and sometimes, cycle cut) only when a re-entrancy arises. The maximum cost of cycle testing is established by the size of the address space. The method is ideal for parallel implementation across private memory domains linked via message-passing, since segmenting the address space abbreviates cycle tests. In particular, while both domains and processors equally shorten worst case execution times, the disposition of domains is a static determination independent of dependencies within a list-structure. Domain balance is thus easier to satisfy than processor load balance.

BACKGROUND

List-structure (henceforth, *LS*) circularities pose a central difficulty in performing the mark phase of a mark-and-sweep garbage collection. While extra tag-bits, stacks, or special address conventions can manage list re-entrancies, very large lists discourage the unbounded use of auxiliary storage, or the moving about of nodes into various address regions. On the other hand, space for a node mark can be found. Memory parity is often disabled and these bits used for marking, true parities being restored in the subsequent sweep.

The Core Marking Algorithm. Lindstrom [4] provides a tag-free algorithm that marks n nodes in average time O(n log n), with worst cases O(n**2); unfortunately, the O(n log n) average time holds whether re-entrancies exist or not, even though tree structures are markable in O(n). Lindstom's method suffers over trees because each newly encountered node could also be, in full generality, a specially-marked node already in the traversal. This possibility must be checked. The challenge has been to devise a general marking that is automatically linear over subtrees of a LISP-like list-structure, LS, that is not ensured free of re-entrancies. Such a solution, the new *Core,* serves henceforth as a vehicle

---

Systems Components Division, National Bureau of Standards, Gaithersburg, MD 20899. A contribution of the National Bureau of Standards. Not subject to copyright.

This work was supported in part by the Defense Advanced Research Projects Agency, Strategic Computing Initiative, Sponsor Task Number 5520.

for discussion [5]. One of the Core algorithm's advantages and strengths is its automatic, linear marking of subtrees. In this respect, it is a partial reply to Standish's comment on marking algorithms for cyclic list structures, "...nobody has yet devised the ideal O(n), bounded-workspace marking algorithm that uses no tag bits" [6, p.213].

Only a few external characteristics of the sometimes convoluted Core algorithm are needed for subsequent discussion. The actual cost of each Core cycle test depends upon the depth of search and the presence or absence of a cycle. Furthermore, the Core algorithm belatedly detects some cycle-causing re-entrancies only after it has scrambled its own bookkeeping. While this damage is easily repaired, extra calculations must be made. As with other tagless solutions, overall worst case markings for the new method are O(n**2), although under circumstances of few re-entrancies Core will do considerably better.

CONSTRUCTION OF A PARALLEL VERSION

Not only is the Core algorithm easily adapted to a message-passing style of parallel execution but it also benefits from the imposed structure. Whenever the next list-structure node in the marking traversal is previously unvisited, it can be placed on a stack as the root of a pending subsearch. While this stacking deferral is treacherous to apply in general (discussion below), its utility is apparent as linkages of the list-structure cross from one private memory domain to another. Here, each processor marks only its private partition in the distributed list-structure, deferring nothing within its domain. However, every processor still maintains a stack for pending searches. Processor x notifies y via message-based *remote stacking* whenever a searched link leaves x's private memory for a location of y; this remote stacking allows y to continue the search abandoned by x.

Notify-and-Reverse. An essential ingredient for a message passing implementation is the Core algorithm's property of *notify-and-reverse*. This property, which can be used optionally on a node-by-node basis, does not depend upon any assumption of parallel processing; however, it is much more practical with the support of private memory domains. At any time in the execution of the (serial) Core algorithm, whenever the next node is *previously unencountered*, the node can be placed on a stack for pending subsearches. This is *notification*. (A heap would work equally well--retrieval order is immaterial.) Having notified the subproblem stack, the algorithm then behaves as if the link were NIL; search direction is set *inward*. This is *reversal*. These two actions together constitute *notify-and-reverse*. There is no particular restriction upon invoking *notify-and-reverse* whenever it applies; the difficulty in a global address space is to ascertain that a node has *not* been visited previously. Such a test is another form of cycle checking, a very expensive nuisance. *The parallel version will use the notify-and-reverse option only in obvious circumstances*.

With notify-and-reverse, whenever a (partial) LS is exhausted (marked), the algorithm must check the auxiliary stack for any remaining sublists. Let z denote such a sublist root. Should the designated root z have been marked in the meantime by another subsearch, no further searching from z can be productive. The pointer to z can be discarded. Alternately, an unmarked z means that all previous marking has failed to reach and, thereby, mark it. Node z is then taken as a new root by the Core algorithm. During root z's marking search other marked nodes trigger cycle testing as usual. Marking of the entire LS terminates when the stack can no longer fulfill a request for a new root.

Thus far no element of parallel computation has been introduced. However, it remains to be demonstrated that notify-and-reverse is something other than a sterile property. Its potential liability is testing for its applicability, which can cost a great deal. Fortunately, notify-and-reverse is an *optional* action. Given circumstances that automatically signal its applicability, it becomes more attractive. Appropriate circumstances do arise with separate memory domains and processors, *i.e.*, parallel processing.

Using Notify-and-Reverse. The true utility of notify-and-reverse is more apparent when it is triggered by a significant implementation detail that renders apparent many unvisited nodes. The obvious circumstances within a loosely-coupled system are LS linkage crossings from one private memory domain to another [Fig. 1]. Imagine the LS partitioned among numerous processors, with each processor supporting a copy of the Core algorithm. Here, each copy knows it cannot visit a node in another processor's memory. (By assigning each processor to mark only private memory, contention problems and LS consistency are also resolved.) Let each core algorithm copy have a private stack for its pending searches. Those LS links that extend beyond the private memory will trigger interprocess messages which, when received, generate entries on pending-search stacks. These *remote stackings* notify the receiver of a subproblem. Processor x notifies another y whenever an LS link leaves $x's$ private memory for one of the locations of y. Notification allows recipient y to resume the search abandoned by x.

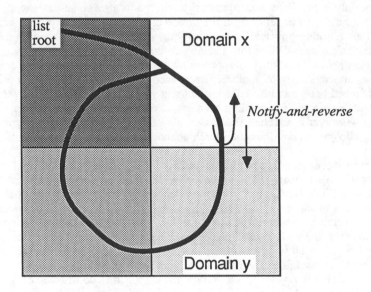

FIG. 1 List circularity that crosses four memory domains.

Worst Case Improvements via Domains. An *estimate* of a worst case marking time for the core algorithm over *n nodes in one address space* is

$$k\, n^2.$$

Now split the single address space in two, distributing nodes evenly among two domains. Having done this, a (serial) worst case estimate for marking is

$$k\,(n/2)^2 + k\,(n/2)^2 + Ck' = k\, n^2/2 + Ck' = k\, n^2/2 + 2nk'$$

where C indicates that some links must leave one space for the other. Given n overall nodes, each node with at most two descendants, communications cannot exceed C = 2n, each with a cost k'.

Further domain splits also improve worst case matters. For example, a split into three domains yields

$$k(n/3)^2 + k(n/3)^2 + k(n/3)^2 + 2nk'$$

$$= k\, n^2/3 + 2nk'.$$

Notice that a 50% increase, from two to three domains, diminishes the quadratic term in direct proportion. In general, d domains will diminish this worst case term by d. The promise of improvement, above, assumes only a uniprocessor with multiple address domains; since no extra processors have been considered, a true parallel version may show more than an "intuitive" speedup.

Adding Parallel Processors. Estimates thus far have not assumed *any* overlapped, parallel computation. Only the address space has been segmented, a common practice in list handling. A next step is to dedicate a processor to each of the address spaces. In the worst possible case the times of the execution are not improved over those just given. This would be for cases with long linear dependencies in the node linkages. However, most list-structures are trees or other interesting hierarchical combinations that provide considerably more opportunity for parallel operations. The best of the worst case estimates (minmax) would be

$$k\, n^2\, d^{-2} + 2nk'$$

for d memory domains and d associated processors. Here, it is assumed that fan-out occurs quickly to all d domains, each with self-contained sublists of the LS. Communication is assumed negligible after the fanout, which might be the case if important sublists are deliberately placed in separate domains. The above expression presents the false impression of a potential $d**2$ improvement in the quadratic term from d processors, whereas in reality, the term reflects contributions of both memory domains and processors. (A message passing paradigm has memory domains and processors bound together.) Furthermore, the estimate is unduly optimistic, since a whole list-structure will not be so ideally parceled among the various memory domains; marking is only one of many competing phases within an application. Static disposition of the LS for the marking phase will have to compete against different LS dispositions which other phases find more useful.

Other points are also important in a parallel implementation. Interprocess messages should be sufficiently fast that the recipient is not starved. This may be a very practical hinderance. Additionally, some convention must hold so that starvation at a node is not confounded with overall termination.

Limits, Measures. In the limit, with n *domains, all* marking becomes at the very worst, linear. Such would be the case when all nodes form *one* linear string, an unlikely event. With n domains, there is *no* LS circularity to worry about: each memory holds but one node. Overall communication, which is linear in nodes, constitutes the entire process. In this same context of likelihoods, *expected worst case* would be a more useful, and considerably more complex, measure than worst case. Although strongly a function of a given application and its concomitant distributions of node linkages, this measure would realistically weight marking penalties. An analytic characterization of expected worst case (or other similarly weighted measures) may be elusive for a broad range of applications. Realistic estimates from empirical studies will be just as satisfactory for achieving good LS balances.

SUMMARY

A parallel, message-based version of the Core algorithm will realize a distinct advantage in having parts of the LS dispersed among private memories. Segmentation only diminishes costs of cycle checking, while the parallel version's remote stackings are a natural match for message transmissions in loosely-coupled architectures. Both memory domains and processors improve worst case expectations, although a good balance of the LS is easier for the domains, involving as it does only node counts. Unlike processor load balance, domain balance is independent of LS internode linkages, at least for a simple worst case measure. Within limits of the measure, the parallel Core typifies a class of algorithms for which protected memory domains play at least as important a role as additional processors.

REFERENCES

(1) D. Gries, *The Science of Programming*, Springer-Verlag, 1981.

(2) M.C. Hamburg, *Two tagless variations on Deutsch-Schorr-Waite*, Information Processing Letters, 22 (1986), pp. 179-183.

(3) G. Lindstrom, *Scanning list structures without stacks or tag bits*, Information Processing Letters, 2 (1973), pp. 47-51.

(4) G. Lindstrom, *Copying list structures using bounded workspace*, Comm. ACM, 17 (1974), pp. 198-202.

(5) G. Lyon, *A tagless marking that is linear over subtrees*, Parallel Processing Group note, NBS, Gaithersburg, MD., December, 1985. 8pp.

(6) T. Standish, *Data Structure Techniques*, Addison-Wesley, 1980.

PART II:
OPERATING SYSTEMS,
LOAD BALANCING AND
PROBLEM MAPPING

The Trillium OS for the FPS T-Series*

ALISON A. BROWN† AND GREGORY D. BURNS†

Abstract An overview of the Trillium operating system, C and Fortran compilers, T-Series simulator, and debugger for parallel programs which the Cornell Theory Center is developing for the FPS T-Series interfaced to one or more Gould UTX-32 (UNIX) hosts. Cites more detailed publications in each of the above areas.

Introduction. The Cornell Theory Center is developing an operating system, a debugging environment, and a suite of development tools for the FPS T-Series attached to one or more Gould UTX-32 (Berkeley UNIX) hosts. Our goal is to provide an environment for development of scientific programs. In developing this software we have assumed that the scientist will be working in an environment which includes UNIX workstations as the "everyday" computational resource, connected by a local area network to larger systems such as the Gould and the FPS T-Series. Our software supports this environment, since it distributes both the user interface and the application across all three types of systems above.

Trillium is layered, so users can request levels of functionality from programming for the "bare" machine to a full operating system with memory management, process management, and I/O support.

Development Tools. The normal UNIX development tools are available on the UNIX host system(s) and the workstation(s). Additional UNIX

---
*Floating Point Systems, Inc., Beaverton, Oregon
† Cornell Theory Center, Cornell University, Ithaca, NY 14853, USA.

processors of the T-Series which have disks attached, as well as all UNIX systems noted above.

The application sees exactly the same environment in all processors -- i.e. the same set of system services, which are requested by identical subroutine calls, are available for all processors and on the host. Not all services will be available on all processors -- e.g. the math library of vector functions will not work on scalar processors nor can you open a file on a local disk if the processor does not have one (you can still use the filesystems of other processors).

Programs are written in either "C" or Fortran and libraries of subroutines are provided to call the system services which support interprocessor communication, passing of data between processes, access to all filesystems, moving processes between processors and other functions necessary to distributed computations. Fortran I/O is not currently supported (i.e., the Fortran READ and WRITE statements) and the Fortran programmer must use the "C" model of calling subroutines for doing I/O.

System services are provided in the area of process management, memory management, message passing, and filesystem I/O. The process management services provide the ability to communicate between running processes, to dynamically create, move and kill processes in any processor (including spawning new copies of running process for dynamic load balancing), and to find out the state of any process (for debugging). The message passing services allow the exchange of data or programs between any processor, including UNIX systems, involved in the computation. The filesystem services provide the normal open/close/read/write/seek operations supported by UNIX filesystems for any processor which has a filesystem and is participating in the computation.

The Trillium User Interface Programs are developed using standard UNIX editors and tools and when complete may be run using either the T-Series simulator or the real T-Series system or a combination of both. The user interface to running a parallel computation using the Trillium system is called the **tshell**.

The tshell provides a set of commands used to start and control the progress of a parallel computation. It is the tshell that provides the ability to load programs into the processors of the T-Series system. The same program may be loaded into all processors or different programs may be loaded into different processors. Because Trillium provides a uniform application interface to all processors, including UNIX processors which are part of the computation, the same program may also be loaded into one or more UNIX systems. You may use the simulator and/or the real T-Series machine to run your computation. No changes to the program itself are required to move between the simulator and the T-Series. You can split the computation, running some of the computation on the real T-Series processors and simulating some of the processors.

development tools include a cross-assembler plus "C" and Fortran cross-compilers for the INMOS Transputer, which is the basic scalar computational unit of the T-Series. There is also a linker which will selectively link in modules from object libraries, as well as facilities for building and maintaining object libraries. A binder is used to produce executable modules.

A T-Series simulator is also provided, which allows an application to run either entirely in the simulator, entirely in the real machine, or with processes split between the two.

The Trillium Operating System. Trillium is a distributed operating system which runs native on the FPS T-Series and also on top of a Berkeley UNIX kernel. It supports computations distributed across the processors of the T-Series, one or more Gould UTX/32 host systems connected directly to the T-Series, and other UNIX systems/workstations connected to the host systems over a network. It provides a normal UNIX command interface with the addition of commands to reserve the T-Series, download programs, and so forth. The applications interface includes routines for requesting operating system services like memory allocation, filesystem I/O, communication with other programs, time and date information, etc.

The applications interface is identical for processes/programs running on T-Series processors and on UNIX processors which are locally or remotely attached to the T-Series. A computation which needs execution-time access to UNIX filesystems need not have part of the computation running on a UNIX system - access to file systems outside the T-Series is available to programs running on T-Series processors as part of the normal system services.

The Trillium Applications Interface In the Trillium system, three types of processors may be used in a single computation:

    a) vector processors of the FPS T-Series (includes scalar processor) b) system processors of the FPS T-Series (scalar only - one per eight
        vector processors)
    c) UNIX systems attached to the T-Series directly or via a network.

The application program may use all these processors, or some subset of them, as appropriate. Each processor may be running one or several programs and all processors may be running the same program(s) or there may be a variety of programs distributed across the processors. It is not necessary for the application to have a program running in the host in order for programs running in the T-Series processors (vector or system) to have access to the host's UNIX filesystem and the user's terminal. The programs running in T-Series processors are automatically provided with the ability to access the host's UNIX filesystem directly, and the processes/programs running in all processors, including those of the T-Series, have defined a standard input source (functional analogue of UNIX stdin) and standard output destination (functional analogue of UNIX stdout) which is the user's terminal by default. The user's terminal may be on a UNIX T-Series host system or a UNIX system which is connected to the T-Series host over a local area network. The standard input and/or output may also be redirected to a file residing on any other processor which has a filesystem. This includes

The location of each part of the computation is provided by a **template** which describes the computation. This template is the basic data structure of the tshell; many of the commands are designed to operate on the templates that describe the computation. Note that the template describes a particular instantiation of an application - there may be several templates describing various ways of running the same program or set of programs.

Using the template you specify which programs are loaded into which processors without regard to whether the processors are real or simulated. Trillium provides the ability to load programs into any processor, and to suspend or kill processes, while the computation is running. The new program can be requested either by a running program in any processor involved in the computation or by a command given to the tshell. The new program will be added (subject to storage limitations) to programs already in the processor.

The Trillium Filesystem All programs that are part of the computation, regardless of which processor they are running in, have access to the filesystems of all processors involved in the computations. UNIX-style pathnames are used in accessing files. Each processor has associated with it a **home directory** which is set to a directory in the UNIX host filesystem by default. This home directory is part fo the template and can be changed as required. For processors with attached disks it may be desirable to make the home directory the root of the filesystem on the local disk. It is also possible to mount the local filesystem at the root of the default home directory on the host. The programs running in any processor can access the files of any other processor via the Trillium open/close/read/write system calls. These calls are provided for both C and Fortran.

The Trillium filesystem in the UNIX host sytem(s) is built on the UNIX filesystem and essentially provides transparent access to the host UNIX files for any processor involved in the computation. The distributed nature of the Trillium filesystem means that no user applications program is required in the host to give programs running in the T-Series processors access to the UNIX files of the host. The T-Series program simply calls open/close/read/write etc. giving the appropriate pathname.

Debugging. Debugging facilities are provided primarily by the simulator, but it is also possible to start up a debugger in a processor where the programs appear to have problems. In this case the debugger need not be loaded into the processor at the time the application program is loaded -- it can be loaded by using the machine shell when it is required. Once the debugger is loaded into one or more processors the tshell is used to enter a debugging environment which provides many of the standard facilities of symbolic debuggers. Unfortunately, it is not possible to provide all facilities, so it may be advisable to rerun the computation on the simulator if possible.

Development Schedule. Currently the cross-assembler, "C" cross-compiler and linker/binder are complete. The innermost Trillium kernel for the FPS T-Series will be complete at the end of 1986, the full kernel is expected to be complete in late summer of 1987. A Fortran comiler is now in progress, and expected to be complete in the first quarter of 1987. The UNIX version of Trillium is operating, as is the simulator. We plan to distribute this software, and the compilers (which are the property of commercial companies) will be sold for a modest cost to academic institutions.

A High Performance Operating System for the NCUBE*

T. N. MUDGE†, G. D. BUZZARD† AND T. S. ABDEL-RAHMAN†

Abstract. This paper examines the existing hypercube array processing node operating system for the NCUBE. Extensions to the operating system that lead to performance increases for important classes of algorithms are described. Performance results are given and are compared to those of other systems.

1   Introduction and Motivation

NCUBE produces a family of commercial hypercube multiprocessors that range in size from 64 processors (NCUBE/six) to 1024 processors (NCUBE/ten). The hypercube array of processing nodes is managed by a host computer (an Intel 80286 based system). Software development for the hypercube is carried out on the host using a multiuser Unix-like operating system called Axis. It allows the hypercube array to be partitioned into subcubes that may be allocated to different users. These subcubes are logically independent of each other and the processing nodes in each subcube are numbered logically beginning at zero. In addition, there is also a run-time executive program called Vertex that executes on the processors of the hypercube array. This paper discusses the design of high performance extensions to Vertex.

The array processors are VAX-class 32-bit microprocessors with IEEE standard floating point capability. Each node has 128 K-bytes of local memory and 22 high speed (1 M-byte per second) unidirectional DMA channels. The channels are paired to provide 11 bidirectional links. Ten of these links can be connected to neighboring processors in the hypercube, thus allowing for systems of 1024 processors. The eleventh link connects to the

---

* NCUBE Corporation, Tempe, Arizona
† Advanced Computer Architecture Laboratory, Department of Electrical Engineering and Computer Science, The University of Michigan.

I/O subsystem which is also connected to the host. More architectural details can be found in [1].

Algorithms that have been proposed for or implemented on hypercube multiprocessors can be classified by their primary mode of communication. In particular, there are three common modes of communication: nearest neighbor, broadcast, and random access. Nearest neighbor (NN) communications are between adjacent processors in the hypercube array. Broadcast (BC) communications originate from a single source and are sent to the remaining processors. Finally, random access (RA) communications, as the name implies, may originate or terminate at any of the processors. Clearly RA communications are the most general. NN communications are subsumed by RA, and BC communications can be achieved by multiple RA communications.

The present version of Vertex implements only RA communications. While this is clearly sufficient, performance of many algorithms can be greatly enhanced by employing a broad set of more specialized communication primitives. In this paper we discuss our initial investigative efforts in this area.

The remainder of this paper is organized as follows. Section 2 contains a concise description of the Vertex run-time executive program. The points of inefficiency inherent in the standard Vertex communication scheme are pointed out in Section 3. Our high performance extensions to Vertex are described in Section 4. Section 5 describes the experiments that we have performed and discusses their results. Finally, concluding comments are given in Section 6.

2 Explanation of Vertex

Vertex is a run-time executive program that executes on the NCUBE array processors. The services provided by Vertex are user program loading, low-level error handling, low-level debugger support, node identification and time call handlers, and communications support that includes message buffer handling. Vertex is compact, requiring only about 5 K-bytes of memory for both code and data (excluding the communication buffers). Entry to Vertex from high level language libraries and user written assembly language routines is via an operating system trap call that saves the current program status word and program counter and branches into Vertex code via an interrupt jump table. A similar mechanism may also be invoked by the hardware in response to an execution exception, or an external interrupt request.

User programs may query Vertex to learn the logical (with respect to the currently allocated sub-cube) node address on which they are executing, the host interface processor address, and currently allocated sub-cube dimension. They may also request the current processor time, which is kept in multiples of 1024 clock cycles since node initialization. These two call handlers, and those of the communication system that will be discussed later, comprise the primary operating system trap call services.

The low-level error handlers, which are invoked by hardware recognized program exceptions, save processor state information and suspend execution of the user process. This allows the low-level debugger, invoked by communication system interrupt handler upon receiving a debugger message, to examine the state of the node as it was when the exception was detected. The debugger then allows the examination and setting of registers and memory, and the setting of breakpoints on any allocated node.

The memory map of an array node divides the 128 K-bytes into four areas: the interrupt jump table; user code and data space; Vertex code and data space; and the communication buffer pool. The interrupt jump table occupies a fixed 2 K-byte region of memory beginning at address zero. The Vertex code and data space occupies about 5 K-bytes of memory. It is statically relocatable and lies between the user code and data space and the communication buffers. Typically about 27 K-bytes of memory is reserved for communications buffers, leaving the remaining 95 K-bytes for the user code and data.

Vertex communications are driven by two events: requests from the user program, via operating system traps; and responses to communication channel interrupts. A brief description of the three calls that comprise the interface to the user program is given here, a more detailed discussion appears later. The node write call is named *nwrite*. It sends a message of a specified type to a designated destination. The *nread* call examines the unclaimed received message queue for a message from the specified source of the desired type. When the desired message is found, it is returned to the caller. The *ntest* call performs a function similar to nread, except that it returns immediately after checking the existing messages and only reports on the success of the search — located messages are not returned.

A pool of communication buffers is maintained by Vertex. These buffers are used on both the sending and receiving nodes. They allow callers of nwrite to be released after a communication buffer is allocated and the user data is copied into it. Therefore, callers are not held up while the system is waiting for access to a communication channel. Furthermore, if the data to be sent is allocated from dynamic stack-based storage, the caller may release that storage immediately after returning from the nwrite call. Similarly, callers of nread are not required to make their calls before messages arrive since all arriving messages are first stored in a communication buffer.

The communication buffer pool begins as a single free buffer. Requests for buffers are satisfied by searching linearly through the doubly linked buffer pool for free buffers of a sufficiently large size. When one is located it is further checked to see if it exceeds the requested size by 32 or more bytes; if so, the free buffer is split so that a buffer of the requested size can be allocated from the end furthest from the front of the list. This policy tends to concentrate free buffers near the beginning of the list. If no buffers of sufficient size are located the request may be queued to search again when another buffer is returned. In addition to attempting to satisfy queued buffer requests, the buffer deallocation routine also collapses adjacent free buffers into a single buffer. Buffers that are in use may be queued on other system queues via a second pair of link fields. Thus, for its own internal use Vertex provides buffer allocate, deallocate, enqueue, and dequeue procedures.

The specific operation of nwrite is to check for valid message length and destination, allocate a communication buffer and copy the user data to it, calculate the outbound channel to use, and, if the channel is inactive, initiate the message transfer protocol. In the case that the channel is busy, the message is queued to be sent as soon as the channel becomes available. In either case, the caller is released to continue execution. When the final step of the DMA controlled message transfer has been completed an interrupt is signalled. The service of this interrupt includes the releasing of the communication buffer. Incoming messages are placed in communication buffers and then queued in an unclaimed message list. Nread checks this queue for a message with a specific source and type, if it is not found it will wait until an appropriate message arrives. When the requested message is located it will be copied to the user data space, dequeued from the unclaimed message list, and the communication buffer will be released. Callers to nread and ntest may specify that messages of any incoming source or type are desired.

Message transmission is controlled via a three way handshake protocol. Simply stated, the sender sends a two byte message to the receiver indicating the number of bytes it wishes to transmit (all inactive channels are set to receive two byte transmissions). The receiver allocates a communication buffer, sets the appropriate DMA channel to receive the indicated number of bytes, and then transmits a two byte acknowledgement back to the sender. Upon receiving this acknowledgement the sender transmits the entire message. This protocol is initiated by a call to nwrite. However, the remaining steps are handled by a sequence of interrupt events. Specifically, the reception of the two byte length message by the receiver and the reception of the two byte acknowledgement by the sender both signal interrupts. An interrupt is also generated on both the sending and receiving nodes when the DMA transfer of the message is completed.

A more detailed description of a message send/receive transaction between two adjacent nodes is given below. Figure 1 expresses this transaction pictorially. In step 1 the sender issues an nwrite call, which generates an operating system trap event. In step 2 the Vertex nwrite trap handler allocates a communication buffer, waiting on a buffer request queue if none are presently available. Once allocated (step 3), the message data is copied from the user process to the communication buffer and the buffer is queued on the send list. The nwrite caller is released at this point. In step 4 the two byte transmission request, indicating message length, is sent. If the channel to the requested destination is not busy this action occurs as the final action of step 3. Otherwise, this transmission request is queued pending an end of message transfer interrupt from the DMA for the message currently using the channel. Reception of the two byte transmission request generates an interrupt on the receiving node. The handler for this interrupt (step 5) attempts to allocate a communication buffer of the requested length. If it is successful, an acknowledgement message is sent back to the sender (step 6). If a buffer is unavailable a buffer request is queued and the acknowledgement message is postponed until after this request is satisfied. It may also be necessary to wait for the channel from the receiver to the sender to become free during step 6 (if a previous message send is still in progress). The reception of the two byte acknowledgement generates an interrupt for the sender. In this interrupt handler (step 7) the DMA transfer of the message is begun. Upon completion of this DMA transfer an interrupt is generated for both the sender and the receiver. On the sender the communication buffer is dequeued from the send queue and released. If another message is ready to be sent on the same channel this procedure is repeated from step 4, otherwise the channel is reset to the inactive state. On the receiver the message is checked to see if this node is the final destination and if this message is a user message. If so, the communication buffer is queued on the incoming unclaimed message list and the channel is reset to its inactive state. If an nread call has been issued for the incoming message, it is dequeued from the incoming unclaimed message list, copied to the user data space, and the communication buffer is released, this corresponds to step 8.

Multi-hop messages are handled in a manner very similar to the above. The following actions, beginning with step 8, occur on each of the intermediate nodes. The receiver

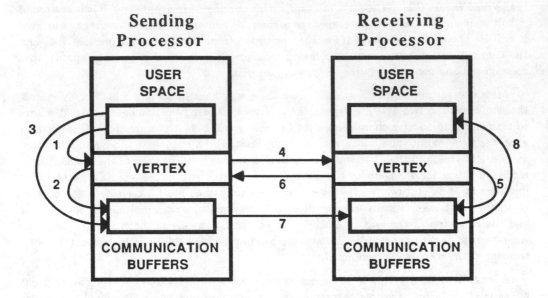

Actions:

1.	Sender:	nwrite call
2.	Sender:	allocate communication buffer
3.	Sender:	copy buffer, release nwrite caller
4.	Sender:	transmission request
5.	Receiver:	allocate communication buffer
6.	Receiver:	transmission request accepted
7.	Sender:	transmit data
8.	Receiver:	if received pending, copy buffer release nread caller

Interrupts:

after 4 on receiver
after 6 on sender
after 7 on sender and receiver

Potential Waits:

at 2 for local buffer
at 4 for use of channel
at 5 for remote buffer and use of channel

Figure 1: Node to Node Communication.

interrupt handler inspects the destination field of the message; calculates the next channel to send it out on in order to get it another step closer to its final destination; queues the communication buffer on the send list; and, if the channel is not busy, sends the two byte transmission request message thus assuming the role of the sender at step 4. This procedure is repeated on each of the intermediate nodes.

System messages (primarily for interactions with the low-level debugger) are also handled in a very similar manner. On the destination receiving node at step 8 the message is checked to see if it is a system message, if it is the appropriate system message handler is invoked.

3   Points of Inefficiency

Two major points of inefficiency can be identified within the communication scheme implemented in Vertex with respect to NN communications. One, is the use of buffer copies, the second is the overhead incurred by the three-way handshake protocol. In many cases, algorithms that fall into the NN classification have *a priori* knowledge of all of their communication requirements; presently this knowledge is unused. With simple extensions to Vertex this knowledge can be exploited to yield much more efficient communications.

While the cost incurred by copying data is obvious, the cost of requiring a more complex communication protocol than is necessary is much harder to quantify. This cost can be traced to two major sources. One, is the overhead incurred by servicing interrupts generated by unnecessary protocol messages. The second, is the loss of the use of the channel from the receiving node to the sending node for the duration of time between the initial transmission length message arriving at the receiver (step 4 in Figure 1) and the acknowledgement arriving back at the sender (step 6 in Figure 1). Notice that this duration may be arbitrarily long if the receiving node does not have sufficient communication buffer space immediately available. These effects are reflected in the experimental results that are presented in Section 5.

Random communications do not incur the buffer copy overhead at intermediate nodes. However, they do have the same protocol overhead on every node that the message traverses. They also incur the additional cost of storing the entire message at each intermediate node before beginning to forward it to the next node.

BC communications are not directly supported in vertex. Broadcasts are typically implemented by a sequence of NN communications arranged in a spanning tree order [2]. Each node (except the root) receives a message from its parent node, then serially relays the message to each of its child nodes. The root node begins the operation by serially sending the message to each of its child nodes. Thus, in addition to the inefficiencies already noted for near neighbor communications, broadcasts also incur a store and forward (with two buffer copies) overhead and a serialization cost associated with sending to only one child node at a time on each of the intermediate (i.e., non-terminal) nodes in the spanning tree. Serialization is unnecessary as a broadcast instruction is implemented in the instruction set of the node processors. The broadcast instruction allows a message to be sent on any subset of the output channels of a node in a single DMA action.

4   Extensions to Vertex

The Vertex operating system has been extended to address both of the major inefficiencies present in NN communications. The new send call, named *send*, and new receive call, named *rcvreq*, do not use communication buffers and are asynchronous. Since return from the send or rcvreq call does not indicate their completion, the caller passes a pointer to a flag variable which is set for this purpose. The indication of completion is signalled by an end-of-DMA interrupt for both send and rcvreq. This protocol places a burden on the caller of send to ensure that the message data is not corrupted before the completion flag is set. It also requires that the receiver make a call to rcvreq before the anticipated message arrives. The latter constraint could be relaxed by allocating a communication buffer if the call to rcvreq has not yet occurred. However, to do so would lead to incompatibilities with the next extension to be discussed. The primary benefit of bufferless communication is that the incremental (i.e., per byte) cost is substantially reduced.

The send and rcvreq call also exploit the *a priori* knowledge that is inherent in most NN class programs by eliminating the three-way handshake protocol. This extension places the additional requirement on the caller of rcvreq to specify the exact number of bytes expected to be received. The chief benefit of this change is a substantial reduction in the fixed overhead of NN communications.

There are three other calls that are presently in available in extended Vertex. Two routines have been added to allow the communication scheme to be switched dynamically. In fact, the communication scheme in use can be selected on a channel by channel basis. These calls are necessary because the extended Vertex communication scheme relies upon different interrupt handlers than standard Vertex. The final extension is a broadcast call that allows a node to send the same message to any set of nearest neighbors simultaneously.

5   Experiments and Results

For programs with simple NN communications we expect the time added by the communications to be approximated by the formula $t_{comm} = mx + f$, where t_{comm} is the total message communication time, m is the length of the message in bytes, x is the incremental (per byte) message cost, and f is the fixed overhead (protocol) cost. Of course, this formula will only hold for simple communications. It does not take into account the positive effect of overlapping message transmission with computation, nor the negative effect of waiting on resources (e.g., communication buffers or channels). Nonetheless, the parameters of this formula are frequently quoted as they do provide a partial indication of expected performance and they are easily measured.

A common technique for measuring the aforementioned parameters is to configure the array nodes into a logical ring, then record the amount of time required to pass a fixed size message around the ring a specified number of times. When this experiment is repeated for messages of differing sizes the parameters m and f can be easily extracted. The results of such an experiment using both standard and extended Vertex communication primitives are given in Table 1. It can be seen that the use of extended Vertex primitives yielded an improvement of 5.6 in fixed overhead and 2.43 in incremental cost over standard Vertex.

	Standard Vertex	Extended Vertex	Speedup
Fixed Overhead	466.40 (μsec/message)	83.20 (μsec/message)	5.60
Incremental Cost	3.14 (μsec/byte)	1.29 (μsec/byte)	2.43

Table 1: Ring Message Results.

Number	NCUBE		iPSC		MarkII(8Mhz)
of bytes	Std. Vtx.	Ext. Vtx.	CrOS	IHOS	CrOS
8	245.76	46.76	160	5960	86.0
64	41.79	10.37	80	777	45.5
256	19.88	6.45	79	202	41.4

Table 2: Values of t'_{comm} (μsec) for the NCUBE, iPSC and MarkII.

Another frequently quoted communication performance parameter is given in [3]. It is also called t_{comm}, but we will henceforth refer to it as t'_{comm} to avoid confusion with our earlier definition. The value of t'_{comm} is conventionally defined as the transfer time of a 32 bit word, and is often given for a range of total message sizes. It can easily be related to t_{comm} by $t'_{comm} = \frac{4t_{comm}(m)}{m}$, where m is the length of the message in bytes. To facilitate comparison with other systems, values of t'_{comm} are given in Table 2. The values for the Intel iPSC and Caltech MarkII were taken from [3]. The iPSC times are reported for both the Intel Hypercube Operating System (IHOS) and the Caltech Crystalline Operating System (CrOS). The values stated for the NCUBE were measured directly, though they could have been derived from the information given in Table 1. As we would expect, the improvement of extended Vertex over standard Vertex ranges from the speedup for fixed overhead towards the speedup for incremental costs as the total message size increases.

The effects of computational overlap and resource contention, mentioned earlier, are often factored into the formula for overall execution time. This formula is given by,

$$T_{exec} = T_{calc} + (1 - \gamma)T_{comm}$$

where $\gamma \in (-\infty, 1]$ is the degree of communication transparency, T_{calc} is the total computation time of the algorithm, and $T_{comm} = \sum t_{comm}$ is the total communication time neglecting the effects of computational overlap and resource contention [4]. When $\gamma = 1$, the effect of T_{comm} is completely hidden by computational overlap. Conversely, negative effects of waiting on resources are expressed by $\gamma < 0$. The parameter γ is very highly dependent on both the communication structure of a given algorithm and the communication support provided by the system.

As a trial application, both sets of communication primitives were used on a common image processing algorithm, the Sobel edge detector. The parallel Sobel algorithm divides an image into a grid of equal size subimages which are distributed on the array nodes (the assignment technique is described in [4]). A 3×3 pixel window operator is convolved with each of the pixels in the subimage. This requires that the pixel values for the 8 neighboring

image size	subimage size	Ext. Vertex speedup over Std. Vertex		Fraction of total execution time spent calculating		Total execution speedup over single node algorithm	
		total	comm.	Ext. Vtx.	Std. Vtx.	Ext. Vtx.	Std. Vtx.
128×128	32×32	1.02	3.83	0.99	0.97	15.9	15.6
64×64	16×16	1.08	5.24	0.98	0.91	16.0	14.8
32×32	8×8	1.34	9.79	0.96	0.72	13.7	10.2

Table 3: Sobel Edge Detector Experiment (16 processors).

pixels (N, S, E, W, NE, NW, SE, and SW) be available. Thus, when calculating the values for pixels on the edge of a subimage, the calculating processor must use pixel values from the edge of the neighboring subimage. A similar requirement exists for the corners. The possibility for computation/communication overlap exists since the interior of the subimage may be processed while awaiting reception of the data needed for the border calculations. Also, the potential for a large number of messages to be active in the system simultaneously leads to some resource contention.

The value of γ is given for both standard Vertex and extended Vertex. The results of the Sobel edge detector experiment are given in Table 3. The advantages of prescheduling resources and extracting as much computation/communications overlap as possible are evidenced by the large speedups achieved with the extended Vertex primitives. For a small subimage size the total program execution speedup was 1.34. As expected, the improvement increases as the communications account for a larger portion of total processing effort.

6   Conclusion

The results that we have produced so far have been encouraging. As shown in Table 3, the use of extended Vertex communication primitives allows the array processors to spend a much higher fraction of their total program execution time calculating results, rather than communicating or waiting for resources. To date, these results have been achieved only for algorithms where the communication mode is nearest neighbor. Work is presently underway to achieve the same type of results for algorithms where the primary communication mode is broadcast or random access.

References

[1] John P. Hayes, Trevor N. Mudge, Quentin F. Stout, Steve Colley, and John Palmer. A microprocessor-based hypercube supercomputer. *IEEE MICRO*, :6–17, October 1986.

[2] Joseph E. Brandenburg and David S. Scott. *Embeddings of Communication Trees and Grids into Hypercubes*. Technical Report 1, Intel Scientific Computers, 15201 N.W. Greenbrier Parkway, Beaverton, OR 97006, 1986.

[3] Geoffrey C. Fox and A. Kolawa. Implementation of the high performance crystalline operating system on Intel iPSC hypercube. In Michael T. Heath, editor, *Hypercube Multiprocessors 1986*, pages 269–271, SIAM, Society for Industrial and Applied Mathematics, 1400 Architects Bldg., 117 South 17th Street, Philadelphia, PA 19103, August 1985.

[4] Trevor N. Mudge and Tarek S. Abdel-Rahman. Vision algorithms for hypercube machines. *Journal of Parallel and Distributed Computing*, 4(2), March 1987 (to appear).

Virtual-Time Operating-System Functions for Robotics Applications on a Hypercube

J. R. EINSTEIN*†, J. BARHEN† AND D. JEFFERSON‡

Abstract. Hypercube multiprocessors used in autonomous robots carrying out time-critical tasks in unpredictable environments require special operating-system functions to provide the capability of rapid response to unforeseen external events. A "virtual-time" shell having such capabilities is under design for the Vertex operating system of the NCUBE hypercube computer.

Introduction. This paper addresses the computing requirements of autonomous robots which must carry out their goals in unpredictable or hostile environments. Here the term "robot" will signify any device having the functions of sensing, effector-control, and intelligence. We are particularly interested in applications in which the robot must be capable of timely responses to numerous events which occur rapidly and unpredictably.

The computer for an autonomous robot must have the power to carry out a large number of asynchronous tasks, many of them at extremely high speeds. Artificial-intelligence tasks are in general very time-consuming, and therefore require powerful computers in order to make real-time responses. Robots may have a number of sensors

---

*Research sponsored by the Office of Military Applications and by the Engineering Research Program of the Office of Basic Energy Sciences, of the U.S. Department of Energy, under contract No. DE-AC05-84OR21400 with Martin Marietta Energy Systems, Inc.

†Center for Engineering Systems Advanced Research, Oak Ridge National Laboratory, Oak Ridge, TN 37831.

‡Computer Science Department, University of California Los Angeles, Los Angeles, CA 90024.

and effectors, each requiring powerful computing. For
example, it may be necessary to solve the inverse dynamics
equations for a multi-link robot arm at rates on the order
of a hundred per second or more.

Hypercube computers possess many of the attributes
required for autonomous robots. As MIMD machines they are
intrinsically suitable for carrying out a large number of
asynchronous tasks, and their distributed-memory,
message-passing architecture makes them scalable to much
larger aggregates of processors than shared-memory
computers. For example, the NCUBE-10 [1] a VLSI-based
hypercube in use at Oak Ridge National Laboratory, can
contain a maximum of 1024 nodes in an enclosure of about
$0.5 m^3$, with design ratings of about 2000 MIPS and 500
Mflops. The large power/volume ratio of such computers
makes them appear especially attractive for use with
autonomous mobile robots.

The use of distributed memory and message passing
makes the hypercube highly scalable, but presents
difficulties for rapid responses of the robot to
unpredictable events in the environment. In particular,
message passing involves significant time delays.
Messages, once sent, are out of reach of the sending node
and cannot directly be changed by it. Messages sent from
various source nodes to a given node may be received out of
their intended time sequence for several reasons including
task migration, which may be necessary because of hardware
failure or desirable for dynamic load balancing.

In this paper we discuss some requirements of a
"virtual-time" (VT) shell for hypercube operating systems,
intended to facilitate real-time responses to unpredictable
events in a robotics application. We also indicate the
status of an on-going effort to implement these
requirements in a VT shell for Vertex, the node operating
system of the NCUBE computer.

Hypercube Communication in a Robotics Application.
Communication between the hypercube and external sensors
and effectors is most efficient when there is a direct I/O
channel between each sensor and the node which processes
its raw data, and one between each effector and the node
which directly controls it. The NCUBE computer can be
equipped with special I/O boards which provide such an
arrangement for serial sensor data and control signals.

A general problem in utilizing a message-passing
multiprocessor for any application, including robotics, is
the mapping of tasks onto nodes so as to minimize message
passing and the time required to complete the tasks. The
time required to pass a message between two nodes varies
directly with the number of links separating them. It will
therefore often be natural to take advantage of the
hypercube's configurability into subcubes by mapping
hierarchical robotics tasks onto subcubes of appropriate
sizes. Then the relatively high rates of message passing

often required between low-level subtasks will take place
between neighboring nodes. A message sent to the top of a
task's hierarchy will cause a "ripple" of messages through
the lower levels of that hierarchy.

Message passing in a hypercube is handled by the
operating system (OS) which resides on each node. For the
NCUBE computer this OS is named Vertex. Message passing in
the NCUBE computer is by direct memory access and uses a
Vertex protocol implemented through interrupts.

Message Passing in Time-Critical Robotics Applications.
When an autonomous robot incorporating a message-passing
computer performs actions in a time-critical setting, or on
moving objects, there is the general requirement that the
planning task send command messages to an effector task
well in advance of the times at which these commands are to
be carried out. (In this paper we assume, for purposes of
clarity, a single centralized "planner", or planning task.)
The minimum lead time for the planner's command is that
required for all calculations by, and message-passing
between, the effector subtasks prior to the command signal
to the external device. However, the time required for
non-synchronous message passing is indeterminate to at
least some extent, for all hypercube computers presently
known to the authors. Messages can be delayed at any node
by the processing of other messages on other serial
channels, or by delays in assigning buffer space. Unusual
circumstances such as the migration of tasks (see below)
can cause much longer delays, also of indeterminate extent.
Therefore, there is normally a requirement for "planning
ahead" -- i.e., sending command messages safely in advance
so as to allow for "maximum" possible delays in
communication. Planning ahead involves the projection into
the future of the "world model": the future positions of
moving objects, etc.

Given the requirement for planning ahead, there will
normally exist at each node of an effector task a queue of
input messages. It is also useful for efficiency that such
queues exist, so that a a node may begin to process a new
message immediately on completing the previous one.

When unpredictable changes take place in the
environment, they are sensed and interpreted by the sensor
task(s) and communicated to the planner, which in many
cases would then have to change its previous plans. If
messages implementing these plans had already been sent to
effector tasks (through planning ahead), they would have to
be corrected or canceled. To do so would also require the
correction or cancellation of any and all ripple messages
sent within the effector subcube as a result of the
original command. In some cases the rate of progress of
such corrections through the effector subcube would not be
sufficiently rapid to prevent the undesired external action
from taking place. Therefore, a facility is required for
emergency communication with the node directly linked to

the external device (the "controller" node).

It is obvious that such corrections, cancellations, and emergency messages must be handled by the operating system itself. For if a correction/cancellation arrives at the input queue of a node while its "mate", the message to be corrected/cancelled, is still in that queue, the operating system can make the necessary changes transparently to the application process. An emergency message must interrupt a running process; this, too, must be a function of the operating system.

An Example: An Autonomous Military Space Platform. As an example of an autonomous robot operating in time-critical fashion in an unpredictable environment, we consider a robot space platform, as for SDI. (The following is not taken from any actual SDI programs, but is purely conjectural.) We assume the platform to be equipped with sensors for measuring the positions of enemy missiles rising from the earth, and with either a kinetic-energy weapon which fires destructive projectiles or a directed-energy weapon (laser). A highly simplified outline of the computer tasks, and of the messages between tasks, is the following.

Sensor tasks
   ↓
   Messages: sequences of (position, time) "fixes" for each
   target; identification of target as real or decoy
      ↓
Path-projection tasks
   ↓
   Messages: for each target, projection of its future
   position as a function of time, and estimated error of
   that projection
      ↓
Planner task: decides in what direction and at what time to
fire at each target
      ↓
   Messages: (orientation, time) commands for firing the
   weapon
      ↓
Effector task: calculates the torques to be used for the
various angular adjustments of the weapon; orients and
fires weapon

One obvious requirement of such a system is the provision of synchronized clocks on all the nodes. This feature is intended for a future version of the NCUBE Computer. Timing registers on the nodes of the present version can be synchronized to within 100-200 microseconds.

We now consider possible reasons for changes of plans. First, suppose that a particular target is identified as a decoy only after the command to destroy it has been sent from the planner to the effector task. When the planner receives this sensor message, it must be able to send a cancellation message to the effector task and avoid, if possible, an unnecessary waste of "ammunition" or stored energy.

Another reason for cancellation would be sensor witnessing of the "mirving" of a missile bus. (Messages related to the new targets would follow.)

A second type of plan change would be called for in case sensor data indicated inaccuracies in previous fixes for a particular target. The planner must then be able to send a correction to the orientation parameter of a previous message.

Non-Conservation of Temporal Logic in Dynamic Multiprocessor Systems. In time-critical applications, it is generally important that messages arriving at a node be processed in a particular order (temporal logic), which is not necessarily that of their arrival at the node. Possible reasons for the arrival of messages out of order include the following.
- Messages may arrive from two or more nodes which differ in their processing loads and therefore "think about the future" at different rates.
- Communication delays, arising from the traversal of additional links or from the temporary busyness of an intermediate node en route, may affect some messages more than others.
- Tasks may need to migrate in the event of a hardware failure, or if dynamic load-balancing is employed. Task migration would cause considerable message delays. (Alternatively, task migration might necessitate clearing and re-starting of the message trains.)

Thus, there is a requirement for the node's operating system to properly order messages in the input queue, as indicated by timestamps in the message headers.

Necessary Extensions to the Node Operating System. The discussion above indicates the necessity of adding to the node's OS (Vertex in the case of the NCUBE computer) a shell which implements (on the basis of codes included in message headers):
- cancellation messages;
- correction messages;
- emergency messages;
- the restoration of temporal logic by ordering messages in the input queue according to their timestamps.

If, on arrival, a cancellation or correction message finds its "mate" in the input queue, the shell actions are: for the cancellation message, to discard it with its mate; for the correction message, to discard it after substituting its data for that of its mate.

Several types of emergency messages are needed. One type causes the shell to trap a particular message upon its (later) arrival and discard it, or, if too late for this, to interrupt the running process and schedule an appropriate alternate such as a "stop" program. Another type of emergency message simply causes an interrupt and "stop".

A requirement for the use of emergency messages is that the planner "know" the locations of the controller node(s).

Possible Actions When Cancellation/Correction Messages Arrive Too Late. When a cancellation/correction message arrives too late -- i.e., its mate has already been processed -- one or more of several possible actions may be taken, depending on the application and the amount of time available before a deadline, and including the following:
- for a cancellation: emergency trap of any output message(s) at the controller node;
- for a correction: emergency trap of any output message(s) at the controller node, followed by recalculation with the corrected input data;
- for either: a procedure which compensates for the error;
- message notifying the planner.

A general discussion of all these possibilities is beyond the scope of this paper. Here we note particularly the possibility of recalculation. For this purpose it is necessary that the shell save (a) the processed messages, for a certain period of time; (b) any local "state" variables. Therefore, two additional functions needed for the OS shell are:
- save input messages for a time after processing;
- store and retrieve state vectors.

Analogies of Operating-System Requirements to "Time Warp" Functions. Time Warp is a methodology developed originally [2] for discrete-event simulations on a distributed-memory, message-passing computer such as a hypercube. In this methodology each node processes the message of lowest timestamp in its input queue, without waiting for possible "stragglers" (messages of even lower timestamp which may arrive later). In case a straggler subsequently arrives, the process "rolls back" to a previous (saved) state, from which it can reprocess the (saved) messages in their correct order. If then it is discovered that messages previously output were incorrect, because of the incorrect order of input, "anti-messages" are sent. When an anti-message meets its mate in the input queue of their destination node, the two mutually "annihilate" each other -- i.e., are discarded by the OS. If an anti-message arrives too late, the destination node performs a roll-back, and may itself be required to send anti-messages.

Clearly, several functions required for our shell have analogies in Time Warp: ordering of messages by timestamp; cancellation (or anti-) messages; saving of previous messages and states; recalculation (or roll-back).

Correction messages may be considered simply an efficient combination of two Time-Warp messages, an anti-message and the corresponding new message.

The use of the name "virtual-time" for the real-time OS shell was first suggested by these analogies to Time-Warp simulations, in which "virtual time" is equivalent to simulation time. "Virtual time" also seems an appropriate name in view of certain additional shell functions to be mentioned below.

Work in Progress. Construction of the virtual-time (VT) shell was begun at ORNL with an early version of the Caltech hypercube simulator, before NCUBE nodes or the Vertex source code were available. This simulator for the Caltech Crystalline Operating System, which runs under VAX/VMS, was kindly made available by Prof. Geoffrey Fox, and was modified at ORNL so as to simulate interrupt-driven message passing, and to allow individual programs to be run on each of the simulated nodes.

Programming of the shell has been in C, in order to facilitate porting to the NCUBE. The NCUBE nodes are proprietary and have a unique assembly language, but C (and Fortran) compilers are available.

The shell in its present form includes new versions of the following Time-Warp functions: ordering of messages in an input queue by timestamp; cancellation (anti-) messages; the saving of previous input and output messages and state vectors; roll-back. Correction messages are implemented. Also, processes which require more than one input message are scheduled to run upon the arrival of the last of the set. Message headers identify source and destination nodes, length and type of message, and include codes which specify the shell functions.

This completed part of the VT shell, with appropriate modifications for the NCUBE node, is in the process of being added to Vertex.

Future Work. The question of how to adapt Time Warp to real-time robotics applications in an optimal manner poses considerable theoretical and practical problems, which we are starting to investigate. In particular, we intend to investigate the integration of the VT shell with hard-real-time scheduling algorithms.

In the nearer term, functions to be added to the shell include:
- emergency messages;
- "clean-out" of over-ridden messages;
- a delay procedure for cases in which changes are necessary and actions can be put off into the future;
- implementation of commands to be executed at specified time increments after an awaited signal -- i.e., at "virtual times". [For example, the command to do action A at time $t_0 + t_A$, action B at time $t_0 + t_B$, ..., where t_0 is as yet unknown.]   The signal might be an

environmental event, the (future) time of which is unpredictable. In certain applications such commands could be utilized for pre-calculation of effector parameters, allowing more rapid action once the signal arrives.

Finally, we shall construct a suitable test bed to excercise thoroughly and with random timings all functions of the VT shell.

REFERENCES

(1) J. Barhen and J. F. Palmer, The Hypercube in Robotics and Machine Intelligence, Comp. Mech. Eng., CIME-5, 4 (1986) pp. 30-38.

(2) D. Jefferson and H. Sowizral, Fast Concurrent Simulation Using the Time-Warp Mechanism, Rand Corporation, June 1983.

Load Balancing and Hypercubes: A Preliminary Look

WINIFRED I. WILLIAMS*

Abstract. Load balancing is an issue of fundamental importance to multiprocessor concurrent systems. In order to have an efficiently running system it is necessary to be able to make transfer decisions based on the current state of the system, and to transfer work from heavily loaded nodes to more lightly loaded nodes.

WaTor (1) is an algorithm which simulates fish and sharks living, moving, breeding, and eating in a two-dimensional ocean. It is an example of simple Monte Carlo dynamics that lends itself well to parallel processing and an investigation of load balancing. The tendency of fish to form schools causes a simple rectangular decomposition to easily become imbalanced. Moreover, schools moving, changing shape, breeding, and eating, provide a constantly fluctuating load.

This paper represents part of a current project being performed jointly by California Institute of Technology and Jet Propulsion Laboratory in an effort to develop a general purpose dynamic load balancer. Described are three possible load balancing policies: simulated annealing, nearest neighbor balancing, and scattered decomposition. Each of the policies is illustrated in terms of its implementation in WaTor. All work presented is being performed on a thirty-two node homogeneous distributed memory hypercube.

Load balancing is an issue of fundamental importance to multiprocessor concurrent systems. For certain types of problems, such as inhomogeneous numeric problems and symbolic problems, without load balancing a parallel system gains little over traditional Von Neumann machines. Moreover, appropriate data decomposition for load balance is not always obvious or

---

*Concurrent Processor Systems Group, Jet Propulsion Laboratory, Pasadena California 91109

consistent. The ability to determine load distribution and to redistribute it is essential for an efficient parallel system.

Currently, load balancing is the responsibility of the applications programmer. All data decomposition must be done before execution as there is no means of data reallocation. We are not using a multi-tasking machine so balancing refers to moving data. If a programmer finds a program imbalanced she must find a better initial decomposition. For homogeneous problems a balanced decomposition may be relatively easy to achieve, but for inhomogeneous problems it may be difficult if not impossible. Often the same program may require different decomposition strategies for different sets of data. For some programs a decomposition strategy that remains balanced throughout the course of a program may be impossible to find.

Our goal is to create a general purpose, automatic, dynamic load balancer. Ideally this would be transparent to the programmer, would work for a wide variety of problems, and would run continuously during program execution.   It would monitor processor activity and redistribute load accordingly. We have begun with problems with a high level of load imbalance, such as irregular finite elements, particle dynamics, non-equilibrium thermodynamics, and evolving population simulations. An example of the latter is WaTor, a problem described by Dewdney in the December 1984 edition of <u>Scientific</u> <u>American</u>. We will look at WaTor to illustrate the operation of three load balancing policies.

WaTor (2) is a program which simulates fish and sharks moving, eating, breeding, and dying in a two-dimensional ocean. For the purposes of further discussion we will define a data item as a fish or a shark   Work on one data item is the computation required to move, eat, breed, and die. In WaTor the work is approximately the same for each fish and shark. The total load is the sum of the work activity needed for each fish and shark, and the necessary inter-node communication. The load changes in each processor when fish and sharks breed, die, leave, or enter the processor. WaTor is good test bed for load balancing because it is representative of a class of problems and provides a dynamically changing and fluctuating load. The tendency of fish to form schools provides excellent out of balance test cases.

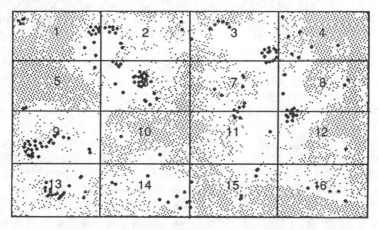

FIG. 1 WaTor in a Rectangular Decomposition

The most straight forward data decomposition in WaTor and many other programs is a rectangular decomposition, in this case breaking up data by ocean regions as pictured above. Fish are represented by small dots and sharks by larger ones. The drawing illustrates how out of balance data can be by the use of this decomposition method. For example processor 9 and 13 have much less work than processors 1 and 5. It would be difficult for a programmer to distribute this data in a balanced manner, particularly one that would remain balanced for the duration of the computation. Therefore it is necessary to establish a dynamic load balancing scheme. The remainder of this paper examines the load balancing policies of simulated annealing, nearest neighbor balancing, and scattered decomposition.

The first load balancing policy examined is known as simulated annealing. Simulated annealing is a technique borrowed from statistical physics. In this method we define the "temperature" of a computing system to be the sum of the computation. The mechanism for restoring balance within a poorly distributed computing system is analogous to that used for attaining minimum temperature and equilibrium in a physical system.

We define a Hamiltonian to express the "temperature" of the computing system:

$$H_{TOTAL} = \Sigma H_{COMM} + \Sigma H_{COMP} \quad (3)$$

As stated this temperature will be the sum of computational and communicational load.

In determining the computational load we consider processes as "particles" free to move about in the " space" of the parallel processor. The load balancing acts as a short-range repulsive "force" causing particles, and thus the computation, to spread out in a balanced manner. Typically one would associate a high velocity with these particles so we need to think of our system as being at a low temperature so processes "stay put" in one place long enough to do useful work. In WaTor the computation performed on each fish or shark is identical. The total load is the sum of the work performed on all the fish and sharks.

While the load balancing spreads out parts of the computation, various parts of the computation must communicate. If communicating parts of the computation are far apart there will be large delays which slow the computation. The communication term acts as a long range attractive force between pairs of particles which must communicate. This force must be made proportional to the amount of communication traffic so heavily communicating parts will coalesce and stay near one another. In the version of WaTor we are using adjacent parts of the ocean are in adjacent processors. Communication is directly proportional to the number of fish to be transferred, and there is no need for long distance communication. Unfortunately, this is not always possible.

With the Hamiltonian defined to represent the "temperature" of our system we begin a simulation of the slow annealing process used in the physical system by the Metropolis Monte Carlo method. We begin with an arbitrary state with the objective of minimizing the energy of the system. We make trial changes which are accepted or rejected on the basis of the probability $\sim e^{-H/T}$ for T>0. By this means we slowly reduce the temperature of the system.

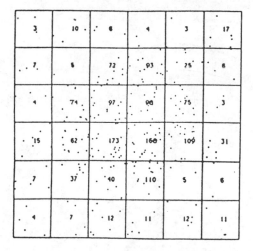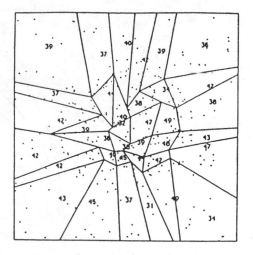

FIG. 2 An example of Simulated Annealing

The diagram above is an example of the effectiveness of the process of simulated annealing. It is not WaTor, but a toy problem drawn from particle dynamics data; the physical likeness to WaTor is apparent. The numerical figures in the left diagram represent the values of the Hamiltonian. The load is redistributed by packaging data and sending it to another node for processing. For clarity the boundaries of the right hand diagram have been moved to represent the movement of data.

The second load balancing policy presented is what we refer to as nearest neighbor balancing. This is a new algorithm in need of further testing and optimization. Initial results have been quite promising.

The nearest neighbor balancing algorithm recognizes the overhead incurred by communication and transfer of data between non-adjacent processors. In this algorithm we have limited ourselves to evaluation and transfer of load with nearest neighbors. This allows a data item to move across the cube in log(n) steps, where n is the number of nodes of the cube.

The algorithm works as follows. Each node of the cube calculates its own load by some means. Each node then communicates its load value to its nearest neighbors and receives and stores the load value of each of its nearest neighbors. The nodes then follow some rather arbitrary rules for redistribution of load. A node takes the average of its load value and each of its nearest neighbors. It evaluates its load in relationship to the average just calculated. If its load is greater than the average it decides to pass a unit of load, a piece or a group of data, to its nearest neighbor with the least load. If its load is less than the average is chooses to take on a unit of load from the most heavily loaded neighbor. Otherwise, it chooses to do nothing. In WaTor the passing of a unit of load would be the passing of the responsibility for a fish or a shark, or a group of fish or sharks. At this time no action has been taken; each processor has only determined the action it cares to take on its neighboring processors. Intended action is exchanged between processors, summed, and executed. This procedure continues until the standard deviation of a processor's load and that of its neighbors is less than some threshold deviation.

NEAREST NEIGHBOR BALANCING
32 NODES
16 NODES
8 NODES
ITERATIONS
0
20
40
60
80
100
120
140
0
10
20
30
40
50
60
STANDARD DEV. (*1000)

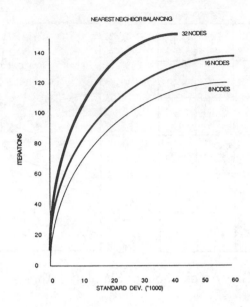

FIG. 3 Results of Nearest Neighbor Balancing

The graph above shows the results of the first test runs of the nearest neighbor balancing algorithm. The algorithm has two particularly promising characteristics. An increase in the number of nodes does not drastically increase the time required to load balance. In addition, after a system reaches a certain standard deviation out of balance, the difference in times to balance even greater out of balance situations is insignificant. Currently the algorithm moves data in single units. We anticipate even better results by altering the algorithm to move larger groups of data dependent upon how out of balance the system is. Further testing of this algorithm continues.

The third load balancing policy presented is known as scattered decomposition. This method uses no algorithm for data reallocation. It is a means of initial decomposition that may remain balanced throughout the course of computation. It divides data into x parts for y processors with each processor controlling x/y non-contiguous parts. This way large groups of data may be split over several processors.

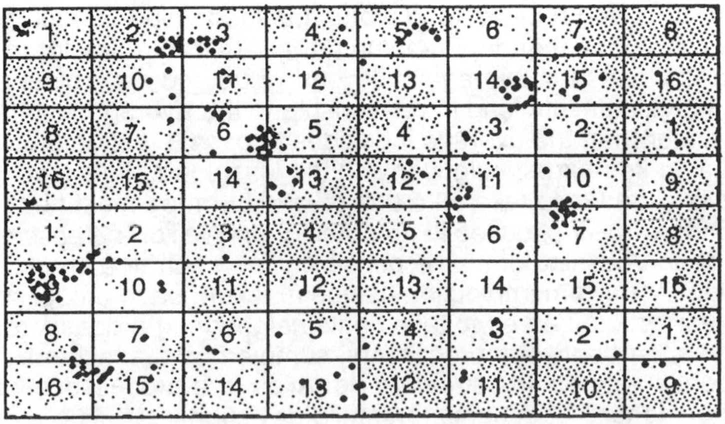

1 2 3 4 5 6 7 8
9 10 11 12 13 14 15 16
8 7 6 5 4 3 2 1
16 15 14 13 12 11 10 9
1 2 3 4 5 6 7 8
9 10 11 12 13 14 15 16
8 7 6 5 4 3 2 1
16 15 14 13 12 11 10 9

FIG. 4 WaTor in a Scattered Decomposition

Figure 4 is the same WaTor ocean shown before. Now the heavily loaded upper left region is controlled by several processors instead of just one. Though processor 10 does much work in this region, in its area in row 6 it does very little. This means of data decomposition could largely eliminate the need to load balance. It does however greatly increase the necessary communication. Work is being done now to compare the cost of increased communication with the cost of load balancing.

Each of the load balancing policies presented works well for some type of problem. No one approach appears to work best for a general class of problems. Simulated annealing balances well but is not particularly efficient computationally or communicationally. Nearest neighbor balancing is very communicationally efficient but requires many iterations to balance a system. Scattered decomposition has the advantage of working continuously without the need to check the load in each processor and redistribute load accordingly, but its communicational overhead is great. There will be a continued investigation of these algorithms and others in an increasingly wider class of problems. JPL and other institutions interested in multiprocessor concurrent systems have come to recognize the importance of the development of load balancing policies and load management tools to an efficiently running parallel system.

REFERENCES

(1) Dewdney, <u>Scientific American</u>, December 1984.

(2)Written by Jon Flower, California Institute of Technology, and Steve Otto, Jet Propulsion Laboratory.

(3) G.C.Fox, S.W. Otto, E.A.Umland, "Monte Carlo Physics on a Concurrent Processor", September 1985.

The Implementation of a Dynamic Load Balancer[*]

G. C. FOX[†], A. KOLAWA[†] AND R. WILLIAMS[†]

ABSTRACT

We discuss the issues involved in the implementing of a simple dynamic load balancer on the hypercube. We use the physics analogy introduced by Fox and Jefferson where load balance corresponds to minimizing an appropriate energy function. We specialize to those problems where the user (problem) can estimate the terms in the energy function and specify a user interface to the load balancer. Our methods apply to a wide class of time synchronized simulations.

1. Introduction

Parallel computers have shown themselves useful in solving many engineering and scientific problems[1]. The advantage of using a parallel computer over the sequential one is that different parts of the user program can be executed at the same time, allowing a reduction in the execution time of the program. Full advantage of running on a parallel computer can only occur if one can ensure that every processor of the computer has equal work loads and that communication between processors is minimized. This is the load-balancing problem: how can one break up (decompose) the problem to maximize the speed up. In some applications the problem has a naturally load-balanced algorithm, as for example in Fourier Transforms, or solutions of partial differential equations on a uniform rectangular grid. However, for many irregular or inhomogeneous problems, this is a difficult problem.

Static load balancing [2] is the process of optimally breaking up the problem at the start, then allowing the user code to run with no further attention. This would be the case of some applications in for instance geodynamics or stress analysis, where a fixed but irregular partitioning of space is made to reflect the structure under investigation. Static load-balancing has already been investigated for the special case of irregular meshes generated by the standard NASTRAN package [2].

[*] Research supported by the Department of Energy grant, DE-FG03-85ER25009, the Parsons Foundation, the Systems Development Foundation, and the office of the program manager of the Joint Tactical Fusion Office.

[†] Concurrent Computation Program, California Institute of Technology, Pasadena, California 91125

In this paper, we discuss dynamic load balancing, where the assignment of work to processors changes to reflect changing conditions. This would be necessary for event-driven simulations, adaptive meshes, many particle dynamics, for $\alpha-\beta$ searching of the game tree in chess, or for simulation of neural networks with time dependent non uniform activity. We must assume that the work-load changes slowly enough that the load-balancer can use past history to extrapolate the future: as discussed elsewhere the scattered decomposition is appropriate for very rapidly varying problems [4,5].

In previous papers, we have discussed load balancing strategies. We review this in section 2 and 3 where we define the Hamiltonian appropriate for a large class of load balancing problems. In the remaining sections, we discuss a simple implementation of these ideas appropriate for time synchronized simulations and similar problems.

In previous static load balancers, we have used a sequential computer to calculate the decomposition of a problem to be run on a hypercube. Here we discuss the more powerful environment where balancer co-exists on the hypercube with the problem code and data. The issues involved in this are discussed in Section 4 while Section 5 describes the user interface and programming model. In Section 6, we describe the implementation of the previous ideas and Section 7 contains the conclusions.

2. The Load-Balancing Hamiltonian

We suppose that the problem can be formulated in terms of a set of 'objects', T. Each object may have different code and data, or may have the same code and only different data, but in any case is supposed to be in some sense self-contained so that it can be moved from processor to processor. The set of objects can be thought of as the vertices of a graph, with objects that communicate connected by an edge of the graph. We assume that these objects communicate with each other at essentially infinite speed (negligible cost) if they are in the same processor, and otherwise through some inter-processor communication protocol, whose details we shall not discuss.

Each object $\alpha \in T$ has a calculation complexity w_α, and we assume that objects α, β need to exchange (communicate) an amount $c_{\alpha\beta}$ of information. $c_{\alpha\beta}$ is typically a large sparse matrix. We assume that the communication is synchronous (i.e. different nodes communicate at the same time) and not overlapped with calculation. This is a valid model for many large scale simulations, matrix problems etc. on current machines. Our methods can easily be extended to asynchronous overlapped communication but we will not discuss this here.

The architecture of the parallel computer can be described in the same form; we have a set of n processors P which are assumed identical, and a communication structure $\bar{c}_{pq}, p, q \in P$ expressing the time taken per unit information transfer from p to q. For the hypercube architecture, of dimension d, $N = 2^d$, and the processor labels are integers from 0 to $2^d - 1$. For current hardware the hypercube communication time has a startup time plus a term proportional to $\bar{c}_{pq}$ the number of bits different between the binary representations of p and q. New hypercubes are being designed with special routing chips which will lead to a $\bar{c}_{pq}$ roughly independent of p and q. Our techniques can easily be adapted for this type of hardware.

The load balancer will partition T into N subsets and put a subset into each processor; we represent, the label of the processor executing object α by $r(\alpha)$.

The total amount of calculation W_p for processor p and the communication time C_{pq} along the path from p to q can be written

$$W_p = \sum_\alpha w_\alpha \, \delta_{p, \, r(\alpha)} \tag{1}$$

$$C_{pq} = \bar{c}_{pq} \sum_{\alpha\beta} c_{\alpha\beta} \, \delta_{p, \, r(\alpha)} \, \delta_{q, \, r(\beta)} \tag{2}$$

We can assume that W_p and C_{pq} are normalized to seconds but of course the absolute scale is irrelevant. (2) ignores the message start up time but this is easy to add if necessary for a particular hardware/software combination. The speed of the concurrent computer is determined by the processor p with the largest amount of work - calculation plus communication.

$$M = \underset{p}{Max} \, [W_p + \sum_q C_{pq}] \tag{3}$$

so that we could define a Hamiltonian (an energy or objective function to be minimized) as the reciprocal of the efficiency:

$$H_{max} = \epsilon^{-1} = M \, / <W_p> \tag{4}$$

where the angle brackets designate the mean value.

There are two reasons why this Hamiltonian is unsuitable for load-balancing purposes. The first is because we are assuming the balancer to work in parallel with the user-code; whenever a change in the processor assignment is made, information from all processors is needed to determine which is maximal, resulting in a sequential bottleneck. The second is that since only one processor is constrained at any one time, the others may have any load assignment as long as it is less than the maximum. When the location of the maximum change, significant work will be needed to rebalance the load as there is no guarantee that the work on non maximal processors is well balanced.

We use a Hamiltonian which does not suffer these deficiencies[4,5]:

$$H = \sum_{pq} C_{pq} + \nu \sum_p W_p^2 \tag{5}$$

where ν is a parameter that expresses the relative importance of calculation compared to communication in the balancing. The value of the parameter ν, for systems with small amount of communication, is derived in ref. [6]. We will survey methods of finding the ground state of H in Section 3. This Hamiltonian is "local" and minimizing it leads to a load that is well balanced over all processors.

The optimization methods described in section 3 can be implemented currently on the hypercube for the simulated annealing and neural net methods. In general one needs to worry about balancing this concurrent balancing operation! However in our initial simple problems this will not be a difficulty; the balancing will be reasonably well balanced by a decomposition that is naturally given by the current decomposition of objects. We will return to this later after we have gained experience with some initial problems.

In section 4, we will point out that one needs to modify equation (5) to include the cost of moving objects between processors. This does not affect the issues determining good optimization algorithms for H.

We note that during the minimization process, the load balancer should only move tokens to the objects and not the objects themselves which take much more time to transfer to between nodes. The minimizer may move an object from p to q and later move it back to p, and only when it is satisfied with the new assignment of objects to processors should the actual transfer of objects take place. In the physics analogy, the use of tokens ensures that the Hamiltonian is conservative, i.e. that it is a function of the initial r (α) and final r' (α) processor assignments but not of the route that the objects take to move (in the minimization process) from r (α) to $r'(\alpha)$. Secondly, the moving of tokens allows the load-balancer to abandon the minimization if it becomes clear that little advantage is to be gained by the reassignment.

3. Algorithms for Generation of Objects and Minimization of the Hamiltonian.

In previous papers, we have developed three techniques for minimizing energy functions such as Eqn. (5). These are

(i) Simulated Annealing. This views H as the energy function of a physical system and uses statistical physics methods to find the minimum i.e. the ground state of H[2–5]. The performance of this method is very sensitive to its formulation [8] and in general can be very time consuming for large systems.

(ii) Neural Networks [9, 10]. Here we use a method introduced by Hopfield and Tank to solve the traveling salesman problem [11]. It roughly corresponds to using a deterministic set of equations to find the ground state instead of the statistical method used in (i). For mesh based problems in D dimensions, this method takes a time

$$T_{min}^{(ii)} \sim [\text{System Size}]^{1+1/D} * \log_2 N \qquad (6)$$

(iii) Graphical Method [12]. This technique does not precisely minimize H but rather works directly from the graph defined by the sparse matrix $c_{\alpha\beta}$. It divides the system into a set of objects such that each object consists of nearby points where proximity is defined in a natural way by the minimum number of edges in the graph needed to connect any two points. This method takes a time

$$T_{min}^{(iii)} \sim [\text{System Size}] * \log_2 N \qquad (7)$$

Although not as precise as (i) or (ii), this method performs surprisingly well in the simple cases in which it has been tested. [12]

If we compare the three methods, we see that the time necessary to minimize H decreases as we go from methods (i) to (ii) to (iii). On the other hand the reliability of the method also decreases with the same ordering of methods. Note the minimization problem is NP-complete and so it is not sensible to hope to obtain the exact minimum. Rather in each case we try (successfully) to find a good approximation to the minimum.

The first two methods are easily implemented in parallel on the hypercube and so are our methods of choice for the dynamic load balancer. We will initially use the simulated annealing method (i) as we have most experience with this.

The graphical method is an attractive possibility for the automatic generation of our objects as a collection of the underlying points/particles in the original problem. This is only necessary in those cases where user cannot naturally find suitable objects. We anticipate that an appropriate number of objects will be about ten times the number of nodes in the hypercube. This will provide fine enough resolution to allow good load balancing and the number of objects is sufficiently small that the load balancer will be quick and that inter-object communication costs will not be great.

4. Interaction of Load Balancer and User Processes

A dynamic load balancer must run together with the user program on the hypercube. There are several design choices involved in this implementation. In this section we describe how the cost of running the load balancer and the cost of moving processes from node to node affect the implementation.

Consider the case where the user code runs for some predetermined time, which is followed by a synchronization of all the processors, and the passage of control to the load-balancer. This will evaluate the current Hamiltonian, based on the estimates of work w_α and communication $c_{\alpha\beta}$. These estimates can either be explicitly found by the user-code, or be evaluated from system monitors controlled by the balancer. As described in section 5, we will only consider the case where the user explicitly calculates w_α and $c_{\alpha\beta}$.

Let us briefly discuss a heuristic strategy to control the load balancer. Initially we will use a 'thermostat': suppose the Hamiltonian had value H_{old} at the end of the most recent load-balancing session, then load-balancing starts again when the present Hamiltonian is greater than a predefined level ηH_{old}, where η is somewhat greater than 1. The minimizer moves tokens for the objects until the Hamiltonian falls below H_{old} again, or the minimizer has run for a predetermined time, whichever is sooner. The objects are then placed in the correct processor according to these tokens, and control is returned to the user code.

We must also add a new term H_T to the Hamiltonian so that the minimizer ' knows' about the present distribution of objects,

$$H \rightarrow H + H_T$$

$$H_T [r, r'] = \mu \sum_{\alpha p q} T_{pq}^{(\alpha)} \, \delta_{p, r(\alpha)} \, \delta_{q, r'(\alpha)} \qquad (8)$$

where $r(\alpha)$ is the present distribution and $r'(\alpha)$ the proposed new distribution. $T_{pq}^{(\alpha)}$ is the cost of moving object α from processor p to processor q, and μ is a parameter expressing the importance of the transfer time. Clearly μ will be inversely proportional to the time that the computation will run before the next load-balancing session, since the advantage from reducing H is integrated over the whole computation time, whereas the cost of the movement of objects is only incurred once at the end of the load-balancing session. In the physics analogy this new term can be considered as an elastic string attaching the new configuration to the old, with an increasing cost associated with more distant moves. This is illustrated in Fig. 1 which indicates as springs the forces on the objects implied by the Hamiltonian.

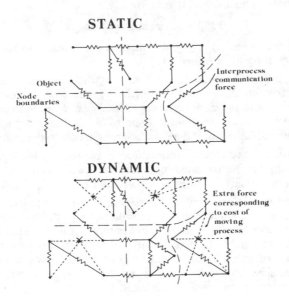

Fig. 1   Physics analogy of the communication terms in Hamiltonian H.
Picture shows two cases:

a) Static - objects are distributed before the program starts to run.

b) Dynamic - objects are distributed before the program starts to run and during the execution some of them are relocated by the load balancer.

Black dots represent objects, strings represent communication costs between objects, short dashed lines and crosses represent cost associated with movement of objects between nodes, boundaries between nodes are shown by dashed lines with longer dashes.

5. Data Structures and Programming Model

We have divided the problem into medium grain size objects where there are several objects in each node of the hypercube. We could in principle perform the balancing at the level of the fundamental grid-points, particles etc. in each object. This has some obvious unattractive features and requires a substantial user coding effort to move data as instructed by the balancer. We will only consider load balancing at the object level.

The user will write the code within each object to define a structure *loadobj* which both contains information from the object, and receives information from the load balancer. This means that the user has to fill all the necessary information in the structure *loadobj* and keep it updated when the load balancer is called during execution of the program. Parts of the structure *loadobj* could be determined automatically by the operating system, but this we will not discuss here.

We initially implement the structure *loadobj* as:

```
struct loadobj {
  int nneigh;
  int neighbor[MAXNEIGH];
  float communicate[MAXNEIGH];
  float work;
  float transfer;
  int procnum;
} object[MAXOBJ];
```

The integer *nneigh* is the number of objects with which this one communicates, the array *neighbor* contains the object labels of these, and the array *communicate* measures how much communication is needed between this object and its neighbors. The floating point variable *work* represents the amount of work which is done in the object. The variable *transfer* indicates how much communication needs to be done to move this object. The integer *procnum* is used by the load-balancer to tell the object in which processor it resides.

The above structure provides enough information to calculate the Hamiltonian. The communication load L can be calculated for a hypercube architecture by,

```
L = 0;
for(i=0; i < MAXOBJ; i++)
  for(k=0; k < object.nneigh; k++){
  dis = object[ object[i].neighbor[k] ] . procnum ^ object[i] . procnum;
  bdis = 0;
  for(l=0; l < dimension_of_cube; l++)
    if((dis & (1 << l)) != 0) bdis++;
  L += bdis * object[i].communicate[k];
}
```

The code presented above calculates the distance between processors in which different communicating objects reside and multiplies it by the weight of the communication channel. The term $\sum W_p^2$ is straightforward to calculate by summing over the squares of all the *work* in every processor.

Currently we are in process of writing a multitasking operating system, MOOOS, which will provide an appropriate environment for implementation of the dynamic load balancer[7]. In MOOOS the user writes the program in terms of different tasks which communicate with each other through a network of pipes. In this system the user can bind together one or more tasks with some external data (shared by the tasks) to form an object. Such an object will be consider as an unit by the load balancer, and will never be split between different nodes.

6. Implementation Issues

The simplest method of implementing the ideas described in the previous sections is *globally*. At the beginning of the run, all the objects transmit w_α and $c_{\alpha\beta}$ to the load balancer and the minimizer is run as a concurrent implementation of the algorithms of section 3 decomposed over the hypercube. One could also implement these algorithms on a single node of the hypercube or an attached host. However this does not seem attractive as we have several powerful minimizing algorithms which are capable of efficient concurrent implementation.

The decision on invoking the load balancer could be based on a global calculation of the current energy function H using the thermostat described in section 4. Alternately one could trigger on a local detection of imbalance to initiate the global load balancer. A more intriguing load balancing method is local. We have the user program and load balancer running asynchronously. One can have just a subset (as small as one) of the nodes involved in the balancing with the decision to invoke the balancer being triggered by a local inhomogeneity in the work load. It is natural to consider nodes that find themselves short of work, being used by the load balancer. In this case one would normally start the problem by a single invocation of the global balancing scheme.

We will explore these various options as our implementations mature.

7. Conclusions

We have described the implementation of a dynamic load balancer within a simple object oriented environment. We have either user or computer generated objects of medium grain size so that each node will contain many objects. These are manipulated by a dynamic balancer which minimizes a local measure of the load imbalance using an inherently concurrent algorithm. The techniques appear sufficient for a variety of important scientific and engineering problems.

We are implementing a system designed along the lines described in this paper and we will report on our experience in later papers.

References

1. "Algorithms for Concurrent Processors", G. C. Fox and S. W. Otto, May 1984 issue of Physics Today, "The Performance of the Caltech Hypercube in Scientific Calculations: A Preliminary Analysis", G. C. Fox at Symposium on "Algorithms, Architectures, and the Future of Scientific Computation", Austin, March 1985; G. C. Fox and S. W. Otto, "Caltech Concurrent Computation Program: A Status Report", to appear Computers in Mechanical Engineering.

2. R. Morrison and S. W. Otto, "The Scattered Decomposition for Finite Elements", C^3P Memo 286; J. W. Flower, S. W. Otto, and M. C. Salama, "A Preprocessor for Finite Elements", C^3P Memo 292.

3. S. Kirkpatrick, C. D. Gelatt, Jr., and M. P. Vecchi, "Optimization by Simulated Annealing", Science **220** (1983) 671.

4   G. C. Fox, S. W. Otto, "Concurrent Computation and the Theory of Complex Systems", Invited talk by G. Fox at Knoxville Hypercube Conference, August 1985.

5   G. C. Fox, D. Jefferson, "Concurrent Processor Load Balancing as a Statistical Physics Problem", Caltech preprint $C^3P\,172$

6   G. C. Fox, unpublished

7   J. W. Flower, S. Callahan, A. Kolawa, J. Salmon, "Specification of MOOOS", paper in preparation.

8   R. D. Williams, "Minimization by Simulated Annealing: Is Detailed Balance Necessary?", C^3P Memo 354

9   G. C. Fox, W. Furmanski, "Load Balancing by a Neural Network", Caltech preprint C^3P-363

10   R. D. Williams, "Optimization by a computational Neural Net", Caltech preprint C^3P-371

11   J. J. Hopfield & D. W. Tank, "Computing with Neural Circuits: A Model," *Science* 233 (1986) 625-639.

12   G. C. Fox, "Load Balancing and Sparse Matrix Vector Multiplication on the Hypercube", Caltech preprint C^3P-327

Embedding of Interacting Task Modules into a Hypercube

MING-SYAN CHEN* AND KANG G. SHIN*

ABSTRACT Each incoming task to an n-cube multiprocessor is represented by a graph, in which each node denotes a module of the task and each link represents inter-module communication. Each module must be assigned to a subcube so as to preserve node adjacencies in the associated task graph. Some mathematical properties of the cube assignment problem are derived. In light of these mathematical results, fast algorithms are developed to determine the size of the cube required for each incoming task, and a heuristic function for the A* search algorithm is derived for the allocation of each task module to subcubes within the cube.

1. INTRODUCTION

In an n-dimensional hypercube, or n-cube, multiprocessor, a task is viewed as a set of interacting modules, which must be assigned to a cube. Thus, processor allocation in an n-cube multiprocessor consists of two sequential steps: (i) determination of the dimension of the cube required to accommodate all the modules of each incoming task and allocation of modules of the task to nodes within the cube, and (ii) assignment of the entire task to a cube of the dimension determined from (i) in the n-cube system. Conventionally, (i) is determined manually by the user, which is often very difficult and results in the under-utilization of processors and degradation of system performance. The automation of step (i) with a rigorous approach is thus very important and will be the focus of this paper.

Each incoming task is described by a graph in which each node denotes a module of the task and each link represents inter-module communication. We want to determine a cube in the system which can accommodate the incoming task subject to the constraint that each module of the task must be assigned to a subcube within the cube while satisfying the *adjacency requirement*, i.e., adjacent modules in the task graph must be

---

* Advanced Computer Architecture Laboratory Department of Electrical Engineering and Computer Science, The University of Michigan, Ann Arbor, MI 48109

assigned to adjacent subcubes. The dimension of the minimal cube required for a given task graph will henceforth be called the *weak cubical dimension* of the graph.

As will be pointed out later, the problem of determining the weak cubical dimension of a task graph is similar to the "squashed embedding problem" [1, 2, 3] in the sense that each node in the concerned graph is mapped into a subcube. But it differs from the squashed embedding problem in that only adjacency, rather than distance between each pair of nodes, has to be preserved under the mapping, and can thus be viewed as a *relaxed squashed* (RS) *embedding* problem. Similarly to the determination of the cubical dimension of cubical graphs, the problem of determining the weak cubical dimension for an arbitrary graph is NP-complete [4]. Therefore, in this paper we will not only propose fast algorithms to determine the RS embedding of a given task graph, but also develop a heuristic function for the A* search algorithm to determine the existence of an RS embedding from a given task graph into a cube. By applying this search algorithm repeatedly, one can determine the weak cubical dimension of an arbitrary graph.

The definitions and notation are given in Section 2. Mathematical properties of the RS embedding problem will be derived in Section 3. Using these properties, fast algorithms for the RS embedding are developed in Section 4. A heuristic search algorithm which determines the existence of an RS embedding from a given graph into a cube of a given dimension is proposed. The paper concludes with Section 5.

2. PRELIMINARIES

The notation and definitions of graphs in [5] will be followed in this paper. Besides, let $\sum$ be the ternary symbol set $\{0, 1, *\}$, where $*$ is the *don't care* symbol. Then, every subcube of an n-cube can be uniquely represented by a sequence of ternary symbols, which is called the *address* of the corresponding subcube. Let q be the address of a subcube and $|q|$ denote the dimension of the subcube. The distance between two subcubes is defined as follows.

Definition 1: The hamming distance, $H : \sum^k \times \sum^k \to I^+$, between $\alpha = a_1 a_2 \cdots a_k$ and $\beta = b_1 b_2 \cdots b_k$ in $\sum^k$ for some integer k is defined as $H(\alpha, \beta) = \sum_{i=1}^{k} h(a_i, b_i)$, where $h(a, b) = 1$ if [a=0 and b=1] or [a=1 and b=0], and $h(a, b) = 0$ otherwise.

Define symbols in $\sum$ as a *partial ordered* set $(\sum, \overset{\bullet}{<})$, in which $0 \overset{\bullet}{<} *$, $1 \overset{\bullet}{<} *$ and $a \overset{\bullet}{<} a$, $\forall$ $a \in \sum$. A subcube $\alpha = a_1 a_2 \cdots a_k$ is said to *contain* another subcube $\beta = b_1 b_2 \cdots b_k$, denoted by $\beta \subseteq \alpha$, iff $b_i \overset{\bullet}{<} a_i$, $\forall i \in \{1,...,k\}$. Besides, we use $\beta \subset \alpha$ to denote the case when $\beta \subseteq \alpha$ and $\beta \neq \alpha$. The *minimal upper subcube* of two subcubes α and β, denoted by lcm(α, β), is defined as the smallest subcube among all the subcubes which contain both α and β. Similarly, the *maximal lower subcube* of two subcubes α and β, denoted by gcd(α, β), is defined as the largest subcube among all the subcubes which are contained in α and β. Let gcd$(\alpha, \beta) = \emptyset$ if $H(\alpha, \beta) \geq 1$.

Definition 2: Let U_1, U_2 be two sets of subcubes. The *merge* operation, denoted by $\odot$, of these two sets is defined as:

$$U_1 \odot U_2 = \left\{ \tau \mid \tau = \text{lcm}(\alpha, \beta) \text{ for } \alpha \in U_1 \text{ and } \beta \in U_2 \right\}.$$

Definition 3: The *exclusion* operation of two sets of subcubes is defined as:

$$U_1 - U_2 = \left\{ r \mid r \in U_1 \text{ and } \gcd(t, r) = \emptyset, \ \forall t \in U_2 \right\}.$$

Definition 4: The *reduced set* of a set of subcubes U is defined as:

$$Rd(U) = U - \left\{ r \mid r \in U \text{ and } t \subset r \text{ for some } t \in U \right\}.$$

Let $D(n_i)$ denote the subcube assigned to module n_i and B_i denote the set of nodes adjacent to n_i in the task graph. For example, $H(00*1*, 1000*) = 2$, $\text{lcm}(*100, 0110) = (*1*0)$ and $\gcd(01**, *10*) = (010*)$. For the example graph of Fig. 1, we get $B_1 = \{n_2, n_3, n_4, n_6\}$. Let $U_1 = \{0**, 0*0, 01*, 001\}$, $U_2 = \{00*, 10*\}$ and $U_3 = \{001\}$. Then, $Rd(U_1) = \{0*0, 01*, 001\}$, $U_1 - U_2 = \{01*\}$ and $U_2 \odot U_3 = \{00*, *0*\}$.

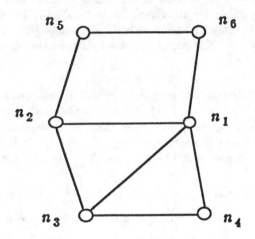

Fig. 1. An example task graph

3. PROPERTIES OF WEAK CUBICAL DIMENSION

3.1. Previous Related Results

In [1], an interesting addressing scheme for loop switching networks [6] was proposed. The problem can be formally stated as follows. Given a connected graph G with n nodes, find the least integer $N(G)$ with which it is possible to assign each node v of G an address $D(v) \in \sum^{N(G)}$ such that $d_G(v_1, v_2) = H(D(v_1), D(v_2))$, $\forall v_1, v_2 \in V_G$, where $d_G(v_1, v_2)$ is the distance between v_1 and v_2 in G, and V_G is the set of nodes in G. This problem has been studied for more than a decade until an important conjecture, $N(G) \leq n-1$, is proved in [3]. As pointed out in [2], this problem is equivalent to the *squashed embedding* problem: embed a task graph into a cube in such a way that each node of the graph is assigned to a subcube while preserving inter-node distances.

Consider the problem of determining the embedding of a given task graph into a cube in such a way that each task node must be assigned to a subcube while satisfying the adjacency requirement. It is easy to see that this problem is a relaxed version of the squashed embedding problem and can thus be viewed as the *relaxed squashed* (RS) *embedding*, since it preserves adjacency instead of inter-node distances. Some useful properties of the RS embedding are derived below, which will then be used for developing solution algorithms in Section 4.

3.2. Mathematical Properties of RS-Embedding

Due to the page limitation, all the proofs in this paper are excluded. The following theorem about the squashed embedding was proven in [2].

Theorem 1 : $N(K_n) = n - 1$, where K_n is a complete graph with n nodes.

When the graph to be embedded is a complete graph, the requirement of preserving distance is the same as the adjacency requirement. This fact results in the following corollary.

Corollary 1.1: Let $wd(G)$ be the weak cubical dimension of G. Then, $wd(K_n) = n-1$.

Consider the case when G_1 is a subgraph of G_2. Clearly, we have less restriction in the RS embedding of G_1 than that of G_2. This leads to the following lemma.

Lemma 1: If G_1 is a subgraph of G_2, then $wd(G_1) \leq wd(G_2)$.

Since every graph with n nodes is a subgraph of K_n, it follows immediately that the weak cubical dimension of a graph with n nodes will be less than or equal to $wd(K_n)=n-1$. In addition, from the fact that the number of nodes in the n-cube system has to be greater than or equal to that of the task graph to be embedded, we get the following corollary.

Corollary 1.2: Let G be a graph with n nodes. Then, $\lceil \log_2 n \rceil \leq wd(G) \leq n-1$.

Theorem 2: Let $G = (V, E)$ be a connected graph and $G_\beta = (V_\beta, E_\beta)$ be a subgraph of G. Suppose the induced subgraph of G with the node set V_S, denoted by $ind_G(V_S)$, can be RS embedded into a Q_m and the removal of all edges in E_S from G results in $|V_S|$ disjoint graphs, $G_i = (V_i, E_i)$, $1 \leq i \leq |V_S|$. Then, $wd(G) \leq \max_{1 \leq i \leq |V_S|} \{wd(G_i)\} + m$.

Corollary 2.1: Let G_i, $1 \leq i \leq k$, be disjoint graphs and $G = \bigcup_{i=1}^{k} G_i$. Then, $wd(G) \leq \max_{1 \leq i \leq k} \{wd(G_i)\} + \lceil \log_2 k \rceil$.

Besides, the effects of join and product operations on the weak cubical dimension of graphs can be described below by Theorems 3 and 4.

Theorem 3: $wd(G_1 + G_2) \leq wd(G_1) + wd(G_2) + 1$.

Corollary 3.1: Let $\{V_1, V_2\}$ be a partition of the node set of a graph G_A, i.e., $V_1 \cap V_2 = \emptyset$ and $V_1 \cup V_2 = V_A$. Let the induced subgraphs of G_A with the node sets V_1 and V_2 be G_{I_1} and G_{I_2}, respectively. Then, $wd(G_A) \leq wd(G_{I_1}) + wd(G_{I_2}) + 1$.

Let $G_{I_{A-S}}$ denote the induced subgraph of G_A with the node set $V_A - V_S$ where $V_S \subseteq V_A$. Then, we have the following corollary.

Corollary 3.2: $wd(G_A) \leq wd(G_{I_{A-S}}) + |V_S|$.

Using Corollaries 3.1 and 3.2, we will propose in Section 4 two fast algorithms for the RS embedding of a given graph. The relationship between the weak cubical dimensions of several graphs and that of their union can be described by the following corollary.

Corollary 3.3: Let $G = \bigcup\limits_{i=1}^{m} G_i$. Then, $wd(G) \leq \sum\limits_{i=1}^{m} wd(G_i) + m - 1$.

It is interesting to compare Corollary 3.3 with Corollary 2.1, which is applicable to disjoint graphs only. This result agrees with our intuition, since there are less restrictions in the RS embedding of disjoint graphs. Moreover, we have the following corollaries for the complement of a graph and a tree.

Corollary 3.4: Let G be a graph with n nodes. Then, $wd(G) + wd(\overline{G}) \geq n - 2$.

Corollary 3.5: Let T be a tree with n nodes. Then, $wd(T) \leq 2\lceil \log_2 n \rceil$.

Using Corollary 3.5, a fast RS embedding algorithm for a given tree will be developed in Section 4.

Theorem 4: $wd(G_1 \times G_2) \leq wd(G_1) + wd(G_2)$.

Theorem 5: Let q be an m-dimensional subcube of a Q_n, where $n \geq m$. Then, q is adjacent to at most $(n-m)2^m$ subcubes within the Q_n.

Corollary 5.1: Let $\{d_i\}$ be the degree sequence of a graph G_A. If $wd(G_A) \leq m$, then $\sum\limits_{i=1}^{|V_A|} 2^{b_i} \leq 2^m$, where for each $1 \leq i \leq |V_A|$, b_i is the least nonnegative integer such that the adjacency number of Q_{b_i} is greater than or equal to d_i.

Theorem 6: Let $m = wd(G_A)$ and $k = \lfloor \log_2 \dfrac{2^m}{|V_A|} \rfloor$. Then,

$$|E_A| \leq \frac{1}{2} \left[(2^{m-k} - |V_A|) \min\left\{ (m-k-1)2^{k+1}, |V_A|-1 \right\} + (2|V_A| - 2^{m-k}) \min\left\{ (m-k)2^k, |V_A|-1 \right\} \right].$$

Theorem 7: The weak cubical dimensions of a cycle C_m, a path P_m and a star S_m can be determined by the following formulas:

(i) $wd(C_m) = \lceil \log_2 m \rceil$,

(ii) $wd(P_m) = \lceil \log_2 m \rceil$,

(iii) $wd(S_m) = \lceil \log_2 (m - 1) \rceil + 1$.

4. ALGORITHMS FOR RELAXED SQUASHED EMBEDDING

The mathematical properties derived in Section 3 are applied to the design of algorithms for the RS embedding. Fast algorithms are presented first, which are efficient but may not offer the minimal cube required for a given task graph. Then a heuristic search algorithm is employed to determine the weak cubical dimension of a graph.

4.1. Fast Algorithms for RS-Embedding

Since every tree is a bigraph, we have an efficient addressing scheme for a tree with n nodes as described below.

Algorithm $A_1(T)$ /* This algorithm uses the property that every tree T is a bigraph and determines an efficient addressing scheme for T. */

Step 1:   Choose an arbitrary node in T. Label it with a symbol +.

Step 2:   Label with –'s all the nodes adjacent to each node labeled with +. **If** every node in T has been labeled with + or – **then** goto Step 4.

Step 3:   Label with +'s all the nodes adjacent to each node labeled with –. **If** every node in T has been labeled with + or – **then** goto Step 4 **else** goto Step 2.

Step 4:   Suppose there are j nodes labeled with + and k nodes labeled with –. Then, encode all the nodes labeled with + with $0* \cdots *B^{(+)}(i)$, $0 \leq i \leq j-1$, where $B^{(+)}(i)$ is a binary representation of the number i with $\lceil \log_2 j \rceil$ bits, which follows $\lceil \log_2 k \rceil$ *'s. Also, encode all the nodes labeled with – with $1B^{(-)}(i)* \cdots *$, $0 \leq i \leq k-1$, where $B^{(-)}(i)$ is a binary representation of the number i with $\lceil \log_2 k \rceil$ bits, which is followed by $\lceil \log_2 j \rceil$ *'s.

By Corollary 3.5, the length of the above addressing scheme must be less than or equal to $2\lceil \log_2 n \rceil$. Although the required length of the addressing scheme used in A_1 may be larger than the weak cubical dimension of the tree, A_1 is favorable in some cases due to its <u>linear</u> complexity, $O(n)$. Consider the case when the task graph is an *arbitrary* graph. We present an algorithms A_2 below, which is derived from Corollaries 3.2.

Algorithm $A_2(G)$ /* Using the technique of node-removing, this is a fast algorithm to determine the size of the cube required for a given task graph. */

Step 1:   Let n^* be the node with the largest degree among all the nodes in G. **If** $d(n^*) \leq 2$ **then** goto Step 2 **else** goto Step 3.

Step 2:   Determine all the cycles in G, denoted by C^1, C^2, $\cdots$, C^m, and the least integer p such that $2^p \geq \sum_{i=1}^{m} 2^{\lceil \log_2 |C^i| \rceil} + 2^{\lceil \log_2 (|V| - \sum_{i=1}^{m} |C^i|) \rceil}$, where $|C^i|$ is the number of nodes in the cycle C^i. Return p.

Step 3:   Let $G_1 := G - \{n^*\}$ and return $A_2(G_1) + 1$.

Using A_2, a graph is reduced by removing the node with the largest degree from the graph. The reduction steps are performed repeatedly until the graph is reduced to the extent that it contains only disjoint cycles and paths. By Corollary 3.2, the size determined in Step 2 plus the total number of nodes removed will be the dimension of a cube required to accommodate the original task graph.

A_2 can be generalized in such a way that in Step 3 a graph can be split into two graphs rather than removing one node at a time. Several heuristic methods can be employed in determining how to partition the node set V into V_1 and V_2 in Step 3. Clearly, a more sophisticated method will lead to an addressing scheme with a shorter length at the cost of higher computational costs.

4.2. An Algorithm for Determining the Weak Cubical Dimension

To facilitate our presentation, the task graph $G_T = (V_T, E_T)$ has to be labeled with n_i, $1 \leq i \leq |V_T|$, in such a way that the induced subgraph with nodes $\{n_1, n_2, \cdots, n_k\}$ $\forall k \leq |V_T|$ is connected. In what follows, we will formulate a heuristic function first and the A^* search algorithm will then be employed to determine the existence of an RS embedding from a given graph into a cube.

Let M^i denote the partial mapping for the task node n_j, $1 \leq j \leq i$. Let $A_{n_j}^{(i)}$ be the set of unoccupied Q_0's which are adjacent to $D(n_j)$ under the partial mapping M^i. Also, define the set of *essential subcubes* of n_j under the partial mapping M^i, denoted by $E_{n_j}^{(i)}$, as the reduced set of unoccupied subcubes which are adjacent to the subcubes assigned to all $n_k \in B_j$, $1 \leq k \leq i$. Then, the $E_{n_k}^{(i)}$ generated under M^i can be expressed as follows.

$$E_{n_k}^{(i)} = Rd\left(\underset{\substack{n_j \in B_k \\ 1 \leq j \leq i}}{\odot} A_{n_j}^{(i)} \right) - \bigcup_{j=1}^{i} D(n_j) \quad \forall k > i. \tag{1}$$

From this formula, we can determine the sets of all essential subcubes of unassigned task nodes. Given a partial mapping M^i, the set of all possible subcubes which can be assigned to the task node n_{i+1} is represented by:

$$Sp(E_{n_{i+1}}^{(i)}) = \left\{ q \,\middle|\, \exists t \in E_{n_{i+1}}^{(i)}, t \subseteq q \text{ and } \sum_{j=1}^{i} |D(n_j)| + |q| < 2^n - (|V_T| - i - 1) \right\} - \bigcup_{j=1}^{i} D(n_j). \tag{2}$$

From Eq. (2), it is easy to see that <u>both</u> (i) more subcubes in $E_{n_{i+1}}^{(i)}$ <u>and</u> (ii) subcubes of smaller dimensions in $E_{n_{i+1}}^{(i)}$ allow more freedom in allocating a required subcube to n_{i+1}. This in turn implies that the sets of essential subcubes of unassigned nodes can be used in determining the heuristic value of the node in the search tree associated with the partial mapping made thus far.

Then, $A_{n_i}^{(i)}$ can be determined by using Theorem 5, and the sets $A_{n_k}^{(i)}$, $1 \leq k < i$, can be updated from their predecessors by Eq. (3) as follows:

$$A_{n_k}^{(i)} = A_{n_k}^{(i-1)} - \{q\}, \quad 1 \leq k < i. \tag{3}$$

Suppose that a node p in the search tree is the one corresponding to the allocation of a subcube q to the task node n_i. Combining all the results and findings discussed thus far, a heuristic function for each node p in the search tree can be constructed as follows:

$$f(p) = g(p) + h(p) \quad \text{where} \quad g(p) = i2^n, \quad h(p) = \sum_{i+1}^{|V_T|} V(E_{n_k}^{(i)}), \quad \text{and} \quad V(E_{n_k}^{(i)}) = \sum_{t \in E_{n_k}^{(i)}} \frac{1}{2^{|t|}} . \quad (4)$$

Applying the above heuristic function to the A* search algorithm, we can determine the existence of an RS embedding of a given graph into a cube. For some graphs whose weak cubical dimensions are in a narrow range, a linear search algorithm is suggested. On the other hand, for those graphs whose bounds for weak cubical dimension are loose, a binary search algorithm is preferred.

5. DISCUSSION AND CONCLUSION

The problem studied in this paper can be generalized by considering both the computation load of each module and the communication load between modules in a task graph. The task graph can then be represented by a labeled graph. The number assigned to a node denotes the dimension of a subcube required for the corresponding module. The number assigned to an edge of the task graph represents the required number of communication links for this edge. Note that two adjacent subcubes could have different numbers of connecting links. Thus, the constraint treated in this paper is a special case of the generalized version, since 1 is assigned to every node and every edge of the task graph. Clearly, the inclusion of computation and communication loads of modules increases the number of constraints to meet and thus makes the RS embedding more realistic but complicated.

REFERENCES

(1) R.L Graham and H. O. Pollark, On the Addressing Problem for Loop Switching, Bell System Tech. J., vol. 50, no. 8, pp. 2495-2519, Oct. 1971.

(2) R. L Graham and H. O. Pollark, On Embedding Graph in Squashed Cubes, Graph Theory and Application, Lecture Notes in Mathematics 303. Springer-Verlag (Proc. of a conference held at Western Michigan University, May 10-13, 1972).

(3) P. M. Winkler, Proof of the Squashed Cube Conjecture, COMBINATORICA, vol. 3, no. 1, (1983) pp. 135-139.

(4) D. W. Krumme, K. N. Venkataraman, and G. Cybenko, Hypercube Embedding is NP-Complete, Proc. of 1-st Hypercube Conf., pp. 148-157, Aug. 1985.

(5) F. Harary, Graph Theory. Mass. Addison-Wesley, 1969.

(6) J. R. Pierce, Network for Block Switching of Data, Bell System Tech. J., vol. 51, no. 6, pp. 1133-1145, July-Aug. 1972.

Automated Problem Mapping:
The Crystal Runtime System

JOEL H. SALTZ* AND MARINA C. CHEN*

Abstract. Very high level language algorithm specification promises to be a crucial factor in the enhancement of software reliability. The ability of this system to map problems onto very large message passing machines in an automated manner should greatly increase the utility of high performance architectures. These architectures may be quite cost effective from the hardware point of view, but unattractive due to the difficulty of providing software able to exploit the potential of the machines.

1 Overview

The effective utilization of multiprocessors, particularly those with architectures that cannot support shared memory in an efficient way, is currently dependent on the ability of the user to map the problem onto the multiprocessor. In order to obtain high levels of efficiency, this mapping must distribute computational load relatively evenly between the machine's processors and must minimize the effects of interprocessor communication delay on algorithm performance. The need to explicitly designate a problem decomposition and to verify that the decomposition is both correct and has the desired performance characteristics can be a time consuming and error prone task. In cases in which the load distribution of an algorithm cannot be predicted sufficiently well in advance to allow a deterministic decomposition to be specified, it may be necessary to specify a family of problem decompositions along with a procedure for run time load management. While the development of methods for dynamically balancing loads is an active area of current research (e.g. see [27] [14] [5] [10] [22] [30]), without the development of automated mapping methods, the implementation of such schemes can be particularly time consuming and difficult [26].

A methodology will be developed that can insulate the user from the considerations required to produce efficient programs for multiprocessor machines while still enabling the user to achieve high levels of performance. Programs will be written in a very high level programming language Crystal.

---

*Department of Computer Science, Yale University, New Haven, CT 06520. saltz@yale, chen-marina@yale. Work supported in part by the Office of Naval Research under Contract No. N00014-82-K-0184 and No. 00014-86-K-0926.

1.1 Language and Compiler

Existing approaches for programming parallel machines can be broadly categorized into two groups:
(1) devising parallelizing compilers for imperative languages (e.g. Fortran) such as the Bulldog
compiler [12,11] and others [21], [2], and (2) devising parallel language constructs and expressing
parallelism explicitly by programmers. The first approach has the advantage that programs can be
written in familiar languages and existing programs can be transformed by parallelizing compilers
for execution on the new machines. One difficulty that has been encountered in the attempt to
exploit large scale data level parallelism in conventional languages is the need to perform extensive
analysis due to interprocedural dependencies. However, useful parallelism may be lost because
the programmer may specify unneeded sequentialization when writing programs in a imperative
language.

Another difficulty is that the parallelism discovered this way is limited by the algorithm embodied by the program. It is unlikely that the transformations provided by the parallelizing compiler
are sophisticated enough for the task of redesigning programs better suited for parallel processing.
Consider, for example, the problem of sorting. Quicksort is a very good sequential method which
can be parallelized by spawning a process for each of the two recursive calls that this sorting algorithm must make. The time complexity is indeed improved from $O(n \log n)$ (average case) in the
sequential version to $O(n)$ (since $O(n)$ comparisons are needed at the top level and the number of
comparisons is halved at every level thereafter) by using $O(n)$ independent parallel processes. However, what can be achieved by various parallel sorting networks (e.g., [32]) with $O(n)$ processors
is $O(\log^2 n)$, which is significantly faster for large n. Numerous other good sequential algorithms
have the same property that they do not lend themselves to efficient parallel implementations, as
exemplified by many of the newly devised parallel algorithms [9] which are significantly different
from their sequential counterparts.

This point leads to the second approach — parallel programming, where parallelism is explicitly
expressed in a program. This is flexible enough to be applied to either class of parallel machines
(shared-memory machines or message-passing machines) as well as any kind of parallel algorithm.
However, parallel programming and debugging can be extremely difficult with thousands of interacting processes. Most parallel languages, either proposed or in use, have explicit constructs for
parallelism. Programmers specify how tasks should be partitioned and which ones can be run in
parallel (e.g., futures in Multilisp [17,18], "in" and "out" in Linda [1]), or they specify explicitly
the communication between processes (e.g., "?" and "!" in CSP [19]). The specification of communication is very tricky because it requires the programmer to keep track of both a processor's
own state and its interactions with other processes. Explicit task decomposition by the user may
yield inefficient code for a large class of problems for which an efficient decomposition cannot be
known until run-time.

A Crystal program is a very high level algorithm specification in which the detailed interactions
among processes in space and time are suppressed. The Crystal compiler and runtime system allow
the generation of instructions to direct an assemblage of communicating processors in the efficient
execution of the specified algorithm.

Crystal is a very-high-level language in which a user program resembles a concise, formal
mathematical description. The language Crystal appears to be quite straightforward to use yet is
designed to have the modularity and freedom from side effects that has been shown to be of substantial benefit in the automatic detection of parallelism. For an overview of the language Crystal,
language constructs, and programming examples, please see [6]. No explicit passing of messages is
needed in the program specification, and task decomposition is done automatically by the Crystal
compiler. The compiler generates as many logical processes as possible and then combines clusters
of logical processes to produce a problem decomposition that possesses a degree of granularity that
is appropriate for the target machine. In cases in which the pattern of computations in a given section of the program is known at compile time, a direct mapping of the algorithm in question may be
performed. When the pattern of computations are fully determined only at runtime, the compiler
constructs a symbolic representation of the data dependencies. This symbolic representation is
used by a run-time system which aggregates the required computations. When enough regularity
is present the runtime system creates a parameterized mapping scheme. Different instances of the
mapping scheme has a range of properties. Using knowledge of target machine characteristics, the

runtime system chooses the appropriate instance of the mapping scheme and dynamically maps the computations onto the target architecture.

1.2 Load Balancing Analysis

The run time system must be designed to require low computational overhead. The way in which the runtime system functions is greatly dependent on the amount of regularity that is detected in a given portion of a crystal program. In many scientific problems, the computations to be performed by a given procedure may be determined in advance once the main data structures of the problem are set up. This set up phase will very often occur at run time. An example of such a code is the preconditioned congugate gradient type linear equation solver described below.

A variety of strategies are used to contain the cost of the run time system in these relatively predictable problems. As much information as possible is obtained from the analysis performed during compilation and when possible, a parameterized mapping function is produced from this information. This mapping function describes how the computation could be mapped onto the processors of a machine and how those computations within each processor would be scheduled. The space of possible problem partitionings is consequently greatly constrained; the mapping chosen is the one that is estimated to give the best results for the given problem and the target machine.

When a given computation must be repeatedly performed, as it might be in an iterative algorithm or in the solution of a time dependent partial differential equation, a problem may be remapped from time to time in search of better performance. Finding the best parameters for mapping given a repetitively executed procedure will often be an iterative process. Performance evaluation mechanisms will be provided to weigh the costs of remapping against possible performance improvements that could be obtained [27],[24], [25]. The control of the remapping can take advantage of the fact that the algorithm is iterative, we can hence employ statistically formulated run time policies for the control of remapping that attempt to minimize expected costs under conditions of uncertainty [27].

There are a large number of problems in which the patterns of data dependency or the distribution of work change during the evolution of the problem. Many of these problems contain enough regularity to make the use of a parameterized problem mapping procedure likely to be advantageous. Examples of such problems include adaptive mesh refinement, particle methods, intermediate and high level image processing and time driven discrete event simulations [4] [3] [24] [16] [15] [28]. The use of policies for dynamic load balancing are vital for the efficient multiprocessor solutions of these problems.

To illustrate the issues involved in balancing load in gradually changing systems, consider the implementation of a time driven discrete event simulator on a message passing multiprocessor. At varying points in the simulation different areas of the simulated domain will have varying levels of activity. These domain regions will consequently require differing amounts of computational work. During the course of the simulation, the majority of the interactions between portions of the domain will be local in character. Consider the tradeoffs that are made in choosing a mapping of domain to processors. A domain decomposition that assigns contiguous regions to processors will lead to relatively low communication costs but may require frequent remappings in order to preserve a good balance of load. Domain decompositions that assign many smaller non contiguous regions of domain to each processor will be subject to higher communication costs but will be less subject to performance deterioration due to developing load imbalances.

A systematic set of policies must take into account tradeoffs between costs of communication and the propensity for loads to become unbalanced, and must also take into account the tradeoffs between the costs and benefits obtained by balancing load at a given point in the computations [24].

There exist classes of problems whose patterns of computations are so irregular that any sort of a-priori problem mapping is likely to be ineffective. Algorithms which attempt to exploit parallelism at the expression level rather than through data decomposition appear to be particularly problematic in this respect. There is a considerable research effort directed towards the investigation of load balancing strategies that could prove to be effective in these less structured contexts [8] [29] [31] [13] [10] [23]. A distributed branch-and-bound mechanism extending some of these principles has been devised as part of the Crystal run-time system for supporting expression level parallelism. Expression parallelism is obtained by interpreting function calls as processes: function calls that do not have any dependency can be executed in parallel. Generally speaking, problems that have fast parallel algorithms (in NC) exhibits a large scale of data level parallelism while NP hard problems exhibits a high-degree of expression parallelism and very little data level parallelism. There exists a potential difficulty in utilizing expression level parallelism: the total number of computations that must be performed may increase as one attempts to gain more parallelism. Many of these computations involve searches of one sort or another; parallelism may be obtained though the investigation of alternatives that the sequential version would be able to identify as being unpromising. This can lead to the anomaly that the sequential processing may out-perform the parallel one because useless computations are performed in the parallel version. It is for this reason branch-and-bound becomes important in a general-purpose programming environment that supports parallelism automatically. The scheduling of work in this case cannot in general be carried out in advance even in a rough sense, and diffusion based load balancing is consequently used.

1.3   Runtime System Control

In the design of a system to automate the run time mapping of work to processors, a number of interacting factors that determine performance must be taken into account. Virtually all non trivial programs are modular in nature. In these programs the computations may be conceived of as occurring in a number of phases. For instance, during the course of computations, a scientific code may calculate a Jacobian, perform local relaxations, perform FFTs, or calculate inner products. We have made the tacit assumption so far that problems consist only of one phase. When problems consist of a sequence of phases, the mappings that are suitable for a given phase cannot be expected to be suitable for all phases. At these interphase transitions, there will often be a choice available between 1) remapping the problem so that suitable mappings may be used for each phase, or 2) avoiding at least some of the work associated with remapping by using mappings that for some phases that may be less efficient [7]. When data dependencies allow the coscheduling of two or more phases, the runtime system must decide whether using this expression level parallelism will be advantageous. Determining the best course of action requires taking into account the costs of remappings, the costs of executing various phases given the mappings under consideration, and the pattern of phase executions. The costs of executing phases given various mappings will be dependent on the run time parameters defining the patterns of computation and the size of the problem to be solved. The pattern of phases may also not be fully pre-determined.

2   Programming in Crystal

Crystal is a general pupose language, and it is particularly powerful for parallel computing in the sense that all fast parallel algorithms — characterized by the class NC [9] (polynomial number of processors and polylogarithmic time complexity) — can be specified in Crystal. A description of Crystal, a discussion of the compiler along with examples of Crystal syntax may be found elsewhere in these proceedings [6].

3   Analysis of a Model Problem

We present a sparse matrix forward solver as a model algorithm. This example is used to illustrate some of the considerations involved in the design of automated problem mapping methods. This solver is taken from a crystal program implementing a preconditioned conjugate gradient type method, orthomin(1) with incomplete LU preconditioning, used to solve sparse linear systems arising from discretizations of partial differential equations. The variables in this problem represent function values at grid points in a two dimensional partial differential equation. The stencil used to discretize the partial differential equation establishes data dependencies between the unknowns.

The incomplete factorization of the matrix A produces sparse lower and upper triangular matrices L and U. One of the crucial features in the parallel implementation of conjugate gradient like methods using this incomplete LU preconditioner is the efficient implementation of the forward and backward solutions involved in the preconditioning. We will restrict attention to the solution of the lower triangular system, considerations involved in the solution of the upper triangular system are virtually identical.

A Crystal program that implements the forward solve is given below:

```
! forward solve:  solving L x = y where L is a sparse lower triangular matrix
! L is in the lower triangle of B

fsolve(B, y) = [x(i) | i = 1:n]
where (
   x(i) = y[i] - (\+ { B(i).value(k) * x(B(i).col(k))
      (k = 1:B(i).ncol) and ( B(i).col(k)<i) })
      )
```

A sparse matrix is represented by a tuple A of records, where each record A(i) represents a row of the sparse matrix and contains three fields. The three fields [A(i).ncol, A(i).col, A(i).value] contain respectively the number of non-zero elements in that row, the column numbers for these elements, and the values of the elements. The notation of a generated set [6] is used in the definition of **fsolve** and is represented by pairs of curly braces. The notation of \+ in front of a set of elements means the sum over those elements. Any binary associative operator $\oplus$ applied to a set of elements can be expressed by $\backslash\oplus$. Using the set notation instead of a do loop has the advantage that sequentiality is not introduced due to the semantics of the programming construct. The absence of such sequentiality allows the straightforward evaluation of the operation to take advantage of the maximum parallelism possible.

3.1   Symbolic DAG Generator

In many scientific problems including the sparse substitution algorithm described above, the computations to be performed by a given procedure may be determined in advance once the main data structures of the problem are set up. A symbolic representation of a directed acyclic graph (DAG) representing the data dependency of an algorithm can be produced by the compiler. For instance, in the subprogram defining the forward solve **fsolve** the symbolic DAG generator produced by the the compiler looks like the following where **nodes** is the set of vertices of the DAG and **edges** is the set of directed edges [u,v] pointed from from vertex **v** to vertex **u**:

```
nodes = {i | i = 1:n}
edges = \union {[ i,B(i).col(k) ] | (k = 1:B(i).ncol) and (B(i).col(k) < i), i = 1:n}
```

When matrix B become available either at compile time or at run time, the explicit DAG can be produced.

3.2   Load balancing: from algorithm designer's view

In the simplest form of incomplete LU preconditioning, the factors L and U have the same sparsity structure as the lower and upper portions of A respectively. A prior knowledge of the sparsity structure will be used to advantage in the generation of the following parameterized problem mapping. Note that this prior knowledge will not be needed when the automated version of the problem mapping is used. This automated version of problem mapping will be described in the next section.

We will assume that we have a rectangular array of grid points, all points are connected with the same stencil. The stencil is assumed to link a given point with it's left, right, upper and lower neighbors in the grid. The matrix is formed by using the so called natural ordering in which grid points are numbered in a row-wise fashion beginning with the first column of the first row of the

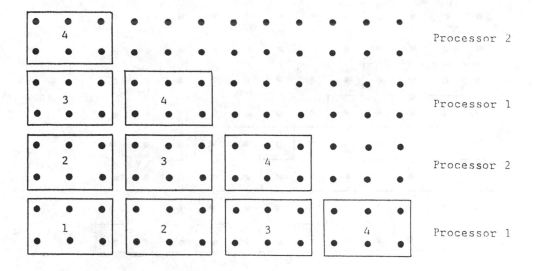

Figure 1: Two processors, five point stencil, block size = 2, window = 3. Numbers designate computational phases.

domain. We assume the same stencil is utilized for all mesh points in the problem. Again, note that these assumptions are used in the description of the explicitly defined parameterized mappings of grid points to processors. The automated mapping techniques to be discussed later is able to directly utilize an arbitrary lower triangular matrix. The automated methods produce the same mappings as the grid oriented techniques to be discussed below when the lower triangular matrix is a representation of a grid that is amenable to the grid oriented techniques.

The data dependency pattern between unknowns in the lower triangular solution may be best understood by refering back to the stencil and the grid utilized in the formulation of the problem [33]. Let $x_{i,j}$ be the location of a mesh point in the two dimensional domain, where $1 \leq i \leq n$ and $1 \leq j \leq n$. In the definition of the problem, a function value at a point $x_{i,j}$ is linearly dependent on function values at a given set of surrounding points. When a system involving a lower triangular matrix with the same sparsity structure as A is solved, the only interactions that need be considered are with variables in the grid that are in rows before i, as well as variables in row i that are before column j.

The grid points in a given row must be solved for sequentially, due to the coupling of each point to it's immediate neighbors. We assume that the stencil is rather small, so that relatively few calculations are involved in obtaining the value for a single grid point of the domain. In these mappings, the smallest unit of work that may be assigned to a particular processor consists of the computations pertaining to a particular row of grid points. The computations in a given row i depend only on results from row $j < i$. Depending on the relative size and properties of the problem and of the machine, better performance may be obtained by using a coarser grained assignment of work in which contiguous blocks of several rows are assigned to each of k processors. When there are more blocks of rows than there are processors, a wrapped assignment is used in which blocks are assigned to processors modulo k.

Given a fixed assignment of grid points to processors, one may be free to schedule the work associated with calculating values at mesh points in a variety of different ways. This processor scheduling has a marked effect on the frequency with which processors must interact to exchange information. When a five point stencil is utilized, a convenient method of scheduling is to partition each block into windows of w columns each. Because of the use of the five point stencil, values for all points in a given window of a block may be computed before any work on the next window is

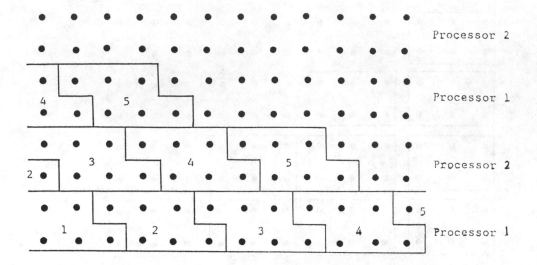

Figure 2: Two processors, nine point stencil, block size = 2, window = 3. Numbers designate computational phases.

begun. If one numbers the windows in each block from left to right, block i may commence work on window j when block $i - 1$ has finished work on window j. This leads to a pattern of computation [33] in which a wavefront of computation is seen to propagate from the lower left portion of the domain (Figure 1). The block size and the size chosen for the window both determine the coarseness of the computation's granularity. A quantitative analysis of this tradeoff in the case where the block size is equal to the window size is given in [33]. For a grid whose points are connected by an arbitrary stencil, the definition of work schedules that maintain data dependency relations yet allow for varying degrees of granularity is somewhat more subtle. Work is begun in the first row of the first block, and in this row the values for w window of grid points are calculated. Following this, values are found for all mesh points in the block for which data dependencies allow calculation. The computation proceeds after this in stages, with the computations that may proceed in a block at a given time being determined by dataflow considerations. Now for an arbitrary but uniform stencil, the computation of the variable at row i column j may require data from rows $i - q$, columns $j - v_q$, for $1 \leq q \leq i - 1$, $v_q \geq 1$. Thus if one wishes to aggregate points in blocks into larger units, with each unit to be calculated sequentially, the partitioning will take on a zig-zag form. Figure 2 depicts the pattern of wavefronts that results from partitioning a domain with a nine point stencil into blocks of size two, and scheduling computation using a window size of two.

3.3   Automated load balancing

In order to automate problem partitioning and work scheduling, it is essential to be able to dispense with as much application dependent information as possible. We have developed and tested a method for generating a parameterized mapping function to partition work possessing data dependencies given by a directed acyclic graph (DAG) generated by the DAG generator of Section 3.1 . In the following, the methods for parameterized mapping will be discussed in the context of solving the lower triangular system of linear equations we have been considering. The methods to be described utilize only the sparsity structure of the lower triangular matrix in the generation of the mapping and scheduling function, no representation of a physical domain is required. Algorithms for inexpensively generating parameterized mappings of acyclic graphs that allow for good performance will be crucial to the overall effectiveness of the crystal run time system.

We will assume that all computations pertaining to a row of the matrix will be assigned to a single processor. Note that this implies a potentially fine degree of granularity as we are dealing with matrices having few non zero elements in a row. The concurrency achievable through the use of this algorithm is largely determined by the dependencies between the rows of the lower triangular matrix. The approach to be taken here is to utilize an analysis of the data dependencies to produce a parameterized mapping. This partitioning process will take place in two stages. The rows of the L will be partitioned into a number of disjoint sets to be called strings. The strings will then be distributed between processors with all computations pertaining to a given string assigned to a single processor.

The partitioning of the rows into strings and the distribution of the strings are performed so as to attempt to satisfy the objectives of maximizing potential concurrency and of minimizing communication costs. In order to reduce the amount of interprocessor communication, we want strings to consist of rows with data dependencies. So as not to compromise potential concurrency, strings should contain only rows that could not under any circumstances be evaluated concurrently.

3.4 Wavefront and String Generator

A general description of how the rows may be partitioned into strings will now be given, details of the algorithm are presented elsewhere [26]. The order in which variables, described by rows in L, can be solved may be depicted by a directed acyclic graph D. The evaluation of rows in the L are represented by the vertices of D, and the data dependencies between the rows by the D's edges. The dependence of matrix row a on matrix row b is represented by an edge going from vertex b to vertex a. A topological sort may be performed which partitions to DAG into wavefronts. This sort is performed by alternately removing all vertices that are not pointed to by edges, and then removing all edges that emanated from the removed vertices. All vertices removed during a given stage constitute a wavefront; the wavefronts are numbered by consecutive integers. An adaptation of a common topological sort algorithm [20] allows the wavefronts of a DAG to be calculated efficiently.

Strings are chosen to be in a rough sense orthogonal to the wavefronts of the DAG D, and so that the graph describing the *inter-string* data dependencies is a directed acyclic graph, to be called here the string DAG. Choosing strings in this way greatly increases the flexibility allowed in the scheduling of computation It should be noted that in cases where the lower triangular matrix in question has been obtained from a rectangular array of grid points with a stencil in the manner described above, the partitioning process will assign a row, a column or a diagonal of grid points to each string. The directed acyclic graph describing inter-string data dependencies is in this case simply a chain with only nearest neighbor relationships. Figure 3 shows the wavefronts and strings assigned to the matrix representing a 12 by 8 point domain with an eight point stencil.

The string DAG may be distributed among processors in a variety of ways. Mapping large contiguous sections of the string DAG onto each processor will tend to minimize communication costs but will also tend to lead to poor load distributions. Scattering or wrapping strings that are contiguous in the DAG may lead to a much better load distribution at the price of increased communication costs [26].

The work associated with each cluster of strings may be scheduled with varying degrees of granularity. The string DAG defines a partial ordering among the strings. The starting strings may be defined as the strings that precede all others in this partial ordering. Computations of rows in these strings are not dependent on information from any other strings in the string DAG.

The granularity of parallelism may be determined by fixing the amount of work starting strings can perform before communicating their data to other strings in the string DAG. Simple relationships involving the wavefronts of *rows* allows the calculation of which rows may be solved for by a processor assigned to a cluster of strings.

The details of the rules for scheduling rows depend on the methods for aggregating strings used by the parameterized mapping function. One particularly straightforward method is to perform a topological sort on the string DAG in order to impose a strict ordering on the strings. Once this ordering is performed, contiguous blocks of strings having constant size b are demarcated, and are assigned to consecutive processors in a wrapped manner.

We make the following observation, with a simple proof by induction given in [26]:

Proposition 1 *Assume we partition the computation into phases p and allow the first string in the first block to compute values for rows between wavefronts $(p-1)w+1$ and pw. At the end*

POINTS

85	86	87	88	89	90	91	92	93	94	95	96
73	74	75	76	77	78	79	80	81	82	83	84
61	62	63	64	65	66	67	68	69	70	71	72
49	50	51	52	53	54	55	56	57	58	59	60
37	38	39	40	41	42	43	44	45	46	47	48
25	26	27	28	29	30	31	32	33	34	35	36
13	14	15	16	17	18	19	20	21	22	23	24
1	2	3	4	5	6	7	8	9	10	11	12

WAVEFRONTS

15	16	17	18	19	20	21	22	23	24	25	26
13	14	15	16	17	18	19	20	21	22	23	24
11	12	13	14	15	16	17	18	19	20	21	22
9	10	11	12	13	14	15	16	17	18	19	20
7	8	9	10	11	12	13	14	15	16	17	18
5	6	7	8	9	10	11	12	13	14	15	16
3	4	5	6	7	8	9	10	11	12	13	14
1	2	3	4	5	6	7	8	9	10	11	12

STRINGS

8	8	8	8	8	8	8	8	8	8	8	8
7	7	7	7	7	7	7	7	7	7	7	7
6	6	6	6	6	6	6	6	6	6	6	6
5	5	5	5	5	5	5	5	5	5	5	5
4	4	4	4	4	4	4	4	4	4	4	4
3	3	3	3	3	3	3	3	3	3	3	3
2	2	2	2	2	2	2	2	2	2	2	2
1	1	1	1	1	1	1	1	1	1	1	1

Figure 3: Points, wavefronts, and strings for a 12 by 8 point domain, eight point stencil

of phase p, all strings in block i may calculate values for rows having wavefronts $(p-i)w+1$ to $(p-i+1)w$.

It is shown [26] that in the special case in which the linearly ordered set of strings have only nearest neighbor data dependencies, the largest wavefront that can be computed by the jth string in block i, during phase p is $w(p+1-i)+(i-1)b+j-1$.

As is documented with experimental work in [26], both the way in which strings are assigned to processors and the degree of granularity in the scheduling of computations within strings influence both load balance and communication costs. Once the decomposition into wavefronts and strings is performed, one has available a range of mapping and scheduling schemes which can be utilized in a way that is appropriate for a given machine and problem.

4   Summary

Very high level language algorithm specification promises to be a crucial factor in the enhancement of software reliability. As described above, we propose an integrated system which has the promise of greatly facilitating the development of large complex high performance software systems. These programs would be executable in an efficient manner on massively parallel architectures. Fault tolerance is an inherent part of the system design since the system incorporates dynamic runtime problem mapping. This mapping allows for execution time system reconfiguration.

References

[1] Sudhir Ahuja, Nicholas Carriero, and David Gelerter. Linda and friends. *IEEE Computer*, August 1986.

[2] F Allen. Compiling for parallelism. In *Proceedings of the IEEE International Conference on Computer Design: VLSI in Computers*, page 126, October 1985.

[3] M. J. Berger and A. Jameson. Automatic adaptive grid refinement for the euler equations. *AAIA Journal*, 23:561–568, 1985.

[4] M. J. Berger and J. Oliger. Adaptive mesh refinement for hyperbolic partial differential equations. *J. Comp. Phys.*, 53:484–512, 1984.

[5] S. Bokhari. *Partitioning Problems in Parallel, Pipelined, and Distributed Computing*. Report 85-54, ICASE, November 1985.

[6] M. C. Chen. Very-high-level parallel programming in crystal. In *The Proceedings of the Hypercube Microprocessors Conf., Knoxville, TN*, September 1986.

[7] T. F. Chen. *On Gray Code Mappings for Mesh-FFTs on Binary N-Cubes*. Report 86.17, RIACS, September 1986.

[8] W. W. Chu, L. J. Holloway, and K. Efe M. Lam. Task allocation in distributed data processing. *Computer*, 13(11):57–69, November 1980.

[9] Stephen A. Cook. A taxonomy of problems with fast parallel algorithms. *Information and Control*, (64):2–22, 1985.

[10] D. L. Eager, E. D. Lazowska, and J. Zahorjan. Adaptive load sharing in homogeneous distributed systems. *IEEE Trans. on Software Eng.*, SE-12:662–675, May 1986.

[11] John R. Ellis. *Bulldog: A Compiler for VLIW Architectures*. The ACM Doctoral Dissertation Award Series, The MIT Press, 1985.

[12] Joseph A. Fisher, John R. Ellis, John C. Ruttenberg, and Alexandru Nicolau. Parallel processing: a smart compiler and a dumb machine. In *Proceedings of the SIGPLAN '84 Symposium on Compiler Construction*, pages 37–47, Association for Computing Machinery, June 1984.

[13] G. J. Foschini. *On Heavy Traffic Diffusion Analysis and Dynamic Routing in Switched Networks*. North-Holland, New York, 1977.

[14] W. Gropp. *Dynamic Grid Manipulation for PDEs on Hypercube Parallel Processors*. Department of Computer Science YALEU/DCS/TR-458, Yale University, March 1986.

[15] W. Gropp. *Dynamic Grid Manipulation for PDEs on Hypercube Parallel Processors*. Department of Computer Science YALEU/DCS/TR-458, Yale University, March 1986.

[16] W. Gropp. *Local Uniform Mesh Refinement on Loosely-coupled Parallel Processors*. Department of Computer Science YALEU/DCS/TR-352, Yale University, December 1984.

[17] Jr. Halstead, Robert H. Multilisp: a language for concurrent symbolic computation. *ACM Transaction on Programming Language and Systems*, October 1985.

[18] Jr. Halstead, Robert H. Parallel symbolic computing. *IEEE Computer*, August 1986.

[19] C.A.R. Hoare. Communicating sequential processes. *Communication of ACM*, 21(8):666–677, 1978.

[20] E. Horowitz and S. Sahni. *Fundamentals of Data Structures*. Computer Science Press, Rockville Maryland, 1983.

[21] K. Kennedy. Compilation for n-processor architectures. In *Proceedings of the IEEE International Conference on Computer Design: VLSI in Computers*, page 15, October 1985.

[22] S. H. Bokhari M. A. Iqbal, J. H. Saltz. Performance tradeoffs in static and dynamic load balancing strategies. In *Proceedings of the 1986 International Conference on Parallel Processing*, 1986.

[23] L. M. Ni, C. Xu, and T. B. Gendreau. A distributed drafting algorithm for load balancing. *IEEE Trans. on Software Eng.*, SE-11:1153–1161, October 1985.

[24] D. Nicol and J. Saltz. *Dynamic Remapping of Parallel Computations with Varying Resource Demands*. Report 86-45, ICASE, July 1986. submitted to Transactions on Computers.

[25] D. M. Nicol and Jr. P. F. Reynolds. *An Optimal Repartitioning Decision Policy*. Report 86-7, ICASE, February 1986.

[26] J. Saltz. Methods for automated problem mapping. In *Proceedings of IMA Workshop on Numerical Algorithms for Parallel Computer Architectures*, 1987.

[27] J. H. Saltz and D. M. Nicol. *Statistical Methodologies for the Control of Dynamic Remapping*. Report 86-46, ICASE, July 1986. to appear in the Proceedings of the Army Research Workshop on Parallel Processing and Medium Scale Multiprocessors, Palo Alto, California, January 1986.

[28] R. Smith and J. Saltz. Performance analysis of strategies for moving mesh control. In *Proceedings of the CMG XV International Conference on the Management and Performace Evaluation of Computer Systems*, pages 301–308, 1984.

[29] J. A. Stankovic. An application of bayesian decision theory to decentralized control of job scheduling. *IEEE Trans. on Computers*, C-34(2):117–130, February 1985.

[30] A. N. Tantawi and D. Towsley. Optimal static load balancing. *Journal of the ACM*, 32(2):445–465, April 1985.

[31] D. Towsley. Queueing network models with state-department routing. *Journal of the ACM*, 27(2):323–327, April 1980.

[32] Jeffrey D. Ullman. *Computational Aspects of VLSI*. Computer Science Press, 1984.

[33] M. Schultz Y. Saad. *Parallel Implementations of Preconditioned Conjugate Gradient Methods*. Department of Computer Science YALEU/DCS/TR-425, Yale University, October 1985.

Mapping Parallel Applications to a Hypercube[*]

KARSTEN SCHWAN†, WIN BO†, N. BAUMAN†, P. SADAYAPPAN†
AND F. ERCAL†

Abstract

Two issues must be addressed when mapping parallel programs to a hypercube architecture: (1) determination of the mapping using application specific and architectural information and (2) efficient run—time support for the mapped application. Regarding (1), we
describe alternative mapping strategies and their effectiveness using a specific parallel application (Finite Element Methods). Regarding (2), we describe some extensions of the basic
hypercube operating system. Specifically, a system mechanism for performing smaller grain
distributed 'services' required by the application is described. These services include the
broadcasting of single values to a subset of the cube's nodes, the computation of norms as
required by the parallel iterative methods used by the FEM application, and others.

1. Introduction

The *mapping problem* for a parallel program can be defined as the binding of program
components to resources of the underlying parallel system. Past research for multiprocessors
and computer networks [13, 19, 18] has concentrated on the allocation and resulting use of
hardware resources, such as processors, memory, and communication links. Our research
considers such allocation problems, and it addresses two additional issues: (1) the provision
of additional mapping choices at the operating system level [15, 14] and (2) the possible

---

[*]This research is being supported by the Small Business Innovative Research Program of the Department
of Defense, monitored by Wright Patterson Air Force Base and in conjunction with Universal Energy Systems
of Dayton, Ohio.

†The Ohio State University, Department of Computer and Information Science, Columbus, OH 43210.

automation of such mappings of program components to operating system constructs [20, 16, 17].

The application domain and target architecture used for this research are finite element methods for metalforming applications [1] parallelized for hypercube architectures [22]. The application's parallel algorithms are described in a companion paper [2]. In this paper, we describe novel operating system constructs now being developed for an Intel iPSC hypercube, and the mapping methods being developed for the finite element methods.

2. The Mapping Problem

In general, the processor mapping problem requires the assignment of a set of parallel tasks to a set of processors such that some desired performance criterion is optimized. Usually, the completion time for the program (or one step of an iterative computation) is used as the performance criterion to be minimized. The general mapping problem, with arbitrary execution and task communication constraints is NP−complete even for small numbers of processors. Hence in practice, heuristic mapping algorithms are often used [10, 3, 11, 5, 7].

We now describe the essence of our processor mapping problem and then discuss our approach to generating good mappings. The application program can be represented as a set of processes that are placed on a regular 2−dimensional grid. The interprocess communication requirement is very regular − each process needs to communicate with each of its nearest neighbors. The outer periphery of the set of processes, however does not necessarily exhibit any regularity, and can be arbitrary. Program execution involves an iterative sequence of alternating phases of computation by all processes followed by communication between neighbors. These processes are to be mapped onto a regular mesh (a 2D−mesh subset of the links of a hypercube are used) of processors. If the overall problem−mesh structure relates to the processor−mesh structure in a simple fashion, then a straightforward mapping of the problem−mesh onto the processor mesh is possible, as shown in figure 1a. However, as is often the case in practice, if the overall problem−mesh does not bear any simple relation to the processor−mesh (as in figure 1b), this scheme will create unbalanced loads in the processors. A mapping scheme is required that will effectively map the processes of the problem−mesh onto the processors in the system so that the computational load is uniformly balanced among the processors and the overhead due to interprocessor communication is minimized.

It is desirable to maximize the speedup obtained by executing the program on the processor mesh, as compared to execution on a single processor. If each process takes time t_{calc} to execute, the total number of processes is N and the total number of processors is P, then on a single processor, time for iteration step completion would be:

$$T_{seq} = N*t_{calc}$$

On the parallel processor system, time for one iteration step for any processor is the sum of the computation time and communication time. The number of processes $N_{calc}(p)$ mapped onto processor 'p' determines the total computation time per iteration step for that processor, T_{calc} as $N_{calc}(p)*t_{calc}$. The amount of time spent by a processor for communication will depend on the number of values that need to be transferred to neighbor processors from processor 'p'. For example, in figure 1a, processor P_4 needs to communicate a total of 9 values per iteration step, 3 to P_5, 3 to P_1 and 3 to P_3. If the communication time per iteration step for processor 'p' is denoted $T_{comm}(p)$, the iteration step completion time on the parallel processor system is given by:

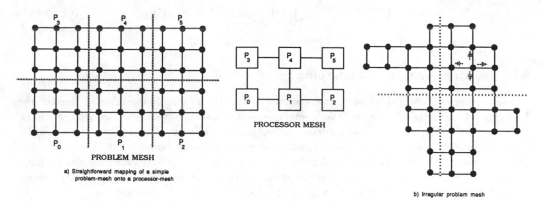

a) Straightforward mapping of a simple
problem-mesh onto a processor-mesh

PROBLEM MESH

PROCESSOR MESH

b) Irregular problem mesh

Figure 1

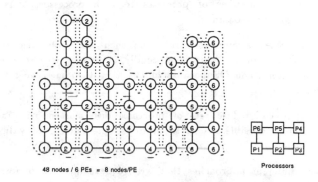

48 nodes / 6 PEs = 8 nodes/PE

Processors

Figure 2. Example to illustrate "strip" method.

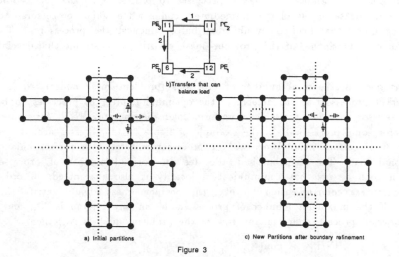

b)Transfers that can
balance load

a) Initial partitions

c) New Partitions after boundary refinement

Figure 3

$$T_{par} = MAX \{ T_{calc} + T_{comm}(p) \} = MAX \{ N_{calc}(p)*t_{calc} + T_{comm}(p) \}$$

$$Speedup = T_{seq}/T_{par}$$

2.1. Heuristic Approach to Mapping

Determining an optimal process–to–processor mapping is quite intractable. Besides the difficulty of accurately modeling the communication times involved (due to set–up times, time for forwarding through intermediate nodes, possible overlap of communication on different channels, possible overlap of communication with computation etc.), even with the simplest communication models used, the determination of optimal assignments is NP–complete. Further, in practice, absolutely optimal assignments are not really necessary; near–optimal assignments that provide very good speedups are perfectly adequate.

A heuristic approach to processor mapping is used, that attempts to separately minimize the maximal T_{calc} and T_{comm} values amongst the processors (rather than minimizing the combined sum of the two), by:

- trying to allocate equal number of processes to each processor, thus achieving minimal T_{calc} through load–balancing.

- trying to allocate processes amongst processors such that only nearest–neighbor communication is ever required (this is especially important with the Intel IPSC running under the Intel Node OS because of the very high message set–up times that are involved).

- trying to collect physically close sets of processes into clusters with as small a perimeter/area ratio as possible, so as to minimize the number of values needing inter–processor communication at each step.

We now describe two different approaches that we are developing to perform problem–to–processor mapping.

2.2. Strip assignment:

The strip method attempts to allocate processes to processors so that each processor only needs to communicate to one of two immediately connected neighbor processors. Additionally, the total computational load is evenly distributed amongst the processors. The method, however can only be applied if the problem–mesh satisfies a constraint that is elaborated on below.

With this method, the total number of processes (problem–mesh nodes) 'N' is divided by the number of processors 'P' to determine the optimum number of processes to be allocated to each processor in order to achieve uniform load distribution ($|N/P|$ for some processors and $|N/P|$ for some processors). In the example of figure 2, 48 processes need to be allocated among the 6 processors, i.e. 8 processes per processor will result in perfect balancing of the computational load. The strip method allocates an optimal number of processes to each processor in such a way that communication locality is also guaranteed. In order that the method guarantees communication locality, the problem–mesh should satisfy the following condition: If the maximum number of process–nodes in any column is N_C, and the maximum number of process–nodes in any row of the problem–mesh is N_R, then

$$|N/P| > min(N_C, N_R)$$

The method groups processes from one or more adjacent rows(columns) into "strips" such that each process needs to communicate only with processes in the same strip or the (single) strip on either side. Starting at one corner of the problem—mesh, processes are counted off, either along the row (if $N_R >= N_C$) or along the column (if $N_C >= N_R$) till all the processes in that row (column) have been selected. Processes are then picked off the next row(s) (column) till the required total number of processes ($|N/P|$ or $|N/P|$) have been obtained. All the processes so picked are allocated to one of the processors. The next strip is formed by continuing to pick processes from the incompletely covered row(column). When that row(column) is completely picked , those processes from the next row(column) are first selected that require communication with any process assigned to the previously allocated processor. If after all such processes are selected, more processes are needed to make up the desired count ($|N/P|$ or $|N/P|$), they are selected from the same row (column), contiguous to the ones already selected, and overflowing to the next row(column) if necessary. Thus, groups of processes are selected in such 'strips,' each containing an optimal number of processes to uniformly balance the computational load. Each strip spans the width(length) of the problem—mesh, so that each strip has exactly one neighbor strip on either side of it. Thus the processes that any given process needs to communicate with will lie either on the same strip or on one of the neighbor strips. Strips are allocated to processors in such a way that neighbor strips are mapped onto adjacent processors, thus guaranteeing complete locality of interprocessor communication.

2.3. 2-Dimensional Mapping Scheme

The 'strip mapping' scheme described above achieves perfect load balancing as well as nearest neighbor communication. However, it is not always applicable. Further, it results in the generation of process clusters that are long and hence have a high perimeter/area as compared to square regions. Thus a different partition that resulted in squarer regions would have fewer boundary nodes, and thus fewer values to be communicated to neighbor proces- sors. Some such schemes have been devised, and have been described elsewhere [1]. These schemes, however, do not generally achieve perfect load—balancing. For such initial assign ments, a 'Boundary Refinement' procedure is applied to improve load—balancing. The final mapping is to be generated using a three—phase process:

1. Generation of an initial partition with 'nearest—neighbor—only' communication requirements

2. Load—balancing by boundary—refinement

3. Secondary refinement,if necessary, to attempt further minimization of combined computation and communication times.

2.3.1. Boundary Refinement

The boundary refinement procedure attempts to equalize the computational load on the processors by refining the boundaries of the partitions obtained by the initial partition. This is illustrated in figure 3 through an example. Figure 3a shows an initial allocation of processes to processors. Processors P_0, P_1, P_2 and P_3 have initial loads of 6, 12, 11 and 11 processes respectively. Since the total number of processes is 40, each processor should be allocated 10 processes to obtain perfect load balancing. This can be achieved by reallocating 4 processes currently allocated to other processors to P_0, reallocating 2 processes currently allocated to P_1 to some other processors, and similarly reducing the loads of P_2 and P_3 by one process each. If these reallocations are always done between neighbor (directly connected) processors, and in such a way that processes transferred are on the edge of the partition separating clusters assigned to the processors, then the new allocations will still satisfy the nearest—neighbor—only communication property.

In general, the determination of the number of processes to be so reallocated from one processor to another can be formulated as an underdetermined (generally) set of simultaneous linear equations in integer—valued variables. Figure 3b shows one of the many possible ways of balancing the load for this example — reallocating 2 of P_1's 12 processes to P_0, real—locating 2 processes from P_3 to P_0, and transferring one process from P_2 to P_3. Figure 3c shows how processes on the partition boundary can be reallocated, resulting in the new load—balanced partitions.

3. Operating System Constructs for Programs Containing Multi-Grain Parallelism

3.1. Multi-Grain Parallelism

When decomposing a large application program into parallel tasks, choices will exist regarding (1) the granularity of each individual task and (2) the required latency and throughput of communication links between tasks. Furthermore, for hypercube architectures, (3) the topology of intertask communications has to be considered. However, in contrast to communication topologies described for sets of processes in shared—memory multiprocessors, for hypercube architectures the individual links among tasks exist and are used not only for the exchange of data or control information relevant to the tasks' computations, but also for message routing or forwarding under program control, for message filtering, etc. Examples of such link usage are especially prevalent in high—performance hypercube applications, such as those written with the Crystalline operating system [6]. For example, this operating system provides provides a broadcast construct embedded as a stub into application code, where a each node processes a global message passing through it and sent to all nodes by the cube manager in order to remove its designated part of that message.

Two problems result. First, the programming of application tasks becomes awkward due to their dual functions as computational activities and as simple message processors. Second, the logical communication topology required by the application's computations is not distin—guished from the physical message communication structure resulting from the mapping of the parallel tasks to the cube's nodes.

It is our aim to provide mechanisms that allow programmers to separately describe and implement the program components performing application—level, computational functions from those performing simple message processing, and to describe explicitly and conveniently the communication topologies used for each application. Such mechanisms must fulfill two requirements. First, since the granularity of simple message processing activities is small compared to typical computational activities performed by an application's parallel tasks, both kinds of activities cannot be represented by a single 'process' construct. Similar problems have been observed and are being dealt with in shared memory machines, where multiple 'threads' of computation or 'light—weight processes' exist within individual processes [12, 15] or where special—purpose hardware is being constructed in order to assist in specific computations performed on data shared between parallel tasks, such as the FetchAndAdd instruction used for task synchronization in the NYU Ultracomputer [21]. Second, communications among message processing activities should be directed at entire communication structures rather than individual message links, so that such structures can be defined and mapped to the cube's nodes separately from the application program. In ad—dition, to balance communication and computation for smaller grain activities, the operating system should support smaller latencies of communication between small grain activities than the latencies existing for larger grain tasks.

An operating system facility to create and delete small grain activities, to construct com—munication topologies linking those activities, and to associate those activities and topologies with an application's computational tasks is presented next. Its usefulness can be demonstrated for homogeneous, large—scale, parallel computations where application tasks are involved in message communication, since this implies that smaller grain message processing activities co—exist with larger grain, computational tasks. Its usefulness is also apparent for applications that exhibit inhomogeneities regarding the computations and communications performed by parallel tasks, such as the large—scale simulations targeted by the TimeWarp operating system [8] or the real—time applications addressed in our previous research [15, 14].

3.2. Communication Topologies and Smaller Grain Activities

An Example. A very simple example of a distributed message processing task in a hyper—cube application is the computation of a global error norm derived by addition of local norm values to partial accumulations of the global norm. In this case, the communication topology used is that of a spanning tree covering all cube nodes possessing local norm values, and the small grain activity at each node consists of the following actions:

wait for all inputs of partial global values
'add' the inputs to each other and to the local norm value
send the new value to all outputs

In any non—trivial node operating system, this simple computation would require at least two system calls (one for message receipt and one for message sending) and the activation of the application process performing the single addition. Such overhead is unacceptable and thus, has led to 'minimal' operating systems like the Crystalline OS that do not offer any of the general constructs recognized as useful in parallel computing [9, 4], such as protection, multi—tasking, etc.

To support smaller grain, application—specific 'activities', we define the following:

- A *service* is a small—grain task defined in conjunction with an application program. A *service mapping* describes the cube processors on which a set of ser—vices should reside.

- A *topology* is a set of communication links defining a logical interconnection structure for a set vertices, which are placeholders for services. Each vertex can have multiple inputs and outputs and it is the responsibility of the service as—sociated with each vertex to define the exact use of inputs and outputs. Vertices are bound explicitly to the physical nodes of the hypercube when a topology is created by specification of a *mapping* of topology to the cube. Each vertex may be mapped to no more than one node. Topologies are not explicitly linked to physical channels of the hypercube. However, since multiple topologies can co—exist on a single cube and single cube node, priorities may be defined between topologies. This results in priorities in the use of the physical communication channels shared by topologies. Since a topology can be defined separately from an application program, a *binding* defines the association of an application process with a topology vertex. Currently, each vertex may be bound to none or one ap—plication process.

- An *operation* on a topology is a request for use of a specific service (thus, ser—vices and topologies are bound dynamically) issued by an application program previously bound to the topology. The available operations are defined below.

3.3. Topology Operations

An application program bound to a topology can perform any one of the following four operations on the topology previously defined and created:

1. **TopoSend (TMB-id, Service-id, Value, Tag)** — this operation makes 'Value' available to the service specified with 'Service—id'. 'TMB—id' is a unique id specifying the topology, its mapping, and its binding. The specified service does not execute until all of its required inputs are available. In our first implemen—tation and to reduce buffering overhead and message latency, the TopoSend operation will either result in an error if buffer space for the 'Value' is not available or is blocked **(TopoSendw)**. In either case, it does not return until the service has been completed. The 'Tag' argument in the call identifies a particular set of input data values for the service routine. Its value is provided by the ap—plication or may be generated by the stub routines embedded with the application's code. To ensure that services which need input data from more than one source are properly sequenced, the tag value should be incremented with each call. Tagged values generated by different processes on different nodes are distin—guished from each other by automatic generation of a processor and process id prefix.

2. **Forwarding-TopoSend (TMB-id, Service-id, Value, Tag)** — the purpose of this operation is to make the output values generated by the service available to the vertex's outputs as well as to the application process bound to the vertex.

3. **Pending-TopoSend (TMB-id, Value, Tag)** — the purpose of this operation is to disable the execution of the service at the vertex and provide the input value to the application process bound to the vertex. The vertex's outputs are also dis—abled. This operation is similar to a normal message send except that the des—tination processes are transparent to the application process.

4. **TopoRecv (TMB-id, Service-id, Result, Tag, Type)** — this operation ob—tains the result of the specified service performed on a set of input data with the tag value specified by 'Tag'. The 'Type' parameter identifies the kind of 'TopoSend' operation for which the 'TopoRecv' is intended. If the values of 'Type' is one, then the result of a 'TopoSend' is sought in the statically allocated buffer of the service used with that 'TopoSend'. If the value of 'Tag' matches a tag value in that buffer, then the result is returned to the application process. Otherwise, an error status and a short history of the tag values of data that have been received are returned. If the value of 'Type' is two or three, then the 'TopoRecv' is intended for a 'Forwarding—TopoSend' or a 'Pending—TopoSend' operation, respectively. In both cases, the result queued for the application process, is retrieved from the appropriate buffers while also checking tag values. If tag values do not match, an error status together with the most recent tag value of the data received is returned. The 'TopoRecv' operation may cause the process to be blocked **(TopoRecvw)** until the matching tag is received or may be set to match any tag value.

To illustrate the use of the topology operations, consider the error norm computation described above. First, a topology describing a spanning tree is defined to cover all hyper—

cube nodes possessing local norm values, is mapped to the appropriate nodes, and the ap—
plication processes that provide the values of local error norms are bound to it. In addition,
a process that obtains the global norm is bound to the root of the tree. To compute the
global error norm, the application processes simply perform local calls to 'TopoSend's with
their local error norm values. The process at the root of the tree can obtain the global er—
ror norm by calling the 'TopoRecv' operation. The actual, distributed additions of local to
partial global norm values are performed by the small—grain service tasks on each node.
Thus, the service task mapped to each topology vertex perform the simple operations shown
at the beginning of this section.

4. Conclusions

The operating system research described in this paper is currently in progress. The design
of the novel constructs has been completed and implementation is now underway using Ver—
sion 3.0 of the node operating system for the Intel iPSC hypercube. Several uses of
topologies and services are planned, in addition to their use for the parallel finite element
computations mentioned earlier. For example, we are using communication topologies for
program monitoring and exception handling, and we are considering their use in implemen—
tation of the object model on the hypercube. In addition, their use for other applications is
being considered, such as high—quality computer graphics (eg. parallel scan conversion
algorithms) and real—time, robotics programs.

References

[1]   C. Aykanat, S.M. Doraivelu, F. Ercal, P. Sadayappan, K. Schwan, and B. Weide.
Parallel Computers for Finite Element Analysis.
In *1986 ASME International Conference on Computers in Engineering, Chicago*
ASME, Aug., 1986.

[2]   C. Aykanat, F. Ozguner, S. Martin, and S.M. Doraivelu.
Parallelization of a Finite Element Application Program on a Hypercube Multiproces—
sor.
In *Second Conference on Hypercube Multiprocessors, Knoxville, Tennessee*. Oakridge
National Laboratories, Sept., 1986.

[3]   S. H. Bokhari.
On the Mapping Problem.
IEEE Trans. on Computers C—30:207—214, March, 1981.

[4]   David R. Cheriton and Willy Zwaenepol.
Distributed Process Groups in the V Kernel.
ACM Transactions on Computer Systems 3(2):77—107, May, 1985.

[5]   J.W.Flower, S.W.Otto and M.C.Salama.
A Preprocessor for Irregular Finite Element Problems.
Technical Report, Caltech Concurrent Cube Project, Report # 292, June, 1986.

[6]   G.C. Fox and A. Kolawa.
*Implementation of the High Performance Cystalline Operating System on Intel iPSC
Hypercube.*
Technical Report, Caltech Concurrent Computational Program and Physics Dept.,
Caltech, Pasadena CA 91125, Hm247, Jan., 1986.

[7]   Geoffrey C. Fox.
       Load balancing and Sparse Matrix Vector Multiplication on the Hypercube.
       Technical Report, Caltech Concurrent Cube Project, Report # 327, July, 1986.

[8]   David R. Jefferson.
       Virtual Time.
       ACM Transactions on Programming Languages and Systems 7(3):404–425, July, 1985.

[9]   A.K. Jones, R.J. Chansler, I. Durham, J. Mohan, K. Schwan, and S. Vegdahl.
       StarOS, a Multiprocessor Operating System.
       In *Proceedings of the 7th Symposium on Operating System Principles, Asilomar, CA*,
           pages 117–127. Assoc. Comput. Mach., Dec.10–12, 1979.

[10]   Virginia Lo and Jane W. S. Liu .
       Task Assignment In Multiprocessor Systems.
       In *Proc. 1981 Intl. Conf. on Parallel Processing*, pages 358–360. IEEE, 1981.

[11]   R.Morison and S.Otto.
       The Scattered Decomposition for Finite Elements.
       Technical Report, Caltech Concurrent Cube Project, Report # 286, May, 1985.

[12]   Mike Acetta, Robert Baron, William Bolosky, David Golub, Richard Rashid, Avadis
       Tevanian, and Michael Young.
       Mach: A New Kernel Foundation for UNIX Development.
       Technical Report, Computer Science Department, Carnegie–Mellon University, Pitts–
           burgh, PA 15213, May, 1986.

[13]   Karsten Schwan.
       Tailoring Software for Multiple Processor Systems.
       UMI Research Press, Ann Arbor, Michigan, 1985.

[14]   Karsten Schwan, Win Bo, and Prabha Gopinath.
       A High–Performance, Object–Based Operating System for Real–Time, Robotics Ap–
           plications.
       In *1986 Real-Time Systems Symposium, New Orleans, Louisiana*. IEEE, Dec., 1986.
       To appear.

[15]   Karsten Schwan, Tom Bihari, Bruce W. Weide, and Gregor Taulbee.
       High–Performance Operating System Primitives for Robotics and Real–Time Control
           Systems.
       Nov., 1986.
       Conditionally accepted to the ACM Transactions on Computer Systems, also available
           as a technical report.

[16]   K. Schwan, R. Ramnath, S. Sarkar, and S. Vasudevan.
       Cool – Language Constructs for Constructing and Tuning Parallel Programs.
       In *International Conference on Computer Languages, Miami Beach, Florida*. IEEE,
           Oct., 1986.

[17]   Karsten Schwan, Thomas E. Bihari, and Ben Blake.
       Adaptable, Reliable Software for Distributed and Parallel, Real–Time Systems.
       In *Sixth Symposium on Reliability in Distributed Software, Williamsburg, Virginia*.
           IEEE, March, 1987.
       To Appear.

[18]   Karsten Schwan and Cheryl Gaimon.
       Automating Resource Allocation in the Cm* Multiprocessor.
       In *Fifth International Conference on Distributed Computing Systems, Denver, Colorado*,
           pages 310–320.   IEEE, Assoc. Comput. Mach., May, 1985.

[19]   Karsten Schwan and Anita K. Jones.
       Specifying Resource Allocation for the Cm* Multiprocessor.
       IEEE Software 3(3):60–70, May, 1984.

[20]   Karsten Schwan and Rajiv Ramnath.
       Adaptable Operating Software for Manufacturing Systems and Robots: A Computer
           Science Research Agenda.
       In *Proceedings of the 5th Real-Time Systems Symposium, Austin, Texas*, pages
           255–262.   IEEE, Dec., 1984.

[21]   J.T. Schwarz.
       Ultracomputers.
       ACM Transactions on Programming Languages and Systems 2(4):484–543, Oct., 1980.

[22]   Charles L. Seitz.
       The Cosmic Cube.
       Comm. of the Assoc. Comput. Mach. 28(1):22–33, Jan., 1985.

PART III:
PERFORMANCE MEASUREMENT
AND COMPARISON

Hypercube Software Performance Metrics

MIKE L. MATHEWS*

ABSTRACT. This paper discusses several descriptive
statistics formulated specifically to analyze and
evaluate the performance of software applications
developed on hypercube multiprocessors in a scientific
and engineering working environment. These statistics
are developed from time stamps placed in the application
software. Evaluation of these timing data aid the
developer in improving the implementation of the
application in the hypercube multiprocessor environment.
Comparison of timing data from applications developed
under different multiprocessing environments is
beneficial to end users and systems analysts in making a
decision about the best environment and best
implementation of the application.

   Included in this paper are discussions regarding the
calculation of speed up for comparison between different
dimension cubes. Many applications in the scientific and
engineering settings use datasets which cannot be
contained in the memory of one node processor.
Therefore, timing a serial run is impossible. Also
discussed are metrics which describe: node busyness and
idleness, use of concurrent resources, node production,
and node wait time. A methodology is also discussed
which allows a software developer to time stamp various
components of an application for comparison with other
implementations or other multiprocessing environments.

*Systems Analyst, General Electric Co.,
Space Systems Division, P.O. Box 8048, Bldg A, Rm 33A30,
Philadelphia, PA 19101

INTRODUCTION. The advent of new technology, such as hypercube multiprocessors, generally leads to an evaluation of the performance of that technology. This paper discusses descriptive statistics specifically formulated to analyze and evaluate the performance of hypercube multiprocessor software. These statistics are derived from timing data collected from time stamps placed in the software. A time stamp consists of reading a processor's clock before an event to be timed occurs and again when the event is complete. Subtracting the former clock reading from the latter yields the elapsed time spent processing the event. During software development, time stamps can be placed strategically throughout the software to time various components of the software. Evaluation of these timing data may aid the developer in improving the implementation of an application using hypercube multiprocessors. Comparison of timing data from applications developed under different hypercube configurations is beneficial to both end users and system analysts in making a decision about the best hypercube configuration for the application (1, 2).

Performance metrics used for evaluation of hypercube multiprocessor software in scientific and engineering environments is a new field. The following paragraphs describe the metrics used for performance evaluation of applications implemented on hypercube multiprocessors (see Table 1). Two fundamental time stamps must be defined before a discussion of the performance metrics. First, is the total elapsed runtime of the host, **M**. This time stamp should be incorporated in the host software as the very first and last executable lines of code. This is the basic metric used for comparison between different hypercube configurations and different implementations of the same application. The second fundamental time stamp is the total elapsed runtime of a node, **Ni**, where i depicts the node number. Like the host time stamp, the node time stamp should be implemented as the first and last lines of executable code; however, time spent communicating with the host should not be included in the node elapsed runtime. Node to host and host to node communications are considered overhead and should be applied to the host elapsed runtime but not the node elapsed runtime. Also, time the node spent idle, as in waiting for a message, etc., is not to be included in the node elapsed runtime. The objective of the node's time stamp is to measure that time spent actively executing code "productive" toward the final answer.

Node and/or host time stamps can be obtained for particular software components for analysis of an application or algorithm. Examples of these components may be: composition and decomposition of data buffers, message passing, computing and sorting. These component time stamps are used in the software development phase to obtain a good distribution of the workload among nodes.

Good distribution of work and few communications results in high utilization of the concurrent resources available in a hypercube multiprocessor.

TABLE 1 Hypercube Software Performance Metrics

M = Total runtime of host
Ni = Total runtime of node i
ΣNi = Total runtime of all nodes

Node Busyness, Npi = $\frac{Ni}{M}$; Node Idleness, Nwi = $1-\frac{Ni}{M}$

Concurrency Factor, CF = $\frac{\Sigma Ni}{M}$

Mean Node Runtime, $\overline{N}$ = $\frac{\Sigma Ni}{n}$

Node Production, Np = $\frac{\overline{N}}{M}$; Node Wait Time, Nw = $1-\frac{\overline{N}}{M}$

Node Deviation, NDi = $\overline{Ni}-N$

Speed-up (Sp, SU). Speed-up is traditionally defined as a comparison of runtimes between serial and parallel machines (3,4). Mathematically, speed-up is:

$$Sp = \frac{Ts}{Tp}$$

where:
Ts = time spent processing an operation in a serial environment,
Tp = time spent processing an operation in a parallel environment.

This equation is useful only if a serial run can be obtained for use in the equation. Some applications implemented on a hypercube multiprocessor can not be configured to run on one processor (node) due to memory constraints of the node processors. Another limitation of the equation is that it cannot be used to calculate speed-up between cube configurations using two or more nodes for each run. These limitations on the traditional definition of speed-up have led to modification of the speed-up definition and calculation. Speed-up modified for use with hypercube multiprocessors is defined as the ratio of host execution times between implementations of the same application/algorithm using a different number of nodes; and is calculated:

$$SU = \frac{Tx}{Ty}$$

where:
Tx = time spent processing an operation with x nodes active,
Ty = time spent processing an operation with y nodes active.

The number of nodes active when Tx was obtained must be
less than the number of nodes active when Ty was
obtained. In most circumstances Tx and Ty will be the
host elapsed runtime, Mx and My, respectively.

Speed-up should be a number greater than one
representing the factor used to define the reduction in
time between the two implementations. For example, a
four-node run of an application took three minutes and an
eight-node run of the same application took two minutes,
SU would equal 1.5, i.e., the eight-node implementation
ran 1.5 times faster than the four-node implementation.
When speed-up is one, no speed-up is gained from the
implementation using additional nodes. If speed-up is
less than one, the use of additional nodes has not
produced a speed-up, rather they have produced a
"slow-down". This case commonly occurs with heavy
message passing applications.

Speed-up, SU, can be calculated for applications as
the dimension of the machine is increased (doubling the
number of nodes). This method lends itself well to a
pairwise comparison of runs. This comparison, when
illustrated graphically or tabularly, summarizes speed-up
between each dimension of the hypercube. The expected
speed-up when doubling the number of nodes would be equal
to two. No speed-up would be equal to one, while a
speed-up less than one would be interpreted as a slow
down.

Node Busyness/Idleness (Npi, Nwi). Node busyness and
idleness describe the percent of time active processing
and inactive, respectively, for a particular node,
relative to the host. Node busyness is calculated:

$$Npi = \frac{Ni}{M}$$

Node idleness is calculated:

$$Nwi = 1 - \frac{Ni}{M}$$

Node busyness and node idleness are useful in software
development because they describe how an individual node
is being utilized. Node busyness can be plotted to
illustrate workload distribution (balance). However, a
separate statistic has been developed to describe balance
(see Node Deviation).

Concurrency Factor (CF). The concurrency factor
describes the amount of time spent completing an
application developed on a hypercube multiprocessor over
and above a serial processor. The concurrency factor is
computed:

$$CF = \frac{\Sigma Ni}{M}$$

The closer this factor is to the number of nodes active
in the hypercube machine, the better the concurrent
resources of the hypercube are utilized. If the

concurrency factor is less than one, the application has performed worse than a serial processor regardless of the number of nodes used in the application. Likewise, if the concurrency factor is equal to one, the hypercube has performed only as well as a serial processor.

Mean Node Runtime ($\overline{N}$). Mean node runtime is nearly self explanatory; it is simply the average node elapsed runtime. Mean node runtime is calculated:

$$\overline{N} = \frac{\Sigma Ni}{n}$$

where n is the number of active nodes.

Node Production/Node Wait Time (Np, Nw) Node production and node wait time are statistics which represent the average node busyness and average node idleness, respectively for all active nodes. Node production is a complement of node wait time. Node production is calculated:

$$Np = \frac{\overline{N}}{M}$$

Node wait time is calculated:

$$Nw = 1 - \frac{\overline{N}}{M}$$

Node production, Np, and the mean node runtime, $\overline{N}$, are correlated numbers where N describes the average in terms of time while Np describes the average as a percentage. Ideally node production should approach one while node wait time approaches zero.

Node Deviation (NDi). The node deviation is computed for each node. It is used specifically to illustrate balance graphically and is computed:

$$NDi = Ni - \overline{N}$$

The deviation can be thought of as a residual in some respects. The sum of the deviations will equal zero. A nodes deviation from the mean node runtime will illustrate how much more or how much less, relative to the mean, a node is productive. This illustrates the balance of the workload. Ideally each NDi should be very close to zero. Nodes which deviate more than ± 20 to 30 percent of N are candidates for redistribution of software components in an effort to better balance the work load of the hypercube (see Figure 1).

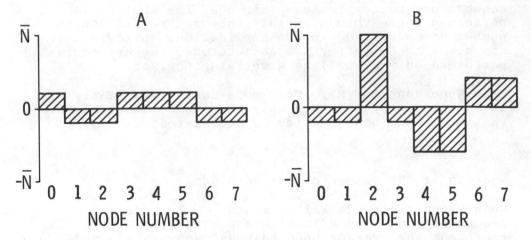

FIGURE 1. Hypothetical plots of NDi's illustrating
applications with good(A) and poor(B) node balance. Zero
represents average node runtime. Negative NDi's indicate
runtimes less then the mean; positive NDi's indicate
runtimes greater than the mean. Figure 1A, Hypothetical
plot of NDi's illustrating an application with good node
balance. All nodes deviate less than 20 percent from the
mean. Figure 1B, Hypothetical plot of NDi's illustrating
an application with poor node balance. Node 2 ran twice
the average time while nodes 4 and 5 ran in half the
average time. Improved balance can be achieved by
reconfiguring software to decrease the runtime of node 2
and increase the runtimes of both nodes 4 and 5.

CONCLUSIONS. The cost of two additional lines of code
for each software module loaded into the nodes and host
is small compared to the potential benefits. The metrics
discussed in this paper represent a means by which an
application implemented on a hypercube multiprocessor
might be evaluated for its performance. This evaluation
can lead to better performance. These metrics also can
be re-utilized in successive implementations until the
desired work distribution, communication topology and
programming techniques are achieved. Admittedly, these
metrics are useful only in a "post-mortem" sense.
However, this is the first step in redefining software
development procedures to include the use of hypercube
multiprocessors. Additional methodologies need to be
developed which address analysis techniques for
identifying how well an application can utilize
concurrent processing, if at all. Mapping the
configuration of an application, which have been
identified as having concurrent traits, into concurrent
processors is defined (5). However, concurrent
architectures are still in an evolutionary state. Also,
techniques need to be developed which allow for the
specification and design of software intended to be
developed on hypercube multiprocessors. These techniques
must also include for management and control of the
software development.

REFERENCES

(1) Y. SAAD and M. H. SCHULTZ, <u>Topological Properties of Hypercubes</u>. Dept. Comp. Sci., Yale Univ., New Haven, CN. Rpt. No. YALEU/DCS/RR-389. 17pp, 1985.

(2) J. E. BRANDENBURG and D. S. SCOTT, <u>Embeddings of Communication Trees and Grids into Hypercubes</u>. Intel Scientific Computers, Beaverton, OR. 7pp, 1985.

(3) C. MOLER, <u>Programming the Intel Personal SuperComputer</u>. Proc. of iPSC Concurrent Programming Workshop. Intel Scientific Computers, Beaverton, OR. np., 1986.

(4) P. MOLLER-NIELSEN and J. STAUNSTRUP, <u>Problem-heap: A Paradigm for Multiprocessor Algorithms</u>. Comp. Sci. Dept., Aarhus Univ., Ny Munkegade, Denmark. 15pp, 1984.

(5) D. P. AGRAWAL and V. K. JANAKIRAM, <u>Evaluating the Performance of Multiprocessor Configurations</u>. Computer 19(5):23-37, 1986.

Communication between Nodes of a Hypercube

ADAM BEGUELIN* AND D. J. VASICEK†

Abstract. Messages on the NCUBE hypercube using the operating system VERTEX are twice as fast as on the Intel cube using the operating system IHOS but slower than the Mark II cube with Cros or Intel iPSC with Cros. Hot spots slow down communication to and from the hot spot on a hypercube. However, hot spots do not impact communication with other nodes of the cube.

Introduction. The Ncube computing system is a hypercube parallel processor capable of supporting 1024 node processors (64 node processors in the Amoco system). The VERTEX operating system supports the transmission of messages between arbitrary nodes of the hypercube as subroutine invocations from Fortran. Using VERTEX, messages are 10 times faster than on the Intel iPSC using Intel's IHOS operating system but slower than the Caltech Mark II or the Intel iPSC running with Caltech's CrOS operating system. The Ncube VERTEX communication rate asymptotically approaches .625 times the node channel communication rate. Contention for communication resources in the presence of imbalance in interprocessor traffic, (hot spot), slows down communication to and from the hot spot but does not greatly impact communication with other nodes of the hypercube.

Comparison of Ncube Internode Communication. The performance of the Ncube can be compared with other hypercube machines by executing the same communication test as that done by Kolawa and Otto in <1>. Kolawa and Otto give results for the Caltech Mark II and the Intel iPSC. K&O configured their hypercube as a ring of processors. Each node writes to its forward neighbor and then reads from its backward neighbor. These operations are repeated n times in a loop. The loop overhead can be estimated by running the loop without sending messages. The loop overhead can then be subtracted from the overall time and the result divided by n, giving the time for a single write/read pair. The time for this operation is dependent on the size of the message being passed. An order 3 hypercube (8 nodes) and 64 bit messages are used in this comparison.

---

* Computer Science Department, U. of Colorado, Boulder, CO 80302.

† Amoco Production Company, Box 3385, Tulsa, Oklahoma 74102.

Machine		Time (microseconds per 64 bit message)
Mark II	(CrOS)	149
iPSC	(CrOS)	320
Ncube	(VERTEX 2.0)	644
Ncube	(VERTEX 2.2)	683
iPSC	(IHOS 3.0)	4,162
iPSC	(IHOS 2.1)	8,910
iPSC	(IHOS 1.0)	11,920

Table 1. Time for a 64 bit write/read pair.

Since the message size is small these results primarily reflect the overhead involved in short messages (i.e. establishing communication links, and allocating buffers). Ncube channels are capable of transmitting 10 bits/μsec. VERTEX achieves .01 of this rate for short messages. It should be noted that since these machines are still very new, their operating systems are undergoing fairly rapid changes. These changes will affect communication times. Results presented here should be considered subject to change.

Communication Time Versus Size and Distance. A relation between communication time, size of message, and distance traveled allows comparison of programming strategies. Each node in the Ncube has its own timer that can be used to time messages, but node timers are not synchronized. Therefore, one way messages are more difficult to measure. So we measure the time required for a message to make a round trip. That is, we read the timer, initiate a round trip message, receive the message, and read the timer again. This is a typical scenario for node communication. We assume that one half of the elapsed time is the average time required for the message to go from its source to its destination. Node timers increment every 1024 machine cycles (146.3 microseconds on our machine) and start when the node is loaded with a program. Therefore, time measurements are in increments of 146.3 microseconds or node timer 'clicks'.

Two programs called SHOUT and ECHO reside on different nodes and make these measurements. SHOUT sends a message to ECHO, and ECHO promptly returns the message. SHOUT sends messages of increasing length and measures how long these messages take to return. Since we have a 64 node hypercube the longest minimal path (VERTEX selects one of the minimal paths) between any two nodes is 6 hops. The SHOUT/ECHO test is done on the cube for distances of 1 through 6.

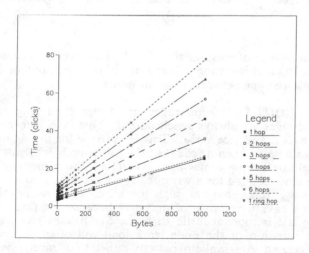

Fig. 1. Node communication time is displayed as a function of the number of bytes sent. One 'click' is 146.3 microseconds.

As Fig. 1 shows, longer messages require more time, and messages take more time to travel longer distances. The information in Fig. 1 can be summarized by the equation (for vertex version 3.2):

```
Msg_time = 1.70 +{Hops*1.53} + {Bytes*0.0128}+ {Hops*Bytes*0.00876},
          {init} {hop ovhd }   {Buffer init }  {Asymptotic rate   }
```

where Msg_time is in clicks (146.3 microsec/click), Hops is the number of edges of the cube the message must traverse, and Bytes is the size of the message in bytes. Theoretically, a message of zero length would require 1.70 clicks or 249 microseconds to travel no distance. The steady state communication rate is 0.00876 clicks/byte/hop or 1.28 microseconds/byte/hop. This is only 50% slower than the node channel speed of 0.8 microseconds per byte.

The average time for the write/read in the ring test was 644 microseconds while the average time reported by the SHOUT/ECHO test for a 64 bit message sent over one link was only 508 microseconds. Fig. 2 shows that messages of all lengths travel more slowly in the ring test configuration than in the SHOUT/ECHO configuration.

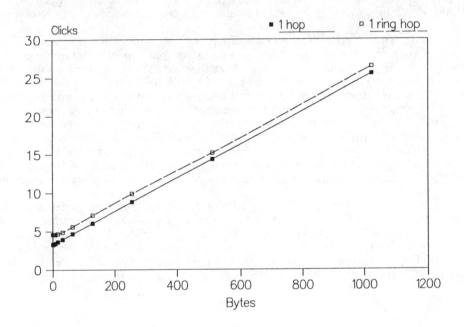

Fig. 2. Comparison of message time for the Ring test with message time for the SHOUT/ECHO configuration. The time given is the number of clicks required to transmit a message between adjacent nodes.

The reason that SHOUT/ECHO messages are faster than ring messages is that SHOUT/ECHO messages are always synchronized. That is, whenever SHOUT sends a message, ECHO reads it and vice versa. This is not true for the ring test. In the ring test each node does a write, then a read, but the target node may not be ready to read a message. It might be writing a message. Therefore, the communication is less synchronized and the time required for a write/read pair averages somewhat longer. In the ring test the message times have a high variance, 90%, while the times of the SHOUT/ECHO test have a variance of only 8% because the ring test requires extra waiting. The ring test is more realistic than the SHOUT/ECHO paradigm for most applications since variation of the node work load will often be essentially random. Messages will be created in a random pattern rather than nicely synchronized. The SHOUT/ECHO test is a benchmark.

The Effect of Hot Spot Contention on a Hypercube. We investigate problems caused by hot spots on the local memory hypercube. Pfister and Norton reported in <2> that slight unbalances in network loads on an Omega network can cause serious degradation in the networks' performance. The problem arises if there is a node in the network which receives more communication activity than the other nodes in the network. The increased activity to this node, or hot spot, causes the times for essentially all the messages in the system to rise dramatically regardless of source or destination. Pfister and Norton describe this as "tree saturation" and propose a solution to the problem by message combining described in <2>. The hypercube's local memory architecture reduces the need for network access and thus the hypercube relies much less on the interconnection network than computers with shared memory such as the NYU Ultracomputer.

We simulate the Omega network with a hypercube by partitioning a 64 node hypercube into two groups of 32 nodes, half of the nodes acting as memory units and the other half acting as processors. Messages travel an average distance of 3.5 hops in this configuration. The processors send 4 byte memory requests to the memories which simply return the messages to the processor. Messages are distributed randomly across the nodes to create a uniform background of message traffic between processors and memories. One node is designated as a hot spot and receives more messages than any other. Messages are timed in the round trip fashion described for the SHOUT/ECHO experiment. The rate at which memory requests are sent out can be varied, as can the percentage of messages going to the hot spot. The above formula for the communication time gives 14.1 clicks for 4 byte messages traveling an average distance of 7.0 hops (a round trip) with the hypercube in the processor/memory configuration. Due to contention for resources, messages will require more than 14.1 clicks. In addition to waiting for message replies, each model processor will check to see if it should be performing other tasks such as generating messages or compiling statistics. As the message rate approaches zero, the message delay levels off at 15.3 clicks per message with uniform distribution of messages. The difference between the 15.3 and 14.1 must be multiprocessing overhead.

The time required for a message should increase as the network gets loaded down. This is shown to be the case in Fig. 3.

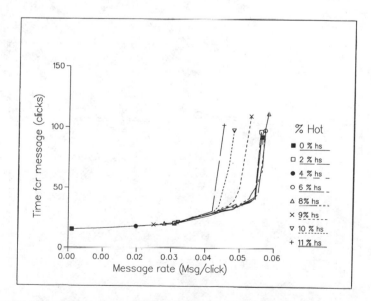

Fig. 3. The number of Ncube node timer clicks required for a message is displayed as a function of the message rate and intensity of hot spot for an Ncube model of the Omega network. One 'click' is 146.3 microseconds.

The 0% hot spot line shows how the message response time increases as the sending rate increases for a uniform distribution of messages. Response time increases as the percentage of messages going to the hot spot increases. This is similar to the results of <2> on Fig. 4, but it differs in several important ways.

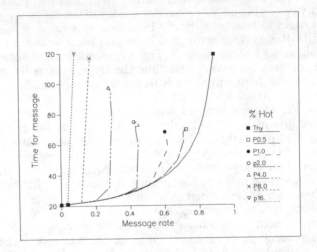

Fig. 4. The number of Omega memory cycles required for a message is displayed as a function of the message rate and intensity of hot spot for the Omega network.

While the message time does increase with the increased traffic to the hot spot, it does not become noticeable until 9% of the traffic is going to one node and messages are being sent out faster than 0.05 messages per click. The other difference is that the messages are not uniformly delayed. Messages to the hot spot are significantly delayed, while messages to the other nodes are unaffected. This can be seen in Fig. 5.

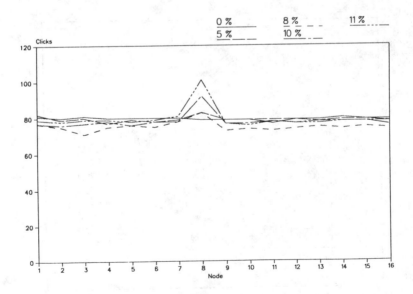

Fig. 5. The average number of Ncube node timer clicks required for a message is displayed as a function of node number and intensity of hot spot for an Ncube model of the Omega network.

The essential difference seems to be the number of connections to each node. The networks are similar in that the maximum distance between nodes is the log of the number of nodes in the network. In the Omega network each node has only one connection to the network, while in the hypercube network each node has log(n) connections where n is the number of nodes in the network. An order 6 hypercube (64 nodes) each node has 6 connections to the network. Each node can send 6 messages and receive 6 messages simultaneously. Each node can support 6 times as much message traffic as the Omega nodes. The 9% hot spot curve on Fig. 3 and the p1.0 curve on Fig. 4 are similar enough to support this argument. In the Omega network the hot spots are a problem because the network connections become overloaded and partition the network. Messages cannot cross saturated links even if they are going to nodes other than the hot spot. The network is partitioned into isolated regions by the saturated paths. Thus, all messages in the network are delayed because of the hot spot. In the hypercube each node has many connections to the network, and so there are fewer chances that a link will be overloaded. The larger number of links available on each node of the hypercube decreases the consequences of one saturated link. However, if all of the links on a node become saturated, then paths of saturated links will divide the hypercube also. As K&O point out the maximum rate of accepting messages for a node with one communication channel is given by $1/(1 + h(p-1))$ where $h =$ hot ratio, and $p =$ number of processors. We modify this for a hypercube. If n is the order of a hypercube then the maximum rate is $n/(1 + h(2^n -1)) \simeq n/(h2^n)$. Thus the order n hypercube is capable of supporting n times greater asymmetry for a given communication rate.

The hot spots do not cause noticeable degradation on the order 6 Ncube hypercube until 10% of the messages are going to the hotspot under nearly maximum network loads. Because of this, message combining or a similar scheme is less useful for the hypercube than it would be for the Omega network.

Direct comparison of the Ncube message time data to the Omega message data requires scaling the message time and rate to comparable values. The message time can be scaled using the message delay for zero message rate. This is 15.28 clicks for the Ncube and 20.8 cycles for the Omega network. Therefore, Ncube delays can be multiplied by the ratio 20.8/15.28 to compare to Omega network delays. If the Ncube message rate is multiplied by 13.10 then the zero percent hot spot Ncube data overlays the Omega zero percent data. Fig. 6 presents Pfister and Norton's Omega network data on the same chart as Ncube message delay data using these two scale factors.

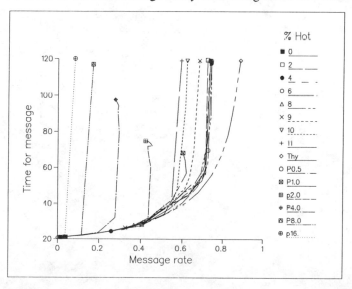

Fig. 6. The normalized time required for a message is displayed as a function of the normalized message rate and intensity of hot spot for the Omega network and Ncube model of the Omega network.

Conclusion. We find that the Ncube hypercube message passing speed for short messages (mostly overhead) is slightly slower than the Caltech Mark II, and the Intel iPSC running the CrOS operating system. The Ncube is 10 times faster than the Intel iPSC running Intel's IHOS operating system. The communication rates for the Ncube can be characterized by the following equation:

```
Msg_time = 1.70 +{Hops*1.53} + {Bytes*0.0128}+ {Hops*Bytes*0.00876},
           {init}  {hop ovhd }   {Buffer init }  {Asymptotic rate   }
```

Where Msg_time is in clicks (146.3 microsec/click). We also find that hot spots in the Ncube hypercube do not cause severe tree saturation.

Benchmarking Hypercube Hardware and Software

DIRK C. GRUNWALD* AND DANIEL A. REED*

Abstract. It has long been a truism in computer systems design that *balanced* systems achieve the best performance. Message passing parallel processors are no different. To quantify the balance of a hypercube design, we have developed an experimental methodology and applied the associated suite of benchmarks to several existing hypercubes. The benchmark suite includes tests of both processor speed in the absence of internode communication and message transmission speed as a function of communication patterns.

Introduction

The appearance of a new computer system always raises many questions about its performance, both in absolute terms and in comparison to other machines of its class. In addition, repeated studies have shown that a system's performance is maximized when the components are balanced (i.e., there is no single system bottleneck). Message passing parallel processors are no different; optimizing performance requires a judicious combination of node computation speed, message transmission latency, and operating system software. Although the interaction of communication and computation can be examined analytically [ReSc83], time varying behavior and the idiosyncrasies of system software can only be captured by observation and measurement.

Because the performance of any system does depend on a combination of hardware and software, our first and primary goal was determining the performance of both the underlying hardware and the fraction of that performance lost due to poor compilers and operating system overhead. Second, we wished to characterize the balance of processing

* Department of Computer Science, University of Illinois, Urbana, Illinois 61801. This work was supported in part by NSF Grant Number DCR 84–17948, NASA Contract Number NAG–1–613 and by the Jet Propulsion Laboratory.

power and communication speed. With these parameters, algorithms can be developed that are best suited to the machine. Finally, we are developing a high–performance, portable operating system for hypercubes, called Picasso, that provides dynamic task migration to balance workloads and adaptive routing of data to avoid congested portions of the network. To meet these goals, it must be possible to rapidly transmit small status messages. Thus, we sought performance data to tune Picasso's algorithms for each hypercube.

Overview

Because any hypercube computation combines both communication and computation [ReFu86], a single number (e.g., MIPS, MFLOPS, or bits/sec) will not accurately reflect the interplay between communication and computation. To explore the interaction of communication and computation, we have developed a hypercube benchmark set and associated methodology. This benchmark set includes four components: simple processor benchmarks, synthetic processor benchmarks, simple communication benchmarks, and synthetic communication benchmarks. The simple processor benchmarks are, as the name implies, simple enough to highlight the interaction between processor and compiler, including the quality of generated code. In turn, the synthetic processor benchmarks reflect the typical behavior of computations and provide a ready comparison with similar benchmarks on sequential machines.

The remainder of the paper examines the processor and communication performance of two commercial hypercubes, the Intel iPSC and Ametek S/14, and the Mark–III prototype developed by the NASA Jet Propulsion Laboratory (JPL). We begin with a brief comparison of these machines.

Hypercube Comparisons

Three of the hypercubes tested are based on the 16–bit Intel 80286 microprocessor. The fourth uses the 32–bit Motorola 68020 microprocessor. Table 1 shows the salient features of each system.

JPL Mark–III. This machine is the latest in a series of hypercubes developed by the California Institute of Technology and JPL. During our tests, a four–node prototype of the Mark–III, running the CrOS–III operating system, was used. CrOS–III provides synchronous, single–hop communication primitives. All test programs were compiled using the Motorola 68020 C compiler provided on the CounterPoint host processor.

Intel iPSC. For all tests, we used a 32–node iPSC system running NX Beta Version 3.0, the latest version of the operating system. This iPSC operating system is derived from

Table 1 Hypercube Hardware Characteristics

	Mark–III	Intel iPSC	Ametek S/14	Ametek S/14 β
Processor	16 MHz 68020	8 MHz 80286	8 MHz 80286	6 MHz 80286
Floating Point	16 MHz 68881	6 MHz 80287	8 MHz 20287	6 MHz 80287
I/O Processor	16 MHz 68020	none	10 MHz 80186	8 MHz 80186
Minimum Memory	4 Mbytes	0.5 Mbytes	1 Mbytes	1 Mbytes
Maximum Memory	4 Mbytes	4.5 Mbytes	1 Mbytes	1 Mbytes
Channels per Node	8	7	8	8
Peak Bandwidth	13.5 Mbits/s	10 Mbits/s	3 Mbits/s	3 Mbits/s

the Cosmic Environment [Seit85] and is functionally equivalent to that system. Programs were compiled using the L–model of the Microsoft C compiler provided with Xenix, the operating system on the hypercube host.

Ametek S/14. A 32–node S/14 system running XOS Version D [Amet86] was used. XOS has capabilities similar to those of CrOS–III. All programs were compiled using the L–model of the Lattice C V3.1 compiler.

Ametek S/14 β. A beta–test version of the S/14 system was used. This machine is functionally equivalent to the S/14, although the processor clocks are slower, and XOS Version 1.1 was used. Programs were compiled using the D–model of Lattice C V2.14 compiler.

Processor Benchmarks

The simple processor benchmarks were based on programs used to evaluate other microprocessors [PaSe82]. The synthetic benchmarks, Dhrystone [Weic84] and Whetstone [CuWi76], were designed to represent typical systems programs and test floating point speeds, respectively. All the benchmarks were written in the C programming language, the only language available on all the machines studied. Unfortunately, this precluded using such standard numerical benchmarks as Linpack [DoBM79].[1] Table 2 describes the tests, their characteristics, and the features they are each designed to test. Table 3, in turn, shows the results of the benchmarks. All results are in seconds unless otherwise noted. In all cases, the 95 percent confidence interval was less than 5 percent of the stated mean.

For those benchmarks involving many procedure calls, in particular the *Fibonacci*, *Sieve* and *Hanoi* tests, the Ametek S/14 provides the best performance of the Intel 80286–based hypercubes. However, all other benchmarks, even the highly recursive *Sort* test, favor the Intel iPSC. Most notably, the Intel iPSC is 4.4 times faster on the Dhrystone synthetic benchmark.

Because the processor architectures for the Intel iPSC and the Ametek S/14 are identical, these dramatic differences must be due to software. To investigate these differences, the *Loops* program was compiled using both the Microsoft and Lattice C compilers and then disassembled. The Intel 80286 provides a 16–bit ALU, while the innermost loop bound in *Loops* requires a 32–bit integer. The Lattice C V2.14 compiler used with the Ametek S/14 β machine invokes a subroutine for 32–bit comparison on each loop iteration. In contrast, the Lattice C V3.1 compiler for the Ametek S/14 expanded the procedure call in–line, providing better performance. Finally, the Microsoft C compiler for the Intel iPSC transformed the innermost loop into two loops, each of which tested a 16–bit integer. The outer loop tested the high–order 16–bits of the loop counter while the inner loop tested the low–order 16–bits.

To further corroborate our view that compiler technology was dominant performance determinant, the *Dhrystone* benchmark was compiled and disassembled using both the C compiler provided with the Ametek S/14 β machine and an Intel 80286 compiler developed by AT&T. The Lattice C compiler yielded 751 lines of assembly code while the AT&T C compiler yielded 467 (unoptimized) and 360 (optimized).

---

[1] With the availability of Fortran compilers for most hypercubes, we are now augmenting the benchmark set.

Table 2 Hypercube Processor Benchmarks

Simple Benchmarks	
Loops	10 repetitions of a 1,000,000 iteration null loop. Tests loop overhead
Sieve	100 repetitions of finding the primes from 1 to 8190. Tests loops, integer comparison, assignment.
Fibonacci	20 repetitions of finding Fibonacci(24). Tests recursion, integer addition, parameter return.
Hanoi	Solve the Towers of Hanoi problem with 18 disks. Tests recursion, integer comparison.
Sort	14 repetitions of quicksorting a 1000–element array of random elements. Tests recursion, comparisons, array references, multiplication and modulus.
Puzzle (subscript)	10 repetitions of Baskett's Puzzle program with subscripts. Tests explicit array subscript calculations and procedure calls.
Puzzle (pointer)	10 repetitions of Baskett's Puzzle program with pointers. Tests use of pointer vs. explicit array subscripts.
Synthetic Benchmarks	
Whetstone	The Whetstone synthetic benchmark. General test of floating point performance, including trigonometric functions, multiplications and divisions.
Dhrystone (no registers)	The Dhrystone synthetic benchmark without register optimization. Tests general integer scalar performance with 'typical' instruction mix.
Dhrystone (registers)	The Dhrystone synthetic benchmark with register optimization. Tests availability and effects of register variables

Table 3 Hypercube Processor Comparison

	Mark–III	Intel iPSC	Ametek S/14	Ametek S/14 β
Loops	8.8	65.6	164.3	263.8
Fibonacci	10.0	39.2	21.3	32.7
Sieve	6.4	21.5	19.3	35.0
Sort	11.8	42.3	83.0	†
Hanoi	4.4	12.5	6.9	†
Puzzle (subscript)	45.5	87.6	97.9	164.3
Puzzle (pointer)	20.2	112.5	491.7	792.4
Whetstone[‡]	684,463	102,637	185,874	7367
Dhrystone (registers)[‡]	3472	724	165	107
Dhrystone (no registers)[‡]	3322	717	167	108

[†]These tests could not be run due to stack size limitations.
[‡]Performance figures in Whetstones or Dhrystones.

Additional conclusions can be drawn from Table 3. The *Puzzle* benchmark exists in two variations. The first variation uses arrays; the second was "optimized" by using explicit pointers and pointer arithmetic rather than implicit array subscript calculations.

On machines with 32–bit integers and pointers, the pointer version typically executes faster because the compiler can more easily optimize the code. On the JPL Mark–III this is the case. With the Intel 80286–based systems, pointer arithmetic is more expensive that array subscript calculations because the former requires 32–bit operations. In contrast, array indexing normally requires only 16–bit quantities.

The floating point performance of the Ametek S/14 is greater than that of the Intel iPSC, primarily due to the faster floating point unit. The Lattice C compiler for the Ametek S/14 β machine uses procedures to implement floating point operations, hence the dramatic performance reduction.

Finally, Table 3 shows that the JPL Mark–III is clearly superior to all machines based on the Intel 80286 microprocessor.[2] Based on the *Dhrystone* tests, a Mark–III node is approximately five times faster than a node based on the Intel 80286. Because of the large performance differential between the Mark–III and the Intel 80286–based hypercubes, it is difficult to compare them.

Simple Communication Benchmarks

To provide a small set of benchmarks that test all link–level characteristics, we have derived three operations that reflect a broad range of common single–link communications. In all the simple communication benchmarks, the programs were structured to provide maximal communication concurrency, using the appropriate idiom in each hypercube operating system. In particular, the Intel iPSC versions use the asynchronous send and recv operations where possible, and the CrOS–III and XOS implementations use such special operations as exchange or exchELT. As with the processor benchmarks, all results are the means of 95 percent confidence intervals, and all intervals are less than 5 percent of the corresponding mean. Figure 1 illustrates the communication patterns tested by each of the simple communication benchmarks.

Simple Transfer

The first test measures transmission speeds across a single link between two processors. Figure 2 compares the four different hypercubes.

If the messages transmitted between nodes are not broken into packets, message transmission time t can be modeled as

$$t = t_l + Nt_c, \tag{1}$$

where t_l is the communication latency (i.e., the startup time for a transmission), t_c is the transmission time per byte, and N is the number of bytes in the message. Statistically, the linear model in (1) is a good fit to experimental data obtained for single link transmissions on all hypercubes we tested. Table 4 shows the result of a least–squares fit of the data to this linear model. Although the measured bandwidth for the JPL Mark–III is higher than the rated peak bandwidth (see Table 1), this anomaly is likely due to the use of a prototype system. The Ametek S/14 has a lower latency than the Intel iPSC, but the higher bandwidth of the Intel iPSC yielded smaller total communication time for messages of more than 150 bytes.

Exchange

---

[2]Informal benchmarks suggest that a single Mark–III node is comparable to a Sun–3/52 workstation.

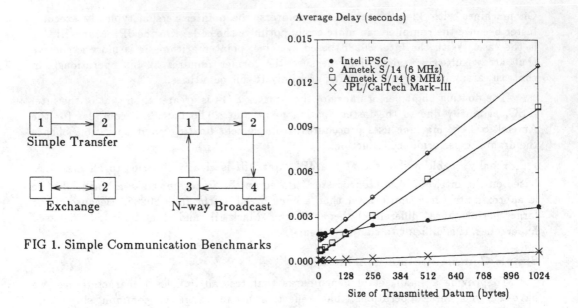

Simple Transfer

Exchange

N-way Broadcast

FIG 1. Simple Communication Benchmarks

FIG 2. Simple Transfer

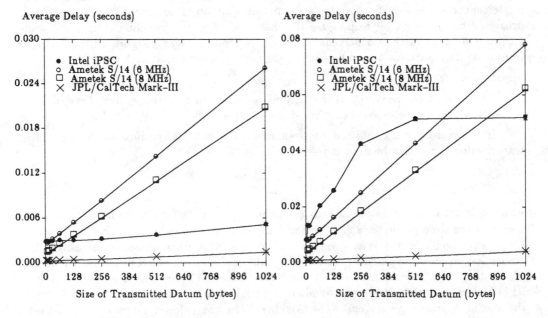

FIG 3. Exchange

FIG 4. N-way Broadcast

Table 5 Hypercube Communication Comparison

	Mark–III	Intel iPSC	Ametek S/14	Ametek S/14 β
Latency (seconds)	9.5×10^{-5}	1.7×10^{-3}	5.5×10^{-4}	1.3×10^{-3}
Transmission time (sec/byte)	5.63×10^{-7}	2.83×10^{-6}	9.53×10^{-6}	1.17×10^{-5}
Bandwidth (Mbits/s)	14.3	2.8	0.84	0.69

The second test was an *exchange* of data values, similar to that in many numerical computations, notably iterative solution of partial differential equations. If full–duplex transmission links were available, this test would measure their effective use.

Comparing the first test, Figure 2, with the second test, Figure 3, shows that, for both the JPL Mark–III and Ametek S/14, the time to complete the exchange is roughly twice that for the simple send operation. However, for the Intel iPSC, the time for the exchange is less than twice the cost of a simple send. Because all four hypercubes provide only simplex communication channels, this differential cannot be attributed to communication overlap. However, the Intel iPSC, with asynchronous message transmissions, can overlap a small portion of buffer allocation time with message transmission; this is the source of the reduced delay. In contrast, the JPL Mark–III provides no equivalent improvement because the CrOS–III operating system permits no asynchrony and executes little code during communication operations.

N–way Broadcast

The third test is an *N*–way broadcast, used when every processor must disseminate a message to all other processors. Because multiple communication links connected to each node can potentially be simultaneously active, this benchmark tests link simultaneity.

The intuitive implementation of this benchmark would use *N* broadcast operations. However, a more efficient approach, for existing hypercubes, uses a *ring broadcast* where node i receives messages from node $i - 1$ and sends messages to node $i + 1$. This requires only $O(N)$ time.

With simplex communication links, the time for a ring broadcast should be approximately six times that for a transmission across a single link. As Figure 4 shows, both the JPL Mark–III and Ametek S/14 exhibit this behavior. Unlike the JPL Mark–III and Ametek S/14, the Intel iPSC has no communication co–processor. This absence is the reason for the iPSC's poor performance.

Synthetic Communication Benchmarks

To study hypercube performance under a variety of communication traffic patterns, we have developed a model of communication behavior. Each hypercube node executes a copy of the model, generating network traffic that reflects some pattern of *spatial* locality. Currently, our model provides three types of spatial locality.

Uniform. Any network node can be chosen as the destination with equal probability. The uniform routing distribution is appealing because it makes *no* assumptions about the type of computation generating the messages; this is also its largest liability. However, because most computations should exhibit some measure of communication locality, it provides what is likely to be an upper bound on the mean internode message distance.

Sphere of Locality. Each node is considered to be the center of a sphere of radius L, measured in hops. A node sends messages to the other nodes inside its sphere of locality with some (usually high) probability ϕ, and to nodes outside the sphere with probability $1 - \phi$. This model reflects the communication locality typical of many programs (e.g., the nearest neighbor communication typical of iterative partial differential equations solvers coupled with global communication for convergence checking).

Decreasing Probability. The probability of sending a message to a node decreases as the distance from the source to the node increases. Specifically, the probability of sending a message l hops is a decreasing power function of the distance. This model reflects the diffusion of work from areas of high utilization to areas of lower utilization.

More detailed descriptions of sphere of locality and decreasing probability routing can be found in [ReFu86]. By choosing parameters for spatial locality, a wide variety of traffic distributions can easily be generated. Finally, additional input parameters control the frequency of message generation and the distribution of message lengths.

Experimental Results

Figure 5 shows the effect of the spatial communication patterns for the Intel iPSC when 16 nodes each sent 3000 messages. For this experiment, the mean message length was 512 bytes, drawn from a negative exponential distribution. As can be seen, the spatial locality distributions can be used to investigate iPSC performance under a variety of conditions. Although space precludes a complete discussion of this and other experiments involving spatial locality, details can be found in [GrRe86].

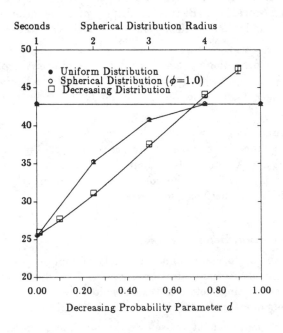

FIG 5. Spatial Communication Locality

Summary

We have defined a collection of benchmarks designed to test both the computation and communication components of hypercubes. These benchmarks include simple processor tests that permit comparison of compilers and synthetic processor benchmarks for comparison with sequential machines. In addition, we defined a series of simple communication benchmarks and used them to determine the transmission latency and communication bandwidth of isolated links. Finally, we outlined a synthetic communication benchmark for testing the communication network when presented with asynchronous, multihop messages.

Acknowledgments

The Concurrent Computation Project at the Jet Propulsion Laboratory provided access to the JPL Mark-III. In addition, Jack Dongarra and Argonne National Laboratory provided access to the Intel iPSC. Their support and help made the benchmarking study possible.

References

[Amet86]   Ametek Computer Research Division, "Ametek System 14 User's Guide: C Edition," Version 2.0, May 1986.

[CuWi76]   H. J. Curnow and B. A. Wichman, "A Synthetic Benchmark," *Computer Journal*, Vol. 19, No. 1, February 1976.

[Denn80]   P. J. Denning, "Working Sets Past and Present," *IEEE Transaction on Software Engineering*, January 1980.

[DoBM79]   J. J. Dongarra, J. R. Bunch, C. B. Moler, and G. W. Stewart, "Linpack Users' Guide," *SIAM Publications*, 1979.

[GrRe86]   D. C. Grunwald and D. A. Reed, "An Experimental Study of Hypercube Performance," Technical Report, Department of Computer Science, University of Illinois at Urbana-Champaign, 1986.

[PaSe82]   D. A. Patterson and C. H. Sequin, "A VLSI RISC," *IEEE Computer*, Vol. 15, No. 9, pp. 8-22, September 1982.

[ReSc83]   D. A. Reed and H. D. Schwetman, "Cost-Performance Bounds on Multimicrocomputer Networks," *IEEE Transactions on Computers*, Vol. C-32, No. 1, pp. 85-93, January 1983.

[ReFu86]   D. A. Reed and R. M. Fujimoto, *Multicomputer Networks: Message Based Parallel Processing*, monograph submitted to *MIT Press*.

[Seit86]   C. L. Seitz, "The Cosmic Cube," *Communications of the ACM*, Vol. 28, No. 1, pp. 22-33, January 1985.

[Weic84]   R. Weicker, "Dhrystone: A Synthetic Systems Programming Benchmark," *Communications of the ACM*, Vol. 27, No. 10, pp. 1013-1030, October 1984.

Hypercube Performance

T. H. DUNIGAN*

Abstract. The performance of three commercially available hypercube parallel processors is analyzed. Computation and communication performance for a number of low-level benchmarks are presented for the Ametek S14 hypercube, the Intel iPSC hypercube, and the Ncube hypercube.

1.1. Introduction. This report summarizes the results of a set of benchmarks run on three commercially available hypercubes. The three cubes are the first generation of the hypercube family of parallel computers, descendants of the pioneering work done at Caltech [9]. The hypercube is an ensemble of small computers interconnected in a communication network with the topology of an n-dimensional hypercube. Each processor, or node, has its own local memory and communication channels to n other nodes. The processors work concurrently on an application and coordinate their computation by passing messages. The architecture is worthy of study because of the wide range of applications that are suitable for the hypercube architecture [4] and because of the attractive cost-performance of the current generation of machines.

We are interested in the performance of hypercubes for several reasons. First, our main area of research is the development of algorithms for matrix computations on parallel computer architectures. To produce algorithms that make effective use of a parallel architecture it is necessary to understand the basic structure of the architecture and the relative performance and capacities of the fundamental components — CPU, memory, and I/O (message passing). Second, a large proportion of our development work is done on hypercube simulators, both to debug and to analyze our algorithms [3]. Performance results from real hypercubes enable us to construct more effective simulators. Finally, a set of benchmarks and performance results can help us evaluate new implementations or architectures.

---

* Mathematical Sciences Section, Oak Ridge National Laboratory, P.O. Box Y, Oak Ridge, Tennessee 37831. Research supported by the U.S. Department of Energy under contract DE-AC05-84OR21400 with Martin Marietta Energy Systems Inc.

In the following section, we summarize the hypercube configurations and programs used in our test suite. Section 2 discusses the three hypercube architectures in more detail, emphasizing the distinctive features of each implementation. Section 3 compares the computational power and memory capacity of the three hypercubes, and section 4 compares their single-channel message-passing capacity. Section 5 illustrates the effect of communication overhead on computations. Section 6 summarizes and looks toward future work.

1.2. Test environment. Three commercially available 64-node hypercubes were used for our benchmark suite. We have both Intel and Ncube hypercubes at Oak Ridge National Laboratory. In addition, Ametek Corporation provided us dial-in access to one of their hypercubes. The configurations utilized in the tests are summarized in Table 1.

Configurations for Tests			
	Ametek	Intel	Ncube
Number of nodes	64	64	64
Node CPU	80286/287	80286/287	custom 32-bit
Clock rate	8 MHz	8 Mhz	7 MHz
Node memory	1024K	512K	128K
Nominal data rate	3 Mbps	10 Mbps	7 Mbps
Node OS	XOS vD1	v3.0	Axis v2.3
C compiler	Lattice C v3.1	Xenix 3.4	CF&G v1.0

Table 1. *Hypercube configurations used in tests.*

The test programs were written in C and were run in the last quarter of 1986. The large model memory option was used with the C compiler for Intel (*-Alfu*) and Ametek (*-ml*), and stack checking was disabled for the Intel and Ncube C compiles. The test suite was selected for simplicity of implementation and widespread use, permitting us to implement the tests with few source changes and to compare the results to other architectures reported in the literature. For the computation tests, the call to the node clock subroutine and the code to send the result back to the host were the only source-code changes made in porting the tests from one vendor to another. Table 2 summarizes the test programs.

2. Configurations. Each hypercube configuration consists of a hypercube attached to a host processor. The host processor is used for program development and as an interface to the outside world for the hypercube. A typical hypercube application program consists of one or more node programs and usually a host program to provide input data and report results. Besides the application program, each node contains a small operating system that manages message passing.

2.1. Ametek System 14. The Ametek System 14 consists of from 16 to 256 nodes attached to a VAX host via a 16-bit parallel interface. Only the corner node, node 0, is attached to the host. The host runs DEC's ULTRIX operating system, and thus provides the full set of software management tools associated with UNIX. The hypercube nodes are Intel 80286/80287 chips running at 8 MHz with one million bytes of memory per node. The node-to-node communication channels are controlled by a separate communication coprocessor, a 10 MHz Intel 80186.

Benchmark Summary	
Caltech	arithmetic operations + - * /
Sieve	finding primes using integer arithmetic
Floatmath	double precision floating point arithmetic
Dhrystone	integer arithmetic and functions
Whetstone	double precision floating point arithmetic and built-in functions
Malloc	free memory test using 1K malloc
Ring	Gray-code ring message passing
Echo	message echo
Spincom	N iterations of a loop timed with simultaneous message routing

Table 2. *Benchmark programs used in tests.*

Each node-to-node data channel is rated by the vendor at 3 million bits per second. Such a vendor rating implies communication shall never exceed that data rate. Only C is supported at present; Fortran eventually will be supported. Since the architecture of the host and nodes are different, a cross-compiler is provided on the VAX for developing node programs. To take advantage of the 80287, however, one must compile C programs on an IBM PC attached via a serial line. A set of command procedures are provided to make this acceptably invisible. The hypercube is presently a single-user subsystem.

The node operating system, XOS, is structured much like the Crystalline system [9]. Communication is synchronous at the application level and only between nearest neighbors. There is no implicit message routing. Message passing is based on 8-byte packets, though multipacket subroutines are provided as well. Various routines are provided for ring and mesh communications as well as full hypercube topology routines [1]. A growing set of application libraries is available. A simulator is provided on the host to assist in program debugging and analysis. Command procedures enable one to switch from simulator mode to hypercube mode with little effort.

2.2. Intel iPSC. The Intel iPSC consists of from 32 to 128 nodes attached to an Intel 310 host processor. The host and node processors are 80286/80287 running at 8 MHz. Each node has 512K bytes of memory and is attached to the host via a global communication channel. (Intel now offers a 4.5 Megabyte/node option as well as an optional vector processing node with 1 Megabyte of memory.) The host operating system is Xenix and supports the typical UNIX program development environment. Since the host and node CPUs are the same, one compiler supports both environments. Fortran and C are supported on the hypercube, and Lisp is supported with the large memory option. The hypercube is presently a single-user subsystem.

The node operating system supports message routing, asynchronous communications, and multi-tasking within each node [6]. A node-to-host logging facility is provided for application debugging and diagnostics. Messages larger than 1024 bytes are broken into 1024-byte segments. A node debugger is provided on the host as well as a simulator. A growing set of application libraries is available.

2.3. Ncube. The Ncube hypercube consists of from 4 to 1024 nodes attached to an 80286/80287 host. The node processor is a 32-bit chip that was designed by Ncube and is presently running at 7 Mhz. It is expected the chip will soon run at 10 Mhz. The chip contains both floating point and message handling facilities. It is surrounded by 128K of memory (soon to be 512K). The chip is also used as the interface processor between the hypercube and the host. The hypercube may be divided into logical subcubes for multi-user use [8].

The host operating system is "UNIX-like" but still lacks many of the features of a mature UNIX environment. Both C and Fortran compilers are provided along with a node-level debugger. The node operating system supports message routing and asynchronous communication. The application library and program development tools continue to grow. A four-node board is available for use on an IBM PC/AT.

3. Computation Benchmarks.
3.1. Arithmetic tests. To compare our test results with earlier hypercube benchmarks performed at Caltech [7], we implemented a series of tests to measure the arithmetic speeds of the CPU for integer and floating point arithmetic. The time to perform a binary arithmetic operation and assignment in a loop was measured for both single and double precision scalars in C. The time for the loop overhead was subtracted, and the resulting time divided by the number of iterations to give a rough estimate of time-per-operation. Table 3 shows the results of those tests. In the table, Fortran notation is used for clarity to describe the data types; the tests were run in C.

Arithmetic Times microseconds				
	Ametek	Intel	Ncube	VAX
INTEGER*2 +	2.5	2.5	4.3	3.3
INTEGER*4 +	5.2	5.0	4.9	1.8
INTEGER*2 *	3.9	4.0	8.7	5.1
INTEGER*4 *	194.0	36.5	8.9	2.4
REAL*4 +	51.2	38.0	18.2	7.1
REAL*8 +	32.4	41.5	11.2	4.6
REAL*4 *	52.4	39.5	20.6	9.3
REAL*8 *	33.9	43.0	14.7	6.5
REAL*4 *+*+*	39.8	23.1	12.0	5.6
REAL*8 *+*+*	28.3	24.1	8.3	4.4

Table 3. *Arithmetic operation times (microseconds).*

For purposes of comparison, times for a DEC VAX 11/780 with FPA and running UNIX 4.3 bsd are included. The times illustrate both CPU speed and compiler differences. The only anomaly is the large INTEGER*4 multiplication time for the Ametek, because it uses a subroutine to perform the computation. The last two entries give the average operation time for a sum of three products. Such an expression permits the arithmetic units to retain intermediate results and get improved performance. It should also be noted that C requires that all floating point expressions be calculated in double precision and that all integer expressions be calculated in the word size of the machine. The default integer word size is 16 bits for the Intel and Ametek machines and is 32 bits for the VAX and Ncube. The degree to which the compilers comply to the C requirement varies. The Ncube is roughly three times faster than the Ametek and Intel hypercubes, operating at 0.12 megaflops to the 80287's 0.04 megaflops.

3.2. Synthetic tests. The results from the arithmetic operation tests are consistent with the next level of tests performed using a simple integer test of finding primes (*sieve*) and a sequence of dependent floating point operations (*floatmath*). The times for 100 iterations of finding the primes from 1 to 8190 and for 256,000 repetitions of the double precision floating point arithmetic operations are illustrated in Figure 1 and Table 4. In the *sieve* variables of type *register int* are used, which means 16-bit arithmetic for the Ametek and Intel machines and 32-bit arithmetic for the Ncube and VAX.

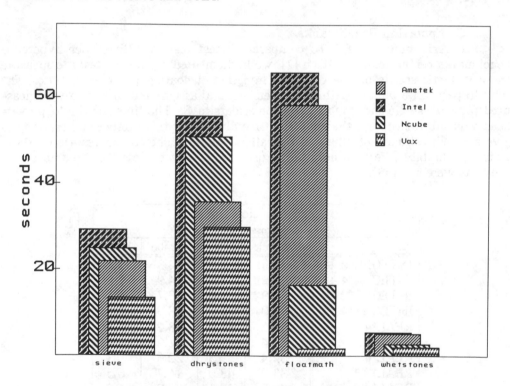

Figure 1. *Synthetic computation tests.*

Figure 1 also shows the times for 50,000 iterations of the Dhrystone test. The test exercises integer arithmetic, function calls, subscripting, pointers, character handling, and various conditionals [10]. There are no floating point calculations. The times are from tests using the *register* storage class of C. The test uses the type *int* which means 16-bit arithmetic for the Intel and Ametek C compilers and 32-bit arithmetic for the Ncube and VAX. The figure also compares times for one million Whetstone operations. The Whetstone test measures double precision

Simple Computation Tests seconds				
	Ametek	Intel	Ncube	VAX
Sieve	22.0	29.3	25.0	13.6
Floatmath	58.5	66.3	17.7	1.9
Dhrystone	35.9	55.9	51.1	30.0
Whetstone	5.3	5.6	2.9	2.2

Table 4. *Execution time in seconds for various test suites.*

floating point performance, conditionals, integer arithmetic, built-in arithmetic functions, subscripting, and function calls [2]. The Intel C generates an additional move instruction for references to external variables which explains the slower performance of the Intel compared to the Ametek.

3.3 Memory utilization. The amount of memory available to an application on a node was measured using the *malloc()* function of C. The test program requested memory in 1,000 byte increments. Table 5 shows the amount of memory available to the application program compared to the total amount of physical memory for the test configuration.

Memory Capacity K Bytes			
	Ametek	Intel	Ncube
Total	1024	512	128
Available	912	366	90

Table 5. *Node memory capacity and usage.*

The difference between the total and available memory gives a rough measure of the amount of memory required by the node for its operating system, message buffers (in the case of Intel and Ncube), and C run-time environment. For the 80286 architectures, memory is managed in 64K segments, so there may be additional small chunks of free memory available. The Intel user also can specify the amount of memory to use for message passing buffers; twenty buffers were specified for the memory test. As was mentioned in section 2, Intel now has a 4.5 million byte memory option, and Ncube will soon provide 512K bytes of memory.

For any computer system, the amount of main memory is a critical metric, and there never seems to be enough. For the hypercube, the amount of node memory can determine the size of problem that might be solved. Shortage of memory is paid for in problem-solution time (due to the I/O or message-passing delays) and in programmer time (due to the additional coding required to multiplex the node memory).

4. Communication Benchmarks.

4.1. Ring test. As a first test of node-to-node communication speed, the time to pass a message 100 times around a 64-node Gray-code ring was measured. The Gray-code mapping ensures that a distance of only one hop is required between each node and its successor in the ring. The Ametek implementation used the *pass*

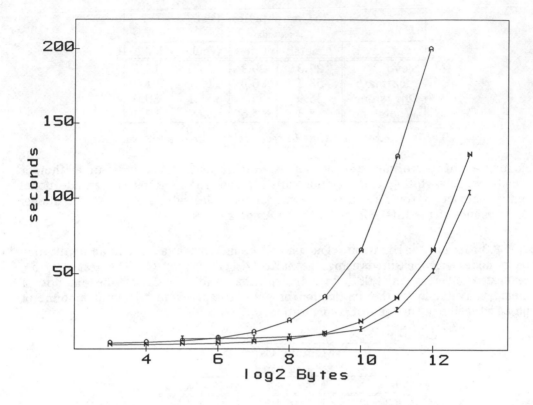

Figure 2. *Times for 100 revolutions of 64-node ring.*

Ring Times			
seconds (KB/s), 64-node ring, 100 revolutions			
Length	Ametek	Intel	Ncube
8	4.0(13)	6.7(8)	3.0(17)
16	4.5(23)	6.8(15)	3.1(33)
32	5.5(37)	6.9(30)	3.3(62)
64	7.4(55)	7.1(58)	3.8(107)
128	11.3(72)	7.5(109)	4.8(170)
256	19.1(86)	8.4(195)	6.8(241)
512	34.7(94)	10.1(323)	10.8(305)
1024	65.9(100)	13.6(482)	18.7(351)
2048	128.2(102)	26.5(494)	34.5(380)
4096	252.8(104)	52.3(501)	66.1(396)
8192	502.2(105)	104.1(504)	129.5(405)

Table 6. *Gray-code ring times in seconds.*

message-passing primitive. *Sendw/recvw* were used on the Intel, and *nwrite/nread* were used on the Ncube. Figure 2 shows the times for messages of size 8 bytes to 8192 bytes. The Ncube is the fastest for small messages, but falls behind the Intel machine for messages larger than 256 bytes — but by less than a factor of two in both cases. The Ametek is slightly faster than the Intel for messages smaller than

32 bytes but is three times slower for messages larger than 1024 bytes. For smaller messages, times increase by only a few percent as the message size is doubled. Table 6 lists the times as well as the node-to-node data rate in bytes-per-second.

4.2. Echo tests. To further measure communication data rates, an echo test was constructed. A test node sends a message to an echo node. The echo node receives the message and sends it back to the test node. The test node measures the time to send and receive the message N times. The nodes utilized the same message-passing functions as in the ring test. Figure 3 shows the data rates for the three hypercubes over various message sizes, where the echoing node is one hop away. Consistent with the ring results, the Ncube is fastest for small messages; the Intel is fastest for large messages. The Ametek peaks out just over 100 KB/s or about 28% of its maximum single-channel bandwidth. The Ncube levels off around at around 405 KB/s or about 46% of its bandwidth. The Intel levels off at around 505 KB/s or about 40% of its maximum bandwidth. The figure also shows the cross-over points where one machine performs better than another. Also evident in the Intel curve is the distinct discontinuity at the 1024 byte message size. Recall from section 2 that Intel breaks messages larger than 1024 bytes into 1024-byte segments. Tables 8, 9 and 10 at the end of this section detail the data exhibited in the figures.

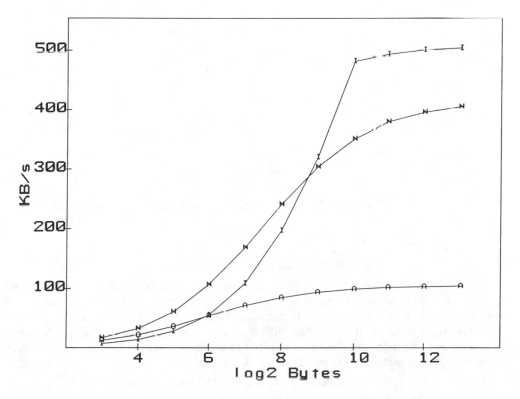

Figure 3. *One-hop data rates.*

The Intel and Ncube node operating systems support message routing so we can use the echo test to measure data rates for passing messages to non-adjacent nodes. Figure 4 illustrates the performance of the Intel and Ncube machines for passing messages of four different sizes to nodes from one to six hops distant. (Tables 9 and 10 give data rates for additional message sizes.) As before, Ncube is faster for smaller messages. The curves are what would be expected from a store-and-forward network, with the data rate decaying in proportion to the number of hops. Of note, however, is the Intel curve for messages larger than 1024 bytes. Segmenting the message into 1024-byte packets will yield higher data rates for multi-hop messages, since a packet may be forwarded while the next packet arrives. But due to the way Intel acknowledges forwarded versus single-hop messages, the data rate is actually higher for a message traveling two hops than for a message traveling just one hop!

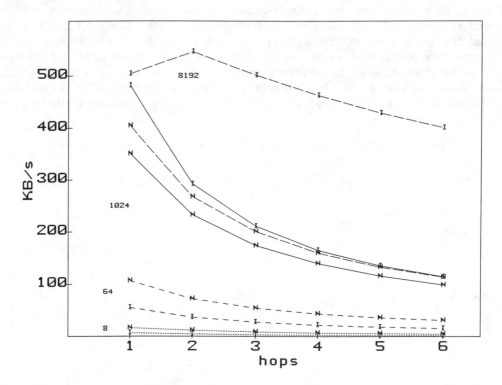

Figure 4. *Multi-hop data rates.*

Measuring the time it takes a node to send a message to itself can give a rough estimate of the amount of software overhead involved in message management, since no actual data transmission is required. Figure 5 shows the data rates for a node sending a message to itself for different size messages. The overhead in passing a message is made up of several components, some fixed and some proportional to the size of the message. Typical components are:

>the application must gather the data into a contiguous area,

>overhead in performing the call to the message-passing subroutine,

>context switch to supervisor mode,

buffer allocation,

copying the user data to the buffer area,

constructing routing and error checking envelopes,

obtaining the communication channel,

DMA transfer with memory cycle stealing,

interrupt processing on transmission completion.

The receiving node must

obtain buffers for message receipt, usually initiated by an interrupt request,

receive the data via DMA cycle stealing,

copy the data to the user area, or, if it is a message to be forwarded, obtain a channel and initiate a DMA output request.

To this is added the delay due to the actual transmission on the hardware medium, delays due to contention for the media, and delays due to synchronization and error checking acknowledgements. For segmented address spaces, like the 80286, additional overhead may be incurred for segment crossings. One or both of the DMA's may directly access the user data area, eliminating a data copy operation.

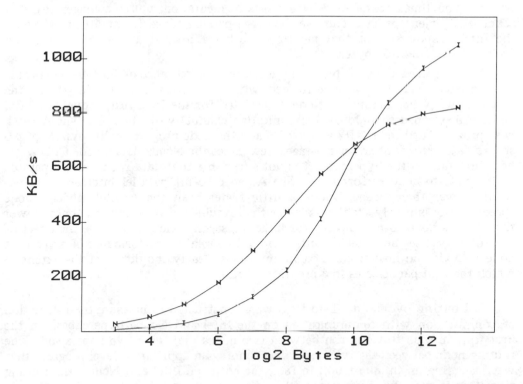

Figure 5. *Node-to-self data rates.*

Empirically for all three hypercubes, the communication time for a one-hop message is a linear function of the size of the message. That is, the time T to transmit a one-hop message message of length N is

$$T = \alpha + \beta N$$

where α represents a fixed startup overhead and β is the transmission time for one byte. Table 7 shows the startup and transmission time coefficients that were calculated from a least-squares fit of the echo data for single-hop messages.

Coefficients of Communication microseconds			
	Ametek	Intel	Ncube
Startup (α)	563.5	862.2	446.7
Byte transfer (β)	9.5	1.8	2.4

Table 7. *Least-squares estimate of communication coefficients.*

The coefficients are in close agreement with data reported by by Grunwald and Reed [5] and show the improvements made in the Intel message-passing software over earlier results reported by Kolawa and Otto [7]. As we have shown, actual transmission times are affected by message segmentation, buffer management, and acknowledgement policy. The fixed message-passing times for small messages on the Intel system suggest that messages are being padded up to some minimum packet size of 32 or 64 bytes.

We also used the echo test to measure the performance of host-to-node communications. The test was performed with the corner node (node 0) for the Ametek and Ncube machines. Node 0 was used for the Intel test, though all Intel nodes are attached to a global communication channel with the host. The Ametek host program utilized *rdnIH* and *wtnIH* and the node program used *pass*. Figure 6 shows data rates for various message sizes. Since the Ncube uses a node CPU as its host interface to the hypercube, it is not surprising that data rates are comparable to its node-to-node performance. The Ametek 16-bit parallel interface is somewhat slower than Ncube, but is a little faster than the Ametek node-to-node speeds. Intel is nearly six times slower than Ncube and is nearly ten times slower than Intel's node-to-node speeds for large messages. One can also see the effect of the 1024-byte segments on the Intel curve. The relative performance of a vendor's node-to-node and host-to-node communications clearly should affect the extent to which the host participates in a problem solution.

5. Routing overhead. Two tests were constructed to measure the interaction of computation with communication on the Intel and Ncube hypercubes. In the first test, an echo test was run between two nodes that were two hops apart. The routing node between the two nodes was running an application level program that was executing an infinite loop. In fact, for both the Intel and Ncube, the routing algorithm is such that the return path of the echo message is different from the initial message path, thus two routing nodes participate. With both routing nodes running the infinite loop, data rates for the two-hop echo were calculated for various message sizes. The data rates were the same as measured when the routing

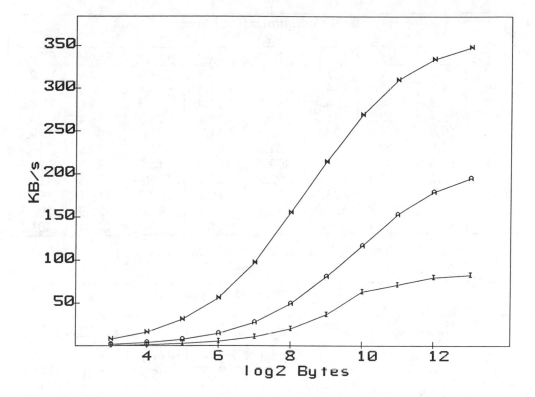

Figure 6. *Host-to-node data rates.*

| Ametek Communication Speeds | | |
| KB/s | | |
Length	Host	1 hop
8	2.0	12.5
16	3.8	22.4
32	7.5	36.9
64	14.6	54.6
128	27.4	71.8
256	49.1	85.3
512	80.1	94.1
1024	114.4	99.2
2048	152.2	102.0
4096	179.5	103.4
8192	196.9	104.2

Table 8. *Ametek host-to-node and node-to-node data rates.*

nodes were idle. Thus the computing an application might be doing on a node will have no effect on the communication throughput of the node. This is due to the high priority given to communication interrupts.

Intel Communication Speeds KB/s								
Length	Host	Self	1 hop	2 hops	3 hops	4 hops	5 hops	6 hops
8	0.7	7.6	7.1	5.0	3.7	2.9	2.4	2.1
16	1.3	15.3	14.2	10.0	7.4	5.8	4.9	4.2
32	2.7	30.5	28.4	19.7	14.5	11.5	9.6	8.2
64	5.3	70.0	55.6	37.1	28.1	22.3	18.4	15.8
128	10.4	116.4	108.9	70.1	51.7	41.3	34.4	29.3
256	19.8	222.6	196.9	124.9	91.4	72.1	59.9	50.9
512	36.6	409.6	320.0	202.8	147.3	115.7	95.2	80.9
1024	63.2	660.7	481.9	292.6	211.1	165.1	135.6	114.7
2048	71.4	835.9	494.5	405.5	318.7	263.4	216.1	190.5
4096	79.8	963.8	501.0	489.1	421.1	369.0	321.9	296.8
8192	82.7	1050.1	504.1	546.1	501.4	462.8	424.4	401.1

Table 9. *Intel single channel data rates.*

Ncube Communication Speeds KB/s								
Length	Host	Self	1 hop	2 hops	3 hops	4 hops	5 hops	6 hops
8	8.0	26.9	17.2	11.7	8.9	7.1	5.9	5.1
16	15.9	52.4	33.1	22.4	16.9	13.7	11.4	9.8
32	30.9	98.9	61.6	41.7	31.4	25.2	21.1	18.1
64	56.4	177.8	106.6	72.1	54.4	43.7	36.5	31.3
128	97.7	293.9	169.5	114.4	86.1	69.1	57.6	49.4
256	155.4	435.4	241.2	162.2	121.4	97.1	81.0	69.5
512	214.2	574.1	304.8	203.4	152.4	121.9	101.6	87.1
1024	269.9	683.6	351.1	233.4	174.9	139.8	116.4	99.8
2048	310.2	755.6	380.0	252.2	188.8	150.8	125.6	107.6
4096	334.2	797.1	396.3	262.8	196.6	157.0	130.7	111.9
8192	347.7	819.9	404.0	268.4	200.7	160.3	133.4	114.3

Table 10. *Ncube single channel data rates.*

A second test was constructed to measure the effect that routing messages had on node computing speed. First, the time for a node program to spin a loop N times was measured with no communications. The node program was then run on the routing nodes of the two-hop echo test. The execution times for the loop were measured for various message sizes of the echo test. Figure 7 shows the degradation in computing speed due to routing for various message sizes for both the Intel and Ncube hypercubes. The vertical axis is the percentage the loop program slowed down from its speed with no communication. For small messages, Intel and Ncube hypercubes exhibit about a 30% loss in "application" computation speed. As the message size increases, the interrupt rate from incoming messages decreases and the slowdown diminishes. For the Intel hypercube, however, the interrupt rate increases again for messages larger than 1024 bytes, since Intel breaks messages in to 1024-byte packets. We have already shown that Ncube can transmit about twice as many 8-byte messages per second as Intel, thus the overhead for routing is even less for Ncube if we were to plot slowdown versus messages-per-second.

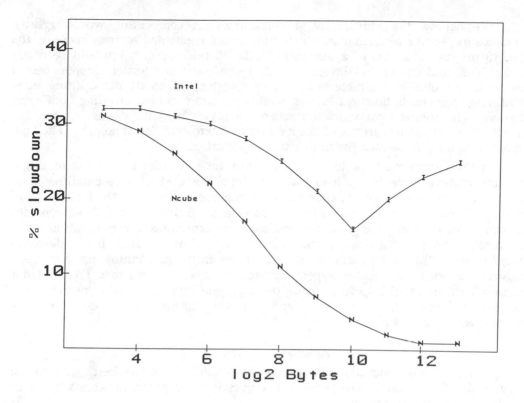

Figure 7. *Application slowdown due to routing.*

6. Conclusions. We have shown that despite differences in hardware and software the three hypercubes have very similar performance characteristics. On the other hand, even with identical computing hardware, computation speeds will differ due to compiler and operating system differences. Table 11 summarizes the performance characteristics of the three hypercubes.

Figures of Merit			
	Ametek	Intel	Ncube
Data rate (KB/s)	104	504	405
Kiloflops	40	40	120
8–byte transfer time (μs)	640	1120	470
8–byte multiply time (μs)	33.9	43.0	14.7
Comm./Comp.	19	26	32

Table 11. *Summary performance figures.*

The data rates represent the 8192-byte transfer speeds, and the kiloflops rate is calculated from compound expression results of the Caltech suite. The 8–byte transfer time is based on the 8–byte, one–hop, echo times. The structure of a hypercube algorithm will be dictated by the amount of memory available on a node, the host-to-node communication speed, and the ratio of communication speed to computation speed. As can be seen from the table, the three hypercubes have roughly equivalent communication–to–computation ratios. The ratio was calculated conservatively using the 8–byte transfer and multiply times.

We believe the addition of a communication coprocessor would greatly enhance hypercube performance. Furthermore, the segmented address space of the 80286 proves somewhat of a nuisance. A 32-bit node processor would be desirable. The need for several levels of node-to-node communication support seems evident. It would be desirable to have a very high speed, small, non-routing, non-buffering communication system as well as a more robust, routing, buffering option. The robust communication scheme could be used for debugging and for applications requiring full use of the hypercube interconnection topology. The high speed option could be used for time-critical applications.

In the future, we hope to expand the test suite in order to test the message-passing systems under heavy load and to measure the total message-handling capacity of a node using multiple channels simultaneously. Running the Caltech Crystalline operating system on the Intel hardware could provide useful performance information on the price paid for buffered, asynchronous communication with automatic routing. Since one of the main thrusts of our research is the development of algorithms for matrix computations, we anticipate running many of these algorithms on the available hypercube architectures. Performance results from these algorithms will help to measure the aggregate throughput of hypercube systems as an ensemble of processors and will supplement the component performance results of this report.

Acknowledgements

The author is gratefully indebted to the Ametek Computer Research Division of Arcadia, California for answering many questions and providing access to one of their System 14 hypercubes.

References

[1] Ametek Computer Research Division, *Ametek System 14 User's Guide*, Ametek V12970, Arcadia, CA, May, 1986.

[2] H. J. Curnow and B. A. Wichman, *A Synthetic benchmark*, Computer Journal, 19 (1976).

[3] T. H. Dunigan, *A Message-passing Multiprocessor Simulator*, Tech. Rept. ORNL/TM-9966, Oak Ridge National Laboratory, Oak Ridge, TN (1986).

[4] G. C. Fox and S. W. Otto, *Algorithms for concurrent processors*, Physics Today, May 1984, pp. 50-59.

[5] Dirk C. Grunwald and Daniel A. Reed, *Benchmarking hypercube hardware and software*, this volume.

[6] Intel, *iPSC User's Guide*, Intel 17455-03, Portland, Oregon, October, 1985.

[7] A. Kolawa and S. Otto, *Performance of the Mark II and Intel Hypercubes*, Hypercube Multiprocessors 1986, ed. M. T. Heath, SIAM, Philadelphia, 1986, pp. 272-275.

[8] Ncube, *Ncube Handbook*, Ncube V1.1, Beaverton, OR, 1986.

[9] C. L. Seitz, *The cosmic cube*, Comm. ACM, 28 (1985), pp. 22-33.

[10] R. Weicker, *Dhrystone: a synthetic systems programming benchmark*, Comm. ACM, 27 (1984), pp. 1013-1030.

On the Performance of
the FPS T-Series* Hypercube[†]

DONNA BERGMARK‡, JOAN M. FRANCIONI§, BRENDA K. HELMINEN§
AND DAVID A. POPLAWSKI§

Abstract. The performance of interprocessor links, vector board memory and vector pipelining of the Floating Point Systems T-Series Hypercube has been measured. The measurements, carried out at Cornell and Michigan Tech on both 16 and 32 node systems, used the Occam language and vendor supplied procedures for performing various communication, vector and I/O operations. The results presented here include the bandwidth and latency of one and two way communications of various size blocks and the megaflop rate of simple vector operations such as DAXPY. The data transfer rates within vector memory have been measured as related to the scatter/gather operations and the machine's restrictions on data placement. The speed of the links under heavy utilization and processor loading, and the performance of more complicated vector and matrix operations were also measured. In addition to the above, reliability of the system, vector memory requirements and availability, and other miscellaneous topics are discussed.

1. Introduction. The FPS T-Series hypercube, announced in the spring of 1986, is a distributed memory multiprocessor in which each processor (node) contains a high speed floating point vector processor. As with all new computers, performance ratings are produced in order to give prospective users an idea of the capabilities of the machine. Early ratings are often given in peak speeds rather than observed speeds under real operating conditions, and many aspects of the performance of the machine are not reported or are presented in gross generalization.

Michigan Technological University was the first paying customer for the FPS T-Series, and has had a 32 node system installed and operating since June of 1986. Cornell University obtained a 16 node system at about the same time. Both groups were interested in the actual capabilities and performance of the machine for our own uses, and we both began benchmarking our machine as soon as they were installed. These studies have focused on the

---
*Floating Point Systems, Inc., Beaverton, Oregon
† This work partially supported by NSF Grant DCS-8404909.
‡ Cornell University, Ithaca, New York 14853
§ Department of Mathematical and Computer Sciences, Michigan Technological University, Houghton, Michigan 49931

measured performance of various components of the machine when running real programs.

This paper summarizes the results of the performance studies done so far. It includes measurements of the speed and latency of the interprocessor communication links, floating point performance in both scalar and vector modes, and the speed of moving data around within a node (most importantly, the speed of scatter/gather).

2. Methodology. Our approach to measuring performance was to write small program segments in the only language available, Occam I [3], and use Occam level procedures and functions provided by FPS for communicating between processors, executing vector operations, and moving data. The functions and procedures are documented by FPS in the T-Series User Guide [1]. We did not try to write any assembly language routines, did not expand any procedures or functions in line to reduce the overhead of the calls, etc. On the other hand, we were in most cases fairly aggressive about finding the best way to do a particular thing, given the above constraints.

In early August, FPS replaced the existing microprocessors (an INMOS Transputer [4]) in the Michigan Tech machine. The new Transputer fixed an important bug in the system and also improved the performance of the machine (in some cases dramatically). The results reported herein are for the new Transputers except in a few cases where the difference in performance is negligible.

Processes in the Transputer run at one of two priority levels. The default priority level is the normal level, but by using the PRI PAR construct in Occam, a process can be run at the higher priority. Priority processes are not time sliced. They run until they complete or block. When a priority process completes or blocks, another priority process is run, or if there are no other priority processes ready to run, a normal process is run. When a blocked priority process becomes unblocked, it preempts a normal priority process if one is running. Normal priority processes are time sliced every 1 millisecond.

All vector processing performance measurements used high priority processes. This is because the result of a vector operation must be stored within a fixed period of time (approx. a millisecond) or the result will be undefined. A normal priority process may get interrupted by a high priority process or because its time slice has expired, and therefore not be able to store the result in the given time. Performance measurements for most other aspects of the machine were made using both normal and high priority processes.

3. Results.

3.1. Communication. Before nodes can communicate in the FPS T-Series, a procedure called **set.links** must be executed. This procedure picks, for a given node, from one to four links which will be enabled for communication. Nodes at the other ends of the chosen links must also execute the set.links procedure. The process executing the procedure will not continue execution until both ends of all communication links specified are *connected*. In effect, this synchronizes those nodes doing set.links to each other. Before a different set of links can be established, the **release.links** procedure must be executed which releases all of the node's links. This procedure must also be executed before communication with the outside world (via RS232 ports on the system board for each module) or disk I/O can be performed. Since every set.links is matched with a release.links, the time to execute both of these procedures was measured (as opposed to each individually).

Set.links/release.links is a fairly time consuming procedure. Table 1 summarizes the time for various combinations of parameters.

Link(s) Established	Milliseconds
1 (within module)	0.327
4 (within cabinet)	0.335
5 (between cabinets)	0.345
1,2	0.436
1,2,3	0.551
1,2,3,4	1.166

Table 1 - Set.links/Release.links Timings

A module in the T-Series is eight nodes whose binary node numbers differ in the lower three bit positions. A cabinet contains two modules. The set.links times for a single link differ only slightly for two nodes within a single module versus two nodes in separate cabinets.

Communication in the FPS T-Series is synchronous. That is, both the sender and receiver must be executing communication commands simultaneously for communication to take place. If the sender executes an output command but the receiver has not executed an input command, the process executing the output command waits. Similarly, if the receiver executes an input command but the sender has not executed an output command, the process executing the input command waits. In both cases, the processes continue only when the communication is complete.

Communication speeds were measured in three ways. The first was where each even numbered node communicated with its corresponding odd numbered node in one direction, i.e., each node was doing one way communication on one link. The second method of communication was where each even/odd numbered pair of nodes communicated in both directions, i.e., two way communication on one link. The third method of communication was where each node communicated with four neighboring nodes simultaneously, i.e., two way communication on four links. Because only four links can be operating simultaneously in the T-Series, this is the maximum bandwidth possible for a given node.

Communication speeds for normal and high priority processes are summarized in Figures 1 and 2 respectively.

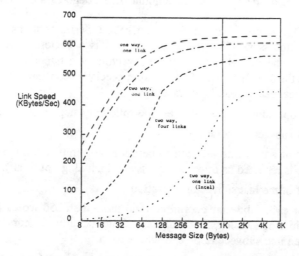

Figure 1 - Communication Speeds (Normal Priority Processes)

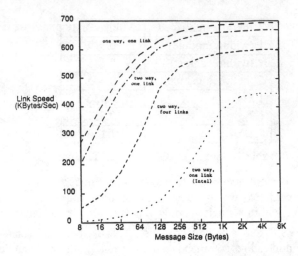

Figure 2 - Communication Speeds (High Priority Processes)

The one-way, single link communication speed for 8192 byte messages using a high priority process is over 694 thousand bytes per second. The performance degrades linearly with the message size, and the latency (i.e., the time to send a 0 length message) was determined analytically to be approximately 19 microseconds. The aggregate bandwidth of a single node occurs when all four links are transmitting in both directions in parallel. For messages of length 8192, the aggregate bandwidth of a single node is 4 * 2 * 603 = 4824 thousand bytes per second (i.e., 4.824 megabytes/second).

For comparison purposes, the speed of two way communication over a single link in a node of the Intel iPSC/d5 was measured. This is shown as the lowest (dotted) line in Figures 1 and 2. The T-Series's communication speeds considerably exceed the Intel's. However, the T-Series has no software for routing, buffering, etc. Consequently it does not pay the overhead in sending extra routing information with every message and does not handle asynchronous communication. If similar software was added to the T-Series, a degradation in the speeds would be expected. At this time the amount of the degradation is not known.

3.2. Floating Point Operations. Each node in the FPS T-Series contains a high speed pipelined floating point processor. The processor can add two vectors at a hypothetical peak speed of 8 megaflops and can also multiply two vectors at a hypothetical peak speed of 8 megaflops. For functions such as DAXPY (double precision constant times a vector plus a vector), the hypothetical peak speed is 16 megaflops.

To perform a vector operation on the T-Series, the following steps must be executed:

(1) Initiate the first subvector operation.

(2) Store the result of a previous subvector operation, and initiate the next subvector operation. This step is repeated as often as necessary (including not at all).

(3) Store the result of the last subvector operation.

The vector length for each subvector operation is no more than 256 words (128 double precision numbers or 256 single precision numbers). Consequently, vectors of more than 256 words must be broken into subvectors of 256 words each.

There are other restrictions on vectors. All vectors must be aligned on a 64 word boundary, and vectors that are not on a 256 word boundary must be shorter than 256 words. The result of any vector operation destroys the previous contents of an entire 256 word block of memory, even if the specified vector length is shorter than 256 words.

The measured performance of vector processing in the T-Series did not approach the hypothetical peak speeds mentioned above. Figure 3 shows the number of megaflops achieved for various vector lengths when adding a vector to a vector (the results are for double precision numbers - single precision did not work at the time). The performance was measured in two ways: one with a loop to repeat the second step described above, and one with the second step completely unrolled (i.e., a sequence of subvector operations repeated as often as required to operate on the entire vector. Note that the highest achieved performance was approximately 4 megaflops for vectors of 8192 elements, as opposed to a peak speed of 8 megaflops.

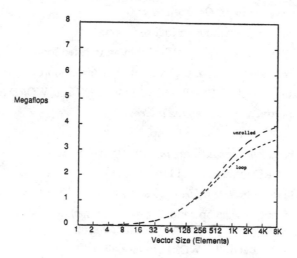

Figure 3 - Vector Performance, Vector + Vector (Double Precision)

Figure 4 shows the number of megaflops achieved for various vector lengths when computing a scalar times a vector plus a vector (DAXPY). The highest achieved performance was approximately 7 megaflops for vectors of 8192 elements, as opposed to a peak speed of 16 megaflops.

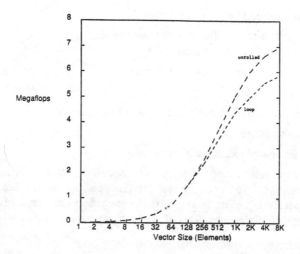

Figure 4 - Vector Performance, Scalar * Vector + Vector (Double Precision)

Scalar floating point performance was also measured. A DAXPY operation ran at approximately 6.8 kiloflops (i.e., 0.0068 megaflops), which was expected considering that scalar operations are implemented by software procedures.

3.3. Data Movement. Moving data around the memory in a node of the T-Series will often be required to meet the alignment and size restrictions for vector operations, and for performing vector operations on non-contiguous data. There are several ways in which to move data from one place in memory to another:

Moving an Occam array to an Occam array:

 (1) Assignment (:=) within an indexed loop.

 (2) PUTWORD and GETWORD within an indexed loop.

 (3) Occam channel IO (! and ?) within an indexed loop.

 (4) Occam channel IO (WORD.SLICE.OUTPUT and WORD.SLICE.INPUT)

Moving an Occam array to an absolute address:

 (6) PUTWORD in an indexed loop.

Moving data from an absolute address into an Occam array:

 (7) GETWORD in an indexed loop.

Moving data from one absolute address to another:

 (8) The identity vector operation. Since this method uses the vector processing unit, it has restrictions on alignment and size.

 (9) GETWORD and PUTWORD in an indexed loop.

Because of the inability to specify the address of a variable in Occam and because the calls to the vector procedures require addresses, only methods (5), (6), (7) or (8) would be used to move data that is used by the vector processing unit. Since method (7) only works for consecutive data, it cannot be used for gather/scatter. The best speeds for the categories above are:

Moving an Occam array to an Occam array:

 0.475 megabytes/second for non-consecutive data.
 4 megabytes/second for consecutive data,

Moving an Occam array to an absolute address:

 0.477 megabytes/second.

Moving data from an absolute address into an Occam array:

 0.463 megabytes/second.

Moving data from one absolute address to another:

 0.432 megabytes/second for non-consecutive data. From 0.05 to 32 megabytes/second for consecutive data, depending on the length (8 to 65536 bytes respectively). The rate is just the megaflop rate for a given vector length (see Figure 3) times the size of a double precision floating point number (8 bytes).

The vector processing speeds approach 4 megaflops for adding vectors of double precision floating point numbers. This translates into two streams of data in and one stream out at 32 megabytes/second per stream. With best speeds for moving non-consecutive data of less than half a megabyte/second, it is clear that the time to do gather/scatter will totally dominate the time to perform the corresponding vector operation.

4. Remarks.   Our experience with the FPS T-Series has led us to several conclusions. First, the machine has very fast and reliable node-to-node communications, especially when compared to other hypercubes such as the Intel iPSC. Each link is very fast, and four links can be communicating simultaneously with very little degradation. However, this high speed communication is possible only once links have been chosen, which was shown to be a very time consuming operation. For applications that need to reset the links often, communication performance is severely degraded since a significant amount of time will be wasted resetting the links.

The machine has good vector floating point performance if the application matches the various data alignment and size restrictions, and if gather/scatter is done very infrequently. If not, then a tremendous amount of time will be spent moving data around, and the performance will be severely degraded (easily by a factor of 100). The alternative of doing scalar instead of vector arithmetic also results in extremely poor performance.

In [2], the relative speeds of communication, moving data and vector arithmetic were shown using the hypothetical peak speeds in the ratios. These ratios are quite different when observed speeds are used. Table 2 shows the results, where the time to communicate a given sized vector is normalized to 1.

	Comm.	Data Move	Vector
Peak	1	10	130
Observed	1	1	100

Table 2 - Peak versus Observed Speed Ratios

In summary, from our limited experience, the FPS T-Series hypercube appears to be a machine that, if the application matches its restrictions on communication and vector processing and does little scalar processing, is quite fast and easy to use. The software supplied with the machine is definitely crude, but should benefit greatly from a period of test and evaluation. Programming in Occam has proven not to be a major problem, although we suspect that users with existing codes in some other language will balk at having to do a rewrite. It is clear, as with many new machines, that there are rough edges that must be smoothed out.

5. References.

1.   FLOATING POINT SYSTEMS, T-Series User Guide 860-0002-004A, May 23, 1986.

2.   J. L. GUSTAFSON, S. HAWKINSON and K. SCOTT, *The Architecture of a Homogeneous Vector Supercomputer*, Proceedings of the 1986 International Conference on Parallel Processing, August, 1986, 649-652.

3.   INMOS LIMITED, *Occam Programming Manual*, Prentice-Hall International, London, 1984.

4.   C. WHITBY-STEVENS, *The Transputer*, SIGARCH Newsletter *13*,3 (June, 1985), 292-300.

Baseline Measurements on the Mark II Hypercube

JIM QUINLAN* AND DAN SIEWIOREK*

Abstract: This paper reports the performance of a collection of test programs run on the Mark II hypercube using the CrOS II operating system. These measurements were taken as a first step towards an architectural evaluation of hypercube based computers. Baseline measurements include the message passing routines for both the synchronous and asynchronous modes of CrOS II. The programs measured include FFT, finite difference, matrix multiplication, and finite element. One program, the finite difference using synchronous Jacobi iterations, was programmed and measured for both modes of CrOS II, providing an interesting comparison between the two methods of communication. Finally, a finite difference program, using asynchronous iterative techniques which cannot be employed in the synchronous communication mode, was measured and showed significant speed-up over synchronous algorithms.

1 Introduction

Performance measurements of a novel architecture such as the hypercube invite comparison to either existing uniprocessors or other concurrent processors. As with any computer architecture, however, the measured performance of a hypercube reflects not only the architecture itself but also a number of obfuscatory factors, including instruction set architecture, compiler proficiency, the operating system, algorithmic differences, and choice of applications. When ignored, these factors make architectural comparisons based on measurements unconvincing if not misleading.

In addition, measurements alone rarely provide enough insight for a comprehensive understanding of an architecture's components, their interactions, and their individual effects on performance. A model of execution of the hypercube, however, would aid the design, refinement, evaluation, and understanding of the hypercube architecture, as well as providing insight for application programmers to decompose their programs. It is our intent to construct a performance model of the hypercube to perform a comprehensive analysis of this architecture, and to possibly use this model as a means of comparison to other multiprocessors.

---

* Department of Electrical and Computer Engineering, Carnegie Mellon University, Pittsburgh PA 15213

Previous modelling work at Caltech [3] is based on simple analytic equations that calculate communication and processing units. This model is accurate for many synchronous applications, but is inadequate for irregular applications, asynchronous applications, or hypercubes employing different communications systems.

As the first step in constructing a hypercube execution model, measurements have been taken on the Mark II hypercube at Caltech. These measurements shall guide the construction of the model and provide validation once it is completed. If necessary, additional measurements will be taken as the construction of this model may be an iterative process. Once the model is completed, its parameters can be varied to reveal new insight into the operation of the hypercube.

Some of the results of the programs measured in this paper have been published in independent studies by Caltech. This paper is unique by presenting the results of many measurements in one succinct and cogent paper, and by presenting new data which has not been published previously.

The rest of this paper is organized as follows. Section 2 briefly describes the Mark II architecture and its corresponding operating systems. Section 3 presents the results of several communication measurements. These measurements are from both the synchronous and asynchronous message passing systems. Section 4 describes the results of four well known programs run on the Mark II: FFT, finite difference, matrix multiply, and finite element. Measurements of these four programs are given for varying data size and hypercube dimension. Section 5 investigates further the finite difference program by employing asynchronous iterative techniques.

2 The Mark II Hypercube

In the Mark II hypercube, there are two computers: the hypercube ensemble and the host. The host, an Intel 310 multitasking computer, performs many functions including program downloading and hypercube I/O. The node processor is an 8 Mhz, 16 bit Intel 8086 microprocessor with an Intel 8087 math coprocessor. Each node has 14 point to point one-way communication lines with adjacent nodes. Each of the 7 adjacent nodes requires two such lines to provide for duplex communication between nodes. Each point to point connection is terminated by an 8 byte FIFO, which allows the processor to write an 8 byte packet and continue processing even if the communication channel is busy. Communication is always done via 8 byte packets whether the communication mode is synchronous or asynchronous. When a packet arrives at a FIFO, it notifies its respective node computer via an interrupt, although for polled communication these interrupts are ignored.

There are two message passing operating systems that run on the Mark II. The first is known as the crystalline operating system, or CrOS II, and is used for most of the applications. In CrOS II, each node can only send messages to adjacent nodes. If a node must send a message to a non-adjacent node it must be explicitly routed by the applications programmer. In CrOS II communications interrupts are disabled: when node i sends a packet to adjacent node j, the packet is not consumed by node j until a read is performed. When node j executes a read call it polls the appropriate communications buffer to see if any packets have arrived. Note that if node j chooses not to read, and node i tries to send a few more packets, node i will be blocked until node j issues a read and makes room for the new packets in the FIFOs. Choosing CrOS II as the communication paradigm has serious implications: CrOS II is suited for applications with synchronous algorithms, since every time a node wishes to send a message it must synchronize with the target node.

The lesser used operating system, IDOS, is asynchronous by nature and can be used to send messages to non-adjacent nodes, transparent to the application programmer. When a packet is received by a FIFO, the FIFO interrupts the main processor which stores it to a receiving buffer, or, when the packet is to be forwarded, to a buffer that is designated to be forwarded to another node.

3 Communication Measurements

This section presents results of timings performed on communication routines for IDOS and CrOS II.

3.1 CrOS II

The smallest unit of communication on the Mark II is a packet, or 8 bytes. CrOS II allows users to read and write single packets by calling two routines, *rdELT* and *wtELT*, which are written in assembly language.

CrOS II has more advanced communications routines that involve more than two nodes and can send more than one packet. For instance, a number of processors may call the *shift* routine and a specified number of packets will be shifted: each processor will shift out a number of packets to an adjacent node and, in the same operation, shift in a number of packets from an adjacent node. The *shift* routine iteratively calls *rdELT* and *wtELT*, and since these routines are blocking, the *shift* routine effectively runs in lockstep across all of the processors. A better description of the *shift* and other routines is given in [2].

Timings were taken for both the *rdELT* and *wtELT* routines. Both routines may block the calling processor, but when taking these measurements the conditions were such that the routines would never block. The *wtELT* routine was measured to take 72 μsec. The *rdELT* routine takes 64 μsec. The end to end transfer time, defined as the time when node *i* calls *wtELT* to the time node *j* returns from its *rdELT* call, was measured to be 93 μsec. In this measurement node *j* calls *rdELT* before node *i* calls *rdELT* so node *j* is already waiting for the packet prior to its arrival.

Three other communication calls, *shift, pass, and pipe*, were timed as a function of the number of packets transferred per processor. These results match those found in an independent report done at Caltech [5].

3.2 IDOS

The asynchronous message passing system IDOS [4] used on the Mark II makes it possible for one node to send a message to any other node using a single operating system call. This action is transparent to the intermediate nodes in the hypercube that store and forward the message to its final destination. Unfortunately, a small packet size (8 bytes) and the absence of an I/O processor on the Mark II node precluded an efficient implementation of a packet switching communications network. As will be shown by the data presented in this section, IDOS is effective for only nearest neighbor communication and performance degrades rapidly for multiple-hop messages or under system conngestion.

When a message is sent in IDOS, the program gives the OS the buffer which contains the message data. The sending processor is blocked until the message is sent to an adjacent node which may or may not be the target node. If the message must go through an intermediate node, the message is reassembled by the intermediate node and flagged for forwarding. The message is reassembled packet by packet; every time a packet arrives at an intermediate node an interrupt is generated and the node stops processing and saves the packet in a forwarding buffer. Because the message is reassembled and forwarded rather than forwarded on a packet by packet basis, the message passing system is most effective for messages to adjacent nodes.

When a message is completely assembled at its destination, a specific message handling routine, written by the application programmer, is called by the OS. This routine may copy the message contents or perform anything desired by the programmer.

Several tests were performed to measure the performance of the message passing system. The time required to send a one packet message is 404 μsec, which is about five times slower than a CrOS II *wtELT*. Figure 1 shows the time per packet taken for messages of distance one, three, and five as a function of message length. These times are end to end: the time taken from when the source node calls the send to the time when the destination node returns from its user supplied service routine. A copy of the message is usually made inside this service routine.

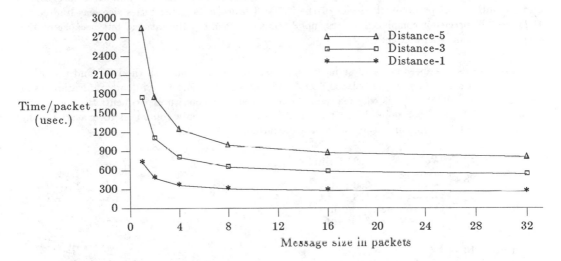

Figure 1:   Timing of IDOS Messages

If two messages need to be forwarded through the same outgoing channel, the node processor actually halts all execution until one of the messages is sent. This deficiency will cause computation speed to plummet if there is much message congestion.

4 Programs

Measurements were taken on four programs: FFT, finite difference, finite element, and matrix multiply. The results of the finite element timings are not presented here; they can be found in [7]. These four programs are both easily understood and useful in ordinary numerical computation. Most measurements were taken on a 32 node hypercube, although at times working and measurements were taken on only 16 nodes due to hardware availibility. Larger hypercubes are operable but were not available for these experiments. Also, sometimes it was impossible to measure single node timings; some programs had excessive single node execution times while other programs required data capacity in excess of that of one node.

Typically, both the execution times and the speed-up figures are given for each program. Speed-up is defined as the time taken for one processor over the time taken for N processors.

Many hypercube research papers use efficiency - defined as the speed-up divided by N - as a performance metric; both speed-up and efficiency are alternative ways of measuring multiprocessor performance.

4.1 FFT

The Fast Fourier Transform (FFT) is an efficient, well known algorithm for computing the Discrete Fourier Transform of a complex valued series whose length is a power of two. A recursive version of the algorithm which performs an in place recursive FFT had been written at Caltech. In this program the complex valued series is distributed across a one dimensional array of processors. The program is by no means optimal; a number of improvements were considered, such as making the program iterative, but never implemented.

The measurements of the FFT were made while varying two factors: the number of processors and the number of points in the series of the FFT. Unfortunately, the series size was limited to 1024 double precision complex numbers, not because of memory limitations, but because of the way the program was written.

Figure 2 plots the speed-up of these measurements. As can be seen with the FFT and the other three programs, emphasis is placed on manifesting the effects of communication and synchronization delays; this is why many of the measurements concern experiments that use small data sizes. Certainly 32 point FFTs have little use; they are only computed to exacerbate the degradation due to communication and synchronization.

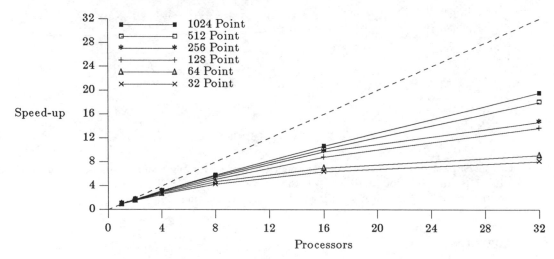

Figure 2: Speed-up of FFT

Figure 2 shows that even for nominal sized experiments (1024 Points), the speed-up is much less than linear. The FFT exhibits the worst performance of the four programs. The reason for this is that the FFT algorithm requires nodes to communicate with non-adjacent nodes: at the end of the FFT the locations of the final results are permuted across the processors, and non-adjacent node communication is required to assemble the FFT series in its proper order. Since the program uses synchronous communications, it explicitly routes the data through intermediate nodes to achieve non-adjacent node communication. The FFT would have been much easier to write using the asynchronous communication system IDOS, although it is unclear whether performance would have improved since IDOS is not efficient.

4.2 PDE: Finite Difference

Many physical phenomena in nature can be expressed in the form of a partial differential equation (PDE). One of the most widely accepted numerical methods to solve PDEs is by finite difference, which is both powerful and straightforward. In this section, the performance of a second order, two dimensional finite difference algorithm is measured for varying grid and hypercube sizes.

For an elliptic PDE, the method of finite differences yields an iterative equation for each grid point: the new value of each grid point is the average of its four neighboring grid points. Because the values needed for this computation are locally obtained and the algorithm used is synchronous, the finite difference program is well suited for implementation on the hypercube.

The finite difference program used in this study performs a synchronous Jacobi iteration on single precision grid points. Other methods are explored in Section 5. The solution of large PDEs on a single node demand the use of single precision due to limited memory capacity.

The grid of the PDE is mapped on a two dimensional node mesh: for 1 processor, a 1 by 1 mesh; two processors, 2 by 1; four processors, 2 by 2; eight processors, 2 by 4; 16 processors, 4 by 4; and 32 processors, 4 by 8. Measurements were also taken for when the grid is mapped on a linear array of processors, but are not presented in this paper.

Figure 3 shows the corresponding speed-ups. As expected, speed-up increases with the grid size. Note that the speed-up decreases as the number of processors increases. This is due to the decreasing communication to computation ratio for each node, which is more evident for smaller grid sizes that already have a small communication to computation ratio.

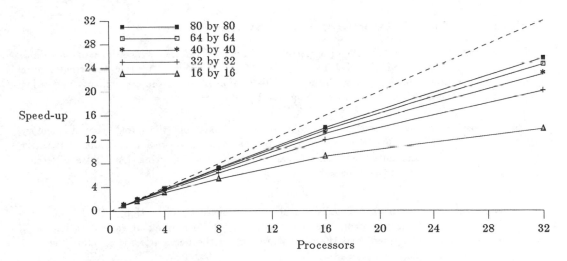

Figure 3:   Speed-up PDE (Jacobi)

4.3 Matrix Multiply

The third program measured in this study was a square matrix multiplier. In this program, the two matrices to be multiplied are stored on a two dimensional mesh of processors. Briefly described, each processor multiplies whatever sections of the two matrices it has at the time, stores the results, and then exchanges its matrix subsections with other processors.

The optimum mesh configuration for this algorithm is a square; in the cases where a square mesh configuration was not possible, the best configuration, defined by perimeter to area ratio, was used instead.

Figure 4 presents the speed-up for the matrix multiply algorithm. The results show that the algorithm performs well except for very small matrices.

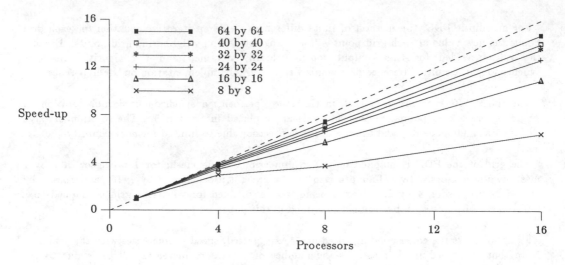

Figure 4:   Speed-up for Matrix Multiply

5   Solution of PDE: Asynchronous vs. Synchronous

This section presents the results of experiments in which different variations of the finite difference method are used to solve Laplace's equation. Section 4.2 presented results of a synchronous Jacobi algorithm using CrOS II. This section presents the experiments measuring asynchronous versions of the finite difference method.

These experiments are based on previous work [6] done on the Cm* shared memory multiprocessor. In this work, finite difference programs with various asynchronous iterative methods were coded and measured. In the same manner, the following four finite difference programs were measured on the hypercube:

- **Synchronous Jacobi I** - This is the algorithm measured in section 4.2. In this algorithm, all of the processors are synchronized at the beginning of each iteration, new values are computed, and the results are sent to the necessary nodes before the next iteration begins.

- **Synchronous Jacobi II** - This is the same algorithm as above except that it is implemented in the asynchronous communication system IDOS.

- **Asynchronous Jacobi** - This is the same as the synchronous version in IDOS except that the processors are not synchronized and one node may update another node's boundary values at any time. However, updates are incorporated only at the beginning of an iteration, so all of the boundary values used for a given node change only at the start of an iteration. The update of a boundary is performed as an atomic action; computation stops and does not resume until all of the points of a boundary are updated.

Determining convergence of the asynchronous algorithms is much more difficult than that of the synchronous algorithms. At each iteration, a token is passed though all of the processors which deposit the value of their maximum residual variable. When the token returns to its sender, the maximum residual is compared to the convergence threshold. This overhead pertains to the asynchronous algorithms only.

- **Asynchronous Gauss-Seidel** - This is the same as the asynchronous Jacobi except that values are used immediately after they are computed. Neighboring nodes may update nodes boundary values at any time, and these new values will be used immediately.

There is nothing novel about these algorithms except that they have been implemented on the hypercube. Even though the hypercube does not have shared memory, IDOS allows a similar paradigm to be implemented, and the algorithms used in the Cm* experiments are equivalent to those used here.

The last two algorithms are identical to those developed in [1]. In this work, Baudet developed sufficient conditions for convergence.

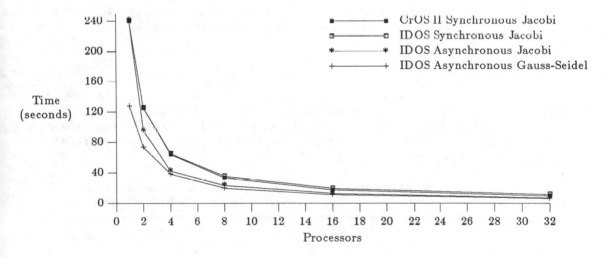

Figure 5:   Times for Finite Difference

Figure 5 shows the execution time for the four different finite difference algorithms. The two synchronous Jacobi algorithms perform roughly equal. The asynchronous Jacobi algorithm performs better than both synchronous Jacobi algorithms but is slower than the asynchronous Gauss-Seidel algorithm.

Figure 6 presents the speed-up of the four different algorithms. Note that the asynchronous Jacobi is superlinear. Although there exists a class of algorithms that exhibit superlinear speed-up, finite difference algorithms are not known to be in this class, and the data shown is more likely the result of either measurement errors, programming errors, or anomalous convergence behavior, rather than the result of true superlinear performance.

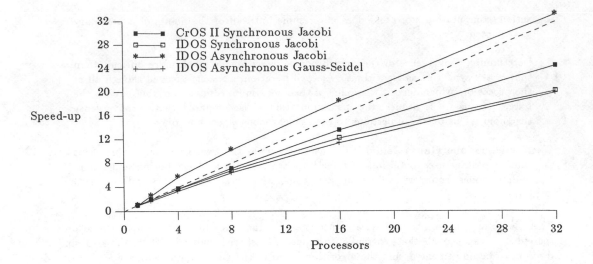

Figure 6:   Speed-up for Finite Difference

Also, previous measurements on Cm* concluded that speed-up grows with the asynchrony of the algorithm. Figure 6 shows no such behavior and the reasons for this remain unexplained.

6 Conclusions

This paper summarizes a set of tests and measurements that were taken on the Mark II hypercube. First, the communication performance was measured for both communications systems, CrOS II and IDOS. Measurements of four programs, the FFT, finite difference, matrix multiply, and finite element, were also taken on the Mark II. The performance of different finite difference algorithms was also explored.

These tests were taken to help guide the construction of a hypercube computation model. The construction of such a model will aid in understanding the dynamics of hypercube computation, and will provide a means to compare and contrast the hypercube to other computer structures.

7 Acknowledgments

This work would not have been possible without the cooperation of Caltech and JPL for allowing me to stay at Caltech to use their hypercubes. All of the people at Caltech and JPL were helpful and friendly; special thanks go to Geoffrey Fox, Jaisim Kim, David Walker, and Barbara Zimmerman. Credit also goes to the authors of the programs used in this study: John Salmon and David Walker for the FFT, finite element, and the finite difference; Steve Otto for the matrix multiply.

This work has been supported in part by the Ballistic Missile Defense Advanced Technological Center and AT&T Bell Laboratories. The views contained in this paper are those of the authors and should not be interpreted as representing the official policies, either expressed or implied, of BMDATC or AT&T Bell Laboratories.

8 References

[1] Gerard M. Baudet.
The Design and Analysis of Algorithms for Asynchronous Multiprocessors.
PhD thesis, Carnegie-Mellon University, April, 1978.
Published as technical report CMU-CS-87-116.

[2] *Nearest Neighbor Concurrent Processor Programmer's Manual*
Caltech/JPL, Pasadena, California, 1986.

[3] Geoffrey Fox et. al.
Solving Problems on Concurrent Processors.
Volume I, to be published.

[4] Mark Johnson.
An Interrupt-Driven Communication System.
Technical Report Hm-137, Caltech, February, 1985.

[5] A. Kolawa and S. Otto.
Performance of the Mark II and Intel Hypercubes.
Technical Report CCCP-254, Caltech, February, 1986.

[6] Levy Raskin.
Performance Evaluation of Multiple Processor Systems.
PhD thesis, Carnegie-Mellon University, August, 1978.
Published as technical report CMU-CS-78-141.

[7] David Walker et. al.
A Comparison of the Performance of the Elxsi 6400 and the CALTECH Hypercube,
in *Second Conference on Hypercube Multiprocessors.* SIAM, September, 1986.
To be published.

A Comparison of the Performance of the Caltech Mark II Hypercube* and the Elxsi 6400†‡

DAVID W. WALKER§, GEOFFREY C. FOX§, ALEX HO§ AND GARY R. MONTRY¶

Abstract. Previous work has investigated the use of the pre-conditioned, conjugate gradient (pcg) algorithm in solving finite element problems on the multi-processor Elxsi 6400, and has shown how the optimal use of cached and shared memory can result in faster code. In this paper the implementation of the algorithm on both the Caltech hypercube and the Elxsi 6400 are discussed. It was found that on both machines the pcg part of the code runs with efficiency greater than 90% for all problems large enough to be of interest. Sequential code can be ported to a shared memory machine without making algorithmic changes, however, extra coding is required to ensure cache coherency. When porting code to a hypercube it is often necessary to make algorithmic changes. A good implementation of the code discussed here on a shared memory machine would use a hypercube type of algorithm, with software support for hypercube message passing.

(1) Introduction

The work presented here arises from an on-going collaboration between researchers at the Sandia National Laboratories and the Caltech Concurrent Computation Project (C^3P). The purpose of this collaboration is to compare the implementation and performance of algorithms on the multi-processor Elxsi 6400 computer and the 32-node, Caltech Mark II hypercube (see, eg., Tuarzon et. al. [1]). This comparison provides insights into the relative merits of shared memory and distributed memory machines, and addresses the issues of efficiency, portability, and programming style.

(2) The Problem

For the initial stages of this study the following simple test problem was chosen :

Solve Laplace's equation, $\nabla^2 \psi = 0$, on the unit sphere, subject to the boundary condition $\psi(1, \theta, \phi) = \cos \theta$.

Since this problem possesses axial symmetry about the $\theta = 0$, $\theta = \pi$ diameter we need only consider a semi-circular domain defined by $0 \leq r \leq 1$, $0 \leq \theta \leq \pi$. The problem is solved using the Galerkin finite element method (Zienkiewicz [2], and Strang and Fix [3]). This results in a set of

---

* The Caltech Mark II hypercube environment is supported by the Department of Energy

† Elxsi, San Jose, California

‡ Caltech acknowledges partial support from Sandia National Laboratories for this work

§ Concurrent Computation Project, 206-49, California Institute of Technology, Pasadena, CA91125.

¶ Advanced Computer Science Project, Fluid and Thermal Sciences Department, Sandia National Laboratories, Albuquerque, NM87185.

linearized residual equations :

$$\mathbf{K\Psi} = \mathbf{b} \tag{1}$$

which are solved using a pre-conditioned, conjugate gradient (pcg) method (Golub and Van Loan [4]). The method of solution divides naturally into three stages:

(1) Initialization, in which storage is allocated, arrays are zeroed, and the problem is decomposed among the processors.
(2) Assembly of the stiffness matrix, $\mathbf{K}$.
(3) The pcg stage in which the pre-conditioned conjugate gradient algorithm is applied iteratively until the solution converges.

The problem is decomposed among the processors as follows. The domain is divided up into a regular grid by making equal sub-divisions in the r and θ directions. In the (r, θ) plane this grid defines a set of $N_r \times N_\theta$ rectangular elements. Each element contains 9 nodes, arranged as a 3×3 grid, with one degree of freedom at each node. The nodes along the $r = 0$ axis are degenerate since the location of each corresponds to the center of the sphere. A physical domain decomposition is used to assign groups of contiguous elements to processors. To ensure good load balancing between the processors approximately the same number of elements are assigned to each processor. It is always possible to ensure that the maximum difference in the number of elements between any two processors is never greater than one. The elements are labelled 0 through $N_e - 1$, starting with the element in the top right-hand corner of the rectangular grid and going down each column. If processor number n is assigned $n_e(n)$ elements, then the first $n_e(0)$ elements go to processor 0, the next $n_e(1)$ elements go to processor 1, and so on. An example is given in figure 1 which shows the decomposition of a 8×4 array of elements between three processors.

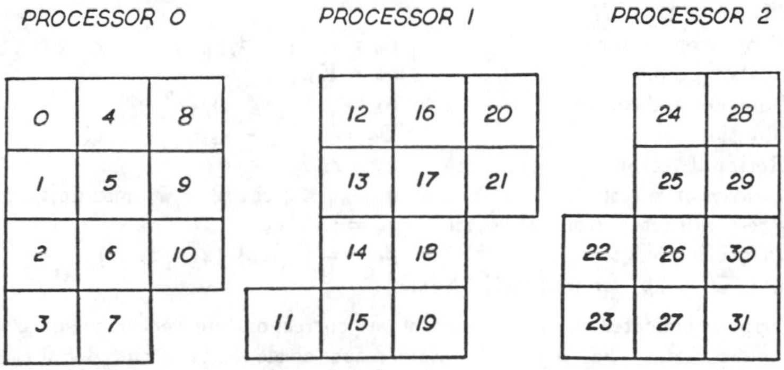

Figure 1. An example of the decomposition of an 8×4 array of elements between three processors. Processors 0 and 1 contain 11 elements, and processor 2 contains 10 elements.

After decomposition and initialization the stiffness matrix is next assembled in packed form using a frontal method to store only the non-zero values. In the frontal method elements are processed in each processor one at a time, starting with the lowest numbered element. At any stage there exists in each processor a boundary between the processed and unprocessed elements. This boundary is referred to as "the front". The following three types of nodes may be identified, and are illustrated in figure 2 :

(a) interior nodes, which lie in processed elements but not on the front
(b) front nodes, which actually lie on the front,
(c) exterior nodes, which lie in unprocessed elements but not on the front.

When a new element is processed some nodes will be added to the front, and others will leave the front to become interior nodes. Once a node becomes interior it will not contribute further to the stiffness matrix, and the row and column in the stiffness matrix corresponding to it will not be changed by subsequent processing. The frontal algorithm maintains an array, called the frontal array, which contains only those contributions to the stiffness matrix from nodes on the front. When a node on the front becomes an interior node the corresponding row and column are extracted from the frontal array and the non-zero values are copied to the packed stiffness matrix. An array of pointers to this matrix is maintained so that its values can later be unpacked.

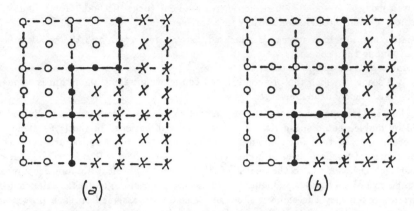

Figure 2. (a) Elements 0 thru 3 have been processed. The front is represented by the heavy solid line. Exterior nodes are represented by crosses, interior nodes by open circles, and front nodes by filled circles. (b) Shows the situation after the next element has been processed.

When the stiffness matrix has been assembled the pcg algorithm solves equation 1 for Ψ as follows (e.g. Golub and Van Loan [4]) :

Initialize: assemble $\mathbf{K}$, $\mathbf{b}$; set $\Psi_0 \equiv 0$, $\mathbf{r}_0 \equiv \mathbf{b}$, $\mathbf{z}_0 \equiv \mathbf{M}^{-1}\mathbf{b}$, $\beta_1 \equiv 0$
Iterate: For $k = 1, \ldots, N_g$

Projection vector	$\mathbf{p}_k = \mathbf{z}_{k-1} + \beta_k \mathbf{p}_{k-1}$
Scalar product	$\mathbf{q}_k = \mathbf{K}\mathbf{p}_k$
Solution update length	$\alpha_k = (\mathbf{z}_{k-1}^T.\mathbf{r}_{k-1})/(\mathbf{p}_k^T.\mathbf{q}_k)$
Solution vector	$\Psi_k = \Psi_{k-1} + \alpha_k \mathbf{p}_k$
Residual vector	$\mathbf{r}_k = \mathbf{r}_{k-1} - \alpha_k \mathbf{q}_k$
Convergence test	if $\|\mathbf{r}_k\| < \delta$ set $\Psi = \Psi_k$ and quit
Pre-conditioned residual vector	$\mathbf{z}_k = \mathbf{M}^{-1}\mathbf{r}_k$
Projection length	$\beta_{k+1} = (\mathbf{z}_k^T.\mathbf{r}_k)/(\mathbf{z}_{k-1}^T.\mathbf{r}_{k-1})$

Terminate: $\Psi = \Psi_{N_g}$ (if arithmetic is exact)

Here subscript k indicates the kth iterate of the corresponding vector or scalar quantity, and the pre-conditioning matrix, $\mathbf{M}$, is just the main diagonal elements of the global stiffness matrix, $\mathbf{M} = diag(\mathbf{K})$. The conjugate gradient algorithm has the property that if the arithmetic is exact then the exact solution is obtained after N_g iterations, where N_g is the total number of nodes.

(3) Implementation on the Elxsi

The Elxsi 6400 is a shared memory multi-processing computer system whose main functional elements communicate via a high speed bus (Olson, Kumar and Leonard [5]). The performance of the Elxsi 6400 has been investigated by Sanguinetti [6]. The machine used in this work has 10 processors each with a write-back cache of 16 Kbytes and a hit ratio typically in the range 90% to 95%. Previous work on problems of this type (Benner et. al. [7]) has shown that efficient use of cache can substantially reduce the mean memory access time. However, as discussed by Montry and Benner [8], the programmer must take care to ensure cache coherency, by manually flushing the caches to main storage at the appropriate times. The use of cached memory increases the risk of bugs creeping into the code, and makes programming somewhat more difficult.

In the assemble stage the boundary elements in two adjacent processors contribute to the same entries in the global stiffness matrix, since nodes lying on the boundary are resident in both processors. This potentially leads to a cache coherency problem. The simplest way to maintain cache coherency in this case is for each processor to first process the elements along its left-hand boundary and then flush the global stiffness matrix data from its cache. Each processor next signals the processor to its left to indciate that the elements along its left-hand boundary have been processed. If no processor is allowed to process the elements on its right-hand boundary until it has received the signal from the processor to its right, then cache coherency will be maintained. When the assemble phase is completed each processor flushes the global stiffness matrix data from its cache and the pcg phase begins.

In the pcg phase cache coherency is important in the evaluation of scalar products. Consider the product $p_k.q_k$. Each processor is responsible for a portion of p_k and q_k, and evaluates the contribution to the scalar product arising from these parts. Each contribution is flushed to main storage. A single processor sums the contributions, and the resulting scalar product is then flushed to main storage. The processors are then synchronized so that each will be able to access the value of the scalar product before continuing. Coherency and synchronization also need to be considered in performing the pcg convergence test. As with the evaluation of scalar products, the convergence test is carried out in a single processor, and the result is stored in shared memory. The processors are then synchronized, and each checks the result of the convergence test and takes appropriate action.

(4) Implementation on the Caltech hypercube

Much of the code for the hypercube implementation is similar to that on the Elxsi, however, there are important differences. For simplicity each processor was assigned a complete segment of the domain. The major difference in the assemble stage is that no values of the global stiffness matrix are communicated between processors. Each processor evaluates the part of the global stiffness matrix arising from its elements, ignoring the boundary elements in other processors. We refer to the matrix evaluated by each processor as the local stiffness matrix. Since no communication takes place between processors during the evaluation of the local stiffness matrix, this phase runs with 100% efficiency. The local stiffness matrix of each processor lies on the main diagonal of the global stiffness matrix. Since nodes lying on the boundaries between processors are processed by both adjacent processors the local stiffness matrices overlap, as shown in figure 3. Each overlap region is an $n_b \times n_b$ matrix, where n_b is the number of nodes along the boundary. The correct value of entries in the global stiffness matrix in the overlap region is just the sum of the corresponding contributions from the two overlapping local stiffness matrices. However, the hypercube implementation of the pcg algorithm does not require each processor to know the correct values for the overlap regions of the global stiffness matrix — the algorithm operates with just the local stiffness matrices. The pcg phase also needs to know the pre-conditioning matrix, M, and the initial residual vector, r_0. Since M is the main diagonal of the global stiffness matrix it can be stored as a vector, d. Each processor evaluates the contributions from its nodes to these two vectors during the assemble phase. At the end of this phase each processor contains a portion of the d and r_0 vectors, and just as with the local stiffness matrices, the portions in neighboring processors overlap. The correct values for entries in the vectors d and r_0 in the overlap regions is just the sum of the corresponding contributions from the two neighboring processors. To ensure that each processor knows the correct values of the portion of the vectors d and r_0 arising from its elements the first and last n_b entries of d and r_0 must be communicated between neighboring processors. This is the only communication between processors in the assemble stage, and takes place after the frontal method has assembled the local stiffness matrix.

The program now enters the pcg stage. The main thing to be borne in mind in the pcg stage is that at all times each processor knows the correct values of the parts of the vectors p_k, q_k, r_k, and d that arise from its elements. We ensure that this is the case by communicating the first and last n_b entries of the vector q_k to the neighboring processors in each iteration. The algorithm for evaluating q_k proceeds as follows in each processor :

(1) Multiply the local stiffness matrix by p_k to give q_k.
(2) Send the last n_b entries in q_k to the processor to the right.
(3) Receive from the processor on the left the last n_b entries from its q_k vector. Add these to the first n_b entries of the local q_k vector.
(4) Send the first n_b entries of the q_k vector to the processor to the left.
(5) Receive from the processor on the right the first n_b from its q_k vector, and replace the last n_b entries of the local q_k vector with these values.

After applying the above algorithm each processor contains a section of the q_k vector arising from the elements in that processor. The last n_b entries of the local q_k vector are the same as the first n_b entries in the processor to the right.

Neighboring processors must also communicate in order to evaluate the scalar products $p_k.q_k$, $z_{k-1}^T.r_{k-1}$, $r_k.r_k$, and $p_k.p_k$. Each of these evaluations requires d single packet exchanges per processor, where d is the dimension of the hypercube.

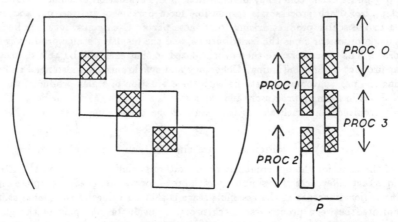

Figure 3. Each square represents the local stiffness matrix from a single processor. The overlap region (shown hatched) corresponds to nodes lying along the boundary of adjacent processors. Also shown is the vector p_k.

(5) Results and Efficiencies

The results for the Elxsi implementation are shown in table 1 for the case of 512 elements. Table 1 shows that if the number of processors is greater than 1 then the efficiency of the assemble process is approximately constant at 72%. The time taken by the assemble process is made up of the time to perform to perform floating point operations plus the memory access time. If T_{fp}^e is the time taken to perform a single floating point operation on the Elxsi, and C_1 is the number of floating point operations performed per element, then the calulation time is $C_1 n_e T_{fp}^e$, where n_e is the number of elements per processor. In the case of a single processor all variables are marked as unshared and cacheable and the cache is controlled by the memory manager by a process that is invisible to the user. If we denote the effective memory access time in this case by T_{cache} and C_2 is the number of memory accesses per element then the time spent accessing memory is $C_2 n_e T_{cache}$. In the multi-tasking case some of the variables are shared, and so the memory manager spends more time fetching data from main memory. In this case we can write the time spent accessing memory as :

$$T_{mem} = (1 - F)C_2 T_{cache} + F C_2 T_{mm} \qquad (2)$$

where T_{mm} is the time taken to access a datum in main memory, and F is a constant in the range 0 to 1 which parameterizes the relative use of cached and shared memory. The time taken by the assemble stage is therefore :

$$T_{asm}^e = n_e \big(C_1 T_{fp}^e + C_2(F T_{mm} + (1 - F)T_{cache}) \big) \qquad (3)$$

The efficiency is defined as the time taken to run on a single processor, divided by N times the time taken by N processors. Thus,

$$\epsilon_{asm}^e = \frac{1}{1 + \frac{FC(t_{mm} - t_{cache})}{1 + Ct_{cache}}} \qquad (4)$$

where $C = C_2/C_1$, $t_{cache} = T_{cache}/T_{fp}^e$, and $t_{mm} = T_{mm}/T_{fp}^e$. For the algorithm employed we assume that F and C are constants, and so the efficiency is a constant whose magnitude is indicative of the relative usage of cached and shared memory.

The time taken for each pcg iteration is dominated by the evaluation of the vector $q_k = Kp_k$, thus we may express the time for each pcg loop as,

$$T_{pcg}^e = n_g(c_1 T_{fp}^e + c_2(f T_{mm} + (1 - f)T_{cache}) \qquad (5)$$

where n_g is the number of nodes per processor. If N_g is the total number of nodes then the efficiency of the pcg stage is,

$$\epsilon_{pcg}^e = \frac{N_g/(Nn_g)}{1 + \frac{fc(t_{mm} - t_{cache})}{1 + ct_{cache}}} \tag{6}$$

Figure 4 shows a plot of ϵ_{pcg}^e against $N_g/(Nn_g)$ for the case of 512 elements. The plot shows the general trend predicted by equation 6, although there is some deviation, which may be due to differences in the mean band-width of the global stiffness matrix for differing numbers of processors, and an over simplistic model of the use of cached and shared memory.

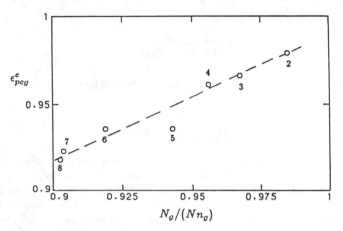

Figure 4. Elxsi results for 512 elements for 2 thru 8 processors. The dashed line represents the type of linear relationship expected from equation 6.

We now consider the efficiency of the hypercube implementation. The assemble stage takes time.

$$T_{asm}^h = n_e G_1 T_{fp}^h + n_b G_2 T_{mess} \tag{7}$$

where G_1 and G_2 are constants, n_b is the number of nodes along each inter-processor boundary, T_{fp}^h is the time for a single floating point operation on the hypercube, and T_{mess} is the time to transfer a single 8-byte packet between two processors. The efficiency for the assemble stage may thus be written as,

$$\epsilon_{asm}^h = \frac{1}{1 + \frac{n_b}{n_e} G t_{mess}} \tag{8}$$

where $G = G_2/G_1$ is a constant, and $t_{mess} = T_{mess}/T_{fp}^h$. This differs from the Elxsi implementation for which the corresponding efficiency is a constant.

In each iteration of the pcg solution the dominant factor in determining the calculation time is the multiplication of the stiffness matrix, $\mathbf{K}$, by the vector $\mathbf{p}_k$. Thus the time for each iteration is,

$$T_{calc} = H_1 n_g b_n T_{fp}^h \tag{9}$$

where H_1 is a constant, n_g is the number of nodes in each processor, and b_n is the mean bandwidth of the stiffness matrix.

The time taken by communication in each loop is due to two transfers of n_b 8 byte numbers, plus four scalar products each of which involve d transfers of one 8 byte number. Here, n_b is the number of nodes along one boundary of each processor, and d is the dimension of the hypercube. Thus the time for communication in each iteration is given by,

$$T_{comm} = H_2 (2d + n_b) T_{mess} \tag{10}$$

where H_2 is a constant.

The total time for each iteration is just the sum of T_{calc} and T_{comm}. In the case of a single processor there is no communication, thus the efficiency is given by :

$$\epsilon_{pcg}^h = \frac{T_{calc}(1)}{N(T_{calc}(N) + T_{comm})} \tag{11}$$

where N is the number of processors. Thus we have :

$$\epsilon_{pcg}^h = \frac{H_1 N_g b_1 T_{fp}^h}{N(H_1 n_g b_n T_{fp}^h + H_2(2d + n_b)T_{mess})} \tag{12}$$

Now, since the nodes on the boundary between processors are processed by both processors, we have :

$$N_g = N n_g - (N - 1)n_b \tag{13}$$

Thus equation 12 may be written as :

$$\epsilon^* = \frac{1}{\left(1 + \frac{H(2d+n_b)}{n_g}\tau b_n\right)} \tag{14}$$

where $H = H_2/H_1$ is a constant, $\tau = T_{mess}/T_{fp}^h$, and ϵ^* is defined by :

$$\epsilon^* = \frac{\epsilon_{pcg}^h}{(1 - (1 - N^{-1})\frac{n_b}{n_g})B} \tag{15}$$

and $B = b_1/b_n$ is the ratio of the band-widths in the two cases. Equation 15 illustrates the component of the inefficiency which arises from the nature of the algorithm itself, rather from the communication process. This algorithmic inefficiency is itself due to two factors. The first arises from the fact that the nodes along processor boundaries reside in both the adjacent processors. The second is the fact that the average band-width of the stiffness matrix is different for different numbers of processors. This algorithmic inefficiency does not necessarily mean that the algorithm is a poor one; the algorithmic inefficiency could be removed, but only by doing more communication, which would itself reduce efficiency.

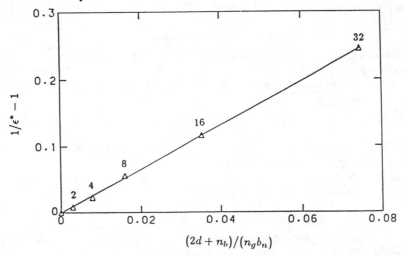

Figure 5. Hypercube results for 128 elements. The number of processors is shown.

The code has been run on the 32-node Mark II hypercube for cases with 128, 256, and 512 elements with various numbers of processors. Because of storage limitations it was possible to run the code on a single processor only in the 128 element case. The results are shown in tables 2, 3, and 4. Table 5 shows the efficiencies, and ϵ^*, for the 128 node case. Equations 14 and 15 show that a plot of $1/\epsilon^* - 1$ against $(2d + n_b)/(n_g b_n)$ should be a straight line. This was checked by solving for 128 elements arranged as a 32 by 4 grid, for $d=0$ thru 5. The results are plotted in figure 5, and as expected, the points lie on a straight line, of slope 3.29. Thus the time for the pcg step of a given problem and requiring n_{iter} iterations run on an N processor hypercube is :

$$T_N = C_1 T_{fp}^h n_{iter}(n_g b_n + 3.29(2d + n_b)) \tag{16}$$

In figure 6 we plot T_N against $n_{iter}(n_g b_n + 3.29(2d + n_b))$ for all the cases considered. As predicted by equation 16, this plot is a straight line of slope 1.53×10^{-4}. We can now write T_N as :

$$T_N = 1.53 \times 10^{-4} n_{iter}(n_g b_n + 3.29(2d + n_b)) \tag{17}$$

Table 1 compares results for the multi-processor Elxsi and the hypercube for the 512 element problem. Since the hypercube could not solve this problem with fewer than 4 processors we use equation 17 to estimate the hypercube times in the 1 and 2 processor cases. The ratio of hypercube cpu time to Elxsi cpu time for the pcg step is about 23, for the same number of processors.

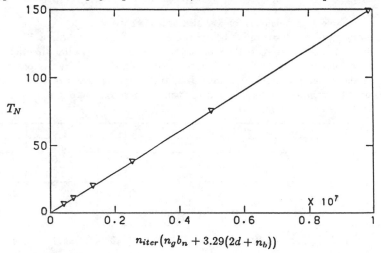

Figure 6. Hypercube timings of the pcg stage for the 128 element case. The straight line thru the points is that given in equation 17.

(6) Conclusions

A sequential algorithm can usually be ported to a shared memory, multi-processing machine without making any algorithmic changes, and as pointed out by McGrogan, Olson, and Toda [9], only a relatively small number of additional lines of code are required. However, indiscriminate use of shared memory will generally result in non-optimal code. Benner et. al. [7] have shown that the efficient use of cached memory can result in speed ups of up to 30% over code that uses just shared memory. However, care must be taken to maintain cache coherency, and this added complication detracts somewhat from the attractiveness of using shared memory machines, although most multi-cache systems maintain cache coherency automatically (cf. Yen et. al. [10]).

When porting a sequential program, or a program from a shared memory machine to a hypercube, algorithmic changes are usually necessary. For the case considered in this work the algorithmic change was not very great — it was merely noted that the product $\mathbf{Kp_k}$ could be evaluated using the local stiffness matrices, and a costly exchange of chunks of the stiffness matrix between processors was avoided, thereby improving the efficiency. If the hypercube algorithm was used on the Elxsi it would lead to a reduction in run time since the local stiffness matrices could be held in local memory, thus reducing memory access time. However, specialized software would be needed to mimic the hypercube's inter-processor message passing capabilities in order to communicate the first and last n_b entries in $\mathbf{q_k}$ between adjacent processors. It appears, therefore, that the hypercube architecture is sufficiently flexible to permit algorithmic enhancements which cannot readily be applied in shared memory machines. The use of machines, such as the *IBM RP3* (Pfister et. al. [11]), which incorporate both shared memory and a mechanism for inter-processor message passing, is currently an area of active research. Software has been developed on the Elxsi which mimics the message passing capabilities of the hypercube, and in the future this will be used to develop algorithms for shared memory hypercubes.

Acknowledgement: Helpful and informative discussions with Jim Quinlan of Carnegie Mellon University are gratefully acknowledged.

N	T_{asm}^e	T_{pcg}^e	T_{pcg}^h	ϵ_{asm}^e	ϵ_{pcg}^e
1	6.50	32.30	691.2	1.000	1.000
2	4.40	16.50	348.3	0.739	0.979
3	3.00	11.15		0.722	0.966
4	2.25	8.40	193.9	0.722	0.961
5	1.75	6.90		0.743	0.936
6	1.51	5.75		0.717	0.936
7	1.28	5.00		0.725	0.923
8	1.14	4.40	100.8	0.713	0.918

Table 1. Efficiencies for 512 elements (141 iterations)

The hypercube timings given for N=1 and 2 have been estimated using equation 17. In tables 1 thru 5 N is the number of processors, n_r is the number of elements in the radial direction, n_θ is the number of elements per processor in the θ direction, n_g is the number of nodes per processor, n_b is the number of nodes along each processor boundary, T_{init} is the time to initialize the problem, T_{asm} is the time to assemble the stiffness matrix, T_{pcg} is the time to perform the pcg iterations, and T_{tot} is the total time. All times are given in seconds.

N	n_θ	n_r	n_g	n_b	T_{init}	T_{asm}	T_{pcg}	T_{tot}
32	1	4	27	9	0.38	1.33	6.50	8.21
16	2	4	45	9	0.42	2.63	11.00	14.05
8	4	4	81	9	0.49	5.19	20.20	25.88
4	8	4	153	9	0.65	10.30	38.50	49.45
2	16	4	297	9	0.97	20.54	75.30	95.84
1	32	4	585	9	1.60	40.97	148.80	191.37

Table 2. Hypercube timings for 128 elements (113 iterations)

N	n_θ	n_r	n_g	n_b	T_{init}	T_{asm}	T_{pcg}	T_{tot}
32	1	8	51	17	0.42	2.67	14.50	17.59
16	2	8	85	17	0.49	5.40	25.20	31.09
8	4	8	153	17	0.64	10.76	46.00	57.40
4	8	8	289	17	0.94	21.43	89.70	112.07
2	16	8	561	17	1.53	42.81	175.90	220.24

Table 3. Hypercube timings for 256 elements (128 iterations)

N	n_θ	n_r	n_g	n_b	T_{init}	T_{asm}	T_{pcg}	T_{tot}
32	1	16	99	33	0.75	5.17	30.70	36.62
16	2	16	165	33	0.89	11.19	54.00	66.08
8	4	16	297	33	1.18	22.80	100.80	124.78
4	8	16	561	33	1.74	45.91	193.90	241.55

Table 4. Hypercube timings for 512 elements (141 iterations)

N	b_n	B	ϵ_{asm}^h	ϵ_{pcg}^h	ϵ^*	$(2d + n_b)/(n_g b_n)$
32	9.44	1.315	0.963	0.715	0.803	7.450×10^{-2}
16	10.69	1.161	0.974	0.845	0.896	3.540×10^{-2}
8	11.52	1.077	0.987	0.921	0.947	1.600×10^{-2}
4	12.01	1.033	0.994	0.966	0.978	0.790×10^{-2}
2	12.27	1.011	0.997	0.988	0.992	0.302×10^{-2}
1	12.41	1.000	1.000	1.000	1.000	0.000×10^{-2}

Table 5. Efficiencies for the hypercube for 128 elements

ϵ_{asm}^h and ϵ_{pcg}^h are the efficiencies for the assembly and pcg steps, respectively. ϵ^* is as defined in equation 15. B is the ratio b_1/b_n where b_1 and b_n are the mean band-widths of the global stiffness matrix for 1 and n processors, respectively. Other quantities are as defined for tables 1-4.

References

[1] J. TUARZON, M. PETERSON, D. LIBERMAN, *Caltech/JPL Mark II Hypercube Concurrent Processor*, Proc. 1985 International Conf. on Parallel Processing, ed. D. Degroot, IEEE Computer Soc. Press, Washington, D.C., 1985.

[2] O. C. ZIENKIEWICZ, *The Finite Element Method*, McGraw-Hill, London, 1977.

[3] G. STRANG, and G. J. FIX, *An Analysis of the Finite Element Method*, Prentice Hall Inc., Eaglewood Cliffs, N.J., 1973.

[4] G. H. GOLUB, and C. F. VAN LOAN, *Matrix Computations*. John Hopkins Univ. Press, Baltimore, 1974.

[5] R. OLSON, B. KUMAR, and L. E. SHAR, *Messages and Multiprocessing in the Elxsi System 6400*, Proc. Comp-Con '83, 28th IEEE-CS Int. Conf., IEEE Computer Soc. Press, Washington, D.C, 1983.

[6] J. SANGUINETTI, *Performance of a Message-Based Multiprocessor*, Computer, Sept. 86, 19:9. Pub. by IEEE Computer Soc, 1986.

[7] R. E. BENNER, G. R. MONTRY, and G. G. WEIGAND, *Concurrent Multi-frontal Methods : Shared Memory, Cache, and Frontwidth Issues*, Int. J. Num. Meth. & Eng. (1986), (submitted).

[8] G. R. MONTRY, and R. E. BENNER, *The Effects of Cacheing on Multi-tasking Efficiency and Programming Strategy on an Elxsi 6400*, Internal Sandia Document, SAND85-2728, 1985.

[9] S. McGROGAN, R. OLSON, and N. TODA, *Parallelizing Large Existing Programs - Methodology and Experiences*, Proc. Comp-Con '86, 31st IEEE-CS Int. Conf., ed. A. G. Ball, IEEE Computer Soc. Press, Washington, D.C., 1986.

[10] W. C. YEN, D. W. L. YEN, K-S FU, *Data Coherence Problem in a Multi-cache System*, IEEE Trans. on Computers, C-34:1, 1985.

[11] G. F. PFISTER, W. C. BRANTLEY, D. A. GEORGE, S. L. HARVEY, W. J. KLEINFELDER, K. P. McAULIFFE, E. A. MELTON, V. A. NORTON, and J. WEISS, *The IBM Research Parallel Processor Prototype (RP3): Introduction and Architecture*, Proc. 1985 International Conf. on Parallel Processing, ed. D. Degroot, IEEE Computer Soc. Press, Washington, D.C., 1985.

PART IV:
COMMUNICATION AND
ARCHITECTURAL ISSUES

Communication Algorithms for Regular Convolutions and Matrix Problems on the Hypercube*

GEOFFREY C. FOX† AND WOJTEK FURMANSKI†

Abstract

We describe a set of communication utilities for the hypercube and illustrate their use in several examples involving long distance messages. We present optimal hypercube decompositions for some matrix algorithms, global scalar products, tree decompositions and the binary Fast Fourier Transform.

Introduction

In a recent detailed paper [1], we introduced a set of hypercube communication utilities which had originally developed as a part of a study of matrix algorithms on the hypercube [2]. In this review, we present a short review of this work and summarize the use of these utilities in some basic matrix algorithms.

In Section 2, we introduce the basic idea behind the *method of ordered cube geodesics* which underlies most of the algorithms presented later. We also describe the general requirements of the hypercube communication system. In Section 3, we discuss those algorithms that apply to homogeneous problems where the data is uniformly distributed throughout the hypercube. These are:

· index
· fold
· expand
· vecadd
· transpose
· global_reverse

In Section 4, we generalize these specific utilities to:

· crystal_router

* Work supported in part by DOE grant DE-FG-03-85ER25009, the office of the program manager of the Joint Tactical Fusion Office, and the Parsons and System Development Foundations.

† Concurrent Computation Program, California Institute of Technology, Pasadena, California 91125

which is a general message routing algorithm appropriate for the *crystalline communication system* (CrOS) which has been very successful in the implementations of many Caltech problems on the hypercube.

In Section 5, we describe a set of inhomogeneous algorithms.

· broadcast

· scatter

· transfer

where the data is **nonuniformly** distributed through the cube at either the beginning or end of the action of the utility.

In the final Section 6, we summarize the performance of some matrix algorithms on the hypercube and indicate how use of the new routines increases the efficiency of the hypercube implementation.

These utilities are currently implemented in terms of CrOS. One can easily implement them in the more general communication systems available on the commercial hypercubes. However, as CrOS is typically higher performance, the utilities are seen at their best in the crystalline environment. This is available on inhouse Caltech hypercubes, the INTEL iPSC [3], the AMETEK S14, and will soon be ported to the NCUBE hypercube. The explicit code for the utilities will be made available in the software supplement to our forthcoming book [4, 5].

2. The Crystalline Environment and Cube Geodesics

The Crystalline environment is a low level synchronous communication system. It provides the capability of transferring data between two adjacent (i.e. connected by hypercube topology) nodes. The CrOS system can cause "long-distance" (non nearest neighbor) transfer of data under user control. In fact, the utilities in this paper provide strategies for certain patterns of long distance communication. *Crystal_router* provides for irregular message traffic but apart from this the other utilities provide optimal implementations of certain regular dataflows. The synchronisity of CrOS implies that all the nodes of the hypercube transmit data at the same time. This is an essential restriction of the crystalline environment. It is adequate for the majority of scientific problems where simulation time or an algorithmic iteration count naturally synchronizes the concurrent program. We note that above and in the following, we always refer to the cube; however, all these utilities can be naturally implemented either over both the full hypercube or any subcube of it. This generalization is, in fact, crucial in many matrix algorithms. However, for clarity in the exposition, we will phrase our discussions in terms of algorithms implemented over the full hypercube.

Let us now discuss the method of ordered cube geodesics. Consider the task of sending a single message between two nodes n_i and n_2 of the hypercube. A shortest path between n_1 and n_2 is a geodesic and there a $h!$ geodesics between n_1 and n_2 if these nodes are h hops apart. This is illustrated in Figure 1. Now consider a general problem where we have a collection of J messages, labelled by j, that we wish to send concurrently from $n_1(j)$ to $n_2(j)$. It is natural to use a geodesic for each message but this leaves two problems unaddressed. Firstly, there are, as discussed above, many geodesics to choose from and secondly, in order to minimize the execution time on the hypercube, it is not sufficient that each message travel along a geodesic. This could lead to communication imbalance or hot spots and corresponding poor concurrent performance. However, we note that if every message travels along a geodesic and the communication is balanced (equal) between processors, then we are guaranteed that our method is optimal. The *method of ordered cube geodesics* is a particular choice of geodesics which does load balance many important problems and is described in the next section. We note that our solution is natural in the *crystalline* environment but not in some other systems. For instance, an alternative approach to this message routing problem is to let each message dynamically find an optimal path based on the current state of the communication channels in the hypercube. This is inappropriate in our case - we do not have each message fighting for survival in a background of otherwise random messages. Rather, we have a large number of messages whose structure is highly correlated. It makes sense to consider the total message traffic and optimize it. This is straightforward in the synchronous environment provided by the crystalline communication system.

In Figure 2, we summarize the action of the utilities to be discussed in the following sections using the simple case of eight data values and four nodes.

3 Homogeneous Communication Utilities

3.1 Data Structures

Many of the crystalline utilities can be usefully applied to convolutions of the general mathematical form:

$$f(\underline{y}) = F(\underline{y}:f(\underline{x})) \tag{1}$$

where F is a functional and f and g functions. The variables $\underline{x}$ and $\underline{y}$ are points in two separate domains, each of which can be decomposed over the hypercube.

A simple example is given by the calculation of a scalar product $\underline{A} \cdot \underline{B}$ where the vectors $\underline{A}$ and $\underline{B}$ are distributed over the hypercube. The components of $\underline{A}$ and $\underline{B}$, $A(x)$ and $B(x)$ are labelled by a variable x decomposed over the hypercube. This global sum is usually performed by mapping the hypercube into a tree. We find a problem of the form (1) by supposing that we have several sets $\underline{A}(y)$, $\underline{B}(y)$ of vectors. Each node holds $A(y,x)$, $B(y,x)$ for all y but only a subset of the x values. We can write the problem as:

$$S(y) = \sum_x A(y,x)B(y,x) \tag{2}$$

Here we start with the variable x fully decomposed and each node containing all of the y values. We will see in the next subsection that the optimal calculation of these several sums, decomposes y so that each node calculates a separate $S(y)$. This corresponds to a democratic decomposition of the hypercube into several trees with the roots of the tree spread over the hypercube. Problems of this type are intrinsically "long-range"; data must travel all over the cube. Let us contrast this with the standard finite difference problem involving local interactions. Here y and x are members of the same domain; $f(x)$ could be the displacement at time t and $g(y)$ that at time $t+dt$. In this case and, in fact, many scientific problems, one is not faced with two variables with inconsistent decompositions; $f(\underline{x})$ and $g(\underline{y})$ naturally use the same decomposition. Correspondingly, we only need nearest neighbor and not long-range communication. As we will see in the next subsection, the FFT is a good example of a problem where $\underline{x}$ and $\underline{y}$ have different decompositions.

For the problem class described above, it is natural to label the data (e.g. the $A,B(\underline{y},\underline{x})$ in Eq. (2)) by three variables i,j, and k. The integer i runs from 0 to N-1 and labels the subsets into which $\underline{x}$ is decomposed; j runs from 0 to N-1 and labels the subsets in which $\underline{y}$ is to be decomposed. Here N is the number of nodes. k supplies any necessary extra labelings; we will typically ignore the k label as the structure is entirely specified by i and j and k is simply looped over as necessary. The situation is illustrated in Figure 3 for the case $N=8$. Each node i holds the data structure labelled by j and k. We will allow degenerate cases when j does not take on the full N values; we let j actually run from 0 to $J-1$.

We now describe various transformations in the $i-j$ plane which form the crystalline communication package discussed in this paper.

3.2 Index

This utility swops the indices i and j and is illustrated in Figure 4. To take a particular example, after *index*, the original contents of node 3 are now decomposed over the whole hypercube but are always stored in the location $j=3$ of each node.

The origin of the name *index* for this utility can be seen from a database example. Let in the formalism of Sec. 3.1, $\underline{x}$ label records in a database and $\underline{y}$ entries in an index to this

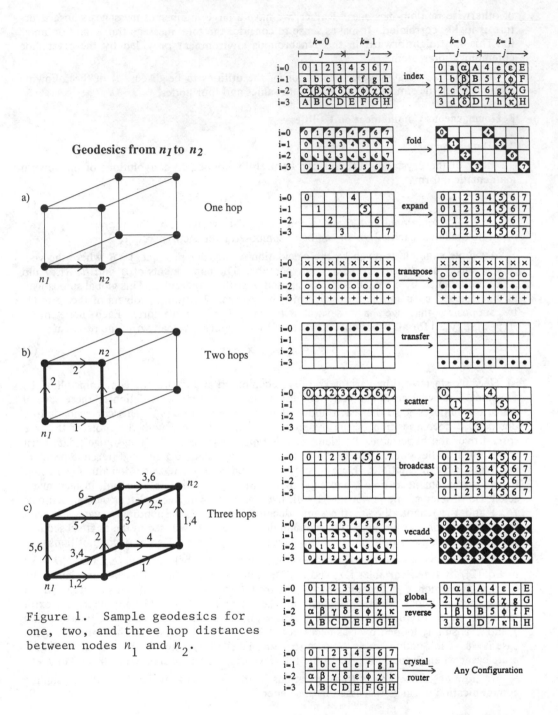

Geodesics from n_1 to n_2

Figure 1. Sample geodesics for one, two, and three hop distances between nodes n_1 and n_2.

Figure 2. A summary for the case of four nodes of the transformations described in this paper. The indices i, j, and k are described in Subsection 3.1.

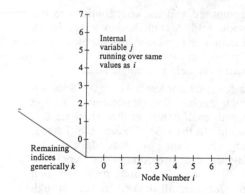

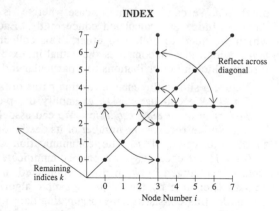

INDEX

Figure 3   The data structure labelled by i, j, and k.

Figure 4   An illustration of *index* for the data structure introduced in Figure 3.   *Index* reflects across the diagonal in the i, j two-dimensional plane.

Cube Geodesics For Index

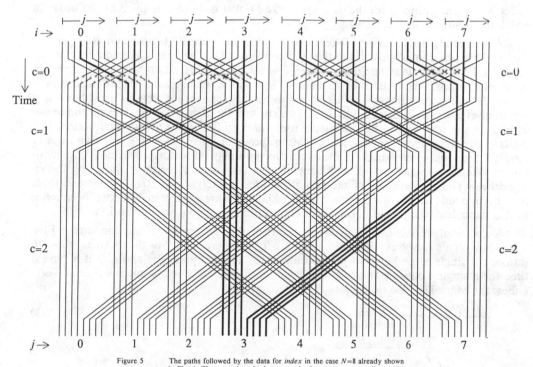

Figure 5   The paths followed by the data for *index* in the case $N=8$ already shown in Fig. 4.   There are three basic communication steps corresponding to the three channels for a three cube.

database. We can consider the case where $\underline{x}$ is decomposed and the contributions to the database index are calculated concurrently. Each node holds a contribution to the index which we need to collect together. This collection action is precisely that performed by *index* which also decomposes the actual index over the hypercube and gives a data structure in which all contributions to a particular index entry are held in a single node.

Figure 5 shows the communication paths of *index* for the same special case $N=8$ shown in Fig. 4. We can use this to exemplify the particular choice of geodesics given by the *method of ordered cube geodesics*. We can associate with each datum in the initial state, a "ticket" which records the number of its destination node. In the case of *index*, the ticket is simply the value of j. The communication strategy has $d=log_2N$ stages labelled by $c=0..d-1$. At each stage, we only communicate along the $c'th$ direction in the hypercube. Data is exchanged between nodes connected in this direction. Each node decides which data to exchange by the following simple algorithm. Consider all data in transit through this node; this consists of any originating data which has yet to be communicated and any data values communicated to this node at a previous step. It excludes all data whose destination is the given node. Data values are communicated at the $c'th$ stage if and only if the binary representation of the ticket and the node number differ in the $c'th$ bit.

The above algorithm clearly transmits all data values along geodesics and in the case where $J=N$ leads to balanced communication. By the argument of Section 2, it follows that this is the optimal communication strategy. For "degenerate" parameter values $J<N$, one can show that the method is still reasonably efficient even though the communication is not fully balanced (the overhead vanishes like $1/d$ for large cubes). The utilities described in the remainder of this paper use variants of the above communication strategy. We will term these generically as the method of *ordered cube geodesics*. The details are given in Ref. 1 and we will not discuss them here.

For comparison with the *crystal_router* algorithm in Section 4, we should note that the ticket is not transmitted with the data value. The ticket is, in fact, implied by the order in which the items are communicated.

An interesting application of index is to a new concurrent FFT algorithm illustrated in Fig. 6. This is a convolution of the type given in Eq. (1). Consider a 32 node decomposition of a $2^{12} = 4096$ point one-dimensional binary FFT. The standard sequential algorithm involves 12 steps, one for each of the binary digits in the representation of a typical $\underline{x}$ or $\underline{y}$ value. In the conventional concurrent algorithm [1], one needs nearest neighbor (in a hypercube) communication for the first five steps and the remainder involves no communication. In the new algorithm, one simply uses *index* to first swap the top and bottom five digits in the decomposition of $\underline{x}$ and $\underline{y}$; this is shown in Fig. 6. Now the first five steps of the FFT are local to each node of the hypercube and may be performed without communication. We now reapply *index* and complete the last seven steps as in the conventional algorithm. The performance of the two algorithms is analyzed in Ref. [1] and one finds that each needs identical communication while the new algorithm is better because it avoids the calculational load imbalance present in the usual concurrent algorithm.

We can analyze this quantitatively in terms of the *efficiency* ϵ of the concurrent FFT algorithm. This involves the ratio $\tau = t_{comm}/t_{calc}$ where t_{comm} is the average time to transmit a single word between neighboring nodes in the hypercube and t_{calc} is a typical time for a single floating point calculation within the nodes. For the initial Caltech hypercubes, the Mark I/II, one finds that $\tau \approx 2$.

$$\frac{1}{\epsilon} - 1 = \frac{[3+2\tau]}{5} \frac{logN}{log(Nn)} \quad - \quad old \tag{3}$$

$$= \frac{2\tau}{5} \frac{logN}{log(Nn)} \quad - \quad new \tag{4}$$

We find it rather striking that one can replace nearest neighbor communication in the old FFT algorithm by long distance communication in *index* and come out ahead!

The above algorithms both lead to a decomposition for the Fourier transform variable $\underline{y}$ that is bit reversed compared to the natural domain decomposition. In Ref. [4], we intro-

a) INDEX for the FFT

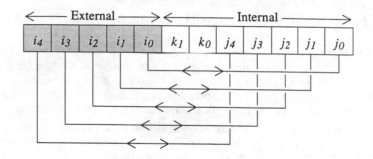

b) GLOBAL REVERSE

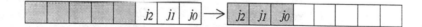

c) DEGENERATE INDEX

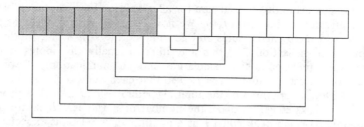

d) DEGENERATE GLOBAL REVERSE

Figure 6   (a) The use of *index* in the concurrent FFT algorithm given in Subsection 3.2. This is compared with *global_reverse* in (b) while (c) and (d) illustrate degenerate cases. Each box corresponds to a single binary digit. Shaded boxes correspond to digits specified in i, the index determining decomposition over the hypercube.

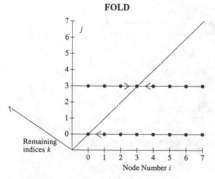

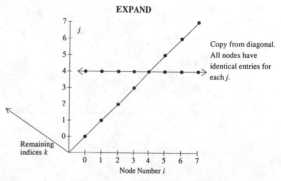

Figure 7   An illustration of *fold* for the data structure introduced in Fig. 3.

Figure 8   An illustration of *expand* for the data structure introduced in Fig. 3.

duce the utility *global_reverse* which transposes the bit reversed to the domain decomposition. *global_reverse* can be shown to be very similar to *index*.

The use of *index* in matrix algorithms will be described in Sections 5.2 and 6.

3.3 Fold and Expand

The next utility, *fold*, is illustrated in Figure 7 and combines all data for a given location, i.e. a given value of j, onto the diagonal of Figure 3 i.e. into the node $j=i$. *fold* can be used with any reasonable arithmetic operation to combine the N values of j into a single value. Obvious operations are multiplication, addition, min/max value etc.

Expand is in some sense the inverse of *fold*; it takes data stored on the diagonal and *broadcasts* them parallel to the x axis in Fig. 3; as illustrated in Fig. 8, for a given j, all nodes hold the same data values after application of *expand*.

fold and *expand* can be used to implement a new algorithm *vecadd* which is the optimal concurrent version of Eq. (2). We first calculate internally to each node the contribution to the scalar products coming from the vector components $A(y,x)$, $B(y,x)$ stored within the node. Each node calculates this partial sum for all y values. In the notation of Section 3.1, the label y is equivalent to the pair (j,k). We now take *fold* with addition as the combining algorithm to add these partial sums and accumulate the $j'th$ scalar product in the $j'th$ node. As described in Section 3.1, this algorithm optimally distributes trees over the hypercube in order to balance the calculation and communication. If we now apply *expand*, we can broadcast the sums $S(y=j,k)$ so that each node receives the values of all scalar products. The performance of the total algorithm *vecadd* is shown in Fig. 9. Note that the efficiency peaks at values of P, the number of y values, which are powers of 2; especially pronounced is the peak when P is a multiple of N. This is expected as, only in the latter case, is the concurrent algorithm totally balanced. However, the method of *ordered cube geodesics* is surprisingly good even in the imbalanced case as shown by the small fluctuations in the efficiencies shown in Fig. 9.

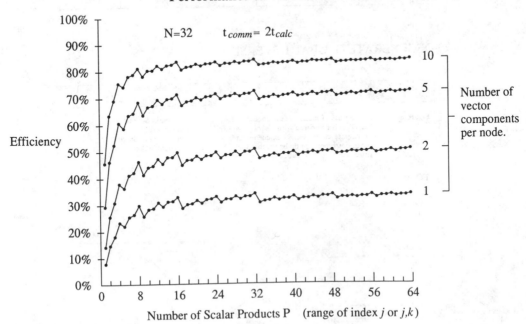

Performance of *VECADD*

Figure 9   The efficiency of the *vecadd* utility as a function of the number of scalar products (number of y values) in Eq. (2). We show curves for a total of N, $2N$, $5N$, and $10N$ x values.

3.4 Transpose and Matrix-Vector Multiplication

Let us illustrate the use of *fold* and *expand* in matrix algorithms by discussing the simple process of matrix-vector multiplication:

$$\underline{y} = A\underline{x} \tag{5}$$

where $\underline{y},\underline{x}$ are vectors of length M and A is an M by M matrix [1, 6]. We are taking the case where A is a full matrix i.e. no significant number of zeros. We take the usual decomposition of A, with a square ($\hat{m} = M/\sqrt{N}$)$\times\hat{m}$ submatrix stored in each node of the hypercube. We can write (5) in block form:

$$\hat{y}_i^{\mu} = \sum_{\nu,j} \hat{A}_{ij}^{\mu\nu} \, \hat{x}_j^{\nu} \tag{6}$$

where μ and ν are block indices running from 0 to $\sqrt{N}-1$. $\hat{y}^{\mu}$ and $\hat{x}^{\nu}$ are $\hat{m}$ dimensional vectors gotten by dividing $\underline{y}$ and $\underline{x}$ respectively into $\sqrt{N}$ separate subvectors:

$$x_{m\nu+j} = \hat{x}_j^{\nu} \tag{7}$$

$$y_{m\mu+i} = \hat{y}_i^{\mu}$$

Figure 10(a) illustrates the storage of both A and $\underline{x}$. In the two-dimensional decomposition of processors, the nodes are labelled by the index pair (μ,ν). Let us suppose we start with the initial state shown in Fig. 10(a); the node (μ,ν) holds the block matrix $\hat{A}^{\mu\nu}$ and all elements of $\hat{x}^{\nu}$.

The algorithm for matrix-vector multiplication is divided into four stages. In the first shown in Fig. 10(a), we form:

$$\hat{y}^{\mu(\nu)} = \sum_j \hat{A}_{ij}^{\mu\nu} \hat{x}_j^{\nu} \tag{8}$$

with no summation over the index ν. $y^{\mu(\nu)}$ are partial contributions to the vector $\hat{y}^{\mu}$. This stage is local to each processor and is load balanced up to differences, of at most one row or column, in the size of the blocks in each processor.

We now use *fold*, illustrated in Fig. 10(b), in each subcube formed by a row of processors. This completes the sum over ν:

$$\hat{y}^{\mu} = \sum_{\nu} \hat{y}^{\mu(\nu)} \tag{9}$$

Now we can follow by *expand* over the same subcubes to broadcast $\hat{y}^{\mu}$ so that each processor in a given row holds the vector $\hat{y}^{\mu}$. This is shown in Fig. 10(c).

This last step depends on the particular way on wants to use (5). Often one needs to iterate $\underline{y} = A\underline{x}$ many times replacing at each iteration $\underline{x}$ by the new $\underline{y}$ on the right hand side. Then the implementation of Eq. (5) is completed by ensuring that $\underline{y}$ is stored in exactly same way as $\underline{x}$. This is achieved by adding a stage before the application of *expand* which transposes the storage of $\hat{y}^{\mu}$ to be along columns rather than rows, [1].

This introduces the next utility *transpose* which transposes information stored in a two dimensional mesh [1, 7, 9]. The transposed vector $\hat{y}^{\mu}$, renamed $\hat{y}^{\mu}\rightarrow\hat{x}^{\mu}$, is now expanded back to the starting storage mode in Fig. 10(a).

The timing of *transpose* is studied in Ref. [1] where it is shown that it takes a time:

$$T_{transpose} = \hat{m} \, t_{comm} \, \frac{\log_2 N}{\sqrt{N}} \tag{10}$$

to transpose the vector where each node holds $\dfrac{\hat{m}}{\sqrt{N}}$ values. The ratio $\log_2 N/\sqrt{N}$, appearing in Eq. (10), can be thought of as the ratio of distances in a hypercube to those in a two-dimensional mesh. This ratio is characteristic of an underlying hypercube. It would be replaced by a number of order unity on a two-dimensional mesh. *Transpose* naturally

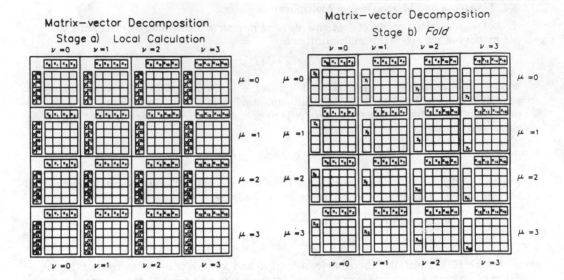

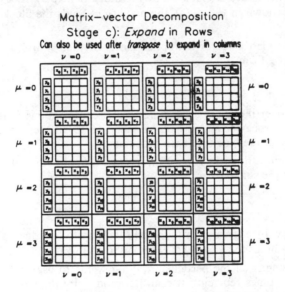

Figure 10   The first three of four stages of matrix vector multiplication discussed in the text and illustrated for a 16 × 16 matrix A decomposed on a 16 node hypercube.

has to transmit information through a distance of order $\sqrt{N}$ in two dimensions.

4 Crystal_Router and General Message Traffic in the Crystalline Environment

In this section, we shall see that the crystalline environment is quite capable of dealing with rather arbitrary message traffic. The only requirement is that the communication be in loose synchronization i.e. that the receiving nodes expect some sort of data. However, we will be able to transmit messages between arbitrary nodes of the hypercube and the size of the messages need not be known by the receiving node, as the basic crystalline read routines only require the user to specify a buffer large enough for the biggest message [4]. We expect that this general crystalline router will offer in many circumstances as much functionality and greater performance than more general message passing systems. In particular, we believe *crystal_router* to be valuable in irregular problems such as particle dynamics and circuit simulation where most communication is local and one wishes to easily accommodate occasional irregularities both in size and destination of messages.

Let us first consider the *ordered cube geodesic* method in the case when a given message is required to be sent from one node to several (more than one) others. A common application of this is to cases where information needs to be broadcast to all nodes of either the cube or a subcube. A complicated example occurs in circuit simulation where the parameters of a given component need to be sent to those nodes which contain components connected to the one in the sending node. It is rarely best to solve this be sending one message to each destination node. Rather it is better to construct a "grand tour" such that the message takes a single path visiting each destination. We see that the routing of multi-destination messages is not an easy problem; it involves the solution of a type of travelling salesman problem that minimizes the path on the hypercube. This illustrates that it is not simple to extend the methods of Section 3 to more general optimal routing methods. Not only is the best route for a given message unknown but also in irregular problems, it is not obvious how to balance the message traffic. In spite of these reservations, we present here a natural generalization of the methods of Section 3 to a general communications in the form of the *crystal_router* algorithm.

We assume that the *loose synchronization* leads to a problem of the following generic form:

At a given stage of the calculation, each node of the hypercube has a set of messages to be sent to other nodes. The destination nodes expect messages but do not know the number of and location of the originating nodes.

This problem is solved by the *crystal_router* which is precisely the algorithm explained in Section 3.2 for *index*. We need to generalize this in two simple ways. First, each message must carry its ticket with it; the destination node is no longer implied by the message position. Secondly, we need to associate several tickets with a given message if there are many destination nodes.

We note that in the case where each message has a ticket to reach every other node, *crystal_router* reproduces the *expand* algorithm of Section 3.3. It also becomes *index* if one gives each message the appropriate single destination. Thus *crystal_router* is optimal for regular communication in both the distributed broadcast (*expand*) and single destination (*index, transpose,* etc.) limits. It is not always optimal in intermediate cases but we are starting to use it in irregular simulations and believe it will be valuable and not far from a practical optimal solution.

5 Inhomogeneous Communication Algorithms

We complete our discussion of useful crystalline communication routines by discussing examples which are intrinsically imbalanced. These include *broadcast* to send information from one to all other nodes; *scatter* to distribute information in one node over all others; and finally *transfer* to send information from one node to a single other one.

5.1 Broadcast, Pipe, and Forest

broadcast is needed in many hypercube algorithms including most full matrix problems. The optimal *broadcast* algorithm depends greatly on the hardware and it is not sensible to give a detailed discussion. We suggest that future hypercubes always be built so that there is special hardware assist for broadcasts both over the full cube and within subcubes. The action of broadcast on the data structure of Section 3.1 is shown in Fig. 11. In Refs. [1] and [8], there is a detailed discussion of the optimal algorithms on machines without special hardware enhancement. On the Caltech Mark I and II hypercubes, the best broadcast algorithm depends on the value of m, the number of words to be sent, and N, the number of nodes. In Fig. 12, we show that one finds three "phases" with separate algorithms dominating in different regions. The *pipe* is typically the best algorithm except for short messages. If the hardware and/or software has significant start-up time for messages, then the pipe is no longer attractive as it requires the message to be broken into several segments - each with its own start-up time - to make up the pipe.

In Fig. 12, one phase is dominated by an algorithm called *forest* in [1] and *personal communication* in [8] (in fact, the algorithm in [8] is slightly more efficient than *forest* and probably optimal). This distributes broadcast trees over the hypercube in a way that leads to less start-up time than *pipe*. However, the cost per word broadcast is lower for the *pipe* which therefore is better as the message length increases. *Forest* generalizes the simplest *broadcast* algorithm which uses a single *tree* decomposed over the hypercube. *Forest* takes the several trees formed by different parts (words/packets) of the message to be broadcast and obtains better load balancing by overlapping the different trees. The third phase shown in Fig. 12 - *scatter* followed by *expand* - uses the algorithm described in the following subsection.

5.2 Scatter

An important utility *scatter* is illustrated in Fig. 13. This takes data stored in a single node and distributes it homogeneously throughout either a subcube or full hypercube forming the set of destination nodes. The algorithm given in [1] uses a combination of ordered cube geodesics and pipes.

An obvious application of *scatter* is to distribute a dataset stored in a given node, say node 0, or more realistically a disk drive attached either directly or indirectly to this node. Then *scatter* will break this data set up into N parts and deliver equal portions to each node. Fig. 14 illustrates another possible use of *scatter*. In many matrix problems, one finds load imbalance because one stage of the algorithm only involves a single row or column. A typical case is LU decomposition where one is finding multipliers from the current column corresponding to the variable to be eliminated. If one is using the optimal two dimensional decomposition for such matrix problems as in Fig. 9, one sees that this step only involves the $\sqrt{N}$ processors in the first column of the node array. Figure 14 shows how we can apply *scatter* to subcubes consisting of rows of nodes and so equalize the load on the nodes. Unfortunately, this method is not practical, as stated, because *scatter* takes time of order $\hat{m}t_{comm}$ where we distribute $\hat{m}$ numbers as $\hat{m}/\sqrt{N}$ packets in $\sqrt{N}$ nodes. The load imbalance that *scatter* is removing is a calculation whose computation time is $\hat{m}t_{calc}$ Thus, in the usual situation where $t_{comm} \gtrsim t_{calc}$, one does not gain. However, one can improve this idea by simultaneously applying the idea of Fig. 14 to the $\sqrt{N}$ columns involved as the "first column" in the next $\sqrt{N}$ steps of LU decomposition. This actually corresponds to applying the *index* algorithm described in Section 3.2. *Index* can be thought of as the homogeneous version of *scatter* just as *expand* is the homogeneous version of *broadcast*. The *index* calculation takes time of order $\hat{m}\log_2 N\, t_{comm}$ which is to be compared with the calculation imbalance which is $\hat{m}\sqrt{N}\, t_{calc}$ for the total of these $\sqrt{N}$ steps. The use of *index* has formally reduced the calculational load imbalance to zero in the limit of large $\sqrt{N}$. Note that the factor $\log_2 N/\sqrt{N}$ is very characteristic of the hypercube and these subtle techniques do not work on simpler architectures such as the two-dimensional mesh.

BROADCAST

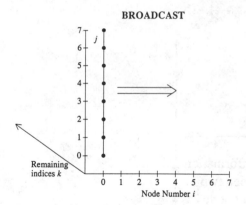

Figure 11
An illustration of *broadcast* for the data structure introduced in Fig. 3.

Broadcast Phase Diagram

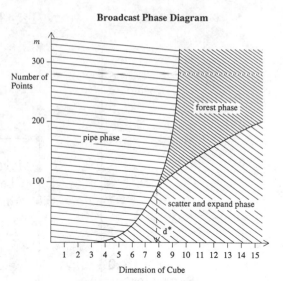

Figure 12

A sketch of the domain spanned by m, the number of words to be broadcast, and $d = \log_2 N$, the dimension of the hypercube. We show three regions where different algorithms dominate. *scatter* followed by *expand* is discussed in Sections 5.2 and 3.3; *pipe* and *forest* are discussed in Section 5.1.

SCATTER

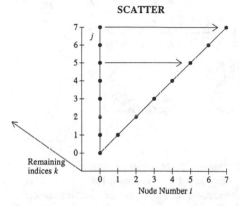

Figure 13
An illustration of *scatter* for the data structure introduced in Fig. 3.

Before

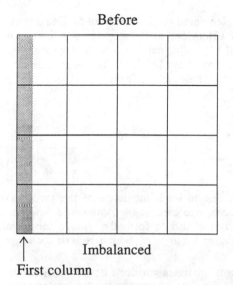

Imbalanced

First column

After SCATTER

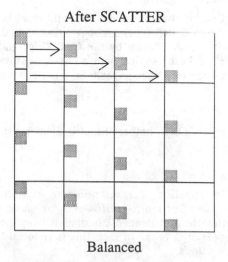

Balanced

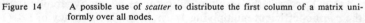

Figure 14   A possible use of *scatter* to distribute the first column of a matrix uniformly over all nodes.

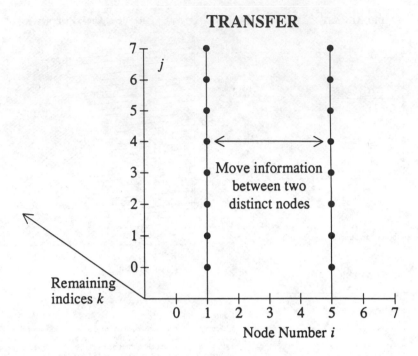

Figure 15   An illustration of *transfer* for the data structure introduced in Fig. 3.

5.3 Transfer

Our final utility *transfer* is perhaps less generally useful, at least in matrix algorithms. As illustrated in Figure 15, it transfers information between two given nodes. *transfer* is needed, when one uses pivoting in LU decomposition. *Transfer* can be implemented optimally as a *dual geodesic pipe* as described in Ref. [4].

6 Matrix Algorithms

Full and banded matrix algorithms are best implemented on the hypercube using a standard two-dimensional decomposition [2,4,10,11,12,13] as long as the message start up is not too large. As shown by the Oak Ridge and INTEL groups, machines with large start up time are best handled with a one-dimensional decomposition [14,15]. For the two dimensional scattered decomposition, one finds typical efficiencies of the form:

$$\frac{1}{\epsilon} - 1 \sim \frac{const}{\sqrt{n}} \tag{11}$$

where n is the number of matrix elements stored in each processor and:

$$const = a + b\frac{t_{comm}}{t_{calc}} \tag{12}$$

In Equation (12), the non-zero value for a is due to load imbalance of the type discussed in Section 5-2. However, as illustrated there, one can, in fact, often use *index* to scatter the imbalanced calculation over the hypercube and so formally remove the term proportional to a. In fact, this is reduced by a factor $\log_2 N/\sqrt{N}$ which is zero for large hypercubes.

These ideas allow one to design an optimal set of matrix algorithms described in detail in Reference [2]. Table 1 records the resultant efficiencies of the hypercube implementations in terms of the *const* coefficient multiplying $1/\sqrt{n}$ in the inefficiency of Eq. (11).

Table 1   Communication Overheads in Optimal Matrix Algorithms

Algorithm	Const (See 11)
Multiplication - Optimal	τ
LU Decomposition*(forward reduction)	
Naive Square Subblock with Scattered Decomposition and No Pivoting	$\dfrac{9}{4} + \dfrac{3\tau}{2}$
Optimal - No Pivoting	$\dfrac{3}{2}\left[1 + \dfrac{1}{2}\,\dfrac{\log_2 N}{\sqrt{N}}\right]\tau$
Optimal - Pivoting	$\dfrac{3}{2}\left[2 + \dfrac{1}{4}\,\dfrac{\log_2 N}{\sqrt{N}}\right]\tau$
Gauss-Jordan Inversion Optimal	$\left[1 + \dfrac{1}{4}\,\dfrac{\log_2 N}{\sqrt{N}}\right]\tau$
Householder Tridiagonalization Optimal	$\dfrac{3}{4}\left[3 + \dfrac{5\log_2 N}{8\sqrt{N}}\right]\tau$
Banded LU Decomposition* (forward reduction)	
Naive - No Pivoting but with Scattered Decomposition	$\tau + 1/2$
Optimal - No Pivoting	$\tau[1 + \dfrac{1}{2}\,\dfrac{\log_2 N}{\sqrt{N}}]$
Optimal - Pivoting	$\tau[2 + \dfrac{1}{4}\,\dfrac{\log_2 N}{\sqrt{N}}]$

*This includes LU decomposition of the matrix and forward reduction of a single right hand side.

References:

1. "Optimal Communication Algorithms on the Hypercube", G. C. Fox, W. Furmanski, C3P-314, July 8, 1986.

2. "Matrix" G. C. Fox and W. Furmanski, C3P-386, December 1986.

3. "The Crystalline Operating System Programmer's Manual for Intel iPSC", A. Kolawa, C3P-287, May 23, 1986.

4. "Solving Problems on Concurrent Processors", Geoffrey C. Fox, Mark A. Johnson, Gregory A. Lyzenga, Steve W. Otto, John K. Salmon, November 1, 1986, to be published by Prentice Hall.

5. Software Supplement to Ref. 4 by D. Walker, G. Fox, and J. Kim.

6. "Iterative Full Matrix-Vector Multiplication on the Hypercube", G. C. Fox, C3P-336, July 29, 1986.

7. "Hypercube Algorithms and Implementations", Oliver A. McBryan, Eric F. Van de Velde (NYU), C3P-266, November 18, 1985. Comparison of Caltech and iPSC Hypercubes.

8. "Distributed Routing Algorithms for Broadcasting and Personalized Communication in Hypercubes", C. Ho and S. Lennart Johnsson, May 1986, Yale University.

9. "Matrix Transposition on Boolean n-cube Configured Ensemble Architectures", C. Ho and S. Lennart Johnsson, September 1986, Yale University.

10. "Matrix Algorithms on the Hypercube I: Matrix Multiplication", G. Fox, A. J. G. Hey, S. Otto, C3P-206, October 1985, to be published in Parallel Computing.

11. "Gauss Jordan Matrix Inversion with Pivoting on the Hypercube", P. Hipes and A. Kuppermann, C3P-347, August 8, 1986.

12. "A Banded Matrix LU Decomposition on the Hypercube", T. Aldcroft, A. Cisneros, G. Fox, W. Furmanski, and D. Walker C3P-348, (in preparation).

13. "Square Matrix Decomposition: Symmetric, Local, Scattered", G. Fox, C3P-97, August, 13, 1984.

14. "Matrix Factorization in a Hypercube Multiprocessor", G. A. Geist and M. T. Heath, in "Hypercube Multiprocessors 1986", edited by M. T. Heath, SIAM, 1986.

15. "Matrix Computation on Distributed Memory Multiprocessors", C. Moler in "Hypercube Multiprocessors 1986", edited by M. T. Heath, SIAM, 1986.

Switching between Interrupt Driven and Polled Communication Systems on a Hypercube[*]

A. CISNEROS[†‡] AND A. KOLAWA[†]

Abstract. We present algorithms to switch between asynchronous and polled communication systems on a hypercube. These algorithms require synchronization routines implemented by message passing on machines without a hardware global line. In switching from asynchronous to polled communications verification that all messages have been received is necessary. The algorithms were implemented on the Caltech/JPL hypercube Mark II model. Timings were taken on the same machine.

April 3, 1986

Introduction. Two types of communication systems are widely used on distributed memory multiple instruction multiple data concurrent computers: a polled system and an interrupt driven system. The polled system is used to send and receive messages between processors connected by a physical communication channel. This system is synchronous in the sense that there must be a corresponding read statement on the receiving end for every write statement on the sending end; programs in different processors proceed in loose lockstep. The interrupt driven system of communications is used to send messages from a processor to any other processor. This system is asynchronous since there is no such restriction on programs executing on different processors. There need not be an explicit read statement for every message received. In one type of asynchronous system, processors are interrupted and a service routine in the user's program decides what to do with the message. In another type of asynchronous system received messages are simply stored in buffers and the user's program looks at messages when it pleases.

At the present stage in the development of hypercubes (both hardware and software), interrupt driven operating systems (IDOS) have not achieved the required communication

---

* Work supported in part by DOE grant DE-FG-03-85ER25009, and the Parsons and System Development Foundations.

† California Institute of Technology, Pasadena, California 91125

‡ On leave from Instituto Politecnico Nacional, Mexico. Supported by Comision de Operacion y Fomento de las Actividades Academicas I.P.N. and by Sistema Nacional de Investigadores, Mexico.

speed to be useful in all applications [2,3]. For most problems, which have been solved on the Caltech/JPL hypercube (Mark II model), it has been sufficient to use a fast synchronous communications system called the Crystalline Operating System (CrOS) [1]. However, some applications use both CrOS and IDOS with frequent switching between them during run time. This requires a switching routine, which enables a proper change between communication systems.

We first present a simple algorithm to synchronize processors before switching from CrOS to IDOS (section 2). We then discuss a synchronization algorithm for IDOS (section 3). This routine synchronizes all processors. However, it is by itself not adequate for use in switching from IDOS to CrOS except in a special case because it does not guarantee that messages are not en route. We then present a general synchronization algorithm based on the previous one (section 4). We assume that we have an asynchronous communication system of the interrupt driven type. If the system is of the type that simply store messages in a memory buffer, a simple modification of the algorithms is necessary (section 5). Timings are given in section 6.

It is necessary to synchronize all processors in passing from IDOS to CrOS, or vice versa, simply because communication errors would occur otherwise. If a processor switches from IDOS to CrOS whenever it is ready, without previous synchronization, another processor still in IDOS may send a message to it, or may send a message that needs to be forwarded through it; a communication error results. Synchronization is necessary but not sufficient to switch from IDOS to CrOS as we will see. To do it properly every node has to have global information about the communication status in the computer. If the machine has a hardware global line, it can be used to synchronize processors and to provide the required information. When a global line is not available, as on the Mark II machine, synchronization must be accomplished by message passing. In both cases the switching routine from asynchronous to polled systems must guarantee that the change occurs when all the messages sent in IDOS have been received in the same system. This is not a trivial task, because in a general use of IDOS processors do not know a priori how many messages they should receive. Communication errors will also occur in switching from CrOS to IDOS if processors are not synchronized first.

Switching from the synchronous to asynchronous communication system. The simplest way to synchronize processors in a hypercube using polled communications is to write and read a message to and from each channel in order. The exchanged messages need to carry no other information content than their presence. The explicit routine is:

1) $i=0$

2) Write a message to channel i.

3) Read a message from channel i.

4) Increment i, exit if i equals dimension of cube. Go to step 2.

This algorithm synchronizes all processors (except for the time delay in processing messages.) This can be seen by noting that once a processor exits step 3 for a value of i, then the subcube connected by channels $0,1,2,...,i$ which contains this processor has been synchronized. No single processor in this subcube can exit step 3 (for this value of i) unless all other processors in the subcube have sent the first $i+1$ messages. We assume that communication channels are full duplex in steps 2) and 3). In case channels are half duplex the routine is slightly complicated by the fact that one of the processors connected to channel i first writes and then reads while the other one must first read and then write. A choice must be made as to which processor writes first.

After processors are synchronized a routine is called to switch to the asynchronous communication system.

A simple synchronization algorithm in an asynchronous communication system. In this section we describe a simple synchronization algorithm, which can be used when the concurrent computer is in the asynchronous mode. (We will call the routine which is used for synchronization *Cube_sync*.) We assume that the system has the ability to distinguish between different types of messages[1]. Synchronization is achieved by sending messages of a special type which we will call SYNC.

The synchronization algorithm looks as follows. We first set up on each processor a number of flags equal to the dimension of cube; one for each physical channel. Flags are initially cleared. (Channel i flag will be set to 1 when a processor receives a SYNC message from channel i.) Whenever the synchronization routine is invoked, a SYNC message is sent to the nearest neighbor through channel 0; the processor then waits until it gets a SYNC message from this channel. It does so by checking the status of channel 0 flag. It now sends a SYNC message through channel 1, waits for a SYNC message from channel 1, and so on.

The strict description of the above algorithm looks as follows:

1) $i = 0$

2) Send a SYNC message to nearest neighbor on channel i.

3) Check channel i flag, wait until it is set. (Wait if processor connected to channel i has not sent a SYNC message)

4) Increment i, exit if i equals dimension of cube. Go to step 2.

This algorithm synchronizes all processors (except for the time delay in processing SYNC messages.) The comment we gave at the end of section 2 applies here to understand the operation of the routine. We propose to call this synchronization algorithm *Cube_sync*.

General algorithm to switch between asynchronous and synchronous communication systems. To switch from IDOS to CrOS it is necessary to synchronize all processors and to verify that all messages have been received. *Cube_sync* cannot by itself be used for this purpose. *Cube_sync* could be called when processors have sent all messages they need to send and then switch, but this will not work. The difficulty lies in the fact that the last non-SYNC messages could still be en route when processors come out of *Cube_sync*. If they switch to polled communications at this point, there will be a communications error. *Cube_sync* can be used for this purpose in the special case when processors know how many messages they will receive in IDOS. The procedure is as follows; processors simply count received messages. After all messages to be sent have been sent, processors check whether all messages to be received have been received before calling *Cube_sync* and switching to CrOS.

A general procedure to synchronize processors in IDOS must make sure that there are no messages en route without a priori knowledge of the number of messages to be sent. There must be a way to access the system itself to find out if a message is being forwarded. We make use of a message flag which is set whenever a message of any type other than SYNC reaches a processor, whether the message is for itself or to be forwarded.

---

[1] This assumption is reasonable because nearly every machine in the market has this ability.

General synchronization routine.

1) Execute *Cube_sync* and during the time of execution set the message flag to one if any message of type different from SYNC has been processed.

2) Copy value of the message flag to some other variable (call it MSG) which will be sent to other processors.

3) Clear message flag.

4) Execute *Cube_sync* exchanging the value of MSG at the same time by sending it as part of the SYNC message. (In our system this is done sending MSG in an unused portion of the SYNC message header.) The value of MSG is *or—ed* with the value of MSG received from a channel and replaces the old value of MSG. The new value of MSG is sent with the SYNC message through the next channel (in step 2 of *Cube_sync*.) If final value of MSG is not zero go to 2, otherwise exit. (This point provides every processor with global knowledge about any message of type different from SYNC being processed anywhere in the machine.)

Note that on exit from *Cube_sync* in step 4 each processor will have the global *or* of the MSG values from all processors. If the value is not zero, at least one processor received a non SYNC message and the procedure must be repeated until all processors report no non-SYNC messages.

Non-interrupt asynchronous systems. We have assumed that we are using an asynchronous system of communications of the interrupt driven type. There is another type of commonly used asynchronous communication system in which the receiving processor is not interrupted to take care of the message. Messages are simply put in a memory buffer; the INTEL hypercube uses this mode, for example. In this case step 3 of *Cube_sync* must be modified to:

3) Search received messages for a SYNC message from channel i, wait until it is seen.

Sync messages are labeled for the channel on which they are sent, or channel number can be deduced from the source processor number which should be part of the header. The channel flags used in *Cube_sync* (section 3) are not necessary.

The implementation of the algorithm presented in the previous section requires modification of the original operating system. In order to execute step 1 of the General Synchronization Routine, the operating system must set the message flag whenever a message is forwarded. In general such a modification is a minor one and easy to implement.

Switching speed timings on the Caltech/JPL Mark II hypercube. We measured the switching speed using the timers on each of the processors of the Mark II hypercube. A simple loop containing the calls async() and sync() was timed. async() synchronizes processors in CrOS and then sets the processor state to IDOS; sync() is the IDOS synchronization routine described in section 4 with a switch to CrOS.

Results

Dimension of cube	time for running async() sync()
3	7.7 ms
4	10.0 ms
5	12.3 ms

The times are closely proportional to the dimension of cube, as they should. Loop overhead is negligible compared to total time in this case. CPU clock speed was 8 MHz.

Conclusions. We have presented general algorithms to switch between synchronous and asynchronous communication systems. The algorithms can be used on any model of hypercube and the ideas presented can be used in implementing switching algorithms in other types of concurrent computers. The implementation of the algorithm is fast enough to be used in applications such as iterative solvers of irregular finite element problems [4].

REFERENCES

(1) G. C. Fox et. al., *Solving Problems on Concurrent Processors*, (to be published by Prentice Hall Englewood Cliffs, New Jersey)

(2) M. Johnson, *An Interrupt Driven Communication System*, January (1985), *Csup* 3*P*-137

(3) G. C. Fox, A. Kolawa, *Concurrent Searching of a Data Base - An Application of the Hypercube to Symbolic Quantum Chromodynamics*, CALT-68-1296 (1985).

(4) A. Cisneros, *A Finite Element-Finite Difference Multigrid Solver for the Hypercube Parallel Computer*, C^3P document to appear.

Increasing Hypercube Communication on Low-Dimensional Problems

JOHN L. GUSTAFSON*

Abstract. We present a simple but powerful hardware technique for greatly increasing interprocessor bandwidth on an arbitrary hypercube of processors. If each processing node has N links to other nodes, then a configuration with only N/M links in use is capable of increasing bandwidth by M-fold for applications requiring only (N/M)-dimensional interconnect. This allows hypercubes to combine the advantages of parallel buses and robust serial interconnections. This is particularly important on hypercubes favoring operations on contiguous vectors, since such machines encourage domain decomposition along "pencils" occupying an entire dimension rather than subregions which minimize the ratio of surface area to volume. A specific example is given for the FPS T Series, which presents the additional challenge of having multiplexed links. T Series configurations up to 128 processors can elect to use a planar (toroidal) interconnect as a linear (ring) interconnect operating at double the communications rate. Examples of increased speed on applications are given.

Introduction. Multiprocessors based on the binary N-cube interconnect contain nearest-neighbor meshes of dimension less than or equal to N. This can be demonstrated by *partitioning* the N-digit binary (Gray code) numbering of each node. Within a partition of n bits, the Gray-code changes in bits represent linear numbering of 2^n processors along a particular dimension. Different partitions represent different dimensions. For example, suppose processors in a 6-dimensional binary cube have numbers represented $b_1b_2b_3b_4b_5b_6$, where b_i is a binary digit. Then the partitioning $(b_1)(b_2)(b_3b_4b_5b_6)$ represents a three-dimensional domain of size 2x2x16 (with wraparound). Thus the extreme cases are N partitions with one bit each (representing an N-dimensional domain with two processors on every edge) and a single partition representing a 1-dimensional domain of 2^N processors.

Physical implementations of hypercube computers require the existence of N physical links out of each processor, but do *not* specify how those physical links are selected or switched out of the CPU. For example, one might be restricted to the use of a single link at any time, and communication across that link might not be able to overlap other CPU activities. This is the situation in the Caltech Cosmic Cube, and in the Intel iPSC productization of that hypercube. The NCUBE design allows simultaneous

---

*Floating Point Systems, Inc., Beaverton, Oregon 97006

operation of many DMA links; roughly 9 of the 22 links (11 input, 11 output) can be active at any time before main memory bandwidth is exhausted. The FPS T Series processors are intermediate between these two, in that 4 out of 15 bidirectional links can be active at any time, and can overlap other CPU activities.

The two preceding paragraphs point to the conclusion that *communications bandwidth is wasted when running problems of low dimensionality* on machines which have the capacity for using several links simultaneously. Interprocessor communication is typically the most precious resource in a hypercube and is often the most important factor in application efficiency. In principle, the hardware connections in a hypercube are entirely point-to-point, implying that there is really no way to recoup the unused links without changing the system framework. In practice, there is a solution which exploits the fact that some systems have a *maximum* configuration which is much larger than the *typical* configuration.

Link Doubling. The FPS T Series provides an example of using link doubling to improve effective communication speed, although the technique is by no means confined to that version of the hypercube. The four bidirectional links embodied in the Inmos Transputer in a node are each software-switchable to one of four interprocessor links. The former are referred to herein as "hard links" whereas the latter are referred to as "soft links". They are organized as shown in Figure 1.

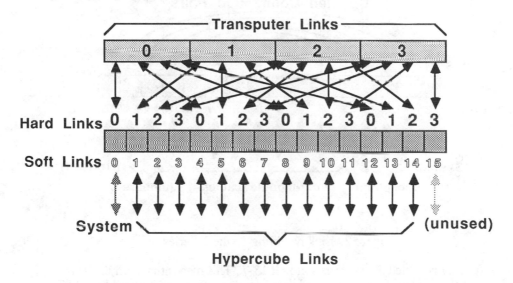

Figure 1. T Series Link Organization

If i is the number of a soft link and j is the number of the hard link to which it maps, then

$$j = i \bmod 4$$

so that the burden on the hard links increases evenly as the system grows. Soft link 0 is used by the "system ring", the one-dimensional interconnect used for such functions as uploading or downloading data and programs. Soft link 15 is not driven. The remaining 14 are available for hypercube interconnections.

Each processor occupies one circuit board, and eight boards are combined with system facilities to form a "module" which consumes the system soft link 0 and the first three hypercube links. Note that there is thus no need to ever multiplex the links for the module, or 3-cube. The packaging is such that all external cabling is module-to-module, using ordinary D-connectors with 8 bidirectional channels (32 wires). Two modules are mounted in a cabinet connected with such a cable combining soft link 4 from every node. At this point there is contention between soft link 4 and soft link 0, since both map to hard link 0. To reassign all four hard links to a different set of soft links takes about 320 μseconds. If no reassignment is needed, message startup time is quite low… approximately 9 μseconds.

Larger systems further increase the number of roles played by the hard links. The largest system so far configured uses up to soft link 6 (64 processors). At any time, the hard links constitute a two-dimensional (toroidal) domain capable of fine-grained parallelism. Applications requiring simultaneous use of more than four soft links tend to be restricted to coarser-grained parallelism because of the time to reconfigure links.

Less than half of the soft links have been used, suggesting that in fact the remaining links can be *doubled up* by adding cables to the system. This need have no impact whatsoever on system software which already ignores those channels on small systems, but provides the applications programmer with additional paths for communication. When links are doubled, the two-dimensional hard interconnect becomes a one-dimensional hard interconnect with *twice the bandwidth* between nearest-neighbor processors. A doubling scheme is shown in Figure 2.

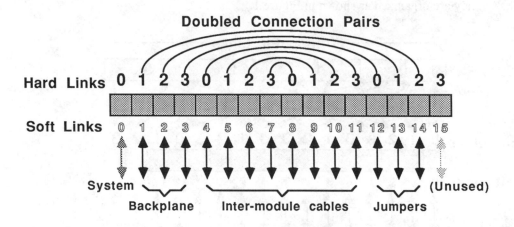

Figure 2. Link Doubling on the T Series

Soft link *j* is cabled the same as soft link 15–*j*. This means that hard link 0 is always doubled by hard link 3, and hard link 1 is always doubled by hard link 2. This is essential for one-dimensional interconnection subsets to have full use of all four links, since hard links 0 and 3 will always connect one side of every processing node to a neighbor and hard links 1 and 2 will always connect the other side. Since soft links 1 to 3 are actually connected across the backplane of a module, the easiest way to double them is to place a *jumper* across corresponding cable sockets for soft links 14 to 12. Schematically, such jumpers can be pictured as shown in Figure 3.

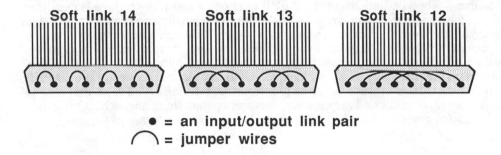

• = an input/output link pair
⌒ = jumper wires

Figure 3. Jumpers to Duplicate Backplane Connections

For a 64-processor system, say, the additional hardware required is simply four cables and 12 jumpers, and insignificant cost compared to the rest of the system. Yet the effect is to double the performance of problems which are badly communication bound! The scheme works up to a 128-processor system, which is a large (and fairly expensive) configuration of the T Series. For larger configurations, one can gradually remove the doubling, resulting in loss of double bandwidth across certain paths resembling "fault lines" in the domain decomposition.

Example: 2D Fourier Transform. On a 16-processor system, the four hard links of a T Series node provide the two-dimensional point-to-point topology shown in Figure 4, where the hollow typeface denotes the soft link numbering.

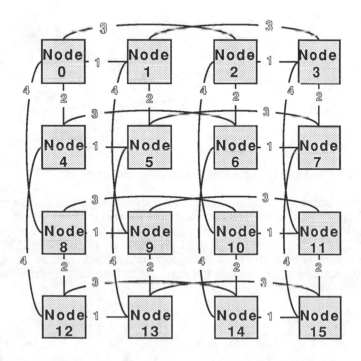

Figure 4. 16-Processor Topology for 2D FFT

However, when performing a radix 2 FFT, only *one dimension at a time* is exercised within the network; in fact, only one of the four possible directions out of a processor is needed to perform the data exchange for the "butterfly" computations which span processors. Now supposed that the application programmer recognizes that there are two paths between each processor pair; one could communicate the real data and the other path the imaginary data, for example. On one x-directional pass of the 2D FFT, soft link 12 is used to attach the same processors as soft link 3, and since they map to hard link 0 and hard link 3 respectively, they can operate simultaneously. On the other x-direction pass, soft link 14 supplements soft link 1 simultaneously.

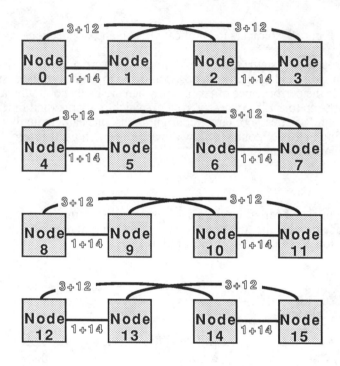

Figure 5. Doubled Links for x-Direction Passes of 2D FFT

Then the links must be reconfigured to perform the y-direction passes, but the amount of computation is large relative to the time to reconfigure the soft links.

Tests have shown this algorithm, without link doubling, to perform at about 12 MFLOPS on a 512x512 FFT, where each of the processors contains a 128x128 point subdomain of complex 64-bit numbers. Communication easily dominates the computation in this case. The link doubling is expected to increase the performance to about 20 MFLOPS.

Significance for Vector Processing. Several hypercubes offer or plan to offer some form of vector arithmetic capability. This affects the domain decomposition in a profound way, as illustrated in Figure 6.

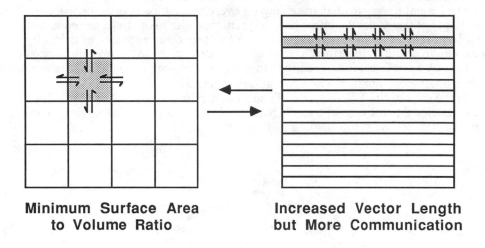

**Minimum Surface Area
to Volume Ratio**

**Increased Vector Length
but More Communication**

Figure 6. Domain Decomposition Tradeoffs

The Caltech paradigm is to minimize the ratio of surface area to volume so as to minimize the penalty for communication; this implies the use of squares or cubes as optimal subdivisions of 2-space and 3-space. However, this can make vectors short enough that the startup time for the vector operation reduces the performance. On a vector hypercube, one attempts to make the domains as long and thin as possible, with the optimal ratio being where the computation on interior points *just barely* overlaps communication of the exterior points.

With simultaneous link operation, the communication time is the *maximum* of the directions communicated, not the sum. In the example in Figure 6, the communication time will be increased four times by using the method on the right. However, the horizontal communication is completely eliminated.

The implication of link doubling for vector hypercubes is simply to reduce the penalty for such long vectors, permitting a higher fraction of peak theoretical speed to be attained without degradation by non-overlapped communication. In the case of the T Series, many two-dimensional problems appear to be optimally solved by making the subdomains long enough to span the entire rectangle and thus eliminating the need to communicate at all across the ends. With link doubling, the two-dimensional problem can be treated with a one-dimensional interconnect as in Figure 6, where each nearest-neighbor connection is twice as fast. A unidirectional transfer currently has an asymptotic speed of 0.691 MBytes/s on the T Series, with half speed achieved for transfers of length 26 bytes. With link doubling, the asymptotic speed on one-dimensional topologies is 1.382 MBytes/s, which brings the ratio of compute speed:link speed down to about 35:1 for 64-bit computations.

Generalization to *M*-Fold Increases. Suppose the existence of a hypercube node capable of N link communications, of which K can be simultaneous, and an application requiring a (K/M)-dimensional nearest-neighbor ensemble, where M divides K evenly and $1<M\leq K$. Then a configuration of dimension (N/M) or less can be configured so that there are M links for every nearest-neighbor connection, effectively increasing communication speed M-fold in any *single* dimension at a time.

The idea of having to change cabling for every application is obviously not appealing, but that is not the intent here. Hypercubes with many links per node have *typical* configurations that use only a fraction of that maximum number of links. It appears quite practical, therefore, to replicate link connections to the maximum degree permitted by a configuration; cabling changes are made when the hypercube is upgraded to more processors, not from one application to another.

In the case of the T Series, $N=14$ and $K=4$, and implying $M=2$ or $M=4$. The latter case is restricted to the case of a single module (8 processors), but in fact one could cable so as to allow 2.7 MByte/s coupling as shown in Figure 7.

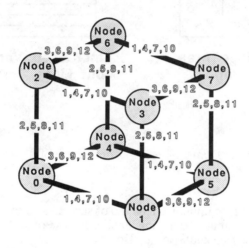

Figure 7. Link Quadrupling on a 3-Cube

Conclusions. The technique of link doubling on hypercubes allows one to recoup one of the features of a bus architecture: smaller configurations can have larger communication bandwidths. Note that this goes completely against the theology of ensemble architectures, since link doubling does not scale! It is difficult to resist such increases in bandwidth, however, since the impact on software appears to be so minor and the additional hardware is very inexpensive compared to the rest of the system. Link doubling could become a standard technique for performance improvement on any commercial hypercube which is available in a wide range of sizes.

Passing Messages in Link-Bound Hypercubes

QUENTIN F. STOUT* AND BRUCE WAGAR*

Abstract: In link-bound hypercubes local processing is ignored, communication time predominates, and all PEs can use all communication links simultaneously. For this model algorithms are developed for a variety of intensive message-passing tasks such as one PE sending a (long) message to another, broadcasting a message from one PE to all others, each PE broadcasting a message to all others, transposing a matrix, and PEs exchanging messages via a fixed permutation. For all problems algorithms are given which achieve a time where the highest-order term is optimal. Our algorithm for exchanging via a fixed permutation can be viewed as a deterministic analogue of Valiant's randomized routing.

Introduction

This paper uses a model of hypercubes in which communication time is assumed to predominate, and local processing time by the processing elements (PEs) can be ignored. We are interested in problems where extensive communication is required because very long messages are being sent, and where all PEs are available to participate in the task and know the communication task being performed. Further, we assume that each processor can utilize all of its communication links simultaneously, where the links between neighboring processors can be used in both directions simultaneously. Thus a processor in a d-dimensional hypercube may be handling $2d$ messages simultaneously, receiving d and sending d. This property we call *link-bound*, as opposed to other possibilites such as processor-bound (in which each PE can do only one operation at a time) or DMA-bound (in which there is an upper bound on the number of

---

*Department of Electrical Engineering and Computer Science, University of Michigan, Ann Arbor, MI 48109-2122, USA. This research was partially supported by National Science Foundation grant DCR-8507851.

messages which can go in and out of a PE at one time). While no hypercube can currently use all of its communication links simultaneously, several manufacturers are trying to attain such ability. The NCUBE machines apparently come the closest, and the FPS T-Series machines have nodes capable of 4 bi-directional communications at the same time.

Throughout, n represents the number of nodes in the hypercube and d represents the dimension, i.e., $n = 2^d$. We assume that it takes $am+b$ time for a PE to send a message of length m to a neighbor, where $a,b > 0$ and b represents the time for start-up and termination. We assume that a PE receiving a packet must finish receiving the packet before any portion of it can be utilized. This is sometimes called the *store-and-forward* or *packet-switched* model, as opposed to a circuit-switched model. In general a and b are treated as constants and the algorithms are analyzed as functions of n (or d) and m. As in [SaSc, HoJo], we ignore the effects of rounding or truncating. Further, because special cases arise for various relative values of the parameters, the exact formulas will be given only for m sufficiently large. Because we are most interested in processing long messages, the term containing the highest power of m will be called the highest-order term.

Several of the problems considered herein, such as broadcasting a message from one PE to all others, have been previously considered by [SaSc] and [HoJo]. Both of these papers use the model used here, but give slightly slower algorithms. In most problems, simple arguments show that our highest-order term is optimal. In a few cases we believe that our algorithms are optimal, but are unable to prove this because our arguments can bound terms involving a, m, and n, or terms involving b and d, but not sums of terms of different types. Due to severe space limitations, this paper states a few problems, gives the times of our best algorithms, and briefly discusses a few of the algorithms. Some related problems for which we have efficient algorithms, but which are not included here because of space limitations, are data balancing (each PE starts with some number of items and the goal is to divide the items evenly among the PEs) and rotating messages (each PE has a message of length m to be viewed by all other PEs, but because of memory limitations no PE can hold more than one such message at a time). We emphasize the techniques used to develop the algorithms rather than the details of specific algorithms. Complete details appear in [StWa].

Algorithm Techniques

In the pursuit of fast message-passing algorithms, a variety of standard techniques can be used. These include:

Pipelining Packets: To send a message of length m over a path with h hops by transmitting the entire message one hop at a time takes exactly $h(am+b)$ time. This can be reduced by dividing the message into packets and sending them in a pipelined fashion. If packets of size p are used, then there will be m/p packets (recall that truncations are ignored to simplify exposition). The last packet starts leaving the originating PE at time $(m/p - 1)*(ap+b)$, and finishes arriving at its destination at time $(h + m/p - 1)*(ap+b)$. This is minimized when $p = [mb/a(h-1)]^{1/2}$, giving a total time of $am + 2[ab(h-1)]^{1/2}m^{1/2} + b(h-1)$.

Multiple Pathways: Different parts of a message can be sent along different paths and reassembled in proper order at their destination, reducing the time needed on each path. Pushing this idea to its extreme, one should try to use nearly all links of the hypercube at once, using symmetry to balance the communication load along different pathways.

Dynamic Packets: Since all PEs know the message-passing task being performed, packets can be partitioned or recombined in transit, not just at the endpoints. If two packets in a PE have to go along the same next hop, combining them reduces the total transmission time by b, i.e., it requires less communication overhead. Further, the packets do not need to contain additional routing or control information which would increase the effective message length.

Completing Algorithms: Algorithms developed for a single source can be converted to ones where each PE is a source by combining stages, typically using dynamic packets. The resulting algorithm is called the "complete" version of the original algorithm. This significantly reduces overhead compared to running multiple copies of the same algorithm. Often it is best to complete an algorithm which is not the optimal single source algorithm, but which has fewer stages.

Broadcasting

In *broadcasting* a PE (assumed to be PE 0) has a message of length m to be sent to all other PEs. This can be accomplished by standard recursive doubling, which takes $d(am+b)$ time and cannot be pipelined because PE 0 is used in all stages. A faster solution can be obtained by using multiple pathways and pipelining. To see this, let C_i denote the set of PEs which are exactly i hops from PE 0, i.e., C_i consists of all PEs with exactly i 1s in their label. A basic algorithm for broadcasting is as follows:
1. Break the data into d equal pieces.
2. At stage i, $0 \le i \le d$, PEs in C_i send pieces forward to neighbors in C_{i+1} and backward to neighbors in C_{i-1}. PEs in C_{i+1} receive $i+1$ pieces and PEs in C_{i-1} receive $d-i+1$, completing their reception of the message. (At stages 0 and 1 only forward sending occurs and at stage d only backwards sending occurs.)

Figure 1 shows the labels of pieces sent along the various directions.

The basic algorithm takes $(d+1)*(am/d + b)$ time, which has a high order term approximately 1/d times the high order term of recursive doubling. The time can be improved by pipelining the pieces into "waves", where each wave has $[m(d-1)a/db]^{1/2}$ items. Further, the last stage (when PE n-1 is sending packets backwards) can be eliminated by having node 0 send out the packets to these destination nodes (in C_{d-1}) via separate paths just after the last wave has left it. (See [StWa] for details.) The time of our algorithm, compared to previous algorithms, is

[StWa] $(a/d)m + 2[ab(d-1)/d)]^{1/2}m^{1/2} + (d-1)b$

[HoJo] $(a/d)m + 2[ab]^{1/2}m^{1/2} + db$

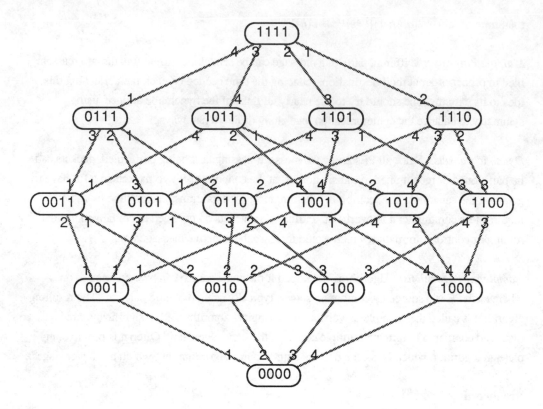

Figure 1. Numbers show pieces sent

Our highest-order term is optimal since it takes at least $(a/d)m + b$ time for PE 0 to send the message anywhere.

Complete Broadcast

In a complete broadcast each PE has a message of length m to be received by all other PEs. This can be efficiently solved by using a slightly slower single source broadcast algorithm with no backwards transmission. At the beginning of stage k, $0 \le k \le d-1$, every PE in C_k has all m items. These are broken into $k+1$ pieces of size $m/(k+1)$ and sent to PEs in C_{k+1} so that each PE in C_{k+1} receives everything. (Notice that this is an example of dynamic packets.) This single source algorithm is then completed, so that at stage k each node does its part of the kth stage for all PEs at distance k. Comparing this to previous algorithms, we obtain

[StWa] $[a(n-1)/d]m + db$

[SaSc] $[a(n+d^2)/d]m + (d+1)b$

Again the highest-order term of our algorithm is optimal because each PE must receive messages with a total length of $(n-1)m$, which takes at least $[a(n-1)/d]m + b$ time.

Opposite Corner Send

In this problem, a PE sends a message of length m to the PE at the opposite corner of the cube (e.g., PE 0 sends to n-1). By combining pipelining and multiple pathways using every edge of the hypercube, we obtain a time of

[StWa] $(a/d)m + 2\{[(d+1)ab]/[d(d-1)]\}^{1/2}m^{1/2} + (d-1)b$.

While this problem has not been explicitly considered by others, it is used repeatedly in our later algorithms. Since it takes at least $(a/d)m + b$ time for a message of length m to leave a PE, the highest-order term is optimal. While each edge of the hypercube is used, only one direction along each edge is used, and thus an exchange of messages between opposite corners can occur in the same time.

Arbitrary Send

In this problem, a PE is sending a message of length m to an arbitrary PE. This generalizes the opposite corner send, using opposite corner sends along multiple pathways. If the nodes are separated by h hops, $h \ge 5$, our algorithm has the following time

[StWa] $(a/d)m + 2\{[(d+1)ab]/[d(d-1)]\}^{1/2}m^{1/2} + (h-1)b$.

Inversion

Here each PE sends a message of length m to the PE in the opposite corner. By completing an opposite corner send algorithm we obtain

[StWa] $am + db$.

The highest-order term can be seen to be optimal by halving the hypercube into 2 subcubes and considering the amount of information which must pass along the $n/2$ wires connecting the halves.

Distribute (also called gather/scatter or personalized communication)

In this problem PE 0 has a different message of length m for each other PE. The inverse problem, collect, involves each PE sending a message of length m to PE 0, and can be efficiently solved by running the distribute algorithm in reverse. By using opposite corner sends to all all PEs (viewing each other PE as the opposite corner of a subcube) and overlapping their stages, we obtain

[StWa]   Less than $[a(n\text{-}1)/d]m + db$

[SaSc] $[a(n\text{-}1)]m + db$

[HoJo]   asymptotically $[a(n\text{-}1)/d]m + db$

Here "asymptotically" means that for fixed a and b, for any d the coefficient of the high order term is slightly larger than that given, but the difference tends to 0 as d tends to infinity. By ours being "less than" the given amount we have an algorithm with a running time strictly less than the indicated time. We can prove a lower bound of $[a(n\text{-}1)/d]m + cdb/\ln(d)$ for some constant $c > 0$.

Complete Exchange

Here each PE has a different message of length m for each other PE. By completing a distribution algorithm we obtain

[StWa] $(an/2)m + db$

[SaSc] $(adn)m + db$

The highest-order term can be seen to be optimal by halving the hypercube into 2 subcubes and considering the amount of information which must pass between the $n/2$ wires connecting the halves.

Permuted Send

Here there is a known permutation π such that PE i sends a message of length m to PE $\pi(i)$. We use the fact that π is known to eliminate having to disseminate its description, which would increase the message length. For our algorithm, each PE breaks its message into n packets of size m/n. These are distributed via a complete exchange to all PEs. Each PE then has a packet for each other PE, so a second complete exchange finishes the algorithm. Breaking a message into small pieces and sending them everywhere is a deterministic analogue of Valiant's randomized routing, which guarantees fast expected time for permuted send by picking random intermediate destinations [Va]. The time of the algorithm is

[StWa] $am + 2db$

The highest-order term is optimal because it includes inversion as a special case.

Matrix Transposition

The PE at $x_1x_2...x_d$ (i.e., its index in binary) sends a message of length m to the PE at $x_{1+d/2}x_{2+d/2}...x_1x_2...x_{d/2}$. This is true matrix transposition when matrices are stored as square submatrices, whether or not Gray coding is used to assign submatrices to PEs. If standard hypercube routing algorithms are used for this problem, where the algorithm picks paths that proceed in a left-right or right-left progression through the bits that differ between the source and destination, then the time will be $\Omega(amn^{1/2})$ since $n^{1/2}$ messages will pass through PE 0 [Va]. Matrix transposition is also analyzed in [SaSc], but they assume that the matrix is initially stored columnwise and the goal is to store it rowwise.. In this case each PE needs to send the same amount of its data to each other PE, and their matrix transposition problem is identical to our complete exchange problem.

Our algorithm breaks the hypercube into edge disjoint "logical hypercubes", where each logical hypercube does an inversion. An edge of a logical hypercube is implemented via a 2-dimensional subcube of the real hypercube. This special case of permuted send can be accomplished in approximately half the time of the general permuted send.

[StWa] $(a/2)m + (2ab)^{1/2}m^{1/2} + b$

The highest-order term can be seen to be optimal by noting that half of the PEs with a 0 as their first digit (the half with a 1 as their $(d/2+1)$st digit) must send data to the half of the PEs with a 1 as their first digit, so $n/4$ messages of length m must pass over the $n/2$ wires separating these subcubes.

Conclusion

We have shown that link-bound hypercubes can make effective use of all of their communication links to perform some common communication-intensive tasks. Since a lower bound for some of these tasks is the time needed to send out the data from an originating node, such tasks would take longer on more restricted machines in which PEs cannot use all their communication links at one time. Thus our algorithms provide support for the belief that it is useful to build machines where PEs can use all of their links simultaneously.

By systematically applying a few message-passing techniques we were able to develop a collection of algorithms giving efficient solutions to a wide range of problems. These algorithms are superior to those appearing earlier, and we believe that some are optimal. Unfortunately good lower bound proofs seem to be difficult since they must incorporate both bandwidth considerations and an accounting of start-up time.

References

[HoJo]   C.-T. Ho and S.L. Johnsson, *Distributed routing algorithms for broadcasting and personalized communication in hypercubes*, Proc. 1986 Int'l. Conf. on Parallel Proc., 640-648.

[SaSc]   Y. Saad and M.H. Schultz, *Data communication in hypercubes*, Yale Univ. Dept. of Computer Science Research Report YALEU/DCS/RR-428, 1985.

[StWa]   Q.F. Stout and B. Wagar, *Algorithms for message passing in link-bound hypercubes*, submitted.

[Va]   L.G. Valiant, *A Scheme for Parallel Communication*, SIAM J. Computing, 11 (1982), pp. 350-361,

Incomplete Hypercubes

HOWARD P. KATSEFF*

Abstract. A widely used topology for the interconnection of computing nodes in multiprocessor systems is the binary hypercube. This topology has the advantage of simple, deadlock-free routing and broadcast algorithms. Since a k-dimensional hypercube has 2^k vertices, these systems are restricted to having exactly 2^k computing nodes. Because system sizes must be a power of two, there are large gaps in the sizes of systems that can be built with hypercubes.

This paper presents routing and broadcast algorithms for hypercubes that are missing certain of their nodes, called *incomplete hypercubes*. Unlike hypercubes, incomplete hypercubes can be used to interconnect systems with any number of processors. The routing and broadcast algorithms for incomplete hypercubes are also simple and deadlock-free.

Introduction. In 1963, Squire and Palais proposed a message-passing multiprocessor computer system with 2^k processing nodes, in which each node is placed at the vertex of an k-dimensional hypercube and the edges of the hypercube are links between the processors [1]. A later paper [2] described simple algorithms for routing and for broadcasting messages between arbitrary nodes of the hypercube. It has been shown that the routing algorithms pass messages without deadlock [3], and have a worst-case path length of k.

A problem with the hypercube topology is that the number of nodes in a system must be a power of 2. In practical terms, this is a severe restriction on the sizes of systems that can be built. This restriction can be overcome by using an *incomplete hypercube*, a hypercube missing certain of its nodes. Unlike hypercubes, incomplete hypercubes can be constructed with any number of nodes. The algorithms presented here for routing and broadcasting on an incomplete hypercube are nearly as simple as

---

*AT&T Bell Laboratories, Holmdel, NJ 07733.

those for the hypercube. Furthermore, the routing algorithm for the incomplete hypercube has similar performance characteristics as the routing algorithm for the hypercube. For example, the algorithm passes messages without deadlock and for an incomplete hypercube with n nodes, have a worst-case path length of $\lceil \log_2 n \rceil$.

Nomenclature. We refer to the processors of a multiprocessor computer system as *nodes*, and the communications links connecting processors as *links*. The processors communicate by passing *messages* on these links. A message sent from one processor to another may be routed through intermediate processors. The ordered list of processors visited by the message is a *path*. The *length* of a path is the number of links in the path.

We use *hypercube* to refer to a boolean hypercube, also known as a boolean n-cube or binary cube. A hypercube with n nodes is constructed by numbering the nodes from 0 to $n-1$ and linking each pair of nodes whose binary representations differ by exactly one bit. If n is a power of two, then this scheme describes a hypercube. Otherwise, it describes an *incomplete* hypercube. We sometimes refer to a hypercube as a *complete* hypercube for emphasis. A link in an incomplete hypercube is said to *exist* if the hypercube contains that link. Note that in a complete hypercube with n nodes, each node has $\log_2 n$ links that exist.

We define the *relative address* of two nodes a and b as the bitwise exclusive-or of their node numbers: $a \oplus b$, and define the *distance* between two nodes as the number of ones in their relative address. A link has *link number* i if it connects two nodes whose numbers differ only in the i-th bit position (starting with the least significant bit as bit 0). For example, the link between nodes 101 and 001 is referred to as link 2 because the two nodes differ in bit 2. Note that the same link number is obtained when computed from either end of the link. For convenience, n is always used to refer to the number of nodes in an incomplete hypercube. Finally, $\log_2(n)$ is defined as $\lceil \log_2 n \rceil$.

Routing Algorithm. We first review the routing algorithm for hypercubes due to Sullivan and Bashkow[2]. The algorithm is a procedure that is executed by the originating node and by every node in the path to the destination. It is described as Algorithm 1.

> **if** ($src == dest$)
>> Send message to local processor.
>
> **else**
>> Compute $reladdr \leftarrow src \oplus dest$.
>> Starting with the most significant bit of $reladdr$:
>>> let i be the bit number of the first 1 in $reladdr$.
>> Send the message on link i.

Algorithm 1. Routing − Complete hypercube[2]
Algorithm to send or forward a message from node src to node $dest$.

Figure 1 shows how a message is routed from node 011 to node 100 in a cube with 8 nodes. It is easy to see that this algorithm correctly routes messages because each step in the routing reduces the distance to the destination by 1.

Surprisingly, a simple variant of this algorithm, described as Algorithm 2, works for incomplete hypercubes.

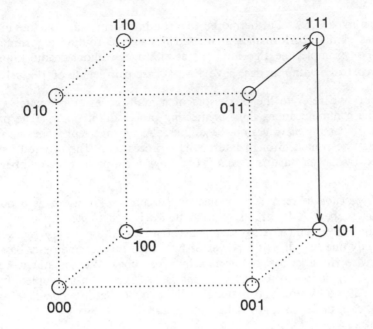

FIG. 1. Routing from 011 to 100 in a cube with 8 nodes.

Figure 2 shows how this algorithm routes a message from node 011 to node 100 in a cube with 7 nodes. It is possible to show that Algorithm 2 always succeeds in finding a link i on which to forward the message. Since no two nodes differ in distance by more than $\log2(n)$, and Algorithm 2 reduces the distance to the source by one each time the message is routed, the maximum path length determined by this algorithm is $\log2(n)$.

A useful property of a message routing algorithm is that it does not deadlock. DeBenedictis has shown that Sullivan and Bashkow's routing algorithm for complete hypercubes does not deadlock[3].

We first examine the issue of buffering in the links between nodes. If the links are not buffered then a node sending a message blocks until the receiving node reads the message. If there is buffering of size k on a link then the sender does not block until k messages are sent on that link that have not been read. It is easy to see that some buffering is necessary to prevent deadlock. Suppose that there is no buffering and each node starts out by sending some message over each of its links. Then each node is blocked sending its messages until the node at the other end of the link reads it. But all nodes are busy sending the message from the local processor, so the messages are not read, causing deadlock.

> **if** ($src == dest$)
>   Send to local processor
> **else**
>   Compute $reladdr \leftarrow src \oplus dest$.
>   Starting with the most significant bit of $reladdr$:
>   let i be the bit number of the first 1 in $reladdr$
>   where link i exists from node src.
>   Send the message on link i.

Algorithm 2. Routing − Incomplete hypercube
Algorithm to send or forward a message from node src to node $dest$.

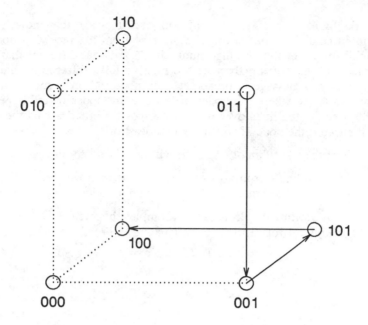

FIG. 2. Routing from 011 to 100 in an incomplete cube with 7 nodes.

It is therefore necessary to assume that there is buffering on every link. It is suffi-cient that each link is able to independently buffer a single message in each direction to show that deadlock does not occur. Algorithm 3, below, is the routing algorithm for incomplete hypercubes modified to explicitly indicate buffering on the links. An instance of this algorithm is connected to each input link of a node. When the algo-rithm blocks waiting for some condition, it stops running and waits for the desired condition to occur. The other instances of the algorithm at the other nodes continue to process incoming data.

One way to prove that Algorithm 3 does not exhibit deadlock is to first show that if there is deadlock, then there must be a cycle among the deadlocked nodes and then show that such a cycle can not occur when using this routing algorithm.

> **if** $(src == dest)$
>> Send to local processor
>
> **else**
>
>> Compute $reladdr \leftarrow src \oplus dest$.
>> Starting with the most significant bit of $reladdr$:
>>> let i be the bit number of the first 1 in $reladdr$
>>> where link i exists from node src.
>>
>> If the previous message that was sent on link i has not been read,
>>> wait until it is read, then send the message on link i.

> **Algorithm 3.** Routing – Incomplete hypercube
>> Algorithm, with explicit buffering,
> to send or forward a message from node src to node $dest$.

Broadcast Algorithm. Sullivan and Bashkow have devised an algorithm for broad-casting a message to all other processors in a hypercube[2]. This algorithm sends the message to all other nodes in $\log2(n)$ steps and sends the message non-redundantly, meaning that each broadcast message is sent to every node exactly once. The algorithm works by sending a *weight* along with each message that indicates how the algorithm should continue broadcasting the message from the receiving node. Algorithm 4 is Sullivan and Bashkow's algorithm. It is somewhat different than the algorithm presented in their paper[2] because we number links differently than they do. Figure 3 shows how a message is broadcast from node 011 in a cube with 8 nodes. The figure shows a tree where the nodes of the tree are nodes of the hypercube and the arcs in the tree are the links over which messages are broadcast by the algorithm. The root of the tree is the node at which the broadcast originates.

Start the algorithm at any node with *weight* set to $\log 2(n)$.

For each link ℓ from this node with ℓ less than *weight*:
    send the message on link ℓ with a *weight* of ℓ.

Algorithm 4. Broadcast − Complete hypercube[2]
Algorithm for forwarding (or originating) a broadcast message

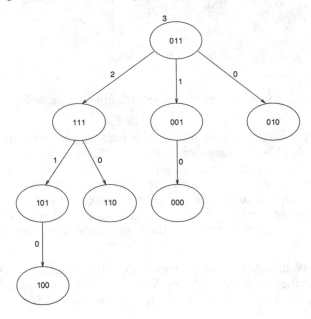

FIG. 3. Broadcast from 011 in an cube with 8 nodes.

A modified version of this algorithm that ignores missing links in an incomplete hypercube successfully broadcasts messages when starting at node 0 because broadcasts messages are always sent from a smaller node number to a larger one. However, it does not work for broadcasting from arbitrary nodes. For instance, in an incomplete hypercube with 3 nodes, a broadcast message sent from node 01 would never arrive at node 10.

To motivate the broadcasting algorithm for incomplete hypercubes, we first describe a version of Algorithm 4 in which the integer *weight* is replaced by a $\log 2(n)$-bit boolean array, *travel*. The elements of the array indicate how the receiver should continue broadcasting as message. If a message is received with *travel*[i] set to TRUE, this indicates that the message should be sent out on link i. See Algorithm 5. Figure 4 shows how this algorithm broadcasts a message from node 011 in a cube with 8 nodes.

Start at any node with all elements in the *travel* array set to TRUE.

for each link ℓ from this node:
    if *travel*$[\ell]$ is TRUE:
        send the message on link ℓ with the array *newtravel*
        computed as:

           for $i \in 0 \cdots \log 2(n) - 1$:
              newtravel$[i] \leftarrow$ TRUE **iff**
                travel$[i]$ is TRUE AND $i < \ell$

Algorithm 5. Broadcast − Complete hypercube (using *travel* array)
Algorithm for forwarding (or originating) a broadcast message

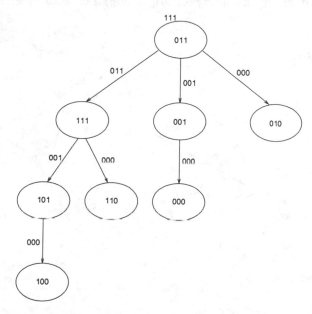

FIG. 4. Broadcast from 011 using *travel* array in an cube with 8 nodes.

The broadcast algorithm for incomplete hypercubes is obtained by modifying Algorithm 5 to remember which links were not traversed because they did not exist. See Algorithm 6. Figure 5 shows how this algorithm broadcasts a message from node 011 in a cube with 7 nodes.

One can show that the broadcast algorithm, Algorithm 6, routes broadcast messages in exactly the same way that the routing algorithm, Algorithm 2, does. More precisely, if a message is broadcast from some node s, then for any other node t, the broadcast algorithm routes the message from node s to node t over exactly one path: the path determined by the routing algorithm to route a message from node s to node t. Given this fact, it should be clear that a message broadcast by Algorithm 6 routes the message to each node exactly once, with a path length no greater than $\log 2(n)$.

Conclusions. We have described simple and effective algorithms for routing and broadcast in incomplete hypercubes. It is thus feasible to build multiprocessor computing systems based on the incomplete hypercube topology. This improves on existing systems based on complete hypercubes because complete hypercubes restrict the

Start the algorithm with all elements in the *travel* array set to TRUE.

for each link ℓ that exists from this node:
    if *travel*[ℓ] is TRUE:
        send the message on link ℓ with the array *newtravel*
        computed as:

        for $i \in 0 \cdots \log2(n)-1$:
            newtravel[i] ← TRUE **iff**
                travel[i] is TRUE AND
                ($i < \ell$ OR link i from this node does not exist)

Algorithm 6. Broadcast − Incomplete hypercube
Algorithm for forwarding (or originating) a broadcast message

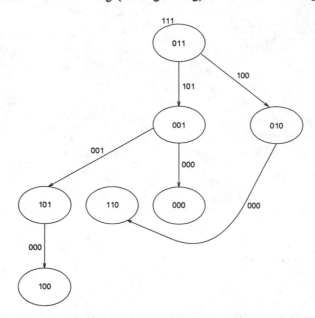

FIG. 5. Broadcast from 011 in an incomplete cube with 7 nodes.

sizes of systems that can be constructed. Systems based on incomplete hypercubes can be built with any number of computing nodes. The routing and broadcast algorithms presented here assume that the network is fault-free. It would be of interest to extend these algorithms to allow deadlock-free routing in the face of faulty nodes or links.

References.
(1) J. SQUIRE and S. M. PALAIS, *Programming and Design Considerations of a Highly Parallel Computer*, Proc. AFIP Spring Joint Computer Conference, 23 (1963), pp. 395-400.

(2) H. SULLIVAN and T. R. BASHKOW, *A Large Scale Homogeneous, Fully Distributed Parallel Machine, I*, Proc. Fourth Symp. on Comput. Arch., (March 1977), pp. 105-117.

(3) E. P. DeBENEDICTIS, *A Communications Operating System for the Homogeneous Machine*, Technical Report Number 4707, Computer Science Department, California Institute of Technology, Pasadena, January 1982.

Alpha Structure Based B-HIVE Multicomputer

W. B. WIKE*, T. K. MILLER* AND D. P. AGRAWAL*

Abstract. This paper describes the design and implementation of the B-HIVE multicomputer, a 24 node generalized hypercube being constructed at North Carolina State University. Each node in B-HIVE consists of a pair of tightly coupled micro computers: a National Semiconductor DB32016 processor with MMU and FPU to serve as the application processor, and an Intel 80186 processor to handle intra-nodal communications. Intra-nodal communications is via dual ported RAM. The hardware is designed to primarily support packet switched communications between nodes, but also has the capability to support a limited number of dynamically configurable circuit switched channels, as well. A demand driven virtual paging mechanism has been incorporated into the design to provide inter-nodal communications which is transparent to the application software. More direct message passing via system call is supported as well.

1 INTRODUCTION

The B-HIVE multi-computer is a 24 node generalized hypercube currently under development at North Carolina State University [1]. The goal of this project is to develop a system for image and digital signal processing, concurrent digital and three dimensional physical simulation, and general research in parallel algorithms. The B-HIVE is a 2x3x4 ALPHA structure architecture [2] and possess the expandability and performance of hypercube multicomputers. Each node in the B HIVE consists of a pair of tightly coupled processors, an application processor (AP) and a communications processor (CP). This structure provides a flexible foundation for interprocessor communications, as well as removing virtually all communications

*Department of Electrical and Computer Engineering, North Carolina State University, Raleigh, North Carolina 27695
This work was supported in part by U.S. Army Research Contract DAAG-29-85-K-0236.

overhead from the AP. The current version of B-HIVE is being implemented from off-the-shelf components and compilers in order to limit development time and costs. Future versions are planned to be built with high speed custom VLSI circuits.

2 THE ALPHA INTERCONNECT STRUCTURE

The ALPHA structure is a generalized hypercube configuration as typified in Figure 1 and described in [2]. The network can be defined for any diameter (maximum path length between any two nodes) for any non-prime number of nodes rather than a number to a power as in hypercubes. There are several disjoint paths between any two nodes. Each node is connected each node with a hamming distance of 1 and to all other nodes along each of its dimensional axes. This means several links or even nodes can be non-operational with little degeneration of performance without yielding the entire system inoperable. In addition, the diameter will determine the maximum inter-nodal communication time even with a high number of faults. The 24 node version yields a diameter of three, with six communication links per node.

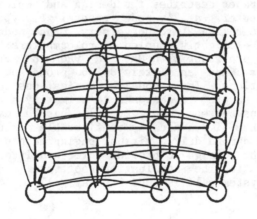

FIG. 1. 2x3x4 Alpha Interconnect Structure

3 NODE STRUCTURE AND COMMUNICATIONS

The B-HIVE nodes are designed to eliminate virtually all communications overhead from the application program. In addition, the use of a general purpose processor to effect interprocessor communications allows the implementation of very simple and flexible user models of interprocessor communications.

The AP and the CP are tightly coupled by a dual ported memory. Each processor also has the ability to interrupt the other. The communications processor manages a set of full duplex, byte oriented, high speed data channels. In the case of our 2x3x4 B-HIVE implementation the number of physical channels per node is six. Node expansion and interface can be implemented through the node multibus.

The B-HIVE node structure supports both packet switched and circuit switched communications at the data link level, and access to the communications at the application level is either by system call or by virtual shared memory. These techniques are combined to provide three distinct modes of communication.

The first mode of communication is via direct system call. The AP issues a CP system call by writing the command into shared memory. Next, the CP will communicate over the network in a packet switched mode and return an acknowledgement to the AP after the requested data is available in the shared memory. A broadcast mode is also available via a system call. In this mode, the CP sends a message one time, but the message is written out to all or any number of ports. This option allows a status message, control message, or application program to be loaded in parallel into buffers for all nodes in a minimum time period.

The second mode of communication is a virtual memory supported remote memory reference. In this mode, the collective physical memory of the APs is mapped into a single virtual address space known to all nodes. Non-local memory references generated by an AP are trapped by its CP, which in turn retrieves the appropriate page from the remote node. This mode has the advantage of transparency to the application program, but has a disadvantage in that operation of the AP must be suspended during the page swap. This disadvantage would be somewhat mitigated if the AP were used in a multi-tasking mode, however this will generally not be the case for the anticipated B-HIVE applications.

The third mode of communication through the network uses circuit switched data links. This mode is accomplished by directly coupling one of the six CP input channels to one of the six output channels via DMA control. The current B-HIVE implementation can support up to two such links per node. This method of communication offers the advantage of minimum latency in interprocessor data transfers. There are two disadvantages, however. The first is that interprocessor links which are configured in this mode are not available for routing of packet switched channels, therefore possibly having an adverse effect on the two communication modes described previously. The second disadvantage is that there is no capability for dynamic re-routing of data around faulty nodes.

4 NODE IMPLEMENTATION

4.1 Overview

In order to implement the communications modes described above, a custom CP board was designed, and a National Semiconductor DB 32016 Development Board is being used as the AP. The CP and AP are connected via Multi-bus to form a B-HIVE node.

The CP is an Intel 80186 microprocessor based computer with six bi-directional network connections or ports. Each port has two uni-directional sixteen bit channels, a transmit and receive channel, in order to eliminate any node link arbitration. In addition, each CP has a local memory for operating system and message storage, decoding, and message error checking. The CP also has all necessary Multi-bus interface and AP virtual support logic as shown in Figure 2. The CP can reset the AP in case of a crash or system reconfiguration. The DB 32016 (AP) is an off-the-shelf full 32-bit single board computer with a MMU (NS32082) for virtual memory support, a floating point co-processor (NS32081), and a 32-bit CPU (NS32016). All of the node's shared memory (128k byte limit) resides on the AP.

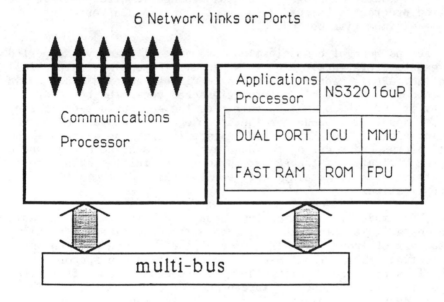

FIG. 2. B-HIVE Node Structure

4.2 Multibus

Multi-bus was chosen for compatibility with the DB 32016 and the availability of a simple interface to the Intel 80186. In addition, Multi-Bus has many compatible support units such as disk drives, data acquisition devices, and host interfaces. In order to optimize the Multi-bus arbitration, the CP and AP use the serial bus arbitration configuration with the AP having the highest priority. This gives the AP the ability to take the bus directly. This occurs when the AP generates a virtual memory reference, at which time which the CP releases the bus, reads the address information generated by the AP, and commences fetching the remote page.

4.3 Communication Processor

The CP has six functional parts as illustrated in Figure 3. The microprocessor is an 8 Mhz Intel 80186. This unit includes two DMA channels, a chip select unit, interrupt controller, and CPU, thereby minimizing the number of peripheral devices required on the board. There are 256K bytes of dual bank sixteen bit local memory that is accessed with no wait states and hardware refresh. This memory is for message coping. This allows for error checking such as check sums; furthermore, if a node or link is non-operational, this allows the last functioning node to re-transmit the message along a different path, rather than re-transmitting from the originating node. Message coping is optional to allow different levels of packet passing latency and error checking. The ports currently consist of six 64 x 8 bit FIFO's as the transmit channels with bus transceivers and ribbon cable inter-connecting the nodes. The FIFO's are asynchronous to eliminate any inter-nodal synchronization. Sixteen bit data is multiplexed and loaded as two bytes plus parity per access with no wait states. This allows a 2 Mbyte per second data transfer rate on each port. In the circuit switched mode, the DMA channels are interfaced to the ports. Data transfers in this mode proceed at a minimum of 1.3 Mbytes per second.

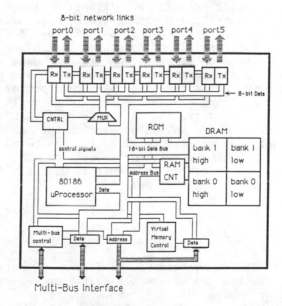

FIG. 3. B-HIVE Communication Processor (CP).

The receive channels are connected to the transmit channels of the connecting nodes. Receive channel logic is a sixteen bit latch that demultiplexes the incoming channel. All port control logic is incorporated into erasable programmable logic devices. The ports are designed to be polled in a round-robin fashion to give equal priority to each port and prevent starvation and lockup. The Multi-bus interface is accomplished with Intel controllers.

4.4 Performance

While actual performance will be somewhat application dependent, minimum network transfer time and optimum performance can be calculated. Since the FIFO's used are 64 bytes deep, the packet size of choice is a multiple of 64 bytes. The clock rate of the CP is 8.0 MHz, and the fall through time on the FIFOs is 1.3 microseconds. Under these conditions a 64 byte packet transfer between adjacent nodes would require a minimum of 53 microseconds. This time assumes immediate availability of the CP and best case positioning in the round-robin polling of the six ports. It includes time for the AP to post the data transfer request, and for address look-up in both the source and destination CP. It does not include error checking or packet acknowledgement.

5 CONCLUSIONS AND FURTHER WORK

The B-HIVE multicomputer has been designed to provide a simple yet flexible repertoire of interprocessor communication modes which can be tailored to a variety of applications. The B-HIVE will serve as a good test bed for developing parallel algorithms for image and signal processing, as well as supporting basic research in parallel computer architecture. The current implementation of the B-HIVE is not intended to yield maximum possible performance, but rather to provide a working model for multicomputer research. In designing the current implementation, however, the possibility of future high performance versions was considered. In keeping with this philosophy, an AP based on the National Semiconductor 32016 was chosen to ensure a highly compatible upward migration to a high performance processor (the NS 32332). Also, hardware interdependencies between the AP and the CP have been kept at a minimum to allow for the development of a high performance, fully custom CP with no impact on the coding of programs run on the AP. Currently an effort is underway to put much of the CP circuitry onto a VLSI chip set.

6 REFERENCES

[1] D.P. Agrawal and W.E. Alexander, "B-HIVE: a heterogeneous, interconnected, versatile and expandable multicomputer system," ACM Computer Architecture News, vol. 12, no. 2, pp. 7-13, June, 1984.

[2] L.N. Bhuyan and D.P. Agrawal, "Generalized hypercube and hyperbus structures for a network of microcomputers," IEEE Transactions on Computers, vol. C-33, no. 4, pp. 323-333, April, 1984.

UNMHC: The Los Alamos and University of New Mexico Hypercube

HOWARD POLLARD*, TAIT CYRUS*, RUSSEL THERMAN*, JUNG HONG†,
RICH KELLNER† AND BOB TOMLINSON†

Abstract The University of New Mexico is building a hypercube which has some unique characteristics. Each node consists of a large compute section and an I/O section, each of which use 32000 series microprocessors to provide compute power. The memory available at a node can be 8 MBytes. The I/O section of each node provides network access and disk storage. The links provide high speed interaction between nodes. The system will be operational soon and provide a platform for a number of application areas.

Introduction The field of hypercube computers has been an exciting area of investigation in recent years, and a number of research teams have been active in pursuing the applications of the architecture[1]. A number of commercial hypercubes are available, and investigation of improvements in nodal architectures is continuing. We have been interested in parallel computing in general, and hypercube computers in particular, for specific application to a number of rather large problems. Our interests include both regular problems, such as hydrodynamics codes, and irregular problems, such as simulations of logic. We are building a machine which will have characteristics both similar and different from other available hypercubes.

One approach at an extensible architecture, such as the hypercube, is to make the elemental building blocks, in this case nodes of the cube, simple machines. This method proposes to make the node inexpensive enough that massive replications of the initial node are possible, and the computational enhancement comes from the multiple copies of the code running, even though each node is a minimal machine. The approach we have taken is to include at each node sufficient resources to allow a single node to

---

* University of New Mexico, Department of Electrical and Computer Engineering

† Los Alamos National Laboratory, Mechanical and Electronics Division, MEE-10, Data Systems

This work supported in part by U.S. Army Ballistic Research Laboratory and Strtegic Defense Initiative, BMc3

accept large sets of data and address a large section of the problem. Thus each node is in itself a complete system, and the amount of data that can be manipulated by the ensemble of nodes can be very large. Each node also has mass storage capabilities and network access capabilities.

This project is being conducted in conjunction with a hypercube effort in the Data Systems group at Los Alamos National Laboratory[2]. The LANL project will include a high performance floating point unit at every node, optimized to address regular problems, capable of but not limited to vectorizable computations. Here we describe the system currently being built at the University of New Mexico, and the status of development.

System Description   We are designing an order ten cube, and will initially build an order five cube with 32 nodes. Each node of the UNM hypercube is a complete computer system, with I/O and mass storage capabilities. The I/O capabilities include RS232 ports for both debug and monitor functions, and an Ethernet connection. Rather than write an operating system for use on the system, we have chosen to implement UNIX at every node. Then, as our experience with the system grows we will streamline the system to optimize the overall capabilities. Thus, normal UNIX facilities are available to users, and computations can proceed in a fairly normal way.

The hardware for the system is broken logically into two sections: the compute section and the I/O section. A block diagram of the compute section is shown in Figure 1. It is composed of a National Semiconductor 32032 microprocessor, 32081 floating point unit, a 32082 memory management unit, a 32202 interrupt control unit, some basic

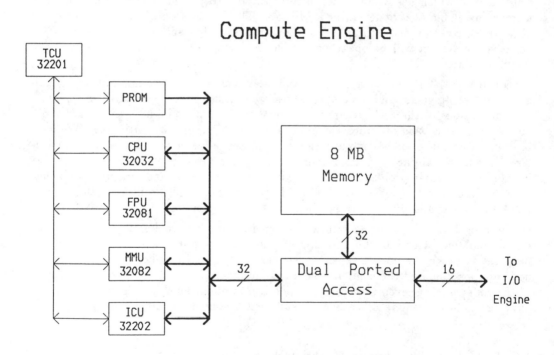

Figure 1. Block Diagram of the Compute Section

routines stored in PROM, and a dynamic RAM section. National Semiconductor is providing support in the form of some parts and system assistance. The RAM memory provides 8 MBytes of storage for data and programs. There are two ports into the memory to allow access for both the compute section and the I/O section.

The I/O section is responsible for transferring data in and out of the system, as well as communication between nodes. A block diagram of the I/O section is shown in Figure 2. The action is controlled by a 32016 processor, which allows both I/O section and compute section to use the same instruction set, compiler, etc., even though the compute section operates on a 32 bit data bus, while the I/O section uses a 16 bit bus. In addition to the processor, the I/O section also includes the 32081 FPU for the few floating point operations which it will need to do, the 32082 MMU, and the 32202 ICU. Programs for the section are stored in PROM, and a local RAM is provided, principally for storage of the system stack and some local variables. Access to the 8 MByte memory is provided through the dual port memory controller.

The Ethernet interface consists of the Advanced Micro Devices Ethernet chip set, and provides access to a communication path common to all nodes. In addition, this provides access to system facilities such as printers and external communications. This path is used by other machines to communicate with the hypercube system.

Mass storage capability is provided by the disk interface. This port provides control and data for an SMD disk. The control signals are provided by programmable peripheral interface chips, and the data path is provided by a National Semiconductor 8466 Disk Data Controller. This path provides data transfer rates to 2.4 MBytes per

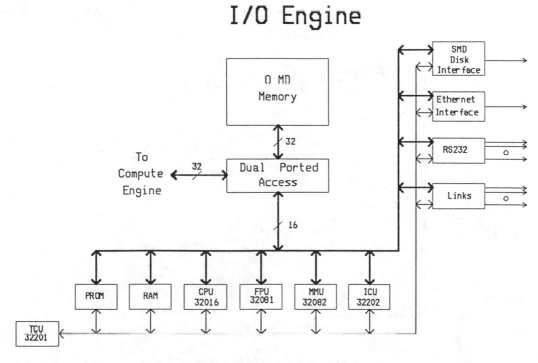

Figure 2. Block Diagram of the I/O Section

second. Currently we are using disks with storage capacities in excess of 300 MBytes. The disks are used for both storage of the operating system and also for data access. This allows for extremely large data sets to be accessed by each node.

The links between the nodes consist of parallel data paths, and a block diagram of a link section is shown in Figure 3. The memory interaction is controlled by a NS 32203 DMA controller over the 16 bit bus of the I/O system. The data is buffered in FIFO storage elements between nodes. The purpose of the FIFO is to allow the DMA controller to work in burst mode, amortizing the bus arbitration time over several transfer cycles. The connections between nodes are bidirectional 16 bit data paths. The direction of transfer is time multiplexed to allow two bytes in each direction every 300 nsec, for a possible data rate of 13.3 MBytes per second. Thus, two nodes can communicate very rapidly, but the overall data rate will be limited by memory access speed, not link speed. In the LANL hypercube, we plan to have a high speed bus and multibank memory, and the overall data rate will be able to approach the speeds possible with these high speed links.

Hardware Status   Currently we have constructed all portions of the node and have checked out many of them. The compute section has been functional for some time, and memory tests and individual checks on the computational capability have been run. We have measured data rates of up to 30 KFlops for compiled C code and up to 80 KFlops for hand optimized single precision codes. These rates were achieved with 6 MHz parts; 10 MHz parts should scale accordingly.

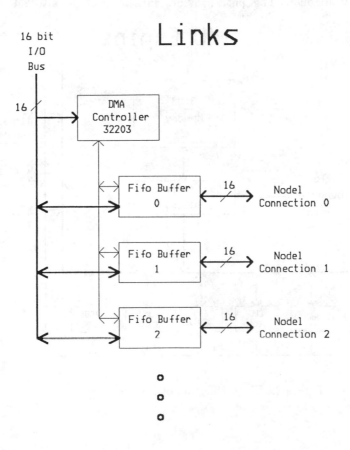

Figure 3. Block Diagram of the Links

The I/O section of the hardware has provided more interesting technical challenges, and hence taken more time. The Ethernet interaction functions and provides capabilities to access information in our local network. The terminal interactions allow access to the system for debugging at rates up to 9600 baud. Our current debugging efforts are centered on the disk interface and the link section. If current debugging rates continue to hold these sections should be functional in about another month. The links have been an interesting challenge since the DMA controller is a new part, and since we have endeavored to transfer multiple words in a single transfer period. We have measured link set up times of about 60 microsec, and transfer rates in excess of 3 Mbytes per second with the 6 MHz parts, node to node with no other conflicts. This will provide both high data rates and low start up delays.

Intended Applications   The immediate application areas for our hypercube include hydrodynamics codes and discrete event simulation. The hydrocodes which we have looked at include non trivial data sets which will require a large portion of the memory, even distributed over all the nodes. Our initial 32 node machine will have a memory capability of 256 MBytes, and disk space excess of 12 gigabytes. This will allow us to perform some very interesting hydrodynamics calculations.

The discrete event simulation is an area of interest for a number of fields. We will experiment with techniques for partitioning the job between the various nodes, and communication methods for ascertaining the progress of the calculations.

One of the purposes of the project has been to improve our abilities at rapid prototyping, allowing quick turnaround from concept to implementation. We have developed tools to aid us in this effort, and these tools have proven very effective. Once a design has been completed to the schematic capture and layout stage, we can produce a wire-wrapped version in about four days (100 ICs, 2500 wires). Computer tools extract the information from the appropriate files and drive a semi-automatic wire-wrap machine, and the result is free from wiring errors. This decreases the debug time as well as the construction time. We are in the process of developing tools to take this to the PCB level, and we will use the compute capabilities of the hypercube to assist in this effort.

Other groups at the University of New Mexico, Los Alamos National Lab, and Sandia National Laboratory have expressed interest in utilizing the capabilities of the hypercube on their problems. These application areas include artificial intelligence, graphics, cognition theory, and interactive simulation.

Conclusion   We are in the process of building a hypercube which has some distinct characteristics. These include a large number of compute resources at each node, mass storage at every node, and high speed links. This combination of capabilities will allow our machine to investigate new application areas and different techniques for machine utilization.

REFERENCES

[1] Michael T. Heath, ed., Hypercube Multiprocessors, 1986, Society for Industrial and Applied Mathematics, Philadelphia, 1986.

[2] J. P. Hong, et. al., A Hypercube Project and a Simulator for a Hypercube of Computers, in Hypercube Multiprocessors, 1986, M. T. Heath, ed, SIAM, Philadellphia, 1986.

A Portable System for Simulating Distributed Parallel Processors on Shared Memory Machines

G. R. MONTRY*

Abstract. A package of FORTRAN communications routines has been developed for use on shared memory multiprocessors. The package allows users to define an arbitrary processor interconnect scheme as though they were working on a distributed memory machine. Data which are not shared between processes or processors may be exchanged via a shared pool of circular buffers. The data messages are physically copied from the sending processor to the receiving processor via the buffers.

The package is portable among shared memory architectures. The only system-dependent capabilities necessary to implement the package are (1) a method of sharing some common memory between all processors, (2) a method of implementing critical sections of shared code, such as locks, and (3) a method of synchronizing tasks, such as semaphores (optional).

The package supports two types of processor-processor communications. The synchronous method, in which cooperating processes must rendezvous in order to exchange data, can be invoked with a single switch. The default method is asynchronous; in which the sending process continues computation without synchronizing with the receiving processor.

A complete post-mortem analysis of the communications statistics for each processor is also available. The post-mortem indicates the efficiency of buffer use and the total read-write latency for each of the processors.

Introduction. The ability to simulate distributed memory systems on shared memory machines is useful for many reasons. First, software development tools are typically more advanced on the current generation of shared memory machines than on their distributed memory counterparts. The availability of interactive de-

---

* Sandia National Laboratories, Albuquerque, NM 87185

bugging facilities for single tasks, and sometimes multitasking, can greatly reduce algorithm development and debug time.

Second, algorithm development, at least in the early stages, is easier on shared memory machines. A necessary step in multitasking algorithm development is the ability to verify the algorithm on a single processor. Shared memory machines are usually large enough, in terms of memory, to execute the whole application on one processor. This capability allows for a smooth transition from the serial version of the algorithm to increasing numbers of processors in arbitrary increments.

Third, algorithm implementation efficiencies can be compared directly for shared memory versus distributed memory architectures with arbitrary processor interconnects. This flexibilty allows for emulation of the mapping of the algorithm to the underlying hardware; in some cases providing the hardware specifications necessary to implement the code in the most efficient way.

Fourth, architectural complexity can be hidden from the user. By using this package on shared and distributed memory machines, it is possible to allocate processors for domain decomposition at the hardware level and let the user communicate between processors by reference to the problem's logical mesh. Thus, source code involving communication does not need to be altered as the code is taken from one class of machine to another.

Implementation. This package was developed on an ELXSI 6400, a bus-connected parallel processor with 10 processing elements (PEs). The ELXSI provides the capability for sharing memory among tasks executing on those PEs through system service calls to declare blocks of memory as shareable. The shared memory must reside in FORTRAN common blocks. For simplicity, we assume that each PE executes one parallel process (a task) at any given time, and that each task is identified by a unique integer starting with zero.

At program run time, an initialization routine is called to define and initialize a block of memory to be shared by all tasks. This block of memory serves as the communication routines' message buffer area. All data communicated between tasks during computation are copied from local unshared memory belonging to the sending task into the shared buffer area and subsequently copied from that area by the receiver.

Each task has its own message buffer area. The buffer area is allocated as a fixed number of *slots* (N_{slots}) of fixed length (L_{slots}) bytes. Each message copied into the buffer is aligned on a slot boundary. The message may be any number of bytes in length, spanning one or more slots if necessary. Buffer memory is always allocated in fixed-length segments to accomodate the whole message. This procedure is wasteful of memory if the preponderance of message lengths are modulo L_{slots} plus a few bytes. However, there are two reasons for this implementation. First, it is very easy to reconfigure the communication package to optimize the use of memory. L_{slots} is an independent value set by a *parameter* statement at compile time. Second, execution efficiency is the most critical factor in producing reasonably worthwhile software communications. Any attempt to reduce the buffer space by stacking messages end-to-end can lead to unacceptable overhead due to garbage collection. The need for garbage collection in the buffers is dependent on the communication protocol used in the message transfers (see Appendix). The fixed-slot method represents a reasonable compromise which retains the flexibility of the package to easily implement other variations of the communications protocol.

The default communications protocol implemented for this package is *synchronous unblocked write – synchronous blocked read*. Here *synchronous* refers to the fact that once the sender (receiver) has exited the *writeto (readfrom)* subprogram, that portion of the communications is complete. There is no need for any status check on the condition of the transfer. Obviously, there is no way to implement asynchronous transfer in software unless the system service which copies the data from one part of memory to another is itself asynchronous. *Unblocked-write* means that the sender does not have to rendezvous with the receiver before completing the write. However, the receiver does block in the *readfrom* routine until it receives notification that the message it is expecting has been sent. For example, if the receiver is expecting a message from task #4, it waits in the *readfrom* routine until that message has been sent, even though messages from other tasks may have already arrived and are awaiting processing. Thus, messages are read by the receiver in a specific order. The receiver specifies the task from which it is expecting the next message.

This determinism has some interesting ramifications. The receiving task has to be able to find the correct message from a possible list of messages which have arrived in pseudo-random order. The maximum length of this list is determined by two parameters. The first parameter (M_{rep}), is the number of times one task can write to another without intervening reads before write-blocking occurs. In other words, it is the number of messages that can be queued in each direction between each pair of communicating tasks. The second parameter is the connectivity of the interconnect, or algorithm, being modeled. The connectivity (N_{conn}) is defined as the number of executing tasks which are physically able to send messages to one particular task. If L_{max} is the longest message sent between tasks, then the buffer must have $N_{slots} \geq (2 \times M_{rep} \times N_{conn} \times (L_{max} + L_{slots} - 1))/L_{slots}$ to ensure avoidance of communication deadlock during execution. The factor of two is necessary because neighbor tasks can race ahead and perform two sets of writes before a receiving task has done any reads.

Even though determinism adds some overhead in the *readfrom* portion of message transfer, it makes for much cleaner source code in the applications program. The lack of generality implied by the determinism is not important for applications involving domain dissection, since all communication paths are known *a priori* and are fixed for the duration of the computation.

For some applications the communication frequency and paths are not constant at run time, so a slight variation of the protocol is required. For these cases, there is a version of the communications package in which the *readfrom* routine picks the first message from the top of a FIFO queue (first-in, first-out) and returns

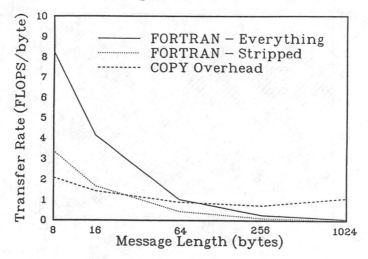

Figure 1: The message transfer overhead is measured in FLOPS for both the complete code and a stripped-down version with no error checking or timers. The copy overhead for the system service routine used to move the data is also shown. (1 FLOP $\approx 1\mu sec$)

with the task identifier of the sender. The receiver then takes the appropriate action depending on the value received. The same buffer sizes are required as in the deterministic case, but the extra overhead of scanning the input queue is eliminated.

Finally, we can institute a rendezvous protocol in conjunction with the FIFO queue mentioned previously. The rendezvous requires that the sending task wait in the sending subprogram *writeto* until the receiving task has entered the *readfrom* subprogram to get the message. This method eliminates the buffer space required in the previous two implementations because only one message can ever be in the buffer at any instant in time.

Results. Figure 1 shows the message transfer overhead for the default case (solid line) measured in double precision FLOPS (floating-point operations/second) for an ELXSI 6400 processor. The dotted line is the overhead for the FORTRAN code after timers and all statistical and consistency checks have been removed. Total transfer time per byte is obtained by adding either of the values for the FORTRAN overhead to the copy overhead, which is the elapsed time to physically move the data from local memory to the buffers. The data shown are for the sending routine *writeto*. The data for the receiving routine are similar; *i.e.*, slightly less efficient for short message lengths but significantly faster for long messages. These variations are probably due to the effect of the different memory used by the sender and receiver. The sender is always copying data from unshared cacheable memory into shared, uncached memory. The receiver, of course, is performing the reverse operation.

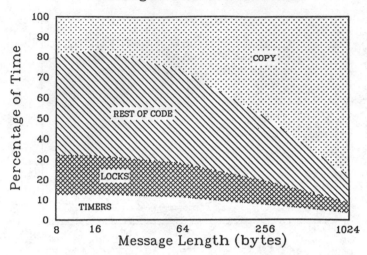

Figure 2: Percent overhead of message transfer as a function of message length.

Figure 2 shows a more detailed breakdown of the overhead, with separate results for the timers and the locks. For messages longer than 256 bytes, the system copy dominates the elapsed time communication overhead. The 'rest of code' time includes subroutine call overhead, message length consistency checks, sending process identity checks, and statistics gathering. The timer overhead was deduced by removing all code except the timers and measuring them separately.

Blocked Communication Queues. There are times when message transfers must be temporarily suspended due to a lack of communication resources. The sender can experience two types of delay. The first type is a spin-wait delay experienced when a sender is trying to send a message to a task which is already in the process of 1) being sent a message by another task, or 2) extracting a message from its queue during a read. The message buffers can be accessible to only one task at a time; so the critical section of code which references these buffers must be protected with locks. This delay is typically no longer than the time it takes one task to execute the *writeto* or *readfrom* subprograms.

The second type of delay occurs when the receiving task's message buffer is full. Now the sender must wait until the reader has emptied enough of its own buffer to accomodate the sender's message. The sender is added to the end of a FIFO write-block queue consisting of a linked list of tasks waiting for buffer space. This situation can always be prevented by making the receiver's buffer of sufficient length, as described earlier.

The reader can also experience the same spin-wait delays as the writer, since access to its buffer space can be controlled by the writer. There are two other situations which block the reader. The first one is when the message buffers are completely empty. In this case the reader is put to sleep via a semaphore. The reader is subsequently awakened by the first task to write a message into its buffer space. However, in the default implementation, this message might not be the correct one, since the receiver is expecting the next message from a particular task. Thus, the reader can be read-blocked even when its message buffer is not empty. In this situation the reader enters a spin-wait state until another message arrives in its buffer. It checks to see if this message is the correct one. If not, it re-enters the spin-wait state and waits again. Eventually, the correct message is processed and the receiving task continues on with a partially full buffer of messages to be processed by later invocations of the *readfrom* subprogram.

Global Communications. Global broadcasts and universal sums, products, minima, maxima, are all handled using a separate message buffer area. The broadcast buffer slot length is chosen independently of the slot length for task-task communications. Here each slot must be long enough to hold the maximum message length expected during computation. A separate semaphore is used to put all entering tasks to sleep after they have deposited their messages into the buffer. The last task to enter the routine performs the necessary arithmetic operations, sets a pointer to the data, and awakens all sleeping tasks. Each task, on exit from the routine, copies the data back into its own local data area. It is difficult to measure the overhead for the universal broadcast for several tasks, since they cannot be exactly synchronized. However, several timing measurements indicate that the maximum overhead is $8 \times N$ FLOPS/byte for a universal sum on a vector of length one (8 bytes) involving N tasks. Experiments are still being conducted to improve the parallelism of the universal operations. It is important to note that for universal operations each task can have its own reserved slot in the message buffer. This allows the copy operations into and out of the buffer to occur simultaneously.

Statistics. Part of the communication package consists of timers and statistics which summarize the status of the communications package during execution. Figure 3 shows the summary printout from the package for a test run in which two tasks were used to transmit messages to one another. In this example, task #1 sent 256 messages to task#2. Task#2 then read all 256 messages from its buffer. The printout for each task shows the amount of buffer space available for accepting messages from other tasks. Notice that we completely filled the space by writing messages of length equal to one slot length (1024 bytes). The summary indicates that we could have written fewer messages of length greater than 1024 bytes. Also tallied are the average buffer utilizations as seen by the sender and receiver. These numbers are useful for adjusting the buffer sizes to maximize transfer efficiency. Another important statistic is the wait time experienced by the writer (reader) because of insufficient buffer space or non-optimally synchronized message transfer. The cumulative wait time allows the user to determine algorithm communication overhead and eliminate communication bottlenecks caused by mis-synchronized message transfer.

```
************** TASK NUMBER   1 **************

********************** INTER-PROCESS COMMUNICATION ****************************
There are 256 slots of  1024 bytes (  262144 = maximum message length allowed)
Average # slots avail on write = 128.5, Average # slots in use on read =    .0
Total bytes written =                262144, Total bytes read =                0
Total time waiting to write =    .000, Total time waiting to read =      .000
Average message queue length at read time =    .0

SECTION  CALLED  ELAPSD TIME   CPU TIME  AVG ET/CALL  AVG MSG LEN  AVG ET/BYTE

writeto     256     .3741      .0604     .0014612     1024.0      .00000143
readfrom      0     .0000      .0000     .0000000        .0      .00000000
*****************************************************************************


************** TASK NUMBER   2 **************

********************** INTER-PROCESS COMMUNICATION ****************************
There are 256 slots of  1024 bytes (  262144 = maximum message length allowed)
Average # slots avail on write =    .0, Average # slots in use on read = 128.5
Total bytes written =                     0, Total bytes read =           262144
Total time waiting to write =    .000, Total time waiting to read =      .000
Average message queue length at read time = 128.5

SECTION  CALLED  ELAPSD TIME   CPU TIME  AVG ET/CALL  AVG MSG LEN  AVG ET/BYTE

writeto       0     .0000      .0000     .0000000        .0      .00000000
readfrom    255     .1563      .0858     .0006107     1024.0      .00000060
*****************************************************************************
```

Figure 3: A sample printout of the communications package statistical summary showing the execution efficiency of message transfers.

Appendix. There are three ways to enforce the protocol to reduce garbage collection overhead. The first way is to force all messages to be a constant length. This method simplifies the communication overhead by eliminating the need for message length checking. Also, buffer space is always freed in pre-determined fixed-length increments. This simplifies the collection for deterministic non-FIFO (first-in, first-out) communication.

The second way is to use a FIFO queue. The receiver always takes the first message, reads it, and determines its source. Thus buffer memory is always freed in consecutive blocks, and the garbage collection reduces to incrementing one or two pointers.

The third way is to force the sender and receiver to rendezvous at the time of message transfer. This protocol ensures that the message expected by the receiver is actually being sent by the intended source. In this case, since the sender is write-blocked until the receiver is ready, buffer space is needed for only one message. There is no garbage collection.

REFERENCES

1. *A Programmer's Guide To Parallel Processing on the ELXSI System 6400* , ELXSI Corporation, 1984.

2. *ELXSI System 6400 System Architecture*, ELXSI Corporation, 1984.

3. G. R. Montry, *A Fortran Multitasking Library for Use on the ELXSI 6400 and the CRAY XMP*, SAND85-1378, Sandia National Laboratories, Albuquerque, 1985.

4. S. Enguehard, *An Advanced Guide to Programming the Hypercube*, Caltech Concurrent Computation Project, #133, December 1984.

PART V:
COMBINATORIAL PROBLEMS
AND ARTIFICIAL INTELLIGENCE

Sorting on Hypercubes*

STEVEN R. SEIDEL† AND LYNN R. ZIEGLER†

Abstract. Two versions of a parallel bitonic sorting algorithm and a parallel version of quicksort are compared on an FPS T-40 and an Intel iPSC d5. Performance measurements show that the parallel bitonic sort exhibits significant speedup on the FPS hypercube for sequences with as few as 2^7 elements and that a speedup is obtained on the Intel hypercube only for sequences of at least 2^{13} elements. In order to create a realistic setting for the evaluation of these algorithms and hypercubes it is assumed that the input to be sorted is initially contained in a single node and that the entire sorted sequence must be returned to that node when sorting is complete. The performance results given here include the costs of distributing the input among the nodes of the hypercube and collecting the results in that node after the sort. The routing algorithm used to accomplish this on the FPS hypercube is also discussed.

1. Introduction. This work studied the performance of algorithms for sorting m elements on hypercubes of $2^d = n$ nodes, where $m \gg n$. The goals were to demonstrate that an observable speedup could be obtained on two currently available hypercubes and to compare the scalar performance of those two hypercubes. In practice, it is likely that the sequence to be sorted is initially contained in a single node of the hypercube or on the host of the hypercube and that the sorted sequence must be returned to that node or to the host. It is assumed here that the elements to be sorted are initially contained in node 0 of the hypercube and that the sorted sequence must be returned to node 0.

The bitonic sorting algorithm for m-processor networks given by Batcher [1] and adapted by Johnsson [4] for hypercubes is theoretically the fastest worst case algorithm and can be easily modified to obtain an algorithm with good expected performance. Johnsson's algorithm assumes that the sequence to be sorted is equally distributed among the n nodes of the hypercube and that when sorting is complete the sequence is left in consecutive nodes of the hyper-

*This work partially supported by NSF Grant DCR-8404909.

† Department of Mathematical and Computer Sciences, Michigan Technological University, Houghton, Michigan 49931

cube. To conform to the assumption above this algorithm was augmented with procedures for subsequence distribution and collection. A third sorting algorithm based on quicksort was also studied. Subsequence distribution is an integral part of this algorithm. Two versions of the bitonic sorting algorithm have been implemented on two 32-node hypercubes: the FPS T-Series and the Intel iPSC. The parallelized quicksorting algorithm has been implemented on a 16-node FPS T-Series.

The sorting algorithms and their analyses are given in Section 2. Section 3 discusses the problem of subsequence distribution and collection on a hypercube with multiplexed links such as the FPS T-Series. Performance measurements are given in Section 4.

2. Algorithms. Three algorithms were studied for sorting a sequence of m elements on a hypercube of $2^d = n$ nodes. It is assumed that $m = 2^q$ for some $q > d$. The nodes of the hypercube are numbered from 0 to $n-1$. The binary representation of a node number is written $b_{d-1}b_{d-2}...b_0$. It is also assumed that the sequence to be sorted is initially contained in node 0 of the hypercube and that the sorted sequence must be returned to node 0.

Two versions of Johnsson's parallel bitonic sort [4] are presented. The difference between the two versions is noted in step 1 of the single algorithm given below. Heapsort can be used by each node in step 1 to locally sort the subsequence of elements it contains. This yields an algorithm with good worst case performance. Alternately, quicksort [7] can be used in step 1 to obtain good expected case performance. An outline of the entire algorithm is given here since the ordering of steps is different than that in [4]. This algorithm has also been augmented with steps to distribute the unsorted sequence contained in node 0 to the other nodes of the hypercube and to collect the sorted sequence back into node 0. In the cost estimates given below $t_{s/r}$ denotes the cost of sending or receiving an element, t_c denotes the cost of comparing a pair of elements, and k denotes the number of channels over which a node can communicate in parallel.

Parallel Bitonic Sort

0.   Node 0 sends each of nodes $1,2,...,n-1$ a distinct subsequence of m/n elements and retains the remaining subsequence. Cost: $(m/k)(1-1/n)t_{s/r}$.

1.   Each node sorts the subsequence of elements it received in step 0 (using heapsort or quicksort). A node sorts the subsequence into ascending or descending order if its node number is even or odd, respectively. Cost: $((m/n-1)\log(m/n)+1)t_c$.

2.   For $i = 0,1,...,d-1$ do steps 3 through 7.

3.   Each node sets *mask* according to the $i+1^{st}$ bit of its node number: node $b_{d-1}b_{d-2}...b_0$ sets $mask = b_{i+1}$. (Assume $b_d = 0$.)

4.   For $j = i,i-1,...,0$ do steps 5, 6 and 7.

5.   Each node sends the first or last $m/(2n)$ elements of its subsequence to its neighbor in dimension $j+1$ if $b_j = 0$ or $b_j = 1$, respectively. Cost: $(m/(2n))t_{s/r}$.

6.   Each node compares the corresponding elements of its two $m/(2n)$-element subsequences. A node keeps the smaller elements in each comparison and sends the larger elements to its neighbor in dimension $j+1$ if $mask = b_j$; otherwise the node keeps the larger elements and sends the smaller. Cost: $(m/(2n))(t_c+t_{s/r})$.

7.   Each node now contains an m/n-element increasing-decreasing or decreasing-increasing bitonic sequence if $b_j = mask$ or $b_j \neq mask$, respectively. Each node merges this sequence into ascending or descending order if $b_{j-1} = mask$ or $b_{j-1} \neq mask$, respectively. (Assume $b_{-1} = 0$.) Cost: $(m/n-1)t_c$.

8.   Nodes $1,2,...,n-1$ send their subsequences to node 0. Node 0 assembles the complete sorted sequence beginning with is own subsequence and followed by the subsequences received, according to the node numbers of the senders. Cost: $(m/k)(1-1/n)t_{s/r}$.

$$\text{The total cost is } 2(\frac{m}{k})(1-\frac{1}{n})t_{s/r} + \left[(\frac{m}{n}-1)\log\frac{m}{n}+1\right]t_c + \frac{d(d+3)}{2}\left[\frac{m}{n}t_{s/r} + (\frac{3m}{2n}-1)t_c\right].$$

The parallel bitonic sorting algorithm itself (steps 1 through 7) promises a linear speedup but the cost of subsequence distribution and collection adds a term of order m to the total cost. Thus an actual speedup will be observed only if $t_{s/r}$ is sufficiently small or k is sufficiently large compared to t_c.

A parallel version of quicksort was also studied. Node 0 initially contains the entire sequence to be sorted. A median-finding algorithm based on quicksort is used to partition this sequence into two $m/2$-element subsequences such that all elements of one subsequence are less than those of the other. Node 0 sends the subsequence with the larger elements to node 2^{d-1}. Nodes 0 and 2^{d-1} split the subsequences they contain and send the larger halves to nodes 2^{d-2} and $2^{d-1}+2^{d-2}$, respectively. This process continues until each node contains a subsequence of m/n elements. Each node quicksorts the subsequence it contains resulting in a sorted sequence stored in consecutively numbered nodes. The subsequences are then collected into node 0.

Parallel Quicksort

0.   For $i = d-1,d-2,...,0$ do step 1.

1.   Each node determines whether $b_i b_{i-1}...b_0 = 00...0$. Such nodes find the median of the $2^{i+1}m/n$-element subsequences they contain and send the largest $2^i m/n$ elements to their neighbor in dimension i. Cost: $(2^{i+1}m/n)t_c + (2^i m/n)t_{s/r}$.

2.   Each node quicksorts the m/n-element subsequence it contains.
      Cost: $((m/n-1)\log(m/n)+1)t_c$.

3.   Nodes $1,2,...,n-1$ send their subsequences to node 0. The sorted sequence is collected into node 0 as in step 8, above. Cost: $(m/k)(1-1/n)t_{s/r}$.

The total cost is $m(1+1/k)(1-1/n)t_{s/r} + 2m(1-1/n)t_c + ((m/n-1)\log m/n+1)t_c$. This cost estimate is larger than that for the parallel bitonic sort. It was ventured that in practice the median-finding algorithm would be of cost comparable to the $d^2 m/n$ terms in the parallel bitonic sort, and that there would be some advantage to making subsequence distribution an integral part of the algorithm, but this turned out not to be the case.

The machine-dependent factors of channel latency and packet size are not included in this estimate. The machine-independent factor of the expected cost of multiple quicksorts performed in parallel is also omitted. The expected cost of running, say, 32 quicksorts in parallel is likely to be greater than the expected cost of a single quicksort because of variations expected in the individual costs of the 32 quicksorts. The authors are not aware of any published estimates of such variations nor whether such variations significantly affect the total cost of parallel sorting algorithms.

3. Distribution and Collection. In practice it is expected that the sequence to be sorted will be contained in the host or in one of the nodes of the hypercube and that the sorted sequence must be returned to that node. It is assumed here that node 0 serves in this role. $n-1$ distinct subsequences of m/n elements each must be distributed to the $n-1$ other nodes of the hypercube and later collected again into node 0. This distribution problem is called the *personalized communication* problem by Ho and Johnsson [3]. As observed there, the source node is a bottleneck for the distribution of messages (subsequences) and so distribution costs on existing hypercubes are significantly affected by the number k of communication links that can be used in parallel. In practice k is often less than d: on the Intel iPSC $k = 1$ and on the FPS T-Series $k = 4$. Ho and Johnsson describe efficient algorithms for personalized broadcast on the iPSC, but the T-Series does not fit their model because of its multiplexed links, as explained below. (These algorithms for the iPSC did not come to the author's attention in time to be included in this work; the node operating system was relied upon for message routing.) This section describes the personalized broadcast algorithm for the T-Series used to obtain the performance data in the next section.

The T-Series has very low channel startup costs (about 14 microseconds [2]) and essentially no limit on the length of a message. On the other hand, the node operating system provides primitives only for nearest neighbor communication so all subsequences must be explicitly routed. Also, communication links between nearest neighbors are multiplexed, complicating efficient routing algorithms in hypercubes of dimension 5 or more. (See [6] for another example of the limitations imposed by multiplexed links on T-Series hypercubes.) Assume that link i connects neighbors differing in bit i. Then all links whose numbers are congruent mod 4 share a multiplexer and only one link on each of the four multiplexers can be selected at any given time. The cost of selecting a link on each of the multiplexers is high (from 0.327 to 1.166 milliseconds, depending on the subset of links selected [2]) and so it is advantageous to select one group of four links and use those exclusively, if at all possible.

In T-Series hypercubes of up to four dimensions there can never be any conflicts between links sharing the same multiplexer. In 5- and higher-dimensional T-Series hypercubes node 0 (as well as all other nodes) is limited to the use of four links at any given time since communication can proceed in parallel on at most that many links. In fact, node 0 must transmit down the same four links in parallel at all but one step to avoid excessive link selection costs. Because of this four-link limitation the distribution paths constructed for the T-Series are significantly longer than optimal paths. The construction of such paths is further complicated by the requirement that the pairs of links used by each node on the paths must not be congruent mod 4. The routing used to obtain the performance results given in the next section is shown in Figure 1. (See [8] for a general solution to this routing problem for hypercubes of 5 or more dimensions.) Node 0 first sends the messages (subsequences) destined for nodes 18, 20, and 24 along links 0, 1, and 2, respectively. Nodes 1, 2, and 4 forward those messages to nodes 3, 6, and 5 while node 0 sends the messages destined for nodes 16, 22, 26, and 21 to nodes 1, 2, 4, and 8, and so on. All messages reach their destinations more or less concurrently at step 8. The collection of messages from the nodes is the inverse of this process. Note that the pair of links used by each node is not congruent mod 4 so that no pair shares the same multiplexer.

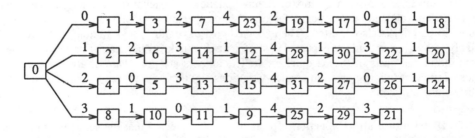

FIG. 1. Distribution paths in 32-node T-Series.

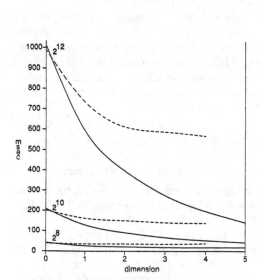

FIG. 2. T-Series: Parallel quicksort
(dashed) and parallel bitonic sort
with local quicksort (solid),
$m = 2^8, 2^{10}, 2^{12}$.

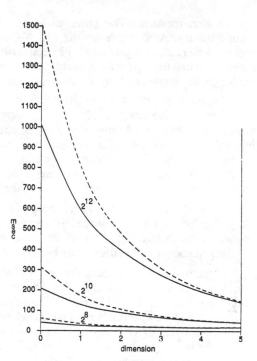

FIG. 3. T-Series: Parallel bitonic sort
with local heapsort (dashed) and
with local quicksort (solid),
$m = 2^8, 2^{10}, 2^{12}$.

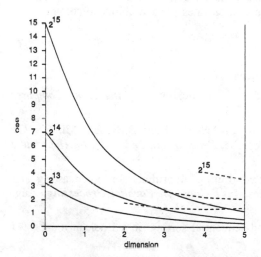

FIG. 4. iPSC (dashed) and T-Series (solid):
Parallel bitonic sort with local heapsort,
$m = 2^{13}, 2^{14}, 2^{15}$.

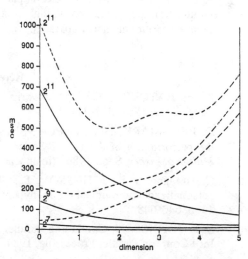

FIG. 5. iPSC (dashed) and T-Series (solid):
Parallel bitonic sort with local heapsort,
$m = 2^7, 2^9, 2^{11}$.

4. Performance. The previous four figures summarize the observed performance of the algorithms discussed above on the FPS T–Series[2] and the Intel iPSC[3]. The elements to be sorted were randomly generated 4-byte integers. Sequences of from 2^6 to 2^{15} elements were sorted although this upper limit could not always be reached on the iPSC because of the limit on the length of messages. Only sequences containing a power of 2 elements were considered.

Figure 2 compares the parallel bitonic sort (using quicksort in step 1) and the parallel quicksort for sequences of 2^8, 2^{10}, and 2^{12} elements on the T-Series. (The latter algorithm was not implemented on a 5-dimensional hypercube so data on that algorithm ends at dimension 4 in the figure.) In all cases the parallel bitonic sort was faster than the parallel quicksort. This is attributable to the cost of finding the medians of subsequences in step 1 of the parallel quick-sorting algorithm. This step contributes a cost of order m and thus the amount of speedup quickly levels off as the number of nodes in the hypercube is increased.

Figure 3 compares the two versions of the parallel bitonic sort on the T-Series. Sequentially quicksorting the sequences is faster by about 30% than sequentially heapsorting the sequences (as expected [5]), but as the length of the hypercube increases the advantage gained by using quicksort all but disappears because of proportionally greater communication costs.

Figures 4 and 5 compare the performance of the iPSC and the T-Series on the parallel bitonic sort (using heapsort in step 1). In both cases the T-Series is faster than the iPSC. (Certain data points for the iPSC are missing in Figure 3 because of that machine's limit on the size of messages.) The apparently anomalous behavior shown for the iPSC in Figure 4 is the result of the domination of various terms in the cost estimate of the algorithm as the dimension of the hypercube is increased. The general increase of cost with dimension is entirely the result of an increase in communication costs. This phenomenon was also observed in the data for the T-Series, though in a much less dramatic fashion; Figure 5 shows a barely discernible increase in the cost of sorting 2^7 elements on 4- and 5-dimensional T-Series hypercubes.

5. Summary. Johnsson's parallel bitonic sorting algorithm has been shown to exhibit nearly linear speedup even when combined with the costs of subsequence distribution and collection. This speedup was obtained on FPS T-Series hypercubes of dimension 5 or less and for sequences of 2^7 to 2^{15} elements. A speedup was observed on the Intel iPSC only for sequences of 2^{13} to 2^{15} elements. This difference in performance is attributable to the T-Series' relatively low communication overhead costs, high communication rates [2] and ability to communicate over as many as four channels in parallel.

References

1. K. E. BATCHER, Sorting networks and their applications, *Spring Joint Computer Conference*, 1968, 307-314.

2. D. BERGMARK, D. A. POPLAWSKI, J. M. FRANCIONI and B. K. HELMINEN, On the performance of the FPS T-Series hypercube, *Proc. of the 2nd Conf. on Hypercube Multiprocessors*, Sept. 1986. (to appear).

3. C. HO and S. L. JOHNSSON, Distributed routing algorithms for broadcasting and personalized communication in hypercubes, *Int'l Conf. on Parallel Processing*, Aug. 1986, 640-648.

4. S. L. JOHNSSON, Combining parallel and sequential sorting on a Boolean n-cube %J Int'l Conf. on Parallel Processing, 1984.

---

[2] The T-Series used B07-series Transputers, software release A00, and all code was written in Occam I.

[3] The iPSC was run under Xenix 286 R3.4 and Node Software R2.1 and all code was written in C.

5.   D. E. KNUTH, in *The Art of Computer Programming, Vol. 3: Sorting and Searching*, Addison-Wesley, Reading, Mass., 1973.

6.   D. A. POPLAWSKI, *Ring connectivity in the FPS T-Series hypercube*, Tech. Rep. 86-10, Dept. of Computer Science, Michigan Technological U., Oct. 1986.

7.   R. SEDGEWICK, Implementing quicksort programs, *Comm. ACM 21*,10 (Oct. 1978), 847-857.

8.   L. R. ZIEGLER, S. R. SEIDEL and D. MACKENZIE, *Personalized broadcast on a link-bounded hypercube*, Tech. Rep. 86-11, Dept. of Computer Science, Michigan Technological U., Nov. 1986.

Hyperquicksort: A Fast Sorting Algorithm for Hypercubes[*]

BRUCE WAGAR[†]

Abstract

This paper considers a new sorting algorithm designed specifically for use in a hypercube network. Based loosely on the underlying principles of quicksort, empirical results done on an NCUBE/ten machine have shown this algorithm to be much faster and more efficient than a similarly coded bitonic sort. Also provided is some detailed analysis of its expected performance to help support the conclusions drawn from its observed behavior.

1 Introduction

Numerous sorting algorithms have been developed for parallel architectures (e.g., [1] and [10]). Many of these have assumed one item per processor, with the understanding that they could be extended to an arbitrary number of items by a method such as that discussed in [2] and [4]. A good deal of them, however, would not be practical to implement on a hypercube, usually because of their limited use of the special architecture available to them. This, then, is an attempt to design, implement, and analyze an efficient sorting algorithm which takes specific advantage of the communication links of a hypercube.

It should be pointed out that, with the advent of actual hypercube machines, this problem is starting to receive more attention (see [3] and [7]).

2 The Sorting Problem

Sorting consists of taking some number, say M, of items, each of which has associated with it a key, and ordering them by their respective keys. It is a well-known fact that any serial sorting algorithm has at least $\Theta(M \log M)$ expected-case time behavior. Given P processors, however, it is not known whether or not it is possible to sort M items using no more than $\Theta((M/P) \log M)$ time (i.e., full linear speedup), at least for practical values of M and P.

[*] This work was supported by NSF Grant No. DCR-8507851.

[†] Department of Electrical Engineering and Computer Science, University of Michigan, Ann Arbor, Michigan 48109

Before going any further, it is necessary to define just what is meant when something is sorted on a multiprocessor machine. There are many possible definitions, each one tailored to particular situations. Therefore, for this paper, a set of items will be assumed to be sorted on a hypercube of 2^D nodes if the items are sorted within each node and, whenever $0 \le I < J \le (2^D - 1)$, every item in node I has a key no greater than any of node J's keys.

Bitonic Sort

Bitonic sort, first described in [1], is a natural sorting algorithm for hypercubes (see [4]). It needs those and only those communication channels present in a hypercube network. Basically, bitonic sort works by sorting the items in individual nodes and then repeatedly merging them together into larger and larger subcubes until the whole cube is sorted.

Given $N = M/P$ items per node and $P = 2^D$ nodes, bitonic sort runs in time

$$\Theta\left(N \log N + \frac{D(D+1)}{2}N\right),$$

expected- and worst-case. Here the $N \log N$ term represents the serial sorting time while the $[D(D+1)/2]N$ term represents the parallel processing time to do the exchanging and merging. While bitonic sort's behavior is very predictable, it's this predictability that makes it inefficient: the merging takes longer and longer to perform as the subcube sizes increase.

Hyperquicksort

Hyperquicksort came about as a way of mimicking the behavior of quicksort on a hypercube architecture. In ordinary quicksort, the median key of the items is "guessed" and then the items broken up into two groups: those whose keys are greater than this "guess" and those whose keys aren't. Then, quicksort is applied recursively to each of these groups until the groups consist of just a single item. Quicksort's main advantage is that, while its worst-case time is $\Theta(M^2)$, its expected time is $\Theta(M \log M)$ and in practice, it outperforms all other serial sorting algorithms.

What follows is a sketch of the Hyperquicksort algorithm.

The Algorithm

1. Distribute the items evenly to all of the nodes.

2. Each node sorts the items it has using quicksort.

3. Node 0 broadcasts its median key K to the rest of the cube.

4. Each node separates its items into two groups: those whose keys are $\le K$ and those whose keys are $> K$.

5. Break up the cube into two subcubes: the lower subcube comprising nodes 0 through $(2^{D-1} - 1)$ and the upper subcube consisting of nodes 2^{D-1} through $(2^D - 1)$. Each node in the lower subcube sends its items whose keys are $> K$ to its adjacent node in the upper subcube. Likewise, nodes in the upper subcube send their items whose keys are $\le K$ to their corresponding adjacent nodes in the lower subcube. When this step is completed, all items whose keys are $\le K$ are in the lower subcube while all those whose keys are $> K$ are in the upper subcube.

6. Each node now merges together the group it just received with the one it kept so that its items are once again sorted.

7. Repeat steps 3 through 6 on each of the two subcubes. This time node 0 will correspond to the lowest-numbered node in the subcube, and the value of D will be one less.

8. Keep repeating steps 3 through 7 until the subcubes consist of a single node (i.e., a total of D times). At that point, the hypercube will be sorted.

Given an even distribution of N items per node to begin with, and with the keys in a fairly random order, it is hoped that reasonably good guesses of the median key for a particular subcube are made in step 3, and that each of the nodes ends up with roughly N items at the end of the corresponding step 5. Then the algorithm should run in expected time

$$\Theta\left(N\log N + \frac{D(D+1)}{2} + DN\right).$$

Basically, the $N\log N$ time is the serial sorting time, which is identical to that of bitonic sort's. The $D(D+1)/2$ term represents the broadcasting in step 3, which is negligible for all but the smallest values of N. Lastly, the DN term represents the parallel processing time for exchanging and merging. Given good splittings, this term should represent a $(D+1)/2$-fold improvement over the corresponding one for bitonic sort.

Note that the items do not have to start out evenly distributed among each of the nodes as is the case with bitonic sort. Unfortunately, there is no guarantee that the items will end up evenly distributed as they do in bitonic sort. In fact, it could be the case that nearly all of them end up in one node. This would certainly happen if the items were sorted to begin with. Thus, this algorithm is not well suited to cases where the items are already in some particular order. This possibility can be greatly reduced by distributing the items in a somewhat random fashion ahead of time.

3   Implementation

Both the bitonic sort and Hyperquicksort algorithms were implemented on an NCUBE/ten machine at the University of Michigan. Some limitations had to be imposed in order to produce clear and consistent results for all sizes of cubes and data sets as well as to take full advantage of the available hardware and software.

All of the code was written in FORTRAN/77. At the time, this was the only high-level language available (C has since been added). Since relative, not absolute, speed was the most important criteria in evaluating performance, it did not seem necessary to resort to any assembly language programming.

Items were limited to two- and four-byte integers, randomly generated using the linear congruential method discussed in [6], and distributed evenly among all of the nodes.

Both sort routines used the same quicksort as a subroutine. This was optimized for the NCUBE and its particular FORTRAN compiler using the suggestions found in [9]. It was also run on the host 80286 for purposes of comparison. The bitonic sort was modified for efficient implementation on a hypercube using [4] as a guide.

4   Results

Included is a series of tables summarizing the important results from the NCUBE implementation. Due to space limitations, only the two-byte item results are provided. The four-byte results are essentially the same. A more complete paper with these and other results is available from the author.

Tables 1 and 2 show the times taken by Hyperquicksort and bitonic sort, respectively, on all of the possible cube and data set sizes, together with the corresponding quicksort times on the host 80286 processor. Each of the Hyperquicksort and host entries represent a mean of 20 separate sample runs, while the bitonic sort times were based on 10 such runs. The times take into account the actual sort processing, and do not include any of the overhead needed to generate the items or distribute them to the nodes. Finally, the times are given to the nearest millisecond.

Table 3 shows the maximum number of items ending up in a single node at the end of a Hyperquicksort run. Again, these entries represent means of the same 20 samples used for Table 1. Although this statistic had greater variances, 20 trials was sufficient to establish a general pattern.

During the time these samples were taken, the host 80286 was running at 10MHz while each of the nodes was running at 7MHz. The node's clock, which produced times accurate to the nearest seventh of a millisecond, was used to time all of the runs.

5   Analysis of Results

Overall, the Hyperquicksort results followed pretty much what was expected. It was nearly two and a half times faster than bitonic sort on 64 nodes. In addition, the minimum and maximum items ending up in any one node differed little from N, the starting allocation.

Tables 4 and 5 give the speedup and efficiencies of the two sort routines for the various subcubes. They are based on the largest data set that could be run on each size subcube.

The 1 node versions are nothing more than a serial quicksort, and their times fit an $N \log N$ curve. From this, their expected times for larger data sets could be extrapolated. These times could then be used to determine the actual speedup as well as efficiency of the algorithms using 8192 items/node as a basis for comparison. Actual speedup is just the ratio of the 1-node time to the many-node time while efficiency is the percentage of linear speedup and can be computed by the simple formula

$$\text{efficiency} = \frac{\text{actual speedup}}{\text{number of nodes}} .$$

Table 6 shows the amount of time spent exchanging and merging for the two routines. Since the initial serial sorting of the routines was identical, this statistic is a better basis for comparison. The ratios of the corresponding bitonic sort to Hyperquicksort times are provided as well. As can be seen, these closely fit the expected $(D + 1)/2$ curve.

At this point, some theoretical analysis of the expected behavior of Hyperquicksort is in order.

6   Theoretical Analysis

As previously observed, several parts of the Hyperquicksort Algorithm are easy to analyze:

- Step 1 (distributing the items) is completely dependent on the intended application of the algorithm and so will not be considered.

Nodes →	host	1	2	4	8	16	32	64
Items								
1	1	0	-	-	-	-	-	-
2	1	0	2	-	-	-	-	-
4	1	0	2	4	-	-	-	-
8	1	0	2	4	7	-	-	-
16	2	1	3	5	7	10	-	-
32	4	3	4	5	7	10	13	-
64	8	6	6	6	8	10	13	17
128	16	14	10	9	9	11	14	17
256	35	32	19	14	12	13	15	18
512	77	71	41	25	18	16	17	19
1024	170	156	87	50	31	23	21	22
2048	372	343	190	103	60	39	29	26
4096	813	747	404	220	121	71	46	35
8192	1758	1611	867	462	250	138	81	54
16384	3774	-	1847	983	521	282	156	94
32768	8129	-	-	2073	1094	582	313	175
65536	-	-	-	-	2291	1211	642	348
131072	-	-	-	-	-	2535	1331	706
262144	-	-	-	-	-	-	2739	1450
524288	-	-	-	-	-	-	-	2994

Table 1: Average Hyperquicksort Times for Two-Byte Items (msec)

Nodes →	host	1	2	4	8	16	32	64
Items								
1	1	0	-	-	-	-	-	-
2	1	0	2	-	-	-	-	-
4	1	0	2	4	-	-	-	-
8	1	0	2	4	7	-	-	-
16	2	1	2	4	7	11	-	-
32	4	3	3	5	7	11	15	-
64	8	6	5	6	8	12	16	21
128	16	14	9	9	11	13	17	21
256	35	32	19	15	15	16	19	22
512	77	71	42	29	24	22	23	25
1024	170	157	90	59	43	35	31	31
2048	372	341	194	123	84	62	49	42
4096	813	747	413	258	171	119	85	65
8192	1758	1606	883	539	351	236	161	113
16384	3774	-	1885	1136	726	477	315	212
32768	8129	-	-	2388	1508	978	634	412
65536	-	-	-	-	3123	2001	1283	822
131072	-	-	-	-	-	4119	2621	1657
262144	-	-	-	-	-	-	5336	3361
524288	-	-	-	-	-	-	-	6831

Table 2: Average Bitonic Sort Times for Two-Byte Items (msec)

Nodes →	2	4	8	16	32	64
Items/Node						
1	2	2	4	5	7	10
2	3	4	6	8	10	15
4	5	7	8	13	15	20
8	10	12	15	19	22	27
16	18	22	25	30	35	41
32	36	39	44	50	59	66
64	67	74	82	88	95	103
128	134	144	151	164	176	187
256	264	279	292	308	320	345
512	522	540	560	576	602	624
1024	1049	1080	1102	1148	1148	1213
2048	2074	2112	2155	2183	2249	2262
4096	4144	4180	4231	4263	4342	4330
8192	8229	8274	8309	8370	8374	8497

Table 3: Average Maximum Number of Two-Byte Items Ending up in a Single Node

Nodes	Time	Extrapolated 1 Node Time	Speedup	Efficiency
2	1847	3469	1.88	0.94
4	2073	7433	3.59	0.90
8	2291	15858	6.92	0.87
16	2535	33697	13.29	0.83
32	2739	71359	26.05	0.81
64	2994	150647	50.32	0.79

Table 4: Hyperquicksort: Two-Byte Items (8192 items/node)

Nodes	Time	Extrapolated 1 Node Time	Speedup	Efficiency
2	1885	3460	1.84	0.92
4	2388	7414	3.10	0.78
8	3123	15816	5.06	0.63
16	4119	33609	8.16	0.51
32	5336	71172	13.34	0.42
64	6831	149842	21.94	0.34

Table 5: Bitonic Sort: Two-Byte Items (8192 items/node)

Nodes	Hyperquicksort	Bitonic Sort	ratio
2	236	278	1.18
4	462	782	1.69
8	680	1517	2.23
16	925	2513	2.72
32	1129	3730	3.30
64	1383	5224	3.78

Table 6: Comparison of Parallel Processing Times for Two-Byte Items (8192 items/node)

- Step 2 (sorting the items within the nodes) takes $\Theta(N \log N)$ expected time.

- Steps 7 and 8 merely iterate Steps 3 through 6 for a total of D times. These iterations will henceforth be referred to as *stages* of the algorithm.

- Step 3 (broadcasting the key) takes total time proportional to $D(D+1)/2$, assuming a standard recursive doubling broadcast.

- Step 4 (breaking the items into two groups) just amounts to a binary search since each node's items are already sorted. Therefore, this Step's time is easily dwarfed by those of Steps 5 and 6.

For Steps 5 and 6 (exchanging and merging the groups), the analysis gets a little trickier. That is because the time these Steps take is proportional to the number of items each node has during each of the stages. If, as is hoped, each node has approximately N items throughout the execution, then the total time contributed by these Steps to the algorithm would be $\Theta(DN)$, which would justify the assumptions made earlier.

What's needed is a careful analysis of just how many items a single node is working on during each stage. A full analysis of this statistic for an arbitrary combination of items and nodes may not be possible, but other useful statistics can be computed. Space limitations permit only a brief summary of the results garnered so far. Techniques found in [5] and [8] were very helpful in doing this work. A more complete and detailed analysis is in preparation.

Summary of Theoretical Results

The problem is most easily approached by looking at what happens to the distribution of items among a pair of adjacent subcubes L and U when the larger cube C they are a part of is split along their common dimension. Assume L contains the lower-numbered nodes. Let i be the total number of items in L and U and j be the number of items in C's lowest-numbered node C_0, which determines the splitting key. Also, assume that all keys are distinct and that all distributions of keys among C_0 and the rest of C are equally likely.

At this point there are two possibilities: either the j sample items are part of L's items or they aren't. Remember, L and U can be *any* two adjacent subcubes about to be split in C, not necessarily the two largest ones which comprise C.

Case 1: $C_0 \in L$

The expected number of items ending up in L (as well as U) is about $i/2$ while the variance is roughly

$$\frac{i(i-j)}{4j} .$$

Of more use is the expected maximum number of items ending up in L or U, which is approximately

$$\frac{i}{2} + \frac{1}{\sqrt{\pi}}\sqrt{\frac{i(i-j)}{2j}} .$$

This last answer is quite powerful, for it leads immediately to an intuitive, but by no means rigorous, proof that in a D-dimensional hypercube containing $2^D N$ items, the expected maximum number of items ending up in a single node after all D stages is no more than

$$N + DN^{1/2} ,$$

which is supported by Table 3.

Case 2: $C_0 \notin L$

The results are similar. The variance in the number of items ending up in L or U turns out this time to be about

$$\frac{i(i+j)}{4j},$$

while the expected maximum number of items ending up in L or U is approximately

$$\frac{i}{2} + \frac{1}{\sqrt{\pi}}\sqrt{\frac{i(i+j)}{2j}}.$$

The most immediate consequence of these results is that when L and U are just single nodes, the number of items ending up in L or U will deviate from the mean by about $\sqrt{3}$ times as much when the splitting key is chosen from a different node's items as it would be if it were chosen from L's. For larger subcubes, the differences between the two cases are much less significant.

References

[1] K. E. Batcher, *Sorting networks and their applications,* Spring Joint Computer Conference, AFIPS Proceedings, vol. 32, 1968, pp. 307-314.

[2] G. Baudet and D. Stevenson, *Optimal Sorting Algorithms for Parallel Computers,* IEEE Transactions on Computers, vol. C-27, no. 1, Jan. 1978, pp. 84-87.

[3] E. Felten, S. Karlin, and S. Otto, *Sorting on a Hypercube,* Caltech/JPL Hm244, California Institute of Technology, 1986.

[4] S. L. Johnson, *Combining parallel and sequential sorting on a Boolean n-cube,* Procedings, 1984 International Conf. on Parallel Processing, pp. 444-448.

[5] D. E. Knuth, *The Art of Computer Programming,* vol. 1 (2nd ed.), Addison-Wesley, 1973.

[6] D. E. Knuth, *The Art of Computer Programming,* vol. 2 (2nd ed.), Addison-Wesley, 1981.

[7] P. Peggi Li, *Parallel Sorting on the Ametek/S14,* Sept. 1986 (available from Ametek).

[8] P. W. Purdom, Jr. and C. A. Brown, *The Analysis of Algorithms,* Holt, Rinehart, and Winston, 1985.

[9] R. Sedgewick, *Implementing Quicksort Programs,* Communications of the ACM, vol. 21, no. 10, Oct. 1978, pp. 847-857.

[10] C. D. Thompson and H. T. Kung, *Sorting on a Mesh-Connected Parallel Computer,* Communications of the ACM, vol. 20, no. 4, Apr. 1977, pp. 263-271.

Multiprocessor Algorithms to Schedule Jobs

SCOTT SHOREY BROWN*

ABSTRACT Three algorithms to solve a scheduling problem
are tested in a hypercube multiprocessor. The scheduling
problem is the maximization of the total value of
scheduled jobs subject to constraints imposed by time
intervals when each job can be performed, the length of
time required to perform a job, and a setup time required
between successive jobs. The schedule is for a single
machine but we find the schedule by adapting standard
optimization algorithms to run on multiple CPUs
(henceforth called nodes). We investigate the performance
of three paradigms on hypercubes. In particular, we
parallelize a dynamic programming algorithm by dividing
the states among the nodes, a queue algorithm with each
node building a schedule in a different time interval, and
a forward reaching algorithm with a controller node
dynamically assigning tasks to other nodes. The run times
for implementations on an Intel iPSC hypercube are
compared.

This paper presents a job scheduling problem which
includes job availability intervals and interjob setup
times. Serial algorithms to obtain near optimal schedules
are adapted to run on a hypercube as follows:

ALGORITHM	Spider	Entry List	Queue
METHOD	Forward reaching	Dynamic programming	Sequential placement
COMMUNICATION	Star	Cube	Ring
CONTROL	Master and slaves	Distributed synchronous	Jobs passed arround ring

---

*General Electric Corporation, Valley Forge, PA.

Each of these algorithms provides an approximation to an optimal job schedule. Since the algorithms which produce higher score schedules require longer run times, we have the usual run time versus score tradeoff. Figure 1 plots run time versus score curves for hypercube configurations of 1, 2, 4, 8, 16, and 32 nodes. These curves show the possibilities for decreasing run time or increasing score with additional nodes. The remainder of this section discusses the algorithms and gives further breakdowns of the performance statistics.

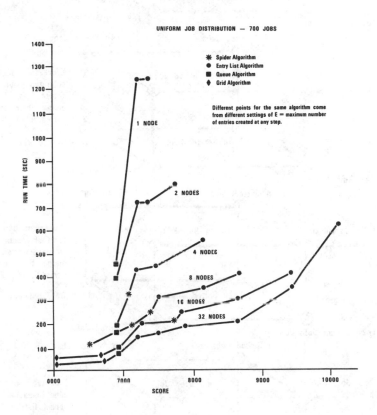

FIG. 1. Performance of Job Scheduling Algorithms

The input to each algorithm is a list of the following values for each of n jobs:
- o earliest time the job can begin and the latest time it can end (called the job's availability interval)
- o time required to perform the job (called the job's duration)
- o value of the job
- o location of the job

The locations of jobs i and j are used to calculate the setup time required when job i immediately precedes job j. Our algorithms do not depend on the details of the setup time calculations but we assume that it takes 1/20 sec. to calculate a setup time on a single hypercube node.

A valid schedule is a sequence of distinct jobs and

N = NUMBER OF NODES = 8

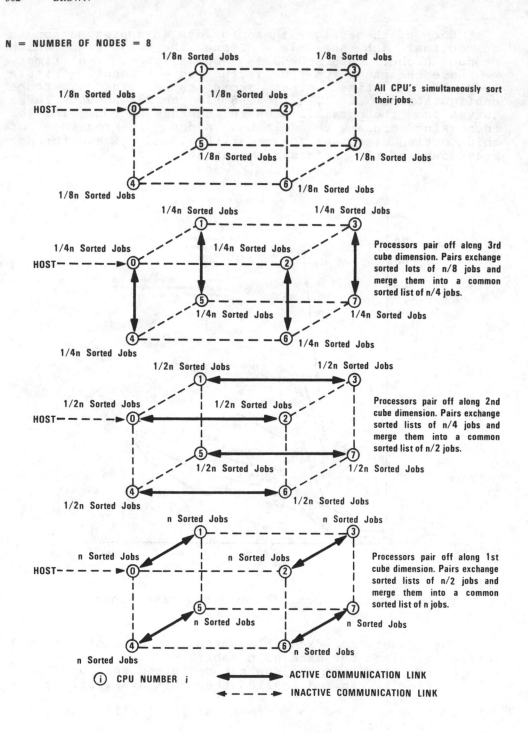

FIG. 2. Merge for Parallel Sort

times for the jobs such that each job is scheduled within its availability interval and the required setup time is allowed between successive jobs. The score of a schedule is the sum of the values of the jobs on the schedule. The job shop problem is to find a valid schedule with maximum score.

The applications we have in mind are similar to those considered by Martin and Poling in reference [1]. They discuss a truck operator who can haul different cargos, one at a time. Each cargo is available for transport in a specific time period, requires a known amount of time to transport, and yields a given fee to the operator. The time to drive between one cargo's destination and the next cargo's pick up point is the setup time in our model.

This problem is as hard as NP-complete problems so any algorithm to produce optimal solutions is likely to have a worst case run time which grows exponentially with the number of jobs. Martin and Poling, reference [1], state that optimal solutions to the job shop problem are feasible only for 20 or fewer jobs. Thus we are led to consider algorithms which approximate optimal solutions. We consider three methods suggested by Martin and Poling and one new method.

All but one of the algorithms begin by sorting the jobs. To sort on a hypercube we first divide the n jobs equally among the N nodes of the hypercube using a broadcast tree where each node sends half the jobs it receives. Next, each node sorts its n/N jobs using a Quicksort. Finally, we merge the N sorted lists of n/N jobs as shown in Figure 2. We have arranged the merges so that the entire sorted list of jobs is left on every node.

Figure 3 shows the time required to sort a randomly chosen sequence of 700 jobs using this algorithm. The run time is broken down into the time spent calculating, communicating, and waiting for other nodes. Note that while the calculation time decreases as additional nodes are used, the communication time increases slightly and the wait time remains nearly constant. The net effect is a decreasing run time but the gain from adding additional nodes diminishes rapidly as more nodes are used.

Figure 3 also shows that the sort time with two nodes is less than half the sort time with one node because our parallel sort algorithm gains speed by using auxiliary storage which the single node Quicksort does not use. For larger numbers of nodes, the low wait and communication times indicate that the load is balanced but there is so much overhead dividing and merging the sublists of jobs that there is little gain in calculation time.

The sort routine forms the initial phase of the Entry List algorithm for the Job Shop problem. Jobs are sorted on the center of their availability intervals and a dynamic programming approach selects the best valid schedule which keeps the jobs in this order. Entry List manipulates intermediate results called entries which contain

    I = identifier of a job
    T = time when job I is scheduled
    S = score, i.e. sum of the values of job I and all
        jobs which precede I on an optimal schedule up
        to time T

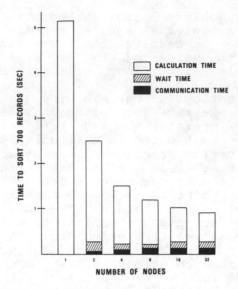

FIG. 3. Run Time for Parallel Sort

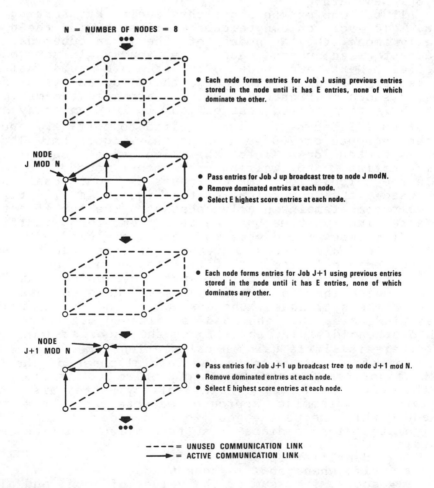

FIG. 4. Two Steps In the Entry List Algorithm

> P = the job which precedes I on an optimal schedule
>   up to time T.

The outer loop of Entry List goes through the sorted list of jobs. For each job, J, it calculates entries by examining potential predecessor entries and scheduling job J as soon after its predecessor as the setup time and the job's earliest start time allow. It also creates a predecessorless entry for J which makes J the first job scheduled.

Entries for job J are discarded if another entry for J has higher score and earlier time. In this case we say the higher score entry dominates the lower score entry. Additionally, to save storage we only retain the E highest score entries for each job. After all entries for job J have been formed we go on to job J+1. After all jobs have been considered the best schedule comes from the entry with the highest score and its predecessors.

In order to implement the Entry List algorithm on a hypercube we divide the list of entries among the N nodes by assigning entry (I, T, S, P) to node I mod N. Each node keeps a list of its entries sorted by score. The nodes compute entries for job J in parallel then send the entries to node J mod N using a broadcast tree rooted at J mod N. See Figure 4 or reference [2] which gives a complete description of broadcast trees. Each node in the broadcast tree removes dominated entries and retains at most E entries for job J. When a node is waiting for a message, it fills the time by precalculating tables of setup times which at anticipates it will need in subsequent entry calculations.

Like the Entry List algorithm, the Spider algorithm constructs a linked list of entries which represent partial job schedules. Spider initializes a list of entries by sorting the jobs on their earliest start time and creating a predecessorless entry for each job at its earliest start time. All newly created entries are marked "unextended." Spider forms additional entries by extending existing entries as follows:

(1) Select one or more unextended entries. Use the earliest unextended entries available.
(2) For each selected entry loop over all jobs J not on the predecessor chain of the entry.
(3) If possible, create a new entry for J scheduling it as early as possible after the old entry.
(4) Mark the old entries "extended."

A list of entries created for each job is maintained with dominated entries deleted.

Because the maintenance of the lists of entries for each job is a significant task, we assign it to a separate group of nodes from the extension of entries. A single control node organizes the work of both the list maintenance and entry extension nodes by passing entries between them. As it passes entries from the entry extension to the list maintenance nodes, the controller builds a table of each entry's predecessor which it uses to attach predecessor chains to entries as it passes entries in the other direction. Figure 5 shows the sequence of messages and calculations and their division among the nodes. The entries for job J are kept by the (J

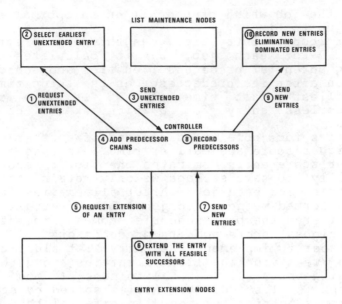

FIG. 5. Messages and Calculations for Spider Algorithm

mod Nl)-th list maintenance node where Nl is the number of list maintenance nodes. Likewise, entries for job J are extended by the (J mod Ne)-th entry extension where Ne is the number of entry extension nodes. When there are no unextended entries, the controller reconstructs the best schedule as the predecessor chain of the highest score entry.

The Spider and Entry List algorithms both examine a variety of tentative schedules and select the best schedule found. The Single Schedule Queue algorithm, on the other hand, builds a single schedule. The jobs are considered in order of decreasing value and assigned a single permanent place in the schedule as they are considered. When a job is considered, the algorithm determines if is can be scheduled in any of the gaps between higher value jobs. If not, the job is discarded. If the job can be scheduled, it is put in the earliest possible gap with the following priorities for its time: (1) the beginning of the gap, (2) the end of the gap, (3) the job's earliest start time. The algorithm terminates when each job has been considered.

To implement the Queue algorithm on a hypercube we divide the gaps among nodes. The nodes are arranged in a ring and jobs are passed around the ring. The first node which finds a gap which can accommodate the job schedules it. Jobs which go all the way around the ring without being scheduled are discarded.

We tested the algorithms described above on a data set of 700 jobs. The data set was constructed by drawing independent uniformly distributed random numbers to represent each job's earliest start time, value, duration,

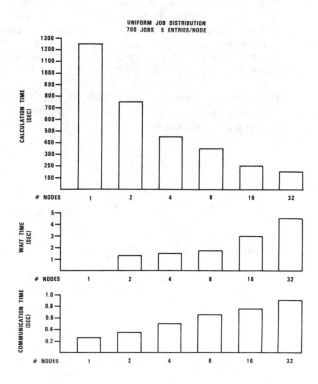

FIG. 6. Run Time For Entry List Algorithm

and slack time. Each job's latest end time was its
earliest start time + duration + slack time.
     Figure 1 shows the scores and run times for each
algorithm. For the Entry List algorithm, a number of runs
are made with different numbers of entries per job.   When
the number of nodes is small, the number of entries per
job is limited by the storage available on each node.
Thus, larger numbers of nodes can achieve higher score
solutions by storing more entries.   The possibility of
sending entries which do not fit in core to the host where
they can be stored on disk has not been investigated.
     Figure 6 shows the run time required for the Entry
List algorithm to get a score of 7200 with increasing
numbers of nodes. While there is always some speedup when
the number of nodes is doubled, the speedup is well below
the full 2 to 1 speedup. As expected, the speedup
decreases with increasing numbers of nodes. Although the
communication and wait times increase when nodes are
added, they play an insignificant role in the total run
time. The low speedups occur because unnecessary
calculations occur when the algorithm is parallelized.
Entries which need not be calculated because there are
higher score entries on other nodes are being calculated.
Additionally, the precalculation of setup times calculates
a significant number of values which are, in fact, not
needed. The lack of need for these values, however, is
not apparent until data is received from other nodes.

REFERENCES

1. C. F. Martin and R. S. Poling, Fast Dynamic Programming Selection Algorithms for the Job Shop Problem with Job Availability Intervals, General Electric Technical Information Series No 78CIS012, June 1978.

2. J. E. Brandenburg and D. S. Scott, Embeddings of Communication Trees and Grids into Hypercubes, Intel Scientific Computers, undated.

Parallel Branch-and-Bound Algorithms on the Hypercube

STEVEN ANDERSON* AND MARINA C. CHEN*

Abstract

A parallel branch-and-bound design for solving NP-hard optimization problems such as Travelling Salesman is presented. The hypercube implementation consists of (1) a distributed manager, which implements a general parallel branch-and-bound method, oversees communication, and balances workload across the network, and (2) problem-specific functions, which tailor the general method to a specific branch-and bound algorithm for a specific problem. The communication costs of workload balancing, incumbent broadcast, and termination detection receive special attention. Worst-case time requirements for this design retain near-linear performance (to within a logarithmic factor) as the number of processors grows large.

1   Introduction

Algorithms can be broadly classified by the amount of expression-level parallelism and the amount of data-level parallelism they contain. Expression-level parallelism models each functional call as a process; function calls that have data dependencies are sequentialized, whereas independent function calls can be executed in parallel. Data-level parallelism models each function call as operating on every data element of a data structure; if the data elements are independent, the operations can proceed in parallel. Scientific computing problems operating on very large data structures typically exhibit a high degree of data-level parallelism. Combinatorial search problems, on the other hand, such as N-queens and Traveling Salesman, operate on relatively small data structures but spawn an enormous number of function calls, exhibiting a high degree of expression-level parallelism.

A parallel branch-and-bound algorithm for problems such as Traveling Salesman cannot get around the inherent NP-hardness of these problems; we can at best get a linear speed-up by increasing the number of processors, whereas the search space grows exponentially in the problem size. A parallel version must retain the power of the sequential algorithm to avoid exploring subtrees that cannot possibly contain an optimal solution.

* Department of Computer Science, Yale University, P.O.Box 2158, Yale Station, New Haven, CT 06520-2158. Work supported in part by the Office of Naval Research under Contract No. N00014-86-K-0296.

However, subtree pruning in sequential branch-and-bound relies on having *global* knowledge available, such as the cheapest solution found so far, or the next "best" subtree to explore. Implementing such global information in a distributed memory system such as the hypercube has a significant cost.

A realistic hypercube implementation cannot assume global information is free; the cost of communication in fact makes it wiser to operate with less than full global information. This paper explores the cost trade-offs inherent in implementing parallel branch-and-bound. A reasonable fear is that near-linear speedup will not hold as the number of processors grows large: a parallel algorithm will explore many subtrees more deeply than would a comparable sequential algorithm, and it is possible that the parallel version will create so much extra work for itself that the advantage of parallel execution is lost. A design is presented, with theoretical arguments showing that even under worst-case assumptions, performance achieves near-linear speedup (with a logarithmic factor) as the number of processors becomes large. An implementation of this design in the parallel language Crystal [1] is a testbed program for the Crystal compiler, soon to be working for the iPSC.

2   Preliminary Review of Branch-and-Bound

Branch-and-bound is a programming technique rather than a single algorithm. It is essentially a refinement of backtracking applied to optimization problems.

In backtracking we are searching a space of possible solutions by recursively subdividing the solution space into smaller subspaces. We do this by building a search tree over the solution space. Each node of the search tree represents a partial solution, governing the subspace of complete solutions derivable from it. Each child represents one possible way to extend its parent's partial solution toward a more complete solution; a child governs a subspace of its parent's solution space. A leaf is either a single feasible solution, or a partial solution that cannot possibly be extended.

For many problems such as travelling salesman we are trying to find not just a *feasible* solution, but the *optimal* solution with respect to some cost function. Branch-and-bound is backtracking with the refinement of using a cost function: this cost function must be defined over all nodes of the search tree, and must have the property that a child's cost is guaranteed to be at least as great as its parent's cost. This means that a node's cost forms a lower bound for its subtree: every node in the subtree must have a cost as least as great as the subtree root's cost. A node that has been reached but whose subtree has not been explored is an *active* node; the current set of all such nodes, ordered by some priority scheme, is called the *active node queue*. The cheapest complete solution found so far is called the *incumbent*; if $cost(incumbent) \leq cost(node)$, then the node cannot possibly lead to a solution cheaper than current incumbent, and we can avoid searching its entire subtree.

A particular branch-and-bound algorithm can be characterized by:

Two termination rules:
       is_a_solution? (node) $\implies$ T or F,
       no_solution_possible? (node) $\implies$ T or F.
An expansion rule:
       expand (node) $\implies$ a set of children nodes.
A selection rule:
       select (active_node_queue) $\implies$ next node to expand.
A bounding rule:
       cost(incumbent) $\leq$ cost(node) $\implies$ T or F.

The termination and expansion rules are specific to a particular algorithm for solving a particular problem. The bounding and selection rules, together with a simple top-level control program, make up the general structure of the sequential branch-and-bound technique.

The selection rule is a heuristic that orders the search tree nodes in the hope that cheaper solutions will be found early, permitting as much subtree pruning as possible.

3 Parallelism in Branch-and-Bound

3.1 A Partially Sequential Strategy

The selection rule, typically either depth-first or best-first search, is by definition sequential, imposing a *total ordering* on the nodes of the search tree. But only the ancestor-descendant ordering is actually required by branch-and-bound's data dependencies. Recall that an active node is one that has been reached but whose subtree has not been explored. Since no pair of active nodes can have an ancestor-descendant relation, all active nodes can potentially be expanded in parallel.

Since, for a sufficiently large problem, the set of active nodes will exceed the available processors, we will need to impose additional ordering upon the nodes that is not strictly required by the data dependencies; in other words, pursue a partially sequential strategy. Therefore we choose to distribute the set of active nodes across the hypercube by maintaining a *local active node queue* on each processor. Each processor will pursue a locally sequential strategy such as best-first search in choosing nodes from its local queue, and will put children from the nodes it expands into its local queue.

The way the active nodes are distributed to the local queues not only determines how the workload is spread across the network, but also determines a global search strategy. A parallel algorithm might explore deeper into subtrees that a sequential algorithm would ignore; we want to be sure that we are not pursuing a global search strategy that generates so much extra work that the hypercube suffers significantly less than linear speedup.

3.2 System Organization

Our system for parallel branch-and-bound consists of a program for each cube processor consisting of a problem-specific user functions and a general manager. A manager executes on each processor, overseeing both local sequential operations and communications with other managers. The distributed manager implements a general parallel branch-and-bound method; it invokes the problem-specific functions, which tailor the general method to a specific algorithm for a specific problem.

The problem-specific functions implement:

> the termination rules,
> the expansion rule,
> the cost function.

The problem-specific functions determine the representation of a search tree node (i.e., a partial solution). These functions are invoked by a processor's manager, and are simply sequential programs, identical to the functions we would write for sequential branch-and-bound.

The manager implements some functions we expect in sequential branch-and-bound:

> the selection rule,
> the bounding rule.

The selection rule interacts with load-balancing in a way described in the next section. The manager also implements various communication functions with other processor managers:

> balancing workload by diffusing active nodes,
> broadcasting new incumbent values,
> processing completion messages involved in global termination.

> The data structures maintained by the general manager are:

> a local active node queue,
> a local incumbent value,
> a set of retired nodes,
> a set of completion messages.

The way that the managers on neighboring processors balance the workload among local active node queues in discussed in the next section. The broadcasting of incumbent values across the network and the implications of broadcast delay are discussed in the incumbent broadcast section. The use of the retired node sets and completion messages in detecting termination and collecting the optimal solution to a known processor are discussed in the final section.

4   Balancing Workload

4.1   Goals

How do we design a global search heuristic that balances work over the network and that interacts well with the local sequential search heuristic? We want to design a global strategy that uses only nearest neighbor information and movement of work, but would be a good approximation of the strategy we would pursue if we could gather the work into a centralized queue, then redistribute it anywhere in the network using perfect global information.

We want the globally "best" nodes, which appear near the beginning of a centralized queue, also to appear near the beginning of the local queues. The intuition is that the "best" nodes are most likely to lead to the cheapest feasible solutions, so if we expand these nodes early, we are more likely to prevent the expansion of non-optimal subtrees.

4.2   Heuristics

A naive view of a particular local queue's workload might be the queue size, but a better view would be some measure of the queue's "goodness" (e.g., for depth-first search, a sum of node depths). Then we have a "goodness" function over the processors; this function has local peaks and valleys. But we would like the "goodness" function to be flat over the space of processors: each processor has about as many "good" nodes (as measured in a centralized queue) early in its local queue as any other processor.

One heuristic for periodically balancing the workload is for each processor to periodically exchange a "goodness" measure with its neighbors, determine a "goodness" gradient in the direction of each neighbor, then make a local decision whether to offload nodes. If processor A's neighbor B has a very poor workload compared with A, then A should send B one or more of A's better nodes. Although A is then left with a slightly less desirable workload, more of A's better nodes will be expanded earlier, with an increased chance of leading to a cheaper incumbent earlier, and more of B's worse nodes have been delayed, with an increased chance that they will never be expanded at all.

4.3 Algorithm

An advantage of this approach is that it only relies on local information from a processor and its immediate neighbors. Since two processors A and B who exchange workload information both know who has the better workload, both know what direction a work offload will go. However, only the potential sender A will know if the offload will actually take place, since A may have other neighbors with even poorer workloads. Therefore A will also need to send the potential receiver B a message informing B no offload will take place.

Initialization: begin by assigning one processor (call it the *root processor*) a singleton active node queue containing the *root node* of the entire search tree. (See the section on termination detection for the special role the root processor plays in termination.) All other processors begin with an empty active node queue.

A compute/communicate cycle looks like this, with computation taking place while waiting for communication to complete. The root node broadcasts a global termination to all other processors when it has determined the algorithm has completed.

0. Initalization:
      root processor gets active queue with root node,
      other processors get empty active queue.
While (no global termination message) {
    1. Process local active nodes.
    2. Send workload summary to neighbors.
    3. Process more local nodes.
    4. Receive workload summary from neighbors.
    5. Send nodes to be offloaded.
    6. Process more local nodes.
    7. Receive offloaded nodes. }

The startup time for iPSC communications is costly, and the iPSC message length can be quite long. Therefore we include other communications, such as incumbent broadcast, subtree completion, and global termination messages (described in the following sections) at the same time we send workload summary and node offload communications.

4.4 Parallel Best-First Search

In depth-first search, A's communicating a single number to neighbor B to represent A's workload is easy: just send the sum of the depths of the nodes in A's active node list. We could do the same for best-first search (sending the sums of the node costs), but comparing these sums for neighbors would be misleading. A could have many cheap nodes and neighbor B could have a few expensive nodes, so that a simple sum of costs gives both A and B approximately equal workloads. However, A obviously has a more valuable workload, and should probably send a few of its cheap nodes to B. For best-first search, it is the *relative order* of A's and B's node costs (not the absolute costs) that determines the relative "goodness" of two local queues.

4.4.1 Exchange Queue Summaries

One way for a processor to get a notion of its neighbor's workload under best-first search is to exchange a *summary* of the active node queue. The active queue contains representations of active nodes, whereas the summary contains only *active node costs*. A processor sends each of it neighbors a summary:

$$queue \ \ a = [5, 19, 23]$$
$$queue \ \ b = [19, 49, 51, 73]$$

then merges its summary with its neighbor's summaries.

$$merge(a, b) = [[a : 5], [a : 19, b : 19], [a : 23], [b : 49], [b : 51], [b : 73]]$$

Weight each node by the reciprocal of its relative position in the merged summary. This has the effect of weighting the best nodes, then nodes appearing earliest in the merged summary queue, most heavily. Each processor computes a weighted sum for itself and each of its neighbors.

$$relative\_load(a) = 1 + 1/2 + 1/3 \qquad = 1.83$$
$$relative\_load(b) = 1/2 + 1/4 + 1/5 + 1/6 = 1.12$$

4.4.2 Threshold workload difference

We do not want to offload nodes from processor A to B unless A's workload exceeds B by some *threshold* value. We impose a threshold to prevent thrashing of active nodes back and forth between A and B. This approach can be generalized to any number of neighbors. It is simplest for A to offload work toward the neighbor with the poorest workload that is less than A's by some threshold.

5 Incumbent Broadcast

5.1 Algorithm

We use the following algorithm for incumbent update. Recall that a cycle is defined in the previous section as the time from one round of workload balancing to the next.

> 0. Initialization: every local incumbent value = $+\infty$.
> While (no global termination message) {
> > 1. Process active nodes:
> > > 1.1 Use local incumbent value to prevent expansion of
> > > > nonoptimal subtrees.
> > > 1.2 Update the local incumbent value if a cheaper solution
> > > > is found.
> > 2. Communicate with neighbors:
> > > 2.1 Send local incumbent value v to each neighbor,
> > > 2.2 Receive each neighbor's local incumbent value v_i.
> > > 2.3 New local incumbent value = $\min(v, v_0, ..., v_{k-1})$
> > > > on the next cycle. }

Ideally, we would like to have a single global incumbent that could be broadcast to all processors instantaneously, so no processor would ever spend effort expanding useless nodes. But on an actual hypercube, we have many local incumbents, and the time to broadcast the cheapest incumbent is $\log n$ cycles, where n = number of processors.

5.2 Worst-Case Analysis of Useless Work

The worst case time wasted per processor on useless work because of incumbent broadcast delay *linear with respect to the cube diameter*. We will assume that killing useless nodes under instantaneous incumbent broadcast costs as much time as expanding these same useless nodes under delayed broadcast; the extra cost under delayed broadcast is spent killing off the *children* of useless nodes that would not have been expanded under instantaneous broadcast. Furthermore, we will assume that the useless children diffuse across the network evenly enough that the cost of killing them off is shared approximately equally by all processors.

Let p be the maximum number of nodes either expanded or killed per processor per cycle, f be the maximum number of children per node. Let us call the processor originating the new incumbent the *origin*. Then for a processor at distance d from the origin, the worst case number of useless nodes that will be expanded (which would not have been expanded if incumbent broadcast had been instantaneous) is $p \cdot d$, and the worst case number of useless children nodes produced that will need to be eliminated is $p \cdot f \cdot d$.

Suppose that some useless child c produced at one processor diffuses to another processor. If c gets chosen at the new processor *after* the new incumbent has arrived, then c gets killed off: it makes no difference to the total cleanup work in the cube whether c gets killed off at its original processor or at some other processor. But if c gets chosen at the new processor *before* the new incumbent arrives, c is merely a useless node that gets expanded (or killed) in place of another useless node that would have been expanded in the worst case if c had not come along. So again the diffusion of c to a new processor makes no difference to the worst case total cleanup work in the cube.

Therefore we can determine the worst case time spent by the cube on cleanup due to incumbent broadcast delay by dividing the number n of cube processors into the worst case number of useless children produced by the cube. Recall that the worst case number of useless children per processor at distance d from the new incumbent origin is pfd. Let $k = \log n$. The number of processors at Hamming distance d from the origin (i.e., the number of processors whose addresses differ from the origin processor's address in d bits) is:

$$\phi(d) = \binom{k}{d}.$$

Proposition 1 *Let n be the number of cube processors. The worst case number $w(n)$ of useless children produced per processor (averaged over the whole cube) because of incumbent broadcast delay is linear with respect to the cube diameter $k = \log(n)$.*

Proof:

$$w(n) \quad = (1/n) \sum_{d=1}^{k} pfd \, \phi(d)$$

$$= (pf/n) \sum_{d=1}^{k} d \binom{k}{d}$$

$$= (pf/n)(k \sum_{d=1}^{k} \binom{k-1}{d-1}) = (pf/n)(k \sum_{d=0}^{k-1} \binom{k-1}{d})$$

$$= (pf/n)(k2^{k-1}) = (pf/n)(\log n)(n/2) = (1/2)pf \log n.$$

So $w(n)$ is $O(\log n)$, linear with respect to cube diameter. Since $w(n)$ is the amount of useless work *per processor*, this result is both pessimistic (useless work per processor increases as we increase network size) and optimistic (it does not increase very fast even in the worst case: doubling n increases $w(n)$ by a constant, so $w(2n) = w(n) + (1/2)pf$). In fact for the average case this result is far too pessimistic: for best-first local heuristic, it assumes that no local queue has *any* active node cheaper than the new incumbent; only the processor originating the new incumbent has any active nodes still worth exploring. This result is encouraging in that even for the worst case it achieves near-linear speedup, within a logarithmic factor.

6   Termination Detection

6.1   Data Representation

Termination detection is easy for a centralized queue (it is empty when we are done), but is harder for distributed queues. When an active node has been expanded (and therefore becomes an internal node), let it be put into a *set of retired nodes*. As active nodes diffuse across the processor network and are expanded, a tree of retired interior nodes gets built up across the network, through which we can upwardly merge messages showing subtree completions.

6.1.1   Active Node

An active node is represented as a tuple containing:

> a problem-specific representation of the node's partial solution,
> the node's cost,
> the node's search tree address, describing the path from the root
>   to this particular node,
> the node's parent's search tree address,
> the node's parent's processor address (i.e., the processor on which
>   the parent was expanded and retired).

If an active daughter node diffuses to another processor before it is expanded, it carries sufficient information to send a message back to its retired parent.

6.1.2   Retired Node

A retired node's representation includes:

> the node's search tree address,
> the node's parent's search tree address,
> the node's parent's processor address.

6.1.3   Completion Messages

Suppose a node is finished rather than expanded; in other words, it is a leaf node that is either a solution, cannot lead to a solution, or else has been killed off by the current incumbent. If a node is finished, do *not* put it in the retirement set, but instead send a completion message to its parent's processor. When a retired node receives a completion message from all daughters, remove the node from the retirement set and send a completion message to its parent. A completion message sent upward from a node represents the complete exploration of the subtree rooted at that node. A completion message is represented as:

> the node's parent's search tree and processor addresses,
> the set of solutions (and their costs) found under this node
>   (may be the empty set).

The algorithm is finished when the root node receives completions from all its daughters. Solution sets can also be merged upward along with the completion messages to collect the optimal solution at the root node.

6.2 Time and Space Requirements for Distributed Termination Detection

The time to detect completion is in the worst case linear in the depth of the tree (which for solutions to TSP is a small polynomial of the number of cities) and is $O(\log n)$, where n is number of processors (assuming that in the worst case we have to cross the entire cube for every child-to-parent completion message).

With regard to the space requirement in each processor, the worst case is that no subtrees get terminated early by incumbents.

Proposition 2 *The number of retired nodes awaiting completion is smaller than the current size of the active node queue.*

Proof: Assume that no nodes have completed yet, that all a active nodes are at the *same* depth d (we have a full tree), and that the number of children per node is f. Then the number of active leaf nodes is $a = f^d$ and the number of retired interior nodes is

$$r = \sum_{i=0}^{d-1} f^i = \frac{f^{d-1} - 1}{f - 1} < f^d = a.$$

Now let us expand one active node. This increases r by 1 and a by $f - 1$. Since $f \geq 2$, the inequality will continue to hold no matter how we choose active nodes to expand.

7 Conclusion

We have presented a hypercube implementation for branch-and-bound problems that consists of a problem-specific function that expands a node into its children nodes, calculates lower-bound costs for nodes, and recognizes a complete solution, and a general manager that schedules nodes for expansion, balances the workload across processors, broadcasts incumbent costs for complete solutions, prevents search of expensive subtrees, and recognizes termination. The paper has focused on the design decisions that went into the manager, in particular demonstrating that it yields near-linear speedup even under worst cast assumptions. An implementation of this hypercube branch-and-bound system has been written and simulated in the parallel programming language Crystal. Experimental results on the iPSC will reported in a sequel.

References

[1] M.C.Chen, *A Parallel Language and Its Compilation to Multiprocessor Machines or VLSI*. 13th ACM Sympos. on Princ. of Prog. Languages, 1986, pp.131-139.

[2] G.J.Li and B.W.Wah, *Computational Efficiency of Parallel Approximate Branch-and-Bound Algorithms*. IEEE International Conference on Parallel Processing, 1984, pp.473-480.

[3] E.M.Reingold, J.Nievergelt, N.Deo, *Combinatorial Algorithms: Theory and Practice*. Prentice-Hall, 1977.

[4] D.R.Smith, *Random Trees and the Analysis of Branch-and-Bound Procedures*. Journal of ACM, Vol.31, No.1, pp.163-188, Jan.1984.

Implementing Best-First Branch-and-Bound Algorithms on Hypercube Multicomputers

MICHAEL J. QUINN*

Abstract. We explore the feasibility of implementing best-first (best-bound) branch-and-bound algorithms on hypercube multicomputers. The computationally-intensive nature of these algorithms might lead a casual observer to believe that their parallelization is trivial. However, as the number of processors grows, two goals must be satisfied to some degree in order to maintain a reasonable level of efficiency. First, processors must be kept busy doing productive work (i.e., exploring worthwhile subproblems). Second, the number of interprocessor communications along the critical path from the original problem to the subproblem yielding a solution must be minimized. It is difficult to improve performance in one of these areas without degrading performance in the other area. A best-first variant of Little et al.'s branch-and-bound algorithm to solve the traveling salesperson problem has been used as a testbed to compare how well four different task allocation strategies meet these criteria. We conclude that the best of these strategies is likely to produce a worthwhile speedup. Our next step will be to solve the traveling salesperson problem on the NCUBE/7 multicomputer, using the most promising task allocation strategy.

Introduction. Combinatorial search is the process of finding "one or more optimal or suboptimal solutions in a defined problem space" [1], and has been used for such problems as laying out circuits in VLSI to minimize the area dedicated to wires, finding traveling salesperson tours, and theorem proving. There are two kinds of combinatorial search problems. An algorithm to solve a *decision problem* must find a solution that satisfies all the constraints. An algorithm that solves an *optimization problem* must also minimize (or maximize) an objective function associated with solutions. The traveling salesperson problem, used as an example in this paper, is an optimization problem.

---

*Parallel Computing Laboratory, Department of Computer Science, University of New Hampshire, Durham, NH 03824

A search problem can be represented by a *state space tree*. The root of the state space tree represents the initial problem to be solved. Traversing an arc from a node representing a problem to its child represents the inclusion of one or more constraints to the problem. Branch-and-bound is a technique often used to search *OR-trees*, state space trees in which the solution to a problem can be found by solving any of its subproblems.

Most interesting combinatorial optimization problems, including the traveling salesperson problem, are NP-hard. No NP-hard problem has yet succumbed to a polynomial time solution. Hence a small increase in problem size usually leads to a dramatic increase in the time needed to solve the problem. For this reason the role of parallelism is more to reduce the solution time of fixed-size problems than to increase the size of solvable problems.

A number of researchers have studied parallel branch-and-bound algorithms. Lai and Sahni [2] and Quinn and Deo [3, 4] have analyzed the speedups theoretically achievable by such an algorithm. Mohan [5] solved the traveling salesperson problem on Cm*, a loosely coupled multiprocessor. Wah et al. [1, 6] discuss combinatorial search on MIMD computers and describe Manip, a computer specifically designed to execute best-first branch-and-bound algorithms.

A *multicomputer* is a multiple-instruction stream, multiple-data stream parallel computer with no shared address space. Synchronization and communication between processors is accomplished entirely through message passing. A *hypercube multicomputer* is a multicomputer containing $p - 2^d$ processors connected as a hypercube. For a more detailed explanation of this architecture, see Quinn [7].

The simulations described in this paper provide evidence that efficient branch-and-bound algorithms can be implemented on a parallel computer without shared memory.

Branch-and-Bound.   Backtrack is a familiar form of exhaustive search. Branch-and-bound is a variant of backtrack that can take advantage of information about the optimality of partial solutions to avoid considering solutions that cannot be optimal. Formally, given an initial problem and some objective function f to be minimized, a branch-and-bound algorithm attempts to solve it directly. If the problem is too large to be solved directly, then it is decomposed into a set of two or more subproblems of smaller size. Every subproblem is characterized by the inclusion of one or more constraints. The decomposition process is repeated until each unexamined subproblem is either decomposed, solved, or shown not to be leading to an optimal solution to the original problem.

The decomposition process applied to the original problem may be represented by a rooted tree, called the *state space tree*. The nodes of this tree correspond to the decomposed problems, and the arcs of the tree correspond to the decomposition process. The original problem is the root of the tree. The leaves of the tree are those partial problems that are solved or discarded without further decomposition.

Recall that the goal of branch-and-bound is to solve the problem by examining a small number of elements in this tree. Assume that a minimum cost solution is desired. A lower bounding function g is calculated for each decomposed subproblem as it is created. This lower bound represents the smallest possible cost of a solution

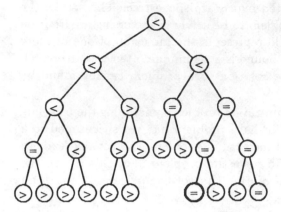

KEY:

   <   Lower bound less than solution cost
   =   Lower bound equal to solution cost
   >   Lower bound greater than solution cost

Figure 1. A portion of a state space tree.

to that subproblem, given the subproblem's constraints. On any path from the root to a terminal node, the lower bounds are always nondecreasing. In addition, the lower bound $g(x)$ at every leaf node x representing a feasible solution is identical to the value of the objective function $f(x)$ for that subproblem.

At any point during the execution of a branch-and-bound algorithm there exists a set of problems that have been generated but not yet examined. A search strategy determines the order in which the unexamined subproblems are examined. The best-first (best-bound) search strategy selects the unexamined subproblem with the smallest lower bound. In case of a tie, the subproblem deepest in the state space tree is chosen. Ties unresolved by the deepness heuristic are broken arbitrarily.

Figure 1 illustrates a portion of a hypothetical state space tree. Every node has been labeled according to the value of the lower bound on the solution cost of the subproblem associated with the node. The "<" symbol denotes a lower bound less than the cost of an optimum solution, the "=" symbol denotes a lower bound equal to the cost of an optimum solution, and the ">" symbol denotes a lower bound greater than the cost of an optimum solution. The heavily circled "=" node represents a subproblem that can be solved directly to yield an optimum solution. In the search for an optimum solution, a branch-and-bound algorithm must examine every subproblem in the state space tree whose value is less than the optimum solution cost, plus at least one node (namely, a solution node) whose value is equal to the cost of the optimum solution. If only solution nodes in the state space tree have a lower bound equal to the cost of the optimum solution, then it is easy to see that a branch-and-bound algorithm using the best-first selection heuristic examines the minimum number of subproblems before finding a solution, because it examines subproblems in nondecreasing order of their lower bound.

Parallelizing Branch-and-Bound. Given a branch-and-bound algorithm that breaks unsolvable problems into k subproblems, and given a parallel computer with p processors, then $\lceil \log_k p \rceil$ levels into the state space tree there will be at least as many subproblems as processors. The rapid generation of unexamined subproblems in the state space tree means that it is easy to get all of the processors active early in the computation. However, two factors put a damper on the speedup achievable through parallelization.

First, it is important to remember that the only processors doing useful work are those which are examining subproblems whose lower bound are less than or equal to the value of the eventual solution. A processor examining a subproblem whose lower bound is larger than the solution cost is actually doing more harm than an inactive processor, since the subproblems it generates cannot lead to a solution and serve only to fill memory.

Second, communication times can be significant on a hypercube multicomputer. It is vital that the examination of subproblems on the path from the root of the state space to tree to a solution node occur with reasonable speed, for this time represents a lower bound on the solution time. This lower bound is not too important when the number of processors is small, because there are likely to be a large number of other worthwhile nodes to explore. However, as the number of processors increases, the importance of this lower bound grows. A communication occurs whenever a subproblem is generated by one processor and examined by another processor. Hence it is important for processors to avoid passing subproblems that are on the path from the root to the eventual solution node.

It is difficult, if not impossible, to ignore one of these goals while optimizing the other. In an ideal situation, one processor would work directly toward the solution, examining only those nodes from the root of the state space tree to a solution node. The other processors would examine only those other nodes in the state space tree whose values were less than the cost of the eventual solution. Of course, since the cost of an optimum solution and the location of valid solution nodes are unknown before the search has terminated, such an ideal situation cannot be orchestrated.

The remaining sections of the paper discuss an experiment used to determine how well a hypercube multicomputer would be able to solve the traveling salesperson problem using some kind of parallel branch-and-bound algorithm.

The Traveling Salesperson Problem.

The traveling salesperson problem is defined as follows: given a set of vertices and a nonnegative cost $c_{i,j}$ associated with each pair of vertices i and j, find a circuit containing every vertex in the graph so that the cost of the entire tour is minimized. Little et al. [8] devised a famous depth-first branch-and-bound algorithm to solve the traveling salesperson problem. When an unresolvable problem is encountered, it is broken into two subproblems representing tours that either must include or exclude a particular edge. The edge that is to be used as the added constraint for the subproblems is chosen so that the lower bound on the cost of the solution of the subproblem excluding that edge is maximized. In other words, when breaking a problem into subproblems, the algorithm examines the minimum increase in the tour length when various edges are excluded, and chooses the edge whose exclusion causes the largest increase in the tour length. See Reingold et al. [9] for an exposition of this algorithm.

Mohan [5] has parallelized a best-first variant of Little et al.'s algorithm for the Cm* multiprocessor. The parallel algorithm creates a number of processes that asynchronously explore the tree of subproblems until a solution has been found. Each process repeatedly removes the unexplored subproblem with the smallest lower bound from the order list of unexplored subproblems, decomposes the problem (unless it can be solved directly), and inserts the two newly created subproblems in their proper places in the ordered list of problems to be examined. This process continues until a process examines a subproblem that is directly solvable, at which time the algorithm terminates.

Parallel Branch-and-Bound Algorithms for the Hypercube.   In this section we present four parallel branch-and-bound algorithms to solve the traveling salesperson problem on hypercube multicomputers. All of these algorithms are based upon the algorithm of Little et al. [8]. They differ in how they allocate unexamined subproblems to processors.

Except where otherwise noted, we assume that the time needed to communicate a subproblem is identical to subproblem expansion time. We also make the simplifying assumption that a single communication channel between processors can accommodate multiple messages.

Algorithm 1.   The first parallel algorithm is a straightforward, naïve adaptation of Mohan's algorithm to the hypercube. Processor 0 contains a heap of the unexamined subproblems. Once there are as many unexamined subproblems as processors, processor 0 begins every iteration of the parallel algorithm by sending the $p - 1$ unexamined subproblems with the smallest lower bounds to the $p - 1$ other processors in such a way that every processor receives a unique subproblem. Once every processor is busy, processor 0 completes every iteration by collecting two newly-expanded subproblems from every other processor. Of course, during the first few iterations of the algorithm, not every processor will be busy.

It is important to note that the communication of subproblems can be pipelined, and hence even those processors a number of communication steps away from processor 0 can be kept busy evaluating a subproblem every time unit, once enough subproblems have been generated.

This algorithm has the advantage of keeping all of the processors busy examining subproblems whose lower bounds are low in a global sense. A disadvantage of this algorithm is that every subproblem examination requires at least two communication steps: at least one step to get the subproblem from the heap to the processor doing the expanding, and at least one step to get its newly expanded subproblems back to the heap. Hence the number of communications occurring on the critical path from the root of the state space tree to the solution node is quite large, putting an unacceptably low ceiling on the potential speedup achievable by this algorithm. Delaying the discovery of the solution through excessive communications also has the effect that the processors have more time to spend examining worthless subproblems. Another disadvantage is the large amount of memory needed by processor 0.

We have simulated the solution of ten 30-city traveling salesperson problems using this allocation strategy, assuming 2, 4, 8, 16, and 32 processors. (At least two processors are needed, since processor 0 does nothing but collect and distribute unexamined subproblems.) The distances between the cities are symmetric and uniformly distributed among the integers between 0 and 99. Figure 2 displays the average number of nodes examined as a function of depth in the state space tree. In other words, the x axis represents the number of constraints added to the original problem, and the y axis represents the average number of subproblems examined for each number of constraints. The curve labeled with a 2 delimits the set of

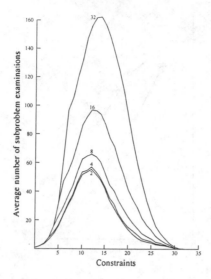

Figure 2. Average number of subproblem examinations made by Algorithm 1.

subproblems whose examination are sufficient to find a solution. Adding processors increases the number of unnecessary subproblem examinations, lowering the overall efficiency.

Algorithm 2.   The second algorithm distributes the heaps containing the unexamined subproblems among the processors. Each iteration every processor with a nonempty heap removes the unexamined subproblem with the smallest lower bound and either solves the problem directly or divides it into two subproblems. If it divides a problem into two subproblems, it puts the subproblem with the edge inclusion constraint into the heap and sends the subproblem with the edge exclusion constraint to the neighboring processor determined by the following formula. Let $p = 2^d$ be the number of processors. On iteration i processor j sends the the message to processor k, where k is found by inverting bit (i mod d) of j. For example, assume that there are 16 processors.

On iteration 12 (0 mod 4) processor 8 sends a subproblem to processor 9.

On iteration 13 (1 mod 4) processor 8 sends a subproblem to processor 10.

On iteration 14 (2 mod 4) processor 8 sends a subproblem to processor 12.

On iteration 15 (3 mod 4) processor 8 sends a subproblem to processor 0.

Note that if processor j sends an unexamined subproblem to processor k on a particular iteration, then processor k sends an unexamined subproblem to processor j. We assume that both of these communications can take place in the time it takes to decompose a single subproblem.

One advantage of this approach is that it reduces the number of communications per subproblem evaluation. In fact, it may be possible for a single processor to examine every node in the state space tree from the root to an optimum solution—in other words, there may be no communications along the critical path. Another advantage of this algorithm is that it distributes the unexamined subproblems among the nodes.

A disadvantage of this approach is that is does not guarantee that processors are working on the globally best candidates. In fact, a processor may never do any

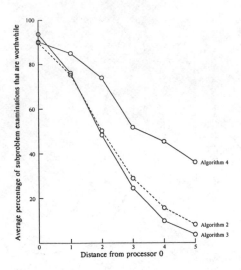

Figure 3. Worthwhile node examinations versus distance from processor 0.

worthwhile work.

Our simulations indicate that this algorithm is likely to achieve far better speedup than the algorithm that keeps all unexamined subproblems in a centralized list.

Algorithm 3.   The third algorithm is a simple variant of the second. Every time a processor expands a subproblem, it looks at the lower bounds of the solutions of each subproblem, keeps the subproblem with the smaller lower bound, and passes the subproblem with the higher lower bound. The motivation behind this change is to reduce the number of communications along the critical path.

Our experimental results indicate that this algorithm is slightly inferior to the previous algorithm, because processors far from node 0 spend less time evaluating worthwhile subproblems. Figure 3 plots the percentage of subproblem evaluations that were worthwhile against distance from node 0 for Algorithms 2 and 3. Passing the newly created subproblem with the higher lower bound results in too few interesting subproblems being passed to the far reaches of the hypercube.

Algorithm 4.   The previous two algorithms distribute unexplored subproblems by passing one of the two most recently created subproblems. The disadvantage of Algorithm 2 is that it is likely to add to the number of communications on the critical path. The disadvantage of Algorithm 3 is that the interesting subproblems are concentrated in too few nodes. An alternative is for the processor expanding a subproblem to put both newly expanded subproblems on its own local heap, and then to pass the unexplored problem with the second-lowest lower bound. Figure 3 also displays for this algorithm the percentage of worthwhile subproblem evaluations as a function of distance from processor 0. Note that this algorithm does a much better job keeping processors busy doing worthwhile work.

Figure 4 contains the average speedup achieved by the four parallel branch-and-bound algorithms solving the 30-city traveling salesperson problem, as computed by our simulation. Of the algorithms discussed, Algorithm 4 shows the most promise for yielding a satisfactory speedup.

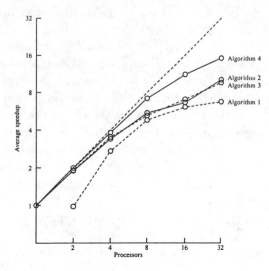

Figure 4. Simulated average speedup achieved by parallel branch-and-bound algorithms solving the 30-city traveling salesperson problem.

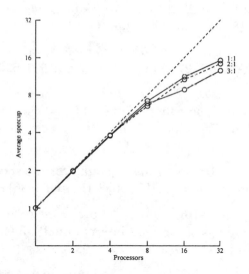

Figure 5. Predicted speedup of Algorithm 4, assuming various ratios of communication time to decomposition time.

How sensitive is this speedup to the communication time? Recall that we assumed subproblem communication time and subproblem decomposition time were identical. We have repeated the ten test cases for various ratios of communication time to decomposition time. The predicted speedup curves appear in Figure 5. The slow decline in speedup achieved is due to the relatively few communications along the critical path,

Conclusions. We have seen that in order for a parallel branch-and-bound algorithm to run with reasonable efficiency on a hypercube multicomputer, two goals must be met. First, the processors must be kept busy examining worthwhile subproblems. Second, the number of communications along the critical path from the original problem to the solution must be minimized. Keeping all of the unexamined subproblems in a central location is clearly an unacceptable strategy. It requires that one processor have an unacceptably large memory, and it leads to an excessive number of communications. Distributing the unexamined subproblems among the processors balances the memory requirements, reduces the number of communications, and allows a large number of the hypercube's communication paths to be busy at once. Our parallel variants of best-first branch-and-bound have shown that a slight change in the distribution rule can have a large impact on the overall speedup achievable by the parallel algorithm. The simulations performed in this study give us confidence that a good implementation of a parallel best-first branch-and-bound algorithm can achieve a respectable speedup on a hypercube multicomputer.

Acknowledgments. This research was supported by National Science Foundation grant DCR-8601209.

REFERENCES

[1] B. W. WAH, G. LI, and C. F. YU, *Multiprocessing of combinatorial search problems*, Computer, 18, 6 (June 1985), pp. 93–108.

[2] T. -H. LAI and S. SAHNI, *Anomalies in parallel branch-and-bound algorithms*, Communications of the ACM, 27, 6 (June 1984), pp. 594–602.

[3] M. J. QUINN AND N. DEO, *An upper bound for the speedup of parallel branch-and-bound algorithms*, in Proceedings of the Third Conference on Foundations of Software Technology and Theoretical Computer Science, Bangalore, India, December 1983, pp. 488–504.

[4] M. J. QUINN AND N. DEO, *An upper bound for the speedup of parallel best-first branch-and-bound algorithms*, BIT, 26, 1 (March 1986), pp. 35–43.

[5] J. MOHAN, *Experience with two parallel programs solving the traveling salesman problem*, in Proceedings of the 1983 International Conference on Parallel Processing, IEEE, New York, NY, 1983, pp. 191–193.

[6] B. W. WAH, G. -J. LI, and C. F. YU, *The status of MANIP—A multicomputer architecture for solving combinatorial extremum-search problems*, in Proceedings of the 11th Annual International Symposium on Computer Architecture, 1984, pp. 56–63.

[7] M. J. QUINN, *Designing Efficient Algorithms for Parallel Computers*, McGraw-Hill, New York, NY, 1987, ch. 2.

[8] J. D. C. LITTLE, K. G. MURTY, D. W. SWEENEY, and C. KAREL, *An algorithm for the traveling salesman problem*, Operations Research, 11, 6 (November-December 1963), pp. 972–989.

[9] E. M. REINGOLD, J. NIEVERGELT, and N. DEO, *Combinatorial Algorithms: Theory and Practice*, Prentice-Hall, Englewood Cliffs, NJ, 1977, ch. 4.

Chess on a Hypercube[*]

E. FELTEN†, R. MORISON†, S. OTTO†, K. BARISH†, R. FATLAND†
AND F. HO†

Abstract. We have implemented computer chess on an Ncube
Hypercube. The program follows the strategy of currently
successful sequential chess programs: searching of an
alpha-beta pruned game tree, iterative deepening, zero
width windows, specialized endgame evaluators, and so on.
An interesting feature is the global transposition table -
for this data structure the Hypercube is used as a shared
memory machine. The search tree is decomposed onto the
Hypercube - loosely speaking, processors race down
different branches of the tree. How one actually does
this is non-trivial, however, since the alpha-beta
technique is in conflict with parallelism.

Our current speedup ranges from 10 to 25 on a 64-node
machine. We are currently (October 1986) attempting to
improve this and discovering how well this scales to even
larger machines.

Motivations. It is becoming fairly clear that Hypercube
connected, MIMD computers are successful in performing a
large class of science and engineering computations. The
problems tend to have regular, homogeneous data sets and
the algorithms are usually "crystalline" in nature. The
second generation of algorithms now starting to be
explored tend towards an amorphous structure and
asynchronous execution. In short, it is less obvious how
well the Hypercube will do.

---

† Caltech, Pasadena, Ca. 91125, Jet Propulsion
Laboratory, Pasadena, Ca. 91109

* We would like to acknowledge Eric Umland, who helped
inspire and lay the initial groundwork for this project.
Wish you were here, Eric.

As an attempt to explore a part of this interesting region in algorithm space, we have implemented chess on a six dimensional Ncube system.   Besides being a fascinating field of study in its own right, computer chess is an interesting challenge for parallel computers because:

1)   It is not clear how much parallelism is actually available - the important method of alpha-beta pruning conflicts with parallelism.

2)   Some aspects of the algorithm require a globally accessed or shared data set.

3)   For the parallel machine, the algorithm has dynamical load imbalance of an extreme nature.

In addition to these easily definable areas of interest, chess is an interesting mix (using Brian Beckman's taxonomy) of "right wing" programming (matrices, PDEs) and "left wing" programming (AI, lisp, prolog). That is, we certainly want a friendly, usable programming environment so that we may rapidly feed "chess knowledge" into the program, but we are unwilling to give up very much performance.

Before going on to the main body of this paper, let us state that our approach to parallelism (and hence, speed) in computer chess is by no means the only one.   Belle, Cray Blitz, and HiTech have shown, in rather spectacular fashion, that fine grained parallelism (pipelining, specialized hardware) leads to impressive speeds [1,2]. Our coarse grained approach to parallelism should be viewed as a complimentary, not a conflicting, method. Clearly, the two can be combined.

Sequential Computer Chess.   In this section we will describe some of the basic aspects of what constitutes a good chess program on a sequential computer.   After this, we will be able to intelligently discuss the parallel algorithm.

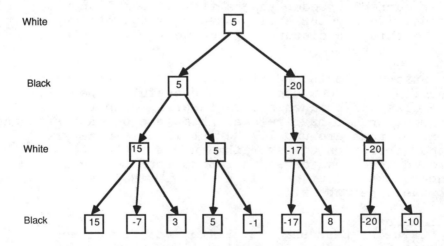

Figure 1.   The method of mini-maxing.
At each level, the player to move picks
the best alternative available: white
maximizes, black minimizes.

It is fair to say that all currently successful chess programs proceed by full-width tree searching. That is, the program starts with the current board position, generates all legal moves from there, for each of these children, generates all legal moves, etc., until some terminal depth is reached. At this depth, an evaluation function, "f", is applied to the boards to give each a rating (a numerical score). These terminal scores are then backed up to the root of the tree (the current, original board position) using the method of "mini-maxing" (see Figure 1). Mini-maxing is just the assumption that, at each level of the tree, the player whose move it is will choose that move which is best for her.

The evaluation function employed is a combination of simple material balance and several terms which represent positional factors. The positional terms are small in magnitude but are important since material balance usually does not change in a move.

The number of legal moves from a typical board position is 35. This means that the size of a depth n chess tree grows as $(35)^n$ - a formidable explosion of work. Alpha-Beta pruning is a technique which reduces the speed of this explosion substantially by pruning the tree. Though alpha-beta is a pruning technique, it is not an approximation. The same answer as in full-width searching is found, but without looking at all of the tree.

The idea is illustrated in Figure 2. On the left-hand side of the tree, we have mini-maxed and found a score of +5 at depth 1. Now start to analyze the right side of the tree. Suppose, as shown, that the first child returns a score of -17 at depth 2. This has an immediate implication for his depth 1 parent. Since the depth 1 parent is trying to minimize the score, we know immediately a bound on his score: it will be less than -17. However, the root node (depth 0) is trying to

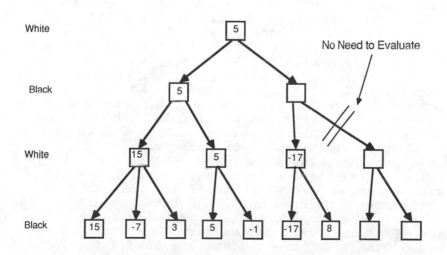

Figure 2. The same as Figure 1, but with alpha-bet pruning.

maximize the score, and -17 is less than +5. Therefore,
no matter what happens with the children of the right half
of the tree, the root will choose the left half branch.
As shown, there is no reason to further analyze the right
half tree, and so we have pruned.

The amount of work saved in this small tree was
insignificant but alpha-beta becomes very important for
large trees. From the nature of the pruning method, one
sees that the game tree is not evolved evenly downward.
Instead, the algorithm pursues one branch all the way to
the bottom, gets a "score to beat" (the alpha-beta
bounds), and then sweeps across the tree sideways. How
well the pruning works depends crucially on move ordering.
If the best line of play is searched first, then all other
branches will prune rapidly. Intelligent move ordering is
accomplished via the techniques of iterative deepening,
hashed transposition tables, and killer heuristics [1].
Our parallel program also employs these tricks.

The Parallel Algorithm. In simple terms, the parallel
search algorithm consists of sending the processors of the
Hypercube (or some other concurrent computer) down the
various branches of the chess tree. Alpha-beta pruning,
in particular, the requirement to search "good" lines of
play first, conflicts with parallelism. One must be
careful in how the scheduling (or allocation) of tasks is
done. It is very easy to produce an algorithm for the
Hypercube which searches an impressive number of chess
boards per second, but which doesn't actually get any
deeper into the tree than a single processor!

Dynamical load imbalance is the other severe problem
which must be faced. The search of substress of identical
depth can take widely varying times. We use self-
scheduling to cope with this. Suppose we are at some
chess board (occuring somewhere in the game tree) which
has 35 children (subtrees) wanting to be searched.
Suppose, further, that we have four processors available
to do the task. We do not simply hand out 35/4 tasks to
each processor and sit back to wait for the answers to
return. Instead, hand out the first 4 tasks to the
processors. Whenever a processor completes, it reports
back to its master process (or processor) and is handed
another task. In this way, if one of the 4 processors
gets stuck in a relatively long search, the other 3 can
race ahead and complete the rest of the job. In the
actual case, the 4 processors may not be single processors
at all, but entire teams of processors.

Our algorithm regards the Hypercube as consisting of
several (4 or 8) teams of processors. Each team is
likewise regarded as consisting of several subteams.
This heirarchy continues until the subteams are single
processors. The chess tree is searched via the recursive
version of the self-scheduling method described above. At
the top of the tree, the 4 teams are handed the first 4
branches of the tree. Within each team, all processors go
down a branch of the tree. At this depth 1 board
position, all legal moves are generated. The first 4

moves are handed out to the 4 subteams. This process
continues until single processors are all running distinct
searches. Figure 3 illustrates this process.

Searching the tree via a heirarchy of teams
accomplishes two things. As described earlier, the self-
scheduling mechanism counteracts load imbalance. The team
concept also concentrates the power of the Hypercube on
the early, good lines of play. This matches the
requirements of alpha-beta: the left side of Figure 2 is
searched first, allowing later searches to cutoff move
rapidly.

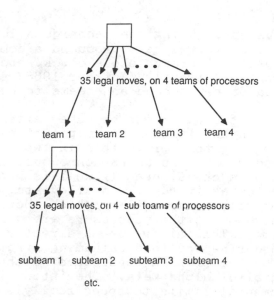

Figure 3. The team/sub-team heirarchy
mapped onto the chess tree.

Global Hash Table. During the game tree search, the same
board position may occur multiple times. This is due to
transpositions: a certain chess board may be reached by
moving the bishop, then a pawn. The same position may
also be reached by moving first the pawn, then the bishop.
To avoid analyzing boards multiple times, a hash table is
constructed and maintained as the search proceeds. This
table stores knowledge gained during the search so that it
may be re-used.

Having a hash table is importantd for sequential
computer chess. We have implemented a global version of
such a table on the Ncube. Normally, the hashing
function, h, takes as input the chess board and returns an
address:

$$h (\square) \ ---> \ 32 \text{ bit address}$$

For the Hypercube, we modify h so that it also gives a
processor number:

$$h (\square) \ ---> \ \text{local address} + \text{procnum}$$

When the program accesses the hash table, it constructs

a special message containing the address and sends it to
processor procnum. The Vertex message system of the Ncube
supports remote reads and writes so that the hash table
accesses happen transparently to the remote processor.
For this part of the computation, the Hypercube is
regarded as a shared memory machine.

Though this crude version of shared memory is
implemented in software (albeit the low-level Vertex
system), it doesn't seem to impact performance by a large
factor. We estimate that if the global requests were,
instead, local requests, the program would speed up by 10-
20%.

Results, Conclusions. Using the techniques loosely
described in the above, we have produced a complete chess
player (with opening library, chess clock, etc.) on the
Ncube. The program currently (October 1986) examines
15,000 chess boards per second and seems to be a 1900
player.

The speedup on the 64 processor cube varies from 10 -
25, dependent upon the initial board position. We are
currently attempting to improve this in two ways. It is
difficult to understand, in an asynchronous, dynamical
computation such as chess, exactly what is happening
inside the machine as it runs. To alleviate this, we have
made a "time correlation profiler" which shows, in a
graphical fashion, what the processors are doing as a
function of time. This allows us to directly study
various move ordering and load balancing strategies. Our
second attack on the problem consists of a theoretical
modeling of parallel alpha-beta. The intent is to define
what the fundamental limits to speed really are and to
compare the theory to the actual behavior of the program.

REFERENCES

(1) P. W. Frey (Editor), <u>Chess Skill in Man and Machine</u>,
Springer Verlag, New York, 1983.

(2) A. K. Dewdney, <u>Computer Recreations</u>, Scientific
American, February, 1986.

Genetic Algorithms on
a Hypercube Multiprocessor

CHRISILA C. PETTEY*, MICHAEL R. LEUZE* AND JOHN J. GREFENSTETTE†

Abstract. Genetic algorithms are adaptive search algorithms, based on principles from population genetics, which have been used in a number of application areas. Genetic algorithms appear to be particularly well-suited for problems with multimodal search spaces. Although genetic algorithms have a significant amount of inherent parallelism, earlier work has tended to focus on sequential implementations. This paper describes a first step toward the development of genetic algorithm implementations for hypercube multiprocessors. Two basic algorithm organizations are discussed: a single parallel genetic algorithm in a master-slave configuration and multiple sequential genetic algorithms cooperating in an asynchronous fashion. Testing is needed to determine the relative merits and areas of applicability of each approach.

1. Introduction. In 1975 a class of algorithms known as *genetic algorithms* was introduced by Holland [9]. Genetic algorithms, hereafter called GA's, are adaptive search algorithms which have been used in many diverse problem areas such as function optimization [1], the traveling salesman problem [4] [7], pattern discrimination [12], image processing [8], and machine learning [3] [10] [13]. Past studies of GA's have tended to focus on sequential implementations. Many problems, however, are of sufficient complexity that sequential GA implementations are not capable of producing useful results in a reasonable period of time. Consequently, there are important problems to which GA's have not yet been applied because of time constraints imposed by sequential execution. An investigation of the opportunities for parallel processing of GA's is needed. In this paper three methods of parallelizing GA's are proposed. These algorithms can be implemented on currently available multiprocessors, such as an MIMD machine with a hypercube interconnection

Research supported in part by the National Science Foundation under Grant DCR-8305693.

* Department of Computer Science, Vanderbilt University, Nashville, Tennessee.

† Navy Center for Applied Research in Artificial Intelligence, Naval Research Laboratory, Washington, D.C.

network.

2. Sequential Genetic Algorithms. This section contains a short introduction to GA's. For a more detailed study of GA's see [1] and [9].

A GA works on a time varying population, $P(t)$, of N structures called *individuals* or *candidate solutions*. Each individual represents a point in the search space and is composed of a set of structures called *genes*. The value of a gene is called an *allele*. A gene may be as simple as a Boolean variable or as complex as a production system rule.

A GA operates on the population of individuals using the algorithm shown in Figure 1. This algorithm is adapted from [1] and is explained in the paragraphs which follow.

```
GA:
    begin
        t:=1;
        initialize P(t);
        evaluate P(t);
        while (not <termination condition>) do
            begin
                t:=t+1;
                select P(t) from P(t-1);
                recombine P(t);
                evaluate P(t);
            end
    end
```

FIG. 1. The Basic GA

The initial population, $P(1)$, can either be randomly initialized or, if something is known about the solution, heuristically initialized. After initialization is completed, the GA evaluates all individuals in the population. The GA then performs the following four steps iteratively: 1) check to see if the termination condition has been met, 2) compute the selection probabilities for each individual and select individuals based on those probabilities (the selection phase), 3) recombine the new population (the recombination phase), and 4) compute the performance of each individual (the evaluation phase, which is the only domain dependent phase). This process continues until the termination condition has been met. With this algorithm, each iteration of the loop produces a generation.

In the selection phase individuals in the old population are chosen based on their performance relative to the whole population, and copies of these individuals, called *offspring*, are placed in the new population.

The key phase of a GA is the recombination phase. The most commonly used operators in this phase are *mutation* and *crossover*. A third operator, *inversion*, is used much less frequently, because it assumes the genes are position independent, when this is generally not the case (i.e., the position of the gene in the individual usually has some meaning). Inversion will, therefore, not be discussed here. Mutation is the assignment of a random allele to a random individual in the population. Crossover is the primary method for adapting the search. To perform a crossover, two individuals are chosen at random with uniform probability. An integer p is chosen such that $1 \le p \le L-1$ (where L is the length, i.e., the number of genes, of an individual). All genes to the right of the pth gene of the first individual are replaced by all genes to the right of the pth gene of the second individual, and vice versa, forming two new individuals. The two original individuals are called *parents*, and the two new individuals are called *children*. The children then replace two individuals in the population. In the example in figure 2, the bits (i.e., genes) are numbered from the left.

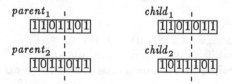

FIG. 2. The Crossover Operator (p = 4)

GA's are an efficient means of search because of their intrinsic parallelism. Intrinsic parallelism refers to the ability of a GA to simultaneously search several areas of the search space. These areas are known as *schemas* [9] or as *hyperplanes* [1]. A schema is a subset of the search space within which a given set of genes has a common combination of alleles.

For example, suppose a GA is trying to minimize the function $f(x)=x$ where $0 \leq x \leq 1.5$. Assume individuals are represented as a sequence of four bits which are interpreted as binary integers and then divided by 10 (i.e., 0000=0.0, 0001=0.1, ..., 1111=1.5). Assume the initial population is randomly distributed between the two schema represented by the binary numbers 0### and 1### (where "#" means "don't care", i.e., either a 0 or a 1). Since the average performance of the individuals in 0### should be higher than those in 1###, the next population should be composed primarily of members of the schema 0###. The two hyperplanes have been tested in parallel, and the better one has been chosen. This effectively reduces the search space to $0 \leq x \leq 0.7$, and the cycle is repeated. At the same time that 0### and 1### are being tested, all other hyperplanes (e.g., #0## vs. #1##) are being tested, and those with superior performance are being chosen over those with inferior performance.

3. Parallel GA's.
There has been very little work done in the study of possible ways of parallelizing GA's. In 1981 Grefenstette [5] made a preliminary study of parallel GA's, in which four possible parallel GA's are suggested. The work proposed in this paper is based on three of Grefenstette's algorithms. The algorithms designated A and B are suitable for problems with a large granularity, i.e., for problems which require a long time to evaluate one candidate solution. The algorithm called C, however, is applicable to problems of any granularity. Discussions of each algorithm, along with questions which require further study and suggestions of methods for testing the performance of the algorithms, are presented in the following paragraphs.

3.1. Synchronous Master-Slave GA's.
Algorithm A, first proposed by Grefenstette, is designed for problems which require a long evaluation. This algorithm is organized in a master-slave configuration with k slaves. The master process maintains a population of k individuals and is responsible for selection and recombination. The slaves evaluate structures which are assigned by the master. The master and slave processes are illustrated in Figure 3.

```
slave i:
    while (not <termination condition>) do
        begin
            evaluate (assigned structure);
        end


master:
    begin
        assign all structures to slaves;
        while (any slave is active) do wait;
        while (not <termination condition>) do
            begin
                compute selection probabilities for P(t);
                generate P(t+1) using selection rules
                    and GA operators;
                assign all structures to slaves;
                while (any slave is active) do wait;
            end
        notify all slaves of termination;
    end
```

FIG. 3. Synchronous Master-Slave GA Processes

An advantage of this algorithm is that it "produces exactly the same sequence of generations as the sequential [GA]" [5], and, therefore, finds the same solution as that found by the sequential GA. A disadvantage of algorithm A is due to its synchronous operation. There are problems for which the time to evaluate an individual is dependent on the individual. Slaves which complete their assigned evaluations early must wait for all other slaves to complete. Furthermore, all slaves are idle while the master performs selection and recombination.

3.2. Asynchronous Master-Slave GA's. Algorithm B is designed to overcome the problem of idle processes caused by the synchronous nature of algorithm A. Algorithm B, like algorithm A, consists of a master process and several slave processes. As in algorithm A, a slave is assigned an individual from the population to evaluate. Whenever any slave finishes evaluating an individual, the master process forms the next generation by means of selection, crossover, and mutation, and then assigns a new individual to the waiting slave process. The slave processes are identical to those of algorithm A. The master process appears in Figure 4.

Algorithm B is somewhat more reliable than algorithm A. If a slave process fails, algorithm B will degrade gracefully. It is anticipated that the performance of algorithm B will be better than that of algorithm A, since a slave never has to wait for other slaves to complete their work. It is important to note, however, that the sequence of generations produced by algorithm B is different from that produced by a sequential GA.

An example of a problem which requires a relatively long evaluation, and is, therefore, suitable for algorithms A and B, is the *robot navigation problem*. A robot is placed in an environment of which it has no prior knowledge. The robot's goal is to navigate around all obstacles in the environment and to find a particular object, such as a door. Each

```
master:
    begin
        while (not <termination condition>) do
            begin
                while (all slaves are active) do wait;
                s := one of the inactive slaves;
                form P(t+1) by inserting the structure
                    evaluated by s into P(t);
                compute selection probabilities for P(t+1);
                generate a new structure via selection rules
                    and genetic operators;
                assign the new structure to s;
            end
        notify all slaves of termination;
    end
```

FIG. 4. Asynchronous Master GA Process

individual in the population will be a rule set. Individuals are evaluated by treating them as production systems (i.e., classifier systems [10]) which govern the movement of the robot in its environment. Each individual rule set is assigned a performance measure based on how well it maneuvers the robot.

3.3. Questions Raised by Algorithms A and B. Since algorithm A produces the exact sequence of generations produced by a sequential GA, an obvious question is whether algorithm A will execute faster than a sequential GA. The answer is, obviously, *yes*, but it is not clear how much faster execution will be. Since most of the overhead of a GA is in the evaluation phase, algorithm A should give near linear speedup, provided the individual evaluations require approximately equal processing time. Preliminary simulations indicate speedups will indeed be nearly linear.

Algorithm B presents an interesting question concerning the effect of frequently updating the selection probabilities. The idea of a generation is no longer applicable. Individuals are selected based on their relative fitness in the population to which they are returned, rather than on their relative fitness in the population in which they are created. Also, an individual returned to a population must replace another individual. It may be necessary to carefully consider which individual should be replaced. One possibility is to use the "crowding factor" approach [1]. This approach says to replace that individual which is most like the incoming individual (i.e., the shortest Hamming distance). Another possibility is to replace the worst individual. Both of these options will be investigated, and the performance of each will be compared with the performance of algorithm A.

Algorithm B motivates another interesting question. What effect does the "short-evaluation-time bias" of algorithm B have on GA's? In algorithm B, the direction of search is initially influenced only by those individuals with a short evaluation time, whereas in a sequential GA, the direction of search is influenced only by the performance of the individuals, regardless of the evaluation time. In many environments -- such as the evaluation of some functions or the evaluation of the length of a tour in the traveling salesman problem -- the same amount of time is required to evaluate any individual. There are, however, environments in which the length of evaluation time depends on the individual. The robot navigation problem is one such problem since individual evaluation is based on the performance of a production rule set. Good production rule sets can be evaluated more quickly than poor production rule sets. Consequently, the shorter the evaluation time, the better the individual. Another problem in which the performance of a structure is related to its evaluation time is image registration [8]. The image registration problem involves finding the warping which will produce one image from another. An individual defines a warping of an image. To evaluate an individual, random pixels from one image are transformed using the individual's warping. The differences in corresponding pixel values are calculated; the mean of these differences defines the performance of the individual. A requirement imposed on the experiment is that the sample mean must be within 10% of the population mean with 95% confidence. It was found that poorer individuals required fewer samples to satisfy this requirement [8]. In the case of image registration, the shorter the evaluation time, the worse the individual. The effects of this "short-evaluation-time bias" on GA's need to be analyzed.

3.4. Cooperating Sequential GA's. Algorithms A and B are good for problems with long evaluations. If, however, the evaluation time is short relative to the other phases, the performance of algorithms A and B degrades due to communication overhead. Algorithm C is an alternative approach which can be implemented on an MIMD architecture regardless of the evaluation time.

In algorithm C, a single GA process runs on each node of a multiprocessor system. Each process maintains a portion of the entire population. A process is responsible for selection and recombination of its portion of the population. Occasionally, an exchange of information takes place during which each process communicates some portion of its population with processes on other nodes. The form of every process is illustrated in Figure 5.

```
process j:
    begin
        t:=1;
        initialize Pj(1);
        evaluate Pj(1);
        while (not <termination condition>) do
          begin
            exchange;
            t:=t+1;
            select Pj(t) from Pj(t−1);
            recombine Pj(t);
            evaluate Pj(t);
          end
    end
```

FIG. 5. Cooperating Sequential GA's

During the exchange phase, a process first sends some number of its own individuals to other nodes in the multiprocessor and then determines whether it has received any individuals from other nodes. The exchange phase can be implemented in a variety of ways. Choices must be made as to the number of individuals exchanged. A process could send only its best individual, it could send a portion of its population, or it could send its entire population. If the algorithm is executing on a message passing system, a process could send to every node in the multiprocessor, or it could send only to nearest neighbors if the machine has an incomplete interconnection network. A final consideration concerns individuals to be replaced by incoming individuals. Possible candidates for replacement are a random individual, the worst individual, or the individual most like the incoming individual (i.e., the smallest Hamming distance).

There is no synchronization among processes in algorithm C. When a process does not receive any individuals during its exchange phase, it continues execution of the GA with its existing population. In order to best utilize processor and communication resources, population sizes and exchange intervals should be set appropriately for the length of the evaluation time. If the evaluation time is very short, the population size could be increased with information exchanged less frequently. For longer evaluation times, a small population with exchanges each generation would be appropriate.

An implementation of algorithm C will be developed for the traveling salesman problem, a problem to which sequential GA's have been applied [4] [6]. This earlier work provides a basis for evaluation of algorithm C. The investigation of algorithm C will involve three types of nearest neighbor exchange. The first approach will be to exchange only the best individual by sending it to each neighbor. The second approach will be to exchange the n best individuals, where n is the number of neighbors. Each individual will be sent to a different neighbor. The third approach will be to exchange the entire population by sending $(1/n)$th of the population to each neighbor.

3.5. Questions Raised by Algorithm C. Several interesting questions will be examined during the study of algorithm C. The effect of isolating pieces of the population during crossover and selection will be considered. The isolation of pieces of the population has a counterpart in the study of population genetics. Algorithm C can be thought of as operating on a "polytypic" species, i.e., a species composed of several subspecies [2], where a species is a group of populations which are capable of interbreeding. The populations in algorithm C are not totally isolated, since the communication of individuals is analogous to migration [11]. The idea of separate populations in GA's is not new. In [12] a vector evaluated genetic algorithm (VEGA) scheme is implemented in order to deal with problems for which the performance measure is multi-dimensional. The goal of VEGA is to develop an individual that performs well in all dimensions. The solution employed by VEGA is a modified selection routine which chooses subpopulations from the total population based on fitness in a single dimension. These subpopulations are then combined to form the new population. If the performance measure has n dimensions, then each subpopulation is $(1/n)$th of the total population. Those individuals which perform well on several tasks (i.e., have high performance evaluations in several dimensions) are more likely to appear in several subpopulations, and, consequently, are likely to appear more often in the new population after combination.

A second question to be dealt with during the study of algorithm C concerns the number of individuals and neighboring nodes to be involved in the exchange process. Exchanging the best individuals only with nearest neighbors could cause the total population to converge at a slower rate than a sequential GA, due to the fact that a "super individual" would be seen by subpopulations instead of by the entire population. Depending on the structure of the interconnection network, it will take one or more exchanges before the entire population will be aware of a super individual. Experience has demonstrated that slower convergence is not necessarily undesirable. Populations sometimes converge quickly to a sub-optimal individual. By avoiding premature convergence a better solution could be achieved. Exchange of all individuals would result in more interaction among processes, but high-performance individuals would propigate more slowly through the entire population, since each neighbor will be sent different information. Thus, the convergence rate could be even slower than for the approach where only best individuals are exchanged.

A third question is whether the selection phase should precede or follow the exchange phase. Should an individual be selected relative to that population within which it was produced or relative to another, perhaps very different, population? The relative performances resulting from the use of these two approaches to selection need to be analyzed.

4. Summary. GA's are a class of adaptive search algorithms that have been used in a variety of applications areas. Little work has been done, however, to develop parallel implementations of GA's for multiprocessor systems. This paper suggests three possible approaches to the parallelization of GA's: synchronous master-slave GA's, asynchronous master-slave GA's, and cooperating sequential GA's. The master-slave GA's appear to be well-suited for problems which require long evaluations of candidate solutions. Cooperating sequential GA's appear to be more generally applicable. Further study is needed to assess the relative merits of these and other techniques for parallelizing GA's.

REFERENCES

[1] K. A. DEJONG, *An Analysis of the Behavior of a Class of Genetic Adaptive Systems*, Ph.D. Dissertation, Dept. of Computer and Communication Sciences, University of Michigan, 1975.

[2] T. DOBZHANSKY, *Genetics of the Evolutionary Process*, Columbia University Press, New York, 1970.

[3] D. E. GOLDBERG, *Computer-Aided Pipeline Operation Using Genetic Algorithms and Rule Learning*, Ph.D. Dissertation, University of Michigan, 1983.

[4] D. GOLDBERG and R. LINGLE, Jr., *Alleles, loci, and the traveling salesman problem*, Proceedings of an International Conference on Genetic Algorithms and Their Applications, J. J. Grefenstette, ed., July 1985, pp. 154-159.

[5] J. J. GREFENSTETTE, *Parallel adaptive algorithms for function optimization* (preliminary report), Technical Report CS-81-19, Computer Science Dept., Vanderbilt University, Nashville, TN, Nov. 1981.

[6] J. J. GREFENSTETTE, *Optimization of control parameters for genetic algorithms*, IEEE Transactions on Systems, Man, and Cybernetics, SMC-16(1) (1985), pp. 122-128.

[7] J. J. GREFENSTETTE, R. GOPAL, B. ROSMAITA, and D. VAN GUCHT, *Genetic algorithms for the traveling salesman problem*, Proceedings of an International Conference on Genetic Algorithms and Their Applications, J. J. Grefenstette, ed., July 1985, pp. 160-165.

[8] J. J. GREFENSTETTE and J. M. FITZPATRICK, *Genetic search with approximate function evaluations*, Proceedings of an International Conference on Genetic Algorithms and Their Applications, J. J. Grefenstette, ed., July 1985, pp. 112-120.

[9] J. H. HOLLAND, *Adaptation in Natural and Artificial Systems*, The University of Michigan Press, Ann Arbor, Michigan, 1975.

[10] J. H. HOLLAND and J. S. REITMAN, *Cognitive systems based on adaptive algorithms*, in Pattern-Directed Inference Systems, Waterman and Hayes-Roth, eds. Academic Press, New York, 1978.

[11] A. JACQUARD, *The Genetic Structure of Populations*, Springer-Verlag, New York, 1974.

[12] D. J. SCHAFFER, *Some Experiments in Machine Learning Using Vector Evaluated Genetic Algorithms*, Ph.D. Thesis, Department of Electrical Engineering, Vanderbilt University, Nashville, TN, 1984.

[13] S. W. WILSON, *Knowledge growth in an artificial animal*, Proceedings of an International Conference on Genetic Algorithms and Their Applications, J. J. Grefenstette, ed., July 1985, pp. 16-23.

MACE: Experimental Distributed Artificial Intelligence Research on the Intel Hypercube

LES GASSER*, CARL BRAGANZA* AND NAVA HERMAN*

Abstract Concurrency can be exploited in AI problem-solving at many different levels: in hardware, in the implementation language (e.g., a production system language), in a problem-solving paradigm, or directly in the application. MACE (Multi-Agent Computing Environment) is an instrumented testbed for building a wide range of experimental Distributed Artificial Intelligence systems at different levels of granularity. MACE computational units (called "agents") run in parallel, and communicate via messages. They provide optional facilities for knowledge representation (world knowledge, models of other agents, their goals and plans, their roles and capabilities, etc.) and reasoning capabilities. The MACE environment maps agents onto processors and handles inter-agent communication. It also provides a language for describing agents, tracing and instrumentation, and a collection of system-agents which construct user-agents from descriptions, monitor execution, handle errors, and interface to a user.

We have used MACE to model lower-level parallelism (a distributed system of production rules without global database or inference engine, where each rule is an agent) and higher-level distributed problem-solving architectures (domain-independent distributed blackboard and contract-net schemes). MACE is implemented on a 16-node INTEL SYM-1 large-memory hypercube, and in a Lisp machine environment. In very preliminary performance tests, the Intel Hypercube has provided up to 7-fold speedups over MACE on a TI Explorer simulating parallelism.

1   Introduction

Distributed Artificial Intelligence (DAI) is a subfield of AI concerned with the problems of describing and constructing multiple "intelligent" systems which interact [4,1,2,3,5,10]. MACE (for Multi-Agent Computing Environment) is a testbed for DAI systems at sev-

---

* Distributed Artificial Intelligence Group, Computer Science Department, University of Southern California, Los Angeles, CA 90089-0782

eral levels of granularity. The goal of the MACE system is to supply a description language, programming environment, simulator, and run-time environment for distributed, intelligent systems. Various parts of the MACE system allow a programmer to simulate and control all levels of the execution process, including both networks of parallel hardware and collections of higher level agents which can run on the hardware. The testbed has been instrumented to allow for changes in execution and simulation parameters for different problems.

MACE provides a language (the MACE *Agent Description Language or ADL*) with which to describe agents. It also provides a language (the MACE *Environment Description Language or EDL*) to describe aspects of the simulation and execution environment such as processors, processor speeds, network interconnections, network communications costs, simulation parameters and data, tracing, etc.

The MACE system environment includes specific MACE agents which serve as interactive tools for building MACE programs. These include agents to build and edit the behaviors and structure of other agents, as well as to change the parameters of the execution environment or simulation[1]. We envision constructing DAI systems which appear to be organizations which solve problems. Programming such a system becomes creating and managing an organization of problem-solvers of varying complexity and power. Thus the primary issues are 3:

- Understanding and specifying the technology to produce the product of the organization (i.e., the solutions to some set of "problems.")

- Staffing and starting up the organization.

- Organizing work and interaction among organization members and the environment dynamically during its operation.

The programmer of a MACE DAI system must develop some of the specifications and technologies for solving the organization's problems, much as the founder of a human organization begins with some initial product ideas and ways of realizing them. In this task, the programmer should have the help of specialists who are experts in known techniques - database technology, compiler technology, domain knowledge for particular applications, etc. The environment should arrive populated with a collection of specialist agents.

Agents themselves should take on much of the burden of actual system construction and operations - the programmer's task should be to establish initial form, directions and policy. Thus programmers become managers of interdependent processes, rather than specifiers and implementers of entire systems in detail. They specify staffing requirements with *job descriptions* - high-level descriptions of the special and general requirements of agents. Agents are assumed to come with basic skills in their domain of expertise. For example, a *Quality-Control* agent might have knowledge about testing techniques, statistical quality control, error-discovery procedures, etc.

---

[1]E.g., an agent called BUILDER constructs agents by interacting with the user through another agent known as USER-INTERFACE.

Programmers direct and organize agents by specifying their relationships to one another and by issuing *policies* and *goals* - high level directives and constraints on behavior. Agents carry out and interpret the policies and goals in the light of their own local circumstances. In this way, agents are problem-solvers, and systems can be adaptive without explicit detailed control by a central actor or overseer.

Since many organizations have similar components (sub-units), MACE comes with a set of existing *System Agents*. One set of starting agents might be:

- Garbage collectors

- Fault-control specialists for error handling

- Organization specialists

- Staffing ("Personnel") specialists

- Communications specialists

- A "Postmaster" who knows routes to other agents

- A collection of "Allocators" which do dynamic load-balancing.

We expect Distributed AI systems to be very complex and difficult to understand[2]. Thus we have chosen to simulate the behavior of our DAI systems before running them on actual parallel networks, to gain repeatability and control. The MACE simulator simulates the execution of high-level MACE agents. It will also simulate errors in the communications and processing in the network, and agent breakdowns, with a specified probability rate. The simulator gathers execution-time behavioral statistics, such as message routing and traffic loads, agent and processor breakdowns, timing and syncronization information, and behavioral trace information. Mace has been designed so that at any point the programmer can "unplug" the MACE simulator and run MACE agents using the MACE runtime environment on concurrent hardware.

2   MACE Agents: Social Actors

MACE is based upon the notion of interacting but autonomous agents. MACE agents can be high-level intelligent objects or simple objects which exhibit low-grain parallelism. MACE agents are inherently "social" in nature: they know about some other agents in their environment, and expect to be able to draw upon and coordinate with the expertise of others they know about. To do this they need to know the identity and location of their acquaintances, something about their capabilities, etc. MACE agents can represent this information in the form of *models of other agents*. In addition, agents may be organized into sub-units or coalitions which act with common interests in response to particular problems. In this sense they respond as organized social groups or composites. The MACE ADL includes facilities for describing composite agents called *organizations*.

---

[2]This expectation is based on experience with existing systems at Rand and UMASS [8,9,7].

Each MACE agent is a *scope* or *name-space* containing and *engine* and a collection of *databases*. The engine and the databases collectively are called the *attributes* of the agent. Thus each agent is represented as a frame-like collection of attributes. All agents share certain standard attributes, and may include optional, user-supplied attributes as well.

Standard attributes include:

- **Type** A description attribute, defining a class of agents described by this agent.

- **Status:** Whether an agent is currently RUNNING, WAITING, NEW, KILLED, or STOPPED, indicating its execution status in the current time.

- **Engine:** Each agent in MACE has a function called its *engine* which describes how it interprest messages and changes its own local state. It may carry along its engine definition as part of its description, or it may draw upon a system-supplied engine. MACE supplies 3 production sytem interpreter engines and a user-interface engine. The engine attribute allows MACE agents to be "heterogeneously-powered."

- **World-Model and Acquaintances:** Specification of other agents known to the current agent. These are the only agents to whom messages can be sent, because all message addresses are extracted from the agents' world-model. The acquaintance system serves as the basic mechanism for encapsulating agents and knowledge in MACE. It also serves as the agents' model of its world, and contains the agent's model of itself.

- **Incoming-Messages:** Incoming-messages is a database which contains messages to be received by the agent. Messages can, in general, be received under agent control (i.e., "When it picks up its mail"). Extractors for Incoming-Messages data guarantee serialization or priority ordering of messages.

MACE Organizations agents have no specialized attributes. Semantically, however, their World-Models always contain forwarding information for messages, rather than means of executing messages themselves.

Messages between MACE agents are simply LISP lists which include the addresses of the sender and receiver (including which processor, for multi-processor or networked configurations), and some message content. Message routing is handled at two levels: The local procedures of MACE agents initiate messages, extracting addresses from the sender agent's *world-model*. The Mace kernel actually routs messages to the appropriate machine and process. To model network breakdowns, some inter-agent communications are checked at the simulator or processor level.

3   MACE Agent Description Language

The MACE agent description language is an extension to LISP. It provides two types of specifications: descriptions of generic agent *types*, and actual agents, called *instances*. Generic descriptions are not executable, while instances are. Agents themselves may be copying descriptions (in order to create new agents), and they are able to specify and generate instance agents using calls to *builder* agents.

Each high-level MACE agent is a self-contained object which inherits nothing from other objects. As such, it is somewhat contrary to the conventional object-oriented approach to programming [12,11] in which objects have some relation to a higher-level but generic class of objects from which they may inherit attributes and behavioral rules. There are several problems with inheritance in a flexible parallel environment:

- **Reliability**: If the superclass object disappears or the machine upon which it resides is disabled, the subclass object cannot inherit.

- **Reference Problems**: If objects are arbitrarily spread across machines, it may be difficult to know the exact whereabouts of parents or children, and inheritance again becomes difficult.

- **Conceptual Problems**: Conceptually, classification is a problem orthogonal to execution - classification of agents and attributes ought to be done as they are specified, but not necessarily as they are executed.

Inheritance and classification are useful for describing agents. There are important research issues which center around how to implement inheritance in a distributed environment[3]. For the moment, however, we consider execution-time inheritance unworkable. Moreover, we often want to make MACE agents *somewhat like* other agents, but not to inherit all attributes of all superclasses. In MACE, *description* is divorced from from *execution*. Each executable MACE agent is a self-contained entity. ADL descriptions of agents used by the BUILDER agent still import attributes or collections of attributes from other agents, making description and classification possible. Any run-time attribute changes are matters for updating (collections of) individual agents.

As an inherently parallel system, MACE presents some execution-time differences from existing object-oriented systems. MACE agents run in parallel, whereas objects in traditional object-oriented languages are sequentially invoked. Messages (E.g. methods) are really procedure calls, and activation is depth-first. The good reasons for this are the ease of implementation, lack of need for synchronization, and the fact that objects retain an interpretation context for return results automatically (See, E.g. ROSS [6].). However, parallel execution of objects is lost. In MACE, agents exhibit truly parallel execution, and we face the problems of synchronization and interpretation contexts. Explicit synchronization can be performed using mailbox-level synchronization primitives and serialization provided by Incoming-Messages database extractors. Retaining interpretation contexts is more difficult, but can be achieved by tagging messages with *computation identifiers* linked to *continuations* in the originating agent.

In MACE, agents can be grouped together into *organizations*. Organizations provide a single message entry point to a collection of agents. A single agent, when delegating work to someone else, need not know whether the other agent is actually a collection of agents. The entry point of an organization is a special agent which acts like a mail-

---

[3]For example, we are currently pursuing another line of thought which treats inheritance as a distributed database problem. Inheritance is only a problem when attributes change - otherwise inherited attributes can be compiled into distributed agents with the only cost being duplicate copies of information. Changes in inherited attributes can be announced via message. The system must have ways, then, of dealing with (not necessarily recovering from!) anomalies caused by action taken before an inheritance-change message is received. The associated costs benefits, and mechanisms are open research questions at the moment.

room, and only handles messages by disseminating them to other agents which are organization members. This provides 2 functions:

- **Encapsulation**: Organizations provide a simple encapsulation mechanism. Interactions among agents are controlled by controlling access to the knowledge of agents, which can only be disseminated via messages. Organizations are communication gateways to their internal agents.

- **Conceptual Modularity** Organizations provide a modular structuring mechanism in a parallel environment. Programs can be constructed modularly and modules can be composed into more complex ones.

Organizations present particular allocation problems. Since encapsulation is entirely based upon communication, sub- or super-agents may reside upon different processors. Thus, processor-agent allocation must take into account the communications requirements of organizations, and try to minimize the communications delay for closely interacting organization-members.

4   MACE Simulator

The MACE system includes a simulator for executing MACE in order to provide a testbed for controlled experimentation. Our primary concerns are ease of experimentation, and having a testbed which exhibits deterministic though flexible behavior. The MACE Simulator is an event-driven parallel simulator, where events are primarily messages sent from agent to agent. The MACE simulator simulates both hardware processors and the kernels which run on them. The simulator is parameterized, and contains several instrumentation facilities as described above.

MACE agents are entirely self-contained, and need only an underlying kernel which can send messages, understands the structure of agents, can execute the engine, and can interpret the local function definitions. This kernel may be part of a simulator, or it may be a kernel running directly on hardware. For the current version of MACE, written in Common Lisp, a LISP processor with a few added functions suffices. Thus MACE agents are portable from the simulator to a network of LISP machines, or a single machine with separate LISP processes running, or a concurrent computer running multiple Lisp processes, as long as those processes can communicate via messages. MACE currently runs on a network comprising Two TI Explorer Lisp Machines and a 16-node Intel Sym-1 Hypercube running CCLisp.

5   Implementation Status

All features described have been implemented in COMMON Lisp, as has the simulator. The simulator is not fully instrumented, though it does a complete trace of messages sent, processors and agents activated, and actions taken.

6   Experimental MACE programs

We have used MACE to build several experimental DAI systems on the Intel Hypercube, including :

- **Distributed Production Systems**: We have built three distributed rule-based production systems in which each rule is an agent, and there is no global database nor centralized inference engine.

- **Robot Planner**: We have built a distributed blocks-world planner for two cooperating robots.

- **Distributed Blackboard System**: We have inmplemented a simple distributed blackboard system where each knowledge source is an agent and each blackboard level is an agent.

- **Contract-Net System**: We have implemented a version of Reid Smith's Contract Net distributed problem-solver [10], using up to 24 agents arranged in groups of 4 agents per Contract-Net node to solve the N-Queens problem. While we do not have a clear way to make direct comparisons, in this application, the Hypercube concurrent showed 7-fold increase in speed over the TI Explorer simulating parallelism.

We have also tested MACE with 3 simultaneously-running communities comprising a total of 60 agents on the Hypercube. These agents were each simple, self-contained production-rule systems.

7   Acknowledgements

We are grateful for Lunze Liu for his help building and documenting an earlier version of MACE, and to Dit-Yan Yeung for his work implementing the Contract Net on MACE. We also thank the Intel Corporation and Prof. Kai Hwang for their support. Part of this research was funded under Lawrence Livermore Laboratory contract number 9094505.

References

[1] Les Gasser. The Integration of Computing and Routine Work. *ACM Trans. Office Information Systems*, Vol. 4:3, pp. 205-225, July, 1986.

[2] Les Gasser, Carl Braganza, and Nava Herman. Mace: A Flexible Testbed for Distributed AI Research, in M. Huhns, Ed., *Distributed Artificial Intelligence*, Pitman, 1987.

[3] Les Gasser, Carl Braganza, and Nava Herman. Implementing Distributed AI Systems Using MACE. *Proc. IEEE Third Conference on AI Applications*, February, 1987 (to appear).

[4] Carl Hewitt. Viewing Control Structures as Patterns of Passing Messages. *Artificial Intelligence,* pp. 323-364, 1977.

[5] Victor R. Lesser and Daniel D. Corkill. The Distributed Vehicle Monitoring Testbed: A Tool for Investigating Distributed Problem Solving Networks. *AI Magazine*, pp. 15-33, 1983.

[6] David McArthur and Philip Klahr. *The Ross Language Manual*. Rand, 1982.

[7] Sanjai Narain, David McArthur and Philip Klahr. Large-Scale System Development in Several LISP Environments. In *Proceedings IJCAI-83*, pp. 859-861. International Joint Conference on Artificial Intelligence, 1983.

[8] Jasmina Pavlin. Predicting the Performance of Distributed Knowledge-Based Systems: A Modeling Approach. In *Proceedings AAAI-83*, pp. 314-319. American Association for Artificial Intelligence, 1983.

[9] Jasmina Pavlin and Daniel D. Corkill. Selective Abstraction of AI System Activity. In *Proceedings AAAI-84*, pp. 264-268. American Association for Artificial Intelligence, 1984.

[10] Reid G. Smith. *A Framework for Distributed Problem Solving*. UMI Research Press, Ann Arbor, Michigan, 1981.

[11] M. Stefik and D. Bobrow. Object-Oriented Programming: Themes and Variations. *AI Magazine*, 6(4), Winter, 1986.

[12] P. Wegner. Language Paradigms for Programming in the Large. 1985. Working Paper, Brown University.

PART VI:
SCIENTIFIC APPLICATIONS

The Caltech Concurrent Computation Program[*]

GEOFFREY C. FOX[†]

I. Introduction

This report describes the current status of the Caltech Concurrent Computation Program (C^3P), which is a major effort at both the Caltech campus and JPL (Jet Propulsion Laboratory). Approximately 100 people are involved in the combined effort, most are part-time and perhaps around 50 full time equivalents are associated with the project.

The major goal of the program is to develop the capability of concurrent processors for general purpose computation with special emphasis on science and engineering. An important feature of our approach is that the members of the project are scientists who lead in the use of computational techniques in their respective research fields, and have already developed state-of-the-art programs on sequential machines. These scientists are motivated to implement problems on concurrent processors because such machines have been demonstrated to be effective computational tools, and capable of solving major computing intensive problems. A further incentive is that we are developing computers whose (hypercube) architectures "scale" to a large number of nodes and, consequently, to much greater computational power than any sequential machines. One advantage of our approach is that we are motivated both to develop efficient ("good") code as well as to implement entire problems. It has been possible to take advantage of advances in computer science and applied mathematics in all three areas of hardware, software and algorithms. The project currently includes researchers in applied mathematics, aerodynamics, astrophysics, biology, chemistry, computer science, condensed matter, earthquake engineering, geophysics, high energy physics, plasma physics, molecular dynamics, nuclear physics, image processing, and structural mechanics. Approximately 20 Caltech faculty are involved in projects on the hypercube which are supported by C^3P.

The impact of our project is partly indicated by the substantial commercial interest in our ideas. Currently at least four different companies are developing hypercubes with INTEL, NCUBE, AMETEK and FPS announcing commercial machine.

---

[*] Research supported by the Department of Energy grant, DE-FG03-85ER25009, the Parsons Foundation, the Systems Development Foundation, and the office of the program manager of the Joint Tactical Fusion Office.

[†] Concurrent Computation Program, California Institute of Technology, Pasadena, California 91125

During the last year, the research has broadened and significantly expanded. Having four years of experience with the hypercube and five years research support from the DOE has allowed us to embark on some high payoff, long term research efforts. Highlights of this year's work include the completion of a beautiful new hypercube based on the Motorola 68020. We have completed the first draft of a book which covers in detail the main body of all but our most recent research. This will be accompanied by a software supplement with several working codes and a hypercube simulator. Recent work has shown, with working examples, how we can solve general finite element codes on the hypercube. Another highlight is the development with UCLA of a new approach to load balancing. We have tested this in several examples and are developing new communications software to support a dynamic load balancer on the hypercube. Academically, much of our research is covered by a new interdisciplinary graduate program, "Computation and Neural Systems," set up by Caltech.

The Campus side of the project has G. Fox as principal investigator. The project was originally funded by the high energy physics section of the Department of Energy (DOE) and DARPA as a collaboration between Fox and Seitz in computer science. The program described here started in summer 1983 and the Campus research is dominantly funded by the applied mathematical sciences section of DOE. Substantial private funding comes from the System Development Foundation, the Parson's Foundation and the Shell Foundation. Industrial support has come in the form of equipment donations from DEC, ELXSI, HITACHI, INTEL, MOTOROLA and TEKTRONIX. We also have industrial participation through our consortium (which offers training and access to our new technology) and sponsored research projects. Currently ALCOA, AMETEK, GENERAL DYNAMICS, GENERAL MOTORS, IBM, INTEL, LOCKHEED and SHELL are involved in this fashion. Further government funding has come from the Joint Tactical Fusion Office and SANDIA.

There is a substantial research effort at JPL, including all the hardware and most of the systems software development. This is supported both by the Campus grants and several additional sponsors.

In the following sections, we describe the status of research in the areas of hardware, systems software, applications software and architectural lessons, respectively. Further documentation on the project may be obtained from:

G. Fox
Mail Code 158-79
Caltech
Pasadena, CA 91125

II. Hardware

Our first hardware--the Mark I hypercube with 64 5 MHz 8086-8087 based nodes--started operation in October 1983. Currently, most of our research is centered on the Mark II machines which are a modest upgrade built at JPL of the original Mark I design of Seitz. Operational is one 128 node and four 32 node Mark II systems which use 8 Mhz 8086-8087 nodes.

We have two commercial hypercubes--a 64 node INTEL iPSC and a 64 node NCUBE/10. We have ported our internal communications software to the iPSC, achieving up to a factor of 50 speed improvement over the INTEL system software.

Our major internal hardware focus is the dual 68020 based Mark III hypercubes constructed at JPL and shown in Figs. 1 and 2. These offer a factor of 5→10 greater performance per node than the original machines.

Key features of the Mark III systems are:

· Large memory
· Separate communications and calculation processors
· Hardware support of cube and subcube broadcasts
· Hardware support of fast message passing

The node board for the Mark III hypercube constructed at JPL.

- Enhanced memory and performance of Mark III allowing a better operating system
- The high performance and user friendliness of these systems will be of interest to more users and funding agencies and so should accelerate the development of hypercube algorithms and implementations.

We have just completed two small four nodes and two 32 node Mark III hypercubes. We are currently seeking funds to build a hypercube supercomputer around the Mark III. Out initial goal is the completion of a 128 node Mark III system with WEITEK based floating point units giving up to a gigaflop performance. Future systems will use an improved node--the IIIe--featuring:

- Pipelined WEITEK based floating point units. These units will be added as daughter boards to existing Mark III systems.
- Serial interconnect with communications controlled by a custom gate array
- 256 node Mark IIIe having better performance than Cray-XMP or Cray-3.
- The Mark IIIe will be designed so that we can upgrade the WEITEK subsystem to 100 megaflops per node VHSIC floating point units.

In Table 1, we summarize the C^3P current hypercube hardware both at present and in the near future.

A 32 node Mark III hypercube.

Table 1: **Current and Near Future** C^3P
Campus Hypercube Hardware

Machine	Nodes	Near Future
Mark II 8086-7 Nodes	128 32 32 (currently configured as 2 16 nodes)	Stable Systems
INTEL iPSC 80286-7 Nodes	64	Stable System
NCUBE Custom Nodes	64	Upgrade to 256 Nodes (~ Dec. 86 → June 87) Upgrade memory to 1/2 megabyte/node when available (1987)
Mark III	32 4	Upgrade to a 64 and two 8 node systems (Fall 87) Upgrade with WEITEK nodes (Fall 87) Seek funds to upgrade to 128 node system
Mark IIIe		Availability 1988-System Size and Performance Dependent on Funding

III. Systems Software

We have described our current software environment in detail in the 1984-85 annual report. Here, we will concentrate on the recent developments.

Most of our hypercube applications have used the Crystalline communications system (CrOS). This is simple and very fast but is only easily used in regular problems. The first volume of our book describes both CrOS and some of the major algorithms that can use it (see Section IV for details). John Salmon has recently significantly improved CrOS with a new library CUBIX which allows the hypercube programmer full access to the C standard I/O library and many UNIX system calls. We have developed and explained in the book a new standard CrOS-III which we believe is portable and can be used on many hypercubes. CrOS-III and CUBIX will soon be available on the internal Mark II and III as well as the commercial INTEL and AMETEK systems. We expect to port this software to the NCUBE hypercube over the summer.

We have seen the difficulties that INTEL and AMETEK had in developing general communication systems that were both user friendly and high performance. We have been developing two new systems that carefully add generality to CrOS but do not impact performance dramatically, i.e., slower by a factor of two with regard to CrOS, not by the factor of 50 seen with the INTEL system. One system, Mercury (the fleet footed messenger), offers all the essential functions of the INTEL system except for multitasking within a node. Mercury is being tested now. A different philosophy is used by MOOOS (Multitasking Object Oriented Operating System) where messages are not queued as in Mercury but rather instantiate tasks. MOOOS is believed to be well suited for such problems as computer graphics and parallel chess; it is also key to the load balancing research described later. A typical use of Mercury is to allow extension of CrOS applications to irregular geometries.

IV. Algorithms and Implementations

In Appendix 1, we list approximately 20 research programs based on the hypercube. We have currently completed about 30 distinct problems on the hypercube; this does not distinguish the 16 distinct lattice gauge theory problems that we have tackled over the last four years. These are displayed in Appendix 2 to illustrate the versatility of the hypercube.

We expect that the development of algorithms and implementations will remain the corner stones of our program. We will continue to encourage complete and efficient implementations by allowing users to both develop code and solve major research problems on the hypercube. These implementations will be accompanied by papers not just on the science but also the algorithms used and lessons learned from the hypercube. Currently our emphasis is on scientific and engineering fields, but we are broadening our research and the projects in neural networks, parallel chess, computer algebra and expert systems illustrate this.

A highlight of our algorithm work is the completion of (a draft of) the first volume of our book on "Solving Problems on Concurrent Processors." The scope of this is best illustrated by a list of chapter titles.

0: Preamble

1: Concurrent Processing

2: Choices and Driving Forces in Concurrent Computation

3: A Particular Approach to Concurrent Computation

4: A Simple Concurrent Programming Environment

5: Introduction to Decomposition and Concurrent Algorithms: Wave Equation

6: Choices in Language and System Environment: CUBIX and the Wave Equation

7: Potential Problems in Two Dimensions I:

8: Potential Problems in Two Dimensions II:

9: Long Range Interactions

10: Elementary Matrix Algorithms: Multiplication

11: The Fast Fourier Transform

12: Generation of Random Numbers

13: Examples of Monte Carlo Methods

14: Crystalline Operating System

15: CUBIX and its Crystalline Implementations

16: Particle Dynamics

17: WaTOR

18: Sorting

19: Scalar Products

20: Matrix Algorithms II: Banded Inversion

21: Communication Strategies and General Matrix Algorithms

22: Conclusions: The Hypercube as a Supercomputer

Appendix: A: Glossary

Appendix: B: Simulator and Demonstration Software

Appendix: C: CrOS III

V. Architecture

A pioneering feature of our research has been the development of a quantitative analysis of the performance of a hypercube. This work is contained in an article in the May 1984 issue of *Physics Today* and a paper appearing in the proceedings of the March 1985 Supercomputer Conference at Austin. We have developed a classification of problems by their homogeneity and the regularity of their geometry. For the special case of homogeneous problems, we have shown that inter-processor communication is the key issue. Performance of any problem depends only on the grain size (amount of data stored at each node) and parameters of the actual node used in the hypercube. This analysis was important in design of our new Mark III hardware.

We have recently formalized these ideas as a general theory of complex systems. We have classified important parameters of general systems that determine the effectiveness of their decomposition onto concurrent computers. One interesting general concept is that of the, typically fractional, dimension of a system. We have also related system properties that affect decomposition to those that determine the functionality of the systems, e.g., we can relate the decomposition of a communications system onto the hypercube to the real-world performance of the system. In the future, we expect an important extension of these ideas to biological systems.

A major outgrowth of this research is a general theory of load balancing which has been developed with Jefferson at UCLA. This corresponds formally to mapping an arbitrary complex system into a physical system and the use of statistical physics techniques to analyze the resultant problem. A recent highlight has been the successful applications of these ideas to finite element problems. The technique can be viewed as an automatic decomposer; in the finite element case, we used it to decompose a mesh generated by the standard package NASTRAN.

In the next 6-12 months, we expect to develop a dynamic load balancer using these ideas. This would allow one to study general, irregular time dependent problems on the hypercube. Applications that we are exploring include finite elements and turbulent finite difference problems, irregular sparse matrices, neural network, particle dynamics and general event and time-driven simulations.

Appendix 1: Current C^3P Hypercube Projects

This lists most of the current algorithm and program implementation work in C^3P. We first list projects which are specific to specific scientific goals. This is organized by Caltech Divisions. We follow with generic algorithm work and some of the related research at JPL.

Table of Contents
Appendix 1: Current C^3P Hypercube Projects

2) Protein Dynamics
W. Goddard, I. Angus

C: Engineering and Applied Science

1) Chaotic Motion in Plasma Physics
J. Theiler (Graduate Student), N. Corngold

2) Plasma Turbulence
R. W. Gould, P. C. Liewer (JPL)

3) Earthquake Engineering
J. Hall, G. Lyzenga (JPL), M. Salama (JPL), A. Cisneros (Postdoc), D. Parsons (Graduate Student)

4) Applied Mathematics
Eric F. Van de Velde (Postdoc), H. Keller, P. Saffman

5) Numerical Measures of Chaotic Behavior
J. Lorenz

6) Computational Aerodynamics
A. Leonard, K. Harstad (JPL)

7) Convolution Decoding
F. Pollara (JPL), R. McEliece, E. Posner

D: Geology and Planetary Science

1) Finite-Difference Wave Simulation
R. Clayton

2) Finite Element Modeling in Geophysics
B. Hager

3) Wave Propagation
R. Clayton

4) Stress, Strain, and Flow Calculations
B. Hager

5) Study of Deep Interior of the Earth by Seismic Waves
T. Tanimoto

E: Physics

1) Computational Astrophysics
R. Blandford, T. Prince, D. Meier (JPL), J. Salmon (Graduate Student)

2) Lattice Gauge Theory
G. Fox, S. Otto (Postdoc), J. Flower, P. Stolorz (Graduate Students)

3) Condensed Matter Physics
M. Cross, G. Fox, S. Callahan, M. Johnson (Graduate Students), F. Fucito, S. Solomon (Postdocs)

4) Sputtering Calculations
T. Tombrello

5) Grain Dynamics
P. Haff, B. T. Werner (Graduate Student)

6) Nuclear Matter Equation of State
S. Koonin, D. Wasson (Graduate Student)

F: Propulsion Laboratory

1) Ray Tracing
J. Goldsmith (JPL), J. Salmon (Graduate Student)

2) Time Warp
D. Jefferson (UCLA) and JPL Collaborators

3) Astronomical Data Analysis
J. Patterson (JPL)

4) Expert Systems and XLISP
A. Bond (UCLA), A. Louie (JPL)

G: General Algorithms

1) Optimal Communication Algorithms
G. Fox, W. Furmanski (Postdoc)

2) Matrix Algorithms
G. Fox, W. Furmanski (Postdoc), A. Cisneros (Visitor)

3) Finite Element Techniques
A. Cisneros (Visitor); D. Walker, S. Otto (Postdocs) R. Morison (Staff), J. Flower (Graduate Student); M. Salama (JPL); G. Montry (SANDIA)

4) Computer Algebra
G. Fox, S. Callahan (Graduate Student)

5) Computer Chess
S. Otto (Postdoc); E. Felten, R. Morison (Staff)

6) Database
G. Fox, A. Kolawa (Staff Scientist)

7) Load Balancing
Jean E. Patterson (JPL), G. Fox, A. Kolawa (Staff Scientist)

8) Optimization Theory
R. Williams (Staff Scientist)

9) MOOOS
J. Salmon, J. Flower, S. Callahan (Graduate Students); A. Kolawa (Staff Scientist)

A: Biology and the New Option - Computation and Neural Systems (CNS)
Modeling of Neural Networks
J. M. Bower

Over the last several years, a growing number of engineers and computer scientists interested in subjects ranging from information storage to pattern recognition have begun to consider "reverse engineering" networks of biological neurons that perform similar functions. Studying the functional characteristics of these networks from either the point of view of engineering or neurobiology has increasingly relied on computer simulation. However, the computational power available for modeling has, in general, limited the complexity of the modeled networks well below that found in the brain. We have implemented on the hypercube a first version of an algorithm for a generic network simulation which can model large networks both of biological neurons and of electronic components. The code is deliberately designed to facilitate transference of information and networks between neurobiologists studying the brain and engineers designing "applied" Hopfield-type networks in silicon.

This "base code" is an object-oriented discrete-time simulation; it is a template that contains no anatomical or physiological information. It assumes that neural systems are made up of cells, which can send information to each other in any desired pattern. A user must overlay two things on this template: equations describing the time behavior of an individual cell, and rules about how those cells are connected together. This code allows for two mappings of neurons to the hypercube: a purely geometric one, where the essentially two-dimensional real systems are mapped onto a planar projection of the hypercube nodes; and a "scattered" decomposition, where the network is broken up into tiles which are distributed regularly among the processors. The first network simulation applications currently are being written on top of the base code.

The hypercube is a good machine for neural network simulation because this is a memory-bound application that does not vectorize well, but parallelizes quite nicely.

Hence, supercomputers that depend on vectorized accessing of memory would run into memory-contention problems simulating the irregularly-connected neural networks, while a distributed-memory machine, like the hypercube, has no such problems. Several thousand average network elements can be modeled on each node of a Mark III hypercube. Since there are thought to be important properties of the networks that are "emergent" which will only appear at certain complexity levels, it is important to be able to model many neurons at once. Hence, this fast access to massive memory is crucial.

We plan to expand the existing base code's capabilities. As it now stands, a user must write several subroutines detailing the internal properties and connectivities of the network elements. We hope to enhance the user interface by developing a "little language" that will allow users to specify their networks more quickly and easily. We also hope to explore the optimization of mapping variously-connected networks on the hypercube by experimenting with various combinations of mappings and routing schemes. Finally, an interesting feature of neural network simulations is that the code is processing input information, by hypothesis the same way the modeled cortex processes its sensory or other input information. This implies that defining neural networks and implementing them on a hypercube provides a general framework for implementing and testing neural-network-derived information-processing artificial intelligence algorithms. Since the brain processes information in parallel, we can only expect to see more synergisms as we expand our neural-network simulation capabilities on the hypercube. We expect this program to be adapted for the research of Koch, a new assistant professor in the computation and neural systems option, and Hopfield. In the latter case, we will model the applied neural networks pioneered by Hopfield.

Machine Vision
D. Fashena (Graduate Student), G. Fox
Goal:

To endow the hypercube with the ability to recognize general three dimensional objects from images.

Work completed:

(1) Image processing environment.

We have developed an efficient image convolution program running on the Mark II 32 node hypercube. General convolutions can be done. Special features exist for the important (Marr) edge detection filters.

We have obtained digitized video images of real world scenes from Alan Bond at the UCLA Robotics Lab. These have been processed by the edge detection routines.

We have written routines allowing fast display of raw and processed black and white images on an IBM PC AT running XENIX with a Professional Graphics display monitor.

Under Development:

(1) A theory of visual recognition.

    (a) Visual Learning.

        Visual images are both complex and extremely arbitrary. What seems familiar and natural to human beings, turtles, fish and slugs is familiar because we have learned them to be so. General guidelines such as connectivity of surfaces and three dimensional structure are abstract structures that are learned, i.e. derived in some way through repeated contact and associations. Fashena proposes that any approach to vision with a pre-categorized "visual vocabulary" of fixed size will never be generally useful and thus that learning is not essential to machine vision. What is important and "memorable" in a visual image? Fashena proposes that the most important primitive objects in an image are edges. Visual memories should arise from interactions of these primitive objects. The convolution program will serve as a "front end" for continuing work by performing edge detection at different scales. In effect, it will do some of the work that a retina does.

(b) Visual Associative Memory.

Given a huge number of visual memories and the large natural variations between similar images, an associative memory is a promising method of correctly matching an observed image to a visual memory. Fashena is currently trying to design such a memory to run on the hypercube.

(2) A development environment running on the hypercube

As presently envisioned, visual information will exist in a distributed fashion throughout the machine. A visual memory system will consist of interlinked communicating parallel processes. Recognition is the statistically probable convergence of many random processes to a subset of active parallel processes which are the representation of an object image.

This requires an asynchronous parallel environment where processes may communicate freely and be easily created and destroyed. The MOOOS operating system presently under development has all of these features. We are communicating with the MOOOS group in order to use the new system for this project.

Relaxation Methods in Computer Vision
A. Bond (UCLA), D. Fashena (Graduate Student)

Current preliminary research were implemented on the hypercube algorithms for recognizing 256 × 240 8bit images. Algorithms coded for the hypercube include:

(i) edge finding by 5 × 5 and 32 × 32 convolution masks, where a separable kernel allows large gains for large masks.

(ii) region finding by intensity histogramming using the Furmanski-Fox technique to aggregate a global histogram, or by using buckets from spatially local histograms.

(iii) direct deduction of 3D surfaces (shape) from 2D distributions of intensity (shading), using a variant of Woodham's cooperative algorithm. Work in progress includes:

(iv) relaxation methods for labelling regions and for model directed segmentation into regions

(v) direct shape extraction using matching of stereoscopic pairs of images.

We intend to extend this work concentrating on relaxation methods - this project is described below.

Background:

In investigating the use of the hypercube for artificial intelligence, it has proved a little premature to try to implement a large rule-based or frame-based expert system, since the rules are not available and hence a rather large effort would be needed to produce the rules as well as to design and implement an expert system. Instead, the use of relaxation methods in computer vision has emerged as a potentially fruitful area of research. Relaxation methods for almost all computer vision mechanisms have been described in some form or other. This includes:

(i) low-level processes such as edge finding and optic flow finding

(ii) low-level surface finding methods such as shape from shading

(iii) region finding by clustering

(iv) region interpretation by labelling, which can be probablistic, of course

however, such methods have not been:

(i) integrated into a unified complete computer vision system

(ii) redescribed as parallel mechanisms

The purpose of our proposed research is to do this.

Aims:

To demonstrate the value of the hypercube for artificial intelligence, more specifically for computer vision, and for hierarchical parallel relaxation.

Objectives:

To investigate parallel relaxation methods, different strategies and approaches, particularly as they relate to computer vision mechanisms.

To produce an experimental complete computer vision system, with edge and feature extraction, clustering and region finding, labelling and interpretation, all using parallel relaxation mechanisms and all integrated into a working computer vision system.

Modeling of the Brain
H. Leong (Graduate Thesis), D. Fender

Leong's thesis involved the modeling of the electromagnetic field within the brain. The numerical calculation involved the calculation of a large number of integrals which were distributed over the hypercube as independent calculations.

B: Chemistry
Chemical Reaction Dynamics
Aron Kuppermann, P. Hipes (Graduate Student)

The objective of this program is to calculate, from first quantum mechanical principles, the state-to-state reaction cross-sections of tri- and tetra-atomic chemical reactions. The program consists of two phases: a) testing, on a sequential computer, a new methodology capable of performing such calculations and b) developing codes for implementing this methodology on a hypercube computer.

Over the last year, significant progress was made on both phases of the work. The new methodology invokes the use of hyperspherical coordinates for formulating the three-dimensional N-body reactive scattering problem. These coordinates involve only one distance, the so-called hyperradius, all the remaining ones being angles. One defines a complete set of local surface functions, which are eigenfunctions of an operator obtained from the system's Hamiltonian by making the hyperradius constant. This defines a bound-state problem which can be solved by finite element or variational approaches. Expansion of the scattering wave function in these local surface functions results in a large set of coupled ordinary differential equations in the hyperradial variable which can be solved numerically to yield the desired results.

Using an FPS-164 attached processor, we programmed a finite element code for generating the surface functions necessary for solving a tri-atomic reactive scattering problem, and then solved the corresponding coupled differential equations using a logarithmic derivative method. The results obtained were of excellent quality and the methodology was shown to be very efficient. We then transferred these codes to a CRAY XMP/48 supercomputer and extended these calculations to an energy twice as high as had been possible previously. The results showed the existence of numerous dynamic resonances in reactive scattering. These resonances are of prime importance in understanding the relation between chemical forces and reaction rates. Finally, we developed a variational method for calculating the surface functions, which promises to be significantly more efficient than the finite element one, and are testing it out on an FPS-164 attached processor.

The hyperspherical coordinate approach is particularly well suited for the hypercube architecture. To implement the solutions of the coupled hyperradial scattering differential equations by a suitable logarithmic derivative approach requires only simple matrix operations: addition, multiplication and inversion. Using a matrix inversion method we developed previously, we programmed for the Mark III hypercube a logarithmic derivative integrator. This code was put into operation and its efficiency determined. We showed that, for a given node size, the efficiency of the algorithm increases with the number of coupled equations, as expected.

We have also developed a new matrix inversion code for the Mark II. It is based on the Gauss-Jordan method rather than the Gauss elimination approach we had used previously, and includes pivoting, which the previous program did not. The Gauss-Jordan approach is particularly well suited for concurrent processing because no matrix rows become inactive during the execution of the algorithm and the load of each node is roughly constant throughout the calculation. As a result of these characteristics, the Gauss-Jordan method results in a significantly more efficient code than the Gaussian elimination approach for hypercube machines. For example, for a 32 node configuration, and excluding pivoting, our efficiency for inversion of a 50×50 matrix by Gauss elimination is 0.54, whereas, it is 0.97 for the Gauss-Jordan code we developed. Including pivoting in the latter decreases its efficiency to 0.57. However, for a 100×100 matrix, the corresponding efficiency increases to 0.75. For the reactive scattering problem we are considering, we can normally use the code which excludes pivoting, with corresponding high efficiencies.

An interesting observation is that, in the process of writing a high efficiency Gauss-Jordan code for the hypercube, we obtained a program which ran somewhat faster on a one node configuration than a sequential code we wrote earlier. From this experience we note that the cost in efficiency of the logic overhead required by a hypercube program is less than the variation in performance found in different implementation of the same sequential algorithm.

Our next project is to rewrite the logarithmic derivative integrator for the Mark III, incorporating in it the Gauss-Jordan matrix inverter. This should lead to a very efficient program which could be used for production runs on that machine and of its upgraded Mark IIIe versions. In addition, once a dense matrix eigenvalue-eigenvector code for the Mark III is available, we will use it to implement on that machine the new variational surface function method. These two Mark III codes should permit us to perform exciting reactive scattering calculations on a 256 node Mark IIIe hypercube which are currently not possible even on the largest available sequential supercomputers.

Reference: Aron Kuppermann and Paul G. Hipes, *J. Chem. Phys.* **84**, 5962 (1986).

Protein Dynamics
W. Goddard, I. Angus

Currently, all efforts are directed toward devising an algorithm for constructing a good initial guess as to what a protein's three dimensional configuration might be. The hope is that this can be achieved by concentrating exclusively on the sometimes present sulphur bridges, and the ubiquitous hydrogen bonds that are known to be crucial to determining the structure. Other effects such as nonbonding interactions are presumed to be unnecessary, at least initially. These conjectures have yet to be proven, success being defined by an algorithm that will work for most practical examples.

Because of the still very crude understanding that we have of the algorithms that we will have to use, all work in the interim will be done on sequential machines. It is not clear whether or not these initial algorithms will have a useful implementation on a hypercube. However, it is known that later steps of the calculation, corresponding to the function of the system BIOGRAF developed at Caltech, will have an efficient concurrent implementation.

C: Engineering and Applied Science
Chaotic Motion in Plasma Physics
J. Theiler (Graduate Student), N. Corngold

Since the work of Lorenz [1], it has become widely known that simple deterministic systems with only a few degrees of freedom can display complicated aperiodic behavior. The experimentalist, confronted with complicated irregular motion, seeks to determine whether that motion is "chaotic," deriving from just such a simple system, or whether it is "stochastic," deriving from a system which itself is complicated and which possesses many degrees of freedom.

The methods proposed for the determination of dimension of a system's trajectory through phase space (any finite piece of the trajectory is, of course, one dimensional - what is actually considered is the limit set of the trajectory in phase space; for an ergodic system that limit set is the phase space itself) provide a means of distinguishing these two kinds of motion.

Theiler has developed an analysis of time series [2,3] which involves the calculation of a correlation function C(r) whose r dependence determines the system dimension. This has been implemented on the hypercube where the algorithm is essentially the same as that used for long-range force problems. The method was applied to experimental TOKOMAK data and the hypercube performed well as expected - the long range force algorithm is intrinsically very efficient.

Theiler has recently improved the algorithm and future plans include implementing this on the hypercube and adding a calculation of the Kolmogorov entropy.

1. E. N. Lorenz, "Deterministic Nonperiodic Flow," J. Atmos, Sci 20 (1963), 130.

2. P. Grassberger and I. Procaccia, "Measuring the Strangeness of Strange Attractors," Physica 9D (1983), 189.

3. J. Theiler, "Spurious Dimension from Correlation Algorithms Applied to Limited Time Series Data", April 30, 1986, C^3P-299 report.

Plasma Turbulence
R. W. Gould, P. C. Liewer (JPL)

Confinement of plasmas for the purpose of energy generation by nuclear fusion is limited by plasma turbulence. Observed confinement times are one to two orders of magnitude less than predicted by collisional diffusion. The origin of the enhanced diffusion is believed to be due to drift-wave turbulence. We are making experimental measurements of density and potential fluctuations of drift-wave turbulence in fusion plasmas. The aim of the calculational program is to determine the behavior of non-linear drift wave equations in two dimensions using different model equations, and to see under what conditions they can reproduce the experimental observations. In particular, we aim to compare the spatial and temporal spectra of the turbulence, its dependence on various parameters, and resulting transport coefficients.

Currently, we are describing the turbulence in terms of the (time-dependent) spatial Fourier components of the density fluctuations. We have developed two codes which evolve these components in time from a specified initial state. One code is a FORTRAN code which runs on the VAX. The other is a code in C (and also compiled BASIC) which runs on a PC. We have found that calculation of the time derivatives takes more than 95% of the computing time because it involves a 2-D convolution. By coding the derivative calculation in assembly language, and by making use of efficient layout of various arrays which occur in the calculation, we have reduced the time for the derivative calculation by a factor of 7. We have also found that by removing the "fast" time scale from the time-evolution of the coefficients, we can reduce the computing time by a factor up to 40, depending on the energy of the system. Other pieces of the calculation are ideally suited for assembly language code. However, this will not increase the overall speed by much. So far our calculations have been limited to a 5×5 grid in the interest of computing time. We are beginning to prepare the program for the hypercube.

Earthquake Engineering
J. Hall, G. Lyzenga (JPL), M. Salama (JPL), A. Cisneros (Postdoc), D. Parsons (Graduate Student)

This project is developing a multigrid method to study three dimensional finite element problems on the hypercube. It uses examples from civil engineering, geodynamics and space craft structural analysis. The basic techniques have been implemented by Cisneros and the testing of the various applications is underway.

Applied Mathematics
Eric F. Van de Velde (Postdoc), H. Keller, P. Saffman

Our hypercube effort is concentrated around the implementation of solvers for incompressible Navier-Stokes equations. Anticipating the availability of powerful hypercubes, we are developing solvers for problems in three spatial dimensions. Typical problems of interest include Taylor-Couette flows and onset of turbulence. For these problems, only two methods are really competitive: conjugate gradient and multigrid. To be efficient, the conjugate gradient method needs preconditioners that are highly problem dependent and difficult to construct (and parallelize). Multigrid methods have the considerable advantage not to need any preconditioning, while obtaining comparable convergence speeds. As a result, programs implementing multigrid methods can be more application independent. From a parallel computation point of view, there are two major issues to resolve. First, the global problem needs to be decomposed over the different processors such that any adaptive strategy can be decided upon locally. To achieve this, a combination of Schwarz's alternating method, a well known domain decomposition method, with multigrid seems ideally suited. Using this strategy, each processor has the task of solving an independent problem over a smaller domain. We will study the global convergence speeds obtained in highly parallel environments. The second issue is related to load balancing: with a locally adaptive grid strategy, the computation may become highly unbalanced. We propose to use the simulated annealing technique, developed specifically for this type of load balancing problems.

We are also implementing a parallel shooting method for the solution of systems of ordinary differential equations. Our interest is to solve large systems as they occur in the study of several fluid dynamics problems, i.e. the Taylor-Couette flow, through the application of the method of lines. In the first stage of the parallel shooting method, the global interval is divided into several subintervals and a fundamental solution set is constructed on each, this is obviously parallel. The second stage combines the local fundamental solutions and finds the correct initial values for each subinterval. To exploit parallelism in this stage, the data needs to be mapped from the representation used in the first stage (domain decomposition), to a more appropriate representation. We are using, at this time, a variant of the scattered decomposition. Other decompositions may need to be explored to find an effective compromise between time necessary to perform the remapping of the data and efficiency of the decomposition. Given the initial conditions found by the second stage, the third stage integrates each interval in parallel to find the correct global solution.

Numerical Measures of Chaotic Behavior
J. Lorenz

Many evolutionary systems of ordinary or partial differential equations exhibit chaotic behavior. Typical trajectories neither approach a stationary state nor a periodic orbit, but are attracted by a set of more complicated structure. Our understanding of turbulence might profit from an investigation of these phenomena, but this remains to be confirmed. It is certain, however, that many equations appearing in engineering and science can show chaotic behavior in certain parameter regions.

A question of continuing interest is the determination of the *dimension* of strange attractors since it gives a lower bound on the degrees of freedom present in the system. Dimension calculations are usually quite time consuming, but it is natural to perform them in parallel to achieve a considerable speedup. A program running on the hypercube has been developed which computes the correlation dimension of a strange attractor as defined by Grassberger and Procaccia (1983). The program was tested for the Lorenz equations for some specific parameter values.

Other concepts of "dimension", different from the correlation dimension of Grassberger and Procaccia, are of interest also;these include, for example, the Lyapunov dimension based on Lyapunov numbers and information dimensions which take into account the *time* which a typical trajectory spends in different parts of the attractor.

In the future work, parallel algorithms to compute values for these dimensions will be developed and applied to numerical and experimental data.

Computational Aerodynamics
A. Leonard, K. Harstad (JPL)

Unsteady, incompressible fluid flows at high Reynolds numbers are being investigated by numerical simulation using vortex methods. In these methods, computational elements of vorticity move with the local fluid velocity. The velocity of each element may be computed as the sum of contributions of all other elements plus additional contributions if solid boundaries are present. Using computing strategies known to be effective for long-range force problems, we have implemented a two-dimensional vortex scheme on a hypercube to study nonlinear interactions of finite-area vortices. Efficiencies are in the 80-100% range depending on the number of elements per processor.

We are now investigating possible schemes to include the effects of solid boundaries and separating boundary layers and to extend the methods to three-dimensional flows. We are also studying two schemes that have recently been proposed that theoretically reduce the computational complexity to O(N log N) or O(N) rather than O(N*N). In particular, we would like to determine how one of these schemes could be implemented efficiently on a hypercube.

Convolution Decoding
F. Pollara (JPL), R. McEliece, E. Posner

The Viterbi Algorithm is a well known method for maximum likelihood decoding of convolutional codes. Its complexity increases exponentially with the number of states of the encoder. For large decoders, it is necessary to use some form of parallel processing by dividing the algorithm into equal parts and minimizing the communication requirements between these parts.

The similarity between the Fast Fourier Transform (FFT) and the proposed Concurrent Viterbi algorithm (CVA) is illustrated by showing the topological equivalence of two network structures: the FFT decimation-in-time graph and the Viterbi trellis. This equivalence is based on a simple recording of the states in the trellis.

Known methods to map the FFT on a hypercube are then applied to the Viterbi Algorithm. The advantage of the FFT-like Viterbi algorithm is that it requires communication only between neighboring vertices of the hypercube.

It is shown how to map codes with m>n states on a n-cube assigning multiple states to each processor. The efficiency ϵ of the concurrent algorithm is given by $\epsilon = 1/(1+rn/m)$, where r is a fixed, machine dependent, ratio of elementary communication time and elementary processing time.

For this algorithm, the hypercube architecture achieves higher efficiency than other structures such as 2-dimensional meshes or rings of processors.

The concurrent algorithm has been programmed and successfully tested on a 64-node hypercube with efficiencies up to 65%, for $6 \leq m \leq 14$.

D: Geology and Planetary Science

There is a major research effort in geophysics on the hypercube. This is a collaboration between Caltech and JPL. Details are given below.

Finite-Difference Wave Simulation
R. Clayton

The simulation of waves in complex media requires direct numerical solutions of the wave equation in its differential or integral form. We have implemented finite-difference solutions for both the 2D acoustic wave equation and the 2D elastic wave equation.

The finite-difference methods we have implemented are accurate to fourth-order in the spatial mesh. This gives substantial accuracy improvements over the usual second-order methods. The fourth-order methods have the same computation-communication balance as the second-order methods. That is, the doubling of the communication requirements is balanced by a doubling of the computation per mesh point. The efficiency is in the 90-100% range depending on the number of mesh points per processor.

Improvements have also been made in the finite-difference technique. A stable method was found for implementing the elastic free surface boundary condition. Source terms have also been modified so that radiation patterns can be included, and also so they mimic the response of a point source rather than a line source.

The codes are being applied to several problems. The most complete is a study of wave propagation in random media. These studies show that it is necessary to consider the earth's randomness as self-similar to predict the travel time and amplitude in distributions that are observed. The codes are also used to simulate exploration geometries, and for limited global wave simulation.

Finite Element Modeling in Geophysics
B. Hager

Finite element calculations of continuum mechanics problems are useful for a range of problems where the geometry of physics of the problem suggests or requires a range in mesh geometries or resolution. We have been concentrating primarily on implementing on the hypercube a difficult finite element problem: slow, creeping thermal convection in an incompressible medium. The motivation is our desire to address large, three-dimensional problems. In three dimensions, the stiffness matrix arising from the finite element description of the equations of motion is best inverted using iterative techniques for which the hypercube architecture is well suited.

Incompressible flow is difficult to treat using iterative techniques. Treating pressure and velocity as independent variables results in a stiffness matrix that is not positive definite, and hence not suitable for standard iterative techniques for inversion. Use of the penalty formulation results in a very stiff stiffness matrix, again unsuitable for efficient interactive solution.

We have approached this problem by using an augmented Lagrangian approach, where the velocity field is solved initially for a slightly compressible medium using a preconditioned conjugate gradient algorithm. (Along the way, we have developed the necessary code to solve compressible elasticity problems.) We have fully implemented the two dimensional augmented Lagrangian and conjugate gradient codes and run them on the Campus Mark II and AMETEK S14 computer. The implementation of the conjugate gradient algorithm has been discussed, and its high efficiency on a hypercube demonstrated. The augmented Lagrangian solution is essentially nested conjugate gradient loops and should have similarly high "hypercube" efficiency, although we have not yet documented this. The thermal equation solver has been fully implemented on a sequential machine and has been coded on the hypercube. It is currently "one last bug" away from being fully operational.

Future Research on Geophysics Applications of Hypercubes

We intend to continue development of the finite-difference and finite-element methods and continue to apply them to "real" problems. We have also expanded our group by one with the addition of Professor Toshiro Tanimoto. His field of expertise is in applying modal decomposition to the study of long-period wave propagation in the earth. Under separate headings the specific research projects are given.

Wave Propagation
R. Clayton

We intend to pursue the coupling of our finite-difference codes to analytic methods. This will allow the time-consuming numerical codes to be used in complex regions and the cheaper analytic methods to be used in simpler regions. In terms of the hypercube, this means we will have to implement several processes per node (probably implemented as subroutines) so that the simulation can shift back and forth between the various schemes. We shall probably have to implement a load balancing scheme to equalize the work per node.

We are also investigating an alternate formulation of the wave equation that allows large 3D simulations on memory limited machines. (All current and near future computers are memory limited for 3D problems.) This technique uses paraxial operators that model waves traveling within an angular cone of a particular direction. This study is motivated by the desire to model strong ground motions in basins such as the Los Angeles or Mexico City basins.

Stress, Strain, and Flow Calculations
B. Hager

We will proceed in our research on implementing geophysical finite-element calculations on the hypercube along three lines: development of improved algorithms, benchmarking of efficiencies, and production runs.

Benchmarking and production runs will use the elastic (conjugate gradient) software, extended to 3D. The particular problem we plan to study in 3D is the concentration of stress around boreholes of arbitrary orientation with respect to the stress tensor. Solutions of this problem are essential to the interpretation of measurements made using Professor T. J. Ahrens' holographic stressmeter. The 1 (4) Mbyte/node memory size of either the Ametek S14 or the (Caltech Mark III) hypercube in geophysics is essential to obtaining reasonable efficiencies in 3D.

The 2D augmented Lagrangian thermal convection code is also almost to the point where benchmarking and production runs are called for.

We are not completely satisfied with the augmented Lagrangian solution to our thermally driven incompressible stokes flow problems, however. The algorithm does not respond well to the good initial guess given by the previous timestep solution in a time dependent convection problem. We are pursuing the Lanczos technique to get better performance.

Finally, in collaboration with a group at Los Alamos, we plan to implement a 3D finite-difference convection using a fast Poisson solver (FFT) on the hypercube.

Study of Deep Interior of the Earth by Seismic Waves
T. Tanimoto

Seismic waves give us the most direct information of the interior structure of the earth. Densities and elastic velocities of the earth are obtained by comparing the seismic data with synthetic seismograms for an earth model.

One of the most time consuming steps in this kind of research is the generation of synthetic seismograms for an earth model. Various methods such as finite difference of finite element methods can be used for this purpose, but normal mode theory has been quite useful in the long-period range (>100 sec). There do not exist many modes in the long-period range (>100 sec) of the earth's oscillation spectra and calculation of a few thousand modes is sufficient to describe motions of the earth in this period range.

In the normal mode analysis, the whole process breaks up into two major steps: One, to calculate eigenfrequencies and eigenfunctions of the model earth and two, to compute the contributions of each mode for a particular source (earthquake or explosion) and receiver (seismometer location) pair. In either step, use of the concurrent processor enchance our capability, since we can let each processor handle one mode at a time and sum up all contributions later.

E: Physics
Computational Astrophysics
R. Blandford, T. Prince, D. Meier (JPL), J. Salmon (Graduate Student)

Two applications were successfully completed in 1984; one by Meier in two dimensional hydrodynamics and another by Salmon on N body simulators of the evolutions of the universe. The latter used the FFT and has led to several physics publications. We expect to extend this work by using new algorithms for fast computation of the gravitational interaction of large numbers of objects. These algorithms partition the particles into a tree and can reduce the calculation time to O (NlogN). It appears that such an algorithm would be a good candidate for implementation in MOOOS and easier than the FFT. Since gravitational systems form tight clusters as well as large empty "voids", load balancing such a simulation poses interesting problems.

Lattice Gauge Theory
G. Fox, S. Otto (Postdoc), J. Flower, P. Stolorz (Graduate Students)
See Appendix 2 for full participants

The fundamental equations of particle physics are a quantum field theory whose complexity has prevented quantitative analytic analysis except in special regimes. Most theoretical work concentrates on symmetry and topological properties which are preserved by the complicated nonlinear infinite dimensional dynamics. Only the perturbative regime allows some analytic prediction of absolute theoretical observables. Thus, the numeric approach to this field is very important. Typically, one sets up a four dimensional grid in space and time and uses a subtle formalism due to Ken Wilson in order to set up the appropriate discrete version of the continuum theory. One can view the resultant numerical problem as a large Monte Carlo integration performed over the boson and fermion field values at the lattice points in space time. Similar techniques are used in some quantum chemistry, nuclear physics and condensed matter calculations. In the latter case, time is not discretized and the integrals "only" run over three and not four dimensions.

Our group, consisting of one to three postdocs and several graduate students, has been working in this area since 1981. Initially, we used a VAX11/780 for our work but one of the original goals of the first (Mark I) hypercubes was the solution of lattice gauge theory problems. Thus, since 1982, the majority of our calculations have been performed on hypercubes; starting with the 4 node Mark I and now using the 128 node Mark II and commercial machines. As shown in Appendix 2, we have completed 13 lattice gauge theory problems while a further three are still in progress. We note that these address a wide range of topics and this illustrates the flexibility and relative ease of programming of the hypercube.

Over the period in which we have been developing the hypercube, access to CRAY's has become quite easy for groups in this area and now most state-of-the-art calculations use between 100 and 1000 hours of CRAY-XMP time. This is available from both DOE and NSF. We decided that our resources were insufficient to optimize algorithms for both the CRAY and the hypercube and so we have chosen to use the cube almost exclusively. Thus, currently we can compete with modest ($\sim$ 100 hours) but not the largest CRAY computations. However, **none** of today's calculations are very convincing. Lack of memory and computational powers force one to approximations and lattice sizes (a $20 \times 20 \times 20 \times 20$ grid is typical of the largest calculations) that are unlikely to lead to reliable answers. It seems certain that only concurrent computers will allow definitive calculations with lattices of order 50^4 and an accurate formalism. Thus, this foresight and the modest power of our current hypercubes implies that our group has concentrated on the development and testing of improved concurrent algorithms rather than major numerical calculations.

Now we can describe the importance of a supercube (hypercube supercomputer) to our research. We would use this to perform the first definitive calculations in this field which should be able to quantify the predictions of quantum chromodynamics (QCD); the proposed theory of the strong interactions. Current algorithms are really only able to calculate what are effectively single particle parameters; most important is the basic meson and baryon mass spectra. Other very interesting calculations which build on our current research (shown in Appendix 2) include the determination of the quark(q)-antiquark and qqq potential. One should be able to extend current potential calculations to include spin effects as well as tracking the potential from the short range perturbative ($\sim$ 0.1 fm) to the "long" range (~ 2 fm) region where one expects to find a linear potential. Current lattice sizes only permit one to follow the spin-averaged potential to a distance of about one fermi, i.e., still effectively inside a hadron and with no account of spin dependence. The meson and baryon potential calculations have been our most interesting work so far on the hypercube and can be directly used to predict heavy meson and baryon spectra (bound states of c,b, t quarks) as well as being of interest in nuclear physics. Other fundamental "single particle" observables of great interest include weak interaction matrix elements, the spectra of so called glueballs (states only containing gluons) and testing of theoretical ideas on the gluon wave function (energy distribution) inside hadrons. We expect to use an improved formalism-the Langevin technique developed by Callahan, Flower, and Otto.

The program outlined above is very ambitious. Using a decent lattice (at least 40^4) for the first time, we should be able to confront the fundamental equations of nature with experiment. This program requires a concurrent supercomputer; a sequential CRAY is insufficient. The minimum memory needs is 1-4 gigabytes, and we could do interesting calculations in approximately 10 gigaflop-months (i.e., ~3 months on an 256 node Mark IIIe). The full program outlined above would take an order of magnitude more time.

The hypercube is well suited to lattice calculations. The topology includes within it the necessary four dimensional mesh. We have found good efficiency (~95%) in most applications because the theory is so complex that calculation easily overwhelms communication even with quite small sublattices in each node.

Condensed Matter Physics
M. Cross, G. Fox, S. Callahan, M. Johnson (Graduate Students); F. Fucito, S. Solomon (Postdocs)

Two condensed matter problems on the hypercube have been completed and written up. A third involving the study of exchange effects in Helium III is under development and will be the thesis of S. Callahan.

M. Johnson completed his Ph.D on the numerical study of the melting of a two dimensional solid using the hypercube. The constraints of detailed balance in an irregular problem required the most sophisticated early (1984) algorithm developed for the hypercube. Johnson developed an optimal communication system and an ingenious algorithm involving time stamping messages to ensure that concurrent updates could be ordered sequentially. Interesting new results were obtained suggesting a first order phase transition; earlier published (sequential) calculations seemed to be in error due to the study of small systems with inadequate statistics.

Fucito and Solomon studied a long range Monte Carlo - the two dimensional Coulomb gas on the hypercube. They developed an algorithm which was efficient but needed new techniques which are different from the particle dynamics long-range force problem. The results of this computation were used to evaluate a Coulomb gas approximation to the two dimensional X-Y model.

Sputtering Calculations
T. Tombrello

The use of molecular dynamics techniques to describe the behavior of solids has been, until recently, limited primarily by the speed and memory size of the computers available. In practice this limitation occurs for systems of $\sim10^3$ atoms, where there are in effect $\sim10^6$ two-body potentials between the pairs of particles. Thus, most simulations suffer from a high surface area to volume ratio that may seriously distort the value of the results.

Our group has been especially interested in the evolution of surfaces and interfaces between different materials under ion/atom bombardment. Our previous work has shown that until the number of atoms can be increased to $>10^4$, there are biases in the computational results that are difficult to remove. During the past year, we have accomplished the following work in using the concurrent processors at Caltech:

1.) We have a working molecular dynamics code running on the 32 node Mark II hypercube. Although this machine is too slow to run systems of 10^4 atoms, the experience obtained in this exercise has been extremely useful in optimizing our technique for parallel processing.

2.) We have just finished a successfully running molecular dynamics code on the NCUBE. The experience obtained on the hypercube has made the transition to this computer relatively easy. Its greater speed (or that of the Mark III, when it is available) makes it possible to run cases of $>10^4$ atoms. Our first efforts will be to investigate ion induced sputtering simulations as a function of target size.

By early fall 1986, we shall be modifying the existing code to include many-body forces among the atoms. (Now we are using only pair potentials.) These forces are obtained from a new technique called the "imbedded atom method", in which the local potential is a function of the local atomic electron density. This electron density is obtained in practice from Hartree-Fock wave functions of the atoms in the solid. Although this modification will require a three fold increase in computing time, it allows a much more accurate representation of the behavior of surface or interface atoms.

Grain Dynamics
P. Haff, B. T. Werner (Graduate Student)

The Caltech Concurrent Processors have been used to study the problem of a macroscopic grain impacting a surface composed of loose grains, a key component of the process by which sand is transported by the wind in short hops, which has been dubbed saltation. The programs to do this simulate the motion of nearly rigid frictional particles. A variety of granular materials phenomena, such as packing, sorting, gravity flow and planetary ring dynamics may be amenable to study using the simulation technique. A recent paper, "The Impact Process in Eolian Saltation: Two-Dimensional Studies", describes the details of the grain-bed impact simulations and the physics we have learned from them. The concurrent algorithms needed are similar to those used in molecular dynamics and the irregular Monte Carlo method of M. Johnson.

Nuclear Matter Equation of State
S. Koonin, D. Wasson (Graduate Student)

Wasson is engaged in an ongoing calculation of the nuclear matter equation of state in the sub-saturation region (nucleon densities from 10% to 100% of the nuclear saturation density) at temperatures up to ~ 10 MeV. One is primarily interested in observing how the topology of the nuclear matter changes as one increases the density. One sees transitions from spherical nuclei to uniform nuclear matter with intervening phases looking like cylinders, slabs, tubes, and bubbles. In the real world, this regime of nuclear matter is encountered during the collapse of stars leading to type II supernova.

Code has been developed on the Mark II cube which calculates the ground state of nuclear matter at a given temperature and density using temperature-dependent Hartree-Fock. This involves determining the single-particle eigenstates of a Hamiltonian and occupying them according to Fermi statistics. The specific Hamiltonian used is generated by the Skyrme force and results in a non-linear, single-particle Schrodinger equation. This equation is solved in a cube with periodic boundary conditions, and the cube size is then adjusted at fixed density to give the minimum free energy per nucleon.

The equation is discretized on a lattice and solved by a local iteration method. The problem is mapped onto the cube by dividing the cubic lattice evenly among the nodes. The primary impedance to full parallelism is the nearest-neighbor communication necessary for the calculation of derivatives, and to a lesser extent, global communication necessary for keeping the wave functions orthonormalized and calculating the chemical potential. The net result is that the program runs at about 85% efficiency.

The primary impedance in running the code is the available memory per node. The current code is only capable of handling densities up to one-third the saturation density for temperatures of a few MeV. This has allowed the observation of the spherical-tocylindrical phase transition but not the higher ones. The code is currently being improved to allow calculation up to the saturation density.

F: Jet Propulsion Laboratory

There is some C^3P associated research at JPL which is not directly related to a particular Campus science or engineering project. Some of this work is listed below.

Ray Tracing
J. Goldsmith (JPL), J. Salmon (Graduate Student)

Ray tracing is a technique used to render computer graphics images of three-dimensional models. It simulates the interaction of light rays with the environment, producing realistic looking refractions, reflections, and shadows.

We have developed a ray tracer that runs on the Mark II hypercube under CUBIX. It also runs on sequential machines, including an ELXSI and VAXes. It performs all the basic functions of a ray tracer, as well as some more complex ones. (See Table 2.) It can render polygons, cylinders, and spheres in numbers currently limited only by the memory space of one node, since the whole program and data base are stored in each node. The pixels comprising the final picture are distributed across the hypercube, thus using all the processors approximately equally.

The ray tracer's object intersection test routine uses the method of hierarchical bounding boxes in order to avoid most testing each object against each ray. This method requires the construction of an extent around each object of a form that is easy to test for intersection with rays. We use rectangular prisms with sides aligned to the coordinate axes. These extents are recursively combined to form a tree with the property that each node is completely contained within its parent. Thus, failure to intersect the parent implies failure to intersect all its children. The shape of these trees is crucial to the performance of the algorithm; we have found new ways to optimize the shape of a tree during its construction.

Currently, we are working on distributing the database, so that very large models can be fit into the machine memory. The tree will be broken up so that each node will have a piece containing the root node and other high-level nodes. The remainder of the tree will be distributed across the hypercube. Processors that do not contain the data of a subtree will contain pointers to the processor that does and will, using MOOOS, execute the intersection test routine on the remote processor for the rest of that subtree. A major consideration in the database distribution is the maintenance of load balance of these intersection calculations. This is done by evaluating the amount of calculation time expected to be expended intersecting with the subtrees and distributing them in approximately equal portions. We are also investigating different pixel distribution strategies, and obtaining timing comparisons on each.

Ray Tracer Features
Unlimited polygons, cylinders, and spheres
unlimited light sources
colored light sources
Variable intensity light sources
Optional falloff curves
Diffuse, ambient, and specular reflection
Metallic or plastic surfaces
Standard viewing transformation
Variable anti-aliasing
Jittered anti-aliasing

Table 2

After the database distribution programs are working, we will implement surface mapping, which will unbalance the database in load versus size and enhance the distribution programs to handle this. We will also investigate use of the techniques of dynamic load balancing in order to implement adaptive anti-aliasing, which will speed up the program considerably.

Time Warp
D. Jefferson (UCLA) and JPL Collaborators

A large effort at JPL has successively implemented on the Mark II hypercube, a novel concurrent discrete event driver simulator (DEVS) using the time warp techniques introduced by Jefferson and Sowizral.

Time Warp is the most ambitious project yet attempted on the Caltech-JPL hypercubes. It is very different in spirit from the regular and near-regular applications that are the staple of hypercube users. Time warp is both an experimental operating system and a programming system. As an operating system, it claims to do for temporal concurrency what Virtual Memory operating systems do for spatial concurrency. As a programming system, Time Warp supports object-oriented programming devoted primarily to DEVS. Object-oriented programming is a methodology for software development that has attracted a great deal of attention in recent years both because it is a good way to organize the work of programming and because it is amenable to distributed processing. DEVS are widely used in government and industry to simulate very complex, irregular systems, such as power plants, commodity markets, armies, digital circuits, and so on.

Our implementation of Time Warp consists of (1) a multi-processing kernel, (2) an executive, and (3) a set of application programs. The application programs are written in a bare-bones, object-oriented dialect of C created by us. Our application set includes (1) the simplest application: **PINGPONG**, (2) a several-dimension family of games of **LIFE** (interrogative/imperative, big/small, toroidal/limited, balanced/unbalanced, etc.), (3) the dining philosopher's problem, and (4) a battlefield communications queueing model, **COMMO**.

The system is now running on the Mark II and being tested and evaluated.

Astronomical Data Analysis
J. Patterson (JPL)

An important computational component (at least 40%) of astronomical data analysis involves matrix inversion associated with the least squares parameter estimation. This is typically done by Householder's transformation which has been implemented on the hypercube.

Expert Systems and XLISP
A. Bond (UCLA), A. Louie (JPL)

A version of Common Lisp written in C (named XLISP) was modified to run on the Mark III hypercube using the Mercury asynchronous communications system. It is now possible to write hypercube programs in LISP just as one can write them in C or FORTRAN. We call it concurrent XLISP or CXLISP.

A CXLISP interpreter runs in the Control Processor (CP) and in every node. The interpreters are in the standard Read-Eval-Print loop; the CP expects input from stdin and the nodes expect input in the form of Mercury messages of a command type. All Mercury messages and the user program evaluates the command messages and the user program evaluates the non-command messages. Commands can be issued from any node to any other node including the CP.

All of the Mercury functions are accessible from CXLISP: sending and receiving messages, searching the queue, etc. A brief CXLISP user guide is expected to be produced in the near future.

The current version of CXLISP cannot handle floating point numbers and future projects include this upgrade and more interestingly the application to simple expert systems.

G: General Algorithms

Apart from the specific science or engineering based projects listed above, there is significant research in genetic algorithms which is listed below.

Optimal Communication Algorithms
G. Fox, W. Furmanski (Postdoc)

The systematic method of "cube geodesics" has been proposed for constructing the optimal mappings on the hypercube, transforming the initial state data distribution f(x) into the final state data distribution g(k) according to some (possibly non-local, non-associative and non-linear) transformations g(k)=F(k,f(x)) where F is a functional.

The explicit algorithms for some practically relevant cases: "fold", "expand", "index", "transpose","scatter", "forest" were described, assembly coded, and timed on Mark II C^3P-314.

The work was inspired by the scalar product algorithm, proposed by G. C. Fox (C^3P-173) and presented in C^3P-314 in its final optimal form as the "fold" algorithm.

An unexpected by-product is a new FFT algorithm with lower communication overheads than the conventional method.

Matrix Algorithms
G. Fox, W. Furmanski (Postdoc), A. Cisneros (Visitor)

We have improved our previous algorithms using the new communication techniques described above. We have applied them to matrix inversion, and eigenvalue determination with tridiagonalization using Householder's method. We have also implemented the banded matrix LU decomposition on the hypercube using less optimal methods; its performance is still good. The efficiency is, for example, 80% on the 64 node Mark II hypercube for a band size of 320.

Finite Element Techniques
A. Cisneros (Visitor); D. Walker, S. Otto (Postdocs) R. Morison (Staff), J. Flower (Graduate Student); M. Salama (JPL); G. Montry (SANDIA)

We have developed several important general techniques for solving finite element problems. These include:

i) General multigrid approach to irregular problems including the appropriate and optimized irregular communication subsystem.

ii) Simulated annealing approach to optimal decomposition of irregular geometry problems. This gave excellent results on sample meshs produced by NASTRAN.

iii) The simpler scattered decomposition approach was also applied to finite element problems and found to be very effective.

iv) We compared the shared memory (ELXSI) with the hypercube for a model finite element problem. Interestingly, the use of the cache or the ELXSI implied that the best method on this machine used the same ideas as the hypercube implementation.

Computer Algebra
G. Fox, S. Callahan (Graduate Student)

We initiated a simple computer algebra program on the hypercube. This is designed to test the basic decomposition ideas and not to be a useful scientific tool. It has become clear that this project needs the MOOOS environment and we are awaiting completion of this new hypercube operating system.

Computer Chess
S. Otto (Postdoc); E. Felten, R. Morison (Staff)

A major effort of the group in parallel AI is the development of a serious chess playing program on the hypercubes. Our intent to produce a high performance chess program forces us to face difficult issues such as the parallel search of an α - β pruned tree and the implementation of a globally hashed lookup table on a distributed memory machine such as the hypercube.

The program follows the approach of the currently successful sequential programs. There is a large opening library, the middlegame proceeds by look ahead into an α - β pruned game tree, the program switches to a specialized evaluation functions (the evaluation function scores a chess board) in the end game. A large transposition table of positions (corresponding to knowledge gained during the search) is kept. The search tree is iteratively deepened so as to produce a reliable principal variation for the deepest tree searched.

The search tree is decomposed onto the parallel computer. Loosely speaking, the processors independently race down the tree, searching different branches. This description is overly simplistic, however, the efficiency of $\alpha-\beta$ pruning is strongly dependent upon the order in which branches of the tree are searched. The point is that $\alpha-\beta$ pruning works most effectively when the good lines of play of the tree are searched first and then these values of α and β (the scores from these lines) are used in searches of the other branches. To mimic this on the parallel machine, we are developing an algorithm which carefully schedules the allocation of processors onto branches of the tree. Roughly speaking, the processors of the parallel machine are first heavily concentrated along the principal variation so as to execute this as rapidly as possible. Once the principal variation is searched, producing good estimates of α and β, the processors "fan out" and search the rest of the tree.

As mentioned previously, a large transposition table, consists of boards and their scores, is constructed and used during the search. This table corresponds to knowledge gained during the search which can be re-used; hence it is worthwhile to store it. The table is stored as a hash table and, on hypercube implementation, we not only hash to a local address but to a processor number as well. In this way, we have a globally hashed lookup table. The necessity of implementing remote memory lookup via software has been observed to not hurt the performance of the program substantially.

Our current goal is to complete a parallel implementation of this "standard, optimal chess program". Beyond this we would like to include some type of learning into the program. Chess boards are scored via an evaluation function which extracts various features of the position such as: material balance, center control, king safety, development, etc., assigns a value to each and then does a linear combination of these to arrive at a score for the board. The choice of relative weights of the various terms is usually done by trial and error by the programmer. Learning can play a role by having the program adjust these weights as it runs so as to dynamically adapt itself to the current game. This method was described by Samuel for the game of checkers and was found to have a definite, positive impact upon the skill of the program. We intend to pursue these ideas in our chess program; part of the code to implement learning is installed in our current program.

We describe the current status of our NCUBE implementation which searches chess game-trees by the traditional full-width alpha-beta strategy. It examines about 20,000 positions per second under tournament conditions (64 NCUBE nodes, 3-4 minutes per move); compare to 100,000 positions/second for Cray Blitz and 200,000 for Hitech. In a complex middlegame situation this corresponds to a depth of 6 ply (half-moves) plus quiescence search (examination of all capture sequence beyond 6 ply, plus extension of the search along lines involving checks). In simple endgames, the search depth can sometimes reach 10 ply or beyond.

Middlegame positions are evaluated by a function which takes into account the following concepts: material, development, piece mobility, attack on the center, attack on opponent's king, attack on advanced squares, and miscellaneous terms such as a penalty for putting knights on the edge of the board. In addition, there is a sophisticated pawn structure term which knows about passed, outside passed, chained, isolated, doubled, and backward pawns, and encourages the program to restrain, blockade, and attack pawn weaknesses and to break up the pawn structure around the opponent's king.

In the endgame, a simpler evaluator is used which encourages king centralization and development and advancement of passed pawns.

The opening is played by consulting a database or "book" of common opening positions. This database currently contains about 17,000 positions. The program plays opening chosen by the programmers for compatibility with its style of play.

The program has been entered in two chess tournaments (against human competition). It scored 3-3 in the Southern California Open (Aug. 30-Sep.1) with a performance rating of about 1540. An improved program was entered in the BVA Volvo Open (Oct 3-5) and scored 5-1 to take second place in the amateur section. The program's performance rating for this tournament was about 1860.

Database
G. Fox, A. Kolawa (Staff Scientist)

A problem encountered in a semi-analytic calculation of the O^{++} glueball in SU(2) gauge theory, required the search of a very long and dynamic list of stakes. This was implemented as a distributed database on the hypercube. We were able to develop a performance analysis which nicely connects this to long range force algorithms.

Load Balancing
Jean E. Patterson (JPL), G. Fox, A. Kolawa (Staff Scientist)

Load balance is a fundamental requirement for the ultimate effectiveness of parallel processing computers. Without the ability to determine the distribution of load within a parallel system and the ability to adjust this distribution, the parallel computing machine will gain little over the traditional von Neumann machine for computation of inhomogeneous numeric or symbolic problems.

Decomposition of a problem for proper load balance can be considered in two parts: static and dynamic. Static load balance occurs at the time when a work is initially distributed among the processing elements of the parallel machine. Decisions on the decomposition of a problem are based on the requirement of computational resource (memory and CPU) and the amount of communication between data elements. Dynamic load balance occurs during the course of a program: as processors become inactive due to unequal distribution of workload, a load balancing mechanism first observes the lack of activity and then modifies the load to improve balance throughout the system.

In the past, it has been the responsibility of the applications programmer to assure that computing tasks were distributed adequately across the hypercube processors. For homogeneous problems sufficient load balance has been relatively easy to achieve; however, for inhomogeneous problems the task has not been as simple. It is often difficult, if not impossible, to predict locations of heavy resource requirements. Once a program demonstrates a lack of balance, the programmer has been required to determine a better initial decomposition of the problem. There has been no automatic means of dynamically moving processing load from overloaded processors to less loaded ones. Moreover, because of the nature of inhomogeneous problems, a distribution strategy which works for one set of input data may not be appropriate for another.

Load balancing is an ongoing task with joint participation by Caltech and JPL funded by the Joint Tactical Fusion Program Office. The objective of this effort is to develop the tools for achieving automatic dynamic load balance throughout the hypercube concurrent architecture. Some of the research into load balancing algorithms has made a strong analogy to physics by drawing a similarity between the statistical methods used to lower temperature of a physical system and those which can be used in a computing system where system temperature is represented as a function of the sum of the computational and communication load.

The current research on load balancing has emphasized experimentation with problems which demonstrate a high level of load imbalance such as irregular finite elements, particular dynamics, non-equilibrium thermodynamics, and an evolving population simulation. This experimentation has included implementation of sequential load balancing algorithms. These algorithms draw an analogy between the mechanism required for restoring balance within a poorly distributed computing system to that used for attaining minimum temperature and equilibrium within a physical system. In the physical system a slow annealing process is used; by using a Monte Carlo technique, the Metropolis algorithm, the same process can be simulated within the computing system.

A second component of the load balancing effort has been in area of operating system enhancement. The MOOOS (Multi-tasking object-oriented) operating system has completed design specifications. This system is the environment for implementation of an automatic dynamic load balancer.

As described below the important aspects of this research are general optimization methods and the development of an appropriate operating system MOOOS for a dynamic load balancer.

Optimization Theory
R. Williams (Staff Scientist)

Williams is working on the theoretical aspects of optimization for load-balancing purposes. In many cases, a problem can be expressed as a set of communicating tasks with different amounts of work and inter-task communication, and the job of the load-balancer is to decide how to position the tasks among the processors of a parallel computer. We can write down a Hamiltonian, which is a function which takes a partitioning and produces the inefficiency of the computation for that partitioning. The load-balancing problem is thus a minimization of the Hamiltonian with respect to assignment of tasks to processors.

Simulated annealing is a stochastic method of minimizing a function of many variables with many local minima, and is analogous to the slow cooling of the system to zero temperature. Random changes are made to the assignment of tasks, and a change is accepted if the Hamiltonian decreases. The change may also be accepted for an increased Hamiltonian: at high temperature such changes are almost always accepted, at low temperature almost never. Gradually the acceptance criterion is tightened (the temperature lowered), so that if the cooling is slow enough, the Hamiltonian will reach its global minimum at zero temperature.

Unfortunately it is not known in general how to choose the cooling schedule to make the Hamiltonian reasonably close to the global minimum in a reasonably short time. Simulated annealing is based on statistical physics, and for any physical annealing process, a condition known as detailed balance must hold, which is equivalent to time-reversal symmetry. For minimization, however, we are not interested in a correct simulation of statistical physics, and we have shown that abandoning detailed balance can lead to much faster convergence.

Simulated annealing is defined in terms of changes of the Hamiltonian resulting from a change in its arguments. If the annealing is taking place in a parallel computer, it is impractical to broadcast the results of each move to all processors affected by it, and would be much easier to make many changes before communicating them. We have shown that this easy method only slightly degrades the performance of the algorithm, for a Hamiltonian derived from a particular class of load-balancing problems.

For a dynamic load balancer the optimization problem is more complicated, since there must be a control system deciding how much and when optimization should be done, and the operation of this system depends on the method of choosing a cooling schedule. In addition, there is a cost associated with moving tasks from one processor to another, which adds a kind of "friction" to the process. Work is in progress on these matters.

MOOOS
J. Salmon, J. Flower, S. Callahan (Graduate Students); A. Kolawa (Staff Scientist)

MOOOS is a multi-tasking operating system under development on the Mark II hypercube. Its primary feature allows the user to schedule asynchronous "tasks" on the nodes of the hypercube. A task is a process with its own local variables, but which shares external names with the other tasks running on the same node. A task may be invoked with arguments, and may return values which are subsequently retrieved either by its creator, or any other task.

Communication in MOOOS is intended to be primarily via task creation and return. Mailboxes are also provided through which tasks may maintain an ongoing dialogue.

Although developed on the Mark II machine, MOOOS is reasonably portable. We have adopted Mark Johnson's protocol for asynchronous communication, often called the "nine routines". This protocol has already been implemented on the Mark III as the lowest layer of the Mercury O/S. It should be straightforward to implement on the NCUBE.

A working version of MOOOS exists, capable of creating tasks on arbitrary nodes, and returning results. Scheduling in not "preemptive", so tasks must cooperate and relinquish control of the CPU of their own accord.

Work is continuing in several directions:

- Implementation of mailboxes

- Design and implementation of a task grouping mechanism, whereby several tasks plus data they share can be bound into a "team". Such a team would constitute an indivisible unit, and would be a candidate for load balancer initiated relocation, on a machine with memory management. The data in a team would be "protected" from outside interference.

- Reanalysis of the design of the communication system. By providing another layer of "pipes" between Mark Johnson's protocol and the multi-tasking system, we may gain a great deal in terms of simplicity, modularity and extensibility with little or no performance penalty.

- Testing a "real" program. The ray tracer will probably be the first program run under MOOOS (not counting toy test programs).

Appendix 2: Quantum Field Theory on the Hypercube

This lists Caltech research using the hypercube for numerical quantum field theory in approximately chronological order.

Authors	Project	Hypercube	Reference
Brooks, Fox, Otto Randeria, Athas De Benedictis, Newton, Seitz	Glueball mass	Mk I 4 node	1
Otto, Randeria	Glueball mass, modified action	Mk I 4 node	2
Otto, Stack	Static quark potential (Meson) 12^3 x 16 lattice	Mk I 64 node	3
Otto, Stolorz	Glueball mass, enhanced statistics 12^3 x 16 lattice	Mk I 64 node	4

Fucito, Soloman	Chiral symmetry breaking | finite Deconfinement transition | temperature Mass spectrum	| pseudo | fermion |	Mk II 64 node	5 5 6
Patel, Otto, Gupta	Monte Carlo renormalization group. Nonperturbative β-function		Mk I 64 node	7
Flower, Otto, Martin	Finite temperature deconfinement | 4 light quark flowers |	Langevin	Mk II 32 node	Unpublished
Flower, Otto	Energy density, heavy meson		Mk II 32 node	8
Flower, Otto	Static quark potential (Meson) 20^4 lattice. Scaling		Mk II 128 node	9
Kolawa, Furmanski	Glueball mass (su(2)). Hamiltonian "loop" formalism		Mk II 32 node	10
Stolorz, Otto	Microcanonical renormalization Group		Mk I 64 node	11
Flower	Static quark potential (Baryon) 20^4 lattice		Mk II 128 node	In progress
Flower	Energy density (Baryon)		Mk II 32 node	In progress
Flower	Restoration of rotational symmetry		Mk II 128 node	12
Flower, Otto, Martin	Static quark potential (Meson). Four light flavors by Langevin method		INTEL iPSC 64 node	In progress

Hypercube Computer Research at the University of Michigan

J. P. HAYES*, R. JAIN*, W. R. MARTIN†, T. N. MUDGE*,
L. R. SCOTT‡, K. G. SHIN* AND Q. F. STOUT*

Abstract Since 1984, the Advanced Computer Architecture Laboratory (ACAL) at the University of Michigan has been developing a research program concerned with the architecture and application of high-performance parallel computers. ACAL operates a 64-processor NCUBE/six hypercube acquired under a beta-site agreement with the manufacturer. This paper describes our early experiences with a hypercube research facility, and also surveys our current research activities in the following areas: performance evaluation, parallel algorithms, fault-tolerant computing, computer vision, and scientific computation.

1. Introduction

The concept of a hypercube computer can be traced to work in the early 1960's by Squire and Palais at the University of Michigan [Squire and Palais 1963]. They carried out a detailed paper design of a 4096-node (12-dimensional) hypercube in which, as noted by Thurber, "hardware considerations and hardware economy were secondary considerations to the ease of programming" [Thurber 1976]. The hardware requirements of the Squire-Palais machine were estimated to be 20 times those of the IBM Stretch, one of the largest and most complex computers then in existence. Although several large hypercube computers were subsequently proposed, notably CHOPP by Sullivan and his colleagues at Columbia University [Sullivan et al. 1977], such machines did not become practical until the 1980's when VLSI technology made it feasible to produce powerful single-chip 16/32-bit microprocessors, and RAM chips in the 1M-bit range. In 1985 three manufacturers, Intel, Ametek and NCUBE, introduced the first commercial hypercubes. Also in that year, the Advanced Computer Architecture Laboratory (ACAL) of the University of Michigan obtained a 64-processor NCUBE/six hypercube made by NCUBE Corp., and has since then served as the sole university-based beta site for this machine.

---
*Department of Electrical Engineering and Computer Science, University of Michigan, Ann Arbor, Michigan 48109. †Department of Nuclear Engineering, University of Michigan, Ann Arbor, Michigan 48109. ‡Departments of Computer Science and Mathematics, Pennsylvania State University, University Park, Pennsylvania 16802.

The organization of ACAL's hypercube research facility is shown in Fig. 1. The hypercube nodes are based on a VAX-like 32-bit microprocessor with full IEEE-standard floating-point capability. Each node has 128K bytes of local RAM storage and 11 high-speed (1M byte/sec) input-output channels. Ten of these channels can be connected to neighboring nodes in the hypercube, thus allowing the NCUBE machine to be expanded to a 1024-node hypercube. An additional channel links each node to a host processor based on the Intel 80286, which manages the I/O system and the UNIX-like AXIS operating system. The programming languages supported are Fortran 77 and C, both with message-passing extensions, and NCUBE assembly language.

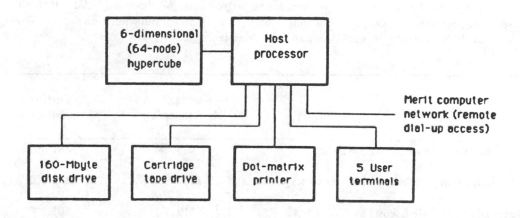

FIG. 1.   The hypercube research facility at Michigan's Advanced Computer Architecture Laboratory as of Sept. 1986.

ACAL is concerned with research into the theory, design, and application of advanced computers, especially massively parallel architectures. It draws its membership primarily from the Computer Science Engineering division of the Electrical Engineering and Computer Science Department at the University of Michigan, but also has participants from the Mathematics and Nuclear Engineering Departments. Current research efforts are concentrated in the following areas: performance evaluation, parallel algorithms, fault-tolerant computing, computer vision, scientific computation. Recent and planned work in each of these areas is discussed in the remainder of this paper.

2. Performance Evaluation

Performance analyses attempt to quantify the behavior of a computer system—how many instructions can be executed per second, how quickly can data be retrieved from secondary storage, and so on. Our work at Michigan is pursuing three approaches to the performance analysis of distributed-memory machines. The first is collecting applications programs to be used as benchmarks. The second involves the creation of synthetic benchmarks, or synthetic workload generators (SWGs), by abstracting representative features from the benchmarks. Finally, the third involves taking the abstraction process further to develop analytical (usually stochastic) models of performance.

An important dichotomy in parallel machine architectures is that between machines with shared memory and those with distributed memory. The NCUBE/six and other hypercubes are representative of the class of parallel machines that have distributed local memories which can be accessed in normal memory access times. In contrast, accessing remote memory, i.e., memory associated with another CPU, takes an order of magnitude longer. Our work in performance evaluation is aimed at determining what limitations, if any, the local memory restriction places on the effectiveness of parallel machines, particularly, hypercubes. The initial phase of our work is concerned with developing a set of programs that can be used as benchmarks. These come from a wide variety of application areas, and draw heavily on the other research being performed at ACAL. Examples of functioning code that we have developed for the NCUBE/six include: synthetic benchmarks, specifically the Whetstone and Dhrystone programs [Hayes et al. 1986a,b]; matrix decomposition using standard Linpack routines; printed circuit board routing [Olukotun and Mudge 1986]; assorted image processing algorithms [Mudge and Abdel-Rahman 1987a,b]; problems in nuclear engineering using Monte Carlo simulation techniques [Martin et al. 1986]; sorting [Wagar 1986]; and machine learning.

Processor	Fortran Dhrystones/s	Fortran Whetstones/s*
NCUBE node processor at 8MHz	999	381,000
NCUBE node processor at 10MHz (est.)	1249	476,000
Intel 80286 (NCUBE host) at 8MHz with 80287 floating-point coprocessor	510	101,000
DEC VAX-11/780 with floating-point accelerator	741	426,000

*Double precision.

FIG. 2. Some performance measurements on the NCUBE node processor.

Figure 2 summarizes the results of some performance experiments, designed by Michigan student D. Winsor that compared the NCUBE node processor to two other CPU's with floating-point hardware: the Intel 80286/80287 (the NCUBE host processor served for this) and the DEC VAX-11/780 with a floating-point accelerator. The measurements were made with the NCUBE node and host processors running at 8 MHz. Extrapolated figures for the planned 10-MHz version of the NCUBE node processor are also given; they assume no wait states. Two widely used synthetic benchmark programs were employed in this study: the Dhrystone and the Whetstone codes. The Dhrystone benchmark is intended to represent typical system programming applications and contains no floating-point or vectorizable code. The original Dhrystone Ada code was translated into a Fortran 77 version with 32-bit integer arithmetic that attempted to preserve as much of the original program structure as possible. The Whetstone benchmark, which aims to represent scientific programs with many floating-point operations, was used in a double-precision Fortran 77 version that closely resembled the original Algol code. The Dhrystone results in Fig. 2 are reported in "Dhrystones per second," each of which corresponds roughly to one hundred Fortran statements executed per second. The Whetstone figures represent the number of hypothetical Whetstone instructions executed per second.

The communication delay associated with neighbor-to-neighbor message passing in the NCUBE/six is indicated by Fig. 3, which is based on measurements made on an image-processing application program. With a 6 MHz clock, each message incurs an overhead of about 0.5 ms, primarily due to message buffer copying and the internode communication protocols employed by Vertex, the resident operating system kernel responsible for the store-and-forward message-passing function in the NCUBE. While this overhead is small compared to that of most other commercial hypercubes, there are applications which require faster message passing. We are developing a set of fast communication routines for these applications that bypass the normal NCUBE message-buffering steps [Mudge, Buzzard and Abdel-Rahman 1986].

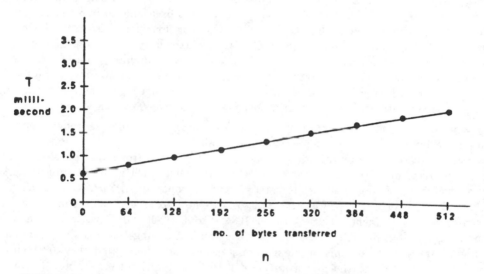

FIG. 3. Node-to-node communication delay T in sending an n-byte message.

3. Parallel Algorithms

The overall objective of this research is to design, analyze, and empirically measure the performance of a variety of parallel algorithms for solving nonumeric problems. It includes algorithms for sorting, routing, mapping graphs onto other graphs, optimization, computational geometry, and image processing. Approximation algorithms for NP-hard optimization problems are being developed with the general goal of obtaining efficient performance on distributed-memory medium-grained parallel machines, and the specific goal of efficient performance on hypercubes.

B. Wagar, a student at the University of Michigan has developed an internal sorting algorithm for the hypercube which has been measured to be significantly more efficient than Bitonic Sort [Wagar 1986]. For a hypercube of n processors each item is moved only $lg(n)$ times, instead of the approximately $lg^2(n)/2$ times required by Bitonic sort.

This sorting technique, which is called Hyperquicksort, is loosely based on Quicksort, and uses estimates for medians to reduce the number of times an individual data item must move. Like Quicksort, the partitioning may not be even, but with only a few hundred items per processor the observed average unevenness is quite small. We intend to push the analysis to prove that this is indeed the expected behavior, and to tune the algorithm for even better performance. We also intend to use Hyperquicksort to develop an external sort in which parallel disk I/O operations are used by the hypercube. The homogeneity of hypercubes encourages one to have a separate I/O channel into each node, but few algorithms have been developed which can utilize such a feature. The NCUBE hardware supports this, as do the FPS T-series machines to a lesser extent, and we expect that it will be widely supported in future hypercubes. For such a machine, efficient sort algorithms are likely to be important tools.

We have studied a variety of routing algorithms for specific message-passing tasks under a model of hypercubes in which the communication channels are the primary limiting factor and where each processor can use all of its channels simultaneously. This model is already approximately appropriate for the NCUBE series of machines, and other hypercube manufacturers are trying to develop nodes with this capability. We have shown optimal or nearly optimal algorithms for tasks such as broadcasting and transposing a matrix [Wagar and Stout 1986], but have not yet been able to implement them to determine the actual times. Slightly less efficient algorithms for these tasks have been developed at Yale [Saad and Schultz 1985]. One particularly interesting algorithm we have developed is a deterministic analogue of Valiant's randomized routing scheme for hypercubes [Valiant 1982]. Currently this requires that all processors know the routing permutation in advance, but we are also trying to find an efficient deterministic algorithm for the situation where the routing permutation is not known in advance.

The mapping of a task graph, where nodes represent modules and edges represent communication, onto a graph representing a parallel architecture, where nodes are processors and edges are communications links, is a well-studied problem in parallel processing. Typically one is trying to optimize some parameter, such as minimizing the maximum stretching of any edge, while satisfying some constraints, such as balancing the computational load of the processors. It is known how to map meshes, some trees, and pyramids onto hypercubes [Harary et al. 1986, Stout 1986], but little is known about mapping general graphs onto hypercubes. Stout and M. Livingston (a visiting scholar at Michigan) are working on this problem from several approaches. First they are trying to provide some bounds on the dimension needed to embed without stretching. For example it is proved in [Garey and Graham 1973] that if a bipartitite graph of n nodes can be embedded into some hypercube without stretching (in which case it is said to be *cubical*), then it can be embedded into a hypercube of dimension $n/2$ without stretching. We have extended this to show that if a graph of n vertices with minimum node degree 2 is cubical, then it can be embedded into a hypercube of dimension $2n/3$ without stretching, and further, this bound is the best possible.

Many computationally important problems in routing, scheduling, and packing are NP-hard optimization problems. Because they are NP-hard, there is an extensive literature on various serial approximation algorithms for such problems. There are also proposals to use special-purpose parallel computers for such problems [Hopfield and Tank 1986]. However, it is not clear how to blend such algorithms together to obtain ones suitable for medium-grained distributed-memory machines, and it seems that several approaches will be needed. In one project we use a 2-tier approach to do wire routing for printed circuit board design [Olukotun and Mudge 1986]. We assign a region of the circuit to each processor, and first use a high-level view which decides which regions each wire would cross. Then we use a local algorithm within each processor to route all the wires in the processor's region, making sure that boundaries matched properly. Once the parallel high-level algorithm has finished, each processor only needs to perform local computations or communications with a neighbor. This approach, which is also used on serial computers, matches medium-grained machines quite well, and seems to be applicable to other problems such as stereo matching of images.

A different approach is being used by a student R. Tanese in another research project. She is examining the neural network model, which has been suggested for optimization problems such as the traveling salesperson problem [Hopfield and Tank 1986]. This model sets up a "neural network" representing an instance of the problem, where some of the synaptic strengths in the network are somewhat randomly chosen, as are the initial neural activation levels. Then the model is iterated to produce a stable situation, which represents a solution which one hopes is legal and nearly optimal. To improve the solution, some of the strengths and/or activation levels are changed and the model is rerun.

4. Fault Tolerance

Fault tolerance, which is the ability to operate reliably in the presence of hardware of software failures, is a key requirement of high-performance computer systems in such areas as vehicle control and medical diagnosis. Its achievement requires comprehensive and fast testing of the system, detection and containment of error propagation, and reconfiguration to recover a fault-free operating condition. We have been conducting research for many years in the areas of fault modeling and test generation [Bhattacharya and Hayes 1985], error handling and fault tolerance models and techniques [Shin and Lee 1984], and recovery techniques for multiprocessors and distributed systems [Yanney and Hayes 1986, Lee and Shin 1984, Krishna and Shin 1986]. We are presently conducting an experimental evaluation [Woodbury and Shin 1986] of the error-handling characteristics of the FTMP and SIFT fault-tolerant multiprocessors at NASA's Langley Research Center. We have begun to study error detection and recovery in massively parallel distributed-memory systems using ACAL's NCUBE/six system. We are also experimenting with the design of test generation and fault simulation programs for execution on both hypercubes and vector processors (the Cray-XMP).

The fault coverage that is achievable by practical testing schemes is severely limited by the computational cost of generating the test patterns; this cost rapidly increases with circuit size. Dramatic improvement in test generation would be possible if many test patterns could be generated in parallel; almost no work has been done to date on such techniques, however. We are investigating the problem of parallel test-pattern generation for very complex digital systems. The major goal of this effort is to obtain extremely high fault coverage i.e., to maximize the percentage of faults that are detected or isolated. A Ph.D. student D. Bhattacharya is developing a new hierarchical approach to this problem that can analyze faults and generate test patterns for them at several different levels of complexity, such as the gate and register levels [Bhattacharya and Hayes 1985]. Thus, instead of dealing with all faults at the conventional single-line or bit level, this methodology can manipulate vectors of lines (buses) or bits so that many faults can be handled in parallel during test-pattern generation. This approach can reduce test generation time, while allowing up to 100 percent of the traditional stuck at-0/1 faults to be detected.

When an error is detected in a multiprocessor system, the source of this error must be quickly identified so as to correctly reconfigure the system and recover from the error successfully. We are attempting to establish an experimentally validated model for the study of error propagation in multiprocessors, including hypercubes, and to use this model for locating faults for a given detection mechanism. The basic component of the model is a unit with a single input and a single output. The error propagation property of the unit is characterized by a triplet (k, L, T), where k represents the pass rate, L the error latency, and T the error delay. The pass rate is the probability that an error in input will eventually induce an error in output. The error latency is measured from the time a fault occurred within the unit till an error was seen in output. The error delay is the time for an error to propagate from input to output within the unit. L and T are both random variables with distribution functions $F_L(\cdot)$ and $F_T(\cdot)$. The unit considered can represent any part of the system, i.e., it is not restricted to represent only processors, memories. It is useful to decompose the whole system into subsystems and model each subsystem as a unit. We are developing rules to combine two units into one larger unit so that once the properties of all subsystems are known, the property of the combined system can be derived. Due to the large number of units in a multiprocessor system, this combination often requires excessive computation. We have developed a parallel algorithm for the NCUBE/six to calculate F_L and F_T for each of n units which interact with one another in an arbitrary way.

Since faults occur randomly and infrequently, it is difficult to study the behavior of faults and errors in a multiprocessor system without an artificial mechanism of injecting faults. Based on our extensive experience in using the fault injector for the FTMP, we are investigating the design of an improved fault injector for a large-scale hypercube multiprocessor. It is to be flexible enough to accommodate the injection of various faults, e.g., permanent faults, transient faults with varying active durations, intermittent faults, and malicious faults. We plan to develop auxiliary software to collect and dump data into a secure device. This data will be used in our parallel investigation of error propagation modeling, system diagnosis, and error containment. As a starting point, we have designed a prototype software fault injector for the NCUBE/six at ACAL.

5. Computer Vision

This research is concerned with a variety of computation-intensive problems related to machine vision, image understanding, and their applications to such areas as sensor-based robot control. A major goal is to develop computer vision algorithms suitable for hypercube architectures in particular, and massively parallel architectures, in general. We are pursuing a new qualitative dynamic approach to image understanding which is based on exploiting redundant information. We wish to compare the performance of distributed-memory versus shared-memory multiprocessors for problems that involve reasoning about images. We are applying our results to problems in real-time control of robots with visual and other sensors as input.

The computational requirements of computer vision systems are extremely demanding, and are well suited to parallel processing. At the signal processing end, the number-crunching requirements may exceed several hundred MIPs (integer arithmetic), while at the cognitive end, very fast processing is also required. We have an extensive research effort at Michigan on dynamic vision [Jain 1984, Sethi and Jain 1986], range image understanding [Besl and Jain 1986] object recognition [Knoll and Jain 1986, Turney et al. 1985], and computer architecture for vision [Agrawal and Jain 1982, Miller and Stout 1985, Mudge and Abdel-Rahman 1987a,b]. We are presently addressing hypercube algorithm design and architectural issues related to some of the more computation-intensive aspects of computer vision.

Fast recognition of objects is one of the major goals of machine vision systems. We are studying object recognition using both range and intensity data. A major long term goal of this effort is to develop techniques that use range information for object recognition and navigation. Range images contain explicit information about surfaces. This explicit information facilitates recognition and location tasks in many applications. Our emphasis in range image understanding is on finding robust symbolic surface descriptors that will be independent of viewpoint. We are developing techniques to characterize surfaces in range images with these symbolic descriptors. We have designed two new methods to recognize objects: the feature-indexed hypotheses method [Knoll and Jain 1986]; and the saliency-based method [Turney et al. 1985]. The first method breaks the recognition process into two phases: hypotheses generation and hypothesis verification. By using features that occur more than once in the possible object set, the number of features in the search can be greatly reduced. This method also has the advantage that unique features, which are difficult or impossible to find if the object set contains many similar objects, are not required.

We view image understanding as a dynamic process, which allows us to cope with the error-filled visual world by exploiting the availability of redundant information in an image sequence. We are currently developing a qualitative approach to this aspect of computer vision. This approach uses relative information available in a sequence to infer the relationships among objects in a scene. In dynamic vision we are addressing the following issues: segmentation, image flow, motion stereo, trajectories, and architecture for dynamic vision. The need to deal with sequences of images makes dynamic scene analysis a strong candidate for parallel processing using hypercubes.

Our past work has shown how many low-level computer vision algorithms (e.g. filtering) and mid-level algorithms can be redesigned to take advantage of hypercube architectures [Miller and Stout 1986, Mudge and Abdel-Rahman 1987b]. We have successfully implemented on the NCUBE/six an algorithm for reconstructing in three dimensions the submicron surface topography of an integrated circuit [Kayaalp and Jain 1986]. Work is also under way to parallelize an existing solder-joint inspection program [Besl, Delp and Jain 1985] for the NCUBE. The inspection technique employed is a statistical pattern analysis method that uses objective dimensionality reduction to select inspection features. It requires us to design and write parallel algorithms for extracting various classes of features from an image. As well as being important to our particular inspection techniques, many of these algorithms are of general use in computer vision. Two other applications being considered are a parallel version of our bin-of-parts algorithm [Mudge and Abdel-Rahman 1983, Turney, et al. 1985], and the development of parallel programs to support our work in dynamic scene analysis.

6. Scientific Computation

This section describes several research projects concerned with the algorithm design and software implementation for scientific computing applications using both hypercubes and conventional vector processors. These projects embrace some of the research issues in areas of scientific computation where supercomputers are most used. The major topics of the current research effort at Michigan are reactor plant simulation, Monte Carlo transport algorithms, logic circuit simulation, and distributed data structures. This work also aims at obtaining new insights into the important question of the relative efficiency of distributed-memory and shared-memory machines for large-scale scientific computations.

We are investigating the development and implementation of a nuclear reactor plant simulation model on hypercube architectures. The goal is to obtain a fast-running (faster than real time), reasonably accurate reactor plant simulation model that can execute satisfactorily on a computer other than an expensive conventional supercomputer.

The cost/performance characteristics of massively parallel architectures such as the hypercube makes them an attractive candidate for such a simulation. The intent is to have an economical and reliable reactor plant model that could be used within an operating plant, perhaps as a standalone plant simulator or as a component within a larger expert system.

The principal research task here is to partition the simulation algorithm across the processors of the hypercubes. Thus, one can assign the reactor to one or more processors or clusters of processors, the steam generator(s) to another cluster, the pressurizer to another cluster, etc., and let each solve the pertinent equations for its specific component. Communication between clusters of processors is necessary due to the flow of the reactor coolant (density, enthalpy, pressure, velocity, etc.) and is being accomplished via message passing. The partitioning of the component models within each cluster of processors requires some new work. Since we have had substantial experience over the past 10 years developing reactor component and plant models [Feng, Lee, and Martin 1981; Baggoura and Martin 1983], this does not pose any major difficulties.

We are conducting research on the implementation of a photon transport Monte Carlo algorithm on the requested parallel processors. As opposed to other types of Monte Carlo methods, particle transport Monte Carlo is characterized by a considerable amount of floating-point arithmetic and is probably one of the most computation-intensive methods in scientific computation. This work is a natural extension of our previous successful efforts to develop vectorized Monte Carlo algorithms for the CDC Cyber-205 vector supercomputer; [Brown and Martin 1985], the Cray-XMP and Cray-2 supercomputers [Martin et al. 1986] and the IBM 3090/200 and /400 supercomputers, [Wan and Martin 1986]. To allow meaningful comparisons with the conventional algorithm, a conventional Monte Carlo code has also been developed and successfully benchmarked against a production-level photon transport code from Lawrence Livermore National Laboratory. At this time we have a series of realistic demonstration codes for Monte Carlo photon transport on vector supercomputers and parallel/vector supercomputers, as well as conventional sequential computers.

We have completed a number of preliminary experiments running a parallel Monte Carlo code for photon transport on the ACAL NCUBE/six [Martin, Wan and Mudge 1986]. As noted in [Martin et al. 1986], two alternative approaches were taken to develop parallelized algorithms for the NCUBE/six which made use of this change. Representative results will be given for one approach - replication of the problem on each of the processors. In this case, the entire code is replicated on each processor and the host processor reads in the input data, sends messages to each node describing the problem and giving the random seed, and receives the results from each node when it is done. Since each node receives a different random seed, it is possible to combine the results a posterior to produce a result which is equivalent to one large simulation. This is one great advantage of Monte Carlo, and this implementation simulates how a user might combine several smaller Monte Carlo calculations to achieve a result with better statistics. It should be noted that this results in a problem size that grows linearly with the number of processors. Figure 4 summarizes the results of simulations with a 49×40 mesh (1960 zones) with approximately 2700 photons per node. As can be seen, the performance is nearly linear with the number of nodes, as might be expected for this approach. Since the total elapsed time for N Monte Carlo calculations (with different random seeds) distributed to N nodes is a constant (approximately 205 s), it is clear that the maximum speedup is being observed, indicating that hypercubes are extremely well-suited to this application. The last column of Fig. 4 lists the number of microseconds to simulate (track) a single photon, a commonly-used performance measure in this area. Comparable figures obtained for the optimal scalar code ($2\times$ faster) on conventional vector processors are 35 μsec/track (Cray-XMP/48) and 40 μsec/track (IBM 3090 and Fujitsu VP-200).

No. of nodes N	Processing time T_S	Elapsed time T_E	μsec/track
1	195	205	4920
2	195	204	2448
4	195	204	1224
8	195	205	615
16	195	205	308
32	195	204	158
64	195	205	78

FIG. 4.   Performance of Monte Carlo photon transport program on the NCUBE/six.

We are also examining ways to automate the programming of algorithms that utilize distributed data structures in scientific computation [Scott, Boyle and Bagheri 1986]. This research involves introduction of language extensions to Fortran that allow code on one processor to access variables explicitly (by name only) that are stored in another processor. In our implementations to date, code written with these extensions is then converted into appropriate message-passing code via a preprocessor. (Implementations have been done for both the NCUBE and Intel hypercubes). Not only does this approach free the programmer from having to write the message-passing code each time, it assures that it will be done correctly. So far, experiments have been carried out for simple iterative and direct methods for solving linear equations, which is the most computationally intensive part of many scientific computation codes. More complex algorithms are currently being coded in the extended language and tested on the NCUBE/six.

References

(1)   B. BAGGOURA and W.R. MARTIN, *Transient Analysis of the TMI-2 Pressurizer System*, Nuclear Technology, vol. 62, 1983, p. 159.

(2)   P. BESL, E. DELP and R. JAIN, *Automatic Visual Solder Joint Inspection*, IEEE J. on Robotics and Automation, vol. 1, no. 1, 1985, p. 42-56.

(3)   P. BESL and R. JAIN, *Invariant Surface Characteristics for 3-D Object Recognition in Depth Maps*, Computer Vision, Graphics and Image Processing, vol. 33, 1986, pp. 33-80.

(4)   D. BHATTACHARYA and J.P. HAYES, *High-level Test Generation Using Bus Faults*, Proc. 15th Fault-Tolerant Computing Symp., June 1985, pp. 65-71.

(5) F.B. BROWN and W.R. MARTIN, *Monte Carlo Methods on Vector Computers*, Prog. in Nuclear Energy, vol. 14, 1985, p. 269.

(6) M.-S. CHEN and K.G. SHIN, *Embedding of Interacting Task Modules Into a Hypercube Multiprocessor*, submitted to SIAM J. on Computer, to appear Sept. 1986.

(7) M.-S. CHEN and K.G. SHIN, *Determination of a Minimal Subcube for Interacting Task Modules*, presented at Second Conf. on Hypercube Multiprocessors, Knoxville, Tenn., Sept./Oct. 1986 (these Proceedings).

(8) Y.C. FENG, J.C. LEE and W.R. MARTIN, *Nonequilibrium Transient Two-phase Flow Modeling and Analysis*, Trans. Am. Nucl. Soc., vol. 39, 1981, p. 505.

(9) M.R. GAREY and R.L. GRAHAM, *On Cubical Graphs*, J. Combin. Theory A, 18, 1973, pp. 263-267.

(10) F. HARARY, J.P. HAYES and P. WU, *A Survey of the Theory of Cube Graphs*, Sept. 1986, submitted for publication.

(11) J.P. HAYES, T.N. MUDGE, Q.F. STOUT, S. COLLEY and J. PALMER, *The Architecture of a Hypercube Supercomputer*, Proc. 1986 Intl. Conf. on Parallel Processing, Aug. 1986a, pp. 653-660.

(12) J.P. HAYES, T.N. MUDGE, Q.F. STOUT, S. COLLEY and J. PALMER, *A Microprocessor-Based Hypercube Supercomputer*, IEEE Micro, vol. 6, no. 5, Oct. 1986b, pp. 6-17.

(13) J.J. HOPFIELD and D.W. TANK, *Computing With Neural Circuits: a Model*, Science, vol. 233, 1986, pp. 625-633.

(14) R. JAIN, *Segmentation of Frame Sequences Obtained By a Moving Observer*, IEEE Trans. PAMI, Sept. 1984, pp. 624-629.

(15) A.I. KAYAALP and R. JAIN, *The Parallel Implementation of an Algorithm for 3-D Reconstruction of IC Pattern Topography Using SEM Stereo on the NCUBE Machine*, presented at Second Conf. on Hypercube Multiprocessors, Knoxville, Tenn., Sept./Oct. 1986 (these Proceedings).

(16) N. KHAN and R. JAIN, *Uncertainty Management in a Distributed Base System*, Proc. Intl. Joint Conf. on Artificial Intelligence, Los Angeles, Aug. 1985, pp. 318-320.

(17) T.F. KNOLL and R. JAIN, *Recognizing Partially Visible Objects Using Feature Indexed Hypothesis*, IEEE J. Robotics and Automation, vol 2, 1986, pp. 3-13.

(18) C.M. KRISHNA and K.G. SHIN, *On Scheduling Tasks with a Quick Recovery from Failure*, IEEE Trans. Computers, vol. C-35, May 1986, pp. 448-455.

(19) Y.H. LEE and K.G. SHIN, *Design and Evaluation of a Fault-tolerant Multiprocessor Using Hardware Recovery Blocks*, IEEE Trans. Computers, vol. C-33, Feb. 1984, pp. 113-124.

(20) W.R. MARTIN et al., *Monte Carlo Photon Transport on a Vector Supercomputer*, IBM Jour. of Res. and Dev., March 1986a.

(21) W.R. MARTIN, D. POLAND, T.C. WAN, T.N. MUDGE and T.S. ABDEL-RAHMAN, *Monte Carlo Photon Transport on the NCUBE*, presented at Second Conf. on Hypercube Multiprocessors, Knoxville, Tenn., Sept./Oct. 1986b (these Proceedings).

(22) R. MILLER and Q.F. STOUT, *Geometric Algorithms for Digitized Pictures on a Mesh-connected Computer*, IEEE Trans. Pattern Analysis and Machine Intelligence, vol. PAMI-7, 1985, pp. 216-228.

(23) R. MILLER and Q.F. STOUT, *Data Movement Operations for Mesh-of-trees and Hypercube Computers*, submitted for publication, 1986.

(24) T.N. MUDGE and T.S. ABDEL-RAHMAN, *Case Study of a Program for the Recognition of Occluded Parts*, Proc. 2nd Annual IEEE Workshop on Computer Architecture for Pattern Analysis and Image Data Base Mangement, Pasadena, CA, Oct. 1983, pp. 56-60.

(25) T.N. MUDGE, *The Next Generation of Hypercube Computers*, Proc. of ARO Workshop on Future Directions in Computer Architecture and Software, May 1986.

(26) T.N. MUDGE, G.D. BUZZARD and T.S. ABDEL-RAHMAN, *A High-Performance Operating System for the NCUBE*, presented at Second Conf. on Hypercube Multiprocessors, Knoxville, Tenn., Sept./Oct. 1986 (these Proceedings).

(27) T.N. MUDGE, and T.S. ABDEL-RAHMAN, *Architectures for Robot Vision*, Specialized Computer Architectures for Robotics and Automation, Ed: J. Graham, Publ: Gordon and Breach, Inc., 1987a, (to appear).

(28) T.N. MUDGE and T.S. ABDEL-RAHMAN, *Vision Algorithms for Hypercube Machines*, Journal of Parallel and Distributed Computer, 1987b, (to appear).

(29) T.N. MUDGE, J.P. HAYES, G.D. BUZZARD and D.C. WINSOR, *Analysis of Multiple-bus Interconnection Networks*, Journal of Parallel and Distributed Computing, 1987, (to appear).

(30) O.A. OLUKOTUN, and T.N. MUDGE, *Parallel Routing on a Hypercube Computer*, submitted to the 24th Design Automation Conf., 1987.

(31) Y. SAAD and M.H. SCHULTZ, *Data Communication in Hypercubes*, Tech. Rept., YALU/DCS/RR-428, Dept. of Computer Science, Yale U., 1985.

(32) L.R. SCOTT, J.M. BOYLE and B. BAGHERI, *Distributed Data Structures* for Scientific Computation, presented at Second Conf. on Hypercube Multiprocessors, Knoxville, Tenn., Sept./Oct. 1986 (these Proceedings).

(33) I.K. SETHI and R. JAIN, *Finding Trajectories of Feature Points in a Monocular Image Sequence*, IEEE Trans. PAMI, Nov. 1986.

(34) K.G. SHIN and Y.-H. LEE, *Error Detection Process: Model, Design, and Its Impact on Computer Performance*, IEEE Trans. Computers, vol. C-33, June 1984, pp. 529-540.

(35) K.G. SHIN and Y.-H. LEE, *Evaluation of Recovery Blocks Used for Cooperating Processes*, IEEE Trans. Software Engineering, vol. SE-10, Nov. 1985, pp. 692-700.

(36) J.S. SQUIRE and S.M. PALAIS, *Programming and Design Considerations for a Highly Parallel Computer*, AFIPS Conf. Proc., vol. 23, 1963 SJCC, pp. 395-400.

(37) Q.F. STOUT and B. WAGAR, *Passing Messages in Link-bound Hypercubes*, presented at Second Conf. on Hypercube Multiprocessors, Knoxville, Tenn., Sept./Oct. 1986 (these Proceedings).

(38) Q.F. STOUT, *Hypercubes and Pyramids*, in Pyramidal Systems for Image Processing and Computer vision, V. Cantoni and S. Levialdi, eds., NATA ASI Series ARW, Springer-Verlag, 1986, to appear.

(39) H. SULLIVAN and T.R. BASHKOW, *A Large Scale, Homogeneous, Fully Distributed Parallel Machine, I*, Proc. 4th Ann. Symp. on Computer Architecture, 1977, pp. 105-117.

(40) K.J. THURBER, *Large Scale Computer Architecture*, Hayden, Rochelle Park, NJ., 1976.

(41)   J.L. TURNEY, T.N. MUDGE and R.A. VOLZ, *Recognizing Partially Occluded Parts,* IEEE Trans. on Pattern Analysis and Machine Intelligence, vol. PAMI-7, July 1985, pp. 410-421.

(42)   L.G. VALIANT, *A Scheme for Parallel Communication,* SIAM J. Computing, vol. 11, May 1982, pp. 350-361.

(43)   B. WAGAR, *Hyperquicksort—a Fast Sorting Algorithm for Hypercubes,* presented at Second Conf. on Hypercube Multiprocessors, Knoxville, Tenn., Sept./Oct. 1986 (these Proceedings).

(44)   T.C. WAN and W.R. MARTIN, *Parallel Algorithms for Photon Transport Monte Carlo,* accepted for presentation at the Winter meeting of the American Nuclear society, Washington, DC, Nov. 1986.

(45)   M.H. WOODBURY and K.G. SHIN, *Performance Modeling and Measurement of Real-time Multiprocessors with Time-shared Buses,* IEEE Trans. on Computers, 1986, (to appear).

(46)   R. YANNEY and J.P. HAYES, *Distributed Recovery in Fault-tolerant Multiprocessor Networks,* IEEE Trans. on Computers, vol. C-35, Oct. 1986, pp. 871-879.

Hypercube Applications at Oak Ridge National Laboratory

MICHAEL T. HEATH*

Abstract. To determine the viability of hypercube architectures for solving a broad spectrum of computational problems typically arising at Oak Ridge National Laboratory, a representative set of applications was chosen for implementation on a hypercube. The projects included finite element fracture analysis, cascade simulation, geochemical contaminant transport, image analysis, molecular dynamics of polymers, density functional theory, and nonlinear magnetohydrodynamics. Each project was a collaborative effort of scientists and engineers from the discipline in which the problem arose and experienced hypercube users from a parallel computing research group. Results of each of these projects and an overall summary are included in this report.

Introduction. Parallel computing is expected to provide the vastly increased computational capacity that will be needed for the complex scientific and engineering problems of the future. That potential remains to be proven, however, in widespread practice. Of course, there have been a few pioneers actively investigating various aspects of parallelism in computation for years, but these efforts have had little concrete impact on the everyday computational work of practicing scientists and engineers.

Our principal past experience with the effect of a major new architectural paradigm on existing "dusty deck" programs was the introduction of vector computers several years ago. Some users have cleverly exploited vector architectures to obtain very high performance, and smart compilers have been devised that do a reasonably good job of vectorizing codes automatically. Nevertheless, the vast bulk of "off-the-shelf" programs do not approach peak performance on vector computers; indeed, efficiencies as low as 10% to 20% are not uncommon.

---

* Mathematical Sciences Section, Oak Ridge National Laboratory, P.O. Box Y, Oak Ridge, Tennessee 37831. Research supported by the U.S. Department of Energy under contract DE-AC05-84OR21400 with Martin Marietta Energy Systems Inc.

Thus, to tap the seemingly unlimited potential performance of multiprocessor architectures, we must face the somewhat daunting prospect of major code conversions and the burden of attaining reasonably efficient use of a large number of processors. Some experience has already been obtained in developing applications codes for multiprocessors, for example in an academic environment at Caltech [9]. Most experience to date in a large research laboratory setting has been with multiprocessors having a small number of very powerful processors sharing a large memory, typified by the Cray X-MP and Cray 2. Much less is known about adapting existing programs to architectures with a much larger number of processors and having only local-memory, so that the data as well as the computational work must be partitioned across processors. In any case, each laboratory and research center must try to anticipate the effect of potential new architectures on its own computational work load.

Oak Ridge National Laboratory (ORNL) has a large and diverse community of scientists and engineers, most of whom use traditional minicomputers, mainframes, and supercomputers for their computational needs. There are a few small research groups within ORNL, however, that have a long-standing interest in more advanced computer architectures. Two groups have taken a particular interest in hypercube architectures, and ORNL was among the first to obtain both Intel and NCUBE hypercubes, which were the earliest hypercubes commercially available. The Intel hypercube is used primarily by the Mathematical Sciences Section for research on parallel numerical algorithms, but is also available for general use throughout ORNL. The NCUBE hypercube is dedicated to robotics research in the Center for Engineering Systems Advanced Research (CESAR). Although the experience of these two groups in using hypercubes has been very favorable, their work is not necessarily representative of the computational needs of the laboratory as a whole.

To determine the viability of multiprocessors in general, and hypercubes in particular, for solving a wide spectrum of general computational problems arising at ORNL, a series of hypercube applications projects was initiated involving participants from throughout the laboratory. The expected benefits of this enterprise were as follows:

- To determine ORNL's degree of interest in future, more powerful hypercubes and other multiprocessors

- To identify difficulties in adapting existing codes and in developing new ones

- To spread multiprocessing expertise throughout the laboratory

- To enhance laboratory readiness for new architectures of the future

- To develop new ideas and uncover new areas for basic research in parallel computing

Project proposals were informally solicited from throughout ORNL. As an inducement for busy researchers to divert their time and resources away from their normal tasks, funding was secured from the Exploratory Studies Program of

ORNL that was adequate to support seven projects at a level of one-half person-year each. The selection of projects was not based on any prior assessment of their suitability for parallel implementation. There may still be some bias in the sample of projects, however, since the volunteer proposers would naturally tend to be exceptionally interested in trying new architectures and would presumably believe their projects were amenable to parallel implementation.

The seven projects represented seven different divisions of the laboratory. Six of the proposers had little prior experience with multiprocessing, and no experience with hypercubes, so a member of the Mathematical Sciences staff was assigned to each project to collaborate with the project originators in developing a hypercube implementation. The one-half person-year total spent on each project included both the Mathematical Sciences personnel and the project originators from the various other divisions. Individual projects involved as few as two or as many as five participants. One proposal, on image analysis, was from CESAR, which had its own hypercube and ample prior experience, so their project was carried out on the NCUBE without a collaborator from Mathematical Sciences. The remaining six projects all used the Intel iPSC hypercube. Most of the projects began with an existing serial Fortran code to convert, at least in part, to the hypercube. Details on the individual projects are given in the following sections.

Finite Element Fracture Analysis. Finite element methods in structural analysis require the solution of a large, sparse, symmetric, positive definite system of linear equations in which a global stiffness matrix relates the unknown displacements to the applied load. The particular problem of interest in this project was the two-dimensional linear elastic stress and fracture analysis of a large steel boiler plate, in which both thermal and mechanical loadings may be included and special crack tip elements are used. A small example is shown in Fig. 1a, in which the plate is modeled by 28 8-node isoparametric elements and has a total of 202 unknown deflections. Once the deflections have been determined, then the stresses along the crack front can be computed.

The existing serial code ORVIRT [2] for solving this problem used the frontal solver of Hinton and Owen [15]. A frontal solver assembles the stiffness matrix element by element, eliminates unknowns as early as possible during assembly, and keeps only a relatively small "active" part of the "front" matrix in fast memory at a given time. Once the matrix has been factored, then the deflections are determined by back substitution. In order to modify the algorithm and data structures as little as possible in adapting this program to a multiprocessor environment, a multifrontal approach was used. The multifrontal approach has become popular in recent years even in serial computing environments because of its ability to reduce the size of the active front matrix, with a consequent reduction in storage requirements [19]. In a multiprocessor environment, the finite element mesh is partitioned among the processors so that there is one front on each processor. Thus, the original single-front code could be used on each processor with minimal modifications. A typical partitioning of the sample problem across four processors is shown in Fig. 1b.

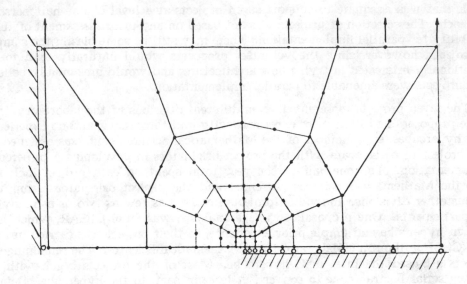

Fig. 1a. Finite element fracture analysis problem.

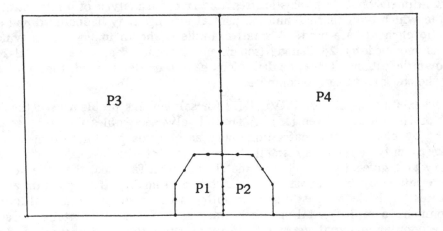

Fig. 1b. Partitioning of sample problem for four processors.

Although the multifrontal approach described above is conceptually simple, the pieces must still be sewn together to obtain the solution to the overall problem. In a distributed-memory architecture such as the hypercube, this phase requires communication among the processors in the form of message passing. The original single-front code running on each processor solves an entire subproblem, but only the host processor knows what the whole problem looks like. Thus, the host must reconstruct the mesh deflections given the deflections computed by individual processors for each piece.

The nodes on boundaries between pieces must be shared between processors. In order for each of the processors to determine its boundary conditions corresponding to these shared nodes, special composite elements, called "super boundary elements," are defined. Super boundary elements are assembled and exchanged pairwise between processors, in effect combining the fronts on the two processors. If there are p processors, then at each stage there are $p / 2$ such exchanges (which can be performed in parallel), and all fronts are combined after $\log_2(p)$ stages. The hypercube network interconnections are ideal for the communications required in this algorithm.

The algorithm just described requires some redundant computation. For example, the final super boundary element is the same for each processor, so all must compute the deflections corresponding to it. An advantage of this approach, however, is that no communication is required during the back substitution phase, and this saving can be significant for problems in which several load cases are applied to the same mesh (i.e., a single factorization followed by several back substitutions).

The ordering of the elements and the partitioning of the problem are critical to the efficiency of the multifrontal algorithm. Ideally, the storage, arithmetic, and communication requirements should all be minimized. This is an extremely difficult combinatorial optimization problem to solve exactly, but some effective heuristics are known. In neither our original serial frontal code nor its parallel multifrontal adaptation has this process been automated as yet; this is an area for future development.

The sample problem shown in Fig. 1a, using the partitioning shown in Fig. 1b, was solved on the Intel iPSC hypercube using four node processors plus the host. The overall execution time for the problem was reduced by 58% compared to that of the serial code running on the host, even though this parallel time includes such purely serial phases as host I/O, host-node communication, and the fracture analysis itself (recall that the parallel finite element phase produces only the deflections). For the purely parallel assembly and factorization portion of the problem, a superlinear speedup of 4.2 was observed. This unexpectedly favorable result was due to the fact that the multifrontal ordering had a somewhat lower operation count than the single-front ordering, so that the parallel code had an advantage beyond simply having more processors. Although this test problem and the number of processors used were quite small, when automated input allows the solution of much larger problems the results are expected to improve even further, since the number of nodes per processor grows much faster than the number of shared nodes as the size of the problem increases.

Participants in this project were John Clinard of the Engineering Technology Division and Al Geist of Mathematical Sciences. For further information, see [4] and [11].

Cascade Simulation. The problem originally posed for this project was the simulation of displacement cascades in radiation damage and similar phenomena such as particle channeling and sputtering of crystals by ion bombardment. The existing code MARLOWE [20] constructs trajectories of atomic particles moving in crystalline solids using the classical binary collision approximation. It is not a Monte Carlo code, but involves particle transport with multiplication so that many particles move simultaneously. The existing code is quite large (about 10,000 lines), having great generality and many detailed options.

Although conceptually this code appears to offer many opportunities for exploiting parallelism, its sheer size was somewhat forbidding considering the relatively "small" target environment of the Intel iPSC hypercube, with its limited access to peripheral resources. In particular, the individual processors have no disk space directly available to them; their only access to the outside world is through communication with the host. When the project began, the host processor had only a 40 megabyte disk and no tape drive, and the host-node communication rate was exceedingly slow (all have since been significantly upgraded, but the basic problem of node access to external data remains). Since the MARLOWE code requires access to a large data base of cross sections and similar information, any meaningful implementation of this code was well beyond the I/O capacity of the available Intel machine.

Having ruled out a direct implementation of the existing serial code, it was decided that the remaining effort on this project would be devoted to another major technical problem that occurs in adapting any Monte Carlo-like "particle pushing" simulation code to a multiprocessor environment, namely the generation of multiple parallel sequences of pseudorandom numbers. Not only should such sequences have suitable statistical properties within themselves, the individual parallel sequences must be independent of one another if the simulation results are to be meaningful. At the same time, one would also like to retain reproducibility of results if possible.

One of the most widely used methods for generating uniformly distributed pseudorandom numbers is the linear congruential method [16], in which, beginning from some initial "seed," each member of the integer sequence is computed by multiplying the previous member by a constant multiplier, adding a constant increment, and retaining only the low-order portion of the result. With suitably chosen constants, such a method yields a reasonably long cyclic sequence of integers with the desired statistical properties. Frederickson *et al* [10] proposed an extension of these methods for generating multiple streams of pseudorandom numbers using the concept of a pseudorandom or Lehmer tree. In addition to the standard "right" sequence generated by the linear congruential method, they also define an auxiliary "left" sequence that in effect generates seeds for each parallel process, and these seeds are guaranteed to yield disjoint sequences.

Although the parallel sequences generated by the Lehmer tree method are disjoint, they still could be highly correlated in practice, in which case they would be of limited use for the intended purpose. Thus, an empirical study was undertaken to determine the extent to which such sequences might be correlated. Two separate test programs were written, one in assembler language for a Data General Eclipse and a second in Fortran that was run on both a DEC VAX 11/780 and a Cray X-MP. Both studies demonstrated substantial correlations among the parallel sequences. These correlations turned out to be a direct consequence of the relatively small number of bits which participate in the left sequences. In this respect the empirical results are consistent with the studies of Marsaglia [17], [18]. Of course, such correlations might not be detrimental to some types of simulations, but it is easy to imagine problems in which underlying symmetries would render the results useless.

In seeking to remedy the correlations observed in the Lehmer tree method, several modifications and alternatives were considered. For example, unrelated left and right sequences could be used. Unfortunately, no conclusions can be drawn concerning disjointness of the resulting sequences, but at least empirically the sequences appear to be uncorrelated. Another approach effectively parcels out a single sequence over multiple processors. This also appears to yield uncorrelated results, but care must be taken to avoid the interprocess communication that is implied, at least conceptually. Although they appear to show promise, these and other alternatives require further study.

This project did not result in a code for the hypercube, but it did identify two important problems that must be solved in order for such an implementation to be possible: massive I/O capability in the hypercube nodes and the generation of parallel sequences of pseudorandom numbers. Progress on the former awaits further developments by hypercube manufacturers. Significant progress on the latter was made, although further study is warranted.

Participants in this project were Mark Robinson of the Solid State Division and Kim Bowman of Mathematical Sciences. For further information, see [1].

Geochemical Contaminant Transport. The disposal and containment of hazardous wastes pose a growing technical and policy-making challenge to society on national and global scales. Evaluation of the migration potential of pollutants requires an understanding of the chemical and hydrologic processes responsible for release, transport, and fixation of contaminants in the environment. Quantitative computer models describing the effects of chemical and hydrologic processes on pollutant mobility help in gaining a better understanding of contaminant transport and are invaluable in selecting disposal sites and assessing alternatives for remedial action. Unfortunately, such models tend to be highly complex and extremely computationally intensive, and therefore are very expensive when applied to realistic problems on conventional computers.

HYDROGEOCHEM [24] is a coupled contaminant transport model that permits calculation of the distribution in space and time of dissolved contaminants as a function of chemical properties and processes responsible for release, transport, and retardation of contaminants (Fig. 2a). It uses a finite element formulation for

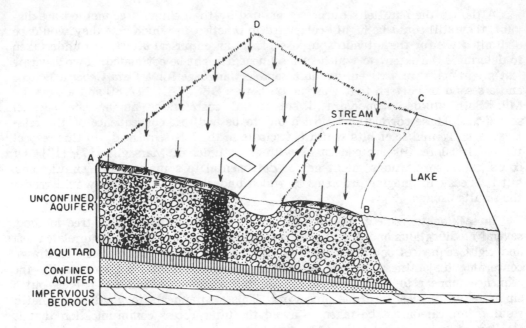

Fig. 2a. Geochemical contaminant transport problem.

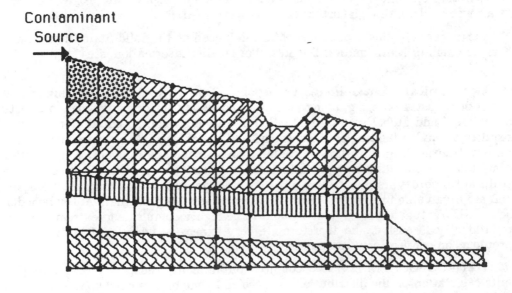

Fig. 2b. Finite element transport model with chemical model at each node.

solving the contaminant transport problem (Fig. 2b). After each time step of the transport problem, the chemical equilibria must be updated. In the serial code, this chemical submodel consumes 90-95% of the execution time. Fortunately, in this model formulation the chemical reactions at a given node of the finite element mesh (representing geographical points) can be computed independently of those at other nodes of the mesh, and thus the costly chemical submodel is an ideal candidate for parallel implementation.

A complete parallel implementation of HYDROGEOCHEM to include the transport submodel was beyond the scope of the immediate project. Thus, the serial transport program was run on the host processor, with the the hypercube being used as an attached processor for updating the chemical submodel. An unfortunate consequence is that, although the chemical submodel requires no communication among the node processors, a significant amount of communication is required between the host and node processors. Initially, a large data base of possible reacting chemicals is sent to each node processor. After this one-time cost, the transport model is updated in successive time steps on the host. After each such step the new concentrations are sent to the node processors, where new chemical equilibria are computed and the results sent back to the host in preparation for the next transport step.

When the project was begun, communication between host and nodes on the Intel iPSC was very slow and somewhat unreliable (this has improved significantly since, but host-node communication remains something of a bottleneck). Thus, a polling discipline was imposed on communication between host and nodes; the host queries each node in turn for results. As expected, the highly parallel chemical submodel attains virtually 100% utilization of the node processors during the chemical update, but the slow and cumbersome communication procedure between host and nodes degrades the overall performance of the code. The chemical submodule, which consumed 90-95% of the execution time in the serial code, now consumes only a small fraction of the total time. Even with the high communication overhead necessitated by this implementation and the modest power of the 80286/80287 processors of the iPSC, the parallel version is competitive with the serial version running on a VAX 8600.

The solution to these difficulties, of course, is a complete parallel implementation of the transport submodule so that the computation would remain distributed among the node processors throughout and host-node communication would be eliminated. A second benefit would be the speeding up of the transport module by using multiple processors on it as well. The finite element nodes could be assigned to the processors by dividing the mesh into strips. Each processor would hold the data associated with a number of finite element nodes and would be responsible for alternately updating the transport and chemical submodels for those nodes. The distributed transport computation would require communication between processors across mesh boundaries, but such communication would be far less in volume than that required by the current implementation, and would itself be performed in parallel (since distinct pairs of nodes would be communicating rather than always involving the host).

Another limitation of the current implementation is imposed by the relatively small amount of memory available on the node processors. Currently, each node must store an active chemical data base in its memory. The chemical data base could conceivably be spread across the processors, but this would entail a significant amount of communication between nodes in order to access it. The memory limitation will become even more severe when the code is fully parallel, since then each node will have to store a portion of the finite element mesh and the code for both the transport and chemical submodels, as well as the chemical data base. Thus, hypercubes with significantly more memory per node would be highly desirable for such applications.

Participants in this project were Vijay Tripathi and George Yeh of the Environmental Sciences Division and John Drake of Mathematical Sciences. For further information, see [21].

Image Analysis. Image analysis is a computationally intensive task that is essential to the development of intelligent robots. Many types of image analysis systems have been developed, but not all of these are suitable for mobile robotics applications. Systems requiring large mainframe computers are appropriate for applications such as satellite surveillance or medical imaging but lack the mobility essential for on-board use in robots. Specialized image processing hardware, on the other hand, lacks the flexibility necessary for the variety of computational tasks that arise in robotics. The purpose of this project, therefore, was to investigate the feasibility of basing an image analysis system on a general-purpose multiprocessor such as a hypercube. A hypercube potentially provides all of the requisite features for robotics applications: compact size for mobile installation, high speed for repetitive sensor sampling, concurrency for handling diverse computational tasks, and dynamic reconfigurability for dealing with a changing environment.

The target machine for implementing the image analysis system was a 64-node NCUBE hypercube. This machine has a number of the requisite features. It has fast 32-bit processors with on-chip floating point and communication capabilities. It is compact, with 64 processors on a single board and the capability to house up to 1024 processors in a single, modest-sized, air-cooled enclosure. The NCUBE system also has the potential for high-bandwidth communication with the outside world through the use of high-speed I/O channels on the nodes connected to multiple I/O subsystem boards. This latter feature is especially important for image processing, since the time to get image data into and out of the hypercube can dominate the computation time. Unfortunately, the system available for the current project had only a single host I/O board, and so image input and output tended to be a bottleneck in this initial system.

Digital images are represented by a two-dimensional array of picture elements, or "pixels," much like a familiar television screen. Each pixel might be a gray level representing the numerical value of intensity or range in a visual scene. The most obvious approach to exploiting parallelism in analyzing such an image is to partition the array into subregions and apply a processor to each piece. A two-dimensional partitioning into squares, much like a checkerboard, is often recommended because it minimizes the perimeter of each subregion. This is important because it also minimizes the volume of communication across boundaries between subregions that is required by many iterative image processing algorithms. Careful analysis shows, however, that partitioning the pixel array into thin strips can be superior for several reasons:

- If image data arrive at the host processor in raster scan lines, it is more efficient to forward the image data directly to the node processors in the same order rather than reorganize them into a two-dimensional format.

- Although a two-dimensional partitioning minimizes the communication volume, it does not minimize the total number of messages sent. When message start-up cost is significant, as it is for the NCUBE, the smaller number of messages required by strips may lead to smaller overall communication time.

- In dynamic applications such as robotics, partitioning into strips allows much greater flexibility in allocating an arbitrary number of processors to image analysis tasks and in redistributing work in an orderly way when the number of processors available changes.

The particular type of image selected for analysis in this project consisted of laser rangefinder data. A typical range image contains 256×256 pixels, each of which is a range measurement taken along a ray at given elevation and azimuthal angles. Fig. 3a shows a sample image. As a first step in identifying objects in the range image, the goal is to detect edges and corners of objects. In this context, discontinuities in the range data are regarded as edges, and discontinuities in the partial derivatives of the range data with respect to the elevation and azimuthal angles are regarded as corners.

The image is partitioned and distributed among the processors by horizontal strips for reasons given above. The strips overlap slightly so that communication between processors is not required during the edge and corner detection. Fig. 3b shows the results obtained from a straightforward edge and corner detection algorithm, based on thresholding simple weighted differences of neighboring pixels, applied to the image of Fig. 3a. The time required to produce the results in Fig. 3b was 200 ms using 64 processors, and the wall clock time to run the program was 10 seconds, including reading the data from disk and writing results back to disk.

Since the edges and corners were not detected very reliably or precisely by the simple algorithm, a more sophisticated detection algorithm was tried, based on transforming the range image into an iso-distance contour map (Fig. 3c). The results of this corner and edge detection scheme are shown in Fig. 3d, which shows significantly greater precision in the location of edges and corners. The processing time for this more complex algorithm was 800 ms using 64 processors. This algorithm is nonlinear in the sense that there are multiple, data-dependent execution paths through the code, a feature that would be difficult to implement with a dedicated SIMD image processor.

The NCUBE hypercube system appears to be a promising candidate for high speed image analysis, especially considering that the system has not yet reached design specifications. Image input is a principal difficulty with the current system; without additional hardware development an image cannot be transferred from the

Fig. 3a. Gray-scale laser image.

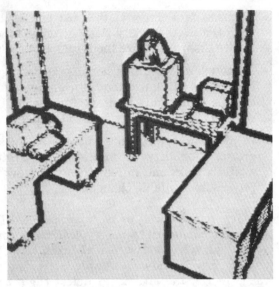

Fig. 3b. Simple edge (■) and corner (+)
detection.

Fig. 3c. Iso-distance contour map.

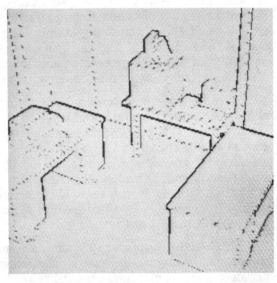

Fig. 3d. Nonlinear edge and corner detection.

host to the node processors in real time. Although this particular application did not test the internode communication capacity of the NCUBE, it did illustrate nicely the value of a general-purpose MIMD multiprocessor system in implementing a nonlinear algorithm for image analysis.

Participants in this project were Matthew Hall and Judson Jones of CESAR in the Engineering Physics and Mathematics Division. For further information, see [13].

Molecular Dynamics of Polymers. Computer simulation techniques of molecular dynamics have long been used to investigate the properties of fluids and solids [8]. Molecular dynamics simulation provides quantities that can be compared directly to experiments or substituted for experimental data when the latter are unavailable. For example, the infrared spectrum of a molecule, the peaks in x-ray or neutron diffraction experiments, and the diffusion coefficient can be obtained from molecular dynamics simulation. Such calculations are typically performed for a few hundred atoms because simulations become increasingly time consuming as the number of particles increases. The study of polymers requires a larger number of particles, however, since a polymer is a macro-molecule consisting of at least a thousand atoms. Furthermore, polymer properties occur over a wider range of time scales than for smaller molecules. For example, the folding of a polymer chain is much slower than the vibration of the chemical bonds in the polymer. To study both types of motion, very long simulation times are required.

These considerations suggest the possible use of parallel computers for molecular dynamics simulations; sharing the work among a large number of processors should permit the solution of larger problems over a longer simulation time span. Most previous uses of parallel computers for molecular dynamics computations have involved special-purpose, one-of-a-kind machines. The goal of this project was to determine the efficiency with which a widely available, general-purpose multiprocessor, such as the Intel iPSC, could solve molecular dynamics problems.

The molecular dynamics technique is conceptually simple. For the collection of particles (atoms) of interest, one solves Hamilton's equations or some other suitable equation system from classical mechanics. Thus, the task is to solve a large system of coupled nonlinear ordinary differential equations subject to a given set of initial conditions. The general methodology is given by the following steps:

1. Specify the initial coordinates and momenta for each atom.

2. Specify the interactions between atoms.

3. Choose a numerical method to solve the differential equation.

4. Choose a time step in the numerical method that is sufficiently small to give accurate results.

5. Solve for the coordinates and momenta for each atom at each time step (these solutions generate the atom's trajectory in phase space).

Rather than attempt to develop general parallel methods for solving initial value problems for ordinary differential equations (such attempts have not met with much success in the past), this study concentrated on exploiting parallelism inherent in the particular problem to be solved. The numerical integration method chosen is due to Verlet [22] and has become a standard technique for molecular dynamics simulations. The specific polymer studied was polyethylene, whose relative simplicity and great commercial importance make it a suitable prototype polymer.

The approach to partitioning the problem for parallel implementation was based on the essentially one-dimensional character (at least on a macroscopic scale) of the long chain of atoms in a polymer. The atoms are partitioned into contiguous groups along the chain. Since interactions among atoms are predominantly along the chain, consecutive groups are mapped onto consecutive processors in a ring embedded in the hypercube by means of a binary reflected Gray code (use of a Gray code ensures that consecutive processors in the ring are physically connected in the hypercube). The only communication required is therefore between immediate neighbors in the ring topology. Two separate computer programs were developed: one with 5-atom coupling that contains only 2- and 3-body interactions, and a second with 7-atom coupling that contains 2-, 3-, and 4-body interactions. The program with 7-atom coupling requires more computation and greater communication volume than the program with 5-atom coupling, but the same number of messages.

Table 1a. Efficiency with 5-atom coupling.

number	number of processors					
of atoms	2	4	8	16	32	64
8	91					
16	96	75				
32	98	87	81			
64	99	94	89	81		
128	99.5	96	95	89	82	
256	99.6	98	97	94	87	79
512	99.8	99.1	98	97	94	88
1024	100	99.6	99.2	98	96	93
2048	100	100	100	99.6	98	95

Results for the two programs for various numbers of atoms and processors are shown in Tables 1a and 1b. Results are given in terms of percent efficiency, which is defined to be speedup divided by the number of processors, where speedup is the serial execution time divided by the parallel execution time. Thus, efficiency measures the percentage of the overall execution time that the processors are busy doing useful work. For a fixed number of atoms, efficiency decreases as the number of processors increases, since the amount of communication increases while the amount of computation remains fixed. For a fixed number of processors, the efficiency increases as the number of atoms is increased, approaching 100% as eventually computation completely dominates communication.

Table 1b. Efficiency with 7-atom coupling.

number	number of processors					
of atoms	2	4	8	16	32	64
16	94					
32	97	89				
64	98	94	90			
128	99	97	95	91		
256	99.5	98.5	97	95	91	
512	100	99.3	99	98	95	91

Due to the relatively modest power of the underlying hardware, the actual execution times observed for the hypercube are not competitive with current super-computers. Nevertheless, the remarkably good results obtained in these experiments demonstrate the great promise offered by multiprocessor architectures for simulating polymer dynamics, especially as more powerful processors are incorporated into these designs. One caveat, however, is that the coupling between atoms in the present model is restricted by the interaction terms to only a few nearest neighbors. More global coupling that is common in molecular dynamics simulations would require increased communication and perhaps a different interconnection topology for efficient parallel solution.

Participants in this project were Elijah Johnson, Don Noid, and George Pfeffer of the Chemistry Division and Andrea Hudson and Skip Thompson of Mathematical Sciences. For further information, see [5].

Density Functional Theory. Density functional theory is a technique for determining fundamental properties of materials from first principles. An example is to calculate the ground state energy and charge density of an arbitrary number of atoms in an arbitrary configuration. Since density functional theory in effect requires the solution of an n-body problem with arbitrary interactions, it can be extremely time consuming computationally. This suggests exploiting inherent parallelism in the n-body problem in order to improve the computational feasibility of this technique. The objective of this project was to develop a simple, yet general, parallel code that could be easily modified to solve problems with various geometries.

Density functional theory expresses the electron interaction energies as a function of electron density, which is determined by the square of the electron wave function. In the Schrodinger equation, the potential energy for the one-particle electron wave function consists of ion-electron and electron-electron interaction terms. The electron-electron interaction is split into a Coulomb term and an exchange-correlation term. In the approach taken here, the resulting system of coupled differential equations is solved by a simulated annealing technique similar to that suggested by Carr and Parrinello [3]. Simulated annealing is a general technique for minimizing a functional with respect to a set of variational parameters.

In this context, artificial classical dynamic equations for the electron wave functions are constructed, then solved by a molecular dynamics simulation technique [22]. Lagrange multipliers are introduced in order to satisfy a normalization constraint on the wave function. The kinetic energy of the system is gradually reduced to zero, at which point the system has annealed into the ground state.

Unlike the other projects described in this report, this project had no serial implementation with which to begin. Thus, to gain experience with and confidence in the simulated annealing technique, a serial code was developed to apply simulated annealing to two cases with known solutions, the one-dimensional harmonic oscillator and the hydrogen atom. Both problems were satisfactorily solved for the ground state and first excited state.

Next a parallel code was developed for computing the charge density and ground state wave functions for a system of atoms using the simulating annealing procedure. To adapt the computation to a parallel computing environment, each ion, together with its associated electron cloud, was assigned to a separate node processor of the Intel iPSC hypercube. The overall computation is controlled and coordinated by the host processor. The host initially sends out information to the nodes to control exchange of boundary faces and multipole moments. During each time step of the annealing procedure, the host updates the Lagrange multipliers and sends them to the nodes along with information on the position of the ion on each node. This information from the host allows computation of the ion–electron and exchange–correlation potentials at each node. The long-range Coulomb term, however, requires that information about the charge and dipole moment of each node be passed to all other nodes. This global communication was implemented by circulating the information from all nodes around a ring. Once the potential has been determined, solving the dynamical equations for the wave function requires the Laplacian of the potential at each point, which necessitates passing boundary information from each node to its adjacent nodes. After the wave function has been determined, information is sent back to the host so that it can update the Lagrange multipliers before a new time step is begun. When the annealing procedure is complete, the entire final wave function can be returned to the host, if desired.

The parallel code was run for a four-atom system on four processors of the hypercube using a $10 \times 10 \times 10$ spatial grid on each node. Only the ion–electron interaction terms were included in this computation. Initial symmetric and antisymmetric wave functions are shown in Fig. 4. Symmetric and antisymmetric wave functions after annealing for 500 steps are shown in Fig. 5 for symmetrically placed and asymmetrically placed ions. These results are in qualitative agreement with band theory. Incorporating the electron–electron interaction terms would have required an estimated 30 hours for a 500 step simulation. To speed up the computation of the Coulomb interaction term, which is simply the solution of Poisson's equation, an FFT technique could be used. An alternative approach is to use the fast multipole algorithm of Greengard and Rokhlin [12]. Even though only the ion–electron interactions were included, these results demonstrate the feasibility of obtaining the electron ground state wave functions for multi-atom systems using density functional theory and simulated annealing on parallel computers. The simplicity and generality of the parallel code should allow it to be adapted readily to solve larger systems in more complex geometries.

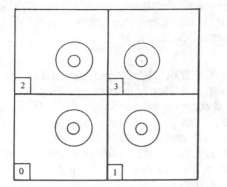 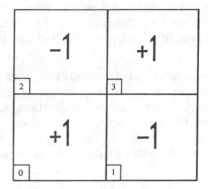

Fig. 4. Initial conditions for symmetric (left) and antisymmetric (right) wave functions.

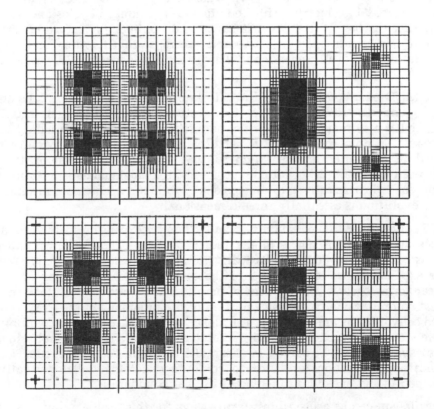

Fig. 5. Symmetric (top) and antisymmetric (bottom) wave functions after annealing for 500 steps with symmetrically (left) and asymmetrically (right) placed ions.

Participants in this project were Richard Ward of the Computing and Telecommunications Division, Bill Butler of the Metals and Ceramics Division, and Al Geist of Mathematical Sciences. For further information, see [23].

Nonlinear Magnetohydrodynamics (MHD). Most magnetically confined plasmas are not quiescent and they are not in strict equilibrium. For controlled fusion, it is essential to understand the dynamics of these plasmas in order to improve their confinement. Resistive instabilities play an important role as a cause of plasma turbulence. Unfortunately, the inclusion of resistivity in the basic fluid equations introduces a disparity of times scales involved in the problem, which is a serious complication for numerical solution techniques. This disparity of time scales, along with a broad range of length scales, makes the computational modeling and simulation of such plasmas extremely costly. Hundreds of hours of computer time have been spent performing these calculations on current supercomputers, and thus there is ample motivation for exploring new parallel architectures.

In selecting a pilot project for hypercube implementation, many choices had to be made regarding the physical detail of the model, the complexity of the numerical solution scheme, and the method of introducing parallelism. The project began with the existing serial code RSF [14], which solves a reduced set of MHD equations in a toroidal geometry. This code includes minimal physics and geometry, but contains the basic three dimensionality and nonlinear structure of the equations. RSF has been in operation for several years, so that its numerical properties and limitations are well understood. These features made the RSF code an ideal testbed for the project.

The MHD equations can be reduced to two time-evolution equations and two Poisson equations. RSF solves the time-evolution equations as an initial value problem with a symmetric equilibrium as initial condition and periodic boundary conditions. To this equilibrium a perturbation is added. The perturbation is expanded in a Fourier representation so that the time evolution of the initial stimulus can be observed. In toroidal geometry, if a single mode is initialized, then the problem is intrinsically two-dimensional, while if two or more are initialized, then the evolution is essentially three-dimensional.

RSF solves the MHD equation system by Fourier expansion in the two angular variables and finite differences in the radial variable. The numerical integration scheme is basically explicit, but dissipative terms are treated implicitly. When the Fourier expansions are introduced into the two-step time integration scheme, the nonlinear terms become convolutions of amplitudes. These convolutions constitute the most computationally intensive portion of the program. In the Cray version of RSF the convolutions are vectorized for higher performance. Radial coupling enters the time stepping procedure through radial derivatives. After each half step, a tridiagonal system must be solved in the radial direction for each mode. Centered difference approximations are used to compute remaining radial derivatives for interior points and one-sided differences at radial boundaries.

Parallelism can be achieved in various ways for this problem, but the simplest is by dividing the geometry of the torus into regions radially. For a distributed-memory multiprocessor such as a hypercube, this has the advantage of requiring very little duplication of data between computational nodes. Dividing unknowns radially among the processors leads to a one-dimensional flow of data between processors. Thus, a ring connectivity suffices for the algorithm. Consecutive sets of contiguous radial grid points are assigned to consecutive processors in the ring, with the first and last processors containing boundary data and the remaining processors containing interior data. Neighboring processors in the ring must exchange data at each time step in order to compute difference approximations to radial derivatives.

The Fourier expansions required to determine the coefficients of the tridiagonal systems can be computed with perfect parallelism (recall that this is the most costly part of the original code). But this leaves the coefficients of each tridiagonal system spread out across all of the processors, and thus communication is required to compute the solutions. A pipelined procedure was developed for solving these multiple systems. The first processor eliminates the portion of the system it owns for the first mode and sends these values to the second processor, which can then begin computing its share of the solution for the first mode. Meanwhile, the first processor has begun the same process for the second mode, and so on. Thus, the entire set of systems is solved in a multistage pipeline fashion and some parallelism is achieved, although there is a startup cost in filling the pipeline. The back substitution algorithm is dealt with similarly, but the flow of data is in the reverse direction across the processors.

Coding details of the adaptation to a parallel environment were not difficult conceptually but required fairly painstaking effort. For example, the initialization of arrays in the node programs was accomplished by creating, on the host, copies of the common blocks that each node needed. The entire common block was then sent in a message and received in place by the nodes, thereby avoiding some of the packing and unpacking of data that would otherwise have been required. The host program maintains overall control of execution, collecting information on the solution from each node after a user-specified number of time steps and storing it in global arrays. As in several of the other projects, the transfer of large volumes of data between host and nodes proved to be a significant bottleneck in the computations.

Table 2. Timing results for MHD test problem.
(times in milliseconds on iPSC)

p	initialize	time step	tridiagonal	collect results
2	30120	21954	1346	595
4	31120	11792	1077	800
8	32605	6490	897	980
16	38325	4239	967	2970
32	49410	3167	1156	11115
64	78580	2992	1579	31655

Table 2 gives timing results for a small test problem with 129 radial grid points and 16 Fourier modes using various numbers of processors. The table shows the one-time costs of initialization from host to nodes and collecting results from nodes to host, as well as the average time spent per time step both on the overall time-stepping procedure and just for solving the tridiagonal systems. All times represent the maximum observed over all nodes, and the averages are taken over ten time steps. As expected, the times for initialization and collection of results grow substantially as the number of nodes increases due to the serial manner in which the host communicates with the nodes. A significant number of time steps would be required to amortize this fixed cost. The time spent on tridiagonal solutions first drops and then grows with the number of processors, as communication eventually dominates computation for this phase of the problem. The overall time per step drops substantially as the perfectly parallel computation of the convolutions is spread over more processors, but eventually the increasing communication overhead of the tridiagonal solutions causes the overall time per step to flatten out. Although the limitations of processor speed and available memory on the iPSC rule out its use for production MHD runs, these results indicate that future implementations of the hypercube architecture — with higher bandwidth I/O, larger memories, and vector processors — may have considerable promise for realistic MHD computations.

Participants in this project were Ben Carreras of the Fusion Energy Division, Richard Hicks and Vickie Lynch of the Computing and Telecommunications Division, and John Drake and Bill Lawkins of Mathematical Sciences. For further information, see [6].

Conclusion. By almost any standard, the overall series of hypercube applications projects would have to be considered a success. No fewer than six of the seven projects actually produced working codes for the hypercube that solved a significant portion of their original problem with reasonable generality and efficiency. This is a remarkably high success rate, given the limited time and resources available for each project. The one project that did not produce a code for the hypercube nevertheless produced both theoretical and empirical results that will be useful in future multiprocessor codes that require parallel sequences of random numbers.

Some general observations on the results of these projects follow:

- None produced a parallel code directly without first having (or in some cases writing) a serial code from which to start. The serial code served as a benchmark for validating the correctness and measuring the efficiency of the parallel code.

- Close examination of the existing serial code in preparation for the parallel adaptation often suggested modifications that caused significant improvements in performance of the serial code. This is not unlike prior experience with vectorization of scalar codes.

- Most concentrated on only a portion of their overall problem, usually the most computationally intensive part. Given the limited time to develop the parallel codes, effort was spent where it would have the greatest impact.

- The coding style most often adopted might be characterized as using the hypercube as an attached processor (albeit a more flexible one than the usual attached array processor), with the host processor controlling the computation and farming out work to the node processors. Since no attempt was made to parallelize some portions of the original code, these serial portions had to be executed on the host.

- An unfortunate consequence of this coding style was that considerable communication was required between host and nodes. Thus, the very slow communication rate between host and nodes was a major bottleneck to good performance. Even in those cases where there was little or no communication between host and nodes during the computation, sending out initial data and collecting final results often required significant amounts of time.

- The coding style could also be characterized as "single program, multiple data" in the sense that none took advantage of the capability of the hypercube to run different programs on different nodes. Of course, the node programs, though identical, still ran asynchronously (i.e., not in lockstep as in an SIMD system).

- None made critical use of the hypercube interconnection topology, as such, but instead either used some other embedded network (e.g., a ring), or used the hypercube as an efficient approximation to a fully connected network, or required no internode communication at all. This should not be construed a negative comment on the hypercube topology, but is instead a strong endorsement of the inherent flexibility of the hypercube interconnection scheme.

- In every case, parallelism arose naturally from the underlying physical problem, specifically through spatial partitioning (including partitioning by particles). Spatial partitioning has the advantage that it not only partitions the computational work, but also partitions the data in a natural way, which is of great importance in a distributed-memory system such as a hypercube.

- The modest processing power, memory, communication speed, and external I/O capacity available in current hypercubes limited the projects to solving rather small test problems. Use of hypercubes for production work will require significant improvements in all of these areas.

- Code development was significantly accelerated by the use of hypercube simulators [7]. These were helpful for debugging hypercube codes and also in alleviating the single-user bottleneck of the iPSC.

- Participation by Mathematical Sciences personnel was critical to the successful completion of most of the projects. It is doubtful that the participants from other divisions could have gotten their applications running on the hypercube in such a short time without the help of these experienced collaborators.

- Many of the participants have expressed an interest in continuing further development of their applications on the hypercube or other multiprocessors.

In summary, the results of these projects indicate that many computational problems in science and engineering are amenable to efficient parallel solutions. The work involved in adapting existing serial programs to a multiprocessor environment is significant but not unmanageable. With the help of experienced collaborators, the scientists and engineers in this sample were willing and able to learn a new parallel architecture and apply it to important computational problems in their respective areas. The problems solved were a diverse and representative cross section of the computational work load of the laboratory. Multiprocessing will almost certainly play an important role in everyday computing at ORNL in the future, quite possibly in the form of more advanced implementations of the hypercube or similar distributed-memory architectures.

References

[1] K. O. Bowman and M. T. Robinson, *Studies of random number generators for parallel processing*, this volume.

[2] J. W. Bryson, *ORVIRT.PC: A 2-D Finite Element Fracture Analysis Program for a Microcomputer*, Tech. Rept. ORNL-6208, Oak Ridge National Laboratory, October 1985.

[3] R. Carr and M. Parrinello, *Unified approach for molecular dynamics and density functional theory*, Phys. Rev. Lett., 55 (1985), pp. 2471-2474.

[4] J. A. Clinard and G. A. Geist, *Implementing Fracture Mechanics Analysis on a Distributed-Memory Parallel Processor*, Tech. Rept., Oak Ridge National Laboratory, in prep.

[5] J. B. Drake, A. K. Hudson, E. Johnson, D. W. Noid, G. A. Pfeffer and S. Thompson, *Molecular Dynamics of a Model Polymer on a Hypercube Parallel Computer*, Tech. Rept., Oak Ridge National Laboratory, in prep.

[6] J. B. Drake, W. F. Lawkins, B. Carreras, H. R. Hicks and V. Lynch, *Implementation of a 3-D Nonlinear MHD Calculation on the Intel Hypercube*, Tech. Rept. ORNL-6335, Oak Ridge National Laboratory, in prep.

[7] T. H. Dunigan, *A Message-Passing Multiprocessor Simulator*, Tech. Rept. ORNL/TM-9966, Oak Ridge National Laboratory, May 1986.

[8] D. Fincham and D. M. Heyes, *Recent advances in molecular dynamics computer simulation*, Adv. Chem. Phys., 63 (1985), pp. 493-575.

[9] G. C. Fox and S. W. Otto, *Algorithms for concurrent processors*, Physics Today, 37, No. 5 (1984), pp. 50-59.

[10] P. Frederickson, R. Hiromoto, T. L. Jordan, B. Smith, and T. Warnock, *Pseudorandom trees in Monte Carlo*, Parallel Computing, 1 (1984), pp. 175-180.

[11] G. A. Geist, *Solving finite element problems with parallel multifrontal schemes*, this volume.

[12] L. Greengard and V. Rokhlin, *A Fast Algorithm for Particle Simulations*, Tech. Rept. YALEU/DCS/RR-459, Yale University, April 1986.

[13] M. C. G. Hall and J. P. Jones, *Use of the NCUBE in Image Analysis for Robotics*, Tech. Rept., Oak Ridge National Laboratory, in prep.

[14] H. R. Hicks, B. Carreras, J. A. Holmes, D. K. Lee and B. V. Waddell, *3D nonlinear calculations of resistive tearing modes*, J. Comp. Phys., 44 (1981), pp. 46-69.

[15] E. Hinton and D. R. J. Owen, *Finite Element Programming*, Academic Press, New York, 1977.

[16] D. E. Knuth, *The Art of Computer Programming*, *Vol. 2*, Addison-Wesley, Reading, MA, 1981, Chapt. 3.

[17] G. Marsaglia, *Random numbers fall mainly in the planes*, Proc. Nat. Acad. Sci., 61 (1968), pp. 25-28.

[18] G. Marsaglia, *Regularities in congruential random number generators*, Numer. Math., 16 (1970), pp. 8-10.

[19] J. K. Reid, *Frontal methods for solving finite-element systems of linear equations*, in Sparse Matrices and their Uses, I. S. Duff, ed. , Academic Press, 1981, pp. 265-281.

[20] M. T. Robinson, *Computer simulation of collision cascades in monazite*, Phys. Rev. B, 27 (1983), pp. 5347-5359.

[21] V. S. Tripathi and J. B. Drake, *A Geochemical Calculation on the iPSC Hypercube*, Tech. Rept., Oak Ridge National Laboratory, in prep.

[22] L. Verlet, *Computer experiments on classical fluids*, Phys. Rev., 159 (1967), pp. 98-103.

[23] R. C. Ward, G. A. Geist and W. H. Butler, *Density functional theory and parallel processing*, this volume.

[24] G. T. Yeh and V. S. Tripathi, *HYDROGEOCHEM: A Coupled Model of Hydrological Transport and Geochemical Equilibrium of Multi-Chemical Components*, Tech. Rept., Oak Ridge National Laboratory, in prep.

Some Graph- and Image-Processing Algorithms for the Hypercube

RUSS MILLER* AND QUENTIN F. STOUT†

Abstract: We give algorithms for a fine-grained hypercube in which one element of an adjacency matrix (for graphs) or one pixel (for images) per processor is stored. By combining the divide-and-conquer paradigm, general data movement operations, and simulations of other parallel architectures, efficient algorithms are developed for a collection of graph and image processing problems. In addition to the standard simulations of meshes, trees, and PRAMs, hypercube simultions of the mesh-of-trees are shown to be quite useful. Problems considered include marking and enumerating the extreme points of figures in an image, determining the diameter of a figure, labeling figures, and deciding if a graph is biconnected. All but one of our algorithms finish in poly-log time.

Introduction

By a *hypercube of size N* we mean a hypercube with N processing elements (PEs). An *image of size N* is an $N^{1/2} \times N^{1/2}$ array of black/white pixels, and an *adjacency matrix of size N* is an $N^{1/2} \times N^{1/2}$ array of 0s and 1s representing the adjacency matrix of an undirected graph with $N^{1/2}$ vertices. Whenever an image of size N or an adjacency matrix of size N is stored in a hypercube of size N it is stored one entry per PE, using standard reflexive Gray coding to map the entries to the PEs. This guarantees that pixels sharing an edge, or adjacent matrix entries, are in adjacent PEs. This also guarantees that a hypercube of size N can simulate any mesh algorithm for an image or adjacency matrix of size N, where one step of the mesh can be simulated by

---

*Department of Computer Science, 226 Bell Hall, State University of New York, Buffalo, NY 14260, USA.

† Department of Electrical Engineering and Computer Science, University of Michigan, Ann Arbor, MI 48109-2122, USA. Partially supported by NSF grant DCR-8507851.

one step of the hypercube (assuming that the hypercube's instruction set includes the instruction set of the mesh).

A *mesh-of-trees of size N* (where N is an even power of 2) has an $N^{1/2} \times N^{1/2}$ mesh computer augmented with a complete binary tree of nodes on each row and column, where the leaves of a tree are the PEs in a given row or column. Except for their leaves, all the trees are disjoint. Figure 1 shows a mesh-of-trees. While the mesh-of-trees (also known as orthogonal trees) has been suggested as a useful VLSI layout for some time [Ul], it is only recently that it has received much attention as a useful architecture for image or graph theoretic problems [Hu, PKEs, MiSt]. We will show that the hypercube can efficiently simulate the mesh-of-trees, and hence all fast algorithms for the mesh-of-trees can be converted to fast hypercube algorithms. In addition, we show several problems which the hypercube can solve strictly faster than the mesh-of-trees.

Because of severe space limitations, this paper will only outline the basic approaches we use, and give a few of the results obtained. Full details of the results mentioned here appear in [MiSt].

Mapping the Mesh-of-Trees onto the Hypercube

To map a mesh-of-trees of size N onto a hypercube of size N, first use the standard reflexive Gray code to map the base mesh onto the hypercube. Next associate each tree node above a row or column with a base node of that row or column, using the simple left-to-right mapping illustrated in Figure 2, and then map the tree node to the same hypercube node that the base node was mapped to. Note that a hypercube node has at most 3 nodes from the mesh-of-trees mapped onto it, namely a base node and a node from that base node's row and column trees.

With this mapping, each tree node p is associated with a base node which has an index which differs by a power of 2 from the index of the base node that p's parent is mapped to. The standard reflexive Gray code mapping has the property that indices which differ by 1 are mapped to adjacent hypercube nodes, while those which differ by any higher power of 2 are mapped to hypercube nodes 2 away from each other. This is to insures that adjacent nodes in the mesh-of-trees are mapped to nodes at most 2 apart in the hypercube. This, coupled with the fact that a hypercube node has at most 3 nodes mapped onto it, shows that there is a small constant C such that any single step of the mesh-of-trees of size N can be simulated in C steps of the hypercube of size N.

Data Movement Operations

For a variety of regular distributed-memory architectures such as mesh or pyramids, the authors have advocated an algorithm development approach which concentrates on writing algorithms in terms of a few data movement operations, and then finding efficient algorithms for performing the operations. In a sense, such data movement operations are very similar to developing standard data structures for serial algorithms.

For the mesh-of-trees it is often useful to concentrate data along the diagonal of the base, for then the disjoint row or column trees can be efficiently used. In the following data movement

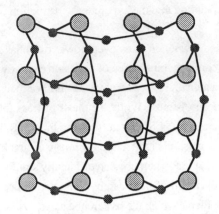

Figure 1 Mesh-of-trees of size 16.
(Mesh connections omitted for clarity)

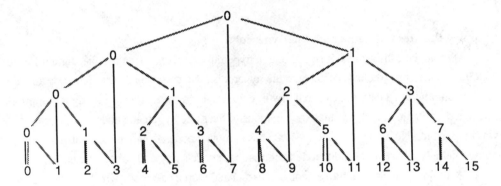

Figure 2. Mapping a tree onto its row/column

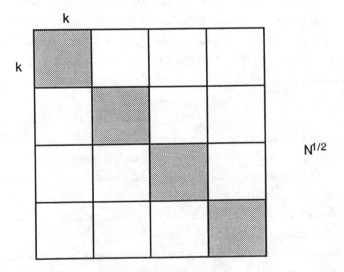

Figure 3. Diagonal squares

operations, *diagonal squares* are part of the base, as illustrated in Figure 3. For the mesh-of-trees, and for the hypercube via simulation, a few of the data movement operations that have proven to be useful are given below. (See [MiSt] for their detailed implementation.) For some of our algorithms, equivalent or slightly slower mesh-of-trees versions were independently presented in [Hu, PKEs].

Compression to the diagonal: Given no more than k items per row, the mesh-of-trees of size N can move the data to $k{\times}k$ diagonal squares in $\Theta(k + \log(N))$ time. It is easy to see that this time is optimal for the mesh-of-trees, but for $k > \log^2(N)$ it is not optimal for the hypercube. (See the comments below concerning sorting and simulating a CRCW PRAM.)

Broadcasting diagonal squares: Assume that the base of the mesh-of-trees has been partitioned into disjoint $k{\times}k$ squares. The data in each diagonal square can be copied to all the squares in the same row or column in $\Theta(k + \log(N))$ time. Again, this time is optimal for the mesh-of-trees but not for the hypercube when $k > \log^2(N)$.

Sorting: The mesh-of-trees of size N can sort $CN^{1/2}\log_4(N)$ items in $\Theta(C \log(N))$ time if there are initially $C \log_4(N)$ items per row. Again this time is optimal for the mesh-of-trees, and this is the largest amount of data the mesh-of-trees can sort in logarithmic time. It is important to notice that if there are N items to be sorted then the mesh-of-trees is not significantly better than its mesh base, and must take $\Omega(N^{1/2})$ time to sort the items. (This time can be attained.) If there are a large number of items to be sorted then the hypercube is superior to the mesh-of-trees since it can sort N items in $\Theta(\log^2(N))$ worst case time by using bitonic sort, or $\Theta(\log(N))$ expected time by using flashsort. Here the probablistic nature of the sort is independent of the initial data distribution, and only depends on intermediate random variables generated by the PEs for routing.

Simulating a CRCW PRAM: The mesh-of-trees of size N, or a hypercube of size N, can simulate T steps of a CRCW PRAM (concurrent read, concurrent write parallel random access machine) with $N^{1/2}\log_4(N)$ PEs and $N^{1/2}\log_4(N)$ memory cells in $O(T \log(N))$ time. Here the concurrent write operation can use a random value, use the largest or smallest value, or use the sum of the values written (or any other semigroup operation which can be computed in unit time). As is usual, sorting is the crucial step of such a simulation, and the time to sort sets a lower bound on the simulation time needed. Therefore the mesh-of-trees cannot efficiently simulate PRAMs with many PEs. A hypercube of size N can simulate T steps of a CRCW PRAM with N PEs and N memory cells in $\Theta(T \log^2(N))$ worst-case time, or $\Theta(T \log(N))$ expected time.

Image Input - Single Figure

In a black/white digitized picture, a connected component of black pixels is called a *figure*. If the picture has a single figure, then many properties of this figure can be rapidly determined by the mesh-of-trees, and hence also by the hypercube. The basic approach for all of the following problems is to realize that each can be solved by knowing only the leftmost and rightmost pixels of a figure in each row. This can be determined in $\Theta(\log(N))$ time by using the row trees, and then the information is moved to the diagonals. From there, CRCW PRAM algorithms are simulated to finish the problem.

Theorem 1: Given a black/white image of size N, the following problems can be solved in $\Theta(\log(N))$ time on a mesh-of-trees of size N or on a hypercube of size N:

    a)   mark and enumerate the extreme points of the black pixels;

    b)   mark the convex hull of the black pixels;

    c)   decide if the black pixels are a convex set;

    d)   determine if the pixels labeled "A" are linearly separable from the pixels labeled "B" (where here each pixel is assumed to have a label with is either "A", "B", or something else);

    e)   decide if the black pixels could have arisen as the digitization of a straight line segment;

    f)   determine a smallest enclosing box of the black pixels;

    g)   determine the diameter of the black pixels;

    h)   determine the smallest enclosing circle of the black pixels.

Image Input - Multiple Figures

When there are multiple figures, typically one first needs to label figures before their properties can be determined. This, and several other problems, can be accomplished by using a divide-and-conquer approach where the image is divided into pieces, the problem is solved in the pieces, and then the pieces are put together using an amount of information proportional to the perimeter of the pieces. Both the hypercube and mesh-of-trees easily accomodate such an approach since each can be subdivided into parts which are themselves hypercubes or mesh-of-trees, respectively. Using this approach, we obtain:

Theorem 2: Given an image of size N on a mesh-of-trees of size N or a hypercube of size N:

    a)   in $\Theta(\log^3(N)/\log(\log(N)))$ time the figures can be labeled;

    b)   given a labeled image, in $\Theta(\log^2(N)/\log(\log(N)))$ time every node can determine the label and distance to the closest neighboring figure to its figure;

    c)   in $\Theta(\log^3(N))$ time the extreme points of each figure can be enumerated, each figure can decide if it is convex, each figure can decide if its convex hull intersects the convex hull of any other figure, and each figure can decide if it could have arisen as the digitization of a straight line segment.

For labeling figures, a different approach can be used by noticing that the trees of the mesh-of-trees can label horizontal or vertical line segments of figures in logarithmic time. If the figures form spirals, or long slanted lines, then this is not of much use since two pixels in the same figure may need many line segments in any path which joins them and consists solely of horizontal and vertical line segments within the figure. However, in many other cases, such as convex figures of bounded elongatedness, any two pixels in the same figure can be joined by such a path with only a few segments.

Theorem 3: Given an image of size N on a mesh-of-trees of size N or a hypercube of size N, suppose that any two pixels in the same figure can be joined by a path of T or fewer horizontal and vertical line segments within the figure. Then the figures can be labeled in $\Theta(T \log(N))$ time.

Image Input - Multiple Figures on a Hypercube

Despite the utility of simulating a mesh-of-trees on a hypercube, when a problem requires that a great deal of information be moved the hypercube may be able to do much better than the mesh-of-trees. A CRCW PRAM can label the figures in $\Theta(\log(N))$ time [ShVi], so the hypercube can label them in $\Theta(\log^2(N))$ expected time. Once figures are labeled, each black pixel creates a record with its label and coordinates. These records are then sorted by label (using a Gray code ordering) so that all representatives of a figure form a region which is essentially a subcube. Within these subcubes operations can proceed independently of other figures, again first reducing each figure to the leftmost and rightmost pixel in each row. Despite the fact that the original geometry of the image has been severely altered, it is possible to use this approach to obtain faster algorithms. Using this approach, we obtain:

Theorem 4: Given a labeled image of size N on a hypercube of size N:
  a) in $\Theta(\log^2(N))$ time the extreme points of each figure can be determined, each figure can decide if it is convex, each figure can decide if its convex hull intersects the convex hull of any other figure, and each figure can decide if it could have arisen as the digitization of a straight line segment;
  b) in $\Theta(\log^2(N))$ time the diameter and a minimal enclosing box can be determined for each figure;
  c) in $\Theta(\log^2(N) + E/N)$ time a minimal enclosing circle can be determined for each figure, where E is the sum over all figures of the cube of the number of extreme points in the figure.

For part c), the most straightforward way to find a minimal enclosing circle of a figure is to take all triples of extreme points and find the circle through each triple, take all pairs of extreme points and find the circle having them as its diameter, and then choose the largest circle found. The total number of calculations which need to be performed by this approach is proportional to E. To minimize the total time first each figure finds its extreme points, then E is determined, and then each figure is allocated a number of PEs proportional to the cube of the number of its extreme points. These PEs then perform the required calculations for their figure.

Graphs

Using mesh-of-trees algorithms from [Hu] and [MiSt], we obtain

Theorem 5: Given a graph G stored as an adjacency matrix of size N on a hypercube of size N, in $\Theta(\log^2(N))$ time:

    a) the connected components of G can be determined (this is equivalent to finding the transitive closure of a symmetric boolean matrix);

    b) a minimal spanning forest of G can be determined (here G is given as a weight matrix);

    c) it can be decided if G is bipartite;

    d) the cyclic index of G can be determined;

    e) all the bridge edges of G can be determined;

    f) all the articulation points of G can be determined;

    g) all the biconnected components of G can be labeled.

For part a), we note that if we are given an unsymmetric boolean matrix and asked to find its transitive closure, then the complexity of the problem is much greater. One reasonable hypercube solution is to simulate a mesh running the algorithm in [VS]. This will result in an algorithm taking $\Theta(N^{1/2})$ time.

Conclusion

We have shown that a collection of image and graph problems can be solved efficiently by utilitzing general data movement operations for the mesh-of-trees and hypercube. While several of these are efficiently solved on the mesh-of-trees, and on the hypercube by simulating the mesh-of-trees, we have also shown that the slow sorting time of the mesh-of-trees is sometimes a bottleneck which the hypercube can avoid. In many cases, we achieve fast algorithms by operations which represent figures in forms which are far removed from their intial geometry.

For many of these problems, it is natural to ask if faster hypercube algorithms are possible, or if problems solvable in fast expected time can be solved in the same time bounds deterministically. For the problems with poly-log time solutions which where not $O(\log(N))$ it is extremely difficult to prove a lower bound greater than $\Omega(\log(N))$, so there are many problems for which the algorithms given herein may not be optimal. One of the most important such problems to consider is sorting, since it is used as the basis of many other algorithms.

It is also of interest to consider hypercubes storing more than one entry per PE. Some of the algorithms used here will not extend well to such situations because they sort too much data, but certainly the divide-and-conquer approach, and the use of general data movement techniques, will be important. It is easiest to obtain linear speed-up with many data items per PE, and none of our algorithms exhibit linear speed-up, so a general question we raise is what is the smallest number of entries per PE needed so that one can have linear speed-up on the problems considered here?

References

[Hu]   M.-D.A. Huang, *Solving some graph problems with optimal or near-optimal speedup on mesh-of-trees networks*, Proc. 26th Symp. on Foundations of Computer Science (1985), pp. 232-240.

[MiSt] R. Miller and Q.F. Stout, *Data movement techniques for the mesh-of-trees and hypercube*, submitted.

[PKEs] V. Prassana-Kumar and M. Eschoghian, *Parallel geometric algorithms for digitized pictures on mesh of trees*, Proc. 1986 Int'l. Conf. on Parallel Processing, pp. 270-273.

[ShVi] Y. Shiloach and U. Vishkin, *An O(log n) parallel connectivity algorithm*, J. of Algorithms 3 (1982), p. 57.

[Ul]   J.D. Ullman, *Computational Aspects of VLSI*. Computer Science Press, MD, 1984.

[VS]   F. VanScoy, *The parallel recognition of classes of graphs*, IEEE Trans. on Computers C-29 (1980), pp. 563-570.

Exploitation of Image Parallelism
via the Hypercube

S.-Y. LEE* AND J. K. AGGARWAL*

ABSTRACT. The time-consuming nature of image processing tasks suggests a parallel computing approach. There are two types of parallelisms in image processing tasks, which can be exploited for speed-up, i.e., image parallelism and function parallelism. In this study, we consider efficient ways to exploit image parallelism using the hypercube structure. Image parallelism here means that the same operation is repeated on every pixel or region throughout an image frame so that the image may be partitioned into a set of subimages which can be processed concurrently by multiple processing elements (PEs). A *pseudo* binary tree, an efficient topology for distributing subimages and combining local results, can be easily embedded in the hypercube. In the computational model, the subimages are loaded from the controller to the processing nodes in the hypercube, processed in parallel, and the local results are collected via the pseudo binary tree. We examine the efficiency of three different schemes in terms of speed-up for different numbers of PEs employed. The results obtained in an implementation of median filtering on the iPSC are provided.

1. INTRODUCTION

Basically, parallel image processing exploits the two fundamental modes of parallelism in image processing tasks: image parallelism and function parallelism [1]. Image parallelism is a kind of spatial parallelism, i.e., the same operation is repeated on each pixel or subregion so that an image frame may be partitioned into a set of subimages which can be processed by multiple processing elements (PEs) for speed-up. On the other hand, function parallelism is a temporal parallelism, i.e., an image processing task (function) consists of several levels of processing. Here we divide an image processing function into subfunctions and utilize the scheme of pipelining. This method is useful when a sequence of images needs to be processed.

The efficiency of exploiting image parallelism is determined by communication overhead. This overhead is mainly due to the distribution of subimages to a set of PEs, data exchange during computation, and the collection of local results. We cannot just keep partitioning an image since as we divide it

---

* Computer and Vision Research Center, College of Engineering, The University of Texas at Austin, Austin, TX 78712.
This research was supported in part by the Air Force Office of Scientific Research under contract F46920-85-K-0007 and in part by IBM.

further the communication overhead increases in general. After some point, the communication over-head might wipe out the advantage of parallel processing and, therefore, the processing time becomes even longer if we employ more PEs. Therefore, it is important to determine the optimum partitioning in terms of the number of PEs employed. In this paper, we address this problem when image parallel-ism is exploited on the hypercube structure.

2. EXPLOITATION OF IMAGE PARALLELISM

2.1. A PSEUDO BINARY TREE

A binary tree is one of the most efficient topologies for collecting or combining local results. It takes $\log_2^N$ steps to combine N items. However, it is wasteful to imbed a (complete) binary tree into the hypercube directly. For example, we need a binary 4-cube (16-node hypercube) to imbed a 3-level binary tree of 7 nodes and a binary 5-cube (32-node hypercube) for a 4-level binary tree of 15 nodes. That is, the utilization of nodes in a hypercube seems to be always below 50 %. A proposed upper bound [2] for the number of levels of a binary tree realizable with a binary n-cube is $\left\lceil \dfrac{n+1}{2} \right\rceil$. In this paper, we propose a *pseudo* binary tree which can perform the same operations as a binary tree does at the expense of a potential delay.

A pseudo binary tree is a binary tree structure imbedded into the hypercube such that a node in the hypercube may represent more than one node in a corresponding (pseudo) binary tree. In Fig.1, a pseudo binary tree of 4 levels imbedded on the binary 3-cube is illustrated. Note that the nodes 0, 4, and 2 (also 6) represent four, three, and two different nodes in the binary tree respectively. The number of levels of a pseudo binary tree imbedded on a binary n-cube is n+1, compared to $\left\lceil \dfrac{n+1}{2} \right\rceil$ of a binary tree.

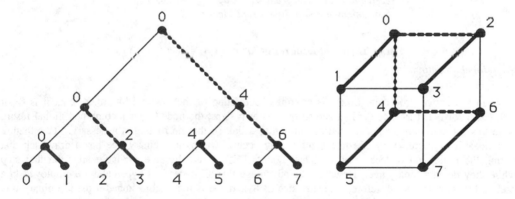

Figure 1   A pseudo binary tree

2.2. A COMPUTATIONAL MODEL

We first describe how to exploit image parallelism using the pseudo binary tree. The system con-sists of a controller and a cube as shown in Fig.2. In many researches, it has been preferred to assume that an image to be processed is already in a processing structure, i.e., ignore the time to load images. However, it would be more realistic to take the loading time into account. The controller acquires an image, sends it to the cube, and get back the result from the cube. The cube, containing 2^k PEs in the hypercube topology, processes a set of subimages concurrently, combines the local results via the pseudo binary tree, and send back the combined result to the controller. These procedures are repeated until all the images are processed. That is, the overall processing consists of three procedures: distribu-tion of the image, parallel computing, and collection of local results.

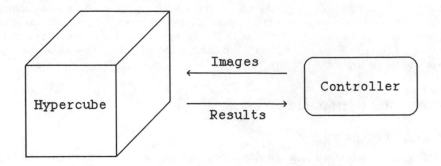

Figure 2   A system configuration

Let us consider a collection of results referring to Fig.1. In the first step, the local results of the nodes 1, 3, 5, and 7 are transferred to the nodes 0, 2, 4 and 6 respectively. In the second step, the combined results in the nodes 2 and 6 are sent to the nodes 0 and 4 respectively. Finally, in three steps, the node 0 will get a global result by receiving the combined result from the node 4. In general, it takes n steps to collect the local results in $N = 2^n$ PEs via a pseudo binary tree of n+1 levels (equivalently a binary n-cube). The procedure of collection which is executed in the node (PE) A = ($a_{n-1}, \dots , a_1, a_0$) may be described as follows:

> *do   label   i = 0, n−1*
>   *if $LB_i(A) = 0$ then*
>   *if $a_i = 0$ then*
>   *receive a local result from $\overline{A} = (a_{n-1} \dots \overline{a}_i \dots a_0)$*
>   and *combine it with its current local result*
>   *else*
>   *send its current local result to $\overline{A} = (a_{n-1} \dots \overline{a}_i \dots a_0)$*
> *label   continue*

In the above procedure, $LB_i(X)$ is a number consisting of the lowest i bits of X, e.g., it is 0 for i=0, (x_0) for i=1, (x_1 x_0) for i=2, and so on. After n steps, the node 0 gets a combined global result. Note that all communications are carried out across a link so that no routing is necessary. This feature is noticeable since no delay due to a conflict may occur. The pseudo binary tree has a drawback that during the collection of local results all leaf nodes (PEs) do not become available after the first step while they do in a binary tree. However, the advantage that all nodes in a hypercube are employed in a pseudo binary tree and, therefore, a smaller size of hypercube is required to imbed a pseudo binary tree of the same level as that of a binary tree should offset the disadvantage. Moreover, half of the total nodes become available after the first step so that the next data may be shipped to those nodes. Three quarters after the second step, and so on. And, in most cases, the collection takes much less time than data processing. Therefore, the performance of the pseudo binary tree is not degraded too much. Obviously, there is no difference in terms of performance between a binary tree and its corresponding pseudo binary tree if only one set of data is to be processed.

We introduce a set of parameters to abstract the computational model described above assuming that all PEs in the cube are homogeneous. First, a variable for computation time is defined. The computation time depends on the size of data and the nature of image processing task. Therefore, we may express the computation time t_c as follows:

$$t_c = f_c (I_s , P) \tag{1}$$

where f_c is a function, I_s the size of an image or subimage to be processed, and P an image processing task. The f_c may be a linear function of I_s as in the case that P is a histogram calculation, a convolution, a median filtering, etc. [3], a quadratic function as in a correlation calculation, or some other forms.

There are two types of communication: one between the controller and a PE in the cube, and one between PEs in the cube. We use t_d to denote the time required for the controller to send (or receive) a set of data to (or from) a PE in the cube. The time required to send a set of data from a PE to an adjacent PE in the cube is represented by t_j. These two variables must depend on the size of data to be sent but seem to be quite independent of a particular image processing task. However, it is reasonable to formulate the two separately since the characteristic of a channel between the controller and the cube is usually different from one between PEs in the cube. Therefore, t_d and t_j are formulated as follows:

$$t_d = f_d (I_s) \tag{2}$$

$$t_j = f_j (I_s) \tag{3}$$

where f_d and f_j are functions for t_d and t_j respectively.

In this study, we assume that there is no communication between PEs during a computation period. In fact, a PE processing a subimage may need some parts of subimages assigned to its neighboring PEs. However, in many cases, we may avoid this type of communication by a careful partitioning of an image *a priori*. This will be addressed in detail later in section 4.

Now we define a measure of performance which is an important factor in parallel image processing, i.e., *processing time per output* denoted by t_o. The processing time per output is a function of the three variables defined above and the number of PEs employed. That is,

$$t_o = f_o (t_c , t_d , t_j , N) \tag{4}$$

where N is the number of PEs.

3. PERFORMANCE

We need to make the formulas (1), (2), and (3) more explicit before deriving f_o. First, it is assumed that t_c is a linear function of I_s. Then we may rewrite the formula (1) as follows:

$$t_c = C_0 + C_1 I_s \tag{5}$$

where C_0 is a constant and C_1 a proportional coefficient.

As mentioned earlier, f_c may be a different function depending on a task. However, the analysis in this section is still applicable by changing the function form for t_c. Let us look into the details of t_d and t_j. The procedure of sending a set of data consists of two subprocedures[4]. We need to prepare the data and acquire a channel, i.e., *set-up* time. Then we can physically transmit the data, i.e., *transmission* time. It is believed that the set-up time is independent of the data size while the transmission time must depend on the size of data. The transmission time may be a linear function of the data size for a certain implementation like circuit switching. But some sort of non-linearity may exist in this component when several packets are to be transmitted. Therefore, as a reasonable approximation, we may adopt a second order polynomial of the data size. Then, the formulas (2) and (3) may be rewritten as follows:

$$t_d = D_0 + D_1 I_s + D_2 I_s^2 \tag{6}$$

$$t_j = J_0 + J_1 I_s + J_2 I_s^2 \tag{7}$$

In equations (6), D_0, D_1, and D_2 are the coefficients to represent the component independent of I_s, the linear component, and the non-linear component, respectively. If the channel between the controller and PEs in the cube has the same characteristic as that of the channel between PEs in the cube, D_i would be equal to J_i for i=0,1,2. In this computational model, the set of parameters of { C_0, C_1, D_0, D_1, D_2, J_0, J_1, J_2 } abstracts the system described above.

Suppose that the data size of the local result in each PE is $I_s = I / N = 2^{-n} I$ where I is the size of a whole image and $N = 2^n$. Then, the size of data to be sent (or received) in the first step of collecting local results is I_s, $2 I_s$ in the second step, $2^2 I_s$ in the third, and then $2^{n-1} I_s$ in the n-th step. Then, the node 0 sends a combined result of size $2^n I_s$ to the controller. Therefore, the time required for collecting local results, T_j, is expressed using Eqs. (6) and (7) in the following form.

$$T_j = \sum_{i=0}^{n-1} (J_0 + 2^i J_1 I_s + 2^{2i} J_2 I_s^2) + D_0 + 2^n D_1 I_s + 2^{2n} D_2 I_s^2$$

$$= n J_0 + (1-2^{-n}) J_1 I + (1-2^{-2n}) J_2 I^2/3 + D_0 + D_1 I + D_2 I^2 \qquad (8)$$

In the following, we compare three schemes in terms of t_o defined earlier. These three are different in that they adopt different methods of distribution. The formula in Eq.(8) is valid for all three cases.

3.1. BROADCAST

Suppose that the controller is capable of broadcasting. We may broadcast a whole image to all PEs involved to reduce the distribution time. Then, each PE takes care of a part of the image assigned to it. This can be effective when D_0 is comparable to $D_1 I_s + D_2 I_s^2$ in Eq.(6). In this case, the time, T_d, required to distribute an image to the cube is written as follows:

$$T_d = D_0 + D_1 I + D_2 I^2$$

SCHEME A-1 : If we have to wait until the collection procedure is finished before distributing another image, t_o is just the sum of distribution, computation, and collection times.

$$t_o = T_d + t_c + T_j$$
$$= n J_0 + 2 D_0 + C_0 + ((1-2^{-n}) J_1 + 2 D_1 + 2^{-n} C_1) I + ((1-2^{-2n}) J_2/3 + 2 D_2) I^2 \qquad (9)$$

SCHEME A-2 : Suppose that a buffer in each PE can store another data set received from the controller while the PE is doing a computation or involved in a collection procedure and the data can be read by the PE after it finishes a current job. Then we may overlap the distribution procedure with the computation and collection procedures to reduce t_o. If the distribution time (broadcast) is longer than the time for computation and collection (but just before PE 0 sends a combined result to the controller), an output is available every $2 T_d$, i.e., a broadcast (T_d) and receiving a result (T_d). Otherwise, it is available every $t_c + T_j$.

$$t_o = \begin{cases} 2 D_0 + 2 D_1 I + 2 D_2 I^2 & \text{if } 2 T_d \geq t_c + T_j \\ n J_0 + D_0 + C_0 + ((1-2^{-n}) J_1 + D_1 + 2^{-n} C_1) I + ((1-2^{-2n}) J_2/3 + D_2) I^2 & \text{otherwise} \end{cases} \qquad (10)$$

3.2. SINGLECAST

A system may not be equipped with a capability of broadcasting or all PEs in the cube may not have a big enough buffer for an entire image. In such a situation, the controller has to partition an image into the same number of subimages as that of PEs employed and distribute them one by one *(singlecast)* to PEs. In this scheme, the time, T_d , to send a subimage to a PE is $D_0 + D_1 I_s + D_2 I_s^2$ where $I_s = I/N = 2^{-n}I$.

SCHEME B-1 : If any of the three procedures, distribution, computation, and collection, cannot be over-lapped with any other as in SCHEME A-1, t_o may be expressed in the formula below.

$$\begin{aligned} t_o &= NT_d + t_c + T_j \\ &= (1+2^n)D_0 + nJ_0 + C_0 + (2D_1 + (1-2^{-n})J_1 + 2^{-n}C_1)I + ((1-2^{-2n})J_2/3 + (1+2^{-n})D_2)I^2 \end{aligned} \qquad (11)$$

SCHEME B-2 : We may overlap the distribution procedure with the computation and collection pro-cedures as in SCHEME A-2. Suppose that we distribute a set of subimages in the order of PE N-1, ... , PE 1, and PE 0. Then saying PE 0 finished the computation implies that all other PEs have already completed the computation. If the distribution time is longer than the time for computation and collec-tion (but except the time for PE 0 to send a result to the controller), an output is collected every $NT_d + D_0 + D_1 I + D_2 I^2$. Otherwise, it takes $t_c + T_j$ to process an image.

$$t_o = \begin{cases} (1+2^n)D_0 + 2D_1 I + (1+2^{-n})D_2 I^2 & \text{if } NT_d \geq t_c + T_j - TD1 \\ nJ_0 + D_0 + C_0 + ((1-2^{-n})J_1 + D_1 + 2^{-n}C_1)I + ((1-2^{-2n})J_2/3 + D_2)I^2 & \textit{otherwise} \end{cases} \qquad (12)$$

where $TD1 = D_0 + D_1 I + D_2 I^2$.

3.3. MODIFIED SINGLECAST

It may be observed that the performance of the singlecast cannot be better than that of the broad-cast mainly due to the component D_0 in t_d. As D_0 becomes comparable to $D_1 I_s + D_2 I_s^2$, the singlecast performs more poorly compared to the broadcast. One way to avoid this degradation is considered here, called a modified singlecast. A set of subimages is distributed to PEs on a certain level l (called *injection level)* in a pseudo binary tree *(injection)*. The root corresponds to $l = 0$, the level right below the root $l = 1$, and the level of leaf nodes $l = n$. An image is partitioned such that the number of subimages is equal to the number of PEs on the injection level. Every PE which receives a subimage divides it into two halves, keeps one and sends the other to its son PE in the pseudo binary tree. This operation is repeated until all leaf PEs receive their subimages *(bisection)*. The number of iterations is $n-l$. This procedure may be described as follows, where $A = (a_{n-1} \ldots a_1 a_0)$ is the address of a PE.

> if $LB_{n-l}(A) = 0$ *then*
>> *receive a subimage from the controller*
> *do label* $i = n-l-1, 0, -1$
>> if $LB_i(A) = 0$ *then*
>>> if $a_i = 0$ *then*
>>>> *send a half of subimage to* $\overline{A} = (a_{n-1} .. \overline{a}_i .. a_0)$
>>> *else*
>>>> *receive a subimage from* $\overline{A} = (a_{n-1} .. \overline{a}_i .. a_0)$
> *label continue*

The performance of this scheme can approach that of the broadcast scheme especially when t_j is much smaller than t_d. Note that the modified singlecast becomes the singlecast scheme when $l = n$. The distribution time T_d consists of two components: injection T_{di} and bisection T_{db}. These two com-ponents are given below.

$$T_{di} = 2^l(D_0 + 2^{-l}D_1I + 2^{-2l}D_2I^2)$$

$$T_{db} = \sum_{i=1}^{n-l} (J_0 + 2^{-(i+l)}J_1I + 2^{-2(i+l)}J_2I^2)$$

$$= (n-l)J_0 + (2^{-l} - 2^{-n})J_1I + (2^{-2l} - 2^{-2n})J_2I^2/3$$

$$T_d = T_{di} + T_{db}$$

SCHEME C-1 : If the three procedures do not overlap one another then t_o may be expressed as follows:

$$t_o = T_d + t_c + T_j$$
$$= (2n-l)J_0 + (1+2^l)D_0 + C_0 + (2D_1 + 2^{-n}C_1 + (1-2^{1-n} + 2^{-l})J_1)I$$
$$+ ((1-2^{2-2n}/3 + 2^{-2l}/3)J_2 + (1+2^{-l})D_2)I^2 \tag{13}$$

SCHEME C-2 : We may employ a similar overlapping technique in this modified singlecast scheme. There are 2^l PEs (or nodes) on the injection level l. If the injection time for 2^l nodes is longer than the time for bisection, computation, and collection (except the transmission of the combined result to the controller), we get an output every $T_{di} + D_0 + D_1I + D_2I^2$. Otherwise, the processing time per output is $T_{db} + t_c + T_j$ since the injection is completed before current local results are combined.

$$t_o = \begin{cases} (1+2^l)D_0 + 2D_1I + (1+2^{-l})D_2I^2 & \text{if } 2^{-l}TD2 \geq T_{db} + t_c + T_j - TD1 \\ (2n-l)J_0 + D_0 + C_0 + (D_1 + (1-2^{1-n} + 2^{-l})J_1 + 2^{-n}C_1)I \\ + (D_2 + (1-2^{2-2n}/3 + 2^{-2l}/3)J2)I^2 & \text{otherwise} \end{cases} \tag{14}$$

where $TD1 = D_0 + D_1I + D_2I^2$ and $TD2 = D_0 + 2^{-l}D_1I + 2^{-2l}D_2I^2$.

3.4. COMPARISON OF PERFORMANCE

We define two measures for the purpose of comparison of the processing schemes described above: *speed-up* and *efficiency*. The speed-up S is the ratio of the processing time per output with a single PE (T_o) to that with N PEs, i.e., $S = T_o / t_o$. The efficiency E is the ratio of the speed-up to the ideal speed-up which is N, i.e., $E = S / N$. If the processing speed is the most important in an application, we may want to maximize S regardless of E. On the other hand, if the efficiency of utilization of the system is as important as the processing speed, we might have to compromise between S and E. In order to show a detailed behavior of the processing schemes, the measures calculated according to the formulas (9)-(14) are tabulated as a function of the number of PEs and the injection level in Table 1. In this calculation, the parameters ($C_i's$ $D_i's$ $J_i's$) measured in an implementation (refer to section 4) are used for a later comparison. In Fig.3, the data in Table 1 are plotted in a graph. For the scheme C-2 in this graph, the injection level giving the largest S is used for each N. Similar graphs are provided for different sets of parameters in Fig.4 and Fig.5.

From Table 1 and Fig.3, the following observations may be made for this particular case: as the number of PEs increases the speed-up of the broadcast and the modified singlecast schemes increases while the efficiency decreases. This is the case since the distribution time is independent of N in the broadcast scheme and it is not affected too much by N in the modified singlecast scheme because t_j is much smaller than t_d, but the computation time is exponentially decreased as N increases. On the other hand, in the case of the singlecast scheme, as N increases the distribution time increases considerably since D_0 is comparable to $D_1I_s + D_2I_s^2$. Therefore, the speed-up increases as N increases but it decreases if N becomes larger than some value since the communication overhead, especially the distribution time, becomes dominant.

SPEED-UP (EFFICIENCY) : THEORETICAL						
$C_1 = 1.212$ $D_0 = 0.255$ $D_1 = 0.0146$ $D_2 = 0.00017$ $J_0 = 0.0041$ $J_1 = 0.0037$ $J_2 = 0.0000035$						
N	A-1	A-2	B-1	B-2	l	C-1	C-2
2	1.816 (.906)	1.901 (.950)	1.821 (.910)	1.901 (.950)	0	1.811 (.906)	1.895 (.947)
4	3.318 (.830)	3.611 (.903)	3.285 (.821)	3.611 (.903)	0	3.292 (.823)	3.580 (.895)
					1	3.323 (.831)	3.601 (.900)
8	5.656 (.707)	6.564 (.821)	5.213 (.652)	6.564 (.821)	0	5.565 (.696)	6.441 (.805)
					1	5.657 (.707)	6.510 (.814)
					2	5.548 (.693)	6.545 (.818)
16	8.731 (.546)	11.100 (.694)	6.439 (.402)	11.100 (.694)	0	8.498 (.531)	10.725 (.670)
					1	8.713 (.545)	10.916 (.682)
					2	8.457 (.529)	11.016 (.689)
					3	7.704 (.481)	11.070 (.692)
32	11.986 (.375)	16.952 (.530)	5.666 (.177)	7.045 (.220)	0	11.530 (.360)	16.055 (.502)
					1	11.929 (.373)	16.487 (.515)
					2	11.456 (.358)	16.716 (.522)
					3	10.115 (.316)	15.645 (.489)
					4	8.042 (.251)	11.155 (.349)
64	14.726 (.230)	20.456 (.320)	3.759 (.059)	4.049 (.063)	0	14.024 (.219)	20.456 (.320)
					1	14.619 (.228)	21.002 (.328)
					2	13.915 (.217)	19.264 (.301)
					3	11.985 (.187)	15.645 (.244)
					4	9.181 (.143)	11.155 (.174)
					5	6.208 (.097)	7.045 (.110)
128	16.619 (.130)	20.456 (.160)	2.134 (.017)	2.187 (.017)	0	15.711 (.123)	20.456 (.160)
					1	16.462 (.129)	21.002 (.164)
					2	15.574 (.122)	19.264 (.151)
					3	13.196 (.103)	15.645 (.122)
					4	9.876 (.077)	11.155 (.087)
					5	6.518 (.051)	7.045 (.055)
					6	3.871 (.030)	4.049 (.032)

Table 1 Comparison of Performance : Theoretical

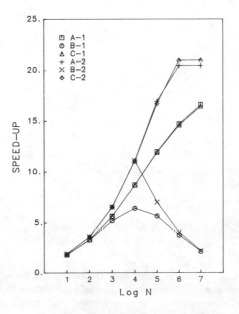

Figure 3 Speed-up : Theoretical
(C_0, C_1, D_0, D_1, D_2, J_0, J_1, J_2) = (.0, 1.212, 0.255, 0.0146, 0.00017, 0.0041, 0.0037, 0.0000035)

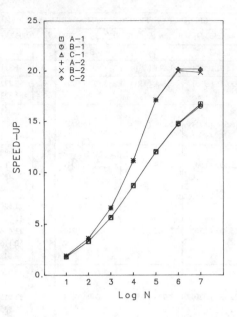

Figure 4   Speed-up : Theoretical
$(C_0, C_1, D_0, D_1, D_2, J_0, J_1, J_2) = (.0, 1.212, 0.0005, 0.03, 0.0, 0.00005, 0.003, 0.0)$

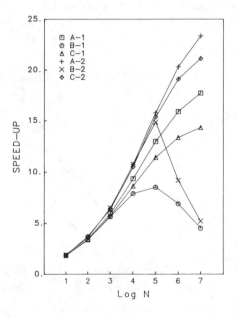

Figure 5   Speed-up : Theoretical
$(C_0, C_1, D_0, D_1, D_2, J_0, J_1, J_2) = (.0, 1.212, 0.1, 0.015, 0.0, 0.1, 0.0015, 0.0)$

The performance of the broadcast scheme is better than the others but the performance of the modified singlecast scheme approaches to that of the broadcast scheme as expected. The overlapping scheme can improve the system performance considerably. It is also noted that there is an optimum injection level in the modified singlecast scheme.

In Fig.4 where the set-up time is negligible compared to the transmission time, we can see that the performances of the three schemes are quite similar. This can be easily seen by noting that in this case the communication time is almost proportional to the size of data to be sent or received. Therefore, the communication time is approximately the same as long as the same amount of data is sent regardless of the scheme adopted. It is not exactly the same since there exist the constant and nonlinear terms in T_d and T_j. Now, suppose that t_j is comparable to t_d. The performance in such a case is shown in Fig.5 where the two components are equal. The advantage of the modified singlecast scheme over the singlecast scheme stems from the parallel bisections and the smaller t_j than t_d. It is observed that the performance of the modified singlecast scheme is degraded compared to the case where t_j is much smaller than t_d. This is the case since the benefit from the small communication time per bisection disappears. However, the modified singlecast scheme is still better than the singlecast scheme because the parallel bisections alone can reduce the distribution time considerably.

4. EXAMPLE

An image processing task has been implemented on the iPSC (intel Personal Super Computer) with 32 PEs to illustrate the schemes described above and to verify the derivations of t_o, Eqs. (9)-(14).

4.1. IMPLEMENTATION

In the iPSC, the controller can access PEs in the cube for distribution of data or collection of local results through multiplexed Ethernet channels. The maximum size of the message which can be sent or received by a PE at a time (by calling a subroutine) is 16 Kbytes. If the data size exceeds the maximum size the subroutine has to be called more than one time.

The image processing task implemented is median filtering, a typical example of a task with image parallelism. The pixels within a window centered at a pixel under consideration are sorted according to their intensities. The pixel is replaced by the median of the sorted pixels. Therefore, when we partition an image, we have to take the boundary problem into account. Otherwise, communication is necessary during computation for each PE to get a certain part of the boundary pixels of subimages assigned to its adjacent PEs. In order to handle this problem, an image is partitioned one-pixel-wide (since a 3x3 window is used) overlapped along the boundary as illustrated in Fig.6 where N = 2. Then, we can avoid the communication during computation, which might degrade the performance to a great extent otherwise.

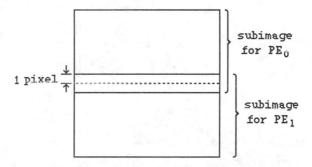

Figure 6 Partitioning of an image for a 3x3 window : N=2

The current version of iPSC does not have a capability of broadcasting data to processes in the cube. Therefore, we had to evaluate t_o for the broadcast scheme by separately measuring the three components, the distribution time, the computation time, and the collection time. Particularly, the distribution (broadcasting) time is replaced by the measured time for sending an entire image to a PE in the cube.

4.2. RESULTS AND DISCUSSIONS

The measured performance is tabulated in Table 2 and plotted in the same format as one used earlier in Fig.7 (but N changes from 1 up to 32). The image size is 256x256 (64 Kbytes). By comparing Table 2 and Fig.7 with Table 1 and Fig.3, we may observe that the measured performance closely follows the calculated one. This tells us that the computational model built in section 2 can abstract a physical system well.

SPEED-UP (EFFICIENCY) : EXPERIMENTAL							
$C_1 = 1.212$ $D_0 = 0.255$ $D_1 = 0.0146$ $D_2 = 0.00017$ $J_0 = 0.0041$ $J_1 = 0.0037$ $J_2 = 0.0000035$							
N	A-1	A-2	B-1	B-2	l	C-1	C-2
2	1.818 (.909)	1.902 (.951)	1.815 (.907)	1.899 (.949)	0	1.815 (.908)	1.890 (.945)
4	3.359 (.840)	3.658 (.914)	3.358 (.839)	3.627 (.907)	0	3.253 (.813)	3.631 (.908)
					1	3.332 (.830)	3.631 (.908)
8	5.816 (.727)	6.776 (.847)	5.212 (.651)	6.769 (.846)	0	5.473 (.684)	5.571 (.696)
					1	5.528 (.691)	6.698 (.837)
					2	5.709 (.714)	6.708 (.838)
16	9.191 (.574)	11.841 (.740)	6.436 (.402)	11.591 (.724)	0	8.505 (.532)	11.647 (.728)
					1	8.531 (.533)	11.675 (.730)
					2	8.779 (.549)	11.861 (.741)
					3	7.797 (.487)	11.724 (.733)
32	12.945 (.405)	18.905 (.591)	5.242 (.164)	7.122 (.223)	0	11.190 (.350)	17.972 (.522)
					1	11.495 (.359)	18.260 (.571)
					2	11.746 (.367)	18.451 (.577)
					3	10.359 (.324)	17.873 (.559)
					4	7.819 (.244)	12.551 (.392)

Table 2 Comparison of Performance : Experimental

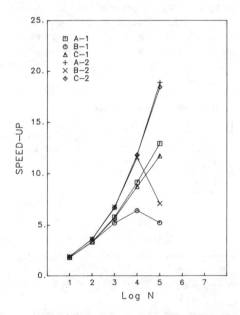

Figure 7 Speed-up : Experimental

$(C_0, C_1, D_0, D_1, D_2, J_0, J_1, J_2) = (.0, 1.212, 0.255, 0.0146, 0.00017, 0.0041, 0.0037, 0.0000035)$

From the results, it is seen that the broadcast scheme (A-2) would be the most desirable processing method to exploit the image parallelism of the type considered here if the broadcasting capability is added to the current system iPSC. In this system, it is also observed that the scheme C-2 can provide as good a performance as the scheme A-2. This is due to the characteristic of the iPSC in that the communication time between PEs is much smaller than that between a PE and the controller. It may be pointed out that the optimum number of PEs for this task (median filtering with 3x3 window for 256x256 image) is 32 for the broadcast and modified singlecast schemes and 16 for the singlecast scheme if only the speed-up is considered.

It should be mentioned that the speed-up and efficiency are determined mainly by the ratio of the computation time to the communication time and, therefore, if a more computationally-intensive task is implemented a larger speed-up would be obtained. Also, the optimum number of PEs employed would increase.

If we take a closer look at the result, we may observe that the optimum injection level is always 2. The reason for this is that the maximum size of a single message is 16 Kbytes in this system. When l is less than or equal to 2 (or equivalently the size of data injected is greater than or equal to 16 Kbytes), the data should be packed into more than one message. Therefore, as l increases from 0 up to 2, the number of the set-up's per injection decreases from 4 down to 1 resulting in a considerable drop in the injection time. However, if l is greater than 2 the number of messages per injection is 1 independent of l since the data size is smaller than 16 Kbytes. The time required per injection decreases slightly while the number of injections increases rapidly and, therefore, the performance is degraded once l becomes larger than 2 in this example.

5. CONCLUSION

In this paper, we consider the schemes to exploit image parallelism using the hypercube structure. First, we propose a pseudo binary tree imbedded in the hypercube, which is an efficient topology to load images into the cube and to collect local results. It takes $\log_2^N$ steps to combine N results just like a binary tree. But a pseudo binary tree requires a hypercube of smaller dimension than its corresponding binary tree. Moreover, all PEs in a hypercube can be utilized for a pseudo binary implementation while only at most half of PEs for a binary tree implementation. A computational model which can abstract a physical system (hypercube) closely enough by a set of parameters is built. Then we derive the formulas of the processing time per output for three processing schemes: the broadcast, singlecast and modified singlecast schemes. The model with the formulas may be used to find the optimum number of PEs to employ for the tasks of the type we considered here.

When the communication time between PEs in the cube is much smaller than that between a PE and the controller, the modified singlecast scheme can give a performance close to that of the broadcast which is an optimum scheme. The performance of the singlecast scheme becomes quite comparable to that of the broadcast scheme if the set-up time is negligible compared to the transmission time.

References

1.   S.-Y. Lee and J. K. Aggarwal, "A Problem-Driven Approach to Parallel Image Processing : System Design and Scheduling," *Proceedings of the IEEE International Conference on Systems, Man and Cybernetics*, pp. 680-686, Tucson, AZ., November 1985.

2.   Y. Saad and M. H. Schultz, "Topological Properties of Hypercubes," *Research Report YALEU/DCS/RR-389, Yale University*, June 1985.

3.   A. Rosenfeld and A. C. Kak, *Digital Picture Processing*, Academic Press, 1982.

4.   W. Stallings, *Local Networks, An Introduction*, Mcmillan, 1984.

Parallel Implementation of an Algorithm for Three-Dimensional Reconstruction of Integrated Circuit Pattern Topography Using the Scanning Electron Microscope Stereo Technique on the NCUBE[*][†]

A. E. KAYAALP‡ AND R. JAIN‡

Abstract. Computer Vision and Image Processing are two areas where one is faced with problems which require processing huge amounts of data in short time. While a number of parallel architectures have been designed for low level vision, parallel architectures for intermediate and high level vision remains an area of active research. In this paper an algorithm for the 3-D reconstruction of sub-micron integrated circuit pattern topography using the SEM (scanning electron microscope) stereo technique will be presented, and its parallel implementation on the NCUBE machine (configured as a 1-D grid) will be discussed. Except for a global optimization process, most computationally intensive operations can be done in parallel for this application. Our experiments show that the parallel algorithm can result in a significant speed up over a serial implementation, with the speedup factor being data-dependent.

Introduction

Speed is one of the critical factors that limit the application of some computer vision techniques in the manufacturing industry. Through the development of special purpose computer architectures, such as pipelined and cellular array processors, significant improvements in speed have been achieved in the area of low level vision (1). Here one performs relatively simple operations on spatially localized, simple data items, such as pixel gray values. The challenge these days is to come up with parallel architectures which can speed up the more higher level computer vision processes where one has to perform more complex operations on more complex data items which may not exhibit spatial locality. 3-D from computer stereo vision is an (intermediate level vision) application which can be formulated to make its parallel implementation on an MIMD machine highly efficient.

In this paper an algorithm for obtaining surface topography information about sub-micron integrated circuit patterns using a binocular stereo algorithm on SEM secondary electron images is presented. A parallel implementation of this algorithm is shown and results obtained on the NCUBE machine are discussed.

---

[*] NCUBE Corporation, Tempe, Arizona

[†] Sponsored by the Semiconductor Research Corporation, under contract number 84-01-045,

‡ Department of Electrical Engineering and Computer Science, The University of Michigan, Ann Arbor, MI 48109

Shape from binocular SEM stereo

Binocular stereo vision is the major mechanism used by humans for obtaining 3-D depth information over close distances. It is based on obtaining 3-D surface information from two images of a scene taken at two different viewing angles. On the SEM, the stereo image pair can be obtained by tilting the specimen and taking its images at two different tilt angles.

The major part of the stereo algorithm involves matching points in the two images, which are projections of the same 3-D scene point onto the image planes of the two cameras. This is known as the "*correspondence problem*". Once this is complete 3-D depth (height) information can be obtained easily by substituting the coordinates of the matching image points into a 3-D reconstruction equation which depends on such factors as the geometry of image formation, and the specific camera set ups used in getting the stereo image pair. Due to space limitations we will not be able to discuss the SEM stereo reconstruction equations here. Details on this can be found in (2).

In the SEM the imaging geometry can be modelled, in general, as a perspective projection of sample surface points onto an image plane, similar to conventional optical imaging using an optical camera. Due to this similarity between optical and electron beam images, several properties (having to do with imaging geometry) that have been developed for optical imaging, are directly applicable to electron beam imaging.

Our view of the 3-D from SEM stereo problem can be stated as coming up with the set of 3-D surface points (among all other such possible sets of points) which best satisfies a number of constraints derived from the imaging geometry, the physics of image formation, and the geometry of the 3-D scene being viewed. The constraints that have been used in the implementation presented here consist of the following, and in general is not limited to only these:

1. the epipolar constraint,
2. uniqueness of a feature point's match,
3. preservation of feature point ordering,
4. boundedness of depth (height) values,
5. the surface smoothness constraint.

The "*epipolar constraint*" arises directly from the imaging geometry. An epipolar plane associated with some 3-D surface point is defined as the plane passing through that point and the focal points of the two cameras. The intersection of this plane with the camera image planes defines two epipolar lines, one on each image. Figure 1 illustrates an epipolar plane and the epipolar lines defined by it. The "*epipolar constraint*" states that the match of an image point on one epipolar line must lie somewhere along the corresponding epipolar line in the other image. This constraint converts a problem of searching over a whole 2-dimensional image into one which involves a series of one-dimensional searches, hence opening the door for possible parallel processing.

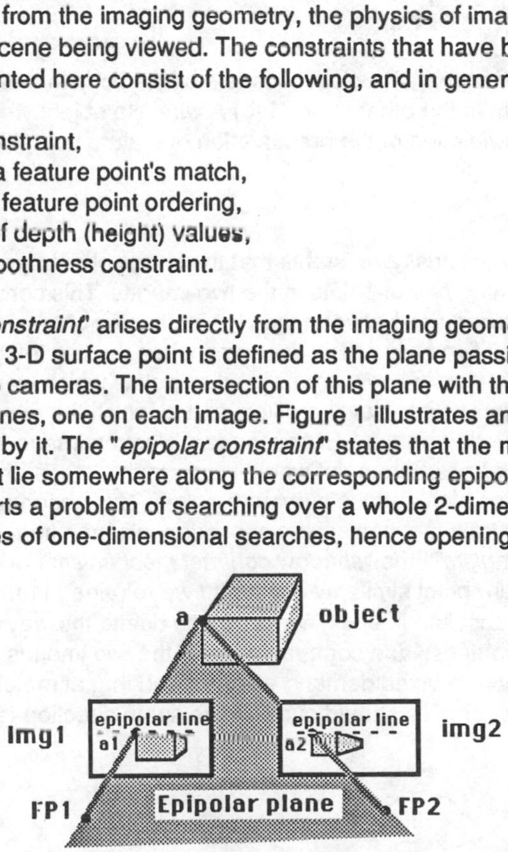

FIG. 1. A 3-D surface point and the epipolar plane and epipolar lines associated with it.

The "*uniqueness of a feature point's match constraint*" states that for each feature point in one image there can be at most one matching feature point in the other image. It arises due to the assumption that the scene being viewed contains no transparent objects. Figure 2a illustrates a case where the presence of a transparent object causes a violation of this rule.

The "*preservation of feature point ordering constraint*" states that the ordering of feature points along an epipolar line in one image should be the same as the ordering of the corresponding match points on the epipolar line in the other image. This constraint comes from the assumption that the surfaces in the scene do not contain any wire-like (narrow) protrusions that could be viewed from one side in one image and from the other side in the other image (see figure 2b).

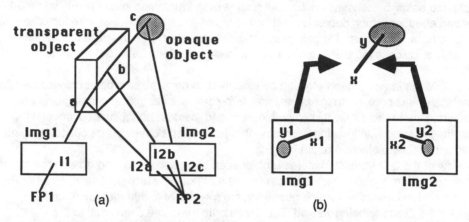

FIG. 2. (a) The presence of a transparent object causes a single point in one image to indeed match with more than one point in the other image., (b) A wire-like object viewed differently in the two images result in the violation of the preservation of feature point ordering constraint.

The "*feature point similarity constraint*" states that the image charecteristics should be similar in the vicinity of a matching pair of points in the two images. This constraint arises from the assumption that the difference between the viewing angles of the two cameras is small and hence the illumination conditions are nearly the same when the two images are obtained. Image feature points along an epipolar line were defined as points which were local curvature maxima of the corresponding image gray level profiles, and at which the curvature value was greater than some threshold. Based on the SEM secondary electron image formation process, it was observed that this choice of a feature point would locate in the image, the projections of important surface points such as high surface curvature points. This observation was based on studying the 3 topographic contrast mechanisms in secondary electron image formation, namely the "*surface tilt contrast mechanism*", the "*shadow contrast mechanism*", and the "*edge effect*" [(3),(4),(5)]. In stating the feature point similarity constraint we refrained from using similarity measures based on absolute intensity values since due to the way we are currently obtaining SEM images, the brightness and contrast levels in the two images can be quite different. Hence we made a more relaxed demand and required that at matching points the corresponding image gray level profiles should curve in the same direction (see figure 3).

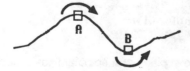

FIG. 3. An image gray level profile and two feature points that were identified. In traversing this profile from left to right, at point A the profile curves to the right and at point B to the left.

The "*depth (height) boundedness constraint*" states that computed depth or height values (with respect to some reference) should lie in a certain range. This constraint is based on the assumption that we have some idea about the scene we are viewing.

Finally, the "*surface smoothness constraint*" states that the computed 3-D surface points should not depict a surface which has abrupt jumps (e.g. surface discontinuities). This constraint comes from the observation that most physical objects have smooth surfaces (when viewed at the proper resolution). In analyzing the surface of an integrated circuit pattern (at very high magnifications), we also do not expect to see a jump in the depth (height) values of two surface points which correspond to two neighboring pixel positions in the images. This constraint is violated at occlusion boundaries, but for the type of images we are dealing with we do not expect to run into this situation very often, if at all.

The serial algorithm

Assuming the two images are aligned in a direction orthogonal to the epipolar line directions and were taken at the same magnification, the algorithm takes image profiles along each epipolar line in one image and attempts to match its feature points with those found along the corresponding epipolar line in the other image. The algorithm consists of the following steps:

1. For all image gray level profile pairs (pi1,pi2) which correspond to each other based on the "epipolar constraint", do:
   a.smooth the two profiles and detect the feature points on each profile,
   b.enforcing the "feature point similarity" and "depth (height) value boundedness" constraints determine the possible matches for each image 1 profile (pi1) feature point,
   c.enforcing the "uniqueness of a feature point's match" and the "preservation of feature point ordering" constraints, enumurate all possible sets of consistent feature point match pairs. Each matching feature point pair defines a particular 3-D surface point. Hence each set of these matching point pairs will define a set of 3-D points and if we were to draw a straight line between neighboring points, we would obtain a "3-D profile" (see figure 4).

FIG. 4. A 3-D profile obtained by drawing straight lines between neighboring 3-D points along the epipolar line direction.

Hence at the end of step 1 we will have obtained (for each epipolar line position in image 1), a set of these 3-D profiles one of which is expected to closely approximate the actual 3-D surface profile at this position.

2.If we were to take one of these 3-D profiles from each epipolar line position and put them side by side we would obtain a 3-D surface. Figure 5a illustrates this idea. Hence in this step our aim is to find the smoothest (in a direction orthogonal to the epipolar line direction) such surface among all possible surfaces that would be obtained considering all possible 3-D profiles at each epipolar line position. This global optimization step is efficiently handled by the deterministic dynamic programming algorithm. The smoothest surface is defined as the one which minimizes the sum (over all epipolar line positions) of the absolute area difference between 3-D profiles at neighboring epipolar line positions (see figure 5b).

(a)   (b)

FIG. 5. (a) A 3-D surface formed by putting together 3-D profiles from each epipolar line position, (b) the cost of a primitive path in the dynamic programming algorithm used (i.e. the cost of simultaneously selecting 3-D profile j at epipolar line position i, and 3-D profile k at position i+1). This cost is defined as the absolute area difference between the two profiles.

The parallel algorithm

The parallel implementation assumes that the processors are connected in a "1-D grid" topology. Corresponding profile pairs one from each of the images are sent to one node, with neighboring nodes on the 1-D grid processing profiles of neighboring epipolar lines in the images. The individual steps of the parallel algorithm follow exactly the steps in the serial algorithm except for the node-to-node communication steps. Figure 6 illustrates the parallel algorithm. As can be seen there are three cases where a nearest neighbor node-to-node communication takes place. The latter two cause the nodes to be globally synchronized, a result of the serial nature of the dynamic programming algorithm.

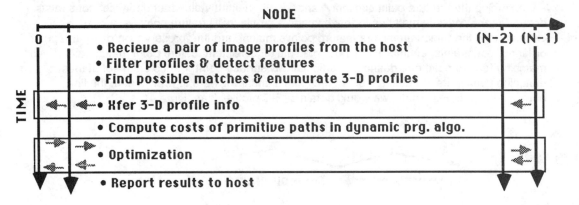

FIG. 6. The parallel algorithm. Each node executes the steps shown above. Arrows show the direction of node-to-node communication at different steps.

Results on the NCUBE

The serial version of the algorithm has been implemented on a VAX-11/780 in C. The parallel version in which each step was coded exactly as in the serial C version, was implemented in Fortran 77 on the NCUBE. More recently a C version of the parallel algorithm was implemented, in which the steps of computing costs of the primitive paths and the transferring of image data onto the host were implemented more efficiently.

Tests were performed on the two images shown in figure 7a using only L x 512 pixel, vertically oriented windows of the images which extend to the right of the horizontal positions marked in figure 7a. The number of lines L that were tried were 8,16 and 32 on 8,16 and 32 NCUBE node processors, respectively. Figure 7b shows the approximate surface that results if one were to connect the computed 3-D points (along each epipolar line) with a straight line.

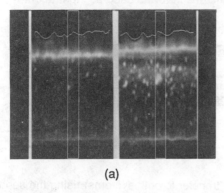
(a)

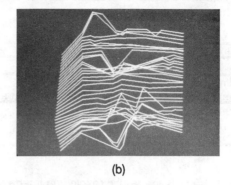
(b)

FIG. 7. (a) A stereo image pair of an aluminum pattern on a substrate (viewed from the top) taken at a magnification of 15K at 7KV and tilt angles of -19 and 1 degrees respectively on a Hitachi S-520 SEM. Only those sections of the two images that fall within the two boxes were used in the run presented here.,
(b) orthographic projection of the approximate 3-D surface that results when computed 3-D surface point are connected to each other by straight lines.The coordinate axis in the direction of the pattern was expanded so as to better see the results. The pattern side wall and the surface bump resulting in the large bright spot in the image are clearly visible, along with some extra topographic features which were the result of incorrect matches.

Table 1 shows the timing results that were obtained. These results clearly reflect the strong influence of the data dependent parts of the algorithm on the node execution time. It was observed that if the nodes were fairly well balanced (i.e. end up with similar number of 3-D profiles on each node), the parallel version can achieve very significant speed up over the serial version. This was the case for the L=8 line run where a speed up factor close to 5 (compared to the optimal value of 8) was obtained when image input times were ignored (see Table 1a). But the L=16 and 32 line data sets caused two neighboring nodes to end up each with a much larger number of 3-D profiles than others, resulting in significant increase in the node execution times for these two cases (see Table 1b). Hence the overall execution time was controlled by the node which had to compute the costs of a very large number of primitive paths. In fact it was observed that this node spent 19371 miliseconds carrying out precisely this step of the algorithm. Note that there was only a minor increase in the execution time obtained for L=32 lines (node) as compared to the 16 line (node) case, since the new data in the 32 line data set did not result in any major load imbalance between the nodes.

In general, as long as the load imbalance is not too severe the parallel version will achieve considerable speed up over the serial version, with the speed up improving as the loads on each node get more and more balanced.

Summary

A SEM stereo algorithm for reconstructing integrated circuit topography has been presented, along with a parallel version of it to be run on a 1-D grid connected multiprocessor. Results from the parallel implementation on the NCUBE reveal that the parallel version can achieve significant speed up over the serial version when the loads on the nodes are not severely imbalanced.

Future work will try to improve the mentioned shortcomings of the parallel version, while at the same time trying to come up with more constraints to reduce the number of feature point mismatches. A new constraint that is being considered is based on the idea that , using our knowledge about the physics of the image formation process, the final 3-D reconstructed surface should be able to "result in" the two stereo images that was used as input to our algorithm.

Serial C on VAX-11/780≈6 sec.   Parallel F77 on NCUBE≈1.25 sec. (mean time on node)

(a)

# of lines (nodes)	Serial C on VAX(ms)	Parallel C version	
		mean time on a node(ms)	maximum time on a node(ms)
8	6000	720-1314	811-1435
16	77000	21604	21923
32	86000	22790	24226

(b)

TABLE 1. (a) L=8 line results (excluding image data transfer to both systems) using the serial C version on the VAX-11/780 and the parallel fortran77 version on the NCUBE (with a 7 MHz clock) using 8 nodes. (b) Results of running the parallel C version on different image sizes. Note, timing data on the nodes were gathered on-line and shipped to the host off-line.

REFERENCES

(1) A. P. REEVES, "Survey: Parallel computer architectures for image processing", CVGIP 25, 1984, pp.68-88

(2) A. E. KAYAALP , R. JAIN, "Obtaining semiconductor wafer surface topography information using SEM stereo", Proc. of the Japan-USA Symposium on Flexible Automation, Osaka, Japan, July 14-18,1986,pp.665-672

(3) J. I. GOLDSTEIN, et al., Scanning Electron microscopy and X-ray Microanalysis, Plenum Press, 1981

(4) L. REIMER, Scanning Electron Microscopy, Springer Verlag, 1985

(5) H. SEILER, "Secondary electron emission in the scanning electron microscope", J. Appl.Phy.54 (11), Nov.1983, pp. R1-18

Studies of Random Number Generators
for Parallel Processing

KIMIKO O. BOWMAN* AND MARK T. ROBINSON†

Abstract. If Monte Carlo calculations are to be performed in a parallel processing environment, a method of generating appropriate sequences of pseudorandom numbers for each process must be available. Frederickson *et al.* proposed an elegant algorithm based on the concept of pseudorandom or Lehmer trees: the sequence of numbers from a linear congruential generator is divided into disjoint subsequences by the members of an auxiliary sequence. One subsequence can be assigned to each process. Extensive tests show the algorithm to suffer from correlations between the parallel subsequences: this is a result of the small number of bits which participate in the auxiliary sequence and illustrates the well-known discovery of Marsaglia. Two alternative algorithms are proposed, both of which appear to be free of interprocess correlations. One relaxes the conditions on the Lehmer tree by using an arbitrary auxiliary multiplier; it is not known to what extent the subsequences are disjoint. The other partitions the main sequence into disjoint subsequences by sending one member to each process in turn, minimizing interprocess communication by defining new sequence generating parameters.

1. Introduction. Numerical solutions to many types of physical problems are based on the so-called Monte Carlo method: for a recent review, see James [1]. Such calculations depend on the availability of a sequence of uniformly distributed pseudorandom numbers, generated by a procedure which, though deterministic, nevertheless yields quantities distributed in a seemingly unpredictable manner. A widely used technique for generating such sequences is the **linear congruential method** [2], which may be represented as:

---

* Engineering Physics and Mathematics Division, P.O. Box Y, Oak Ridge National Laboratory, Oak Ridge, Tennessee 37831-2009

† Solid State Division, P.O. Box X, Oak Ridge National Laboratory, Oak Ridge, Tennessee 37831-6032

(1.1) $x_i = ax_{i-1} + c \, , \, \bmod m \, , \quad i \geqslant 1 \, .$

Each integer member of the sequence x_i is found by multiplying the previous member by a constant integer multiplier a, adding a constant integer increment c, and then retaining only the low-order portion of the result. When suitable choices are made for the parameters a, c, x_0, and m, a reasonably long cyclic sequence of integers is produced which has many of the desired statistical properties. The procedure for selecting these parameters is well-illustrated by the recent work of Fishman and Moore [3], who also review many of the problems with such generators.

If Monte Carlo methods are to be applied in a parallel processing environment, a technique is required for supplying appropriate portions of sequences such as (1.1) to each of the parallel processes in a timely and efficient manner. In addition to having suitable statistical properties within themselves, the individual parallel sequences must be independent of one another. Frederickson et al. [4] have proposed an elegant algorithm for this purpose, based on the concept of pseudorandom or Lehmer trees. They show that it is possible, under certain conditions on the parameters of sequence (1.1), to define a related sequence whose members divide (1.1) into a set of disjoint subsequences. They term (1.1) the 'right' sequence and the auxiliary sequence the 'left' sequence. Figure 1 illustrates the relation between the two sequences: the cyclic right sequence is represented by

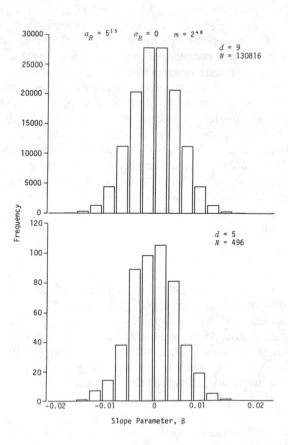

Figure 1. Division of a Pseudorandom Number
Sequence Into Disjoint Subsequences

the solid circle, the elements of the cyclic left sequence by the cusps in the dotted hypocycloid. The left sequence is used to generate 'seeds', that is, values of the parameter x_0, for each parallel process and these can then be used to initiate sequences of pseudorandom integers which are guaranteed to be disjoint. As they point out, the property of disjointness may not be necessary to successful generation of pseudorandom numbers in parallel processes, but unfortunately, as we will show here, it is not sufficient either.

2. Frederickson *et al*'s Theorem. The proposal of Frederickson *et al*. may be summarized as follows: the right sequence is (1.1) with the values

(2.1) $a_R = 1 \bmod 4$, $c_R = 2 \bmod 4$, $x_0 = 1 \bmod 2$.

The left sequence is then defined as (1.1) with the values

(2.2) $a_L - 1 = 6k$ or $10k$, mod $16k$, $c_L = 0$, $x_0 = 1 \bmod 2$,

where

(2.3) $k \leqslant m / 16$.

The essence of the proof is to note that the conditions on the parameters of the right sequence guarantee that it consists of the $m / 2$ possible odd numbers and that the left sequence generates a small number of these which can be shown to divide the right sequence into $m / 2k$ disjoint sequences, each of length k. We believe that the theorem applies also when $c_R = 0$: the period of the generator is reduced to $m / 4$ by omitting half of the odd numbers; one is left with $m / 2k$ sequences, each of length $k / 2$ which appear to be disjoint.

A question left unanswered by the work of Frederickson *et al*. is the extent, if any, to which the generators assigned to parallel processes are correlated. Even though the parallel sequences are disjoint, they may yet be correlated. This question has been addressed empirically.

3. Implementation. The pseudorandom, or as we shall say, the Lehmer tree concept was implemented in two independent programs. One was written in assembler language for a Data General Eclipse MV/10000 computer. The program allowed free selection of the initial seed, the multiplier, and the increment of the right sequence, and of the initial seed, the 'dimensionality', and the 'algorithm' of the left sequence, but the modulus was fixed at $m = 2^{48}$. By 'algorithm' is meant the choice of the '6k' or '10k' multiplier: by 'dimensionality' is meant d, where

(3.1) $n = m / 2k = 2^d$, $d \geqslant 3$.

The terminology reflects our interest in pseudorandom numbers for use on a parallel computer with the hypercube architecture. One would anticipate using the dimensionality of the hypercube for d. The other implementation was based on a published [5] machine-independent FORTRAN random number generator (a similar generator is described by James [1]) and was used on both a Cray X-MP and a VAX 11/780 computer, with the intention of simulating an INTEL Hypercube computer with 64 nodes. Calculations with the two programs gave essentially similar results.

Study of these generators revealed systematics of the Lehmer trees which must be kept in mind. First, as can be seen by inspection of the definitions above, only the high-order d bits participate in the changes associated with the left sequences. If $m = 2^f$, the low-order $f - d$ bits are unaffected by the left-sequence operations and are consequently the same in the initial seeds supplied to each parallel process. The lower-order bits are determined entirely by the right-sequence multiplier and increment: while they change from one subsequence member to the next, for any given position in the subsequence they are the same in all parallel processes. Thus, even though the right sequences may show ideal statistical behavior, the left sequences are such that correlations between processes are not unlikely. Second, the two algorithms in (2.2) generate exactly the same subsequences, but the order in the two is different; that is, a particular subsequence is assigned to a particular process in the '6k' algorithm, but to a different process in the '10k' algorithm. Third, for any value of $d > 3$, all subsequences for processes of lower dimensionality reappear, interleaved with new ones. Thus any correlations in Lehmer trees of low dimensionality will be repeated for all higher dimensions.

4. Study of Correlation. To study correlations, a series of parallel processes of the desired dimensionality was established and a linear regression was run between the subsequences generated in pairs of these processes. Calling the two subsequences y and x, respectively, a least squares determination was made of the intercept and slope of the linear function

$$(4.1) \qquad y \mid m = \alpha + \beta x \mid m$$

assuming equal weight for all data. If the two sequences were truly uncorrelated, the least squares analysis would be expected to yield $\alpha = 0.500 \pm 0.577 \cdot r^{-\frac{1}{2}}$ and $\beta = 0 \pm r^{-\frac{1}{2}}$, where r is the number of generated values in each sequence. The slope β is closely related to the ordinary correlation coefficient. For each of the $N = n(n - 1)/2$ regressions that could be obtained for any dimensionality, the value of β was scored in a histogram. Two examples are shown in Fig. 2, using the much studied [6] generator with $a_R = 5^{15}$ and $c_R = 0$, here implemented with $m = 2^{48}$. For each sequence, $r = 50{,}000$ values were generated. Many similar calculations were performed with other multipliers and increments with similar results. The whole is summarized by the following paragraphs.

For a given value of d, $n/2$ pairs of processes show values of β close to -1/2; another n have β near -1/8; another $2n$ have β near -1/32; and so on, the series limited only by N. The first group consists of pairs separated by $n/2$ in the left sequence (process 1 with process $1 + n/2$, etc.), the second of those separated by $n/4$ (process 1 with processes $1 + n/4$ and $1 + 3n/4$, etc.), and so on. Detailed examination of examples from the first group show that for these

$$(4.2) \qquad y_i = x_i + m/2, \bmod m .$$

A plot of y_i vs. x_i consists of a single straight line (folded where it leaves the unit square) from which there is no dispersion at all. In many situations, the occurrence of this kind of correlation would destroy the usefulness of the calculations in one of the parallel processes.

The second group includes similar cases where

$$(4.3) \qquad y_i = x_i \pm m/4, \bmod m .$$

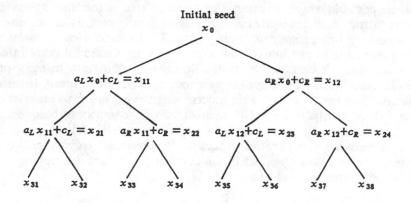

Fig. 2. Histogram of the Regression Coefficient β for
the Lehmer Tree Algorithm

As d increases, more complex relationships appear in which two or more sets of lines appear in the correlation plots. Eventually, for large enough d and for processes nearly adjacent in the left sequence, the correlation plots appear to be fairly random. This does not imply that the Lehmer tree is a suitable basis for parallel process Monte Carlo, however, since the strongly correlated pairs are still present.

The behavior described above is yet another example of Marsaglia's famous discovery [7], [8] that groups of numbers generated by any linear congruential generator define vectors which fall in only a limited number of hyperplanes. The maximum number of such planes was shown by Marsaglia to be

$$(4.5) \qquad\qquad M = (j!m)^{1/j}$$

where j is the dimensionality of the vectors and m is the modulus of the generator. In the present case, for correlations between parallel processes, we take the vectors to be defined by the members of the parallel subsequences. Then, $j = 2$ and $m = 2^d$, so that $M = 2^{(d+1)/2}$. For $3 \leqslant d \leqslant 9$, $4 \leqslant M \leqslant 32$. Thus, it is not at all surprising that the algorithm (2.2) produces sets of sequences with strong pair correlations. These correlations are the direct consequence of the very small numbers of bits which participate in the left sequences. The algorithm (2.2) thus appears to be a rather efficient way of locating some of the Marsaglia planes for this system.

5. **Remarks on the Frederickson Algorithm.** The question of whether (2.2) supplies a useful algorithm for random number generation is rather complicated and depends on the application. In cases where x, $x + m/2 \bmod m$, $x \pm m/4 \bmod m$, and so on, are related to some symmetry of the problem, (2.2) would be entirely useless. This is likely to be true in many applications in solid state physics and crystallography where the underlying symmetry of crystalline solids would interact very unfavorably with the random number generator symmetries outlined above. On the other hand, there may be applications where these symmetries are not particularly significant and for which (2.2) could perhaps supply a useful algorithm. Our results warn, however, that the burden of proof would lie on the user of the algorithm!

Another possible way of using the Lehmer tree algorithm stems from the observation that the interprocess correlations are destroyed if the parallel subsequences are not exactly in step. Thus, if the processes consume numbers from the generators at randomly fluctuating rates, any residual correlations might be small enough to tolerate. Or, if the subsequences remain in step, one might remove the correlations by stepping each one a different amount before starting calculations. For instance, the j th process might be caused to start calculations with the j th or the $(n + 1 - j)$th member of the generator subsequence, instead of the first one. Both of these schemes were tested and in both cases the correlations between the parallel processes disappeared. However, the fact that strong correlations could reappear if the parallel generators did not remain in step is a matter of considerable concern.

6. Modified Lehmer Tree Methods. Our second program was modified to use the tree sequences sketched in Fig. 3. The right sequence uses the generator (1.1) with $c_R = 2 \mod 4$ and the left sequence uses the generator (2.2). In this scheme, each step doubles the number of branches, so that after six steps there are 64 seeds for 64 processes. We used both small and extremely large c_R. The results obtained for the correlations between parallel processes were similar to those obtained for the Frederickson method.

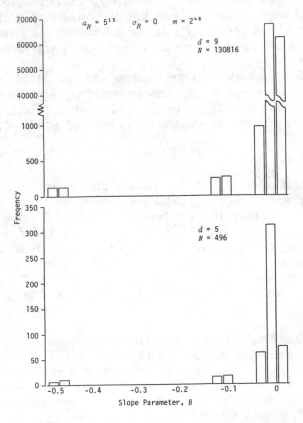

Fig. 3. A Scheme Illustrating a Random Tree

Another possibility that was explored is to relax the conditions of the generator (2.2) altogether and to generate the left sequences using (1.1), but with entirely different multipliers a_L and a_R. In this case, the selection of the multipliers is necessarily very important. Fishman and Moore [3], for instance, found only 414 acceptable multipliers among more than 534 million candidates for modulus $2^{31} - 1$. The choices made were

$$(6.1) \qquad a_R = 5^{15} \quad a_L = 13147^3 \quad c_R = c_L = 0 \quad m = 2^{48}$$

and 64 parallel processes were constructed. Samples of $r = 10,000$ random numbers were generated for each process and the 2016 correlations were analyzed. The resulting correlation coefficients were distributed according to expectations for independent samples, that is, with mean zero and variance approximately $1/r$. Unfortunately, this does not guarantee that correlation is absent in all cases, nor do we know anything at all about the disjointness of the parallel sequences.

The last method shows promise, but more detailed study would be necessary to optimize the choices of the two multipliers for various numbers of processes and for various sorts of problems. Detailed studies of the statistical properties of the individual subsequences, including internal correlations, would be required also.

7. The 'Leapfrog' Method.

Another algorithm which is easily implemented produces disjoint sequences of pseudorandom numbers in each of several parallel processes, but, unlike the Lehmer tree algorithm, the subsequences are not linear congruential generator, one value at a time to each of the parallel processes in turn.

In order to minimize the implied interprocess communications, the following property of linear congruential generators is used [2]:

$$(7.1) \qquad x_{i+n} = A_n x_i + C_n , \mod m ,$$

where:

$$(7.2) \qquad A_n = a^n , \mod m ,$$

$$(7.3) \qquad C_n = c(a^{n-1} + a^{n-2} + \cdots + 1), \mod m ,$$

and a and c are the parameters of (1.1). For n parallel processes, the first n values from the sequence (1.1) are delivered as initial seeds to each of the processes, along with the 'jump' multiplier and increment defined in (7.2) and (7.3). Then, each process generates its own subsequence according to (1.1) with A_n and C_n replacing a and c. Each subsequence consists of every nth member of the original sequence, starting in each process at a different point. Figure 1 illustrates the situation with the cusps of the hypocycloid now representing the successive members of one particular subsequence. Only the starting information need be passed as interprocess communications (and even this could be built into the programs running the parallel processes, if necessary).

This 'leapfrog' algorithm was subjected to an analysis of correlation, exactly as was done for the Lehmer tree algorithm. The choices $a = 5^{15}, c = 0$, and $m = 2^{48}$ were again made and 50,000 numbers were generated in each parallel sequence for analysis by linear regression. From 8 to 512 parallel processes were examined. No significant correlations were found between pairs of processes. The individual β values were distributed according to a normal distribution with mean value zero and variance 2×10^{-5}, independently of the dimension. An example is shown in

Fig. 4. Note that the scale of the abscissa has been expanded by a factor ten as compared with Fig. 2.

The leapfrog algorithm shows great promise, but further detailed study, particularly of the statistical properties of the individual subsequences is needed. The optimal choice of multiplier may well be different from what it would be for a single sequence generator.

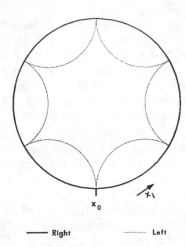

———— Right   ·········· Left

Fig. 4. Histogram of the Regression Coefficient β for
the "Leapfrog" Algorithm

8. Conclusion. We have studied the Lehmer tree algorithm [4] as a basis for pseudorandom number generation in a parallel processing environment. The algorithm produces parallel pseudorandom subsequences which are strongly correlated. We have also described two alternative methods, one based on random trees with unrelated left and right multipliers, the other on a different method of partitioning a single sequence. Both seem to be free of the correlations that made the Lehmer tree method unsatisfactory, but more thorough and careful study of both algorithms is warranted to assure that they have adequate statistical properties in all circumstances.

If none of these methods should prove workable, the 'truly random' numbers of Frigerio et al. [9], [10] could always be used. It would be necessary to read the Frigerio magnetic tape and to pass segments of its contents to each parallel process as a series of interprocess communications. Although lacking perhaps in elegance, this method would assuredly avoid the statistical problems encountered with the Lehmer tree algorithm.

This research was sponsored jointly by the Division of Material Science and the Applied Mathematical Sciences subprogram of the Office of Energy Research, U.S. Department of Energy under contract DE-AC05-84OR21400 with Martin Marietta Energy Systems, Inc.

REFERENCES

[1] F. JAMES, *Monte Carlo theory and practice*, Rep. Prog. Phys., 43 (1980), pp. 1145–1189.

[2] D. E. Knuth, *The Art of Computer Programming*, Vol. 2, Addison Wesley, Reading, Ma, (1981), Chapter 3.

[3] G. S. FISHMAN and L. R. MOORE III, *An exhaustive analysis of multiplicative congruential random number generators with modulus $2^{31} - 1$*, SIAM J. Sci. Stat. Comput., 7 (1986), pp. 24–45.

[4] P. FREDERICKSON, R. HIROMOTO, T. L. JORDAN, B. SMITH, and T. WARNOCK, *Pseudo-random trees in Monte Carlo*, Parallel Computing, 1 (1984), pp. 175–180.

[5] E. J. MCGRATH and D. C. IRVING, *Techniques for Efficient Monte Carlo Simulation*, Vol. II, Oak Ridge National Laboratory Report ORNL-RSIC-38, April 1975, pp. 105–110.

[6] R. R. COVEYOU and R. D. MACPHERSON, *Fourier analysis of uniform random number generators*, J. Assoc. Comput. Mach., 14 (1967), pp. 100–119.

[7] G. MARSAGLIA, *Random numbers fall mainly in the planes*, Proc. Nat. Acad. Sci., 61 (1968), pp. 25–28;

[8] G. MARSAGLIA, *Regularities in congruential random number generators*, Numer. Math., 16 (1970), pp. 8–10.

[9] N. A. FRIGERIO and N. CLARK, *A random number set for Monte Carlo computations*, Trans. Amer. Nucl. Soc., 22 (1975), pp. 283–284.

[10] N. A. FRIGERIO, N. CLARK and S. TYLER, *Toward Truly Random Numbers*, Argonne National Laboratory Report ANL/ES-26, part 4, 1978.

Monte Carlo Photon Transport on the NCUBE[*]

WILLIAM R. MARTIN[†], TZU-CHIANG WAN[†], DOUG POLAND[†],
TREVOR N. MUDGE[‡] AND TAREK S. ABDEL-RAHMAN[‡]

Abstract. Parallelized Monte Carlo algorithms for the analysis of photon transport in an inertially-confined fusion (ICF) plasma are considered. Algorithms have been developed for both shared memory and distributed memory parallel processors. The shared memory algorithm has been implemented on the IBM 3090/200 and timing results have been obtained for a dedicated run with two processors. Two alternative algorithms have been developed for the distributed memory processor – a *replication* algorithm and a *dispatching* algorithm. The former approach takes advantage of the unique feature of Monte Carlo particle transport which allows the *a posteriori* combination of separate Monte Carlo runs while the latter approach is identical to the shared-memory algorithm and partitions a single Monte Carlo simulation across multiple processors. Results for both approaches are given for the NCUBE/six hypercube parallel processor for cube orders one through six (1-64 nodes). Essentially full efficiency is observed for the replication algorithm, and the absolute performance with the 64 node configuration is nearly the same as with the Cray X-MP/2. For the dispatching algorithm, results are obtained for different problem sizes as well as different cube sizes. Efficiencies above 80% are observed for a large simulation for a 64 processor NCUBE configuration.

---

[*] NCUBE Corporation, Tempe, Arizona

[†] Department of Nuclear Engineering
University of Michigan, Ann Arbor, Michigan 48109

[‡] Department of Electrical Engineering and Computer Science
University of Michigan, Ann Arbor, Michigan 48109

Introduction. The Monte Carlo method has been utilized for years to solve complex problems in particle transport applications, such as the transport of neutrons in a nuclear reactor shield or the transport of photons in a inertially-confined fusion (ICF) plasma. The advantage of the Monte Carlo method is its generality – it can be used to simulate almost any particle transport problem, regardless of geometry or physical complexity, as long as the geometry can be described mathematically and the physical process can be represented by equations or probability distributions. The basic approach is to simulate the transport of particles in a medium by letting the particle move on trajectories in accordance with the appropriate laws of motion. Particle interactions are handled statistically by sampling from the probability distributions describing the interaction of the particle with the medium. For example, neutral particles will travel on straight lines between collisions with a background medium, whereas electrons moving in a semiconductor device will travel on curved trajectories. The usual complaint against the Monte Carlo method is computational time – the time required to simulate the requisite number of particle histories (to achieve reasonable statistics) may be exorbitant on conventional computers. Modern-day computer architectures are providing some relief – the natural parallelism of Monte Carlo would seem tailor-made for massively parallel architectures such as hypercube parallel processors. This paper investigates the development and implementation of photon transport Monte Carlo algorithms on both shared-memory and distributed-memory parallel processors. Timing results for both the IBM 3090/200 and the NCUBE hypercube parallel processor are discussed.

Previous Work. The vectorized photon transport Monte Carlo code VPHOT was originally developed to assess whether or not this application could be successfully adapted to a vector supercomputer. To provide a comparative tool, the SPHOT code was created which solves the identical problem as VPHOT but with the conventional (inherently scalar) Monte Carlo algorithm. The VPHOT/SPHOT Monte Carlo codes solve the specific problem of photon transport in an ICF plasma. The geometry is constrained to be two-dimensional with azimuthal symmetry, and individual zones are bounded by at most four conic sections. Reference [1] may be consulted for a detailed description of the capabilities of the codes as well as a description of the physics, Monte Carlo methodology, and the database which describes the interaction of photons with the ICF plasma. The results [1] indicate that this Monte Carlo application can be successfully vectorized, with speedups in the range of 5–6 versus the optimal scalar algorithm on the same computer.

Sequential Algorithm. The scalar algorithm contained in SPHOT is similar to the conventional Monte Carlo algorithm found in production-level codes such as MCNP or MORSE, where

particles are emitted one at a time from a known source
distribution and followed until "terminated", such as by an
absorption or escape from the geometry. For the specific
case of photon transport in an ICF plasma, the photons are
created within a specific zone via Planckian emission, and
are followed throughout the plasma. The photons may be
absorbed or scattered (Thomson) by the plasma. The specific
algorithm utilized for SPHOT is depicted in Figure 1 below.

- Read input
- Generate geometrical mesh
- Calculate zone properties (e.g., opacities)
- For zones **z** = 1,2,......NZONES
    - For energy groups **g**=1,2,...NGROUPS
        - Determine number of photons N_{zg} to be emitted in
          zone **z**, energy group **g**
        - For photons n=1,2,...N_{zg}
            - Emit photon (Planckian emission)
            - Simulate photon history
            - Accumulate tallies
            - Next photon **n**
        - Next energy group **g**
    - Next zone **z**
- Report results
- End

Figure 1. Sequential Algorithm   (SPHOT)

Parallel Algorithm - Shared Memory. The initial effort to
develop a parallelized algorithm was targetted for the IBM
3090/200 shared-memory parallel processor. As described in
[2], a "dispatching" algorithm has been developed that
partitions the photons by the zone in which they were born
(emitted). That is, a separate process is defined for all
photons *emitted* in a given zone. The process then emits the
photons and follows them, regardless of where they happen
to travel. The advantage of partitioning by zone of emission
is that it was relatively straightforward to implement this
algorithm on the IBM 3090/200 with the IBM Multitasking
Facility (MTF), which requires communication between the
main task and slave tasks via argument list only. However,
it should be emphasized that this partitioning is arbitrary
and clearly not optimal, because it is not load-balanced
(the workload depends on the zone properties and location)
and is relatively fine-grained. The algorithm is described
in Figure 2.

```
MAIN →      • Read input
TASK        • Generate geometrical mesh
            • Calculate zone properties (e.g., opacities)
            • Determine initial random seeds for each zone z
            • For  zones z = 1,2,......NZONES

SLAVE →       • Create process (Call to MTF)
TASKS         • Determine total number of photons N_z to be
                emitted in zone z
              • For photons n=1,2,...N_z
                • Emit photon
                • Simulate photon history
                • Accumulate partial tallies
                • Next photon n

MAIN →      • Next zone z
TASK        • Accumulate global tallies from partial tallies
            • Report results
            • End
```

Figure 2. Dispatching Algorithm (Shared Memory)

In this algorithm, the work in the loop over zones is completely parallel and the sequential portion is simply the input, initialization, and output. The fraction of work that is done in parallel depends on the number of photon histories. For the standard ICF simulation [1], there are ~240,000 photons emitted in the plasma and the vast bulk of the work is done in the parallel section. The sequential fraction was determined to be approximately .03% by simulating the parallel algorithm on a uniprocessor and taking synchronization delays into account by timing each process individually. Of course, as will be noted below, even this *negligible* sequential fraction (.0003) has severe implications for a massively parallel architecture.

This algorithm was implemented on an IBM 3090/200 and a dedicated run yielded a speedup of 1.93, where the speedup S is defined

$$S = \frac{\text{elapsed time for single processor}}{\text{elapsed time for two processors}} \qquad (1)$$

The performance with the optimal sequential algorithm was essentially the same as the parallel algorithm on a single processor, because the overall algorithms are similar and the MTF is not utilized for one processor. Therefore, the definition of speedup in Equation (1) is consistent with the usual definition - the ratio of the optimal sequential elapsed time to the elapsed time for multiple processors. Elapsed times were used because the IBM 3090/200 was run in dedicated mode.

However, this measured speedup of 1.93, while encouraging, is not consistent with the predicted speedup using Amdahl's Law,

$$S = \frac{1}{f + (1-f)/N} \tag{2}$$

where f is the sequential fraction and N is the number of processors. Equation (2) yields S = 1.999 for f = .0003. One possible explanation might be the operating system overhead imposed by the MTF, which spawns the tasks and assigns them to the next available processor (one of two processors for the IBM 3090/200). Defining the total overhead as f_{op} times the total workload, one obtains the a revised version of Equation (2) which accounts for the postulated fractional overhead,

$$S = \frac{1}{f + (1-f)/N + f_{op}} \tag{3}$$

If one assumes f = .018, which implies that the operating system adds an additional 1.8% of the total computation to the overall workload, then the predicted speedup becomes 1.93. Thus, a plausible explanation of the discrepancy between the measured and predicted results is the effect of operating system overhead to implement the multitasking.

It is interesting to project what the speedup would be for N processors assuming that the 1.8% overhead held for any number of processors. Table 1 illustrates the sensitivity of the predicted speedups to the presence of the seemingly modest 1.8% overhead. Thus even for an inherently parallel application such as Monte Carlo, where the degree of parallelization is close to 100%, the impact of a relatively small overhead due to the operating system will be significant. It should be stressed, however, that these results are for only one possible partitioning of the simulation - by zone of emission - which is fairly fine-grained (1960 tasks for the test problem) and is not load-balanced as explained earlier. We are currently examining alternative partitioning schemes for the shared memory algorithm which are load-balanced and coarser-grained.

N	$S(f_{op}=0.0)$	$S(f_o=.018)$
2	1.999	1.93
3	2.998	2.84
4	3.996	3.73
8	7.98	6.98
16	15.9	12.4
32	31.7	20.2
64	62.8	29.5
128	123	38.3
256	238	45.0
512	444	49.4
1024	784	51.9
∞	3333	54.6

Table 1.   Effect of Operating System Overhead

Parallel Algorithm - Local Memory. A parallelized algorithm for the 64-node NCUBE hypercube parallel processor at the University of Michigan [3] has been developed. Three approaches were examined, stemming from the relatively modest memory (128K Bytes) per node that made it impossible for the SPHOT code to be replicated on each node. These versions are denoted A, B, and C :

    Version A - the DIMENSION statements in SPHOT were reduced to allow a maximum of 20 zones versus 2000 zones for the original version of SPHOT. The entire code (except for I/O) was replicated in each processor and the host merely read in the input data, broadcast it to the nodes, and then received the results from each node and printed out separate results for each calculation. A Lehmer tree was utilized to start out each node calculation with a different random seed [4], allowing the separate Monte Carlo runs to be combined to yield results equivalent (statistically) to one large run with the same total number of photons. Table 2 summarizes the results for the reduced-dimension algorithm as a function of N, the number of nodes. Note that the overall simulation speed for the 64 node NCUBE is nearly as fast as a Cray X-MP/2 with the optimal scalar algorithm (SPHOT) for the same 5 x 4 problem. Here we are using an absolute measure of performance which is proportional to the time to achieve a result - the "microseconds (μsec) per track", which is the CPU time to follow a photon from one position in phase space to its next position.

N^a	$\tau_N{}^b$	$\tau_{tot}{}^c$	$\mu sec/track^d$
1	13.5	14	2481
2	13.5	14	1242
4	13.4	14	624
8	13.4	14	312
16	13.4	14	156
32	13.4	14	80.4
64	13.4	14	39.6

Notes: [a] N = number of nodes.

[b] τ_n = average CPU time per node (s)

[c] τ_{tot} = total time from posting of first message
to receipt of last message

[d] Comparison - 37.5 $\mu sec/track$ on Cray X-MP/2

Table 2.   Results for Version A (5x4)

Version B - the uniform and homogeneous mesh (in the ICF
test problem) was taken advantage of by calculating the zone
vertices and material composition as a function of the zone
index .   This eliminated the need to store the zone vertices
and composition for each zone. Since the zone vertices are
needed constantly throughout the simulation, this resulted in
a significant increase in the computational time (nearly
double) versus the original algorithm. The rationale for
this was to allow the analysis of the "standard" test problem
with the 49x40 mesh, which could not be fit into the NCUBE
node if the zone vertices and compositions were to be stored.
Other than this change to eliminate the stored arrays,
Version B is identical to Version A. Table 3 summarizes the
results for the "small" mesh (5x4) analyzed with Version A
and Table 4 contains the results for the "standard" ICF test
problem with the 49x40 mesh. A comparison of Tables 2 and 3
indicates that the modified algorithm to compute the zone
vertices and composition is nearly a factor of two slower
than the original algorithm in SPHOT which stores these zonal
quantities. Table 4 indicates the effect of the 49x40 mesh
versus the 5x4 mesh - a significant increase in computational
time due to the additional boundaries that are crossed by the
photons. However, the measure $\mu sec/track$ remains nearly the
same, indicating the usefulness of this absolute performance
measure for Monte Carlo.

N	τ_N	τ_{tot}	µsec/track
1	22.7	24	4279
2	22.8	24	2130
4	22.8	24	1065
8	22.8	24	532
16	22.8	24	266
32	22.8	24	137
64	22.8	24	67.6

Table 3.   Results for Version B (5x4)

For Versions A and B, it is important to note that the problem size grows linearly with the number of nodes, because the same problem is simply run on more processors. However, since the random seeds for each problem are different, the overall simulation does represent a meaningful calculation because the results from each simulation can be combined to yield overall results with statistics improved by the ratio $1/\sqrt{N}$, where N is the number of nodes. It should be clear that essentially full efficiency is being obtained with Versions A and B as a function of the number of nodes. That is, since the overall simulation time is a constant and the problem size is growing linearly with the number of nodes, then the observed speedup is also linear.

N	τ_N	τ_{tot}	µsec/track
1	194.7	205	4920
2	194.7	204	2448
4	194.7	204	1224
8	194.7	205	615
16	194.7	205	308
32	194.7	204	158
64	194.7	205	78.1

Table 4.   Results for Version B (49x40)

Version C - the "dispatching" algorithm developed for the shared memory parallel process was modified to be operational on the NCUBE. In this case, the algorithm is shown in Figure 3.

Version C is different from Versions A and B in that a single Monte Carlo simulation is being spread out over the N processors in the cube, rather than replicating the same calculation (with different random number sequences) in each of the N processors. However, the method used in Version B to eliminate the stored arrays is also used in Version C. Tables 5-7 summarize the performance results for algorithm C as a function of the number of nodes and the problem size (the number of photons simulated).

HOST →   • Read input
          • Generate geometrical mesh
          • Calculate zone properties (e.g., opacities)
          • Determine initial random seeds for each zone **z**
          • For zones **z** = 1,2,......NZONES
            • Dispatch index **z** and input data to next
              available processor
              (via message from **HOST** to **NODE**)

NODES →   • Determine total number of photons N_z to be
              emitted in zone **z**
          • For photons **n**=1,2,...N_z
            • Emit photon
            •Simulate photon history
            • Accumulate partial tallies
            • Next photon **n**
          • Send message "ALL DONE" back to **HOST**

HOST →   • Next zone **z**
          • Accumulate global tallies from partial tallies
          • Report results
          • End

Figure 3. Dispatching Algorithm (Local Memory)

As opposed to the replication approach taken in Versions A
and B, the Version C algorithm partitions the workload
internally, dispatching work (batches of particles emitted
within a specific zone) to the next available processor.

N^a	$\tau_N{}^b$	Speedup[c]	μsec/track[d]	Efficiency[e]
1	207	---	----	---
2	142	1.46	3206	.73
4	72	2.88	1626	.71
8	46	4.50	1039	.56
16	26	7.96	587	.49
32	16	12.9	361	.40
64	13	15.9	294	.25

Notes: [a] N = number of nodes
        [b] τ_N = total time (s) for simulation excluding I/O
                (host clock resolution = 1 second)
        [c] Speedup = τ_1 / τ_N
        [d] See text
        [e] Efficiency = Speedup/N

Table 5. Results for Version C (~2700 photons)

N	τ_N	Speedup	μsec/track	Efficiency
1	1773	---	---	---
4	563	3.15	1406	.79
8	337	5.26	841	.66
16	167	10.6	417	.66
32	85	20.9	212	.65
64	39	45.5	97	.71

Table 6. Results for Version C (~24,000 photons)

N	τ_N	Speedup	μsec/track	Efficiency
1	18124	---	4376	---
16	1596	11.4	387	.71
32	873	20.8	212	.64
64	348	52.1	84	.81

Table 7. Results for Version C (~240,000 photons)

As can be observed from Tables 5-7, the efficiency increases with the problem size, with the largest problem (Table 7) representative of typical applications of interest. Thus, for 64 processors, we see an efficiency in excess of 80%, with an absolute performance almost half that of a Cray X-MP/2 with the optimal scalar algorithm, which is nearly twice as fast as the one used in the above hypercube algorithms.

Acknowledgements. This work was supported by Los Alamos National Laboratory , Lawrence Livermore National Laboratory and IBM Corporation (Kingston Laboratory).

References.

[1] W.R. Martin, P.F. Nowak, and J.A. Rathkopf, *Monte Carlo Photon Transport on a Vector Supercomputer*, IBM Journal of Research and Development 30, 193(1986).

[2] T.C. Wan and W.R. Martin, *Parallel Algorithms for Photon Transport Monte Carlo* , to be presented at the Winter Meeting of the American Nuclear Society, Washington, DC (Nov. 1986).

[3] J.P. Hayes, et al., *Hypercube Computer Research at the University of Michigan* , presented at the Second Conference on Hypercube Multiprocessors, Knoxville, TN, Sept. 1986 (these proceedings).

[4] P. Frederickson, R. Hiromoto, T.L. Jordan, B. Smith, and T. Warnock, *Pseudo-Random Trees in Monte Carlo*, Parallel Computing 1, 175 (1984).

Adaptation of a Large-Scale Computational Chemistry Program for the Intel iPSC* Concurrent Computer

A. R. LARRABEE† AND R. G. BABB†

Abstract. A study was made of some of the characteristics, capabilities, and limitations of the Intel iPSC concurrent computer. Because of the relatively large overhead of messages passing, programs adapted to run concurrently will have the greatest speedup over the same program executed serially if the computational time is large relative to the time spent passing messages. A large-scale computational chemistry program (named ECEPP83) that calculates the global minimum energy of peptide structures (a peptide is a small protein) was ported and adapted to execute on a 32 node iPSC computer. The data entry and checking portion of the original code was ported to the 286/310 Intel computer that serves as a manager of the nodes. The data for each structure is sent by the manager to a separate node which reports its results back to the host or system manager and then is assigned another structure. This version is able to concurrently minimize the energy for 32 chemical structures 17 times faster than serial execution on a VAX 11-780 computer. A user manual was written to assist the user in assembling the input data file.

Introduction. Many computer scientists believe that present machines based on "von Neumann" architecture are approaching a physical limit for the speed obtainable with computers having only one central processing unit (CPU). One approach to solving this problem is to build machines with multiple CPU's that can attack various aspects of a problem concurrently. Such parallel architectures offer the potential for achieving more computational operations per unit time, but also introduce new problems , such as determining which aspects of a serially executed algorithm are amenable to parallel computation, coordinating the results of the various processors, avoiding race conditions, and reducing contention for resources [1]. The level of parallelism

---

*Intel Company, Santa Clara, California

† Department of Computer Science and Engineering, Oregon Graduate Center, Beaverton, Oregon 97006.

can vary from fine-grained parallelism, (e.g. a single executable statement), to an entire subroutine or program. Although it is possible for compilers to detect some opportunities to calculate do loops and array manipulations in parallel, in general, existing programs written in conventional programming languages can be difficult to parallelize [1]. Thus, in order to move into parallel computations, either other languages more suited to concurrency must become popular [2], or existing code must be restructured [3,4]. For certain applications, radical architectures and approaches may prove effective [5].

Rationale and Early Studies. Since the iPSC we used consists of 32 nodes, the best speedup attainable for the time to solve a single problem would be 32 times the speed of a machine with only a single node. For a program to take maximum advantage of the iPSC, it must require enough CPU time to justify the extra time spent in initializing and loading the nodes, and especially in coordinating the computation on the nodes via message passing.

Messages between any two nodes can be up to 16K (K=1024) bytes long, but are sent in 1 Kbyte packets and then reassembled after reception. Early test programs executed on a 32 node iPSC showed that message passing between nodes is time consuming, and message passing from the nodes to the cube manager is even slower. Moreover, the time depends upon the number of internode connections a message must pass over to reach its destination. Measurements of the time required to send messages (Version 2.1) are shown in Figure 1. Current versions of the system software afford somewhat faster transmission times than these figures.

Internodes	Message Length(Kbytes)	Time(msec)
1	1	8.0 ± 0.5
1	2	11.5 ± 0.1
1	3	16.0 ± 0.5
1	4	23.0 ± 1.4
2	1	11.1 ± 0.3
2	2	27.3 ± 1.2
2	3	43.5 ± 3.1
2	4	61.3 ± 3.5

Figure 1. Time for message sending (blocked).

Because of the relatively high overhead of message passing, the creation of too many parallel process, (e.g. creation of slave nodes to attempt to ease the bottleneck of a rate-limiting subroutine), can actually increase the throughput time of the program relative to that of one with a smaller number of slave nodes. If the number of messages is constant, the fraction of time devoted to message passing decreases as the computational load increases. Thus, for programs to be suitable for the iPSC, they must require relatively large amounts of processor time, must be intrinsically "parallelizable", and most important, must have a high ratio of computational operations to message passing.

Additional test programs demonstrated that if messages were generated at a rate faster than they could be received, the system would "hang" as apparently the node buffers were filled to capacity. The explanation for this is that the node operating system (NOS version 2.0) does not do any flow control. Nodes are not able to alter running programs with the goal of letting the number of unreceived messages decrease. Similarly, many messages arriving at the host can cause the message reception apparatus to become a bottleneck and messages may "time out" if they are not received within a certain time span. This latter problem has been greatly lessened by later versions of the software. As will be seen, this flow control problem arose during the implementation of the program for this work.

A major parameter in parallel processing is the size of the "granule" of computation that is executed in parallel. In traditional programs for Von Neumann computers, a granule corresponds to an entire application program, and little parallelism within an application program can be exploited. On the other hand, in most dataflow work to date, the grain size chosen for parallel scheduling has been at the level of a single arithmetic or logical operator [3,4].

The program chosen for the present work ran twice as slow on a single node of the iPSC compared to the VAX 11-780 at the Oregon Graduate Center. Thus, a 100% improvement of program execution would bring the performance of the hypercube and 11-780 close to the same value. Therefore, a search was made for a scientific application program that 1) is in current use, 2) is computationally intense rather than input-output intense, 3) requires enough execution time on a VAX class machine to justify an improvement effort, and 4) is amenable to parallel execution. Such a program could then be utilized to study concurrent computations in general, and the advantages and disadvantages of a particular hardware approach to current computers, viz., the Intel iPSC hypercube.

After some searching among chemistry programs, an ideal candidate for meeting the above goals was found—a program that computes the energy of peptides (a peptide is a small protein) as a function of the three-dimensional conformation (i.e. structure of the molecule) utilizing a torsional angle minimizer and rigid geometry calculations [6,7]. The initial program used for experiments with the iPSC is the property of the Polygen Corporation, Waltham, Massachusetts and is called ECEPP83 (Empirical Conformational Energy Program for Peptides-1983 edition). An earlier version, without the minimizer, is available through the "Quantum Chemistry Program Exchange"[8]. The version of the program modified for the iPSC is called ECEPP83-iPSC. This and similar programs have been used extensively to calculate the global energy minimum of peptide hormones and peptide effector molecules [6,7]. Chemists believe that the native structure or conformation of proteins and peptides is the one(s) with the lowest free energy. ECEPP83 and earlier versions enjoy relatively wide use since some small peptides are not crystallizable and thus their structures are not determinable by X-ray crystallography. Moreover, spectroscopic methods at present can only yield vague attributes of structures as complex and variable as peptides. In many cases, computational methods, such as the one provided by ECEPP83, are the only means available to study this problem.

The search for a global minimum for one peptide can easily require many hours, or even days, of VAX speed CPU time [6 and the references quoted there]. The complexity for the minimumization algorithm embodied in ECEPP83 is $O(nr^2)$, where n is the number of conformers whose energy is sought and r is the length of the peptide, i.e. the number of amino acid residues.

ECEPP83 requires the user to define an initial structure for a particular peptide whose structure is to be calculated. This is done by defining an initial value for each dihedral angle of the molecule. The user then specifies the number of passes through the minimizer and what angles are to be allowed to change in the subsequent energy minimization algorithm. Lastly, the number of iterations is chosen and from this point on the program requires no I/O until a local minima is found.

Initial studies of ECEPP83 (with gprof[9] on the 11-780) showed that 33 to 40% of the CPU time was spent in calculating square roots. Moreover, there were many loop functions which had the potential for concurrency. The energy interactions between pairs of atoms are independent and therefore could possibly be calculated on separate processors. On the other hand, each such calculation would require a message to be sent back to the host, or sent to a node dedicated to data collection and task assignment. However, a consideration of how ECEPP83 is used by peptide chemists led to an ideal solution to this problem. ECEPP83 is an iterative energy minimizer, but it is not able to escape from local minima. In other words, it travels down into an "energy valley"—but there is no assurance the the valley is the one of lowest global "elevation". Users must supply many starting conformer structures, minimize each one, and hope that they have hit the lowest valley or energy minima. This corresponds to feeding a series of structures to a "von Neumann" computer. The approach taken here is to run the computational part of the ECEPP83 program on every node of the iPSC concurrent computer and thus be able to calculate up to 32 structures concurrently.

The input and data checking part of ECEPP83-iPSC is run in the cube manager. The user creates an input file which defines the structures of a series of conformers (one conformer is one defined chemical structure). The necessary arrays are initialized with the information for a conformer. The cube manager maintains and updates, via messages from the nodes, an array which stores information as to the availability of nodes. The cube manager reads the array to find a node that is not presently assigned a conformer, sends the data for a conformer, and looks for a node for the next conformer data, etc.

Development of the Program. By implementing the major part of the ECEPP83-iPSC program on every node of the hypercube, the best match between the serial use of the program and the inherent advantages of the iPSC hypercube was obtained. Since this program is used in a SPMD (Single Program Multiple Data) mode, implementation of the program on every node is close to the ultimate in large grain parallelism, i.e. a collection of computers under the control of another computer.

The initial task was to port the entire program onto the cube manager. The program as obtained from the Polygen Corporation ran correctly on the OGC VAX 11-780 with no modifications. The necessary minor changes were made to port the code to the Intel (ftn286) 286/310 computer that serves as the host for the 32 nodes of the iPSC.

The final version of the cube manager program behaves as follows: ECEPP83 originally could obtain the data for a conformer either interactively or via an input file. The version resulting from this work is called ECEPP83-iPSC and is shown schematically in Figure 2. The program uses DATA statement initialization to specify the force field data for the calculation of charge interactions. The data for amino acid angles and bond lengths is read from an external file. The only user input after the host program is initiated is to answer a request for the number of conformers to be input. The conformer data is then read from a user prepared input file named "ecpdat".

If no input errors for a conformer are detected, the required data, most of which is contained in arrays and variables in COMMON statements, is sent to the lowest numbered node available. The free node is chosen after consultation of an array named "freelist" which contains the information as to the availability of nodes ready for assignment. Once a node is sent the pertinent data for one conformer, successive iterative cycles of minimization are initiated and repeated as specified. When the nodes finish their calculations, the results are written into an output file named "mylog" via a node operating system utility named *syslog*.

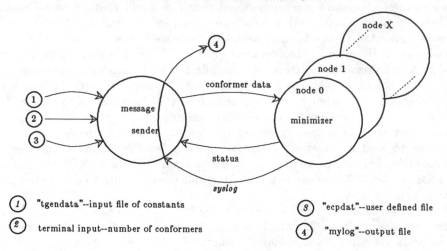

1 "tgendata"--input file of constants   3 "ecpdat"--user defined file

2 terminal input--number of conformers   4 "mylog"--output file

Figure 2. Data flow view of ECEPP83-iPSC loaded on the iPSC.

Alternatively, the initial data and the data for the minimization of each conformer could have been managed by a master node. This node would be the only one corresponding with the host. Such an arrangement would have the advantage that 60% of the information required to define a conformer is the same for all conformers and thus this information could be sent in one message to the master node for dispersal to the nodes via a minimum cost spanning tree connection network. As implemented, the host uses its slower message mechanisms to disperse this common information to each node separately. Aside from the loss of a "slave" node there are several other problems with the master node concept in the present case. The resulting data from each node is several lines long and if the minimization data for two structures arrived at the master node concurrently, the resulting data would be interspersed. The master node could be loaded with software that separated the data from two or more incoming nodes based on the "type" variable that accompanys each message. However, the test programs mentioned alerted the possibility that such an arrangement could lead to message timeouts or program interruption if the number of messages unreceived became large. It was decided not to implement a master node, rather to produce the final results via the *syslog* function, which does not exhibit flow control problems. The data from two or more nodes written into the output file by *syslog* still can be interspersed and this problem was handled by processing the output file with the Xenix *sort* and *awk*[10] functions to sort and convert the final results into a more readable format.

Testing showed that conformers whose energy calculations are caught in local minima, can sometimes be further minimized (jump out of local minima) by increasing the number of minimization "cycles" requested. Thus, once caught in a local minima, the user can generate a new set of conformers to test, or alternatively, initially request more minimizer passes for each conformer (this latter, of course, involves hindsight).

Assessment. The approach outlined here has several distinctive characteristics which are summarized below.

(1) the ECEPP83-iPSC program depends on "brute force" calculations involving much CPU time. Research is in progress [11,12] to construct expert systems for intelligent selections of starting conformers.

(2) the simplified approach and the large grain parallelism suggested here afford nearly ideal load balancing.

(3) Although the parallelization strategy suggested for ECEPP83-iPSC will not generalize to all scientific calculations, the approach presented here will have applicability to other problems, is relatively easy to understand, implement, and easy to use.

(4) Most important, the speedup potential will be maximized.

The major problem in implementation of the ECEPP83-iPSC code was the management of the large amount of data that must be sent from the manager to the nodes. As mentioned above, there is a flow control problem in that messages cannot be allowed to be issued by the manager *ad libitum* without the possibility of "hanging" the system. When the message passing was implemented, it was indeed found prudent to send a few messages to a node, have the node respond that it was ready for more data, then to proceed with more host to node messages.

During node initialization, a message may arrive from another node signaling that the node is finished with calculations on a particular conformer and ready for another assignment. Such a message must wait until the next flow control message arrives. During each pause generated by 12 additional flow control messages from the node to the host, the host is able to receive pending messages of any type. The type accompanying the message allows the software to determine whether the message is a flow control message, one concerning an available node, or a message signaling that a node has an interrupt from which it cannot recover. If the message is the first type, the program continues to send conformer data. If it is the second type, the freelist array is updated in the appropriate position, the program loops back to receive another message. This cycle continues until a flow control message is received. If it is of the last type, the program loops back to receive another message, the freelist is not updated, and the host program will not send any new data sets to this now nonfunctional node.

Results. ECEPP83—the original program, running on the VAX 11-780, and ECEPP83-iPSC—the original program modified for the iPSC, yield similar but not absolutely identical results. A number of conformer data sets have been processed by each machine. The greatest difference between the two machines each processing the same data involved two passes through the minimizer of 100 cycles each. In one cycle, each angle of the peptide (i.e. the angles the user wishes varied) is varied at least once and then varied again continuously until the energy value for the peptide no longer decreases. The VAX 11-780 produced a value of 68402 Kcal and the iPSC a value of 68406 Kcal. This difference is attributed to the effects of accumulated roundoff and is acceptable. Similarly, it was noticed in one part of one calculation, that after only 30 cycles, the two machines value for one angle differed by 0.30 degrees. In this case, the energy values were identical as apparently this amount of rotation in a side chain bond did not affect the free energy.

In one case, initially terrifying, the two machines produced totally different answers starting from the same data set. However, if each final set of angles was fed to the other machine, the same answer was obtained. In other words, although the two machines obtained different minimized structures from the same data, each one appeared to have traveled down to a different energy valley. There are many local minima but only one lowest energy structure. Each machine, when fed the final set of angles calculated by the other, verified the energy values. A study of each pass through the minimizer indicated that initially the two machines were minimizing along the same path. The investigation was sufficient to show that the divergence occurred at a point where the calculated energy as a function of the omega angle in question was constant on one machine and had a very slight downward slope on the other. Apparently, one machine (the 11-780) persisted in changing this same angle while the iPSC switched to varying another angle. Thus, each proceeded down a different solution path. Such a result does not constitute a "flaw" in parallel computation, but certainly is a consequence that must be considered with algorithms that deal with problems that have many solutions. One could consider an algorithm that calculates chess moves as analogous to the one discussed here. There may be several minima for a particular peptide that differ only by a few Kcal and thus may be thermally interconvertible. Similarly, there may be several chess moves of similar desirability. In both cases, the algorithms presently known are incomplete as far as finding the perfect answer.

Performance Measurements After loading the entire program, modified as described, onto the cube manager (not utilizing any of the nodes), a test program required 251 to 298 seconds to run (with no other users). The same program run on the VAX 11-780 (using gprof to yield meaningful times) required 84 to 89 seconds. Thus, for this example, the Intel 286/310 is slower than the VAX 11-780 by about a factor of three. If the nodes proved to be the same speed as the 286/310, we could expect a theoretical speedup of 32/3 or about 10 for a d = 5 iPSC hypercube (fully loaded) over that of the 11-780. This value can be compared to the actual speedup obtained after the program was implemented on the nodes.

In all the test cases utilized in this study and for ECEPP83-iPSC, blocked messages were used exclusively. For the test cases, programs with unblocked messages did not execute faster than the same program with blocked messages. Apparently, the time required to send the messages in these cases was the same order of magnitude as that required to execute a *status* check to determine if the communication channel could be reused. Because of the flow control problem mentioned, no attempt was made to use unblocked messages in the ECEPP83-iPSC program code.

The starting data for three test conformers was fed to ECEPP83 running on the 11-780 execution profiled with gprof [9]. The CPU time measured for the three test conformers was 31, 88, and 220 seconds for a total of 339 seconds. The cube could calculate the same three serially on one node in 535 seconds. The 11-780 is approximately 1.58 times faster with these three calculations than a single iPSC node. In spite of the fact that the ECEPP83 version running on the 11-780 has slightly more printout than the hypercube version, the hypercube has the potential to calculate peptide conformers roughly 20 times faster(32/1.58) than the 11-780. In another test case, 64 sets of the above data which took 339 seconds to run on the 11-780, was run on the iPSC concurrently. Ignoring the fact that the cube was only fully loaded less than half of the time, the speedup for the iPSC over the 11-780 was 11.6. It is expected that more detailed measurements (i.e. the fully loaded time is increased relative to the partially loaded time) would show that the iPSC hypercube can achieve close to a 20 fold speedup with some SPMD applications such as the ECEPP83-iPSC program studied here.

After these measurements were taken, the f77 library function *frexp()* has been improved. The f77 *sqrt()* function uses this function and currently the program mentioned above that required 220 seconds, now runs in 184 to 188 seconds. For the ECEPP83 program running on the VAX 11-780, this represents a 15% improvement. A recalculation of the possible speedup of the iPSC hypercube over the VAX 11-780 yields a new value of 17 (32/1.86). It is expected that each new version of either machine will continue to move this figure up or down. As long as such perturbations are relatively small, the results reported here will have the same relevance.

Conclusions For any person considering writing original code for parallel execution or converting existing code from serial to parallel execution, several considerations can be suggested. The following suggestions are made on the assumption that it is more difficult to construct parallel computations than serial ones.

(1) What is the potential for speedup when a comparison is made between the parallel machine in question and the existing serial machine?

(2) Whether writing new or porting existing code, what debugging tools are available?

(3) What is the stage of development of the parallel machine, and what is the reliability of the software and its documentation?

(4) On parallel machines, the results of one processor must be communicated to other processors and/or to a computer controlling the processors either by message passing or shared memory. What is the overhead involved or contention problems associated with processor cooperation?

(5) For existing code, how well documented is the code, and what depth of understanding is required to modify the serial code for parallel execution?

(6) How difficult will be the thorough testing of the parallel implementation for correct output and normal termination?

(7) What is the granularity of parallelization that can be applied to the algorithm? What is the ratio of computation effort to the effort mentioned in item 4 above?

(8) Is expertise available to deal with the problems that seem to arise in any effort to improve an existing application code?

The present study has pointed out that for the case of the Intel iPSC computer, items (2) to (4) above had negative aspects which increased the implementation time or tended to minimize the gains achievable. In the case of item (5) above, it was usually the case that it was sufficient to know what the various subroutines accomplished, rather than how they were designed, in order to construct the parallel version of ECEPP83. On the other hand, the in program documentation was not updated each time the code was improved. The formal documentation was written in 1975 for the first implementation on an IBM 370 computer. In the case of the present study, positive effects of readily exploitable large grain parallelism and help from the code's developers served to mask these difficulties and those associated with items (2) to (6). The large grain parallelism implemented here matches well the single program multiple data use of the ECEPP83-iPSC program. The number of messages required did not grow with the size of the problem, and although relatively slow, the message passing overhead is a small fraction of the computation time.

Consideration should be given to all of the above items when implementing any algorithm on a parallel machine. The completed parallel implementation must be tested extensively to help assure that the output will be compatible with the program executed serially.

References

(1)   J.R. McGRAW and T.S. AXELROD, *Exploiting Multiprocessors: Issues and Options*, Preprint from the Lawrence Livermore National Laboratory, Livermore, CA, 1984.

(2)   E. SHAPIRO and A. TAKEUCHI, *Object Oriented Programming in Concurrent Prolog*, New Generation Computing, 1, (1983), p 25.

(3)   R.G. BABB and L. STORC, *Parallel Processing on the Denelcor HEP with Large Grain Data Flow Techniques*, Technical Report CS/E 85-010, Oregon Graduate Center, 1985.

(4)   R. G. BABB, *Programming the HEP with Large-Grain Data Flow Techniques*, in *MIMD Computation: HEP Supercomputer and Its Applications*, J. S. Kowalik, ed., The MIT Press, Cambridge, MA, 1985.

(5)   D. HAMMERSTROM, D. MAIER, and S. THAKKAR, S., *The Cognitive Architecture Project*, Computer Architecture News, 14 (1986), pp. 9-21.

(6)   H. CHUMAN, F.A. MOMANY, and L. SCHAFER, *Backbone Conformation, Bend Structures, Helix Structures and Other Tests of an Improved Conformational Energy Program for Peptides: ECEPP83*, Int. J. Peptide Protein Res., 24 (1984), pp. 233-248.

(7)   A.T. HAGLER, *Theoretical Simulation of Conformation Energies and Dynamics of Peptides*, Preprint from the Agouron Institute, La Jolla, CA.

(8)   *Quantum Chemistry Program Exchange*, Program No. QCPE 286. Chemistry Department, Indiana University, Bloomington, IL 47401. phone: 812-337-4784.

(9)   *Unix Programmer's Manual 4.2 Berkeley Software Distribution*, Computer Science Division, Department of Electrical Engineering and Computer Science. University of California, Berkeley, CA 94720, 1979.

(10) *Xenix 286 Reference Manual*, Intel Corporation, 3065 Bowers Ave., Santa Clara, CA. 95051, 1984.

(11) *Biopolymers*, in press.

(12) Conversations with Dr. Frank Momany, Polygen Corporation, Waltham, MA.

Density Functional Theory and Parallel Processing[*]

RICHARD C. WARD†, G. A. GEIST† AND W. H. BUTLER†

ABSTRACT. We demonstrate a method for obtaining the ground state energies and charge densities of a system of atoms described within density functional theory using simulated annealing on a parallel computer.

INTRODUCTION. Density functional theory [1,2] is a technique which, in principal, allows one to calculate the ground state energy and charge density of an arbitrary number of atoms in an arbitrary configuration. Materials scientists, solid state physicists, and chemists have devoted a tremendous amount of effort to develop specialized codes that apply density functional theory to various types of problems. The objective of the work described here is the application of parallel processing to develop a general technique for calculating the properties of molecules and materials from first principles using density functional theory. The philosophy is to use a very simple but general code which can be made parallel, with the hope that any losses in efficiency due to the simple and general nature of the code can be overcome by applying more processors.

We apply density functional theory to a cluster of atoms with each atom assigned to a separate node of the parallel processor (the INTEL Hypercube). The resultant set of coupled differential equations is solved by a simulated annealing procedure similar to that suggested recently by Carr and Parrinello [3]. In simulated annealing artificial classical dynamic equations for the electron wave functions are constructed. These are then solved using the molecular dynamics

* Research supported by the Exploratory Studies Program of the Oak Ridge National Laboratory which is operated by Martin Marietta Energy Systems Inc., under contract DE-AC05-84OR21400 with the U. S. Department of Energy.

† Oak Ridge National Laboratory, Oak Ridge, Tennessee, 37831

computer simulation technique [4]. The kinetic energy of the system is gradually reduced to zero, at which point the system has "annealed" into the ground state. In contrast to previous applications of simulated annealing [3], our calculations were done in real space to obtain the actual wave functions.

This paper will first present a short description of density functional theory. Following this we describe simulated annealing and apply it to obtain the solution of two well-known problems, the linear one-dimensional harmonic oscillator and the hydrogen atom. We then describe how a parallel code was constructed to obtain the ground state energies and charge densities for a system of atoms within density functional theory. Finally we will present results for the simulated annealing of a system of four atoms in a plane (a two-dimensional Hypercube geometry).

DENSITY FUNCTIONAL THEORY.   Density functional theory expresses the electron interaction energies (Coulomb and exchange-correlation) as a functional of the electron density which is determined by the square of the electron wave function [1,2]. The Schrödinger equation for the one-particle electron wave function, ψ_j, in density functional theory is (in Rydberg units):

$$-\nabla^2 \psi_j + V(\vec{r})\psi_j = \epsilon_j \psi_j \qquad\qquad 1.$$

where ϵ_j is the eigenvalue of the jth state. The potential energy, $V(\vec{r})$, consists of ion-electron and electron-electron interaction terms. The electron-electron interaction is split into a Coulomb term, which describes the direct electron-electron interactions, and an exchange-correlation term:

$$V(\vec{r}) = V_{ie}(\vec{r}) + V_c(\vec{r}) + V_{xc}(\vec{r}) \qquad\qquad 2.$$

Ion-Electron: $\qquad\qquad V_{ie}(\vec{r}) = -\sum_{ion} 2 Z / |\vec{r} - \vec{r}_{ion}|$

Coulomb: $\qquad\qquad V_c(\vec{r}) = 2 \int d^3 r' n(\vec{r}') / |\vec{r} - \vec{r}'|$

Exchange-Correlation: $\quad V_{xc}(\vec{r}) = -\alpha\, n(\vec{r})^{1/3}.$

Here we have taken a typical form [5] for the exchange-correlation energy in the local density approximation. The electron charge density is the sum over all electron states up to the Fermi energy, ϵ_f:

$$n(\vec{r}) = \sum_j \psi_j^*(\vec{r}) \, \psi_j(\vec{r}) \qquad\qquad 3.$$

The charge density, $n(\vec{r})$, is required to obtain $V(\vec{r})$ and since $n(\vec{r})$ depends on ψ the set of three equations (Equs. 1 - 3, referred to as the Kohn-Sham equations) must be solved self consistently. In the past [6] this was done by an explicit iterative procedure of first guessing a charge density, then computing $V(\vec{r})$ and the wave function to obtain an updated value of the charge density. The simulated annealing procedure will do this for us automatically. We need only provide initial forms for the wave functions to begin the process.

DESCRIPTION OF SIMULATED ANNEALING. In simulated annealing, one desires to minimize a functional with respect to a set of variational parameters [3]. For the purposes of demonstrating the procedure, we assume that the variational parameter is a single wave function. The functional to be minimized is the total energy, E, the sum of the kinetic and potential energies:

$$E[\psi] = -\int \psi^*(\vec{r}) \, \nabla^2 \psi(\vec{r}) \, d^3r + V[n(\vec{r})] \qquad\qquad 4.$$

where V is the potential energy and $n(\vec{r})$ is the density, $|\psi(\vec{r})|^2$. In simulated annealing we consider the wave function to be described by a set of dynamical equations (Newton's equations) with the energy functional E as the Hamiltonian:

$$\mu \, \ddot{\psi}(\vec{r}) = -\delta E/\delta \psi^*(\vec{r}) + \lambda \psi(\vec{r}). \qquad\qquad 5.$$

where μ is a fictitious mass and the Lagrange multiplier λ is introduced to satisfy the constraint:

$$\int |\psi(\vec{r})|^2 \, d^3r = 1. \qquad\qquad 6.$$

The molecular dynamics technique [4] is used to solve the set of Newton's equations. The minimization of these equations is accomplished by reducing the velocity of the wave function at each discrete lattice point following an annealing schedule. At equilibrium, when the kinetic energy of the system has been reduced to zero, $\ddot{\psi}$ is zero and the dynamical equation becomes identical to the Schrödinger equation (Equ. 1) with the Lagrange parameter, λ, equal to the eigenvalue, ϵ.

The Verlet algorithm [4] was used to carry out the molecular dynamics simulation and the values of the Lagrange multiplier were determined by the method of Ryckaert, Ciccotti and Berendsen [7]. For a single wave function this required solving a single quadratic equation:

$$A \lambda^2 + B \lambda + C = 0 \qquad \qquad 7.$$

where

$$A = \Delta t^4 \int \psi^2 \, d^3 r / \mu^2 \quad , \quad B = \Delta t^2 \int \psi \, \hat{\psi} \, d^3 r / \mu \quad \text{and} \quad C = \int \hat{\psi} \, \hat{\psi} \, d^3 r.$$

$\hat{\psi}$ is the solution to the unconstrained Newton's equation and Δt is the time step.

If there are two wave functions, as in the case for the two electron example considered further on, the total density (Equ. 3) is obtained by summing over the density due to each wave function and the constraint equation is replaced by the set of equations:

$$\int \psi_j^*(\vec{r}) \, \psi_k(\vec{r}) \, dr^3 = \delta_{j,k} \qquad \qquad 8.$$

where j and k designate the wave functions. In this case there will be four Lagrange multipliers, λ_{11} , λ_{22} , λ_{12} and λ_{21}. By symmetry, the off-diagonal elements will be the same. Equation 7 becomes a 2X2 matrix equation which is solved by non-linear iteration to yield the Lagrange multipliers. On annealing, the Lagrange multipliers, λ_{11} and λ_{22}, become the eigenvalues for the ground state and first excited state and the off-diagonal element λ_{12} $(=\lambda_{21})$ will approach zero.

PROBLEMS WITH KNOWN SOLUTIONS - HARMONIC OSCILLATOR AND HYDROGEN ATOM. A serial code was developed to apply simulated annealing to two problems with known solutions - the one-dimensional harmonic oscillator and the hydrogen atom. The potential for the one-dimensional harmonic oscillator is: $V(x) = k x^2/2$, where k is the spring constant (here chosen to be 1), and x is the displacement from the origin.

The problem was solved over the range x(-4.,4.) with a spatial step size of 0.02. The boundary condition on the wave functions at the limits of the range was that they be equal to zero. The initial wave function is shown in Fig. 1a (solid line). After annealing for 2000 time steps with $\Delta t = 0.01$ the ground state of the harmonic oscillator (Fig. 1b) was obtained. The serial code was then modified to allow for solution of two wave functions. Beginning with the initial symmetric and antisymmetric wave functions shown in Fig. 1a, we obtained both

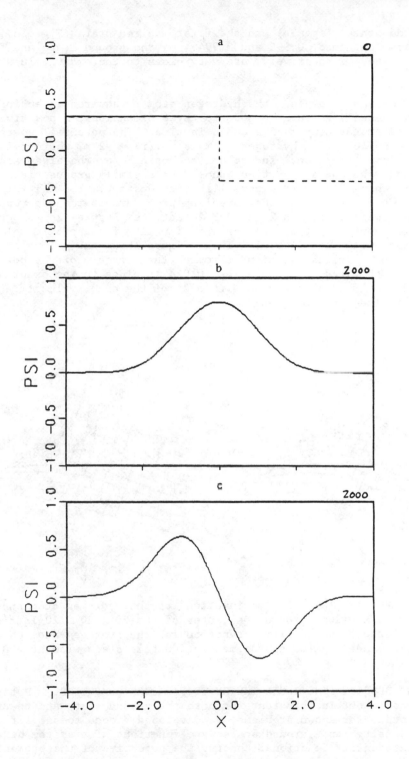

Fig. 1. (a) Initial symmetric (solid) and antisymmetric (dashed) wave functions for linear harmonic oscillator. (b) Ground state and (c) first excited state of the linear harmonic oscillator obtained by simulated annealing for 2000 time steps with $\Delta t = 0.01$.

the   ground state (Fig. 1b) and the first excited state (Fig. 1c). The
eigenvalues   obtained, 0.996 and 2.994, for the ground state and first
excited   state,   respectively, are very close to the exact values of 1
and 3.

The   second   example - the hydrogen atom - required extending the
simulated   annealing   serial   code to three dimensions. A positive ion
was   placed at the center of a cubic lattice.   The potential energy of
the   electron   of   the   hydrogen atom is: $V(r) = -2/r$, where r is the
distance   from   the   ion.   In the units chosen here, the eigenvalue is
unity   and   the   wave   function   should be a simple exponential, ψ =
A exp(-r)   where   A   is   the   normalization constant.   The initial wave
function   used   to   start   the annealing procedure is the cap function
(Fig.   2a)   defined over a 20 X 20 X 20 lattice. Figure   2b   shows the
results   of annealing the electron wave function for approximately 500
time   steps   with Δt = 0.01.   This   figure shows the values of wave
function   on   a   cross   section   through   the   center   of the box. The
eigenvalue   obtained   by   annealing (0.93) is close to the exact value
(1.)   and   could be obtained to within 2% of the exact value if a 64 X
64 X 64 lattice had been used.

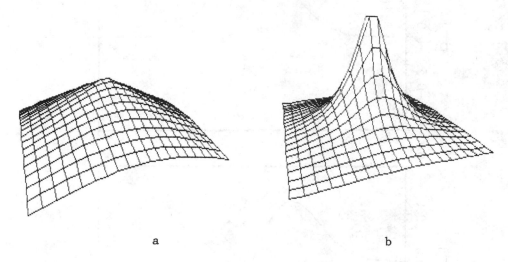

a   b

Fig. 2.   (a) Initial wave function for the hydrogen atom shown on
a cross section through the center of the 20 X 20 X 20 lattice.
(b)   Ground   state   wave   function for the hydrogen atom obtained
after annealing for approximately 500 time steps with Δt = 0.01.

ADAPTING   DENSITY FUNCTIONAL THEORY TO PARALLEL COMPUTERS.   Satisfied
that we could obtain solutions for both the ground state and the first
excited state for known problems, we developed a code to solve for the
charge   density   and   ground state wave functions of a system of atoms
within the density functional theory. The objective of the project was
to   develop   a   parallel   code   that would use the simulated annealing
procedure   as described above to solve for the electron wave functions
within density functional theory.

To adapt the computation to the parallel computing environment, each ion and its associated electron cloud was physically assigned to a separate node of the parallel computer (an INTEL Hypercube). As an example we chose to consider four atoms in a plane (Fig. 4), a configuration of nodes which corresponds to a two-dimensional Hypercube geometry.

The computation of the ion-electron potential can be carried out on each node as long as the position of the ion on each node is known by all the other nodes. This information is passed to all the nodes at each time step to allow for possible ion motion (although none is considered in the calculations presented here). Since the exchange-correlation potential is determined in the local density approximation, it can be determined on each node with no additional information being exchanged between nodes.

The Coulomb term, however, is long-range and to account approximately for the interaction between electron wave functions on separate nodes, the contribution from neighboring nodes was approximated by a multipole moment expansion:

$$V_c(\vec{r}) = 2\int_{node} d^3r' \; n(\vec{r}')/|\vec{r} - \vec{r}'| + \sum_{j \neq node} M(q_j, \vec{d}_j) \qquad 9.$$

where expansion (M) is a function of the charge (q_j) and the dipole moment ($\vec{d}_j$) of the jth node. Thus to calculate the potential, information about the charge and dipole moment of each node must be passed to all other nodes. This was accomplished using the E2E (Everybody to Everybody) subroutine, wherein the information from each node is packed into a vector and passed around to the nodes in a ring configuration.

Solving the dynamical equations for the wave function (Equs.4-6) requires that we obtain the Laplacian at each point. This requires passing boundary information from one node into its adjacent nodes. This was carried out by another communications subroutine (EXCHANGE). Thus the computation of the potentials and the solution of the dynamical equation for the wave function at each step required two exchanges between nodes (Fig. 3). In each case however, a relatively small amount of information was interchanged.

```
HOST PROGRAM:                           NODE PROGRAM:

SEND information to control             RECEIVE information
     exchange of boundary faces
     and multiple moments
time loop - - - - - - - - - - - - -time loop
SEND λ                                  RECEIVE λ
                                        use λ to find new
                                        wave function
                                        EXCHANGE faces
                                        compute moments
                                        EXCHANGE moments
                                        compute potentials and forces
                                        obtain A,B,C
RECEIVE A,B,C                           SEND A,B,C
update λ
end time loop - - - - - - - - - -end time loop
RECEIVE wave function                   SEND wave function
end                                     end
```

Fig. 3. Schematic for the parallel code to solve for the electron wave functions in density functional theory using simulated annealing. This schematic indicates when communications are occurring between the host and nodes and when the nodes are exchanging information amongst themselves.

Examination of the schematic of the parallel code (Fig. 3) also reveals that the node need not return the values of the wave functions at each lattice point to the host, but only lattice sums of wave functions. For the one-dimensional case these are the parameters A,B,C discussed above and for the three dimensional case there are nine of these parameters. When the energy calculations are completed, the host will collect the information, compute the eigenvalues and proceed to the next time step. The values of the wave functions at each lattice point need to be returned to the host only at the very end of the simulation, if a plot of the wave function is desired.

The parallel code was run on the Hypercube using a 10 X 10 X 10 lattice on each node, with a lattice spacing of 0.8 and a time step of 0.01. Due to the time consuming nature of the computation for the Coulomb and exchange-correlation terms, these were ignored. The initial wave functions are shown in Fig. 4. The symmetric wave function consisted of hydrogenic wave functions ($A\exp(-r)$) on each ion, the antisymmetric wave function consisted of all values of +1 or all values of -1 on alternating nodes.

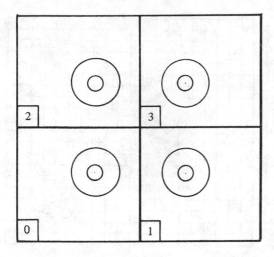

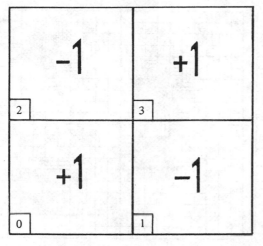

Fig. 4. Initial Conditions for the symmetric (top) and anti-symmetric (bottom) wave functions for four atoms in a plane. Each atom is assigned to a particular node of the Hypercube, designated by the number in the lower left corner. The symmetric wave functions are hydrogenic wave functions (A exp(-r)) and the antisymmetric wave functions are all +1 or all -1 on alternating nodes.

The resulting symmetric and antisymmetric wave functions, after annealing for 500 time steps with $\Delta t = 0.01$, are shown in Fig. 5a. The eigenvalues were -1.93 and -1.81 for the symmetric and antisymmetric wave functions, respectively. We would expect that the energy of the antisymmetric or excited state would be less negative (less bound) than that of the symmetric or ground state as we see in this example. A longer run (1000 steps) indicated that while the ground state was stable, the excited state tended to oscillate between two values. A shorter time step and longer annealing time might have eliminated this oscillation.

Moving the ions to non-symmetric positions, and starting again with the same initial conditions, we obtained Fig. 5b, with eigenvalues -2.09 and -1.81 for the ground state and first excited state, respectively. We see that the charge density in the ground state has concentrated on the clustered pair of ions, leaving the further removed ions deficient in charge. The charge density is more

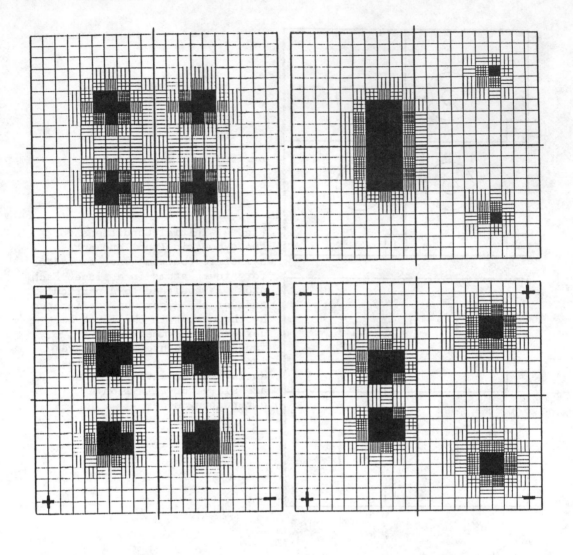

a   b

Fig. 5. (a) Symmetric (top) and antisymmetric (bottom) wave functions after annealing for 500 steps with $\Delta t = 0.01$. The antisymmetric wave function is positive on nodes 0 and 3 and negative on nodes 1 and 2. (b) Symmetric (top) and antisymmetric (bottom) wave functions for case where the ions are placed asymmetrically. The antisymmetric wave function is positive on nodes 0 and 3 and negative on nodes 1 and 2.

uniformly distributed for the first excited state. These results are qualitatively in agreement with band theory arguments.

We have not as yet attempted to do simulated annealing incorporating the electron-electron interaction terms using the parallel algorithm as the computational time required is excessive (30+ hours for a 500 step simulation). To speed up the computation of the Coulomb electron-electron interaction term, which is simply the solution of the Poisson equation, a fast fourier transform (FFT) can be used. This modification has been made to a serial version of the code but there were problems in obtaining the solution to Poisson's equation for an isolated charge distribution [8]. Furthermore, it appears that it will be very difficult to adapt the FFT to the parallel processor. An alternative solution is to use the fast multipole algorithm of Greengard and Rokhlin [9] to compute the Coulomb term.

We are confident that the example discussed above, incorporating only the ion-electron interactions, demonstrates the feasibility of applying simulated annealing to obtain the electron ground state wave functions for multi-atom systems and that, eventually, in combination with the density functional description, the technique could solve for the ground state energies and charge densities of atomic, molecular and solid systems of arbitrary geometry.

CONCLUSIONS. We have discussed the use of simulated annealing to solve for the electronic properties of a system of atoms described using density functional theory on a parallel computer. In simulated annealing the dynamical equations for the electron wave functions are constructed. These equations reduce to Schrödinger's equations if the accelerations are zero. The dynamical equations are solved using the molecular dynamics computer simulation technique. The kinetic energy of the system is gradually reduced to zero, at which point the system has "annealed" into the ground state.

First we constructed a serial code that would solve for the ground state and first excited state of the one-dimensional, linear harmonic oscillator, by simulated annealing. The code was then generalized to three dimensions and used to solve for the ground state of the hydrogen atom.

Having obtained confidence in applying simulated annealing to problems with known solutions, we developed a parallel code to solve for the ground state energies and charge densities of multi-atom systems within the framework of density functional theory. On the parallel computer each atom was assigned to its own processor. Results were presented for the ground state wave functions for four atoms neglecting the electron-electron interactions. These results establish the feasibility of solving this problem with the electron-electron interactions included provided that the Coulomb term is computed using a fast multipole expansion algorithm.

This project is important to understanding the fundamental behavior of atoms, molecules and solids since it will allow the solution of the electron wave functions for a multi-atom system of general geometry. In addition the parallel code is remarkably simple in construction allowing for easy modification upon extending to a larger geometry.

(1.) P. Hohenberg and W. Kohn, Inhomogeneous Electron Gas, Phys. Rev. 136, (1964), pp. B864-871.

(2.) W. Kohn and L.J. Sham, Self Consistent Equations Including Exchange and Correlation Effects, Phys. Rev. A, 140, (1965), pp. 1133-1138.

(3.) R. Carr and M. Parrinello, Unified Approach for Molecular Dynamics and Density Functional Theory, Phys. Rev. Lett., 55, (1985), pp. 2471-2474.

(4.) L. Verlet, Computer "Experiments" on Classical Fluids. I. Thermodynamical Properties on Lennard-Jones Molecules, Phys. Rev. 159, (1967), p. 98.

(5.) W. Kohn, A New Formulation of the Inhomogeneous Electron Gas Problem, in Many Body Theory - Part 1, Ryogo Kubo, ed., W. A. Benjamin, New York, 1966, pp. 71-85.

(6.) J. P. Dahl and J. Avery, eds., Local Density Approximations in Quantum Chemistry and Solid State Physics, Plenum Press, New York, 1984.

(7.) J. P. Ryckaert, G. Ciccotti, and H. J. C. Berendsen, Numerical Integration of the Cartesian Equations of Motion of a System with Constraints: Molecular Dynamics of n-Alkanes, J. Comput. Phys. 23, (1977), 327.

(8.) J. A. Maruhn, T. A. Welton and C. Y. Wong, Remarks on the Numerical Solution of Poisson's Equation for Isolated Charge Distributions, J. Comput. Phys, 20, (1976), 326.

(9.) L. Greengard and V. Rokhlin, A Fast Algorithm for Particle Simulations, Yale University Research Report, YALEU/DCS/RR-459, April 1986.

Implementation of Capacitance Calculation Program CAP2D on iPSC*

CHEN-PING YUAN†

Abstract. CAP2D is a fortran program which computes interconnect capacitances in VLSI circuits. Green's function approach and moment method were employed to solve two-dimensional static poisson's equation. The implementation and the result showed that Green's function approach lends itself quite nicely to parallel processing. Instead of solving a large sparse matrix, a dense symmetric matrix was solved. The most CPU intensive computation in the approach is the calculation of each matrix element which can be very easily distributed among the processors. The result showed a 15.2 speed-up on 16 node iPSC system, and utilization over 90%. It can not be overemphasized that the Green's function approach provides an easy and natural way to parallel processing.

Introduction. Interconnect capacitance has gradually become an integral part of VLSI circuits. Along comes the need to accurately model them and compute all the resulting capacitances, including both self capacitances with respect to the ground plane and the coupling capacitances among interconnects. One way would be to set up Poisson's equation as a boundary value problem. First discretize the region of interest into grids by finite difference method, then solve the resulting algebraic equation for potentials. From these potentials and charges, all capacitances can then be computed. This usual approach has been used in [1,2] to compute the capacitances.

*Intel Company, Santa Clara, California
†Technology Development CAD, Intel Company, Santa Clara, California 95052

Green's function Approach.   The approach taken in the simulation program CAP2D is instead based on Green's function, and the method of moments [3].   First the Green's function to the Poisson's equation G(r, r') will be derived [4,5].   In the derivation, the multiple layers of dielectrics will be taken into account.   Then the potentials can be expressed as a convolution integral as follows :

$$\Phi(r) = \int_S \rho(r')G(r, r')\, dr' \tag{1}$$

where $\Phi(r)$ is the potential at observation point r, and $\rho(r')$ is the charge density over the source surface designated as S.   In the above equation, the potential $\Phi(r)$ can be evaluated at a boundary point with a known value, and the only unknown in the equation is the charge density $\rho(r')$.   Hence, eq.(1) becomes an integral equation.

Eq. (1) can be solved by employing the method of moments. Assuming that the unknown charge density function $\rho(r')$ can be expressed in terms of a set of "basis" functions, $w_i(r')$, i=1,2,...,n as

$$\rho(r') = \sum_i \alpha_i w_i(r') \tag{2}$$

Then the unknowns in the equation are transformed into a set of n unknown coefficients, since the basis fucntions are known functions. This is similar to orthogonal function expansion. Substitute eq.(2) back to eq.(1), we have

$$\Phi(r)\,|_S = \sum_i \alpha_i \int_S w_i(r')G(r, r')\, dr'.$$

Analogous to orthogonal function expansion, another set of "testing" functions t_j, j=1,2,...n, usually the same basis functions, is multiplied, then integrated on both sides of the above equation.   In other words, inner products with testing functions are then taken on both sides of the equation.   (Inner product is defined as $\int f(r)g(r)dr$.) Finally, the integral equation in eq.(1) are transformed into a set of linear algebraic equations as follows :

$$b_j = \sum_i A_{ij}{}^* x_i \tag{3}$$

where

$$b_j = \int_S \Phi(r) |_S t_j(r) dr$$

$$A_{ij} = \int_S dr \int_S dr' \; w_i(r') G(r,r') t_j(r)$$

Since all the integrands in b_j and A_{ij} are known, they can be evaluated straightforwardly. To avoid numerical integration, the basis functions can be chosen in such a way that b_j and A_{ij} will all have closed-form evaluation. Also in choosing the same testing functions as the basis functions, the matrix A_{ij} becomes a positive-definite, symmetric one. This will further reduce the computation complexity.

Parallel Implementation. After monitoring and profiling the run-time statistics of CAP2D, it was found that majority of process time, over 90%, was spent on the evaluation of the elements of matrix Aij. It is obviously very easy to parallize the computation of matrix elements. Each processor was allocated its equal share of elements to be computed. After the evaluation, the results are sent back to cube manager to solve the matrix and then compute the capacitances as on serial computers. However, it should be emphasized that it is not this parallization of matrix element computation is any different or difficult but rather the Green's function approach which results in this ease of parallelization is of interest.

As a comparsion, the usual finite difference approach with grids and five-point stencil will result in a large but sparse matrix, and the majority of process time will be spent in solving this matrix. To parallelize this algorithm, we have to device a way to parallelize the solution of this sparse matrix which will be more difficult than the parallelization of matrix element evaluation. From another point of view, the finite difference approach solves Poisson's equation directly, straightforward discretization into grids, then solution without any derivation; while in Green's function approach the Poisson's equation was manipulated and transformed into an integral equation. The effects of dielectrics, external boundary conditions can be thought of being consolidated into a kernel, the Green's function. Then the moment method merely discretizes the source region. Since each subdivision in the source region is independent of one another, they become easily parallelizable as described above. Hence, we can argue that it is the Green's function approach which results in this ease of parallelization.   Along this line of thinking, we can attempt to parallelize computation employing an approach with more "independent" computation like the Green's function approach here.

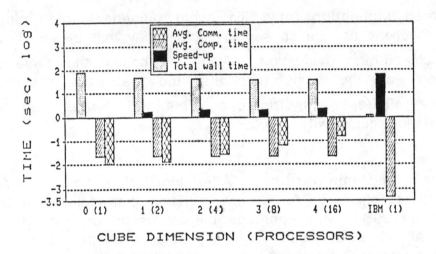

FIG. 1. Run Times of CAP2D on iPSC with One Layer Dielectric.

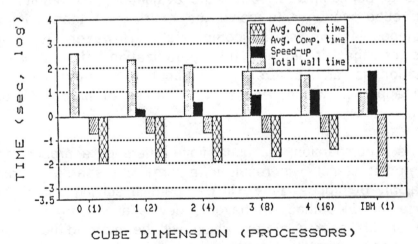

FIG. 2. Run Times of CAP2D on iPSC with Two Layer Dielectric.

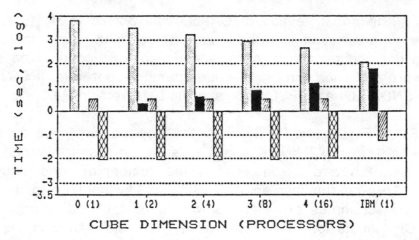

FIG. 3.   Run Times of CAP2D on iPSC with Three Layer Dielectric.

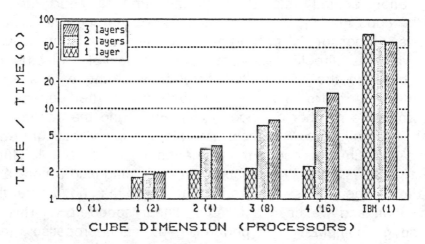

FIG. 4.   Speed-up comparison.

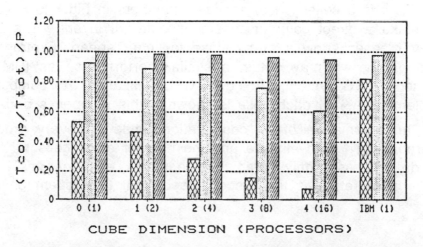

FIG. 5.   Percentage of Time spent on Matrix Element Computation.

Results.   The serial version of CAP2D was ported to INTEL's iPSC. Since the parallelization is rather easy, it took only about three days to add in the communication calls, and debug the code.   The results shown were obtained on a 16-node memory-upgraded iPSC (d4m) running XENIX R3.4 and iPSC node execute beta version R3.0.

Fig.1, Fig.2 and Fig.3 show the elapsed run times of running CAP2D with 1 layer, 2 layers and 3 layers of dielectrics, respectively. The abscissae showed the increase of the number of node processors from 1 to 16, and the last entry is IBM 3090 without using its vector facility.   The ordinates are elapsed wall times for iPSC numbers, but process CPU times for IBM results since the tests were running under time-sharing condition.   Also showed in the graphs are average computation time and average communication time.   The only communication actually monitored is the time to send the results back to the cube manager. On the other hand, the computation time on each node processor is proportional to the complexity of Green's function which is directly related to the number of dielectric layers. In Fig.1, because the computation time on each node is short for 1 layer dielectric, there may be contention in the communication channel when the number of node is increased, and the speed-up stays flat after 4 processors.   In contrast, Fig.3 shows that the average communication time is about the same as in Fig.1, but it stays flat for 1 to 16 processors. With about 2 order of magnitude more average computation time, it is apparent that there is no contention in communication and we have a close to linear speed-up.   This shows that if enough computation is performing on each processor, the less likely will the contention on the communication channel occur.

Fig.4 is a collection of speed-up numbers in Fig.1 to Fig.3, and we can make a direct comparison among different layers. The 2-layer and 3-layer cases show a pretty close to linear speed. Exptrapolating from the graph, we may obtain a similar performance as IBM 3090 with 64-node iPSC system. In Fg.5, "CPU utilization" (to compute the matrix element A_{ij}) of each case is shown. This number is derived by dividing the summation of all computation times on every processor to the product of total wall time and the number of processors. Since each node processor only computes the matrix element, this number should be interpreted as the precentage of toal time spent on matrix

should be interpreted as the precentage of toal time spent on matrix element computation. In the case of IBM serial computation, it also only include the time on matrix element computation and exclude the time like matrix solve and data set-up. Hence, in 1-layer case, it shows only 80% utilization for IBM run. And only about 8% utilization on 16-processor iPSC run.

Conclusion. We can further refine the aforementioned parallelization algorithm to exclude the inefficiency in 1 layer case. "Lincube" or similar type of parallel linear algebraic equation solver may be used to decompose and solve the matrix A_{ij} on the whole cube, thus eliminating the possibility of communication contention in sending back the matrix element to one processor, in this case the cube manager. Then we may arrive at a truely parallel computation with close to linear speed-up for all dielectric cases. It can not be overemphasized that this parallelization should be attributed to the Green's function approach in solving Poisson's equation.

References.

[1]   R.L.M. Dang and N. Shigyo, "Coupling Capacitances for Two-Dimensional Wires", *IEEE Electron Device Letters,* Vol.EDL-2, No.8, pp.196-197, Aug. 1981.

[2] P.E. Cottrell, E.M. Buturla andD.R. Thomas, "Multi- Dimensional Simulation of VLSI Wiring Capacitance", *IEEE International Electron Devices Meeting Proceedings*, San Francisco, CA., Dec. 1982.

[3] R.F. Harrington, *Field Computation by Moment Methods*, R.E. Krieger Publishing, Malabar, FL. 1982.

[4]   W.T. Weeks, "Calculation of Coefficients of Capacitance of Multiconductor Transmission Lines in the Presence of a   Dielectric Interface", *IEEE Trans. on Microwave Theory and Techniques*, Vol.MTT-18, No.1, pp.35-43, Jan. 1970.

[5] C.P. Yuan, "Modeling and Extraction of Interconnect Parameters in VLSI Circuits", PhD Thesis, University of   Illinois, Urbana, IL. 1983

PART VII:
NUMERICAL METHODS

An Implementation of a 2^d-Section Root Finding Method for the FPS T-Series Hypercube[*]

JOAN M. FRANCIONI† AND JAY ALAN JACKSON†

Abstract. This paper is a case study of implementing a parallel algorithm which calculates the root of a function on the FPS T-series computer. The algorithm is a generalization of the bisection method to a 2^d-section method, where d is the dimension of the hypercube. It involves communication between the nearest neighbor nodes of the hypercube arranged in a ring topology as well as a general broadcast from any one node to all others. The characteristics of the FPS T-series architecture, together with the programming language Occam, impose certain restrictions on the manner in which these communications can be performed. In addition to discussing the implementation of the 2^d-section method, the results of running the algorithm on various size hypercubes are reported. The effectiveness of the hypercube for this problem is evaluated with respect to the size of the cube, the computational expense of the particular function, and the communication overhead.

1. Introduction. For any numerical problem, even very simple ones, efficient parallel programs are highly dependent on effective communication. It is also the case that an algorithm's communication structure can be very efficient for one kind of computer architecture but not for another. With these concepts in mind, we present a case study of an implementation of a parallel algorithm for finding the root of a function.

The major objectives of this study were

to determine the effectiveness of extending the bisection root finding method to a parallel n-section method;

to determine the effectiveness of a hypercube for this problem with respect to the dimension of the cube (hence, the name "2^d-section method"); and

to examine the features and limitations of the FPS T-series hypercube as related to algorithms of this nature.

---

*Floating Point Systems, Inc., Beaverton, Oregon 97006

†Department of Mathematical and Computer Sciences, Michigan Technological University, Houghton, MI 49931

This work was assisted by research equipment supported by NSF Grant No. DCR-8404909

In section 2, we describe the n-section method in general. Mapping this algorithm onto a hypercube architecture is discussed in section 3, where we also address general and specific communication issues. Section 4 includes results from an implementation of the algorithm on both the FPS T-20 and T-40 computers. Our conclusions are given in section 5.

2. Algorithm for the n-Section Root Finding Method. The n-section method is a straight-forward extension of the bisection method for finding the root of a function. However, instead of only dividing the interval in half on each iteration, the interval is divided into n subintervals. Given that there are n processors available, these subintervals can be processed in parallel. We assume that the function being evaluated has one root in the interval of interest. The following is the pseudo code for the algorithm.

(Note: The same program runs on every processor.)

```
        Sequential Begin
    1   Set up interval on an initial start-node;
    2   Set up number of iterations;
    3   Determine left and right neighbor nodes;

        For (number of iterations) do
    4       Broadcast the interval from start-node to all other nodes;
    5       Determine the subinterval to be evaluated;
    6       Compute the function at the right endpoint, x_r, of the subinterval;
    7       Pass f(x_r) to right neighbor;
    8       If root is in subinterval then
    9               this node is the new start-node;
        (End For)
        (End Seq)
```

Algorithm 1. n-Section Root Finding Method

In this algorithm, communication between processors is involved in steps 4 and 7. In step 4, information is broadcast from one processor to all other processors involved in the program. The receiving processors do not know which processor will initiate the broadcast. This type of communication is known as broadcasting from an unknown source. The communication involved in step 7 facilitates each processor only having to compute the function at one endpoint. If the time to communicate the functional value to a neighbor is less than the time to compute the function, this will be an effective strategy. The details of the communication steps are discussed in the next section.

We are interested in finding out if and when this method is better than the simple bisection method. Hence, we compare

$T_n(k)$, the run time of the n-section method, with

$T_b(k)$, the run time of the bisection method.

For our analysis, we let

n   = number of processors

t_{cp} = computation time per iteration

t_{cm} = communication time per iteration

Assume the initial interval of concern is of length 1, and let $\frac{1}{k}$ be the length of the interval at termination. Therefore we will determine the root of the function with an accuracy of $\frac{1}{k}$. To make the analysis easier, we assume k is a power of 2^d for some d. That is,

$$k = (2^d)^i, \quad \text{for } i = 1, 2, \cdots; \quad d = 1, 2, \cdots. \tag{2.1}$$

and hence,

$$\log_2 k = di. \tag{2.2}$$

In the bisection method, each iteration reduces the length of the interval by $\frac{1}{2}$. Reducing the interval to $\frac{1}{k}$ will require di iterations, where no communication is involved. Therefore

$$T_b(k) = (di)t_{cp} + c_0. \tag{2.3}$$

In the n-section method, each iteration reduces the length of the interval by $\frac{1}{2^d}$ if $n = 2^d$. Therefore, it takes i iterations to do the same amount of work as the bisection method does in equation (2.3). However, for the n-section method, communication is necessary on each iteration for both broadcasting and for passing values to neighbors. Hence,

$$T_n(k) = i(t_{cp} + t_{cm}) + c_1. \tag{2.4}$$

Using equations (2.3) and (2.4), the n-section method is better than the bisection method when

$$T_n(k) < T_b(k)$$
$$i(t_{cp} + t_{cm}) < (id)t_{cp}$$
$$t_{cm} < (d - 1)t_{cp}.$$

And with $n = 2^d$

$$t_{cm} < (\log_2 n - 1)t_{cp}. \tag{2.5}$$

By this derivation, we can see that the ratio of communication time to computation time necessary for the n-section method to be effective is

$$\frac{t_{cm}}{t_{cp}} < \log_2 n - 1. \tag{2.6}$$

It can also be seen that the speedup of the n-section method over the bisection method is

$$\frac{T_b(k)}{T_n(k)} = \frac{(\log_2 n)t_{cp}}{t_{cp} + t_{cm}}. \tag{2.7}$$

The maximum speedup possible would be when the communication time is negligible compared to the computation time. In that case,

$$\frac{T_b(k)}{T_n(k)} = (\log_2 n). \tag{2.8}$$

3. The n-Section Algorithm Mapped to a Hypercube.

The number of nodes, n, in a hypercube is equal to 2^d, where d is called the dimension of the hypercube. Thus, the n-section algorithm mapped to a hypercube can be called a 2^d-section algorithm.

There are two communication issues that have to be dealt with in order to effectively map the 2^d-section algorithm onto a hypercube architecture. These are the right-neighbor communication and the broadcast communication steps. Passing information to a right neighbor in a hypercube requires that a ring structure be embedded in the cube. The most common way of accomplishing this is to use the binary-reflected Gray code ordering of the nodes. For any d, this code ensures that each node is directly linked to its rightmost and leftmost neighbors.

The broadcast that is necessary for this algorithm is a bit more complex. Basically, the problem of broadcasting from an unknown source can be stated as follows:

to broadcast information from any one node to all other nodes, where the destination nodes do not know which node is the source node.

There exist a number of methods for accomplishing a broadcast on a hypercube that take $\Theta(\log_2 n)$ steps. The most common of these are the embedded spanning tree, and the method of recursive doubling [3, 5]. However, a direct implementation of these methods implies that all destination nodes must be ready to receive the information on any link. In particular, on the FPS T-series this means that each node must actually receive something on every link; and hence each node must send something on every link. Based on these restrictions, a modified recursive doubling technique can be used. The modification is that all nodes participate in communicating on all links, passing dummy information until they have the real information and then passing on the real information. Algorithm 2 gives the pseudo-code for the broadcast of step (4) in Algorithm 1.

```
    Sequential Begin
1       For i := 1, d  do
2           PAR Begin
3               send real or dummy information on link i;
4               receive information on link i;
            (End PAR)
        (End For)
    (End Seq)
```

Algorithm 2. Broadcasting from an Unknown Source

On the FPS T-series computer, it is possible to communicate simultaneously in both directions over the same link. This allows the use of the PARallel statement in step 2 of the above algorithm. On a machine where this type of communication is not possible, steps 3 and 4 would have to be done sequentially. Either way, the run time of the algorithm is still $\Theta(\log_2 n)$.

In addition to using the PAR statement as above, the two-way communication also facilitates an asynchronous broadcast method [2]. Although this method is somewhat slower than the recursive doubling method on the FPS T-Series, it is faster for broadcasting to $n - 1$ nodes when messages are longer than 128 words. A fast broadcast to $n - 1$ nodes is useful in problems where the nodes can go on with their computations as soon as they receive the information, without having to wait for the last node to also receive the information. It turns out that the 2^d-section method has this property, but the length of the broadcasted message is too small for the asynchronous broadcast to be effective on this computer.

4. Implementation of 2^d-Section Algorithm on FPS T-20 and T-40. On the FPS T-20 machine, it is possible to set up a hypercube of dimension 3 or 4. To compare the bisection, 2^3-section and 2^4-section methods on a T-20, we set up the following:

Case 1. $k = 2^{24}$;   and
$f(x) = x - c.$

Using this function in our implementation ensures that t_{cp}, the computation time, is minimal. This way the effects of the communication involved are obvious. Table 1 shows the run times of the three algorithms doing the same amount of work, i.e. reducing the interval to $1 / 2^{24}$. For the bisection method this requires 24 iterations; for the 2^3-section method this requires 8 iterations; and for the 2^4-section method it requires 6 iterations.

	Bisection	2^3-section	2^4-section
iterations	24	8	6
communication time	0	49.2	43.6
computation time	12	3.8	2.9
total time	12	53	46.5
t_{cm}	0.0	6.150	7.267
t_{cp}	0.5	0.475	0.483

(times given in clock ticks; 64 μs/tick)

Table 1. Run Times for Algorithms on FPS T-20

Using equation (2.5), it can be seen that the 2^4-section method is better than the bisection method when

$$t_{cm} < (\log_2 n - 1)t_{cp}$$
$$7.267 < (4 - 1)t_{cp}$$
$$7.267 < 3t_{cp}$$
$$2.422 < t_{cp}$$

$$155\mu s < t_{cp}$$

As can be seen from Table 1, it is also the case that the 2^4-section method is always more efficient than the 2^3-section method.

If the ratio of t_{cm} for the 2^3-section method to t_{cm} for the 2^4-section method had been less than 3/4, then the 2^4-section method would only be faster than the 2^3-section method for sufficiently complex functions. As it turned out, the ratio was greater than 3/4, which suggests that the 2^5-section method should be even faster still. The implementation for dimension 5 on the T-40, however, required two major changes in the code, directly related to the FPS architecture. For one, all nodes must communicate on links 1 through d for the broadcast communication (d = dimension).[1] On the FPS T-series, it is necessary to reconfigure the link connections of a node between communications on links i and j when (i mod 4) = (j mod 4). This reconfiguration is done via the *set.links* command. If d is less than or equal to 4, no reconfiguration is necessary. When d = 5, the broadcast procedure requires two set.links for the proper configuring, which takes approximately 2 ms to execute [1]. Hence, the communication time, for each iteration of the algorithm, is increased by 2 ms. As we shall see, this greatly affected the run time for the 2^5-section method.

The second change required was also related to reconfiguring the links of the nodes. The communication for passing f(x) to the right (step 7 in Algorithm 1) requires a parallel send and receive to be effective. Otherwise, this communication would take *n* steps. As it turns out, if a binary-reflected Gray code is used to embed a ring structure in a 5-dimensional hypercube, then some nodes will have one neighbor connected on link 1 and the other neighbor on link 5. Hence, this code does not facilitate parallel nearest-neighbor communications on the FPS T-40. It is, however, possible to set up the ring so that no node has nearest neighbors on both links 1 and 5. A procedure to generate such a ring ordering is described by Poplawski [4]. This procedure can be used to generate a cyclic code for any dimension, however, the same code generated for dimension 5 can not also be used for dimension 4. (Theoretically at least, this was the advantage of using the Gray code.) Hence, this change only affected the generality of the program and did not adversely affect the run time.

Incorporating both of the changes described above, the 2^5-section implementation was run on the FPS T-40 using the following:

---

[1] On the FPS computers, the link numbers are from 1 to d rather than from 0 to d-1.

Case 2. $k = 2^{20}$;   and

$\qquad f(x) = x - c.$

The run times for this method are shown in Table 2 along with comparable-work runs for the bisection and 2^4-section methods.

	Bisection	2^4-section	2^5-section
iterations	20	5	4
total time	10	39	210

(times given in clock ticks; 64 μs/tick)

Table 2. Run Times for Algorithm on FPS T-40

The major result here is that although the 2^5 method will be better than the bisection method for sufficiently large t_{cp}, it will never be better than the 2^4-section method. Therefore, it is not worthwhile on this machine to use a 5-cube over a 4-cube for this problem.

5. Concluding Remarks. The conclusions from this case study are enumerated as follows.

(1)   The parallel 2^d-section method is an effective root finding method when the ratio of the communication time to the computation time is less than ($\log_2 n - 1$).

(2)   The hypercube architecture is effective for this problem because the amount of information passed between nodes is small; and an $\Theta(\log_2 n)$ broadcast is possible.

(3)   Theoretically, the 2^d-section method exhibits a linear speedup with respect to the dimension of the hypercube.

(4)   Being able to overlap communication with computation on the FPS T-series machines is of limited usefulness for this problem.

(5)   Having to reconfigure the node links when $d = 5$ on the FPS T-40 results in longer communication times; and prevents using a general Gray code for all nodes passing information to a nearest neighbor in parallel.

(6)   For the FPS T-series, the 4 dimensional hypercube was the most effective.

REFERENCES

1.   D. Bergmark, J. M. Francioni, B. K. Helminen and D. A. Poplawski, On the Performance of the FPS T-Series Hypercube, *Proceedings of the Second Conference on Hypercube Multiprocessors*, 1986.

2.   J. M. Francioni, Broadcasting from an Unknown Source on a Hypercube, Computer Science Technical Report 86-13, Michigan Technological University, October 1986.

3.   C. Ho and S. L. Johnsson, Distributed Routing Algorithms for Broadcasting and Personalized Communication in Hypercubes, *Proceedings of the 1986 International Conference on Parallel Processing*, August 1986, 640-648.

4.   D. A. Poplawski, Ring Connectivity in the FPS T-Series Hypercube, Computer Science Technical Report 86-10, Michigan Technological University, October 1986.

5.   Y. Saad and M. H. Schultz, Topological Properties of Hypercubes, Technical Report YALEU/DCS/RR-389, Department of Computer Science, Yale University, June 1985.

Solving Polynomial Systems of Equations on a Hypercube

ALEXANDER P. MORGAN* AND LAYNE T. WATSON†

Abstract. Certain classes of nonlinear systems of equations, such as polynomial systems, have properties that make them particularly amenable to solution on distributed computing systems. Some algorithms, considered unfavorably on a single processor serial computer, may be excellent on a distributed system. This paper considers the solution of polynomial systems of equations via a globally convergent homotopy algorithm on a hypercube. Some computational results are reported.

1. Introduction. The purpose of this work is to study solving polynomial systems on a hypercube computer, using homotopy continuation. Continuation methods have been applied at GMR to a variety of engineering problems. The SYMPOL code [7] has been used in GMSolid, in combustion chemistry simulations, and in solving the inverse kinematics of manipulators. (See [11, 6, 15], respectively.) Recently, POLSYS [18] has been developed at GMR as an alternative to SYMPOL. SYMPOL and POLSYS are particularly amenable to parallel implementation, and we have developed a version of POLSYS for Intel's iPSC-32 hypercube computer.

Generally, computational capacity can be increased in several different ways: by increasing the speed of the hardware, by using vector processors, and by exploiting parallelism. Many different computer architectures are available, and computational experience on these machines is accumulating. But very fast hardware is very expensive (for example, Cray computers). Further, many supercomputer systems – like the Goodyear MPP, the CMU WARP, the NYU Ultracomputer, the Illinois Cedar, and the BBN Butterfly – have both severely limited access and formidable programming problems.

---

* Mathematics Department, General Motors Research Laboratories, Warren, MI 48090-9055.

† Departments of Electrical Engineering and Computer Science, Industrial and Operations Engineering, and Mathematics, University of Michigan, Ann Arbor, MI 48109. Current address: Department of Computer Science, Virginia Polytechnic Institute & State University, Blacksburg, VA 24061. The work of this author was supported in part by AFOSR Grant 85-0250.

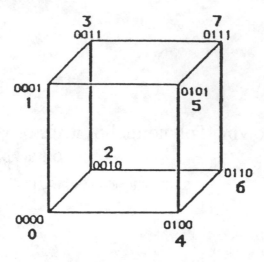

Figure 1. 3-cube structure and node labelling.

A hypercube computer uses independent processors connected together in a reasonably efficient, yet still manageable, network. A hypercube consists of 2^n processors (nodes), each with memory, floating-point hardware, and communication chips. The nodes are independent and asynchronous, and connected to each other the way the corners of an n-dimensional cube are connected by its edges.

Section 2 briefly sketches the hypercube computer architecture. Section 3 presents an overview of the path-tracking strategy that is fundamental to the POLSYS algorithm. Section 4 discusses polynomial systems. Computational results on an Intel iPSC–32 and several other machines are contained in Section 5.

2. The hypercube. The word "hypercube" refers to an n-dimensional cube. Think of a cube in n dimensions as sitting in the positive orthant, with vertices at the points

$$(v_1, \ldots, v_n), \quad v_i \in \{0, 1\}, \quad i = 1, \ldots, n.$$

There are thus 2^n vertices, and two vertices v and w are "adjacent", i.e., connected by an edge, if and only if $v_i = w_i$ for all i except one. The associated graph, also sometimes referred to an an "n-cube", has 2^n vertices (which can be labelled as above with binary n-tuples) and edges between vertices whose labels differ in exactly one coordinate (Figure 1).

A "hypercube computer architecture" is a computer system with 2^n (node) processors, corresponding to the 2^n vertices (nodes), and a communication link corresponding to each edge of the n-cube. Thus each processor has a direct communication link to exactly n other processors. We define the "distance" between any two nodes to be the number of edges that must be passed through to go from one node to another. Then, the distance between any two of the $P = 2^n$ hypercube processors is at most n. This can be viewed as a compromise between total connectivity (distance = 1) and ring connectivity (distance $\leq P/2$).

Typically the node label $(v_1, \ldots, v_n)$ is viewed as a binary number $v_1 v_2 \ldots v_n$, and in this view two nodes are adjacent if and only if their binary representations differ in exactly one bit. Typically node addresses are computed in programs by a "gray code", a bijective function

$$g : \{0, \ldots, 2^n - 1\} \to \{0, \ldots, 2^n - 1\}$$

such that the binary representations of $g(k \pmod{2^n})$ and $g(k+1 \pmod{2^n})$ differ in exactly one bit for all k (cf. [4]).

Realizations of this abstract architecture have one additional feature: a "host" processor with communication links to all the node processors. This host typically loads programs into the nodes, starts and stops processes executing in the nodes, and interchanges data with the nodes. In current hardware implementations only the host has external I/O and peripheral storage; the nodes consist of memory, a CPU, and possibly communication and floating-point hardware.

The Intel iPSC has 32, 64, or 128 nodes. Each node is an 80286/80287 with 512K bytes of memory. The host is also an 80286/80287, but with 4 MB of memory, a floppy disk drive, a hard disk, an Ethernet connection, and a Xenix operating system. The nodes have only a minimal monitor for communication and process management.

3. Homotopy continuation and path tracking. Let V^n denote n-dimensional real or complex Euclidean space, and let $F : V^n \rightarrow V^n$ be a smooth (twice continuously differentiable) function. The general problem is to solve the nonlinear system of equations

$$F(x) = 0.$$

The basic homotopy continuation approach is to find a simplified version of F, called G, and to define a homotopy system such as

$$\rho(\lambda, x) = \lambda F(x) + (1 - \lambda)G(x) \qquad (1),$$

so that $\rho(0, x) = G(x)$ and $\rho(1, x) = F(x)$. Now, if G is chosen so that ρ obeys certain technical conditions, then the solutions to $\rho = 0$ will consist of smooth paths in V^n connecting solutions of $G(x) = 0$ to solutions of $F(x) = 0$. See, for example, [7,9,10,16,17] for various formulations of the technicalities.

The general idea of the numerical algorithm is then simple. Let x_0 be a solution to $G(x) = 0$ and follow the zero curve γ emanating from $(\lambda, x) = (0, x_0)$ until a zero $\tilde{x}$ of $F(x)$ is reached (at $\lambda = 1$). Of course, not all choices of G and x_0 will work, and it is nontrivial to develop a viable numerical path-tracking algorithm. But, at least conceptually, the algorithm for solving the nonlinear system of equations $F(x) = 0$ is clear and simple. We do not assume that λ increases monotonically from 0 to 1 as the continuation is carried out. The continuation parameter λ is permitted to both increase and decrease along γ; that is, turning points present no special difficulty. Also G can be chosen so that there are never any "singular points". Thus, γ does not "get stuck" at an interior point of $[0, 1) \times V^n$. (See the previously cited references.)

The zero curve γ of the homotopy map $\rho(\lambda, x)$ in (1) can be tracked by many different techniques; refer to the excellent survey [1] and recent work [18], [19]. The numerical results here were obtained with preliminary versions of HOMPACK [18], a software package currently under development at Sandia National Laboratories, General Motors Research Laboratories, Virginia Polytechnic Institute and State University, and the University of Michigan. There are three primary algorithmic approaches to tracking γ : 1) an ODE-based algorithm, 2) a predictor-corrector algorithm whose corrector follows the flow normal to the continuation path (a "normal flow" algorithm); 3) a version of Rheinboldt's linear predictor, quasi-Newton corrector algorithm [12] (an "augmented Jacobian matrix" method).

Only the ODE-based algorithm will be discussed here. Alternatives 2) and 3) are described in detail in [19] and [2], respectively. Assuming that the zero curve, γ , (beginning at x_0) is well defined, it is continuously differentiable and can be parametrized by arc length s. Thus $\lambda = \lambda(s)$, $x = x(s)$ along γ, and

$$\rho(\lambda(s), x(s)) = 0 \qquad (2)$$

identically in s. Therefore

$$\frac{d}{ds}\rho(\lambda(s), x(s)) = D\rho(\lambda(s), x(s)) \begin{pmatrix} \dfrac{d\lambda}{ds} \\[4pt] \dfrac{dx}{ds} \end{pmatrix} = 0, \qquad (3)$$

and

$$\left\| \left(\frac{d\lambda}{ds}, \frac{dx}{ds} \right) \right\|_2 = 1. \qquad (4)$$

If we take

$$\lambda(0) = 0, \quad x(0) = x_0, \qquad (5)$$

the zero curve γ is the trajectory of the initial value problem (3–5). When $\lambda(\bar{s}) = 1$, the corresponding $x(\bar{s})$ is a zero of $F(x) = 0$. Thus all the sophisticated ODE techniques currently available can be brought to bear on the problem of tracking γ [14], [17].

Typical ODE software requires $(d\lambda/ds, dx/ds)$ explicitly, and (3), (4) only implicitly define the derivative $(d\lambda/ds, dx/ds)$. (It might be possible to use an implicit ODE technique for (3–4), but that seems less efficient than the method proposed here.) The derivative $(d\lambda/ds, dx/ds)$, which is a unit tangent vector to the zero curve γ, can be calculated by finding the one-dimensional kernel of the $p \times (p+1)$ Jacobian matrix

$$D\rho(\lambda(s), x(s)),$$

which can be shown to have full rank under reasonable conditions. It is here that a substantial amount of computation is incurred, and it is imperative that the number of derivative evaluations be kept small. Once the kernel has been calculated, the derivative $(d\lambda/ds, dx/ds)$ is uniquely determined by (4) and continuity. Complete details for solving the initial value problem (3–5) and obtaining $x(\bar{s})$ are in [16] and [17]. A discussion of the kernel computation follows.

The Jacobian matrix $D\rho$ is $n \times (n+1)$ with (theoretical) rank n. The crucial observation is that the last n columns of $D\rho$, corresponding to $D_x\rho$, may not have rank n, and even if they do, some other n columns may be better conditioned. The objective is to avoid choosing n "distinguished" columns, rather to treat all columns the same. (This is not possible for sparse matrices. Also, polynomial systems are somewhat special because γ is monotonically increasing in λ. Our comments here should be taken as general guidelines only.) There are kernel finding algorithms based on Gaussian elimination and n distinguished columns [5]. Choosing and switching these n columns is tricky, and based on *ad hoc* parameters. Also, computational experience has shown that accurate tangent vectors $(d\lambda/ds, dx/ds)$ are essential, and the accuracy of Gaussian elimination may not be good enough. A conceptually elegant, as well as accurate, algorithm is to compute the QR factorization with column interchanges [3] of $D\rho$,

$$Q\, D\rho\, P^t P z = \begin{pmatrix} * & \cdots & * & * \\ & \ddots & \vdots & \vdots \\ 0 & & * & * \end{pmatrix} P z = 0, \qquad (6)$$

where Q is a product of Householder reflections and P is a permutation matrix, and then obtain a vector $z \in \ker D\rho$ by back substitution. Setting $(Pz)_{n+1} = 1$ is a convenient choice. This scheme provides high accuracy, numerical stability, and a uniform treatment of all $n + 1$ columns. Finally,

$$\left(\frac{d\lambda}{ds}, \frac{dx}{ds}\right) = \pm \frac{z}{\|z\|_2},$$

where the sign is chosen to maintain an acute angle with the previous tangent vector on γ. There is a rigorous mathematical criterion, based on a $(n + 1) \times (n + 1)$ determinant, for choosing the sign, but there is no reason to believe that would be more robust than the angle criterion.

Several features which are a combination of common sense and computational experience should be incorporated into the algorithm. Since most ordinary differential equation solvers only control the local error, the longer the arc length of the zero curve γ gets, the farther away the computed points may be from the true curve γ. Therefore when the arc length gets too long, a "correction" in G can be computed so that the continuation can be restarted on a nearby continuation path, along which the path tracking continues. A full description and justification for this strategy is given in [17].

Remember that tracking γ is merely a means to an end, namely a zero $\tilde{z}$ of $F(x) = 0$. Since γ itself is of no interest (usually), one should not waste computational effort following it too closely. However, since γ is the only sure way to $\tilde{z}$, losing γ can be disastrous. The tradeoff between computational efficiency and reliability is very delicate, and a fool-proof strategy appears difficult to achieve. None of the three primary algorithms alone is superior overall, and each of the three beats the other two (sometimes by an order of magnitude) on particular problems. Since the algorithms' philosophies are significantly different, a hybrid may be hard to develop.

4. Polynomial systems. A system of n polynomial equations in n unknowns,

$$F(x) = 0, \tag{7}$$

will generally have many solutions. It is possible to define a homotopy so that all geometrically isolated solutions of (7) have at least one associated homotopy path. It is this sort of homotopy we shall consider.

Sometimes, (7) will have solutions at infinity, which forces some of the homotopy paths to diverge to infinity as λ approaches 1 [8, 10]. However, (7) can be transformed into a new system which, under reasonable hypotheses, can be proven to have no solutions at infinity. Then the homotopy paths will be bounded. Because scaling can be critical to the success of the method, a general scaling algorithm is applied to scale the coefficients and variables in (7) before anything else is done. For technical reasons, we must take $V^n = C^n$; that is, the continuation must be carried out in complex space. See [10], Chapter 1.

Since the homotopy map is complex analytic, the homotopy parameter λ is monotonically increasing as a function of arc length [7, 9, 10]. The existence of an infinite number of solutions or an infinite number of solutions at infinity does not destabilize the method. Some paths will converge to the higher dimensional solution components, and these paths will behave the way paths converging to any singular solution behave. Practical applications usually require a subset of the solutions, rather than all solutions [6, 10, 11, 15]. However, the sort of generic homotopy algorithm considered here must find all solutions and cannot be limited without, in essense, changing it into a heuristic.

Define $G : C^n \to C^n$ by

$$G_j(x) = b_j x_j{}^{d_j} - a_j, \qquad j = 1, \ldots, n, \tag{8}$$

where a_j and b_j are nonzero complex numbers and d_j is the degree of $F_j(x)$, for $j = 1, \ldots, n$. Define the homotopy map

$$\rho_c(\lambda, x) = (1 - \lambda)\, G(x) + \lambda\, F(x), \tag{9}$$

where $c = (a, b)$, $a = (a_1, \ldots, a_n) \in C^n$ and $b = (b_1, \ldots, b_n) \in C^n$. Let $d = d_1 \cdots d_n$ be the *total degree* of the system.

Theorem [9]. For almost all choices of a and b in C^n, $\rho_c^{-1}(0)$ consists of d smooth paths emanating from $\{0\} \times C^n$, which either diverge to infinity as λ approaches 1 or converge to solutions to $F(x) = 0$ as λ approaches 1. Each geometrically isolated solution of $F(x) = 0$ has a path converging to it.

A number of distinct homotopies have been proposed for solving polynomial systems. The homotopy (9) is from [9]. As with all such homotopies, there will be paths diverging to infinity if $F(x) = 0$ has solutions at infinity. These divergent paths are (at least) a nuisance, since they require arbitrary stopping criteria. Solutions at infinity can be avoided via the following "projective transformation".

Define $F'(y)$ to be the homogenization of $F(x)$:

$$F_j'(y) = y_{n+1}{}^{d_j}\, F_j(y_1/y_{n+1}, \ldots, y_n/y_{n+1}), \qquad j = 1, \ldots, n. \tag{10}$$

Note that, if $F'(y^0) = 0$, then $F'(\alpha y^0) = 0$ for any complex scalar α. Therefore, "solutions" of $F'(y) = 0$ are (complex) lines through the origin in C^{n+1}. The set of all lines through the origin in C^{n+1} is called complex projective n-space, denoted CP^n, and is a smooth compact (complex) n-dimensional manifold. The solutions of $F'(y) = 0$ in CP^n are identified with the solutions and solutions at infinity of $F(x) = 0$ as follows. If $L \in CP^n$ is a solution to $F'(y) = 0$ with $y = (y_1, y_2, \ldots, y_{n+1}) \in L$ and $y_{n+1} \neq 0$, then $x = (y_1/y_{n+1}, y_2/y_{n+1}, \ldots, y_n/y_{n+1}) \in C^n$ is a solution to $F(x) = 0$. On the other hand, if $x \in C^n$ is a solution to $F(x) = 0$, then the line through $y = (x, 1)$ is a solution to $F'(y) = 0$ with $y_{n+1} = 1 \neq 0$. The most mathematically satisfying definition of *solutions to $F(x) = 0$ at infinity* is simply *solutions to $F'(y) = 0$ (in CP^n) generated by y with $y_{n+1} = 0$.*

A basic result on the structure of the solution set of a polynomial system is the following classical theorem of Bezout:

Theorem. There are no more than d isolated solutions to $F'(y) = 0$ in CP^n. If $F'(y) = 0$ has only a finite number of solutions in CP^n, it has exactly d solutions, counting multiplicities.

Recall that a solution is *isolated* if there is a neighborhood containing that solution and no other solution. The multiplicity of an isolated solution is defined to be the number of solutions that appear in the isolating neighborhood under an arbitrarily small random perturbation of the system coefficients. If the solution is nonsingular (i.e., the system Jacobian matrix is nonsingular at the solution), then it has multiplicity one. Otherwise it has multiplicity greater than one. (See [10], Chapter 3.)

Define a linear function

$$u(y_1, \ldots, y_{n+1}) = \xi_1 y_1 + \xi_2 y_2 + \cdots + \xi_{n+1} y_{n+1}$$

where $\xi_1, \ldots, \xi_{n+1}$ are nonzero complex numbers, and define $F'' : C^{n+1} \to C^{n+1}$ by

$$\begin{aligned}
F_j''(y) &= F_j'(y), \qquad j = 1, \ldots, n, \\
F_{n+1}''(y) &= u(y) - 1.
\end{aligned} \tag{16}$$

So $F''(y) = 0$ is a system of $n+1$ equations in $n+1$ unknowns, referred to as *the projective transformation of* $F(x) = 0$. Since $u(y)$ is linear, it is easy in practice to replace $F''(y) = 0$ by an equivalent system of n equations in n unknowns. The significance of $F''(y)$ is given by

Theorem [8]. If $F'(y) = 0$ has only a finite number of solutions in CP^n, then $F''(y) = 0$ has exactly d solutions (counting multiplicities) in C^{n+1} and no solutions at infinity, for almost all $\xi \in C^{n+1}$.

Under the hypothesis of the theorem, all the solutions of $F'(y) = 0$ can be obtained as lines through the solutions to $F''(y) = 0$. Thus all the solutions to $F(x) = 0$ can be obtained easily from the solutions to $F''(y) = 0$, which lie on bounded homotopy paths (since $F''(y) = 0$ has no solutions at infinity).

The projective transformation functions essentially as a scaling transformation. Its effect is to shorten arc lengths and bring solutions closer to the unit sphere. Coefficient and variable scaling are different, in that they directly address extreme values in the system coefficients. The projective transformation works well with these more conventional scaling schemes. See [6, 10, 18].

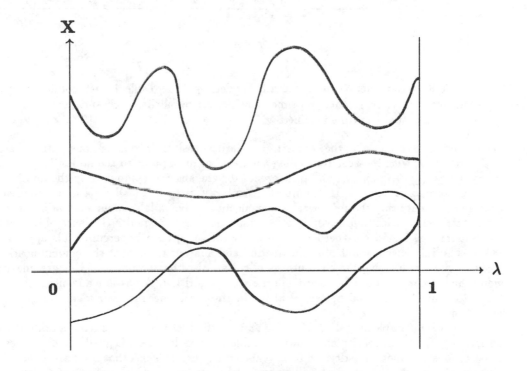

Figure 2. The set $\rho_a^{-1}(0)$ for a polynomial system.

Figure 2 illustrates the qualitative characteristics of the zero curves for a polynomial system. There are d (the total degree of F) of them, they are monotone in λ, and have finite arc length. (This last characteristic assumes that the hypothesis of the above theorem holds.)

5. Computational results. In solving a polynomial system using continuation, a number of homotopy paths must be tracked. There are two extreme approaches to implementing this on a hypercube.

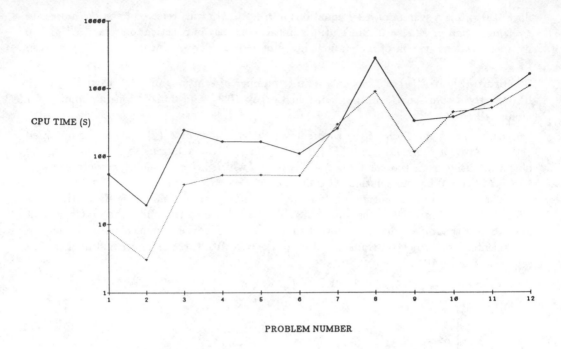

CPU TIME (S)

PROBLEM NUMBER

Figure 3. Graph comparing column 3 divided by 32 of Table 1 with column 4. The lower curve represents cpu times for "perfect parallelization" and the upper curve the actual cpu time attained.

The first extreme, with the coarsest granularity possible, is to assign one path to each node processor, with the host controlling the assignment of paths to the nodes, keeping as many nodes busy as possible, and post-processing the answers computed by the nodes.

The second extreme, with the finest granularity, is to track all d paths on the host processor, distributing the numerical linear algebra, polynomial system evaluation, Jacobian matrix evaluation, and possibly other things amongst the nodes. Because of the high communication overhead (whether hardware or software) on a hypercube, this approach requires an immense amount of sophistication and analysis to prevent the communication costs from overwhelming the computational costs. Also the algorithm at this granularity would have to be a major modification of the serial algorithm. A possible advantage is that the load could be balanced better, resulting in an overall speedup over a coarser grained algorithm.

Our current implementation of POLSYS uses the first approach, having a node track an entire path. Some results are shown in Table 1. (Problem data is available on request. Most of these problems are derived from real engineering problems that have arisen at GM and elsewhere.) Further research will be required to determine which aspects of the second approach may be worthwhile. Perhaps eventually certain intermediate schemes will prove to work best.

The third and fourth columns of Table 1 compare a single processor of the iPSC-32 hypercube with the 32-node hypercube itself. If parallelism were perfect, then dividing column 3 by 32 would yield column 4. This is not so because generally the workload is not balanced perfectly between processors (especially in the smaller problems) and communications between the host and nodes takes some time. Also, our timer is subject to the usual variations. Figure 3 compares column 3 divided by 32 with column 4.

Table 1. Execution time (secs).

Problem number	total degree	80286/ 80287	iPSC-32	VAX 11/750	VAX 11/780
1	4	255	54	41	18
2	4	84	19	14	6
3	12	1200	243	325	152
4	16	1655	163	216	112
5	16	1657	162	216	112
6	16	1628	108	216	112
7	60	9450	257	1707	796
8	60	28783	2795	4332	2054
9	64	3669	335	703	334
10	81	14336	378	1884	999
11	256	16257	645	2438	1248
12	625	34692	1616	5260	2656
13	256	—	11527	29779	16221
14	576	—	11786	49736	27815

Let us comment here on some realities of parallel computation. The parallel computation scheme of assigning a path to a node seems completely transparent and straightforward. Why this turned out not to be so is illustrative of difficulties in the field of parallel computation generally. The following is a list of tasks that should be trivial, with comments as to why they were not.

1. Assigning paths to nodes.

There are exactly d paths and starting points, completely determined by the parameters in the homotopy map ρ_c. (Here, "d" is the total degree of the system.) Once ρ_c is chosen, these starting points are fixed, and may not be changed in any way. In production use of HOMPACK, not every solution may be desired, so only some of the paths may need to be tracked. Thus the parallel computer code has to keep track of all the paths, which of those are being tracked and have been assigned to a node, and which are to be tracked but have not yet been assigned to a node. This is further complicated by the fact that the number of paths does not equal (in general) the number of nodes. Also the nodes are finishing paths at random (thus becoming available to track another path), and so must be reused in random order. Now all this bookkeeping can, of course, be done, but the point is that these considerations do not even arise for the serial program.

2. Transmitting data to the nodes.

In the serial version of HOMPACK, all work arrays (below the level of the main program) have variable dimensions, and there are absolutely no static arrays limiting the size of the problem. Current hardware implementations of the hypercube architecture have nodes with relatively small memories (128K or 512K), and the nodes do *not* support virtual memory. Furthermore, what executes on the nodes is a "main program", not a "subroutine". Thus memory is tight, and arrays cannot be dynamically allocated. Since the actual storage needed depends on several factors–dimension, total degree, number of terms, etc.–it is difficult to fit a problem into the available memory optimally. Another annoyance is that only short messages may be sent, so the data defining the problem must be broken up and transmitted in pieces. All this communication sending, receiving, queueing, blocking, and unblocking is currently (and unfortunately) the responsibility of the application programs.

3. Transmitting answers to the host.

To appreciate the situation here, consider the following three facts: 1) the complete answer (the point at end of the path and concomitant path statistics) cannot be sent all in one message; 2) the nodes finish tracking their assigned paths asynchronously; 3) for hardware and software reasons, the host cannot just "listen" to one node. No matter how the host resolves this situation, it is going to be nontrivial.

One possibility is to maintain a huge data structure, and as the answer pieces arrive, insert them in the correct slot in the structure. This requires an identification stamp with each message, and some blocking and unblocking overhead at the ends. A second possibility is to establish a "handshake" protocol, whereby each node simply informs the host that its path is complete, and does not transmit its solution until the host requests it. Even in this case an answer reception may be punctuated by completion notices from other nodes, which must be queued. This second approach was the one used for the times reported in Table 1. There are many other reasonable approaches to this issue; more research is needed.

4. Replicating performance measurements.

Message transmission is a combination of hardware and software, and may involve several (intermediate) nodes between the sender and recipient. All this happens asynchronously in real time, and the temporal order of events may depend on such things as buffer status, free space list size, timer interrupts, and even random (corrected) hardware errors. The state of the node operating systems and disk file fragmentation on the host can affect durations and the temporal order of events, sometimes by as much as 10%. Obtaining performance data is difficult, and for complex, realistic codes, replicating performance results may be impossible.

REFERENCES

[1] E. ALLGOWER AND K. GEORG, *Simplicial and continuation methods for approximating fixed points*, SIAM Rev., 22 (1980), pp. 28–85.

[2] S. C. BILLUPS, *An augmented Jacobian matrix algorithm for tracking homotopy zero curves*, M.S. Thesis, Dept. of Computer Sci., VPI & SU, Blacksburg, VA, Sept., 1985.

[3] P. BUSINGER AND G. H. GOLUB, *Linear least squares solutions by Householder transformations*, Numer. Math., 7 (1965), pp. 269–276.

[4] INTEL CORPORATION, *iPSC Users' Manual*, 1985.

[5] M. KUBICEK, *Dependence of solutions of nonlinear systems on a parameter*, ACM-TOMS, 2 (1976), pp. 98–107.

[6] K. MEINTJES AND A. P. MORGAN, *A methodology for solving chemical equilibrium systems*, Appl. Math. Comput., to appear. Also available as Res. Pub. GMR-4971, Mathematics Dept., G.M. Research Labs., Warren, MI 49090, 1985.

[7] A. P. MORGAN, *A method for computing all solutions to systems of polynomial equations*, ACM Trans. Math Software, 9(1983), pp. 1–17.

[8] ——, *A transformation to avoid solutions at infinity for polynomial systems*, Appl. Math. Comput., 18(1986), pp. 77–86.

[9] ——, *A homotopy for solving polynomial systems*, Appl. Math. Comput., 18(1986), pp. 87–92.

[10] ——, *Solving Polynomial Systems Using Continuation for Scientific and Engineering Problems*, Prentice-Hall, Englewood Cliffs, NJ, to appear in 1987.

[11] A. P. MORGAN AND R. F. SARRAGA, *A method for computing three surface intersection points in GMSOLID*, ASME paper 82-DET- 41 (1982). Also available as Res. Pub. GMR-3964, Mathematics Dept., G.M. Research Labs., Warren, MI 49090, 1981.

[12] W. C. RHEINBOLDT AND J. V. BURKARDT, *Algorithm 596: A program for a locally parameterized continuation process*, ACM Trans. Math. Software, 9 (1983), pp. 236-241.

[13] C. L. SEITZ, *The cosmic cube*, Commun. ACM, 28 (1985), pp. 22–33.

[14] L. F. SHAMPINE AND M. K. GORDON, *Computer Solution of Ordinary Differential Equations: The Initial Value Problem*, W. H. Freeman, San Francisco, 1975.

[15] L.-W. TSAI AND A. P. MORGAN, *Solving the kinematics of the most general six- and five-degree-of-freedom manipulators by continuation methods*, ASME J. of Mechanisms, Transmissions and Automation in Design, 107(1985), pp. 48-57.

[16] L. T. WATSON AND D. FENNER, *Chow-Yorke algorithm for fixed points or zeros of C^2 maps*, ACM TOMS, 6 (1980), pp. 252–260.

[17] L. T. WATSON, *A globally convergent algorithm for computing fixed points of C^2 maps*, Appl. Math. Comput., 5 (1979), pp. 297–311.

[18] L. T. WATSON, S. C. BILLUPS, AND A. P. MORGAN, *HOMPACK: A suite of codes for globally convergent homotopy algorithms*, Res. Pub. GMR-5344, Mathematics Dept., G.M. Research Labs., Warren, MI 49090, 1986.

[19] L. T. WATSON, *Numerical linear algebra aspects of globally convergent homotopy methods*, Tech. Report TR-85-14, Dept. of Computer Sci., VPI&SU, Blacksburg, VA, 1985.

Implementation of Two Control System Design Algorithms on a Message-Passing Hypercube

JUDITH D. GARDINER* AND ALAN J. LAUB*

Abstract. Frequency response calculation and solution of the algebraic Riccati equation, both for linear time-invariant multivariable state space models, have been implemented on an Intel iPSC hypercube. Frequency response is computed using Laub's Hessenberg algorithm; Riccati equations are solved by means of the matrix sign function algorithm. The principal components of both algorithms are the solution of linear systems and matrix multiplication. We have adopted a column-oriented approach, assigning each processor node several columns of each matrix. High level functional parallelism in the algorithms is exploited to maximize processor utilization.

Introduction. Two key computational problems which arise in the design and analysis of control systems are frequency response calculation and the solution of algebraic Riccati equations. Riccati equations are particularly ubiquitous and play a central role in optimal estimation and filtering, as well as in optimal control. These particular problems were chosen for parallel implementation for three reasons: 1) They are important in control systems engineering, 2) they are computationally expensive, and 3) straightforward (i.e., easily parallelized) algorithms were already available for them. Reference [1] gives further background in control design computations.

Both problems are based on the linear, time-invariant, multivariable state space model

$$\dot{x} = Ax + Bu \qquad\qquad (1)$$

$$y = Cx$$

where

$$x \in \mathbb{R}^n , \quad u \in \mathbb{R}^m , \quad y \in \mathbb{R}^r , \quad A \in \mathbb{R}^{n \times n} , \quad B \in \mathbb{R}^{n \times m} , \quad C \in \mathbb{R}^{r \times n} .$$

The coefficient matrices A, B, and C range in size from rather modest, say on the order of 10-100, through quite large, say on the order of 500-1000. We shall further assume these matrices to

---

* Dept. of Electrical and Computer Engineering, University of California, Santa Barbara, CA 93106 This research was supported in part by the Office of Naval Research under contract number N00014-85-K-0553 and the National Science Foundation (and AFOSR) under grant number ECS84-06152.

be dense, with no exploitable structure. Such a model might represent, for example, a large space structure (LSS) as approximated by the finite element method (FEM).

The solutions to these problems have been implemented on an Intel iPSC/d5 hypercube, with quite satisfactory results.

Frequency Response. Given the linear system (1) we want to compute the $r \times m$ complex-valued frequency response matrix

$$G(j\omega) = C(j\omega I - A)^{-1}B$$

for N values of the scalar parameter ω, where typically $N \gg n$. An efficient and reliable algorithm for this computation is:

1. Transform A to Hessenberg form using orthogonal similarity transformations, also transforming B and C appropriately.

2. For each value of ω, "solve $G(j\omega)=C(j\omega I-A)^{-1}B$", where (A,B,C) is the system resulting from step 1. This step will be described further below. For additional details, see [2], [3]. Under the assumption that $N \gg n$, most of the computation time is spent on this step.

An analysis of this algorithm, which is the one we chose for hypercube implemention, reveals a considerable amount of parallelism on several levels. After the Hessenberg reduction has been done, the computations at the N different frequencies ω are independent. Assuming that the coefficient matrices are small enough, the processing nodes can work independently on different frequencies, making the problem almost perfectly parallel. If the matrices must be split among multiple nodes, then they are allocated by columns (column wrapped distribution). Each processor receives approximately n/p columns of A, m/p columns of B, etc., and produces m/p columns of G, where p is the number of processors.

In reality we combine these two approaches. Let d be the dimension of the smallest subcube capable of computing $G(j\omega)$ for a single value of ω, and let $d_{\max}$ be the dimension of the entire cube. We treat the system as $2^{d_{\max}-d}$ independent subcubes of dimension d. The subcubes receive identical matrices but different frequency ranges. The columns are distributed among the nodes of each subcube. With this implementation the Hessenberg reduction step is performed redundantly by all the subcubes, but it is an insignificant part of the total computation.

The Hessenberg reduction is accomplished by Householder similarity transformations:

$$A \longleftarrow P_{n-2} \cdots P_2 P_1 A P_1 P_2 P_{n-2}$$

$$B \longleftarrow P_{n-2} \cdots P_2 P_1 B$$

$$C \longleftarrow C P_1 P_2 \cdots P_{n-2}$$

where

$$P_j = I - \sigma_j u_j u_j^T, \qquad \sigma_j = \frac{u_j^T u_j}{2}.$$

Each u_j is selected to zero out the elements of column j below the subdiagonal, without affecting the previously processed columns.

The key step is the computation of PAP, which can be written (dropping all subscripts) as

$$PAP = (I - \sigma u u^T) A (I - \sigma u u^T)$$

$$= A - \sigma u v^T - \sigma w u^T$$

where

$$v = A^T u$$

$$w = \bar{A}u$$

$$\bar{A} = A - \sigma u v^T$$

Note that

$$w = \bar{A}u = [\bar{a}_1 \ \cdots \ \bar{a}_n] \begin{bmatrix} \mu_1 \\ \cdot \\ \cdot \\ \cdot \\ \mu_n \end{bmatrix} = \sum_i \mu_i \bar{a}_i$$

(We are following Householder's notational conventions. Thus $\bar{a}_i$ is a column of the matrix $\bar{A}$, μ_i is an element of the vector u, and v_i is an element of v.) The parallel algorithm is:

For $j = 1, \ldots, n-2$

1)   Owner of a_j: Compute u and σ from a_j as for sequential algorithm
     Others: wait *

2)   Broadcast u, σ *

3)   All: Compute $v_i = a_i^T u$ for each local a_i †

4)   All: Compute $a_i \longleftarrow a_i - \sigma v_i u$ for local a_i (Now have $A - \sigma u v^T$) †

5)   All: Compute w (partial sum) $:= \sum \mu_i a_i$ for local a_i †

6)   Global add: Add up pieces of w from all nodes *

7)   Broadcast w *

8)   All: Compute $a_i \longleftarrow a_i - \sigma \mu_i w$ for local a_i †

Updating B is similar to steps 3 and 4; updating C resembles steps 5 through 8.

The steps marked with * involve idle time for some nodes, because of either communication delays or a sequential portion of the algorithm. The steps marked with † possess another level of parallelism that could be exploited by a vector processor.

Next consider the computation of the frequency response matrix

$$G = C (j\omega I - A)^{-1} B$$

for a single value of ω. Defining

$$H = j\omega I - A ,$$

we have

$$G = CH^{-1}B$$

$$= C(LU)^{-1}B$$

$$= (CU^{-1})(L^{-1}B)$$

$$= YX$$

where

$$H = LU$$

$$YU = C$$

$$LX = B$$

The factorization of the complex Hessenberg matrix H is done by Gaussian elimination with partial pivoting, although another possiblilty is to use QR factorization by Givens transformations.

Examining the problem for high level functional parallelism, we immediately see that Y and X can be computed in parallel. Next we consider the factorization of $H =: [\eta_{ij}]$, which has the form

For $j=1, \ldots, n-1$

1) Compute a transformation L_j to eliminate $\eta_{j+1,j}$ (based on η_{jj} and $\eta_{j+1,j}$)

2) Apply L_j to the $(n+1-j) \times (n+1-j)$ trailing submatrix of H (affects only rows j and $j+1$)

3) Output L_j and the jth row of U

Output $\mu_{nn} := \eta_{nn}$ (the last row of U)

Each factor of L can be applied to B as soon as it is produced, affecting rows j and $j+1$ of B and yielding the jth row of X.

The triangular system $YU = C$ can be written in the form

$$y_i = \frac{1}{\mu_{ii}} [c_i - \sum_{j=1}^{i-1} \mu_{ji} y_j].$$

So if we define

$$y_i^{(0)} = c_i \, , \, i=1, \ldots, n$$

then at step j we can compute

$$y_j = \frac{1}{\mu_{jj}} y_j^{(j-1)}$$

$$y_i^{(j)} = y_i^{(j-1)} - \mu_{ji} y_j \, , \, i=j+1, \ldots, n$$

Finally, since Y emerges by columns and X emerges by rows, G is naturally computed as an outer product.

Figure 1 shows a data flow diagram for the entire procedure. This structure can be regarded as data pipelining at a high level. Ideally each box should execute whenever it has input available, without regard to what the other boxes are doing internally. As implemented, the processing within each node is synchronous, but the overlap is still important for minimizing wasted time.

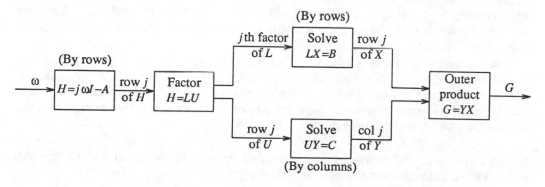

FIG. 1. Data Flow Diagram for Frequency Response Calculation

The parallel algorithm, given $H = j\omega I - A$, is:

For $j=1,...,n-1$

1)   Owner of h_j, c_j: Compute transformation L_j; compute y_j †
Others: wait *

2)   Broadcast L_j and y_j *

3)   All: Apply L_j to local h_i , $i=j+1,\ldots,n$ and local b_i , $i=1,\ldots,m$ †

4)   All: Update local y_i , $i=j+1,\ldots,n$ †

5)   All: Update local $g_i \longleftarrow g_i + x_{ji}y_j$ (outer product) †

Again, * indicates idle time and † indicates additional parallelism.

The actual code consists of a host program and a node program. The node program runs on as many nodes of the cube as are to be used, normally all of them but always a power of 2.

The host program reads the input matrices and determines the size of the smallest subcube, $p=2^d$, capable of computing the frequency response at a single frequency. The node programs are then loaded and configured to operate as 2^{d_m-d} independent subcubes of dimension d.

The A, B, and C matrices are sent to all the subcubes and distributed by columns to the nodes within the subcube. Each subcube transforms the system to Hessenberg form. If there are multiple subcubes this results in duplicated work, but it is insignificant if a large number of frequencies are to be used. The duplication of work could be avoided by having all the nodes work together on the Hessenberg reduction, then redistributing the matrices for the appropriate subcube configuration. This would increase both the complexity of the program and the amount of communication between nodes. Some speedup advantage might be seen, especially for large problems, but we have not investigated this option.

The host gets the desired frequency range and number of points from the user and divides the range among the subcubes. Each subcube computes the frequency response at logarithmically spaced frequencies within its range and returns the results to the host. Choice of the frequencies is still an open problem.

Communication within the cube is limited to broadcasts and "global operations", the dual of broadcasts. Both are accomplished by means of a spanning tree. Each subcube has its own spanning tree, so its communication is independent of any other subcube.

By pipeling data through the program and not estimating condition numbers, we avoid storing the complex matrix $H := j\omega I - A$ and its factors L and U. No storage is required for X since a column of Y and a row of X are used directly to form G. The storage requirement per node is approximately $(n+3r+4)(n_{loc}+m_{loc})+4(n+r)$ double words. The terms n_{loc} and m_{loc} refer to the number of columns of A and B, respectively, owned by the node. Recall that n_{loc} is approximately n/p.

Some timing results are provided in Table I. VAX times are for a VAX 11/780 with floating-point accelerator. Hypercube times are for an iPSC/d5 (32 processors). All computations were done in Fortran (f77 compiler on the VAX, ftn286 on the iPSC) using double precision or double precision complex arithmetic. Note that problems large enough to require more than one node on the cube are too large to be practical on the VAX.

Riccati Equations. The continuous-time generalized algebraic Riccati equation (GARE), which arises in linear quadratic optimal control and filtering problems, is

$$A^TXE + E^TXA - E^TXGXE + Q = 0. \tag{2}$$

The coefficients A, E, G, and Q and the solution X are $n\times n$ real matrices; G and Q are symmetric nonnegative definite; E is nonsingular. Under certain technical conditions, (2) has a unique symmetric nonnegative definite solution. For details, see [5].

Table I. Timing Results for Frequency Response Calculation

n	m	r	subcube dim.	# of subcubes	Hessenberg reduction			Freq. resp. (per freq)		
					iPSC time	VAX time	speedup	iPSC time	VAX time	speedup
10	3	2	0	32	<1	.1	-	.0146	.05	3.4
50	10	10	0	32	16	8.2	.5	.367	2.7	7.4
100	15	15	0	32	118	56	.5	1.82	13	7.1
180	20	20	1	16	334	*	*	7.13	*	*
300	32	32	3	4	444	*	*	63	*	*
520	32	32	4	2	1175	*	*	91	*	*

* (too large for VAX)
Note: Times are in seconds.

The best sequential algorithm for solving the GARE is the Schur vector method described in [5], which is based on the QZ algorithm. Since this method does not lend itself readily to parallel implementation, we have chosen to use an alternative algorithm based on the matrix sign function. For details, see [6] and references contained therein.

The sign function algorithm is an iterative algorithm related to the Hamiltonian pencil associated with (2). With

$$Z_0 = \begin{bmatrix} -Q & -A^T \\ -A & G \end{bmatrix}$$

and

$$F = \begin{bmatrix} 0 & E^T \\ -E & 0 \end{bmatrix}$$

the iteration is

$$Z_{k+1} = \frac{1}{2}(\frac{1}{c}Z_k - cF^T Z_k^{-1} F)$$

$$= \frac{1}{2}(\frac{1}{c}Z_k - cF^T U^{-T} D^{-1} U^{-1} F)$$

$$= \frac{1}{2}(\frac{1}{c}Z_k - cYD^{-1}Y^T)$$

where

$$c = \left[\frac{|\det Z_k|}{|\det F|} \right]^{\frac{1}{2n}}$$

$$Z_k = UDU^T$$

$$UY^T = F$$

Note that Z_k is symmetric at each step, and that F is skew-symmetric. Under the technical conditions already alluded to, it can be shown that the sequence $\{Z_k\}$ converges. Let the final value of Z_k be

$$\bar{Z} = \begin{bmatrix} \bar{Z}_{11} & \bar{Z}_{12} \\ \bar{Z}_{12}^T & \bar{Z}_{22} \end{bmatrix}$$

The solution to (2) is then defined by the linear equation

$$(\bar{Z}_{12} + E^T)XE = -\bar{Z}_{11} \tag{3}$$

The only operations involved are very basic ones: solution of linear systems, matrix multiplication, scaling, and addition. We have again chosen a column-oriented approach for our implementation and column-wrapped distribution for the matrices Z, F, and Y.

For the decomposition $Z_k = UDU^T$ we parallelized the LINPACK [4] algorithm for factoring symmetric indefinite matrices (DSIFA). U is unit upper triangular and D is block diagonal with 1×1 and 2×2 blocks. Unfortunately, the symmetric matrix factorization involves a lot more communication among nodes than the unsymmetric LU factorization. Pivoting requires column exchanges (exchanges between nodes) as well as row exchanges (within a single node).

Figure 2 shows the data flow diagram for computation of Z_{k+1} from Z_k. U is generated in factored form, and the factors can be applied to F as they emerge. Y emerges by columns. The outer product $\sum \delta_k^{-1} y_k y_k^T$ is accumulated to give $YD^{-1}Y^T$. All the nodes compute the determinant of Z_k from D and then compute the scale factor c.

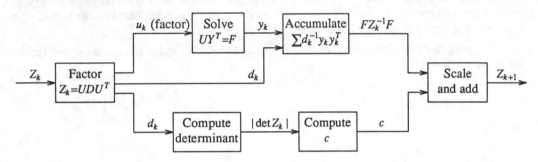

FIG. 2. Data Flow Diagram for Sign Function Iteration

To check for convergence, each node computes its portion of the difference $|Z_k - Z_{k+1}|$. A global addition is used to compute the total difference, which is broadcast to all the nodes. The iteration terminates when the difference is small enough.

After the sign iteration is done, the Riccati solution XE is computed from (3).

Some timing results are given in Table II. VAX times are for a VAX 11/780 with floating-point accelerator using Laub's Schur vector method for standard algebraic Riccati equations. Hypercube times are with 32 processors. All computations were done in Fortran (f77 compiler on the VAX, ftn286 on the iPSC) in double precision arithmetic.

Table II. Timing Results for Riccati Equation Solution

n	Hypercube time (sec.)	VAX time (sec.)	Speedup
20	47	32	0.68
40	84	210	2.5
80	253	1547	6.1
100	383	too long	*

Continuing and Future Work. Work continues on several aspects of the parallel frequency response and Riccati equation algorithms. We plan to convert the frequency response code to run on the Butterfly and Culler parallel computers. This will give us an informal benchmark to compare the performance of different machines on a practical controls problem.

For the sign function algorithm we are investigating an updating scheme that will replace the repeated symmetric indefinite matrix factorization. This approach requires an initial factorization of the form $Z=UDU^T$. It then uses orthogonal and hyperbolic rotations to update the factors U and D, requiring much less interprocessor communication than the current algorithm. The updating approach was suggested by Paul Van Dooren [private communication].

Work remains also on the discrete-time generalized algebraic Riccati equation. It can be solved by the sign function method but, in contrast to the continuous-time case, it does not lead to a symmetric sign iteration. Another alternative being studied is a discrete-time doubling algorithm.

REFERENCES

[1]   A.J. LAUB, *Numerical linear algebra aspects of control design computations*, IEEE Trans. Aut. Contr., AC-30(1985), pp. 97-108.

[2]   A.J. LAUB, *Efficient multivariable frequency response computations*, IEEE Trans. Aut. Contr., AC-26(1981), pp. 407-408.

[3]   A.J. LAUB, *Algorithm 640: Efficient calculation of frequency response matrices from state space models*, ACM Trans. Math. Softw., 12(1986), pp. 26-33.

[4]   J.J. DONGARRA, J.R. BUNCH, C.B. MOLER, G.W. STEWART, *LINPACK Users' Guide*, SIAM, Philadelphia, 1979.

[5]   W.F. ARNOLD and A.J. LAUB, *Generalized eigenproblem algorithms and software for algebraic Riccati equations*, Proc. IEEE, 72(1984), pp. 1746-1754.

[6]   J.D. GARDINER and A.J. LAUB, *A generalization of the matrix sign function solution for algebraic Riccati equations*, Int. J. Control, 44(1986), pp. 823-832.

Parallel Iterative Methods for the Solution of Fredholm Integral Equations of the Second Kind

LOTHAR REICHEL*

Abstract

Atkinson [3] and Brakhage [5] analyzed several two-grid schemes for solving Fredholm integral equations of the second kind. Let n be the number of unknowns in the algebraic linear system of equations obtained by discretizing the integral equation by a Nyström method. We show that the size of the preconditioning matrix in the two-grid schemes can be chosen so that the operation count for iteratively solving the algebraic linear system of equations is only $O(n^2)$ arithmetic operations, i.e. the operation count is of the same order of magnitude as for multigrid schemes. These two-grid schemes are easy to implement efficiently on a computer with several processors. We also show that many integral equations in applictions and in the numerical analysis literature have a structure that reduces the operation count for their solution to $O(n \log n)$ arithmetic operations.

1. Introduction

Many problems of Applied Mathematics can be formulated as Fredholm integral equations of the second kind. In order to keep the notation simple, we formulate our results for one-dimensional integral equations,

$$u(x) - \int_0^1 k(x,y)u(y)dy = f(x), \quad 0 \le x \le 1, \tag{1.1}$$

but the iterative schemes we propose are applicable to higher dimensional problems as well. We assume that (1.1) has a unique solution $u^*(x)$, and that $k(x,y)$ satisfies a Hölder condition, see (2.1) below. The discretization of (1.1) typically gives rise to a large linear system of algebraic equations,

$$(I - K_n)\mathbf{u}_n = \mathbf{f}_n, \quad \mathbf{u}_n, \mathbf{f}_n \in \mathbb{R}^n, \quad K_n \in \mathbb{R}^{n \times n}, \tag{1.2}$$

with a filled matrix K_n. The solution of (1.2) by Gaussian elimination requires $O(n^3)$ arithmetic operations. Atkinson [3] and Brakhage [5] suggested iterative solution of (1.2) by two-grid methods, which require $O(n^2 \log n)$ arithmetic operations in order to yield an approximate solution $\tilde{\mathbf{u}}_n$ of (1.2) with an error of the same order of magnitude as the discretization error in (1.2). This operation count stems from that each iteration requires $O(n^2)$ arithmetic operations, and the number of iterations is $O(\log n)$, see [7] for details.

*Department of Mathematics, University of Kentucky, Lexington, Kentucky 40506

Recently multigrid schemes have been proposed for the solution of (1.2), see Hackbusch [6], Hemker and Schippers [7] and Schippers [9]. Multigrid schemes require only $O(n^2)$ arithmetic operations in order to determine an approximate solution of the same accuracy as $\bar{u}_n$. The number of iterations required by the multigrid schemes is independent of n.

In Section 2 we present a modification of the two-grid schemes of Atkinson [3] and Brakhage [5]. The modified schemes require only $O(n^2)$ arithmetic operations in order to determine an approximate solution with an error of the same order of magnitude as the discretization error in (1.2). The number of iterations is independent of n. Our modification consists of letting the size of the preconditioning matrix in the two-grid scheme be a slowly increasing function of n. These two-grid schemes are easy to implement efficiently on a computer with several processors. In particular, they are simpler to implement than multigrid schemes.

In many applications and in many examples in the numerical analysis literature, the kernel $k(x,y)$ has a structure that makes it possible to split the matrix K_n into a sum of products of Toeplitz or Hankel matrices. In Section 3, we show how such integral equations can be solved in $O(n \log n)$ arithmetic operations by the two-grid schemes of Section 2. Section 4 contains computed examples.

2. Two-grid schemes

Let $[\alpha]$ denote the integer part of $\alpha \geq 0$, and let $C^\alpha[0,1]$ be the set of $[\alpha]$ times continuously differentiable functions, whose derivative of order $[\alpha]$ satisfies a Hölder condition with Hölder constant $\alpha - [\alpha]$. Assume that for some constant $\alpha > 0$ the kernel $k(x,y)$ satisfies, with $l := [\alpha]$,

$$\begin{cases} \max_{0 \leq x \leq 1} | \frac{\partial^l}{\partial y^l} k(x,y_1) - \frac{\partial^l}{\partial y^l} k(x,y_2) | \leq c \, | y_1 - y_2 |^{\alpha - l} \\ \max_{0 \leq y \leq 1} | \frac{\partial^l}{\partial x^l} k(x_1,y) - \frac{\partial^l}{\partial x^l} k(x_2,y) | \leq c \, | x_1 - x_2 |^{\alpha - l} \end{cases} \qquad (2.1)$$

for some constant c and all $0 \leq x_1, x_2, y_1, y_2 \leq 1$.

We describe the two-grid schemes in detail when (1.1) is discretized by the Nyström method based on the trapezoidal rule. The use of other quadrature rules is discussed in the end of this section. Define the trapezoidal operator $T_n : [0,1] \to \mathbb{R}$ by

$$T_n u := \sum_{j=0}^{n-1} w_{jn} u\left(\frac{j}{n-1}\right), \qquad (2.2)$$

with $w_{on} := w_{n-1,n} := (2(n-1))^{-1}, w_{jn} := (n-1)^{-1}, \ 2 \leq j \leq n-2$. For any $u \in C^\beta[0,1]$, we have for some constant c dependent on u but independent of n,

$$| T_n u - \int_0^1 u(x)dx | \leq cn^{-\gamma}, \ \gamma := \min\{2, \beta\}. \qquad (2.3)$$

We obtain the matrix

$$K_n := \tilde{K}_n D_n, \qquad (2.4)$$

where

$$\tilde{K}_n = \left[k\left(\frac{s}{n-1}, \frac{t}{n-1}\right) \right]_{s,t=0}^{n-1}, \quad D_n = \operatorname{diag}(w_{on}, w_{1n}, \ldots, w_{n-1,n}).$$

Introduce the restriction operator $R_n : C[0,1] \to \mathbb{R}^n$,

$$R_n u := (u(0), u\left(\frac{1}{n-1}\right), u\left(\frac{2}{n-1}\right), \ldots, u(1))^T, \qquad (2.5)$$

and define the prolongation operator $P_n : \mathbb{R}^n \to C[0,1]$ by piecewise linear interpolation. For $\mathbf{u}_n = (u_0, u_1, \ldots, u_{n-1})^T$, let

$$(P_n \mathbf{u}_n)(x) := \sum_{j=0}^{n-1} u_j \phi_j(x), \tag{2.6}$$

where

$$\phi_j(x) := \begin{cases} 1 - |(n-1)x - j|, & \dfrac{j-1}{n-1} < x < \dfrac{j+1}{n-1} \\ \\ 0 & , \text{ otherwise.} \end{cases} \tag{2.7}$$

Equip $C[0,1]$ with the uniform norm

$$\| u \| := \max_{0 \le x \le 1} |u(x)|. \tag{2.8}$$

Assume that $k(x,y)$ satisfies (2.1) for some $\alpha > 0$, and that f in (1.1) satisfies $f \in C^\beta[0,1]$ for some $\beta > 0$. Then the solution u^* of (1.1) satisfies $u^* \in C^\gamma[0,1]$ for $\gamma := \min\{\alpha, \beta\}$. Equation (1.2) has a unique solution $\| \mathbf{u}_n^* \|$ for n sufficiently large, and we obtain the discretization error, see, e.g., Atkinson [3] for details,

$$\| u^* - P_n \mathbf{u}_n^* \| = O(n^{-\kappa}), \quad n \to \infty, \quad \kappa := \min\{2, \alpha, \beta\}. \tag{2.9}$$

A preconditioning matrix $I - K_m \in \mathbb{R}^{m \times m}$ is obtained by discretizing the integral operator (1.1) by the trapezoidal rule T_m for some $m << n$. Introduce the prolongation $p : \mathbb{R}^m \to \mathbb{R}^n$ and restriction $r : \mathbb{R}^n \to \mathbb{R}^m$,

$$p := R_n P_m \text{ and } r := R_m P_n. \tag{2.10}$$

If $n-1$ is a multiple of $m-1$ then

$$rp = I. \tag{2.11}$$

The two-grid schemes that Atkinson denotes "Method 1" and "Method 2", see Atkinson [3, pp. 139-147], can be written, in order,

$$\begin{cases} \mathbf{w}_n^j := \mathbf{f}_n - \mathbf{u}_n^j + K_n \mathbf{u}_n^j \\ \mathbf{u}_n^{j+1} := \mathbf{u}_n^j + (I + p(I - K_m)^{-1} K_m r) \mathbf{w}_n^j \end{cases} \quad j = 0,1,2 \cdots \tag{2.12}$$

$$\begin{cases} \mathbf{w}_n^j := \mathbf{f}_n - \mathbf{u}_n^j + K_n \mathbf{u}_n^j \\ \mathbf{u}_n^{j+1} := \mathbf{u}_n^j + \mathbf{w}_n^j + (I + p(I - K_m)^{-1} K_m r) K_n \mathbf{w}_n^j \end{cases} \quad j = 0,1,2 \cdots \tag{2.13}$$

where the superscript denotes the iteration number. In Section 4 we use the starting approximation

$$\mathbf{u}_n^0 := p(I - K_m)^{-1} \mathbf{f}_m. \tag{2.14}$$

The vector and matrix norms used in this paper are the maximum norms, e.g. $\| \mathbf{v}_n \| := \max_{0 \le j < n} |v_j|$, where $\mathbf{v}_n = (v_0, v_1, \ldots, v_{n-1})^T$. It can be shown that for all $m \ge m_0$, for some constant m_0, $(I - K_m)^{-1}$ exists and that there is a constant $\rho := \rho(m_0)$ such that

$$\| (I - K_m)^{-1} \| \le \rho, \ m \ge m_0, \tag{2.15}$$

see Atkinson [3, pp. 88-106]. In the derivation of (2.12-13), we also used that

$$(I - pK_m r)^{-1} = I + p(I - K_m)^{-1} K_m r, \ m \ge m_0, \tag{2.16}$$

which holds if (2.11) is satisfied. We remark that Atkinson used Nyström interpolation to define p and q instead of defining them by (2.10).

Theorem 1. Assume that (1.1) has a unique solution, that (2.1) holds for some $\alpha > 0$ and that (2.11) and (2.15) are satisfied. For $n > m \geq m_0$, we write (2.12) as

$$\mathbf{u}_n^{j+1} = M'_{nm}\mathbf{u}_n^j + N'_{nm}\mathbf{f}_n, \tag{2.12'}$$

and (2.13) as

$$\mathbf{u}_n^{j+1} = M''_{nm}\mathbf{u}_n^j + N''_{nm}\mathbf{f}_n. \tag{2.13'}$$

There is a constant c, independent of m and n such that

$$\|(M'_{nm})^2\| \leq cm^{-\gamma}, \quad \|M''_{nm}\| \leq cm^{-\gamma}, \quad n > m \geq m_0, \tag{2.17}$$

where $\gamma := \min\{2, \alpha\}$. Choose $m = m(n)$ such that

$$\max\{m_0, c_0^{1/\gamma} n^\delta\} \leq m \leq c_1 n^{2/3} \tag{2.18}$$

for some constants c_0, c_1, δ satisfying $c_0 > c$, where c is defined by (2.17), $c_1 > c_0^{1/\gamma}$ and $0 < \delta \leq 2/3$. We assume that n is sufficiently large so that m satisfying (2.18) exist. Then an iterate $\mathbf{u}_n^j$ can be determined from (2.12) or (2.13) in $O(n^2)$ arithmetic operations, such that for any constant $c_2 > 0$ independent of n, m and j,

$$\|\mathbf{u}_n^* - \mathbf{u}_n^j\| \leq c_2 n^{-\kappa}, \quad \kappa := \min\{2, \alpha, \beta\}, \tag{2.19}$$

where $f \in C^\beta[0,1]$. The error in $\mathbf{u}_n^j$ is of the same order of magnitude as the discretization error (2.9) as n increases. In particular, the number of iteration necessary to determine an $\mathbf{u}_n^j$ satisfying (2.19) depends on c_2 and u^* but is independent of n.

Proof. From (2.12-13) we obtain, using (2.11),

$$M'_{nm} = (I + pK_m(I - K_m)^{-1}r)(K_n - pK_m r), \tag{2.20}$$

$$M''_{nm} = (I + pK_m(I - K_m)^{-1}r)(K_n - pK_m r)K_n. \tag{2.21}$$

We first bound M''_{nm}. There are constants c_3, c_4, c_5 independent of m and n, such that

$$\|p\| \leq c_3, \quad \|r\| \leq c_4, \quad \|K_m\| \leq c_5, \quad m \geq m_0. \tag{2.22}$$

By (2.15) it now follows that $\|I + p(I - K_m)^{-1}K_m r\|$ is uniformly bounded for $m \geq m_0$. It remains to bound $(K_n - pK_m r)K_n$. Let $\mathbf{u}_n = [u_j]_{j=0}^{n-1} \in \mathbb{R}^n$ satisfy $\|\mathbf{u}_n\| \leq 1$. Element q of the vector $K_n K_n \mathbf{u}_n$ has the form

$$(K_n K_n \mathbf{u}_n)_q = \sum_{l=0}^{n-1} k\left(\frac{q}{n-1}, \frac{l}{n-1}\right) w_{ln} \sum_{j=0}^{n-1} k\left(\frac{l}{n-1}, \frac{j}{n-1}\right) w_{jn} u_j$$

$$= \sum_{j=0}^{n-1} \left[\sum_{l=0}^{n-1} k\left(\frac{q}{n-1}, \frac{l}{n-1}\right) k\left(\frac{l}{n-1}, \frac{j}{n-1}\right) w_{ln}\right] w_{jn} u_j$$

$$= \sum_{j=0}^{n-1} \int_0^1 k\left(\frac{q}{n-1}, t\right) k\left(t, \frac{j}{n-1}\right) dt \, w_{jn} u_j + \sum_{j=0}^{n-1} e_{qjn} w_{jn} u_j,$$

where, by (2.1) and (2.3), there is a constant c_6 independent of j, q and n, such that

$$|e_{qjn}| \leq c_6 n^{-\gamma}, \quad n > m_0, \quad \gamma := \min\{2, \alpha\}.$$

Hence,

$$\left|\sum_{j=0}^{n-1} e_{qjn} w_{jn} u_j\right| \leq c_6 n^{-\gamma} \sum_{j=0}^{n-1} |w_{jn}|.$$

Therefore, uniformly for $0 \leq q < n$ and $\|\mathbf{u}_n\| \leq 1$,

$$(K_n K_n \mathbf{u}_n)_q = \sum_{j=0}^{n-1} \int_0^1 k\left(\frac{q}{n-1}, t\right) k\left(t, \frac{j}{n-1}\right) dt \, w_{jn} u_j + O(n^{-\gamma}). \tag{2.23}$$

Consider $pK_m r K_n \mathbf{u}_n$ and let $\mathbf{v}_m = [v_j]_{j=0}^{n-1} := r K_n \mathbf{u}_n$. $\mathbf{v}_m$ is a discretization of a function in $C^\alpha[0,1]$. For any $\|\mathbf{u}_n\| \le 1$, we have $\|\mathbf{v}_m\| \le c_7 := c_4 c_5$. By (2.1) and (2.3) we obtain, uniformly for $0 \le q < n$ and $\|\mathbf{u}_n\| \le 1$,

$$|(pK_m \mathbf{v}_m)_q - \sum_{j=0}^{m-1} k\left(\frac{q}{n-1}, \frac{j}{m-1}\right) w_{jm} v_j| \le c_8 m^{-\gamma} \sum_{j=0}^{m-1} |w_{jm} v_j| \le c_7 c_8 m^{-\gamma} \sum_{j=0}^{m-1} |w_{jm}|. \tag{2.24}$$

Formula (2.24) shows the difference between using the prolongation p defined by (2.5-6), (2.10) and prolongation by Nyström interpolation.

We next compare $r K_n \mathbf{u}_n$ to the vector obtained when Nyström interpolation is used. When $n-1$ is a multiple of $m-1$ then r is an injection, $(r\mathbf{u}_n)_q = u_{q(n-1)/(m-1)}$, $0 \le q < m$. For general m and n, there is a constant c_9, such that

$$|(r K_n \mathbf{u}_n)_q - \sum_{j=0}^{n-1} k\left(\frac{q}{m-1}, \frac{j}{n-1}\right) w_{jn} u_j| \le c_9 n^{-\gamma} \|\mathbf{u}_n\| \sum_{j=0}^{n-1} |w_{jn}|. \tag{2.25}$$

We obtain from (2.22) and (2.24-25), uniformly for $0 \le q < n$ and $\|\mathbf{u}_n\| \le 1$,

$$\begin{cases} (pK_m r K_n \mathbf{u}_n)_q - \sum_{l=0}^{m-1} k\left(\frac{q}{n-1}, \frac{l}{m-1}\right) w_{lm} \sum_{j=0}^{n-1} k\left(\frac{l}{m-1}, \frac{j}{n-1}\right) w_{jn} u_j = \\ O(n^{-\gamma}) + O(m^{-\gamma}) = O(m^{-\gamma}), \quad n > m \ge m_0. \end{cases} \tag{2.26}$$

Similarly as we derived (2.23), we obtain

$$\begin{cases} \sum_{l=0}^{m-1} k\left(\frac{q}{n-1}, \frac{l}{m-1}\right) w_{lm} \sum_{j=0}^{n-1} k\left(\frac{l}{m-1}, \frac{j}{n-1}\right) w_{jn} u_j \\ = \sum_{j=0}^{n-1} \int_0^1 k\left(\frac{q}{n-1}, t\right) k\left(t, \frac{j}{n-1}\right) dt \, w_{jn} u_j + O(m^{-\gamma}), \end{cases} \tag{2.27}$$

uniformly for $0 \le q < n$. Combining (2.23) and (2.26-27) yields

$$\|(K_n - pK_m r)K_n\| = O(m^{-\gamma}), \tag{2.28}$$

uniformly for $n > m \ge m_0$. This establishes (2.17) for M''_{nm}. In order to show (2.17) for M'_{nm}, we use a trick employed by Atkinson [3, pp. 139-140] when proving a related result: bound the norm of $B_{nm} := (M'_{nm})^2$. We write B_{nm} as

$$B_{nm} = (I + pK_m(I-K_m)^{-1}r)(K_n - pK_m r)[(I + pK_m(I-K_m)^{-1}r)K_n - (I + pK_m(I-K_m)^{-1}r)pK_m r].$$

Let $\mathbf{v}_n \in \mathbb{R}^n$, $\|\mathbf{v}_n\| \le 1$, and introduce

$$\mathbf{u}_n := (I + pK_m(I-K_m)^{-1}r)K_n \mathbf{v}_n. \tag{2.29}$$

By (2.15) and (2.22) there is a constant c_{10} independent of n and m, such that $\|\mathbf{u}_n\| \le c_{10}$. Since $\mathbf{u}_n = K_n \mathbf{v}_n + pK_m r \mathbf{u}_n$, we obtain, using (2.11) and (2.28),

$$\|(K_n - pK_m r)(I + pK_m(I-K_m)^{-1}r)K_n \mathbf{v}_n\|$$

$$\le \|(K_n - pK_m r)K_n \mathbf{v}_n\| + \|(K_n - pK_m r)pK_m r \mathbf{u}_n\| \tag{2.30}$$

$$\le O(m^{-\gamma}) + \|(K_n - pK_m r)pK_m r \mathbf{u}_n\|, \quad n > m \ge m_0.$$

By (2.11), we obtain

$$(K_n - pK_m r)pK_m r \mathbf{u}_n = K_n pK_m r \mathbf{u}_n - pK_m K_m r \mathbf{u}_n.$$

In $K_n pK_m r \mathbf{u}_n$ we first replace p by Nyström interpolation, and then replace a sum by an integral. By (2.1) and the boundedness of $\|\mathbf{u}_n\|$, we obtain, uniformly for $0 \le q < n$, $n > m \ge m_0$,

$$(K_n p K_m r \mathbf{u}_n)_q = \sum_{l=0}^{n-1} k\left(\frac{q}{n-1}, \frac{l}{n-1}\right) w_{ln} \sum_{j=0}^{m-1} k\left(\frac{l}{n-1}, \frac{j}{m-1}\right) w_{jm}(r\mathbf{u}_n)_j + O(m^{-\gamma})$$

$$= \sum_{j=0}^{m-1} \int_0^1 k\left(\frac{q}{n-1}, t\right) k\left(t, \frac{j}{m-1}\right) dt \; w_{jm}(r\mathbf{u}_n)_j + O(m^{-\gamma}).$$

Similarly,

$$(p K_m K_m r \mathbf{u}_n)_q = \sum_{j=0}^{m-1} \int_0^1 k\left(\frac{q}{n-1}, t\right) k\left(t, \frac{j}{m-1}\right) dt \; w_{jm}(r\mathbf{u}_n)_j + O(m^{-\gamma}),$$

uniformly for $0 \le q < n$, $n > m \ge m_0$. Therefore,

$$\| (K_n - p K_m r) p K_m r \| = O(m^{-\gamma}), \quad n > m \ge m_0. \tag{2.31}$$

This shows that (2.30) is bounded by $O(m^{-\gamma})$, $n > m \ge m_0$. Analogously to (2.29), we next introduce for $\mathbf{v}_n \in \mathbb{R}^n$, $\|\mathbf{v}_n\| \le 1$,

$$\mathbf{u}_n := (I + p K_m (I - K_m)^{-1} r) p K_m r \mathbf{v}_n. \tag{2.32}$$

We note that $\mathbf{u}_n$ is bounded and write $\mathbf{u}_n$ as

$$\mathbf{u}_n = p K_m r \mathbf{v}_n + p K_m r \mathbf{u}_n. \tag{2.33}$$

From (2.32-33) it follows that

$$(K_n - p K_m r)(I + p K_m (I - K_m)^{-1} r) p K_m r \mathbf{v}_n$$

$$= (K_n - p K_m r) p K_m r (\mathbf{u}_n + \mathbf{v}_n).$$

By (2.31) and by the boundedness of $\mathbf{u}_n$ and $\mathbf{v}_n$, we obtain

$$\| (K_n - p K_m r)(I + p K_m (I - K_m)^{-1} r) p K_m r \| = O(m^{-\gamma}), \tag{2.34}$$

uniformly for $n > m \ge m_0$. By (2.15), (2.30-31) and (2.34) it follows that

$$\| B_{nm} \| \le c_{11} m^{-\gamma}, \quad \gamma := \min\{2, \alpha\}, \quad n > m \ge m_0,$$

where c_{11} is a constant independent of n and m. This establishes (2.17) for M'_{nm}.

Finally, let $c_0^{1/\gamma} n^\delta \le m \le c_1 n^{2/3}$ for some constants $c_0 > 0$, $c_1 > 0$, $0 < \delta \le 2/3$ independent of m and n. Then $I - K_m$ can be LU-factored with less than or equal to $O(n^2)$ arithmetic operations. Computing the matrix elements in (2.12-13) requires $O(n^2)$ arithmetic operations, and so does each iteration. We next show that the number of iterations required is independent of n. We first consider scheme (2.13). By (2.17), we have

$$\| \mathbf{u}_n^* - \mathbf{u}_n^j \| \le c^j m^{-\gamma j} \| \mathbf{u}_n^* - \mathbf{u}_n^0 \|,$$

and require (2.19), i.e. we want

$$c^j m^{-\gamma j} \| \mathbf{u}_n^* - \mathbf{u}_n^0 \| \le c_2 n^{-\kappa}. \tag{2.35}$$

Let $\tilde{c} := c_2(\| \mathbf{u}_n^* - \mathbf{u}_n^0 \|)^{-1}$. Since $\kappa \le \gamma$, and $m \ge c_0^{1/\gamma} n^\delta$, (2.35) is satisfied if

$$\frac{c^j n^\gamma}{c_0^j n^{\delta j \gamma}} \le \tilde{c},$$

and therefore for $j \ge \max\{\delta^{-1}, \ln(\tilde{c})/\ln(c/c_0)\}$. Hence, j is determined independently of n. Iteration with scheme (2.12) requires no more than twice the number of iterations that scheme (2.13) requires at most. This follows from (2.17). □

Theorem 1 has been shown for the Nyström method based on the trapezoidal rule and the prolongations and restrictions defined by (2.5-6) and (2.10). With obvious modifications the theorem also holds for other convergent integration rules and other prolongation and restriction operators. Atkinson [3] chooses, for instance, to carry out prolongation and restriction by Nyström interpolation. Piecewise polynomial prolongation and restriction are used by Hackbusch [6].

The dominating computational work in schemes (2.12-13) is the computation of K_n, and in each iteration the multiplication of K_n by a vector. Both tasks can be carried out in parallel on a computer with several processors by assigning several rows of K_n to each processor. Other parts of the computations in (2.12-13) can also be carried out in parallel. For instance, in (2.12), we can compute $K_m r (\mathbf{f}_n - \mathbf{u}_n^j + K_n \mathbf{u}_n^j)$ in parallel.

Scheme (2.13) requires roughly twice the computional work of scheme (2.12) for each iteration. In the computed examples in Section 4 iterations (2.13) converge twice as rapidly as iterations (2.12), as suggested by (2.17). The bounds (2.17) are, however, not sharp. A comparison of the schemes based on the smoothing properties of K_n is given by Atkinson [3].

3. Iteration with Toeplitz and Hankel matrices

In many applications $\tilde{K}_n$ in (2.4) is a Toeplitz matrix, a Hankel matrix or can be written as the sum of products of such matrices. For such $\tilde{K}_n$, $K_n \mathbf{u}_n$ can be computed in $O(n \log n)$ arithmetic operations for any $\mathbf{u}_n \in \mathbb{R}^n$.

Ex 3.1: Toeplitz matrices. Love's integral equation

$$u(x) + \frac{1}{\pi} \int_{-1}^{1} \frac{d}{d^2 + (x-y)^2} u(y) dy = f(x), \quad -1 \le x \le 1,$$

arises in electrostatics, see Baker [4, p. 258], Atkinson [3]. Discretization with equidistant nodes gives rise to a matrix $K_n = \tilde{K}_n D_n$ with $\tilde{K}_n$ being a Toeplitz matrix. It is well known that for any $\mathbf{v}_n \in \mathbb{R}^n$, $\tilde{K}_n \mathbf{v}_n$ can be computed in $O(n \log n)$ arithmetic operations using the fast Fourier transform method (FFT), see, e.g., Ammar and Gragg [1] or Strang [10]. Implementation of the FFT method on multiprocessor computers is discussed by Swarztrauber [11]. In order to solve (1.2) in $O(n \log n)$ arithmetic operations we choose $m = m(n)$, such that

$$\max\{m_0, c_0^{1/\gamma} n^\delta\} \le m \le c_1 n^{1/3}. \tag{2.18'}$$

The conditions on c_0, c_1 are the same as for (2.18) and δ is required to satisfy $0 \le \delta \le 1/3$. The LU-decomposition of $I - K_m$ can then be carried out in $O(n)$ arithmetic operations by Gaussian elimination. Further speedup can be achieved by replacing Gaussian elimination by a factorization method requiring only $O(m^2)$ arithmetic operations, see Ljung and Ljung [8]. Other examples of integral equations with Toeplitz kernels can be found in [2],[3],[4],[8]. □

Ex 3.2: Hankel matrices and generalization. Let $k(x,y) = k(x+y)$ and discretize (1.1) using equidistant nodes. Then $\tilde{K}_n$ is a Hankel matrix. Let J_n be the $n \times n$ matrix with ones on the skew-diagonal and with zero elements otherwise. Then $J_n J_n = I$ and $\tilde{K}_n J_n$ is a Toeplitz matrix. For any $\mathbf{v}_n \in \mathbb{R}^n$, $\tilde{K}_n \mathbf{v}_n$ is computed in $O(n \log n)$ arithmetic operations from $\tilde{K}_n \mathbf{v}_n = (\tilde{K}_n J_n) J_n \mathbf{v}_n$. Consider the equation,

$$u(x) - \int_0^1 \cos(xy) u(y) dy = \log(1+x), \quad 0 \le x \le 1. \tag{3.1}$$

Equations of this form are discussed in [3],[6],[7]. From $xy = \frac{1}{2}(x+y)^2 - \frac{1}{2}x^2 - \frac{1}{2}y^2$, we obtain

$$\cos(xy) = \cos\frac{1}{2}x^2 \cos\frac{1}{2}(x+y)^2 \cos\frac{1}{2}y^2 - \sin\frac{1}{2}x^2 \cos\frac{1}{2}(x+y)^2 \sin\frac{1}{2}y^2$$

$$+ \cos\frac{1}{2}x^2 \sin\frac{1}{2}(x+y)^2 \sin\frac{1}{2}y^2 + \sin\frac{1}{2}x^2 \sin\frac{1}{2}(x+y)^2 \cos\frac{1}{2}y^2.$$

Hence, when discretizing (3.1) by a Nyström method with equidistant nodes, $\tilde{K}_n$ can be written as $\tilde{K}_n = \sum_{j=1}^{4} D^{(j)} H^{(j)} \tilde{D}^{(j)}$, where the $H^{(j)}$ are Hankel matrices and the $D^{(j)}$ and $\tilde{D}^{(j)}$ are diagonal matrices. $\tilde{K}_n \mathbf{v}_n$ can therefore be computed in $O(n \log n)$ arithmetic operations. The system (1.2) obtained can be solved in $O(n \log n)$ arithmetic operations provided that m satisfies (2.18'). □

4. Computed examples

Let $\mathbf{u}_n^G$ denote the approximate solution of (1.2) determined by Gaussian elimination. Introduce

$$r_n^G(x):=(P_n(\mathbf{u}_n^G-K_n\mathbf{u}_n^G))(x)-f(x),$$

$$r_n^j(x):=(P_n(u_n^j-K_n u_n^j))(x)-f(x).$$

Generally the solution u_n^* of (1.2) is not known, but the condition number of $I-K_n$ is bounded as $n \to \infty$, and we therefore expect $\mathbf{u}_n^G$ to be a good approximation of $\mathbf{u}_n^*$. We stop to iterate when $\| r^j \|_d$ is very close to or smaller than $\| r^G \|_d$, where $\| \ \|_d$ denotes the discrete maximum semi-norm

$$\| r_n^G \|_d := \max_{0 \le j \le 6(n-1)} | r^G(\frac{j}{6(n-1)}) |.$$

u_n^0 is determined by (2.14). The computations were carried out on a MicroVAX II computer in double precision arithmetic, i.e. with 15 significant digits.

Ex 4.1 Equation (3.1) is solved by the iterative schemes (2.12-13). We let $m:=(n-1)^{1/3}+1$. For the values of n chosen in Tables 1-5, (2.11) is satisfied.

n	m	$\| r_n^G \|_d$	$\| r_n^0 \|_d$	$\| r_n^2 \|_d$	$\| r_n^4 \|_d$	$\| r_n^6 \|_d$	$\| \mathbf{u}_n^6 - \mathbf{u}_n^G \|$
28	4	1.7(-4)	6.2(-2)	4.0(-3)	3.0(-4)	1.7(-4)	2.0(-4)
65	5	3.0(-5)	3.8(-2)	1.4(-3)	5.7(-5)	3.1(-5)	2.3(-5)
126	6	7.9(-6)	2.5(-2)	5.9(-4)	1.6(-5)	8.1(-6)	4.0(-6)
217	7	2.7(-6)	1.8(-2)	2.9(-4)	5.3(-6)	2.7(-6)	9.5(-7)
344	8	1.1(-6)	1.3(-2)	1.6(-4)	2.1(-6)	1.1(-6)	2.8(-7)

Table 1: Method (2.12)

n	m	$\| r_n^G \|_d$	$\| r_n^0 \|_d$	$\| r_n^1 \|_d$	$\| r_n^2 \|_d$	$\| r_n^3 \|_d$	$\| \mathbf{u}_n^3 - \mathbf{u}_n^G \|$
28	4	1.7(-4)	6.2(-2)	5.3(-3)	4.9(-4)	1.7(-4)	4.5(-4)
65	5	3.0(-5)	3.8(-2)	1.9(-3)	1.0(-4)	3.0(-5)	5.3(-5)
126	5	7.9(-6)	2.5(-2)	8.2(-4)	2.8(-5)	8.0(-6)	9.5(-6)
217	7	2.7(-6)	1.8(-2)	4.1(-4)	9.8(-6)	2.7(-6)	2.3(-6)
344	8	1.1(-6)	1.3(-2)	2.2(-4)	4.0(-6)	1.1(-6)	6.8(-7)

Table 2: Method (2.13)

For both iteration methods the number of iterations required in order to achieve $\| r_n^j \|_d \le \| r_n^G \|_d$ is seen to be independent of n. The computational work required to compute r_n^6 of Table 1 is roughly the same as the work required to determine r_n^3 of Table 2. $\square$

Ex 4.2 Consider the equation

$$u(x)+\int_0^1 \sqrt{1+xy}\ u(y)dy =\log(1+x),\ \ 0\le x \le 1.$$

Each iteration requires $O(n^2)$ arithmetic operations, and we choose $m=(n-1)^{2/3}+1$.

n	m	$\|r_n^G\|_d$	$\|r_n^0\|_d$	$\|r_n^1\|_d$	$\|r_n^2\|_d$	$\|u_n^2 - u_n^G\|$
28	10	1.7(-4)	1.0(-3)	4.5(-4)	1.7(-4)	5.4(-7)
65	17	3.0(-5)	3.3(-4)	1.3(-4)	3.0(-5)	6.3(-8)
126	26	7.9(-6)	1.4(-4)	4.9(-5)	7.9(-6)	1.1(-8)
217	37	2.7(-6)	6.7(-5)	2.3(-5)	2.7(-6)	2.7(-9)
344	50	1.1(-6)	3.7(-5)	1.3(-5)	1.1(-6)	7.8(-10)

Table 3: Method (2.12)

n	m	$\|r_n^G\|_d$	$\|r_n^0\|_d$	$\|r_n^1\|_d$	$\|u_n^1 - u_n^G\|$
28	10	1.7(-4)	1.0(-3)	1.7(-4)	2.0(-7)
65	17	3.0(-5)	3.3(-4)	3.0(-5)	2.2(-8)
126	26	7.9(-6)	1.4(-4)	7.9(-6)	3.8(-9)
217	37	2.7(-6)	6.7(-5)	2.7(-6)	9.1(-10)
344	50	1.1(-6)	3.7(-5)	1.1(-6)	2.6(-10)

Table 4: Method (2.13) □

Ex 4.3 The solutions u^* of Examples 4.1-2 were analytic. This example illustrates that fast convergence can be obtained for non-smooth solutions, also. Consider

$$u(x) - \int_0^1 \sqrt{xy}\ u(y)dy = \frac{1}{2}\sqrt{x},\ 0 \le x \le 1,$$

with solution $u^*(x) = \sqrt{x}$. Let $m = (n-1)^{2/3} + 1$.

n	m	$\|r_n^G\|_d$	$\|r_n^0\|_d$	$\|r_n^1\|_d$	$\|u_n^1 - u_n^G\|$
28	10	2.35(-2)	8.10(-2)	2.35(-2)	3.7(-3)
65	17	1.53(-2)	6.24(-2)	1.53(-2)	1.1(-3)
126	26	1.09(-2)	4.94(-2)	1.09(-2)	5.1(-4)
217	37	8.30(-3)	4.11(-2)	8.30(-3)	2.6(-4)
344	50	6.59(-3)	3.55(-2)	6.59(-3)	1.5(-4)

Table 5: Method (2.12) □

Acknowledgement

This work was carried out in part while I visited Argonne National Laboratory. I would like to thank Danny Sorensen and Jack Dongarra for making my stay there possible and enjoyable.

References

[1]   G.S. Ammar and W.B. Gragg, *The implementation and use of the generalized Schur algorithm*, in Computational and Combinatorial Methods in Systems Theory, C.I. Byrnes and A. Lindquist, eds., North-Holland, Amsterdam, 1986, pp. 265-279.

[2]   K. Atkinson, *The numerical solution of integral equations on the half-line*, SIAM J. Numer. Anal., **6** (1969), pp. 375-397.

[3]   K.E. Atkinson, *A survey of numerical methods for the solution of Fredholm integral equations of the second kind*, SIAM, Philadelphia, 1976.

[4]   C.T.H. Baker, *The numerical treatment of integral equations*, Clarendon Press, Oxford, 1977.

[5]   H. Brakhage, *Über die numerische Behandlung von Integralgleichungen nach der Quadraturformel-Methode*, Numer. Math., **2** (1960), pp. 183-196.

[6]   W. Hackbusch, *Multigrid methods of the second kind*, in Multigrid methods for integral and differential equations, D.J. Paddon and H. Holstein, eds., Clarendon Press, Oxford, 1985.

[7]   P.W. Hemker and H. Schippers, *Multiple grid methods for the solution of Fredholm integral equations of the second kind*, Math. Comput., **36** (1981), pp. 215-232.

[8]   S. Ljung and L. Ljung, *Fast numerical solution of Fredholm integral equations with stationary kernels*, BIT, **22** (1982), pp. 54-72.

[9]   H. Schippers, *Multiple grid methods for equations of the second kind with applications in fluid mechanics*, Mathematical Centre Tracts **169**, Mathematisch Centrum, Amsterdam, 1983.

[10] G. Strang, *A proposal for Toeplitz matrix calculations*, Studies in Appl. Math., **74** (1986), pp. 171-176.

[11] P.N. Swarztrauber, *Multiprocessor FFTs*, Report, National Center for Atmospheric Research, Boulder, Colorado, 1986.

Performance of the One-Dimensional Fast Fourier Transform on the Hypercube

STEPHEN R. WALTON*

Abstract. The implementation of the Fast Fourier Transform algorithm on a hypercube multiprocessor computer is discussed. Performance measurements on an AMETEK System 14 are given for a straightforward port of a serial FFT subroutine which show high efficiency (75%). Theoretical calculations of the amount of speedup are shown, based on models of the communication time and calculation time required. These calculations show that the speed of an FFT almost always increases with the number of processors used. The FFT's communication requirements are such that faster floating-point calculations on a given node do not result in a proportionate increase in FFT times.

Algorithms. I will not discuss the details of the FFT here. Interested readers are referred to any of a number of works on the subject. I am particularly fond of Nussbaumer's 1982 book[1].

There is a very small literature at present dealing with hypercube FFT's. Swarztrauber[2] discusses FFT's on vector processing machines (multiple processors with shared memory) and on the hypercube. He derives a technique for generalized index reordering of a multi-dimensional array on a hypercube and applies it to the FFT problem. Essentially all other discussions of multiprocessor FFT's focus on vector processors.

In an elegant analysis, Swarztrauber[2] shows that arbitrary subscript reordering of a multiply-subscripted array can be accomplished on a d-dimensional hypercube with no more than $1.5d$ communications per node, each of which exchanges $N/(2P)$ elements between adjacent nodes, where N is the total number of complex elements in the transform and P is the number of processors in the hypercube. In the case of simple index reversal, such as the bit-reversal reordering of an FFT, only d communication calls are required. This method is faster than the more common one in which each node creates one "package" of data for each of the other nodes and transfers it, with (possibly manual) forwarding by intermediate nodes. Each node sends and receives the same amount of data with either algorithm, but Swarztrauber's method does so in fewer total commu-

---

*AMETEK Computer Research Divsion, 610 N. Santa Anita Ave., Arcadia, CA 91006

nications, thus incurring fewer of the fixed startup times associated with an individual call to the hypercube's communication subroutines.

Swarztrauber is also able to show that naturally ordered data can be converted to its naturally ordered transform in $2d+1$ exchanges (he calls them "parallel transmissions"), of $N/(2P)$ points, provided that $d \leq r/2$ where $r = \log_2 N$, that is, provided there are at least as many complex points per node as there are nodes. All of the calculations required for an FFT can be accomplished in d exchanges with no restriction on the relative size of d and r. However, the result here is a transform which is in a very non-standard order, and which might require $1.5d$ exchanges to reorder, or a total of $2.5d$ exchanges to go from an ordered input to an ordered output. This algorithm is excellent, however, for work in which one does not need an ordered transform, such as convolutions, in which two transforms of equal length have operations done on corresponding elements, followed by an inverse transform.

Performance. I have implemented an FFT subroutine in both C and Fortran for the AMETEK System 14 hypercube. Both are parallel versions of the FOUR1 subroutine[3]. A bit-reversal step coded according to Swarztrauber's algorithm is performed first, requiring d communications of $N/(2P)$ complex values. Then two loops are executed. The first loop calculates the partial transforms for pairs separated by $2^0, 2^1, \ldots, 2^{r-d-1}$, This loop requires no exchanges between processors. The second loop calculates equation (2) for pairs separated by $2^{r-d}, 2^{r-d+1}, \ldots, 2^{r-1}$. In each pass through this loop, each processor exchanges $N/2P$ points with one of its neighbors at two points, once to obtain the data for the next step of the transform, and again to send the partially transformed data "home." While this algorithm is not optimum, it has the advantage of ease of coding, and was in fact a fairly straightforward port of the serial subroutine.

The following table compares times for various implementations of the above algorithm in single precision (4 byte real numbers). The VAX times are CPU times for a VAX 780 running 4.3BSD UNIX and the FORTRAN version of the original serial subroutine; the hypercube times are for an AMETEK System 14 with 16 nodes, each node containing an 80286/80287 pair running at 8 MHz. N is the number of complex points in the transform; each complex point consists of two 4-byte real numbers. The test data consisted of different psuedo-random numbers in the real and imaginary parts.* The two versions of the Lattice C compiler used were the UNIX cross-compiler, version 1.24, and the native compiler, version 3.10. Finally, the FORTRAN version was compiled with version 2.01 of Ryan-McFarland's FORTRAN compiler for MS-DOS.

The System 14 times are internal elapsed times; a special synchronization routine was called immediately before starting the timer. Lattice V1.24 is the version of the Lattice C 8086 cross-compiler currently available for UNIX and distributed with the System 14; it is essentially equivalent to V2.15 for MS-DOS. A cross compiler version of Lattice 3.10 has arrived, but these calculations were done before the cross compiler was available, so compilation was done on an IBM PC. Ryan-McFarland FORTRAN is available only as a native compiler for MS-DOS, and the FORTRAN programs above were also generated on an IBM PC. Transforms of 256K and 512K were not done using FORTRAN on the hypercube due to that language's lack of dynamic memory allocation. The VAX, equipped with 4 MB of memory, could not calculate transforms larger than 256K complex points without spending most of its time in swapping pages. The large-problem times correspond to a rate of about 230 kiloflops for C and 300 kiloflops for

* It is important to use non-zero data when benchmarking the 8087 family, since these chips are significantly faster at handling operations involving zero.

N	μVAX	Lattice V1.24	Lattice V3.10	FORTRAN
64	0.01	0.32	0.06	0.04
128	0.03	0.38	0.07	0.05
256	0.06	0.47	0.11	0.08
512	0.15	0.63	0.19	0.14
1024	0.35	0.93	0.34	0.26
2048	0.73	1.55	0.65	0.50
4096	1.54	2.81	1.31	1.01
8192	3.38	5.43	2.65	2.06
16K	7.23	10.9	5.45	4.23
32K	15.8	22.3	11.2	8.71
64K	32.5	—	23.1	18.02
128K	69.6	—	47.6	37.13
256K	150.0	—	98.3	—
512K	—	—	202	—

FORTRAN.

Efficiency Model. The calculation of an FFT of N complex points requires $3N \log_2 N$ real additions and $2N \log_2 N$ real multiplications. These operations can be distributed evenly over the P nodes of a hypercube. Assuming that both these operations require roughly the same amount of time δ, we have

$$t_{calc} = \frac{5\delta N \log_2 N}{P} \qquad (1)$$

The FFT's communications on a hypercube consist entirely of exchanges between adjacent nodes, with no "pipelining" (forwarding) of data required. Different algorithms are available with various communication requirements[2]. The communication time per node can be written as

$$t_{comm} = k \log_2 P (\alpha + \beta \frac{N}{P}) \qquad (2)$$

where α is the startup time for a node-node exchange, and β is the time to exchange a *real* number between nodes. For AMETEK's System 14, which cannot simultaneously send and receive on the node-node communication channels, α in equation (2) would be twice what is customarily called "overhead," and β would be twice the per-byte rate times the size of a real number in bytes (4 for single precision). k is a multiplier for the communications required for various ordering options. The minimum communication required corresponds to $k = 1$, in the sense that it represents the communication used to convert an ordered input into a scrambled output. If an ordered transform is desired, k should be 2 or 2.5, depending on the relative size of N and P. For the implementation discussed above, $k = 3$, as it is somewhat less than optimum.

The total time for an FFT on a hypercube then, is

$$t_{FFT} = \frac{5\delta N \log_2 N}{P} + k \log_2 P (\alpha + \beta \frac{N}{P}) \qquad (3)$$

Swarztrauber[2] differentiates the above with respect to P, and thus derives an equation for the number of nodes P_{opt} which minimizes t_{FFT} given α, β, δ, and N. P_{opt} satisfies

$$\alpha P_{opt} - \beta N \ln P_{opt} = 5\delta N \ln N + \beta N \qquad (4)$$

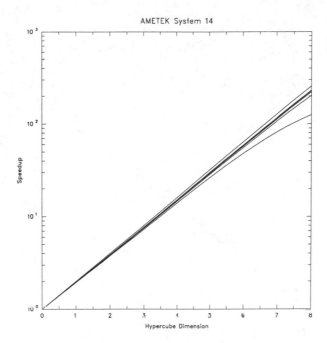

FIG. 1. Speedup S_p versus hypercube dimension for the fastest possible hypercube FFT, calculated using equation (3) of the text with $k = 1$. Hardware parameters are for the AMETEK System 14. From bottom to top, the curves are for transforms of length 1K, 8K, 64K, 512K, and 4096K complex points. The straight line at the top represents 100% efficiency.

for $k = 1$. Swarztrauber shows that for a hypercube with a reasonably small α, less than about 100 times δ, the fastest FFT is always accomplished on the largest possible hypercube, namely $P = N/2$. The FFT may be unique among algorithms for the hypercube studied so far. All other algorithms which have been studied in detail have a limiting hypercube size, in the sense that using a larger cube actually increases the execution time due to increased communication overhead. This is not the case for the FFT; the largest hypercube always yields the fastest execution times provided communication startup time is reasonably small.

For System 14, $\alpha = 1\,\mathrm{ms}$ (that is, roughly 500 microseconds for a unidirectional startup) and $\beta = 75\,\mu s$ (send and receive a real, 4 bytes of data, at 9.5 μs per byte). The nodes run at roughly 20 kiloflops, so δ is 50 μs.

Actual performance on hypercubes is best shown by speedup curves. The speedup S_P is defined as simply the ratio of the single-node calculation time to the P-node calculation time. Figures 1 and 2 are plots of S_P vs. P for hypercube dimensions of 0 to 8 and transform sizes of 1K, 8K, 64K, 512K, and 2048K complex points (1K = 1024). Two curves for System 14 are shown, one for the calculation of a (reversibly) scrambled transform from an ordered input, and the other for the implementation described above; that is, $k = 1$ and $k = 3$, respectively.

These curves do not reach a maximum speedup, again showing that P_{opt} is large, and they do not approach a speedup of 1 for large problems. The latter feature can be understood by considering the ratio of calculation time to communication time:

$$\frac{t_{comm}}{t_{calc}} = \frac{\log_2 P(\alpha + \beta N/P)}{5\delta N \log_2 N/P} \qquad (5)$$

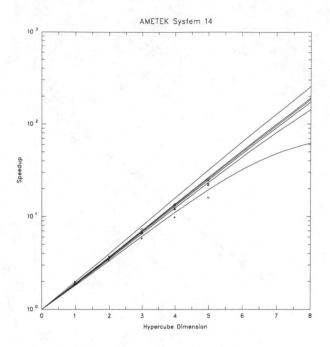

FIG. 2. Speedup S_p versus hypercube dimension for an actual FFT implementation. The solid curves the same as those of Figure 1 with $k = 3$. The points
are measured performance on an AMETEK System 14 using FORTRAN, for
transforms of length 1K (+), 8K ($\star$), and 64K ($\circ$) and for hypercubes containing
1 to 32 nodes.

If N is sufficiently large that the inequality

$$\frac{\alpha}{\beta} << \frac{N}{P} \tag{6}$$

holds, the second term in the numerator of equation (6) dominates. For the asymptotes
in the speedup curves, $\log_2 N / \log_2 P$ is at least 2 and the ratio in (6) becomes

$$\frac{t_{comm}}{t_{calc}} \approx \frac{\beta}{10\delta} \tag{7}$$

Equation (7) gives a value of approximately 0.3 for this ratio for System 14. The efficiency
for large problems, then, is

$$\epsilon = \frac{t_{calc}}{t_{calc} + t_{comm}} = \frac{1}{1 + t_{comm}/t_{calc}} \approx 0.75 \tag{8}$$

Note that the ratio scales linearly with node calculation speed. For example, if a hypothetical new floating-point unit improved System 14 floating-point performance to
200 kiloflops (a factor of 10) per node while the communication rate remains the same,
t_{comm}/t_{calc} would increase to about 1.5 and the peak efficiency would be about 0.40,
and the speedup for the entire hypercube would be only about half of the per-node improvement. However, if the communication time could be halved, the full factor of 10
improvement would be realized. In cases where there is a large discrepancy between
floating-point speed and per-byte communication rates, it is likely that no improvement

in FFT times would be realized by increasing the former in the absence of an increase in the latter; a further factor of 10 improvement in System 14, to 2 megaflops per node, would improve FFT times by only a factor of 1.5 or so.

Conclusions. We can draw the following conclusions from the above results:
 (1) The FFT is extremely well suited to fine-grain decomposition on a hypercube with many nodes, provided the communication startup time is less than about 100 times the floating-point rate.
 (2) The maximum FFT speedup in the case of a large number of points per node is approximately 10 times the ratio of the time for a floating-point calculation to the time to exchange a floating point number between adjacent nodes.
 (3) High efficiencies, 75% or higher, can be easily achieved for the FFT even with an algorithm which uses more than the optimum amount of communication.
 (4) Simultaneous send and receive on the node-node communications channels on a hypercube has the potential for a large performance improvement.

UNIX is a trademark of AT&T. VAX is a trademark of Digital Equipment Corporation. MS-DOS is a trademark of Microsoft, Inc. IBM PC is a trademark of International Business Machines, Inc.

REFERENCES

(1) II.J. Nussbaumer, *Fast Fourier Transform and Convolution Algorithms*, Springer-Verlag, Berlin, 1982.

(2) P.N. Swarztrauber, *Multiprocessor FFTs*, preprint, National Center for Atmospheric Research, Boulder, Colorado, 1986.

(3) W.H. Press, B.P. Flannery, S.A. Teukolsky, and W.T. Vetterling, *Numerical Recipes*, Cambridge University Press, Cambridge, 1986.

PART VIII:
MATRIX COMPUTATIONS

A Parallel Triangular Solver for a Hypercube Multiprocessor[*]

GUANGYE LI[†‡] AND THOMAS F. COLEMAN[†§]

Abstract: We consider solving triangular systems of linear equations on a hypercube multiprocessor. Specifically, we propose a fast parallel algorithm, applicable when the triangular matrix is distributed around the cube by column in a wrap fashion. Numerical experiments indicate that the new algorithm is very efficient.

A theoretical analysis confirms that the total running time varies linearly, with respect to the matrix order, up to a threshold value of the matrix order, after which the dependence is quadratic.

NOTE: This paper is an abbreviated version of a complete report by Li & Coleman [1986] which has been submitted for publication elsewhere.

Introduction

Recent work on hypercube algorithms for numerical linear algebra has resulted in efficient parallel methods for the factorization of dense matrices (eg. Geist & Heath[1986], Moler[1986]). However, the discovery of methods for the efficient parallel solution of the

---

[*]This report represents a summary of a complete paper of the same name, Technical Report TR 86-787, Department of Computer Science, Cornell University.

[†]Computer Science Department and Center for Applied Mathematics, Cornell University, Ithaca, New York 14853. Research partially supported by the U.S. Army Research Office through the Mathematical Sciences Institute, Cornell University.

[‡]Permanent address: Computer Center, Jilin University, People's Republic of China.

[§]Research partially supported by the Applied Mathematical Sciences Research Program (KC-04-02) of the Office of Energy Research of the U.S. Department of Energy under grant DE-FG02-86ER25013.A000.

resulting triangular systems has lagged behind somewhat. This is especially true in the case where matrices are distributed by column (instead of by row). For example, Geist & Heath [1986] recently demonstrated that the best parallel triangular solver (at that time) was essentially no better than a distributed sequential solver. While there has been some very recent progress on this problem (Romine & Ortega [1986]), we propose to further close this gap with a new and efficient column-oriented parallel triangular solver.

We have implemented our triangular solve algorithm on an Intel iPSC hypercube multiprocessor with 16 nodes. However, it should be noted that the full hypercube architecture is not needed by this algorithm: only ring connectivity is used. Therefore, the algorithm can be used on any local memory message-passing multi-processor in which a ring can be embedded provided **send** and **receive** primitives are available. We assume that when control of a node program passes to a **send** statement, the **send** is executed immediately, in time zero, and then control passes on to the next executable statement in this node program. Of course this does not imply the message is received immediately - we discuss this transfer time below. We also assume that when control passes to a **receive** statement in a node program, execution of this node program is suspended until the message is physically received which happens when the appropriate transfer time elapses.

Message passing speed plays an important role in the execution time of algorithms for the solution of triangular systems of linear equations. This contrasts with the factorization stage (Moler [1986]) in which floating point computations clearly dominate. In order to quantify message-passing speed in our analysis, we use a quantity t:

> t is the maximum number of flops that can be executed on a single processor during the time in which a single 'small' message is **sent** by one node and then **received** by a waiting adjacent node.

In this context we define 'small' to be a message of size less than or equal to p double precision words (64 bits each), where p is the number of processors. On the Intel iPSC (release 2.0) with $p \leq 16$, we have estimated t to be approximately 100 flops, where a flop is the operation

$$y \leftarrow ax + y$$

We estimated t in the following way. First, a message of size $p = 16$ was forwarded around a 'ring' of 16 processors for a total of 1000 round-trips. That is, processor i sent the message to node $i+1$; node $i+1$ received the message and then sent it to node $i+2$, ... The total time for these 1000 circuits was recorded as T_1. Second, the time to execute the loop

    for $i=1:1000$
        $y \leftarrow ax + y$

was recorded as T_2. Then t was estimated:

$$t \cong \frac{T_1}{16 \times T_2}.$$

Notice that the 'ring' used above is defined by the natural ordering of the nodes. Since the natural ordering does not define a true ring, t is overestimated by this computation: we feel that this difference is relatively insignificant and we ignore it.

Our paper is organized as follows. Section 1 describes the column algorithm and provides numerical results and comparisons. Section 2 provides an expression for the running time as a function of $n,t,$ and p. This expression is most illuminating and we discuss this result at length. Concluding remarks and possible extensions are given in Section 3.

1. The Column Algorithm: Description and Numerical Results

In this section we describe a new algorithm to solve the upper triangular system $Ux = b$ on a hypercube multiprocessor where the n columns of the matrix U are distributed to the p nodes (processors) in a wrap fashion. A wrap mapping is used because it seems a very reasonable choice for the factorization stage (e.g. Geist & Heath[1986]). The order in which the nodes are visited in the wrap assignment is arbitrary; however, the algorithm is most reasonable when the nodes form a ring. We refer to the node containing column j as $P(j)$. Therefore, due to the wrap assignment, $P(j) = P(k)$ if and only if $j = k \pmod{p}$.

1.1A Parallel Column Triangular Solver (PCTS)

Mechanically, the algorithm is simple: the p 1 array SUM passes around the ring going from $P(j)$ to $P(j-1)$ for $j=n:2$. When SUM arrives at node $P(j)$, $P(j)$ determines $x(j)$, modifies SUM (p flops), and then forwards SUM to node $P(j-1)$. Finally, node $P(j)$ modifies the first $j-p$ elements of array $PSUM$ using column j of U ($j-p$ flops).

The procedure PCTS is executed by every node: the following initial conditions are assumed.

If $\mathbf{myname} = P(n)$: $SUM(1:p) = b(n:n-p+1)$

                $PSUM(1:n-p) = b(1:n-p)$

If $\mathbf{myname} \neq P(n)$: $SUM(1:p) = 0$

                $PSUM(1:n-p) = 0$

Also: For brevity, we follow the convention that if an array index is out of bounds, the returned value is assumed to be zero. Each node has at most $m = \left\lceil \dfrac{n}{p} \right\rceil$ columns of the upper triangular matrix U.

Procedure PCTS ($x[1{:}m]$, $SUM(1{:}p)$, $PSUM(1{:}n-p)$, $U(1{:}n,[1{:}m])$)

For $j = n{:}1$

    If myname $= P(j)$

        Receive $SUM(1{:}p-1)$ [if $j < n$]

        $x(j) \leftarrow (SUM(1) + PSUM(j))/U(j,j)$

        $SUM(1{:}p-2) \leftarrow SUM(2{:}p-1) - U(j-1{:}j-(p-2), j)\times x(j)$

                $+ PSUM(j-1{:}j-(p-2))$

        $SUM(p-1) \leftarrow -U(j-(p-1), j)\times x(j) + PSUM(j-(p-1))$

        Send $SUM(1{:}p-1)$ to node $P(j-1)$ [if $j > 1$]

        $PSUM(1{:}j-p) \leftarrow PSUM(1{:}j-p) - U(1{:}j-p, j)\times x(j)$

End

We have listed all the arrays used, and their dimensions, in the procedure statement. The square brackets indicate indirect addressing. For example, $x[1{:}m]$ says that there are at most m components of the vector x on this node but they are not necessarily the first m components of the n-vector x. In particular, the components of x are assigned to the nodes in a wrap mapping consistent with the assignment of columns. Rather than introduce indirect indexing in the body of the procedure, we refer to components directly. So for example, $x(j)$ refers to the jth component of the solution x, not the jth component of the array $x[1{:}m]$ on this node. Of course for this reference to be valid, this component must be assigned to this node.

The mechanism behind *PCTS* can be described as a distributed outer product. On each node k the array *PSUM* holds part of the outer product corresponding to processed columns on that node; the travelling array *SUM* funnels the distributed sums together, as needed.

1.2 Numerical Experiments with PCTS

Our experiments were performed on an Intel hypercube iPSC (release 2.0) with 16-nodes using Fortran ftn286. All computations were performed in double precision. This cube is operated by the Theory Center at Cornell University. This particular system has extra memory boards so that the total available memory per node is approximately 4 megabytes. Hence, the total available memory on a 16-node cube is approximately 64 megabytes: we were able to run experiments on dense matrices up to order approximately $n = 2000$.

The megaflop rate is the number of millions of floating point operations (megaflops) per second. *Note: Megaflop rate does not refer to millions of flops per second but rather millions of floating point operations per second. One flop requires two floating point operations.* Experimentally, we determined the maximum megaflop rate per node, $mflp_1^*$, to be .033 megaflops per second. Hence, the maximum megaflop rate for the cube on 16 nodes, $mflp_{16}^*$, is approximately .53 megaflops per second. $mflp_1^*$ was determined by executing $PCTS$ on one node for large n; then,

$$mflp_1^* = \frac{n^2 \times 10^{-6}}{T}$$

where T is the execution time.

For all our experiments, we used a single test problem where the matrix A is

$$A(i, j) = \frac{1}{n - i - j + 1.5}$$

and $b(i) = n - i + 1$.

Pivoting is required for stability purposes when solving this system.

One final remark concerning our reported results: we did not, in fact, use a ring ordering for our experiments. The natural ordering of the nodes of the cube was used. Hence we expect a modest improvement in the performance of $PCTS$ when implemented on a real ring .

In the Context of LU Solve

Our original motivation for pursuing this research was to develop a column based parallel triangular solver whose running time was insignificant relative to the LU factorization time for all reasonably large n. A distributed sequential triangular solver such as $DSEQ$ (described in Li & Coleman [1986]) does not have this property.

In Table 1.1 we present numerical results obtained on a cube of size $p = 16$. The LU factorization program used is due to C. Moler (Intel Scientific Computers) but modified slightly: in our version, row interchanges are explicitly performed on the whole row rather than just on the part of the row in U. This has no noticeable effect on the running time of the LU factorization but allows for the separation of the tasks 2 and 3 mentioned in Section 1.2.

The triangular solve times listed include the application of the permutation matrix to the right-hand-side, 2 triangular solves, and the collection of the final solution in node $P(1)$ For comparison we have also listed the running time for algorithm $DSEQ$ (a distributed sequential solver described in Li & Coleman [1986]). In both cases we used an assembler version of the BLAS (Basic Linear Algebra Subroutines, Lawson et. al [1979]), as implemented by C. Moler.

N	LU	DSEQ	PCTS
100	5.216	2.496	2.080
200	23.248	14.992	4.144
400	125.552	56.992	8.352
600	363.376	112.464	12.416
800	801.424	213.440	16.656
1000	1491.024	286.656	20.592
1200	2509.840	439.296	24.768
1500	4759.842	628.080	30.960
2000	10974.032	1122.624	41.696

LU Factorization Versus
Triangular Solve [seconds]

Table 1.1 $(p = 16)$

As evidenced above, the total running time is clearly dominated by the factorization stage when the new parallel triangular solver is used. For example, when $n = 600$, *DSEQ* takes about 1/3 of the factorization time, whereas *PCTS* takes 1/30 of it.

Time as a Function of Problem Size n

An important concern is the way in which the running time of *PCTS* varies with n. As we establish in Section 2, the dependence is linear up to a threshold value of n, and then quadratic. We explain this transition in Section 2.

Graphs of the running times of the triangular solve stage, for different n, are shown in Figures 1.1 & 1.2. Note: the times reported represent the sums of the times to apply the permutation matrix, execute both the lower and upper triangular solves, and then collect the solution on node $P(1)$.

In Figure 1.1 the transition from linear to quadratic is clear. The threshold value occurs at approximately $n = 400$ which is close to the theoretical value established in the next section.

Figure 1.2 shows that T varies linearly for n up to its maximum possible value when $p = 16$. In this case the threshold value of n, demarking the transition from linear to quadratic performance, is beyond the storage capacity of the 16-node cube.

In Figures 1.3 and 1.4 we chart the megaflop rates obtained for different values of n for both the 4-node and 16-node cubes. The megaflop rate is computed as follows. For each run the system clock records the running time, T, for the triangular solution stage (ie. apply P, two triangular solves, collect solution on node $P(1)$). Then, the megaflop rate on a p-node cube is :

$$mflp_p = \frac{2n^2 \times 10^{-6}}{T}$$

We use $2n^2$ because this is the total number of floating point operations to solve the lower and upper systems. The maximum megaflop rate, $mflp_p^*$, was determined as described previously.

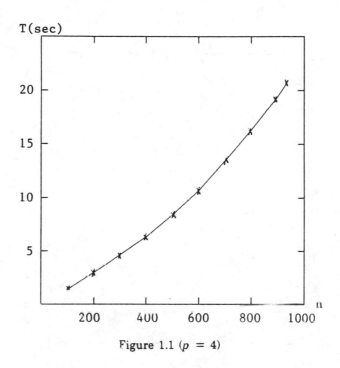

Figure 1.1 ($p = 4$)

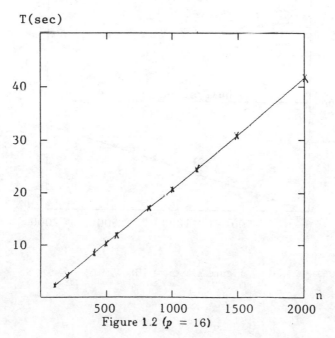

Figure 1.2 ($p = 16$)

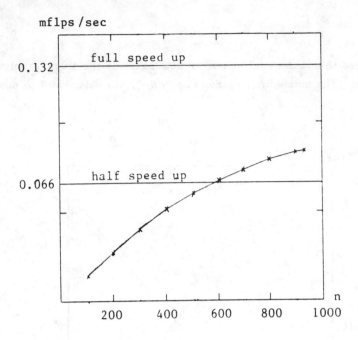

Figure 1.3 ($p = 4$)

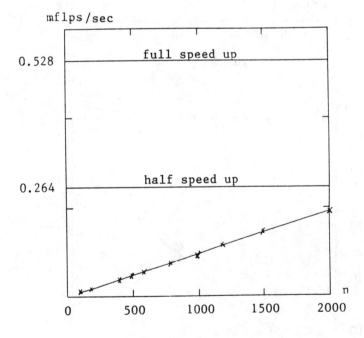

Figure 1.4 ($p = 16$)

Notice that, in Figure 1.3, the linear quadratic transistion is evident. In Figure 1.4, the curve remains linear because the quadratic stage demands a matrix of size exceeding the storage capacity.

Comparisons

In this section we experimentally compare our new triangular solver, *PCTS*, to an alternative parallel column solver, *CPIP*, suggested by Romine & Ortega [1986] and implemented by C. Moler. (We used C. Moler's implementation in our experiments. We believe it represents a careful and efficient implementation of the algorithm described by Romine & Ortega [1986]. It is written in the same style as *PCTS*: e.g. the 'BLAS' were used wherever possible. We should note that the assembler versions of the BLAS were not used in these particular experiments. The reason is that the assembler codes available to us did not allow for step increments ('INCX') different from unity: hence, *CPIP* could not benefit from an assembler implementation. Therefore, to be fair, we used only Fortran code in both cases.)

This algorithm complements *PCTS* in the sense that while *PCTS* is a distributed outer-product method, *CPIP* computes a distributed inner-product.

Results of our experiments comparing our implementation of *PCTS* with Moler's implementation of *CPIP* follow in Table 1.2.

N	CPIP	PCTS
100	3.904	2.192
200	7.744	4.432
400	16.480	8.880
600	25.424	13.360
800	35.328	17.776
1000	45.568	22.432
1200	56.208	26.576
1500	73.744	33.840
1765	90.688	40.624

Comparison of new method (*PCTS*) versus
inner product method (*CPIP*)   [seconds]

Table 1.2 ($p = 16$)

2. Analysis of Column Method

A full analysis of algorith *PCTS* is given by Li & Coleman [1986]. Here, we state and discuss the major result. We derive an expression for the time complexity T -measured in flops - as a function of n, t, and p. (Recall that t is a measure of the time (in flop units) to send a message of size p from one node to an adjacent node.) Expression T accounts for total computation time, including communication costs. Our theory is completely consistent with, and explains, the emperical evidence reported in Section 1.

2.1 Complexity Analysis

The major result in this section is an expression for the total time T, expressed in number of flops.

For simplicity, let us assume that $n = mp$ for some integer $m > 2$ where p is the number of nodes (processors) and n is the matrix dimension. Further, we assume that the columns are dealt out to the nodes in a wrap fashion; the nodes are 'configured' to form a ring. Let $P(i)$ be the node housing column i. Hence $P(i+1)$ is adjacent to $P(i)$ for $i = 1:n-1$ and $P(1)$ is adjacent to $P(n)$.

For convenience, we have taken some freedom with the definition of the term 'flop'. In general, 1 flop represents the operation $y \leftarrow ax + y$ which is 2 floating point operations. However, algorithm $PCTS$ does not cleanly break up into flops: for example, the update of $SUM(i)$ for $1 \leq i \leq p-2$, requires slightly more than 1 flop. We have decided to ignore these deviations in our analysis: we decree that every assignment statement in $PCTS$ costs 1 flop. This assumption allows for a much cleaner presentation and obscures no important information. (Alternatively, we could count floating point operations - every multiply, add, subtract, and divide counts as 1. We have decided not to present this analysis because it is very clumsy and no more insightful than the 'flop' approach.)

Theorem 2.1. If $n \leq p(t+p)$ then

$$T = (t+p)n - \frac{p(p-1)}{2} - t$$

else

$$T = \tfrac{1}{2}\{\frac{n^2}{p} + n + p(t+p)^2 - pt - p^2 + p\} - t.$$

Proof: Li & Coleman [1986].

Theorem 2.1 provides considerable insight into algorithm $PCTS$ and its expected behaviour - Li and Coleman [1986] discuss this at length.

3. Concluding Remarks

We have presented a new parallel algorithm, $PCTS$, for the solution of triangular systems of linear equations, applicable when the columns of the matrix are distributed amongst the nodes of a hypercube computer, in a wrap fashion. The running time is clearly dominated by matrix factorization time for all reasonable n. Moreover, our numerical results suggest that algorithm $PCTS$ may be significantly faster than the recently proposed fan-in method of Romine and Ortega[1986], which uses a more sophisticated message passing technique (ie. fan-in).

Perhaps there is a global message here. In particular, a distributed triangular system necessitates relatively high communication costs - at least np traffic units (approximately) and $n-1$ total messages - compared to total floating point computation requirements which are of order n^2. In such a situation it appears to be advantageous to use simpler communication methods (e.g. a ring versus a global fan-in) - at least this seems to be true for a modest number of processors.

Indeed, in a recent private communication, M. Heath (Oak Ridge National Laboratory) reported another example in support of this thesis: apparently it is possible to solve distributed triangular systems using an inner-product **ring** algorithm. Heath's experiments indicate that this method may be competitive with *PCTS* in some cases. Once again simple communication methodology appears to win.

On the other hand, the ring mechanism exhibits some advantage even when n is large. In such a case, the computations are essentially pipelined, thus masking communication costs entirely (except at the ends). This contrasts with the fan-in type algorithm in which communication is never masked by computation.

In any event, it now appears that triangular systems can be efficiently solved on hypercube computers either when matrices are distributed by rows or by columns. The choice between row or column distribution should definitely not be based on the resulting efficiency of the triangular solution step.

For fixed p and t, as $n \to \infty$, the difference between the running times of *PCTS* and *CPIP* goes to infinity: ie.

$$T(CPIP) - T(PCTS) \to +\infty.$$

This is easy to see because $T(CPIP)$ is approximately $\dfrac{n^2}{2p} + tn \cdot logp$ flops whereas $T(PCTS)$ is approximately $\dfrac{n^2}{2p} + \dfrac{n}{2}$ flops, for large n. On the other hand, this difference becomes relatively less important as $n \to \infty$. The total computational cost is growing with n^2, but the difference $T(CPIP) - T(PCTS)$ grows only linearly with n.

If p is varied, the situation becomes less clear though recent experiments by C. Moler indicate that the gap between $T(CPIP)$ and $T(PCTS)$ narrows as p increases and n grows more modestly. This seems quite reasonable to us; however, as we mention in the next section, we believe *PCTS* can be modified to increase efficiency when p is large but n is modest. We will experiment with this scheme when we have a 'large' cube available.

The effect of variation in t is difficult to predict. It is worth noting that t is a relative quantity, balancing processor speed with communication time. In the future, we can expect t to fluctuate, as advances are made in message-passing technology and processor speed.

Future Work

There are at least two possible ways to improve *PCTS* is some circumstances.

First, for very large n, and fixed p and t, *PCTS* is not well-balanced. In particular, at the beginning of a run with large n, *PCTS* is computation bound because the vectors are long; later in the computation, vectors are short and therefore the processors are idle much of the time. However, it is possible to re-arrange the work in *PCTS* to achieve an evenly-balanced work profile. For example, work on the upper half of the last $\frac{n}{2}$ columns can be postponed until columns in the first half are being processed. In such a fashion a rectangular work profile can be achieved.

Second, it is possible to exploit the fact that for fixed t and n there is an optimal p: i.e. it is not always advantageous to have p as large as possible. With the help of Richard Chamberlain (Chr. Michelsen Institute), we have discovered that it is possible to divide the 'great ring' on p nodes into several small pieces - each of 'optimal size' - and then revise *PCTS* accordingly. This technique should lead to significant gains in efficiency when p is large and n is not significantly larger than p

Acknowledgements

We are grateful to a number of people who read a draft of the full report. In particular, we thank Chris Bischof, John Gilbert, Doug Moore, and Earl Zmijewski.

We are also grateful to Cleve Moler and David Scott of Intel Scientific Computers for supplying us with various subroutines and help when needed. We also thank Mike Heath of Oak Ridge National Laboratory for alerting us to the interesting paper by Romine and Ortega, and for being generally available for consultation and discussion.

Finally, we express our appreciation to Cornell University's Theory Center - and the Advanced Computing Facility in particular - for the use of the Intel iPSC hypercube computer.

References

R.M. Chamberlain [1986], *An Algorithm for LU Factorization with Partial Pivoting on the Hypercube*, Technical Report CCS 86/11, Chr. Michelsen Institute, Bergen, Norway.

G.A. Geist and M.T. Heath [1985], *Parallel Cholesky Factorization on a Hypercube Multiprocessor*, Technical Report ORNL-6211, Oak Ridge National Laboratory, Oak Ridge, Tennessee.

G.A. Geist and M.T. Heath [1986], *Matrix Factorization on a Hypercube Multiprocessor*, in Hypercube Multiprocessors 1986, M. Heath ed., SIAM Publications, Philadelphia, PA.

C. Lawson, R.Hanson, D. Kincaid, and F. Krogh [1979], *Basic Linear Algebra Subprograms for Fortran Usage*, ACM Transactions on Mathematical Software, 5, 308-371.

G. Li & T. Coleman [1986], *A Parallel Triangular Solver for a Hypercube Multiprocessor*, Technical Report TR 86-787, Dept. of Computer Science, Cornell University, Ithaca, NY.

O.A. McBryan and E.F. Van de Velde [1985], *Hypercube Algorithms and Implementations*, Technical Report, Courant Institute of Mathematical Sciences, New York University, New York, N.Y.

C. Moler [1986], *Matrix Computation on Distributed Memory Multiprocessors*, Technical Report, Intel Scientific Computers.

C.H. Romine and J.M. Ortega, *Parallel Solution of Triangular Systems of Equations*, Technical Report RM-86-05, Department of Applied Mathematics, University of Virginia.

The Parallel Solution of Triangular Systems on a Hypercube

C. H. ROMINE*

Abstract. It has been suggested by several authors that the parallel solution of an $n \times n$ triangular system of equations in which the coefficient matrix is assigned to the processors by columns is inherently inefficient on a local-memory multiprocessor. In this paper, a parallel inner-product formulation of the solution of a column-stored triangular system on a hypercube multiprocessor is presented and analyzed. Assuming synchronous, logarithmic communication, our model predicts that the inner-product algorithm should be nearly as efficient as the usual column-sweep algorithm applied to a row-stored system. The better performance exhibited empirically by the inner-product algorithm is attributed to the difference in the fan-in and fan-out operations. Empirical results for pipelined, ring communication are also given, showing that the two algorithms with ring communication are roughly equivalent in efficiency.

1. Introduction. Romine and Ortega [6] introduced a parallel implementation of the classical inner-product formulation for the solution of a triangular system of linear equations. Their analysis showed that the algorithm applied to a lower triangular matrix that is assigned to the processors by columns should be reasonably efficient. This work can be considered a sequel to that paper, in which the effectiveness of the parallel inner-product algorithm is demonstrated on an Intel iPSC hypercube multiprocessor. In addition, results from a ring implementation of the algorithm show that using ring communication enhances the algorithm's performance.

Throughout the paper, we assume that the $n \times n$ lower triangular matrix L is full. Sections 2 and 3 are short descriptions of the column-sweep and inner-product formulations (respectively) for the solution of a lower triangular system of equations. Further details can be found in Romine and Ortega [6]. In section 4, we analyze and compare the expected performance of the two algorithms on a

---

*Engineering Physics and Mathematics Division, Mathematical Sciences Section, Oak Ridge National Laboratory, Oak Ridge, Tennessee 37831-2009. Research supported by the Applied Mathematical Sciences Research Program, Office of Energy Research, U.S. Department of Energy under contract DE-AC05-84OR21400 with Martin Marietta Energy Systems Inc.

hypercube multiprocessor. Section 5 presents results obtained by implementing the two algorithms on the Intel iPSC hypercube. Finally, section 6 contains conclusions and suggestions for future work.

2. The Column-Sweep Formulation. The column-sweep parallel algorithm for the solution of a triangular system (see Kuck [4]) is an adaptation of the classical immediate-update algorithm given below.

$$
\begin{aligned}
&\text{for } j = 0 \text{ to } n-1 \\
&\quad x_j = b_j / l_{jj} \\
&\quad \text{for } i = j+1 \text{ to } n-1 \\
&\qquad b_i = b_i - l_{ij} x_j
\end{aligned}
$$

At each stage j, x_j is computed and then immediately eliminated from all succeeding equations, thereby reducing to a triangular system of one lower order. We assume that the coefficient matrix L is distributed to the processors of the hypercube by a row-wrapped mapping; that is, if the rows are numbered 0 to $n-1$, and the processors are numbered 0 to $p-1$, then row j is assigned to processor $j \, (\text{mod } p)$. The load-balancing advantages of wrapped mapping for matrix calculations are well documented (see Geist and Heath [2], O'Leary and Stewart [5] and Ipsen, Saad and Schultz [3], for example). Under row-wrapped mapping, the following pseudo-code describes the column-sweep algorithm:

$$
\begin{aligned}
&\text{for } j = 0 \text{ to } n-1 \\
&\quad \text{if } (\, j \, (\text{mod } p) == \text{mynode}) \\
&\qquad x_j = b_j / l_{jj} \\
&\quad \text{fan-out } (x_j) \\
&\quad \text{for all rows } i > j \text{ which I own} \\
&\qquad b_i = b_i - l_{ij} x_j
\end{aligned}
$$

Note that the fan-out operation contains all of the communication in the algorithm. The fan-out is implemented by communication along the edges of a minimal spanning tree, a common technique for broadcasting information in logarithmic time on a hypercube.

3. The Inner-Product Formulation. The classical inner-product formulation for solving $L x = b$ is given below.

$$
\begin{aligned}
&\text{for } i = 0 \text{ to } n-1 \\
&\quad \text{for } j = 0 \text{ to } i-1 \\
&\qquad b_i = b_i - l_{ij} x_j \\
&\quad x_i = b_i / l_{ii}
\end{aligned}
$$

The j-loop in the above pseudo-code computes the inner-product of the ith row of L and the first i elements of the vector x. The inner-product algorithm is a natural dual of the column-sweep algorithm in which all computation that affects row j is delayed until stage j. We therefore categorize the inner-product algorithm as a delayed-update algorithm.

If we assume that the columns of L are distributed to the processors in a column-wrapped fashion, and that the elements of b (and hence x) are distributed to the processors so that b_i is assigned to processor $i \pmod{p}$, then the partial inner-products $l_{ij} x_j$ can be performed in parallel. These are then collected and summed using a fan-in operation, whereupon x_i can be calculated by processor $i \pmod{p}$. The resulting parallel pseudo-code looks like the following.

```
for i=0 to n−1
    s = 0
    for all columns j <i which I own
        s = s + l_{ij} x_j
    t = fan-in (s)
    if ( I own b_i )
        x_i = (b_i − t)/ l_{ii}
```

Again, note that the only communication required in the algorithm is contained in the **fan-in** operation, which is also implemented using a minimal spanning tree in a hypercube.

4. Algorithm Analysis. In order to obtain upper bounds on the execution times of the algorithms described, we make the following assumptions:

(a) Each floating-point operation requires one *time step*.

(b) The cost of a **fan-out** broadcast is $C \log p$ for some constant C.

(c) The cost of a **fan-in** sum operation is $(1+C) \log p$.

(d) $n = kp$ for some integer k.

Assumption (d) is for convenience and does not materially affect the results. An upper bound for the execution time of each algorithm is now obtained by summing the largest execution time of any processor for each stage.

In the column-sweep algorithm, during stage j, there is a maximum of $1 + 2 \lceil \dfrac{n-j-1}{p} \rceil$ floating-point operations performed in any processor. Adding this to the $C \log p$ cost of the fan-out and summing over all stages, we obtain an upper bound of

$$T_{cs}(p) = (n-1)C \log p + \frac{1}{p}(n^2 + 2np - 2n).$$ (4.1)

Since the serial operation count for the triangular solution is n^2, equation (4.1) yields a *lower* bound on the speedup of the algorithm:

$$S_l(p) = \frac{n^2}{T_{cs}(p)} = \frac{n^2}{(n-1)C \log p + \frac{1}{p}(n^2 + 2np - 2n)}$$ (4.2)

$$\approx p \left[\frac{n}{Cp \log p + n + 2p - 2} \right].$$

In the inner-product algorithm, the computation cost during stage i is given by $1+2\lceil\frac{n-i-1}{p}\rceil$ (excluding the cost of the sums computed during the fan-in). Including the cost of the fan-in sum at stage i yields

$$T_{ip}(p) = (n-1)C\log p + \frac{1}{p}(n^2 + 2np + np\log p - 2n) \tag{4.3}$$

as the upper bound on the execution time for the inner-product algorithm. Notice that the difference in the bounds is

$$T_{ip}(p) - T_{cs}(p) = n\log p, \tag{4.4}$$

indicating that the column-sweep algorithm might perform slightly better than the inner-product algorithm.

As before, the upper bound (4.3) induces a lower bound on the speedup of the inner-product algorithm, given by

$$S_l(p) = \frac{n^2}{T_{ip}(p)} = \frac{n^2}{(n-1)C\log p + \frac{1}{p}(n^2 + 2np + np\log p - 2n)} \tag{4.5}$$

$$\approx p\left[\frac{n}{Cp\log p + n + p\log p + 2p - 2}\right].$$

A graph of the lower bounds in (4.2) and (4.5) is given in Figure 4.1, showing that they are nearly equivalent.

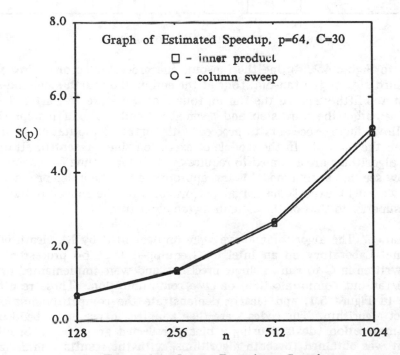

Figure 4.1. Lower Bounds on Speedups.

There is a fundamental difference between the costs of a fan-out and a fan-in for which we have not accounted in the models above. During the $\log p$ stages of a fan-out, nearly all of the processors are either busy or are awaiting information. However, during the $\log p$ stages of a fan-in, half of the processors at each stage become free immediately, and can then proceed to the next computation. A simple illustration of this idea is given in Figure 4.2, which shows the six steps, or half stages, required for a fan-out or fan-in on a three-dimensional (8 node) hypercube.

Fan-out Processor Utilization Chart								
Step	P0	P1	P2	P3	P4	P5	P6	P7
1	$S \to 1$	Wait	Wait	Wait	Wait	Wait	Wait	Wait
2	$S \to 2$	$R \leftarrow 0$	Wait	Wait	Wait	Wait	Wait	Wait
3	$S \to 4$	$S \to 3$	$R \leftarrow 0$	Wait	Wait	Wait	Wait	Wait
4	Done	$S \to 5$	$S \to 6$	$R \leftarrow 1$	$R \leftarrow 0$	Wait	Wait	Wait
5		Done	Done	$S \to 7$	Done	$R \leftarrow 1$	$R \leftarrow 2$	Wait
6				Done		Done	Done	$R \leftarrow 3$

Fan-in Processor Utilization Chart								
Step	P0	P1	P2	P3	P4	P5	P6	P7
1	Wait	Wait	Wait	Wait	$S \to 0$	$S \to 1$	$S \to 2$	$S \to 3$
2	$R \leftarrow 4$	$R \leftarrow 5$	$R \leftarrow 6$	$R \leftarrow 7$	Done	Done	Done	Done
3	Wait	Wait	$S \to 0$	$S \to 1$				
4	$R \leftarrow 2$	$R \leftarrow 3$	Done	Done				
5	Wait	$S \to 0$						
6	$R \leftarrow 1$	Done						

Figure 4.2. Processor Utilization Charts.

Referring to Figure 4.2, during the fan-out, one processor becomes free at the end of the third step of the fan-out, four at the end of the fourth step, and seven at the end of the fifth step. In the fan-in, four processors are free after the first step, six at the end of the third step, and seven at the end of the fifth step. Hence, the fan-in allows more processors to proceed with further computation at an earlier stage than the fan-out. In the models of execution time presented, all processors in both algorithms are assumed to require the full $\log p$ time for communication. We now see that such a model is less appropriate for the inner-product algorithm, and we might expect the actual performance of the inner-product algorithm to be superior to that of the column-sweep algorithm.

5. Performance. The algorithms above were implemented by M. Heath of Oak Ridge National Laboratory on an Intel iPSC equipped with 64 processors. The codes were written in C to run in single precision, and were implemented first by using fan-in/fan-out communication, or *cube* communication. These results are summarized in Figure 5.1, and clearly demonstrate the competitiveness of the inner-product algorithm. The codes were then adapted to use an embedded ring for the communication (devised using a binary reflected gray code). Significant improvement was obtained for both algorithms, with the results summarized in Figure 5.2. The improvement is due to the effect of pipelining (or overlapping) the communication and computation, which unfortunately also serves to make the algorithms difficult to analyze.

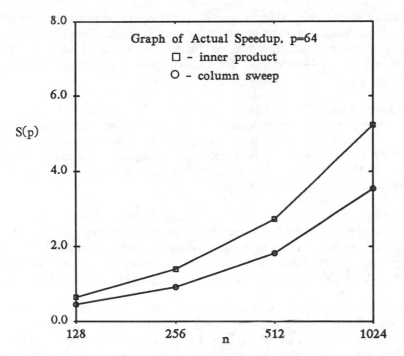

Figure 5.1. Results Using *Cube* communication.

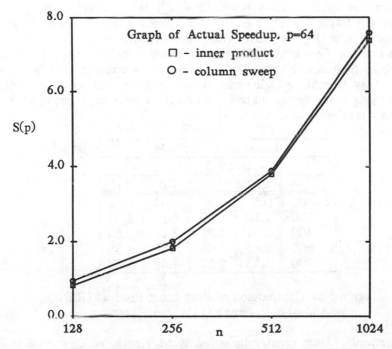

Figure 5.2. Results Using *Ring* communication.

Several points should be made concerning the results given in Figures 5.1 and 5.2. First, the low speedups obtained on the iPSC with these algorithms (<8 on 64 processors) are typical of parallel algorithms which are communication bound.

In the algorithms above, only $O(n^2)$ floating-point operations are performed, not enough to mask the high degree of communication required. However, the speed-ups reported for these algorithms are, as far as we know, among the highest speedups obtained on a 64-node iPSC for the solution of a dense triangular system.

The second point, directly related to the first, is the amount of improvement obtained by using a ring communication scheme rather than the minimal spanning-tree. Figure 5.2 shows a dramatic increase in the speedup of both algorithms; however, this increase is only a small percentage of the maximum speedup which is theoretically possible. The scale of the vertical axis in Figures 5.1 and 5.2 is somewhat misleading in this respect.

Finally, the figures indicate that the inner-product algorithm is superior to the column-sweep algorithm if cube communication is used, whereas the column-sweep algorithm is superior for ring communication. The reason for this behavior is currently under investigation; however, the execution times for both cases are sufficiently close that we consider them to be roughly equivalent in efficiency.

6. Future Work. There have been a number of algorithms introduced since [6] for the solution of a column-stored triangular system. Many of these have been implemented on the Oak Ridge iPSC, and a comparison of their performance is underway. For example, our implementation of the algorithm introduced at the present conference by Li and Coleman (see [1] and these proceedings) appears to be a solid winner for small values of p ($p \leqslant 32$); for $p \geqslant 64$, other algorithms (including the ring implementation of the inner-product algorithm described here) appear preferable (see Figure 5.3). Our future work includes attempting to explain these results. One major goal is to provide a sufficient analytical framework to analyze pipelined algorithms, since our experience is that pipelining is often the best way to achieve high performance. Finally, the solution of triangular systems arising from sparse matrix factorization may be improved by one or more of the new methods under study.

Times are in Seconds				
	p=16		p=64	
	RIP	LC	RIP	LC
n=100	0.53	0.30	0.62	0.56
200	1.10	0.60	1.10	1.33
400	2.37	1.22	2.16	2.86
600	3.85	1.83	3.30	4.39
800	5.53	2.57	4.49	5.93

Figure 5.3. Comparison of Ring Inner Product (RIP)
and Li & Coleman (LC) algorithms.

Acknowledgements. I am greatly indebted to M. Heath, A. Geist and E. Ng of Oak Ridge National Laboratory for their valuable contributions; I particularly want to thank M. Heath for his efficient iPSC implementations of the algorithms discussed.

REFERENCES

(1) G. Li and T. F. Coleman, *A Parallel Triangular Solver for a Hypercube Multiprocessor*, Technical Report TR 86-787, Cornell University, October 1986.

(2) G. A. Geist and M. T. Heath, *Matrix Factorization on a Hypercube Multiprocessor*, in Hypercube Multiprocessors 1986, M. T. Heath, ed., SIAM, Philadelphia, 1986, pp. 161-195.

(3) I. C. F. Ipsen, Y. Saad, M. H. Schultz, *Complexity of Dense Linear System Solution on a Multiprocessor Ring*, Linear Algebra Appl., 77 (1986), pp. 205-240.

(4) D. J. Kuck, *Parallel Processing of Ordinary Programs*, in Advances in Computers, M. C. Youvits, ed., Academic Press, New York, 1976, pp. 119-179.

(5) D. P. O'Leary and G. W. Stewart, *Assignment and Scheduling in Parallel Matrix Factorization*, Linear Algebra Appl., 77 (1986), pp. 275-300.

(6) C. H. Romine and J. M. Ortega, *Parallel Solution of Triangular Systems of Equations*, Applied Mathematics Technical Report RM-86-05, University of Virginia, August 1986.

A Lower Bound on the Communication Complexity of Solving Linear Tridiagonal Systems on Cube Architectures*

S. LAKSHMIVARAHAN† AND SUDARSHAN K. DHALL†

Abstract: A comprehensive analysis of the communication complexity in mapping four well known parallel algorithms for solving linear tri-diagonal systems on cube architectures is presented. In particular, a lower bound on the communication complexity is derived. Using this lower bound, we prove the optimality of mapping due to Johnsson based on binary reflected Gray-Codes. Our analysis provides a framework using which similar lower bounds on the communication complexity of mapping virtually any parallel algorithm on the cube architecture can be derived.[2]

1. INTRODUCTION: Distributed memory architecture based on (binary or base-2) hypercube interconnection schemes has gained widespread acceptance in the literature [1], [2], [3]. For a comprehensive analysis of the topological properties of cube interconnection schemes refer to [1]. Generalizations of the binary hypercube interconnection schemes to base-b ($b \geq 2$) hypercube is described in Lakshmivarahan and Dhall [2]. Similar generalizations are also studied in Bhuyan and Agrawal [4]. In this paper we focus our attention on the problem of solving linear tridiagonal systems on the cube architectures. We analyze four different methods: (a) odd-even (cyclic) reduction [5], [7], (b) odd-even elimination [5], [7], (c) recursive doubling [9] and (d) a new method due to the authors [10]. Since the computational complexity of these algorithms are well understood [3], [5], [9], [10], in this paper we concentrate only on the communication

---

*The research reported in this paper was supported in part by the AMOCO Research Center in Tulsa, Oklahoma and the Energy Resource Institute, University of Oklahoma.
†Parallel Processing Institute, School of Electrical Engineering and Computer Science, University of Oklahoma, Norman, OK 73019

complexity. This relates to the analysis of mapping of the above algorithms on the cube. A lower bound on the complexity of mapping each of these four algorithms on the cube is derived. A comparison of these algorithms along with the implications of solving related class of problems such as prefix problems etc. are discussed. For a comprehensive survey of parallel algorithms refer to [5], [6].

2. ODD-EVEN (CYCLIC) REDUCTION [5], [7]

In this section we analyze the communication complexity of any (arbitrary) mapping of the odd-even reduction algorithm for solving tridiagonal systems on cube architectures. Let $M = N - 1, N = 2^n$. Consider a linear tridiagonal system $Ax = d$

where

$$A = \begin{bmatrix} b_1 & c_1 & 0 & 0 & \ldots & 0 & 0 & 0 \\ a_2 & b_2 & c_2 & 0 & \ldots & 0 & 0 & 0 \\ 0 & a_3 & b_3 & c_3 & \ldots & 0 & 0 & 0 \\ \vdots & \vdots & \vdots & \vdots & \ldots & \vdots & \vdots & \vdots \\ 0 & 0 & 0 & 0 & \ldots & a_{M-1} & b_{M-1} & c_{M-1} \\ 0 & 0 & 0 & 0 & \ldots & 0 & a_M & b_M \end{bmatrix}$$

and $x = (x_1, x_2, \ldots, x_M)^t$ and $d = (d_1, d_2, \ldots, d_M)^t$ where t denotes the transpose. The odd-even reduction algorithm [5], [7] consists of two phases: (a) the reduction phase and (b) the back-substitution phase.

(a) The Reduction Phase:

In this phase, in the first step all the odd indexed variables are eliminated. In the second step, variables with indices that are odd-multiples of 2 are eliminated. At the jth step, all the variables with indices that are odd multiples of $2^{(j-1)}$, are eliminated. Thus, after the $(n-1)^{th}$ step, $x_{2^{n-2}}$ and $x_{3.2^{n-2}}$ are eliminated leaving behind only one equation in the unknown $x_{2^{n-1}}$.

The interaction between various parallel computations for $M = 15$ are graphically represented in figure 1. In this graph, basic computations involving index i are associated with node i. The labels of the edges correspond to the computation step of the reduction phase. Notice that the computation of node i involves node i, node $i - h$ and node $i + h$ where $h = 2^j$, $j = 0, 1, \ldots, n - 1$. This fact is denoted by the directed edges from nodes $i + h$ and $i - h$ to node with label j. Since this graph describes only the logical connections needed between various interacting computations, henceforth, we refer to these graphs as communication graphs.

(b) The Back Substitution Phase:

This phase is initialized by first computing $x_{2^{n-1}}$.

The rest of this phase consists of $(n - 1)$ steps and for convenience we number steps starting from $(n - 1)$ to 1 in steps of -1.

At the $(n - 1)^{th}$ step two variables with indices that are odd multiples of 2^{n-2} that is, $x_{2^{n-2}}$ and $x_{3.2^{n-2}}$ are recovered. In general, at the $(n - j)^{th}$ step, 2^j variables with indices that are odd multiples of 2^{n-j-1}, that is $x_{2^{n-j-1}}$,

$x_{3 \cdot 2^{n-j-1}}, \ldots x_{(2-1)2^{n-j-1}}$ are recovered. At the step 1, 2^{n-1} variables with odd indices that is $x_1, x_3, x_5, \ldots x_{2^{n-1}}$ are all recovered. The interaction between the various parallel computations for $M = 15$ are again graphically illustrated in figure 1 with the directions of the edges reversed. Henceforth, in view of this similarity, the communication graphs of the two phases are combined to give an undirected labelled graph. Further, in the following we restrict our attention only to the reduction phase. All the results would immediately apply to the back-substitution phase as well.

The following result due to Johnsson [3] on the mapping of the communication graph on to the base-2 cube is fundamental. If the computation involving the index i is assigned to a node in a base-2 cube whose label (in binary) corresponds to the ith code word in the binary reflected Gray Code [8], then all the communications in any step of the reduction phase is restricted to processors that are at a distance no more than two apart. In other words, under this mapping the nodes that are logically adjacent (in the communication graph) are not mapped on to processors that are physically adjacent on the base-2 cube. Counting the cost of one communication between processors at d distance apart as d units, it can be shown [3] that the total communication cost of the reduction phase resulting from the above said mapping is $(2n - 3)$. While this is of the same order of magnitude as the computational complexity, since communication in the contemporary architectures is many times more expensive compared to basic arithmetic operations, it is interesting to ask if there exists a mapping of the reduction phase with still lower communication cost. Recall that the absolute minimum for the communication cost is equal to the number of steps in the reduction phase. This discussion immediately leads to the following definition. A mapping of the cyclic reduction is said to be desirable if it achieves the minimum communication cost. Notice that under desirable mapping the communications are restricted to physically adjacent processors. Our first result of this section relates to non-existence of desirable mapping of the odd-even reduction on the base-2 cube.

Theorem 2.1: In any mapping of the reduction phase on a base-2 cube, it is necessary that at least $((n/2) - 1)$ steps of the reduction phase must involve communication between processors that are at distance two or more apart.

Proof: Consider an arbitrary mapping of the reduction phase on to the base-2 cube. Let m be the label of a nodal processor that is responsible for the computation involving $i = N/2$. It is clear from the communication graph that this nodal processor needs to communicate with two distinct processors in each of the $(n - 1)$ steps of the reduction phase. If each of these communications are to be restricted to processors that are at a unit distance from m, then clearly this designated nodal processor m must necessarily have $2(n - 1)$ neighbors. But, in a base-2 cube there are only n neighbors to each node. Thus, the nodal processor m needs to communicate with at least $(n - 2)$ processors that are at distance two or more. Since each step involves a pair of processors, the theorem follows.

The following corollary is immediate [2].

<u>Corollary 2.2</u>: The mapping of the cyclic reduction on to the base-2 cube based on the binary reflected Gray Code is optimal.

We now turn to analyze the existence of <u>desirable</u> mapping of the reduction phase on base-b cubes for $N \geq b > 2$. Recall that the basic requirement of the desirable mapping is to consider the logical neighbors of the communication graph as physical neighbors as well. From this consideration, the following theorem is rather immediate [2].

<u>Theorem 2.3</u>: There exists a desirable mapping of the reduction phase on to the complete $(M, M) - 1$ cube.

<u>Lemma 2.4</u>: Any three node graph connected in a triangle can be mapped on to three mutually adjacent nodes (say with labels x, y and z) on a complete (L,b)-k cube if and only if x, y and z differ in the same base-b digit position, that is, x, y and z belong to the same basic projection [2].

<u>Proof</u>: Let G = (V,E), with V = {a,b,c} and E = {(a,b), (b,c), (c,a)} be the given three node (undirected) graph. Let f be a mapping such that f(a) = x, f(b) = y, f(c) = z. Clearly x and y are neighbors if and only if $x = x_k x_{k-1} \ldots x_{j-1} x_j x_{j+1} \ldots x_1$ and $y = x_k x_{k-1} \ldots x_{j-1} y_j x_{j+1} \ldots x_1$ and $x_j \neq y_j$. Let $z = z_k z_{k-1} \ldots z_1$ where $z_q \neq x_q$ and $z_i = x_i$ for all $i \neq q$, that is, z is a neighbor of x. But, clearly, both $h_b(x, z)$ and $h_b(y, z)$ are unity if and only if $q = j$ and $z_q \neq y_j \neq x_j$. Hence the lemma.

The following corollary is widely applicable [2].

<u>Corollary 2.5</u>: Consider a set of four nodes a,b,c and d connected in the form of two triangles with a common edge. Under the desirable mapping the fourth node (say d) belongs to the same projection as the first three nodes (a,b,c) do.

To understand the relevance of this lemma, observe that the basic (structural) building block of the communication graphs given in figure 1 is a triangle of a simple cycle of length 3. From the lemma, it is clear that any desirable mapping must map the three nodes of every simple cycle of length 3 on to the same basic projection. Since there are no odd cycles in a base-2 cube, this lemma further <u>seconds</u> the conclusion of our Theorem 2.1. Base-4 cube, on the other hand, admits a variety of odd cycles (including cycles of length 3, refer to section 3 for details). This observation might lead one to suspect the existence of desirable mapping on the base-4 cube. However the following theorem implies that for $N \geq 16$, there does <u>not</u> exist a desirable mapping on a base-4 cube either [2].

<u>Theorem 2.6</u>: There does not exist a desirable mapping of the reduction phase on to a complete (L,b)-k cube where $L \geq N, K \geq 2$ and $2 < b < N$ unless $b \geq (N/4) + 1$.

Notice that this theorem only provides a necessary condition for the existence of desirable maps. The actual map, if it exists still has to be found by other means. To further understand the importance of this theorem, recall that a complete $(L, ((N/4) + 1)) - 2$ cube has $L = (N/4 + 1)^2$ nodes and $(N/4)(N/4 + 1)^2$ edges. The complete $(M, M) - 1$ cube on the other hand, has

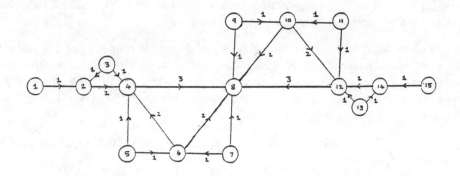

Figure 1. Communication graph of the Reduction Phase. M=15

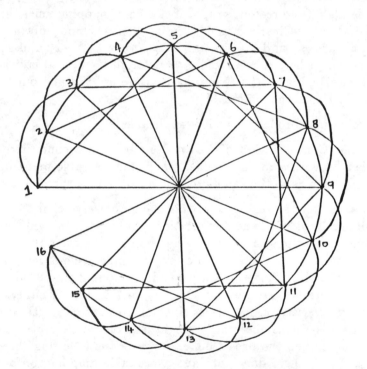

Figure 2. Communication graph of the odd-even elimination.

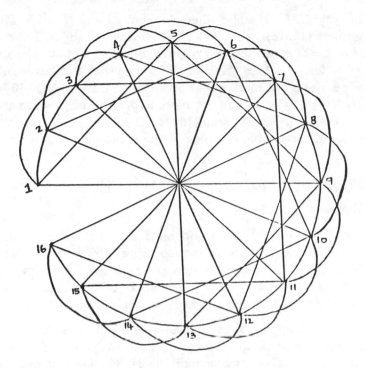

Figure 3. Communication graph of recursive doubling-
linear first order recurrence.

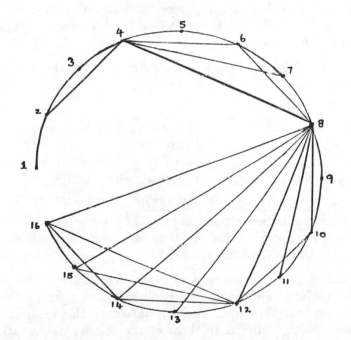

Figure 4. Communication graph of the New Algorithm-
Linear first order recurrence.

M nodes and $(1/2)M(M-1)$ edges where $M = N-1$ and $N = 2^n$. Thus, when $N = 16$, a complete $(15, 15)$-1 cube has 15 nodes and 105 edges. But a complete $(L,5)$-2 cube has L=25 nodes and 100 edges. An example of a desirable map on the $(25,5)$-2 cube for $M = 15$ is given in [2]. Notice that this latter cube at the cost of <u>five</u> edges needs <u>ten</u> more nodal processors. But for $N > 16$, since the complete $(L, ((N/4) + 1)) - 2$ cube has more nodes and edges compared to the (M,M)-1 cube, it is obvious that complete (M,M)-1 cube is the most economical of the cubes on which desirable mapping of the reduction phase exists.

3. <u>ODD-EVEN ELIMINATION ALGORITHM [5], [7]</u>

Let $M = N = 2^n$ in (2.2).

The communication graph for this algorithm for $N = 16$ is given in figure 2. From these graphs it is clear that each node communicates with <u>no more than two</u> distinct (logical) neighbors in a given step and that the maximum degree of a node is $(2n - 1)$. Since there are only n neighbors to a node in a base-2 cube, the following analogue of Theorem 2.1 and Corollary 2.2 is immediate.

<u>Theorem 3.1</u>: In any mapping of the odd-even elimination on to a base-2 cube it is necessary that at least $(n/2) - 1$ steps must involve communication between processors that are at distance two or more apart. Further, the mapping based on binary reflected Gray Code is also optimal for odd-even elimination.

Comparing the algorithm for the reduction phase of the odd-even reduction with the odd-even elimination, it readily follows that the communication graph for the reduction phase is a subgraph of that of the odd-even elimination. While it follows from this fact that the Theorem 2.6 also holds good for odd-even elimination as well, the following Theorem is a direct analogue of Theorem 2.6 for the odd-even elimination [2].

<u>Theorem 3.2</u>: There does not exist a desirable mapping of the odd-even elimination on to a complete (L,b)-k cube where $L \geq N, K \geq 1$ and $2 < b \leq N$ unless $b = N, k = 1$ and $L = N$.

The proof is very similar to that of Theorem 2.6 and essentially follows by repeated application of the Lemma 2.1 and Corollary 2.5.

Thus for all $N \geq 2$, the complete (N,N)-1 cube is the most economical topology on which desirable mapping of this algorithm exists.

4. <u>RECURSIVE DOUBLING ALGORITHM [9]</u>:

The Gaussian elimination algorithm provides the mathematical framework for both the <u>recursive doubling</u> due to Stone [9] and a new class of algorithm due to the authors [10] analyzed in section 5.

The communication graph of the recursive doubling algorithm for $N = 16$ is given in figure 3. Now comparing the graph in figure 3 with that in figure 2, it is readily seen that the communication pattern of this recursive doubling algorithm is astonishingly similar to those of the odd-even elimination. Thus all the conclusions of section 3 are directly applicable to the recursive doubling algorithm.

5. A New Algorithm [10]:

The new algorithm due to the authors is described in [10].

The communication graph of the new algorithm for $N = 16$ is given in figure 4. It can be shown that, in general, the node $(N/2)$ of this graph has the maximum degree of $(N/2) + (n - 1)$. Clearly, there does not exist any desirable mapping of this algorithm on a base-2 cube. Another peculiarity of this algorithm is that even under binary reflected Gray Code mapping on a base-2 cube, the maximum distance between communicating processors is not limited to 2. In fact, under any coding on a base-2, this maximum distance is equal to the diameter of the cube. Further, using the argument similar to those in Theorem 2.6 the following result can be proved and the proof is omitted.

Theorem 5.1: There does not exist a desirable mapping of the new algorithm on to a complete (L,b)-k cube where $L \geq N, k \geq 1$ and $2 < b \leq N$ unless $b \geq (N/2) + 1$ and $k \geq 2$.

From this Theorem it readily follows that for $N \geq 2$, the complete (N,N)-1 cube is the most economical cube topology permitting desirable mapping of the new algorithm.

6. A Comparison:

This section provides a number of comments relating to the four algorithms discussed above. To our knowledge this is the first comprehensive analysis of the communication complexity in mapping all the four well known algorithms for solving linear tridiagonal systems on a cube architecture. (1). Except for the actual schedule of computations, both the odd-even reduction and odd-even elimination essentially follow from the same first principle namely elimination of variables. Likewise, both the recursive doubling and the new algorithm follow from another related first principle that of LU factorisation of the given tridiagonal matrix. (2). In spite of the differences, it is interesting to note that the binary reflected Gray Code mapping of the odd-even reduction, odd-even elimination and recursive doubling on to a base-2 leads to optimal communication complexity. With respect to the new algorithm the binary reflected Gray Code mapping is not optimal. Thus, the new algorithm is not suitable for cube architectures. (3). Since there does not exist any desirable mapping of any of these algorithms on a base-2 cube, the question of the relative performance between three competing algorithms namely odd-even reduction, odd-even elimination and recursive doubling must be settled only by actual simulation. (4). From section 4 it is clear that the communication pattern in solving first-order linear recurrences by recursive doubling is intimately related to those that arise in solving tridiagonal systems using odd-even elimination. A special case of the first order linear recurrence is called the prefix or the cascade sum problem. Thus, an analysis in section 4 is directly applicable to the prefix or the cascade sum problem.

REFERENCES

[1] Y. Saad and M.H. Schultz. " Topological Properties of Hypercubes". Research Report -RR - 389, Yale University, June 1985.

[2] S. Lakshmivarahan and S.K. Dhall. " A New Hierarchy of Hypercube In-

terconnection Scheme for Parallel Computers: Theory and Applications". Technical Report-OU-PPI-TR-86-02, Parallel Processing Institute, School of EECS, University of Oklahoma, August, 1986.

[3] L. Johnsson. "Odd-even cyclic reduction on Ensemble Architectures and the Solution of Tridiagonal Systems of Equations", Research Report - RR-339, Yale University, October 1984.

[4] L.N. Bhuyan and D.P. Agrawal. "Generalized Hypercube and Hyperbus Structures for Computer Networks", IEEE Transactions on Computers, Vol. 33, pp. 323-333, 1984.

[5] D. Heller. "A Survey of Parallel Algorithms in Numerical Algebra". SIAM Review, Vol. 20, pp. 740, 777, 1978.

[6] A.H. Sameh. "Numerical Parallel Algorithms - A Survey"
in High Speed Computers, Algorithms and Organization (Edited by) D. Lawrie and A.H. Sameh. Academic Press, New York, pp. 207-228, 1977.

[7] A.W. Hockney and C.R. Jesshope. Parallel Computers, Adam Hilger, 1981.

[8] E.M. Reingold, J. Nievergelt and N. Deo. Combinatorial Algorithms, Prentice Hall, 1977.

[9] H.S. Stone. "An Efficient Parallel Algorithm for the Solution of Tridiagonal System of Equations". Journal of ACM, Vol. 20, pp. 27-38, 1973.

[10] S. Lakshmivarahan and S.K. Dhall. "A New Class of Parallel Algorithms for Solving Linear Tridiagonal Systems". Proceedings of the Fall Joint Computer Conference, November 1986 (To appear).

An Alternative View of LU Factorization with Partial Pivoting on a Hypercube Multiprocessor

R. M. CHAMBERLAIN*

Abstract. An algorithm for the solution of linear equations using a variant of Gaussian elimination with partial pivoting is presented. Rows are distributed among the processors and column pivoting is done so no communication between processors is necessary to calculate the pivots. Alternatively the same ideas can be applied to provide a normal Gaussian elimination algorithm with the matrix stored by columns. The elimination and the choice of pivots can be overlapped, and the work of pivot selection and distribution of the pivot rows can be shared among the processors. The location of the rows of the triangular matrices is free to be chosen. By distributing them in a wrap manner, the workload of the processors is balanced and a Gray code ordering is chosen to aid the back substitution. This work is based on the same ideas as Chamberlain and Powell[3], which describes an algorithm for QR decomposition using Givens rotations.

1. Introduction. The solution of linear equations is a fundamental tool on any general-purpose computer. The choice on a sequential or vector machine is usually a simple one between a direct or an iterative method. If a direct method is chosen, then a library subroutine is usually available and this subroutine has often been optimised. However on parallel machines it is not so clear-cut. The 'best' method depends on the number of processors, the number of equations, the communication time and computational speed of the processors. The user may have the matrix stored by rows, columns, blocks or some other way and so the provision of a general-purpose subroutine is not feasible.

There has been recent work on the solution of linear equations on a hypercube multiprocessor when the matrix is stored by rows (Geist[6] and Geist and Heath[7]) and by columns (Davis[5]). There are two approaches to doing the factorisation with pivoting. In the first approach the processors combine in the work of the pivoting selection. This method is "synchronised", because the processors all do the pivoting simultaneously. This approach has been investigated by Geist and Heath[7]. In the second approach one processor does the pivot selection. Here the pivoting is carried out while the other processors are performing eliminations using previous pivotings. Because one processor is doing the pivoting, the

---

* Chr. Michelsen Institute, Fantoftveien 38, N-5036 Fantoft, Norway.

amount of communication is reduced.

This paper shows that both approaches can be used, irrespective of whether the matrix is stored by rows or columns. Normal Gaussian elimination picks the maximal element in a column as the pivot, but the pivot can be taken as the maximal element in a row. Thus, if the storage of the matrix is by rows, then the pivoting can be done within a processor if the maximal element in a row is taken as the pivot and the processors can combine to do the pivoting if the maximal element in a column is chosen as the pivot. The position is reversed if the storage is by columns.

Similarly there are two approaches to the back substitution and both ways are applicable when the matrix is stored by rows or by columns. Firstly there are the "fan-in/fan-out" algorithms of Geist[6] for row storage and of Romaine[9] for column storage. This approach uses a global broadcast or gather. Alternatively there is the "ring" algorithm of Coleman and Li[8] for column storage and the analogous algorithm used by Chamberlain[2] for row storage. The "ring" algorithms require less communication, which can be important when the message passing is relatively slow.

This paper describes an implementation of a method where the matrix is stored by rows and the maximal element in a row is taken as the pivot. The pivoting is carried out by one processor. Exactly the same ideas apply to a matrix stored by columns where normal Gaussian elimination is applied. The implementation in this paper, which does pivoting within a processor and uses a ring algorithm for the back substitution, is suitable for hypercubes where the communication is "relatively slow". This certainly applies to early versions of the INTEL iPSC and to the vector processor extension of this machine.

2. LU Factorisation. The system of linear equations is denoted by

$$A\underline{x} = \underline{b}$$

where $\underline{x}$ is a vector of n variables and the matrix A is a general $n \times n$ non-singular matrix, which is assumed to be dense. In normal Gaussian elimination zeroes are introduced column by column starting from the left-hand column and working to the right. The zeroes in a column are produced by adding a multiple of the row containing the diagonal element to each of the rows below it in the matrix.

To produce the desired zeroes, the element on the diagonal must be non-zero and it may be necessary to alter the ordering of the equations by swapping either two rows or two columns. This process is called pivoting. Pivoting is also desirable to ensure that the solution process is stable, because small values of the diagonal element in relation to other elements in the row or column may lead to unacceptably large elements of the L or U matrix. Full pivoting is done by finding the element of largest absolute value in the remaining submatrix to be factored and swapping two rows and columns to put it in the diagonal position. This is the so-called pivot for this column. This requires considerable manipulation of the matrix, and so partial pivoting is usually performed. Here the pivot is chosen to be the element of maximal absolute value in either the leading column or the leading row. This just requires the swapping of two columns or two rows respectively. When the maximal element in a column is chosen as a pivot and two rows are interchanged, we call this *row pivoting*. When the maximal element in a row is found and two columns are interchanged then it is called *column pivoting*.

An algorithm for Gaussian elimination using partial pivoting on the hypercube has been proposed by Geist[6] and modifications to this algorithm have been suggested by Chu and George[4] and Geist and Heath[7]. In Geist's algorithm, the rows are distributed among the processors and the pivoting is done by finding the maximum element in each column (i.e. row pivoting). This is achieved by using a separate host processor, which is normally used to load programs and store data, and has a direct link to all the processors. The host processor collects the maximal element in each processor from all the processors, calculates the pivot element and then passes a message to all the processors informing them of whether they contain the pivot row. The processor which contains the pivot row sends the pivot row to all the other processors through a tree structure, while the other processors wait to receive the pivot row and then contribute towards distributing it through the tree structure. The processors then calculate their possible values for the next pivot element before completing the elimination on the rows in their processors. The purpose of this is that the host has nothing else to do during the calculation and can calculate the pivot while the processors are completing the elimination for the column. Chu and George[4] suggest that the pivot row is exchanged with a row in a designated processor so that all the processors have the same number of equations still to be factored (to within one equation). This balances the load of the processors.

This approach has two drawbacks. Firstly there must be a host processor available which has a direct link to all the processors. Even if this processor exists, it may be carrying out other jobs associated with being part of a network and providing a service to the hypercube. It seems more important to develop algorithms for a general hypercube architecture alone. The second drawback is the large number of messages to and from the host processor. For a large hypercube the cost for this will become prohibitive.

Geist and Heath[7] propose that the determination of the pivots is done by the nodes. Each processor works out the maximum element in their part of the column. Communication is then required to combine this information to determine the pivot row. Further communication is then needed to distribute the identity of the pivot row and then the pivot row itself must be distributed. The algorithm in this report requires no communication to determine the pivot, and so the only communication is the distribution of the pivot rows. The algorithm also overlaps the pivoting and the eliminations so that processors avoid waiting for pivot rows to be distributed, for much of the calculation.

The main difference in our algorithm is that column pivoting is done. The maximal element in a row is taken as the pivot element, as in Barrodale and Stuart[1], and columns are interchanged to put the maximal element on the diagonal. Linear combinations of the pivot row are added to the other rows to produce the desired zeroes and this is discussed later. No communication is required to determine the pivot element so the number of messages is usefully reduced. In this way the determination of the pivot is done entirely sequentially in one processor. The columns are physically interchanged and the information about which columns to interchange is transmitted in the message containing the pivot row. The pivot element is determined after the processor holding the row has completed the elimination on the pivot row and before this processor does the eliminations for the remaining rows that it holds. Thus the pivot row starts to be distributed while the other processors are still working on eliminations in the previous column. This overlaps the pivoting and the elimination and avoids the problem that all the processors are waiting for one processor to calculate the pivot, at least while all the processors have several rows which require further work.

In [3] the processors carried on with internal work while they waited for messages necessary to do so-called merges. There is an analogous idea for the LU factorization. The main objective of each processor is the distribution of the next pivot row. Eliminations are carried out until a new pivot row arrives when the processor does what is necessary to distribute the new pivot row through the tree. This requires that there is a subroutine available to check whether there is a message in the communications buffer (PROBE on the INTEL iPSC), or an interrupt mechanism. Each processor has an array for pivot rows. While there is room in this pivot array, it collects any pivot row it receives, places it in the pivot array and forwards it through the tree. On the INTEL machine it is sensible to use PROBE to check the message buffer after completing the calculations on each row. It is beneficial to have storage for at least two pivot rows so that the distribution of the next pivot row can be carried out during the elimination in the current column. A large pivot array may be useful so that several modifications to array elements can be made at the same time. There may also be some advantage to having a large pivot array when the communications are very slow, so that the pivot rows are distributed as quickly as possible.

The above algorithm applies to any architecture of loosely coupled processors, which have only local memory and use message passing to communicate between processors. The algorithm is specific to hypercubes only when the choice of the tree structure and the choice of the processors to hold the rows of U is made. This choice should be made to keep the loads balanced in two ways. Firstly the calculations that the processors do to introduce zeroes should be shared evenly amongst the processors. Secondly the extra work involved in pivoting and passing messages through the tree should be balanced among the processors. This balancing should happen locally as well so that no processor is heavily loaded with extra work on several consecutive columns.

When the processors combine to do the pivoting (as in Geist and Heath[7]), the pivot row is randomly distributed and this leads to the workload of the processors being somewhat unbalanced. In the above algorithm the processors to hold the final rows of the matrix U are free to be chosen. A wrap mapping is chosen to ensure that each processor has the same number of rows remaining to be factored (to within one row). In this way the calculations of the processors are balanced. As with the QR factorization [3], we have chosen the rows to be distributed according to a Gray code so that the neighbouring rows are in neighbouring processors for the forward and back substitution. This ensures that the communication necessary for the back substitution is minimised. Chamberlain[2] discusses methods for the back substitution. The particular Gray code chosen is the binary reflected Gray code (see [3]).

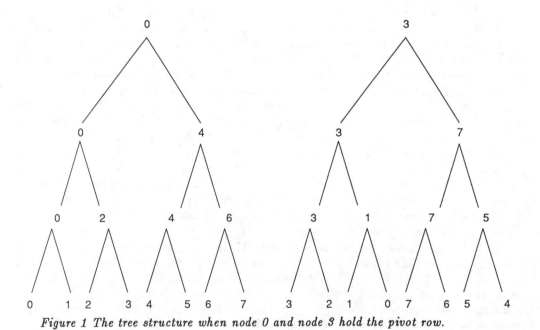

Figure 1 The tree structure when node 0 and node 3 hold the pivot row.

The chosen tree structure is also the same as the one used in the QR factorization (see Figure 1). However it is now used from the top down. So in the left hand diagram node 0 holds the pivot row and passes it first to node 4, then to node 2, and then to node 1. Node 4 receives the row from node 0 and passes it to node 6 and then to node 5. The tree on the right in Figure 1 shows the way in which the pivot row is distributed when processor

3 holds the pivot row. A requirement for the tree is that no node is high up on the tree for several consecutive columns, because then that processor has to send many messages and gets behind. It is straightforward to show that for the processor containing the pivot row for one column (and so the one with most work to do), there is a neighbouring column where the processor is at the bottom of the tree and so has only one receive to do. The combination of this tree structure and the binary reflected Gray code was found to be efficient and had some good properties for the QR factorization [3]. These properties also provide good local load balancing in this problem.

This algorithm contains several desirable features. The choice of the pivot requires no communication, and the only communication is the distribution of the pivot rows. There is an overlapping of the elimination and the distribution of the pivot rows, which reduces the time a processor spends waiting for pivot rows. The extra work involved in finding the pivot, scaling the pivot row and distributing the pivot row is shared among the processors. The rows of the upper triangular matrix are distributed among the processors according to a Gray code, which is appropriate for the back substitution and ensures that the workload of the processors is balanced.

3. Implementation and results. A simple implementation of the ideas in the previous section was implemented on an INTEL iPSC with memory extension boards. The 32 node hypercube was running under version 2.1 of the node operating system so the communications were still relatively slow.

The implementation uses two pivot buffers. One is used for the eliminations in the current column and the second buffer is used for the distribution of the pivot row for the next column. The pseudo-code for the implementation which overlaps the pivoting and the elimination is:

```
            if i hold first pivot row then
                    do pivoting
                    distribute pivot row to my neighbours
            end if
            loop over columns
                    if i have not received pivot row for current column then
                            receive pivot row
                            distribute pivot row to my children in tree
                    end if
                    interchange columns
                    carry out elimination for my first row
                    if i hold next pivot row then
                            do pivoting
                            distribute pivot row to my neighbours
                    end if
                    loop through remaining rows
                            carry out elimination for a row
                            if next pivot row has arrived then
                                    receive next pivot row
                                    distribute pivot row to my children in tree
                            end if
                    end loop
            end loop
```

Three versions of a factorisation program were tested. The first two were variants of the ideas in this paper. The first version was a direct implementation of the above pseudo-code. The second version omitted the if test on the arrival of the next pivot row in the innermost loop. Thus the processor holding the pivot row calculates the pivot row as early as possible and distributes it to its neighbours. Any further distribution of the pivot row is not overlapped with the elimination and the processors receive the next pivot row and pass it on to their children in the tree only when they are ready to use it. The difference in timing of these two versions shows the advantage of the overlapping of the distribution of pivot rows and the pivoting. The third version uses row pivoting and there is a fan-in to a processor who determines the pivot, a fan-out to inform everybody of the holder of the pivot row and then a fan-out of the pivot row. All the processors complete the eliminations for the previous column before they proceed to the pivoting. The test matrix was a random matrix and so the location of the pivot rows was random for the row pivoting algorithm. This led to an imbalance in the workload between the processors in this case.

The results for the experiments are shown in Table 1. The numbers are milliseconds. The main feature of the results is the slowness of the row pivoting algorithm. This is explained by considering the time required for the communication. Each pivoting step requires 3 fan-ins/fanouts and thus 15 messages on a 32-node hypercube. Even taking the conservative estimate of 4.5 milliseconds for each message, this means that the message passing for the pivoting takes at least 20,000 milliseconds for the case n=300. This communication overhead is very noticeable on the smaller problems but is less significant on the larger problems. The overlapping of the pivoting and the distribution of the pivot rows is seen to lead to a speed-up of between 5 and 10 percent.

Number of variables	Column pivoting with overlap	Column pivoting without overlap	Row pivoting
300	27888	29600	55600
400	57872	62592	101424
500	105536	111408	170384
600	175920	184672	264960

Table 1 The solution of linear equations on a 32-node hypercube

4. Conclusions. An algorithm for Gaussian elimination with partial pivoting on the hypercube has been described. If the matrix is stored by rows, column pivoting is used so that no communication is needed for the calculation of the pivot elements. Similar ideas can be used to perform the usual Gaussian elimination when the matrix is stored by columns. The processors which hold the rows of the upper triangular matrix U are free to be chosen and we have let the rows be distributed among the processors according to a binary reflected Gray code. This ensures the workload of the processors is balanced and is also advantageous for the back substitution. The work of pivoting and distributing the pivot rows is shared among the processors, and the elimination and distribution of the pivot row are overlapped. Numerical results show that this method provides substantial gains over the normal row pivoting when the communications are relatively slow.

Acknowledgments. The author would like to express his warm thanks to Clifford Addison for his helpful comments on an earlier version of this paper.

REFERENCES

(1) I. BARRODALE and G.F. STUART, *A new variant of Gaussian elimination,* Journal of the Institute of Mathematics and its Applications, 19 (1977), pp 39-47.

(2) R.M. CHAMBERLAIN, *An algorithm for LU factorisation with partial pivoting on the hypercube,* CMI Centre for Computer Science report no. CCS/11, June 1986.

(3) R.M. CHAMBERLAIN and M.J.D. POWELL, *QR factorization for linear least squares problems on the hypercube,* CMI Centre for Computer Science report no. CCS/10, July 1986.

(4) E. CHU and J.A. GEORGE, *Gaussian elimination with partial pivoting and load balancing on a multiprocessor,* Tech. Rept., Department of Computer Science, University of Waterloo, Canada, 1986.

(5) G.J. DAVIS, *Column LU factorization with pivoting on a hypercube multiprocessor,* Oak Ridge National Laboratory report ORNL-6219, 1985.

(6) G.A. GEIST, *Efficient parallel LU factorization with pivoting on a hypercube multiprocessor,* Oak Ridge National Laboratory report ORNL-6211, 1985.

(7) G.A. GEIST and M.T. HEATH, *Matrix factorization on a hypercube multiprocessor,* in Hypercube Multiprocessors, M.T. Heath, ed., SIAM, Philadelphia, 1986, pp. 161-180.

(8) G. LI and T.F. COLEMAN, *A parallel triangular solver for a hypercube multiprocessor,* Cornell University Computer Science Report, 1986.

(9) C.H. ROMAINE and J.M. ORTEGA, *Parallel solution of triangular systems of equations,* University of Virginia Applied Mathematics Report No. RM-86-05, 1986.

Communication Reduction in Parallel Sparse Cholesky Factorization on a Hypercube*

ALAN GEORGE†, JOSEPH LIU‡ AND ESMOND NG†

Abstract. We consider the problem of reducing data traffic among processor nodes in the parallel factorization of a sparse matrix on a hypercube multiprocessor. A task assignment strategy based on the structure of an elimination tree is presented. This assignment is aimed at achieving load balancing among the processors and also reducing the amount of processor-to-processor data communication. Some experimental results on the performance of this scheme are presented.

1. Introduction

This article deals with the problem of factoring a large sparse positive definite matrix A on a multiprocessor system. It is assumed that the system supports message passing among individual processors, and that each processor has a substantial amount of local memory, but that there is no globally shared memory. These assumptions are appropriate for a number of recent commercially available machines, such as the binary hypercube multiprocessors marketed by Ametek, Floating Point Systems, Intel and NCUBE corporations.

In [2] a parallel algorithm was developed for solving sparse positive definite systems on such machines. In this paper we consider the problem of reducing data

---

* Research was supported in part by Canadian Natural Sciences and Engineering Research Council under grants A8111 and A5509, by the Applied Mathematical Sciences Research Program, Office of Energy Research, U.S. Department of Energy under contract DE-AC05-84OR21400 with Martin Marietta Energy Systems Inc., and by the U.S. Air Force Office of Scientific Research under contract AFOSR-ISSA-85-00083.

† Mathematical Sciences Section, Oak Ridge National Laboratory, Oak Ridge, Tennessee 37831. The first author is also a member of the Departments of Computer Science and Mathematics, The University of Tennessee, Knoxville, Tennessee 37996.

‡ Department of Computer Science, York University, Downsview, Ontario, Canada M3J 1P3.

traffic between processor nodes during the execution of this algorithm. We present a task assignment strategy based on the structure of an elimination tree which is aimed at achieving load balancing among the processors and also reducing the amount of processor-to-processor data communication.

An outline of the paper is as follows. Section 2 contains some background information on the algorithm mentioned above and describes some basic ideas about elimination trees. Section 3 contains our main contribution, which is to show how the assignment of tasks can be done to preserve the load balancing characteristics of the original algorithm, while reducing the communication traffic. Section 4 contains some numerical experiments conducted on an Intel iPSC hypercube showing that the new allocation scheme does reduce communication traffic and lead to corresponding improvements in performance.

2. Background on Parallel Sparse Cholesky Factorization

2.1. Dense Case: the Basic Algorithm

We begin by providing a column-oriented version of the basic Cholesky factorization algorithm, described in the following algorithmic form. Note that A is overwritten by L in the code.

```
for j := 1 to n do
begin
    for k := 1 to j−1 do
        for i := j to n do
            a_ij := a_ij − a_ik *a_jk
    a_jj := √(a_jj)
    for k := j +1 to n do
        a_kj := a_kj / a_jj
end
```

It is shown in [2] that this form of Cholesky factorization, the so-called column-Cholesky formulation, is particularly well suited to medium- to coarse-grain parallel implementation. Following [2], we let $Tcol(j)$ be the *task* that computes the j-th column of the Cholesky factor. Each such task consists of the following two types of subtasks:

1. $cmod(j,k)$: modification of column j by column k $(k < j)$;
2. $cdiv(j)$: division of column j by a scalar.

Thus, in terms of these sub-tasks, the basic algorithm can be expressed in the following condensed form.

```
for j := 1 to n do begin
    for k := 1 to j−1 do
        cmod(j,k)

    cdiv(j)
end
```

There is considerable potential for parallelism in the above formulation of the algorithm. Note that $cdiv(j)$ cannot begin until $cmod(j,k)$ has been completed for all $k < j$, and column j can be used to modify subsequent columns only after $cdiv(j)$ has been completed. However, there is no restriction on the order in which the $cmod$ operations are executed, and $cmod$ operations for different columns can be performed concurrently. For example, after $cdiv(1)$ has completed, $cmod(2,1)$ and $cmod(3,1)$ could execute in parallel.

2.2. Parallel Sparse Column-Cholesky and the Effect of Ordering

The main difference between the sparse and dense versions of the algorithm stems from the fact that for sparse A, column j may no longer need to be modified by *all* columns $k < j$ of L. Specifically, column j is modified *only* by columns k for which $l_{jk} \neq 0$, and after $cdiv(j)$ has been executed, column j needs to be made available only to tasks $Tcol(r)$ for which $l_{rj} \neq 0$. This can be understood easily by examining the basic form of the algorithm displayed at the beginning of section 2.1. In the code, if a_{jk} (which is really l_{jk}) is zero, it is obviously unnecessary to execute the loop on i, since it has no effect.

In order to gain insight into the role that sparsity plays here, it is useful to introduce the notion of elimination trees for sparse Cholesky factors [1,6,8].

Consider the structure of the Cholesky factor L. For each column $j \leqslant n$, if column j has off-diagonal nonzeros, define $\gamma[j]$ by

$$\gamma[j] = \min\{ i \mid l_{ij} \neq 0, i > j \} \quad ;$$

that is, $\gamma[j]$ is the row subscript of the first off-diagonal nonzero in column j of L. For convenience, we assume that A is irreducible, so that $\gamma[j] > j$ for $1 \leqslant j < n$. We set $\gamma[n] = n$. If A is reducible, then it can be permuted into block diagonal form, having irreducible diagonal blocks. The ideas in this paper can then be applied to each of the blocks.

We now define an *elimination tree* corresponding to the structure of L. The tree has n nodes, labelled from 1 to n. For each j, if $\gamma[j] > j$, then node $\gamma[j]$ is the *parent* of node j in the elimination tree, and node j is one of possibly several *child* nodes of node $\gamma[j]$.

An example to illustrate the notion of elimination trees is provided by the structure of the Cholesky factor shown in Figure 1, with the associated elimination tree being shown in Figure 2.

The elimination tree provides precise information about the column dependencies. Specifically, $cdiv(i)$ cannot be executed until $cdiv(j)$ has completed for all descendant nodes j of node i.

Trees that are "short" and "wide" are typical of those generated by orderings that are good in the sense of yielding low fill and low operation counts. It should be clear that trees with such properties and their associated orderings lend themselves well to parallel computation.

Specifically, in the elimination tree, if node i and node j belong to the same level of the tree, the tasks $Tcol(i)$ and $Tcol(j)$ can be performed independently so long as the tasks associated with their descendant nodes have all been completed. In order to gain high processor utilization, it is therefore desirable to assign, if possible, nodes on the same level of the tree to different processors. An overall

$$L = \begin{pmatrix} x & & & & & \\ & x & & & & \\ x & & x & & & \\ & & x & x & & \\ x & x & x & x & x & \\ & x & & x & x & x \end{pmatrix}$$

Fig. 1: Structure of a Cholesky factor.

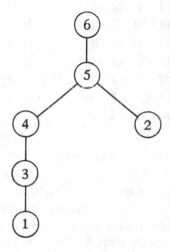

Fig. 2: The elimination tree associated with the Cholesky factor in Fig. 1.

task assignment scheme will then correspond to assigning the $Tcol(i)$ tasks to successive processors in a breadth-first bottom-up manner from nodes of the elimination tree.

Some of the practical fill-reducing orderings can be modified so that they order the nodes of the elimination tree in this desirable sequence. These include the recent implementation of the minimum degree ordering using multiple elimination [5] and a version of the nested dissection ordering [3]. In such cases, the task assignment scheme corresponds to the straightforward *wrap-around assignment*, where task $Tcol(i)$ will be assigned to the processor s, given by $s = (i-1) \bmod p$.

3. Case Study: k by k Regular Grid

3.1. Task Assignment: Subtree-to-Subcube

It is well known that a *nested dissection* ordering [4] is an optimal ordering of the k by k regular grid with respect to both operations and fills for the (serial) sparse Cholesky factorization of the corresponding sparse matrix. The number of multiplicative operations is $9.87 \, k^3$ and the number of nonzeros in the Cholesky factor is $7.75 \, k^2 \log_2 k$.

Assume that a given k by k grid is ordered by a nested dissection ordering. Consider the parallel solution of the associated sparse linear system on a hypercube using the task assignment strategy described in the previous section. Basically, tasks are assigned to the processors of the hypercube in a wrap-around manner, level-by-level starting from the bottom level of the elimination tree. An example of this assignment scheme for $k = 7$ and $p = 4$ is illustrated in Figure 3, where column numbers are shown on the left, and corresponding processor numbers are shown on the right.

1	25	2	43	3	28	4		0	0	1	2	2	3	3
17	26	18	44	19	29	20		0	1	1	3	2	0	3
5	27	6	45	7	30	8		0	2	1	0	2	1	3
37	38	39	46	40	41	42		0	1	2	1	3	0	1
9	31	10	47	11	34	12		0	2	1	2	2	1	3
21	32	22	48	23	35	24		0	3	1	3	2	2	3
13	33	14	49	15	36	16		0	0	1	0	2	3	3

Fig. 3: Nested dissection ordering and task assignment by wrapping.

This parallel sparse factorization scheme is shown in [2] to be quite effective in achieving load-balancing and communication-balancing. The amount of computation performed by each processor is roughly the same, and the amount of data transmitted and received by each is also about the same. It is important to note, however, that using this task assignment scheme, the $7.75 \, k^2 \log_2 k$ nonzeros have to be sent to p processors (actually $p-1$), so that the total amount of traffic is $O(p \, k^2 \log_2 k)$. In other words, even though balancing is achieved in communication, each processor still requires $O(k^2 \log_2 k)$ communication.

We now propose a task assignment strategy based on the idea of mapping a subtree of the elimination tree to a subcube of the hypercube. Figure 4 illustrates such a mapping on a 7 by 7 grid, using the same column numbering as in Figure 3.

In general, given the k by k grid problem and p processors, we assign (as indicated above) the first level of "+"-separator nodes to the p processors in a

0	0	0	2	1	1	1
0	0	0	3	1	1	1
0	0	0	0	1	1	1
0	1	2	1	3	0	1
2	2	2	2	3	3	3
2	2	2	3	3	3	3
2	2	2	0	3	3	3

Fig. 4: Subtree task assignment on 7 by 7 grid.

wrap around manner. In what follows, we refer to this as a *level-one separator*, and the original grid as a level-0 (sub)grid.

This level-1 separator creates four level-1 subgrids of size $k / 2$ by $k / 2$, each of which will be assigned to a disjoint set of $p / 4$ processors. In particular, if the hypercube being used is of dimension d, then the four sets of processors will be chosen to be the four $d - 2$ dimension subcubes of the hypercube. Each of these subgrids will be further subdivided by a level-2 "+"-shaped separator, whose nodes will be assigned to that grid's $p / 4$ processors. Each of the 16 level-2 subgrids of size $k / 4$ by $k / 4$ so created will be allocated to disjoint sets of $p / 16$ processors, each consisting of a $d - 4$ dimension subcube of the $d - 2$ dimension subcubes mentioned above. This process will continue until the number of subgrids at some level is equal to or exceeds p.

The reader should be aware that the processor allocation just described is slightly different from the one actually used in our experiments. Our description here employs "+"-shaped separators because they simplify what is already a fairly complicated analysis. For our experiments, however, we employ "line separators", which involve successive "halving" a subgrid at each stage. For this strategy, the dimension of the subcubes drops by only one at each stage.

3.2. Recursive Communication Analysis

In this section, we provide an analysis of the total amount of communication required using the subtree-to-subcube assignment described in the previous subsection. As before, let k be the size of the grid and p be the number of parallel processors available. Let $comm(k, p)$ be the total number of nonzeros that need to be communicated among the processors in the factorization of the associated sparse matrix. We give a bound for this communication in the following theorem.

Theorem 3.1: $comm(k, p) = O(p \, k^2)$.

Before presenting the proof, we need to prove several lemmas. In what follows, for convenience we implicitly assume that $p < k$, although the results can be obtained in a similar way if $p \geqslant k$.

A key fact in the proof of the theorem is that the processors that are assigned to a level-r subgrid G form a *subset* of the processors assigned to the level-r "+"-shaped separator that created G from a grid four times the size of G. Note that G may have other processors associated with segments of its boundary comprised of parts of level-s separators for $s < r$.

Now consider an i by i subgrid of the k by k grid. This subgrid is surrounded by nodes that may be residing in other processors.

Lemma 3.2:   The number of nonzeros from columns associated with the i by i subgrid that are required by nodes on the subgrid boundary (for column modifications) is bounded by $\frac{341}{12} i^2$.

Proof: For an i by i grid which is bordered on four sides, let $f(i, 4)$ be the number of nonzeros from this subgrid that are required by nodes on the four sides. Also define $f(i, 2)$ and $f(i, 1)$ to be the number when the subgrid is bordered on two and one side respectively. The meaning of these functions is depicted by the pictures in Figure 5, where the lines in the figure denote grid lines whose columns are involved in the function. It should be clear that $f(i,4)$ is the required nonzero count in the lemma.

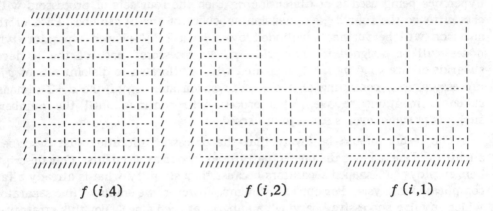

$$f(i,4) \qquad\qquad f(i,2) \qquad\qquad f(i,1)$$

Fig. 5: Illustration of the functions $f(i,j)$, $j=1,2,4$.

First note that the number of nonzeros in the columns associated with the first level of "+"-separator on this subgrid is bounded by

$$\frac{31}{4} i^2.$$

The recurrence relations on $f(i,*)$ can then be formulated as follows:

$$f(i,4) = \frac{31}{4} i^2 + 4 f(\frac{i}{2},2)$$

$$f(i,2) = \frac{31}{4} i^2 + f(\frac{i}{2},2) + 2 f(\frac{i}{2},1)$$

$$f(i,1) = \frac{31}{4} i^2 + 2 f(\frac{i}{2},1)$$

On solving them, we have

$$f(i,1) = \frac{31}{2} i^2,$$

$$f(i,2) = \frac{62}{3} i^2,$$

$$f(i,4) = \frac{341}{12} i^2.$$

Note that the result above provides only the volume of traffic that is needed by the columns residing on the boundary. If those columns are all contained in one processor, then the bound on the communication traffic associated with the boundary nodes will be $\mu = \frac{341}{12} i^2$. One the other hand, if the boundary nodes are distributed among t different processors, a bound on the total communication to the boundary nodes will be $t\,\mu$. (This bound can be sharpened somewhat, since in general not all processors will need all the data, but the bound used here is adequate for our purposes. In particular, sharpening it would change only the constant in the final result.)

Now consider an i by i subgrid (at level r, say) and suppose that q processors are assigned to the tasks associated with this subgrid. From the previous discussion we know that part of the boundary of this grid is comprised of a level r separator, and the processors associated with this separator form a superset of the q processors assigned to the subgrid. Furthermore, the size of this superset is bounded by $4q$.

Figure 6 attempts to depict the situation being described. The width of the lines depicting the separators is intended to denote set inclusion in the sense that a line of width w denotes columns whose processors form a subset of those associated with a line of width $w+1$. Thus, for example, the hashed subgrid would be assigned q processors which would form a subset of the $4q$ processors assigned to the "+"-shaped separator marked "S".

We assume for the moment that the volume of communication σ from the q grid processors to *other* processors associated with the boundary nodes is *known*. The following lemma provides a bound, which we denote by $traffic(i,q)$, for the total *additional* traffic among the q processors associated with this i by i grid. Thus the *total* traffic associated with the grid is $\sigma + traffic(i,q)$.

Lemma 3.3: $traffic(i,q) < 152 \, q \, i^2$.

Proof: We claim that

$$traffic(i,q) \leqslant \frac{341}{3} q \, i^2 + 4 \, traffic(\frac{i}{2}, \frac{q}{4}).$$

To see this, first note that by Lemma 3.2, we need to send at most $\frac{341}{12} i^2$ nonzeros to the $4q$ superset processors on the boundary.

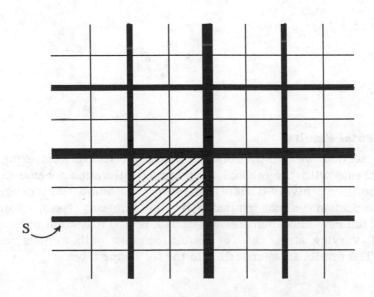

Fig. 6: Illustration of the allocation of processors.

Now consider the problem as partitioned into four parts. Each part has $q/4$ processors assigned to it, and the number of nonzeros sent from this $i/2$ by $i/2$ subregion to its q superset processors is $traffic(\frac{i}{2}, \frac{q}{4})$. Thus, we obtain the desired recurrence relation and

$$traffic(i, q) \leqslant \frac{341}{3} q \, i^2 (1 + \frac{1}{4} + \frac{1}{4^2} + \cdots)$$

$$< 152 \, q \, i^2.$$

It is important to note in the proof above that the analysis does indeed account for all of the traffic associated with the grid. At any given level t in the recursion, the subgrid under consideration is surrounded by a boundary that consists of parts of separators that are either at level r (the boundary of the original i by i grid), at level s where $r < s < t$, or at level t. It is sufficient to consider only the traffic to the processors associated with the level t part since traffic to processors associated with other nodes has already been accounted for at lower levels of recursion, or is incorporated into σ.

Proof of Theorem 3.1:

Consider the given k by k grid and p processors. The first level of "+"-separator nodes are assigned to the p processors. There are at most $\frac{31}{4} i^2$ nonzeros associated with this separator and they have to be sent to at most p processors (actually $p-1$). Now we have four subgrids of size $i/2$. Each will be assigned $p/4$ processors and the boundary nodes are located in at most p processors. Therefore,

$$comm(k, p) \leqslant \frac{31}{4} p \, k^2 + 4 \, traffic(\frac{k}{2}, \frac{p}{4}).$$

Applying Lemma 3.3, we have

$$comm(k, p) \leqslant \frac{183}{4} p \, k^2.$$

---

4. Experimental Results

In this section we present some experimental results comparing the new allocation scheme with the original wrap-around allocation scheme used in [2]. Our first experiments involved simply computing the number of messages and the total communication volume generated by the Cholesky factorization for the original and the new allocation scheme, using a nested dissection ordering on grid problems of varying sizes, and for multiprocessors with various numbers of processors. The results are summarized in the following table.

Communication counts and volume					
k	p	wrap mapping		subtree mapping		percentage reduced (in volume)
		count	volume	count	volume	
31	4	2829	49802	1127	28601	42.6
63	4	11745	285326	3031	134049	53.0
31	8	5786	108947	2653	68323	37.3
63	8	24460	638204	7553	333253	47.8
31	16	9461	197648	4949	131979	33.2
63	16	41184	1219769	15111	697088	42.9

Table 1. Communication counts and volume for the two allocations.

The results in the table above confirm that the new processor allocation scheme does indeed lead to significant savings in communication volume and numbers of messages. Note that for fixed p, the improvement (in terms of communication volume) over the original wrap mapping scheme increases with n. This is because the subgrid assigned to a single processor (in the new scheme) is larger for larger n and the number of columns in this subgrid which are required by other processors is smaller compared to the number of columns in the subgrid. On the other hand, for fixed n, the improvement (again in terms of communication volume) over the original wrap mapping scheme decreases with p. This is due to the fact that the subgrid assigned to a processor in the new scheme becomes smaller as p increases.

Wrap mapping vs Subtree mapping. ($k = 15$, $n = 225$) (Execution times in seconds.)			
p	wrap	subtree	% reduced
1	3.90	3.90	0.0
8	1.97	1.67	15.7
16	1.79	1.43	20.4
32	1.57	1.38	12.1
64	1.58	1.48	6.6

Wrap mapping vs Subtree mapping. ($k = 31$, $n = 961$) (Execution times in seconds.)			
p	wrap	subtree	% reduced
8	11.29	8.64	23.5
16	10.32	6.96	32.6
32	8.62	6.01	30.2
64	6.85	5.41	21.0

Wrap mapping vs Subtree mapping. ($k = 63$, $n = 3969$) (Execution times in seconds.)			
p	wrap	subtree	% reduced
16	62.34	42.17	32.4
32	51.17	32.63	36.2
64	38.58	26.68	30.8

Table 2. Improvement in execution time for the Cholesky factorization.

In Table 2, timing results for Cholesky factorization are presented for various grid problems run on an Intel iPSC multiprocessor, using various numbers of processors. Again we observe that the improvement increases as n increases for fixed p. It is interesting to note that as p increases for fixed n, the improvement shows a peak. It is not surprising that the improvement trends down as p becomes large, since for large enough p, there is no difference between the two allocation schemes. However, the initial upward trend in the improvement is still being studied. A final comment is that the grid problems used in the experiments are not large enough for the improvements using the new mapping scheme to be significant. This is because the last subgrid that is assigned to a single processor will be relatively small. For large problems, we expect the improvements in execution times to be big.

5. References

[1] I. S. Duff and J. R. Reid, *"The multifrontal solution of indefinite sparse symmetric linear equations"*, ACM Trans. on Math. Software, 9 (1983), pp.302–325.

[2] J. A. George, M. T. Heath, J. W-H. Liu, E. G-Y. Ng, *"Sparse Cholesky factorization on a local-memory multiprocessor"*, Technical report ORNL/TM-9962, Oak Ridge National Laboratory, Oak Ridge, Tennessee (1986).

[3] J.A. George and J.W-H. Liu, *"An automatic nested dissection algorithm for irregular finite element problems"*, SIAM J. Numer. Anal., 15 (1978) pp.1053–1069.

[4] J. A. George and J. W-H. Liu, *Computer Solution of Large Sparse Positive Definite Systems*, Prentice-Hall, Englewood Cliffs, NJ, 1981.

[5] J. W-H. Liu, *"Modification of the minimum-degree algorithm by multiple elimination"*, ACM Trans. Math. Software, 11 (1985), pp.141–153.

[6] J. W-H. Liu, *"A compact row storage scheme for sparse Cholesky factors using elimination trees"*, ACM Trans. on Math. Software (1986). (To appear.)

[7] J. W-H. Liu, *"Computational models and task scheduling for parallel sparse Cholesky factorization"*, Parallel Computing, 3 (1986), pp. 327–342.

[8] R. S. Schreiber, *"A new implementation of Gaussian elimination"*, ACM Trans. on Math. Software, 8 (1982), pp. 256–276.

Orthogonal Factorization on a Distributed Memory Multiprocessor

ALEX POTHEN*, SOMESH JHA* AND UDAYA VEMULAPATI*

Abstract

We design and analyze algorithms for computing the orthogonal factorization on a distributed memory multiprocessor. The factorization is computed by means of a sequence of Givens rotations. The freedom available in the order in which rotations are applied is used to design different algorithms. Three Givens sequences are explored: the standard Givens sequence, the greedy Givens sequence, and recursive fine partition. Analysis of the arithmetic and communication complexity shows that the latter two algorithms have promise.

1 Introduction

We design and analyze algorithms for computing the orthogonal factorization of an $M \times N$ matrix A on a distributed memory multiprocessor. The matrix A is factored as $A = QR$, where Q is an orthogonal matrix, and R is upper trapezoidal. The orthogonal matrix Q is computed as a product of a sequence of Givens rotations. We consider only Givens sequences in which zeros once created in the matrix are preserved during the rest of the factorization.

Givens sequences are promising in this context, since disjoint rotations can potentially be computed concurrently. There is a great deal of freedom in the order in which the Givens rotations in a sequence are applied to the matrix. This freedom can be exploited to design algorithms which differ in processor interconnection requirements, data mapping, and arithmetic and communication complexity. We study three different Givens sequences:

- The standard Givens sequence (sgs), has been discussed by Gentleman [4], who showed that the grouping of rotations in this sequence led to tighter error bounds, and by Sameh and Kuck [6], who designed a parallel orthogonalization algorithm for SIMD machines using this sequence.

---

* The Pennsylvania State University, University Park, PA 16802.

- The greedy Givens sequence (ggs) is inspired by a greedy algorithm to compute the orthogonal factorization studied by Modi and Clarke [5], and by Cosnard, Robert, and Muller [2]. In the greedy algorithm, the rotations are organized into groups such that as many disjoint rotations as possible are included in each group. In the first group, for instance, $\lfloor M/2 \rfloor$ rotations can be included. However, data mapping considerations preclude the concurrent computation of all the rotations in a group by processors in a distributed architecture.

  In the ggs, each processor introduces as many zeros as possible into the submatrix it holds without communicating with another processor. The remaining nonzeros in a column are eliminated by cooperating processors in a recursive elimination phase. The algorithm described in this section is a variant of an algorithm designed and implemented by Chamberlain and Powell [1].

- In the recursive fine partition sequence (rfp), the matrix is partitioned into submatrices, rather than rows as in sgs and ggs. These submatrices are assigned to the processors. Each processor introduces zeros into a column block it holds to make it upper trapezoidal. The transformation of a column block is completed by recursive elimination, when processors cooperate to eliminate the residual upper triangular matrices on a column block.

We assume that M, N are much greater than the number of processors P, and consider the design of medium-grain algorithms. For arithmetic, we assume that the time required for a flop is τ. For communicating m words from one processor to another, we assume that time $m\lambda + \beta$ is required, where β is the start-up time, and λ is the time needed to transfer a word. All logarithms are computed with base 2.

$$
\begin{array}{cccc}
\times & & & \\
7 & \times & & \\
6 & 8 & \times & \\
5 & 7 & 9 & \times \\
4 & 6 & 8 & 10 \\
3 & 5 & 7 & 9 \\
2 & 4 & 6 & 8 \\
1 & 3 & 5 & 7 \\
\end{array}
$$

Figure 1: The standard Givens sequence for a matrix.

2   The standard Givens sequence

2.1   Introduction

In sgs, an element a_{ij} is annihilated by a rotation between rows i and $i-1$; the tuple (i, j) will denote this rotation. The sequence is illustrated for an 8×4 matrix in figure 1. An integer k in place of a matrix element indicates that the element is zeroed by a rotation in the k-th group. There are $M + N - 2$ groups for an $M \times N$ matrix.

The entire sequence can be divided into two phases: an *increasing* phase when the number of rotations in successive groups increases (more precisely, does not decrease), and a *decreasing* phase when the number of rotations in successive groups decreases. Groups 1 through 7 belong to the increasing phase, and groups 8, 9, and 10 to the decreasing phase for the matrix illustrated.

To implement sgs, we use a ring of P processors numbered from 0 to $P - 1$. The ring topology is obtained by finding a Hamilton cycle in the hypercube by means of binary reflected Gray codes. The *predecessor* of processor k is $k - 1 \bmod P$, and its *successor* is $k + 1 \bmod P$.

The rows of the matrix are numbered 1 to M. The matrix is mapped by rows onto the processors by wrapping; row M is mapped onto processor 0, row $M - 1$ to processor 1, etc. Each processor has approximately $\lceil \frac{M}{P} \rceil$ rows. The *top row* on a processor is the lowest numbered row it holds, and the *bottom row* is its highest numbered row.

2.2   The algorithm

Zeros are introduced into the matrix from bottom to top, and from left to right. To zero an element in row i, a processor receives row $i - 1$ from its successor, computes the rotation, and updates row i. Concurrently, its successor receives row i, computes the rotation, and updates row $i - 1$. The processors which communicate with each other are neighbors in the hypercube. The node program on a processor is shown in figure 2.

The variable *col* corresponds to the column position of row i in which a zero is introduced by the Givens rotation. Since zeros are introduced from left to right in a row, the value of *col* increases from 1 to the column position of the last zero.

The algorithm uses the concept of *active* rows. If rotation $(i, 1)$ belongs to group k, then row i becomes active only when the processor it is on has completed all rotations in groups previous to k. Thus a row becomes active when a zero can be introduced in

```
repeat as long as active rows exist
   for each active row i
      1.   { zero (i + 1, col) }
           send row i to predecessor;
           receive row i + 1 from predecessor;
           update row i;
      2.   { zero (i, col) }
           send row i to successor;
           receive row i − 1 from successor;
           update row i;
   rof
end
```

Figure 2: The sgs algorithm.

its first column by a rotation in the group currently executed by a processor. Once a row is made active, it remains so till the row is completely processed.

Initially, the only active row on a processor is its bottom row. From the definition of the sgs, rotations to zero elements $(i, j + 1)$ and $(i - 2j, 1)$ belong to the same group. Since the next highest numbered row on a processor holding row i is $i - P$, after $\lceil \frac{P}{2} \rceil$ zeros have been introduced in row i, row $i - P$ is made active.

During each iteration of the **repeat** loop, the node program makes new rows active, and updates the count of the number of its active rows. In the increasing phase, this number increases. Once the top row has been completely processed, the processor enters the decreasing phase, and this number starts decreasing. When it becomes zero, the node program terminates. These details are not shown in figure 2.

For each row it holds, a processor keeps track of the next column in which a zero is to be introduced. It also keeps track of the column up to which its predecessor has zeroed, using this row. This information is readily available from the number of times it sends this row to its predecessor. Hence a processor can infer the status of its predecessor and successor from the rows sent and received. Thus the only messages required in the algorithm are the rows, and no explicit synchronization messages are necessary. Hence, at a given instant, different processors may be executing rotations belonging to different groups.

2.3   Complexity

We bound the time required for a group of rotations in the sgs sequence, and then multiply the resulting time by the number of groups in the sequence. This estimate will be an upper bound on the complexity of the algorithm, since in the distributed implementation we have described, computations in different groups can overlap.

The maximum number of rotations in a group is N, one in each column. Hence the number of rows in a group that need to be updated by a processor is no more than $X \equiv \lceil \frac{2N}{P} \rceil$. When a zero is introduced in the j-th column, there are $N - j$ elements in the row that need to be updated. Let $\pi \equiv \frac{P}{2}$. Since the rows are wrapped onto the processors, the number of elements that a processor updates in a group is bounded by

$$\nu \equiv \quad N + (N - \pi) + (N - 2\pi) + \cdots + (N - (X-1)\pi)$$
$$= NX - \frac{\pi}{2}X(X-1).$$

Simplifying, we get $\nu = \frac{N^2}{P} + \frac{N}{2}$. The number ν is also an upper bound on the number of elements a processor needs to communicate to its neighbor for the rotations in a group.

Updating a row segment of j elements requires $2j\tau$ time ($2j$ multiplications and j additions) on a processor. Each group hence takes time less than $2\nu\tau$. since there are $M + N - 2$ groups in the algorithm, the arithmetic time is bounded by $2\nu(M+N-2)\tau$. This is approximately $\frac{2N^2}{P}(M + N - 2)\tau$.

The communication time of a group is proportional to the number of elements communicated by a processor, ν. By similar reasoning, the communication time is $\frac{2N^2}{P}(M + N - 2)\lambda + \frac{2N}{P}(M + N - 2)\beta$.

For a square matrix of order N, a similar analysis yields arithmetic time to be $\frac{5N^3}{3P}\tau$, and the communication time to be $\frac{5N^3}{3P}\lambda + \frac{N^2}{P}\beta$. Note that optimally the coefficient of the leading term should be 4/3, so that there is some degradation of performance.

3   The greedy Givens sequence

3.1   Introduction

In this sequence, the matrix is partitioned by rows and mapped onto the processors. In each column of the submatrix it holds, a processor introduces zeros until only one nonzero remains. Processors cooperate pairwise, in a recursive elimination phase, to zero the remaining elements in a column. Communications between processors is required only in this second phase, and hence the communication cost in this sequence is low.

This sequence can be implemented on differing processor architectures such as a binary tree or ring. We describe the ring implementation for two reasons: The recursive elimination phase is used in the rfp algorithm also, and the ggs ring algorithm provides a simpler setting for its description. Also, there are close connections between the ggs ring and rfp algorithms.

A minor variant of the ggs ring algorithm described here has been implemented on a six dimensional hypercube by Chamberlain and Powell [1] recently. They have incorporated several features in their algorithm to optimize running time. Their results clearly demonstrate the usefulness of distributed memory multiprocessors in the computation of orthogonal factorization.

As in sgs, a ring of P processors numbered from 0 to $P - 1$ is used. The rows of the matrix are numbered from 0 to $M - 1$. The first N rows are wrapped onto the processors, such that row 0 is on processor 0, row 1 on processor 1, etc. The rest of the $M - N$ rows can be equally distributed among the processors in any manner.

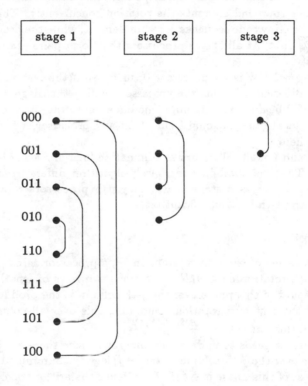

Figure 3: The recursive elimination phase.

3.2   The algorithm

Zeros are introduced into the submatrix on a processor from bottom to top, and from left to right. A column of the matrix is transformed into a column of a triangular matrix by means of two phases: an internal rotations phase (IP), and a recursive elimination phase (RP).

Consider the transformation of the j-th column of the matrix. Before this column can be completely transformed, the transformation of the previous column $j - 1$ has to be completed. Rows 0, ..., $j - 1$ have also been completely processed by now, and only the remaining rows need to be updated. Without loss of generality, let the diagonal row j be on processor 0. The *top row* on a processor at this stage is its lowest numbered row which is numbered greater than or equal to j.

In IP, each processor zeros elements in the j-th column by using the rows it holds. This phase ends when the only nonzero in the j-th column is on the top row.

In RP, processors cooperate to eliminate the rest of the nonzeros in column j. This phase is divided into $\log P$ stages. In each stage, pairs of processors exchange their top rows to zero an element on one of them. In $\log P$ stages, all the nonzeros below the diagonal row j will be eliminated.

Processor pairing in RP is shown in figure 3. The first column in the figure shows the processor id's on a ring of 8 processors, when the binary reflected Gray code is used to embed the ring. In the k-th stage of this phase, processors that differ in id's in the k-th most significant bit pair up to perform the elimination. Processors in a pair exchange their rows and compute the rotation concurrently. The processor that appears later in the Gray code sequence zeros its element, while the processor appearing earlier updates its row. At all stages processors that form pairs are neighbors on the hypercube.

Since the diagonal row is on processor 0, in figure 3 the last nonzero is held by processor 0. For different columns, the processor holding the diagonal row and hence the last nonzero will be different. A simple modification to the survival strategy shown in the figure can locate the diagonal element on any processor, which, however, will not be discussed here.

Chamberlain and Powell call recursive elimination 'merging according to a (binary) tree structure'. The Chamberlain and Powell algorithm differs from that described above only in that in the k-th stage of RP, they pair processors which differ in their processor id's in the k-th least significant bit.

3.3   Complexity

Consider the processing of the j-th column. In IP, a processor zeros $\lceil (M - j)/P \rceil - 1$ elements, and each rotation costs $4(N - j)\tau$ since two rows of length $N - j$ need to be updated. The cost of this phase over the j-th column is the product of the number of rotations and the cost of a rotation. Summing this over all columns, we get the arithmetic cost of this phase to be $\frac{2N^2(M-N/3)}{P}\tau$.

In RP, a processor needs to update only one row. Since there are $\log P$ stages, the cost of this phase over the j-th column is $2(N - j)\log P\,\tau$. Summing over all columns, the arithmetic cost of this phase is $N^2 \log P\,\tau$. Hence the arithmetic complexity of the ggs algorithm is the complexity of IP.

During recursive elimination on the j-th column, the cost of sending a row is $(N - j)\lambda + \beta$. This cost multiplied by the $\log P$ stages is the cost of this phase for the j-th column. Summed over all columns, we obtain the communication complexity to be

$$\frac{N^2}{2}\log P\,\lambda + N \log P\,\beta.$$

4   The recursive fine partition sequence

4.1   Introduction

For ease of exposition, we consider a square matrix of order N. A $p \times p$ processor grid is employed, and the grid is embedded in the hypercube in the usual manner by means of binary reflected Gray codes. The processors form a ring along each column and row of the grid. Also, each row and column of processors is a subcube of dimension $\log p$. We will denote by p_{ij} a processor on the the i-th row and j-th column of the grid, where $0 \leq i, j \leq p - 1$. The total number of processors is $p^2 \equiv P$.

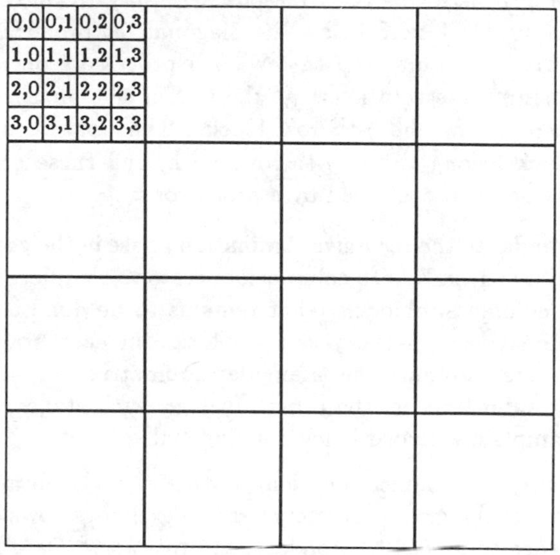

0,0	0,1	0,2	0,3
1,0	1,1	1,2	1,3
2,0	2,1	2,2	2,3
3,0	3,1	3,2	3,3

Figure 4: The fine partition of a matrix.

The matrix is coarsely divided into p *column blocks* and p *row blocks*, which partitions A into p^2 *coarse submatrices*, each square of order N/p. These column and row blocks are numbered from 0 to $p - 1$. Each coarse submatrix is further divided into p *column subblocks* and p *row subblocks* which partitions it into p^2 *fine submatrices*. Each fine submatrix is thus square of order $N/p^2 \equiv n$. Within each coarse submatrix, denote by (i, j) the fine submatrix formed by the i-th row subblock and j-th column subblock, where $0 \leq i, j \leq p - 1$. The fine submatrix (i, j) is assigned to the processor p_{ij}. This partitioning and mapping are illustrated in figure 4.

One could avoid fine partitioning, and map the p^2 coarse submatrices onto the processor grid; we call this coarse partitioning. The drawback to this simpler mapping is that a row and column of processors become idle as each column block is transformed. This load imbalance leads to greater computational costs. However, coarse mapping can lead to an $O(N \log^2 N)$ algorithm for orthogonal factorization, if $P = N/k$, where k is a constant of order 1.

4.2   The algorithm

The columns of the matrix are transformed into columns of a triangular matrix from left to right. Zeros are introduced into the lower triangle of column blocks in the order $0, \ldots, p - 1$. Within each column block, zeros are introduced into the lower triangle of column subblocks also in the order $0, \ldots, p - 1$.

Assume that the column blocks $0, \ldots, j - 1$ have been transformed; at this stage, the row blocks $0, \ldots, j - 1$ have been completely processed, and only the remaining row blocks need to be updated. Each processor now holds a submatrix of order $(p - j)n$ that requires further transformation.

We describe how the algorithm transforms the zeroth column subblock of the column block j. Processors $\{p_{i,0} : i = 1, \ldots, p - 1\}$ on the zeroth column of the grid hold the submatrices of this column subblock. The algorithm has two phases: a diagonalization phase (DP), and a recursive elimination phase (RP).

DP Each processor $p_{i,0}$ performs the rotations necessary to make its portion of the zeroth column subblock zero below the diagonal. It broadcasts these rotations to the other processors on the i-th row. All processors on a row update their submatrices using these rotations. At the end of this phase, the zeroth column subblock is zero below the j-th row block. The nonzero submatrices of this column subblock belong to the j-th row block, and these are upper triangular submatrices of order n, each held by a processor $p_{i,0}$.

RP This phase is similar to the recursive elimination phase in the ggs algorithm. In this phase, processors on the zeroth column cooperate to complete the transformation of the zeroth column subblock. What remains to be done is the zeroing of the triangular submatrices on the j-th row block. In each stage of this phase, a pair of processors eliminate the triangular submatrix on one of them by using the triangular submatrix on the other. In $\log p$ such stages, the zeroth column subblock is completely zeroed below its diagonal.

This phase requires communication along both row and column directions in the grid. Along a column of the grid, processors need to exchange rows of the submatrices, and along a row, processors need to broadcast the rotations. Care has to be exercised in implementing row exchange along the column direction. Call the processor whose submatrix gets zeroed, the *zeroing processor*, and the other, the *updating processor*.

The two processors initially exchange the top rows of their submatrices. Both processors compute the rotation to zero the element in the first column of the zeroing processor's top row, and each processor updates its row. Now the zeroing processor can zero its diagonal elements. Next, the updating processor sends its second row, while the zeroing processor sends its (modified) first row. The latter can now zero the element in the second column of its top row, and afterwards, zero its first superdiagonal. In the k-th such exchange, the zeroing processor sends its top row, while the updating processor sends its k-th row. Other processors in these rows need to exchange the same sets of rows to update their submatrices.

4.3   Complexity

We analyze the complexity of the diagonalization and recursive elimination phases separately. We compute the cost of each phase on a column subblock of the the j-th column block, and then sum over all column subblocks in a column block, and then over all column blocks, to get the complexity of the phase over the entire algorithm.

A processor computes $(p - j)n^2 - n^2/2$ rotations to transform a column subblock of the j-th column block. Processors that update using these rotations have two rows of length $(p - j)n$ each to update. The arithmetic for DP costs

$$\{4(p - j)n\tau\}\{(p - j - 1/2)n^2\}.$$

Summing this over the column subblocks and the column blocks, we obtain the arithmetic complexity of DP to be $\frac{4}{3}p^4 n^3 \tau + 2p^3 n^2 \tau$.

In each stage of RP, the zeroing processor computes $n^2/2$ rotations, and each rotation involves two rows of length $(p - j)n$ each. The arithmetic cost of a stage of RP is then $\frac{n^2}{2}(4(p - j)n\tau)$. Multiplying by $\log p$ stages, we obtain the cost of RP over a column subblock, and summing over column subblocks and column blocks, we get the arithmetic complexity of RP to be $p^3 \log p \, n^3 \tau$.

The arithmetic complexity of the algorithm is the sum of the complexities of DP and RP. Using $n = N/P$, and $P = p^2$, we get this to be

$$\frac{4N^3}{3P}\tau + \frac{N^3 \log P}{2P^{3/2}}\tau.$$

The analysis of communication complexity follows along similar lines. In DP, a processor needs to broadcast $(p - j - 1/2)n^2$ rotations while transforming a column subblock of the j-th column block; this costs $2(p-j)\log p \, n^2 \lambda + \log p \, \beta$. After the sums over the subblocks and blocks, this phase is found to cost $p^3 \log p \, n^2 \lambda + p^2 \log p \, \beta$.

Each stage of RP requires a processor to broadcast $n^2/2$ rotations along a row, and costs $n^2 \log p \, \lambda + n \log p \, \beta$. Multiplying this cost by $\log p$, we get the cost over a subblock. Multiplying by p^2 gives the cost over all subblocks. Hence the communication complexity of RP is $p^2 \log^2 p \, n^2 \lambda + p^2 \log^2 p \, n\beta$.

The communication complexity of the algorithm is hence

$$\frac{N^2}{\sqrt{P}}\lambda + \frac{N^2 \log^2 P}{4P}\lambda + \frac{N \log^2 P}{4}\beta.$$

4.4 Rectangular matrices

We sketch the modifications necessary for an $M \times N$ matrix. The submatrix formed by the first N rows are mapped as in the square case. The submatrix formed by the remaining $M - N$ rows are partitioned into column subblocks as before, but partitioned into p row blocks of $(M - N)/p$ rows each. The resulting $(M - N)/p \times N/p^2$ submatrices are mapped on the processors. The only change in the algorithm is in the diagonalization phase, when each processor has a larger submatrix to work with. The complexity of the algorithm is shown in table 1.

5 Conclusions

The complexity of the three algorithms is tabulated in table 1. For each algorithm, the 'A' row shows the arithmetic complexity, and the 'C' row, the communication complexity. Only leading terms are shown.

The arithmetic costs of the ggs and rfp algorithms are optimal in the leading term, while the sgs algorithm is not. The high communication cost in the sgs algorithm is caused by a rotation (i, j) being computed between rows i and $i - 1$. Relaxing this requirement brings the costs down by an order of magnitude in the ggs and rfp algorithms.

The M dependence in the communication complexity of the rfp algorithm is because we used a square grid. With a rectangular grid, it is possible to change the leading term to $N^2/2\sqrt{P}$. Partitioning by submatrices distributes the communications over the processors better, as evidenced by the $\sqrt{P}$ term in the denominator in the rfp algorithm.

We implemented the sgs, ggs, and a variant of the rfp algorithm, the recursive coarse partition algorithm, on a hypercube simulator developed by Dunigan [3] at Oak Ridge National Laboratory. The code was written in C. The timing results we obtained on random matrices of order up to 128 were in agreement with the analysis here. We are currently engaged in porting these algorithms to a hypercube, and in gathering computational results.

Algorithm		Complexity
sgs; ring;	A	$\frac{2N^2}{P}(M + N - 2)\tau$
wrap rows	C	$\frac{2N^2}{P}(M + N - 2)\lambda + \frac{2N}{P}(M + N - 2)\beta$
ggs; ring;	A	$\frac{2N^2}{P}(M - N/3)\tau$
wrap first N rows	C	$\frac{N^2}{2}\log P\,\lambda + N\log P\,\beta$
rfp; square grid;	A	$\frac{2N^2}{P}(M - N/3)\tau$
wrap blocks	C	$\frac{(2M-N)N}{2\sqrt{P}}\log P\,\lambda + \frac{N}{4}\log^2 P\,\beta$

Table 1: Algorithms and their complexity.

We have explored the algorithmic possibilities that result from different Givens sequences. Our analysis indicates that both the ggs and rfp algorithms are promising. Our description of the algorithms has been at a fairly high level; in efficiently implementing these, several choices in computational strategy had to be made. These will be described together with our results in a future report.

References

[1] R. M. Chamberlain and M. J. D. Powell, QR factorization for linear least squares problems on the hypercube, Tech. Report CCS 86/10, Chr. Michelsen Institute, Bergen, Norway, July 1986.

[2] M. Cosnard, J. -M. Muller, and Y. Robert, Parallel QR decomposition of a rectangular matrix, *Num. Math.*, **48** (1986), pp. 239–249.

[3] T. H. Dunigan, A message passing multiprocessor simulator, Tech. Report 9966, Oak Ridge National Lab., Oak Ridge, TN, May 1986.

[4] W. M. Gentleman, Error analysis of QR decomposition by Givens transformations, *Linear Algebra and Appl.*, **10** (1975), pp. 189–197.

[5] J. J. Modi and M. R. B. Clarke, An alternative Givens ordering, *Num. Math.*, **43** (1984), pp. 83–90.

[6] A. H. Sameh and D. J. Kuck, On stable parallel linear system solvers, *J. ACM*, **25** (1978), pp. 81–91.

Fast Parallel Algorithms for the Moore-Penrose Pseudo-Inverse

MAURICE W. BENSON* AND PAUL O. FREDERICKSON†

Abstract.

We employ the concept of an approximate pseudo-inverse (API) of a singular linear operator A to construct algorithms that yield the Moore-Penrose pseudo-inverse solution $x^+ = A^+y$ to the singular system $Ax = y$. Such an algorithm is a nonmatrix representation of the Moore-Penrose pseudo-inverse A^+ of A. We are particularly interested in fast algorithms [executable in $O(n)$ operations] that are fully efficient on parallel computers. One result presented concerns the construction of APIs for consistent problems and is applied to the two-dimensional free-boundary spline interpolation problem. For this problem, the conjugate gradient algorithm, preconditioned with an API, proves to be very effective. The V-cycle multigrid algorithm FAPIN is shown to be an API if the smoother satisfies a certain condition and proves to be very effective for Poisson's problem on a two-torus. We have demonstrated our algorithms for n close to one million on the iPSC hypercube at Christian Michelsen Institute, Bergen.

1. Introduction

If the large sparse linear operator $A: \mathcal{X} \to \mathcal{Y}$ is singular, then the linear system

$$Ax = y \tag{1}$$

may have no solution, which is the case when $y \notin \mathcal{R}(A)$. In this situation, our task is often to find a *best approximate solution*, or a *least squares fit* to the data y, which is any x such that $\| y - Ax \|$ is minimized. When $\mathcal{X}$ and $\mathcal{Y}$ are finite dimensional Hilbert spaces, our primary concern in numerical computation, not only do such best approximate solutions

---

* *Department of Mathematical Sciences, Lakehead University, Thunder Bay, Canada.*

† *Los Alamos National Laboratory, Los Alamos, New Mexico.*

x always exist, but there is a unique best approximate solution of minimum norm. This we denote x^+ and refer to as the Moore-Penrose solution of equation (1). The operator $A^+ : Y \to X : y \mapsto x^+$ turns out to be linear and is called the Moore-Penrose pseudo-inverse of A. For more details see Moore [14], Penrose [15], or Ben-Israel and Greville [1].

Our task is to derive fast parallel algorithms for A^+, algorithms which will allow us to evaluate $x^+ = A^+ y$ as efficiently as possible on a parallel computer. Our approach is to define an *approximate* pseudo-inverse to A and show that these can sometimes be constructed efficiently on a parallel computer. When they can, they provide an effective construction of the exact Moore-Penrose pseudo-inverse A^+.

Definition 1. *The linear operator $Z : Y \to X$ is an ϵ-approximate pseudo-inverse (ϵ-API) of the linear operator $A : X \to Y$ if $\epsilon < 1$ and*

$$\| (Z - ZAZ)v \| \le \epsilon \| Zv \| \quad \forall v \in Y , \qquad \mathcal{N}(Z) \perp \mathcal{R}(A) , \text{ and } \mathcal{R}(Z) \perp \mathcal{N}(A) . \quad (2)$$

Using the concept of an ϵ-API, we can state a simple defect correction (DC) algorithm for the solution of (1) as the following:

---

algorithm API-DC

$$r^n = y - Ax^n, \quad x^{n+1} = x^n + Zr^n$$

Theorem 1. *If Z is an $\epsilon-$ approximate pseudo-inverse of A, then algorithm API-DC converges at the geometric rate ϵ, for any initial approximation x^0, to an x such that $\| y - Ax \|$ is minimized. If $x^0 = 0$, then x is the Moore-Penrose pseudo-inverse solution $x^+ = A^+ y$.*

A detailed proof may be found in Frederickson and Benson [9]. For a fuller discussion of the iterative solution of singular systems, see Ben-Israel and Greville [1] and Keller [12]. Our primary interest in this paper is to show that there are highly parallel algorithms which implement the concept of an API and therefore, through Theorem 1, provide a fast representation of A^+. In the next section, we show that the orthogonality condition in X is handled easily for consistent systems. In Section 3, we show that a preconditioned conjugate gradient algorithm can be an effective representation of A^+ if an API is used as a preconditioner. Phrased another way, CG-acceleration of the API–DC algorithm is possible under certain conditions. We demonstrate this on a rather large singular problem, one of dimension 500,000 and with a null space of dimension 3000, on an iPSC hypercube. For details see Section 5. In Section 4, we show that the multigrid algorithm FAPIN (fast approximate pseudo-inverse) can provide an effective representation of an API on a hypercube.

2. Construction of APIs in the Consistent Case

Consistent, but underdetermined, linear systems are particularly easy to handle because we are able to concentrate on the inequality in the definition of API and ignore the orthogonality conditions.

Theorem 2. *If the linear operator $A : X \to Y$ is onto, that is $R(A) = Y$, and the linear operator $B : Y \to X$ satisfies the inequality*

$$\| x - BAx \| \le (\sqrt{1 + \epsilon} - 1) \| x \| \qquad \forall x \perp N(A) \tag{3}$$

for some $\epsilon < 1$, then $Z = A^* B^* B$ is an $\epsilon - API$ of A.

Proof: $R(Z) \perp N(A)$ follows from the fact that $R(Z) = R(A^*)$. For any $x \perp N(A)$

$$\| (I - A^* B^* BA)x \| = \| (I - (I - (I - A^* B^*))(I - (I - BA)))x \|$$

$$\le \| (I - A^* B^*)x \| + \| (I - BA)x \| + \| (I - A^* B^*)(I - BA)x \| \le \epsilon \| x \|.$$

Since $R(A) = Y$, $N(Z) \subset R(A)$. Thus if $N(Z) \ne 0$, we can find $x \in X$ such that $ZAx = 0$, violating the inequality. ∎

As demonstrated on the spline interpolation problem below, the above approach can provide an effective solution method. For related results, see Björck and Elfving[4] or Elfving [6], where a symmetric successive overrelaxation technique is used as a preconditioner for the conjugate gradient method applied to $AA^* z = y$.

3. Approximate Inverses

Suppose now that the linear spaces X and Y have bases $\{x^i, i \in I\}$ and $\{y^j, j \in J\}$, with respect to which the linear operator A has a sparse matrix representation. In some cases, we are able to construct an API that also has a sparse matrix representation, perhaps with the same sparsity as A^*. One way to do this generalizes the concept of an LSQ approximate inverse [2,3] that has proven quite effective for nonsingular linear systems.

Definition 2. *The LSQ approximate pseudo-inverse of A is the operator $Z = \Pi_X B \Pi_Y$, where Π_X projects onto $N^\perp(A)$, Π_Y projects onto $R(A)$, and B minimizes the Frobenius norm*

$$\| I - BA \|_F \tag{4}$$

subject to the constraint that B have the same graph (non-zero structure) as A^*.

For example, the bicubic spline interpolation operator on a two-torus is defined by the 9-point operator

$$A = \frac{1}{36} \begin{pmatrix} 1 & 4 & 1 \\ 4 & 16 & 4 \\ 1 & 4 & 1 \end{pmatrix}, \tag{5}$$

which is both sparse and diagonally dominant. An elementary calculation shows that

$$Z = LSQ(A) = \begin{pmatrix} 0.1541 & -0.6603 & 0.1541 \\ -0.6603 & 2.830 & -0.6603 \\ 0.1541 & -0.6603 & 0.1541 \end{pmatrix}. \tag{6}$$

Note that Z has the same cartesian product structure as A. Even in the variable coefficient case, this construction is inexpensive and parallel because the variational equations that define B decouple so that the equations for the rows of B are independent. Moreover, for some interesting problems (such as the Laplacian on a two-torus, which we consider in Section 4), the projections Π_X and Π_Y are inexpensive. In other cases, the method suggested by Theorem 2, which does not rely on the availability of efficient projection operators, is more appropriate. This is what we use to precondition the conjugate gradient operator in the next section.

4. API-CG: An API-Preconditioned Conjugate Gradient Algorithm

If the operator $A: X \to Y$ is nonsymmetric as well as singular, we can be sure that the standard conjugate gradient algorithm will have difficulty. The recent papers of Faber and Manteuffel [7] and [8] contain a clear discussion of the limitations of the standard conjugate gradient algorithm and the class of generalizations that they refer to as orthogonal error methods. On the other hand, Kammerer and Nashed [11] and Björck and Elfving [4] and [6] have shown that the preconditioned conjugate gradient algorithm of Concus, Golub, and O'Leary [5] may be used, under certain conditions, to solve singular linear systems. We will see that when Z is an API of A with the additional property that $ZA: X \to X$ is symmetric, the following preconditioned conjugate gradient algorithm converges.

---

algorithm API-CG

$$
\begin{aligned}
initiate: \quad & r^0 = y - Ax^0 \\
& q^0 = Zr^0 \\
& p^0 = q^0 \\
iterate: \quad & a^i = \langle q^i, r^i \rangle / \langle p^i, Ap^i \rangle \\
& x^{i+1} = x^i + a_i p^i \\
& r^{i+1} = r^i - a_i Ap^i \\
& q^{i+1} = Zr^{i+1} \\
& b_i = \langle q^{i+1}, r^{i+1} \rangle / \langle q^i, r^i \rangle \\
& p^{i+1} = q^{i+1} + b_i p^i
\end{aligned}
$$

We have obtained particularly good convergence rates using the inner product $\langle x, y \rangle = (x, A^+ y)$ in conjunction with an API of the form $Z = A^* B^* B$. The evaluation of both inner products required by the API-CG algorithm is easy in this situation. To understand this, note that

$$\langle q^i, r^j \rangle = (Zd^i, A^+ r^j) = (r^i, B^* BAA^+ r^j) = (Br^i, Br^l), \tag{7}$$

with the last reduction using the fact that $r^j \in \mathcal{R}(A)$. Observing that $p^j \in \mathcal{R}(Z) = \mathcal{R}(A^*)$, we compute

$$\langle p^i, Ap^j \rangle = (p^i, A^+ Ap^j) = (p^i, p^j), \tag{8}$$

which is certainly easy to evaluate.

Theorem 3. *If Z is an $\epsilon-$ approximate pseudo-inverse of A and $ZA: \mathcal{X} \to \mathcal{Y}$ is symmetric, then the API-CG algorithm converges, for any $y \in \mathcal{Y}$ and any $x^0 \in \mathcal{X}$, to an x such that $\| y - Ax \|$ is minimized. The error at the nth iterate satisfies the inequality*

$$\| x - x^n \| < 4(\epsilon/2)^{2n} \| x^0 \| . \tag{9}$$

If $x^0 = 0$, then the limit x is the Moore-Penrose pseudo-inverse solution $x^+ = A^+ y$. Thus the API-CG algorithm with $x^0 = 0$ is an effective representation of the Moore-Penrose pseudo-inverse A^+ of A.

For a proof we refer the reader to Reference [9].

5. The Fast Approximate Pseudo-Inverse FAPIN

If the linear operator $A : \mathcal{X} \to \mathcal{Y}$ is very poorly conditioned as well as singular, we may expect it difficult to find an ϵ–API that is powerful enough to make even the API–CG algorithm converge as fast as we would like. We do, however, know how to deal with discretizations of elliptic partial differential equations: the antithesis of their ill-conditioning is the multigrid algorithm in one of its many variants. We describe one V-cycle of a multigrid algorithm as an approximate inverse. If the smoothing is done properly, using an API of A, and if a projection is inserted in the right place, the result is an approximate pseudo-inverse, which we refer to as a *fast approximate pseudo-inverse*, or FAPIN. Choosing the correct smoothing step is the key to building this algorithm.

Definition 3. *The linear operators $Z_k: \mathcal{Y}_k \to \mathcal{X}_k$ are an ϵ-nested approximate pseudo-inverse (ϵ-NAPI) of the linear operators $A_k: \mathcal{X}_k \to \mathcal{Y}_k$ if $\epsilon < 1$ and*

$$\| (I - Z_k A_k)u \|^2 \leq \epsilon^2 \| u' \|^2 + \| u'' \|^2 \quad \forall u \perp \mathcal{N}(\mathcal{X}_k) ,$$

$$\mathcal{N}(Z_k) \perp \mathcal{R}(A_k) , \quad and \quad \mathcal{R}(Z_k) \perp \mathcal{N}(A_k) ,$$

where $u = u' + u''$, $u' \in \mathcal{N}(A_{k-1})$, $u'' \perp \mathcal{N}(A_{k-1})$.

---

algorithm FAPIN(k, r_k)

  if $k > 0$, *then*

$$r_k = \Pi_k r_k$$
$$r_{k-1} = P_k r_k$$
$$w_{k-1} = FAPIN(k - 1, r_{k-1})$$
$$w_k = Q_k w_{k-1}$$
$$s_k = r_k - A_k w_k$$
$$w_k = w_k + Z_k s_k$$

  else

$$w_k = Z_0 r_0$$

  endif

  return w_k

Theorem 4. *If for some $\epsilon < 1$ and all $0 \leq j \leq k$, Z_j is a nested approximate pseudo-inverse of A_j, then $FAPIN(k, *)$ is an ϵ–API of A_k, and may be used in either API–DC or API–CG to provide an effective representation of the Moore-Penrose pseudo-inverse A^+ of A.*

The interested reader is referred to Reference [9] for a detailed proof.

6. Hypercube Computations

We study a free boundary spline interpolation problem in the plane. Consider a discrete mesh with spacing h in the x and y directions and with n_x and n_y points in the x and y directions, respectively. At each *interior* point, a value for the function to be interpolated is provided. Thus, applying the bicubic spline interpolation operator at these points yields $(n_x - 2)(n_y - 2)$ equations in $n_x n_y$ unknowns, a consistent system for any data because the operator is of full rank.

We have implemented the algorithms presented here on the 32-node iPSC hypercube at Christian Michelsen Institute in Bergen, Norway. We used the high-level CMI library as the basis for our computations and added an efficient procedure that evaluated any of the operators A, A^*, B, and B^*, using a 7 by 7 array of 3 by 3 arrays to store the coefficients. The API–CG algorithm requires more communication cost than the API-DC algorithm because of the inner products. As shown in Table I, this is more than offset by the enhanced performance.

Table I. Computational Results for the Free-Boundary Spline Problem*

N	API–DC			API–CG		
	$per(1)$	$per(8)$	$T(8)/N$	$per(1)$	$per(8)$	$T(8)/N$
2^{11}	0.332	0.271e-3	4.69	0.125	0.732e-5	5.88
2^{13}	0.341	0.321e-3	3.36	0.123	0.754e-5	4.02
2^{15}	0.344	0.325e-3	2.98	0.119	0.716e-5	3.50
2^{17}	0.346	0.328e-3	2.86	0.120	0.674e-5	3.34
2^{19}	0.347	0.332e-3	2.83	0.119	0.629e-5	3.29

*Free-boundary spline problem results using the linear stationary iterative process API-DC and the API-CG algorithm. N is the number of unknowns. $per(n) = \| r^n \|_2 / \| r^0 \|_2$. $T(n)$ is the time for n iterations in milliseconds.

7. Conclusion

The concept of an approximate pseudo-inverse provides a useful tool for the implementation of the exact Moore-Penrose pseudo-inverse A^+ of a singular linear operator A and, in some circumstances, allows an $O(N)$ implementation of A^+. We have described a simple construction technique for an API that is useful for consistent singular problems and have applied such APIs to the large sparse underdetermined system arising from free-boundary spline interpolation. The rate of convergence was independent of the order of the problem in this example, which was demonstrated for orders up through a half million, showing that we indeed had an $O(N)$ implementation of A^+. We also demonstrated the effectiveness of the fast approximate pseudo-inverse FAPIN, a V-cycle multigrid algorithm using an API as a smoother, on Poisson's problem on a two-torus of size a quarter million. These APIs proved to be almost perfectly parallelizable, which we demonstrated using the iPSC hypercube at the Christian Michelsen Institute in Bergen. They also proved to be very effective preconditioners for the conjugate gradient algorithm, and allowed the API-CG algorithm to be applied to a nonsymmetric problem, such as the free-boundary spline interpolation problem.

8. Acknowledgements

This work was done in part while M. Benson was visiting the Center for Non-Linear Studies, Los Alamos National Laboratory and while both authors were visiting Christian Michelsen Institute, Bergen, Norway. Support from the U.S. Department of Energy, Norges Teknisk-Naturvitenskapelige Forskningsråd, and the Natural Sciences and Engineering Research Council of Canada (Grant no. A5031) is gratefully acknowledged.

REFERENCES

[1] A. Ben-Israel and T. N. E. Greville, *Generalized Inverses: Theory and Applications*, John Wiley & Sons, Inc., New York, 1974.

[2] M. W. Benson and P. O. Frederickson, *Iterative solution of large sparse linear systems arising in certain multidimensional approximation problems*, Utilitas Math.,**22** (1982), pp. 127–139.

[3] M. W. Benson, J. Krettmann, and M. Wright, *Parallel algorithms for the solution of certain large sparse linear systems*, Int. J. Comput. Math., **16** (1984), pp. 245–260.

[4] A. Björck and T. Elfving, *Accelerated projection methods for computing pseudoinverse solutions of systems of linear equations*, BIT, **19** (1979), pp. 145–163.

[5] P. Concus, G. H. Golub, and D. P. O'Leary, *A generalized conjugate gradient method for the numerical solution of elliptic partial differential equations*, in Sparse Matrix Computations, J.R. Bunch and D.J. Rose, eds., Academic Press, New York, 1976.

[6] T. Elfving, *Block-iterative methods for consistent and inconsistent linear equations*, Numer. Math., **35** (1980), pp. 1–12.

[7] V. Faber and T. A. Manteuffel, *Necessary and sufficient conditions for the existence of a conjugate gradient method*, SIAM J. Numer. Anal., **21** (1984), pp. 352–362.

[8] V. Faber and T. A. Manteuffel, *Orthogonal error methods*, SIAM J. Numer. Anal. (to appear).

[9] P. O. Frederickson and M. W. Benson, *Fast parallel solution of large sparse singular systems*, Chr. Michelsen Institute, Centre for Computer Science report 86/9 (1986).

[10] P. O. Frederickson and M. W. Benson, *Fast parallel algorithms for the Moore-Penrose pseudo-inverse solution to large sparse consistent systems*, Chr. Michelsen Institute, Centre for Computer Science report 86/19 (1986).

[11] W. J. Kammerer and M. Z. Nashed, *On the convergence of the conjugate gradient method for singular linear operator equations*, SIAM J. Numer. Anal., **9** (1972), pp. 165–181.

[12] H. B. Keller, *On the solution of singular and semidefinite linear systems by iteration*, SIAM J. Numer. Anal., **2** (1965), pp. 281–290

[13] O. A. McBryan and E. F. Van de Velde, *Hypercube algorithms and implementations*, Courant Mathematics and Computing Laboratory Report DOE/ER/03077-271 (1986).

[14] E. H. Moore, *On the reciprocal of the general algebraic matrix*, Bull. Amer. Math. Soc., **26** (1919), pp. 394–395.

[15] R. Penrose, *A Generalized Inverse for Matrices*, Proc. Cambridge Philos. Soc., **51** (1955), pp. 406–413.

On Using the Jacobi Method on the Hypercube

P. J. EBERLEIN*

Abstract. We describe an implementation of a 'one-sided' Jacobi Method for solving the symmetric eigenproblem on the hypercube. This implementation is a modification of the Hestenes procedure and uses only columns of the matrix. We determine the Jacobi angle from columns of the factored matrix and columns of the vector matrix. We also describe a new formation of Jacobi rotation sets. These require only one send and one receive per set, and a complete set is found in the minimal n-1 steps.

1. Introduction Let A be an n x n symmetric matrix. The classical Jacobi method generates a sequence $A_0 = A$, $A_{i+1} = R_i^T A_i R_i$ where the rotations, R_i are chosen to annihilate the off-diagonal element in the plane of the rotation. The angle which accomplishes this is:

$$(1) \qquad \tan 2\phi = 2a_{km}/(a_{kk} - a_{mm}).$$

A necessary condition for convergence is that all of the $n(n-1)/2$ possible pivot pairs, (k_i, m_i), are used for the planes of rotation. A full set of these is called a sweep.

Block Jacobi methods, [1], [2], [3], [5], [6], [12], [14], [15], [16], [17] designed for parallel computation generally assign blocks, or patches, of the matrix to a square mesh of processors. As is well-known, n/2 rotations, called rotation sets, may be computed in parallel.

---

*Department of Computer Science, State University of New York at Buffalo, Buffalo, New York 14260

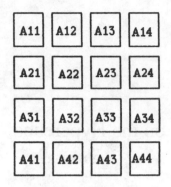

Each ☐ represents a processor which contains an mxm submatrix, Aij. The diagonal processors generate the rotations which must be sent both across and down to the off–diagonal processors which complete the rotations.

Because of the cost involved in sending small packets of rotational information, both horizontally and vertically, to the off–diagonal processors, we look at the one–sided Jacobi methods, [1], [3], [4], [7], [9], [10], [13].

2. One sided Jacobi. This method is usually associated only with the singular value problem, and has been rediscovered many times. A different sequence of transformations is used:

$$A_0 = A, \quad A_{i+1} = A_i R_i.$$

In this case, the requirements for the pivot pairs remains the same as that in the classical case, but the angle is chosen to make the rotated columns of A^{i+1} orthogonal, ie:

$$(2) \qquad \tan 2\emptyset = \langle a^k, a^m \rangle / (\langle a^k, a^k \rangle - \langle a^m, a^m \rangle).$$

where $\langle \, , \, \rangle$ denotes inner product and A is represented by its column vectors: $A = (a^1, a^2, \ldots a^n)$. Matrix updates for this iteration involve only columns and not rows. In this case, it is natural to assign columns, or strips, to processors as follows:

A1	A3	A5	A7		A15
A2	A4	A6	A8	...	A16

Each strip represents a processor containing two blocks of columns of A. We arrange the planes of the rotations so that all the information necessary for a rotation is available within each processor. Special communication is not necessary.

Corresponding to each column, a^i of A, we initialize, in the processors, vectors v^i, $i=1 \ldots n$, to unit vectors, which are updated by $V^{i+1} = V_i R_i$, where $V = (v^1, v^2, \ldots v^n)$.

The limiting matrix of the sequence $A_{i+1} = A_i R_i$ with the angle defined by (2) converges to a matrix having columns which are orthogonal. If we denote this limiting matrix by B, then $R_i^T B$ does <u>not</u> always converge to a diagonal matrix (as it does when the eigenvalues are distinct in absolute value). Instead, [8], $R_i^T B$ converges to a block diagonal form where the blocks are multiples of unitary matrices.

We redefine the one-sided Jacobi procedure by using a different angle, as follows:

$$(3) \quad \tan 2\emptyset = <v^k,a^m>/(<v^k,a^k> - <v^m,a^m>).$$

where $V = (\ v^1,\ v^2,\ \dots\ v^n)$ is the vector matrix. One can easily see that the angle defined by (3) is identical to the classical Jacobi angle, (1).

We summarize. The columns of the symmetric matrix A are sent in blocks to individual processors, and the columns of V initialized. For appropriate pivot pairs the angle defined by (3) is computed, and A' = AR, and V' = VR are computed. We have for the pair (k,m):

$$a^{k\prime} = ca^k + sa^m \qquad\qquad v^{k\prime} = cv^k + sv^m$$
$$a^{m\prime} = -sa^k + ca^m \qquad\qquad v^{m\prime} = -sv^k + cv^m.$$

After this update, blocks of pairs of columns a and v are sent to adjacent processors, forming a new pivot pairing.

3. Rotation Sets. We describe several possibilities for the determination of the $n(n-1)/2$ pivot pairs, developed as Jacobi Rotation sets which can be performed in parallel.

We first used the Brent-Luk [3], [11] ordering to generate independent Jacobi sets. The pairs of vectors (a and v) are transmitted to neighboring processors as indicated in the diagram below for n=8.

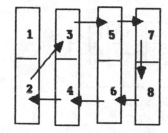

$$(1,2)\ (3,4)\ (5,6)\ (7,8)$$
$$(1,4)(2,6)(3,8)(5,7)$$
$$(1,6)(4,8)(2,7)(3,5)$$
$$(1,8)(6,7)(4,5)(2,3)$$
$$(1,7)(8,5)(6,3)(4,2)$$
$$(1,5)(7,3)(8,2)(6,4)$$
$$(1,3)(5,2)(7,4)(8,6)$$
$$(1,2)(3,4)(5,6)(7,8).$$

Here the integers 1, 2, ... 8 represent eight blocks of columns. The successive pairings are shown at the right. Note that all pairs in each set are independent. After n-1 sets, the sweep is completed and, we are returned to the initial set.

We wish to avoid the double sends and receives, so we may also trying the 'tractor-tread' or 'caterpillar' algorithm, [11], [12], [15], [17], which alternates between the following two schema:

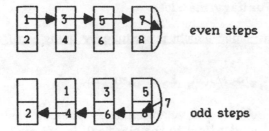

even steps

odd steps

The rotation sets for this schema are:

$$(1,2) \ (3,4) \ (5,6) \ (7,8)$$
$$2 \ (1,4) \ (3,6) \ (5,8) \ 7$$
$$(2,4) \ (1,6) \ (3,8) \ (5,7)$$
$$4 \ (2,6) \ (1,8) \ (3,7) \ 5$$
$$(4,6) \ (2,8) \ (1,7) \ (3,5)$$
$$6 \ (4,8) \ (2,7) \ (1,5) \ 3$$
$$(6,8) \ (4,7) \ (2,5) \ (1,3)$$
$$8 \ (6,7) \ (4,5) \ (2,3) \ 1$$
$$(8,7) \ (6,5) \ (4,3) \ (2,1)$$

which is equivalent to the original rotation set. Note here that n sets (instead of n-1) are required per sweep, and that one processor is idle every other set, but we do have one send and one receive per rotation set.

We prefer to have one send and one receive at each change of rotation sets, and, if possible to keep all processors occupied, ie, to return to the original set after n-1 steps. So, assuming a loop of even length, which is easily implemented in Gray code, we use the following scheme,[8] which has the desired properties:

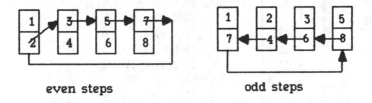

even steps   odd steps

Here the rotations sets are:

$$(1,2) \ (3,4) \ (5,6) \ (7,8)$$
$$(1,7) \ (2,4) \ (3,6) \ (5,8)$$
$$(1,4) \ (2,6) \ (3,8) \ (5,7)$$
$$(1,5) \ (4,6) \ (2,8) \ (3,7)$$
$$(1,6) \ (4,8) \ (2,7) \ (3,5)$$
$$(1,3) \ (6,8) \ (4,7) \ (2,5)$$
$$(1,8) \ (6,7) \ (4,5) \ (2,3)$$
$$(1,2) \ (8,7) \ (6,5) \ (4,3)$$

4. Numerical experiments. We have had limited access to a hypercube, and therefore our experiments are sketchy. We report two here. The first was done with   matrices of varying order, using the Brent-Luk Jacobi sets. The first set of results is done with matrices taken from a chemical application for which the roots were known. The second set are for matrices with random elements. np denotes the number of processors.

n	chemical	random	np
32	10.4	12.4	16
48	21.7	23.2	24
64	44.6	38.0	32
96	81.3	92.2	48
128	158.7	136.6	64

The timings are taken from the time the last node receives its share of the data until the computation in that node is completed.

The next example was written using the Jacobi rotation sets with one send and one receive. However, the loop of even length was not used so that the communication for at least one node per rotation set is not optimal. Here, a single matrix of order 64 was run on a varying number of processors. Only 32 nodes were up, so we were limited to that number. In this case the timings were taken over an average of the finishing times of the different nodes. The time for one node was taken from a serial program (of necessity different from that used by the rest).

np	time	'speedup'	time/(n^3/np)	(assuming time = c x n^3/np.	
				525.6/np	time-525.6/np
1	525.6		.0020		
2	353	1.5	.0027	262.8	90.2
4	168.7	3.11	.0057	131.4	37.3
8	86.97	6.05	.0026	65.7	21.27
12	71.77	7.33	.0033	43.8	27.97
16	49.07	10.7	.0030	32.8	16.27
20	58.07	9.06	.0044	26.28	31.87
24	55.21	9.53	.0051	21.9	33.31
28	52.08	10.1	.0055	18.77	33.31
32	34.87	15.1	.0043	16.43	18.44

Conclusions. Berry and Sameh reported recently [1] that what we have called '**block**' Jacobi (on the Alliant FX/8) outperformed EISPACK routines for n<100.

They also report that '**one-sided**' Jacobi (using the Hestenes angle) outperformed "the most efficient" EISPACK routines for all orders considered, (≤400) and LINPACK routines for the singular value problem 2-3 times. Since our one-sided Jacobi is of identical complexity to theirs (see the definition of the angles defined by (2) and (3), one may hope that the use of Jacobi algorithms on the hypercube will be profitable when carefully implemented.

For serial computation, the Jacobi process (for a dense matrix, with all eigenvalues and eigenvectors required) takes approximately three to four times longer than the standard QR/bisection method (more for the Dongarra procedure and inverse iteration for the vectors) for comparable problems. However, for matrices of fixed order, the EISPACK routines seem to show little speedup, for matrices of fixed size, as the number of processors is increased beyond ten or so. Thus we could consider

$$n^3/10 \text{ versus } 4n^3/np,$$

and, even if the constant 4 is wrong, Jacobi promises to improve with an increasing number of processors.

We wish to thank Neil Ostlund at the University of Waterloo, and his students, for the use of their hypercube, and for their help and patience in our getting anything to run.

Bibliography

[1]*   M.Berry and A.Sameh, Multiprocessor Jacobi Algorithms for Dense Symmetric Eigenvalue and Singular Value Decompositions, Proc. of the '86 Int. Conf. on Parallel Processing, Aug. '86.

[2]   C. Bischof, A Parallel Ordering for the Block Jacobi Method on a Hypercube Architecture, TR 96-740, Cornell University, Dept. of Comp. Sci. 1986.

[3]   R. Brent and F.T.Luk, The Solution of Singular-Value and symmetric Eigenvalue Problems on Multiprocessor arrays, SIAM J. Sci. Stat Comput, 6, #1, 1985, pp. 69-84.

[4]   B.Chartres, Adaption of the Jacobi method for a Computer with Magnetic Backing Store, The Computer Journal, 5,1962, pp. 51-60.

[5]   K. Chen and K. Irani, A Jacobi Algorithm and its Implementation on Parallel Computers, Proc. of the 18th Annual Allerton Conf. on Communication Control and Computing, 1980.

[6]   P.J.Eberlein, On the Schur Decomposition of a Matrix for Parallel Computation, Technical Report, Dept. Comp. Sci., SUNY/Buffalo, 1985.

[7]   P.J.Eberlein, On One-sided Jacobi Methods for Parallel Computation, Tech Report 86-15, Dept. Comp. Sci., SUNY/Buffalo, 1986.

[8]   P.J.Eberlein, Comments on Some Parallel Jacobi Orderings, Tech Report 86-16, Dept. Comp. Sci., SUNY/Buffalo, 1986.

[9]   M.R.Hestenes, Inversion of Matrices by Biorthogonalization and Related Results, SIAM J. App.Math., 6, 1958, pp. 51-90.

[10]   H.F.Kaiser, The JK method: A Procedure for Finding the Eigenvectors and Eigenvalues of a Real Symmetric Matrix, The Computer Journal, **15**, 1972, pp. 271–273.

[11]   F.T.Luk, and H.Park, On Parallel Jacobi Orderings, EE-CEG-86-5, Cornell University, 1986.

[12]   J.J.Modi and J.D.Pryce, Efficient Implementation of Jacobi's Diagonalization Method on the DAP, Num. Math., 46, 1985, pp 443–454.

[13]   J.C.Nash. A One-sided Transformation Method for the Singular Value Decomposition and Algebraic Eigenproblem, The Computer Journal **18**, 1977 , pp.74–76.

[14]   A. Sameh, On Jacobi and Jacobi-type Algorithms for a Parallel Computer, Math. Comp., v. 25, 1971, pp. 579–590.

[15]   D.Scott, M.T.Heath, and R.C.Ward. Parallel Block Jacobi Algorithms Using Systolic Arrays, TR-85-01, Dept. of Comp. Sci., Univ. Texas, 1985.

[16]   G. W. Stewart, A Jacobi-like Algorithm for Computing the Schur Decomposition of a Non-Hermitian Matrix, Technical Report 1321, Dept. Comp. Sci., U of Md., 1983.

[17]   R.A. Whiteside, N.S.Ostlund, and P.G. Hibbard, A Parallel Jacobi, Diagonalization Algorithm for a Loop Multiple Processor System, IEEE.

The Two-Sided Block Jacobi Method on a Hypercube

CHRISTIAN BISCHOF*

Abstract. Jacobi methods are ideally suited for multiprocessor environments due to their inherent parallelism. In this paper we show how the two-sided block Jacobi method can be used to efficiently compute the singular value decomposition of a matrix on a hypercube. We suggest a new parallel ordering that is based on recursively embedding rings into the hypercube and results in the lowest communication overhead possible. We discuss why we expect the Block Jacobi method to perform very favorably on machines with vector nodes such as the Intel iPSC VX.

1. Introduction. The singular value decomposition (SVD) of an $m \times n$ matrix A (assume $m \geq n$) is a very versatile decomposition and perfectly stable to compute (see Golub and Van Loan (1983)). In the SVD we seek orthogonal matrices $U \in \mathbb{R}^{m \times m}$ and $V \in \mathbb{R}^{n \times n}$ such that

$$U^T A V = diag(\sigma_1, ..., \sigma_n)$$

The σ_i are called the singular values of A; the columns of U and V are called left and right singular vectors, respectively. It is normally assumed that $\sigma_1 \geq ... \geq \sigma_n \geq 0$, but we will not insist on this normalisation. To set the stage for the block Jacobi algorithm, consider A as a $k \times k$ block matrix (A_{ij}), $i, j = 1,...,k$. The ith block column of A is denoted by A_i. The idea behind the two-sided block Jacobi approach is to make A increasingly more block diagonal by solving a series of subproblems. To measure how

---

* Dept. of Computer Science, Cornell University, Ithaca, NY 14853. This work was supported by the U.S. Army Research Office through the Mathematical Sciences Institute of Cornell University and by the Office of Naval Research under contract N00014-83-K-0640. Computations associated with this research were partially performed on the Theory Center Facility at Cornell University.

close A is to the desired block diagonal form, we define OFF(A) as the Frobenius norm of the off-diagonal blocks, i.e.

$$\text{OFF}(A) \equiv \text{sqrt}(\sum_{i \neq j} \|A_{ij}\|_F^2).$$

We consider A to be block-diagonal if OFF(A) is of the order of machine precision. Once A is block diagonal, it is straightforward to compute the SVD of A by computing the SVD of each diagonal block.

To decrease OFF(A) we repeatedly compute the SVD of two-by-two block subproblems S_{ij} of the form

$$S_{ij} \equiv \begin{bmatrix} A_{ii} & A_{ij} \\ A_{ji} & A_{jj} \end{bmatrix}.$$

If W_{ij} and Z_{ij} are chosen such that

$$(1.1) \qquad W_{ij}^T S_{ij} Z_{ij} = \begin{bmatrix} D_{ii} & 0 \\ 0 & D_{jj} \end{bmatrix} \equiv \Sigma_{ij}$$

is block diagonal and if B is the matrix we obtain by updating block rows and block columns i and j of A with W_{ij}^T and Z_{ij} respectively, then it is not hard to see that

$$(1.2) \qquad \text{OFF}(B)^2 = \text{OFF}(A)^2 - \|A_{ij}\|_F^2 - \|A_{ji}\|_F^2.$$

So by solving a judiciously chosen sequence of two-by-two block subproblems we will be able to reduce A to block diagonal form. See Bischof and Van Loan (1986) for the details associated with solving a subproblem.

In section 2 we will introduce the parallel block Jacobi algorithm. In section 3 we discuss a scheme for zeroing the off-diagonal blocks that allows for maximal concurrency with minimal communication overhead on a hypercube architecture. In section 4 we summarize our results and discuss why we expect this method to perform well on parallel architectures with vector nodes.

2. The Block Jacobi Method on a Multiprocessor. The block Jacobi method has been studied in detail by several researchers. For reference see Van Loan (1985) and Scott, Heath and Ward (1985). The method proceeds in *sweeps*. In a sweep, each off-diagonal block A_{ij} gets annihilated exactly once. Note however, that off-diagonal blocks A_{ij} that have been zeroed in one subproblem will be filled in later when another subproblem updates block rows and columns i or j of A. To guard against pathological cases and ensure convergence of the algorithm, it is necessary to incorporate a threshold criterion into the algorithm We skip solving for the S_{ij} subproblem if

$$\mu_{ij} \equiv \text{sqrt}(\| A_{ij} \|_F^2 + \| A_{ji} \|_F^2)$$

is small according to a subproblem threshold τ. Now if we are given an ordering

$$(i_1, j_1),...,(i_r, j_r) , r = \tfrac{1}{2}k(k-1)$$

of the off-diagonal index pairs, the block Jacobi algorithm on one processor is described by algorithm 2.1. Here I_m denotes the $m \times m$ identity. For simplicity, we have assumed that the order in which subproblems are solved is the same in each sweep. Van Loan (1985) has proved the convergence of this algorithm and in practice it converges quadratically.

Algorithm 2.1. Given a subproblem threshold $\tau \leq \varepsilon \| A \|_F / k$, the following algorithm computes orthogonal U and V such that OFF($U^T A V$) $\leq \varepsilon \| A \|_F$. The original A gets overwritten with $U^T A V$.

$U \leftarrow I_m ; V \leftarrow I_n ;$
while OFF(A) $> \varepsilon \| A \|_F$ do
    for $l = 1$ to $k(k\text{-}1)/2$ do
      $(i,j) \leftarrow (i_l, j_l)$
      if $\mu_{ij} \geq \tau$ then
        Compute W_{ij} and V_{ij} that block diagonalize S_{ij}.

$$\left. \begin{array}{l} [A_i, A_j] \leftarrow [A_i, A_j] Z_{ij} \\ [U_i, U_j] \leftarrow [U_i, U_j] W_{ij} \\ [V_i, V_j] \leftarrow [V_i, V_j] Z_{ij} \end{array} \right\} \quad (2.1)$$

        for $q = 1$ to k do

$$\begin{bmatrix} A_{i,q} \\ A_{j,q} \end{bmatrix} \leftarrow W_{ij}^T \begin{bmatrix} A_{i,q} \\ A_{j,q} \end{bmatrix} \quad (2.2)$$

        end for
      end if
    end for
end while

If we have $p = \tfrac{1}{2}k$ processors available, then we distribute A,U and V such that each processor holds two block columns (assume k even from now on). Each processor now has enough information to solve the subproblem that is defined by the two block columns of A it holds. The updates (2 1) can also be performed concurrently as each processor holds the required columns of A, U and V. Only for the update (2.2) each processor has to broadcast its W_{ij} to each other processor since rows of A are distributed over all the processors. Then we have to redistribute block columns between processors to be able to solve a different set of subproblems in the next step.

To complete a sweep, we have to solve each of the $p(k-1)$ subproblems once. Each grouping of the set $\{1,..,k\}$ in pairs of two defines a *rotation set*, i.e. a set of $p=\frac{1}{2}k$ subproblems that can be solved concurrently. By convention the ith processor P_i solves the subproblem defined by the ith tuple. The computations associated with one rotation set are referred to as *stage*. A *parallel ordering* is now an ordering of subproblems such that a sweep is completed in $(k-1)$ stages and the redistributing of columns between stages requires only nearest-neighbour communication. A parallel ordering is *optimal*, if each processor exchanges only one set of block columns between stages. Each processor has to exchange at least one set of block columns as otherwise it would solve the same subproblem again.

3. A New Optimal Parallel Ordering for the Hypercube.
Various parallel orderings have been suggested for different topologies. Luk and Park (1986) give a framework for several previously known orderings on a linear array of processors using a "caterpillar track" scheme. The linear array does not seem to allow for an optimal ordering, however. For a ring topology, Eberlein (1986) suggests an optimal ordering. We here present a new optimal ordering for the hypercube architecture. In our ordering we will have to embed rings in the hypercube such that processors adjacent in the ring will be adjacent in the hypercube. The *binary reflected Gray code* fulfills this specification (see Saad and Schultz (1985)). To define it, let $G(d)$ be a 2^d-vector whose ith entry g_i^d is the encoding of i ($i = 0,...,2^d-1$) in the Gray code for 2^d numbers. Then

$$G(1) = (0, 1)$$

and recursively

$$(3.1)\quad G(d) \equiv (g_0^{d-1}0, g_0^{d-1}1, g_1^{d-1}1, g_1^{d-1}0, ..., g_{r-2}^{d-1}0, g_{r-2}^{d-1}1, g_{r-1}^{d-1}1, g_{r-1}^{d-1}0)$$

where $r \equiv 2^{d-1}$. So if i and j are successive numbers (modulo 2^d) then g_i^d and g_j^d differ in exactly one bit. Now let

$$S_1 \equiv \{g_i^d \mid i = 0 + 4l \ or \ i = 3 + 4l, l \in \{0,1,2,...,2^{d-2}-1\}\}$$

and

$$S_2 \equiv \{g_i^d \mid i = 1 + 4l \ or \ i = 2 + 4l, l \in \{0,1,2,...,2^{d-2}-1\}\}.$$

From (3.1) it is easy to see that processors with labels in S_1 and processors with labels in S_2 lie on two smaller rings of size 2^{d-1} since the last bit in each group is identical and the first $d-1$ bits are numbered according to $G(d-1)$. If we now look just at the first $d-1$ bits in S_1 or S_2, we can repeat this procedure and embed the processors within each group onto two rings of size 2^{d-2}. Continuing this argument recursively, we can altogether embed 2^{d-l} rings of length 2^l in the hypercube, $l = 0,1,...,d$.

From now on assume that the block dimension k of A is a power of two, i e $k = 2^{d+1}$ and that we have $p = 2^d$ processors in a d-dimensional hypercube. Further let the processors be labelled according to the Gray code labelling for a d-dimensional hypercube. So processor P_i has binary label $g_i{}^d$, $i = 0,..,2^d - 1$. To generate the parallel ordering for the hypercube, we recursively embed successively smaller rings in the hypercube. The idea is demonstrated by going through one sweep for a 16×16 block matrix distributed over the 8 processors of a 3-cube. Assuming that initally processor P_i contains block column sets $2i + 1$ and $2i + 2$, $i = 0,..,7$, we have the set-up shown in figure 1. Each processor P_i is labelled by $g_i{}^d$.

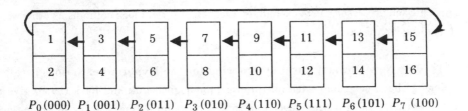

$P_0 (000)$ $P_1 (001)$ $P_2 (011)$ $P_3 (010)$ $P_4 (110)$ $P_5 (111)$ $P_6 (101)$ $P_7 (100)$

FIG. 1. *The Ring Shuffle*

So the first rotation set is

$$(1,2), (3,4), (5,6), (7,8), (9,10), (11,12), (13,14), (15,16).$$

To prepare for the next stage, we use the 8-ring and send the "upper" block column set to the left neighbour and receive a new one from the right neighbour as indicated by the arrows in figure 1. So we obtain rotation set

$$(3,2), (5,4), (7,6), (9,8), (11,10), (13,12), (15,14), (1,16).$$

Using the same idea of just moving the upper columns on the ring, we can now generate 6 more stages solving subproblems

$$(5,2), (7,4), (9,6), (11,8), (13,10), (15,12), (1,14), (3,16)$$
$$(7,2), (9,4), (11,6), (13,8), (15,10), (1,12), (3,14), (5,16)$$
$$(9,2), (11,4), (13,6), (15,8), (1,10), (3,12), (5,14), (7,16)$$
$$(11,2), (13,4), (15,6), (1,8), (3,10), (5,12), (7,14), (9,16)$$
$$(13,2), (15,4), (1,6), (3,8), (5,10), (7,12), (9,14), (11,16)$$
$$(15,2), (1,4), (3,6), (5,8), (7,10), (9,12), (11,14), (13,16).$$

Then the configuration is

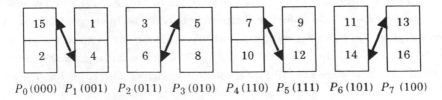

$P_0 (000)$ $P_1 (001)$ $P_2 (011)$ $P_3 (010)$ $P_4 (110)$ $P_5 (111)$ $P_6 (101)$ $P_7 (100)$

FIG 2 *Splitting the Ring*

Now every subproblem involving an "upper" and "lower" block column set has been solved and continuing the computation in this way would just reproduce the first rotation set. So to generate the next rotation set, we split the ring of 8 processors into two smaller rings consisting of processors { 0,3,4,7 } and { 1,2,5,6 }, respectively. The block column sets are exchanged in a zig-zag manner as indicated by the arrows in figure 2. The rotation set we obtain is

$$(4,2), (1,15), (3,5), (6,8), (12,10), (9,7), (11,13), (14,16).$$

Note that the subcube consisting of processors 0, 3, 4 and 7 now contains all the previously "lower" block columns, whereas the second subcube contains all the previously "upper" columns. We now continue in each subcube recursively, using the ring shuffle until we would regenerate a rotation set and then splitting the ring into two smaller ones. The remaining subproblems are solved in the following order where next to each stage it is denoted whether it resulted from a ring shuffle or a split.

$$(6,2), (3,15), (9,5), (12,8), (14,10), (11,7), (1,13), (4,16) \quad \text{ring}$$
$$(12,2), (9,15), (11,5), (14,8), (4,10), (1,7), (3,13), (6,16) \quad \text{ring}$$
$$(14,2), (11,15), (1,5), (4,8), (6,10), (3,7), (9,13), (12,16) \quad \text{ring}$$
$$(8,2), (5,15), (1,11), (4,14), (6,12), (3,9), (7,13), (10,16) \quad \text{split}$$
$$(10,2), (7,15), (3,11), (6,14), (4,12), (1,9), (5, 13), (8,16) \quad \text{ring}$$
$$(16,2), (13,15), (9,11), (12,14), (4,6), (1,3), (5,7), (8, 10) \quad \text{split}$$

At this point we are finished with one sweep and to generate the first rotation set for the next sweep we use the 2^d- ring to generate subproblems

$$(13,2), (9,15), (12,11), (4,14), (1,6), (5,3), (8,7), (16,10)$$

and from there we continue as described.

This example shows that this method for generating the subproblems in a sweep conforms to our definition of an optimal parallel ordering: We generate $k - 1$ rotation pairs and every processor exchanges only one set of block columns between each rotation set. Due to the Gray code labelling we only communicate between neighbours at any point. Note that the orderings generated by this method differ from sweep to sweep. This algorithm does not sort the singular values but if that is required, a variant of bitonic sort can be used to sort the singular values in time that is negligible compared to the overall cost of the algorithm (see Johnson (1984)).

4. Conclusions. We have demonstrated how the two-sided block Jacobi method can be implemented with minimal communication overhead on a hypercube architecture. We have chosen the block Jacobi method over the scalar Jacobi method (where each block A_{ij} is just a scalar entry a_{ij}) for several reasons. The block algorithm exhibits a more favorable computation-to-communication ratio. It also allows for graceful handling of rectangular problems and architectural constraints (like $k = 2^{d+1}$ above) as blocks needn't be of the same size. Brent, Luk and Van Loan (1985) discuss some of these difficulties with the scalar algorithm.

In addition the block Jacobi method is ideally suited for parallel architectures where each node has special vector hardware. The reason is that block column updates (2.1) and (2.2) are straightforward matrix-matrix multiplications - the operation guaranteed to fully exploit the vector unit. Solving the subproblems on the other hand involves matrix-vector multiplications, rank-one updates and a good deal of quite complicated scalar code. But the size of the subproblem is proportional to $1/p^2$, the size of the block columns to be updated is proportional to $1/p$. So as we increase the number of processors while keeping the problem size fixed, the computational load is shifted from solving the subproblems to updating the block columns.

REFERENCES

C. H. BISCHOF and C. F. VAN LOAN (1986), *Computing the Singular Value Decomposition on a Ring of Array Processors*, in Large Scale Eigenvalue Problems, J. Cullum and R. A. Willoughby, eds. Vol. 127, Mathematics Studies Series, North-Holland, Amsterdam, the Netherlands.

R. P. BRENT, F. T. LUK and C. F. VAN LOAN (1985), *Computation of the singular value decomposition using mesh-connected processors*, J. VLSI Computer Systems, 1 (1985), pp. 242-270.

P. EBERLEIN (1986), *Comments on Some Parallel Jacobi Orderings*, SUNY Buffalo, Computer Science Report TR 86-16.

G. H. GOLUB and C. F. VAN LOAN (1983), *Matrix Computations*, John Hopkins University Press, Baltimore.

S. L. JOHNSON (1984), *Combining Parallel and Sequential Sorting on a Boolean n-Cube*, Proc. Int. Conf. on Parallel Processing, Shanty Creek, Michigan.

F. T. LUK and H. PARK (1986), *On Parallel Jacobi Orderings*, Cornell University, School of Electrical Engineering Report EE-CEG-86-5.

Y. SAAD and M. H. SCHULTZ (1985), *Topological Properties of Hypercubes*, Yale University, Dept. of Computer Science Report YALEU/DCS/RR-389.

D. SCOTT, M. T. HEATH, R. C. WARD (1985), *Parallel Block Jacobi Eigenvalue Algorithms using Systolic Arrays*, University of Texas at Austin, Dept. of Computer Science Report TR 85-01.

C. F. VAN LOAN (1985), *The Block Jacobi Method for Computing the Singular Value Decomposition*, Cornell University, Dept. of Computer Science Report TR 85-680.

A Hypercube Implementation of the Implicit Double Shift QR Algorithm

G. J. DAVIS*, R. E. FUNDERLIC† AND G. A. GEIST‡

Abstract. A parallel implementation of the implicit double shift QR algorithm for finding the eigenvalues of dense unsymmetric matrices is presented along with an algorithm to reduce the original matrix to upper Hessenberg form on a hypercube multiprocessor. Our preliminary results show that these algorithms can achieve reasonable efficiencies even with slow hypercube communication.

1. Introduction. For sequential machines, the method of choice for calculating all the eigenvalues of a dense matrix is to reduce the matrix to an equivalent Hessenberg form and then performing QR iteration on the Hessenberg matrix. We expect parallel implementations of the best sequential algorithms to be important benchmarks. The methods of choice for serial computers usually have considerable literature on both analysis, (e.g., error analysis) and practice.

The reduction to Hessenberg form is usually carried out by *orthogonal* similarity transformations, though this requires about twice as many operations than for a non-orthogonal reduction that uses elementary triangular and permutation matrices. The EISPACK User's Guide [6] reports a factor of 2.3 improvement in speed by using the nonorthogonal reduction. In a parallel setting, we expect users to risk the rare instability [7], [9], [1] of the nonorthogonal

---

* Mathematics and Computer Sciences, Georgia State University, Atlanta, Georgia 30303-3083

† Department of Computer Science, North Carolina State University, Raleigh, North Carolina 27695-8206

‡ Engineering Physics and Mathematics Division, Mathematical Sciences Section, Oak Ridge National Laboratory, Oak Ridge, Tennessee 37831-2009

reduction for a faster algorithm. Of a further consideration for us is that we (Geist [5], Davis [2]) have had considerable experience in the solution of systems of equations using elementary triangular and permutation matrices. This experience has allowed us to quickly extend the Geist LU code [5] to a similarity reduction code.

Section 2 describes the mathematics of the reduction to Hessenberg form and describes the action of QR iterations on Hessenberg matrices. Sections 3 and 4 outline the parallel implementations of the Hessenberg reduction and the QR iteration respectively. Communication is quite intensive for the QR iteration, $O(n^2)$, whereas it is only $O(n)$ for the Hessenberg reduction. Section 5 gives timing results. The concluding Section 6 suggests some future work.

Our codes were developed in Fortran for the Intel iPSC. We tried to develop and adhere to good programming principles. For example, we used a top down, small subroutine approach and checked out our global communication with an artificial QR iteration subroutine. Wherever possible, we used ideas and parts of existing systems in our implementation, e.g., communication utilities. Of course, we used the Oak Ridge simulators [3] extensively in the development of our programs.

2. Mathematics of the Algorithms.

Gaussian elimination for the solution of systems of equations can be thought of as premultiplying a system $Ax = b$ by elementary permutation and elementary triangular matrices. These matrices have the form of the identity matrix with one column being nonzero below the diagonal, e.g., at the *second* stage for $n = 6$

$$\begin{pmatrix} 1 & 0 & 0 & 0 & 0 & 0 \\ 0 & 1 & 0 & 0 & 0 & 0 \\ 0 & -m_1 & 1 & 0 & 0 & 0 \\ 0 & -m_2 & 0 & 1 & 0 & 0 \\ 0 & -m_3 & 0 & 0 & 1 & 0 \\ 0 & -m_4 & 0 & 0 & 0 & 1 \end{pmatrix} . \tag{2.1}$$

A Gauss similarity reduction of a full dense real matrix to upper Hessenberg form, i.e., upper triangular with one nonzero subdiagonal, can also be accomplished by elementary permutation and triangular matrices. The *first* step can be regarded as finding the pivot among the second to n th elements of the first column. The Hessenberg matrix is then premultiplied by the appropriate elementary permutation matrix P_1 and then an elementary triangular matrix M_1 of the form of (2.1). This is followed by postmultiplication of $P_1^{-1} = P_1$ which interchanges columns, and then postmultiplication by M_1^{-1} which has the same form as (2.1) with the signs on the multipliers, m_i, changed. Postmultiplication does not introduce nonzeros where zeros have been produced by the premultiplication.

Francis [4] first described an economical method of performing two steps of the QR algorithm with complex conjugate shifts without using complex arithmetic. The description of this similarity transformation algorithm applied to Hessenberg matrices would require too much space to be described here. It is, however, important for our purposes to describe what happens to the Hessenberg matrix H as the iteration proceeds.

As the QR iteration proceeds on H, zeros (in practice, "small enough" numbers) appear on the subdiagonal. In the early stages of the iteration, the "zeros" tend to appear toward the lower right corner. As the iteration proceeds, some zeros usually appear higher on the subdiagonal. This lessens the necessary computation and makes the parallel implementation of QR on H more interesting.

Let l be defined as one plus the column number of the rightmost subdiagonal zero, and let $l = 1$ if there are no subdiagonal zeros. Some of the possibilities will be illustrated by three Hessenberg matrices of order six. Suppose the QR iteration has just produced a zero in h_{65} in

$$
\begin{bmatrix}
x & x & x & x & x & x \\
x & x & x & x & x & x \\
  & x & x & x & x & x \\
  &   & x & x & x & x \\
  &   &   & x & x & x \\
  &   &   &   & 0 & \lambda
\end{bmatrix} . \tag{2.2}
$$

In this case, l would change from 1 to 6. The occurrence of $l = n$ signals that one root has been found, i.e., the eigenvalue $\lambda = h_{66} = h_{nn}$. In this case, n is reduced by one, l is reset to one and we proceed with the leading principal submatrix of order five. The situation just described, and that of $l = n - 1$, are the two most common cases. The latter case can be depicted by

$$
\begin{bmatrix}
x & x & x & x & x & x \\
x & x & x & x & x & x \\
  & x & x & x & x & x \\
  &   & x & x & x & x \\
  &   &   & 0 & x & x \\
  &   &   &   & x & x
\end{bmatrix} .
$$

The occurrence of $l = n - 1$ signals that two eigenvalues have been found. The quadratic formula is used to calculate the eigenvalues of the trailing principal submatrix of order two. In this case, n is reduced by two, l is reset to one and we proceed with the leading submatrix of order four. If a zero appears higher on the subdiagonal, a useful reduction of computation can be utilized. For example, if $h_{32} = 0$ in

$$
\begin{bmatrix}
x & x & x & x & x & x \\
x & \alpha & x & x & x & x \\
  & 0 & \beta & x & x & x \\
  &   & x & x & x & x \\
  &   &   & x & x & x \\
  &   &   &   & x & x
\end{bmatrix} \tag{2.3}
$$

then l changes from one to three and we can proceed with the trailing submatrix of order four. There is considerable potential savings as (2.3) may be the trailing principal submatrix of a very large matrix which allows us to iterate with a matrix of order four rather than a much larger one. However, some of the savings is lost since working with the entire matrix tends to reduce the number of iterations required for the new eigenvalues to be found.

The test for a negligible subdiagonal element is the standard one [8] for Hessenberg matrices which can be illustrated by:

$$ |h_{32}| \leqslant \epsilon \{ |\alpha| + |\beta| \}. $$

Standard routines which implement QR for Hessenberg matrices on serial machines allow for a further economy when two successive subdiagonals elements are small enough. We expect that the large communication costs necessary for a parallel implementation of this test would outweigh the benefits. Therefore, we do not check for two small successive subdiagonal elements.

3. Implementation of the Hessenberg Reduction. We expected and found that partitioning the original matrix A by rows and mapping these onto the processors in a wrapped fashion produced a very efficient algorithm. By wrapped, we mean that if the processors are numbered from 0 to $p - 1$, then row j of A is on processor $(j - 1) \bmod p$.

Since each processor has n/p rows, the search for the pivot can be done in parallel and then a fan-in process determines the pivot row. Though there is bookkeeping to be done, row interchanges are done implicitly rather than actually moving data. Once the pivot row is determined for a particular stage of the reduction, the pivot row is broadcast to all the other processors. The divisions to form the multipliers and the eliminations are then carried out in parallel. Column interchanges are explicitly performed since the partitioning is by rows. At the i th stage, a multiplier vector of length $n - 1 - i$ must be assembled and distributed which is done in a fan-in and fan-out manner. This vector at stage one for a matrix of order six would be (m_1, m_2, m_3, m_4), see (2.1). Once the multiplier vector is received, the postmultiplication can be done in parallel. Only one column is affected at each stage, but all the elements in that column are modified so that each processor modifies in parallel n/p elements.

4. Implementation of QR on H. Sequentially, and from a programming standpoint, the implicit double shift QR iteration on a Hessenberg matrix can be regarded as a loop with the index k going from 0 to $n - 2$; in actuality, the beginning index is $l - 1$. At each step k, except for the last, three rows and then three columns are modified. Figure 3.1 depicts a Hessenberg matrix of order 8 at the third step, $k = 2$. At this step, rows 3, 4 and 5 in the solid figure, are modified and then columns 3, 4 and 5 inside the dashed rectangle are modified. Understanding the communication in the parallel implementation is facilitated by realizing the communication of a typical processor. We will take as an example, a matrix of order 8 and assume a hypercube of dimension 3 so that there is one column per processor; in general, several columns will be wrap mapped onto the processors. On processor P_4 which contains column 5, and at step $k = 2$ in Figure 3.1, we have that P_4 receives data from P_1 and then does its row modification work on h_{35}, h_{45} and h_{55}. P_4 then sends its column to P_2, as does P_3. P_2 calculates a vector v of length $k + 4$, and sends v to P_3 and P_4 to use to modify their columns. At the next step, $k = 3$, P_4 receives data from P_2 for modifying its three elements in the solid box, sends its column to P_3, receives a new v from P_3 and then modifies its entire column. At step $k = 4$, Figure 3.2, P_4 receives its row modification data from P_3, then receives column vectors from P_5 and P_6 to form its vector v, sends v to P_5 and P_6, and then modifies its column 5. Finally, P_4's last task is performed for $k = 5$ when it broadcasts row modification data to P_5, P_6 and P_7.

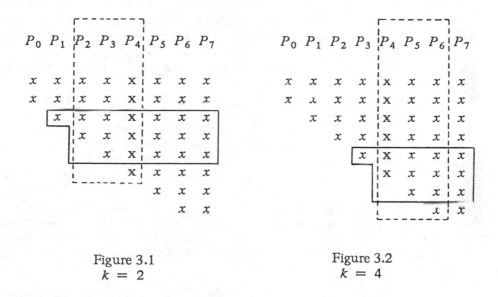

Figure 3.1
$k = 2$

Figure 3.2
$k = 4$

5. Results. We have tried to measure both the serial execution time as well as the parallel execution times of the Hessenberg and QR algorithms. Measurement of the parallel execution times was done on an Intel iPSC running the NX node kernel. Various size problems were run in 1 through 5 hypercube dimensions and the results are presented in Table 5.1. Although the parallel Hessenberg code runs very fast, requiring about two hours to reduce a 2000 × 2000 matrix using 64 processors, the QR code is estimated to take several days.

In analyzing any parallel algorithm, the first thing to realize is that the real serial time, T_1, is a function of the size of the problem, in our case, n, and the implementation of the algorithm. The ideal T_1 is a fair and reasonable time that is comparable to a single time of a parallel run, T_p. Often, the value of n is restricted in determining T_1 leading researchers to extrapolate pseudo-T_1's for large n. The second problem involves the use of inferior serial implementations to determine T_1. This gives the illusion that the parallel implementation is better than it really is.

In the Hessenberg reduction phase, we used the EISPACK routine ELMHES for the serial implementation. It was run on one hypercube node for $32 \leqslant n \leqslant 192$. A matrix of order about 200 is the largest that can fit in one node.

TABLE 5.1. Execution Times for $n = 128, n = 256$

	$n = 128$		$n = 256$	
P	Hess	QR	Hess	QR
1	120	1470 (sec)	1128	11880 (sec)
4	38.9	535	279	2840
8	24.4	468	156	2819
16	17.9	530	94	2755
32	16.5	582	67	2798

In the QR phase, we were not able to determine any real T_1's. Instead, pseudo-T_1's were determined by running the EISPACK routine HQR on the host processor which has more operating system overhead. It was also necessary to compile the serial code with another compiler (the ftn286 compiler) which doesn't produce as optimized code. The obvious solution of compiling the parallel code with ftn286 failed due to compiler bugs.

Figure 5.1 shows the speedup of the Hessenberg reduction for two problem sizes, $n = 128$ and $n = 256$. The results are quite good considering the small size of the test problems. Speedup was over 7 using 8 processors and over 16 using 32 processors when $n = 256$. The reason we did not run larger problems was that HQR already required four hours to find the 256 eigenvalues serially. We felt it was impractical to wait for larger pseudo T_1's. The speedups for the parallel QR code are shown in Figure 5.2. Unlike the Hessenberg results, the speedup appears to be roughly constant for a given n. We suspect this is caused by the $O(n^2)$ communication complexity. Thus, for $n = 256$, we see a speedup of 4 using either 4 processors or 32 processors. The speedup increases as n increases as we expected since the communication complexity is lower than the computational complexity. In this case, computational complexity is $O(n^3)$.

6. Future Work. We expect to improve the efficiency of the QR iteration. These improvements will take the form of various programming modifications and possibly pipelining. Perhaps QR combined with some other method will prove to be effective in a parallel setting for Hessenberg matrices. Other methods are suggested in Wilkinson's book [8].

So far, we have not incorporated the exceptional shift strategy [8] which allows convergence in some special cases that cycle. This modification is expected to be easy. It is known that the double precision accumulation of inner products helps the numerical stability of the reduction to Hessenberg form [8]. We will consider this inner product implementation. Gene Golub suggested that we try to devise a method to monitor the errors in the reduction to Hessenberg form. In addition, it can be important for the initial matrix to be balanced. We will consider a parallel implementation of the standard balancing code [8]. On the other end of the codes, much work needs to be done to provide for the parallel computation of eigenvectors.

Presently, we have no interface between the Hessenberg reduction and the QR iteration. It appears that the communication problems with QR are identical whether the Hessenberg matrix is stored across the processors, by rows or by columns. Therefore, we expect to convert our QR implementation to row mapping to better facilitate the interface of our routines.

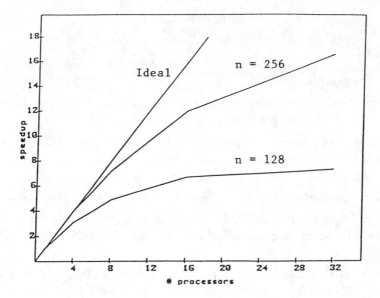

Figure 5.1. Speedup for Hessenberg Reduction

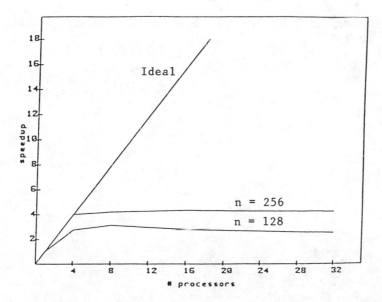

Figure 5.2. Speedup for QR Iteration

REFERENCES

(1) P. A. Businger, *Reducing a Matrix to Hessenberg Form*, Mathematics of Computation, 23 (1969), pp. 819-822.

(2) G. J. Davis, *Column LU Factorization With Pivoting on a Message Passing Multiprocessor*, SIAD, 7(4) (October 1986), pp. 538-550.

(3) T. H. Dunigan, *A Message-Passing Multiprocessor Simulator*, Technical Report ORNL/TM-9966, Oak Ridge National Laboratory, May 1986.

(4) J. G. F. Francis, *The QR Transformation - A Unitary Analogue to the LR Transformation*, Computer Journal, 4 (1961/1962), pp. 265-271 and 332-345.

(5) G. A. Geist, *Efficient Parallel LU Factorization with Pivoting on a Hypercube Multiprocessor*, Technical Report ORNL-6211, Oak Ridge National Laboratory, October 1985.

(6) B. T. Smith, J. M. Boyle, J. Dongarra, B. S. Garbow, Y. Ikebe, V. C. Klema and C. B. Moler, *Matrix Eigensystem Routines - EISPACK Guide*, Heidelberg: Springer (1974).

(7) G. W. Stewart, *Introduction to Matrix Computations*, Academic Press, New York, 1973.

(8) J. H. Wilkinson, *The Algebraic Eigenvalue Problem*, Clarendon Press, Oxford, 1965.

(9) J. H. Wilkinson and C. Reinsch, *Handbook for Automatic Computation*, Springer Verlag, New York, 1971.

Two Methods for Solving the Symmetric Tridiagonal Eigenvalue Problem on the Hypercube

ILSE C. F. IPSEN* AND ELIZABETH R. JESSUP*

Abstract

Several algorithms have been conceived specifically for determining eigenvalues and eigenvectors of symmetric, tridiagonal matrices on single processors. These include the QR algorithm, Cuppen's divide-and-conquer strategy, and bisection with Sturm sequences combined with inverse iteration. Cuppen's method and multisection, a generalization of bisection, have been implemented successfully on *shared*-memory multiprocessor architectures and their simulators. While significant speedups over the sequential versions have been reported for these cases, it remains to be determined which multiprocessor configuration is most advantageous for the solution of the symmetric, tridiagonal eigenvalue problem. We investigate the suitability of the *distributed*-memory hypercube architecture, in general, and its instantiation in the form of Intel's iPSC, in particular, for the parallel solution of the symmetric tridiagonal eigenvalue problem. Two methods will be discussed: a parallel version of Cuppen's method, and multisection together with inverse iteration. We present numerical tests of both methods on the iPSC.

1. Introduction

The symmetric eigenvalue problem is an important one in many contexts. In quantum physics, for example, the probabilities of transition of a dynamical system from one energy state to another are recorded as the entries of a symmetric matrix. The distribution of the eigenvalues of the transition matrix indicates whether or not chaotic dynamics can be expected. Properties of its eigenvector matrix give further information about the system [8]. Best results for this problem are obtained from a transition matrix of order 1000 or greater. Determination of the eigenvalues and eigenvectors of such large matrices by standard numerical techniques is, however, a time-consuming process demanding extensive

*Department of Computer Science, Yale University, P.O. Box 2158 Yale Station, New Haven, CT 06520, USA

memory. The above and similar applications thus provide motivation for the study of parallel interpretations of the symmetric eigenvalue problem: the increased computing and storage resources provided by multiprocessors can allow efficient solution of large order problems.

One traditional approach to the symmetric eigenproblem involves the initial reduction of the symmetric matrix to a more easily solvable tridiagonal form. The eigenvalues and eigenvectors of the original matrix are then determined from those of the tridiagonal matrix. Algorithms for computing eigensystems of symmetric, tridiagonal matrices on conventional uniprocessors include Cuppen's divide-and-conquer strategy [2] and multisection, a generalization of bisection, combined with inverse iteration [13]. Both have been implemented successfully on *shared*-memory multiprocessor architectures and their simulators [1, 3, 9]. While significant speedups over the sequential versions have been reported for these cases, the most advantageous multiprocessor architecture for the solution of the symmetric, tridiagonal eigenvalue problem has yet to be determined.

In this paper, we present parallel implementations on a hypercube multiprocessor for Cuppen's method and multisection. In contrast to previous implementations of parallel eigensolvers, each processor has direct access to its own local memory only. Without common memory, exchange of data between processors is accomplished through passing of messages. After a brief outline of the parallel implementations on the hypercube timings for both methods on the Intel iPSC/d5M are given. For more detailed descriptions and complexity analyses see the forthcoming paper [7]. The characterizations and topological properties of the hypercube graph used in the next sections are derived in [11].

2. Communication Routines for the Hypercube

In order to implement Cuppen's method and multisection on the hypercube, it is necessary to devise efficient ways of exchanging data among processors. To this end, two algorithms are presented: one is for broadcasting data from every processor to all others, and the other is for multiplying matrices distributed by columns among the processors. The latter is used for computing eigenvectors in Cuppen's method and for determining residuals for both Cuppen's method and multisection.

2.1. Data Transmission on the Hypercube

The *Alternate Direction Exchange Algorithm* (ADE) was first presented in [10]. It appeals to the recursive structure of the hypercube to bring about a total exchange of the data held by the processors of a cube. All processors in a d-cube whose binary labels agree in the same bit position form a $(d-1)$-cube. Because there are d bits in each binary label, there are d ways of dividing a d-cube into two $(d-1)$-cubes.

The process of broadcasting a vector of length k from one processor to all others in a d-cube requires d steps of data transmission where the amount of data doubles in size during each step.

Algorithm ADE.

For $l = 1, 2, \ldots, d$

1. Processors are divided into two $(d-1)$-cubes S_0 and S_1 according to the value of bit $l - 1$ in their binary labels.

2. Processors in corresponding positions of S_0 and S_1 exchange vectors of length $2^{l-1}k$.

3. Each processor concatenates its own vector with the one received in order to form a vector of length $2^l k$.

The above algorithm is also used when data are broadcast within a subcube S of dimension $i \leq d$. The cube S is then made up of all processors of the d-cube whose binary labels agree in exactly the same $d - i$ bit positions. Broadcasting within 2^{d-i} disjoint i-cubes can occur simultaneously without interference.

2.2. Matrix Multiplication on the Hypercube

The parallel implementations of Cuppen's method and multisection take advantage of the fact that the processors along with their interconnections form a ring within the hypercube [11].

The following algorithm, *Ring Matrix Multiplication* (RMM), performs the multiplication $C = AB$ of two $N \times N$ matrices A and B both distributed by columns among the processors of a d-cube. For simplicity, the matrix order N is assumed to be a multiple of the number of processors, $N = k2^d$. RMM takes full advantage of the distributed memory on the cube and keeps the amount of storage per processor to a minimum. Initially, processor j, $0 \leq j \leq 2^d - 1$, contains the columns $jk, \ldots, (j+1)k - 1$ of A and of B, and upon completion columns $jk, \ldots, (j+1)k - 1$ of A, B, and C. During the formation of C, the columns of B remain in their original places while the columns of A are passed cyclically from processor to processor along the ring, overwriting the previously held columns of A in each processor.

Let $\hat{A}_{ij}$ denote the $k \times k$ block-matrix held in position (i, j) of A, $0 \leq i, j \leq 2^d - 1$, and let

$$\hat{A}_j = \begin{pmatrix} \hat{A}_{0j} \\ \vdots \\ \hat{A}_{2^d-1,j} \end{pmatrix}$$

represent the k columns $jk, \ldots, (j+1)k - 1$ of A. Algorithm RMM proceeds as follows (indices should be taken modulo 2^d).

Algorithm RMM.

In parallel, do on all processors j, $0 \leq j \leq 2^d - 1$:
$\hat{C}_j = 0$
For $i = 0, \ldots, 2^d - 1$:

    1. Compute $\hat{C}_j = \hat{C}_j + \hat{A}_{j-i}\hat{B}_{j-i,j}$

    2. Send $\hat{A}_{j-i}$ to processor $j + 1$

    3. Receive $\hat{A}_{j-i-1}$ from processor $j - 1$

3. Cuppen's Method

The first scheme to be discussed is a divide-and-conquer method described by Cuppen that determines all eigenvalues and all eigenvectors of a symmetric tridiagonal matrix [2].

3.1. Algorithm

Cuppen's method is based on the fact that a symmetric tridiagonal matrix T of even order N can be divided into a pair of equal-sized symmetric tridiagonal submatrices as follows

$$T = \begin{pmatrix} \hat{T}_0 & \alpha e_{N/2}e_1^T \\ \alpha e_1 e_{N/2}^T & \hat{T}_1 \end{pmatrix}$$

$$= \begin{pmatrix} T_0 & \\ & T_1 \end{pmatrix} + \begin{pmatrix} \theta\alpha e_{N/2}e_{N/2}^T & \alpha e_{N/2}e_1^T \\ \alpha e_1 e_{N/2}^T & \theta^{-1}\alpha e_1 e_1^T \end{pmatrix} \quad (3.1)$$

$$= \begin{pmatrix} T_0 & \\ & T_1 \end{pmatrix} + \theta\alpha \begin{pmatrix} e_{N/2} \\ \theta^{-1}e_1 \end{pmatrix} \begin{pmatrix} e_{N/2}^T & \theta^{-1}e_1^T \end{pmatrix},$$

where α is the off-diagonal element of T at position $N/2$, e_i is the ith unit vector of length $N/2$, and T_0 and T_1 are of order $N/2$. The sign and magnitude of θ are selected to ensure that subdivision of the matrix can be performed at this position without cancellation [3]. The original problem has now been split into two eigenproblems of half its order.

If the solutions to the two smaller eigensystems are $T_0 = X_0 D_0 X_0^T$ and $T_1 = X_1 D_1 X_1^T$, then

$$T = Q \left[D + \alpha\theta \begin{pmatrix} l_1 \\ \theta^{-1}f_2 \end{pmatrix} \begin{pmatrix} l_1^T & \theta^{-1}f_2^T \end{pmatrix} \right] Q^T$$

where

$$Q = \begin{pmatrix} X_0 & \\ & X_1 \end{pmatrix}, \quad D = \begin{pmatrix} D_0 & \\ & D_1 \end{pmatrix},$$

$l_1^T = e_{N/2}^T X_0$ is the last row of X_0, and $f_2^T = e_1^T X_1$ is the first row of X_1. Computation of the eigensystem of T is accomplished via a rank-one updating technique described in [5] that determines the eigenvalues and eigenvectors of a diagonal plus rank-one matrix $D + \rho z z^T = Q^T T Q$. Here, $z^T = \sqrt{\frac{\alpha\theta}{\rho}}\left(l_1^T \quad \theta^{-1}f_2^T\right)$, and ρ is selected so that $\| z \|_2 = 1$.

The subdivision or 'tearing' process can be applied recursively to compute the eigensystem of T: during the ith division, submatrix T_{ij} is split into

$$T_{ij} = \begin{pmatrix} T_{i-1,2j} & \\ & T_{i-1,2j+1} \end{pmatrix} + \alpha_{ij}b_{ij}b_{ij}^T, \quad 0 \le j \le 2^{d-i} - 1,$$

where matrix $b_{ij}b_{ij}^T$ has a form similar to that shown in equation (3.1). It is this recursive nature of Cuppen's method that suggests its suitability to parallel implementation on the hypercube architecture. A high-level description of a parallel version of Cuppen's method is given as Algorithm C.

Algorithm C: Cuppen's method for a Matrix of Order $N = k2^d$ on a d-Cube.

Recursively divide the matrix d times so that processor j contains submatrix T_{0j} of order k, $0 \leq j \leq 2^d - 1$.

Step 0.   Each processor (0-cube) independently computes the eigensystem of its order-k submatrix.

Step i, $1 \leq i \leq d$. Each $(i - 1)$-cube pairs with another $(i - 1)$-cube to form an i-cube by exchanging information about the eigensystems of $T_{i-1,2j}$ and $T_{i-1,2j+1}$ of order $k2^{i-1}$ that were computed in step $i - 1$. Each i-cube independently computes the eigensystem for its matrix T_{ij} of order $k2^i$. The 2^{d-i} i-cubes at step i are enumerated according to the index j, $0 \leq j < 2^{d-i}$.

Note that the number of updating steps in Algorithm C is equal to the dimension of the hypercube. At step i, 2^{d-i} i-cubes independently solve eigensystems of order $k2^i$. Upon completion of step d, each processor contains k of the $N = k2^d$ eigenvalues of the original matrix T as well as the k corresponding eigenvectors (of length N). If N is not a multiple of the number of processors, T is recursively divided so that the orders of the smallest submatrices T_{0j} differ by no more than one.

The remarkable speed of Cuppen's method on sequential and shared-memory machines is due to the frequent occurrence of 'deflation': a component of z that is zero or close to zero may be disregarded in the rank-one updating process since the corresponding eigenvalue and eigenvector remain unchanged. When multiple elements occur along the diagonal of D, the eigenvector basis is rotated to zero out the corresponding elements of z thereby leading to additional deflation.

3.2. Experimental Results

To demonstrate the influence of deflation on the hypercube implementation two symmetric, tridiagonal eigenvalue test problems are examined. The first matrix [1,2,1] has all off-diagonal elements equal to 1, all diagonal elements equal to 2, and zeros everywhere else. The second matrix [1,ι,1], has the value 1 in each off-diagonal position and the value $\iota \times 10^{-6}$ in the $\iota - th$ diagonal position. Substantial deflation occurs for [1,2,1], while little takes place for [1,ι,1].

Speedup is defined as the time required to solve a problem with the fastest sequential method on one processor divided by the time required to solve the same problem on $p \geq 2$ processors. We measured speedup with respect to the subroutine SESUPD, a sequential implementation of Cuppen's method. SESUPD is the fastest available routine that determines all eigenvalues and (orthogonal) eigenvectors of a symmetric tridiagonal matrix to high accuracy [3]. The speedup of Cuppen's method on the hypercube is strongly dependent on the matrix at hand. Figure 1 shows speedup on a 5-cube as a function of matrix order for the two test problems. Data points marked with circles indicate matrix orders equal to a multiple of 32. The points marked with a square correspond to matrix order 100. Although speedup is almost maximal in case of little deflation, it drops to about 50 percent when deflation is prevalent.

For two reasons, the savings incurred from deflation on a sequential machine do not necessarily carry over to a hypercube. Due to communication and additional computational

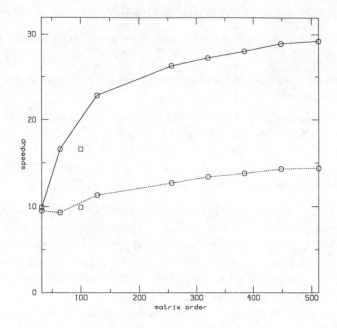

Figure 1: Cuppen's Method on a 5-Cube: Speedup for $[1,\iota,1]$
(Solid Line) and $[1,2,1]$ (Dotted Line) versus Matrix Order.

overhead of the hypercube code the actual eigensystem computations represent a smaller fraction of the total time than in the sequential case. Therefore, time savings from deflation are not as dramatic for the hypercube as for the sequential version. In addition, matrix partitioning results in non-identical subproblems for the various processors. Although a single processor may encounter savings when significant deflation occurs for its own sub-problem, the gain may not be shared by the cube as a whole due to the strict processor synchronization and the *static* task scheduling.

An alternate design for Cuppen's method on the hypercube would allow for *dynamic* task scheduling during the updating phase. As noted in [7], however, the loss of efficiency due to redundant arithmetic and communication bottlenecks inherent in such an approach suggests that significant improvement is not possible through dynamic scheduling.

Figure 2 shows the communication time on the iPSC as a fraction of the total time for a 5-cube versus matrix order. Computation time is seen to be greater than communication time for matrix orders as small as 64. For eight or more eigenvectors per processor, the communication cost on the iPSC levels off at about 16 percent of the total time.

4. Multisection and Inverse Iteration

The method to be described in this section is based on the determination of eigenvalues of a symmetric, tridiagonal matrix T by multisection and the subsequent computation of eigenvectors via inverse iteration. Its suitability for parallel implementation is based on independent computations within the different sections.

4.1. Algorithms

The method of bisection locates eigenvalues of a matrix T by repeatedly halving an

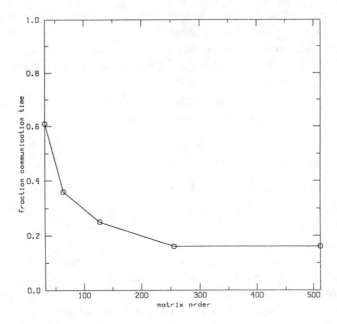

Figure 2: Cuppen's Method for Matrix [1,2,1] on a 5-Cube: Communication Time on the iPSC as a Fraction of the Total Computation Time versus Matrix Order.

interval (on the real line) known to contain one or more eigenvalues. The number of eigenvalues in each half is determined from Sturm sequence evaluations at its endpoints [4].

A generalization of bisection known as *multisection* consists of dividing the interval into $p \geq 2$ sections of equal size. Again, Sturm sequence evaluations at the endpoints of each of the p sections provide an eigenvalue count for each section. As in [9], a section containing more than one eigenvalue is in turn subjected to multisection in order to *isolate* individual eigenvalues. A section containing no eigenvalues is removed from the search area. Multisectioning is continued until all sections either consist of only one eigenvalue or else contain several eigenvalues and have been reduced to a width no larger than a given tolerance δ. In the latter case, the confined eigenvalues are considered to represent a *cluster* of computationally coincident eigenvalues of T. The refinement of an eigenvalue or cluster of eigenvalues to a specified tolerance, δ, is termed *extraction*.

To achieve a reasonable numerical accuracy for the computed eigenvectors requires attention to the eigenvalue distribution. For a set of well-separated eigenvalues, inverse iteration converges quickly and generates orthogonal eigenvectors. However, the closer an eigenvalue is to other eigenvalues the slower inverse iteration converges to the corresponding eigenvector. In addition, the computed eigenvectors corresponding to close eigenvalues are no longer necessarily orthogonal, and an additional orthogonalization step must be included. If the close eigenvalues form a cluster, i.e. are actually computationally coincident, then standard inverse iteration, which converges to a single eigenvector, cannot be employed to find the eigenspace corresponding to a cluster.

One remedy in case of clusters is to perturb close eigenvalues to a non-problematic distance. Wilkinson [13] maintains that a separation of neighboring eigenvalues on the order of three times machine precision is sufficient to produce independent eigenvectors. These vectors do suffer the loss of orthogonality associated with close eigenvalues, so the modified Gram-Schmidt procedure is recommended for orthogonalizing the vectors. This version of perturbed inverse iteration has gained acceptance as implemented in the routine TINVIT of EISPACK. [12]

The procedure for finding all eigenvalues of a symmetric, tridiagonal matrix using multisection and the corresponding eigenvectors with inverse iteration is summarized in Algorithm M below.

Algorithm M: Multisection for a Matrix of Order $N = k2^d$ on a d-Cube.

Step 0.   *Determination of Initial Search Area.*
          Each processor contains the entire matrix and determines intervals containing all eigenvalues by computing all Gerschgorin disks.

Step 1.   *Isolation of Eigenvalues.*
          Each interval I containing more than one eigenvalue is divided into $p = k2^d$ equal sized sections. Processor i determines the number of eigenvalues in the ith section of interval I and sends its results to all other processors. Hence, all processors know the eigenvalue counts of all intervals and can maintain identical queues of those intervals that need further dividing.

          The processors work in lock step and the next interval I they divide is the one currently at the head of the queue. This process continues until all single eigenvalues are isolated (and the queue is empty) or until the resulting sections are of width less than $p\delta$ and thus are too small to be evenly divided among all p processors.

Step 2.   *Extraction of Eigenvalues.*
          The isolation phase produces two sets of intervals. The first set is made up of intervals that contain a single eigenvalue, the width of those intervals is not known. The eigenvalue of such an interval is extracted via bisection in a single processor to precision δ. (As shown in [9], on one processor it is more efficient to divide intervals with single eigenvalues via bisection rather than multisection.)

          The second set is made up of intervals that contain several eigenvalues, the width of those intervals is less than $p\delta$. A single processor performs one multisection step on such an interval to confine its eigenvalues to subintervals of width δ or less.

          As in the previous isolation step, efficient extraction necessitates explicit distribution of the work load. The two sets of intervals define two distinct sets of extraction tasks. The simple synchronization-communication load balancing scheme of the first step is no longer applicable, instead a static task assignment is employed. As each processor knows all intervals and their eigenvalue counts, it can estimate the time required to extract all eigenvalues. Each then selects and performs its 'fair share' of tasks.

          After all eigenvalues have been extracted to precision δ they are suitably grouped together and perturbed in preparation for the following step.

Test Matrix	Isolation	Extraction	Eigenvectors
[1,2,1]	0.52	0.41	0.07
[2,2,2]	0.42	0.50	0.08

Table 1: Multisection on a 5-Cube: Fraction of Total Computation Time Spent in Different Steps.

Step 3.   *Computation of Eigenvectors.*

The previous step results in two sets of eigenvectors. The first set is made up of eigenvectors corresponding to well-separated eigenvalues. These vectors can be computed in a small number of inverse iterations. If there are M of them effective load balancing is achieved by having each processor compute M/p vectors. No communication is required, and an equal number of eigenvectors is stored in each processor. If M is not a multiple of p, some processors are required to compute one more vector than others.

The second set is made up of eigenvectors corresponding to a cluster. To achieve orthogonality in this case, the computed eigenvectors for a cluster are orthogonalized against each other by means of the modified Gram-Schmidt process. Although the time for the Gram-Schmidt process can be estimated the increased number of iterations for inverse iteration cannot be predicted. At best, an approximate 'weighting' of eigenvector computing tasks based on cluster size is possible. The method chosen for load balancing is based on the cyclic distribution of computing tasks around a ring: processor g computes eigenvectors indexed $g, g + p, g + 2p, \ldots$, where the eigenvalues (and hence eigenvectors) are numbered according to their location on the real line.

The most appealing feature of cyclic distribution is its regularity: eigenvectors are systematically distributed across processors and memory allocation is uniform since the numbers of eigenvectors computed per processors differ by at most one. Hence, cyclic distribution provides good balancing of processor workload and storage. Although extensive communication is necessary for the orthogonalization of vectors within a cluster, cyclic distribution assures that the message size is independent of the number of eigenvalues per cluster. Furthermore, a processor can perform inverse iteration on one set of eigenvectors while awaiting messages for orthogonalization of another set. This overlap of communication and computation keeps idle time to a minimum.

Our objective first and foremost has been to devise a simple and robust implementation of multisection for the hypercube. On account of its regularity, simplicity and good performance cyclic distribution seems to be the only load balancing strategy able to achieve this goal.

4.2. Experimental Results

The fraction of the total time of multisection spent in each of the steps depends on the problem to be solved. The following two test problems indicate the difficulties in assessing the contribution of the different steps towards the total time.

Table 1 summarizes results for test matrices [1,2,1] and [2,2,2] of order 64. Both test problems are $N \times N$ Toeplitz matrices of the form [e,d,e] with eigenvalues $\lambda_j = \mathrm{d} + 2\mathrm{e}\cos\frac{j\pi}{N+1}$, $1 \le j \le N$ [6]. The eigenvalues of [1,2,1] exhibit a closer spacing than those of [2,2,2]. Hence, a larger proportion of time is spent in the isolation phase for [1,2,1]. Despite

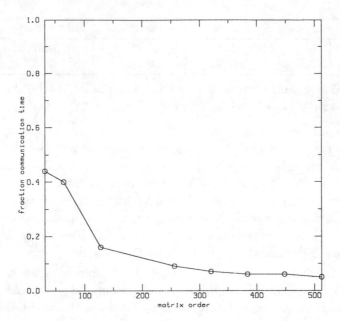

Figure 3: Multisection for Matrix [1,2,1] on a 5-Cube: Communication Time on the iPSC as a Fraction of the Total Computation Time versus Matrix Order.

a larger initial search area from the Gerschgorin disks, the more widely spaced eigenvalues of [2,2,2] are more rapidly confined to individual intervals. However, the resulting intervals are wider than those produced for [1,2,1] and thus lead to a proportional increase in extraction time for [2,2,2].

All steps of multisection involve communication, yet computation time dominates communication time even when only one eigenvector is computed per processor. As Figure 3 shows the pure communication time for matrix [1,2,1] levels off at only 5 percent of the total time on the iPSC as the matrix order exceeds 300.

For large matrix orders, the combination of EISPACK routines BISECT (bisection) and TINVIT (inverse iteration) on a single processor determines all eigenvalues and eigenvectors of the test matrix [1,2,1] more quickly than Cuppen's method – at the expense of lower accuracy. As the accuracy from multisection is of the same order as that of bisection, speedup is measured with respect to BISECT/TINVIT. Figure 4 shows the speedup results as a function of matrix order for a 5-cube. Maximal speedup is not even observed for large matrix orders. Identical scheduling calculations performed in parallel in all processors as well as other redundant computations involved in the hypercube code significantly reduce the efficiency during eigenvalue computations.

5. Comparison and Conclusion

In summary, we can conclude from our hypercube implementation that multisection is slightly faster but less accurate than Cuppen's method with static assignmetnt of tasks. As can be seen from the given measures of residual and orthogonality, introduction of communication for the hypercube does not alter the numerical properties of the methods. As

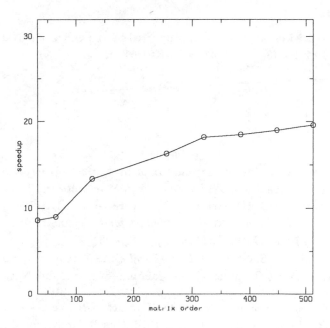

Figure 4: Multisection for Matrix [1,2,1] on a 5-Cube: Speedup versus Matrix Order.

Method	Time Seconds	Residual $\|TX - \lambda X\|$	Orthogonality $\|X^T X - I\|$
Cuppen's	10.48	1.860544e-15	1.938191e-15
Multisection	8.54	2.403447e-14	1.496798e-13

Table 2: Comparison for Matrix [1,2,1] of Order 100 on a 5-Cube.

an example, Table 2 shows the residual and deviation from orthogonality for both methods for the matrix [1,2,1] of order 100.

Because speedup curves for the test matrices level off with increasing order the expected speedup will not be maximal in the case when multisection is applied to problems of large order, and when Cuppen's method encounters significant deflation in some but not all subproblems. In either method efficient task scheduling is crucial for good performance. However, the extensive communication requirements of a dynamic scheduler or the parallel execution of an explicit scheduler on all processors reduces processor utilization on the hypercube. Consequently, both methods exhibit lower efficiency on the distributed-memory hypercube than on the shared-memory machines.

Nevertheless, the hypercube implementations are promising. The communication time represents a small portion of the total time for both Cuppen's method and multisection. The lack of any communication bottlenecks indicates that matrix order is not an obstacle to performance on the hypercube: the large distributed memory is available without contention problems.

Acknowledgements

The work presented in this paper was supported by the Office of Naval Research under contracts N000014-82-K-0184 and N00014-85-K-0461.

References

[1] H.J. Bernstein and M. Goldstein, *Parallel Implementation of Bisection for the Calculation of Eigenvalues of Tridiagonal Symmetric Matrices,* Technical Report 129, Computer Science Department, New York University, 1984.

[2] J.J.M. Cuppen, *A Divide and Conquer Method for the Symmetric Tridiagonal Eigenproblem,* Num. Math., 36 (1981), pp. 177–95.

[3] J.J. Dongarra and D.C. Sorensen, *A Fully Parallel Algorithm for the Symmetric Eigenvalue Problem,* Technical Memorandum 62, Argonne National Laboratory, 1986.

[4] W. Givens, *Numerical Computation of the Characteristic Values of a Real Symmetric Matrix,* Technical Report ORNL-1574, Oak Ridge National Laboratory, 1954.

[5] G.H. Golub, *Some Modified Matrix Eigenvalue Problems,* SIAM Review, 15 (1973), pp. 318–34.

[6] R.T. Gregory and D.L. Karney, *A Collection of Matrices for Testing Computational Algorithms,* John Wiley and Sons, Inc., 1969.

[7] I.C.F. Ipsen and E.R. Jessup, *Solving the Symmetric Tridiagonal Eigenvalue Problem on the Hypercube,* Research Report in Preparation, Computer Science Department, Yale University, 1986.

[8] R.V. Jensen and R. Shankar, *Statistical Behavior in Deterministic Quantum Systems with Few Degrees of Freedom,* Phys. Rev. Lett., 54 (1985), pp. 1879–1882.

[9] S. Lo, B. Phillipe and A. Sameh, *A Multiprocessor Algorithm for the Symmetric Tridiagonal Eigenvalue Problem,* Technical Report, Center for Supercomputing Research and Development, University of Illinois at Urbana-Champaign, 1986.

[10] Y. Saad and M.H. Schultz, *Data Communication in Hypercubes,* Research Report 428, Computer Science Department, Yale University, 1985.

[11] ———, *Some Topological Properties of The Hypercube Multiprocessor,* Research Report 389, Computer Science Department, Yale University, 1984.

[12] B.T. Smith, J.M. Boyle, J.J. Dongarra, B.S. Garbow, Y. Ikebe, V.C. Klema and C.B. Moler, *Matrix Eigensystem Routines–EISPACK Guide, Lecture Notes in Computer Science, Vol. 6,* Springer-Verlag, 1976.

[13] J.H. Wilkinson, *The Algebraic Eigenvalue Problem,* Clarendon Press, Oxford, 1965.

A Divide and Conquer Algorithm for the Unitary Eigenproblem

W. B. GRAGG* AND L. REICHEL†

Abstract

In divide and conquer methods for eigenproblems, the original problem is split into several smaller subproblems by using rank one modifications of the matrix. This approach has been shown to be efficient for the symmetric eigenproblem, in particular, when implemented on a parallel computer. The present paper describes a divide and conquer method for the eigenproblem for unitary matrices.

1. Introduction

In the divide and conquer (DC) methods for the symmetric eigenproblem [Cu], [DS], one first reduces the given real symmetric matrix into a symmetric tridiagonal matrix by an orthogonal similarity transform. This tridiagonal matrix is then split into two symmetric tridiagonal matrices by rank one tearing. The new tridiagonal matrices can again be split by rank one tearing. One keeps splitting until only trivial eigenproblems remain [Cu], or until one, after k splittings, solves 2^k eigenproblems by the QR method for symmetric tridiagonal matrices [DS]. Since the 2^k eigenproblems are independent, the algorithm is well suited for implementation on a parallel computer. When the 2^k eigenproblems have been solved, they are assembled pairwise to yield 2^{k-1} independent eigenproblems. The assembly requires the computation of the zeros of certain rational functions, the zeros being the eigenvalues of the assembled matrices. Eigenvectors of the 2^k matrices are updated to yield eigenvectors of the 2^{k-1} larger matrices. The assembly is repeated until the eigenvalues

*Department of Mathematics, University of Kentucky, Lexington, Kentucky 40506. Research sponsored, in part, by the National Science Foundation under Grant DMS-84-04980 and by the University of Umea, Sweden.

†Department of Mtahematics, University of Kentucky, Lexington, Kentucky 40506. Research supported by the Applied Mathematics Division, Argonne National Laboratory.

and eigenvectors of the original tridiagonal matrix have been determined. For the symmetric eigenproblem DC methods have been shown to be competitive [Cu], [DS]. They are based on previous work in [L], [W], [Go], [BNS].

The present paper describes a DC scheme for *unitary* matrices $H \in \mathbb{C}^{n \times n}$. H is unitarily similar to a right Hessenberg matrix with real nonnegative subdiagonal elements. If a subdiagonal element vanishes, then the eigenproblem splits into eigenproblems for smaller Hessenberg matrices. We therefore may assume that H is a right Hessenberg matrix with *positive* subdiagonal elements. Then all eigenvalues of H are simple. It is easy to show that H can be written as a product of Given's reflections $G_j \in \mathbb{C}^{n \times n}$:

$$H = H(\gamma_1, \gamma_2, \ldots, \gamma_u) = G_1 G_2 \ldots G_{n-1} G_n , \qquad (1.1)$$

where

$$G_k = \begin{bmatrix} I_{k-1} & & & \\ & -\gamma_k & \sigma_k & \\ & \sigma_k & \bar{\gamma}_k & \\ & & & I_{n-k-1} \end{bmatrix},$$

$$\gamma_k \in \mathbb{C}, \quad \sigma_k \in \mathbb{R}, \quad |\gamma_k|^2 + \sigma_k^2 = 1, \quad \sigma_k > 0, \quad |\gamma_k| < 1, \quad 1 \le k < n ,$$

and

$$G_n = \begin{bmatrix} I_{n-1} & \\ & -\gamma_n \end{bmatrix},$$

with $|\gamma_n| = 1$. Here I_j denotes the $j \times j$ identity matrix, $\sigma_1, \sigma_2, \ldots, \sigma_{n-1}$ are the subdiagonal elements of H, $\gamma_1, \gamma_2, \ldots, \gamma_n$ are the so-called *Schur parameters* of H, and $\bar{\gamma}_k$ denotes the complex conjugate of γ_k. We compute the γ_k as follows. Let M_{jk} denote element (j,k) of a matrix M. From (1.1), we obtain

$$\gamma_1 = -H_{11},$$

$$\gamma_j = (G_{j-1}^H \ldots G_2^H G_1^H H)_{jj}, \quad 2 \le j \le n .$$

Now

$$H = G_1 \ldots G_{s-1} G_s G_{s+1} \ldots G_n$$

$$=: \begin{bmatrix} H_1 & \\ & I_{n-s} \end{bmatrix} G_s \begin{bmatrix} I_s & \\ & H_2 \end{bmatrix}, \qquad (1.2)$$

where $H_1 \in \mathbb{C}^{s \times s}$ and $H_2 \in \mathbb{C}^{(n-s) \times (n-s)}$ are unitary. Assume for the moment that $H \in \mathbb{R}^n$. Then the γ_j are real and G_s is a Householder transformation or a Householder transformation with reversed sign. Let

$$\omega_1 := \left(\frac{1 + |\gamma_s|}{2} \right)^{1/2}, \quad \omega_2 := -\text{sign}(\gamma_s) \frac{\sigma_s}{2\omega_1},$$

and define

$$w := e_s \omega_1 + e_{s+1} \omega_2 \in \mathbb{R}^n \ .$$

Throughout this paper e_j denotes the jth column of an identity matrix of appropriate size. Then

$$G_s = \text{sign}(\gamma_s)(I - 2ww^T)$$

and H is unitarily similar to

$$H' := \begin{bmatrix} H_1 \\ & H_2 \end{bmatrix} (I - 2ww^H) =: \tilde{H} - 2\tilde{H}ww^H \ . \tag{1.3}$$

This is the first step in the divide and conquer scheme for unitary matrices. How the splitting (1.3) should be carried out when $\gamma_s \in \mathbb{C} \backslash \mathbb{R}$ is described in Section 2. The eigenvalues and eigenvectors of H_1 and H_2 are computed first, and are then used to determine the eigenvalues and eigenvectors of H'. This assembly phase of the algorithm requires the determination of zeros of a certain trigonometric function. A method for finding these zeros is described in Section 3. The computation of eigenvectors is treated in Section 4. Sometimes H_1 and H_2 have very close eigenvalues. This reduces the computational work and is discussed in Section 5. There we also show how the computation can be sped up when the vector w is nearly orthogonal to an eigenvector of $\tilde{H}$.

Similarly as for the symmetric eigenproblem, the DC method can be applied in two different ways for unitary eigenproblems. Either the DC scheme is applied recursively until the original eigenproblem has been reduced to the solution of many trivial eigenproblems, which then need be assembled, or the DC scheme is used to divide the original problem into only a few independent subproblems, each of which is solved by the unitary QR method [Gr1] or by reduction to some bidiagonal singular value problems [AGR].

Among the applications of the unitary eigenproblem are the computation of Pisarenko frequency estimates [Cy] and the generation of Gaussian quadrature rules for the unit circle [Gr2].

2. Partitioning by rank one tearing

This section generalizes (1.3) to $\gamma_s \in \mathbb{C}$, $|\gamma_s| < 1$, for which G_s is not a real Householder transform. G_s is, however, diagonally unitarily equivalent with a real Householder transform. Let

$$\gamma_s' := \begin{cases} \gamma_s / |\gamma_s|, & \gamma_s \neq 0 \\ 1, & \gamma_s = 0 \end{cases} \ .$$

Then $|\gamma_s'| = 1$ and

$$\begin{bmatrix} I_{s-1} \\ & \bar{\gamma}_s' \\ & & I_{n-s} \end{bmatrix} G_s \begin{bmatrix} I_s \\ & \gamma_s' \\ & & I_{n-s-1} \end{bmatrix} = I - 2ww^H, \tag{2.1}$$

where

$$w := e_s \omega_1 + e_{s+1} \omega_2 \tag{2.2a}$$

with

$$\omega_1 := \left(\frac{1+|\gamma_s|}{2} \right)^{1/2} \quad \text{and} \quad \omega_2 := \frac{-\sigma_s}{2\omega_1} . \tag{2.2b}$$

Substitution of (2.1) into (1.2) yields

$$H = \begin{bmatrix} H_1 & \\ & I_{n-s} \end{bmatrix} (I - 2ww^T) \begin{bmatrix} I_s & \\ & H_2 \end{bmatrix} \tag{2.3a}$$

with

$$\begin{aligned} H_1 &:= H(\gamma_1, \gamma_2, \ldots, \gamma_{s-1}, -\gamma_s') \\ H_2 &:= H(\bar{\gamma}_s' \gamma_{s+1}, \bar{\gamma}_s' \gamma_{s+2}, \ldots, \bar{\gamma}_s' \gamma_n) . \end{aligned} \tag{2.3b}$$

After a unitary similarity transform of (2.3a) we obtain a formula analogous to (1.3),

$$H' := \begin{bmatrix} H_1 & \\ & H_2 \end{bmatrix} (I - 2ww^H) =: \tilde{H} - 2\tilde{H} ww^H . \tag{2.4}$$

Let

$$H_k = W_k \Lambda_k W_k^H, \quad k = 1, 2, \tag{2.5}$$

be spectral resolutions, i.e., the W_k are unitary and the Λ_k are diagonal. Then $\tilde{H}$ has the spectral resolution $\tilde{H} = \tilde{W} \Lambda \tilde{W}^H$ with

$$\tilde{W} = \begin{bmatrix} W_1 & \\ & W_2 \end{bmatrix}, \quad \tilde{\Lambda} = \begin{bmatrix} \Lambda_1 & \\ & \Lambda_2 \end{bmatrix} = \mathrm{diag}(\lambda_1, \lambda_2, \ldots, \lambda_n) . \tag{2.6}$$

Here $|\lambda_k| = 1$, $1 \leq k \leq n$. In the next section, we describe how the spectrum of H' can be determined from Λ, the last row of W_1 and the first row of W_2.

3. The spectrum of H

Let H be a unitary right Hessenberg matrix (1.1) and let H' and $\tilde{H}$ be defined by (1.2-3) or (2.1-4). Introduce the characteristic polynomial

$$\chi(\lambda) := \det(\lambda I - H) = \det(\lambda I - H') = \det(\lambda I - \tilde{H} + 2\tilde{H} ww^H)$$

$$= \det(\lambda I - \tilde{H}) = \det(I + 2(\lambda I - \tilde{H})^{-1} \tilde{H} ww^H) =$$

$$= \psi(\lambda)(1 + 2w^H (\lambda I - \tilde{H})^{-1} \tilde{H} w) =$$

$$= \psi(\lambda)(1 + 2w^H \tilde{W} (\lambda I - \tilde{\Lambda})^{-1} \tilde{\Lambda} \tilde{W}^H w),$$

where $\tilde{W}$ and $\tilde{\Lambda}$ are defined by (2.6), and w is given by (2.2). Let $z = [\varsigma_j]_{j=1}^n$ be defined by

$$z = \tilde{W}^H w = \begin{bmatrix} W_1^H e_s \omega_1 \\ W_2^H e_1 \omega_2 \end{bmatrix} \tag{3.1}$$

and introduce the *spectral function*

$$\phi(\lambda) := \frac{\chi(\lambda)}{\psi(\lambda)} = 1 + 2 z^H (\lambda I - \tilde{\Lambda})^{-1} \tilde{\Lambda} z = 1 + 2 \sum_{j=1}^n |\varsigma_j|^2 \frac{\lambda_j}{\lambda - \lambda_j} = \sum_{j=1}^n |\varsigma_j|^2 \frac{\lambda + \lambda_j}{\lambda - \lambda_j}, \tag{3.2}$$

where we have used that $z^H z = 1$. Since all $|\lambda_j| = 1$, the linear fractional transformations $(\lambda + \lambda_j)/(\lambda - \lambda_j)$ map the unit circle onto the imaginary axis, and therefore $\operatorname{Re} \phi(e^{i\theta}) = 0$ for $\theta \in \mathbb{R}$. Setting

$$\lambda_j =: \exp(i\theta_j), \quad \lambda =: \exp(i\theta), \tag{3.3}$$

we obtain

$$\phi(\lambda) = i \sum_{j=1}^n |\varsigma_j|^2 \cot\left(\frac{\theta_j - \theta}{2}\right) =: i\, \Phi(\theta), \tag{3.4}$$

where $\Phi(\theta) \in \mathbb{R}$ for $\theta \in \mathbb{R}$. Using $z^H z = 1$ yields

$$\Phi'(\theta) = \frac{1}{2} \sum_{j=1}^n |\varsigma_j|^2 / \sin^2\left(\frac{\theta_j - \theta}{2}\right) \geq \frac{1}{2} \left[\max_\theta \sin^2\left(\frac{\theta_j - \theta}{2}\right) \right]^{-1} = \frac{1}{2}. \tag{3.5}$$

We may assume that the θ_j are distinct and that all $|\varsigma_j| > 0$ because otherwise we can make these conditions hold by deflation, see Section 5. Let θ_j' denote the zeros of $\Phi(\theta)$. They are the arguments of the eigenvalues of H. The sets $\{\theta\}_{j=1}^n$ and $\{\theta_j'\}_{j=1}^n$ strictly interlace.

We turn to the description of a rootfinder. By (3.5) the zeros of $\Phi(\theta)$ can be computed accurately. Denote an initial approximation of a zero of $\Phi(\theta)$ by θ^0. We may assume that $0 < \theta_1 < \theta_2 < \cdots < \theta_n < 2\pi$ and that $\theta^0 = 0$. Then $\theta_n - 2\pi < \theta^0 < \theta_1$. Until otherwise stated, assume further that

$$\Phi(\theta^0) < 0. \tag{3.6}$$

By the strict interlacing property of the sets $\{\theta_j\}_{j=1}^n$ and $\{\theta_j'\}_{j=1}^n$, $\Phi(\theta)$ has precisely one zero, say θ_1', in $]\theta_n - 2\pi, \theta_1[$. Introduce

$$\hat{\Phi}(\theta) := \rho + \sigma \cot\left(\frac{\theta_1 - \theta}{2}\right), \tag{3.7}$$

where ρ and σ are determined by osculatory interpolation, i.e.,

$$\rho + \sigma \cot\left(\frac{\theta_1}{2}\right) = \Phi(0),$$

$$\frac{\sigma}{2} \left[\sin\left(\frac{\theta_1}{2}\right) \right]^{-2} = \Phi'(0),$$

from which it follows that

$$\rho = \Phi(0) - \Phi'(0)\sin\theta_1 ,$$

$$\sigma = 2\Phi(0)\sin^2\left(\frac{\theta_1}{2}\right) . \tag{3.8}$$

The zero θ^1 of $\hat{\Phi}(\theta)$ in $]\theta_n - 2\pi, \theta_1[$ is our next approximation of θ_1'. New approximations θ^{j+1} of θ_1' are computed from θ^j, $j \geq 1$, in a similar fashion. This defines a sequence $\{\theta^j\}_{j=1}^\infty$ of approximations of θ_1'. We next consider some properties of this sequence. Introduce

$$E(\theta) := \hat{\Phi}(\theta) - \Phi(\theta) = \rho + (\sigma - |\varsigma_1|^2)\cot\left(\frac{\theta_1 - \theta}{2}\right) - \sum_{j=2}^n |\varsigma_j|^2 \cot\left(\frac{\theta_j - \theta}{2}\right) . \tag{3.9}$$

Lemma 3.1 Let the θ_j, $1 \leq j \leq n$, be distinct in $[0, 2\pi[$. Then $\left\{1, \cot\left(\frac{\theta_1 - \theta}{2}\right), \ldots, \cot\left(\frac{\theta_n - \theta}{2}\right)\right\}$ is an extended Chebyshev system on $[0, 2\pi[\setminus \{\theta_j\}_{j=1}^n$, i.e.,

$$\alpha_0 + \sum_{j=1}^n \alpha_j \cot\left(\frac{\theta_j - \theta}{2}\right), \tag{3.10}$$

with not all $\alpha_j = 0$, has at most n zeros in $[0, 2\pi[$ counting multiplicities.

Proof. $\text{span}\left\{1, \cot\left(\frac{\theta_1 - \theta}{2}\right), \ldots, \cot\left(\frac{\theta_n - \theta}{2}\right)\right\} = \text{span}\{1, (\lambda_1 - \lambda)^{-1}, \ldots, (\lambda_n - \lambda)^{-1}\}$, where λ, λ_j, θ and θ_j are related by (3.3). Moreover, $\text{span}\left\{1, \cot\left(\frac{\theta_1 - \theta}{2}\right), \frac{\partial}{\partial\theta}\cot\left(\frac{\theta_1 - \theta}{2}\right), \ldots, \frac{\partial^j}{\partial\theta^j}\cot\left(\frac{\theta_1 - \theta}{2}\right)\right\} =$ $\text{span}\{1, (\lambda_1 - \lambda)^{-1}, (\lambda_1 - \lambda)^{-2}, \ldots, (\lambda_1 - \lambda)^{-j}\}$. The Hermite interpolation problem for $\{1, (\lambda_1 - \lambda)^{-1}, \ldots, (\lambda_n - \lambda)^{-1}\}$ with interpolation in $n+1$ interpolation points in $(\mathbb{C} \cup \{\infty\}) \setminus \{\lambda_j\}_{j=1}^n$ has a unique solution [SL, Section 1.1.1]. Therefore (3.9) has at most n zeros, counting multiplicity. $\square$

Lemma 3.2 From (3.6) follows that $\hat{\Phi}(\theta) \geq \Phi(\theta)$ for $\theta_n - 2\pi < \theta < \theta_1$.

Proof. $E(\theta)$ has at least a double zero at θ^0. By continuity of $E(\theta)$ in $]\theta_j, \theta_{j+1}[$, $2 \leq j < n$, and by the fact that the coefficients of $\cot\left(\frac{\theta_j - \theta}{2}\right)$, $2 \leq j \leq n$, all are of the same sign, it follows that $E(\theta)$ has at least one zero in each subinterval $]\theta_j, \theta_{j+1}[$, $2 \leq j < n$. By Lemma 3.1, $E(\theta)$ has precisely one zero in each subinterval $]\theta_j, \theta_{j+1}[$, $2 \leq j < n$, and $]\theta_n - 2\pi, \theta_1[$. The zero in the latter subinterval is of multiplicity two. From $|\varsigma_n|^2 > 0$ and $\sigma - |\varsigma_1|^2 > 0$ it follows that $\lim_{\theta \downarrow \theta_n - 2\pi} E(\theta) = \lim_{\theta \uparrow \theta_1} E(\theta) = \infty$. This proves the lemma. $\square$

Theorem 3.3 Let (3.6) hold, and denote the zero of $\Phi(\theta)$ in $]\theta_n - 2\pi, \theta_1[$ by θ_1'. Then θ^j converges monotonically and quadratically towards θ_1' as $j \to \infty$, and $\theta^j \leq \theta_1'$ for all $j \geq 0$.

Proof. The result follows from Lemma 3.2 and the osculatory interpolation. $\square$

Let $\theta_n - 2\pi < \theta^0 < \theta_1$ and assume that $\Phi(\theta^0) > 0$. Then we use

$$\hat{\Phi}(\theta) := \rho + \sigma \cot\left(\frac{\theta_n - \theta}{2}\right)$$

instead of (3.6), and obtain a sequence $\{\theta^j\}_{j=1}^n$ such that θ^j converges monotonically and quadratically towards θ_1' as $j \to \infty$, and $\theta^j \geq \theta_1'$ for all $j \geq 0$.

We note that if $H \in \mathbb{R}^n$, then the nonreal eigenvalues appear in complex conjugate pairs. Only half of them need to be determined with the rootfinder.

4. Spectral resolution of H

Given the spectral resolutions of H_1 and H_2, see (2.5), we describe the computation of the spectral resolution

$$H = W \Lambda W^H, \quad \Lambda = \text{diag}(e^{i\theta_1'}, e^{i\theta_2'}, \ldots, e^{i\theta_n'}). \tag{4.1}$$

In the assembly phase of the algorithm the rootfinder needs the last and/or first rows of the eigenvector matrix. In the end of this section we show how the computations simplify if only the first and last row of W are required.

From (2.3a) and (2.4), we obtain

$$H = \tilde{H} - 2u\tilde{u}^H, \quad u = \begin{pmatrix} H_1 e_s \omega_1 \\ e_1 \omega_2 \end{pmatrix}.$$

Let $\lambda = e^{i\theta'}$ be an eigenvalue of H and let $Hv = \lambda v$. Then

$$(\tilde{H} - 2u\tilde{u}^H)v = \lambda v,$$

or, equivalently,

$$(\tilde{H} - \lambda I)v = u\alpha, \quad \alpha = 2\tilde{u}^H v.$$

This shows that any normalized eigenvector v of H associated with λ is a normalization of

$$v' = (\tilde{H} - \lambda I)^{-1} u = \begin{bmatrix} (H_1 - \lambda I)^{-1} H_1 e_s \omega_1 \\ (H_2 - \lambda I)^{-1} e_1 \omega_2 \end{bmatrix} =$$

$$= \begin{bmatrix} H_1 W_1 & \\ & W_2 \end{bmatrix} \begin{bmatrix} (\Lambda_1 - \lambda I)^{-1} W_1^H e_s \omega_1 \\ (\Lambda_2 - \lambda I)^{-1} W_2^H e_1 \omega_2 \end{bmatrix} = \begin{bmatrix} W_1 & \\ & W_2 \end{bmatrix} \begin{bmatrix} (I - \lambda \Lambda_1^H)^{-1} W_1^H e_s \omega_1 \\ (\Lambda_2 - \lambda I)^{-1} W_2^H e_1 \omega_2 \end{bmatrix}.$$

By $\|W_1\|_2 = \|W_2\|_2 = \|\Lambda_1\|_2 = 1$, (2.6), (3.1) and (3.5), we obtain

$$\delta(\lambda) := \|v'\|_2 = \|(\tilde{\Lambda} - \lambda I)^{-1} z\|_2 = \left(\sum_{j=1}^n \frac{|\varsigma_j|^2}{|\lambda_j - \lambda|^2}\right)^{\frac{1}{2}} = \left[\frac{1}{2}\Phi'(\theta')\right]^{\frac{1}{2}} \geq \frac{1}{2}.$$

We can take

$$
v = \begin{bmatrix} W_1(I-\lambda\Lambda_1^H)^{-1}W_1^H e_s \omega_1 \\ W_2(\Lambda_2-\lambda I)^{-1}W_2^H e_1 \omega_2 \end{bmatrix} / \delta(\lambda) \ . \tag{4.2}
$$

The lower bound for δ suggests that the computation (4.2) is numerically stable.

If the eigenvectors are not required, we saw in Section 3 that the rootfinder requires Λ and, generally, the first and last rows of W in order to determine the spectrum of the next larger problem. We call the triple $(\Lambda, e_1^H W, e_n^H W)$ the *partial spectral resolution* of H. The first and last elements of v can easily be determined from

$$
e_1^H v = e_1^H W_1(I-\lambda\Lambda_1^H)^{-1}W_1 e_s \omega_1/\delta(\lambda)
$$

$$
e_n^H v = e_{n-s}^H W_2(\Lambda_2-\lambda I)^{-1}W_2 e_1\omega_2/\delta(\lambda) \ .
$$

5. Deflation

In Section 3 we assumed that all components of z are nonzero and the eigenvalues of $\tilde{\Lambda}$ are distinct. These conditions are not satisfied in general, but deflation techniques can be employed to arrange their satisfaction. The techniques discussed here are similar to those in [BNS], [Cu], [DS] for the symmetric eigenproblem.

First assume that ς_l vanishes. By (2.4-6) and (3.1),

$$
\tilde{W}^H H' \tilde{W} = \tilde{\Lambda} - 2\tilde{W}^H \tilde{H} w w^H \tilde{W} = \tilde{\Lambda}(1-2zz^H) \ . \tag{5.1}
$$

From $e_l^H z = 0$, we obtain

$$
\tilde{\Lambda}(1-2zz^H)e_l = \tilde{\Lambda}e_l = e_l\lambda_l \ , \tag{5.2}
$$

and, by (5.1),

$$
H'\tilde{W}e_l = \tilde{W}e_l\lambda_l \ .
$$

Therefore, by (2.3),

$$
H\begin{bmatrix} W_1 & \\ & W_2\Lambda_2^H \end{bmatrix}e_l = \begin{bmatrix} W_1 & \\ & W_2\Lambda_2^H \end{bmatrix}e_l\lambda_l \ . \tag{5.3}
$$

By (5.2), H has an eigenvalue λ_l and (5.3) shows the corresponding eigenvector. The term $|\varsigma_l|^2\cot\left(\dfrac{\theta_l-\theta}{2}\right)$ is removed from (3.4).

We turn to deflation due to multiple eigenvalues. Let $\tilde{\Lambda} = \text{diag}(\lambda_1, \lambda_2, \ldots, \lambda_n)$ with $\lambda_1 = \lambda_2 = \cdots = \lambda_m \neq \lambda_j$, $j > m$. For any unitary matrix $R \in \mathbb{C}^{m\times m}$, we have

$$
\tilde{H} = \tilde{W}\begin{bmatrix} R^H & \\ & I_{n-m} \end{bmatrix}\tilde{\Lambda}\begin{bmatrix} R & \\ & I_{n-m} \end{bmatrix}\tilde{W}^H \ .
$$

We can now let the vector z used in (3.2) be defined by, c.f. (3.1),

$$z = \begin{bmatrix} R \\ & I_{n-m} \end{bmatrix} W^H w =: \begin{bmatrix} Rz_0 \\ & z_1 \end{bmatrix}.$$

Choose R so that $Rz_0 = e_1 \|z_0\|_2$. Then $e_j^H z = e_j^H Rz_0 = 0$, $2 \leq j \leq m$, and deflation as described above can be carried out. In actual computations, deflation is carried out when $|\varsigma_l|$ or $|\lambda_j - \lambda_k|$ are "tiny" for any l, j and k. [Cu] and [DS] noted that deflation may speed up the computations considerably.

This paper shows the feasibility of solving the unitary eigenproblem by a divide and conquer method. Numerical experiments will be presented in a forthcoming paper.

References

[AGR] G.S. Ammar, W.B. Gragg and L. Reichel, *On the eigenproblem for orthogonal matrices*, in Proc. 25th IEEE Conf. on Decision and Control, Athens, 1986.

[BNS] J.R. Bunch, C.P. Nielsen and D.C. Sorensen, *Rank-one modification of the symmetric eigenproblem*, Numer. Math. **31** (1978) 31-48.

[Cu] J.J.M. Cuppen, *A divide and conquer method for the symmetric eigenproblem*, Numer. Math. **36** (1981) 177-195.

[Cy] G. Cybenko, *Computing Pisarenko frequency estimates*, in Proceedings of the Princeton Conference on Information Science and Systems, Department of Electrical Engineering, Princeton, 1985.

[DS] J.J. Dongarra and D.C. Sorensen, *A fully parallel algorithm for the symmetric eigenvalue problem*, SIAM J. Sci. Stat. Comput., to appear.

[Go] G.H. Golub, *Some modified matrix eigenvalue problems*, SIAM Rev. **15** (1973) 318-334.

[Gr1] W.B. Gragg, *The QR algorithm for unitary Hessenberg matrices*, J. Comput. Appl. Math. **16** (1986) 1-8.

[Gr2] W.B. Gragg, *Positive definite Toeplitz matrices, the Arnoldi process for isometric operators and Gaussian quadrature on the unit circle* (in Russian), in Numerical Methods in Linear Algebra, E.S. Nikolaev, ed., Moscow University Press, 1982.

[L] K. Löwner, *Über monotone Matrixfunktionen*, Math. Z. **38** (1934) 177-216.

[SL] V.I. Smirnov and N.A. Lebedev, Functions of a Complex Variable, M.I.T. Press, Cambridge, MA, 1968.

[W] J.H. Wilkinson, The Algebraic Eigenvalue Problem, Clarendon Press, Oxford, 1965.

PART IX:
PARTIAL DIFFERENTIAL EQUATIONS

A High-Level Library for Hypercubes

R. M. CHAMBERLAIN*, P. O. FREDERICKSON†, J. LINDHEIM* AND
J. PETERSEN*

Abstract. We have constructed a high level subroutine library for hypercubes to make them easier for a non-specialist to use. At the primary level we have included an assortment of elementary communications primitives. At the next level up we have included subroutines which establish various global data structures for use in problems which have spatial extent in one, two, or three dimensions. We have also included an assortment of discrete differential operators. The library is written so that the user does not need to know the details of the communication mechanisms, as all communications are hidden in a small number of subroutines. This means that the library will be portable to other parallel machines by simply changing the communications primitives.

An example is given which demonstrates the use of the library in solving the wave equation. The library is being extended to include other useful matrix and vector operations and operations specific to the formulation and solution of partial differential equations. The ultimate aim of such a high-level library is to make the hypercube no more difficult to use than an ordinary sequential machine. Should the scientist or engineer with a difficult problem to solve really need to know that he is programming for a hypercube?

1. Introduction. There has been much recent interest in hypercube multiprocessors. It is now important to assess the hypercube and determine for what problems and applications the power of the hypercube can be used. However for the user with a large scientific problem to solve and little hypercube knowledge, the job of developing his application on the hypercube can be a long and frustrating experience. As manufacturers work to improve the hypercube environment and to provide debugging tools, the user still requires a number of basic tools to ease his job. It is thus preferable that users share the tools that they develop, and that a general design and framework is established for programs to be easily distributed and used.

At Chr. Michelsen Institute we have been developing a high level library for hypercubes.

---

* Chr. Michelsen Institute, Fantoftveien 38, N-5036 Fantoft, Norway.

† Los Alamos National Laboratory, Los Alamos, New Mexico, U.S.A.

There are four important reasons why there is a need for such a library. Firstly it allows the user to work at a higher level and achieve significant results more easily and more quickly. In this way more users can develop their applications on a hypercube and so a wider assessment of the suitability of hypercubes can be made. Secondly it avoids the duplication of effort in the development and debugging of large programs. There are many fundamental operations, which require non-trivial programs because the data is distributed among the processors, and it is important to have tested versions available for general use. Thirdly some of the complexities of the machine can be hidden from the user. This makes the hypercube attractive for the new user or non-specialist in parallel computing. Fourthly a high level library allows programs to be moved from one hypercube to another. A number of the lower-level library subroutines will vary between the two hypercubes but the application program is then portable across both machines.

There are a number of high-level libraries for sequential machines, e.g. LINPACK, EISPACK, NAG and IMSL and the goals of these libraries are similar to ours. However the added complexity of parallel machines (and in our case hypercubes) means that it is important to provide a library for general use which hides this complexity. There has been work on general-purpose software for hypercubes in the CALTECH library[2] and by McBryan and Van der Velde[6]. However it is important that this work is unified to provide a single high-level library which enables hypercubes to be widely and efficiently used. This unified library would provide an easy method for the distribution of software for hypercubes.

In this paper we describe briefly our library and the design principles behind it. An application is given to illustrate the use of the library and show the simplicity of the user's program. The example is taken from partial differential equations and the library has been specifically intended for the solution of partial differential equations. The library has been developed on the INTEL iPSC hypercube, but has been written so that it should be able to run on other hypercubes with only a small number of changes. The authors welcome comments and discussion both on the design and contents of the library.

2. Design Principles. The main guideline in writing subroutines has been that they should be modular, simple and clear. In this way a simple algorithm may be preferred to an optimal one, so that at least a version is available to the user. As long as the design has been modular it is easy to replace the first version with a faster but perhaps more complicated version later. The need for clarity is always present in developing software, but perhaps is more necessary when working with parallel machines as there are new ways of introducing errors.

The library has been written in standard FORTRAN 77. Comments, indenting and standard constructs are used to make the code as portable and understandable as possible. There are simple calling sequences for the library subroutines, so that the user need only supply the few necessary parameters. Many lower-level parameters, e.g. variables required for communication, are hidden in small common blocks. These hidden variables are available to the user through a subroutine call, if he requires them for his main program. Otherwise they are passed between the relevant system subroutines through these small common blocks. The machine-specific variables and functions have been limited to a few library subroutines.

There are many important features which these design principles are intended to provide. The library must be quick to develop so that users can program their applications on hypercubes now. It must be simple to change and maintain, so that new and modified subroutines can be added and any problems with existing subroutines quickly found. It must be simple to use to attract users and the machine-dependent features must be isolated in a small number of places to ensure easy portability.

3. The library. The CMI library has been divided into two parts. There is a communications library (COM-LIB), which contains a number of basic communication subroutines and a collection of subroutines (PDE-LIB) which are helpful for the solution of partial differential equations.

In COM-LIB there are an assortment of higher-level communications primitives, including global broadcast and gather. There are also subroutines which establish and use various global data structures for use in problems which have spatial extent in one, two, or three dimensions, particularly partial differential equations. When solving a partial differential equation, the domain is often divided into blocks and each processor works on one block. If a finite difference or finite element method is used then most of the calculations of a processor use values for points in the block. However it is also necessary to update boundary elements and for that an exchange of boundary data between neighbours is required. A subroutine in COM-LIB does precisely this exchange for neighbours in a 2-dimensional grid. Another important pair of subroutines are *hsgive* and *hstake*. These subroutines call the system communication subroutines to do the message passing. In this way *hsgive* sends a message and *hstake* receives a message. The purpose of these subroutines is to ensure portability so that all the subroutines in PDE-LIB call *hsgive* and *hstake* and it is only these two subroutines that require changing between hypercubes.

In PDE-LIB there are an assortment of discrete differential operators, such as *grad* and *div*, for use when these data structures represent scalar or vector fields, and we have included the corresponding global norms. There are also global operations, such as minimum, and various data initialisation subroutines. The subroutines in PDE-LIB call only subroutines in COM-LIB, so that PDE-LIB is a portable high-level library. The subroutines in COM-LIB will need to be changed for different hypercubes.

The motivation for this split is similar to that for the Basic Linear Algebra Subroutines (BLAS)[4] and Extended BLAS[1]. By separating out the machine-dependent part, this can be efficiently implemented on a variety of hypercubes, while the rest of the library requires no changes for different hypercubes. Our purpose is also similar to Rice[7], Lusk and Overbeck[5] and Frederickson, Jones and Smith[3] who propose extensions to Fortran, implemented as subroutine calls. These machine-dependent subroutines hide the complexities of the communication and synchronisation primitives in the hardware vendor-supplied operating system. In this way more easily understood, and therefore more probably correct, high-level programs can be developed.

There are programs both for the processors and for a host in the library. Programs for the host processor are used for data input and output. This allows for graphical output and for interactive use. Though this part of the library will run on other hypercubes, it has been designed specifically for the INTEL hypercube. Here communications between the processors is much faster than the communications between the host and the processors and so these programs have been written to minimise the number of messages between the host and the nodes.

4. An example: the wave equation. Our first demonstrations of the library included the construction of seismic pressure waves through an inhomogeneous medium. The problem is to find the solution of the wave equation

$$\frac{\partial \vec{U}}{\partial t} = \kappa \, grad \, P$$

$$\frac{\partial P}{\partial t} = \gamma \, div \, \vec{U}$$

initialized with a gaussian distribution potential

$$P(\vec{x}, 0) = \alpha \, exp(-\beta < \vec{x} - \vec{x}_0, \vec{x} - \vec{x}_0 >)$$

$$\vec{U}(\vec{x}, 0) = 0$$

as the wave passes through an inhomogeneous medium

$$\gamma = \gamma(\vec{x}), \quad \kappa = \kappa(\vec{x}).$$

What are the effects of discretization in time and space? The variable coefficient fields κ and γ are initialised and multiplied by dt

$$kapdt \longleftarrow \kappa(\vec{x}) \, dt$$

$$gamdt \longleftarrow \gamma(\vec{x}) \, dt$$

using a special purpose subroutine. Then, using library calls, the main part of the user's program which calculates the solution is:

```
c Initialise the hypercube and set up the 2-d grid
        call hinit(2)
c Initialise the pressure with a Gaussian with half-width halfwd
        call hsgaus(p, nx, ny, halfwd, x0, y0)
c Set the velocity to zero initially
        call hvzero(u, nx, ny, d)
c Send initial wave to host for plot
        call hzoom(p, nx, ny, 0.0, 1.0, 0.0, 1.0))
        do 100 it = 1 , tsteps
c Do ten time steps between each plot
        do 50 j = 1,10
        call hograd(gradp, p, nx, ny, delta)
        call hvaxpy(u, kapdt, gradp, nx, ny)
        call hodiv(divu, u, nx, ny, delta)
        call hsaxpy(p, gamdt, divu, nx, ny)
50      continue
c Send data to host for plotting
        call hzoom(p, nx, ny, 0.0, 1.0, 0.0, 1.0)
100     continue
```

The output of this program is shown in Figure 1, where the pressure is plotted and the pulse is seen as it disperses across the domain. In this program subroutine *hinit(2)* sets up the two-dimensional grid and determines the neighbours of each processor. Communication is needed in subroutine *hograd*, where the boundary data in each processor has to be passed to its neighbours, and this is done using a subroutine in COM-LIB. All the processors combine to send a plot to the cube manager when *hzoom* is called. In this example the values for the whole domain (the unit square) are sent to the cube manager, but particular areas can be studied by changing the last four parameters.

This example shows the user working at a higher level on the hypercube. The user need not concern himself with the mechanics of generating the grid or the details of the communications.

5. Conclusions. For many people it is still unclear whether the processing power of hypercubes can be used in large scale scientific computations. It is vital that users are given as much help as possible in developing applications on hypercubes. In this way the suitability of hypercubes for various applications can be more quickly ascertained.

We have developed a high level library for users at CMI. Although our library is only small at present, we believe it is an important step to helping users to develop their application

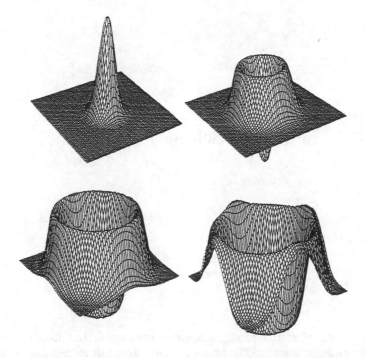

Fig.1. The pressure, p, as the wave propagates through the medium at four different times. The plots are normalised to the maximum and minimum values of p.

on the hypercube. We have shown an example of the modelling of the wave equation. Other applications of the library have included a multigrid application, block matrix-vector multiplication and the analysis of changing scenes using optical flow.

REFERENCES

[1] J.J. DONGARRA, J. DUCROZ, S. HAMMARLING and R.J. HANSON, *A Proposal for an Extended Set of Fortran Basic Linear Algebra Subprograms*, NAG report TR3/86, NAG Limited, Oxford, 1986.

[2] G.C. FOX et. al., *Concurrent Computation Project Annual Report 1983-1984*, Cal Tech/JPL, Passadena, 1984.

[3] P.O. FREDERICKSON, R.E. JONES, B.T. SMITH, *Synchronization and Control of Parallel Algorithms,* Parallel Computing, 2 (1985), pp. 255-264.

[4] C. LAWSON, R.J. HANSON, D. KINCAID and F. KROGH, *Basic Linear Algebra Subprograms for Fortran Usage*, ACM Transactions on Mathematical Software, 5 (1979), pp. 308-323.

[5] E.L. LUSK and R.A. OVERBECK, *Implementation of Monitors with Macros: A programming aid for the HEP and other parallel processors*, ANL-83-87, Argonne National Laboratory, 1983.

[6] O.A. MCBRYAN, E.F. VAN DE VELDE, *Hypercube Algorithms and Implementations,* Courant Mathematics and Computing Laboratory Report DOE/ER/03077-271, New York University, 1986.

[7] J. RICE, *FORTRAN Extensions for Parallel and Vector Computation*, Purdue University Report CSD-TR 470, 1984.

Solving Finite Element Problems with Parallel Multifrontal Schemes[*]

G. A. GEIST[†]

Abstract. A parallel multifrontal scheme is presented that uses a method we call the super boundary element technique. This technique reduces the amount of communication required during the factorization to $\log_2(p)$ sends, where p is the number of processors. Furthermore, no communication is required in the parallel back substitution using this technique. A finite element fracture analysis problem is used to illustrate this method. Results from this small problem show a decrease in execution time of 58% while larger problems are expected to have even better improvements.

1. Introduction. The use of finite element methods in structural analysis typically involves solving a large system of linear equations:

$$K\delta = b$$

where K is the global stiffness matrix for the structure and is usually sparse, symmetric, and positive definite. By far the most popular method of solving this system for the displacement, δ, is by Gaussian elimination. In particular, engineers have favored banded solvers or its variants skyline and frontal solvers, to determine δ. These methods are popular because the data structure is simple and they are easy to implement out of core. (Solving the system out of core allows one to solve much larger problems than can fit in the main memory.) In the last few years, general sparse matrix solvers have been developed which use much better orderings than the banded solvers. The effect of these improved orderings is to significantly reduce the operation count and storage requirement in solving the system of equations. The drawback is a more complex code and data structure.

---

* Research supported by the Exploratory Studies Program of the Oak Ridge National Laboratory

† Engineering Physics and Mathematics Division, Mathematical Sciences Section, Oak Ridge National Laboratory, Oak Ridge, Tennessee 37831-2009

We began by looking at an existing finite element code [1] which used the frontal solver of Hinton and Owen [5]. Since we did not wish to change the data structure in the rest of the code, we sought to parallelize the frontal method. In the next section we will look at the frontal method and its extension to multifrontal methods. In section 3 we will discuss our implementation of a p-front method and its advantages. Finally, we will present some results from a sample problem.

2. Multifrontal Methods. The frontal method was first described by Irons [6] to solve finite element problems, and is based on the observation that Gaussian elimination can begin before the assembly of K is complete. In fact a node in the finite element mesh can be eliminated as soon as all the elements it is associated with are assembled. Since the assembly and factorization of K proceed together, this method is more natural for element problems [7]. In order for the frontal method to be efficient, it is important that the front width be kept as small as possible, but for irregular or complex meshes this can be a difficult task. This is illustrated by the mesh of Figure 2.1. While this mesh is composed of members whose widths are only 4 nodes, the width of the front must grow to at least 18 nodes during the factorization.

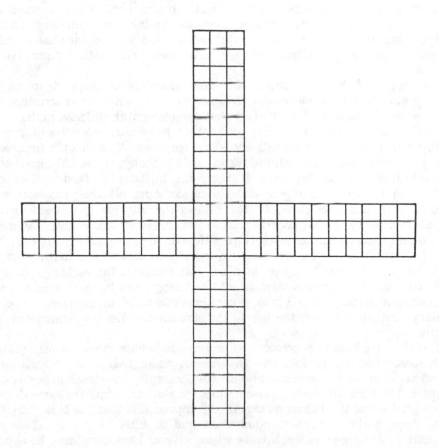

Figure 2.1. The Frontal Method Performs
Poorly on This Simple Mesh.

One way to keep the front widths small was proposed by Duff and Reid [4]. They allowed multiple fronts to exist at any time. Thus, in Figure 2.1, a separate front could begin at the ends of each of the branches and remain narrow until the hub is reached. In order to determine when fronts would start and stop, Duff used a minimum degree ordering of the nodes and constructed an assembly tree. An assembly tree describes which nodes are in a front and the order in which the fronts are assembled and written back into memory. In doing this they combined the good general sparse orderings with the advantages of frontal techniques. Using these ideas they developed a sequential multifrontal code called MA27 [3].

3. Parallel Implementation. The obvious approach of using a frontal solver on a local-memory multiprocessor is to have one front on each processor. We will call this the p-front approach. It is the first approach we implemented. The major advantage of this approach was the ability to use the original frontal solver on each processor, thus avoiding the problem of changing the data structure in the entire code.

The p-front approach is designed so that each processor solves an entire subproblem. In reality only the host processor knows what the whole problem looks like. It is the host's job to reconstruct the mesh deflections given the deflections of the individual processors' pieces. The nodes shared between processors play an important role in both this reconstruction and in the solution. In order for each of the processors to determine its boundary conditions corresponding to these shared nodes, various combinations of the shared nodes are combined into special elements. We call these elements "super boundary elements."

It is unlikely that the super boundary elements correspond to an actual element, and thus their elemental stiffness matrix cannot be determined in the normal way. Instead we use the fact that the elemental stiffness matrix is some permutation of the frontal matrix on another processor. So pairs of processors assemble super boundary elements and exchange them. The effect is to essentially combine the two fronts on each processor. This exchange is the only node-to-node communication that is required. If there are initially p fronts, they can be combined in $\log_2(p)$ exchanges. After each exchange all the processors proceed normally with this next element. This allows the solution to proceed to the end without developing special code to handle the shared nodes. As an example, if p equals 8 and the problem is suitably partitioned, then processor pairs 0-1, 2-3, 4-5, and 6-7 exchange on the first step. On the second step the exchange pairs are 0-2, 1-3, 4-6, and 5-7. And on the third and last exchange the exchange pairs are 0-4, 1-5, 2-6, and 3-7. In each step the $p/2$ exchanges can be performed in parallel. And between exchanges all the processors compute in parallel. The super boundary element has been the key to the efficient parallel implementation of the algorithm.

In order for each processor to solve its subproblem some redundant calculations must be performed. In general, some redundant calculations are performed after each communication. For example, the final super boundary element is the same for each processor thus they all calculate the same deflections for this final element. The advantage of the approach is that the back substitution can be done without any communication and is thus very fast. This can be important in finite element problems where several load cases may be applied to the same mesh.

The most difficult task in this approach is determining a good partitioning of the mesh into p independent blocks and reorganizing the global problem into p smaller complete problems. The original serial code required the engineer to set up the data files in the way he wanted the problem to be solved. Our initial approach has been to require the same. The routines read the reorganizing information from a data file set up by the engineer. Automation of the partitioning and reordering of the problem is under investigation. The problem can be simply stated. The original problem must be partitioned into p problems such that the communication is minimized and the operation count is minimized while maximizing the parallelism among the p problems.

The communication is minimized in two ways. First only mesh information is passed between the host and the nodes instead of the entire K matrix. Second, the number of shared nodes between processors at each of the log p exchanges must be minimized. The number of shared nodes is a property of how the original problem has been partitioned and the order in which the exchanges are performed.

The operation count is a function of the shape of each of the subproblems which is dictated by the partitioning of the elements. Since K is sparse the operation count can often be reduced by reordering the elimination of the element nodes. Initially we have used a profile minimization ordering because this is the best ordering for a frontal solver. Recently there has been evidence that a minimum degree ordering coupled with a multi-frontal solver can dramatically reduce the operation count and thus the execution time of finite element analysis codes. We have begun investigating the possibility of using a multi-frontal solver, together with a good ordering on each of the p problems.

In summary there are three major stages to the reorganization of the original problem. First, the mesh must be partitioned into p blocks such that the number of shared nodes is minimized and each of the blocks contains approximately the same amount of work. Second, the super-boundary elements and partners must be determined for each of the subproblems in such a way that the amount of computation between exchanges is balanced across the processors. Third, the individual subproblems must be numbered (ordered) in a way that will minimize the number of operations in each of them. Once the reorganization is complete, the host processor sends one subproblem to each hypercube processor.

4. Results for a Sample Problem. The sample problem arose from a fracture analysis of a large steel boiler plate. The plate is modeled by 28 8-node isoparametric elements shown in Figure 4.1 and has a total of 202 unknown deflections. In order to have a reasonable number of elements on each processor we decided to manually partition the problem into four pieces. The partitioning is shown in Figure 4.2. The results from running the sample problem are very encouraging. As seen in Table 4.1, the overall execution time for the original problem has been decreased by more than 58%. Even more impressive is the fact that this time includes all the host I/O, host-to-node communication, and the fracture analysis. Looking at the two parts of the code that were parallelized, the assembly/factorization of K and the solution of $K\delta=b$, the results need some explaining. Notice that the parallel assembly/factorization step is performed 4.2 times faster than the serial step. This is due to the fact that the p-frontal ordering has a slightly lower operation count than the frontal ordering so the parallel code has an advantage above and beyond having more processors. A similar but less dramatic improvement can be seen in the solution time for the same reason. We also ran the sample problem through MA27 on the host processor and found it required about 29 seconds to perform the factorization.

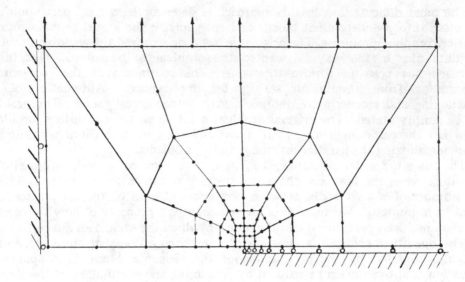

Figure 4.1.   Finite Element Mesh of Sample
Fracture Analysis Problem.

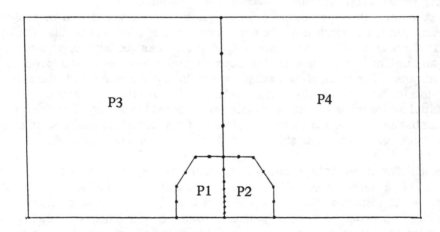

Figure 4.2.   Partitioning of Sample Problem
Into 4 Blocks.

The reason MA27 does not perform much better than the original serial time is due to the problem's small size (order 202) and high density (up to 40 nonzeros per row).

Another point the reader may notice is that the actual saving is greater than the serial factorization time minus the parallel factorization time. This is due to the host processor performing useful work while the nodes are computing the deflections. So, effectively $p+1$ processors are working in parallel on different parts of the problem.

Table 4.1. Performance Results for Sample Problem

Code	assemble / factor	solv	total time*
Serial on host	32.2	0.88	55 (sec)
Parallel w/4 nodes	7.6	0.27	24 (sec)

*Total time includes I/O, Host to Node communication, and fracture analysis.

As the problem size grows, the number of nodes on an individual processor grows much faster than the number of shared nodes. Thus it is expected that the performance of this algorithm will continue to improve as the problems get larger. We are in the process of automating the problem partitioning. When this is complete, larger problems will be run to verify that the performance improves with problem size.

For the interested reader, more details about this method can be found in [2].

REFERENCES

(1) Bryson, J. W., *ORVIRT.PC: A 2-D Finite Element Fracture Analysis Program for a Microcomputer*, ORNL-6208, October 1985.

(2) Clinard, J. A. and Geist, G. A., *Implementing Fracture Mechanics Analysis on a Distributed-Memory Parallel Processor*, ORNL Technical Report (in preparation).

(3) Duff, I. S. and Reid, J. K., *MA27 - A Set of FORTRAN Subroutines for Solving Sparse Symmetric Sets of Linear Equations*, Report AERE R 10533, Harwell, 1982.

(4) Duff, I. S. and Reid, J. K., "The Multifrontal Solution of Indefinite Sparse Symmetric Linear Systems," *ACM Trans. on Math. Software*, Vol. 9, pp. 302-325.

(5) Hinton, E. and Owen, D. R. J., *Finite Element Programming*, Academic Press, New York, 1977.

(6) Irons, B. M., "A Frontal Solution Program," *International Journal of Numerical Methods in Engineering*, Vol. 2, pp. 5-32, Jan.-March, 1970.

(7) Reid, J. K., "Frontal Methods for Solving Finite-Element System of Linear Equations," in *Sparse Matrices and Their Uses*, ed. I. S. Duff, Academic Press, New York, 1981.

Parallelization of a Finite Element Application Program on a Hypercube Multiprocessor

C. AYKANAT*, F. ÖZGÜNER*, S. MARTIN† AND S. M. DORAIVELU†

Abstract. *In this paper, a description is given of the work being done to parallelize ALPID, a finite element modelling program based on a rigid viscoplastic formulation, on a hypercube multiprocessor. The computationally intensive components in ALPID can be broadly classified into : a) generation of the global stiffness matrix of the linear system of equations to be solved and b) the solution of the linear system of equations generated in (a).*

Concurrency in the global stiffness matrix generation is achieved easily since the elemental stiffness matrix of each finite element can be generated independent of the others. Processors of the hypercube compute the elemental stiffness matrices of different finite elements in parallel and then add these contributions in parallel to generate the global stiffness matrix. Complete locality of communication is achieved during this computation step.

The Conjugate Gradient(CG) method is chosen due to various numerical and concurrency considerations for the solution of the linear system of equations. The basic CG method and its variant methods are being implemented on the hypercube. The CG algorithm introduces a large amount of inter-processor communication overhead and concurrency limitation due to its strong data dependencies during iteration steps. In order to overcome these difficulties a large grain parallel partial CG algorithm with reduced data dependencies is presented in this paper.

1. Introduction. The synergistic development of the computer and the finite element method (*FEM*) has established *FEM* as the predominant method of solution of linear boundary value problems and it is also rapidly penetrating into areas requiring the solution of nonlinear problems, such as metalworking. Metalforming operations, such as extrusion, and forging involve large plastic deformations of the material involved.

---

* Department of Electrical Engineering,The Ohio State University, Columbus, Ohio 43210.

† Universal Energy Systems, Dayton, Ohio 45432.

In general, the elastic strains are inconsequential when compared with the plastic ones, presenting the possibility of ignoring elastic strains in the solutions. This line of reasoning lead to the development of the rigid-viscoplastic approach by Lee and Kobayashi [1]. This approach has been successfully applied to analyze forming problems such as solid cylinder upsetting, sheetbending [2], extrusion and ring compression and has been extended to include thermal effects(thermo-viscoplastic analysis [3]).

ALPID (Analysis of Large Plastic Incremental Deformation) is a finite element code which embodies the approach of Kobayashi and co-workers. It was developed under the Air Force Processing Science Program by Oh [4] of Columbus Battelle Laboratories. Oh implemented the *FEM* formulation and developed convenient features such as capabilities for handling arbitrary die geometries and remeshing. The details of the implementation and some of its applications are available in numerous publications [5].

The nonlinearities in *ALPID* arise from both material and geometric sources. The geometric nonlinearities are dealt with using an updated Lagrangian approach. The material nonlinearities must however be dealt with directly. This means that the objective function to be minimized is nonlinear and a system of simultaneous nonlinear equations must be solved to achieve this.

Two methods are used for the solution of the nonlinear finite element equations in *ALPID* ; Direct Iteration and Newton-Raphson. The Direct Iteration method has a larger radius of convergence but is at best linearly convergent. The Newton-Raphson method is quadratically convergent but has a smaller radius of convergence. Direct Iteration is used in situations where there is a poor initial guess for the solution and the Newton-Raphson is used where a good initial guess(possibly generated by Direct Iteration) exists. One of two different stiffness matrices are generated according to the method chosen but this has a minimal impact on the parallelization of the stiffness matrix generation and its subsequent solution. Each of the methods requires solving a system of linear subproblems to produce a sequence of iteration vectors which converges to the solution of the nonlinear system of equations. Each of these linear subproblems involves the determination of a matrix representing a linearized version of the nonlinear system of equations and the solution of the generated matrix eqution to produce the next iteration value.

The Conjugate Gradient(*CG*) method([6]) has recently become increasingly popular to solve large, sparse, positive definite linear system of equations. The symmetric and positive definite nature of the coefficient matrices arising in the finite element problems [7] makes the *CG* method a good choice for implementation. It has been also observed that the convergence rate of the direct iteration process, is not very sensitive to the accuracy levels of the solutions to the sequence of linear system of equations generated. Hence, the tolerance value for the convergence of a linear system of equations can be held reasonably high and the number of *CG* iterations can be lowered.

The *CG* method can be implemented very efficiently on the hypercube. The only drawback of the method for parallelization is the requirement for the computation of two global scalar parameters at each iteration step. In this paper a restructuring of the basic *CG* algorithm to overcome this global communication bottleneck is proposed.

2. Parallel K-Matrix Generation. *ALPID*, in many respects is a standard finite element program and thus shares many features with them. A typical finite element mesh is shown in Figure 1, consisting of 10 elements(circled numbering) and 18 nodes(normal numbering). The finite element method produces a solution over the entire mesh domain as a function of the values of one or more degrees of freedom at the nodal points. The elemental stiffness equations give relationships between each of the nodes associated with the element. All of the nodes associated with an element are connected(i.e. they are interrelated). The normal formulation requires the solution of equations of the form $K\mathbf{x} = \mathbf{b}$, where K is the global stiffness matrix, $\mathbf{x}$ is the vector of nodal degrees of freedom and $\mathbf{b}$ is the applied nodal forces. The global K matrix is merely superposition of the individual elemental K matrices. Therefore, the individual elemental K matrices may be computed independently and this portion of the generation of the global K matrix can be done completely in parallel.

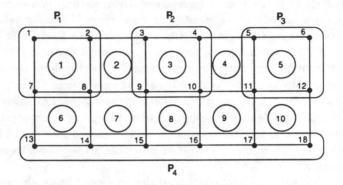

Figure 1: *Finite element mesh and mapping of nodes onto 2 dimensional hypercube*

It is important to note that the adjacency matrix associated with the finite element graph is identical in its zero-nonzero structure to the global K matrix. This knowledge is of great importance in achieving the greatest degree of compaction when using an iterative solution scheme.

For an iterative method, it is natural to define a row partitioning of the global K matrix. This corresponds to mapping a set of nodes onto each processor of the hypercube. The mapping determines which rows of the K matrix need to be resident on a processor in order to perform the necessary matrix-vector product operations in the CG method. The operations to be performed in parallel are then the construction of these matrix rows. The question to be answered has become : what is the relationship between the elemental stiffness matrices and the rows of the global K matrix? It is obvious that the elemental stiffness matrices which contribute to a global stiffness matrix row-i are those which have node-i associated with them. Figure 1 defines a nodewise mapping onto processors 1,2,3 and 4. Processor 2 requires matrix rows 3,4,9,10 and Processor 4 requires 13,14, 15,16,17,18 in order to perform their portion of the matrix vector product required in the CG method. Examination of the lists of necessary elements for the two processors reveals that elemental K matrices for 7,8 and 9 provide data relevant to row constructions on both processors.

Let the set of all elements which contain nodes in the mapped node set for a processor be known as the associated element set for that processor. The set of elements whose related nodes are contained entirely in the mapped node set are defined as interior elements(e.g. finite element 3 for processor 2). The difference between the associated element set and the interior element set of a processor is called the boundary element set. This set provides results for the construction of rows mapped on at least two different processors and thus represents data that must be either communicated or calculated redundantly.

In order to scrutinize the feasibility of redundant calculation versus communication their relative costs must be weighed. Two factors affect the relative costs : the nature of the communications themselves and the mapping of the rows(nodes) onto the processors. The time performance model for the node-to-node(neighbors) communication in a hypercube multiprocessor can be given as $t_{comm} = t_{su} + b * t_{transf}$ where t_{su} is the set-up(zero byte latency) time, b is the number of bytes transferred and t_{transf} is the actual data transmission rate per byte over the channel. The two bounding cases to be examined are when the communication time is dominated by either the set-up time or the transmission time. If t_{su} is dominating then it is desirable to minimize the number of communications per processor and if $b * t_{transf}$ is dominant then it is preferable to minimize the volume of data to be communicated. In terms of mappings, the number of communications a processor must perform is represented by the number of other processors that it shares boundary elements with. The volume of data to be transmitted is proportional to the size of the boundary element set. Therefore, to maximize performance for the two bounding cases the mapping must try to optimize with respect to one of these two properties of the boundary element set. Since the amount of redundant work necessary to prevent communication is directly proportional to the number of elements in the boundary element set, a mapping that is good for minimizing communication volume is preferable for this case also.

In the present implementations of the hypercube(Intel's iPSC, Ametek's hypercube and the Ncube), the communications are best approximated by the set-up time domination model. Since there are many communications during the CG algorithm the mappings must try and minimize the number of communications per processor. Thus, there is a conflict between the mapping goals for redundant calculation and CG. But t_{su} is still large enough that, even with a mapping designed to reduce the number of communications , redundant calculation is still faster. A desirable mapping for this situation would produce a minimal number of communications per processor, produce proper load balancing between processors and under the two previous constraints minimize the size of the boundary element set on each processor.

3. Parallel CG Algorithm on the Hypercube.

The basic steps of the CG algorithm can be given as follows ;

Initially, choose $\mathbf{x}_0$

$$\mathbf{r}_0 = \mathbf{p}_0 = \mathbf{b} - K\mathbf{x}_0 \qquad (1)$$

for $k = 0, 1, 2, \ldots$

1. $a.$ $form$ $\mathbf{u}_k = K\mathbf{p}_k$ $(local\ comm.)$
    $b.$ $form$ $< \mathbf{p}_k, \mathbf{u}_k >$ $(global\ sum)$

    $c.$ $\alpha_k = \frac{<\mathbf{r}_k, \mathbf{r}_k>}{<\mathbf{p}_k, \mathbf{u}_k>}$ $(global\ broadcast)$

2. $\mathbf{x}_{k+1} = \mathbf{x}_k + \alpha_k \mathbf{p}_k$

3. $\mathbf{r}_{k+1} = \mathbf{r}_k - \alpha_k \mathbf{u}_k$ (2)

4. $a.$ $form$ $< \mathbf{r}_{k+1}, \mathbf{r}_{k+1} >$ $(global\ sum)$

    $b.$ $\beta_k = \frac{<\mathbf{r}_{k+1}, \mathbf{r}_{k+1}>}{<\mathbf{r}_k, \mathbf{r}_k>}$ $(global\ broadcast)$

5. $\mathbf{p}_{k+1} = \mathbf{r}_{k+1} + \beta_k \mathbf{p}_k$

Here, $\mathbf{r}_k$ is the residual error associated with the trial vector $\mathbf{x}_k$, $i.e.$ $\mathbf{r}_k = \mathbf{b} - K\mathbf{x}_k$ which must be null when $\mathbf{x}_k$ is coincident with $\mathbf{x}^*$ which is the solution vector. $\mathbf{p}_k$ is the direction vector at the k-th iteration. A suitable criterion for halting the iterations is $[< \mathbf{r}_k, \mathbf{r}_k > / < \mathbf{b}, \mathbf{b} >]^{\frac{1}{2}} < tolerance.$

As it is seen from these equations, the parallel CG algorithm has three basic kinds of operations : matrix vector product required in step 1.a ; inner products required in step 1.b and step 4.a ; vector additions required in step 2, step 3 and step 5. As is discussed in Section 2, the rows of the coefficient matrix K are distributed amongst the processors for parallel K matrix generation. The corresponding elements of the vectors **b, x, p, u** and **r** are also distributed amongst the processors accordingly in order to perform these basic operations in parallel. Each processor is responsible from updating the values of those vector elements assigned to itself.

During distributed matrix vector product computation, processors need the most recently updated values of the direction vector elements which are assigned to neighbor processors. Hence, local interprocessor communication is required during distributed matrix vector computation. The pattern of this local interprocessor communication step strongly depends on the mapping strategy chosen.

Each processor can compute concurrently the partial sum corresponding to the slices of the vectors assigned to itself. Then a global sum communication step is taken to accumulate the inner product term on the root processor from these partial sums resident on each processor. This step requires $\log_2 P$ concurrent nearest neighbor communication steps where P is the number of processors. Then the root processor computes the global scalar α or β in terms of these inner products. A global broadcast communication step is taken for the root processor to send the updated scalar to all the processors. This step also requires $\log_2 P$ concurrent nearest neighbor communication steps.

After each processor receives the updated global scalar values α and β, the distributed vector addition can be performed concurrently without involving any communications.

4. Data Dependencies in the CG Algorithm.

Calculation and broadcast of the global scalars α(in steps 1.b, 1.c) and β(in steps 4.a, 4.b) introduce strong data dependencies in the basic CG algorithm. These inner product calculations require global information and thus are inherently sequential. The inner product steps introduce a large number of communications and constrain most processors of the hypercube to be idle during these calculations.

The idea of restructuring the basic CG algorithm to minimize data dependencies is first proposed in [8]. However, the restructuring given in [8], is proposed for a hypothetical multiprocessor with negligible communication cost. Therefore, this is not a feasible assumption for message passing multiprocessors such as hypercubes. Hence, in this work a different restructuring scheme is proposed to minimize the interprocessor communication costs.

As was previously pointed out, set up time is the real dominating factor in the overall communication cost. Due to the data dependencies in inner product computations only one inner product term can be accumulated during one global sum communication step and hence only one global scalar can be broadcasted during one global broadcast communication step. Hence, only one floating point word is transferred between neighbor processors during the $2\log_2 P$ concurrent local communication steps of the global sum and the gloabal broadcast communication steps. The frequency rather than the volume of the communication degrades the performance of the algorithm during the computation of the global scalars. The basic CG algorithm is restructured in such a way to increase the number of inner products that can be accumulated during one global sum communication step. Hence, the number of global scalars that can be broadcasted in one global broadcast communication step is also increased.

5. A Large Grain Parallel Partial CG Algorithm. The CG method recursively generates the sequence of conjugate direction (K-orthogonal) vectors $\mathbf{p}_k$. It makes use of this sequence of direction vectors to generate the sequence $\mathbf{x}_k$ which minimizes the the quadratic objective function $f(\mathbf{x}) = \frac{1}{2} < \mathbf{x}, K\mathbf{x} > - < \mathbf{b}, \mathbf{x} >$ over the linear variety $E_k = \mathbf{x}_0 + Sp\{\mathbf{p}_0, \mathbf{p}_1, \ldots, \mathbf{p}_{k-1}\}$. Here, $Sp\{\mathbf{p}_i\}_{i=0}^{i=k-1}$ represents the subspace spanned by the vectors $\{\mathbf{p}_i\}_{i=0}^{i=k-1}$. Hence, for a positive definite K matrix, the sequence $\mathbf{x}_k$ approaches to the unique minimum of the above objective function which is also the unique solution to the linear system of equations $K\mathbf{x} = \mathbf{b}$.

The CG theorem is given below without proof(see [6] for proof).

Theorem 1 (CG Theorem) If the CG algorithm does not terminate at $\mathbf{x}_k$(i.e. $< \mathbf{r}_k, \mathbf{r}_k > \neq 0$) then

  a: $E_k = Sp\{\mathbf{p}_0, \mathbf{p}_1, \ldots, \mathbf{p}_{k-1}\} = Sp\{\mathbf{r}_0, \mathbf{r}_1, \ldots, \mathbf{r}_{k-1}\} = Sp\{\mathbf{r}_0, K\mathbf{r}_0, \ldots, K^{k-1}\mathbf{r}_0\}$

  b: $\mathbf{p}_k$ is K-orthogonal to E_k, i.e. $< \mathbf{p}_k, K\mathbf{p}_i > = < \mathbf{p}_k, K\mathbf{r}_i > = 0$ for $i = 0, 1, \ldots k - 1$

  c: $\mathbf{r}_k$ is orthogonal to E_k, i.e. $< \mathbf{r}_k, \mathbf{p}_i > = < \mathbf{r}_k, \mathbf{r}_i > = 0$ for $i = 0, 1, \ldots k - 1$

Hence, due to a) of the CG theorem the sequence $\mathbf{x}_{k+1}$ generated according to

$$\mathbf{x}_{k+1} = \mathbf{x}_0 + \sum_{i=0}^{k} \alpha_i \mathbf{p}_i \tag{3}$$

can be also generated using

$$\mathbf{x}_{k+1} = \mathbf{x}_0 + \sum_{i=0}^{k} \eta_i \mathbf{q}_i \tag{4}$$

where $\mathbf{q}_i = K^i \mathbf{r}_0$ for $i = 0, 1, \ldots, k$.

The desirable property of this alternative formulation is that the generation of the sequence $\mathbf{q}_k$ does not depend on the result of any inner product terms in contrast to the generation of the sequence $\mathbf{p}_k$ in the basic CG algorithm. The sequence of matrix vector products $\mathbf{q}_k$ can be generated using the recurrence relation

$$\mathbf{q}_i = K\mathbf{q}_{i-1} \tag{5}$$

for $i = 1, 2, \ldots, k$ where $\mathbf{q}_0 = \mathbf{r}_0$.

By equating Equation (3) to Equation (4) one can obtain $\sum_{i=0}^{k} \alpha_i \mathbf{p}_i = \sum_{i=0}^{k} \eta_i \mathbf{q}_i$. Due to a) of the CG theorem, the sequence of direction vectors $\mathbf{p}_i$ can be expressed in terms of the sequence of vectors $\mathbf{q}_i$ as $\mathbf{p}_i = \sum_{j=0}^{i} d_{i,j} \mathbf{q}_j$. Hence,

$$\eta_i = \sum_{j=i}^{k} \alpha_j d_{j,i} \tag{6}$$

for $i = 0, 1, \ldots, k$. can be obtained. Now, the problem is to find the recurrence relations for the scalars $\{\alpha_i\}_{i=0}^{k}$ and $\{\{d_{i,j}\}_{j=0}^{i}\}_{i=0}^{k}$. It is clear from the recurrence relations in the basic CG algorithm that, for the vectors $\mathbf{r}_i$ and $\mathbf{p}_i$

$$\mathbf{r}_i = r_i(K)\mathbf{r}_0 \tag{7a}$$
$$\mathbf{p}_i = p_i(K)\mathbf{r}_0 \tag{7b}$$

holds where $r_i(t)$ and $p_i(t)$ are matrix polynomials defined by the recurrence formulas

$$r_i(t) = r_{i-1}(t) - \alpha_{i-1}tp_{i-1}(t) \tag{8a}$$
$$p_i(t) = r_i(t) + \beta_{i-1}p_{i-1}(t) \tag{8b}$$

where $r_0(t) = p_0(t) = 1$.

Hence the coefficients of the polynomials $p_i(t) = \sum_{j=0}^{i} d_{ij}t^j$ and $r_i(t) = \sum_{j=0}^{i} f_{ij}t^j$ can be generated using the recurrence relations

$$f_{i+1,j} = f_{i,j} - \alpha_i * d_{i,j-1} \ for \ j = 1, \ldots, i+1 \tag{9a}$$
$$d_{i+1,j} = f_{i+1,j} + \beta_i * d_{i,j} \ for \ j = 0, \ldots, i \tag{9b}$$

where, $f_{i+1,0} = 1$ and $d_{i+1,i+1} = f_{i+1,i+1}$ and $f_{0,0} = d_{0,0} = 1$.

Now, the problem is to find the recursive expressions for the scalars α_i and β_i that arises in the above recurrence relation. A corollary of the CG Theorem, results of which will be used for the derivation of these expressions, is stated below.

Corollary 1

  a: $< p_k, K^j p_i > = < p_k, K^j r_i > = 0$ for $i + j \leq k$ and $j \neq 0$

  b: $< r_k, K^j p_i > = < r_k, K^j r_i > = 0$ for $i + j < k$

PROOF a: p_i and $r_i \in Sp\{r_0, Kr_0, \ldots, K^i r_0\}$ due to a) of the CG theorem. Hence, $K^{j-1}p_i$ and $K^{j-1}r_i \in Sp\{r_0, Kr_0, \ldots, K^{i+j-1}r_0\} = Sp\{p_0, p_1, \ldots, p_{i+j-1}\}$. Thus,

$$< p_k, K^j p_i > = < p_k, K(K^{j-1})p_i > = 0$$
$$< p_k, K^j r_i > = < p_k, K(K^{j-1})r_i > = 0$$

for $i + j \leq k$ and $j \neq 0$ due to b) of the CG theorem. *Q.E.D.*

PROOF b: This part of the corollary can be similarly proven using the results a) and c) of the CG theorem. *Q.E.D.*

Now the results of the CG theorem and the corollary will be used to derive the expressions for the scalars α and β. From the equations of the basic CG iterations

$$\alpha_i = \frac{< r_i, r_i >}{< p_i, Kp_i >} \tag{10a}$$
$$\beta_i = \frac{< r_{i+1}, r_{i+1} >}{< r_i, r_i >} \tag{10b}$$

Hence, expressions for the inner products $< r_i, r_i >$ and $< p_i, Kp_i >$ are required. Now, using the recurrence relation defined for r_i in the basic CG algorithm

$$< r_i, r_i > = < r_i, r_{i-1} > -\alpha_{i-1} < r_i, Kp_{i-1} >$$
$$= (-\alpha_{i-1}) < r_i, Kp_{i-1} >$$

$< r_i, r_{i-1} > = 0$ by c) of the CG theorem. By use of the recurrence relation defined for p_{i-1} in the basic CG algorithm

$$< r_i, r_i > = (-\alpha_{i-1})[< r_i, Kr_{i-1} > +\beta_{i-2} < r_i, Kp_{i-2} >]$$
$$= (-\alpha_{i-1}) < r_i, Kr_{i-1} >$$

$< r_i, Kp_{i-2} > = 0$ by b) of the corollary. Therefore, using the recurrence relation defined for r_{i-1} in the basic CG algorithm

$$< \mathbf{r}_i, \mathbf{r}_i > \; = \; (-\alpha_{i-1})[< \mathbf{r}_i, K\mathbf{r}_{i-2} > -\alpha_{i-2} < \mathbf{r}_i, K^2\mathbf{p}_{i-2} >]$$
$$= \; (-\alpha_{i-1})(-\alpha_{i-2}) < \mathbf{r}_i, K^2\mathbf{p}_{i-2} >$$

$< \mathbf{r}_i, K\mathbf{r}_{i-2} >= 0$ by b) of the corollary Hence, repeating the above recursive procedure i times it can be shown that :

$$< \mathbf{r}_i, \mathbf{r}_i >= (\prod_{j=0}^{i-1}(-\alpha_j)) < \mathbf{r}_i, K^i\mathbf{q}_0 > \tag{11}$$

where $\mathbf{q}_0 = \mathbf{r}_0 = \mathbf{p}_0$. Similarly, it can be shown that

$$< \mathbf{p}_i, K\mathbf{p}_i >= (\prod_{j=0}^{i-1}(-\alpha_j)) < \mathbf{p}_i, K^{i+1}\mathbf{q}_0 > \tag{12}$$

Inserting $\mathbf{r}_i = r_i(K)\mathbf{q}_0$ and $\mathbf{p}_i = p_i(K)\mathbf{q}_0$ into the above equations

$$< \mathbf{r}_i, \mathbf{r}_i > \quad = \quad (\prod_{j=0}^{i-1}(-\alpha_j)) < (\sum_{j=0}^i f_{i,j}K^j)\mathbf{q}_0, K^i\mathbf{q}_0 >$$

$$= \quad (\prod_{j=0}^{i-1}(-\alpha_j)) \sum_{j=0}^i f_{i,j} < K^j\mathbf{q}_0, K^i\mathbf{q}_0 >$$

similarly,
$$< \mathbf{p}_i, K\mathbf{p}_i > \quad = \quad (\prod_{j=0}^{i-1}(-\alpha_j)) \sum_{j=0}^i d_{i,j} < K^j\mathbf{q}_0, K^{i+1}\mathbf{q}_0 >$$

These inner products $< \mathbf{q}_0, K^j\mathbf{q}_0 >=< K^v\mathbf{q}_0, K^w\mathbf{q}_0 >=< \mathbf{q}_v, \mathbf{q}_w >$, where $v + w = j$ can be accumulated in a single global sum communication step after the sequence of vectors $\{\mathbf{q}_j\}_{j=0}^{i+1}$ are computed. Now, defining $\ell_j =< \mathbf{q}_0, K^j\mathbf{q}_0 >=< K^v\mathbf{q}_0, K^w\mathbf{q}_0 >=< \mathbf{q}_v, \mathbf{q}_w >$, where $v + w = j$

$$< \mathbf{r}_i, \mathbf{r}_i > \quad = \quad (\prod_{j=0}^{i-1}(-\alpha_j)) \sum_{j=0}^i f_{i,j}\ell_{i+j} \tag{13a}$$

$$< \mathbf{p}_i, K\mathbf{p}_i > \quad = \quad (\prod_{j=0}^{i-1}(-\alpha_j)) \sum_{j=0}^i d_{i,j}\ell_{i+j+1} \tag{13b}$$

is obtained. Hence, inserting these expressions for the inner products into Equations (10a)-(10b)

$$\alpha_i \quad = \quad \frac{\sum_{j=0}^i f_{i,j}\ell_{i+j}}{\sum_{j=0}^i d_{i,j}\ell_{i+j+1}} \tag{14a}$$

$$\beta_i \quad = \quad \alpha_i * \frac{\sum_{j=0}^{i+1} f_{i+1,j}\ell_{i+j+1}}{\sum_{j=0}^i f_{i,j}\ell_{i+j}} \tag{14b}$$

is obtained. Note that, the expression for the scalar α_i in Equation (14a), is given in terms of the coefficients of the matrix polynomials $p_i(t)$ and $r_i(t)$ and the sequence of inner products $\{\ell_j\}_{j=i}^{2i+1}$. Similarly, the expression for the scalar β_i in Equation (14b), is given in terms of α_i, the coefficients of the matrix polynomials $r_i(t)$ and $r_{i+1}(t)$ and the sequence of inner products $\{\ell_j\}_{j=i}^{2i+2}$. Hence, the coefficients of the sequence of polynomials $\{p_i(t)\}_{i=0}^k$ and the sequence of scalars $\{\alpha_i\}_{i=0}^k$ can be recursively calculated using the recurrence relations in Equations (14a),(9a), (14b),(9b)(in the given order).

The steps for the large grain parallel partial CG algorithm with step size s is given below as

Initially : let $\mathbf{r}_0 = \mathbf{b} - K\mathbf{x}_0$ and let $\mathbf{q}_0 = \mathbf{r}_0$

STEP 1 : Compute s matrix vector products

$$\mathbf{q}_i = K\mathbf{q}_{i-1} \tag{15}$$

for $i = 1, \ldots, s$

STEP 2 : Compute $2s$ inner-products

$$\ell_j = <\mathbf{q}_u, \mathbf{q}_v> \tag{16}$$

for $j = 0, 1, \ldots, 2s - 1$ where $u + v = j$.

STEP 3.A : Compute the coefficients of the polynomials
$p_i(t) = \sum_{j=0}^{i} d_{ij} t^j$ and $r_i(t) = \sum_{j=0}^{i} f_{ij} t^j$ from

$$\alpha_i = \frac{\sum_{j=0}^{i} f_{i,j} \ell_{i+j}}{\sum_{j=0}^{i} d_{i,j} \ell_{i+j+1}} \tag{17}$$

$$f_{i+1,j} = f_{i,j} - \alpha_i * d_{i,j-1} \; for \; j = 1, \ldots, i+1 \tag{18}$$

$$\beta_i = \alpha_i * \frac{\sum_{j=0}^{i+1} f_{i+1,j} \ell_{i+j+1}}{\sum_{j=0}^{i} f_{i,j} \ell_{i+j}} \tag{19}$$

$$d_{i+1,j} = f_{i+1,j} + \beta_i * d_{i,j} \; for \; j = 0, \ldots, i \tag{20}$$

for $i = 0, 1, \ldots, s - 1$ where $f_{i+1,0} = 1$ and $d_{i+1,i+1} = f_{i+1,i+1}$. and where $d_{0,0} = f_{0,0} = 1$.

STEP 3.B compute scalars η_i for $i = 0, 1, \ldots, s - 1$ where

$$\eta_i = \sum_{j=i}^{s-1} \alpha_j d_{j,i} \tag{21}$$

for $i = 0, 1, \ldots, s - 1$

STEP 4 : compute s vector additions

$$\mathbf{x}_s = \mathbf{x}_0 + \sum_{i=0}^{s-1} \eta_i \mathbf{q_i} \tag{22}$$

STEP 5 : compute

$$\mathbf{r}_s = \mathbf{b} - K\mathbf{x}_s \tag{23}$$

and let

$$\mathbf{q}_0 = \mathbf{r}_s \tag{24}$$

then GO TO STEP 1

In STEP 1, s distributed matrix vector products are computed to generate the sequence of vectors $\{\mathbf{q}_i\}_{i=0}^{s}$. In this step, s local interprocessor communications are required. At the end of STEP 1 each processor contains its own slice of the sequence of vectors $\{\mathbf{q}_i\}_{i=0}^{s}$. In STEP 2, each processor concurrently computes $2s$ partial sums. Then, in a single global sum communication step, these $2s$ inner products $\{\ell_i\}_{i=0}^{2s-1}$ are accumulated in the root processor. In STEP 3.A, the root processor recursively computes the coefficients of the sequence of direction vector polynomials $\{p_i(t)\}_{i=0}^{s-1}$ in terms of the sequence of inner products $\{\ell_i\}_{i=0}^{2s-1}$. Next, in STEP 3.B the root processor computes the sequence of scalars $\{\eta_i\}_{i=0}^{s-1}$ in terms of the sequence of scalars $\{\alpha_i\}_{i=0}^{s-1}$ and the coefficients of the sequence of direction vectors $\{p_i(t)\}_{i=0}^{s-1}$ already computed in STEP 3.A. Then, the root processor broadcasts this sequence of s scalars in a single global broadcast communication step. In STEP 4, after each processor receives these s scalars, a sequence of s distributed vector addition steps are performed without involving any communications.

6. Performance Analysis of the Algorithm. In the proposed algorithm, the approximate solution vector $\mathbf{x}_s$ is generated starting from $\mathbf{x}_0$ in a single global sum and global broadcast communication step without generating the intermediate sequence of direction and residual vectors. Thus, the parameter, s can be thought of as a look-ahead parameter. Now, assume that the step size parameter s can be chosen such that the convergence is obtained in the first s iterations of the basic CG algorithm $(i.e.\ [<\mathbf{r}_s, \mathbf{r}_s>/<\mathbf{b}, \mathbf{b}>]^{\frac{1}{2}} < tolerance)$. Then, the performance model of the proposed algorithm can be given as

$$
\begin{aligned}
T &= s(C+3)\frac{N}{P}t_{calc} &+& \; 2.5(s^2-s)t_{calc} &+& \; [2\log_2 Pt_{su} + 3s\log_2 Pt_{transf} + sL_c] \\
&= \quad parallel &+& \quad sequential &+& \quad\quad communication
\end{aligned}
$$

where N is the number of equations, C is the number of nonzero entries per row of the K matrix, P is the number of processors in the hypercube, t_{calc} is the time taken per single floating point addition and multiplication, t_{transf} is the data transmission rate per single floating point word over the channel and L_c is the total local communication time required during a single matrix vector product.

For the sake of comparison, the performance model of the basic CG algorithm for s iterations is also given below.

$$
\begin{aligned}
T &= s(C+5)\frac{N}{P}t_{calc} &+& \; [4s\log_2 P(t_{su}+t_{transf}) + sL_c] \\
&= \quad parallel &+& \quad\quad communication
\end{aligned}
$$

The following results can be deduced from the comparison of these performance models :

1. the frequency of the global communication is reduced 2s times from $4s\log_2 P$ to $2\log_2 P$ per s iterations of the basic CG algorithm.

2. the volume of global communication is reduced from $4s\log_2 P$ to $3s\log_2 P$ per s iterations of the basic CG algorithm.

3. the parallel computation time is reduced from $s(C+5)\frac{N}{P}$ to $s(C+3)\frac{N}{P}$ per s iterations of the basic CG algorithm.

4. a sequential computational overhead proportional to s^2 is introduced per s iterations of the basic CG algorithm.

5. memory requirement is increased from $(C+5)\frac{N}{P}$ to $(C+3+s)\frac{N}{P}$ floating point words.

By equating the reduction in parallel computation to the overhead in sequential computation $s \simeq \frac{4}{5}\frac{N}{P}$ is obtained. This value for the parameter s represents the case with no computational overhead and with the reduction in communication indicated in 1 and 2.

The performance comparison given above is made under the assumption that the step size parameter s can be chosen arbitrarily large. However, there exist some limitations concerning the selection of the parameter s. The first limitation is the fact that the sequential computational overhead increases with the square of the parameter s. The second limitation is the fact that if the coefficient matrix K has any eigenvalue with modulus greater than one, then the norms of the moments of the matrix K will increase exponentially. Since, $\| q_i \| = \| K^i q_0 \| \leq \| K \|^i \| q_0 \|$, the upper bound for the norms of the sequence of vectors q_i increases exponentially. Hence, for sufficiently large s, the sequence of inner products generated may cause overflow. The third limitation is the fact that the new formulation is more sensitive to round-off errors then is the basic CG algorithm. For sufficiently large s, the sequence of direction vectors generated in the proposed algorithm may begin to diverge from the true direction vectors. Hence, the step size parameter s should be chosen considering these factors each of which greatly depends on the application.

If the convergence is not obtained during the first pass of the algorithm for the chosen step size s, the residual vector r_s is computed in STEP 5. Then the algorithm is restarted by assigning r_s to q_0. Hence, the algorithm effectively performs s iterations of the CG procedure during the first pass and then rather than continuing the CG iterations it restarts from the current solution vector x_s and performs s more CG iterations during the second pass. This procedure is repeated until the convergence is obtained. Hence, the method is a partial CG method [9]. The special case of $s = 1$ corresponds to the standard method of steepest descent while $s = N$ corresponds to the full CG method. If however, convergence is obtained during the first pass, it effectively shows the numerical performance of the full CG method. It has been shown in [9] that for sufficiently large m the result of applying $\frac{m}{s}$ passes of the partial CG with step size s gives better approximation then $\frac{m}{s-1}$ passes of the partial CG with step size $s - 1$. Hence, in order to increase the convergence rate of the method, the step size should be chosen as large as possible.

As is indicated above, the proposed algorithm may increase the total number of effective CG iterations required for convergence if the convergence is not obtained during the first pass of the algorithm. Therefore, in this case the performance comparison given previously does not hold since extra computation and communication steps have to be performed due to the extra iterations required for convergence. However, as long as the decrease in the convergence rate is not very large, the performance of the proposed algorithm can be still much better on the hypercube due to the reduction in the global communication costs. The performance analysis of the proposed algorithm with different s for different sample FEM application problems is still underway. The results of these performance measurements will be given in a later work.

If the performance of the proposed algorithm does not give satisfactory results for a class of application problems of interest, then STEP 5 of the algorithm can be modified to continue the basic CG iterations. In this case however , the increase in the performance will be only due to the reduction in the global communication costs during the first s iterations of the basic parallel CG algorithm.

Acknowledgements   This work was supported by the SBIR Program Phase II(F33615-85-C-5198) of Universal Energy Systems Inc. with the Air Force Materials Laboratory, AFWAL/MLLM, WPAFB, Ohio 45433. Special thanks to Dr. Harold L. Gegel, senior scientist, and Mr. James C. Malas, project manager of this SBIR Program at the analytical process modeling WUD, Metals and Ceramics Division, WPAFB, Ohio 45433. They provided extensive support for the project.

REFERENCES

[1] C. Lee and S. Kobayashi, "Analysis of axisymmetric upsetting and plane-strain side processing of solid cylinder by finite-element method," *ASME Journal of Engineering for Industry*, vol. 93, pp. 445–454, 1971.

[2] S. Oh and S. Kobayashi, "Finite element analysis of plane-strain sheet bending," *International Journal of Mechanical Sciences*, vol. 22, pp. 583–594, 1980.

[3] S. Kobayashi, "Thermoviscoplastic analysis of titanium alloy forging," Technical Report AFWAL-TR-81-4130, Air Force Wright Aeronautical Labs., 1981.

[4] S. Oh, "Finite element analysis of metal forming processes with arbitrary shaped dies," *International Journal of Mechanical Science*, vol. 24, pp. 479–493, 1982.

[5] C. Chen and S. Kobayashi, "Rigid-plastic finite element analysis of plastic deformation in metal-forming processes," Technical Report AFML-TR-79-4105, Air Force Wright Aeronautical Labs., 1979.

[6] D. Luenberger, *Introduction to Linear and Nonlinear Programming*. Addison Wesley, 1973.

[7] G.A.Lyzenga, A.Raefsky, and G.H.Hager, "Finite element and the method of conjugate gradients on a concurrent processor," in *ASME International Conference on Computers in Engineering*, pp. 393–399, 1985.

[8] J. Rosendale, "Minimizing inner product data dependencies in conjugate gradient iteration," in *Proceedings of the IEEE International Conference on Parallel Processing*, pp. 44–46, August 1983.

[9] D.K.Faddeev and V. Faddeeva, *Computational Methods of Linear Algebra*. San Fransisco: W.H. Freemand and Company, 1963.

A Survey of ADI Implementations on Hypercubes

DAVID S. LIM* AND REX V. THANAKIJ*

Abstract. Implementations of the ADI method to solve the two dimensional heat equation on hypercubes are presented. In solving the tridiagonal systems imbedded in the ADI, six different algorithms are used. They are Scattered Decomposition (SD), Serial Cyclic Reduction (SECR), Parallel Cyclic Reduction (PACR), and three variants of Substructured Gaussian Elimination (GE). The variants include pipelined Thomas's algorithm (GETH), Serial Cyclic Reduction (GESE), and Parallel Cyclic Reduction (GEPA). The speedup curves derived both experimentally and theoretically for each method are presented for the AMETEK System 14 Hypercube. Comparisons of these curves identify the best speedup regions for each method. Our results show that SD, GETH, and GESE are the best three methods. They form a triple point plot that can be used to identify which method to use, given problem size and number of processors for a particular hypercube processor.

1. Introduction. The Alternating Direction Implicit (ADI) method by Peaceman and Rachford, and Douglas is used extensively today to solve parabolic and elliptic partial differential equations. There are several proposed implementations of the ADI method onto a hypercube. In this research, we are interested in the following algorithms: Serial Cyclic Reduction, Parallel Cyclic Reduction, Scattered Decomposition, and three variants of Substructured Gaussian Elimination. Our objective is to evaluate each of the implementations and determine which method is best suited for a given set of parameters. The choice of implementation

---

*AMETEK Computer Research, 610 North Santa Anita Ave., Arcadia, California 91006 USA

depends on the problem size, the number of processors, communication overhead time, communication per-byte rate, floating-point rate, and available memory per processor. The various implementations are actually coded up and timed on an AMETEK System 14 (S14) and compared with predicted curves.

2. Model Problem. The two-dimensional heat equation was used as the model problem for evaluating the various implementations. A plate is subjected to a heat source at the upper right hand corner. The plate has adiabatic boundary conditions at the edges, and is cooled convectively over its face. In addition, the plate has directional thermal conductivities. The thermal conductivity in the horizontal direction is nine times greater than in the vertical direction. In the sections below, the problem size refers to the number of grid points on one side of the plate.

3. Serial Cyclic Reduction. The Serial Cyclic Reduction (SECR) was originally proposed to solve block tridiagonal matrices [1]. For the ADI method, SECR is used to solve tridiagonal matrices in parallel [2][3]. Although SECR requires more arithmetic operations and array indexing than Thomas's algorithm, it is more "parallelizable." In this implementatation, the method is restricted to solving tridiagonal systems with 2^n-1 equations.

4. Parallel Cyclic Reduction. The Parallel Cyclic Reduction (PACR) is a variant of SECR [3]. It has more "parallelism" than SECR but requires more arithmetic operations. Furthermore, PACR is communication-intensive and requires heavy array indexing; therefore, we anticipate PACR to have poor speedup. PACR is also restricted to solving 2^n-1 equations.

5. Scattered Decomposition. Unlike the other implementations described here Scattered Decomposition (SD) can only be used to solve multiple tridiagonal systems [4][5]. It reduces to Thomas's algorithm on one processor. One restriction is the problem size cannot be less than the number of processors.

6. Substructured Gaussian Elimination. Substructured Gaussian Elimination reduces the number of equations in each processor to a single equation. The reduced equations form an intermediate tridiagonal system that needs to be solved. The three variants of GE differs only in the way that the intermediate tridiagonal system is solved. The single tridiagonal system can be solved using the Serial Cyclic Reduction (SECR), Parallel Cyclic Reduction (PACR), or a pipelined Thomas's algorithm (GETH) [6][7].

7. Results and Discussion. Figure 1a shows the speedup curves for SD indicating reasonable agreement between the experimental and theoretical curves. SECR's speedup curves

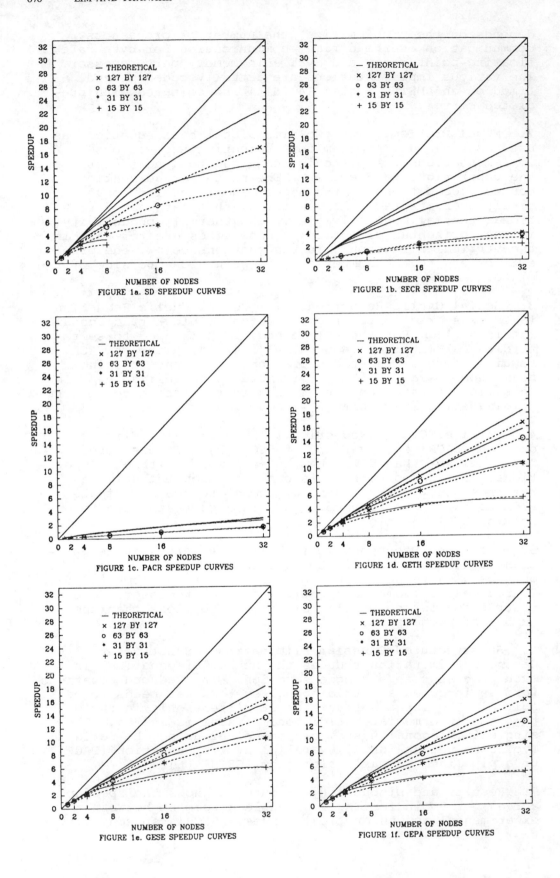

FIGURE 1a. SD SPEEDUP CURVES

FIGURE 1b. SECR SPEEDUP CURVES

FIGURE 1c. PACR SPEEDUP CURVES

FIGURE 1d. GETH SPEEDUP CURVES

FIGURE 1e. GESE SPEEDUP CURVES

FIGURE 1f. GEPA SPEEDUP CURVES

are shown in Figure 1b. The discrepancy between the theoretical and experimental curves is quite large. This discrepancy arises from the fact that there is a lot of indexing operation in coding up the SECR, more so than any other
method. This array indexing makes SECR less efficient than
expected. Our theoretical result only involves the floating point calculation and communication rate. This difference suggests that the array indexing can become large and
should be included in the future prediction to obtain a
good agreement between the theoretical and experimental
values.

       As seen in Figure 1c PACR has poor speedup. This can
be attributed to being too communication-intensive as well
as heavy array indexing. The speedup curves for the GETH,
GESE, and GEPA are shown in Figure 1d, 1e, and 1f, respectively. In general the theoretical and experimental values
are in good agreement. Figure 2 theoretically compares all
the methods for a problem size of 63. This figure suggests
that within the range shown, SD and GETH are the two best
methods.

       The theoretical curves are calculated using the float-
ing-point rate of 20 kflops per node, obtained from the
Linpack LU benchmark. In predicting the speedup curves for
all the methods, we assume this floating-point rate to be
constant. The difference between the theoretical and experimental curves can be attributed to the flaw of this
assumption as well as the indexing operations. In certain
cases, the experimental results show better speedup than
predicted. Since this is physically impossible, the logical explanation is that the floating-point rate is not as
high as we expected. In benchmarking Thomas's algorithm on
one processor, the value of 13 kflops was obtained, which
is lower than what was expected. It does make sense that
each method has its own effective floating-point rate because different algorithms have different patterns of calculation. However, to standardize the curves the value of
20 kflops was used with the realization that each method
has a different floating-point rate. It appears that the
best thing to do is to benchmark each method on a single
processor and find the effective floating-point rate for
each method when calculating the theoretical speedup
curves.

       Figure 3 shows the theoretical comparison of different
methods. Within the range shown, SD, GETH, GESE, and SECR
seem to be the best algorithms to use. Our experimental
results, however, indicate that SD, GETH, and GESE are the
best methods. They form a triple-point plot showing an
overview of which implementation is best, given the problem
size and number of processors. SECR's region does not manifest itself in our result due to the array-indexing problem stated earlier. The theoretical calculation of SECR
needs to be changed to reflect the array indexing. If we
leave SECR out of the theoretical triple-point plot, we
should get a more realistic result. Figure 4 is a plot of
theoretical values without SECR and the experimental values. This figure indicates the theoretical and experimental values are in good agreement.

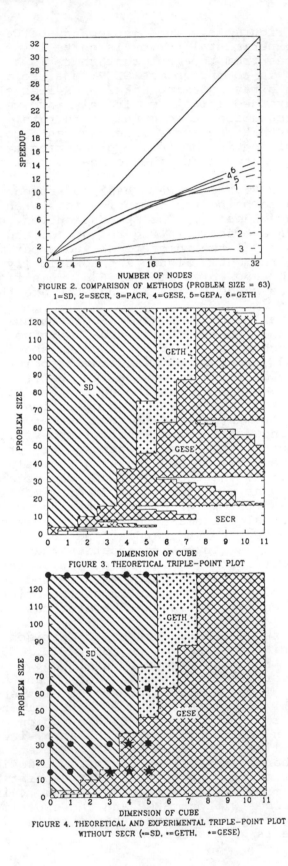

FIGURE 2. COMPARISON OF METHODS (PROBLEM SIZE = 63)
1=SD, 2=SECR, 3=PACR, 4=GESE, 5=GEPA, 6=GETH

FIGURE 3. THEORETICAL TRIPLE-POINT PLOT

FIGURE 4. THEORETICAL AND EXPERIMENTAL TRIPLE-POINT PLOT
WITHOUT SECR (•=SD, ■=GETH, ★=GESE)

8. Conclusion. The object of the research was to obtain the triple-point plot shown. The results show that different methods are best depending on the number of processors and problem size. For large-grain parallelism, SD is the best method, for medium-grain parallelism, GETH, and for small-grain parallelism, GESE. If one wants to code up only one method, we would recommend GESE; when it is slower it is not significantly slower than the other methods, and it can also be used to solve a tridiagonal system.

The research was done only for a specific hypercube machine. Further research is required to evaluate the effect of communication overhead time, communication per-byte rate, and floating-point rate on the triple-point plot. The available memory per processor is a key factor: methods that require significantly more memory than others may be excluded from consideration; as may large problems for small numbers of processors. A more concrete measure of the ratio of problem size to number of processors is required. This data would be helpful in choosing an implementation for a specific hypercube, or for designing a hypercube machine.

9. Acknowledgement. We would like to thank NCAR for the use of their GKS-Compatible Graphics System.

REFERENCES

[1] Buzbee, B.L., Golub, G.H., and Neilson, C.W., On Direct Methods for Solving Poisson's Equations, SIAM J. Numer. Anal., Vol.7, No.4, Dec 1970.

[2] Johnsson, S.L., Odd-Even Cyclic Reduction on Ensemble Architectures and the Solution of Tridiagonal Systems of Equations, YALE Research Report YALEU/CSD/RR-339, Oct 1984.

[3] Hockney, R.W., and Jesshope, C.R., Parallel Computers, Adam Hilger Ltd., Bristol, 1981.

[4] Saad, Y., and Schultz, M.H., Alternating Direction Methods on Multiprocessors: An Extended Abstract, YALE Research Report YALEU/DCS/RR-381, Apr 1985.

[5] Chan, T.F., Saad, Y., and Schultz, M.H., Solving Elliptic Partial Differential Equations on the Hypercube Multiprocessor, YALE Research Report YALEU/DCS/RR-373, Mar 1985.

[6] Johnsson, S.L., Solving Tridiagonal Systems on Ensemble Architectures, YALE Research Report YALEU/DCS/RR-436, Nov 1985.

[7] Johnsson, S.L., Saad, Y., and Schultz, M.H., Alternating Direction Methods on Multiprocessors, YALE Research Report YALEU/DCS/RR-382, Oct 1985.

Solving Schrödinger's Equation on the Intel iPSC*
by the Alternating Direction Method

FAISAL SAIED†, CHING-TIEN HO†, S. LENNART JOHNSSON† AND
MARTIN H. SCHULTZ†

Abstract. We consider the numerical solution of the Schrödinger's equation and investigate several different algorithms for implementing the Alternating Direction Method on hypercubes. We indicate the relative merits of the algorithms depending on cube parameters such as arithmetic speed, communication latency, transfer rate, the packet size, and the cost of reordering data locally. We present timings for the Intel iPSC that show that Alternating Direction Methods can be implemented efficiently on hypercubes.

1 Introduction

In this paper, we discuss implementations of the Alternating Direction Method on the Intel iPSC. The implementations are for the time-dependent, two-dimensional Schrödinger equation on a rectangular domain. Schrödinger's equation is a fundamental equation in quantum mechanics. We focus on the efficiency of the Alternating Direction Method. The results reported here were obtained on a 32 node configuration of the Intel iPSC.

The structure of this paper is as follows. We describe the problem in which we are interested, and mention several numerical techniques for its solution. In this paper we investigate only the Alternating Direction Method. We briefly discuss the architectural features of the Intel iPSC that are relevant for our implementations. We outline several methods for solving multiple tridiagonal systems on a hypercube, indicate their relative performances on the iPSC and compare them on the basis of model times. We describe the basic approach towards the parallel implementation of the ADM that we have followed, and discuss several variants. Finally we present the results of some experiments on the iPSC.

---

* Intel Company, Santa Clara, California

† Department of Computer Science, Yale University, New Haven, Connecticut 06520.

2   The Model Problem

We consider a time-dependent partial differential equation of the following form:

$$i\frac{\partial u}{\partial t} = \frac{\partial^2 u}{\partial x^2} + \frac{\partial^2 u}{\partial y^2} + V(x,y,t)u \text{ in a rectangular region, } R, \qquad (1)$$

where $u = u(x,y,t)$ satisfies

$$u(x,y,0) = \phi(x,y) \text{ for } (x,y) \in R, \text{ and } u(x,y,t) = \psi(x,y) \text{ for } (x,y) \in \partial R.$$

This equation is essentially the time-dependent, two-dimensional Schrödinger's equation in quantum mechanics.

3   Numerical Schemes for the Model Problem

Some of the methods that have been applied to (1) are the following.

- Explicit methods

- Crank-Nicolson

- ODE techniques (method of lines)

- ADM (alternating direction methods)

An explicit scheme that is conditionally stable with first order accuracy in time was proposed in [1] for Schrödinger's equation. With two space dimensions, the computational stencil involves eight neighboring grid points. Each time step involves a matrix-vector product only, with local communication involving the stencil neighbors only. However, a larger number of time steps is required to achieve a given accuracy at a fixed point in time than with methods that are second order in time. Thus, an efficient parallel implementation of this method is probably not competitive with the ADM.

The Crank-Nicolson scheme is unconditionally stable, second order accurate in time and implicit. It requires the solution at each time step of a linear system whose matrix has the non-zero structure of the discrete Laplacian. Solving such a system can be costly, especially if the form of the function V precludes the use of fast Helmholtz solvers. The efficient parallel implementation of iterative solvers of this class is a topic of current research, but is not considered in this paper.

In the ODE approach, one discretizes the space variables and solves the resulting coupled system of ordinary differential equations, which are typically stiff, by some implicit method, which again requires solving large sparse linear systems, defined by the stencils, at each time step.

Alternating Direction Methods were developed for solving parabolic partial differential equations [6]. They have the advantage of being unconditionally stable, second order accurate in time and require $O(P^2)$ operations per time step on a $P \times P$ grid. In applying the ADM to our model problem the spatial operators are approximated by their discrete equivalents, which for 3-point central differences yields an equation of the form

$$\frac{du}{dt} = \tilde{A}_x u + \tilde{B}_y u + f(x, y, t)u, \tag{2}$$

where $\tilde{A}_x$ and $\tilde{B}_y$ with the appropriate orderings, are block diagonal matrices, each block being a tridiagonal matrix. One ADM step for this equation consists of two half steps,

$$(I - \frac{1}{2}\Delta t A_x)u^{i+\frac{1}{2}} = (I + \frac{1}{2}\Delta t B_y)u^i,$$

$$(I - \frac{1}{2}\Delta t B_y)u^{i+1} = (I + \frac{1}{2}\Delta t A_x)u^{i+\frac{1}{2}}.$$

Here, A_x and B_y are obtained from $\tilde{A}_x$ and $\tilde{B}_y$ by modifying the diagonal entries to account for the last term in (2). In the first half step, we form P tridiagonal matrix-vector products in the y-direction, corresponding to $(I + \frac{1}{2}\Delta t B_y)u^i$, to get the right hand sides for the P tridiagonal solves in the x-direction which involve $(I - \frac{1}{2}\Delta t A_x)$. The second half step requires the same operations to be performed, with the roles of the x- and y-directions interchanged. It is usual to transpose the data at each half step in sequential implementations, to make the tridiagonal solves in both directions equally efficient.

For the applications we are interested in, the $P \times P$ grid vector u is complex. We give the operation counts in terms of real, floating-point operations, even though complex arithmetic is used. Thus, a complex add is counted as two flops, etc. Let C_{MVP} and C_{TRID} be the number of real single precision operations required per unknown for each matrix-vector product and tridiagonal solve respectively. Further, let t_a be the time to perform one floating-point operation. Then the sequential time for one ADM step on a $P \times P$ grid is

$$T(P) = 2(C_{MVP} + C_{TRID})P^2 t_a.$$

4   Solving Tridiagonal Linear Systems on Hypercubes

In this section, we discuss the problem of solving multiple independent tridiagonal systems on a hypercube. We first give a brief description of the methods we have considered and then compare them, in terms of actual performance on the iPSC and on the basis of model times.

The choice of the method for solving the tridiagonal systems is influenced by the size of the cube and the size of the local memories relative to the problem size, in addition to depending on other cube parameters like the arithmetic rate, the communication latency, the transfer rate, etc.

4.1   Outline of the Methods

Suppose that we have P tridiagonal systems, each of order Q, and a hypercube with N processors. For simplicity, we assume that P and Q are powers of 2. We will initially outline the methods for the case $N \leq P$ and using "one-dimensional domain decomposition". We will indicate the modifications that are necessary to implement them when more processors are available $(P < N)$, using two-dimensional domain decomposition. Two-dimensional domain decomposition can also be applied when $N \leq P$, and will be discussed in the next section.

The simplest approach to the problem is to move P/N systems to each processor, solve them locally, using standard Gaussian elimination and move the solutions back to their original distribution. Since the data movement is equivalent to a transpose (of a distributed, rectangular matrix), we will refer to this method as **TGET** [4] ("Transpose-GE-Transpose"). For Gaussian elimination, the number of floating point operations per row required is 8.

The transpose operation can be implemented efficiently as follows. Assume that there are P systems each of order Q spread identically across N processors, each processor having Q/N rows of each system. At the first step, each processor whose node number has its lowest order bit equal to zero, sends its rows of systems $(P/2) + 1, \ldots, P$ to its neighbor whose node number differs in the lowest order bit. That neighbor sends its rows of systems $1, \ldots, P/2$ in exchange. All processors then reorder the unsent part of their original data and the received data so as to make the data for each system contiguous and ordered. This process is repeated for the other bits in the node numbers, going from low to high. At each step, the number of systems in each processor is halved and the number of rows of each system in a processor is doubled. Thus in each of $\log N$ steps, each processor sends and receives messages equal to half its local data, and reorders all of its local data. Let $T_{comm}(B)$ be the time to send or receive a message consisting of B bytes. The cost of the above transpose procedure for a real $P \times Q$ matrix spread across N processors is given by

$$T(P,Q,N) = \log N \ [4\frac{PQ}{N}t_{copy} + 2T_{comm}(2\frac{PQ}{N})] \tag{3}$$

The parameter t_{copy} denotes the time to move one byte of data in the local memory. This data movement is implemented in FORTRAN by a pair of nested loops and can have an appreciable cost. Note that t_{copy} will be smaller for complex arrays than for real arrays due to the lower loop overhead *per byte*. Unrolling the inner loop reduces the value of this parameter somewhat. An optimized variant of the transpose operation on a hypercube has been devised [2] that reduces local copying at the cost of more sends/receives and reduces the overall run-time.

A different approach is to use substructuring. By substructuring (SS) we mean reducing each system down to one equation per processor using what is essentially block Gaussian elimination in the manner described in [7], [3]. For substructuring, the number of floating point operations required per row is 17. In methods applying substructuring the load is perfectly balanced during this phase, and there is only one nearest neighbor communication between adjacent partitions in a subcube. We consider three alternative approaches for solving the reduced tridiagonal systems.

1. **SS/TGET**: This methods applies TGET to the reduced systems, after performing substructuring. The Gray code is not required for the transpose [2].

2. **SS/"Naive" CR**: Solve the reduced systems by cyclic reduction (CR), with all systems converging to the same processor. We do not recommend this method because of its poor load balancing properties.

3. **SS/BalCR**: The CR process is balanced, in the sense that an equal number of systems converge to each processor [4]. Each step of CR requires 17 floating point operations per row. The reduction phase and the substitution phase take $\log N$ steps each in CR. The number of rows modified in each processor is halved on successive steps. Each step in balanced CR requires shipping half as much data as the previous step, in contrast to the transpose, where the the amount of data shipped is the same for all steps. However, each step of BalCR requires twice as many start-ups as a step of the transpose. One potential advantage of SS/BalCR is the fact that for "sufficiently" diagonally dominant systems, the cyclic reduction process can be terminated in fewer than $\log N$ steps, where N is the number of processors.

We now discuss the modifications that are required to implement the methods described above when $P < N$. Note that this regime is not important on small hypercubes such as the iPSC with 32 or 64 nodes, but will be relevant for larger cubes. To use more than P processors, we must use two-dimensional domain decomposition. However, this involves separating the tridiagonal systems into groups that are confined to disjoint subcubes, and the problem on each subcube corresponds to one-dimensional domain decomposition, with more processors than systems. When $N > P$, TGET will involve moving one single system to each of P processors, leaving the remaining $N - P$ processors idle while Gaussian elimination is being applied. This requires that the local memories be sufficient to hold an entire system. Even when sufficient memory is available, this approach will be unattractive when too many processors are idle. Similar considerations apply to SS/TGET, except that the local memory requirements are lower, since only the reduced systems are being solved by TGET. With SS/BalCR, after $\log P$ steps, we end up with single systems on subcubes of dimension $\log N - \log P$. We can then apply any method that is appropriate for solving single tridiagonal systems on hypercubes, for example cyclic reduction [4].

4.2 Comparison of Methods for Multiple Tridiagonal Systems

In the following, we compare TGET, SS/TGET and SS/BalCR. We first present the results of experiments on the iPSC and then use model times to predict the relative performance of the methods on cubes with different parameters.

We use the following simplified model of communication on the hypercube. The time to send or receive a message consisting of B bytes is

$$T_{comm}(B) = Bt_c + \left\lceil \frac{B}{B_m} \right\rceil \tau,$$

where τ ($\approx 1.5\ msec$) is the start-up time, t_c ($\approx 0.001\ msec$) is the transfer time per byte, and B_m is the maximum packet size. $B_m = 1k$ bytes on the iPSC. This is different from the maximum message size, which is 16k bytes on the iPSC. This model neglects the difference between "internal" start-ups that occur between packets in the same message, and the "external", or initial start-up for the first packet. The considerable variability in the measured communications times for different runs with the same code and input parameters represents a significant difficulty in applying this model, or any other performance related model.

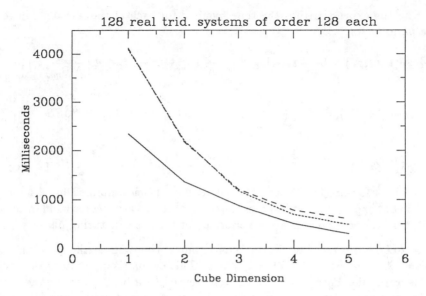

Figure 1: Solving 128 real tridiagonal systems of order 128 on the Intel iPSC with one-dimensional domain decomposition. Solid line: TGET, Dotted line: SS/TGET, Dashed line: SS/BalCR.

Figure 1 shows the time needed to solve 128 real independent tridiagonal systems, each of order 128 on the iPSC using one-dimensional domain decomposition, on cubes of dimension up to 5, using SS/BalCR, SS/TGET and TGET. Note that the amount of substructuring and the order of the reduced systems vary with the cube dimension, but all times are for solving the same problem. For this problem, TGET was the fastest, followed by SS/TGET, with SS/BalCR being the slowest.

We now discuss the relative merits and shortcomings of each method, to explain the ranking that is displayed in Figure 1, and why one can expect the ranking to change as parameters such as cube size, problem size, ratio of arithmetic to communication speed, etc. are varied. The advantage of TGET over SS/TGET is that SS/TGET has to pay the "substructuring penalty" of 17 floating arithmetic operations per row as opposed to 8 for Gaussian elimination in TGET. This is the primary factor that leads to the superiority of TGET for this problem. This advantage will be offset by the the fact that TGET transposes the entire data, whereas SS/TGET transposes only the data associated with the reduced systems as the problem size is increased. SS/BalCR also pays the substructuring penalty and in addition, requires twice as many start-ups as as SS/TGET (these two methods do not incur internal start-ups for this problem), which is why it is the slowest in Figure 1. However, since the amount of data communicated at each step is halved on successive steps for SS/BalCR and remains constant for TGET and SS/TGET, balanced cyclic reduction will be at an advantage for large cubes, and large problems. If the computational speed is increased relative to communication speed (e.g. by using vector boards), SS/BalCR and SS/TGET will benefit more than TGET because the substructuring penalty will be less crucial. Finally, reducing the copying time, t_{copy}, will help TGET and SS/TGET.

We state the expressions for the time required for each of the methods, in terms of the cube parameters.

$$T_{TGET}(P,Q,N) = 8\frac{PQ}{N}t_a + \log N \left(8\frac{PQ}{N}t_{copy} + 8\frac{PQ}{N}t_c + 4\left\lceil\frac{2PQ}{NB_m}\right\rceil\tau\right), \quad (4)$$

$$T_{SS/TGET}(P,Q,N) = 17P(\frac{Q}{N}-1)t_a + 8Pt_a + \log N\left[20Pt_{copy} + 20Pt_c + 4\tau\right], \quad (5)$$

$$T_{SS/BalCR}(P,Q,N) = 17P(\frac{Q}{N}-1)t_a + 17P(1-\frac{1}{N})t_a + 80P(1-\frac{1}{N})t_c + 8\log N\tau. \quad (6)$$

The expressions for SS/TGET and SS/BalCR have been simplified by assuming that messages do not exceed B_m bytes, i.e. no internal start-ups are incurred and by neglecting the nearest neighbor communication performed in the substructuring phase.

Figure 2 compares the three methods using model times under the following assumptions: $P = Q$, $N \le P$, $\tau = 1000$ and $t_c = 1$. This comparison assumes that sufficient memory is available. Each (P, N) pair is represented by a box, which is shaded to indicate which method is fastest for that pair. The four plots, (A) through (D), represent different choices of the parameters t_a and t_{copy}. SS/BalCR is the fastest for sufficiently large P and N, but reducing the copying time shifts the crossover boundary in favour of TGET (or SS/TGET). Reducing the arithmetic cost (going from (B) to (C)), clearly favours the methods that apply substructuring. Note that plot (B) in Figure 2 corresponds approximately to the current parameters for the Intel hypercube.

5   ADM on Hypercubes

In this section, we discuss our implementations of the Alternating Direction Methods. We embed a two-dimensional processor mesh (torus) in the hypercube [5]. The $P \times P$ computational grid is mapped onto an $N_x \times N_y$ processor grid, with all processors receiving equal, contiguous blocks of grid points. $N = 2^n = N_x \times N_y$ is the total number of processors in the cube and N_x and N_y are powers of 2. We point out that for $N_y = 1$, this scheme reduces to embedding a linear array in the hypercube, or one-dimensional domain decomposition. For simplicity, we assume that P is also a power of 2.

We recall that for Schrödinger's equation we use complex arithmetic. The tridiagonal matrix-vector products at each half step involve $C_{MVP}(P^2/N)$ arithmetic operations and nearest neighbor communication. The methods discussed in the preceeding section are central to the parallel implementation of the ADM. In going from real to complex arithmetic, with the grid size fixed, the arithmetic costs increase approximately by a factor of 5 and the data volume in each communication is doubled compared to the real case. Based on our experience with multiple real tridiagonal systems, where SS/BalCR was close to but slower than SS/TGET, we only report results for the ADM using the TGET and SS/TGET algorithms.

When we consider the complexity of a full ADM step, using a two-dimensional processor mesh, it is interesting to note that several terms in the final expression depend on N, but not on N_x or N_y. These include the total arithmetic for the matrix vector products (MVP), for substructuring in SS/TGET and for Gaussian elimination in

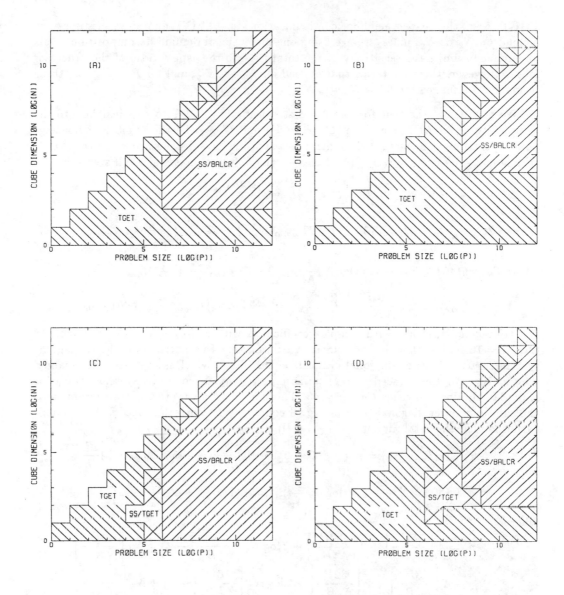

Figure 2: Comparison of TGET, SS/TGET and SS/BalCR based on model times for solving P tridiagonal systems of order P, on N processors. $N \leq P, \tau = 1000$ and $t_c = 1$. (A): $t_a = 25$, $t_{copy} = 10$, (B): $t_a = 25$, $t_{copy} = 5$, (C): $t_a = 5$, $t_{copy} = 5$, (D): $t_a = 5$, $t_{copy} = 1$.

TGET. Also, the nearest neighbor communications in the MVP and SS phases does not depend on N_x or N_y, unless we are using one-dimensional domain decomposition. This phenomenon limits the sensitivity of the total time to the aspect ratio of the processor mesh. However, there are terms that depend on N_x and N_y, and for $P \times P$ grids, these terms are minimized for $N_x = N_y = \sqrt{N}$.

We now derive the time for one ADM step using SS/TGET to give insight into the complexity of an ADM step. Let C_{MVP}, C_{SS} and C_{TRID} be the number of floating-point operations per point for the matrix-vector products, substructuring and the (local) tridiagonal solves respectively. The times for the different phases of a full step are

$$T_{MVP} = 2C_{MVP}\frac{P^2}{N}t_a + 2T_{comm}\left(8\frac{P}{N_x}\right) + 2T_{comm}\left(8\frac{P}{N_y}\right),$$

$$T_{SS} = 2C_{SS}\frac{P^2}{N}t_a + 2T_{comm}\left(32\frac{P}{N_x}\right) + 2T_{comm}\left(8\frac{P}{N_x}\right) + 2T_{comm}\left(32\frac{P}{N_y}\right) + 2T_{comm}\left(8\frac{P}{N_y}\right),$$

$$T_{RS} = \left(40 \log N_x \frac{P}{N_y} + 40 \log N_y \frac{P}{N_x}\right)t_{copy} + C_{TRID}\left(\frac{P}{N_x} + \frac{P}{N_y}\right)t_a$$

$$+ 2 \log N_y\left[T_{comm}\left(\frac{16P}{N_x}\right) + T_{comm}\left(\frac{4P}{N_x}\right)\right] + 2 \log N_x\left[T_{comm}\left(\frac{16P}{N_y}\right) + T_{comm}\left(\frac{4P}{N_y}\right)\right].$$

For tridiagonal matrices with complex coefficients with constants on the off-diagonals, $C_{MVP} = 16$ real arithmetic operations. Assuming that the matrices for the tridiagonal system solution have off-diagonal elements equal to -1, which is the case after scaling, $C_{SS} = 70$. For the reduced system we assume a general, complex, system, which for Gaussian elimination yields $C_{TRID} = 46$. This constant reduces to 24, if we assume that the sub- and super-diagonals entries are all equal to -1. With the simplified communication model, the total time is

$$T_{ADM}(P, N, N_x) = n_s \tau + (96 + 40 \log N_y)\frac{P}{N_x}t_c + (96 + 40 \log N_x)\frac{P}{N_y}t_c$$

$$+ \left(40 \log N_y \frac{P}{N_x} + 40 \log N_x \frac{P}{N_y}\right)t_{copy}, + \left(172\frac{P^2}{N} + 46\frac{P}{N_x} + 46\frac{P}{N_y}\right)t_a$$

where

$$n_s = 4\left\lceil\frac{8P}{N_x B_m}\right\rceil + 2\left\lceil\frac{32P}{N_x B_m}\right\rceil + 2 \log N_y\left\lceil\frac{16P}{N_x B_m}\right\rceil + 2 \log N_y\left\lceil\frac{4P}{N_x B_m}\right\rceil$$

$$+ 4\left\lceil\frac{8P}{N_y B_m}\right\rceil + 2\left\lceil\frac{32P}{N_y B_m}\right\rceil + 2 \log N_x\left\lceil\frac{16P}{N_y B_m}\right\rceil + 2 \log N_x\left\lceil\frac{4P}{N_y B_m}\right\rceil$$

is the total number of start-ups incurred, under our communication model. If we choose $N_x = N_y = \sqrt{N}$, n_s decreases like $(\log N_x)/N_x$ as N increases, but is bounded below by $12 + 4 \log N$.

We now consider the case $N_y = 2$, which is a special case in the sense that when we apply TGET in the y direction, each tridiagonal system is distributed over two processors. By using "two-way" Gaussian elimination, we can avoid the two transposes (which would have required just one step each) and replace them by one small exchange, involving just one row per system. Even though for larger cubes and larger problems with square grids, we expect a square processor mesh to be optimal, in our experiments we found $N_y = 2$ to be faster than $N_x = \sqrt{N}$. For a one dimensional cube, the tridiagonal solves in one direction are entirely local and this special case applies to the other direction. For a two dimensional cube, this special case applies for both directions.

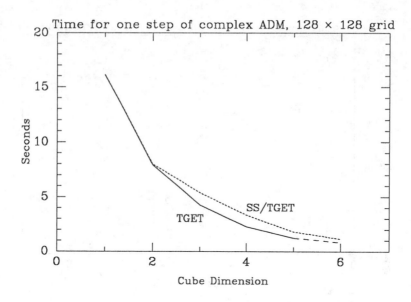

Figure 3: Cost of one step of ADM on the iPSC. Solid line: Using TGET (Dashed line: Extrapolation to 6-cube), Dotted line: Using SS/TGET.

6   Experimental Results on the Intel iPSC

In our experiments we used hypercubes of up to 5 dimensions. The floating-point capacity of each node is approximately 35 kflops (measured). The standard version of the Intel iPSC comes with 512k bytes of memory per node, but the Yale iPSC is currently configured with 4.5 Megabytes of memory per node. The Intel times reported here were obtained with the NX operating system, which has a reduced communication latency ($\approx$ 1.5 milliseconds) and the Ryan-MacFarland Fortran compiler, which handles complex arithmetic much more efficiently than the previous compiler.

In our experiments, we found that TGET with $N_y = 2$ was faster than SS/TGET for the 128 × 128 grid on cubes up to dimension 5 and the results reported correspond to this case, rather than $N_x = N_y$.

Figure 3 gives the time to perform one ADM iteration on a 128×128 grid, as a function of the cube dimension. With a 5-cube, TGET took 1.24 seconds, which represents a speed-up of 25.8 over the same code on a single node of the hypercube, and is faster than the VAX 8600 which took 1.4 seconds for the same problem. The code for TGET was not run on a 6-cube, and we have used an extrapolated value (0.8 seconds). The predicted time on a 7-cube is $\approx$ 0.6 seconds. Figure 4 shows the efficiencies corresponding to the times in Figure 3. The efficiencies are based on a running time of 32 seconds on a single node. For both methods, the efficiency falls off as the cube size is increased, but the deterioration is more rapid for SS/TGET because of the substructuring. Finally, Figure 5 shows the variation in the total time as N_x is varied. As one can see, the "edge effect" of choosing $N_y = 2$ yields the best results for a 5-cube. TGET is less sensitive to variations in the aspect ratio of the processor mesh than SS/TGET.

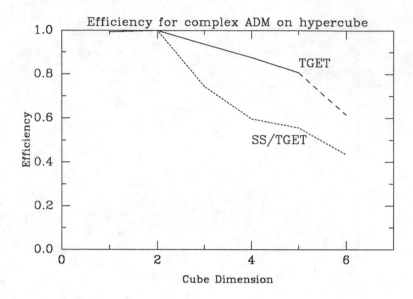

Figure 4: Efficiency of an ADM step. Solid line : Using TGET, Dotted line: Using SS/TGET.

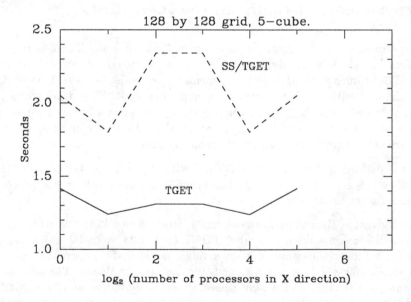

Figure 5: Effect of varying the aspect ratio of the processor mesh for a 5-cube. Time for one ADM step vs. N_x. Solid line: Using TGET, Dashed line: Using SS/TGET

7   Conclusion

The ADM scheme can be implemented efficiently on hypercubes. This is due to the fact that the method has regularity and a considerable degree of parallelism. The best iPSC time for a 128×128 grid is 1.24 seconds on a 5-cube, which represents a speed-up of 25.8, or an efficiency of 81%. Our predicted time on a 6-cube for the same problem is $\approx$ 0.8 seconds, which represents a speed-up of 40, or an efficiency of 63%. The time on a 7-cube is expected to be less than 0.6 seconds. The same problem takes 1.4 seconds on a VAX 8600.

The ADM scheme, due to its desirable numerical properties and the effectiveness with which it can be parallelized, can be recommended for the solution of Schrödinger's equation on hypercubes. However, future work on some of the other solution methods mentioned may lead to comparable or better parallel methods for the model problem.

Acknowledgement

This work was supported in part by the following: ONR grant N00014-84-K-0043, ONR grant N00014-82K-0184, NSF/CER grant DCR 8106181 and ARO FSP DAALO3-86-G-0029.

References

[1] T.F. Chan, D. Lee and L. Shen. *Stable Explicit Schemes for Equations of Schrödinger Type*. Technical Report YALEU/DCS/RR-305, Department of Computer Science, Yale University, 1984.

[2] C.-T. Ho and S.L. Johnsson. *Matrix Transposition on Boolean n-cube Configured Ensemble Architectures*. Technical Report YALEU/CSD/RR-494, Yale University, Dept. of Computer Science, September 1986.

[3] S.L. Johnsson. *Odd-Even Cyclic Reduction on Ensemble Architectures and the Solution Tridiagonal Systems of Equations*. Technical Report YALE/CSD/RR-339, Department of Computer Science, Yale University, October 1984.

[4] S.L. Johnsson. Solving tridiagonal systems on ensemble architectures. *SIAM J. Sci. Stat. Comp.*, 8:, May 1986. Report YALEU/CSD/RR-436, November 1985.

[5] S.L. Johnsson, Y. Saad and M.H. Schultz. Alternating direction methods on multiprocessors. *SIAM J. on Sci. Stat. Comp.*, ():, 1986. Yale University, Dept. of Computer Science, August, 1985, YALEU/CSD/RR-382.

[6] D.W. Peaceman and H.H. Rachford Jr. The numerical solution of parabolic and elliptic differential equations. *J. Soc. Indust. Appl. Math.*, 3:28–41, 1955.

[7] H.H. Wang. A parallel method for tridiagonal equations. *ACM Trans. Math. Softw.*, 7:170–182, 1981.

The SSOR Preconditioned Conjugate Gradient on a Hypercube

COURTENAY T. VAUGHAN* AND JAMES M. ORTEGA*

Abstract. This paper gives model and computational results for SSOR preconditioned conjugate gradient on a 64 processor Intel iPSC. Results for conjugate gradient and SOR are also given. All three methods are applied to two model problems: a Poisson-like equation with a mixed derivative term and a plane stress problem.

1. Introduction. We consider the implementation of the m-step SSOR preconditioned conjugate gradient (PCG) method on a 64 processor Intel iPSC hypercube. For comparison, we also implement the CG method, with no preconditioning, and the SOR iteration. Our implementations of the SOR iteration and the SSOR preconditioning are based on multicolor orderings [2] and we follow Adams [1] who implemented these methods for the same model problems on the Finite Element Machine. Our results on the conjugate gradient method complement those of [6].

In our experiments we use two model problems. The first is the usual nine-point finite difference discretization of the elliptic equation

$$u_{xx} + u_{yy} + \beta u_{xy} = f \tag{1.1}$$

on the unit square with Dirichlet boundary conditions. The second is a two dimensional plane stress problem, described in [1] and [3], in which a plate is fastened to a rigid body along one side and a load applied at the opposite end. Here, the rectangular domain is discretized by triangular finite elements

---

*Department of Applied Mathematics, University of Virginia, Charlottesville, Virginia 22901

Research Sponsored in part by the National Aeronautics and Space Administration grant NAG-1-46 and the Applied Mathematical Sciences Research Program, U.S. Department of Energy, under contract DE-AC05-84OR21400 with Martin Marietta Energy Systems, Inc.

on which linear basis functions are defined. At each grid point, there are two unknowns, the displacements u and v in the x and y directions.

2. Implementations and Computational Models. We describe in this section our implementations and, at the same time, develop models which allow us to predict running times as well as Mflop rates. We assume a $p = 2^q$ processor hypercube with the processors numbered from 0 to p−1.

SOR. By means of multicolor orderings, SOR may be implemented by γ Jacobi iterations, where γ is the number of colors [2]. For the mixed derivative problem (1.1), four colors are required. For the plane stress problem three are sufficient but the two unknowns at each grid point remain coupled so that 2×2 systems are solved in carrying out an SOR step. The particular colorings used for the two problems are shown in Figure 2.1.

1	2	1	2	1	2	1	2		2	3	1	2	3	1
3	4	3	4	3	4	3	4		3	1	2	3	1	2
1	2	1	2	1	2	1	2		1	2	3	1	2	3

        a) Mixed Derivative   b) Plane Stress

Figure 2.1. Multicolor Orderings

For both model problems, the grid points are partitioned to the processors as illustrated in Figure 2.2. For 2^q processors, we assume a $2^i \times 2^j$,

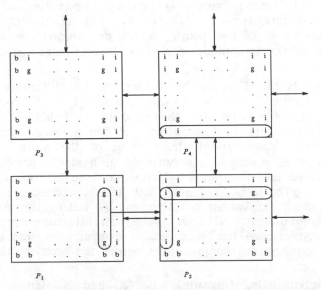

Figure 2.2. Data Distribution to Hypercube Processors

i+j=q, processor grid, and partition the differential equation grid accordingly. Figure 2.2 shows a subset of four processors of such a partition in which processors 1, 2 and 3 hold boundary values, denoted by the b's, and P_4 holds only unknowns. Unknowns corresponding to the grid points are denoted by g. Each processor also holds a copy of neighboring unknowns from adjacent processors. These are denoted by i's and are called *internal boundary unknowns*. It is these internal boundary unknowns that are transmitted between processors, as will be described shortly. We note that with the plane stress problem, two unknowns are associated with each grid point.

For the mixed derivative problem, it is not necessary to store the coefficient matrix since the coefficients in each equation are identical. For the plane stress matrix, however, the coefficient matrix is stored. Each unknown is coupled to at most thirteen other unknowns and, utilizing symmetry, A can be stored as eleven diagonals. We note that all storage in both problems is handled by one-dimensional arrays.

An SOR iteration proceeds as follows. All unknowns of color 1 are updated by a Jacobi sweep and use of the relaxation parameter, and then the internal boundary unknowns of color 1 are transmitted to neighboring processors. Next, the color 2 unknowns are updated and internal boundary unknowns transmitted, and so on. In the communication steps, processors send first to their east and west neighbors and then to their north and south neighbors. This is illustrated in Figure 2.2. The unknowns of color 1 in the circled column of grid unknowns in processor 1 are transmitted to their corresponding positions as internal boundary unknowns in processor 2. Then the unknowns of color 2 in the top circled row of processor 2 are transmitted to the corresponding internal boundary unknown positions in processor 4. This transmission also includes the values of the adjacent internal boundary unknowns on that row. This eliminates the need for a special transmission of corner points, which are needed for the 9-point and 7-point stencils of the two model problems, to non-neighboring processors.

Convergence is tested using the ∞-norm of the difference of the current and previous iterates. The ∞-norm is calculated as follows. First, each processor computes the norm for the variables it holds. Then a fan-in is initiated in which, at the first stage, half of the processors send their values to the other half, which update their value of the norm. The process is repeated until, after q stages, the norm is in a single processor. Then the process is reversed and the norm is fanned out to all processors, which all make the convergence test. We note that if the processors had an interrupt capability, we could implement a faster test by testing the norm in the processor which computes it and then sending an interrupt signal to the other processors if convergence has occurred. However, the test as implemented also serves to synchronize the processors before the next iteration.

We next give timing formulas. Let N_x and N_y denote the number of interior grid points in the x and y directions and p_x and p_y the number of processors in each direction. Then the largest subset of grid points that each processor holds is $n_x n_y$, where $n_x = \lceil \frac{N_x}{p_x} \rceil$ and $n_y = \lceil \frac{N_y}{p_y} \rceil$. Also, define $\eta_x = 0$

if $p_x = 1$, $\eta_x = 1$ if $p_x = 2$ and $\eta_x = 2$ otherwise, and define η_y similarly using p_y. Then η_x and η_y are just the number of neighbor processors that a processor has in each direction.

At the end of updating the unknowns of a given color, the internal boundary unknowns of that color are transmitted to neighbor processors. For the mixed derivative problem each processor either sends or receives, but not both since neighbor grid points must be different colors. Hence, there will be $\eta_x + \eta_y$ sends or receives per color per iteration. Each processor makes four data transmissions in the east-west direction, one after the update of each color; the total number of words sent is n_y except for those processors that contain $n_y - 1$ grid points in the vertical direction. For the north-south transmission, $n_x + 2$ words are sent since the corner points are transmitted also. Thus, the communication time per iteration for the mixed derivative problem with four colors is approximately

$$4(\eta_x + \eta_y)S + [\eta_x(n_x + 2) + \eta_y n_y]\alpha \qquad (2.1)$$

where S is the start-up time and α is the incremental time per word. We have included in α the time to gather into contiguous memory locations the data to be sent as well as scatter it to the proper locations after the transmission.

For the plane stress problem there are three colors and two unknowns at each grid point. Because there are only three colors, data transmissions must be made in both directions after each color is updated. Therefore, the communication time per iteration is

$$3(\eta_x + \eta_y)S_2 + 2[\eta_x(n_x + 1) + \eta_y n_y]\alpha \qquad (2.2)$$

where S_2 is the start-up time for communication between two processors in both directions. Note that $n_x + 1$ is used in (2.2) for the data volume in the y direction because the seven point stencil for the plane stress problem requires the transmission of only one internal boundary unknown.

Fan-outs are implemented by a spanning tree broadcast as described in [5] and the fan-in proceeds in reverse. $\text{Log}\, p$ stages are required and thus $2(S + \alpha_0)\log p$ communication time is required to do both the fan-in and fan-out used in the convergence test. Here α_0 is the incremental time when no gather-scatter is needed. In the convergence test, the absolute value of the difference of successive iterates must be taken and compared. We use comparisons to compute the absolute value so a total of two comparisons per unknown plus one comparison each stage of the fan-in are required. Therefore, the time for the convergence test is $2n_x n_y c + (2S + c)\log p$ for the mixed derivative problem and $4n_x n_y c + (2S + c)\log p$ for the plane stress problem where c is the time for a compare. There is also a wait time introduced by the interaction of the communication of the internal boundary unknowns and the convergence test. This interaction is almost linear in the number of processors and can be modeled by $(p - 1)w$, where w is a wait time.

For the mixed derivative problem, there are $13n_x n_y$ arithmetic operations per iteration, including the introduction of the relaxation parameter, while for the plane stress problem there are $66 n_x n_y$. Hence the total time per iteration for the mixed derivative problem is approximately

$$(2S+2\alpha_0+c)\log p+4(\eta_x+\eta_y)S+[\eta_x(n_x+2)+\eta_y n_y]\alpha+13n_x n_y a+2n_x n_y c+(p-1)w \quad (2.3)$$

and for the plane stress problem is

$$(2S+2\alpha_0+c)\log p+3(\eta_x+\eta_y)S_2+2[\eta_x(n_x+1)+\eta_y n_y]\alpha+66 n_x n_y a+4n_x n_y c+(p-1)w \quad (2.4)$$

where a is the time for a floating point operation, and includes the time for fetch and store. Also, for simplicity, we assume that all arithmetic operations, including division, require the same time.

Conjugate Gradient. For the conjugate gradient method, the unknowns at the grid points are stored as in SOR. We also need to store in the same way the residual, r, and the direction vector, p. In the CG method, multicoloring is neither needed nor used. However, in preconditioning by SSOR, the coloring is used as in SOR. More precisely, an SSOR sweep is implemented by updating the unknowns color by color and then repeating the updating in the reverse order of colors. No specific ordering of the unknowns of a particular color is necessary since they can all be updated independently. Since the last color updated on the forward pass is the same as the first color on the reverse pass, it suffices to use a relaxation parameter $\omega(2-\omega)$, in place of ω, on a single updating of this color. The same can be done in combining the last color on the reverse pass with the first color of the forward pass of the next iteration. We also use the procedure of [4] in which some of the colors used to update a color on the forward pass are not updated until after the color is updated on the backward pass. Therefore, the information from these colors can be saved and used again on the backward pass.

If M is the preconditioning matrix corresponding to m SSOR steps, then $M^{-1}r^k$ is the modified residual. The inner product $(r^k, M^{-1}r^k)$ is used in the conjugate gradient iteration and we base an initial convergence test on this quantity; that is,

$$(r^k, M^{-1}r^k) \leq \epsilon \quad (2.5)$$

When this test is met, we then test on the residual itself: $(r^k, r^k) \leq \epsilon$. If this test is not met, we re-enter the iteration. In this way, the convergence test is carried out with very little additional work but still yields a final residual based on the usual inner product rather than the inner product defined by M^{-1}.

We next give timing formulas for the conjugate gradient method. The matrix vector multiply requires communication of internal boundary unknowns in both directions and this requires the larger start-up time S_2. However, since colors are not used, there are only $\eta_x + \eta_y$ start-ups. For the mixed derivative problem there are $10 n_x n_y$ arithmetic operations and so the total matrix vector multiply time is approximately

$$(\eta_x + \eta_y)S_2 + [\eta_x(n_x + 2) + \eta_y n_y]\alpha + 10 n_x n_y a$$

The plane stress problem requires $54 n_x n_y$ arithmetic operations and its matrix vector multiply time is approximately

$$(\eta_x + \eta_y)S_2 + 2[\eta_x(n_x + 1) + \eta_y n_y]\alpha + 54 n_x n_y a$$

The CG algorithm also requires three linked triads and two inner products. The former each require $2 n_x n_y$ arithmetic operations and no communication. An inner product is computed by first calculating the partial inner products within each processor; these require $2 n_x n_y$ arithmetic operations. Then a fan-in is initiated which is implemented by a spanning tree, as in the calculation of the ∞-norm, and requires a cost of $(S + \alpha_0 + a)\log p$. After the inner product is complete it must be sent back to the processors by a fan-out which requires $(S + \alpha_0)\log p$ time. We note that there is an interaction between the matrix-vector multiply and the inner product; this is similar to the interaction of the transmission of the internal boundary unknowns and the convergence test for SOR, and can also be modeled by the addition of a $(p-1)w$ term.

Collecting the above parts gives the following approximate timings for the CG iteration on the two model problems:

$$4(S + \alpha_0)\log p + (\eta_x + \eta_y)S_2 + [\eta_x(n_x + 2) + \eta_y n_y]\alpha + (20 n_x n_y + \log p + 2)a + (p-1)w \quad (2.5)$$

$$4(S + \alpha_0)\log p + (\eta_x + \eta_y)S_2 + 2[\eta_x(n_x + 1) + \eta_y n_y]\alpha + (74 n_x n_y + 2\log p + 2)a + (p-1)w \quad (2.6)$$

We consider next the m-step SSOR preconditioning. The first step of SSOR requires $2\gamma - 1$ Jacobi steps, where γ is the number of colors. At each Jacobi step, internal boundary unknowns must be communicated just as for the SOR iteration. For the mixed derivative problem there are six start-ups and the total communication volume per step is $3/2$ times that for SOR while the computation time is $\frac{47}{4} n_x n_y a$ plus $\frac{19}{4} n_x n_y a$ for the use of the relaxation parameter. Hence, the total time for the first SSOR step on the mixed derivative problem is

$$6(\eta_x + \eta_y)S + \frac{3}{2}(\eta_x n_x + \eta_y n_y)\alpha + \frac{33}{2} n_x n_y a \quad (2.7)$$

For the plane stress problem, there are three colors and hence 4 Jacobi steps per SSOR step. The volume of data communicated is then $\frac{4}{3}$ that of an

SOR step and the computation time is $\frac{208}{3}n_x n_y a$ plus $\frac{16}{3}n_x n_y a$ for the use of the relaxation factor. Hence, the time for the first SSOR step for the plane stress problem is

$$4(\eta_x+\eta_y)S + \frac{8}{3}(\eta_x n_x + \eta_y n_y)\alpha + (\frac{224}{3})n_x n_y a \tag{2.8}$$

Therefore, the time for one complete iteration of 1-step SSOR PCG in the mixed derivative problem is (2.5) plus (2.7), and similarly for the plane stress problem. Subsequent SSOR steps require only $2\gamma-2$ Jacobi steps. Hence, the time for these steps is somewhat less than that given by (2.7) or (2.8). Therefore, for m-step SSOR PCG, the iteration time is somewhat less than (2.5) plus m times (2.7) for the mixed derivative problem, and similarly for the plane stress problem.

3. Computational Results. We now report on computational results on a 64 processor Intel iPSC. Tables 1-6 give actual and predicted times for the three methods on the two model problems for several problem sizes. The problem sizes are given in the left most column in terms of the grid size as well as the total number of unknowns. As the problem size increases, the data can no longer be held in the memories of fewer than the number of processors indicated; for example, in Table 1, the problem with 7396 unknowns cannot be handled by two processors. Note that the predicted values compare very well with the actual values. The percentage error is given in the third line in each box and is less than 9% with most errors well below 5%.

To obtain the predicted times in these tables, we have used the formulas of the previous section with the following values of the parameters in milliseconds:

$$S = 1.497, \; S_2 = 3.054, \; c = 0.084$$

$$\alpha_0 = 0.012 \; , \; \alpha_1 = 0.363 \; , \; \alpha = \alpha_0+\alpha_1 = 0.375$$

$$a = .027-.035 \qquad\qquad w = 1.1-3.2$$

The parameters S, S_2, α, α_0, and α_1 were measured independently using a program that just did communication between two neighboring nodes and are only valid for nearest neighbor communication with messages less than one kilobyte in length. The parameter c was also measured independently by a program just doing compares. The parameters a and w vary from program to program because of the way the computations are done for a and because of the different communication patterns for w.

The tables also give the Mflop rates which are computed by using the timing formulas without communication to obtain the total number of arithmetic operations for each problem, and then dividing by the actual running time. Note that the Mflop rate on a single processor varies between 0.025 and 0.031 which is consistent with results for Choleski's method reported in

size		Number of processors						
		1	2	4	8	16	32	64
60×60 3600	time/iter	1.893	0.964	0.501	0.293	0.205	0.161	0.171
	pred	1.892	0.968	0.518	0.297	0.198	0.162	0.172
	% error	0.07	−0.36	−3.40	−1.54	3.03	−0.45	−0.62
	MFLOPS	0.025	0.049	0.093	0.160	0.229	0.310	0.312
86×86 7396	time/iter		2.010	1.049	0.580	0.341	0.220	0.197
	pred		1.970	1.027	0.568	0.345	0.233	0.206
	% error		2.02	2.13	2.04	−1.16	−6.33	−4.88
	MFLOPS		0.048	0.092	0.170	0.295	0.458	0.512
120×120 14400	time/iter			1.927	1.022	0.588	0.346	0.260
	pred			1.960	1.029	0.576	0.352	0.267
	% error			−1.70	−0.70	2.10	−1.58	−2.76
	MFLOPS			0.097	0.183	0.318	0.541	0.720
172×172 29584	time/iter				2.047	1.085	0.640	0.418
	pred				2.046	1.094	0.627	0.414
	% error				0.08	−0.84	1.94	0.98
	MFLOPS				0.188	0.355	0.615	0.964
240×240 57600	time/iter					2.019	1.103	0.655
	pred					2.039	1.095	0.644
	% error					−0.99	0.74	1.70
	MFLOPS					0.371	0.679	1.142
344×344 118336	time/iter						2.116	1.167
	pred						2.122	1.162
	% error						−0.24	0.38
	MFLOPS						0.727	1.318
480×480 230400	time/iter							2.079
	pred							2.108
	% error							−1.40
	MFLOPS							1.441

Table 1. SOR, Mixed Derivative

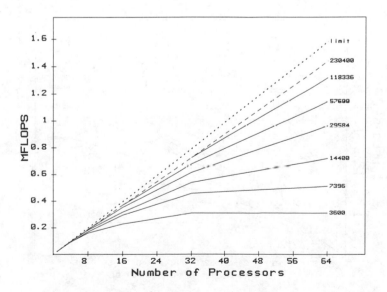

Figure 3. SOR, Mixed Derivative

size		Number of processors						
		1	2	4	8	16	32	64
32×32 2048	time/iter	2.257	1.149	0.613	0.361	0.250	0.213	0.213
	pred	2.270	1.162	0.622	0.357	0.242	0.195	0.211
	% error	−0.58	−1.08	−1.40	1.15	3.31	8.30	0.65
	MFLOPS	0.030	0.059	0.110	0.187	0.270	0.318	0.318
44×44 3872	time/iter		2.167	1.131	0.623	0.384	0.277	0.249
	pred		2.177	1.136	0.619	0.377	0.278	0.262
	% error		−0.49	−0.49	0.63	1.77	−0.28	−5.15
	MFLOPS		0.059	0.113	0.205	0.333	0.503	0.611
64×64 8192	time/iter			2.307	1.223	0.696	0.446	0.326
	pred			2.349	1.232	0.692	0.426	0.330
	% error			−1.79	−0.76	0.63	4.44	−1.17
	MFLOPS			0.117	0.221	0.388	0.606	0.830
88×88 15488	time/iter				2.250	1.215	0.711	0.461
	pred				2.261	1.215	0.692	0.465
	% error				−0.50	−0.02	2.60	−0.85
	MFLOPS				0.227	0.421	0.719	1.109
128×128 32768	time/iter					2.405	1.313	0.772
	pred					2.442	1.313	0.779
	% error					−1.56	−0.00	−0.91
	MFLOPS					0.450	0.823	1.400
176×176 61952	time/iter						2.334	1.289
	pred						2.351	1.303
	% error						−0.73	−1.07
	MFLOPS						0.876	1.586
256×256 131072	time/iter							2.481
	pred							2.530
	% error							−1.97
	MFLOPS							1.743

Table 2. SOR, Plane Stress

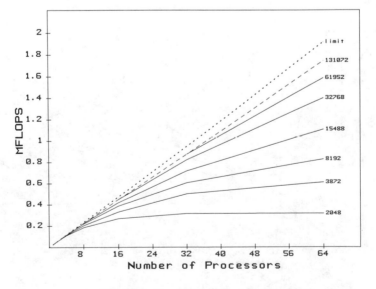

Figure 4. SOR, Plane Stress

size		Number of processors						
		1	2	4	8	16	32	64
60×60 3600	time/iter	2.312	1.172	0.603	0.347	0.230	0.181	0.176
	pred	2.318	1.181	0.624	0.349	0.222	0.173	0.173
	% error	−0.29	−0.73	−3.62	−0.47	3.59	4.76	2.00
	MFLOPS	0.031	0.061	0.120	0.208	0.314	0.426	0.470
86×86 7396	time/iter		2.389	1.212	0.651	0.385	0.264	0.218
	pred		2.408	1.245	0.678	0.399	0.259	0.214
	% error		−0.77	−2.75	−4.19	−3.60	2.04	1.88
	MFLOPS		0.062	0.122	0.233	0.402	0.588	0.715
120×120 14400	time/iter			2.335	1.232	0.673	0.413	0.289
	pred			2.386	1.241	0.679	0.402	0.287
	% error			−2.17	−0.74	−0.90	2.64	0.77
	MFLOPS			0.123	0.234	0.428	0.699	1.000
172×172 29584	time/iter				2.457	1.292	0.728	0.451
	pred				2.483	1.310	0.736	0.464
	% error				−1.05	−1.34	−1.06	−2.99
	MFLOPS				0.241	0.458	0.832	1.377
240×240 57600	time/iter					2.423	1.301	0.748
	pred					2.463	1.305	0.744
	% error					−1.66	−0.27	0.59
	MFLOPS					0.476	0.886	1.540
344×344 118336	time/iter						2.615	1.415
	pred						2.556	1.375
	% error						2.25	2.84
	MFLOPS						0.905	1.673
480×480 230400	time/iter							2.602
	pred							2.528
	% error							2.86
	MFLOPS							1.771

Table 3. CG, Mixed Derivative

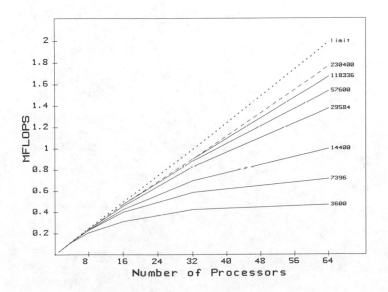

Figure 5. CG, Mixed Derivative

size		Number of processors						
		1	2	4	8	16	32	64
32×32 2048	time/iter	2.428	1.237	0.640	0.356	0.230	0.188	0.174
	pred	2.425	1.235	0.653	0.363	0.230	0.172	0.169
	% error	0.12	0.12	-1.88	-2.02	0.02	8.37	2.91
	MFLOPS	0.031	0.061	0.118	0.213	0.330	0.406	0.440
44×44 3872	time/iter		2.337	1.199	0.645	0.378	0.262	0.220
	pred		2.320	1.201	0.642	0.374	0.260	0.223
	% error		0.75	-0.18	0.41	0.99	0.97	-1.22
	MFLOPS		0.061	0.119	0.222	0.380	0.597	0.779
64×64 8192	time/iter			2.489	1.304	0.706	0.427	0.300
	pred			2.495	1.296	0.709	0.417	0.295
	% error			-0.23	0.58	-0.34	2.25	1.68
	MFLOPS			0.122	0.233	0.429	0.711	1.013
88×88 15488	time/iter				2.421	1.272	0.707	0.442
	pred				2.394	1.267	0.701	0.439
	% error				1.11	0.39	0.96	0.62
	MFLOPS				0.237	0.451	0.811	1.299
128×128 32768	time/iter					2.581	1.367	0.771
	pred					2.575	1.363	0.774
	% error					0.23	0.33	-0.37
	MFLOPS					0.470	0.887	1.574
176×176 61952	time/iter						2.493	1.342
	pred						2.469	1.332
	% error						0.97	0.80
	MFLOPS						0.919	1.709
256×256 131072	time/iter							2.661
	pred							2.640
	% error							0.78
	MFLOPS							1.823

Table 4. CG, Plane Stress

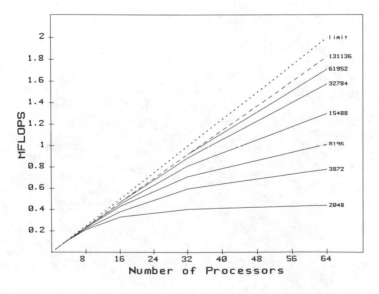

Figure 6. CG, Plane Stress

size		Number of processors						
		1	2	4	8	16	32	64
60×60 3600	time/iter	4.578	2.341	1.213	0.722	0.490	0.403	0.389
	pred	4.573	2.336	1.247	0.708	0.466	0.377	0.401
	% error	0.12	0.22	-2.85	1.83	4.76	6.54	-3.02
	MFLOPS	0.029	0.056	0.108	0.182	0.269	0.348	0.386
86×86 7396	time/iter		4.780	2.460	1.330	0.816	0.545	0.462
	pred		4.759	2.477	1.364	0.821	0.551	0.485
	% error		0.44	-0.69	-2.50	-0.68	-1.05	-5.02
	MFLOPS		0.056	0.110	0.208	0.347	0.519	0.614
120×120 14400	time/iter			4.628	2.464	1.367	0.875	0.631
	pred			4.733	2.479	1.380	0.837	0.632
	% error			-2.28	-0.61	-0.93	4.31	-0.09
	MFLOPS			0.114	0.213	0.385	0.601	0.834
172×172 29584	time/iter				4.884	2.615	1.486	0.949
	pred				4.939	2.634	1.505	0.987
	% error				-1.13	-0.71	-1.26	-4.07
	MFLOPS				0.221	0.413	0.744	1.193
240×240 57600	time/iter					4.814	2.618	1.520
	pred					4.922	2.637	1.546
	% error					-2.25	-0.70	-1.70
	MFLOPS					0.437	0.803	1.384
344×344 118336	time/iter						5.046	2.775
	pred						5.121	2.800
	% error						-1.47	-0.88
	MFLOPS						0.856	1.557
480×480 230400	time/iter							4.970
	pred							5.088
	% error							-2.36
	MFLOPS							1.692

Table 5. PCG, Mixed Derivative

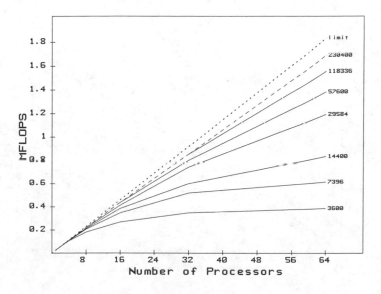

Figure 7. PCG, Mixed Derivative

size		Number of processors						
		1	2	4	8	16	32	64
32×32 2048	time/iter	5.026	2.564	1.342	0.783	0.529	0.414	0.410
	pred	5.039	2.574	1.369	0.773	0.506	0.390	0.403
	% error	−0.26	−0.37	−2.08	1.26	4.30	5.73	1.76
	MFLOPS	0.030	0.059	0.113	0.194	0.288	0.368	0.373
44×44 3872	time/iter		4.825	2.484	1.377	0.829	0.587	0.494
	pred		4.828	2.512	1.355	0.808	0.575	0.515
	% error		−0.06	−1.14	1.58	2.51	2.05	−4.38
	MFLOPS		0.060	0.116	0.209	0.348	0.535	0.696
64×64 8192	time/iter			5.141	2.727	1.521	0.941	0.663
	pred			5.205	2.719	1.507	0.905	0.667
	% error			−1.24	0.30	0.89	3.84	−0.60
	MFLOPS			0.118	0.223	0.401	0.648	0.919
88×88 15488	time/iter				5.027	2.677	1.534	0.977
	pred				5.005	2.671	1.497	0.969
	% error				0.44	0.21	2.37	0.82
	MFLOPS				0.229	0.430	0.751	1.180
128×128 32768	time/iter					5.364	2.888	1.662
	pred					5.398	2.878	1.668
	% error					−0.63	0.33	−0.37
	MFLOPS					0.454	0.844	1.466
176×176 61952	time/iter						5.193	2.820
	pred						5.185	2.832
	% error						0.14	−0.43
	MFLOPS						0.887	1.633
256×256 131072	time/iter							5.515
	pred							5.559
	% error							−0.81
	MFLOPS							1.767

Table 6. PCG, Plane Stress

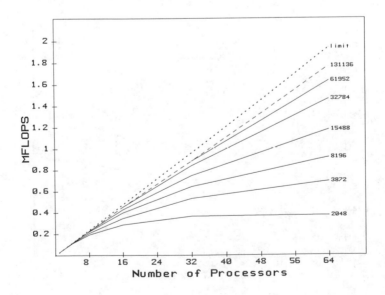

Figure 8. PCG Plane Stress

[5] and for Gaussian elimination reported in [7].

These Mflop rates are also plotted in Figures 3–8. In each figure, the Mflop rate is plotted for several problem sizes as a function of the number of processors. As expected, the smaller the problem size the more rapidly the speedup falls off as the number of processors increases. However, the speedup as the problem size increases in proportion to the number of processors is given by the dashed lines and is almost perfect. The problem sizes have been chosen so that each requires approximately twice the floating point arithmetic per iteration as the next smaller one. Hence, as we double the number of processors the amount of floating point computation per processor per iteration remains roughly constant. Therefore, if there is no increasing loss to communication time as the problem size increases we expect the increase in the Mflop rate to be linear in the number of processors and this is what we indeed observe.

References

[1]   L. Adams, *An m-step Preconditioned Conjugate Gradient Method for Parallel. Computation*, Proc. 1983 Int. Conf. Par. Proc., pp. 36–43.

[2]   L. Adams, and J. Ortega, *A Multi-color SOR Method for Parallel Computation*, Proc. 1982 Int. Conf. Par. Proc., pp. 53–56.

[3]   E. Becker, G. Carey and J. Oden, *Finite Elements: An Introduction. Vol. 1*, Prentice Hall, Englewood Cliffs, N.J., 1981.

[4]   V. Conrad and Y. Wallach, *Alternating Methods for Sets of Equations*, Numer. Math. 32 (1979), pp. 105–108.

[5]   A. Geist and M. Heath, *Matrix Factorization on a Hypercube Multiprocessor*, Hypercube Multiprocessors 1986 (M. Heath, ed.) SIAM, Philadelphia, 1986, pp. 161–180.

[6]   O. McBryan and E. van de Velde, *Hypercube Programs for Computational Fluid Dynamics*, Hypercube Multiprocessors 1986 (M. Heath, ed.) SIAM, Philadelphia, 1986, pp. 221–243.

[7]   C. Moler, *Matrix Computation on Distributed Memory Multiprocessors*, Hypercube Multiprocessors 1986 (M. Heath, ed.) SIAM, Philadelphia, 1986, pp. 181–195.

Numerical Computation on
Massively Parallel Hypercubes[*]

OLIVER A. McBRYAN[†][‡]

Abstract. We describe numerical computations on the Connection Machine, a massively parallel hypercube architecture with 65,536 single-bit processors and 32 Mbytes of memory. A parallel extension of COMMON LISP, provides access to the processors and network. The rich software environment is further enhanced by a powerful virtual processor capability, which extends the degree of fine-grained parallelism beyond 1,000,000.

We briefly describe the hardware and indicate the principal features of the parallel programming environment. We then present implementations of SOR, multigrid and pre-conditioned conjugate gradient algorithms for solving partial differential equations on the Connection Machine. Despite the lack of floating point hardware, computation rates above 100 megaflops have been achieved in PDE solution. Virtual processors prove to be a real advantage, easing the effort of software development while *improving* system performance significantly. The software development effort is also facilitated by the fact that hypercube communications prove to be fast and essentially independent of distance.

---

[*] Research supported in part by DOE contract DE-ACO2-76ER03077 and by NSF grant DMS-83-12229.

[†] C-3, MS-B265, Los Alamos National Laboratory Los Alamos, NM 87545.

[‡] Permanent address: Courant Institute, 251 Mercer Street, New York, NY 10012.

1. Introduction

This paper is part of an ongoing effort to exploit parallelism in the solution of equations arising in Computational Fluid Dynamics. We have previously presented implementations of conjugate gradient and multigrid solvers on other parallel architectures, including the Denelcor HEP shared memory computer[1, 2, 3, 4, 5, 6], the 32 processor Caltech Mark II Hypercube and the Intel iPSC d7 processor, a 128 processor Hypercube[7, 8, 9, 10, 11]. We have also developed an extensive portable linear algebra package for such systems, see[10, 11]. The current work extends these studies to the range of massively parallel architectures, beginning with the Connection Machine, a 65,536 processor hypercube architecture. The Connection Machine (CM in the sequel) is different from other architectures we have worked with in several respects. We will discuss some of these differences in this introduction. For a more complete discussion of the Connection Machine, and of the implementation of numerical algorithms on the machine, we refer to our paper[12].

Most significantly, the CM is a massively parallel machine. The CM therefore requires that applications be decomposed at a very fine level, presenting an interesting challenge in implementing applications. The CM processors are simple one-bit processors. Floating point operations, which are supported in micro-code, consume many (up to 1,000) machine cycles, with resulting floating point performance on the order of 1 kflops per processor. Despite this, peak rates of 120 Mflops have been attained on 32-bit vector operations using 64k processors, demonstrating the power achievable with massive parallelism. Each processor is associated with only 512 bytes of memory. This is compatible with the fine-grained parallelism, although it ensures that inter-processor communication is required more frequently on the CM than on coarser-grained machines. Fortunately communication on the CM is fast and has minimal communication startup cost.

The CM is an SIMD machine rather than the MIMD architecture of other hypercubes. While all processors receive identical instructions on each cycle, some processors may choose to ignore an instruction, depending on the setting of an internal flag. Logical expressions are implemented using this facility, although some care is required as each nested binary branch will incur an effective increase in execution time for the expression of a factor of 2.

The current CM software environment is entirely LISP based, with the standard programming language being *LISP, a parallel extension of COMMON LISP. The powerful user-friendly software environment of the CM is unique among current parallel processors. Support for parallelism is fully integrated into the programming language. To a large extent the message passing characteristics of the hypercube network are hidden from the programmer. The system provides support for distributed data types and has facilities for parallel global memory reference.

A final feature of the CM architecture is the possibility of using *virtual processors,* extending the apparent degree of parallelism to over a million. Virtual processors perform more slowly and with less local memory than physical processors, but total machine throughput may actually be increased. The ability to program complex applications in terms of very fine-grain parallelism should not be underestimated. We illustrate with the example of a typical grid-based computation. On medium-scale machines, it is necessary to perform two independent decompositions of data and associated code. First, the data is broken into blocks of grid points, with one block associated to each processor. Within each processor a further decomposition is required down to the single point level. On the CM, with up to a million virtual processors, one can generally avoid the first step entirely.

For the rationale behind the CM design see the book by Hillis[13]. Further information on the CM architecture is available in documents from Thinking Machines Corporation, for example[14].

Sections 2 and 3 introduce the CM hardware and software in more detail. Sections 4 and 5 describe the implementation of the multigrid and conjugate gradient algorithms on the CM, while section 6 presents performance measurements for the CM in PDE solution.

2. Connection Machine Hardware

The CM is accessed through a standard architecture front end computer, currently the Symbolics 3600, though a VAX interface is about to be released. Connection machine programs contain two types of statements - those operating on single data items, which are executed in the front end, and those operating on whole data sets which are executed in the CM. *LISP instructions for the CM are sent first to a micro-controller which expands them into a series of machine instructions. Floating point instructions are expanded in this way.

The CM consists of 4096 chips, each with 16 processors plus associated memory, for a total of 65536 processors. The chips form a 12 dimensional hypercube. Within each chip the processors are fully connected. Each chip also has a *router* module, a communication processor that allows any on-chip processor to communicate with any remote processor.

In addition to the router hypercube network there is a separate communication facility called the *NEWS grid*. Each processor is wired to its four nearest neighbors in a two-dimensional rectangular grid. Communication on the NEWS grid is extremely fast and is encouraged for those processes that can avail of the limited interconnections involved. Long range communication, even on a grid, is best done however with the router system.

An important feature of the CM system is support for *virtual processors*. The user may specify that each physical processor is to simulate a small rectangular array of virtual processors. The current machine provides up to 1,048,576 virtual processors. All system facilities are transparent to virtual processes, except that such processors appear to be correspondingly slower and have only a fraction of the 512 bytes of memory of a physical processor. The NEWS grid and hypercube communication facilities are supported between arbitrary virtual processors.

3. The CM Programming Environment

The programming languages available on the CM are a parallel extension of COMMON LISP, called *LISP, and an assembly language called PARIS. For a complete description of COMMON LISP see the book by Steele[15]. For further details of the *LISP language see the Thinking Machine Corporation's *LISP manual[16].

*LISP is an extension to COMMON LISP that includes facilities for utilizing parallelism. The primary data extension is the concept of a *pvar,* or parallel variable. Pvars are defined using the *defvar* function, in the same way as *defvar* is used for defining ordinary LISP variables. A pvar can be thought of as a sequence of ordinary LISP variables, one per processor. Parallel constants are supported with a special function "!!": if c is a LISP object, then (!! c) returns a pvar which contains the value c in every processor. Parallel versions of many standard LISP operators are defined, typically with !! appended to the LISP name. For example:

$$(*!! \ (!! \ 2) \ p \ )$$

applies the parallel multiply operation *!! to the constant pvar (!! 2) and the pvar p. Similarly there are parallel versions of logical operators such as <!! , *and*!! , and so on.

Logical and looping constructs parallel those in LISP and allow an operation to be performed over any subset of processors. This *selection* mechanism is very powerful and is a primary mechanism for providing non-homogeneous SIMD instructions. Selection scoping is block structured.

Since pvars are distributed across the CM, it is essential to be able to locate neighboring elements of a pvar, and to communicate in parallel with other processors. This is accomplished by a set of pvar functions which provide parallel global memory references. Processor addressing in these functions may be either absolute or relative, and may be performed using either grid or hypercube indexing.

4. Parallel Multigrid

The basic multigrid idea[17, 18, 19, 20, 21, 22, 7] involves two aspects - the use of relaxation methods to dampen high-frequency errors and the use of multiple grids to allow low-frequencies to be relaxed inexpensively. For the Connection Machine, there is an important difference in approach from that on other parallel machines. The CM has only 512 bytes of memory per processor, which means that it is not possible to store a substantial subgrid of points per processor as was done in our other implementations[7]. Instead, we have chosen to assign only one grid point per processor. This may seem wasteful of memory, but is not really so because of the CM's virtual processor ability. By using sufficiently many virtual processors all memory may be fully utilized.

In our multigrid implementation, the coarse grid points are always assigned to the same processor as their corresponding fine grid points. Because of memory limitations this implies a restriction on the number of multigrid levels that can be accommodated. When relaxation is performed on coarse grids, most processors are idle. As a result, V-cycles are more favored than W-cycles on the CM, and multigrid iterations with more than about 5 levels are also undesirable. This is borne out by our experiments presented in the results section.

We have used parallel versions of modified Jacobi relaxation and of red-black Gauss-Seidel relaxation. There is little obvious advantage to using red-black relaxation on the CM since it requires 2 successive sweeps each involving only half of the grid points. Consequently half of the processors are unused at any time. Thus the known improved convergence rate of red-black Gauss-Seidel iteration, which is twice as fast for the Poisson Equation, is canceled by the 50% reduction in attainable CM utilization. We note however that if 2 or more virtual processors are used per physical processor, then this disadvantage disappears - all of the physical processors may remain active at all times. We also note that with one grid point per processor, and a completely parallel execution, lexicographic Gauss-Seidel relaxation reduces to ordinary Jacobi relaxation.

We accomplish the distribution of data to various grid levels, by representing the solution, error, and right-hand-side on each grid level as a *LISP pvar. In particular the hypercube is organized as a rectangular mesh of virtual processors. Each grid is associated with a selection pvar called *domain* which is simply a 1-bit pvar initialized to be true at all virtual processors that contain a grid point of that grid, and false elsewhere. Relaxation is performed only for domain points for that grid. The same mechanism allows irregular rectangular grids to be handled as easily as regular grids.

The fine-grid residual equation is projected to the coarse grid using full injection in the modified Jacobi case or half-injection in the red-black Gauss-Seidel case. As discussed previously, no communication is involved here since the relevant fine-grid point is in the same processor as the target coarse-grid point.

To control termination of iteration, norms of error values or residuals need to be calculated. These are evaluated by using the *LISP function *sum* which tree-sums the elements of a pvar over a set of processors. In terms of *sum* we can define a *norm-vector* function, to evaluate the norm of a vector stored as a pvar on an arbitrary subset of processors, again specified by selection.

Having solved the error equation on the coarse grid, the solution on the fine grid has to be updated by addition of a suitable interpolation of the computed coarse grid error. We have used linear interpolation at this point. This step does involve communication, in fact over long distances in the case of very coarse grids, in which case hypercube communication channels are used.

5. Parallel Conjugate Gradient

Discretization of elliptic partial differential equations by finite element or finite difference methods leads to systems of equations with sparse coefficient matrices. The parallel conjugate gradient method we have developed on the CM, solves systems of equations with such coefficient matrix structures. This allows us to parallelize the solution of finite element discretizations of arbitrary and even variable degree with high efficiency.

The preconditioned conjugate gradient method[23, 24, 25, 26, 27, 28] finds the solution of the system of equations $Ax = f$ (A is assumed to be positive definite symmetric) to a specified accuracy ε by performing an iteration on the vector x, which has been appropriately initialized. Apart from simple vector linear algebra, this iteration involves only the operations $x \to Ax$, $x \to Bx$, $<x,y>$, and simple vector linear algebra operations. Here B is an approximate inverse of A, which is also assumed to be positive definite symmetric, and $<x,y>$ denotes the inner product of vectors x and *y.* A carefully chosen *preconditioning* operator B can be effective in improving substantially the convergence rate of the unpreconditioned algorithm (case $B=I$)[25].

We parallelize the algorithm by exploiting parallelism in every operation of the iteration. All of the vectors in the algorithm are allocated as *LISP pvars. The communication-intensive operation $p \rightarrow Ap$ is implemented as a *LISP function which stores the value of Ap into a pvar *ap*. For our Poisson equation test problem with a 5-point discretization on a rectangle, this function is easily written using the global memory access functions mentioned in section 3. For simplicity we have chosen the pre-conditioning operator to be the identity operator. The other communication intensive operations in the conjugate gradient algorithm are the several inner products of vectors which are required. These are trivially implemented using the *sum* *LISP function.

6. Computational Results

As a test problem we have solved a Poisson equation on a rectangle using SOR relaxation, multigrid and conjugate gradient methods. Zero Dirichlet boundary conditions were imposed on all sides. Iterations were continued until the initial residual was reduced by a specified factor, usually .001. Most of the results reported were obtained on a 16k processor CM, with some measurements on 32k processors. However all indications are that results demonstrated here on 16k and 32k systems scale essentially linearly to the 64k system.

We performed various tests using 4 and 8 virtual processors per physical processor, with up to 256k virtual processors. Such a configuration provides an excellent test of the ability to effectively use very fine-grained parallelism. We plot two quantities that describe system performance. The *megaflops* attained in a computation is the average number of millions of floating point operations executed per second. We count only standard floating point arithmetic operations such as addition and multiplication. A closely related quantity methods is the *time per iteration,* defined by taking the total computation time for a solution and dividing it by the number of iterations used. The *grid size* label on the following graphs denotes the number of grid points in each dimension.

6.1. Relaxation

In Figure 1 we present the results for solution of the equations using straight SOR relaxation. The relaxation parameter $\omega = .8$ for successive over-relaxation in Jacobi iteration has been used. Two curves are presented in Figure 1, the shorter one

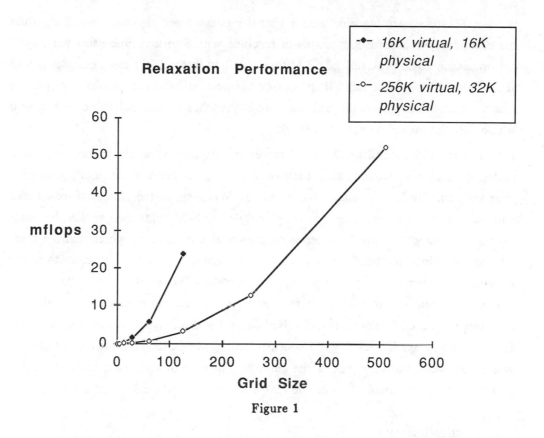

Figure 1

Relaxation using 128*128 processor grid and
optimal choice between News and Hypercube

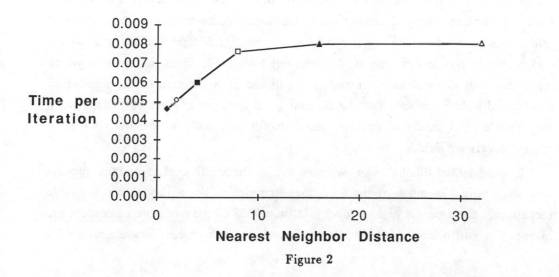

Figure 2

is for a 16k processor machine with 1 virtual processor per physical processor, while the second curve is for a 32k processor machine with 8 virtual processors per physical processor. The peak rate of 52 Mflops obtained in the latter case, corresponds to about 104 Mflops for a full 64k processor Connection Machine. Relaxation performance improves rapidly with grid size, until it reaches its optimal value with a grid which fills the virtual processor network.

The relaxation results in Figure 1 involved only nearest neighbor communication patterns. Multigrid requires relaxation on coarser grid levels, where communication over substantially longer distances is required. We measure the effects of long range communication in Figure 2, where we plot time per SOR relaxation versus the interprocessor distance involved. A series of grids was used each of which had the same number of points, but with the distance between grid-points, which we refer to as the *nearest neighbor distance,* successively increasing. We used 32 different nearest neighbor distances. As mentioned previously, there are two distinct communication facilities on the CM - the rectangular NEWS grid and the hypercube Router network. Each of the relaxation tests was performed using whichever communication method was faster. The flat later part of the curve in Figure 2 indicates the remarkable fact that hypercube communication on the CM is essentially independent of distance.

6.2. Multigrid Results

All multigrid solutions were obtained using V-cycles, with 3 modified Jacobi relaxations per grid level. The coarsest grid level was treated identically to the other levels. In Figure 3 we present measurements of multigrid performance on a 16k processor machine. All computations were on a 112×112 grid which allows for even sub-divisions down to 5 levels. The *curve* in Figure 3 shows the time required for the complete multigrid solution as a function of the number of levels used in solution. In standard multigrid fashion the solution time drops rapidly as the number of grid levels increases. One might conclude that multigrid is performing well on the CM. This is not in fact true as is borne out by the bar chart in Figure 3 which represents megaflops attained in multigrid solution as a function of the number of levels used. Here one sees that the maximum performance of over 19 Mflops when only one level is used (i.e. straight relaxation), drops rapidly to just over 3 Mflops when 5 levels are used.

To understand this behavior, we note that in the multi-level cases most processors are sitting idle much of the time, thus diminishing the ability to use available megaflops. Even on the highest level grid only 75% of the available processors are in use. On a fifth-level grid, only 49 of the available 16k processors are active. Yet

Multigrid on 112*112 Grid using 16K processors

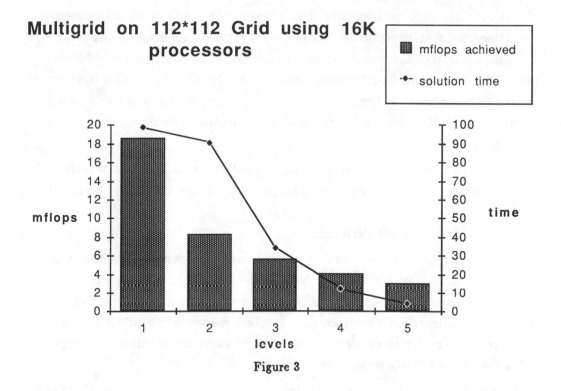

Figure 3

Conjugate Gradient Performance

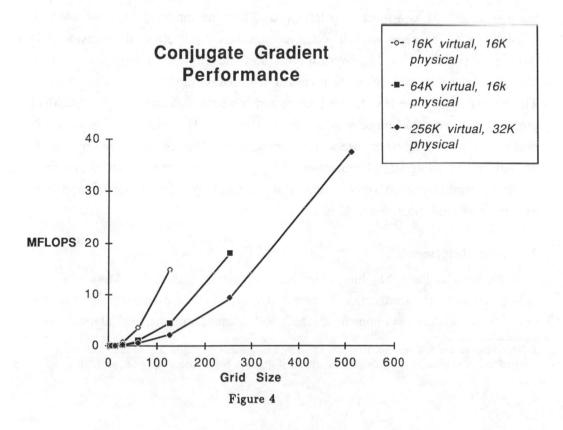

Figure 4

the algorithm spends the same amount of *time* on such a grid as it does on the finest grid since the CM is an SIMD machine. It is actually remarkable that megaflops rates do not decay even more severely than indicated. Another feature of Figure 3 is the rather sharp drop in performance between level 1 and level 2. This is explained by the fact that in going from a 1-level problem (relaxation) to 2 levels a variety of overheads are incurred, including residual computations and coarse-to-fine grid transfers.

We conclude that standard multigrid as implemented here is not a particularly good algorithm for a massively parallel machine such as the Connection Machine[1].

6.3. Conjugate Gradient Performance

Conjugate gradient performance is much more satisfactory than for multigrid because all processors may be kept busy most of the time, with the exception that during evaluation of the many inner products required by conjugate gradient most processors are inactive. This leads to a reduction in attained megaflops as compared to relaxation, but overall performance is still quite satisfactory, being in the region of 80 Mflops for a full 64k machine.

We present the results for conjugate gradient solution in Figure 4, where again we plot megaflops as a function of grid size. There are three curves, corresponding respectively to the cases (i) 16k virtual processors on 16k physical processors, (ii) 64k virtual processors on 16k physical processors and (iii) 256k virtual processors on 32k physical processors. Note in particular the relationship of the first two curves. The top point on these two curves both correspond to computations on 16k *physical* processors in which all processors are in use - in the first case computing with 16k grid points, and in the other case with 64k grid points. We see that higher megaflops are attained by using virtual processors. With virtual processors, much of the inter-processor communication is occurring within a single physical processor and thus external communication overhead is lower.

7. Acknowledgements

We wish to thank Thinking Machines Corporation, Cambridge, Mass., for providing access to the Connection Machine. We also benefited enormously from the uniquely stimulating environment at TMC, and acknowledge the help of many who

1. This observation has prompted further research into parallel multigrid algorithms, and has resulted in a new class of multiple grid algorithms with much better megaflops rates, see[29].

were instrumental in providing hints to using the system.

References

1. O. McBryan, E. Van de Velde, and P. Vianna, "Parallel Algorithms for Elliptic and Parabolic Equations," *Proceedings of the Conference on Parallel Computations in Heat Transfer and Fluid Flows*, University of Maryland, November 1984.

2. O. McBryan, "State of the Art of Multiprocessors in Scientific Computation," *Proceedings of European Weather Center Conference on Multiprocessors in Meteorological Models, Dec. 1984*, EWCMF, Reading, England, 1985.

3. O. McBryan and E. Van de Velde, "Parallel Algorithms for Elliptic Equation Solution on the HEP Computer," *Proceedings of the Conference on Parallel Processing using the Heterogencous Element Processor, March 1985*, University of Oklahoma, March 1985.

4. O. McBryan and E. Van de Velde, "Parallel Algorithms for Elliptic Equations," *Commun. Pure and Appl. Math.*, vol. 38, pp. 769-795, 1985.

5. O. McBryan and E. Van de Velde, "Parallel Algorithms for Elliptic Equations," in *New Computing Environments: Parallel, Vector and Systolic*, ed. A. Wouk, SIAM, 1986.

6. O. McBryan and E. Van de Velde, "Elliptic Equation Algorithms on Parallel Computers," *Commun. in Applied Numerical Methods*, vol. 2, pp. 311-316, 1986.

7. O. McBryan and E. Van de Velde, "The Multigrid Method on Parallel Computers," in *Proceedings of 2nd European Multigrid Conference, Cologne, Oct. 1985*, ed. J. Linden, GMD Studie Nr. 110, GMD, July 1986.

8. O. McBryan and E. Van de Velde, "Hypercube Algorithms for Computational Fluid Dynamics," in *Hypercube Multiprocessors 1986*, ed. M. T. Heath, pp. 221-243, SIAM, Philadelphia, 1986.

9. O. McBryan and E. Van de Velde, "Architectural and Software Issues for Medium Scale Multiprocessor Systems," *Proceedings of the ARO workshop on Parallel Processing for Medium Scale Multiprocessors, Stanford University, Jan 1986*, SIAM, to appear.

10. O. McBryan and E. Van de Velde, "Hypercube Algorithms and Implementations," *Proceedings of the 2nd SIAM Conference on Parallel Processing for Scientific Computation, Norfolk, Nov. 1985*, SIAM, March 1987, to appear.

11. O. McBryan and E. Van de Velde, "Matrix and Vector Operations on Hypercube Parallel Processors," *Parallel Computing*, Elsevier, Jan 1987, to appear.

12. O. McBryan, "The Connection Machine: PDE Solution on 65536 Processors," Los Alamos National Laboratory Preprint, Aug 1986.

13. W. Daniel Hillis, *The Connection Machine*, MIT Press, Cambridge, Mass, 1985.

14. "Introduction to Data Level Parallelism," Thinking Machines Technical Report 86.14, Cambridge, Mass., April 1986.

15. G. L. Steele Jr., S. E. Fahlman, R. P. Gabriel, D. A. Moon, and D. L. Weinreb, *Common Lisp: The Language*, Digital Press, Burlington, Massachusetts, 1984.

16. *The Essential *LISP Manual, Release 1, Revision 7*, Thinking Machines Corporation, Cambridge, Mass., July 1986.

17. A. Brandt, "Multi-level adaptive solutions to boundary-value problems," *Math. Comp.*, vol. 31, pp. 333-390, 1977.

18. W. Hackbusch, "Convergence of multi-grid iterations applied to difference equations," *Math. Comp.*, vol. 34, pp. 425-440, 1980.

19. K. Stuben and U. Trottenberg, "On the construction of fast solvers for elliptic equations," *Computational Fluid Dynamics*, Rhode-Saint-Genese, 1982.

20. A. Brandt, "Multi-Grid Solvers on Parallel Computers," ICASE Technical Report 80-23, NASA Langley Research Center, Hampton Va., 1980.

21. O. McBryan, "Fluids, Discontinuities and Renormalization Group methods," *Physics 124A*, pp. 481-494, North-Holland Publishing Company, Amsterdam, 1984.

22. D. Gannon and J. van Rosendale, "Highly Parallel Multi-Grid Solvers for Elliptic PDEs: An Experimental Analysis," ICASE Technical Report 82-36, NASA Langley Research Center, Hampton Va., 1982.

23. C. Lanczos, "An Iteration Method for the Solution of the Eigenvalue Problem of Linear Differential and Integral Operators," *J. Res. Nat. Bur. Standards*, vol. 45, pp. 255-282, 1950.

24. M. R. Hestenes and E. Stiefel, "Methods of conjugate gradients for solving linear systems," *J. Res. Nat. Bur. Standards*, vol. 49, pp. 409-436, 1952.

25. M. Engeli, Th. Ginsburg, H. Rutishauser, and E. Stiefel, *Refined Iterative Methods for Computation of the Solution and the Eigenvalues of Self-Adjoint Boundary Value Problems*, Birkhauser Verlag, Basel/Stuttgart, 1959.

26. J. K. Reid, "On the method of Conjugate Gradients for the Solution of Large Sparse Systems of Linear Equations," in *Large Sparse Sets of Linear Equations*, ed. J. K. Reid, pp. 231-54, Academic Press, New York, 1971.

27. P. Concus, G. H. Golub, and D. P. O'Leary, "A Generalized Conjugate Gradient Method for the Numerical Solution of of Elliptic Partial Differential Equations," in *Sparse Matrix Computations*, ed. D. J. Rose, Academic Press, New York, 1976.

28. G. H. Golub and C. F. Van Loan, *Matrix Computations*, John Hopkins Press, Baltimore, 1984.

29. P. Frederickson, O. McBryan, and Parallel Superconvergent Multiple Scale PDE Solvers, Los Alamos National Laboratory Preprint, to appear.

Performance Studies of the Multigrid Algorithms Implemented on Hypercube Multiprocessor Systems

VIJAY K. NAIK* AND SHLOMO TA'ASAN*

ABSTRACT

In this paper we analyze and compare the performance on a hypercube multiprocessor of some of the major multigrid techniques used in practice. The model problem considered here is that of solving the 2-D incompressible Navier-Stokes equations representing the flow between two parallel plates. Results obtained by implementing the different multigrid schemes on an iPSC are presented. Effects on the overall performance of various parameters of the algorithms, of the partitioning strategies employed, and of some of the characteristics of the underlying architecture are discussed.

1. Introduction

Multigrid algorithms are found to be optimal and efficient for solving a large class of problems involving partial differential equations on sequential machines. Recently there has been increased interest in parallelizing these algorithms. Although the multigrid methods exhibit a high degree of parallelism in the individual operations involved, it is not necessarily true that these algorithms perform optimally on multiprocessor systems as well. The performance of a multiprocessor system solving a given problem depends on several parameters. These include architecture dependent parameters, algorithm dependent parameters, and implementation dependent parameters. In this paper we discuss some of the performance issues involved in the parallel implementation of these algorithms and present some experimental results obtained by solving the 2-D Navier-Stokes equations for incompressible fluid flow on the Intel's Personal SuperComputer (iPSC). All the experimental results presented here are obtained with the Release 3.0 iPSC operating system. In the following section we briefly describe the idea behind the multigrid methods and present

*Institute for Computer Application in Science & Engineering Hampton, VA 23665. Research supported by the National Aeronautics and Space Administration under NASA Contract Nos NAS1-17070 and NAS1-18107 while the authors were in residence at ICASE, NASA Langley Research Center, Hampton, VA 23665.

three different algorithms based on this idea. In Section 3 the model problem is given. In Section 4 the performance issues involved are discussed and some experimental results are presented. Conclusions are given in Section 5.

2. Multigrid Algorithms

Consider a differential equation given by $LU = F$ with boundary conditions $BU = g$ defined on an n-dimensional domain in R^n. For simplicity of exposition let L be an elliptic operator. Let the difference scheme $L^h U^h = F^h$ with boundary condition $B^h U^h = g^h$, approximate this differential equation.

Now suppose we are solving the difference scheme by relaxation (Gauss-Seidel in lexicographic order, for instance). The error here can be written as $e_n^h = U^h - u_n^h$ where, u_n^h is the current approximation after the n-th relaxation sweep. Now consider the ratio $\mu_n = \|e_{n+1}^h\| / \|e_n^h\|$ where, $\| \cdot \|$ denotes the L_2-norm. From numerical experiments it is seen that the above ratio increases with n from some value $\mu_0 < 1$ and approaches a number that may be very close to one. That is, convergence is fast in the first few steps and then slows down.

A closer study reveals that whenever the error e_n^h is not smooth, μ_n is small, giving a good convergence rate. When e_n^h is smooth the resulting convergence rate becomes poor. That is, relaxation smoothes the error. The main idea of multigrid is this: if the error is smooth , approximate it by a coarse grid, say of mesh size $2h$. Applying this idea recursively one arrives at a multigrid algorithm. It involves relaxation sweeps on all levels, transfer of residuals from a fine to coarse level, and interpolation of correction from coarse to fine level. An important property of such an algorithm is that the rate of convergence remains independent of the size of the problem if the order and the frequency with which the grids are visited are chosen properly.

The recursive idea described above for reducing the error in the solution of the problem gives rise to a cyclic order of computation and these are referred to as the multigrid cycles. Different multigrid algorithms have been developed depending on the order and the frequency with which the grids are visited within a cycle. The most commonly used ones are the V and W cycles. In addition to these two types there is another type of cycle called F cycle which is less well known. A scheme called Full MultiGrid (FMG), in which the first approximation on the fine level is obtained by solving a similar problem on a coarser level, yields optimal performances. A detailed description of the various multigrid techniques and the algorithms based on these cycles is given in [Brandt 1984]. For the sake of clarity, we will refer to the algorithms based on these three cycles as the V, F, and W algorithms. All three algorithms make use of the FMG scheme. Furthermore, the basic multigrid operations in these algorithms remain the same, but the number of times a given grid is visited within a multigrid cycle is different. We will see that the relative performance of these three algorithms on multiprocessor systems is not the same as on the sequential machines.

From the performance point of view the parameters that characterize these algorithms are the amount of computational work done per cycle, the number of cycles required for achieving the desired accuracy, and the order and the relative frequency with which different grids are visited. The last parameter is not so important for the sequential implementations but is a crucial factor for parallel applications.

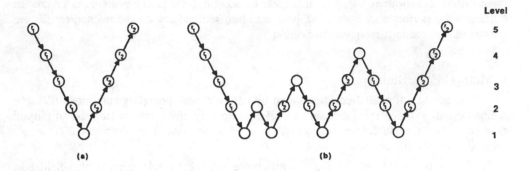

Fig. 1 (a) V Cycle (b) F Cycle

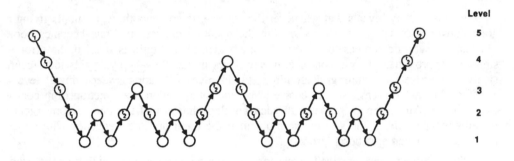

Fig. 2 W Cycle

If w_L denotes the total amount of computational work on the highest level L then it can be shown that the total work per FMG cycle for the V algorithm is asymptotically less than or equal to $\frac{16}{9} \cdot w_L$. It is less than or equal to $\frac{64}{27} \cdot w_L$ and $4 \cdot w_L$ for the F and W algorithms, respectively. These calculations assume that the number of relaxation sweeps on each grid is a small constant. If the number of multigrid cycles necessary to achieve the desired accuracy is also a small constant then all three algorithms perform optimally, i.e., in time $O(w_L)$, on sequential machines.

Characterizing the convergence properties of these algorithms is difficult, but experimental results suggest that in general the convergence rates per cycle for the W algorithm are the best and those of the V algorithm are mediocre. The F algorithm is somewhere between the two, usually slightly worse than the W algorithm. So the W algorithm is almost always preferred over the other two on sequential machines.

Figures 1 and 2 illustrate the order in which the three algorithms visit the different levels within a cycle. Here the increasing level numbers indicate finer mesh sizes. The letters within circles denote the number of relaxation sweeps on the corresponding levels. On levels with empty circles $r_1 + r_2$ number of relaxations are performed. It can be easily verified that for the V algorithm each level is visited exactly once within a multigrid cycle. For the F algorithm, level i is visited $l - i + 1$ times where l is the highest level for that cycle. For the W algorithm, level i is visited 2^{l-i} times. Thus, the number of visits to the coarsest level grows exponentially for the W algorithm, whereas for the F algorithm it grows linearly. The significance of this property will become clearer in Section 4 where we discuss performance issues.

3. Model Problem

The model problem considered here is that of solving the 2-D steady state incompressible Navier-Stokes equations. Such equations arise, for example, in studying the fully developed flow between two parallel plates where one plate may be moving with respect to the other plate. Their solutions present some of the difficulties involved in solving real life problems, but at the same time are simple enough for experimentation on currently available multiprocessor systems.

The equations in terms of vorticity ω and stream function ψ are:

$$\Delta\psi = \omega$$
$$u\,\omega_x + v\,\omega_y = \frac{1}{\text{Re}}\,\Delta\omega.$$

Re is the Reynold's number of the fluid flow and u and v are the velocity components in the X and Y directions, respectively. The velocity components are given in terms of the stream function ψ by,

$$u = -\psi_y \text{ and } v = \psi_x.$$

If the domain of computations is $\Omega = \{(x, y) \mid 0 \le x \le 1,\ 0 \le y \le 1\}$ and if U_0 is the velocity of the moving plate, then the boundary conditions for such a flow are given by,

$$u = v = 0 \qquad \text{at } y = 0$$
$$u = U_0, \quad v = 0 \quad \text{at } y = 1$$

Periodicity is imposed in the X direction and
a constant pressure gradient is imposed on the flow.

The details of discretizing and solving these equations using the multigrid methods on the hypercube multiprocessor system are given in [Naik 1986a].

4. Performance Issues in the Parallel Implementation

There are several parameters that affect the performance of a multiprocessor system employed to solve a given problem. These parameters are algorithm and implementation dependent as well as architecture dependent. One must take into account all these parameters before making a decision about the suitability of a particular algorithm for solving a problem on a multiprocessor system. In the following, we describe the interaction of some of these parameters. For a more detailed discussion on the performance issues involved see [Naik 1986b].

4.1 Partitioning Scheme

First we describe the effect of partitioning the domain on the distribution of the computational load. For the sake of simplicity consider a 2-D square domain with $2^L \times 2^L$ points on the highest level L. We divide the domain on the finest level into 2^x partitions along the X direction and 2^y partitions along the Y direction. Thus we get 2^{x+y} partitions with each partition having 2^{L-x} points along the X direction and 2^{L-y} points along the Y direction. We map the partitions onto the hypercube nodes in a one-to-one fashion using the binary reflected grey code scheme [Chan 1986]. We further assume that the *fixed region* partitioning strategy [Naik 1986a] is used, i.e., on the successive coarser levels each partition contains regions of the domain, formed by the points that are the coarse level counterparts of the fine level points of the partition. Under this partitioning scheme, in moving from level L to level $\max(x, y)$ the number of points associated with each partition decreases by a factor of four. Below level $\max(x, y)$ each partition has at most one line of points. With further coarsening the number of points per partition is halved until level $\min(x, y)$ is reached. On that level each partition has at most one point of the domain. Furthermore, in moving from level l to level $l-1$, where $\max(x, y) \geq l > \min(x, y)$, the number of partitions having any points and hence any computational work reduces by a factor of two. When l is less than or equal to $\min(x, y)$ this number reduces by a factor of four.

With the above described properties of the partitioning scheme, it is possible to make some predictions about the performance of the various multigrid algorithms under some assumptions about the communication costs. Specifically, it is possible to develop some analytical bounds on the speedups or efficiency of the system with a given set of communication parameters. Here we consider some simple cases and present some experimental results. For more details on the analytical results see [Naik 1986b].

Consider the case where there are as many partitions as there are points on the finest level i.e., each processor is assigned one point of the domain. In the above notation this means that $x = y = L$. Assume that there are no communication costs and so the evaluated performance parameters will represent the upper bounds. We consider speedup or efficiency of the system as a measure of the performance. We define the speedup of a system with N processors as the ratio of the time taken by a single processor to solve a problem to the time taken by N processors to solve the same problem using the same algorithm. The efficiency of this system is obtained by dividing the speedup by N.

The total computational cost incurred with N processors is bounded by the computational cost of the processor that performs work on all the levels. Now for the case considered here the work on any level is equal to the work associated with a single point and so, the total computational cost C_N of the system is given by,

$$C_N = \sum_{i=1}^{L} V_i \cdot w_i$$

where, V_i is the total number of visits to level i and w_i is the maximum work per processor on level i - a constant in this case. Thus,

$$\text{speedup} = \frac{c \cdot N}{\sum_{i=1}^{L} V_i}$$

$$\text{where, } c = \begin{cases} \dfrac{16}{9} & \text{for } V \text{ Algorithm} \\[2mm] \dfrac{64}{27} & \text{for } F \text{ Algorithm} \\[2mm] 4 & \text{for } W \text{ Algorithm} \end{cases}$$

Note that here $N = 4^L$. Depending on the type of algorithm chosen, the sum over total number of visits varies. It can be shown that for the V algorithm this sum is $O(L^2)$. It is $O(L^3)$ and $O(2^L)$ for the F and W algorithms, respectively. Thus, the maximum speedup with N processors for the V algorithm is $O\left[\dfrac{N}{\log_4^2 N}\right]$, for the F algorithm it is $O\left[\dfrac{N}{\log_4^3 N}\right]$, and for the W algorithm it is $O(N^{\frac{1}{2}})$. This shows that when there are as many processors as there are number of points on the fine level, the speedup for the W algorithm is far from being optimal even when the communication costs are ignored.

For the cases where the number of points assigned to each partition on the highest grid is more than one, the expressions for the speedups are more complex. In general the bounds improve. The effects of the algorithm properties and of the partition size on the computational efficiency are shown in Fig. 3. The results shown in this figure are obtained by measuring only the computational costs on the iPSC. Clearly, the sensitivity to the partition size is different for the three algorithms; V algorithm is the least sensitive and W algorithm is the most sensitive. Another point to be noted is that for the smaller size hypercubes i.e., when the partition size is large, all three algorithms show improvements in efficiency and the difference in the efficiencies of the three algorithms decreases. The effect of the size of the partitions is shown explicitly in Fig. 4 for the F algorithm. The other two algorithms show similar trends. As in Fig. 3 the measurements are made without including the communication costs. The results presented in these two figures suggest that even if communication is instantaneous, the attainable speedup or efficiency is low if the amount of work per partition is small. If the communication costs are included in the measurements then the performance deteriorates as shown by Fig. 5 for the F algorithm.

The efficiency discussed above represents a measure of the ability of an algorithm to keep the processors of the system busy. It does not include the numerical properties of the algorithm. If one is interested in the minimum overall cost of solving the problem, then both of these properties must be taken into account. The numerical properties are usually dependent on the problem being considered and so cannot be characterized easily. For the V algorithm these properties sometimes depend on the mesh size also. For the problem we are considering here both the F and W algorithms need about two FMG cycles to solve a 128 x 128 problem to the level of discretization error, whereas the V algorithm takes about seven cycles for the same. To compare the three algorithms more accurately we compute the efficiencies using the best sequential timings. In all cases the problem is solved to get the same level of numerical accuracy. We refer to such an efficiency as the normalized efficiency. Here the sequential timings of the F algorithm are used for normalization. These results are shown in Fig. 6. Note that here the communication costs are included in computing the normalized efficiency. It can be seen that when the partition sizes are large and the hypercube size is small, both the F and W algorithms perform better than the V

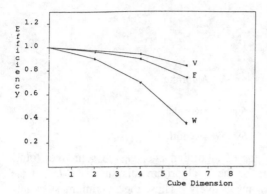

Fig. 3: Effect of Algorithm Characteristics
on Computational Efficiency
Square Partitions,   128x128 Domain

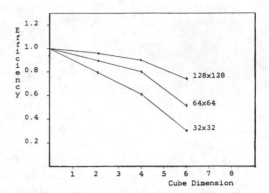

Fig. 4: Effect of Partition Size
on Computational Efficiency
Square Partitions, F Cycle

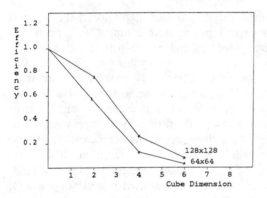

Fig. 5: Efficiency vs. Cube Dimension
Square Partitions,   F Cycle

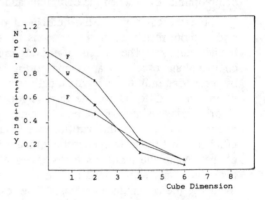

Fig. 6: Effect of Normalizing Efficiency
(Communication Costs Included)
Square Partitions,   128x128 Domain

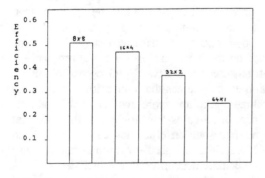

Fig. 7: Effect of Partition Shape
on Computational Efficiency
64x64 Domain, 64 PEs, F Cycle

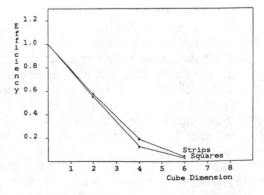

Fig. 8: Effect of Partition Shape
on Efficiency (Communication Costs Inc.)
64x64 Domain   F Cycle

algorithm in spite of the adverse communication costs. For small partition sizes the V algorithm may perform better even though its convergence properties are inferior.

4.2 Partition Shape

When the number of points per partition on the finest level is more than one, the shape of the partitions is another parameter that has to be taken into account. Reed et al. [Reed 1986] have discussed in detail the combined effect of the iteration stencil, the partition shape, and the communication parameters of the underlying architecture on the total communication cost. Their discussion concentrates on minimizing the communication cost assuming that the computational work is evenly distributed and remains the same through out the computation. For multigrid algorithms, the fact that the computational work decreases on the coarser levels must also be taken into account. We explain this point with the help of an example. Consider a domain with 64 by 64 points on the fine level. Assume that 64 partitions are to be made on the fine level. In the fixed region partitioning scheme, if we use square partitions, then each partition has at least one point on levels 3, 4, 5, and 6. (Level 1 is the coarsest level.) On the other hand if one were to partition the domain in strips (one column of 64 points in each partition, for example), then only on level 6 would all partitions have some points assigned to them. Note that in both cases each partition has the same computational work on the finest level. Thus among squares, rectangles, and strips, squares balance the computational load best.

Experimental results showing the efficiency of partitions with different shapes in balancing the computational load are shown in Fig. 7. Note that the communication costs are not taken into account. Here a domain with 64x64 points on the fine level is subdivided into 64 partitions. The four different cases considered consisted of partitions with 8x8 points (8 points in x direction and 8 in y direction), 16x4 points, 32x2 points, and 64x1 points on the fine level. In the first case we get square partitions whereas in the last case we get strips. As expected the squares balance the computational load better than any other shapes considered. The results shown here correspond to the F algorithm. For the W algorithm these will be more pronounced, but less so for the V algorithm.

When communication costs are introduced the shape of the partitions may affect the performance differently. For the iPSC the cost of initializing a message is orders of magnitude higher than sending a single byte across a channel. A single packet can contain up to 1024 bytes. In addition, all the channels leaving or entering a node cannot be effectively utilized for simultaneously sending or receiving messages. For the problem sizes we have considered here, it turns out that the communication costs on the iPSC for the strips are less than those for the squares. This is shown in Fig. 8 for the F algorithm applied to a problem with 64x64 points on the highest level. Here the efficiency is based on the computation plus communication cost. It is obvious from Figures 7 and 8, that for the problem sizes we are considering, the communication costs incurred with strips are much less than those for the squares. In general this is not true. The problem sizes considered here are special cases and it can be easily shown that for strips, asymptotically, the total number of packets for the two messages sent out per exchange of information with the neighboring partitions is greater by a constant factor than those for the four messages sent out by the square partitions when the number of interior points per partition is the same.

4.3 Schemes for Reducing the Communication Costs

In the partitioning schemes considered above, the regions of the domain are permanently assigned to the processors on all the levels even when the associated computational work is small. Sometimes it is advantageous to resort to a *shifting region* partitioning scheme [Naik 1986a]. In this scheme below a certain level l^* the work on the entire domain is shifted to one node so that on all the successive coarser levels there is no communication cost. On levels l^* and above the computational work is uniformly distributed among all the partitions, but below level l^* the computation is serialized. Thus every time there is transition between levels l^* and $l^* - 1$ either the data has to be gathered to one partition or scattered to all partitions from one partition. This scheme performs well if l^* is such that

$$\sum_{l=1}^{l^*-1} \left[C_{part_l} + C'_{part_l} \right] > \sum_{l=1}^{l^*-1} C_{Dom_l} + G_{l^*} + S_{l^*}.$$

where, C_{part_l} and C'_{part_l} denote the computation and communication costs, respectively, associated with a partion on level l. C_{Dom_l} is the computation cost associated with the entire domain on level l. G_{l^*} and S_{l^*} are the costs of gathering and scattering the domain on level l^*, respectively.

Experimental results showing the performance improvements brought about by serializing the work below level l^* by moving all the regions to a single node, are shown in Fig. 9. In this figure $l^* = 1$ corresponds to the fixed region partitioning scheme i.e., no moving takes place. It can be seen that the performance peeks out at a particular value of l^*. Note that when the problem size is small or when the size of the partitions assigned to each processor is small, the gains are higher. Here each partition has a smaller piece of work on the highest level and so the communication costs are more dominant. By serializing the computation below a certain level, the percentage reduction in the total cost is higher than that in the bigger size problem. In Fig. 10 we show the effect of the above described partitioning scheme when the computing power is increased by adding more processors. Note that for the larger size hypercube, the cost of scattering and gathering the data is also higher. But now the computational work associated with each partition has decreased and so the communication costs form a higher proportion of the total cost.

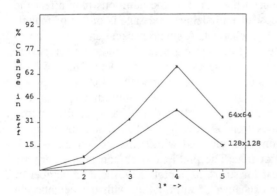

Fig. 9: Percent Change in Efficiency by
Serializing Computation Below Level 1*
Square Partitions, F Cycle, 16 PEs

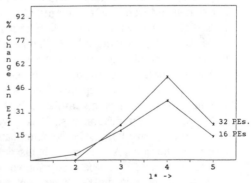

Fig. 10: Effect of Cube Size on
Serializing Computation Below Level 1*
Square Partitions, 128x128 Domain, F Cycle

Conclusions

We have considered the performance issues involved in implementing the multigrid methods on a hypercube multiprocessor system. It is shown that both algorithm dependent as well as implementation dependent parameters affect the performance considerably and the selection of an algorithm or of a partioning scheme must be based on the combined effect of these parameters. We demonstrate by some experimental and analytical results that the best sequential algorithm may not always be the most suitable algorithm for parallel processing. At the same time an algorithm that gives the best speedups may not be the most suitable candidate either. By using the problem of solving the 2-D Navier-Stokes equations as a model problem we show that a less well known method given by the F algorithm gives the best performance. We have also shown that when the communication costs are high instead of balancing the computational load it may be advantageous to sequentialize some parts of the work and avoid communication costs in those sections.

ACKNOWLEDGEMENT

We would like to thank the Mathematics and Statistics Research Section at Oak Ridge National Laboratory for generously granting us the use of their iPSC. We are particularly indebted to Tom Dunigan for his assistance during the course of this work. We are grateful to Bob Voigt for constant support and encouragement and to Merrell Patrick for invaluable assistance in editing this paper. Thanks to Amr Fahmy for his time and and help in preparing the figures.

REFERENCES

(1) A. Brandt, *Multigrid Techniques: 1984 Guide*, GMD Studien 85, Gesellschaft fur Mathematik und Datenverarbeitung, St. Augustin, 1984.

(2) T. F. Chan and Y. Saad, *Multigrid algorithms on the hypercube multiprocessor*, IEEE Trans. Comput., 35 (1986), pp. 969-977.

(3) V. K. Naik and S. Ta'asan, *A methodology for implementing multigrid methods in solving Navier-Stokes equations on a hypercube multiprocessor system*, in preparation, 1986a.

(4) V. K. Naik and S. Ta'asan, *Performance studies of multigrid algorithms implemented on message passing architectures*, in preparation, 1986b.

(5) D. A. Reed, L. M. Adams, M. L. Patrick, *Stencils and problem partitionings: Their influence on the performance of multiple processor systems*, IEEE Trans. Compt., to appear.

Implementation of Multigrid Algorithms on Hypercubes*

TONY F. CHAN† AND RAY S. TUMINARO‡

Abstract.

We discuss the implementation of multigrid algorithms for the solution of partial differential equations on a hypercube multiprocessor. We show how the topology of the hypercube fits the data flow of the multigrid algorithm, and therefore allows efficient parallel implementations. We present a timing model for the execution time which predicts accurately experimental results obtained from runs on an Intel iPSC system.

1. Introduction.

The multigrid algorithm is a fast efficient method for solving elliptic partial differential equations on serial computers. The algorithm consists of "solving" a series of problems on a hierarchy of grids with different mesh sizes. For many problems, one can prove that its execution time is asymptotically optimal in that it takes $O(n^2)$ operations to solve the equations corresponding to an n x n grid [11, p 50-51]. No algorithm can do better than $O(n^2)$ since there are n^2 unknowns. Not only is it asymptotically optimal but when properly implemented it is competitive with other algorithms on grids of a modest size [5]. Multigrid is now found in many areas of scientific computation (such as computational fluid dynamics [10]). Given its success on serial computers, it is natural to consider its performance characteristics on parallel machines.

In this paper, we consider an implementation of the basic multigrid method on a distributed memory, message passing hypercube multiprocessor. It would appear that the mapping of the multigrid algorithm to a multiprocessor would be as simple as it is for most other iterative solvers (like the Jacobi method). However, the hierarchy of grids in the multigrid algorithm complicates the flow of data. This in turn may make it difficult to efficiently map the algorithm to parallel machines. We illustrate, however, how the hypercube interconnection topology "naturally" corresponds to the multigrid data flow and thereby makes an efficient parallel implementation possible. Further, it is argued that the multigrid algorithm in a certain sense achieves the optimal execution time for solving an elliptic partial differential

* This work is supported by the Research Institute for Advanced Computer Science, NASA Ames, Moffett Field, Ca. and the Department Of Energy under contract DE ACO2 81ER 10886.

† Department of Mathematics, University of California - Los Angeles, Los Angeles, Ca. 90024.

‡ Department of Computer Science, Stanford, Stanford, Ca. 94305.

equation on a hypercube. Finally, we present a model of the communication and computation for the parallel multigrid algorithm. Using this model, we can predict the performance of the multigrid algorithm on a variety of hypercubes as well as analyze variations of the basic algorithm. We compare this execution model with our computer implementation of the parallel multigrid algorithm on an intel hypercube and find excellent agreement.

2. Jacobi Method.

Before considering parallel multigrid, we briefly outline the Jacobi algorithm which will serve as a typical iterative procedure to compare with multigrid. To simplify the description we restrict our attention to the 1d Poisson equation: $u_{xx} = f(x)$ on $0 \leq x \leq 1$. The ideas extend naturally to other problems and to higher dimensions. We discretize Poisson's equation by a central difference approximation on a mesh with spacing h, and obtain

$$\frac{u(x_{i+1}) - 2u(x_i) + u(x_{i-1})}{h^2} = f(x_i) \qquad i = 1, \cdots, n-1 \tag{1}$$

which can be written as

$$Au = h^2 f \tag{2}$$

where A is an $(n-1)$ x $(n-1)$ matrix, and u and f are $n-1$ vectors.
Rewriting equation (1) we get :

$$u(x_i) = [u(x_{i+1}) + u(x_{i-1}) - h^2 f(x_i)]/2 \qquad i = 1, \cdots, n-1 \tag{3}$$

One Jacobi iteration consists of using an approximate solution u to evaluate the righthand sides of equation (3) to obtain a new approximation for each $u(x_i)$.

One nice aspect of the Jacobi algorithm is that it parallelizes easily. If, for example, there are $n-1$ processors, we can put one grid point per processor and evaluate all $n-1$ righthand sides of equation (3) in parallel. In the general case when there are more grid points than processors, each processor is responsible for updating a block of contiguous points. Notice that to apply the formula each processor needs to know the old values of u at the points in its contiguous block as well as the points which border its block. This implies that each processor must communicate with the processors that are assigned to points which are adjacent to its own points. Thus a processor interconnection which topologically matches the difference stencil is sufficient for the parallel Jacobi algorithm. It is well known that when a gray code is used to number contiguous regions, this defines a mapping to the hypercube where adjacent domains are mapped to neighboring processors [4]. Therefore the Jacobi iteration can be made to run with high efficiency on the hypercube.

The major disadvantage of the Jacobi method is its slow rate of convergence. For Poisson's equation it will typically require $O(n^2)$ iterations to converge to the solution for an n x n grid of unknowns. It is this slow rate of convergence that leads us to consider the multigrid algorithm.

3. Multigrid Algorithm.

Only a brief sketch of the multigrid algorithm follows. A detailed description of the algorithm can be found in [1], [7], [8] and [11]. The basic steps are:
   1. Apply a couple of iterations of a standard iterative method (for example Jacobi) to produce an approximation : u_1.
   2. Set up a system of equations for the error in u_1.
   3. "Solve" these equations for the correction on a coarser grid.
   4. Interpolate the coarse grid correction and add the correction to u_1 to define the new approximation.

Notice that step 3 involves "solving" a set of equations on a coarser grid for which we can recursively call the same algorithm (ie. use multigrid to solve this coarser set of equations). Below we give the skeleton of a computer code for the basic "V cycle" multigrid algorithm that we have described [8]. The term level is used to denote the grid on which we are currently working on. Level one corresponds to the finest grid. Level two corresponds to the next coarser grid, etc.

```
proc multigrid(f,u,level,pre_relax,post_relax)
{
        if ( level = coarsest level ) then u = (A_level)^{-1} h^2 f
        else
                for k = 1 to pre_relax do Jacobi(f,u,level)
                compute_residual(f,u,level,residual)
                project_residual(level,residual,proj_res)
                multigrid(proj_res,v,level+1,pre_relax,post_relax)
                interpolate(level,v,correction)
                u = u + correction
                for k = 1 to post_relax do Jacobi(f,u,level)
        endif

}
```

The main advantage of multigrid is that it converges in a constant (ie. independent of the mesh size) number of iterations and each iteration costs only a constant factor more than that of Jacobi. For large n, this is considerably better than the $O(n^2)$ rate of convergence of the Jacobi method.

Let us consider a parallel implementation of a 1d multigrid algorithm. The basic idea is similar to the Jacobi algorithm. We assign grid points to different processors using a gray code mapping. Specifically, we look at the case when there are $n-1$ processors and $n-1$ unknowns (where $n = 2^k$). We look at this case in detail for two reasons. First, it is less complicated than the case where we have many points per processor and second even if n is greater than the number of processors on the fine grid as we continue to form coarser grids eventually the number of points on the coarse grid will be equal to the number of processors. In this case we assign one point per processor like in the Jacobi algorithm. The coarse grid is defined by taking every other point from the fine grid. Notice this implies that we will have many idle processors on the coarser grids. Let's look at processor $n/2$. To perform the residual projection, interpolation, and Jacobi iterations, this processor has the following communication needs:

finest grid level 0 : communicates with processors $n/2 - 1$ and $n/2 + 1$.
grid level 1 : communicates with processors $n/2 - 2$ and $n/2 + 2$.
grid level i : communicates with processors $n/2 - 2^i$ and $n/2 + 2^i$.

Thus the multigrid algorithm requires more sophisticated communication links than Jacobi. In other words, a simple processor grid which matches the stencil of the partial differential equation is not sufficient for an efficient multigrid algorithm. We state without proof the following result. If a particular gray code (specifically the binary reflected gray code) is used to assign grid points to processors on a hypercube, then the processors that must communicate with each other in the multigrid algorithm are at most a distance of two away from each other (regardless of the level of the grid and the size of the hypercube). Further, there is a simple and efficient algorithm that allows one to shuffle the grid points to different processors before moving to a different level so that we can maintain communication links of a distance one. We omit the details and refer the reader to [3]. The key point is that by properly mapping a problem on a hypercube, our communication needs remain local no matter how coarse the grid is compared to the size of the hypercube.

4. A Lower Bound Based on Data Flow in Solving PDE's.

In this section, we shall introduce a data flow view of algorithms for solving elliptic pde's and use it to derive a lower bound on the execution for solving such equations on hypercube computers.

The solution of an elliptic pde at any point in the domain requires some knowledge of information on the boundary. We know for example that by changing the boundary conditions we change the solution inside the domain at all points. Therefore, when we consider the convergence of numerical methods to the solution of elliptic problems, we can get a lower bound by determining the time it takes for the boundary information to reach all points in the interior. For example, consider the Jacobi method applied to the 1d Poisson equation. It takes $O(n)$ iterations before this information propagates to all the interior points. Thus a lower bound for the convergence of the Jacobi method is $O(n)$. Note that it actually takes $O(n^2)$. From this point of view, we can see why the multigrid algorithm yields such rapid convergence. One multigrid iteration propagates the boundary information to all the points in the interior. Thus the lower bound on the convergence of multigrid is $O(1)$ which is the actual convergence rate.

The principle advantage of the hypercube interconnections is that they allow one to efficiently communicate the boundary information globally. For example, if we have one point per processor and the processor $i_1 i_2 i_3 \cdots i_n$ contains some boundary information, it will take log n steps to propagate this information to processor $\bar{i}_1 \bar{i}_2 \bar{i}_3 \cdots \bar{i}_n$ (where the overhead bar denotes complement). Thus we can conclude that the optimal asymptotic time for solving an elliptic problem with one point per processor on a hypercube is $O(\log n)$. We shall see in Sec 5 that the multigrid algorithm achieves this optimal time as it takes $O(\log n)$ time to perform one multigrid iteration on a hypercube of size n (see also [2] and [6]).

The need for efficient global communication is not particular to multigrid. For example, any numerical algorithm which requires convergence checking needs to be able to communicate global information. Notice that convergence checking within the multigrid algorithm can be performed with almost no overhead. For example if we use the residuals as a measure of convergence, which are already computed in the multigrid algorithm, the norm of the residual vector on the finest grid can be accumulated at the coarsest level using a tree sum method which can be integrated into the multigrid algorithm. In fact by clever programming, the norm of the fine grid residual can be sent in the same messages which are used to transmit the residuals on the lower levels. This method implies that convergence will be determined after one additional multigrid iteration has been performed.

5. Modeling Communication and Computation.

We model the execution time of the parallel multigrid algorithm on a two dimensional $n \times n$ point grid using a $p \times p$ processor grid. The execution of one multigrid iteration consists of performing the Jacobi sweeps, interpolation, residual projection, and "solving" the coarse grid equation. There are two separate cases in the parallel multigrid implementation which must be analyzed slightly differently. Specifically when $n > p$, each processor has ($n/p \times n/p$) points. Thus when we communicate with our nearest neighbor we send messages of length n/p. On the other hand when $n < p$ we have some idle processors and those processors which are not idle contain only one point. So communication with our nearest neighbor requires messages of length one to be sent. Notice that even if $n > p$ on the fine grid, eventually on some level (ie. on some coarse grid) n will be less than p.

We define the following notation:

$T(n)$: time to perform one multigrid iteration on an $n \times n$ grid using p^2 processors.

$\alpha + \beta n$: time to communicate a message of length n between neighboring processors.

t : time to compute one Jacobi sweep at one point on the grid.

v : total number of Jacobi sweeps that are performed on each multigrid level
   (ie. pre_relax + post_relax).

r : time to compute the residual at one point.

ρ : time to project one point of the residual onto the coarse grid.

i : time to interpolate from the coarse grid and apply the correction to the previous approximation.

$M = vt + r + \rho + i$. The computation time on one level for one point.

We assume in this analysis that the hypercube has bi-directional simultaneous send and receive. If we count the arithmetic operations for the case $n > p$, we have:

Jacobi sweeps : $v(t(n/p)^2 + 4(\alpha + \beta(n/p)))$.

   - receive information on all four boundaries and compute new approximation at all $(n/p)^2$ points.

compute residual : $r(n/p)^2 + 4(\alpha + \beta(n/p))$.

   - receive information on all four boundaries and compute residual at all $(n/p)^2$ points.

project residual : $\rho(n/p)^2 + 4(\alpha + \beta(n/p))$.

   - receive information on all four boundaries and project residual at all $(n/p)^2$ points.

interpolate : $i(n/p)^2 + 4(\alpha + \beta(n/2p)) + 4(\alpha + \beta)$.

   - receive information on all four boundaries as well as information on the corners to interpolate the correction at all $(n/p)^2$ points.

We can now combine these to obtain a recurrence relation for the execution time of the multigrid algorithm. For $n > p$

$$T_1(n) = T_1(n/2) + M(n/p)^2 + [4\nu + 10]\beta(n/p) + ([4\nu + 16]\alpha + 4\beta).$$

For $n = p$ we have the initial condition

$$T_1(p) = T_2(p)$$

Doing a similar analysis for the case $n \leq p$ (using the Chan-Saad shuffle algorithm) we get :

$$T_2(n) = T_2(n/2) + M + [20 + 4\nu](\alpha + \beta)$$

with initial condition

$$T_2(2) = C_1$$

where C_1 is the time to solve the system corresponding to a 2 x 2 grid with one point per processor (and the processors are nearest neighbors). Note these formulas are only valid for $p > 2$ as the assumptions of sending and receiving on four boundaries are not valid for smaller systems. To analyze smaller systems we must modify our assumptions. Solving the above recurrence relations we get

$$T_1(n) = (4/3)M[(n/p)^2 - 1] + d_1[(n/p) - 1] + d_2\log(n/p) + T_2(p)$$

and

$$T_2(p) = d_3\log(p/2) + C_1$$

where

$$d_1 = (8\nu + 20)\beta, \quad d_2 = (4\nu + 16)\alpha + 4\beta, \quad d_3 = M + (20 + 4\nu)(\alpha + \beta).$$

When the ratio n/p is large, the first term dominates and so $T_1(n) \approx (4/3)M(n/p)^2$. Thus when the number of points per processor is large, the execution time is reduced by almost p^2 which is in fact the maximum attainable speed up on a p^2 node hypercube. Considering the optimal nature of serial multigrid, parallel multigrid can also be considered asymptotically optimal $O((n/p)^2)$. At the other extreme when n is large and $n = p$ (ie. one point per processor), then $T_1(n) = O(\log n)$. Our previous discussion concluded that $O(\log n)$ is the optimal execution time for solving elliptic partial differential equations on a hypercube with one point per processor. Thus multigrid is also asymptotically optimal when there is one point per processor and a large number of processors. It is interesting to note that this optimal behavior is achieved even with the many idle processors that result when "solving" on the coarse grids.

The results of the preceding paragraph are encouraging, but they do not indicate the performance of the parallel multigrid algorithm on practical grid sizes and realistic hypercubes. Toward this end, we can use the execution model to predict the actual execution of the parallel multigrid algorithm under different assumptions. Figure 1 shows the predicted runtimes for one multigrid iteration using the machine parameters for both the intel iPSC and the Caltech Mark II hypercube (using sixteen nodes) for different grid sizes. The values for α and β were obtained from data in [9]. For the Caltech Mark II machine $\alpha = 8.8 \times 10^{-4}$ and $\beta = 8.4 \times 10^{-4}$. The efficiency plots shown in figure 2 indicate how large the ratio (n/p) must be before we are close to the maximum attainable speedup. For the Caltech machine, we see that for $n/p \approx 16$ we reach 80 percent efficiency. This is an indication that the ratio n/p does not have to be large before we get almost p^2 speed up.

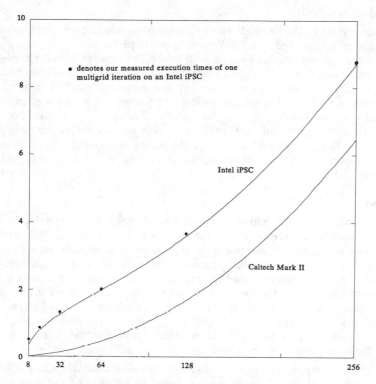

figure 1 : predicted execution time of one multigrid iteration vs. n
using 16 processors for grids of size n x n

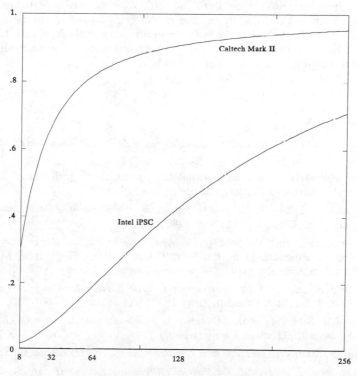

figure 2 : predicted efficiency of one multigrid iteration vs. n
using 16 processors for grids of size n x n

6. Numerical Experiments.

A computer code of the parallel multigrid algorithm was implemented on the intel iPSC hypercube. This code was used to solve Poisson's equation ($u_{xx} + u_{yy} = f(x,y)$) on a square grid. The Dirichlet boundary conditions as well as the function $f(x,y)$ were chosen so that the exact solution was $u(x,y) = x^2 + y^2$. In the current version of the multigrid code there is no convergence checking. Timing experiments of the parallel multigrid algorithm were run using four nodes as well as using sixteen nodes. The processors were assigned to subdomains using the binary reflected gray code (in the x and y directions). The execution runtimes for one multigrid iteration (averaged over a sequence of iterations) of this code on grids of various sizes is shown in figure 1. The close correspondence between the actual runtimes and the predicted runtimes is an indication that the execution time model accurately reflects the runtimes of the parallel multigrid algorithm.

7. Conclusion.

It is well known that the multigrid algorithm is among the most effective methods for solving elliptic partial differential equations on serial computers. In this paper, we have shown that it can be effectively mapped to a hypercube so as to maintain its optimal properties. When there are many grid points compared to the number of processors, it is possible to attain almost the maximum possible speed. When there are many processors and only a few points per processor, the multigrid algorithm is also optimal. Specifically, if the ratio of points per processor is fixed at one and the number of processors p is varied, the multigrid algorithm achieves the asymptotically lower bound, $O(\log p)$ for solving pde's. This implies that for large processor systems multigrid is optimal and that for small processor systems where there are many points per processor, multigrid is still optimal.

To determine estimates of execution times on realistic machines and realistic size problems, we presented a model of the communication/computation of the multigrid algorithm. The accuracy of the model was verified by a comparison with the timing results of our multigrid implementation on an Intel iPSC 32 node system. Using the model, it is possible to predict the execution time of the multigrid algorithm on various hypercubes (ie. with different machine parameters). In addition, the model can be used to compare the execution time of different variants of the algorithm. Our preliminary analysis, illustrates that a parallel multigrid can be efficiently mapped to a hypercube and therefore execute significantly faster than on a serial machine.

References

[1] A. Brandt, *Multi-level Adaptive Solutions to boundary-value problems*. Math Comp 31 (1977) 333-390.

[2] A. Brandt, *Multi-grid Solvers on Parallel Computers,* Technical Report 80-23, ICASE, NASA Langley Research Center, Hampton, VA, 1980.

[3] T. Chan, and Y. Saad, *Multigrid Algorithms on the Hypercube Multiprocessor,* IEEE Trans. Comp. Vol. C-35, No. 11, Nov 1986, pp969-977.

[4] T. Chan, Y. Saad, and M. Schultz, *Solving Elliptic Partial Differential Equations on Hypercubes.* In: Proceedings of the First Conference on Hypercube Multiprocessors, M. Heath (ed), SIAM, Knoxville, Tennessee, August, 1985, pp 196-210.

[5] T. Chan, and F. Saied, *A Comparison of Elliptic Solvers for General Two-Dimensional Regions,* Siam J. Sci. Stat. Comput., July 1985, Vol 6, No 3. pp 742-760.

[6] T. Chan, and R. Schreiber, *Parallel Networks For Multi-grid Algorithms: Architecture and Complexity,* Siam J. Sci. Stat. Comput., July 1985, Vol 6, No. 3. pp 698-711.

[7] W. Hackbusch, *Multi-grid Methods and Applications*, Springer-Verlag,1985, Berlin.

[8] D. Jespersen, *Multigrid Methods for Partial Differential Equations.* In: Studies in Numerical Analysis, G Golub (ed), MAA Studies in Mathematics Vol 24, 1984. pp 270-318.

[9] A. Kolawa, and S. Otto, *Performance of the Mark II and Intel Hypercubes*, Caltech Concurrent Computation Group - report 254. Pasadena, CA, Feb 1986.

[10] R. Peyret, and T. Taylor, *Computational Methods for Fluid Flow*, Springer-Verlag, New York, 1983.

[11] K. Stuben and U. Trottenberg, *Multigrid Methods: Fundamental Algorithms, Model Problem Analysis and Applications*. In: Multigrid Methods, Hackbusch, W. and Trottenberg, U. (eds), Koln-Porz, Nov 1981. Lecure Notes in Math 960. Springer, Berlin 1982.

Hypercube Implementation of Domain-Decomposed Fast Poisson Solvers

TONY F. CHAN* AND DIANA C. RESASCO†

Abstract: We present some parallel fast direct solvers derived from domain decomposition techniques for the solution of the Poisson equation in two and three spacial dimensions. The domain is divided into parallel strips or boxes, uncoupled fast solves are performed on each subdomain, and then the interface variables are computed exactly by fast Fourier transform. Finally, the solution on the interior of the subdomains can be computed by one more fast solve on each subdomain. While the algorithm lends itself easily to parallelization, a naive implementation would double the leading order term of the complexity of conventional fast direct solvers, because *two* problems must be solved on each subdomain. We shall show how this increase in complexity can be avoided by taking into account the special structure of the subdomain solvers. Experiments carried out on an Intel Hypercube multiprocessor system show times that are very close to linear speed up.

1. Introduction

The method of *domain decomposition* is a class of techniques for the solution of elliptic problems on a domain that is decomposed in smaller and often regular subdomains. Some of the applications of the method are the solution of elliptic problems on irregular domains that can be broken up into regular subdomains, the solution of very large problems on machines with limited storage and problems where the domain is naturally partitioned, for example, when some parameters have different values on the various subdomains.

In particular, we are interested in the application of domain decomposition techniques to constant coefficient problems on regular domains, in order to derive fast direct solvers that can be implemented on parallel machines. We use a uniform mesh with grid size h on the domain Ω with n internal grid points in the x–direction, i.e. $h = \frac{1}{n+1}$ and m internal grid points in the y–direction. We consider the system of algebraic equations

$$Au = f \tag{1.1}$$

---

* Department of Mathematics, UCLA, 405 Hilgard Ave., Los Angeles, California 90024

† Department of Computer Science, Yale University, Box 2158, Yale Station, New Haven, Conn. 06520.

resulting from applying a standard difference approximation to the differential operator. Consider a partition of the domain Ω into subregions Ω_i, $i = 1$ to k. If we order the unknowns for the internal points of the subdomains first and then those in the interfaces Γ between subdomains, then the discrete solution vector u can be partitioned as $u = (u_\Omega, u_\Gamma)$ and the linear system (1.1) can be reordered and expressed in block form as follows:

$$\begin{pmatrix} Q_\Omega & P \\ P^T & Q_\Gamma \end{pmatrix} \begin{pmatrix} u_\Omega \\ u_\Gamma \end{pmatrix} = \begin{pmatrix} f_\Omega \\ f_\Gamma \end{pmatrix} . \tag{1.2}$$

Since there is no coupling between internal gridpoints on the subdomains, Q_Ω is a block diagonal matrix, each diagonal block corresponding to the discretization of the differential operator on each subdomain Ω_i. Therefore, every time a system with Q_Ω must be solved, it corresponds to solving independent problems on the subdomains.

By applying block Gaussian Elimination to (1.2), we obtain the following system for the interface unknowns:

$$Cu_\Gamma = g \tag{1.3}$$

where

$$g \equiv f_\Gamma - P^T Q_\Omega^{-1} f_\Omega \tag{1.4}$$

and

$$C \equiv Q_\Gamma - P^T Q_\Omega^{-1} P . \tag{1.5}$$

C is sometimes called the *capacitance matrix*. The solution u_Ω can then be computed by solving

$$Q_\Omega u_\Omega = f_\Omega - P u_\Gamma . \tag{1.6}$$

In section 2, we apply domain decomposition to the case where the domain Ω is partitioned into parallel strips and we will show that for this particular case, the interface system (1.3) can be solved by a fast direct solver (matrix decomposition) using fast Fourier transforms. The method is naturally suited for parallel implementation, because most of the computation is reduced to solving independent problems on the subdomains, and the solution of (1.3) will need communication among the processors that involves only those gridpoints near the interfaces. However, a naive implementation based on (1.4) and (1.6) requires solving two systems with the matrix Q_Ω, which introduces a factor of two in the leading term of the complexity analysis. In section 3 we discuss some efficient implementations of the algorithm that save such factor of two. In section 4 we discuss the parallel implementation of the methods; in particular, we discuss details of the implementation on hypercube architectures and give some experimental results obtained on an Intel iPSC hypercube multiprocessor system.

2. Domain Decomposed Fast Poisson Solvers

Consider the solution of the Poisson equation:

$$\Delta u = f \qquad \text{on} \quad \Omega \tag{2.1}$$

with Dirichlet boundary conditions on a rectangular region Ω. By the method of Domain Decomposition, the domain Ω is partitioned into strips Ω_i, for $i = 1, \ldots, k$ and the solution of the system (1.1) resulting from the discretization on a regular grid is reduced to the solution of problems in the subdomains and the linear system (1.3) for the interface unknowns. In this case, a fast direct solver can be derived, which can be very naturally implemented on a multiprocessor system with k parallel processors. Each subdomain Ω_i contains an n by m_i grid and each interface Γ_i between Ω_i and Ω_{i+1} contains n grid points. In order to simplify notation, we will assume that all subdomains have the same dimension, i.e. $m_i \equiv m_0$, and therefore, $m = km_0 + k - 1$. We note that this is not an important assumption, since similar results can be easily applied to different values of m_i.

In order to decouple the system, we solve for the unknowns at the interfaces first. The discrete solution vector $u = (u_\Omega, u_\Gamma)$ satisfies the linear system (1.2), where Q_Ω is the block diagonal matrix $diag(L)$, with k diagonal blocks of dimension nm_0, each block L corresponding to the discrete Laplacian on each subdomain Ω_i. Q_Γ is the block diagonal matrix $diag(T)$, with $k - 1$ diagonal blocks. Each diagonal block is the n by n tridiagonal matrix $T = tridiag\,(1, -4, 1)$. Finally, the matrix P has the following block bi-diagonal form:

$$P = \begin{pmatrix} P_1 & & & \\ P_2 & P_1 & & \\ & & \ddots & \\ & & P_2 & P_1 \\ & & & P_2 \end{pmatrix}. \tag{2.2}$$

The block P_1, of dimension nm_0 by n, corresponds to the coupling between the unknowns in each subdomain Ω_i with those in the interface Γ_i and it has the form

$$P_1 = (0 \;\; \cdots \;\; 0 \;\; I)^T \;, \tag{2.3}$$

where I represents the identity matrix of dimension n. The block P_2 corresponds to the coupling between the unknowns in each subdomain Ω_i with those in the interface Γ_{i-1} and it has the form

$$P_2 = (I \;\; 0 \;\; \cdots \;\; 0)^T \;. \tag{2.4}$$

Since Q_Ω is block diagonal, the vector $z = Q_\Omega^{-1} f_\Omega$, needed for the computation of the right hand side (1.4), can be partitioned into k components, the solution of k independent Poisson problems given by the restriction of equation (2.1) to the subdomains Ω_i, $i = 1, \ldots, k$ with zero Dirichlet boundary conditions on the interfaces Γ_{i-1} and Γ_i, for $i = 1, \ldots, k - 1$. This corresponds to solving the independent linear systems $Lz_i = f_{\Omega_i}$ for $i = 1, \ldots, k$.

Once (1.3) is solved, the problem is decoupled and the solution u_{Ω_i} at the subdomains can be computed by (1.6). Again, since Q_Ω is block diagonal, equation (1.6) can be written as k independent subproblems of the form:

$$Lu_{\Omega_i} = f_{\Omega_i} - P_2 u_{\Gamma_{i-1}} - P_1 u_{\Gamma_i} \tag{2.5}$$

for $i = 1, \ldots, k$. This is nothing more than solving for u_{Ω_i} on each subdomain Ω_i with the computed $u_{\Gamma_{i-1}}$ and u_{Γ_i} as boundary conditions.

We will next show that, for the constant coefficients case, the interface system (1.3) can be solved by fast direct methods using Fourier analysis. By substituting the expressions for Q_Ω, Q_Γ and P in (1.5), we can see that the matrix C has the following block tridiagonal form:

$$C = \begin{pmatrix} H & B & & \\ B & H & \ddots & \\ & \ddots & \ddots & B \\ & & B & H \end{pmatrix}. \tag{2.6}$$

The matrices H and B, given by $H = T - P_1^T L^{-1} P_1 - P_2^T L^{-1} P_2$ and $B = -P_2^T L^{-1} P_1$, have the same eigenvectors, namely $w_j = \sqrt{\frac{2}{n+1}} (\sin j\pi h, \sin 2j\pi h, \cdots, \sin nj\pi h)^T$. The eigenvalues of H are given by

$$\lambda_j^C = -2 \left(\frac{1 + \gamma_j^{m_0+1}}{1 - \gamma_j^{m_0+1}} \right) \sqrt{\sigma_j + \frac{\sigma_j^2}{4}} \tag{2.7}$$

and the eigenvalues of B,

$$\delta_j = \sqrt{\gamma_j^{m_0}} \left(\frac{1 - \gamma_j}{1 - \gamma_j^{m_0+1}} \right), \tag{2.8}$$

for $j = 1$ to n, where $\sigma_j = 4\sin^2 \frac{j\pi h}{2}$ and $\gamma_j = \left(1 + \frac{\sigma_j}{2} - \sqrt{\sigma_j + \frac{\sigma_j^2}{4}} \right)^2$. The system (1.3) can thus be solved by matrix decomposition [2] using fast Fourier transforms.

In the three dimensional case, we can obtain similar expressions for C, H, and B, with σ_j replaced by the eigenvalues of the two-dimensional Laplacian operator. These results can also be easily generalized to the case of strips of different sizes and other operators, such as Helmholtz equation and variable coefficients elliptic operators with coefficients that take constant values on each subdomain [3]. The eigenvalues of H and B will depend on these coefficients and can be easily derived from the operator. Operators of this last form are used as preconditioners for more general variable coefficients elliptic problems.

2.1. The Algorithm

By replacing H and B by their eigenvalue decompositions $H = W\Lambda W^T$ and $B = WDW^T$ in (1.3), we get the transformed system:

$$\hat{C}\hat{u}_\Gamma = \hat{g} \quad, \tag{2.9}$$

where $\hat{C}$ is the block tridiagonal matrix $tridiag(D, \Lambda, D)$ and $\hat{u}_\Gamma = (\hat{u}_{\Gamma_1}, \hat{u}_{\Gamma_2}, \ldots, \hat{u}_{\Gamma_{k-1}})^T$, $\hat{g} = (\hat{g}_{\Gamma_1}, \hat{g}_{\Gamma_2}, \ldots, \hat{g}_{\Gamma_{k-1}})^T$, with $\hat{u}_{\Gamma_i} = W^T u_{\Gamma_i}$ and $\hat{g}_{\Gamma_i} = W^T g_{\Gamma_i}$. The new right hand side $\hat{g}$ can be computed by fast Fourier transforms. By reordering the unknowns, $\hat{C}$ becomes block-diagonal, with n tridiagonal blocks of dimension $k - 1$. After solving (2.9), the solution at the interfaces can be computed by applying inverse sine transforms to $\hat{u}_\Gamma$, i.e., $u_{\Gamma_i} = W\hat{u}_{\Gamma_i}$. The Domain-Decomposed fast Poisson solver can then be summarized as follows:

ALGORITHM DDFAST

Step 1: Solve $Q_\Omega z = f_\Omega$, which is equivalent to solving the following Poisson problem on each subdomain:

$$Lz_i = f_{\Omega_i} \tag{2.10}$$

Step 2: Form the right hand side for the interface system, $g = (g_{\Gamma_1}, g_{\Gamma_2}, \ldots, g_{\Gamma_{k-1}})^T$, where each component of g is given by

$$g_{\Gamma_i} = f_{\Gamma_i} - P_1^T z_i - P_2^T z_{i+1} \quad. \tag{2.11}$$

Step 3: Solve the interface system (1.3) as follows: compute $\hat{g}_{\Gamma_i} = W^T g_{\Gamma_i}$ for $i = 1, \ldots, k - 1$ by FFT's, then solve the transformed system (2.9) and finally compute $u_{\Gamma_i} = W\hat{u}_{\Gamma_i}$. for $i = 1, \ldots, k - 1$ using FFT's.

Step 4: Solve (2.5) on each subdomain, with $u_{\Gamma_0} = u_{\Gamma_k} = 0$

The algorithm is naturally suited for parallel implementation, because the k systems in step 1 can be solved in parallel, as well as the k systems in step 4.

By (2.4) we can see that the vector $P_2^T z_{i+1}$ in (2.11), corresponds to selecting the computed values of z_{i+1} at the first row of internal grid points in Ω_{i+1} and by (2.3), $P_1^T z_i$ corresponds to selecting the computed values of z_i at the last row of internal grid points in Ω_i. The system (2.9) is reordered to get a block-diagonal system with n tridiagonal blocks of size $k - 1$.

The above algorithm has the advantage of its modularity. On a multiprocessor system with k processing units, the Poisson problems in steps 1 and 4 can be solved on each processor by any sequential fast direct solver (*"black box"*). The price to be paid for this modularity is an increase of a factor of two in the leading term of the arithmetic complexity with respect to other fast Poisson solvers. This factor of two is due to the fact that two Poisson problems must be solved on each subdomain, namely steps 1 and 4. We point out, however, the following two important facts about these two subdomain solves: first, in (2.10), only the values of z_i at the gridpoints near the interfaces are needed for the computation of g in (2.11); second, the right hand side in (2.5) differs from the right hand side in (2.10) only at the mentioned gridpoints. These two facts can be often exploited, at the cost of sacrificing modularity, to save the factor of two in the leading term of the arithmetic complexity. For a few standard sequential methods applied to solve the subdomain problems, we will discuss in the next section some efficient implementations of DDFAST that save this factor of two.

3. Implementations of Algorithm DDFAST with different subdomain solvers

In this section we analyze combinations of Algorithm DDFAST with various fast solvers for the solution of the subproblems in steps 1 and 4. We will consider fast solvers using Fourier analysis (matrix decomposition) and a combination of odd-even block cyclic reduction with Fourier analysis (FACR).

3.1. Subdomain solvers using Fourier Analysis I: FFT's in the direction parallel to the strips

We will first analyze Algorithm DD1, wich consists of algorithm DDFAST, where the subdomain problems (2.10) and (2.5) are solved by a fast Poisson solver based on computing sine transforms in the direction parallel to the strips and solving tridiagonal systems of equations in the other direction. We will assume that the reader is familiar with this technique, called matrix decomposition [2].

The naive implementation of Algorithm DD1 would require the computation of $4m+2$ sine transforms of vectors of dimension n on each processor, but the algorithm can be modified so that only $2(m+1)$ transforms are needed. This is achieved by solving the interface system in Fourier space, thus saving two intermediate Fourier tranform phases. We will denote by $\tilde{L}$ the transformed operator $diag(W)\, L\, diag(W)$. After reordering the gridpoints, $\tilde{L}$ becomes block-diagonal, with tridiagonal diagonal blocks. We outline the algorithm as follows:

ALGORITHM DD1

Step 1: a) Compute $\hat{f}_{\Omega_i}$ for $i = 1, \ldots, k$ and $\hat{f}_{\Gamma_i}$ for $i = 1, \ldots, k-1$, the n-sine transforms of the right hand side f.
   b) Solve $\tilde{L}\hat{z}_i = \hat{f}_{\Omega_i}$ for $i = 1, \ldots, k$.

Step 2: Form the (transformed) right hand side for the interface system $\hat{g}_{\Gamma_i} = \hat{f}_{\Gamma_i} - P_1^T \hat{z}_i - P_2^T \hat{z}_{i+1}$ for $i = 1, \ldots, k-1$.

Step 3: Solve the interface system in Fourier space, (2.9). By reordering equations, this corresponds to solving n tridiagonal systems of dimension $k-1$, given by the matrices $tridiag(\delta_j, \lambda_j^C, \delta_j)$ for $j = 1, \ldots, n$, with λ_j^C and δ_j given by (2.7) and (2.8).

Step 4: a) Compute $\hat{u}_{\Omega_i}$ for $i = 1, \ldots, k$ by solving $\tilde{L}\hat{u}_{\Omega_i} = \hat{f}_{\Omega_i} - P_1 \hat{u}_{\Gamma_i} - P_2 \hat{u}_{\Gamma_{i-1}}$
   b) Compute the solution u_{Ω_i} for $i = 1, \ldots, k$, at the interior of the subdomains

and u_{Γ_i} for $i = 1, \ldots, k-1$, at the interfaces, by computing the inverse sine transforms of $\hat{u}_{\Omega_i}$ and $\hat{u}_{\Gamma_i}$.

The above algorithm is almost equivalent to a well known parallel implementation of a fast direct solver, which consists of computing the FFT's locally and solving the tridiagonal systems by substructuring (sometimes called GECR). GECR can be described as follows: Gaussian elimination (GE) is applied locally to obtain a reduced system that is distributed among the processors, one equation per processor. The reduced system is then solved by balanced cyclic reduction (CR) or other method for solving multiple tridiagonal systems in parallel. For the case of the Poisson equation with constant coefficients, it can be shown that the reduced system obtained in GECR is in fact the same as the transformed interface system (2.9). The elimination phase has been simplified in algorithm DD1, since the reduced system does not need to be computed, except for the right hand side.

3.2. Subdomain solvers using Fourier Analysis II: FFT's in the direction orthogonal to the strips

We next consider the case where the strips are narrow, i.e. $m_0 < n$. The method that consists of applying FFT's in the direction perpendicular to the strips will give a lower complexity $\mathcal{O}(nm_0 \log m_0)$ algorithm for the subdomain solves. In this case, however, saving the factor of two due to the two subdomain solves is not straightforward, since the FFT's needed for the solution of the capacitance system are in the direction perpendicular to those needed for the subdomain solves.

Suppose that the interior nodes on each subdomain are numbered by columns instead of by rows. Then, a Poisson problem on one of the strips can be solved with $2n$ Fourier transforms of dimension m_0 and the solution of m_0 tridiagonal systems of dimension n. After reordering the unknowns and applying FFT's in the y-direction, an equation of the form $Lu = f$ is transformed into $\tilde{L}\hat{u} = \hat{f}$, which can be reduced to solving m_0 tridiagonal systems of dimension n. We outline the algorithm as follows:

We will call Algorithm DD2 the combination of Algorithm DDFAST with the subdomain solver just described. We outline the algorithm as follows:

ALGORITHM DD2
Replace steps 1 and 4 of Algorithm DDFAST by the following
Step 1: a) Compute sine transforms of the right hand side f_{Ω_i} (dimension m_0).

   b) Solve $\tilde{L}\hat{z}_i = \hat{f}_{\Omega_i}$ for $i = 1, \ldots, k$.

   c) Compute (only) inverse FFT's of
$P_1^T z_i = (z_{1m_0}^i, \ldots, z_{nm_0}^i)$ and $P_2^T z_i = (z_{11}^i, \ldots, z_{n1}^i)$.

Step 4: a) Update the sine transform $\hat{h}_{\Omega_i}$ of the right hand side h_{Ω_i} for the second solve (2.5), by transforming only $-P_2 u_{\Gamma_{i-1}} - P_1 u_{\Gamma_i}$, which is a sparse vector (direct calculation, i.e. no FFT's).

   b) Solve the m_0 tridiagonal systems $\tilde{L}\hat{u}_i = \hat{h}_{\Omega_i}$
   c) Compute u_{Ω_i} by FFT's.

We note that Algorithm DD2 only requires $2n$ FFT's of dimension m_0 as opposed to $4n$ for the naive implementation and the complexity of steps 1-(c) and 4-(a) is $\mathcal{O}(nm_0)$ instead of $\mathcal{O}(nm_0 \log m_0)$.

3.3. Other Subdomain Solvers

Similarly, we can consider combinations of DDFAST with other subdomain solvers, such as odd-even block cyclic reduction and FACR(s), which consists of applying s steps of block cyclic reduction and then solving the resulting reduced system by Fourier Analysis [5]. As is well known, the arithmetic complexity of FACR(s) can be minimized with respect to s, giving an $O(nm_0 \log\log m_0)$ algorithm for the subdomain problems. We refer the interested reader to [4] for a discussion about saving the factor of two due to the two subdomain solves.

A very special case is given by R. Bank and D. Rose's Generalized Marching algorithm (GMA) [1], which can be viewed as a special instance of the algorithm DDFAST, where the marching method is applied for the solution of the subdomain problems. While in the above implementations of DDFAST the number of strips k can be chosen arbitrarily, in the case of GMA, the value of k is chosen in order to prevent instability. The marching method, as a subdomain solver, has optimal order $O(nm_0)$, but it becomes unstable for large values of m_0.

4. Some Numerical Experiments and practical considerations

Numerical experiments were carried out on an Intel Hypercube multiprocessor system, with a number of processors ranging from one to sixty four. We solved the Poisson equation in two and three dimensions on the unit square (cube), with Dirichlet boundary conditions. Regular $N \times N$ ($N \times N \times N$) grids were used, with the five (seven) point discretization scheme. The domain was divided into k identical strips, where k is the number of processors involved. For the two dimensional case, we implemented algorithms DD1 and DD2 and compared their speed-up with perfect speed-up, which was defined as the ratio of the time to solve the problem on one processor by using a standard fast Poisson solver and the number of processors. The fast Poisson solver used was matrix decomposition, applying FFT's in the x-direction and solving tridiagonal systems in the y-direction. Fig. 1 shows speed-up curves for DD1 and DD2 on a grid of dimension $N = 255$, for cube dimensions varying from 2 to 6.

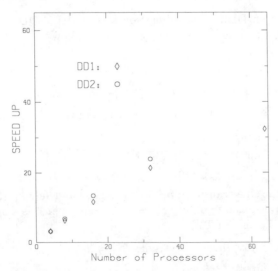

Fig. 1: Speed-up for DD1 and DD2

Fig. 2 shows speed-up curves for DD2 with increasing gridsizes. As we can see, the curves approach linear speed-up as N gets large. We note that we could, potentially, obtain super-linear speed-up with DD2, since in theory, a sequential version of DD2 has lower complexity than the standard $\mathcal{O}(N^2 \log N)$ fast solver. In practice, however, super-linear speed-up is not observed. One important reason for this is that a large overhead in computing FFT's, which is not considered in the complexity analysis, will make the advantage of computing N FFT's of dimension N/k over computing N/k FFT's of dimension N not visible for small values of N.

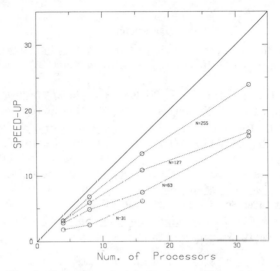

Fig. 2: Speed-up curves for increasing grid sizes

Fig. 3 shows some preliminary results for the three dimensional case. In this case, a naive version of DD2 in three dimensions was implemented. In general, we can observe a maximum efficiency of fifty per cent, which is not surprising, given that no optimizations were applied to the code in order to save some computations during the two subdomain solves.

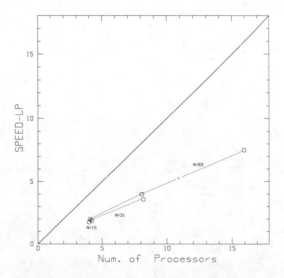

Fig. 3: Speed-up for a 3-D fast Poisson solver

Acknowledgments:

The authors were supported in part by the Department of Energy under contract DE-AC02-81ER10996. Part of this work was carried out while the first author was on sabbatical leave at the Research Institute of Advanced Computer Science, NASA Ames, California.

References

[1] R. Bank and D. Rose, *Marching Algorithms for Elliptic Boundary Value Problems I The Constant Coefficient Case*, SIAM J. Numer. Anal., 14/5 (1977), pp. 792–828.

[2] B. L. Buzbee, G. H. Golub and C. W. Nielson, *On Direct Methods for Solving Poisson's Equations*, SIAM J. Numer. Anal., 7 (1970), pp. 627–656.

[3] T.F. Chan and D.C. Resasco, *A Survey of Preconditioners for Domain Decomposition*, Technical Report YALEU/DCS/RR-414, Yale Computer Science Department, 1985.

[4] T.F. Chan, D.C. Resasco and F. Saied, *Implementation of Domain Decomposed Fast Poisson Solvers on Multiprocessors*, Technical Report YALE/DCS/RR-456, Yale Computer Science Department, 1986.

[5] R. W. Hockney, *A Fast Direct Solution of Poisson's Equation using Fourier Analysis*, J. ACM, 12 (1965), pp. 95–113.

On the Implementation of
Kernel Numerical Algorithms for
Computational Fluid Dynamics on Hypercubes

TONY F. CHAN*

Abstract: We discuss some issues that arise in the implementation of numerical algorithms for computational fluid dynamics (CFD) on multiprocessor systems such as hypercubes. We identify several important kernel numerical algorithms from CFD that map well onto the hypercube architecture. We emphasize the importance of considering the optimal mapping for a collection of kernel algorithms used in an application program rather than just on individual optimal mappings. Several examples illustrating the trade-offs between rearranging data to fit a particular kernel algorithm and using suboptimal mappings will be discussed.

1. Introduction

The field of computational fluid dynamics (CFD) has been a primary motivating force behind the recent interest in parallel computing. CFD demands lots of compute power, primarily due to the presence of wide scales of physical phenomenon that need to be modelled. Since CFD applications are already stretching the limits of sequential processing, many people believe that the computing power needed for major advances in CFD can only be delivered by parallel processing.

This trend has already been recognized for many years at CFD research centers such as the NASA Ames Research Center, which developed one of the earliest parallel computers, the ILLIAV IV. Recent developments there include the NAS project (Numerical Aerodynamics Simulation) one of whose goals is to bring the most powerful supercomputer at any given time to applications in CFD. Currently, it operates a 4 processor Cray 2 system. Looking into the future, NAS sees computers with massive parallelism. With this trend, the interplay between architecture and algorithms becomes more important.

* This work is supported by the Research Institute in Advanced Computer Science, NASA Ames Research Center and the Department of Energy under Contract DE AC02 81ER 10996 while the author is on sabbatical leave from Yale University. Current address: Dept. of Mathematics, UCLA, 405 Hilgard Av., Los Angeles, CA 90024.

For this reason, the Research Institute for Advanced Computer Science (RIACS) has initiated a research program to bridge the gap. Efforts so far include studies of CFD on the MPP parallel computer and the Intel iPSC hypercube multiprocessor computer by John Bruno [2,3] and a workshop headed by Jack Dennis on the use of data flow architectures in CFD [1].

This article describes a preliminary study on the use of hypercubes to CFD. Our approach here is to identify and study kernel algorithms in CFD in detail in order to provide a scientific basis for implementation into future production codes. A main issue we study is the optimization of load balancing and communication cost by careful mapping of data (domain). We put a special emphasis on selecting optimal mappings for a collection of algorithms used in a typical application rather than on mappings for individual kernels. We also study the tradeoffs between the cost of using a suboptimal mapping and that of rearranging the data to obtain an optimal mapping. Several examples from CFD will be used to illustrate our points.

2. Kernel Algorithms in CFD

CFD can be classified by the various versions of the Navier Stokes equations that it solves: e.g. incompressible flows, compressible flows, transonic flows, turbulence modelling etc. Due to the different mathematical characteristics of the governing equations, these variants usually require different computational algorithms for their solutions. In this section, we identify some of the commonly used kernel algorithms in each case.

First of all, most methods require some sort of nearest neighbor mesh (NN-mesh) computations defined by the discretization stencil, such as for the computation of the residual and in relaxation methods.

In compressible flows, alternating direction implicit methods (ADI) are popular. These methods require the solution of block tridiagonal linear systems in each coordinate direction at each time step. A representative code is ARC3D developed at NASA Ames [19].

In incompressible flow, there is usually a Poisson equation to be solved at each time step (for the pressure in the primitive variable formulation and for the stream function in the stream function vorticity formulation), which often consumes most of the computation time. Thus a fast Poisson solver is an important kernel for these applications.

Spectral methods are becoming more widely used in CFD. In turbulence modelling [18], they are particularly predominant. Combined with their applications to other kernels such as fast Poisson solvers, this makes the fast Fourier transform (FFT) an extremely important kernel for CFD.

Transonic flows are usually modelled by equations which have different type (hyperbolic or elliptic) in different regions of the computational domain. Since the location of these type transitions depends on the solution itself, the discretization may change during the solution procedure. This feature leads to iterative methods (usually relaxation methods) which makes successive sweeps across the domain to update the solution. These iterative methods are often accelerated by techniques such as multigrid and preconditioned conjugate gradient methods, which are finding increasing application in other areas of CFD as well. The most well-known codes in this area are perhaps the series of codes starting from FLO52 by A. Jameson [13]. Recent versions of this code use the ADI method with multigrid acceleration.

3. Mapping of Algorithms to Hypercube Architecture

Part of the reason for the popularity of the hypercube architecture is the fact that many other topologies, such as meshes, trees, pyramids and butterflies, are embeddable in the hypercube topology [21]. By this we mean the graphs representing these other topologies can be mapped onto the binary n-cube graph with small dilation (the relative increase in the distance between vertices) and expansion (the relative increase in the total number of vertices) [20]. In practice, this implies that computations involving data flow graphs taking the form of the previously mentioned topologies can be carried out with minimum communication overheads on binary n-cube computers. In this section, we shall briefly discuss the problem of mapping some of the kernel algorithms in CFD identified in the last section onto the hypercube. These include FFT (butterfly), cyclic reduction (tree), multigrid (pyramid) and computations on NN-meshes.

3.1. FFT

We shall restrict our discussions to the radix-2 FFT algorithm. The data flow graph for the FFT is usually referred to as the "butterfly". Let the array elements be x_j, where the index j ranges from 0 to $2^d - 1$. These array elements are updated at each of d stages of the computation. At the i-th stage of the computation, the array element with index j must communicate with another element with index k, whose binary representation differs from that of j in the i-th most significant position. On a hypercube, the natural mapping is to map x_j to node number j of the cube [9]. To be mathematically precise, let $M : I \rightarrow N$ be the class of mapping functions, where I denotes the set of indices of the array elements and N the set of node numbers of the hypercube. Then the FFT mapping $f \in M$ is given by

$$f(j) = j. \tag{1}$$

With this mapping, it is easy to see that at every stage of the computation, the necessary communication will be between neighboring nodes. Moreover, all such communications at a given stage can be carried out in parallel. Each stage can be viewed as "collapsing" the hypercube in one of its coordinates. In fact, the hypercube is *isomorphic* to the butterfly of the same dimension.

Note that after the completion of the forward transform, the data elements are not arranged in the natural order. Rather, they are in what is known as bit-reversed order. This is unimportant if the inverse transform of the data array is to be computed next, perhaps after some computations on the transformed array itself, which is typical in many applications. If needed, the array elements can be permuted into natural order in d steps with only nearest neighbor communication [23].

3.2. NN Mesh

Another very common data flow graph is the nearest neighbor (NN) mesh, which occurs naturally in the solution of partial differential equations. We shall limit our discussion here to one dimensional meshes, since higher dimensional meshes can be easily built from tensor products of one dimensional ones[7,21]. If the array elements are denoted by x_j, then the NN-mesh graph with the x_j's as vertices contains all edges connecting a given vertex x_j with its nearest neighbors on the mesh. In one dimension, these are the two vertices x_{j-1} and x_{j+1}. (Throughout this paper, all indices are to be taken modulo 2^d, where d is the dimension of the hypercube.)

It is well-known that the NN-mesh graph with 2^d vertices can be mapped into a d-dimensional hypercube with no dilation or expansion via Gray codes. The natural mapping $m \,\varepsilon M$ for the NN-mesh to a d-dimensional hypercube is

$$m(j)=g_j, \tag{2}$$

where g_j is the j-th member of a d-dimensional Gray code. It is important to note that Gray codes are not unique but any d-dimensional Gray code will work here.

3.3. Multigrid

Multigrid algorithms can be viewed as methods for accelerating relaxation methods by performing extra iterations on a hierarchy of coarser grids in addition to the fine grid on which the solution is sought. On the finest grid, only NN-mesh computations are performed and therefore the tensor product Gray code mapping discussed in the last section can be used effectively. On the coarser grids, however, NN-mesh computations require communication between grid points that are increasingly becoming farther apart. Thus a little bit more care must be used to map the grid onto the hypercube so that coarse grid communications can be made efficient. In [6], it is shown that, if the grid coarsening factor is 2, then by using a special Gray code (namely the binary reflected Gray code (BRGC)) to map the finest grid to the hypercube, all coarse grid communications are exactly distance 2 apart (which is optimal), independent of the size of the grid or that of the hypercube. We emphasize that this is a special property of the BRGC and does not hold for many other Gray codes. Thus, the same mapping which is optimal for NN-meshes is also optimal for multigrid.

3.4. Cyclic Reduction

Odd Even Cyclic Reduction (CR) is one of the most efficient parallel algorithm for solving tridiagonal systems [12]. In the first stage of the algorithm, the odd numbered equations are used to eliminate the odd numbered unknowns in the neighboring even numbered equations, resulting in a new tridiagonal system of half the original size governing only the even numbered unknowns. Subsequent stages are recursive applications of the same principle. If the size of the system n is a power of 2, this leads to one equation in one unknown after $\log_2 n$ stages, which can be solved trivially. This is followed by a backsolving phase reversing the data flow of the forward elimination phase. The communication requirement is similar to the multigrid algorithm: starting from NN-mesh at the first stage, communications are between nodes that are at increasing powers of 2 apart. Therefore, it is easy to see that if the BRGC is used to map the equations to the hypercube, then all communications in subsequent stages are exactly at distance 2 apart [15], which is optimal.

4. Suboptimal Mappings Versus Data Rearrangement

In the last section, we saw that the optimal mapping for many kernel algorithms in CFD are easy to define and implement. However, what is often not appreciated is the fact that different algorithms require different mappings. Moreover, in applications where the same data set must be operated on by more than one algorithm, situations may arise where the optimal mappings for the individual algorithms are not compatible with one another. What is ideal for one could be disastrous for the others. In such situations, we have two alternatives: rearrange the data between algorithms or use only one mapping which may be suboptimal for some of the algorithms. The suboptimality could be either due to communication delays or to imperfect load balancing. The tradeoff between these two approaches depends on the relative frequency each algorithm in the collection is executed. In this section, we shall illustrate these issues by several examples in CFD.

4.1. The Incompatibility Of the FFT and the NN-Mesh Mappings

The most natural mapping for the FFT algorithm, namely f in equation (1), turns out to be inefficient for NN-mesh computations. If the data array x_j is mapped onto the hypercube using the FFT mapping f, then a nearest neighbor computation on the same data array requires communication over a distance d (equal to the diameter of the hypercube) for some nodes, e.g. between node $2^{d-1}-1$ and node 2^{d-1}. Thus, as far as the NN-mesh computation is concerned, the FFT mapping f is the *worst* possible mapping. For higher dimensional hypercubes, this may cause a significant reduction in the efficiency of algorithms using the nearest neighbor data flow graph.

On the other hand, the NN-mesh mapping m in equation (2) can be made suitable for FFT computations. To see this, note that the FFT butterfly involves pairs of array elements separated by strides of diminishing powers of 2 and thus if the array elements are mapped to the hypercube using a BRGC, then the communications occur between nodes at most a distance two apart. This is optimal because a distance of one would create a cycle of odd length in the hypercube (the power of 2 stride plus the nearest neighbor connection), which is impossible [21].

Alternatively, one can consider rearranging the data before the execution of each algorithm according to the most natural mapping for that algorithm, especially if the algorithm is to be executed many times. It turns out that one can convert from a BRGC NN-mesh mapping to a FFT mapping (and vice versa) with $d-1$ nearest neighbor exchanges [5,15], which is comparable with the communication cost of one FFT computation. Thus if many FFTs are to be performed, then it may pay to carry out the conversion to the optimal FFT mapping. For a detailed analysis of which mapping is best for a particular application and the tradeoffs between rearranging data and using a suboptimal mapping, the reader is referred to [5].

Applications employing both the FFT and the NN-mesh data flow graphs are very common in CFD. A finite difference discretization of the Navier Stokes equation often produces a nearest neighbor stencil. Thus the NN-mesh mapping is natural for computation of residuals. On the other hand, if a spectral method or a fast Poisson solver is used to solve the difference equations, then the FFT mapping is called for.

4.2. The Parallel Exchange Multigrid Algorithm

Sometimes it may be beneficial to rearrange data even between different parts of the *same* algorithm. In the parallel implementation of multigrid methods on hypercubes as described in Section 3.3, by using a BRGC NN-mesh mapping of the finest grid, communication on coarser grids are at distance exactly 2 apart. If many NN-mesh operations are to be performed on a coarse grid, then one can consider rearranging the data on it to reduce this distance to 1. In [6], it is shown how this can be achieved by a simple exchange communication between certain neighboring nodes on the fine grid before starting computations on the coarse grid. A similar exchange must be used when coming back from a coarse grid to a fine grid. This remapping thus pays if more than 2 smoothing sweeps are performed on the coarse grid. See [8] for more details on the implementation of this algorithm.

4.3. Transpose in ADI Methods

Another example of the tradeoff between using a suboptimal mapping and rearranging data to an optimal mapping is in the parallel implementation of Alternating Direction Implicit Methods (ADI) on hypercubes [16]. We shall restrict our discussion to two dimension regions. Each iteration of the ADI method consists of solving independent tridiagonal systems on grid lines in each of the two coordinate directions. If the grid is partitioned into groups of grid lines along one coordinate direction and each group mapped onto the hypercube according to the BRGC, then the solution of the tridiagonal systems in this chosen direction are all within the same processor and requires no communication. The solves in the other direction can be solved by the cyclic reduction algorithm described in Section 3.4, with communication between processors at distance 2 apart after the first reduction stage. By a similar exchange operation as in the multigrid algorithm described earlier in Section 4.2, this distance can be reduced to one [15]. By a more costly transpose operation of the grid, this distance can be further reduced to zero (solves within the same processor). Which alternative is best is still an open research problem and probably depends on the sizes of the grid and the hypercube and the relative cost of computation and communication [11,17,22].

4.4. Load Balancing in Parallel FFT

The previous examples show situations where remapping can reduce the communication cost of an algorithm. Sometimes, remapping can improve load balancing. Consider the parallel implementation of the Gentleman-Sande version of the FFT [24]. The original sequence is divided into contiguous blocks and each block mapped onto the processors of the hypercube using the FFT mapping f discussed earlier. At each stage, two kinds of computations must be performed: (1) the sum of two intermediate transformed values and (2) their difference, multiplied by appropriate powers of certain roots of unity. In the early stages, these two computations are performed on neighboring processors requiring communication whereas in the latter stages, they are performed in the same processor requiring no communication. In [10], it is pointed out that in the early stages the computations are not perfectly balanced: some processors must compute (or look up) the roots of unity and perform a complex multiplication whereas others do not. This imbalance can be eliminated by permuting the data at every stage so that only local FFTs of the same size are performed in each processor. For more details, the reader is referred to [10].

4.5. Particle in Cell Methods

Another example of remapping to improve load balancing is in certain parallel implementation of particle in cell methods [4]. These methods typically consists of two stages: the solution of a Poisson equation for the field on a regular grid and then "particle pushing" of the individual particles. The Poisson equation is usually handled by a "fast solver" which prefers a regular mapping, e.g. the tensor product BRGC NN-mesh mapping. However, if the particles are distributed nonuniformly in the computational domain, then the particle pushing phase prefers a nonregular mapping which would produce better load balancing in the sense of having roughly the same number of particles in each processor. Again the tradeoff is between the cost of remapping and that of using a suboptimal mapping.

5. Concluding Remarks

A typical CFD program contains several kernel algorithms working on the same data. One of the main purposes of this article is to emphasize the need to go beyond studying the optimal implementation of the individual algorithms and look at the whole collection as a whole. The reason is simply that what is best for one algorithm may not be optimal for the others. Very often, a remapping of the data to perfectly suit an algorithm should be considered. The tradeoff is between the cost of the remapping and the benefits of reduced communication and better load balancing. We have shown in this article several such examples arising naturally in CFD applications. The optimal choice of mapping depends on many factors, such as the frequency the algorithms are to be executed and the ratio of the arithmetic speed to the communication speed.

Reference

[1] G.B. Adams, R.L. Brown, P.J. Denning, *Report on an Evaluation Study of Data Flow Computation*, RIACS Technical Report 85.2, Research Institute in Advanced Computer Science, 1985.

[2] J. Bruno, *Final Report on the Feasibility of Using the Massively Parallel Processor for Large Eddy Simulation and other Computational Fluid Dynamics Applications*, RIACS Technical Report 84.2, Research Institute in Advanced Computer Science, 1984.

[3] J. Bruno, *Report on the Feasibility of Hypercube Concurrent Processing Systems in Computational Fluid Dynamics*, RIACS Technical Report 86.7, Research Institute in Advanced Computer Science, March 1986.

[4] C. Catherasoo, *The Vortex Method on a Hypercube*, paper presented at the 2nd Conference on Hypercube Multiprocessors, Knoxville, Tennessee, September 29 - October 1, 1986.

[5] T.F. Chan, *On Gray Code Mappings for Mesh-FFTs on Binary N-Cubes*, RIACS Technical Report 86.17, Research Institute in Advanced Computer Science, September, 1986.

[6] T.F. Chan, Y. Saad, *Multigrid Algorithms on the Hypercube Multiprocessor*, IEEE Trans. on Comp., Nov., 1986, pp. 969-977.

[7] T.F. Chan, Y. Saad, M.H. Schultz, *Solving Elliptic Partial Differential Equations on Hypercube Multiprocessors*, Proceedings of 1st Conference on Hypercube Multiprocessors, ed. M. Heath, pp. 196-210, SIAM, Philadelphia, 1986.

[8] T.F. Chan, R. Tuminaro, *Implementation of Multigrid Algorithms on Hypercubes*, RIACS Technical Report 86.30, Research Institute in Advanced Computer Science, November, 1986. To appear in the proceedings of the 2nd Conference on Hypercube Multiprocessors, Knoxville, Tennessee, September 29 - October 1, 1986.

[9] G. Fox, S. Otto, *Decomposition of Scientific Problems for Concurrent Processors*, Physics Today, May, 1984.

[10] G. Fox, W. Furmanski, *Some Highlights of Hypercube Research at Caltech*, paper presented at the 2nd Conference on Hypercube Multiprocessors, Knoxville, Tennessee, September 29 - October 1, 1986.

[11] C.T. Ho, S.L. Johnsson, F. Saied, M.H. Schultz, *The Three Dimensional Wide Angle Wave Equation, Tridiagonal Systems and the Intel iPSC*, paper presented at the 2nd Conference on Hypercube Multiprocessors, Knoxville, Tennessee, September 29 - October 1, 1986.

[12] R.W. Hockney, C.R. Jesshope, *Parallel Computers*, Adam Hilger Ltd., Bristol, 1981.

[13] A. Jameson, *Solution of the Euler Equations for Two Dimensional Transonic Flow by a Multigrid Method*, Appl. Math. and Comp., vol.13, pp.327-355, 1983.

[14] L.S. Johnsson, *Odd-Even Cyclic Reduction on Ensemble Architectures*, Research Report YALEU/DCS/RR-339, Yale Univ., Dept. of Comp. Sci., Oct. 1984.

[15] L.S. Johnsson, *Communication Efficient Basic Linear Algebra Computations on Hypercube Architecture*, Research Report YALEU/DCS/RR-361, Yale Univ., Dept. of Comp. Sci., Sept. 1985.

[16] L.S. Johnsson, Y. Saad, M.H. Schultz, *Alternating Direction Implicit Methods on Multiprocessors*, Research Report YALEU/DCS/RR-382, Yale Univ., Dept. of Comp. Sci., Oct., 1985.

[17] D. Lim, R.V. Thanakij, *Alternating Direction Implicit Methods on a Hypercube*, paper presented at the 2nd Conference on Hypercube Multiprocessors, Knoxville, Tennessee, September 29 - October 1, 1986.

[18] R.S. Rogallo, *An ILLIAC Program for the Numerical Simulation of Homogeneous Incompressible Turbulence*, NASA Document No. NASA TM-73, 203, 1977.

[19] T.H. Pulliam, J.L. Steger, *Implicit Finite Difference Simulations of Three Dimensional Compressible Flow*, AIAA J., vol. 18, p.159, 1980.

[20] A. Rosenberg, *Data Encoding and Their Costs*, Acta Inform. 9 (1978), pp.273-292.

[21] Y. Saad, M.H. Schultz, *Some Topological Properties of the Hypercube Multiprocessor*, Research Report YALEU/DCS/RR-428, Yale Univ., Dept. of Comp. Sci., October, 1985.

[22] F. Saied, *ADI Methods for Schrodinger's Equations on Hypercubes*, paper presented at the 2nd Conference on Hypercube Multiprocessors, Knoxville, Tennessee, September 29 - October 1, 1986.

[23] J. Salmon, *private communication*. See also Chapter 8 of the book "*Solving Problems on Concurrent Processors*" by G. Fox et al, to be published.

[24] P. N. Swarztrauber, *Multiprocessor FFTs,* paper presented at the International Conference on Vector and Parallel Computing, Loen, Norway, June 2-6, 1986.

The Vortex Method on
a Hypercube Concurrent Processor

CHRISTOPHER J. CATHERASOO*

Abstract. The vortex method in fluid mechanics, in which the vorticity transport equation is solved numerically in the Lagrangian reference frame by following the motion of elementary vortices, is ideally suited to concurrent processing on the hypercube. This stems from the fact that the algorithms used, especially the direct-summation algorithm for computing the pair-wise interactions between the spatially localized vortices, can be sped up by exploiting the computer architecture. The method has been used at NASA Ames to simulate turbulent flows over arbitrary bluff bodies at high Reynolds numbers. The NASA code combines a number of different procedures and algorithms, which include Gaussian elimination with pivoting, back solving, numerical integration using Simpson's rule, sorting, many-body interactions, and solution of ordinary differential equations using a second-order Adams-Bashforth method. This work discusses the implementation of the code on an AMETEK System 14 hypercube concurrent processor. Timing results and speedups are given for two different sizes of problems on hypercubes ranging from 1 through 64 nodes.

1. Introduction. Vortex interactions in both two and three dimensions define a class of problems that are of considerable interest in fluid mechanics. Presently, the basic 'bottleneck' in vortex calculations is the large amount of work required at any timestep in order to calculate the velocities of the Lagrangian, circulation-carrying elements from their instantaneous positions and strengths. With N Lagrangian elements, this work scales as N^2. This is due simply to the long-range nature of the velocity interaction between the points, which requires that every element is influenced by every other. This scaling is independent of whether one is using classical point vortices or some kind of vortex 'blob' with a smoothed-out core in two dimensions, or nodes on a set of filaments in three dimensions. (Most calculational schemes use some kind of smoothing of the vortex filament core, although there are sharply divided opinions on which one is best). Ultimately, this operation-count scaling is what forces vortex-method practitioners to settle for a relatively small number of computational

---

*AMETEK Computer Research Division, 610 North Santa Anita Avenue, Arcadia, California 91006, USA.

elements, which in turn limits the flow regimes that the method can access with confidence.

Ingenious ways have been found to attempt to circumvent the N^2 operation-count problem. In the so-called 'vortex-in-cell' method, an Eulerian grid is introduced and used in parallel with the Lagrangian variables to solve the stream function-vorticity field equation. By familiar arguments, not be be repeated here, this technique essentially reduces the operation count from N^2 to $N\log_2 N$ in two dimensions. However, this 'cell' method of reduction incurs several auxiliary problems, all of which are associated more or less directly with the properties of the underlying grid. For example, it is not difficult to see that the basic interaction between vortices acquires an unphysical orientation dependence following the coordinate directions of the grid. Although this can be cured to some extent, it is an unpleasant 'aliasing' error that takes considerable experience and 'overhead' to deal with. Also, grids invariably introduce dissipative and/or dispersive mechanisms of non-physical origin at scales on the order of a grid spacing or less. For all these reasons, it is usually necessary to repeat calculations of the same physical problem using many different grid resolutions. This is both expensive and time-consuming. For a lead into the literature on vortex flows and vortex methods, the reader is referred to reviews by Leonard [1], [2], and Aref [3]. The vortex-in-cell method is well described in the original paper by Christiansen [4].

Recent developments have also occurred in other areas such as stellar dynamics and plasma physics, where problems involving many interacting particles must be dealt with. Appel [5] has suggested a number of improvements to the direct-summation algorithm, including a gridless method of clumping 'nearby' and 'far away' particles through the use of tree-like data structures to reduce the computational complexity to $O(N\log N)$. Also, Greengard and Rokhlin [6] have developed an algorithm that uses multipole expansions to compute the potentials or forces for which the work is proportional to N. Very little is known about how well these methods are suited for fluid dynamics computations or about their resultant accuracies.

It is on this background that the concurrent processing option becomes particularly attractive. As discussed by Fox and Otto [7] and by Seitz [8], long-range pairwise interactions between spatially localized particles defines a problem format for which concurrent processing realizes its full potential. Hence, what is offered is an option for retaining the more accurate $O(N^2)$ direct-summation algorithm, but speeding it up via the computer architecture and attendant programming. Thus one need *not* use methods that in principle sacrifice isotropy or other very desirable properties of the basic interaction.

Engineering implementations of the vortex method on sequential computers have been performed at NASA Ames and are described by Spalart, Leonard and Baganoff [9] and Spalart [10]. These implementations have been used to simulate flows around bluff bodies, helicopter blades, stalled airfoils and cascades of blades. Research into the application of the vortex method to airfoils and to shear layers is also being undertaken at Caltech and UC San Diego.

2. The Fluid Mechanics. The program that has been implemented is the NASA Ames code. A brief description of the physics of the problem will be given here, but for full details, the reader is referred to [9]. The program simulates the unsteady flow field around a bluff body as it evolves in time. A bluff body is one whose shape or alignment with the flow is such that the fluid passing over it is unable to follow the geometrical contours of the body. The fluid separates from the body, and forms a wake consisting of large turbulent eddies.

Two restrictions are imposed on the fluid in order to simplify the full Navier-Stokes equations, namely that the fluid must be incompressible and inviscid. Incompressible means that there is negligible change in volume with change in pressure, while inviscid means that viscosity is unimportant. Experiments have shown that, in general, viscosity becomes important only in a very thin layer at the body surface. This layer is called a *boundary layer* or inner flow. Inside the boundary layer, the fluid velocity changes from zero at the wall (the 'no-slip' condition) to the free-stream velocity at the edge of the layer. Within the boundary layer, the fluid is in shear, and hence viscous effects become important. It is this viscosity which introduces vorticity into the flow and results in the formation of turbulent eddies.

The vorticity in the flow is modelled as *vortices* or discrete blobs of fluid carrying circulation. These vortices are introduced into the flow at specific points on the body surface which are referred to as the *creation points*. Each vortex induces a velocity at every point in the flow field and, in two dimensions, this induced velocity is proportional to $1/r$, where r is the distance from the center of the vortex. (This investigation has been limited to the two-dimensional case, although this is not a limitation on the method in general). Hence each vortex induces a velocity on every other vortex in the flow field. The total velocity of each vortex is the sum of all the induced velocities plus the freestream velocity, and the total velocity is integrated with respect to time to give the displacement of the vortex. Thus, as time progresses, the number of vortices in the flow increases, and the older vortices are swept downstream.

3. The Concurrent Implementation. The main calculation loop of the code can be divided up into five sections as follows: (a) new vortices are injected into the flow at specific vortex creation points so as to satisfy certain boundary conditions on the velocity field at the body surface; (b) the velocity induced on each vortex by every other vortex in the flow is calculated, and the new vortex positions are determined by integrating these velocities with respect to time; (c) the vortices that have crashed into the wall are detected and removed from the flow; (d) suitably matched pairs of vortices are merged so as to keep the total number of vortices in the flow down to a desired level, and finally, (e) the vortices in the flow are shared out equally among all the processors so as to achieve an even load balance.

In the concurrent implementation, parallelism is achieved mainly by sharing the creation points and the vortices among the processors. In addition to this, the matrix decomposition is performed by splitting the matrix by rows among the processors, and the back solution is also performed in parallel. Calculation of the boundary layers on the upper and lower halves of the body are performed on alternate processors and the results shared among all the nodes.

4. Results. For the purposes of making timing runs, it was decided to vary two main parameters — the number of creation points at the body surface, and the number of vortices. The times measured were the times taken for each iteration, that is, the time taken to complete one loop of the calculations described in Section 3. The results are presented as speedup curves in Figure 1, where Figure 1(a) is for 32 creation points,

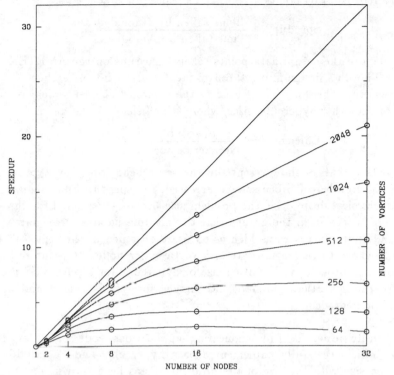

Figure 1(a). Speedup curves for 32 creation points.

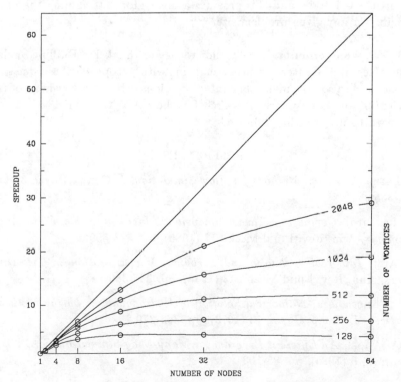

Figure 1(b). Speedup curves for 64 creation points.

while Figure 1(b) is for 64 creation points. The speedup is defined as

$$\text{Speedup} = \frac{\text{Time taken by 1 node}}{\text{Time taken by } N \text{ nodes}}.$$

The circles denote the actual data points taken from runs on the AMETEK System 14 hypercube. The 45° line running through the 1-node point on each of the graphs is the ideal speedup. This line can be used as the standard against which to measure the efficiencies of the other hypercube sizes, where the efficiency is defined as

$$\text{Efficiency} = \frac{\text{Speedup}}{\text{Number of nodes}}.$$

Both sets of curves show essentially the same behavior. For a given number of vortices, as the number of processors is increased, the speedup first increases and then displays the classical drop-off as the problem size becomes too small for the size of the hypercube. It is seen from the graphs that the maxima lie at approximately 8 vortices per node, and that efficiencies as high as 85% are obtained in the region to the left of the maxima, where there are more than 8 vortices per node. It is interesting to note that this number provides the limiting size of hypercube for a particular problem size, and that for fewer vortices per node, no further speedup is gained and, in fact, the speedup will be degraded.

5. Conclusions. A full engineering applications code based on the vortex method has been successfully implemented on a hypercube, and by suitably matching the hypercube size with the size of the problem, it has been shown that efficiencies as high as 85% can be realized. It is found that the speedup curves peak at approximately 8 vortices per node, and this provides a means for determining the limiting size of a hypercube for any given problem size.

6. Acknowledgements. The author wishes to thank Dr. Phillipe Spalart of the NASA Ames Research Center for providing him with a copy of the sequential vortex method code and also for many helpful discussions. He also wishes to thank the National Center for Atmospheric Research for their AUTOGRAPH graphics package which was used to prepare the graphs.

REFERENCES

[1]   A. Leonard, *Vortex Methods for Flow Simulation*, J. Comp. Phys., 37 (1980), pp. 289-335.

[2]   A. Leonard, *Computing Three-Dimensional Incompressible Flows with Vortex Elements*, Ann. Rev. Fluid Mech., 17 (1985), pp. 523-559.

[3]   H. Aref, *Integrable, Chaotic and Turbulent Vortex Motion in Two-Dimensional Flows*, Ann. Rev. Fluid Mech., 13 (1983), pp. 345-389.

[4]   J.P. Christiansen, *Numerical Solution of Hydrodynamics by the Method of Point Vortices*, J. Comp. Phys., 13 (1973), pp. 363-379.

[5]   W.A. Appel, *An Efficient Program for Many-Body Simulation*, SIAM J. Sci. Stat. Comput., 6 (1985), pp. 85-103.

[6] L. Greengard and V. Rokhlin, *A Fast Algorithm for Particle Simulation*, YALEU/DCS/RR-459, Yale University, 1986.

[7] G.C. Fox and S.W. Otto, *Algorithms for Concurrent Processors*, Physics Today, 37 (1984), pp. 50-59.

[8] C.L. Seitz, *The Cosmic Cube*, Commun. ACM., 28 (1985), pp. 22-33.

[9] P.R. Spalart, A. Leonard and D. Baganoff, *Numerical Simulation of Separated Flows*, NASA TM-84328, 1983.

[10] P.R. Spalart, *Two Recent Extensions of the Vortex Method*, AIAA Paper 84-0343, 1984.